WARNER MEMORIAL LIBRARY
EASTERN COLLEGE
ST. DAVIDS, PA. 19087

D1295651

HANDBOOK OF DEVELOPMENT ECONOMICS
VOLUME I

HANDBOOKS
IN
ECONOMICS

9

Series Editors

KENNETH J. ARROW

MICHAEL D. INTRILIGATOR

NORTH-HOLLAND
AMSTERDAM · NEW YORK · OXFORD · TOKYO

HANDBOOK OF DEVELOPMENT ECONOMICS

VOLUME I

Edited by

HOLLIS CHENERY
Harvard University

and

T.N. SRINIVASAN
Yale University

WARNER MEMORIAL LIBRARY
EASTERN COLLEGE
ST. DAVIDS, PA. 19087

1988

NORTH HOLLAND
AMSTERDAM · NEW YORK · OXFORD · TOKYO

12/12/89

© ELSEVIER SCIENCE PUBLISHERS B.V., 1988

All rights reserved. No part of this publication may be reproduced, stored in a retrieval system, or transmitted in any form or by any means, electronic, mechanical, photocopying, recording or otherwise, without the prior permission of the copyright owner.

ISBN North-Holland for this set 0 444 70339 X
ISBN North-Holland for this volume 0 444 70337 3

Publishers
ELSEVIER SCIENCE PUBLISHERS B.V.
P.O. Box 1991
1000 BZ Amsterdam
The Netherlands

Sole distributors for the U.S.A. and Canada
ELSEVIER SCIENCE PUBLISHING COMPANY, INC.
52 Vanderbilt Avenue
New York, N.Y. 10017
U.S.A.

Library of Congress Cataloging-in-Publication Data

Handbook of development economics.

  (Handbooks in economics ; 9)
  Includes bibliographies.
  1. Economic development—Handbooks, manuals, etc.
I. Chenery, Hollis Burnley. II. Srinivasan, T. N.,
1933–   . III. Series: Handbooks in economics ;
bk. 9.
HD82.H275 1988   338.9   87-34960
ISBN 0-444-70337-3 (U.S.)

HD 82 .H275 1988
Handbook of development
economics

PRINTED IN THE NETHERLANDS

INTRODUCTION TO THE SERIES

The aim of the *Handbooks in Economics* series is to produce Handbooks for various branches of economics, each of which is a definitive source, reference, and teaching supplement for use by professional researchers and advanced graduate students. Each Handbook provides self-contained surveys of the current state of a branch of economics in the form of chapters prepared by leading specialists on various aspects of this branch of economics. These surveys summarize not only received results but also newer developments, from recent journal articles and discussion papers. Some original material is also included, but the main goal is to provide comprehensive and accessible surveys. The Handbooks are intended to provide not only useful reference volumes for professional collections but also possible supplementary readings for advanced courses for graduate students in economics.

CONTENTS OF THE HANDBOOK

VOLUME I

PART 1: ECONOMIC DEVELOPMENT – CONCEPTS AND APPROACHES

Introduction
T.N. SRINIVASAN

Chapter 1
The Concept of Development
AMARTYA SEN

Chapter 2
The Roots of Development Theory
W. ARTHUR LEWIS

Chapter 3
Alternative Approaches to Development Economics
PRANAB BARDHAN

Chapter 4
Analytics of Development: Dualism
GUSTAV RANIS

Chapter 5
Economic Organization, Information, and Development
JOSEPH E. STIGLITZ

Chapter 6
Long-run Income Distribution and Growth
LANCE TAYLOR and PERSIO ARIDA

PART 2: STRUCTURAL TRANSFORMATION

Introduction
HOLLIS CHENERY

Chapter 7
Patterns of Structural Change
MOSHE SYRQUIN

Chapter 8
The Agricultural Transformation
C. PETER TIMMER

Chapter 9
Industrialization and Trade
HOWARD PACK

Chapter 10
Saving and Development
MARK GERSOVITZ

Chapter 11
Migration and Urbanization
JEFFREY G. WILLIAMSON

PART 3: HUMAN RESOURCES AND LABOR MARKETS

Introduction
T.N. SRINIVASAN

Chapter 12
Economic Approaches to Population Growth
NANCY BIRDSALL

Chapter 13
Education Investments and Returns
T. PAUL SCHULTZ

Chapter 14
Health and Nutrition
JERE R. BEHRMAN and ANIL B. DEOLALIKAR

Chapter 15
Labor Markets in Low-Income Countries
MARK R. ROSENZWEIG

Chapter 16
Credit Markets and Interlinked Transactions
CLIVE BELL

VOLUME II

PART 4: PLANNING AND RESOURCE ALLOCATION

Introduction
HOLLIS CHENERY

Chapter 17
Short-Run Macroeconomics
PERSIO ARIDA and LANCE TAYLOR

Chapter 18
Multisectoral Models
SHERMAN ROBINSON

Chapter 19
Income Distribution and Development
IRMA ADELMAN and SHERMAN ROBINSON

Chapter 20
Technological Change
LARRY WESTPHAL

Chapter 21
Taxation for Developing Countries
NICHOLAS STERN and EHTISHAM AHMAD

Chapter 22
Project Evaluation in Theory and Practice
LYN SQUIRE

PART 5: INTERNATIONAL ASPECTS

Introduction
T.N. SRINIVASAN

Chapter 23
International Cooperation
PAUL STREETEN

Chapter 24
Trade and Development: Theoretical Issues and Policy Implications
CHRISTOPHER BLISS

Chapter 25
Alternative Perspectives on Trade and Development
DAVID EVANS

Chapter 26
Foreign Public Capital Flows
JONATHAN EATON

Chapter 27
Foreign Private Capital Flows
RUDIGER DORNBUSCH

Chapter 28
Transnational Corporations and Direct Foreign Investment
GERALD HELLEINER

Chapter 29
Disequilibrium and Structural Adjustment
SEBASTIAN EDWARDS and SWEDER VAN WIJNBERGEN

PART 6: COUNTRY EXPERIENCE WITH DEVELOPMENT

Introduction
HOLLIS CHENERY

Chapter 30
The Experience of Primary Exporting Countries
STEPHEN R. LEWIS

Chapter 31
Import Substitution as a Development Strategy
HENRY BRUTON

Chapter 32
Outward Orientation
BELA BALASSA

Chapter 33
Large Countries: The Influence of Size
DWIGHT H. PERKINS and MOSHE SYRQUIN

PREFACE TO THE HANDBOOK

The scope of the Handbook

Development economics has been defined as the study of the economic structure and behavior of poor (or less developed) countries [W.A. Lewis (1984)]. It is generally agreed that "development" encompasses the reduction of poverty, improvements in the health and education of the population, and an increase in productive capacity as well as rising per capita income. Although the core concerns of development economics are clear enough, its outer boundaries are difficult to establish and essentially arbitrary.

Earlier empirical work in this field focused on changes in the composition of demand, production, employment, and international trade that were observed in the comparative studies done by Kuznets and others. This led to a description of development issues in structural terms, such as the transformation of a poor, stagnant rural society into a more diversified, urbanizing economy capable of sustained growth. The processes associated with this transformation include capital accumulation, human resource development, and the evolution of political and economic institutions, including markets.

In approaching the study of development, it is natural to examine the applicability of conventional analytical tools of economics to the features characteristic of less developed economies. Although the salient problems of a traditional peasant society, a rapidly industrializing economy and a mature nation may be quite different, and countries enter their development stage in varying historical contexts, these differences may not have much impact on the choice of analytical concepts. In its extreme form, this hypothesis is tantamount to a denial of the usefulness of a separate economics of development. Whether neoclassical economics can serve this unifying role is one of the central issues discussed in this Handbook.

Since development economics is explicitly characterized by competing paradigms, rather than by a dominant orthodoxy, we have organized the Handbook around the implications of different sets of assumptions and their associated research programs. While we follow Lewis in identifying the field of development with the problems and behavior of poor countries, we leave open the question of the extent to which this implies a need for a distinctive analytical framework. Exploration of this issue has been ensured by selecting authors known to have different views.

The focus of development economics on problems of poverty and growth makes some branches of conventional economics more relevant than others. Explaining the stylized facts of development involves both the microeconomic behavior of households and production units and the macroeconomics of saving, investment, and financial development. Sectors of the economy that undergo substantial changes during the transformation – such as agriculture, manufacturing, and infrastructure – require particular attention. Perhaps most important of all is the changing international economy within which national development takes place. Indeed, international trade is often described as an engine of growth and development.

Finally, the role of the state is at least as important in the early stages of development as it is later on. Although governments have chosen to intervene in the mobilization and allocation of resources in a variety of ways, their performance of these functions is one of the crucial aspects of a development strategy. We have therefore included in Part 6 a comparison of the experience of countries following different strategies.

Organization

The simplest way to organize the Handbook would be to adopt the traditional division of economics, devoting a chapter to each of the more relevant branches. While we have followed this pattern to a considerable extent, it had to be supplemented to give a more integrated view of related development processes. Thus, we have divided the Handbook into two volumes, each with three parts which focus on the broad processes of development. Each part has an introduction, describing its unifying themes and summarizing its contents.

Volume I starts with a part of six chapters dealing with the concept of development, its historical antecedents, and alternative approaches to the study of development broadly construed.

Part 2 of Volume I is devoted to the structural transformation of economies as they develop over time. Chapter 7 introduces the overall patterns of structural change. Subsequent chapters in Part 2 cover the major development processes: agricultural transformation, industrialization and trade, saving, migration, and urbanization. The main themes of Part 2 are the relations among these development processes and the ways in which they vary from country to country.

The role that human resources play in economic development is the theme of Part 3. As development gains momentum, the quality of the labor force improves through accumulation of human capital in terms of better health, nutrition, and education. The efficiency with which labor markets function in allocating various (skill) categories of labor across sectors and occupations is an important aspect of development. At the early stages, agriculture is the major sector of employment.

The tenurial arrangements under which land is cultivated, and the functioning of credit markets influence resource allocation as well as the pace of technical progress in agriculture. Among other related topics, the five chapters in Part 3 cover the determinants and consequences of population growth, the process of human capital formation (education, health, and nutrition), and labor and credit markets.

In Volume II, the emphasis shifts toward policy issues. Part 4 examines techniques of resource allocation and policy planning at both macro and micro levels. The use of multisectoral models for development policy is first surveyed in general terms and then applied to problems of income distribution. Separate chapters are devoted to macroeconomic management, technical change, taxation, and the microeconomics of project selection.

Part 5 consists of seven chapters dealing with the international aspects of development and their effects on policy. Policy issues are introduced in a chapter on international cooperation, which discusses the global institutions needed to integrate developing economies into the world economy. Neoclassical and alternative approaches to studying the role of international trade in the development process are each the subject of a chapter. The role of international capital flows is discussed, with separate chapters devoted to public lending, private lending, and transnational corporations. Since smooth adjustment to shocks is important if development is not to be jeopardized, a separate chapter is devoted to the process of adjustment by which economies handle the experience of unanticipated shocks.

The final part of Volume II looks at the experience of countries pursuing different development strategies and draws lessons for policy. One strategic choice concerns the orientation towards the outside world. An outward-oriented strategy is neutral between production for home use and for export, and between earning foreign exchange through exports and saving foreign exchange through import substitution. An inward-oriented strategy emphasizes production for home use and import substitution. The four chapters of part 6 deal in turn with the experience of primary product exporters, the contrast between countries that have followed an import substitution strategy and those that have had an outward orientation and the special features of large countries.

Acknowledgements

We owe a deep debt of gratitude to the authors of the two volumes for their diligence in preparing their chapters, and in particular for revising them to take account of comments received from other authors and the editors. We thank them for commenting on each others' chapters and on our introductions. Thanks are also due to the Harvard Institute for International Development for sponsoring the conference where authors discussed their preliminary drafts, and to its editor, James Ito-Adler. Our assistants, Melissa Davy at Harvard and Louise Danishevsky at Yale, bore the brunt of keeping various drafts of each chapter in order, typing comments, and generally seeing to it that the preparation of the volumes was kept on an even keel.

HOLLIS CHENERY
Harvard University

T.N. SRINIVASAN
Yale University

Reference

Lewis, W.A. (1984) 'The state of development theory', *American Economic Review*, March: 1–10.

CONTENTS OF VOLUME I

Introduction to the Series   v

Contents of the Handbook   vii

Preface to the Handbook   xii

PART 1: ECONOMIC DEVELOPMENT – CONCEPTS AND APPROACHES

Introduction
T.N. SRINIVASAN   3

Chapter 1
The Concept of Development
AMARTYA SEN   9

   1.   The Background   10
   2.   Production, growth, and development   12
   3.   Characteristics, functionings, and living   15
   4.   Freedom and capability   16
   5.   Weights and rankings   18
   6.   Values, instruments, and objects   20
   7.   Conclusion   23
   References   24

Chapter 2
The Roots of Development Theory
W. ARTHUR LEWIS   27

   1.   Introduction   28
   2.   Sectoral imbalance   28
   3.   Overall balance   31
   4.   Organization   34
   5.   Conclusion   36
   References   37

Chapter 3

Alternative Approaches to Development Economics
PRANAB BARDHAN   39

  1. Introduction   40
  2. Theory of the household   40
  3. Institutions and resource allocation   45
  4. Income distribution and growth   51
  5. Trade and development   57
  6. Economic policy and the state   63
  7. Concluding remarks   66
     References   68

Chapter 4

Analytics of Development: Dualism
GUSTAV RANIS   73

  1. Introduction   74
  2. Dualism in the history of economic thought   75
  3. The modern analytics of closed dualism   76
  4. Dualism in the open economy   86
     References   91

Chapter 5

Economic Organization, Information, and Development
JOSEPH E. STIGLITZ   93

  1. Introduction   94
  2. Basic tenets and objectives of analysis   96
      2.1. Stylized facts   96
      2.2. Alternative approaches   96
  3. The theory of rural organization   105
      3.1. The organization of the family   105
      3.2. The landlord–tenant relationship: The sharecropping puzzle   115
      3.3. Unemployment in the rural sector   125
      3.4. The rural sector as a whole: The interlinkage of markets   133
  4. The urban sector   134
  5. Market equilibrium   136
  6. Government pricing policies, wage subsidies, and cost–benefit analysis   140
  7. The development process   142
      7.1. Factor supplies   142
      7.2. Technical change and entrepreneurship   147
      7.3   Development strategies   150

8. Concluding remarks 153
   8.1. Choice of managers 153
   8.2. Market failures and government failures 153
References 157

Chapter 6
Long-Run Income Distribution and Growth
LANCE TAYLOR and PERSIO ARIDA 161

1. Introduction 162
2. The heirs of Schumpeter 163
3. Demand-driven models 165
4. Resource limitations and reproduction 169
5. Shades of Marx 174
6. The neoclassical resurgence – trade 178
7. Structuralists versus monetarists 184
8. Patterns of growth 187
9. Conclusions 189
References 190

PART 2: STRUCTURAL TRANSFORMATION

Introduction
HOLLIS CHENERY 197

Chapter 7
Patterns of Structural Change
MOSHE SYRQUIN 203

0. Introduction 205
1. The study of structural change 206
   1.1. Structural change in economic history 209
   1.2. Structural change in development economics 211
   1.3. The need for a typology 214
2. Empirical research on the structural transformation 216
   2.1. Bases for comparative analysis 216
   2.2. A unique path of development? 217
   2.3. The methodology of comparative analysis 218
   2.4. Time-series vs. cross-section studies 221
3. Patterns of growth and accumulation 223
   3.1. Growth patterns 223
   3.2. Accumulation 225

4.   Changes in sector proportions   228
     4.1.   The accounting framework   230
     4.2.   Final demand   231
     4.3.   Intermediate demand   231
     4.4.   Trade   232
     4.5.   Structure of production: Broad sectors   235
     4.6.   Post-war patterns   239
     4.7.   Manufacturing: Disaggregated results   242
5.   Structure and growth   243
     5.1.   Sectoral contributions to growth   244
     5.2.   Typology of development patterns   248
6.   Accounting for the transformation   250
     6.1.   Growth accounting: Demand side decomposition   250
     6.2.   Growth accounting: Supply side   254
     6.3.   Resource shifts and productivity growth   255
7.   Relative prices and exchange rate conversions   258
     7.1.   Relative prices   259
     7.2.   Exchange-rate conversions   262
8.   Approaches to policy   265
     References   268

Chapter 8
The Agricultural Transformation
C. PETER TIMMER   275

1.   Introduction   276
2.   The process of agricultural transformation   279
     2.1.   Evolving stages   280
     2.2.   Agriculture and economic development   283
     2.3.   The role of the agricultural sector   288
3.   Why agriculture is different   291
     3.1.   Decision-making in agriculture   292
     3.2.   Characteristics of agricultural production functions   294
     3.3.   The farm household as both producer and consumer   299
     3.4.   What difference does the difference make?   300
4.   Transforming agriculture   302
     4.1.   The sources and dynamics of technical change   302
     4.2.   Unresolved issues   313
5.   Agricultural development strategy   321
     5.1.   Policies for "getting agriculture moving"   321
     5.2.   Alternative strategies for maintaining the transformation process 323
     5.3.   Agricultural policy and structural change   327
     References   328

Chapter 9

Industrialization and Trade

HOWARD PACK   333

1. Introduction	334
2. A retrospective	336
2.1. The compression of the industrialization process	336
2.2. Initial conditions	337
2.3. The elasticity of factor supplies	338
2.4. The role of rationality	341
2.5. The role of international trade	341
3. The evolving structure of production	342
3.1. Normal patterns	342
3.2. The impact of policy intervention	344
3.3. Import substitution, exports, and the patterns of growth	344
4. The impact of trade on industrial performance	346
4.1. Industrial productivity – a key variable	346
4.2. The costs of protection	347
4.3. Trade orientation and the growth of total factor productivity	348
4.4. The empirical evidence	352
4.5. Cross-country models	356
4.6. The large country puzzle	357
5. Micro studies of productivity	358
5.1. Early intercountry comparisons of productivity levels	358
5.2. The Hirschman hypothesis	359
5.3. Firm-level productivity studies in the less developed countries	360
6. Employment creation in the manufacturing sector	365
6.1. The choice of technology	366
6.2. Factor market distortions and information costs	369
6.3. The aggregate gains from improved technology choice	370
7. Conclusions	371
References	372

Chapter 10

Saving and Development

MARK GERSOVITZ   381

1. Introduction	382
2. Personal savings	383
2.1. A simple model of individual saving	384
2.2. Evidence on the simple model	385
2.3. Uncertainty and saving	390
2.4. Borrowing constraints	392
2.5. Education and asset choice	394

	2.6.	Health, nutrition and savings	396
	2.7.	Bequests and savings	400
	2.8.	The family and savings	401
3.	Savings at the national level	403
	3.1.	Aggregation over cohorts	404
	3.2.	Income distribution and aggregate savings	407
	3.3.	Corporate savings	411
	3.4.	The role of government	412
	3.5.	Evidence at the aggregate level	413
4.	Conclusions	418
References	419

Chapter 11

Migration and Urbanization

JEFFREY G. WILLIAMSON   425

1.	The problem	426
2.	The urban transition	427
	2.1.	Quantifying the urban transition	427
	2.2.	Migrant selectivity bias	430
	2.3.	Selectivity bias, the brain drain, and remittances	431
	2.4.	City growth, migration, and labor absorption	433
3.	Disequilibrating labor market shocks and equilibrating migrant responses	433
	3.1.	Disequilibrium and wage gaps	433
	3.2.	Are migrants rational?	435
	3.3.	Are there too many city immigrants?	437
4.	What does "overurbanization" mean?	439
	4.1.	Push, pull, and the engines of city growth	439
	4.2.	The urban bias	441
5.	How do urban labor markets work?	442
	5.1.	The evolution of conventional wisdom	442
	5.2.	The Todaro model	443
	5.3.	Critique: How do urban labor markets really work?	445
	5.4.	Some evidence	446
6.	Migration and city growth in general equilibrium: What are the driving forces?	449
	6.1.	What drives Third World migration and city growth?	449
	6.2.	Modeling migration and city growth	453
	6.3.	Understanding the past and projecting the future	455
7.	Where do we go from here?	459
References	461

PART 3: HUMAN RESOURCES AND LABOR MARKETS

Introduction
T.N. SRINIVASAN   469

Chapter 12
Economic Approaches to Population Growth
NANCY BIRDSALL   477

1.   Introduction and overview   478
2.   Recent demographic change in the developing world   479
3.   Macroeconomic analyses of the economic consequences
    of population growth   483
    3.1.   Malthus and successor pessimists   486
    3.2.   The optimists   490
    3.3.   The revisionists   493
4.   Microeconomic foundations: The determinants of fertility   501
    4.1.   Economic models of fertility behavior   503
    4.2.   Fertility models: Differences, conceptual limitations   509
    4.3.   Empirical studies of fertility behavior   512
    4.4.   Endogenous fertility, optimal population size, and social welfare   522
5.   The welfare economics of public policies to reduce fertility   523
    5.1.   Externalities   523
    5.2.   Fertility control and market failure   525
    5.3.   Specific policies   526
6.   Summary and conclusions   529
References   535

Chapter 13
Education Investments and Returns
T. PAUL SCHULTZ   543

1.   Introduction and preview   544
    1.1.   An overview   545
    1.2.   Problems: Conceptual and empirical   547
2.   National educational systems: Interpretation of aggregate patterns   550
    2.1.   World trends   551
    2.2.   Adjustment of the educational system to demand and supply   557
    2.3.   A model of the educational system   562
    2.4.   An empirical decomposition of educational expenditures   564
    2.5.   Estimates of school expenditure equations   568
    2.6.   Sex differences in school enrollment rates   571
    2.7.   Regional patterns in residuals   573
    2.8.   Cross-sectional findings and time-series forecasts   575

3. Alternative models of education and earnings, data,
and policy implications   577
4. Rates of return to schooling in market activities   585
   4.1. Student ability, parent background, and school quality   587
   4.2. Labor supply and unemployment   591
   4.3. Occupational choice   593
   4.4. The education and productivity of farmers   597
   4.5. Migration   599
   4.6. Male–female comparisons of returns   602
   4.7. Interactions with educational returns   605
   4.8. Efficiency and equity   606
5. Nonmarket production and schooling   607
6. Policy   610
7. Conclusions   615
Appendix   618
References   621

Chapter 14
Health and Nutrition

JERE R. BEHRMAN and ANIL B. DEOLALIKAR   631

1. Introduction   633
2. Theoretical framework   637
   2.1. Micro considerations: Household production functions and reduced-form
      demands for health and nutrients   637
   2.2. Supply considerations   649
   2.3. Macro or aggregate considerations   649
3. Measurement and estimation problems in health and
nutrition relations   650
   3.1. Measurement of health status   650
   3.2. Measurement of nutrient intakes and nutritional status   653
   3.3. Measurement of non-nutrient health-related inputs   656
   3.4. Measurement of prices, health-related inputs, and assets   657
   3.5. Estimation problems   658
4. Empirical studies of determinants of health and nutrition
in developing countries   660
   4.1. Determinants of health   660
   4.2. Determinants of nutrients   674
5. Empirical studies of the impact of health and nutrition
in developing countries   683
   5.1. Impact on labor productivity   683
   5.2. Impact on schooling productivity   688

5.3.   Impact of female nutrition on fertility 689
5.4.   Impact of infant mortality on fertility 690
6.   Empirical studies on supply considerations and related policies 692
6.1.   Food subsidies 692
6.2.   Other health goods and services subsidies 696
6.3.   Impact of macro adjustment policies on health and nutrition 697
7.   Summary and conclusions 698
7.1.   Summary of available studies 698
7.2.   Directions for future research 702
References 704

Chapter 15
Labor Markets in Low-Income Countries
MARK R. ROSENZWEIG 713

1.   Introduction 714
2.   Employment and wage determination in rural labor markets 715
2.1.   Surplus labor, disguised employment and unemployment 715
2.2.   The family enterprise model and agricultural dualism 728
3.   Rural labor contracts: Risk, information and incentives problems 733
3.1.   Casual and permanent laborers: Spot and future markets for labor 736
3.2.   Tenancy contracts 738
4.   Geographic mobility 743
4.1.   The basic human capital model of migration 744
4.2.   Information and capital market constraints on mobility 745
4.3.   Two-sector unemployment equilibrium models 746
4.4.   Risk, remittances and family behavior 751
4.5.   Heterogeneity and selective migration 753
5.   Urban labor markets 754
5.1.   Diversity and unemployment 754
5.2.   Urban dualism and dual labor markets 756
6.   Conclusion 757
References 759

Chapter 16
Credit Markets and Interlinked Transactions
CLIVE BELL 763

1.   Introduction 764
2.   Credit markets 766
2.1.   The credit contract 769
2.2.   Innovation and the rate of interest 782
2.3.   Public policy 783
2.4.   Some evidence 791

3. Interlinked transactions   797

    3.1. The causes of interlinking   798

    3.2. The interlinking of tenancy with credit: The principal–agent approach   803

    3.3. An alternative to contract-taking equilibrium: The Nash bargaining solution 810

    3.4. Interlinking and innovation   813

    3.5. Welfare and income distribution   816

    3.6. Policy reforms   823

4. Concluding remarks   826

References   828

Index   831

PART 1

ECONOMIC DEVELOPMENT – CONCEPTS AND APPROACHES

INTRODUCTION TO PART 1

T.N. SRINIVASAN

Yale University

Part 1 of this Handbook is, appropriately enough, concerned with the concepts of and approaches to the study of the economics of development. Development, as contrasted with mere growth of the economy, is, according to Schumpeter, "a distinct phenomenon, entirely foreign to what may be observed in the circular flow or in the tendency towards equilibrium. It is spontaneous and discontinuous change in the channels of flow, which forever alters and displaces the equilibrium previously existing" [Schumpeter (1961)]. While Schumpeter wrote in 1911 and, therefore, did not have contemporary developing countries in mind, economists writing after the Second World War viewed the developing economies as being caught in an equilibrium variously described as a "vicious circle of poverty", "low-level equilibrium trap", and so on. The problem of development was described as taking the economy out of this equilibrium and setting it on a path of self-sustaining growth.

Unlike Schumpeter, who emphasized the role of innovations and the concomitant private anticipation of entrepreneurial profit as major factors explaining development, most development economists writing in the late 1940s and 1950s visualized a dominant role for the state in initiating and sustaining the development process. A corollary view was the advocacy of comprehensive national development planning under state auspices. This view, however, came to be tempered considerably by the sobering experience of the decades following the Second World War with disappointing, if not entirely counterproductive, state interventions in the economy in one developing country after another.

In the dominant neoclassical paradigm of the postwar era, Adam Smith's parable of the invisible hand was rigorously restated in terms of the two fundamental theorems of welfare economics. First, under a set of mild restrictions on production technology and individual preferences, the equilibrium of a laissez-faire market economy is a Pareto optimum. Pareto optimality obtains if any departure from it cannot make everyone better off, that is, benefit for some can come only at the expense or loss in welfare of others. The fact that a laissez-faire equilibrium is Pareto optimal does not of course imply that it is fair in some well-defined sense. More simply put, the distribution of income or

Handbook of Development Economics, Volume I, Edited by H. Chenery and T.N. Srinivasan
© *Elsevier Science Publishers B.V., 1988*

welfare associated with a laissez-faire Pareto optimum could be highly unequal. Second, given a set of rather restrictive assumptions, including the absence of technological externalities and increasing returns to scale in production of goods, and convexity of consumer preferences, any Pareto optimum is also a competitive equilibrium provided income (or initial endowments) of individuals can be redistributed through lump-sum transfers or other non-distortionary means. Thus, both efficiency of resource allocation and distributional equity (in the sense of Pareto optimality) can be achieved in a competitive equilibrium, albeit one with redistribution of incomes or endowments, rather than one that is laissez-faire.

The "static" or "certainty" version of the theorems stated above was extended by Arrow and Debreu to cover resource allocations in time, space, and in uncertain states of the world. The essential feature of this extension is that a complete set of markets for the purchase or sale of goods contingent on each possible combination of time, space, and the (uncertain) state of nature is assumed to exist. In both the original and extended versions there was no room for strategic behavior and no costs of transactions by assumption.

Early development economists based their analytical case for state intervention in the developing economies on the exceptions to the validity of the static version of the second theorem. They argued that, in early stages of development, externalities are pervasive and scale economies are significant, particularly in sectors such as transport and communications which provide the infrastructure for the functioning of an economy. Capital markets are likely to be segmented and imperfect; and the financial system primitive and not performing intermediation to any significant extent. The entrepreneurial class is likely to be miniscule, if not altogether absent or alien and unassimilated. But even if entrepreneurs were believed to exist in adequate numbers, the markets for risk pooling and sharing were thought likely to be absent, so that the scope for entrepreneurial activity would be severely circumscribed. Under such circumstances, it was argued, market failure was the rule rather than an exception. The state would then have to perform the role of the Schumpeterian entrepreneur as well as intervene in existing markets, through appropriate taxes and subsidies, to ensure that externalities were appropriately reflected in private calculations. Recent theoretical work on development has taken the exceptions to the extended version of the second theorem as its point of departure, in emphasizing the absence of a complete set of contingent markets and asymmetries in information and strategic behavior. This research investigates the origins and consequences of incomplete markets, imperfect information, transactions costs, and imperfect competition. One important consequence is that the allocation of resources through existing markets may not be Pareto optimal, and once again a role for government intervention can emerge.

In contrast to the neoclassical approach to development which is ahistoric and based on virtual time, there is the historical, real-time Marxian approach that is perhaps closer to the spirit of Schumpeter's analysis. In this approach, the forces of production, represented by available technology at any point in historical time, and the existing relations of production, represented by the institutions governing ownership and access to the means of production, determine an "equilibrium". Exogenous technical progress, i.e. shifts in the forces of production, disturbs such an equilibrium inducing a realignment of relations of production that replaces those of the pre-existing equilibrium which are no longer functional. In this linear view of history, capitalistic production relations supplanted feudal relations in the historical context because changes in technology (particularly after the industrial revolution) made the feudal relation obsolete. In turn, the recurrent crises that Marx so confidently predicted for mature capitalism were expected to lead to socialism and, eventually, to communism. As will be noted below, the recent rational-choice school of Marxism (perhaps it should be called neo-classical Marxism) does not view the world in the rigidly deterministic way described above and allows some scope of action for individuals.

In the structuralist view of development, rigidities of various kinds preclude the rapid and quantitatively significant response of the economy to changing incentives as conveyed by market signals. Thus, for example, the supply response to improved terms of trade for agriculture, the dominant sector in the early stages of development, was said to be negligible, at least in the short to medium run. The prospects of acquiring growing amounts of foreign exchange deemed essential for obtaining or financing vital imports through exports of traditional products were considered poor and so on. Even if market failures in the neoclassical sense were absent, development will be hampered unless strategies (e.g. import substituting industrialization) that alleviate the structural rigidities are adopted. Dualism between the traditional and rural agriculture and urban and modern industries is another example of a structural rigidity. However, neither the origin of the rigidities nor their persistence is adequately explained in behavioral terms by structuralists.

All three approaches to development – neoclassical, Marxian, and structuralist – are represented, at least minimally, in this Handbook. Part 1 elaborates some of the more prominent features of each approach and compares their explanations of some of the stylized facts of development. It is fair to say that most development economists, and certainly the authors of this Handbook, would not wish to be tied down exclusively to one approach. They would rather apply that approach which is most suited to the analysis of each problem. Besides, the divergence in the explanations of stylized facts as put forth by different schools appears to be narrowing.

In much of neoclassical analysis, inter-personal comparison of welfare is avoided so that for comparing situations in which the welfare of different individuals may be affected differently only a partial ranking by appealing to Pareto optimality is used. That is, unless in one situation every individual is better off (or worse off) compared to another, two situations are not ranked. Sen's philosophical analysis of the concepts and indicators of development in Chapter 1 makes it plain that a major difficulty with the concept of development arises from value-heterogeneity, i.e. that people differ in their views as to what things are valuable to promote, and value-endogeneity, i.e. in fact that the process of change involved in development alters the valuations of people. Yet, Sen strongly argues that it is often possible and desirable to separate the relatively uncontroversial judgements from the controversial ones related to value-heterogeneity and value-endogeneity. In his view much of development policy analysis involves valuation problems that are not excessively problematic.

Arthur Lewis (Chapter 2) traces the historical roots of development thought in the writings of economists of the pre-Adam Smith era and finds them to be surprisingly modern in identifying constraints on growth imposed by agricultural growth, foreign exchange, and saving. Rudiments of the theory of bank credit, human capital, and public finance are also found in these early writings.

Bardhan (Chapter 3) compares three alternative approaches, which he terms "neo-classical", "Marxist", and "structuralist-institutionalist", to five broadly defined problems: theory of household behavior, resource allocation, income distribution and growth, trade and development, and economic policy and the state. His discussion of Marxist approaches is heavily weighted in favor of a so-called "rational-choice" Marxism as contrasted with traditional Marxism, the former being closer to neoclassical economics in positing that individuals have room for choice and are not completely constrained by technology and history. He argues that although superficially the three approaches may appear very different there is a significant measure of methodological similarity among the more sophisticated versions of each. Institutions and modes of behavior such as share-cropping and interlinkages between markets that were once condemned by Marxists as exploitative and by neoclassicists as inefficient, may turn out to be rational responses to individuals to problems of risk, moral hazard, and/or costs of monitoring work-effort. While Marxists tended to emphasize the role of ideology as legitimizing exploitation or false consciousness as masking it, and while neoclassicists ignored it altogether, recent work on political economy views ideology as a resource-saving way of keeping free riders in check in the provision of public goods of all kinds.

Another area where Bardhan argues that modern Marxian and neoclassical analysis are converging is in explaining the existence of unemployment in equilibrium. While Marxists suggest that the threat of unemployment disciplines workers and enables the capitalists to extract labor power from them, neoclassicists point out that compared to the alternatives of monitoring workers closely or making them put up bonds for good behavior, the threat of unemployment may be an instrument for reducing shirking by workers, thus extracting effort from them at a reasonable cost. Another area of convergence of views can be discerned in the waning enthusiasm for centralized bureaucratic planning for economic development and a grudging recognition of the efficiency of the market mechanism on the part of some Marxists and structuralists and the recognition by neoclassicists of a role for government for reasons other than the standard one of market failure.

Labor markets are likely to be segmented and imperfect in early stages of development when more than two-thirds of the labor force is employed in agriculture. Development, almost by definition, involves a transfer of labor from agriculture to manufacturing and services. Following in the footsteps of Arthur Lewis, development economists have lavished analytical attention on this transfer and the factors that influence it. Ranis (Chapter 4) elaborates the influential dual-economy model of development in which an essentially market-oriented and capitalistic urban manufacturing sector expands by drawing labor from an agricultural sector based on traditional family farms. Until a unified labor market emerges, the real wage in urban manufacturing is related to the agricultural wage by such factors as rural–urban terms of trade, the cost associated with moving from rural to urban areas, and any wedge introduced by public policy intervention. The rate of capital accumulation in urban manufacturing determines the pace of withdrawal of labor from agriculture in the Ranis model.

In no real world economy, developed or otherwise, does a complete set of contingent commodity markets exist. The non-existence of some markets as well as the imperfect functioning of others are characteristic of the state of underdevelopment. Stiglitz (Chapter 5) analyzes the causes and consequences of these phenomena. According to him the two important consequences are: first, equilibria based on transactions in existing markets need not be Pareto optimal, and second, contractual arrangements other than "arm's length" market transactions between anonymous parties may be widespread. The absent markets most often cited are those related to insurance against risks and those related to financial intermediation, broadly construed. One of the major factors contributing to the non-existence of markets is the problem of asymmetric information leading to moral hazard, adverse selection, etc. Stiglitz is able to provide a rationale for share-cropping (often with a 50–50 split of output between the landlord and tenant whatever be the crop grown), for inter-linking of share-cropping with credit and marketing, and sharing of costs with sharing of output, etc. An important but troublesome implication of his analysis is that although laissez-faire equilibria in such contexts are not Pareto optimal, and thereby a role for government intervention exists, there is no presumption that Pareto-superior equilibria can always be achieved through government intervention.

Stiglitz is also concerned with efficiency wage theories. Efficiency problems arise from a number of sources including: incentives for shirking due to imperfect monitoring and supervision of workers, self-selection considerations in a context of asymmetric information about worker productivity, and the possibility that workers' productivity depends on their nutritional status, the latter being positively related to their consumption out of their wages.

Taylor and Arida (Chapter 6) study the macroeconomics of growth by identifying Schumpeter's circular flow equilibrium with long-run steady state growth. Five versions of the steady state are elaborated, three of which are constrained from the supply side and two from the demand side. The three supply-constrained models include Solow and Swan's neoclassical models of growth. In these models the exogenous steady growth of labor in efficiency units determines the growth rate of the system. In contrast, in another supplied-constrained model the growth rate of one sector's output is exogenously specified to which rate the growth of output of other sectors converge, inter-sectoral equilibrium being maintained through relative price changes. In the demand-determined models of Taylor and Arida, output and capacity utilization respond to changes in demand with no presumption of full employment or full capacity utilization. The constraint on growth in demand arises because the pattern of income distribution needed to sustain a full capacity equilibrium differs from that associated with existing production relations. Implicit in this story is a whole host of structural rigidities, and inflexibilities that either prevent prices from adjusting or resources from being reallocated in response to price changes. Taylor and Arida explore the implications of rigidities of technology and in behavior of agents.

Reference

Schumpeter, J. (1961) *The theory of economic development*. New York: Oxford University Press.

Chapter 1

THE CONCEPT OF DEVELOPMENT

AMARTYA SEN*

Harvard University

Contents

1. The background   10
2. Production, growth, and development   12
3. Characteristics, functionings, and living   15
4. Freedom and capability   16
5. Weights and rankings   18
6. Values, instruments, and objects   20
7. Conclusion   23
References   24

*For helpful discussions and comments, I am most grateful to Hollis Chenery, T.N. Srinivasan and Paul Streeten.

Handbook of Development Economics, Volume I, Edited by H. Chenery and T.N. Srinivasan
© *Elsevier Science Publishers B.V., 1988*

1. The background

"The French grow too fast", wrote Sir William Petty in 1676. Whether or not this was in fact the first recorded expression of what is clearly a traditional English obsession, it was certainly a part of one of the earliest discussions of development economics. Petty was concerned not merely with the growth of numbers and of incomes, but he also took a broad view of development problems, including concern with the exact content of the standard of living. Part of his statistical analysis was meant "to show" that "the King's subjects are not in so bad a condition as discontented Men would make them". While Petty had estimated national income by using both the "income method" and the "expenditure method", he had also gone on to judge the conditions of people in a broad enough way to include "the Common Safety" and "each Man's particular Happiness".[1]

Petty is regarded, with justice, as one of the founders of modern economics, and specifically a pioneer of quantitative economics.[2] He was certainly also a founder of development economics. Indeed, in the early contributions to economics, development economics can hardly be separated out from the rest of economics, since so much of economics was, in fact, concerned with problems of economic development. This applies not only to Petty's writings, but also to those of the other pioneers of modern economics, including Gregory King, Francois Quesnay, Antoine Lavoisier, Joseph Louis Lagrange, and even Adam Smith. *An Inquiry into the Nature and Causes of the Wealth of Nations* was, in fact, also an inquiry into the basic issues of development economics.

The fact that in the early writings in economics there was this noticeable congruence of development economics and economics in general is a matter of some interest, especially in the context of investigating the nature of "the concept of development". Interest in development problems has, traditionally, provided one of the deepest *motivations* for the pursuit of economics in general, and this broad basis of development economics has to be borne in mind when investigat-

---

[1]*Political Arithmetick*, in which these passages occur, was written by Petty around 1676 but it was published posthumously in 1691. The text could be found in Hull (1899, vol. I). The passages referred to can be found on pages 241–242, 311.

[2]It may be remembered that it was Petty, the anatomist and musicologist, turned economist, who had insisted at the Royal Society that in discussions in the society, "no word might be used but what marks either number, weight, or measure" [Hull (1899, vol. I, p. lxiv)]. Those who complain about the "recent craze" for mathematical economics might have to put up with the fact that the recent times began a long time ago.

ing the details of the concept of development. Having started off, rightly, with an ell, development economics can scarcely settle for an inch.

It is not hard to see why the concept of development is so essential to economics in general. Economic problems do, of course, involve logistic issues, and a lot of it is undoubtedly "engineering" of one kind or another. On the other hand, the success of all this has to be judged ultimately in terms of what it does to the lives of human beings. The enhancement of living conditions must clearly be an essential – if not *the* essential – object of the entire economic exercise and that enhancement is an integral part of the concept of development. Even though the logistic and engineering problems involved in enhancing living conditions in the poor, developing countries might well be very different from those in the rich, developed ones, there is much in common in the respective exercises on the two sides of the divide [on this see Bauer (1971)].

Sometimes development economists have been rather protective of their own domain, insisting on separating development economics from the rest of economics. While the underlying motivation behind this effort is easy to understand, it is important not to make too much of the divide, nor to confuse separateness with independence. Tools of standard economics may have much fruitful use in development economics as well, even when the exact problems addressed happen to be quite specialized. It is, however, arguable that for one reason or another, a good deal of standard economics has tended to move away from broad issues of poverty, misery and well-being, and from the fulfilment of basic needs and enhancing the quality of life. Development economists have felt it necessary to emphasize and justify their involvement with these – rather "old-fashioned" – problems, even though the relevance of these problems is by no means confined to development economics. There are also institutional differences that separate out the logistic issues in developing countries from those of developed ones, in the pursuit of economic development and the enhancement of living conditions.

Certainly, the systematic differences in institutional features is a matter of great moment in arriving at policies and deriving practical lessons regarding what is to be done. But the first issue – the emphasis on development objectives – is not a matter only for development economics as such, but of importance for economics in general [see Hirschman (1970)]. In this respect, too, insisting on a sharp division between development economics and other types of economics would be rather counter-productive. Development economics, it can be argued, has to be concerned not only with protecting its "own" territory, but also with keeping alive the foundational motivation of the subject of economics in general. The literature on the "concept of development" – whether explicitly put forward or discussed by implication – has to be examined in this broad perspective related to economics in general, rather than only in terms of "development economics" narrowly defined.

2. Production, growth, and development

The close link between economic development and economic growth is simultaneously a matter of importance as well as a source of considerable confusion. There can scarcely be any doubt that, given other things, an expansion of opulence must make a contribution to the living conditions of the people in question. It was, therefore, entirely natural that the early writings in development economics, when it emerged as a subject on its own after the Second World War, concentrated to a great extent on ways of achieving economic growth, and in particular increasing the gross national product (GNP) and total employment [see Rosenstein-Rodan (1943), Mandelbaum (1945), Dobb (1951), Datta (1952), Singer (1952), Nurkse (1953), Dasgupta (1954), Lewis (1955), Baran (1957), Hirschman (1958)]. The process of economic development cannot abstract from expanding the supply of food, clothing, housing, medical services, educational facilities, etc. and from transforming the productive structure of the economy, and these important and crucial changes are undoubtedly matters of economic growth.

The importance of "growth" must depend on the nature of the variable the expansion of which is considered and seen as "growth". The crucial issue, therefore, is not the time-dimensional focus of growth, but the salience and reach of GNP and related variables on which usual measures of growth concentrate. The relation between GNP and living conditions is far from simple.[3] To illustrate the problem, figures for GNP per head and life expectancy at birth in 1984 are given in Table 1.1 for five different countries, namely, China, Sri Lanka, Brazil, Mexico, and South Africa. South Africa, with about seven times the GNP per

Table 1.1
GNP and life expectancy

	GNP per head, 1984 (U.S. Dollars)	Life expectancy at at birth, 1984 (years)
China	310	69
Sri Lanka	360	70
Brazil	1,720	64
Mexico	2,040	66
South Africa	2,340	54

Source: World Bank (1986).

[3] For discussions on this, see Adelman and Morris (1973), Sen (1973), Adelman (1975), Grant (1978), Morris (1979), Kakwani (1981), Streeten (1981), Streeten et al. (1981), Stewart (1985), Anand and Harris (1986).

head of China and Sri Lanka, has a substantially lower expectation of life than the latter countries. Similarly, Brazil and Mexico also with many times the income of China and Sri Lanka have achieved considerably less in longevity than these two much poorer countries. To point to this contrast is not, of course, the same thing as drawing an immediate policy conclusion as to exactly what should be done, but the nature of the contrast has to be borne in mind in refusing to identify economic development with mere economic growth. Even though an expansion of GNP, *given other things*, should enhance the living conditions of people, and will typically expand the life expectancy figures of that country, there are many other variables that also influence the living conditions, and the concept of development cannot ignore the role of these other variables.

Life expectancy is, of course, a very limited measure of what has been called "the quality of life". Indeed, in terms of what it directly measures, life expectancy is more an index of the "quantity" of life rather than of its quality. But the forces that lead to mortality, such as morbidity, ill health, hunger, etc. also tend to make the living conditions of the people more painful, precarious, and unfulfilling, so that life expectancy may, to some extent, serve as a proxy for other variables of importance as well. Furthermore, if we shift our attention from life expectancy to these other important variables, the relationship with GNP per head does not become any more immediate. Indeed, some of the variables related to living conditions, e.g. the prevalence of crime and violence, may sometimes have even a perverse relationship with average material prosperity.

This is a problem that applies not only to the poor, developing countries, but also to the richer ones. In fact, various studies of perception of welfare done in western Europe have suggested a rather limited role of real income in self-assessment of personal welfare [see van Praag (1978), Allardt (1981), van Herwaarden and Kapteyn (1981), Erikson, Hansen, Ringen and Uusitalo (1986)]. Reliance of self-assessment based on questionnaire information does, of course, have some problematic features also, but nevertheless there is enough evidence here to question the rather straightforward connection between material prosperity and welfare that is sometimes taken for granted in standard economic analysis.

In drawing a distinction between development and growth, a number of different sources of contrast have to be clearly distinguished from each other. First of all, insofar as economic growth is concerned only with GNP per head, it leaves out the question of the *distribution* of that GNP among the population. It is, of course, possible for a country to have an expansion of GNP per head, while its distribution becomes more unequal, possibly even the poorest groups going down absolutely in terms of their own real incomes. Noting this type of possibility does not question the relevance of income considerations as such, but argues against taking only an aggregated view of incomes. Undoubtedly, some of the cases in which achievements in living conditions fall far behind what might be expected on the basis of average per capita GNP (e.g. in South Africa, and to a lesser extent in Brazil and Mexico, as reflected in Table 1.1) relate closely to the distributional question. Indeed, the contrast can be brought out even more sharply by looking also at the distribution of life expectancy (and of mortality and morbidity rates) over the population (e.g. between the racial and class groups in South Africa, and class and regional categories in Brazil and Mexico).

A second source of difference between growth and development relates to the question of *externality* and *non-marketability*. The GNP captures only those means of well-being that happen to be transacted in the market, and this leaves out benefits and costs that do not have a price-tag attached to them. Even when non-marketed goods are included (e.g. peasant outputs consumed at home), the evaluation is usually restricted to those goods which have a market and for which market prices can be easily traced.[4] The importance of what is left out has become increasingly recognized, as awareness of the contribution of the environment and natural resources to our well-being has grown [see Dasgupta and Heal (1979), Dasgupta (1982)]. The argument can be applied to the social environment as well as to the physical one [see Hirschman (1958, 1970)].

Third, even when markets do exist, the valuation of commodities in the GNP will reflect the *biases* that the markets may have. There are important problems in dealing with different relative prices in different parts of the world. As has been shown by Usher (1968, 1976) and others, this can make quite a substantial quantitative difference. Even for a given economy, the relative importance that is attached to one commodity compared with another may be distorted vis-à-vis what might be achieved under perfectly competitive conditions if the market operations happen to be institutionally "imperfect", or if equilibrium outcomes do not prevail. There is an extensive welfare-economic literature on this, and the connection of that range of issues with the concept of development is obvious enough.

Fourth, the real income enjoyed by a person in a given year reflects at best the extent of well-being enjoyed by that person at that period of time. However, in assessing what kind of a life the person has succeeded in living, we have to take a more *integral* view of that person's life. The issues to be considered include interdependences over time [e.g. inter-period complementarities emphasized by Hicks (1965) among others], as well as the more elementary question of the *length* of that life. It is easy to construct two scenarios in which the time series of *per capita* GNP as well as *aggregate* GNP (and, of course, the population size) happen to be exactly the same in the two cases (period by period), but in one society people live twice as long as those in the other. There are difficult evaluative problems in judging what the "trade-off" should be between larger number, on the one hand, and longer life, on the other, but no matter in which

---

[4]Even when such market prices exist, reflecting the balance of actual demand and supply, the proper valuation of the non-traded units of tradeable variables may be far from easy. On the problem of including the value of leisure and leisure time expended at home, in the light of wage rates, see Nordhaus and Tobin (1972).

direction one argues, there is an issue here of great importance to the assessment of development that is completely obscured by the GNP information. Even if GNP did everything it is expected to do (and there are very strong reasons for doubting this possibility), even then the information provided by GNP must remain fundamentally inadequate for the concept of development.

Finally, it must be noted that GNP is, in fact, a measure of the amount of the *means* of well-being that people have, and it does not tell us what the people involved are succeeding in getting out of these means, given their ends. To take a crude example, two persons with different metabolic rates and consuming the same amount of food will quite possibly achieve rather different levels of nourishment. Insofar as being well nourished is an important end, their actual achievements will be different, despite the congruence of their command over the *means* of achieving nourishment. As it happens, "poverty lines" have typically been defined in developing countries in the light of the "requirements" of some basic commodities, in particular food, and the inter-personal as well as the intra-personal variability in the relationship between food and nourishment have been, in this context, a major problem to deal with.[5]

Ultimately, the assessment of development achieved cannot be a matter only of quantification of the *means* of that achievement. The concept of development has to take note of the actual achievements themselves. The assessment of development has to go well beyond GNP information, *even when* the other difficulties referred to earlier (such as distributional variation, presence of externalities and non-marketabilities, imperfect price mechanisms, etc.) were somehow overcome.

3. Characteristics, functionings, and living

Insofar as development is concerned with the achievement of a better life, the focus of development analysis has to include the nature of the life that people succeed in living. This incorporates, of course, the *length* of the life itself, and thus life expectancy data have an immediate relevance to the living standard and through that to the concept of development. But the nature of the life that people succeed in living in each period is also a matter of importance. People value their ability to do certain things and to achieve certain types of beings (such as being well nourished, being free from avoidable morbidity, being able to move about as desired, and so on). These "doings" and "beings" may be generically called "functionings" of a person.

The well-being of a person can be seen as an evaluation of the functionings achieved by that person. This approach has been implicitly used by Adam Smith (1776) and Karl Marx (1844) in particular, and more recently in the literature on

[5] For arguments on different sides of this debate, see Bardhan (1974), Sukhatme (1977), Srinivasan (1982), Lipton (1983), Gopalan (1983), Dasgupta and Ray (1986), Kakwani (1986), Osmani (1987).

"the quality of life" [see, for example, Morris (1979), Streeten (1981)].[6] It can be more explicitly developed, conceptually defended, and empirically applied [on this see Sen (1980, 1985a)]. The functioning achievements are, of course, causally related to commodity possession and use, and thus the constituent elements of the GNP do enter the *determination* of functioning achievements. Indeed, these elements are the means of which the functionings are the ends – a point of view clearly presented by Aristotle in *Nicomachean Ethics* and *Politics*.

In recent departures in consumer theory, developed by Gorman (1956, 1976) and Lancaster (1966, 1971), commodities are viewed in terms of their characteristics. This is clearly a move in the right direction as far as well-being is concerned, since the functionings achieved by a person relate to the characteristics of the commodities used. On the other hand, no index of characteristics as such could possibly serve as an indicator of the achievements of a person, since the conversion of characteristics into functionings can and does vary from person to person. Characteristics of commodities are impersonal in a way that functionings cannot be, since the latter are features of *persons*, whereas the former are features of *commodities*. The relationships between commodities, characteristics, and functionings, and the sources of variations in their interconnections, have been discussed elsewhere [see Sen (1980, 1985a, 1985b)].

The achievement of functionings depends not only on the commodities owned by the person in question, but also on the availability of public goods, and the possibility of using private goods freely provided by the state. Such achievements as being healthy, being well-nourished, being literate, etc. would depend naturally also on the public provisions of health services, medical facilities, educational arrangements, and so on. In recognizing this, there is no need yet to enter into the debate, which is important but need not be pursued here, as to whether provision by the state is a cost-effective way of enhancing the relevant functionings involved. That debate about development strategy will involve logistic and engineering issues, which require careful assessment. What is being pointed out here is the importance of judging development in terms of *functionings achieved*, and of seeing in that light the availability and use of the *means* to those functionings (in the form of possession of commodities, availability of public goods, and so on).

4. Freedom and capability

One of the functionings that may be thought to be particularly important in assessing the nature of development is the freedom to choose. Sometimes this

---

[6] See also Sen (1973, 1985b), Adelman (1975), Scanlon (1975), Gwatkin, Wilcox and Wray (1980), Floud and Wachter (1982), Fogel, Engerman and Trussell (1982), Gopalan (1983), Panikar and Soman (1984), UNICEF (1986), Chen (1986), Williams (1987).

concept is used in a rather narrow and limited way, so that the *actual* freedom to choose is not assessed, but instead the focus is on whether there are *restraints* imposed by others that hinder the actual freedom. That "negative" perspective, much pursued in the libertarian literature, does have, of course, philosophical standing of its own [see Hayek (1960), Berlin (1969), Nozick (1974)]. However, what is important to recognize in the present context is the fact that the "negative" emphasis on the absence of restraint is part of a moral approach that does not judge the goodness of a society in terms of the actual qualities of life *achieved* by the members of the society, and concentrates instead on the correctness of the *processes* through which these and other achievements come about. It is possible to debate whether the particular insistence on *processes* that do not involve such restraint is, in fact, as convincing as it clearly is to some exponents of this point of view. But in the present context, we need not enter into that large and important debate. It is sufficient here to note that as far as the living standards of the people are concerned, there is no escape from focusing on *achievements*, and processes come into all this mainly as means to and antecedents of those achievements, rather than being *independently* valuable in this context.

However, the *positive* freedom to be able to choose is, in fact, an important functioning on its own rights. Two persons who have identical achievements of *other* functionings may not still be seen as enjoying the same level of well-being if one of the two has no option to choose any other bundle of functionings, whereas the second person has significant options. Being able to freely choose to lead a particular life may be a point of a richer description of the life we lead, including the choices we are able to make [on this perspective, see Sen (1985a)].

A person's capability can be seen as the set of alternative functioning n-tuples any one of which the person can choose. One way of introducing the importance of freedom in the determination of well-being is to see well-being as a function not only of the actual functioning achievement, but also of the capability set from which that n-tuple of functionings is chosen. In this way of formally characterizing the problem, the list of functionings need not include "choosing" as such, but the value of choosing will be reflected in the evaluation by making that evaluation depend both on the chosen n-tuple of functionings, *and* on the nature and the range of the capability set itself.

There are difficult analytical problems involved in the evaluation of a set, in the light of the freedom it offers [on this see Koopmans (1964), Kreps (1979), Sen (1985b)]. But insofar as the assessment of the quality of life and of development achievements involves these considerations, it is important not to lose sight of this perspective, even though it may not be immediately possible to make extensive use of this approach in actual empirical exercises.

A different way of looking at this problem involves incorporating the freedom to choose in the nature of the functionings themselves by defining them in a "refined" way [see Sen (1985a)]. Choosing to do x when one could have chosen any member of a set S, can be defined as a "refined functioning" x/S. The point can be brought out by considering the functioning of "fasting". When a person fasts he is clearly starving, but the nature of that functioning includes the choice *not* to so starve. A person who has no option but to starve (because, say, of his extreme poverty) cannot be said to be fasting. In assessing the achievements of the persons and of the society, the distinction between fasting and willy-nilly starving may well be very important. The route of "refined functionings", taking note of substantive exercise of choice, provides one particular way of incorporating the aspect of freedom in the assessment of functionings.

5. Weights and rankings

It should be clear that the perspective of functionings and capabilities specifies a *space* in which evaluation is to take place, rather than proposing one particular formula for evaluation. The exercise has to begin with an identification of valuable functionings. In the context of economic development, there might well be considerable agreement as to what functionings are valuable, even though there might be disagreement on the *relative* values to be attached to the different functionings. When an agreed list has been arrived at, the approach of "dominance" provides a *minimal* partial order on that space (in terms of greater achievement in *every* respect).

To go further than this will require more articulate evaluation functions. But these evaluations need not be based on a unique set of "indifference curves". The relative values may be specified as belonging to particular ranges, and corresponding to such specification of ranges, the overall ranking may be a partial order more extensive than the minimal dominance order but probably well short of a complete ordering. As the ranges of relative values are narrowed, the partial ordering will be extended. The mathematical technology involved in such evaluation (based on "intersection partial orderings") has been extensively used in other contexts [see, for example, Sen (1970), Blackorby (1975), Fine (1975), Basu (1979)]. The important thing to note here is that the problem of evaluation need not be seen in an all-or-nothing way. It is possible to extend the partial order by narrowing the ranges of weights, and how far one can go on the basis of agreement on evaluation will depend contingently on the nature of the exercise in question.

Even the specification of the space of functionings and capabilities does, however, have considerable cutting power. Achievements of real income and opulence may differ quite substantially from that of functionings and capabilities. To give just one example, in a comparison of the states in India, Kerala always figures as one of the poorest, in terms of GNP per head. On the other hand, in terms of many of the more important functionings, including living long, being educated, etc. Kerala does better than any other Indian state. Given this contrast, it is interesting to ask whether Kerala should be seen as having *more* achievement *or* rather *less* than the other Indian states. This relates to a question of considerable importance to the formulation of the concept of development. The argument for placing Kerala at the high end, rather than the low end, turns on the evaluation of functionings and capabilities as the right approach to development.

A crude assessment of functionings and capabilities in terms only of a few indicators like longevity, literacy, etc. will, of course, be inadequate and have to be revised and extended, but the exercise can be systematically done if and only if the concept of development is seen in terms of ends rather than means. As it happens, use of information regarding *morbidity* detracts somewhat from Kerala's high record, since the extent of illness seems to be rather large in Kerala, in comparison with some other Indian states, even after taking note of the greater "awareness" of health conditions in a population that is more educated and better served by public health services [on this see Pankar and Soman (1984), Kumar (1987)]. The adoption of the perspective of functionings and capabilities will call for a great deal of empirical as well as theoretical work being done within that general format.

As was argued earlier, that format is, of course, an old one in economics, even though the focus on opulence on the one hand and utility on the other has tended to deflect attention from that fundamental concern. Aside from discussions by Aristotle, Smith, and Marx, to which reference was made earlier, it should be mentioned that ad hoc uses of this perspective can be found extensively in the economic literature. In many planning exercises, the specification of objectives has included a clear recognition of the importance of certain functionings, e.g. in the specification of a "minimum level of living" [see Pant (1962)]. The literature on development indicators has also brought in some of these functionings, along with many other types of variables [see, for example, Adelman and Morris (1973), Adelman (1975), Kakwani (1981), Streeten (1981)].

The literature on "basic needs" also relates to this question, since the specification of basic needs of commodities has to be related to the recognition of their role in the achievement of functionings. Even though the *space* in which the basic needs have typically been specified has been that of commodities rather than of functionings and capabilities, the motivation clearly does relate to attaching importance to the latter [see, for example, Streeten (1981), and Streeten et al. (1981)].

The literature on basic needs has been growing rapidly in the recent years, but clear discussions of this question can be found even in Pigou's classic book *Economics of Welfare* (1952). Of course, Pigou related his focus on the command over a minimal basket of commodities to the utilitarian perspective, whereas in the modern literature quite often the foundational features have not been specified. It is arguable that these foundational questions are ultimately quite important for the concept of development, and it is precisely in that context that the capability approach provides a different strategy of assessment, more clearly geared to the evaluation of living as such rather than merely of the happiness generated by that living (as in the utilitarian approach). This is not the occasion to pursue the philosophical differences further [I have tried to do this elsewhere; Sen (1985a)], but there is no escape from recognizing the importance of this foundational question underlying the concept of development.

6. Values, instruments, and objects

One of the difficulties in adequately characterizing the concept of development arises from the essential role of evaluation in that concept. What is or is not regarded as a case of "development" depends inescapably on the notion of what things are valuable to promote.[7] The dependence of the concept of development on evaluation becomes a problem to the extent that (1) the valuation functions accepted by different people differ from each other, and (2) the process of change involved in development alters the valuations of the people involved. These two problems may be called respectively "value-heterogeneity" and "value-endogeneity".

The problem of value-heterogeneity was already addressed earlier in the context of valuations of functionings and capabilities. It was pointed out that even when there are disagreements on the relative values to be attached to different functionings and capabilities, it is still possible to get uncontroversial partial orderings, based minimally on "dominance", but more extensively on "intersections" of the class of acceptable valuation functions. It is, of course, a matter of substantive normative analysis to argue in favor of some valuation functions against others, and insofar as the ranges of disagreement could be reduced through this means, the scope and reach of "intersection partial orderings" can be correspondingly enhanced.

Much of traditional development economics has proceeded on the basis of implicitly assuming a fairly large intersection of valuations related to objects of development. Even though the original discussions of economic development had tended to concentrate on the GNP and real income as such, the evaluation underlying that approach was implicitly based on assuming a widespread agreement on the *ends* to which real income and opulence are *means*. The shift in the focus of attention to basic needs, quality of life, and functionings and capabilities in general, would not change the assumed agreement on the underlying basis of

---

[7]On this general question, see Marglin and Marglin (1986).

development analysis. The problem of value-heterogeneity is undoubtedly serious, but it is by no means absurd to think that the actual extent of agreement is indeed quite large. Most of the debates on development policy have tended to concentrate on the relationship between policy instruments and *agreed* ends (accepted in the analysis of policy).

It is, however, possible that a more explicit characterization of well-being and of people's freedom to achieve what they would value achieving will increase the demand for data and information in the conceptualization of development. For example, the scope for using more demographic and health-related information is certainly great in assessing the real achievements of development, and recent works dealing with the past as well as the present have outlined the necessity of seeking this type of information, neglected in traditional development analysis.[8]

It is possible that once these informational needs are recognized, there might again emerge a fair degree of consensus on what is to be valued and how. On the other hand, it is also possible that there might be much disagreement regarding the respective importance of different aspects of well-being. Some of these differences might involve scientific argumentation as to the precise role of different variables in human functioning. For example, whether an expansion of body size related to the process of economic development is an achievement of importance can be disputed in terms of the alleged presence or absence of relations between body size and performance. The conversion of nutrients into body characteristics *and* the role of body characteristics in achieving valuable functionings both call for close scrutiny.[9]

Other disputes may turn not on factual relations, but on what is to be regarded as an important part of a valuable life and how valuable it is. It would be idle to pretend that disputes on the relative importance of different types of functionings can be fully resolved on the basis of scientific argument alone. It is, therefore, particularly important to build into the concept of development the possibility of persistent incompleteness in ranking. Seeing the agreed ranking as the intersection of the partly divergent valuation functions must, of necessity, entail this.

The value-endogeneity problem raises issues of a somewhat different kind from those raised by value-heterogeneity. With value-heterogeneity the intersection partial ordering may have to be silent on some comparisons, but insofar as judgements are possible, they can be made on the basis of a *given* valuation function (whether or not complete). Value-endogeneity, on the other hand, raises what is, in some ways, a deeper problem, to wit, the *dependence* of the valuation function on the thing that is being valued. The process of development may bring about changes in what is regarded as valuable and what weights are attached to

---

[8] See, in particular, Sen (1973, 1985b), Floud and Wachter (1982), Fogel, Engerman and Trussell (1982), Gopalan (1983), Panikar and Soman (1984), UNICEF (1986), Williams (1987).

[9] For different views on this subject, see, for example, Sukhatme (1977), Srinivasan (1982), Gopalan (1983), Fogel (1986), Dasgupta and Ray (1986), Kakwani (1986), Osmani (1987).

these objects. There are complex philosophical issues involved in judging changed conditions, when those changes bring about alterations in the values attached to these conditions.[10]

However, in this problem too there is a possibility of using an "intersection" technique. A change may be judged to be an improvement if it is superior *both* in terms of the antecedent values *and* subsequent values, i.e. prospectively better than the available alternatives and also retrospectively better than the rejected alternatives. In this case, there may be at least a pragmatic argument in favor of regarding this to be a genuine improvement, even though a purist might doubt whether such judgements can at all be taken as definitive when they are *generally* volatile (even though not, as it happens, in a way that affects the judgement of *this particular* change). Even this pragmatic justification will not obtain if the judgements based on antecedent values differ on the particular issue under discussion from those based on subsequent ones. It is possible for a change to be regarded as worse in terms of the earlier values, but better in terms of valuations made after the event.

In the more philosophical literature, the case for seeing valuations as having a certain measure of objectivity has increasingly gained ground compared with the situation that obtained some decades ago.[11] The "objectivist" position is, in fact, in line with very old traditions in ethics and political economy (going back at least to Aristotle), even though it was extremely unfashionable at the time development economics emerged as a subject, when the dominant schools of methodology were "positivism" of various types. The "objectivist" position would tend to support the possibility of resolving the conflicts involved in intertemporal changes in values by rational assessment.

These foundational issues will not be purused further here. It is sufficient for the present purpose to note that no matter what view is taken of the nature of valuation, the practical problems of making judgement in the situation of value-heterogeneity and value-endogeneity must be enormous. Even if these differences could in principle be resolved through rational assessment, the possibility of actually resolving these differences in practice may be severely limited. Given that fact, the necessity of settling for partial orders in response to value-endogeneity as well as value-heterogeneity is, to some extent, inescapable.

Explicitly facing these problems of valuation has some advantages which should be emphasized. First, separating out relatively uncontroversial judgements from the controversial ones related to value-heterogeneity and value-endogeneity, helps to clarify what can be asserted with some confidence, and what can be said only with much greater hesitation. A lot of the debates on policy making in the

---

[10] For an interesting discussion of this question, see Elster (1979, 1983). Some similar issues are raised in consumer theory when tastes are taken as endogenous [see, for example, von Weizsacker (1971), Pollak (1978)]. See also Hirschman (1970).

[11] See in particular, McDowell (1981), Nagel (1980, 1986), Hurley (1985), Wiggins (1985).

context of economic development relates to valuation problems that are not unduly problematic. Whether state intervention or reliance on the market may be better means of enhancing living conditions is, of course, both important and controversial, but the controversy has typically centered, rightly, on the relationship between means and achievements, rather than on differences in valuation. By explicitly facing the sources of the difficulties in valuation, it is possible to give those debates a deeper foundation, without compromising the broad motivation underlying development economics.

Second, in some parts of the development literature, values have been treated as if they are simply *instrumental* to economic development, rather than the ultimate basis of judging the nature of development itself. For example, encouraging the valuation of profits and that of enterprise has often been seen as good *means* of development. Certainly, in terms of the dependence of economic growth on particular motivations these propositions can be helpfully presented and assessed. On the other hand, it is also important to recognize that values are not *just* instruments, but also views about what should or should not be promoted. This dual role of values – both important and neither sacrificable – was recognized clearly enough by pioneers of modern economics, including Adam Smith (1776, 1790) and Karl Marx (1844, 1875). The foundational role of values can be neglected in favor of an instrumental view only by trivializing the basis of the concept of development.

7. Conclusion

The concept of development is by no means unproblematic. The different problems underlying the concept have become clearer over the years on the basis of conceptual discussions as well as from insights emerging from empirical work. Insofar as these problems have become clearer, something of substance has in fact been achieved, and the demise of the brashness which characterized the initiation of development economics need not be seen entirely as a loss. A clearer recognition of the difficulties and problems is certainly a step in the direction of enhancing our ability to tackle them.

Work on valuational problems will undoubtedly continue. Meanwhile, the agreed valuations in the form of emphasizing the importance of certain basic achievements in life make it possible for us to pursue practical debates on policy and action on the basis of an acceptable valuational foundation. Since many of these debates relate to matters of life and death, well-being and illness, happiness and misery, freedom and vulnerability, the underlying objectives are perspicuous enough and command broad agreement. Work on development economics need not await a complete "solution" of the concept of development.

References

Adelman, I. (1975) 'Development economics – a reassessment of goals', *American Economic Review, Papers and Proceedings*, 65.

Adelman, I. and C.T. Morris (1973) *Economic growth and social equity in developing countries*. Stanford: Stanford University Press.

Allardt, E. (1981) 'Experiences from the comparative Scandinavian welfare study, with a bibliography of the project', *European Journal of Political Research*, 9.

Anand, S. and C. Harris (1986) 'Food and living standard: implications for food strategies', WIDER, Helsinki, mimeo.

Baran, P. (1957) *Political economy of growth*. New York: Monthly Review Press.

Bardhan, P.K. (1974) 'On the incidence of poverty in rural India in the sixties', in: T.N. Srinivasan and P.K. Bardhan, eds., *Poverty and income distribution in India*. Calcutta: Statistical Publishing Society.

Basu, K. (1979) *Revealed preference of government*. Cambridge: Cambridge University Press.

Bauer, P.T. (1971) *Dissent on development*. London: Weidenfeld and Nicholson.

Berlin, I. (1969) *Four essays on liberty*. Oxford: Clarendon Press.

Blackorby, C. (1975) 'Degrees of cardinality and aggregate partial ordering', *Econometrica*, 43.

Chen. L.C. (1986) 'Primary health care in developing countries: Overcoming operational, technical, and social barriers', *Lancet*, 2.

Dasgupta, A.K. (1954) 'Keynesian economics and underdeveloped countries', *Economic Weekly*, 6 (January 26). Reprinted in *Planning and economic growth*. London: Allen & Unwin (1965).

Dasgupta, P. (1982) *The control of resources*. Oxford: Blackwells.

Dasgupta, P. and G. Heal (1979) *Economic theory and exhaustible resources*. London: James Nisbet; Cambridge: Cambridge University Press.

Dasgupta, P. and D. Ray (1986) 'Adapting to undernutrition: Clinical evidence and its implications', WIDER, Helsinki, working paper. Forthcoming in Drèze and Sen (1988).

Datta, B. (1952) *Economics of industrialization*. Calcutta: World Press.

Dobb, M.H. (1951) *Some aspects of economic development*. Dehli: Dehli School of Economics.

Drèze, J. and A. Sen (1988) *Hunger: Economic and policy*. Oxford: Clarendon Press. To be published.

Elster, J. (1979) *Ulysses and the sirens*. Cambridge: Cambridge University Press.

Elster, J. (1983) *Sour grapes*. Cambridge: Cambridge University Press.

Erikson, R., E.J. Hansen, S. Ringen, and H. Uusitalo (1986) *The Scandinavian way: Welfare state and welfare research*. Forthcoming.

Fine, B. (1975) "A note on 'interpersonal comparisons and partial comparability'", *Econometrica*, 43.

Floud, R. and K.W. Wachter (1982) 'Poverty and physical stature: Evidence on the standard of living of London boys 1770–1870', *Social Science History*, 6.

Fogel, R.W. (1986) 'Nutrition and the decline in mortality since 1700: Some additional preliminary findings', National Bureau of Economic Research, Cambridge MA, working paper 182.

Fogel, R.W., S.L. Engerman, and J. Trussell (1982) 'Exploring the use of data on height: The analysis of long-term trends in nutrition, labour productivity', *Social Science History*, 6.

Gopalan, C. (1983) 'Measurement of undernutrition: Biological considerations', *Economic and Political Weekly*, 19 (April 9).

Gorman, W.M. (1956) 'The demand for related goods', Iowa Experimental Station, Ames, IA, journal paper J3129.

Gorman, W.M. (1976) 'Tricks with utility function', in: M.J. Artis and A.R. Nobay, eds., *Essays in economic analysis*. Cambridge: Cambridge University Press.

Grant, J.P. (1978) *Disparity reduction rates in social indicators*. Washington, DC: Overseas Development Council.

Gwatkin, D.R., J.R. Wilcox, and J.D. Wray (1980) 'The policy implications of field experience in primary health and nutrition', *Social Science and Medicine*, 14C.

Hayek, F.A. (1960) *The constitution of liberty*. London: Routledge & Kegan Paul.

Hicks, J.R. (1965) *Capital and growth*. Oxford: Clarendon Press.

Hirschman, A.O. (1958) *The strategy of economic development*. New Haven: Yale University Press.

Hirschman, A.O. (1970) *Exit, voice and loyalty*. Cambridge, MA: Harvard University Press.

Honderich, T., ed. (1985) *Morality and objectivity*. London: Routledge.

Hull, C.H., ed. (1899) *The economic writings of Sir William Petty*. Cambridge: Cambridge University Press.

Hurley, S. (1985) 'Objectivity and disagreement', in: T. Honderich (1985).

Kakwani, N.C. (1981) 'Welfare measures: An international comparison', *Journal of Development Economics*, 8.

Kakwani, N.C. (1986) 'On measuring undernutrition', WIDER, Helsinki, working paper. Forthcoming in *Oxford Economic Papers*.

Koopmans, T.C. (1964) 'On the flexibility of future preferences', in: M.W. Shelly and G.L. Bryan, eds., *Human judgements and optimality*. New York: Wiley.

Kreps, D.M. (1979) "A representation theorem for 'preference for flexibility'", *Econometrica*, 47.

Kumar, B.G. (1987) 'Poverty and public policy : Government intervention and levels of living in Kerala, India', D. Phil. dissertation, Oxford University. To be published.

Lancaster, K.J. (1966) 'A new approach to consumer theory', *Journal of Political Economy*, 74.

Lancaster, K.J. (1971) *Consumer demand: A new approach*. New York: Columbia University Press.

Lewis, W.A. (1955) *The theory of economic growth*. Homewood, IL: Irwin.

Lipton, M. (1983) *Poverty, undernutrition and hunger*, World Bank Staff Working Paper. Washington, DC: World Bank.

McDowell, J. (1981) 'Noncognitivism and rule-following', in: S.H. Holtzman and C.M. Leich, eds., *Wittgenstein: To follow a rule*. London: Routledge & Kegan Paul.

McMurrin, S. (1980) *Tanner lectures on human values*, vol. I. Cambridge: Cambridge University Press.

Mandelbaum (Martin), K. (1945) *The industrialization of backward areas*. Oxford: Blackwell.

Marglin, F. and S. Marglin, eds. (1986) 'Development and technological transformation in traditional societies: Alternative approachers', papers presented at a WIDER conference. To be published.

Marx, K. (1844) *The economic and philosophic manuscript of 1844*, English translation. London: Lawrence & Wishart.

Marx, K. (1875) *Critique of the Gotha programme*, English translation. New York: International Publishers.

Morris, M.D. (1979) *Measuring the conditions of the world's poor: The physical quality of life index*. Oxford: Pergamon.

Nagel, T. (1980) 'The limits of objectivity', in: S. McMurrin (1980).

Nagel, T. (1986). *The view from nowhere*. Oxford: Clarendon Press.

Nordhaus, W. and J. Tobin (1972) 'Is growth obsolete?', in: National Bureau of Economic Research, *Economic growth: Fiftieth anniversary colloquium*. New York: NBER.

Nozick, R. (1974) *Anarchy, state and utopia*. Oxford: Blackwell.

Nurkse, R. (1953) *Problems of capital formation in underdeveloped countries*. Oxford: Blackwell.

Osmani, S.R. (1987) 'Nutrition and the economics of food', WIDER, Helsinki, working paper. Forthcoming in Drèze and Sen (1988).

Panikar, P.G.K. and C.R. Soman (1984) *Health status of Kerala*. Trivandrum: Centre for Development Studies.

Pant, P. et al. (1962) *Perspective of development 1961–1976. Implication of planning for a minimum level of living*. New Delhi: Planning Commission of India.

Parfit, D. (1984) *Reasons and persons*. Oxford: Clarendon Press.

Petty, W. (1676) *Political arithmetick*. Republished in: C.H. Hull (1899).

Pigou, A.C. (1952) *The economics of welfare*, 4th ed., with eight new appendices. London: Macmillan.

Pollak, R.A. (1978) 'Endogenous tastes in demand and welfare analysis', *American Economic Review, Papers and Proceedings*, 68.

Rosenstein-Rodan, P. (1943) 'Problems of industrialization in Eastern and Southeastern Europe', *Economic Journal*, 53.

Scanlon, T.M. (1975) 'Preference and urgency', *Journal of Philosophy*, 73.

Sen, A.K. (1970) 'Interpersonal aggregation and partial comparability', *Econometrica*, 38; 'A correction', *Econometrica*, 40.

Sen, A.K. (1973) 'On the development of basic income indicators to supplement GNP measures', *Economic Bulletin for Asia and the Far East (United Nations)*, 24.

Sen, A.K. (1980) 'Equality of what?', in: S. McMurrin (1980).

Sen, A.K. (1985a) 'Well-being, agency and freedom: The Dewey lectures 1984', *Journal of Philosophy*, 82.

Sen, A.K. (1985b) *Commodities and capabilities*. Amsterdam: North-Holland.

Singer, H.W. (1952) 'The mechanics of economic development', *Indian Economic Review*. Reprinted in: A.N. Agarwala and A.P. Singh, eds., *The economics of underdevelopment*. London: Oxford University Press.

Smith, A. (1776) *An inquiry into the nature and causes of the wealth of nations*. Republished; edited by R.H. Campbell and A.S. Skinner. Oxford: Clarendon Press (1976).

Smith, A. (1790) *The theory of moral sentiments*, rev. ed. Republished; edited by D.D. Raphael and A.L. Macfie. Oxford: Clarendon Press (1975).

Srinivasan, T.N. (1982) 'Hunger: Defining it, estimating its global incidence and alleviating it', in: D. Gale Johnson and E. Schuh, eds., *Role of markets in the world food economy*.

Stewart, F. (1985) *Planning to meet basic needs*. London: Macmillan.

Streeten, P. (1981) *Development perspectives*. London: Macmillan.

Streeten, P. et al. (1981) *First things first: Meeting basic needs in developing countries*. New York: Oxford University Press.

Sukhatme, P.V. (1977) *Nutrition and poverty*. New Delhi: Indian Agricultural Research Institute.

UNICEF (1986) *The state of the world's children 1986*. New York: United Nations.

Usher, D. (1968) *The price mechanism and the meaning of national income statistics*. Oxford: Clarendon Press.

Usher, D. (1976) 'The measurement of real income', *Review of Income and Wealth*, 22.

Van Herwaarden, F.G. and A. Kapteyn (1981) 'Empirical comparison of the shape of welfare functions', *European Economic Review*, 15.

Van Praag, B.M.S. (1978) 'The perception of welfare inequality', *European Economic Review*, 10.

von Weizsacker, C.C. (1971) 'Notes on endogenous changes in tastes', *Journal of Economic Theory*, 3.

Wiggins, D. (1985) 'Claims of need', in Honderich (1985).

Williams, A. (1987) 'What is wealth and who creates it?', York University, mimeo.

World Bank (1986) *World Development Report 1986*. New York: Oxford University Press.

Chapter 2

THE ROOTS OF DEVELOPMENT THEORY

W. ARTHUR LEWIS

Princeton University

Contents

1.	Introduction	28
2.	Sectoral imbalance	28
3.	Overall balance	31
4.	Organization	34
5.	Conclusion	36
	References	37

Handbook of Development Economics, Volume I, Edited by H. Chenery and T.N. Srinivasan
© Elsevier Science Publishers B.V., 1988

1. Introduction

The theory of economic development established itself in Britain in the century and a half running from about 1650 to Adam Smith's *The Wealth of Nations* (1776). The purpose of this chapter is to investigate how much of the development theory of today is already to be found in the writings of the eighteenth century.

There was of course voluminous writing before 1650, but this differs so much in objective and in methodology that it would prove rewarding only to specialist historians. Jumping back a hundred years we are amongst the schoolmen. Their purpose was to reconcile modern economic life and institutions (especially trading, interest, profit-making, and the right to hold private property) with ethics and religion; and their method was to quote from the Bible and the writings of the early Church. The early mercantilists, who follow, are concerned with strengthening the military power of the state, in part to unify the country, and in part to fight external enemies (especially the Dutch and the French). The military problem is as acute now for some Third World states as it was at that time; although their remedy – to keep the king's war chest full of gold – would not in these days command much support. By the time we have crossed 1650 our economists are no longer occupied with military power. The wealth of the king moves from center stage, and the income of the nation, as reflected in the balance of trade, has taken its place. Economics has also begun to be quantitative, under the leadership of Sir William Petty.

The writers of the seventeenth and eighteenth centuries are often disparaged for being confused and confusing. Much of this is due to misuse of words, as in treating as synonyms for wealth: money, gold, treasure, balance of trade, and balance of payments. With hindsight it is easy to recognize anomalies of language, and to correct for them. We can also deal with misunderstandings due to changes in institutional backgrounds. With such adjustments eighteenth-century economics was surprisingly advanced. We also reduce the burden by concentrating on the writings of the three superstars of the eighteenth century, Hume, Steuart and Adam Smith, and two whose influence was more restricted, Cantillon and Wallace. We have also set aside the French and German authors. [See Hume (1748), Cantillon (1755), Steuart (1767), Smith (1776), Wallace (1753).]

2. Sectoral imbalance

We approach the subject by assuming that a manufacturer hires more employees and increases his output, and that the relevant elasticities are such that he must buy more raw materials and sell more manufactures. If this is a closed economy, the terms of trade will move against manufactures, and if this goes far enough, the revenue required to sustain the increase in the output of manufactures will not materialize. The size of the non-farm population depends on the size of the agricultural surplus.

This doctrine goes back very far. Its main proponents in the eighteenth century are Hume, Steuart, and Adam Smith. Here, in a nutshell, is Smith's formulation:

> It is the surplus produce of the country only, or what is over and above the maintenance of the cultivators, that constitutes the subsistence of the town, which can therefore increase only with the increase of the surplus produce [Smith (1776, p. 357)].

But there is a way out. Remove the assumption of a closed economy and the towns are no longer limited by the size of the domestic agricultural surplus. They can import and export instead, leaving it to the agricultural community to do the same, or to ignore what is happening in the manufacturing sector or both (this depends on the size of the export multiplier). This alternative is recorded by Adam Smith:

> The town indeed may not always derive its whole subsistence from the country in its neighborhood, or even from the territory to which it belongs, but from very distant countries; and this, though it forms no exception from the general rule, has occasioned considerable variations in the progress of opulence in different ages and nations [Smith (1776, p. 357)].

The existence of the alternative shifts the constraint on growth of output from the size of the agricultural surplus to potential foreign exchange earnings. But there is also much dispute as to the strength of the foreign exchange constraint. Structuralists maintain that it is very hard to raise the rate of growth of exports, or to cut imports; while "market" economists claim that elasticities are adequate, and that failure to rely on them is mistaken. The two-gap model was invented in the 1950s to illustrate the difficulty of earning foreign exchange. Presumably the facts of each case must be considered separately. It seems likely that the recent years (1973–1988) have been more difficult to manipulate than the two preceding decades.

The debate on the gains from trade had been in progress for two centuries, and would still be in progress two centuries later. Here is Hume on the subject:

> There seems to be a happy concurrence of causes in human affairs, which checks the growth of trade and riches, and hinders them from being confined entirely to one people; as might naturally at first be dreaded from the advantages of an established commerce. Where one nation has gotten the start of another in trade, it is very difficult for the latter to regain the ground it has lost; because of the superior industry and skill of the former, and the greater stocks, of which its merchants are possessed, and which enable them to trade

on so much smaller profits. But these advantages are compensated in some measure, by the low price of labor in every nation which has not an extensive commerce, and does not much abound in gold and silver. Manufactures therefore gradually shift their places, leaving those countries and provinces which they have already enriched, and flying to others, whither they are allured by the cheapness of provisions and labor; till they have enriched those also, and are again banished by the same cause [Hume (1748, "Of Money", pp. 34–35)].

Whatever may be the individual case, the general principle remains the same. Foreign exchange and foreign exchange reserves are a potential constraint on growth. This was not fully appreciated after the Second World War. Some Development Plans were made, for instance, in the 1950s without checking that the proposed allocation of resources would provide enough foreign exchange. The consequences of this neglect are painful. As the country runs short of foreign exchange, it is forced ultimately to reduce the import of raw materials and machinery, so factories close and unemployment swells.

I speak of foreign exchange and foreign exchange reserves, but this is an anachronism. Reserves were held in gold or silver, not in paper (bills, notes). The practice of major countries holding their reserves routinely in the form of entries in bankers' books in some other country did not begin until the twentieth century [Lindert (1969)]. When the Mercantilists say that one should have an adequate stock of gold, they sound confused, but when a twentieth-century LDC seeks to increase its foreign exchange reserves, it appears to be highly sensible.

Fundamentally what they were saying was that export industries, or, as we would say, "tradeable goods", are more valuable than non-tradeable goods because they can be turned into foreign currency. They felt for this distinction, but they never quite reached it. On the way they got bogged down in other distinctions. A favorite track led to the question whether agriculture or manufacturing was the more important. The Physiocrats voted for agriculture, since manufacturing does not add to the embodied physical resource; whereas the Mercantilists voted for manufacturing partly because its output was easily tradeable at a profit. Twentieth-century development economists are not caught in such a trap because we do not answer questions involving all-or-nothing. We operate at the margin. So our question is by how much to increase both agriculture and manufacturing, respectively, and our answer depends on time, place, and elasticities. But even today non-professional writing and debating are fascinated by this choice in the language of all-or-nothing. We would also not accept that services are inferior to commodities, because there is no tangible product. This trapped even Adam Smith:

The labor of some of the most respectable orders in the society is, like that of menial servants, unproductive of any value, and does not see or realize itself in any permanent subject or vendible commodity which endures after that labor is past, and for which an equal quantity of labor could afterwards be procured [Smith (1776, p. 315)].

Services add value (in our language) whether they are tradeable, invisible, or permanent. Governments need to be warned about services because they tend to expand health, housing, education, and welfare services much faster than national income grows; but the error turns not on the nature of services but on failure to equilibrate that part of the Development Plan that projects the balance of payments.

In sum, the eighteenth-century economists did not find the precise distinction between tradeable and non-tradeable goods and services, but this was what they were feeling for. They were also conscious of the difficulties of exporting imposed constraints on the growth of the economy. If they were obsessed with the balance of payments, it may also be said that mid-twentieth-century economists underestimated the importance of this constraint, and paid the penalty in almost continual international currency crises from 1913 to the time of writing (1985).

3. Overall balance

Now let us close the economy, and concentrate on internal balance. Suppose that there is a balanced expansion (balanced sectorally as between industry and agriculture), and financed by a proportionately equal increase in the quantity of money. Will the money so spent turn up as income more or less equal to that which was originally expanded? In the language of Keynes: Will aggregate demand equal aggregate supply? This is one of the oldest questions in economic development.

The first point to note is that the money would circulate. Harvey discovered the circulation of the blood in 1616, and this image was in the mind of most economists from then onwards. Nearer home, the idea of circulation is inherent in Quesnay's *Tableau Economique*, but this was not published until 1758. What is known as Say's Law was not formulated until 1821, but the question is much older.

That all costs become equivalent incomes is tautological. The question is: What happens to the incomes? Adam Smith's proposition that: "What is annually saved is as regularly consumed as what is annually spent" [Smith (1776, p. 321)] assumes that all income will be re-spent, if not for consumption, then on investment. But this need not be so. Income receivers may hoard; savers may fail to invest; the chain of expenditure, to use a different metaphor, may break.

Smith would not accept that the level of employment would depend on the division of expenditure between savings and consumption, but he did put forward his own distinction, which is effective in the long run but not in the short. This was the distinction between "productive" and "unproductive" labor. Labor, whose product was sold for a profit, was productive because it yielded an investible surplus. Thus, if a man hires a maid to work in his hotel, her labor is productive, but if he hires her to work in his house, her services are unproductive. So if labor was transferred from productive to unproductive output, the short-term level of employment would not change, but the long-run rate of growth would diminish because of slower growth of the stock of accumulated capital. At the next stage of this argument the sum paid in wages is transmuted into a "fund for the employment of labor". Any change in the structure of national income will alter the proportion of productive to unproductive in the wages fund, and so raise or reduce the growth rate of output in the long run. For example, in our day it was proposed that "surplus labor" be used in the slack agricultural season to build, in parts of India, useful local infrastructure, such as irrigation channels, farm to market roads, schools, etc. Surplus labor can be converted to saving when the labor is willing to work without pay; but if it is not, then extra food and other consumer goods must be mobilized for the villagers along with extra pay. So the program absorbs savings instead of generating savings. One can state this in terms of Smith's formula: unproductive workers are being converted into productive ones, but nothing is gained by doing this, beyond recognizing that the need for savings is a further constraint upon growth even when using surplus labor. The wages fund model spurred a lot of argument among the classical economists but it was confusing and did not contain any useful insight. The fact that it survived into the second half of the nineteenth century is rather surprising. Other writers did not accept Smith's assumptions or his conclusion that output was unaffected by the ratio of consumption to national output. They insisted that what we now call "aggregate demand" might fall short of or exceed aggregate supply, and that it was therefore necessary to bolster consumption if full employment was to be maintained. This was the position taken by Mandeville in his *The Fable of the Bees*, but it was also the opinion of highly regarded economists like Hume, in whose words: "Luxury, when excessive, is the source of many ills; but is in general preferable to sloth and idleness, which would commonly succeed in its place, and are hurtful both to private persons and to the public" [Hume (1748, "On Refinement in the Arts", p. 32)]. This, freely translated, means: unemployment (idleness) is bad, and needs to be minimized by spending on consumer goods; but spend on matters that give general pleasure (art museums, etc.) rather than on loose living.

These economists needed to have a theory of wages, since the level of wages would determine the size of the surplus available for investment after paying off the laborers. The model was already established in which net saving was done only out of profits income, and not out of rent or wages: the formula that would continue to be used over the next century. Here is Hume's version of it:

> There is no other profession, therefore, except merchandise, which can make
> the monied interest considerable, or, in other words can increase industry and,
> by also increasing frugality, give a great command of that industry to particu-
> lar members of the society. Without commerce the state must consist chiefly of
> landed gentry, whose prodigality and expense make a continual demand for
> borrowing; and of peasants who have no sums to supply that demand. The
> money never gathers into large stocks or sums which can be lent at interest. It
> is dispersed into numberless hands, who either squander it on idle show and
> magnificence, or apply it in the purchase of the common necessaries of life.
> Commerce alone assembles it into considerable sums [Hume (1748, "Of
> Interest", p. 54)].

The wage level also determined the supply of labor in the short run, since the
workers were "slothful" and offered themselves for full employment only as
wages fell. Adam Smith thought the opposite, namely that workers worked more
as wages rose. He also thought that wages would rise above subsistence level if
the economy were growing fast. As he said: "It is not the actual greatness of
national wealth, but its continual increase, which occasions [high wages]" [Smith
(1776, p. 69)]. Adam Smith favored a wage level beyond subsistence, but other
economists, preoccupied with the balance of trade, wanted wages to be as close to
subsistence as possible so that exports be stimulated and imports choked by low
British prices. Their position was not unlike that of twentieth-century seekers
after a prices and incomes policy that will enable a country to keep its money
costs per unit of output rising no faster than costs in closely competing countries.

So far we have not considered the effects of money on output. Seventeenth-
and eighteenth-century economists wrote copiously on this subject, establishing
how it would be approached until the twentieth century. We can therefore be
brief.

The Quantity Theory of money was well known to economists throughout the
eighteenth century, on account of its formulation by John Locke [Locke (1691)].
It was familiar in its simplest form, where an increase in the quantity of money
leads to an equal proportionate increase in prices. But it was also debated in its
more sophisticated form, where some increase in employment would occur, as
well as more work become available for those already at work but not fully
occupied (the disguised unemployed). This was Steuart's position. The synthesis
was provided by David Hume in his essay "Of Money". The increase in money
would first raise prices by more than costs, but in the long run costs would catch
up:

> We find that in every Kingdom, into which money begins to flow in greater
> abundance than formerly, everything takes a new face; labor and industry gain

life, the merchant becomes more enterprising, the manufacturer [i.e. industrial worker] more diligent and skillful, and even the farmer follows his plow with greater alacrity and attention... At first no alteration is perceived; by degrees the price rises, first of one commodity, then of another; till the whole at last reaches a just proportion with the new quantity of specie which is in the Kingdom. In my opinion it is only in this interval or intermediate situation, between the acquisition of money and rise of prices that the increasing quantity of gold and silver is favorable to industry [Hume (1748, "Of Money", p. 37)].

Hume took the same "intermediate" position on the effects of an increase in the quantity of money on the rate of interest; he thought that the rate would fall at first, but thereafter return to its previous level. He was flanked by Cantillon and Smith on the one side, insisting on the neutrality of money, and by Locke and Steuart on the other side, establishing the monetary case. This debate continues.

Note the apparent expectation that in normal times the labor market is slack, and that it comes to full employment only in response to a monetary stimulus. As Petty put it, "There are spare hands enough among the King of England's subjects to earn two million more per annum than they do now" [quoted from Johnson (1937, p. 113)]. There was, however, no suggestion of a regular trade cycle, even though with hindsight we' can see that money and commerce were already showing such a pattern (industry was still too small to matter in this context).

Population theory was still in confusion. While there was not much dispute about the short-term effects on wages of an increase in the demand for labor, the long-run effects were disputed by at least three groups: those who believed in increasing returns, those who saw an infinitely elastic supply of labor, and a third group that expected diminishing returns. The issues would not be clearly sorted out until the nineteenth century.

4. Organization

Economic institutions were different then from now, and this is reflected in the shape of development theory.

First, in the pure model the economy consists of landlords, capitalists, and wage earners, and the theory of distribution explains how the product is divided amongst these classes. English agriculture did indeed have that pattern, but in other countries the labor force consisted of small farmers, working in various legal forms, from near slavery upwards. Their ways of living were not represented in current theory.

Similarly, the farmer in this model represents the entrepreneur, and also the bearer of innovations. The entrepreneur as such seems to have had his function and procedures analyzed by only one economist of our period, namely Richard Cantillon. He stressed the risk-bearing function, instead of capital provision, which was in those days more common. One can understand the general lack of interest. The typical entrepreneur at this time was neither a farmer nor an industrial tycoon, but a merchant adventurer in foreign trade. His capital was working capital rather than fixed capital; and his ability to supplement it by borrowing was restricted by the fact that financial institutions were rather rudimentary. We do not have to ask, like Max Weber, where all these capitalists came from. Once the schoolmen had given their blessing to commerce, there would be no shortage of merchant adventurers. Many countries today are in the situation that they have an "unlimited supply" of businessmen while sorely lacking industrial entrepreneurship. Adam Smith detested businessmen; Cantillon and Hume thought they were wonderful [Smith (1776, p. 250), Cantillon (1755, pp. 63–73), Hume (1748, "Of Interest", p. 52)].

The economics of land tenure invited interest from the time of Cromwell's conquest of Ireland, but did not blossom until the nineteenth century. Part of this problem is that the Law of Diminishing Returns, which would dominate distribution theory until the 1960s, was not formulated until after the end of our period [West (1815)].

The eighteenth century could not contribute spectacularly to the monetary theory of the twentieth century since the institutional background differed so greatly as between the two periods. Ours is an age of paper money – banknotes checks and so on – whereas theirs was still an age of precious metals circulating as money. But the transition to paper had begun. Banks were issuing notes and creating credit (though denying the latter). And the ambiguity of deciding what was and what was not to be included in the count as money had already begun. How far apart we are is illustrated by Adam Smith's pronouncement that:

> The whole paper money of every kind which can easily circulate in any country can never exceed the value of the gold and silver of which it supplies the place, or which (the commerce being supposed the same) would circulate there if there was no paper money [Smith (1776, p. 284)].

This statement is either a tautology or false.

The role of government occupied eighteenth-century economists as much as it occupies our own generation. Government was indeed much smaller, almost certainly not exceeding 5 percent of national income, including defense. They argued as to where to draw the line between private enterprise and ownership and government enterprise and ownership, and possible mixtures; the argument turning principally on inefficiency and corruption, much as it does in the Third World today. Adam Smith uses the concept of external economies in describing human capital, but does not develop it:

> [The capital of the country consists] fourthly of acquired and useful abilities of all the inhabitants or members of the society. The acquisition of such talents, by the maintenance of the acquirer during his education, study or apprenticeship always costs a real expense, which is a capital fixed and realized, as it were, in his person. Those talents, as they make a part of this fortune, so do they likewise of that of the society to which he belongs [Smith (1776, pp. 265–266)].

The duty of the government to do whatever was needed to improve the economy was not challenged; this, after all, was implied in two centuries of argument about foreign trade. We look for a theory of shadow prices, but this was still a century ahead. Monopoly was denounced not so much for reasons of allocation, as because it was seen as an obstacle to the division of labor and also an unjust tax upon the public.

Finally, a note on public finance. Our economists created the mold within which this subject would live for the next hundred and fifty years. There was no theory of public expenditure; the emphasis was rather on the theory of the incidence of different kinds of taxes.

5. Conclusion

We set out to see how much of modern development theory was already available in the year 1776. By development theory I mean those parts of economics that play crucial roles when one tries to analyze the growth of the economy as a whole. There was quite a good beginning, that gave us the constraints imposed on growth by the agricultural surplus, or foreign exchange, or saving. Also we had Say's Law, the "Quantity Theory of Money", inflation, continual unemployment, entrepreneurship as a separate factor of production, the theory of bank credit, human capital, and the incidence of taxes. Just ahead of us in the first half of the nineteenth century would come the law of diminishing returns, the law of comparative cost, population theory, and the theory of land tenure. After that, interest in development theory would almost die out until the theoretical explosion of the 1950s and after.

Finally, economics may change, but not economists. Let us give the last word to Adam Smith:

> The annual produce of the land and labor of England, for example, is certainly much greater than it was, a little more than a century ago at the restoration of Charles II. Though at present, few people, I believe, doubt of this, yet during this period five years have seldom passed away in which some book or

pamphlet has not been published, written too with such abilities as to gain some authority with the public, and pretending to demonstrate that the wealth of the nation was fast declining, that the country was depopulated, agriculture neglected, manufacturers decaying, and trade undone. Nor have these publications been all party pamphlets, the wretched offspring of falsehood and venality. Many of them have been written by very candid and very intelligent people; who wrote nothing but what they believed, and for no other reason but because they believed it [Smith (1776, p. 327)].

References

Cantillon, Richard (1755) *Essai sur la nature du commerce en general.* London: Fletcher Gyles.

Hume, David (1748) *Essays moral and political* (edited by Eugene Rotwein; London: Nelson, 1955).

Johnson, E.A.J. (1937) *Predecessors of Adam Smith.* New York: Prentice Hall, Inc.

Lindert, P.H. (1969) *Key currencies and gold, 1900–1913,* Princeton Studies in International Finance, no. 24, Princeton University.

Locke, J. (1691) *Some consideration of the consequences of lowering the rate of interest.* Reprinted in: M. Cranston, ed., *Locke on politics, religion, and education.* New York: Collier Books, 1965.

Smith, Adam (1776) *The wealth of nations* (edited by Edwin Cannan; New York: The Modern Library, 1937).

Steuart, James (1767) *Enquiry into the principles of political economy* (edited by Andrew S. Skinner; London: Oliver & Boyd, 1966).

Wallace, Robert (1753), *A dissertation on the numbers of mankind in ancient and modern times.* Edinburgh: Hamilton & Balfour.

West, Sir Edward (1815) *Essay on the application of capital to land.* Reprinted as: *Sir Edward West on the application of capital to land 1815.* Baltimore: The Lord Baltimore Press, 1903.

Chapter 3

ALTERNATIVE APPROACHES TO DEVELOPMENT ECONOMICS

PRANAB BARDHAN*

University of California at Berkeley

Contents

1.	Introduction	40
2.	Theory of the household	40
3.	Institutions and resource allocation	45
4.	Income distribution and growth	51
5.	Trade and development	57
6.	Economic policy and the state	63
7.	Concluding remarks	66
	References	68

*I am grateful for comments on an earlier draft by Clive Bell, Hollis Chenery, David Evans, Steve Marglin, Alan Richards, T.N. Srinivasan, and Suresh Tendulkar. The remaining blemishes are no doubt due to my laxity in following up on all of their suggestions.

Handbook of Development Economics, Volume I, Edited by H. Chenery and T.N. Srinivasan
© *Elsevier Science Publishers B.V., 1988*

1. Introduction

Development economics as a separate branch of economics originated in a widespread perception of the limited usefulness of orthodox economics, and even though its pristine separatism has mellowed over the years it retains to this day its contrary, unruly, if somewhat flaky, image in the eyes of mainstream economists. Standard neoclassical economics is mainly on the defensive in this terrain and a number of alternative approaches clash and contend for our attention. In my subsequent discussion I shall primarily deal with three major approaches, what can be classified somewhat loosely as neoclassical, Marxist, and structuralist-institutionalist. These are, of course, portmanteau categories, each containing widely diverse strands of methodology and analytical assumptions and results. There is, for example, a world of difference between Marxists who believe in methodological individualism and other Marxists, just as there is between the neoclassicals in the Walras–Debreu tradition and those of the Akerlof–Stiglitz vintage. Yet they are usually clubbed together in an undifferentiated group by their adversaries: larger targets make shooting practice easier. What is more, with the lines of mutual communication between contending schools largely blocked by years of misunderstanding and jargon-mongering, easy " victories" are often unilaterally claimed and hailed after setting up essentially a straw man to represent the opposing viewpoint and comfortably shooting it down. I happen to believe that the differences between the more sophisticated versions of alternative approaches, even though substantial, are narrower than is generally perceived.

In this chapter I shall not attempt a comprehensive examination of all aspects of the alternative approaches. Instead, I shall focus on a few, highly selective, areas of enquiry with a brief, impressionistic, comparative assessment of some major contributions in each area. The following five sections deal with five such distinct but not entirely unrelated areas: (a) theory of the household; (b) institutions and resource allocation; (c) income distribution and growth; (d) trade and development; and (e) economic policy and the state. While these five certainly do not exhaust the arenas of conflict among the different approaches, in my judgment they involve some of the core issues of development economics and may represent a fair cross-section of some of the active disputes. I should also note that for considerations of space as well as personal competence I have excluded a discussion of short-run macroeconomic issues; for example, some of the major policy disputes relating particularly to Latin America between structuralists and monetarists will remain entirely unrepresented in this chapter.

2. Theory of the household

2.1. Maximization, even by peasant households in traditional agriculture, is a basic presumption in neoclassical development economics. Marxists, on the other hand, often emphasize the overwhelming importance of structural constraints, leaving little scope for freedom of action or rational choice. As Elster (1979), a "rational-choice" Marxist, comments, clearly they mean this to apply with some asymmetry, members of ruling classes, for example, supposedly having more choice and being less hemmed in by structural constraints than the subordinate classes. And in their choice, even if not all members of the former classes are maximizers, the competitive process will tend to weed out the non-maximizers. This biological model of the survival of profit-maximizers is, for example, implicit in the Marxian assumption of equality of profit rates through competition of capital. But when competition is lacking, when markets are "thin" or highly segmented or inadequately formed, non-maximizers (like large landowners wastefully using their land) can survive for a prolonged period. The plausibility of the assumption of maximization is thus not entirely independent of the market structure or even the mode of production.

A large empirical literature has now accumulated confirming intimations of peasant rationality, particularly when one is careful to take into account the insurance motivation under the pervasive uncertainty in the physical and social environment. In the neoclassical empirical literature rationality has often been interpreted in the very narrow sense of price responsiveness. But even when a farmer is not very sensitive to market prices or the markets themselves are inadequately formed, there may still be ample evidence of a coherent pattern in his behavior which indicates his attempt, by and large, to improve his condition under the given constraints. Even patron–client relations, which are often cited as a mark of a traditional custom-bound social system or a "moral" economy, may sometimes be viewed as a form of rational response to a situation of desperate need of subsistence insurance and protection on the part of the client, and that of ready availability of cheap labor services for the patron. It may also be quite rational for a landlord or an industrial monopolist to "waste" some resources in activities and rituals enhancing his social status or political power, which (in terms of current industrial organization theory) may often be regarded as investment in entry barriers to particular markets. The presumption of rationality, in this extended sense, may thus be a good starting hypothesis to work with, even if one ends up by finding it to be violated in many particular cases.[1] As Elster (1979) comments:

> This presumption is a "principle of charity" similar to the one often used in textual interpretation. One should never take textual contradictions at their

---

[1] There are, of course, many cases of *systematic* cognitive errors like the ones analyzed in the work of Tversky and Kahneman (1986). In a world of incomplete information it is also difficult to distinguish between irrational and uninformed behavior. One should also keep in mind that while the neoclassical maximand is usually income or utility, the objective of self-realization is more central to Marxism: thus, work, which invariably yields disutility in neoclassical models, may be a channel for self-realization under appropriate organizational conditions. Sometimes self-esteem, following certain culturally specific codes of honor, is more important to the individual than the usual neoclassical maximands.

face value, but consider whether the context might not give a clue to consistency. Similarly, one should always look very closely at apparently irrational behavior to see whether there could not be some pattern there after all.

Development economics is full of examples of how apparently irrational behavior may be successfully explained as an outcome of more complex exercises in rationality, particularly with deeper probes into the nature of the feasibility constraints or the preference patterns.

At the same time the rigid maximization in the formal neoclassical models clearly ignores the manifold ambiguities of interest perception among individual agents in the real world, particularly in situations of poverty and deprivation. Marxists in this context have emphasized (though not analyzed at sufficient depth) the social determination of preference patterns and the role of ideology in legitimizing existing systems of exploitation. The poor often internalize the severe constraints they face (and their earlier generations have faced) and its expressions may take the form of fatalism, low aspirations, low perception of needs, high rate of time discount, and so on. And as Sen (1984) reminds us, "many of the inequities of the world survive by making allies out of the deprived and the abused".

2.2. Most rational-choice Marxists as well as neoclassical economists take the household as a compact decision-making unit and, until recently, have underemphasized intra-household conflicts of interest, particularly among members in different age–sex categories. Household behavior in response to changing prices and income may not, for example, be easily explained if the same changes affect the relative bargaining power (or fall-back options) of different household members in different ways. Similarly, the expansion of a market may expand the choices for some members of the family while limiting them for others. This has important implications for the impact of the development process, particularly on the conditions of women.

One variant of the neoclassical household economics, following Becker (1981), treats the family as composed of what Sen (1984) calls "super-traders" relentlessly pursuing their individual utilities without constraints of norms or duty. Not merely intra-family allocation of work and goods, but complex institutions like marriage or extended family, are sought to be explained in this way. To analyze family relationships as if they are market transactions at implicit prices, with the focus on income and substitution effect of price changes on these relationships, is to ignore the complex of institutions on which contracts in actual markets crucially depend and to oversimplify the mix of cooperative and conflicting elements in family relations. The Marxist literature, since the appearance of Engels' *The Origin of Family, Private Property and the State* in 1884, has also been full of simplistic and economic-reductionist generalizations on family relations, but usually they are somewhat more sensitive to historical and institutional variations across different modes of production. I should also note here that Marxists (or anyone else for that matter) have not been able to provide a satisfactory explanation of why rules of family formation and inter-generational property transfer ("modes of reproduction") have sometimes been extraordinarily persistent over several centuries of changes in forces of production. Primogeniture, for example, gained wide acceptance in Europe with the spread of feudalism, but it has long outlived feudalism and helped capitalist accumulation.

2.3. There are elegant neoclassical models of agricultural households taking inter-dependent decisions on production, consumption, and labor supply.[2] One of the striking results in this literature is the separability of the consumption and production decisions. For example, in these models farm labor and other input demands can be solved as functions of market prices, technological parameters of the production function and factor endowments, and consumption depends on market prices and full income. Preferences, prices of consumer goods, and income do not affect production decisions. This separability property makes econometric estimation easier, since all prices can be taken as exogenous to the household.

But the separability result crucially depends on the assumption of perfect markets. If some markets are non-existent or incomplete or imperfect, as is often the case in developing countries, the household may be constrained to equate consumption with own production for some commodities. These constraints will be associated with a set of shadow prices (in general different from market prices) which will depend on the household's endowments, technology, and preferences. Output supplies, production techniques, and input demands will thus depend on household preferences and endowments through these shadow prices. The imperfect marketability of labor, for example, leads to the differential labor intensity in different size classes of farms, as is often emphasized in the literature on size and productivity. There are also other important (e.g. dynamic) ways in which the household consumption and production decisions may interact which the standard static models do not capture.

2.4. The peasant household in the orthodox Marxist literature belongs to what Shanin has called an "awkward class". Both Lenin and Rosa Luxemburg pointed to the tenacity of peasant survival delaying capitalist take-over in European agriculture. In the much more densely populated agriculture of Asia, this delay has often been prolonged enough to raise doubts about the transitional nature of the mode of peasant proprietorship. While Marxists often see in this tenacity peasants' astonishing capacity to take punishment or "self-exploitation", always adjusting to the labor adsorption rate in secondary and tertiary sectors, writers like Boserup (1965) have pointed to many cases of improvement in traditional

---

[2] For a good survey, see Singh, Squire and Strauss (1986, ch. 2).

agricultural practices on peasant farms induced by population growth (Marxists usually ignore such effects of demography on the development of the forces of production) and Geertz (1963) has pointed to the related demographic–ecological processes of "agricultural involution" providing a surprising elasticity to the system. While orthodox Marxists usually associate capitalist agriculture with large-scale capital-intensive methods of production, more recent advances in biochemical technology associated with the so-called green revolution have shown possibilities of successful adoption on small farms. The main constraint here is not the small-scale nature of production as such, but more the availability of public infrastructural facilities like irrigation, power, extension services, and credit, and the acute problem of externalities generated by a crazy quilt of petty private property rights, underlining the need for community cooperation in land consolidation, water allocation, soil conservation, and so on. In parts of East Asia (Japan, Taiwan, etc.) where the public infrastructure, cooperative organizations and communal rules have provided these services, small-scale labor-intensive peasant farms have thrived for a long time. In densely populated countries the Japanese road to agricultural development may be a historical alternative to Lenin's oft-quoted "Prussian" or "American" roads.

In the more recent Marxist literature on what de Janvry (1981) calls "functional dualism", it is claimed that the coexistence of peasant farms is functional to the on-going process of agricultural and industrial capitalism since the former lower the wage costs to the capitalists. I am not sure I quite understand this argument. It appears to me that the wage costs for the capitalists may be even lower if the peasant farms are wiped out and the erstwhile self-employed peasants now crowd the wage labor market (unless one introduces high supervision costs that the employers have to incur).

2.5. In the theory of peasant households while Chayanov emphasizes demographic differentiation among the peasantry (on the basis of variations in resource balance over the family life-cycle), and classical models like that of Arthur Lewis focuses only on family farmers in agriculture, Marxists give much more importance to class differentiation. Roemer (1982) has provided an endogenous determination of class structure on the basis of differential ownership of means of production.[3] Extending his model to introduce the limited access of agents to working capital and the requirement, necessitated by moral hazard, that the supervisor of the farming activity be the residual claimant of output, Eswaran and Kotwal (1986) have developed a model where four agrarian classes (laborer-cultivators, self-cultivators, small and large capitalists) emerge as a result of the utility-maximizing activities of individual agents bound by time (strictly, imper-

---

[3] For an application of the Roemer classification scheme and a discussion of its limitations in the context of Indian agriculture, see Bardhan (1984a, ch. 13).

fect substitutability between own time and unsupervised hired labor) and capital constraints. Class hierarchy, and the attendant misallocation of resources (with land-to-labor ratios differing across farm sizes), are thus the direct outcome of imperfections in labor and capital markets. This is a good example of how Marxist results can be derived rigorously with neoclassical methods. There is a growing recognition among rational-choice Marxists of the methodological necessity of tracing the microfoundations of class analysis in postulates of individual behavior.[4]

Neoclassical economics with its traditional preoccupation with competitive equilibrium, of course, avoids the key Marxian concept of class struggle as a mechanism of historical change. Nevertheless, the recent advances in the application of bargaining theory in neoclassical microeconomics may be fruitfully used in the analysis of class struggle, just as the literature on collective action gives us some clues in studying what blocks class formation particularly among the poor.

3. Institutions and resource allocation

3.1. A persistent theme in Marxist and other institutionalist writings in development economics is how certain institutions or production relations act as "fetters" on the development of forces of production. The most frequent examples here are drawn from the retarding effects of agrarian institutions in many poor countries, like the elaborate hierarchy of rent-extracting land rights, sharecropping, usury, speculative trading, and so on.[5] The nature of these effects, however, needs to be clearly spelled out. It is easy to see that the direct cultivator, squeezed by layers of landlords in the subinfeudation process, has limited incentive to fully utilize or develop the forces of production. But the primary question is why the landlord does not use his surplus in productive accumulation. To answer this by showing that the rate of return to rentier activities or usury or speculation is high is somewhat circular; one still has to show (a) why the rate return to productive investment is low, and (b) why and particularly how yield-increasing innovations, potentially raising the latter rate of return, will be blocked by the unproductive

---

[4] One common criticism of such methodological individualism is its alleged oversight of the fact that individual actions are sometimes derived from supra-individual entities (like a kinship group, caste, community, nation, etc.). But the doctrine of methodological individualism does not preclude such substantive facts of individual human nature. It only gives explanatory priority to individuals and claims, to quote Elster (1985) again, "that all social phenomena – their structure and their change – are in principle explicable in ways that only involve individuals – their properties, their goals, their beliefs and their actions". These need not be individualistic individuals.

[5] In pre-capitalist economies there is also a tendency, as Brenner (1985) puts it, of the dominant class to invest in the development of the means of coercion at the expense of developing the means of production. But as the level of available production technology improves, the *relative* rate of return from investment in coercion should drop.

landlord, money-lender or trader interests. In large parts of the world where some of the poorest people live (for example in regions of monsoon paddy or unirrigated dryland cultivation) the basic technology has remained extremely backward and ecologically fragile, not always because easily available technological improvements have been undercut by vested interests, but often because prerequisites for such improvements involve massive public investment in irrigation and flood-control, research and extension, and the privately inappropriable externalities they generate. In areas or crops where high-yielding (and disease-resistant) seeds are available, along with a public network of irrigation and drainage, the merchant-moneylender resistance to adoption of innovation has not been significant and even rentier landlords have often converted themselves, in the style of later Prussian junkers, into enterprising farmers.[6]

Even when economic betterment following from adoption of innovations is to increase the general bargaining power of agricultural workers or reduce the political control of landlords over them, in an environment of competition no individual landlord will be rationally deterred from such adoption.[7] But in a situation of market segmentation and territorial monopoly, a local landlord can get away with delaying adoption. (Even when there are a few local landlords the theory of repeated games shows how collusive arrangements may be attained even in non-cooperative situations.) Similarly, it is not enough to point out that land-saving biochemical technology (as in the case of much of the so-called green revolution) may reduce the scarcity rent of land, unlike labor-saving mechanical innovations, and hence the landlords will adopt the latter over the former. An individual landlord will economize both on land and labor costs. But agricultural technology is often primarily generated in public research institutions and its diffusion is seriously dependent on public extension, credit, and hydraulic works. If the landed oligarchy, sufficiently small and cohesive (overcoming the collective action problem), can influence state policies regarding research and diffusion, the nature of technological development may be affected, as has been claimed in the case of Argentine agriculture by de Janvry (1978). The neoclassical literature on induced innovations emphasizing factor scarcity and market prices usually ignores

---

[6] In this context I do not find Bhaduri's (1983) predator–prey model (with antagonistic relationship between merchant-moneylender class and the class of rich farmers) very plausible, either on theoretical or empirical grounds. Theoretically, he has not shown why and how entry from one of these classes to the other is restricted; empirically, he ignores the substantial evidence of portfolio diversification of the rural rich in farming, lending, trading, and other businesses and services, nor does he cite any evidence that in recent years productive investment by rich farmers has been resisted by professional moneylenders or traders.

[7] Braverman and Stiglitz (1986) have drawn attention to some special cases where a productivity-raising innovation may be resisted by an individual landlord if such an innovation at the same time accentuates the incentive problems. See also the discussion on interlinking and innovation by Clive Bell in Chapter 16 of this Handbook.

the interaction between dominant class interests and the relevant state policies. The Marxist literature, on the other hand, displays much too often a functionalist and conspiratorial attitude, suggesting that the absence of (or a particular bias in) technical progress must be there because it serves the interests of a particular class, without bothering to show the mechanism through which the class attempts and achieves the intended results.

3.2. The major claim of orthodox neoclassical economics that given well-defined property rights efficient resource allocation is independent of institutional arrangements or relations of production is largely irrelevant in the context of developing countries. That the serious and pervasive cases of market failures, incomplete markets, information asymmetry, and moral hazard problems falsify the presumption of efficiency of resource allocation and make the latter crucially dependent on asset ownership structures and property relations is now well recognized, for example, in the neoclassical economics of (imperfect) information.[8] The terms and conditions of (implicit or explicit) contracts in various transactions critically depend on the distribution of assets and the former have important effect on the efficiency of resource allocation. The inefficiencies, for example, of share-cropping contracts (in terms of suboptimal worker effort and choice of technique) arising in a second-best situation of moral hazard problems can, under certain circumstances, be eliminated if the peasants own the land they till or have full access to credit to buy it (a land reform or credit reform). If all individuals had the same wealth (and the associated local risk-aversion characteristics), the need to transfer risks and hence the moral hazard problems of many principal–agent game situations in contractual arrangements would have disappeared.

Similarly, as we have already noted in Section 2, differential access of farmers to working capital and own time endowment leads to a misallocation of resources, with land-to-labor ratios varying across farm sizes. Again, in the efficiency theory of wages and unemployment relating particularly to poor countries (with the crucial non-convexity in the consumption–ability relation of a worker at low consumption levels) one implication[9] is that a more egalitarian distribution of assets, by reducing the malnourishment particularly of the currently unemployed, is likely to lead to a rise in aggregate output in the economy. One could give many other examples, but by now it is fairly obvious that by giving up on the separability between equity and efficiency considerations many neoclassical economists have now come a long way towards the position of the institutionalists.

---

[8] For brief but excellent surveys of the issues, see Stiglitz (1985a, 1985b).
[9] For the development of this implication, see Dasgupta and Ray (1986).

3.3. Marxists and other institutional economists often refer to certain institutional constraints, taken as frozen data from history, and concentrate on their adverse effects on the use and development of the forces of production, overlooking the economic rationale of the formation of these institutions as well as how in the historical-evolutionary process the underlying rationale changes and the same institutional forms adapt and mutate in response to the changed circumstances. I shall give two examples from peasant agriculture, one from the profuse literature on land tenure and the other from that on labor transactions. First take again the case of share-cropping, which is often cited as an institutional obstacle to development. In their zeal for institutional change the Marxists usually ignore the origin and nature of this institution as an imperfect economic response to incomplete markets and market failures:[10] under a set of constraints, share-cropping does serve a real economic function, and its simple abolition without taking care of the factors that gave rise to this institution in the first place may not necessarily improve the conditions of the intended beneficiaries of the abolition program. There are some important political lessons here from what may be called the economics of second-best reformism.

The models of institutionalists also suffer from inadequate specificity. While they may give a convincing reason why a particular institution exists or persists, they often fail to explain variations in the detailed structures and terms of contracts over time or across space. Blanket references to the "power" of dominant classes cannot explain, except in a question-begging way, important differences in institutional arrangements. Marxists have also a tendency to equate share-cropping tenancy mechanically with the "feudal" or "semi-feudal" mode of production, thus ignoring how in the real world the same institution adapts itself to the development of the forces of production, with numerous cases of capitalist share-tenant farmers (as, for example, in Punjab) or more widespread cases of cost-sharing and other forms of landlord–tenant partnership in adoption of the new technology of high-yielding varieties in agriculture. Thus, while Marxists have been most vocal in raising the issue of agrarian institutions and their interaction with technological development, the more substantive contributions in development theory in this respect have been carried out with neoclassical methodology looking into the micro foundations of their rationale, drawing upon the growing literature on imperfect information, uncertainty, incentives, and principal–agent games.

My other example relates to the case of labor-tying arrangements in agriculture. Historically, agrarian labor-tying brings to mind the blatant cases of obligatory service by the tenant–serf to the lord of the manor (as in the classic

---

[10] For a review of the literature relating sharecropping to market failures and imperfections in credit, risk, and human and animal labor markets and costly monitoring of worker effort, see Newbery and Stiglitz (1979), Bardhan (1984a, ch. 7), and Singh's chapter in Bardhan (forthcoming).

instances of European feudalism) or those of debt–peonage to moneylender-cum-landlord as prevailed in many parts of the world. These are clearly cases where tying involves a continuing lack of freedom on the part of the laborer and the sanctions underlying the employer's authority are based primarily on social or legal coercion. This is to be distinguished from the case where the laborer voluntarily enters long-duration contracts with his employer and reserves the right to leave unconditionally at the end of the specified period. This latter type of (implicit) labor-tying contracts is quite significant in agriculture in many areas. Neoclassical methodology has been quite useful in exploring their rationale[11] (in terms of "labor-hoarding" for tight peak seasons, risk-sharing, productivity effects of continued relationships, incentive effects of selective exclusion, etc.), and in some cases it is not difficult to show why such contracts may even increase in importance with yield-increasing improvement and capitalist development in agriculture at least in the early phases. Yet most Marxists continue to identify all forms of labor-tying as "bonded labor" and characterize them as symptoms of economic stagnation.

Many such implicit futures contracts in labor or land-lease markets of poor agrarian economies are cemented by credit relationships. By their very nature such interlocking transactions are often highly personalized.[12] Such personal ties between transacting agents are automatically described as pre-capitalist in the Marxist development literature, while in contrast the literature on implicit contracts and imperfect information in the context of industrially advanced economies often emphasizes the importance of what Okun (1981) called "customer" (as opposed to "auction") markets. Neoclassical economists who discuss the rationale of personalized interlinked contracts in these terms often, in their turn, overlook that the elaborate market segmentation which such personalization involves in poor economies frequently leaves the weaker partner in these transactions with virtually all-or-nothing choices. Of course, if the peasant is already pressed down to his reservation utility level, as in the principal–agent models of non-cooperative games, he cannot by assumption be worse off as a result of contract interlinkage. But in a bargaining framework, as in the Bell–Zusman (1976) tenancy model of Nash cooperative games, the peasant may be worse off with an interlinked set of transactions than with a set of separate bilateral bargains (even when the utility-possibility frontier itself shifts outward with interlinking). Neoclassical economists also fail to emphasize that personalized interlocking of labor commitments and credit transactions often divide the workers and effectively emasculate their collective bargaining strength vis-à-vis

---

[11] See Bardhan (1983), and Eswaran and Kotwal (1985).

[12] For a review of the literature on this, see Bardhan (1984a, ch. 12), and the chapter by Clive Bell in this Handbook (Chapter 16).

employers, who use this as an instrument of control over the labor process (as well as command of social and political loyalties).

Neoclassical economists [e.g. Ruttan and Hayami (1984)] who emphasize endogenous institutional innovations in response to changes in factor endowments or technology, usually presume such innovations to take the general direction of greater efficiency. A faith in such a unilinear progress of history is also shared in some Marxian teleological schemes. Apart from the ambiguities in the welfare effects of improvements in efficiency when in the political process gainers usually do not compensate the losers, these views incorporate a kind of functionalism which is often indefensible and ahistorical. An institution may benefit a group and yet the latter may have very little to do with its origin or maintenance; its mere function of serving the interests of beneficiaries is inadequate in *explaining* an institution. Dysfunctional institutions often persist for a long period. Akerlof (1984) has built models to show how economically unprofitable or socially unpleasant customs may persist as a result of a mutually sustaining network of social sanctions when each (rational) individual conforms out of fear of loss of reputation from disobedience. Another self-reinforcing mechanism for the persistence of socially suboptional institutions may be in operation when *path-dependent* processes are important, as is now recognized in the literature of the history of technological innovations. As Arthur (1985) has emphasized, when there are increasing returns to adoption of a particular (technological or institutional) innovation – i.e. the more it is adopted the more it is attractive or convenient for the others to join the bandwagon – a path chosen by some initial adopters to suit their interests may "lock-in" the whole system for a long time to come, denying later, more appropriate, technologies or institutions a footing. The process is *non-ergodic*; there are multiple outcomes and historical "small events" early on may well decide the larger course of structural change. The historical-evolutionary process thus does not always move inexorably to the "fittest" institutional form.

A movement towards a more efficient institution may also be blocked by the superior social, political, and military power of the potential losers and by the problems of collective action that limit the ability of the potential gainers to get their act together. In an incisive analysis of European history, Brenner (1977) focuses on substantially different paths of transition from feudalism (the contrasting experiences of Western and Eastern Europe, of British agricultural capitalism and French small peasant proprietorship even within Western Europe) in which specific historical processes of class capacity for resistance and struggle play the crucial role, in comparison with factors like demography (changing factor endowments) or expansion of markets (and associative changes in specialization, scale economies, and trade). Changes in factor endowments or market size or technology change the costs and benefits of collective action on the part of different classes, but cannot predetermine the balance of class forces or the outcome of social conflicts.

It is also important to note that the neoclassical emphasis on the locally efficient ("second-best") nature of some of the contractual arrangements under the existing set of constraints should not divert our attention from the basic issue of removing those constraints (through, for example, appropriate asset redistribution). It is also underemphasized in the literature on the economics of information or that of transaction costs that moral hazard problems leading to work-shirking, costly monitoring, etc. are themselves partly the results of a specific and mutable set of social institutions: as Bowles (1985) notes, a more democratic organization of the work process and more egalitarian distribution of output may significantly reduce the Hobbesian malfeasance problems which form the staple of much of the principal–agent literature. Related is the important question of the role of ideology in the economic theory of institutions. North (1981) is the rare neoclassical economic historian who underlines the importance of social ideology in its function of reducing free-riding, shirking, and venality so that the individual supervises himself and often behaves in a way contrary to the standard presumptions of principal–agent games. Marxists usually offer some useful clues (and some functionalist red herrings) about the structural roots of different ideological systems, but it is easy to see that we do not yet have a good theory of the formation, maintenance, and institutionalization of ideology which lends some regular predictive ability to a model of institutional change that incorporates ideology. Among economists' infrequent attempts to analytically understand ideology, the ones that may be most useful towards explaining institutions in poor countries are those by Akerlof (1984), particularly his work on class loyalty ("loyalty filters"), cognitive dissonance (how people handle unpleasant conditions by adjusting their beliefs to their constraints), and the concept of fairness (in wage and work norms, for example).

In the propagation of ideology and the socialization process, as in defining and enforcing property rights, the state plays the authoritative role. Neoclassical explanations of institutional arrangements usually are not very sensitive to the linkages between such arrangements at the local level and macro political forces and to the frequent fact that the state for reasons of maintaining its own support structures may prolong socially inefficient property rights. By drawing pointed attention to the role of ideology and the state in his explanation of the processes of institutional change North (1981) has brought the neoclassical theory of economic history very much closer to the Marxian.

4. Income distribution and growth

4.1. A fundamental difference in orthodox neoclassical theory from Marxist or structuralist-institutionalist theory relates, of course, to the determination of income distribution. In the former, factor markets clear to determine factor prices, while in the latter they depend on class struggle or are given exogenously (with vaguely defined "institutional" wage rates or mark-up rates). Contrary to popular impression, the difference does not lie in the neoclassical use of marginal-productivity relationships – as Marglin (1984) emphasizes, Marxian as well as Keynesian theories are quite consistent with the marginal-productivity equation, which is merely an implication of the competitive profit-maximization assumption – or of continuous factor substitution along production functions (which is, again, nothing inherently neoclassical).[13] It is the presumption (or model outcome) of markets not clearing, of involuntary unemployment, and, in some cases, of excess capacity that distinguish the other theories from neoclassical.

Here again the neoclassical theory and some of the Marxian theorizing have come close to each other. In the labor market, while most Marxists start with the presumption of a reserve army of labor (replenished whenever necessary by an unlimited supply from other sectors of the economy with petty modes of production), Marxists like Bowles (1985) have now tried to provide micro foundations to Kalecki's (1943) suggestion that capitalism uses unemployment as a worker discipline device: given a positive cost of surveillance and a conflict of interest between employer and worker over work effort (extraction of labor power from laborers), the wage rate offered even by the competitive profit-maximizing employer will exceed the market-clearing wage and equilibrium entails unemployment. This is, of course, very similar to the models of involuntary unemployment in Calvo (1979), Eaton and White (1982), Stoft (1982), and Shapiro and Stiglitz (1984). While these models· were not specifically designed to represent labor markets in developing countries, one may say that in these markets the possible substitutes for the threat of unemployment (in creating work incentives) in the form of job entry fees or employment bonds or fines are less likely to operate, whereas threats in the form of losing credit from the employer-cum-lender if caught shirking work are more plausible.

Employers may also offer wages in excess of market clearing to reduce costly labor turnover, as in the urban labor market model with training costs in Stiglitz (1974) or the rural labor market model with recruitment costs in the peak season in Bardhan (1984a, ch. 4). These are all special cases of a general relationship[14] between labor productivity (or costs) and the real wage paid by the employer, in which case it is possible that market equilibrium will be characterized by unemployment. The original model where this hypothesis was first advanced was that of Leibenstein (1957) where a nutritional relationship between worker efficiency and wage was posited. But Bliss and Stern (1978) and Bardhan (1984a,

---

[13] Elster (1983) takes some pains to show convincingly that the widely held view that Marx presumed fixed coefficients of production in industry is false. He cites many passages from Marx which imply that the capitalist has a choice of techniques and that he makes the choice on the basis of relative prices.

[14] For a review of the issues in the context of developed and developing countries, see Yellen (1984) and Binswanger and Rosenzweig (1984), respectively.

ch. 4), have raised theoretical and empirical doubts in the cases both of permanent and, particularly, casual labor contracts.

Analogous to the case of unemployment equilibrium in labor markets, the neo-neoclassical theory provides an explanation of equilibrium in the capital markets, characterized by credit rationing and excess demand for capital. In a situation of imperfect information, as Stiglitz and Weiss (1981) show, the expected utility of the lender may go down even as the interest rate increases on account of adverse selection effects and higher risks of default on the part of all borrowers. In the closed face-to-face village communities some of the information problems and adverse selection effects are less acute; repeated situations, reputation effects, and interlinked contracts (between credit and tenancy or wage labor) relieve some of the default risks. On the other hand, strong covariate income risks and synchronic timing in agriculture limit local deposit banking and financial intermediation.[15] Such intermediation on any substantive scale has to come from outside, but for an outsider the information problems mentioned above reappear. With such information and other transaction costs acting as barriers to entry, the local lender may enjoy territorial monopoly powers in charging usurious interest rates and in undervaluing collateral assets provided by the borrower.[16] Of course, in these situations the monopoly power of the lender need not always be reflected in usurious interest rates (even abstracting from the fact of social control that the lender may like to exercise over his borrowers instead, as some Marxists emphasize), just as in commodity markets when monopolists know their customers' demand schedules, they may not charge monopoly prices; they may instead lower prices to the level that would prevail in competition and extract the additional consumer surplus by imposing flat entry charges or by some tie-in mechanism like interlinked contracts.[17]

The Marxist economist's emphasis on class power and class alliances in understanding income distribution is clearly crucial, as long as one keeps in mind that class formation (particularly in the sense of what Marx called class-for-itself) among the poor in many parts of the world is as yet in its infancy. But to leave wage theory entirely up to the political process and the balance of class forces is analytically unsatisfactory for an economist, particularly in the face of accumulating evidence[18] that wage rates are often quite sensitive to market pressure even when markets do not clear. When class struggle takes the form of some formal or informal collective bargaining, the good old neoclassical demand–supply framework may provide indispensable clues in understanding the "disagreement

---

[15]See Binswanger and Rosenzweig (1986) on this point.

[16]Bhaduri (1977) has emphasized undervaluation of collateral as a way of turning lender's risk into borrower's risk.

[17]For an application of this idea in the rural credit market, see Basu (1984) and Bardhan (1984a, ch. 6).

[18]See Bardhan (1984a, ch. 4).

pay-offs" in any bargaining game and in delimiting the possible range of wage indeterminacy. It may also be useful in assessing the nature and intensity of pressures in the political lobbying process on incomes policy. Again, Marxists usually leave the domain of class struggle unspecified; information costs and moral hazard problems may, for example, delimit the "moral" boundaries of a village community and partly explain how the consequent territorial segmentation[19] of the labor and credit markets blocks supra-village class solidarity.

4.2. While in neoclassical growth models distribution of income responds to growth, in the demand-driven models of structuralists income distribution clearly affects the rate and pattern of growth. In the development literature in Latin America and India existing income inequality and mass poverty in the countryside are sometimes found to pose severe limits to the expansion of home market for manufactured goods. As Lustig (1980) points out, this market insufficiency theory is quite different from Marxist realization crisis theories, and is more akin to the underconsumption thesis of Sismondi and later some Russian populists (like Nicolai-on and Vorontsov). In Dutt's (1984) model, with differential saving propensities of capitalists and workers, a regressive income distribution lowers consumption demand, which through an accelerator effect depresses investment demand, profits, and growth. Some of the Latin American structuralist writers, however, imply quite the opposite: increased income concentration may solve the problem of underconsumption in the key consumer durables sector. In the model of de Janvry and Sadoulet (1983) there is a critical level of income inequality above which such a process of what they call "social disarticulation" always obtains. The results are more ambiguous in the more general two-sector growth models of Taylor (1983a, ch. 9; 1983b). One sector produces wage goods while the other produces consumption goods for profit recipients and capital goods. Shifts in distribution in response to shifts in demand composition are shown to depend on labor intensity of the sectors (as in neoclassical models), while growth effects depend on the sectoral sensitivity of investment demand functions to profit rates. An increased income inequality may induce faster growth if the investment response of the non-wage good sector capitalists to higher profits is strong enough. While in a system with excess capacity it is important to take account of the dependence of growth on investment demand, it is not clear, as Buffie (1984) comments, why and how the degree of excess capacity and the average profit rate influence the *current* investment demand in Taylor's long-run model. The ad hoc specification of mark-ups which is customary in these models is also unsatisfactory.

4.3. Let us now turn to the impact of growth on income distribution. The differences in the alternative approaches are quite familiar on this question and

---

[19] For empirical evidence on such territorial segmentation, see Bardhan and Rudra (1986).

we shall be brief. Neoclassical economists, apart from pointing to the equalizing impact over time of concave saving functions – as in Stiglitz (1969) – and the opposite effect of a higher rate of population growth among the poor, usually offer the comforting hypothesis of "trickle-down". They are invariably most scathing on the possibility of immiserizing growth under policy-induced price distortions. Marxists and the structuralists usually emphasize the existing institutions which perpetuate and reinforce inequalities with capitalist growth. A major focus is on differential access to capital, which tends to result in differential flow of benefits from technical progress (as, for example, in the case of the so-called green revolution). Similarly, unequal initial endowments and "connections" lead to unequal benefits from human investment and migration, to entry deterrence in quality jobs, and to further polarization. The rich can take better advantage of economies of scale (in production, in marketing and other transaction costs, and in mobilization of finance) in ways which the constant returns to scale assumption of many neoclassical models cannot handle, and the distance from the poor widens. If preferences are socially determined, as Marxists claim, the experience of the poor makes them less future oriented and hence less likely to be full participants in the growth process.

Differential consumption propensities and sectoral demand composition have been used in the well-known Bacha–Taylor (1976) model of "unequalizing spiral" of growth. It is a three-sector model (wage goods, luxury goods, capital goods) with production requiring fixed ratios of capital to "effective labor" in all sectors, fixed relative wages of skilled to unskilled labor, infinitely elastic supply of unskilled labor, the latter consuming only wage goods while the skilled also consume luxuries as well as save, and investment demand functions in the non-wage good sectors responding readily to output. In such a model growth starts a whole cumulative process in which a rise in skilled employment, in relative demand for luxury goods, and in investment in the luxury sector feed on one another, accentuating inequalities all along. While the behavioral foundations of such models need to be spelled out more clearly, I find them yielding more insights into the distribution process than all the fine tuning of some neoclassical models.

On the question of income distribution effects of capitalist growth the Marxists and institutionalists are usually on the same side vis-à-vis the neoclassicals. But there is some tension between the Marxists and other institutionalists (whom the Marxists, echoing Russian debates of the late nineteenth century, sometimes disparagingly call neopopulists) on some implications of large-scale capital-intensive capitalist or state-socialist industrialization. These implications often involve "inappropriate" technology,[20] shrinking of employment prospects particularly for marginal groups in the labor force, urban bias, squeezing of surplus from the

---

[20] For a simple theoretical model of the adverse distributional implications of inappropriate technology in the context of localized technological progress, see Lapan and Bardhan (1973).

poorer agricultural sector, "de-skilling" of artisans in traditional handicrafts, marginalization and pauperization of small proprietors, and so on. Most Marxists are sensitive to these problems, but some problems are regarded by Marxists as inevitable costs of the development of the forces of production. As Emmanuel (1982) bluntly puts it, "if capitalism is hell there exists a still more frightful hell: that of less developed capitalism". In the advocates of small-scale labor-intensive production and of "basic needs" Marxists often detect an anti-industrialization bias and a nostalgia for the vanishing petty modes of production (this is reminiscent of Marx's comments on the so-called Utopian socialists and anarchists of his time). Some Marxists, however, are more sympathetic: on capital-intensive technology they even point out that machine-paced operations may be introduced by capitalists not for higher direct productivity but for larger control over the labor process and work discipline; in response to comments like that of Emmanuel above some Marxists reject the unilinearity of the stages of history, regard the social and human costs of capitalism avoidable, and envisage leap-frogging from pre-capitalism direct to socialism.[21]

But the questions of the distribution effects of inappropriate technology and sectoral bias in production and investment allocation remain even under socialism and state-led industrialization. Some critics of socialist industrialization programs in the mixed economies of some developing countries trace an alleged bias towards squeezing the agricultural sector to the net effects of the legacy of the 1920s Soviet discussion of the problems of what Preobrazhensky (1926/1965) called "primitive socialist accumulation" on early planning literature and of the traditional Marxian distrust of peasants. But at an analytical level the price or tax policies (of Preobrazhensky and his latter-day followers among development economists) aimed at mobilizing agricultural surplus essentially incorporate not an anti-peasant bias as such, but the imputation of a relatively large social weight to investment as compared to current consumption.[22] The same imputation of a low social rate of time discount calls for the choice of relatively capital-intensive techniques in industrial production even in the face of a large supply of underemployed labor (which may look like the working of an anti-worker bias), as has been shown in Dobb (1960), Sen (1960), and Marglin (1967); or in

---

[21] There is growing evidence that in the last decade of his life Marx himself was, hesitatingly, toying with such ideas, favorably reacting to Russian populists, of skipping the stage of capitalism. Let me quote one example from a letter he wrote in 1878 to the Editor of *Otechestvennye Zapiski* refuting an article by Mikhailovski:

> He (Mikahilovski) absolutely insists on transforming my historical sketch of the genesis of capitalism in Western Europe into a historico-philosophical theory of the general course fatally imposed on all peoples, whatever the historical circumstances in which they find themselves placed.... But I beg his pardon. That is to do me both too much honor and too much discredit.

An English version of this letter is now published in Shanin (1984).

[22] For a lucid demonstration of this, see Sah and Stiglitz (1984).

investment allocation with sectoral non-shiftability of capital for an emphasis on basic capital goods industries as opposed to consumer goods industries, as is suggested in the planning models of Feldman (1928/1964) and Mahalanobis (1953). The presumption of a low social rate of time discount and the consequent consumption sacrifices on the part of workers and the peasants for the sake of investment in capital-intensive industrialization programs are, however, hard to justify[23] in situations of increasing inequality, unemployment, and the government's frequent inability to control conspicuous consumption of the rich and wastage and graft in the public bureaucracy, and the white elephants in the state-run industrial sector.

5. Trade and development

5.1. A major point of apparent conflict between neoclassical (or classical) and Marxist views that looms large in development economics centers around the idea of gains from trade and specialization. Liberal economists never tire of emphasizing the benefits of voluntary exchange based on comparative advantage (with appropriate qualifications for learning by doing, externalities, diversification as insurance against market risks, and so on). At the other end there is a large number of development economists, some, though certainly not all, of whom are associated with the Latin American dependency school (both Marxist and non-Marxist), who are deeply suspicious of trade contacts and foreign economic "intrusions", based on the historical experience of oppressive relationships between the "center" and the "periphery". Some of the heat generated in the debates between the two sides is, of course, attributable to misunderstanding of each other's position and talking at cross-purposes. For example (if we leave aside international relations of plunder or tribute and focus on market exchange), it is quite consistent for the "periphery" to gain from trade with the "center" (in the Samuelsonian sense of having the opportunity to trade as better than being denied that opportunity), and yet for the former to be exploited by the latter in the Marxian sense (that the former would have been better off in the counterfactual world of a more egalitarian international distribution of assets),[24] just as in a capitalist society the assetless worker gains from trading his labor power (as opposed to not working for the capitalist), and yet is exploited in the Marxian sense. There is also often an elementary confusion among some Marxists about the meaning of a nation's "gain" that the liberal economist imputes to trade: he means *potential* gain with appropriate inter-group redistribution. In the absence

[23] For an analysis of the suboptimality of collective savings and the "prisoners' dilemma" aspect of the social rate of time discount, see Sen (1984, chs. 4 and 5).

[24] For a rigorous exposition of this idea in the context of the unequal exchange literature, see Roemer (1983).

of such redistribution, the gain may accrue only to a "comprador" class with the majority of people actually losing from trade. To the extent Emmanuel's (1972) idea of unequal exchange refers to a transfer of value from the capital-poor periphery to the capital-rich center in the process of international trade, it thus does not negate the neoclassical idea of potential gains from trade.

This is not to deny the very important differences between the Marxian and neo-Ricardian models[25] of trade on the one hand, and the neoclassical on the other, particularly in terms of the role of circulating capital as an independent determinant of comparative advantage and of income distribution, which in the neoclassical model is endogenously determined but in the other models depends on different historical and institutional processes in the trading countries (including differential worker bargaining power and modes of production in the center and the periphery). It should also be noted that the standard neoclassical treatment of gains from trade, which involves a comparison of hypothetical autarchic equilibria, usually underplays the fact that such a comparison may not be meaningful when the process of trade itself changes factor availabilities, utilization of scale economies, technologies, and even demand patterns.

To the extent that unequal exchange refers to the real possibility of unfavorable terms of trade for the periphery, this has long been recognized in standard trade theory, given the high income elasticity of import demand in the periphery, relatively low world demand for many of its exportables and the monopoly power of giant trading companies of the center. Bacha (1978) has thus couched this aspect of Emmanuel's problem in an extended Prebisch–Singer framework. If, however, prices in this model cannot be relied upon to ensure balance of payments equilibrium and one allows for quantity adjustments, Ocampo (1986) shows that there may be a trade-off between terms of trade and employment level in the periphery, so that less unequal exchange may entail higher unemployment.

5.2. Marxist theory, of course, goes beyond static distribution effects of trade and other transactions with foreign countries. The theory of imperialism emphasizes the dynamic effects (some positive, some negative) of foreign capitalist penetration of underdeveloped economies. Marx and Engels primarily stressed (though with growing reservations in their later years) the historically progressive role of colonialism and trade, with their "brutal but necessary" function of destroying pre-capitalist structures. Marxist writers on imperialism at the turn of the century (Lenin, Luxemburg, and others) pointed to the ambiguous role of foreign capital, the weak and dependent nature of local bourgeoisie, and the tendency of the international division of labor to confine colonial production to mineral and agricultural primary products. In more recent years writers like Baran (1957) and

[25]See the chapter by David Evans (Volume II, Chapter 25) in this Handbook for a discussion of neo-Ricardian trade models.

many of his direct or indirect followers in the dependency school[26] have gone farther and seriously questioned the viability of capitalist development in under-developed countries integrated into the world economy, in view of surplus expropriation by foreign capital in alliance with domestic pre-capitalist oligarchies. Ironically, pessimism about prospects of peripheral capitalism reached new heights among these writers of the dependency school precisely in the decades when many of these less-developed countries were experiencing a substantial expansion in capitalist growth and trade. As Cardoso (1977) remarks, "history had prepared a trap for pessimists". Foreign capital and transnational enterprise have led to a rapid capitalist transformation of some of these econo-mies (e.g. pre-debt-crisis Brazil, Mexico, Malaysia); on the other hand, industrial growth was very slow in countries like Burma which adopted a policy of virtual delinking with foreign trade and investment interests, or like India which, compared to most other major non-socialist developing countries, followed a substantially autarchic policy. The dramatic cases of growth in some of the East Asian "open" economies (like South Korea or Taiwan) have even started posing a competitive challenge to the industrially advanced economies in many sectors.

Much of this growth cannot be described as "dependent" development. In this process, as in the earlier phase of nationalization of foreign investment in the extractive industries and public utilities in most countries, the state along with the domestic capitalist class has played the decisive role. Even in Brazil, where the military regime had a strong commitment to the internationalization of the domestic market with a substantial involvement of the transnationals, a tight integration of state and local private capital transformed some of the leading sectors in Brazilian growth, most notably the petrochemical sector [see Evans (1982)]. Of course, many critics have elaborately commented on the negative consequences of the uneven, lopsided, "disarticulated" pattern of growth in these countries, but the issue of unpleasant aspects of capitalist growth should surely be kept separate from that of viability of capitalism. Some Marxists now recognize the overemphasis in the dependency literature on the process of *circulation*[27] (as opposed to the process of production), its unduly stagnationist perspective, and the neglect of the complex role of the state. Neoclassical economists, on the other hand, completely ignore the historical role of foreign trade and investment in altering the structure of property rights in the economy, the balance of class forces in civil society, and the nature of the state.

Largely inspired by the Marxist and structuralist comments on the history of international transactions between the center and the periphery, there now exists

---

[26] Palma (1978) has traced the Marxist origin of the main ideas of this school to the Sixth Congress of the Communist International in 1928.

[27] For Marxist criticisms on this line, see Laclau (1971), Brenner (1977), and Cardoso and Falleto (1979).

a large theoretical literature on the so-called North–South models, focusing on the asymmetry in structure and performance of the two aggregative trading groups of countries. In different models one or more of the following kinds of asymmetries in the features of the center and the periphery have been assumed:

(a) differential income elasticities of demand of importables and exportables as in the standard Prebisch argument;

(b) asymmetry in product market structure, with mark-up pricing and monopoly rent from product innovations in the center;

(c) asymmetry in labor market conditions, with inelastic labor supply in the center and unlimited labor supply in the periphery, as in the Solow–Lewis model of Findlay (1980), and with wages in the periphery equal to average productivity of labor in the food sector and strong unions in the production of exportables in the center, as in the extended Lewis model of Bardhan (1982);

(d) rigidities in output in the periphery, whereas the center is a demand-driven Keynes–Kalecki economy, with supply perfectly elastic at a price equal to a mark-up on variable costs and employment and output determined by investment, as in the models of Taylor (1983a, ch. 10) and Kanbur and Vines (1986);

(e) the larger initial capital stock in the center allowing for larger external economies of scale in the production of manufactures, and with profits reinvested larger cumulative advantage in manufacturing, as in the model of Krugman (1981);

(f) asymmetry in the generation and diffusion of technical progress in the form of both product and process innovations.

Many of these models confirm the original Prebisch insight that productivity improvements in export production may be transferred through a worsening of the barter terms of trade for the periphery, but retained through higher real incomes in the center. In the Solow–Lewis model improvements in productivity or thrift benefit the periphery in the form of larger employment. As expected, in the Keynes–Kalecki economy thrift is not a blessing. As contributions to the literature on uneven development, items (e) and (f), seem much more promising, particularly emphasizing the cumulative process involved in economies of scale in production, information gathering, and acquisition of technological capability. The advantage of backwardness emphasized in Findlay's (1978) model of technological diffusion is often more than outweighted by the localized nature of technical progress in advanced countries and the entry deterrence involved in the large fixed costs in learning and adaptation of new technology.

5.3. One major difference in the structuralist literature on trade and development from the neoclassical has traditionally been the empirical pre-judgment in the former of price inelasticities of demand and supply and of varying degrees of export pessimism. Chenery's famous two-gap model was an early attempt to theoretically examine the consequences: how the ex ante desired level of investment may not be realized due to lack of foreign exchange to pay for imported intermediate and capital goods. In the neoclassical literature the investment level implied by the savings constraint can always be reached through reductions in competitive imports (or increases in competitive exports) which free the necessary foreign exchange for investment purposes. Neoclassical economists also point out that even when there are serious restrictions on expansion of exports of all developing countries taken together, an individual country's exports may be more price-sensitive and may depend more on domestic factors of demand, supply, and trade policy. To this the structuralist answer is that in a non-Walrasian world even a "small" country can face a foreign exchange bottleneck, with its exports restricted by Keynesian unemployment in other countries, not necessarily by domestic excess demand. The foreign effective demand constraint on exports may ease over time if domestic prices go down as unused capacity emerges; a lower real exchange rate may then improve exports. Bacha (1984) has extended the two-gap model to the case where capital movements assume the form of interest-bearing foreign debt: credit rationing in world capital markets may still keep a developing country under a binding foreign exchange constraint. In a disequilibrium macroeconomic model Arida and Bacha (1987) show that the structuralist viewpoint correctly apprehends the nature of disequilibria when the goods market is in excess supply, but, on the other hand, an economy can present unemployment, external deficit, and excess supply of goods, apparently confirming the structuralist diagnosis, and yet, a Walrasian equilibrium may exist, suggesting that exchange rate devaluations may be called for.

5.4. A superb result of neoclassical trade theory, attributable largely to the Bhagwati–Ramaswami (1963) model of domestic distortions and optimum trade policy, has delinked the traditional association between the advocacy of liberal trade policy and that of laissez-faire in domestic economic policy. It became easier to be an avid interventionist in domestic economic matters, and yet remain a liberal trade theorist maintaining the position that trade restriction is not the first-best policy to tackle most problems of a (small) economy. Since then – as Little (1982) reports in a triumphant account – a formidable combination of neoclassical trade theory, project evaluation theory, empirical studies of the high cost of restricted foreign trade regimes, and glowing accounts of "outward-oriented" East Asian success stories has effectively challenged and undercut the basis of a pronounced anti-trade bias in the early structuralist development literature. While the latter definitely needed the challenge of clear rigorous thinking and the neoclassical offerings indisputably contain many gems of first-best wisdom, I think in the nth best world of practical politics, industrial strategy, imperfect tradability, incomplete markets, and costly acquisition of technological capability the clear-headed structuralist need not concede too much (even though he will have to give up vestiges of any "knee-jerk" protectionism).

The standard neoclassical prescription of "getting the prices right" and bringing them in line with international prices, even though desirable in many cases, is not a necessary, and certainly not a sufficient, condition for successful industrialization.[28] The neoclassical presumption of perfect tradability is invalid in the case of many industrial products and elements of technology to be assimilated, with some of them actually inherently non-tradable. This may call for selective government intervention, rather than the neutral incentive regime of neoclassical policy literature. Welfare losses from lack of coordination and integrated decision-making with imperfect tradability under increasing returns may be relatively large, even in comparison with the empirical estimates of losses of misallocation under policy-induced distortions that the neoclassicals have marshalled. If managing the local acquisition of technological capability, more than factor accumulation or allocation, is at the core of industrialization, the catalytic role of strategic and selective intervention is imperative in information gathering, in encountering indivisibilities in effective assimilation of new knowledge, in bargaining terms of technology agreements, in underwriting risks and raising credit, in providing marketing infrastructure, in coordinating rationalization in established industries, in minimizing the social costs of dislocation in industrial reorganization, and, in general, in sailing the unchartered waters of potential dynamic comparative advantage, as the recent history of Japan and South Korea amply demonstrates.

It is by now well known[29] that the favorite neoclassical showcase of South Korea is not predominantly one of market liberalism but of aggressive and judiciously selective state intervention. The Korean state has heavily used the illiberal compliance mechanisms of selective command and administrative discretion, restricting imports for industrial promotion, disciplining the private sector through control over domestic credit, foreign exchange and underwriting of foreign borrowing, and public enterprises leading the way in many areas. It is not that the South Korean state has always (or even primarily) used the first-best policies of the neoclassical distortion literature, some of their policy instruments are basically the same as the ones that have drawn neoclassical wrath in slow-growing "inward-looking" economies. But they have used these instruments with speed and flexibility, tackling economic targets like a military operation. Neoclassical economists are, of course, right in pointing out that the export-orientation of the Korean state has allowed for larger utilization of scale economies in promotion of infant industries and that the state's alertness in using the signals emanating from world markets to judge dynamic efficiency has helped in keeping firms on their toes.

---

[28]A good analysis of some of the main issues, particularly in relation to technological change, that we have drawn upon is that of Pack and Westphal (1986).

[29]See Jones and Sakong (1980), Pack and Westphal (1986).

6. Economic policy and the state

6.1. The immediately preceding discussion has already brought us to the question of policy-making and the state. Early development economics often displayed an unquestioning faith in the ability of the state to correct market failures and imperfections and to effectively direct the economic process towards development goals. After the experience of massive government interventions of the last few decades in many developing countries, the literature has now turned full circle; it is now full of gory neoclassical accounts of "public failures" of regulatory, interventionist states. The neo-neoclassical economists emphasizing transaction costs and imperfect information see problems on both sides: on the one hand, the traditional neoclassical models ignore that under information-theoretic considerations the market equilibrium is in general not Pareto efficient, that it may not be possible to decentralize efficient resource allocations, and that information exchange often takes place through signals other than prices; on the other hand, the information problems involved in adverse selection and moral hazard are no less acute for the planning or regulatory authorities than for the private sector. While there are problems on both sides and they sharply differ from one historical situation to another, one need not always take an agnostic position on this matter, even on an a priori basis. Of the different items of transaction costs, identification costs, and enforcement costs may be lower under private market institutions (individual actors may locate one another more easily than government agencies and self-interest rather than command may be a better enforcer), but negotiation costs may be lower under administrative institutions and there may also be some economies of scale in administrative enforcement. In particular, when prisoners' dilemma type collective action problems are important or economies of coordination, as in situations of industrial and technological strategy discussed in the preceding section, are significant, private market mechanisms are particularly deficient. Similarly, in risk-pooling and in concentrating resources to start a process of cumulative causation, as is often the case in early industrialization, central mediation and planning have important functions to perform. Even in more general cases, Farrell (1987) has constructed a plausible rigorous example of how under incomplete information and imperfections of the bargaining process private property rights and voluntary negotiation can be less efficient than even an uninformed and bumbling bureaucrat. It should also be stressed that our discussion should not be confined to the polar opposites of private market and centralized bureaucracy; there may be many small-group cooperative institutions which may avoid some of the "failures" of the two poles and adequately reconcile problems of equity and efficiency.

6.2. Much of the policy discussion (neoclassical or institutionalist) in development economics is often conducted in a political vacuum. Economists are quick with their suggestions for improving allocation efficiency, accumulation or income distribution, but governments are frequently slow in implementing them or sometimes even inclined to go in the opposite way, not necessarily because they lack the awareness or the advice. Our theories of economic policy need a good theory of the state. Marxists are usually more forthcoming in spelling out their theory of the state than the others, but more often than not it is of a rather crude instrumentalist variety, with the state as a direct tool of the dominant class (or in the slightly more sophisticated version, the state has "relative autonomy", acting not at the behest of, but on behalf of, that class).

The state is also passive in the recent neoclassical theories of political economy (whether in the public choice or the international trade literature)[30] where the state passively responds to rent-seeking behavior or directly unproductive profit-seeking activities of various interest groups and lobbies. The neoclassical emphasis is on the social wastage of resources involved in such political processes.[31] This waste is measured as a deviation from the competitive equilibrium – a hypothetical alternative without any information, transaction, or political costs. This seems to me a comparison of very limited value; as North (1984) points out in this context, "there is no meaningful standard of Pareto efficiency possible, since one cannot specify a least-cost structure of government for any given economic output". One can, however, allow for costs of government and define wastage as occurring only when resources are diverted beyond what is accounted for by these costs. The use of a Pareto criterion is inappropriate also because the major focus of political processes is distribution. The neoclassicals routinely show how, given the outcome of the political process, one could do better since it is away from the utility-possibility frontier, but that does not prove that any given market outcome, which is presumably on the frontier, is necessarily better: the two actual outcomes may be, and often are, Pareto incomparable.

More important than the static misallocation effects of the politics of clientelism are its dynamic effects on the processes of accumulation. Olson (1982) has emphasized the prisoners' dilemma type problems that arise in the context of a multiplicity of pressure groups and the consequences they have for the performance of an economy over time. Bardhan (1984b) has extended this to the case of a large and heterogeneous coalition of dominant classes (with multiple veto powers) in contemporary India and used this collective action problem as part of an explanation of the frittering away of investible surplus in the form of public

---

[30] For a collection of articles in these and other strands of the neoclassical literature, see Collander (1984).

[31] As Milgrom and Roberts (1987) point out, within the hierarchical organization of the capitalist firm, where there is a great deal of centralization of authority, the costs of various kinds of "influence activities" can also be considerable.

subsidies and of indifferent management of public capital, resulting in slow industrial growth.

The Indian example also suggests that the state today is much more powerful than is visualized in the Marxian or neoclassical political economy of class or pressure group politics. In many developing countries, the state controls the "commanding heights" of the economy, owning a large part of the non-agricultural economy and regulating the flow of credit, foreign exchange, and investment licenses. To a large extent it can play one class against another, local capital against foreign, one transnational company against another, all for the purpose of furthering its own goals. This is not to deny that the articulated interests of organized classes and pressure groups act as serious constraints on policy formulation and, particularly, implementation, but to focus exclusively on them is to ignore the large range of choices in goal formulation, agenda setting, and policy execution that the state leadership usually has. I think both Marxist and neoclassical political economies err in taking the state merely as an arena of group competition and in not including the state itself as a strategic actor in a game of mixed conflict and cooperation with other groups. The state as an autonomous actor should not be identified with the bureaucracy (as is usually done in the neoclassical political economy literature). One should distinguish between the top political leadership representing the state (let us call it the state elite) which takes the general political decisions, and the hierarchy of agents, the bureaucracy, which is supposed to implement those decisions. The process of implementation often generates various kinds of rental income which, to a significant extent, accrues to the bureaucracy and the latter forms a pressure group to secure this income flow, with goals which are often much narrower than those set by the state elite. The impulses that shape major policies and actions by the latter are fuelled not merely by motives of self-aggrandizement but quite often also by what Miliband (1983) calls its "conception of the national interest" in a way that the neoclassical theories of predatory or rentier state or North's (1981) revenue-maximizing discriminating-monopolist state or the simple Marxist class-driven state somehow fail to capture. In many cases of state-directed industrialization this leadership genuinely considers itself as the trustee of the nation's deeply held collective aspirations and derives its political legitimacy from them. In a world of international military and economic competition, one, though not the only, form these aspirations often take is to strive for rapid economic development.

None of the existing theories of the state, however, provides a satisfactory general theoretical explanation of how different interventionist states with command over roughly similar instruments of control end up being a developmental state in some cases (e.g. South Korea) as opposed to a primarily regulatory one in some others (e.g. India), or for the same country (say, South Korea) pass from a preoccupation with zero-sum rent-seeking (in the Rhee regime) to a dynamic entrepreneurial state (as in the Park and Chun regimes). Clearly, many international and historical conjunctural forces and path-dependent sequences (like those we have emphasized at the end of Section 3) are important here.

In general discussions of policy implementation it is customary to ascribe chronic failures to a lack of "political will" (whatever that means) or a lack of "social discipline" – with which Myrdal (1968) characterized his "soft" states. In the context of economic growth it is rather the capacity of the system to *insulate* economic management from the distributive demands of pork-barrel politics that seems to make the crucial difference. The South Korean state under an authoritarian military regime has centralized decision-making power in the executive branch, granted considerable operational space to economic technocrats and carried out a corporatist restructuring of relations with labor, business, and the rural sector to an extent unmatched even by the Latin American states at the peak of their so-called bureaucratic-authoritarian phase. But authoritarianism is neither necessary nor sufficient for the insulation process. Japan manages to have a high degree of such insulation with a reasonably liberal democratic government. Myrdal's own Sweden is another such example. On the other hand, the authoritarian regimes of many developing countries have not succeeded in isolating the management of the public economy from the ravages of rent-seeking processes. It is sometimes suggested that if the politics of a given developing country is "messy" and the state lacks the ability to insulate, then it better be non-interventionist and leave things to neoclassical first-best rules, so the least amount of vested-interest structures are created. I find this naive, as the very reasons why insulation is infeasible are often also the ones which will make first-best policies inoperative and, in the inevitable absence of lump-sum redistribution, a policy of relative inaction may be distributionally unacceptable.

7. Concluding remarks

In conclusion let me briefly refer to Hirschman's (1982) sad account of development economics, reeling, as he describes it, under "attacks" from neo-Marxist as well as neoclassical writings, and "wounded" by a series of political disasters in developing countries. In response to Hirschman's premature obituary of development economics, it is, of course, easy to point out that it is alive and well, at least its vital signs are no less pronounced than those in the rest of economics. But what Hirschman was really referring to was the marked decline in the initial tempo and expectations (at least those in the minds of the pioneers of the subject, of which he was clearly one), and in the confidence of a brash young subdiscipline that "it could slay the dragon of backwardness virtually by itself". In some sense it is better that the subject gets over its initial delusions of grandeur sooner than later, and settles down to its enormously complex, concrete, if mundane, tasks. "We may have gained in maturity", as Hirschman consoles himself, "what we have lost in excitement."

In this maturation process not merely have we seen the "big-push" enthusiasm of some of the development economists of the 1950s dampened by the subsequent *dirigiste* excesses, autarchic inefficiencies, and adverse distributional consequences of some industrialization programs, but we have also seen the feet of clay of some of their neo-Marxist and neoclassical challengers. In contrast to the missionary zeal of these contending early protagonists, we are now somewhat more circumspect in rallying to partisan causes and more sensitive to problems and pitfalls on all sides. In our heretical eclecticism we have even suggested in this paper that the differences between alternative approaches are now narrower than are generally perceived[32] and that there is some scope for culling valuable insights from all of them, without underplaying their still substantially different perspectives.

In development economics, as in much of social science in general, the most valuable contribution of the Marxist approach is the sense of history with which it is imbued, its focus on the tension between property relations and productive potential in a given social formation, and on the importance of collective action and power in enhancing or thwarting processes of institutional change to resolve that tension, its insistence on bringing to the forefront of public policy debates an analysis of the nature of the state and the constellation of power groupings in civil society, and, of course, its abiding commitment to certain normative ideas on questions of exploitation and injustice. Its processes of reasoning, however, leave much to be desired, with its frequent substitution of convenient teleology for explanatory mechanisms and of a kind of murky institutionalism for a rigorous rationale of (formal or informal) contractual arrangements, and its failure to base aggregative results firmly on consistent actions of economic agents at the micro level, ignoring as a consequence incentive compatibility problems, issues of contract enforement in a world of imperfect information, strategic interaction of agents (even with commonality of class interests), the free-rider problem in class formation and action, and the disequilibrium dynamics of adjustment paths. Neoclassical economics has, of course, made substantial contributions in some of these areas and Marxists, who are not unduly worried about "tainted" tools, can profitably borrow from neoclassical methodology. There is no denying that the "great" questions of economics or history are usually asked first by the Marxists, even though we may not always accept their pre-digested answers or may insist on explanatory mechanisms and processes even when the answers are broadly acceptable. The neoclassicals, who are usually more refined

---

[32] Chenery (1975) already suggested that the differences between these approaches are relatively narrow when it comes to specifying the alternative empirically testable hypotheses.

in their spelling out of the causal mechanism in an implicit social process of "natural" selection, are often insensitive to their institutionally aseptic assumptions and ahistorical categories; in their obsession with the minutiae of "getting the prices right" they often get their historical and institutional environment wrong. As we have mentioned before, some of the neo-neoclassical models now fully recognize the crucial dependence of efficiency of resource allocation on asset ownership structures and property relations. Similarly, some of these non-Walrasian models have given up on market-clearing factor prices and explored the microeconomics of equilibria with involuntary unemployment and rationing. Similar bridge-building between the alternative approaches has been attempted by rational-choice Marxists in tracing the micro foundations of class analysis in postulates of individual behavior and in general in using the techniques of game theory in understanding social interaction and historical change in situations of interest conflicts. Such attempts at exploration of each other's territory, in spite of the withering scorn of purists on both sides of the barricade, are refreshing and likely to increase in future. But at the same time we should recognize that the economists on *both* sides are better equipped to handle "interests", rather than "passions" (to use Hirschman's eloquent distinction) that move individuals and social groups, and that both usually share a limiting vision of the goals of development, ignoring ways of expanding human capabilities beyond improvements on the technological frontier. Both sides are also prone to claim too much, in the generality of laws of motion of history (as in the case of Marxists) or of the supposedly universalistic postulates of human behavior (as in the case of neoclassicals), overlooking important historical specificities and localized contexts of culture and ecology.

References

Akerlof, G. (1984) *An economic theorist's book of tales*. Cambridge: Cambridge University Press.
Arida, P. and Bacha, E. (1987) 'Balance of payments: A disequilibrium analysis for semi-industrialized economies', *Journal of Development Economics*, October.
Arthur, B. (1985) 'Competing technologies and lock-in by historical small events', CEPR Publication no. 43, Stanford.
Bacha, E. (1978) 'An interpretation of unequal exchange from Prebisch–Singer to Emmanuel', *Journal of Development Economics*, December.
Bacha, E. (1984) 'Growth with limited supplies of foreign exchange: A reappraisal of the two-gap model', in: M. Syrquin, L. Taylor and L. Westphal, eds., *Economic Structure and Performance*. New York: Academic Press.
Bacha, E. and Taylor, L. (1976) 'The unequalizing spiral: A first growth model for Belindia, *Quarterly Journal of Economics*, May.
Baran, P. (1957) *The political economy of growth*. New York: Monthly Review Press.
Bardhan, P. (1982) 'Unequal exchange in a Lewis-type world', in: M. Gersovitz et al., eds. *The theory and experience of economic development*. London: Allen and Unwin.
Bardhan, P. (1983) 'Labor tying in a poor agrarian economy: A theoretical and empirical analysis', *Quarterly Journal of Economics*, August.

Bardhan, P. (1984a) *Land, labor and rural poverty: essays in development economics*. New York: Columbia University Press.

Bardhan, P. (1984b) *The political economy of development in India*. Oxford: Blackwell.

Bardhan, P., ed. (forthcoming) *The economic theory of agrarian institutions*. Oxford: Oxford University Press.

Bardhan, P. and Rudra, A. (1986) 'Labor mobility and the boundaries of the village moral economy', *Journal of Peasant Studies*, April.

Basu, K. (1984) *The less developed economy*. Oxford: Blackwell.

Becker, G. (1981) *A treatise on the family*. Cambridge, MA: Harvard University Press.

Bell, C. and Zusman, P. (1976) 'A bargaining theoretic approach to cropsharing contracts', *American Economic Review*, September.

Bhaduri, A. (1977) 'On the formation of usurious interest rates in backward agriculture'. *Cambridge Journal of Economics*, March.

Bhaduri, A. (1983) *The economic structure of backward agriculture*. London: Academic Press.

Bhagwati, J. and Ramaswami, V.K. (1963) 'Domestic distortions, tariffs and the theory of optimum subsidy', *Journal of Political Economy*, February.

Binswanger, H. and Rosenzweig, M. (1984) 'Contractual arrangements, employment and wages in rural labor markets: A critical review', in: H. Binswanger and M. Rosenzweig, eds., *Contractual arrangements, employment and wages in rural labor markets in Asia*. New Haven: Yale University Press.

Binswanger, H. and Rosenzweig, M. (1986) 'Behavior and material determinants of production relations in agriculture', April.

Bliss, C.J. and Stern, N.H. (1978) 'Productivity, wages and nutrition', *Journal of Development Economics*, December.

Boserup, E. (1965) *The conditions of agricultural growth: The economics of agrarian change under population pressure*. New York: Aldine Publishers.

Bowles, S. (1985) 'The production process in a competitive economy: Walrasian, neo-Hobbesian, and Marxian models', *American Economic Review*, March.

Braverman, A. and Stiglitz, J.E. (1986) 'Landlords, tenants and technological innovations', *Journal of Development economics*, October.

Brenner, R. (1977) 'The origins of capitalist development: A critique of neo-Smithian Marxism', *New Left Review*, July–August 1977.

Brenner, R. (1985) 'The social basis of economic development', in: J. Roemer, ed., *Analytical Marxism*. Cambridge: Cambridge University Press.

Buffie, E. (1984) book review of *Structuralist macroeconomics*, by L. Taylor, *Journal of Development Economics*, September–October.

Cardoso, F.H. (1977) 'The originality of the copy: ECLA and the idea of development', *CEPAL Review*.

Cardoso, F.H. and Falleto, E. (1979) *Dependency and development in Latin America*. Berkeley: University of California Press.

Calvo, G. (1979) 'Quasi-Walrasian theories of unemployment', *American Economic Review*, May.

Chenery, H.B. (1975) 'The structuralist approach to development policy', *American Economic Review*, May.

Collander, D., ed. (1984) *Neoclassical political economy*. Cambridge, MA: Ballinger.

Dasgupta, P. and Ray, D. (1986) 'Inequality as a determinant of malnutrition and unemployment', *Economic Journal*, December.

Dobb, M. (1960) *An essay on economic growth and planning*. London: Routledge and Kegan Paul.

Dutt, A. (1984) 'Stagnation, income distribution and monopoly power', *Cambridge Journal of Economics*.

Eaton, B.C. and White, W. (1982) 'Agent compensation and the limits of bonding', *Economic Inquiry*, July.

Elster, J. (1979) *Ulysees and the sirens: Studies in rationality and irrationality*. Cambridge: Cambridge University Press.

Elster, J. (1983) *Explaining technical change*. Cambridge: Cambridge University Press.

Elster, J. (1985) *Making sense of Marx*. Cambridge: Cambridge University Press.

Emmanuel, A. (1972) *Unequal exchange*. New York: Monthly Review Press.

Emmanuel, A. (1982) *Appropriate or underdeveloped technology?* New York: Wiley.

Eswaran, M. and Kotwal, A. (1985) 'A theory of two-tier labour markets in agrarian economies', *American Economic Review*, March.

Eswaran, M. and Kotwal, A. (1986) 'Access to capital and agrarian production organization', *Economic Journal*, June.

Evans, P. (1982) 'Reinventing the bourgeoisie: State entrepreneurship and class formation in the context of dependent capitalist development', *American Journal of Sociology*, supplement.

Farrell, J. (1987) 'Information and the Coase theorem', *Journal of Economic Perspectives*, Fall.

Feldman, G.A. (1964) 'On the theory of growth rates of national income', 1928, translated in: N. Spulber, ed., *Foundations of Soviet strategy for economic growth*. Bloomington, IN: Indiana University Press.

Findlay, R. (1978) 'Relative backwardness, direct foreign investment and the transfer of technology: A simple dynamic model', *Quarterly Journal of Economics*, February.

Findlay, R. (1980) 'The terms of trade and equilibrium growth in the world economy', *American Economic Review*, June.

Geertz, C. (1963) *Agricultural involution: The process of ecological change in Indonesia*. Berkeley: University of California Press.

Hirschman, A. (1982) 'The rise and decline of development economics', in: M. Gersovitz et al., eds. *The theory and experience of economic development*. London: Allen and Unwin.

De Janvry, A. (1978) 'Social structure and biased technical change in Argentine agriculture', in: H. Binswanger and V.W. Ruttan, eds., *Induced innovation: Technology, institutions and development*. Baltimore, MD: Johns Hopkins University Press.

De Janvry, A. (1981) *The agrarian question and reformism in Latin America*. Baltimore, MD: Johns Hopkins University Press.

De Janvry, A. and Sadoulet, E. (1983) 'Social articulation as a condition for equitable growth', *Journal of Development Economics*, December.

Jones, L.P. and Sakong, I. (1980) *Government, business and entrepreneurship in economic development: The Korean case*. Cambridge, MA: Harvard University Press.

Kalecki, M. (1943) 'Political aspects of full employment', *Political Quarterly*, October–December.

Kanbur, S.M.R. and Vines, D. (1986) 'North–South interaction and commod control', *Journal of Development Economics*, October.

Krugman, P. (1981) 'Trade, accumulation and uneven development', *Journal of Development Economics*, April.

Laclau, E. (1971) 'Feudalism and capitalism in Latin America', *New Left Review*, 67.

Lapan, H. and Bardhan, P. (1973) 'Localized technical progress and transfer of technology and economic development', *Journal of Economic Theory*, December.

Leibenstein, H. (1957) *Economic backwardness and economic growth*. New York: Wiley.

Little, I.M.D. (1982) *Economic development: Theory, policy and international relations*. New York: Basic Books.

Lustig, N. (1980) 'Underconsumption in Latin American economic thought: Some considerations', *Review of Radical Political Economics*, spring.

Mahalanobis, P.C. (1953) 'Some observations on the process of growth of national income', *Sankhya*, September.

Marglin, S. (1967) 'The rate of interest and value of capital with unlimited supplies of labor', in: K. Shell, ed., *Essays on the theory of optimal economic growth*. Cambridge, MA: MIT Press.

Marglin, S. (1984) *Growth, distribution and prices*. Cambridge, MA: Harvard University Press.

Milgrom, P. and Roberts, J. (1987) 'Bargaining and influence costs and the organization of economic activity', working paper no. 8731, Berkeley.

Miliband, R. (1983) 'State power and class interests', *New Left Review*, 138.

Myrdal, G. (1968) *Asian drama: An enquiry into the poverty of nations*. London: Pelican.

Newbery, D. and Stiglitz, J.E. (1979) 'Sharecropping, risk-sharing and the importance of imperfect information', in: J.A. Roumasset et al., eds., *Risk, uncertainty and agricultural development*. SEARCH/ADC.

North, D.C. (1981) *Structure and change in economic history*. New York: Norton.

North, D.C. (1984) 'Three approaches to the study of institutions', in: D. Collander (1984).

Ocampo, J.A. (1986) 'New developments in trade theory and LDC's', *Journal of Development Economics*, June.

Okun, A.M. (1981) *Prices and quantities: A macroeconomic analysis*. Washington, DC: Brookings Institution.

Olson, M. (1982) *The rise and decline of nations: Economic growth, stagflation, and social rigidities*. New Haven, CT: Yale University Press.

Pack, H. and Westphal, L.E. (1986) 'Industrial strategy and technological change: Theory versus reality', *Journal of Development Economics*, June.

Palma, G. (1978) 'Dependency: A formal theory of underdevelopment or a methodology for the analysis of concrete situations of underdevelopment?', *World Development*, July–August.

Preobrazhensky, E. (1965) *The new economics*, 1926, English translation. Oxford: Clarendon Press.

Roemer, J. (1982) *A general theory of exploitation and class*. Cambridge, MA: Harvard University Press.

Roemer, J. (1983) 'Unequal exchange, labor migration and international capital flows: A theoretical synthesis', in: P. Desai, ed., *Marxism, central planning and the Soviet economy*. Cambridge, MA: MIT Press.

Ruttan, V.M. and Hayami, Y. (1984) 'Toward a theory of induced institutional innovation', *Journal of Development Studies*, July.

Sah, R.K. and Stiglitz, J.E. (1984) 'The economics of price scissors', *American Economic Review*, March.

Sen, A.K. (1960) *Choice of techniques*. Oxford: Blackwell.

Sen, A.K. (1984) *Resources, values and development*. Oxford: Blackwell.

Shanin, T. (1984) *Late Marx and the Russian road*. London: Routledge and Kegan Paul.

Shapiro, C. and Stiglitz, J.E. (1984) 'Equilibrium unemployment as a worker discipline device', *American Economic Review*, June.

Singh, I., Squire, L. and Strauss, J., eds. (1986) *Agricultural household models*. Baltimore, MD: Johns Hopkins University Press.

Stiglitz, J.E. (1969) 'Distribution of income and wealth among individuals', *Econometrica*.

Stiglitz, J.E. (1974) 'Alternate theories of wage determination and unemployment in LDC's: The labor turnover model', *Quarterly Journal of Economics*, May.

Stiglitz, J.E. (1985a) 'Information and economic analysis: A perspective', *Economic Journal*, supplement.

Stiglitz, J.E. (1985b) 'Economics of information and the theory of economic development', NBER working paper, February.

Stiglitz, J.E. and Weiss, A. (1981) 'Credit rationing in markets with imperfect information', *American Economic Review*, June.

Stoft, S. (1982) 'Cheat threat theory: An explanation of involuntary unemployment', mimeo.

Taylor, L. (1983a) *Structuralist macroeconomics*. New York: Basic Books.

Taylor, L. (1983b) 'Demand composition, income distribution and growth', mimeo.

Tversky, A. and Kahneman, D. (1986) 'Rational choice and the framing of decisions', *Journal of Business*, October.

Yellen, J. (1984) 'Efficiency wage models of unemployment', *American Economic Review*, May.

Chapter 4

ANALYTICS OF DEVELOPMENT: DUALISM

GUSTAV RANIS

Yale University

Contents

1. Introduction 74
2. Dualism in the history of economic thought 75
3. The modern analytics of closed dualism 76
4. Dualism in the open economy 86
References 91

Handbook of Development Economics, Volume I, Edited by H. Chenery and T.N. Srinivasan
© Elsevier Science Publishers B.V., 1988

1. Introduction

Definitions of dualism abound. There is, for example, a so-called sociological dualism which stresses cultural differences between Western and non-Western types of economic organizations usually associated with the name of Boeke. Such dualism emphasizes the differences in societal objectives, with Western economies driven by economic goals and Eastern societies by social or non-material goals. Most economists have been very critical of cultural/sociological dualism and its corollary of a backward-bending supply curve of labor – which in empirical reality may or may not exist – as well as its essentially static nature. The literature also contains the concept of technological dualism associated with the names of Higgins (1968) and Eckaus (1955) which focuses on the differences in technology between two sectors, one traditional with variable technical coefficients, the other, modern, with fixed coefficients. Others, e.g. Singer (1970), extend this notion to the international arena to trace the impact of international dualism on domestic Third World development in the Myrdal (1968)/Prebisch (1971) tradition.

The concept of dualism that will be utilized in this chapter is both more narrowly economic and dynamic. It focuses on the coexistence of two sectors which are basically asymmetrical – and thus dualistic – in terms of both product and organizational characteristics. The production asymmetry relevant here is that while traditional agriculture disposes over something approaching "fixed" inputs of land, very little capital, with large pre-existing inputs of labor, the modernizing manufacturing sector requires virtually no land, while capital can be accumulated and labor absorbed as needed. This asymmetry is also characterized by essentially one-way flows of labor and resources from agriculture to non-agriculture, as will be discussed below. Organizational asymmetry resides in the fact that, as a consequence of the different initial endowment conditions of the two sectors, their spatial characteristics, as well as their differential potential deployment of technology, asymmetrical rules of the game are in place in the labor market when the curtain rises on the development effort. Finally, our concept of dualism will be intrinsically dynamic since we will endeavor to trace the interactions between the two sectors over time in the closed economy context and, ultimately, with each other and the rest of the world, in the open economy context.

Section 2 briefly reviews the place of dualism in economic history and in the history of economic thought. Section 3 presents an examination of modern-day dualism in the closed economy, focusing on the main elements of linkage between the agricultural and non-agricultural sectors as well as on the normative problem of defining developmental success and non-success with the help of the concept of dualism in its dynamic version. Section 4 considers open dualism, focusing on the triangular relationships between domestic agriculture, domestic non-agriculture and the rest of the world, distinguishing between dualism in a colonial context from dualism in a developmental context.

2. Dualism in the history of economic thought

Undoubtedly the first clear manifestation of our concept of dualism appears in the tableau economique of the physiocrats. Although the emphasis there is on one preponderant "productive" sector, agriculture, the physiocrats also clearly envisioned its coexistence with a small non-agricultural (to them "non-productive") sector producing services, artisanal goods and other requirements of the ruling nobility – if the "produit net" of the soil (read agricultural surplus) was large enough to permit some labor reallocation. This essentially circular flow mechanism may yield slow increases in real per capita income over time as the productivity-enhancing results of "father teaching son" plus inter-regional specialization and an enhanced division of labor lead to increases in agricultural productivity. But these represent limited amendments to what is basically a fixed technological schema. It should be noted that the "serfs" in the system, mostly agricultural, a few allocated elsewhere, continue to maintain a virtually constant consumption standard.

Agrarian dualism which emphasized the fundamental primacy of agriculture, the importance of an agricultural surplus and the long run prognosis of stagnation gave way to the concept of classical dualism more or less coincident with the advent of the so-called industrial revolution in Western Europe. This classical concept à la Ricardo (1815) focused on the coexistence of still overwhelmingly dominant agricultural activities subject to diminishing returns to labor on the fixed land – and without benefit of technological change – and non-agricultural activities, later recognized as important and growing as a consequence mainly of the accumulation of fixed capital. While the classical school did not carefully model the interactions between these two sectors, it is clear that the main fuel for the reallocation of workers and the accumulation of industrial capital goods was seen as coming from the "profits" of agricultural capitalists, i.e. the agricultural surplus left over after agricultural workers and landlords (who consumed everything) had been paid off. It should be noted that the classicists introduced the related assumption of the near fixity of land combined with Malthusian population pressures in agriculture and that they retained the notion of an institutionally determined real wage in agriculture – even though the laboring class was now free and could bargain with the capitalists in setting the level of that wage.

While the classicists differed amongst themselves with respect to their overall prognosis for the dual economy as a whole, Ricardian–Malthusian pessimism with respect to the agricultural sector's ultimate stagnation was a dominant feature of their overall analytical work. In the absence of marked technology change, either generated within agriculture or via modern inputs from non-agriculture, agricultural stagnation and thus the drying up of the needed agricultural surplus represented the long-term outlook. Whether technology change and the exploration of economies of scale within the industrial sector would be sufficiently strong to provide enough industrial profits to rescue the situation remained controversial.

While the classicists deployed the analytics of dualism in this way the world around them was changing rapidly. What Kuznets (1966) later called the transition to modern growth was under way in Europe, i.e. more and more countries, having emerged from agrarianism into dualism, following England's lead, were now undergoing a transition from a dualistic structure into a one-sector modern economic growth system. This transition could be observed by means of structural changes in terms of value added, as agriculture (A) declines relative to manufacturing (M) and services (S), or in terms of the reallocation of labor from A to non-A until the agricultural sector ultimately becomes a mere appendage to the system as a whole. The same phenomenon spread geographically not only across Western Europe and to the so-called late comers, Japan, Germany, the United States, etc. but also to the so-called "overseas territories", or the developing countries, in post-World War II terminology. It is in this context that the post-war revival of analytical interest in development and in the usefulness of the dualism concept should be examined.

3. The modern analytics of closed dualism

The modern concept of dualism continues to be based on the notion of a "meaningful" asymmetry between two sectors, agriculture and non-agriculture. Taking our cue from the physiocrats, dualism arises in a situation in which the agricultural sector still plays a dominant role in the total economy, with a substantial proportion of the population, perhaps as much as 80 percent, living in dispersed conditions in the rural areas, while non-agricultural activities, in contrast, take place in relatively concentrated urban centers. In this context, the asymmetry arises both from the product characteristics as well as the organizational characteristics of the two sectors. Let us examine one at a time.

First, with respect to the product characteristics, agricultural products and non-agricultural products are different in kind and cannot readily be substituted for each other. It is well known that food is an essential component of consumption for both rural and urban households even as the urban industrial sector provides inputs for both, plus its share of total final consumption. In this sense, in the closed economy agriculture is a necessary condition for industry, while the converse does not hold. This early stage of necessarily asymmetric one-way flows termed "primitive socialist accumulation" by Preobrazenskii (1924) stands in contrast to the later emergence of balanced intersectoral growth in the dual economy. Because agriculture dominates the economy in terms of both employment and output generation early on, its performance not only conditions the overall development possibilities via savings, foreign exchange earnings and markets for non-agricultural goods, but it also interacts in a vital way with the non-agricultural sector through flows in the intersectoral financial, intersectoral commodity, and intersectoral labor markets. While these essential functions of the agricultural sector are, with time, increasingly shared by the industrial sector, the importance of product dualism during the early transition growth period needs to be remembered [see Kanbur and McIntosh (1985)].

Figure 4.1 provides an operational perspective of such a dualistic system showing the interrelationships between its agricultural and non-agricultural sectors in the closed economy context. Each of the sectors has been divided into a production sector and a household sector. The intersectoral linkages at this level of aggregation may be classified into three types, as shown by the three circles at the center of the diagram, i.e. (1) the intersectoral commodity market; (2) the intersectoral financial market; and (3) the intersectoral labor market. In our diagram the arrows indicate the direction of the flow of real goods and services, while movements in the opposite direction, of course, would imply the flow of money payments.

Let us begin with the intersectoral commodity market. Note that a part of the total output of the agricultural sector A goes to agricultural households for self consumption, A_a, and a part flows to the non-agricultural sector, a flow we have labeled as TAS or total agricultural surplus. This is a commodity surplus, i.e. the agricultural output available in excess of the traditional consumption of those working in agriculture. Part of it is consumed by non-agricultural households, A_n, and part of it flows as an intermediate input into the non-agricultural sector, A_m.

Turning to the non-agricultural sector, here total output, Q, is partly consumed by the non-agricultural households, Q_n, while the rest of the non-agricultural output takes the form of investment goods, I, or of goods purchased by the agricultural sector, Q_a, either for consumption by agricultural households, Q_c, or as modern inputs into agricultural production, Q_m.

The agricultural production sector receives land and labor services, Y_a, as well as modern inputs, Q_m. The incomes received by agricultural households are either spent on consumption, $A_a + Q_c$, or saved, S_a. Similarly, in the non-agricultural household sector factor payments Y_n are either consumed ($Q_n + A_n$) or saved, S_n. Together $S_a + S_n$ constitute the total available savings fund of the closed dualistic economy to finance investments via the intersectoral financial market.

In order to gain a full understanding of the role of the agricultural sector in this context we should note that the contribution of that sector to the rest of the economy can be measured in the first instance, and in a most basic sense, in

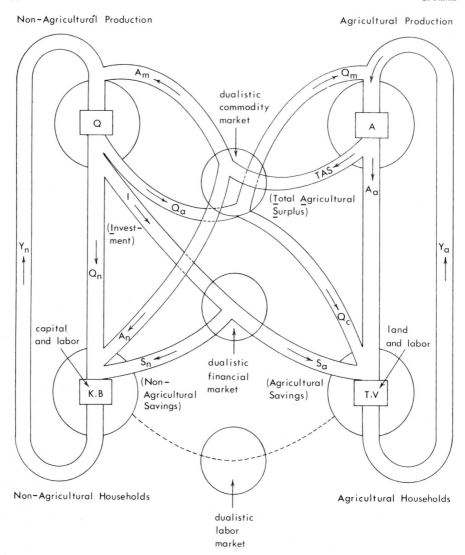

Figure 4.1. The operation of closed dualism.

terms of net real resources transferred, i.e. the difference between the truckloads
of food and raw materials delivered to the industrial sector and the truckloads of
industrial goods which are sent in the opposite direction. Shipments in both
directions flow through the intersectoral commodity market and thus, in this
physical sense, the agricultural sector's export surplus may be seen as the net
contribution of that sector to the industrialization process over time in terms of

the net resources flow. This net contribution of the agricultural sector may be labeled $B = TAS - Q_m - Q_c$. If we think of the two sectors as equivalent to two countries, B represents the export surplus of the agricultural sector or, equivalently, the import surplus of the non-agricultural sector, on the assumption that there is likely to be a net flow of resources from A to Q over time in the developing economy, even if not necessarily in every year, especially at the early stages.

Turning to the financial counterpart of this real resources contribution of the agricultural sector, we must next examine the dualistic financial market. Once again, as in the case of two countries, the savings of the agricultural sector may lead, aside from possible investments back in the same sector, to new capital formation in the other. In terms of financial intermediation we have the creation of a claim against non-agriculture the magnitude of which is determined by the size of the export surplus. In other words, the investment fund of the dualistic economy available for next period's capital accumulation derives from the savings out of the agricultural surplus in this period plus the possible profits or savings of the non-agricultural sector. With S_a and S_n providing the total savings in the closed economy, the financial intermediation network, either formal or informal, then helps to match up savers and investors and thus to finance the investment goods produced by the non-agricultural sector, as indicated in Figure 4.1. If we accept the simplifying (but not necessary) assumption that land and labor are the only factors of production in agriculture, and capital and labor the only factors of production in non-agriculture, we may, for convenience, hold that all industrial capital goods are destined for investment back in the non-agricultural sector. S_a thus represents the full amount of the financial credit extended by the agricultural sector to the non-agricultural sector.

In the dualistic type of developing economy, given an initially large agricultural sector, we can then assume that the savings out of the agricultural surplus serve as the principal fuel for the continued growth of the dualistic economy. This is so even taking into account the various possible leakages we have shown, plus the added possibility of a leakage in the form of a slightly higher standard of consumption over time for the agricultural workers themselves. For this reason it is likely that agricultural savings will constitute a major source of the economy's investment fund, dwarfing the savings of the non-agricultural sector in the early stages.

As to the intersectoral commodity market, the participants are, on one side, the owners of the agricultural surplus who sell surplus agricultural food and, on the other, the newly allocated industrial workers who may be thought of as possessing wage income in the form of non-agricultural goods and anxious to exchange these for the food "left behind". Once these transactions are completed the newly allocated industrial workers find themselves in possession of the agricultural goods which they need to consume. In this way the intersectoral commodity market is indispensable for transforming the consumption bundle of some of the agricultural labor force into a wages fund for newly allocated non-agricultural workers. At the same time the owners of the agricultural surplus obtain ownership of, or a claim against, a portion of the newly formed industrial output. Depending on the availability and diversity of the financial intermediation network, which should permit an increasing separation of ownership and control over time, such claims will be maintained in the form of savings and bank deposits, postal savings deposits, stocks and bonds, and, of course, direct ownership. The financial intermediation network must be sufficient in reach and diversity to provide the financial assets acceptable to various owners of the agricultural surplus and, in this way, enable the dualistic economy to convert its rural savings into productive non-agricultural investments. The satisfactory performance of these two markets must clearly be viewed as an interrelated package.

The third intersectoral market is the labor market through which some of the low, possibly – but not likely – even zero, marginal product agricultural labor force can be reallocated to more productive employment elsewhere. As we have seen earlier, the empirical reality is that up to 80 percent of the initial labor force may find itself in agriculture, with 20 percent in non-agriculture; in the context of a successful development effort those proportions can be reversed over a few decades. It is in the intersectoral labor market, moreover, that the second important analytical dimension of dualism, i.e. organizational dualism, is likely to be of major importance. It is based on the initial condition of an agricultural sector facing very high man/land ratios, traditional technology and production units frequently coincident with households – while in the non-agricultural sector we find fully capitalistic commercialized activities predominating, especially in reference to the urban large-scale activities operating on the basis of modern technology and specialization.

Organizational dualism as first put forward by the classical school, and by Lewis (1954) in his revision of classicism, insists that the determination of the real wage in the agricultural sector, given heavy population pressure on the scarce land in the presence of traditional technology, approaches that of a traditional or subsistence related consumption standard. Given the large number of spatially dispersed farmers facing low marginal products, this wage is based on some institutional sharing arrangement rather than on the marginal productivity calculus. In the commercialized non-agricultural sector the usual competitive principle can be expected to operate. It should be understood that the really guiding principle of organizational dualism is "commercialized" versus "non-commercialized", with "agricultural" versus "non-agricultural" serving as a short-hand. To the extent there is commercialized plantation agriculture and non-commercialized service or small industry activity, there is a less than complete mapping between product and organizational dualism.

Notice that this notion of an institutional wage in agriculture does not require that some of the agricultural labor force must be redundant in the sense that it can be removed, under assumptions of constant technology, without affecting agricultural output adversely – only that some proportion of the agricultural population receive a food allocation in excess of its marginal product. It is in this sense that organizational dualism is an important feature of the labor market. Given the abundance of labor and the relative scarcity of cooperating factors, mainly land, this is what is meant by the phenomenon of underemployment, i.e. a situation in which productive employment opportunities are limited not because of a lack of effective demand but because of technological and resource constraints. Even though technology is flexible, i.e. variable proportions obtain, the initially heavy endowment of labor relative to land means that a substantial portion of the agricultural labor force faces a low, or possibly even zero, marginal product condition which may well require a wage above the neoclassical marginal product to be agreed upon by the community, the family, the commune, or whatever organizational or tenurial structure exists within the particular agricultural system. Such a wage in excess of the marginal product may be set equal to the average product or – in order to leave a surplus, say for the head of the family – at some percentage of the average product. Nor do we need to assume that this institutional or bargain wage is constant over time. Such determination is likely to persist as long as the supply of agricultural labor remains in surplus in the sense that there are too many people on the land to permit a sharing nexus to be replaced by competitive rules. As Nurkse (1953) and Lewis (1954) have pointed out, given the heavy hand of history, while everyone has to be fed and no one can be fired, some people can be reallocated to higher productivity activities elsewhere and thus, by transferring labor from the traditional to the commercialized sector, an important existing slack in the economy can be taken up or "hidden rural savings" mobilized. This is all the more realistic when seen in the context of simultaneous changes in agricultural technology.

The existence of an institutional wage in agriculture should thus not be confused either with assertions about a zero marginal product – sometimes used only for convenience in formal modeling – or equated to the average product, again a matter of sheer convenience. Instead, the basic assertion is that wages in the traditional sector contain a strong dosage of output "sharing", largely a function of the fact that people cannot as readily be dismissed when households and production units coincide and/or when decisions are still made on a collective basis. Inter-household sharing has its roots in a village agrarian tradition where it serves as a form of insurance, given that bad times can strike any family and few are living far from the margin of subsistence [Scott (1976)].

This also does not mean, of course, that the institutional wage is likely to be constant, especially as agricultural productivity increases – only that the wage continues to lag behind a rising marginal product. The empirical record of labor-abundant countries which have experienced sustained agricultural productivity increases is certainly consistent with that hypothesis.

While, by its very definition, this institutional real wage cannot be scientifically determined, it is likely to be related to the consumption standard as a floor. Any institutional explanation of the level of agricultural real wages, of course, is not very satisfactory to economists, and many efforts have been made in recent years to link up such determination with specific peculiarities of rural organization, tenure arrangements, linked market features, etc. as an alternative to the acceptance of an eroding sharing nexus [Binswanger and Rosenzweig (1984)]. Nevertheless, the empirical reality of a gently upward-sloping supply curve of agricultural real wages, even in periods of rapid labor productivity increase, remains above controversy, for example, as Sen (1966) has demonstrated. Its significance is three-fold. First, it has distributional significance, especially when combined with classical savings behavior, i.e. savings that are mainly attributed to property. Secondly, in the dual economy context it has important allocation significance, e.g. as utilized in the work of Lewis, it is the main regulator of the allocation of the labor force as well as, when combined with product dualism, in the determination of the intersectoral terms of trade and intersectoral commodity exchange. Thirdly, the agricultural real wage, of course, has an impact on technology in both sectors. With an unlimited supply of labor in agriculture, the unskilled industrial real wage will tend to be tied to, though certainly not equal to, the agricultural real wage.

Consequently, the existence of relatively constant or gently sloping real wages in both sectors, with a gap between the two, should induce labor-intensive technology choices and, more importantly, labor using technology change over time in both the agricultural and non-agricultural sectors of the dual economy. Once the two wages are given within a general equilibrium context, the reallocation of agricultural labor to non-agricultural activities – occurring simultaneously with the generation of the agricultural surplus – is part of a static balanced growth context which needs to be explored more realistically in a dynamic setting. The so-called wage gap for unskilled labor in the two sectors is partly required to induce the typical agricultural worker to overcome his traditional attachments to soil and family, partly to meet transport costs, and partly also as a consequence of institutional factors affecting the level of wages in non-agriculture, i.e. minimum wage legislation, unionization, etc. which usually do not extend to the agricultural sector.

The heart of the development problem in the dual economy is thus the ability of the agricultural sector to yield sufficiently large agricultural surpluses and to preserve a sufficiently large part of such surpluses for productive investment in non-agriculture. Simultaneously, the non-agricultural sector, financed by this agricultural surplus plus the reinvestment of industrial profits, must grow fast enough to absorb the labor force being reallocated. Over time there clearly must thus result something of a balance between capital accumulation, allocated mainly to non-agriculture, and technology efforts in both sectors so as to approach a concept of balanced growth. Such balanced growth must, moreover, proceed at a pace in excess of additions to the population or labor force which continually tends to add to the pool of the underemployed, i.e. those whose wage exceeds their marginal product.

Balanced growth may thus be defined by two criteria. One is that the volume of agricultural workers freed up through agricultural productivity increase must not be too far out of line with the new employment opportunities created in non-agriculture; and the other is that markets for agricultural and non-agricultural goods in the intersectoral commodity market clear without a major change in the intersectoral terms of trade. Dixit (1969) has suggested the existence of an optimal balanced path for the accumulation of capital in both the agricultural and industrial sectors. Using a simple model with fixed technology in both sectors and with labor the only factor which is mobile between sectors, he seeks to minimize the time for reaching a minimum capital base target in industry alone. He finds that this sometimes requires an initial specialization in agricultural capital accumulation to reach the balanced-growth "turnpike" if agricultural output is too low at very early stages of development. The reason it may not be optimal to attempt capital accumulation for the industrial sector via accumulation in the industrial sector alone is simply that the price of food for industrial workers acts as a constraint, through minimally acceptable wages, on the pace of capital accumulation in industry.

In the context of the market economy, where relative prices provide the signals for investment opportunities and technological efforts in the two sectors, the dynamics of the dual economy's balanced-growth path can be illustrated by reference to consumer preference as between agricultural and non-agricultural goods in the context of the setting we have outlined. Figure 4.2 should be helpful in illustrating the meaning of balanced growth in the dual economy within a simplified setting – i.e. without intermediate input flows between the two sectors. Total population L is shown on the horizontal axis in quadrant II, with agricultural output and the institutional consumption standard $c = W_a$, measured in terms of agricultural goods, on the vertical axis. The curve OQ^* describes per capita food availability for the total population, or Q/L, at a given level of technology, for various possible proportions of the total population already allocated to other activities ($\theta = B/L \geq 0$). Curve OQ^* may have a horizontal portion if some part of the agricultural population or labor force is "redundant" in the sense of having an extremely low or even zero marginal product. One equilibrium point along a balanced growth path may then be defined as follows:

Let initial consumption $c = W_a^0$, and the terms of trade between W_a^0, the "wage in terms of agricultural goods" (A), and W_{na}^0 the "wage in terms of non-agricultural goods" (NA) be given. For simplification only, we assume there is no wage gap between unskilled agricultural and non-agricultural labor. The price-consumption curve (PC) in quadrant I of Figure 4.2 then indicates all

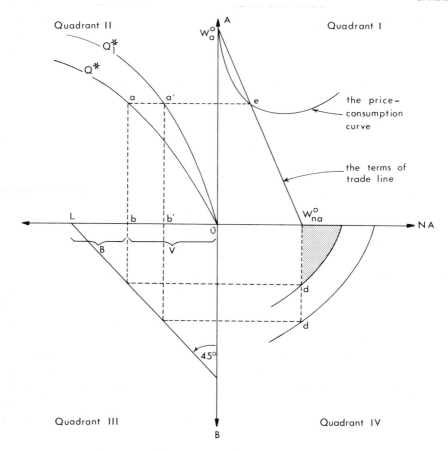

Figure 4.2. Balanced growth in the dualistic economy.

possible points of tangency between changing terms of trade and a given typical worker's consumer preference map between agricultural and non-agricultural goods. Point *e* is the consumption equilibrium point for the typical worker in society, given the terms of trade shown, regardless of whether he is engaged in agricultural or non-agricultural activities. Point *b* represents one consistent allocation of population between agricultural and non-agricultural activities. *B* is the population outside of agriculture and the remaining agricultural population *V* produces enough food to meet everyone's consumption requirements at the institutional wage.

The auxiliary 45° line in quadrant III transposes workers already allocated to non-agricultural work onto the vertical axis. The consistent equilibrium point for employment in the non-agricultural sector is point *d*, located at the intersection between the "horizontal" supply curve of non-agricultural labor, at wage level W_{na}^0, and the demand curve for non-agricultural labor, or the marginal productivity curve corresponding to a particular level of the capital stock and technology in that sector. Assuming no upward adjustment of the agricultural real wage and, thus, of the non-agricultural real wage which is "tied" to it, balanced increases in agricultural and non-agricultural productivity resulting from capital accumulation and technology change – shown by a shift of the per capita food availability curve to OQ_1^* in quadrant II and of the marginal productivity of labor curve in quadrant IV – would result in a new equilibrium position at $a'b'd'$. Such a growth path would clearly meet the labor market equilibrium condition, and this is the meaning of "balanced growth" in the labor market sense. Moreover, a little more work would show that equilibrium in the commodity market sense as previously defined permits agricultural and non-agricultural workers to exchange some of the goods they produce for the goods they want at the given terms of trade, enabling everyone to remain at the same equilibrium point e. The landlords or the government, whoever owns the agricultural surplus, would end up with some part of the non-agricultural capital stock. Industrial profits are represented by the shaded area in quadrant IV of Figure 4.2. This is the meaning of balanced growth in the commodity clearing sense.

The investment fund for the next period is composed of this period's non-agricultural profits and savings from the agricultural surplus. The allocation of the society's investment fund, plus innovative energies, as between the sectors, would be guided by the relative shortages between agricultural and non-agricultural goods, as reflected, in the case of a market economy, in changes in the intersectoral terms of trade. In a non-market economy the role of changes in the terms of trade as a signaling device would be taken over by evidence of unplanned shortages or surpluses in the material balances sense.

As we have already noted, the entire process must not only be balanced but also proceed at a pace in excess of population growth if the initial reservoir of surplus labor is to ultimately be exhausted and neo-classical wage determination to take over. Moreover, if balanced growth, as indexed by the rate of labor reallocation, just marginally exceeds the rate of population growth, on average, the length of time it takes to arrive at that turning point, marking the end of dualism, must also be politically acceptable.

The real world, of course, does not quite operate in this fashion. There are times when, under the impetus of an "industry first" strategy, non-agricultural productivity increases for some time at a rate in excess of agricultural productivity growth, leading to food shortages and the shifting of the terms of trade in favor of agriculture. The reverse can also occur, although empirically there seems to be less danger of this. Most successful dualistic developing societies have experienced something approaching constancy in the terms of trade. In any case, progress along a balanced growth path at a rate in excess of population growth – and sufficiently in excess to guarantee a socially acceptable time perspective – is essential to a society's successful escape from dualism into a modern growth regime.

Balanced growth as an analytical concept in the dual economy context thus addresses itself to the identification of a set of necessary and sufficient conditions. While the real world, of course, never functions smoothly and in a fully "balanced" fashion, the search for these underlying conditions as a basic framework for our thinking has led us to focus on the more or less synchronized real resources functions which need to be performed by both sectors if "success" is to be achieved. Success is defined as the end of labor surplus and consequently the end of organizational dualism in the labor market. Once balanced growth has proceeded long enough and fast enough labor shortage will appear in both sectors which means that the marginal productivity calculus of wage determination will take over. At this point organizational dualism disappears; and, given considerable increases in per capita incomes and the workings of Engel's Law, product dualism also atrophies over time as agriculture gradually becomes an appendage to the economy, or just another smooth or symmetrical sector within the system's input–output matrix. Increasingly the economy is then ready to perform according to the rules of modern economic growth as described by Kuznets (1966).

4. Dualism in the open economy

Thus far we have examined dualism in the closed economy context to get the basic analytics right. The open economy or trade-related dimensions of dualism are, of course, important enough to warrant substantial amendment to the dualistic framework we have presented. Even before post-independence dualism, as we have defined it, appears, foreign trade, is, of course, likely to be an important consideration, i.e. during what might be called the "open agrarian" or colonial phase of development. Typically during this colonial period part of the economy is tied to foreign markets by virtue of some of the labor force being weaned away from food production and into some other land-based, but export-oriented, activity, e.g. minerals and other primary products of interest to foreigners. There may also be an urban component to this enclave consisting of ancillary services, banks, ports, transportation networks, etc. required to make the colonial system function effectively. A triangular relationship is thus established among the cash crop export sector, the foreign sector, and the food-producing domestic agricultural sector. Cash crops are sent abroad in exchange for producers' goods intended to further the expansion of the export enclave activities, plus industrial consumer goods to induce agricultural workers to move out of food-producing agriculture and into the export-oriented cash crop activities.

Once the economy subsequently moves out of its colonial "overseas territory" phase and into a development oriented transition growth phase the dualism analyzed earlier must now be amended to take openness into account. To do so, we must first recognize that the export-oriented cash crop agricultural subsector continues to generate foreign exchange earnings but that these are now used to import capital goods for the construction of a new industrial sector producing, for the domestic market, the previously imported non-durable consumer goods, i.e. to fuel so-called primary or "easy" import substitution. These exports, converted into industrial capital goods imports, now provide a second source of agricultural surplus – possibly supplemented by the inflow of foreign savings – to help finance non-agricultural growth in a balanced-growth context. Thus, a triangular relationship between two kinds of commercialized activities, one agricultural and one non-agricultural, and the food-producing agricultural hinterland replaces the colonial triangle.

We can demonstrate this "opening up" of the closed dual economy model of Figure 4.2 with the help of Figure 4.3. Notice that now, given a per capita output of agricultural goods indexed by Q^* (and assuming, for convenience, only one type of agricultural output), at equilibrium, i.e. with Ob workers still in agriculture and Lb workers already allocated to non-agriculture, per capita agricultural exports in the amount of ac (or total exports in the amount of the thatched area in quadrant II) are available after the consumption requirements of the total population have been met. Given the same terms of trade nationally and internationally – only for convenience – this permits the importation of the thatched area of industrial goods in quadrant IV for subsequent investment in the non-agricultural sector. In this sense the system's agricultural supply has both a domestic and a foreign component, each contributing to the further growth of the dualistic economy. If this growth in the open dualistic economy is to proceed in a balanced fashion once again, as in the closed economy case, what must result is approximate equilibrium in the labor market and near-constancy in the terms of trade. A second equilibrium along the balanced growth path is also depicted in Figure 4.3; with higher agricultural productivity, depicted by curve Q_1^* in quadrant II, we see that an additional $bb' = dd'$ units of labor can be reallocated while keeping constant both the domestic consumption and exports of agricultural goods. It is, of course, entirely possible, as was noted earlier, that increases in agricultural labor productivity can lead to at least somewhat higher agricultural real wages (w_a shifts up) and/or to higher per capita (and total) exports. But the simplifying assumptions underlying Figure 4.3 already permit us to highlight the analytics of open dualism.

Thus far we have assumed balanced trade. But it is entirely possible, in fact likely, that the developing open dual economy will run an import surplus during much of its transition growth effort. Beyond the additional possibilities of trade and capital movements there is, of course, also the new capacity to import

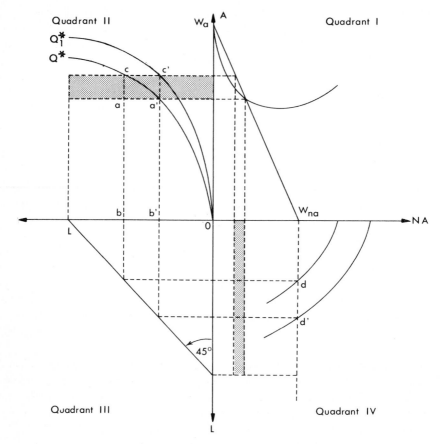

Figure 4.3. Balanced growth in the open dualistic economy.

technology, not available in the closed dual economy case. In fact, the presence of production functions outside the system – even if not always used to best advantage either in terms of technology borrowing or adaptation – represents the single most important feature of the open economy landscape. The additional opportunities represented by trade, capital imports and technology imports in the open economy setting of course render the development task easier ceteris paribus, i.e. balanced growth can proceed at a faster pace and all development objectives, including the ultimate termination of dualism, can be reached earlier.

As is well known, this first import substitution subphase of transition growth is customarily accompanied by a number of government interventions in the foreign exchange, capital and other markets, all directed to assist, through protection and windfall profits, the new industrial entrepreneurial class. In the process domestic balanced growth as we have previously defined it becomes more difficult to achieve as there is a built-in tendency for relative agricultural neglect. But this is an empirical observation, not a theoretical necessity, as some successful real world cases have demonstrated. If we view the early import substitution phase as possibly desirable on infant industry grounds – and it certainly has been shown to be virtually inevitable empirically – much depends, of course, on its severity, i.e. the extent to which various government interventions discriminate against the agricultural sector, for instance, as well as on how long the syndrome is allowed to persist over time.

What is more critical for our purposes here is what happens at the end of this primary import substitution phase, i.e. once domestic markets for the "easy" non-durable consumer goods are saturated. It is apparent that in the relatively natural resource rich countries of the Third World there is a tendency to continue with import substitution, now shifting from labor-intensive light industries to more capital-intensive durable consumer goods, the processing of raw materials and the production of capital goods. In the minority of countries which have a relatively poor exportable natural resources base to fuel the process, on the other hand, we observe a shift, from a domestic to an export market orientation for the same non-durable consumer goods. This may be called export substitution, or the early utilization of the system's human resources to replace land-intensive exports as a way to secure the needed raw materials and machinery for the continued growth of the dual economy.

First and foremost, as we have already noted, the export sector now constitutes a powerful new production function available to the economy through which traditional and, later, non-traditional (industrial) exports can be converted into imported capital goods and raw materials. The availability of this additional production function permits the developing country to harvest the gains from trade or, as Smith (1880) and Myint (1958) put it, to benefit from the "vent for surplus" of previously under-utilized resources in both agriculture (raw materials) and non-agriculture (unskilled labor). Secondly, the openness of the economy permits foreign capital to provide additional finance in support of the balanced growth process. While such flows also existed during the colonial period, they were really circumscribed in both direction and impact. Thirdly, an important advantage accruing as a direct consequence of the economy's openness is, of course, the whole range of technological alternatives available abroad to help, after suitable modification and adaptation, achieve successful balanced growth as previously described. Picking and choosing from the formidable shelf of technology, the less developed dualistic economy is at least in a position to import the type of capital equipment more suited to its resource endowment, as well as, dynamically, more subject to the appropriate direction of technology change. Finally, and related, there are more indirect dynamic benefits associated with openness to competitive forces and ideas from abroad which permeate the entire economy and are undoubtedly of great importance, even though much more difficult to capture and analyze.

In some ways the successful transition of the open dualistic economy where a large fraction of the population is initially engaged in agricultural activities still consists mainly of the effort to mobilize the agricultural sector and to have the kind of balanced interaction with domestic non-agriculture previously described. In the large economy, for instance, which, even when "opened", still features domestic balanced growth as the centerpiece, this agricultural/non-agricultural interaction remains the dominant development focus, since the export oriented enclave, although of help, cannot affect outcomes profoundly. In the small dualistic economy, on the other hand, the development problem focuses more on the importance of the capacity to move flexibly from consumer goods import substitution fuelled by traditional raw material exports to either the path of a continued import substitution or to export substitution.

This choice, of course, matters a great deal because the open economy context presents additional opportunities for accomplishing the basic societal tasks under dualism, i.e. rapid labor reallocation associated with productivity increases in agriculture, industrialization and growth. Continued secondary import substitution (in the Latin American style) represents the temptation to try to short-cut the always difficult problem of agricultural mobilization by importing food, even when there exists rural slack, i.e. substantial reserves of productivity, while moving directly from consumer non-durables into the production of capital goods and consumer durables, mainly for the domestic market. Yielding to this temptation has caused many historically efficient food exporters to become increasingly dependent on food imports at a substantial cost in foregone savings, foreign exchange and growth.

Moreover, such temptations can be less well resisted when there exists a relatively ample natural resource endowment, regardless of the size of the country, because more "expensive" industrial growth paths can then be "afforded". In such cases the system becomes less dualistic, i.e. it gives up domestic balanced growth, thus does without the substantial potential contribution of the domestic agricultural surplus to the nation's savings fund, and without the full contribution of its human resources both in terms of its agricultural labor and entrepreneurship. This effort to essentially "skip" its labor-intensive export phase usually means paying a price in terms of lower growth rates and a less favorable distribution of income. But it can be done if there are enough natural resource bonanzas around and/or enough foreign capital can be attracted to pay for the process.

Ceteris paribus, one would assume that a dualistic economy with a substantial initial labor surplus in agriculture would be better off with plentiful natural resources of the cash crop variety and/or ready access to foreign capital than without these. Nevertheless, both the narrowly defined effects of the "Dutch

Disease" on tradeables and the exchange rate as well as its broader impact on overall decision-making may be quite perverse. A strong market for traditional and primary exports may lead to an overvalued exchange rate, making it more difficult to diversify into competitive industrial exports, as we have seen in the case of the oil bonanzas and their aftermath in Indonesia, Nigeria, Mexico and Venezuela. But, in the broader sense, the relatively easy availability of earnings from natural resource exports or foreign capital inflows may lull a society into believing it can avoid the difficult policy changes often required to move a system from import to export substitution. As we have seen, a dualistic economy, to be successful, must utilize its major potential resource, its unskilled labor and its entrepreneurial capacities, to satisfy domestic balanced growth demands and, subsequently, to penetrate international markets competitively while maintaining the domestic balanced-growth effort. The end of dualism then occurs when the process has succeeded in reallocating enough workers to render unskilled labor a scarce commodity, indexed by marked rises in real wages which are now neoclassically determined.

While this discussion may approach the realm of political economy, it is understandable that governments, like individuals, simply do not lightly tackle entrenched interest groups as long as there are ready alternatives at hand, at least over the limited time horizon under which many governments operate. Ultimately, continued growth based on traditional exports entailing a disregard of domestic balanced growth, and thus the neglect of the domestic agricultural sector in our dualistic context, is likely to run into difficulties because of worsening employment and income distribution results. But "ultimately" may not be just around the corner. On the other hand, mobilizing the dualistic economy in a balanced, sustained fashion, with the open economy opportunities representing the second important strand of that balance, has called for sustained changes in entrenched protectionist and interventionist habits in various markets. The ability to resist the temptation of continuing on the import substitution track when one is not forced to consider a change in policy may require a considerable degree of statesmanship. It may well make the difference between ultimate success and failure in the typical dualistic economy.

References

Binswanger, H.P. and Rosenzweig, M.R., eds. (1984) *Contractual arrangements, employment and wages in rural labor markets in Asia*. New Haven: Yale University Press.

Dixit, A. (1969) 'Marketable surplus and dual development', *Journal of Economic Theory*, 1:203–219.

Eckhaus, R.S. (1955) 'The factor proportions problem in underdeveloped countries', *American Economic Review*, 45:539–565.

Higgins, B. (1968) *Economic development: Principles, problems, policies*. New York: Norton.

Kanbur, R. and McIntosh, J. (1985) 'Dual economy models', in: *The new Palgrave: A dictionary of economic theory and doctrine*. New York: Macmillan.

Kuznets, S. (1966) *Modern economic growth: Rate, structure and spread*. New Haven: Yale University Press.

Lewis, W.A. (1954) 'Economic development with unlimited supplies of labor', *Manchester School*, 22:139–191.

Myint, H. (1958) "The 'classical' theory of international trade and the underdeveloped countries", *Economic Journal*, 68:317–337.

Myrdal, G. (1968) *Asian drama*. New York: Pantheon.

Nurkse, R. (1953) *Problems of capital formation in underdeveloped countries*. Oxford: Blackwell.

Prebisch, R. (1971) *Change and development: Latin America's great task*, Report submitted to the Inter-American Development Bank. New York: Praeger.

Preobrazenskii, E. (1924) *The new economics*, translated by B. Pearce. Oxford: Clarendon Press (1965).

Ricardo, D. (1815) *Works and correspondence of David Ricardo*, Vols. 1–4. Cambridge: Cambridge University Press.

Scott, J.C. (1976) *The moral economy of the peasant*. New Haven: Yale University Press.

Sen, A.K. (1966) 'Peasants and dualism with or without surplus labor', *Journal of Political Economy*, 74:425–450.

Singer, H.W. (1970) 'Dualism revisited: A new approach to the problems of dual society in developing countries', *Journal of Development Studies*, 7:60–75.

Smith, A. (1880) *The wealth of nations*. Oxford: Clarendon Press.

Chapter 5

ECONOMIC ORGANIZATION, INFORMATION, AND DEVELOPMENT

JOSEPH E. STIGLITZ*

Princeton University

Contents

1.	Introduction	94
2.	Basic tenets and objectives of analysis	96
	2.1. Stylized facts	96
	2.2. Alternative approaches	96
3.	The theory of rural organization	105
	3.1. The organization of the family	105
	3.2. The landlord–tenant relationship: The sharecropping puzzle	115
	3.3. Unemployment in the rural sector	125
	3.4 The rural sector as a whole: The interlinkage of markets	133
4.	The urban sector	134
5.	Market equilibrium	136
6.	Government pricing policies, wage subsidies, and cost–benefit analysis	140
7.	The development process	142
	7.1. Factor supplies	142
	7.2 Technical change and entrepreneurship	147
	7.3 Development strategies	150
8.	Concluding remarks	153
	8.1. Choice of managers	153
	8.2. Market failures and government failures	153
	References	156

*Financial support from the Hoover Institution and the National Science Foundation is gratefully acknowledged. I am indebted to B. Salonie, T.N. Srinivasan, J. Swinkels, and N. Stern for their helpful comments.

Handbook of Development Economics, Volume I, Edited by H. Chenery and T.N. Srinivasan
© *Elsevier Science Publishers B.V., 1988*

1. Introduction[1]

The central questions facing development economics are: Why is it that some countries are so much poorer than others? What can be done to make them grow faster?[2] Faster growth is needed if the gap in living standards is not to be widened even further.

Many of our earlier insights into these questions came from looking at the process of growth as it developed in Europe and North America, and contrasting patterns observed there with those observed elsewhere, trying to identify which among the many differences were crucial. Many economists took the position that there were certain stages of economic growth through which an economy had to go into the process of becoming a mature economy; just as a child has to go through certain stages in becoming an adult. Thus, urbanization and industrialization were taken to be virtually synonymous with development.

This view is, I think, fundamentally incorrect. The central problem facing England, France, and the United States was one of innovation, of developing new techniques and technologies, and of diffusion of these recently developed technologies through the economy. The "economics" of this process of innovation, though discussed by Schumpeter, Hicks, and Robinson, among others, is not as well understood as that of the production and allocation of goods and services using known techniques. Only recently has it become once again the center of attention [Nelson and Winter (1982), Dasgupta and Stiglitz (1980a, 1980b)]. But from what we already have learned, we know that issues of appropriability and pre-emption are central. These are not the central issues facing less developed countries (LDCs). The LDCs are in the position of imitators.[3] For them, the questions of concern are much closer to those addressed in the classical theory of comparative advantage, modified by certain important dynamic considerations. The rapid improvements in agricultural technology during the past two decades mean that significant improvements in standards of

[1]Parts of this chapter represent an extension of Stiglitz (1985a, 1986c).
[2]For a recent discussion of what has been happening to the gap in living standards, see Baumol (1986). Earlier neo-classical growth models [Solow (1956)] predicted a convergence in rates of growth and, if capital were mobile, even in levels of income. For attempts to construct models which are consistent with this non-convergence, see Lucas (1985) or Stiglitz (1987c).
[3]This is not to say that at times, there were industries in each of the major developed countries that were in a position of being followers. But much of the dynamic force of the economies came from those sectors which were at the leading edge of innovation. Still, the LDCs may have something to learn from the developed countries: but perhaps more from studying the lagging sectors, the imitators, than the leaders.

living can occur without industrialization and urbanization. The LDCs thus face a choice about the appropriate path of development.

By the same token, I view much of the discussion of capital accumulation as misplaced. It is true that significant increases in the capital stock are likely to be accompanied by some increase in output per head. But the differences in output per head between the developed and less developed countries cannot be explained on the basis of differences in capital stock alone; for if that were the case, the return to capital in the LDCs would be much higher than in developed countries, and the natural avarice of capitalists would lead to capital flows which would tend to equalize per capita incomes. A major source of the difference between developed and less developed countries lies in the efficiency with which the available supplies of capital are used. The evidence for this statement, the explanations for this, and its implications for the design of policy are, or should be, central concerns of development economics, and I shall return to these questions in the concluding sections of this chapter.

Most of the recent analytical work in development economics, of which this chapter is supposed to be a survey, has been concerned with a narrower, albeit important set of questions. It has been concerned with describing and analyzing what may be referred to as the micro foundations of development economics, with how labor gets allocated between and within sectors, with how workers get compensated in the rural sector or wages get determined in the urban sector. It is concerned with such questions as: In what ways do markets work differently in LDCs than in developed countries? To what extent can what we learned about markets in the latter case carry over to LDCs? It is essential to answer these questions if we are to have any confidence in policy recommendations concerning, for instance, wage subsidies, pricing policies, or project selection (cost–benefit analysis). At the same time, we should keep in mind that we are more concerned here with tactics, rather than strategy. Still, the kind of analysis presented here is a necessary prelude to any systematic account of the consequences of alternative development strategies.

The chapter is organized as follows. In Section 2 we set out the basic tenets of our theory, and contrast these with some alternative hypotheses. Section 3 is concerned with the theory of rural organization, which attempts to describe the organization of economic activity within the rural sector. Section 4 is concerned with the urban sector within LDCs. Section 5 is devoted to describing the market equilibrium. Section 6 describes recent research devoted to analyzing the consequences of alternative policies within this structure. The analysis in Sections 2–6 is basically static. But the development process itself is dynamic. Thus, Section 7 is concerned with growth, technical change, and entrepreneurship. Section 8 presents some concluding remarks, including some observations concerning the role of the government in the development process from this broader perspective.

2. Basic tenets and objectives of analysis

This chapter (and the research on which it is based) begins with the hypothesis that there are certain regularities to be found within LDCs, and that economic theory should be able to explain, or at least shed light on these regularities. Let me emphasize what I mean by regularities: not phenomena that are *universal* among LDCs, but phenomena that occur with sufficient frequency that they cannot simply be dismissed as anomalies, for which an explanation based on the peculiar circumstances and history of the economy in question will suffice.

At the same time, one needs to emphasize the diversity among LDCs; one is not looking for a single model which will describe all LDCs, but a general framework, which, with appropriate adaptation, can be made relevant to most LDCs.[4]

2.1. Stylized facts

Among the regularities which we seek to explain are:

(1) Widespread urban unemployment within LDCs, suggesting that wages are set at levels above market clearing.

(2) Large wage differentials for laborers of seemingly equivalent skill levels.

(3) Extensive migration from the rural to the urban sector, in spite of the high level of unemployment.

(4) The use of sharecropping within the rural sector. Sharecropping often (but not always) entails some form of cost sharing for other inputs between the landlord and the tenant.[5]

(5) In economies which make use of sharecropping, interlinkage of credit and land markets (and sometimes of other markets): the landlord is frequently also the supplier of credit.

2.2. Alternative approaches

There have been a number of alternative approaches to understanding LDCs.

---

[4] I should also note that there is not universal agreement among economists about the prevalence of several of the so-called regularities which I seek to explain. Thus, while I follow a good deal of the literature in seeking to explain widespread urban unemployment, there are some who claim that open unemployment and rural–urban migration are not of central importance in many LDCs. Later chapters of this Handbook will illuminate these empirical controversies.

[5] We shall present a more detailed discussion of the stylized facts concerning rural organization below.

2.2.1. *The neo-classical model: The rational peasant with well functioning markets*

One approach views LDCs as being very much like competitive developed economies: peasants are rational "maximizers".[6] But not only do individuals act rationally to pursue their own interests, the economic system as a whole acts "rationally": markets, while perhaps not perfect, function reasonably well.[7] And even in the absence of markets, individuals can, and will, get together to design efficient economic relationships.[8] In this view, then, traditional neo-classical economics may be applied directly (with obvious adjustments in the relevant parameters) to LDCs.

There is a contrasting view that traditional neo-classical economic theory has little, if any, relevance to the problems of less developed economies. Some of the important developments in theory during the past quarter of century have provided considerable justification for that view. Though the Fundamental Theorem of Welfare Economics has shown rigorously that there is a set of conditions under which Adam Smith's conjecture concerning the invisible hand has some validity, the conditions required seem particularly inapplicable to the circumstances of most LDCs. In particular, there is not the full set of markets – whether for risks, capital (futures markets), or products – that the theorem requires; information is far from perfect; the assumption of a fixed and known technology seems particularly incongruent with an attempt to understand

---

[6] We beg the question of what rationality means. Typically, economists' formal models simply impose a weak set of consistency conditions that individuals not choose at one time commodity bundle A when commodity bundle B is obtainable while at another time they choose commodity bundle B when A is obtainable. Unfortunately, in laboratory experiments individuals frequently exhibit inconsistencies, particularly in contexts of making choices under uncertainty.

There is a stronger sense of rationality which we shall discuss in the text below.

[7] That is, while the conditions which ensure the Pareto efficiency of the market economy (the Fundamental Theorem of Welfare Economics) are not satisfied perfectly, the model provides a sufficiently close approximation to reality that we should feel confident that the market, if not Pareto efficient, is at least not far from it.

[8] This is sometimes loosely referred to as the Coase conjecture. Advocates of this view maintain that even externalities do not pose a problem for economic efficiency: so long as there are well defined property rights, those affected by the externality will bribe the producers of the externality to behave in a socially efficient manner.

This is not the appropriate place for a complete discussion of the Coase conjecture. [For a brief overview of the arguments, see, for instance, Farrell (1987) or Stiglitz (1986b).] Here we simply note that the standard arguments for it ignore free rider (public good) problems and inefficiencies arising in bargaining situations with imperfect information. (The examples cited by Coase in his classic paper suggest that he was concerned with bargaining situations involving two, or in any case, a limited number of parties; in that case, the free rider problems do not arise, but the imperfect information problems still do. But by the same token, it is not apparent that Coase believed that bargaining would resolve the kinds of market failures associated with, say, systemic externalities.)

the processes by which LDCs adopt more advanced technologies,[9] and by which new technologies diffuse through the economy; and the early stages of development require the provision of infrastructure, which is a public good, and/or is characterized by strong non-convexities.[10]

The problems I have listed are, of course, well recognized, and they are widely discussed under the rubric of "market failures". The liberal doctrines of the 1960s and the early 1970s held that a certain amount of tinkering by a benevolent government could remedy these deficiencies in the marketplace, and with these limited interventions, the market economy would function well, in the way that the classical theory had said it would all along.

Indeed, many of the believers in the market mechanism believed that many if not most of the so-called market failures would not turn out to be market failures once they were subjected to close enough scrutiny. Was it, for instance, a market failure if markets did not exist because transactions costs were sufficiently high that the gains from establishing a market were less than the costs? Under these circumstances, should not the absence of a market be taken as evidence of the rationality of the market economy, not of its failure?[11]

To believers of neo-classical theory, the difference between LDCs and developed countries was a matter of degree: the market failures were perhaps more pronounced and thus stronger government interventions might be called for. To critics, the qualifications were of central importance.

Two developments during the past decade have, however, necessitated a reshaping of these views. The first is well known: many of the attempts by governments, both in the LDCs and in developed countries, to remedy certain apparent market failures have been less than successful. There were two responses to the increasing perception of "government failure". Those who were committed to a basic reliance on the market mechanism felt their views reinforced. The traditional approach to defining market failures attempted to identify circumstances under which government intervention could result in a Pareto improvement. These economists maintained that, accordingly, the "correct" definition of a market failure ought to be limited to those circumstances under which a "real" government intervention – not that of some Utopian idealization of government – could achieve a Pareto improvement. Thus defined, market

---

[9] The assumption of a given set of available technologies may, of course, be more appropriate for LDCs than for developed countries, who spend considerable resources trying to develop new technologies. But the problem of diffusion of knowledge about the available technologies is central to the development process, and an analysis of these questions is precluded in a model in which it is assumed that all individuals have perfect information about the set of available technologies.

[10] These problems obviously arise in developed countries as well. The point is that while there may be some debate about the relevance of the Arrow–Debreu model for a developed economy, these market failures are so large within LDCs as to make it not even a matter of debate.

[11] Indeed, it was maintained that even non-convexities which were so large that only one firm would operate in equilibrium need not interfere with the efficient workings of the economy. This was the spirit of the Baumol, Panzer and Willig (1982) analysis of contestable markets.

failures were viewed likely to be a rarity. (These economists often sought to explain government failures using traditional neo-classical tools. Rent-seeking behavior, with all of its consequences, was to be expected from rational individuals, including those comprising the government.) At the very least, the perception of widespread government failure meant that the set of circumstances under which government actions were desirable was far more limited than the traditional market failures approach might have led one to believe.

The alternative response to the widespread perception of government failure did not disagree that the existence of government failure implied that simply identifying circumstances under which some idealized government could attain a Pareto improvement did not provide an adequate basis for government policy. Whether it meant that the set of circumstances under which government action might be desirable was *much* more limited was an empirical question. But it did mean that great care needed to be taken both in identifying circumstances where government policy was likely to effect an improvement and in structuring government policies and the ways to implement them, so that the intended objectives were actually achieved.

The development of ideas is influenced not only by events – here the apparent failure of so many government policies. Ideas have a life of their own. The market failures perspective of the 1960s has thus been altered by some important developments in economy theory. At the same time that the standard neo-classical theory was continually being refined, a number of economists were attempting to construct models of the economy using neo-classical tools of analysis, but introducing more realistic assumptions: they were concerned with investigating the causes and consequences of incomplete markets, imperfect information, transactions costs and imperfect competition.[12] In many cases, these studies were motivated by an attempt to provide models with a greater relevance to LDCs; but the models which worked well for LDCs have, it has turned out, provided considerable insight into the functioning of developed economies as well.[13]

---

[12]Among the earlier studies of imperfect information were George Akerlof's Theory of Lemons (1970), which became the forerunner of innumerable analyses of markets characterized by adverse selection, in which prices convey information (his work was motivated in part by observations concerning information problems he noted during an extended stay in India); Gary Fields' (1983) models of the education market, and Stiglitz's (1975) study of education as a screening device, both of which were motivated by their experiences in Kenya [though Michael Spence independently derived a quite similar theory of education as a signal (1974)].

[13]It may be worth noting at least two important instances of this. The analysis of sharecropping [Stiglitz (1974a)] has provided the basis of the general analysis of incentives (the so-called principal agent problem). The role of wage differentials between the urban and rural sectors in giving rise to urban unemployment [Todaro (1968), Harris and Todaro (1970)] has provided the basis for Hall's analysis of differences in unemployment rates across cities. And generalizations of the efficiency-wage model [Leibenstein (1957), Mirrlees (1975), Stiglitz (1974b, 1976a, 1982a, 1982c)] have provided an explanation of wage rigidities giving rise to unemployment in developed countries [see, for example, Stiglitz (1976b, 1986a, 1987b), Weiss (1980), Calvo (1979), Akerlof (1984), Yellen (1984), Bulow and Summers (1985), Shapiro and Stiglitz (1984)].

These two developments, one in the world of ideas, the other in the world of events, are not unrelated: the Economics of Information has focused on the information and incentive problems which are common both to public and private organizations; it has provided at least part of the rationale for Public Failures as well as Private Failures, and has provided a framework within which a more rational basis for the assignment of responsibility to each sector can be made.

2.2.2. The information-theoretic approach

These developments have provided the basis of the second approach to under-standing LDCs which, for want of a better name, I shall refer to as the information-theoretic approach.[14]

2.2.2.1. Central tenets. There are five central tenets of the information-theoretic approach:

(1) Individuals (including peasants in the rural sectors of LDCs) are rational, that is, they act in a (reasonably) consistent manner, one which adapts to changes in circumstances.

(2) Information is costly. This has numerous important implications: individuals do not acquire perfect information, and hence their behavior may differ markedly from what it would have been had they had perfect information. When individuals engage in a trade (buying labor services, extending credit, renting land or bullocks), there is imperfect information concerning the items to be traded; thus, transactions which would be desirable in the presence of perfect information may not occur.[15] Similarly, certain contracts, e.g. to perform certain services at a certain standard, may not be feasible, if it is costly to ascertain, ex post, whether or how well those services have been performed.

(3) Institutions adapt to reflect these information (and other transaction) costs. Thus, institutions are not to be taken as exogenous, but are endogenous, and changes in the environment may lead, with a lag, to changes in institutional structure.

---

[14]Some economists would include much of what is contained in this second perspective under the general rubric of "neo-classical analyses". They would simply distinguish between economic analysis based on rational behavior, and that in which an important role is given to irrational behavior and to rigidities and inflexibilities which are not derived as a consequence of rational behavior.

While to some extent this is a semantic quibble, there is, I believe, a fundamental distinction between those who believe that economic systems (as opposed to just individuals) function in a "rational" way, so that outcomes are Pareto efficient, and those who believe that even when individuals behave in an individually rational way, economic systems may not be Pareto efficient, as they may not be when, for instance, there are important costs of information.

[15]By the same token, some transactions may occur which would not do so with perfect information; but the general result is that the extent of trade will be less. See, for instance, Akerlof (1970).

(4) The fact that individuals are rational and that institutions are adaptable does not, however, imply that the economy is (Pareto) efficient. The efficiency of market economies obtains only under the peculiar set of circumstances – including the assumption of a complete set of markets and perfect information – explored by Arrow and Debreu. With imperfect information and incomplete markets, the economy is almost always constrained Pareto inefficient, i.e. there exists a set of taxes and subsidies which can make everyone better off. [See Greenwald and Stiglitz (1986, 1988).] It is important to emphasize that this result on the inefficiency of market economies takes into account the costs of transactions and information. Even if it is optimal not to have some risk market (say, because of transactions costs), the allocation of resources, *given* the absent risk market, is not Pareto efficient. There are taxes and subsidies, employing only publicly observable variables, which can effect a Pareto improvement.

(5) This implies that there is a *potential* role for the government. The fact that there is a potential role for the government neither means that in any particular circumstance governments are likely to effect a Pareto improvement, or even that government policies ostensibly designed to effect an improvement are likely to succeed. Government policies are, of course, more likely to succeed if those responsible for designing and implementing government policy have the incentives to direct policies to effect Pareto improvements, rather than, for instance, to redistribute income (either from the poor to the rich or vice versa, or from everyone else, to themselves), often at considerable loss to national output.

Informational problems, including incentive problems, are no less important in the public sector than in the private; the fact that we have studied them well in the latter does not mean that they are not present in the former. The consequence of these remarks is to make us cautious in recommending particular government actions as remedies for certain observed deficiencies in the market.

2.2.2.2. Related approaches. My emphasis on information in the preceding discussion should not be taken to exclude the importance of other market failures, several of which we have already noted. In particular, the absence or limitations (for whatever reason) of certain markets – risk markets, rental markets, credit markets – may have profound effects on behavior in LDCs; though we would argue that many of these market failures can, in turn, be explained by imperfect information, some of them may not be; and in any case, the consequences may be the same, regardless of the cause (although the policy implications may differ).

2.2.2.3. Transactions costs. There is one other approach, closely related to the one I have advocated, that has received some attention: the transactions cost approach, which attempts to understand economic relations by focusing on transactions costs. Information costs are an important part of transactions costs (though information problems arise in other contexts as well). My reservations concerning the transactions cost approach lies in its lack of specificity: while the information paradigm provides a well-defined structure which allows one to derive clear propositions concerning, for instance, the design of contracts, the transactions cost paradigm does not. Thus, the transactions cost approach might provide some insight into why cost sharing is employed, but not into the terms of the cost sharing agreement. The transactions cost paradigm might say that economies of scope provide an explanation for why the landlord also supplies credit, but it does not provide insights into when the landlord-cum-creditor would subsidize credit, or when he would "tax" it. Moreover, while the information paradigm identifies parameters which affect the magnitude of the externalities between landlords and creditors, and thus enables, in principle, the identification of circumstances under which interlinkage is more likely to be observed; the transactions cost paradigm can do little more than to say that there are circumstances in which the diseconomies of scope exceed the economies, and in these circumstances there will not be interlinkage.

2.2.3. The irrational peasant hypothesis

The two approaches presented so far share the view of the peasant as a rational agent. The differences between the standard neo-classical view and what I have called the information theoretic view have to do with the nature of the environment; in what I have characterized as the neo-classical model, the peasant is assumed to be working in an environment with reasonably complete information and complete and competitive markets. By contrast, the information-theoretic approach emphasizes the importance of limitations on information and on markets, and argues that many of the institutions within LDCs can best be understood as responses to these problems. Moreover, it is concerned with the costs and benefits of acquiring information, of adopting new technologies, and is concerned with understanding the barriers which inhibit the diffusion of more productive technologies.[16]

The similarities and differences between the alternative approaches may be illustrated by their view of sharecropping. In both views, sharecropping is a rational response to the problems faced by peasants. In the "neo-classical view" the focus is on transactions costs and risk taking; incentives are not relevant: with perfect information and perfect enforceability of contracts, the sharecropping contract can enforce the desired level of labor supply and the choice of technique which is efficient. These theories have had little to say about some of the other phenomena which I have noted: interlinkage, technical change, cost

---

[16]Some recent work, for instance, has stressed the problems of learning to learn (or adapt). Thus, even if peasants are efficient in the use of current technologies, they may not have the same capabilities for adopting new technologies as, say, farmers in more developed countries. See Sah and Stiglitz (1986b) and Stiglitz (1987c).

sharing.[17] In the "information-theoretic approach" while risk sharing and transactions costs are relevant, incentives are central: sharecropping is a rational response to an incentive problem caused by informational imperfections and a risk problem caused by the absence of insurance markets; it represents a balancing of risk and incentive considerations.

There are those, however, who disagree with both of these views: they see the peasant as irrational, with his behavior dictated by customs and institutions, which while perhaps serving a useful function at some previous time, may no longer do so. This approach (which I shall refer to, somewhat loosely, as the institutional-historical approach) may attempt to describe the kinds of LDCs in which there is sharecropping, interlinkage, or cost sharing. It may attempt to relate current practices to earlier practices. In particular, the institutional-historical approach may identify particular historical events which lead to the establishment of the sharecropping system, or to the development of the credit system. But the question of why so many LDCs developed similar institutional structures, or why in some countries cost shares equal output shares, while in others the two differ, is largely left unanswered. More fundamentally, a theory must explain how earlier practices developed, and to provide an explanation of these, one has to have recourse to one of the other theories. Thus, by itself, the institutional-historical approach is incomplete.

Some economists have emphasized the departures from competition in the rural sector, and the consequent ability of the landlords to exploit the workers. In some cases, workers are tied to their land; legal constraints may put the landlord in a position to exploit the worker. But in the absence of these legal constraints, one has to explain how the landlords exercise their allegedly coercive powers. In many LDCs there is a well-developed labor market. Many landlords need laborers at harvest time and at planting time. The worker has a choice of for whom he can work. It is important to recognize that the exploitation hypothesis fails to explain the mechanisms by which, in situations where there are many landlords, they exercise their exploitive power.[18] More generally, it fails to explain variations in the degree of exploitation over time and across countries. The fact that wages in some village at some time appear low (relative to wages at other locations and/or other times) is not necessarily evidence of exploitation: the competitive market will yield low wages when the value of the marginal product of labor is low.

---

[17] Interlinkage might be explained in terms of the advantages in transactions costs, but if transactions costs were central, one should only have observed simple cost sharing rules (with cost share equalling output share).

[18] Note that recent advances in repeated games have shown how collusive outcomes can be attained even in non-cooperative settings. Thus landlords in rural economies where mobility is limited and in which there are only a few landlords in any community may well act collusively. The circumstances in which these non-cooperative collusive arrangements work well has, however, not been well studied.

The exploitation hypothesis also fails to explain the detailed structure of rural organization: why cost shares are the way they are, or why (or how) landlords who can exploit their workers use the credit market to gain further exploitive capacity.

There may be some grain of truth in all these approaches. Important instances of currently dysfunctional institutions and customs can clearly be identified. Institutional structures clearly do not adapt instantaneously to changed circumstances – in developed or less developed countries.[19] Yet, as social scientists, our objective is to identify the systematic components, the regularities of social behavior, to look for general principles underlying a variety of phenomena. It is useful to describe the institutions found in the rural sector of LDCs, but description is not enough.

I thus view the rationality hypothesis as a convenient starting point, a simple and general principle with which to understand economic behavior. Important instances of departures from rationality may well be observed. As social scientists, our objective is to look for *systematic* departures. Some systematic departures have been noted, for instance in the work of Tversky, in individual's judgments of probabilities, particularly of small probability events; but as Binswanger's (1978, 1980) studies have noted, departures from the theory appear less important in "important" decisions than in less important decisions. Many of the seeming departures from "rationality" that have been noted can be interpreted as "rational" decision-making in the presence of imperfect information.

I also view the competition hypothesis as a convenient starting point.[20] Many of the central phenomena of interest can be explained without recourse to the exploitation hypothesis. Some degree of imperfect competition is not inconsistent with the imperfect information paradigm: The imperfect information paradigm provides part of the explanation for the absence of perfect competition; it can help identify situations where the landlords may be in a better position to exploit the workers. Moreover, to the extent that imperfect information limits the extent to which even a monopoly landlord can extract surplus from his workers, the imperfect information paradigm can provide insights into how he can increase his monopoly profits. The theory of interlinkage described below can thus be applied to help understand the behavior of a monopolist landlord.

---

[19]Of course, there may be costs of changing institutions, and the benefits may be less than those costs. And there is always uncertainty about the consequences of any institutional change; with sufficient risk aversion, one can justify the maintenance of the status quo so long as there is any probability that the change will lower welfare.

[20]Indeed, with limited labor mobility, in small villages the labor markets are unlikely to be perfectly competitive; at the same time, the landlord is far from a labor monopolist. (But see footnote 18 above.) The real world is probably better described by a model of "monopolistic competition" than either of the polar models, monopoly or perfect competition.

3. The theory of rural organization

The theory of rural organization is divided into three parts: (a) the organization of the (often extended) family; (b) the tenant–landlord relationship; and (c) credit markets, and the relationship among land, labor, credit, and other markets.

3.1. The organization of the family

Conventional economic theory takes the "individual" as the basic unit of analysis. Yet for many purposes the decision unit is not the individual, but the family; or perhaps more accurately, one cannot understand the behavior of the individual in isolation from his relationship with other members of his family. (Of course, understanding family structure is also important for developed countries, e.g. for understanding female labor participation rates; but it is central for understanding economic behavior in LDCs, partly because the family constitutes the basic production unit, partly because the absence of insurance (and other) markets necessitates the family undertaking the functions which otherwise would be served by these markets.)

There are three broad categories of models of the family. The first is the "family welfare" model; the family acts *as if* it were maximizing an (equalitarian) family social welfare function (frequently, the utilitarian social welfare function, where family welfare is just the sum of the utilities of the members of the family). The work described below by Mirrlees (1975) and Stiglitz (1976a) falls within this mold. The second is the "household as a market" view; the members of the family form a sub-market, linked by transactional convenience, with the distribution of work and consumption within the family determined by competitive forces (outside opportunities) in much the same way that it would be determined in the absence of the family. The third represents hybrids of the two views. The family acts cooperatively in some dimensions, non-cooperatively in others. These hybrid models have played an important role in earlier discussions of misallocations within the rural sector of LDCs; unfortunately, the reason that some decisions are taken cooperatively, others non-cooperatively, is never spelled out; though the models may have some superficial semblance to actual practices, the question is: Are there alternative, more consistent ways of interpreting the observations?

The models of household behavior have been used most extensively to explain fertility behavior. Though we shall comment briefly on this aspect, our concern here is primarily with the implications of the alternative models for labor supply and output.

3.1.1. Models with family welfare functions

For simplicity, in the ensuing discussion we shall assume families have a utilitarian social welfare function, but none of the results would be altered, provided the family has an equalitarian social welfare function. Utilitarian families allocate goods and labor so as to maximize the sum of the utilities of the members of the family. In the absence of wage–productivity effects (see below), this implies equating the marginal utility of income to all members of the family, while those with greater productivity work more. That is, if all individuals have the same utility function (a strong hypothesis) $U^i(C_i, L_i)$, where C_i is consumption and L_i is labor supply, and if the productivity of the ith family member is w_i (that is, individual i can do in an hour what individual j can do in w_i/w_j hours[21]) then the family

$$\underset{\{C_i, L_i\}}{\text{maximizes}} \sum_i U^i(C_i, L_i) \tag{3.1}$$

subject to

$$\sum_i C_i \leq \sum_i w_i L_i.$$

That is, it sets

$$U_1^i = U_1^j, \tag{3.2}$$

and

$$U_2^i/w_i = U_2^j/w_j, \tag{3.3}$$

where U_1^i is the marginal utility of consumption and U_2^i is the marginal disutility of work. The marginal disutilities of work are proportional to the worker's productivity. Thus, if we postulate a separable utility function,

$$U = u(C) - v(L), \tag{3.4}$$

then (3.2) implies that *income should be shared equally within the family*, while (3.3) implies that the more productive should work harder. An immediate implication of this is that the more able members of the family are actually worse off.[22]

---

[21] This assumes that individuals differ in a pure labor augmenting way; that is, some individuals are not more productive in using capital or land than others. The extension to the more general case is straightforward [see Stiglitz (1982b)].

[22] This result does not require the strong separability assumptions we have made. It will be true, for instance, so long as both leisure and consumption goods are "normal".

Many observers believe, accordingly, that this degree of cooperation is implausible. Of course, within the broader perspective of an individual's lifetime, in which he is more productive during certain periods of his life, less productive in others, the magnitude of the redistributions involved may be much smaller than those observed at any moment. Moreover, the gains from other aspects of the family life (including the purely economic gains from the implicit insurance provided by the family,[23] which is not obtainable elsewhere) means that even those who are net "subsidizers" over their lives, redistributing the most, may be better off than if they were not members of the family. In this perspective, then, utilitarianism provides a way of allocating the gains to be had from family cooperation.

Families must decide not only how much each individual should work, but where they should work. In this view, then, the decision to migrate is based on an assessment of the benefits and costs to the family from migration [see Stiglitz (1969)]. The family provides the capital to finance the individual's job search; and in return the individual who is successful in obtaining a job in the urban sector remits back a certain amount to his family. Thus, with the separable utility function, the remittances will be determined to equate the marginal utility of income of the urban migrant with those remaining in the rural sector. This does not mean that incomes will be equal; the remittances will take account of differences in prices. Moreover, in deciding on how to allocate family members between the urban and the rural sector, they will take into account the differences in cost of living as well as the differences between the marginal productivity of the (marginal) family member in the rural sector and his (her) expected income in the urban sector, taking into account the probability of not obtaining a job.[24,25]

---

[23] It would obviously be preferable to spread the risks more widely than just within the family. We do not provide here an analysis of why individuals cannot or do not obtain market insurance for so many important risks. *One* explanation has to do with the importance of moral hazard and adverse selection; these informational problems are less important within the family, and accordingly there are distinct advantages in family-provided insurance (though, obviously, risk cannot be spread as well within the family as it can be by an insurance firm). For a discussion of the role of family and other non-market institutions in insurance, see Arnott and Stiglitz (1984).

[24] Formally, let N be the number of individuals in the family, N_r the number "assigned" to the rural sector, Ew_u the expected urban wage, $Q(L_r \ N_r)$ the output on the farm, a function of total labor hours of labor supplies, where L_r is the hours supplied by each worker, then the utilitarian family maximizes:

$$U(C_u, L_u; p_u) N_u + U(C_r, L_r; p_r) N_r$$

subject to

$$p_r Q + Ew_u N_u L_u = p_u C_u N_u + p_r C_r N_r,$$

where N_u and N_r are the number of workers assigned by the family to the urban and rural sectors,

This view has several very important consequences:

First, urban–rural wage differentials may have no significant implications for inequality: the families themselves engage in redistribution.

Secondly, the supply price of labor to the urban sector is determined not by the average level of consumption in the rural sector, but by the marginal productivity of labor in the rural sector (and in particular, by the marginal productivity of the marginal migrant). There is, in other words, no distortion caused by the fact that workers in the rural sector receive the average product (there is income sharing).

Thirdly, unlike the standard neo-classical model, the urban wage (received by those who obtain employment) is not equal to the value of the marginal product of a worker in the rural sector. This presents important problems for calculating the opportunity cost of hiring an additional worker in the urban sector.[26] (If prices in the urban and rural sector are identical, then the marginal productivity of a worker in the rural sector will equal the *expected* urban income, if hours worked in the two sectors are the same. But if these conditions are not satisfied,

---

respectively ($N_u + N_r = N$, the total number of members in the family) and where C_i is consumption of an individual in the ith sector. (In the formulation, we have assumed that the family can choose the number of hours it wishes its urban members to work; in fact, L_u may be set exogenously.) N_r is set so that

$$U_r - U_u = v\left(Ew_u L_u - p_u C_u - \left(p_r (\mathrm{d}Q/\mathrm{d}N_r) - p_r C_r \right) \right),$$

where U_i is the utility of an individual in the ith sector and where v is the shadow price on the family's budget constraint. It is thus apparent that so long as there are net remittances from the urban to the rural sector, so that rural consumption exceeds average output in the rural sector, which equals or exceeds the marginal productivity of the marginal rural worker, migration will continue to the point where the level of utility of those remaining in the rural sector exceeds that of the urban migrant.

Thus, under the assumption of separability, if hours worked in the urban and rural sector are the same, consumption levels will be equal, if prices are equal, in which case we obtain the standard result of equating the marginal productivity of a worker in the rural sector to the expected urban wage. If urban prices exceed rural prices, urban consumption will be lower, though urban expenditure may be higher or lower. In the case of a utility function which is separable between leisure and goods, and in which the utility of consumption is logarithmic, expenditures will be the same; but since rural utility will be higher, the expected wage in the urban sector will exceed the rural wage. These results hold a fortiori if marginal utility of consumption has greater than unitary elasticity.

[25]This is not quite correct, unless the labor market is a spot market. If workers are hired for extended periods of time, the worker will normally remain unemployed for a period after arriving in the urban area. If there is a positive discount rate, the decision to migrate will take account of this. The migration decision will also be affected by capital market constraints, risk aversion, transportation costs, and differences in the amenities in the urban and rural sectors. See below for a discussion of these and other refinements to the theory of migration.

[26]One striking result should perhaps be noted: when the urban and rural wages are both fixed, under the conditions given below where the value of the rural marginal product equals the expected urban wage, then the opportunity cost of hiring an additional worker in the urban sector – that is, the reduction in output in the rural sector – is just equal to the urban wage. See Harberger (1971), Stiglitz (1974b) or Sah and Stiglitz (1985a).

then the marginal productivity of a worker in the rural sector may either be greater or less than the expected urban income. If, for instance, hours worked are the same, but prices are higher in the urban sector, then the marginal product in the rural sector will exceed the expected urban income, provided the elasticity of marginal utility with respect to consumption is greater than or equal to unity.)

Two related questions which have been of considerable concern in LDCs are:

(1) Under what conditions will the supply function of labor to the urban sector be horizontal, i.e. the urban sector can (at least over a relevant range) obtain close to an unlimited supply of labor at a given wage? Obviously, if the urban sector can obtain an unlimited supply of labor at a fixed wage, the major constraint on its growth will not be labor, but capital, entrepreneurship, or some other factor.

(2) Under what conditions will the output in the rural sector not decrease as workers migrate from the urban sector? Obviously, if the marginal product of labor is zero, removing labor from the rural sector will have no effect on output. But in most LDCs most workers are gainfully employed at least some of the time. The question then becomes: If some workers leave, will the remaining workers increase their labor supplies (effort) enough to compensate, so that output does not decrease, or does not decrease significantly? (Some economists, e.g. Sen, have labeled situations where, when workers migrate from the rural sector, output does not decrease, as exhibiting disguised unemployment. I am not sure that this nomenclature is very helpful.)

In our utilitarian family, as workers migrate the number of workers remaining on the fixed amount of land decreases, and this increases their marginal productivity. Thus, to induce further migration requires an increase in the expected urban wage (taking into account the periods of unemployment). Moreover, the higher expected urban wage increases family utility. This has the important consequence that though each member of the family is likely to work slightly harder, they will not increase their effort sufficiently to compensate for the loss in labor input from the migrant.[27] It thus follows that unless the marginal product of labor is fixed, i.e. *unless there is surplus labor or surplus land* (in the former case, the marginal product of labor remains at zero[28]) *the supply function of labor to the urban sector will be upward sloping and output in the rural sector will be*

---

[27]For assume they did. Then the value of the marginal product from working an additional hour would be the same for any remaining worker; but because of the higher income the marginal utility of consumption is lower. Hence, the family would decide that it is working too hard.

If there are remittances from the urban to the rural sector, output is likely to be decreased even more, because of the income effect.

[28]We also need to assume either that no capital is required in production, or that there is surplus capital.

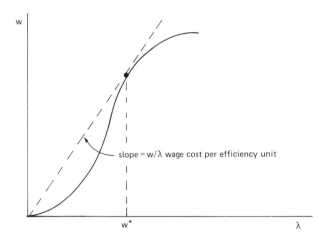

Figure 5.1. The relationship between wages and productivity and the efficiency wage (the wage which minimizes wage costs per efficiency unit).

reduced as labor migrates to the urban sector.[29] Of course, this is a qualitative proposition: this theoretical analysis cannot answer the question of the elasticity of the labor supply function or by how much rural output (surplus) falls with migration, though it can help us to identify the relevant parameters, e.g. the elasticity of rural output with respect to labor input (unity in the case of land surplus).

Wage productivity effects. In many LDCs, nutritional levels are sufficiently low that workers' productivity may be significantly increased by an increase in consumption [Bliss and Stern (1981a, 1981b)]. The wage–productivity relationship is often depicted as taking the form of Figure 5.1, with a region in which there is increasing returns. We write:

$$\lambda = \lambda(c), \quad \text{with } \lambda > 0, \ \lambda'' < \text{ or } > 0 \text{ as } c > \text{ or } < c', \tag{3.5}$$

where λ is the productivity of a worker consuming c.[30] Assume that if income

---

[29] We have focused attention on what we view to be the "normal" case. In certain special cases, the results could be reverse. For instance, if the marginal utility of income is much higher in the urban sector, then it is conceivable that workers in the rural sector would subsidize (net) those in the urban sector; in which case those remaining in the rural sector might be induced to work harder. Alternatively, if we had postulated a non-separable utility function, with an increase in consumption decreasing the marginal disutility of work, then it may be possible for output to increase. For an extreme case of this, see below.

[30] For our analysis here, it makes no difference what the *source* of the dependency of productivity on wages. It could be effort, where it is assumed that the family cannot monitor (control) the effort of family members directly. In this interpretation, (5) is a supply of effort function.

were equally divided c would be less than c^*, the level of consumption at which $\lambda(c)/c$ is maximized. [c^* is the point of tangency of a line through the origin to the wage–productivity curve. It is characterized by

$$\lambda(c)/c = \lambda'(c),$$

the marginal increase in productivity from an increase in consumption equals the ratio of productivity to consumption.] That is, assume that the rural production function is of the form:

$$Q = G(E)$$

where E is the effective supply of labor; if all workers are identical, and receive the same consumption, then

$$E = \lambda(c)N,$$

where N is the number of individuals in the rural sector (family). In an equalitarian family, one which insists on dividing income equally, then c is the solution to

$$c = Q/N = G(\lambda(c)N)/N.$$

Differentiating G/N with respect to N,[31] we immediately see that there exists a $c'' < c^*$, such that consumption is reduced as a result of an increase in the number of workers, if $c > c''$. More to the point, however, is the fact that if $c'' < c < c^*$, total output, Q, is reduced: *rural output increases as workers migrate from the rural sector.*[32]

In the utilitarian analysis, similar results would obtain if the marginal cost of exerting effort increases markedly at low levels of nutrition. Then the levels of effort could presumably be those "assigned" by the family.

[31] Differentiating c with respect to N, we obtain (using the fact that $c = G(\lambda(c)N)/N$):

$$dc/dN = (G'E - G)/(1 - G'\lambda')N^2.$$

The numerator is negative with diminishing returns. The denominator is positive near $\lambda = \lambda(c^*)$, for at c^*, $\lambda' = \lambda/c = \lambda N/G$. Substituting into the denominator, we have that the sign of the denominator is that of $(G - EG')/G > 0$, with diminishing returns. It follows that, since for $c > c'$ (with $c' < c^*$), $\lambda'' < 0$, there exists a $c'' < c^*$, such that for $c > c'$, the denominator is positive. Moreover, if $\lim_{c \to 0} \lambda' > 0$, $\lim_{c \to 0} \lambda = 0$, $\lim_{E \to 0} G'(E) \to \infty$, then there exists a c''' such that for $c < c'''$, $1 \cdot G'\lambda' < 0$.

[32] $dQ/dN = d(cN)/dN = c + Ndc/dN = G'[E - G\lambda']/(1 - G'\lambda')N$

$$= G'(\lambda - c\lambda')/(1 - G'\lambda').$$

For $c < c^*$, the numerator is negative, while, as we have already argued, there exists a $c'' < c^*$, such that for $c > c''$, the denominator is positive.

In general, however, a utilitarian family will not divide its income equally among its members, even if all of its members are identical, when faced with wage–productivity relationships of the form (5). In particular, it can be shown [Stiglitz (1976a)] that some workers will receive a higher level of consumption than others. Stiglitz provides a simple characterization of the optimal distribution of consumption. First, he shows that there will be only two levels of consumption. We can think of each worker as getting a wage, equal to his marginal product, plus a share of the rent (the difference between the total output of the firm, and the "implicit" wage payments).[33] The more productive workers have a higher marginal product. The question is: How are rents to be divided? He shows that within the utilitarian family the more able individual receives a share of the rent that is greater than $1/N$, where N is the number of individuals in the family; but less than his proportionate contribution to effective labor supply.[34]

The extreme case of this model is that in which the family simply maximizes the value of output. In that case, a fraction of the family will get zero consumption (and have zero productivity); and the remainder will be at the efficiency consumption level, c^*. In that extreme case, rural output will be completely unaffected by the number of workers in the rural sector: additional workers are simply unemployed, even though employed workers have a strictly positive marginal productivity. (Thus, the result we obtained above, that with egalitarian families, output increases with out-migration, turns out to be general; only if the family is completely indifferent to the distribution of welfare will output not increase.)[35]

3.1.2. Market-oriented families

The analysis of extreme market oriented families is fairly straightforward. In this view, how income is divided within the family depends simply on market power,

---

[33] Rents thus equal $G - G'E$.

[34] This model ignores labor supply (effort), while the previous model focused on precisely that issue. The question is: How can these models be reconciled? The simplest way is to think of the workers in this model as having zero marginal disutility of working up to their capacity, $\lambda(c)$, and infinite disutility beyond that. Their capacity is determined by their level of consumption.

[35] The discussion here has focused on rural output, not marketed surplus. With fixed prices, it is easy to translate these results into results concerning marketed surplus: if rural output increases, so will marketed surplus, unless there are interactions between labor supplies and the relative demands for agricultural and urban goods. With a separable utility function, letting Q be total rural output, Q^* marketed surplus, and p be the relative price of urban and agricultural goods,

$$Q^* = S(p, Q).$$

Since generally as workers migrate from the rural sector, each worker's labor supply will increase (assuming that the increase in productivity results in a substitution effect outweighing the income

or opportunity costs. The family can be thought of as a firm. As in the traditional theory of the firm, it makes little difference whether capital hires workers, or workers rent capital, in this view, it makes little difference whether the husband is thought of as employing the wife, or the wife the husband. There is a market price (the bride-price, or the dowry).

Just as we often assert that to understand what goes on in developed countries we need to see through the veil of the corporation, here we need to see through the veil of the household. In this view, then, there is little if any redistribution that occurs within the family. (What often is mistaken for redistribution is nothing more than the pay-offs on certain implicit insurance policies. Remittances are nothing more than the pay-offs on certain loans.)

Note that in this view, then, urban–rural wage inequality is of concern; if the migrants are mainly young males, there is no presumption that they are remitting a sufficient amount to eliminate differences between their welfare and that of those remaining in the rural sector. On the other hand, it remains likely that the supply schedule of workers to the urban sector is upward sloping and that rural output would be reduced (in the absence of wage–productivity effects) as a result of migration. To see this, assume that claims on rents were unchanged and that output was unchanged. Then, wages (the marginal product of labor in the rural sector) will be the same, rents will be the same, and hence consumption will be the same; but labor supply will be increased (for each individual) and hence the marginal rate of substitution cannot be equal to the wage. This argument is obviously strengthened if output were increased and/or if migrants lose (part of) their share in rents; for then labor must have increased, wages decreased, and consumption increased; if leisure is a normal good, this is not possible.[36]

An important aspect of the analysis of market-oriented families is the determination of property rights, particularly in the face of migration. Does the migrant lose his rights to the land, or to the (often implicit) rents to the land? In many instances he seems to. This may give rise to some important distortions. The worker, in deciding whether to leave, must compare his current wage, plus his share of the rents, with his expected urban income. Thus, if the expected urban income correctly measured the worker's opportunity costs in the urban sector, there would be too little migration. In the case where all workers are identical, and within the rural sector receive an equal share of the rent, then this yields the familiar result that the supply price of labor to the urban sector is the *average product* of labor in the rural sector. But note that if there is a group of landless workers, these workers will migrate as soon as the rural wage equals the

---

effect), if the decreased leisure reduces the marginal rate of substitution between urban and rural goods enough, it is conceivable that marketed surplus will decrease, even though rural output has increased; we view this case to be unlikely.

[36]Obviously, if leisure is not a normal good, these results may not hold.

expected urban wage. If the marginal migrant is a landless worker, the supply price of labor to the urban sector represents the workers' opportunity cost.[37]

In some situations, urban migrants will continue to migrate back to the rural sector in order to maintain their property rights, even though such migratory activity is inefficient.

3.1.3. Hybrid families

Models in which families act cooperatively in some dimensions but not in others have played an important role in earlier analyses. For instance, it is frequently assumed that while income is shared, effort decisions are made non-cooperatively. Since each worker knows that he will receive only $1/N$ (where N is the number of members of the family) of the value of the marginal product of his effort, he puts out too little effort. Migration has a further benefit in this case: it reduces the distortion associated with the undersupply of effort.

The question that is naturally raised at this juncture is: If output is divided equally, why cannot labor supply be decided cooperatively? One possible answer is that while output is observable, effort is not easily monitorable. The worker goes out to the field (an observable event) but day-dreams while out there. The importance of the non-observability of effort will play an important role in our discussion below of landlord–tenant relationships, and accordingly I do not want to underestimate its importance. At the same time, work on family farms often is organized in such a way as to minimize its importance. For instance, the family goes out together to the rice paddy to plant the seedlings. They are then in a position to observe each other.

Moreover, since the members of a family are in a long-term relationship (and there are often severe social sanctions for the severance of these relationships), even if there was no altruism, cooperative outcomes could be enforced,[38] provided, of course, that it is possible to observe deviations from cooperative actions. Even in instances in which deviations cannot be directly observed, it may be possible to make inferences concerning these deviations if some individual consistently undersupplies effort. In general, in the presence of uncertainty and positive discount rates, although it may not be possible to do as well as one could do with perfect monitoring [see Abreu (1985)], nonetheless, the outcomes may be closer to those described under the "utilitarian family" than under the "market-

---

[37]In the absence of capital market imperfections and risk aversion, the marginal migrant would, of course, be the landless worker, so long as there remained any landless workers in the rural sector. But with capital market imperfections these workers may not be able to finance the period during which they remain unemployed or the transportation costs required to go the urban sector. See Kanbur (1981). And there is always some risk of obtaining a job; the landless workers, being poor, may not be willing to undertake this risk. (On the other hand, there is risk within the rural sector; what is of concern is the relative magnitudes of the two risks.) Finally, if there are important wage–productivity effects, and if landlessness is observable, then urban employers will discriminate against the landless.

[38]See, for instance, Abreu for a discussion in a somewhat different context of how cooperative solutions may be enforced in repeated relationships.

oriented family".[39] In particular, it is not apparent how much attention should be paid to the peculiar distortions which arise in hybrid families, with income sharing but without work sharing.

The previous discussion focused on the consequences of different family structures, primarily in the context of a family-owned farm. Similar issues arise under systems of wage labor or sharecropping. In the next section we focus on the consequences of alternative systems of land tenancy, ignoring, however, the subtleties concerning the organization of the family upon which we have focused in this section.

3.2. The landlord–tenant relationship: The sharecropping puzzle

A variety of contractual relationships between landlords and tenants can be observed. Here, we focus on sharecropping contracts,[40] in which the landlord receives a fraction of the output of the land as compensation for its use, on why these contracts are so widely observed, on the forms these contracts take, and on the efficiency of sharecropping arrangements.

The persistence of sharecropping has been a continuing source of puzzlement to economists. Economists are used to thinking of institutions, or at least institutional arrangements with the universality that sharecropping has, as serving particular economic functions, and if not serving those functions optimally, at least not doing "too badly". Yet sharecropping has long been vilified for its failure to provide adequate incentives for work (and for the application of other inputs). While workers bear the entire costs, they receive only a fraction of the output, and this reduces their incentives for work.

Recent advances, described below, show that there is indeed a good economic rationale for sharecropping, though the terms of the sharecropping contract may well be such as to reduce output from what it would be under an alternative contractual relationship.

3.2.1. Equivalency result

Agricultural output is risky. Farmers can seldom buy insurance against these risks.[41] In sharecropping, the risks of output fluctuations are shared between the

---

[39] It should be clear that for sufficiently high discount rates, the threat of future punishment for non-cooperative behavior looses its bite. Thus, the question of whether a cooperative equilibrium can be maintained within the family depends on the discount rate and the ease of monitoring.

[40] For other recent surveys, see Binswanger and Rosenzweig (1984).

[41] In some situations, they can buy insurance against specific risks, such as hailstorms, but they cannot obtain insurance against output fluctuations in general. Part of the reason for this has to do with the standard problems facing insurance markets: moral hazard (the provision of insurance

landlord and the tenant.[42] It appears as if sharecropping can be thought of as a risk-sharing mechanism.

An important qualification on this view was provided by the fundamental *equivalency* theorem [Cheung (1969), Stiglitz (1974a)] which showed that workers, by mixing wage and rental contracts (i.e. working for wages for one landlord, and renting some land) could exactly replicate the risk–return patterns associated with sharecropping, provided labor was perfectly monitorable, and provided there were no costs associated with mixing. This theorem lead to two alternative explanations of sharecropping.

In Cheung's (1969) analysis, sharecropping was justified as having advantages in transactions costs. He assumed that labor was monitorable and, accordingly, the dead weight loss associated with the undersupply of effort simply did not arise. The landlord, in signing a contract with a tenant, knows that his return depends critically on the labor input of his tenant; hence, he specifies precisely what the tenant is to do. There is, in this approach, no difference between wage labor and sharecropping labor, or between the labor supplied on rented land.

By contrast, in Stiglitz's (1974a) analysis, labor was assumed not to be monitorable. Again, the landlord knows that what he (the landlord) receives depends on the labor input of his tenant, but it is assumed that he cannot control that directly. (Even if he could monitor whether the worker was in the fields, he could not without great cost monitor the effort the worker put out while in the field, what fraction of the weeds were removed, etc.) Thus, he attempts to affect *indirectly* the labor input of his tenant by the terms of the contract. As he increases the share that the tenant receives, the tenant has greater incentives for work, but at the same time, he bears greater risk. There is thus a fundamental trade-off between incentives and risk bearing. The equilibrium contract balances these off; it will clearly depend on the worker's elasticity of labor supply and his degree of risk aversion. [See Stiglitz (1974a) for precise formulae.] Even if the landlord is risk neutral, the worker will bear some of the risk; for if his income does not depend at all on output, he will have no incentives.[43] The sharecropping contract thus is viewed as a compromise between pure rental contracts, in which the worker does have good incentives, but in which the worker has to bear all the risks; and the pure wage contract, in which the landlord, who is in a better

---

affects individual's incentives to avoid the risk, here a low output); and adverse selection (the insured knows more about the risks he faces than the insurance firm; variability in weather may be quite local, and individuals may be much more well informed concerning the consequences of this for the crops than the insurance company). These do not provide a complete explanation of the absence of insurance markets; they probably do not explain, for instance, the absence of insurance against hail.

[42] Both, of course, still face price risks.

[43] This analysis has served as a general paradigm for a large literature which developed subsequently, referred to as the principal–agent literature. See also Ross (1973).

position to bear risks than the tenant, does so; but the worker has no incentives to work.[44]

There is another advantage of sharecropping contracts, which Johnson (1950) has emphasized. If rents are paid at the end of the production period, there is some probability that the landlord will not be paid; thus, he still bears some risk. If the tenant has to borrow to pay the rent at the beginning of the period, the problem is essentially unaffected; the risk is now borne not by the landlord, but by the creditor. But not only do rental contracts thus not really avoid all risk, they may provide the tenant with incentives for risk taking which are adverse to the interests of the landlord (at least without threats of bonding tenants who default on their rents). The tenant is only concerned with what he gets, over and above what he has to pay the landlord in rents. He does not care what the landlord (creditors) get in the event of a default.[45]

An alternative resolution of the incentives/risk sharing problem is for the landlord to use direct supervision; one must then compare the economic costs of this supervision with the dead weight loss associated with the risks which the worker must bear, and the undersupply of effort, associated with the sharecropping contract.

3.2.2. Equilibrium contracts

It is, of course, not only the share, but all the terms of the contract which affect the worker's incentives. Thus, the equilibrium sharecropping contract (in an economy with homogeneous workers, homogeneous land, and no outside wage opportunities) is assumed to be the solution to the problem of maximizing the expected utility of the landlord subject to the worker's obtaining a given level of expected utility.

Formally, we represent the equilibrium share, α, as the solution to the following problem. Let $Q(l, e, \theta)$ be the output per acre of a farm with l workers per acre in state θ (θ is the state of nature, specifying, among other things, the weather, whether there is an insect infestation, or some infestation of a disease), where the worker exerts effort (labor supply) e, and let $U(Y, e)$ denote the utility

---

[44] There is an alternative resolution to the incentives problem: if there are long-term contracts, then even if effort cannot be directly monitored, the landlord can make fairly accurate inferences concerning the level of effort by observing output over an extended period of time. If individuals were infinitely lived, discount rates were low, and unbounded punishments could be imposed upon shirkers, once one becomes confident that they were in fact shirking, this would enable the design of contracts with almost perfect incentives and the landlord bearing almost all of the risk. But discount rates are not low, individuals are finitely lived, and there are finite bounds on punishments. Long-term relationships may thus ameliorate the incentive problems, but they do not eliminate them.

[45] For a discussion of the effect of this form of contractual arrangement on incentives for risk taking, see Stiglitz and Weiss (1981).

function of the worker; the equilibrium contract is the solution to

$$\max_{\{l,\alpha,\beta\}} (1-\alpha)Q + \beta \tag{3.6}$$

subject to

$$\max_{\{e\}} EU(\alpha Q l - \beta, e) > \overline{U}, \tag{3.7}$$

where $\overline{U}$ is the expected utility that the worker can receive on any other farm and β is a fixed payment from the tenant to the landlord, and where the landlord recognizes that the level of effort that will be supplied by the tenant will be the solution to (3.7), i.e.

$$e = e(\alpha, \beta, l).$$

Thus, we replace the wage-taking hypothesis of standard competitive theory with the utility taking hypothesis. The solution to this will yield α, β, and l all as a function of $\overline{U}$. l determines the demand for tenants. (A landlord with T acres will want to have Tl tenants.) There is a given supply of tenants. If we postulate that there are no outside job opportunities, then clearly if there are T acres in aggregate and N farmers, in equilibrium farm size must be T/N. Thus, the market equilibrium is that value of $\overline{U}$ for which

$$l = N/T.$$

Notice that we have thus described in full the equilibrium for this economy: we have solved not only for the equilibrium share, but also for the equilibrium level of expected utility of workers, and the equilibrium expected income of landlords. One can use the model to analyze the consequences, for instance, of an increase in population pressure (which will presumably lower the expected utility of workers; the effects on α are, however, not so obvious).[46]

3.2.3. Two extensions

3.2.3.1. Outside wage opportunities. The extension to the case with outside wage opportunities is straightforward. If workers are restricted to working either on the sharecropping farm or on the outside wage opportunities, then we can postulate a supply function of workers (tenants) to the sharecropping sector; equilibrium is simply the intersection of demand and supply.

---

[46] Notice the problem that one encounters if one fails to note the central role that farm size plays in determining the attractiveness of a contract. Each landlord would then seek, at any fixed $\{\alpha, \beta\}$ to squeeze as many tenants onto a plot of land as he could. His demand for tenants would be infinite. It is hard, in this context, to know what is meant by an equilibrium to the market.

If workers can work both on and off the farm, then the analysis is basically unaffected, except that now, the dependence of effort on the terms of the contract is altered;[47] it is still the case that a reduction in α, the share the worker receives, is likely to reduce the worker's effort on the field.[48]

3.2.3.2. Labor heterogeneity. The introduction of labor heterogeneity complicates the analysis in one important way. If differences in workers' productivity were easily observed, the analysis would be essentially unaffected. But if landlords are imperfectly informed concerning the abilities of potential tenants, they may use the terms of the contract to help them sort out (screen) more productive from less productive workers. In particular, workers who are willing to accept a larger share (and make a correspondingly larger fixed payment β) are likely to be more productive [see Newbery and Stiglitz (1979)]. Thus, if it is observed that output on rental contracts is higher than on sharecropping contracts, or that output on sharecropping contracts is higher than on wage contracts, only part of the increased output should be attributed to the beneficial incentive effects. Some of the increased output may be attributable to the fact that those who have chosen the rental contract are more productive than those who have chosen the sharecropping contract, and these, in turn, are more productive than those who have chosen the wage system. (To put it another way, though a land redistribution might have positive incentive effects, the magnitude of the gains may not be as much as one might infer on the basis of currently observed differences in productivity across tenancy arrangements.)

3.2.4. Uniformity

As we shall see, not only has the persistence of sharecropping posed a puzzle for economists, but so too has some of its characteristics. In this and the next section, we consider two of these puzzles. Here we are concerned with the

---

[47] Of course, the landlord will recognize that effort will be reduced if the worker spends some of his time on other employment activities; as in other situations where such "moral hazard" (incentive) issues arise, he may attempt to restrict his tenant, e.g. from working off the farm, say during harvesting or planting times. There are costs to monitoring such exclusivity provisions.

[48] With a separable utility function between consumption and effort, but with effort on and off the job entering additively, i.e.

$$U = u(c) - v(e_1 + e_2),$$

where e_1 is effort on the farm; e_2 is work effort at the wage job, we obtain:

$$Eu'(c) = v'(e_1 + e_2)/w = \alpha Eu'Q_e/w.$$

One suspects that, in general, the additional opportunities for earning will increase the elasticity of effort with respect to α.

widespread uniformity in sharecropping rates. The theory presented above would seem to suggest that under different conditions (different crops, different labor supply elasticities, etc.) one ought to observe different values of α, the crop share. Some variations in α are observed, but it is surprising, nonetheless, that 50 percent (or 60 percent) shares are so commonly observed.

One explanation has recently been provided by Allen (1985). He observes that a basic problem in all contractual arrangements is that of enforcement: the landless peasant can abscond with all the output if the landlord demands too much. For simplicity, assume that the contract is simply described by its share, α. If the worker absconds, he keeps the full output, but must then seek alternative employment elsewhere. If he never regained employment, then α would be constrained by the relationship (assuming that he would have remained on the plot forever, if he did not abscond),

$$\alpha Q(1+r)/r > Q$$

or

$$\alpha > r/1+r.$$

On the other hand, if he were to remain unemployed only for one period, and thereafter was able to obtain a job which was not much worse than his current contract, α is constrained by the relationship

$$\alpha Q(1 + 1/1+r) > Q$$

or

$$\alpha > (1+r)/2+r,$$

i.e. for small r, $\alpha \sim 0.5$.[49] It is possible that this is the binding constraint, in which case α will be equal to $(1+r)/(2+r)$, regardless of technology, risk aversion, etc. Critics of Allen's view claim that because landlords are aware of the possibility of absconding, they watch crops very carefully. Moreover, they claim that one seldom sees farmers absconding, perhaps partly because the social ostracism that would result acts as a far more effective deterrent than any economic punishment. The fact that one seldom sees tenants absconding is not, however, a convincing criticism of the theory; for if the terms of the tenancy

---

[49] Note that this and the previous equation can be thought of as imposing bounds on the relevant values of α; that is, if the new job that the individual gets is just as good as the old, α must exceed $(1 + r)/(2 + r)$; while if he fails to obtain any job, α need only exceed $r/1 + r$.

contract are set appropriately, the contract is designed to be self-enforcing, i.e. tenants will not in fact abscond. And the fact that landlords attempt to monitor tenants implies that the tenant can only "cheat" by stealing a limited fraction of the crop; the equilibrium share can then be adjusted accordingly. To the extent, however, that monitoring as well as the nature of the gains and punishments (economic and social) from absconding vary across countries and over time, Allen's model does not succeed in accomplishing what was intended – a theory to explain the uniformity of the terms of the sharecropping contract.

A rather different explanation has been recently noted by Braverman and Stiglitz (1986a). They ask what happens if the actual output of the farm is not monitorable; what is monitorable are the supplies the farm has available for sale. These could have been produced on the farm, or purchased from other farms. In that case, if any landlord were to lower the share he paid his tenants, they would all market their output through their neighbors. This explains downward rigidity in shares. Similarly, if any landlord were to attempt to raise the share he paid relative to those paid by his neighbors, he would find that all of the neighbors would market their share through him. This would give him enormous advantage, but it is unlikely that they would not respond. There are two reasons that a landlord might desire to increase the share he pays his tenant (other than diverting the output of his neighbors to himself). He may wish to attract tenants from other landlords, and he may wish to elicit greater effort out of his current tenants. If he believes that his neighbors will respond, he will find that he will not be able to recruit any tenants from his neighbors. Thus, he will increase the share only if the elasticity of output with respect to share is greater than unity. These considerations suggest that once a share gets accepted, it may be sustained, in spite of considerable variations in economic conditions. This theory does not explain, however, how the same share got to be accepted across different regions.

Non-competitive equilibrium. A slight variation around this theme suggests that in many situations it may be inappropriate to view the share as that determined by competitive equilibrium. If labor mobility across villages is limited, and if there are a limited number of landlords, cooperative equilibrium can be enforced non-cooperatively, by imposing sanctions against those who fail to cooperate (and indeed, simply by the belief that sanctions will be imposed against those who do not cooperate).[50] Thus, deviations from an established "normal" share

---

[50] In standard game theoretic formulations, these "reputation equilibrium" beliefs need not be based on experience (since, if individuals believe them, they will not deviate from the cooperative solution, and hence punishments will never need to be imposed).

Recent work in oligopoly has attempted to use similar arguments to explain why prices do not vary over the business cycle, i.e. why prices do not vary much with changing economic conditions. See, for example, Rotenberg and Saloner (1986).

Whether these models are very persuasive in the context under discussion here remains a moot question.

may not arise, even in the presence of an excess demand for tenants, particularly if that excess demand is viewed to be temporary.

3.2.5. Cost sharing

So far we have focused on only three dimensions of the share tenancy contract: the output share, the fixed fee, and the plot size. Another important dimension of the share tenancy contract is the cost share. Many sharecropping contracts specify a cost share. Why? And what determines the cost share?

In the absence of cost sharing, tenants will have insufficient incentives to apply inputs (such as fertilizer) since they will receive only a fraction of the benefits. One solution [suggested, for instance, by Heady (1947)] was for the landlord to provide a share of costs equal to the share he takes of the output, since then tenants will receive the same share of output as the fraction of the costs they bear, there will be an efficient allocation of inputs. This simple argument seems plausible; yet systematic deviations from this rule are observed. Since the rule of equating output shares and cost shares seems both simple, and to engender economic efficiency, these deviations are particularly disturbing.

The problem posed by cost shares is all the more puzzling, once it is recognized that for cost sharing to be feasible, inputs must be observable; but if inputs are observable, there is no reason to employ cost sharing. The landlord could, as well, simply specify the level of inputs.[51]

Indeed, Braverman and Stiglitz (1986a) have established a general equivalency result, analogous to the equivalency result established earlier between wage, rental, and sharecropping contracts: any outcome that can be obtained by a cost share can be obtained by an equivalent contract with input specification; with the output shares in the two contracts being identical; and the fixed payments adjusted to reflect differences in expenditures on inputs in the two situations.

The resolution of these seeming paradoxes lies in the differential information available to the landlord and the tenant. There are great variations in the productivity of inputs, both over time and across space. The tenant may be better informed concerning the particular plot of land he works on; and since information becomes available to the tenant after the "signing" of the contract, the

---

[51] Of course, he would presumably have to specify these inputs prior to the agreement on the contract; if the landlord were given discretion in imposing requirements (arguing that the input requirements need to vary with circumstances) he would always have an incentive to impose the maximal requirements allowed. This problem may be mitigated with long-term contracts, and if landlords worry about their reputations affecting the terms at which future tenants will be willing to agree to contracts. There may also exist self-selection devices which induce "truth telling" on the part of the landlord, but as usual there are costs associated with implementing these self-selection equilibria.

tenant is in a position to use this information to make better allocative decisions.[52] Thus, contracts which specify an input share allow more *flexibility*; they allow the adjustment of the level of input to reflect differences in circumstances. One can show, accordingly, under fairly weak conditions that a cost sharing contract will dominate a contract which specified a fixed level of input; and more generally, if a contract does specify a fixed level of inputs, it will also supplement this with a cost sharing provision.

In setting the cost share, the optimal contract will take account of two considerations: first, lowering the cost to the tenant of the monitorable input will normally lead to an increase in the purchase of these inputs. If this increases the value of the marginal product of the non-monitorable inputs (labor),[53] then it pays the landlord to provide a share of the costs that is in excess of the share of output that he receives; and conversely if this decreases the value of the marginal product of the non-monitorable inputs. Secondly, since inputs have to be purchased prior to the production period, making the tenant bear a larger fraction of the costs imposes a greater risk on him. In some cases, where the fixed fee can be adjusted, this effect can be offset; but in other cases, it may not be.

There is a quite distinct argument for cost sharing. Though purchases of inputs may be monitored, it is difficult to monitor their actual application; and it is difficult to monitor resale among farms. Thus, if the landlord did provide the inputs, if there is heterogeneity among the farms, the tenants would have an incentive to resell the inputs, to equate the value of the marginal product. A similar analysis provides an argument for why cost shares should be uniform within a region: if cost shares differed, there would be scope for arbitrage. The tenant whose landlord paid a larger share of the costs would purchase the inputs, for resale to other farms.

3.2.6. Efficiency of market equilibrium

The way we have formulated our equilibrium has misled some into believing that the market equilibrium is efficient. After all, we have maximized the welfare of one of the agents (say the landlords) subject to the level of the other agent

---

[52] The second effect is perhaps more important than the first, since presumably the landlord would eventually learn about the nature of the land that he owns, i.e. he will be equally or even better informed than his tenant.

Note that if the landlord were better informed about the varying productivities of inputs, then if landlords are less risk averse, they would presumably simply provide the tenant with the inputs, rather than imposing a requirement that he purchase the inputs. This will avoid the problem we noted earlier that if the landlord has discretion in specifying input requirements after the contract has been agreed to, he will have an incentive to impose the highest requirements allowed.

[53] By the same token, subsidizing inputs may affect the choice of technique (risk taking) and the landlord will take this into account as well.

(tenants) being at a particular level. It thus appears that, by definition, the equilibrium must lie along the "contract curve". The contract is locally efficient; but the market equilibrium may not – and in general will not – be Pareto efficient; for each firm takes prices as given; and those prices do not correctly reflect opportunity costs [see Greenwald and Stiglitz (1986)].[54]

Critics of sharecropping were concerned, however, not so much with its Pareto efficiency, but with a much simpler view of efficiency: because tenants received only a fraction of their output, they exerted less effort than they would have exerted had they received the total value of their marginal product (keeping income fixed), and thus output will be lower. Sharecropping arises largely from the disparity between the ownership of capital (land) and labor endowments.[55] A land reform, which redistributed the land which each tenant worked to the tenant, would, unless the supply curve of labor is backward bending, cause output to increase. Of course, even after a land reform, as time evolves some farmers will work harder, be smarter, or be luckier, and accumulate wealth, purchasing land from those who do less well. Inequality of land ownership – and sharecropping – might re-emerge. Policies which attempt to limit land ownership are not only often of limited effectiveness, but they weaken the incentives for exerting effort and for saving.

Our discussion of sharecropping has identified several other factors (besides the disparity between wealth and land ownership and labor endowments) which determine the extent to which it is employed. Under some circumstances (in plantation farms), it may be possible to monitor workers' efforts, in which case wage labor may be employed. Under other circumstances, risk may be limited, and default on rental contracts may be relatively unimportant, which will favor the employment of rental contracts. As tenants become wealthier, and savings institutions develop where they can invest their funds in a relatively safe manner, they become better able to bear the risks, and they have access to credit to further smooth the fluctuations in their incomes. This again is favorable to rental contracts. On the other hand, innovations or public expenditures, such as irrigation, which make it advantageous to make more extensive use of capital in farming, make tenancy arrangements more desirable.

---

[54]Of the various market failures which they study in their paper, the sharecropping model with homogeneous labor provides examples of two: there is an incomplete set of risk markets, which, with more than one commodity generically generates market equilibrium which are not constrained efficient; and there are moral hazard (incentive) problems, which results in outcomes which are not constrained Pareto efficient, either when there is more than one commodity, or when exclusivity arrangements cannot be enforced. [See Arnott and Stiglitz (1984, 1986).]

[55]Thus, in these models there is not the conventional separation between efficiency and equity issues which characterized the simpler models of competitive economies. With equal ownership of wealth, for instance, the economy might be Pareto efficient, while with unequal ownership, with sharecropping, the economy may not be Pareto efficient.

3.3. Unemployment in the rural sector

Rural unemployment has been a persistent concern of economists, both because of the social and economic losses it engenders, and because it poses a puzzle for the theorist: how can unemployment persist in competitive markets. In the previous analysis we have assumed full employment in the rural sector. (One should not confuse low incomes, rural poverty, with unemployment; nor should one confuse seasonal unemployment with unemployment. Fluctuations in productivity may easily lead to variations in labor utilization – a telephone operator can be viewed as unemployed as she waits to handle another call. Efficiency requires some variability in the utilization of labor. This can be mitigated by providing counter-seasonal job opportunities; but the capital required may be such as to make such job opportunities not viable. Still, unless the marginal productivity falls to zero, one would expect that competitive markets would clear; and even if marginal productivity falls to zero, competitive markets clear, though at a wage of zero.)

There is a variety of situations where, when the landlord maximizes his (expected utility of) income, subject to the (expected) utility constraint associated with workers, the constraint will not be binding. That is, the landlord may find it profitable to offer terms that are better than the individual's reservation utility level. These situations give rise to unemployment. That is, there will exist workers who are willing to work at the terms being offered by employers (landlords), but they cannot get hired.

Unemployment can be generated whenever the productivity of the worker is affected by the terms of the contract: a lower share or a lower wage results in a more than offsetting reduction in productivity, so that labor costs are actually increased.[56] There are four basic reasons for this.

3.3.1. The nutritional wage–productivity model

At low utility levels, the individual may not be very productive. We have discussed this efficiency–consumption relationship above, in our analysis of the allocation of consumption within the family. The same arguments suggest that at low levels of utility, the effort that the tenant may be able to exert may be so low that the landlord's expected income will be increased if he pays more than the minimal utility level at which he can obtain workers. There will, in this case, be unemployment: some workers will obtain employment, while seemingly identical

---

[56] For a general discussion of the consequences of the dependence of productivity on wages, see Stiglitz (1987b).

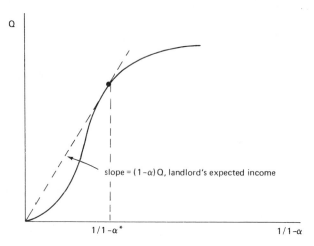

Figure 5.2. Optimal share.

workers fail to do so.[57] They cannot undercut the wages of the employed, however, because the landlords know that their output would then be less.

This result holds, of course, whether the worker is hired on a wage system, or within a share tenancy contract. Thus, if the worker is paid a wage, and his wage productivity curve appears as in Figure 5.1, then the wage which minimizes labor costs, i.e. minimizes the wage divided by productivity, is w^*, at the tangency of a line through the origin to the wage productivity curve. By the same token, assume that with sharecropping the output of the farm is an increasing function of the share paid the worker. For simplicity, we plot output, Q, as a function of $1/1 - \alpha$. If it appears as in Figure 5.2, then the optimal share is α^*, again at the tangency of the line through the origin to the "share-productivity curve". For the slope of the line is just $Q/(1/1 - \alpha) = (1 - \alpha)Q$, the income of the landlord. And this is maximized at the point of tangency.

w^* is called the efficiency wage and, by analogy, α^* is called the efficiency share. If the supply of available workers is greater than the demand, w^* (α^*) is still the equilibrium.

For it to be worthwhile for an employer to pay higher wages so that his employee will be more productive requires the higher wage actually be spent in prouctivity-enhancing ways. Expenditures on other members of the family may

---

[57]When all workers are, ex ante, identical, and the employer or landlord randomly chooses among them which to employ, then their ex ante expected utility will be the same. Their ex post utility will, however, differ.

For a brief discussion of how these models differ from the standard Arrow–Debreu model (which assumptions of that model are not satisfied) see Stiglitz (1987b).

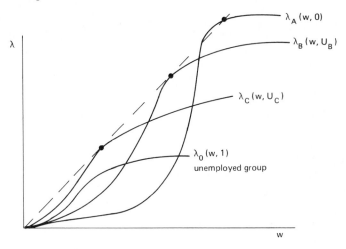

$\lambda_i = \lambda_i\ (w_i, U_i)$, i th group's productivity depends on
wage and group's unemployment rate

Figure 5.3. Wage–productivity curves may differ across groups. Group specific unemployment rates will adjust to ensure that in equilibrium all groups which are partially employed have same costs per efficiency unit. Fully employed groups have higher wages reflecting higher productivities. Low productivity groups may be totally unemployed.

have a very limited effect in increasing the worker's productivity. Thus, landlords have an incentive to provide meals on the job. More generally, the fact that only a fraction of higher wages goes into productivity-enhancing expenditures alters the relationship between productivity and wage, but does not change the qualitative result (so long as the productivity-wage curve has the shape of Figure 5.1).

Moreover, if nutrition affects productivity largely through affecting general physical strength and health, and this is a function not of consumption at any one moment but of consumption over an extended period, it is only in long-term relationships that one should observe employers (landlords) paying wages in excess of what they need to pay to obtain labor, for nutritional-productivity reasons. Under these circumstances the productivity–consumption relationship will be irrelevant for casual laborers, hired on a daily basis.

The nutritional efficiency wage model has one further implication. If there are different groups in the population, with different wage–productivity curves, then in equilibrium we can divide the population into three categories, represented by the three wage productivity curves depicted in Figure 5.3. All of those hired must receive a wage which is proportional to their productivity. Thus, there will exist some groups which are paid more than their efficiency wage, such as group A. Then there are other groups, such as group C, for which, at no wage, is there productivity/wage ratio sufficiently high that it pays to employ them. Workers in these groups do not succeed in getting jobs. Finally, there is group B, which is paid its efficiency wage. Some of the members of group B are employed, while others remain unemployed.

One way in which workers differ is the amount of land which they own. Some workers may have some land of their own, yielding them rents. These workers will be more productive than the landless. Thus, unemployment will be concentrated among the landless and the near landless. (By the same token, if the landless and the near landless do obtain employment, the wages they receive may be less than that received by the landed, not because there is any discrimination, but simply because they are less productive.)[58] This analysis assumes, of course, that the employer cannot hire workers on a piece-rate basis. The problem of doing so is precisely that noted earlier: the difficulty of monitoring output.[59]

As the economy becomes wealthier, this nutritional wage efficiency unemployment will disappear. [Note that in this version of what is called the efficiency wage model, if all workers were identical, the wage, or the expected utility in a share-tenancy contract, would be fixed (say in food terms) until the economy became wealthy enough for the wage to exceed the efficiency wage. On the other hand, if the population is heterogeneous, e.g. in land ownership, then as the

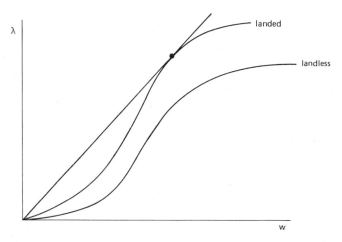

Figure 5.4. If the landless have a lower productivity at each wage, they will face higher unemployment rates.

[58]This application of the general principles of market equilibrium with efficiency wages was noted by Bliss and Stern (1981) and has been further developed by Dasgupta and Ray (1986a).
[59]Even if it were possible to pay workers on a piece rate, there could be unemployment; an unemployed worker could not offer to undercut the going, efficiency wage (piece rate).

economy becomes wealthier, successively less productive groups (here, those who own less land) get employment; and the wage (expected utility) of the more productive increases.]

Note that in this version of the efficiency wage model, non-price-rationing devices cannot be used to substitute for price rationing; that is, not only is the landlord constrained from reducing the share (lest the productivity of the worker be reduced), but he is also constrained from reducing plot size or changing the other terms of the contract in a way which reduces the expected utility.

Also, note that a land reform (land redistribution) can have significant effects both on efficiency and unemployment. Thus, in Figure 5.4, there are two groups, the landed and the landless; the landed receive an (implicit) rent of R^* (per capita) on their land, which shifts their efficiency wage curve to the left. In this example, the landless remain unemployed, while the landed receive a wage in excess of their efficiency wage. A land redistribution program results in an efficiency wage curve lying between the zero rent and the R^* rent curves; with the new efficiency wage curve there may be full employment.

This property – the impossibility of the separation of efficiency and equity issues, and the possible efficiency gains from redistribution – is a general property of the efficiency wage models [see, for example, Shapiro and Stiglitz (1984)].

3.3.2. Incentive-efficiency wage models

The second class of efficiency wage models is that where workers' incentives depend on the terms of the contract (and possibly the existence of unemployment). We have already noted that lowering the tenant's share attenuates his efforts. The question is: Are there other terms of the contract which can be adjusted if there is an excess supply of workers? There are two possibilities.

3.3.2.1. Reducing the amount of land. This has a negative substitution effect (the reduced land means that the worker's marginal product is lowered); and a positive income effect (the lower income induces the worker to work harder). (There actually may, in some circumstances, be a negative income effect: though the worker works harder, what the landlord cares about is how hard he works on the farm's cash crops, assuming that consumption of non-cash crops on the farm is difficult to monitor. For as the farmer becomes poorer, he may switch a greater fraction of his effort into subsistence crops; and indeed, the greater degree of risk aversion at the lower level of income may induce him to take whatever wage labor jobs he can get.) Although under some conditions [see Braverman and Srinivasan (1981)] the income effect outweighs the substitution effect, so that unemployment would never arise; under other conditions – particularly when there are alternative wage opportunities available – the substitution effect dominates; and then it is possible that there will be unemployment.

3.3.2.2. Increasing the fixed payment. This has a beneficial incentive effective on work in general (the income effect on work is positive); but there are three possible negative effects. One of these we have already noted: at the lower income, though the worker may work harder, he may allocate a larger fraction of his effort to subsistence crops and to off-the-farm jobs.

The second negative effect (which can arise whenever the terms of the contract adversely affect the worker) can occur whenever there is more than a single decision variable (effort) under the control of the worker. In most circumstances the worker also has some control over the choice of technique; these choices affect both the average output and the riskiness of the output (when effort is exerted; if the crop is harvested earlier, the average size of the drop may be smaller, but the likelihood of losing the entire crop because of adverse weather conditions is also reduced). By our assumption of risk neutrality, the landlord is just concerned about the average output, while the worker cares about the riskiness of output as well. The induced risk which he must bear corresponding to the increased fixed payment may lead him to undertake less risky production, which in turn may reduce the landlords expected income.[60]

The third negative effect is that, at contract terms which are less attractive to workers, the landlord only attracts the less productive workers. We discuss these adverse selection effects below. Before turning to these, we should make two other remarks concerning the incentive–efficiency wage model. First, we have already noted that the importance of these incentive effects may be reduced as a result of the long-run relationship which landlords and tenants have; a tenant who does not apply himself repeatedly, year after year, will find that eventually the landlord will terminate his lease.

Because of the adverse incentive effects of, for example, reducing the worker's share, the landlord is more likely to respond to a worker that he believes is shirking by terminating the relationship than by reducing the worker's share [see Stiglitz and Weiss (1983)].

The cost imposed on the tenant by the termination of the lease depends on how easy it is for the worker to obtain outside employment opportunities. Thus, the presence of unemployment serves itself a positive incentive effect. This is

---

[60] The increased fixed payment makes the tenancy contract closer to a rental contract, in which the worker bears all of the risk.

Note again that what is at issue is, at least in part, a monitoring problem. If the landlord could costlessly monitor all of the worker's actions, and could write a contract specifying what he should do in each contingency, there would be no problem. But in fact, many of the actions are not monitorable except at great cost; and it is virtually impossible to have (even an implicit) contract specifying what the tenant should do under each contingency.

On the other hand, some actions, such as the use of fertilizer or the allocation of land among different crops may be monitorable.

particularly important in wage contracts, where the only incentive is provided by the threat of the termination of the contract [see Shapiro and Stiglitz (1984)].[61]

In this analysis, the incentives of the worker depend on the returns he obtains, and his alternative opportunities. There is another version of the wage–productive–incentives model, where "morale" effects are crucial [Stiglitz (1973, 1974c), Akerlof (1984), Yellen (1984)]. Workers' effort (productivity) depends on whether they believe that they are being fairly treated. If, for whatever reason, they believe that they are not being fairly treated, they will put in less effort. It is natural to hypothesize that views of equity are based on one's (perceptions of one's) pay relative to what others receive. These perceptions may or may not be correct. More generally, they may be based on irrelevant comparisons, e.g. on what a skilled worker receives. This view explains rigidities in relative wages. (An employer may not reduce the wage of his unskilled workers relative to that of the skilled workers, even though changes in supply or demand conditions may have created an excess supply of unskilled workers.)

Land reform in this model, as in the previous one, may have significant beneficial effects: this is not to claim that land reform would be Pareto improving (those who have lost their land may indeed be worse off). But providing workers with their own land removes the deleterious incentive effects associated with sharecropping. Several qualifications on this result should be noted:

(a) The welfare gains to the tenants are less than the gains in expected output, since the tenants now must bear more risk. This has two consequences. First, tenants may change their choice of technique, in a way which reduces mean output. Secondly, the desire to transfer risk to those who are more able or willing to bear it may result in contractual arrangements which have deleterious incentive effects, not unlike those of sharecropping.

(b) If other inputs (such as capital or fertilizer) are required, then the formerly landless peasants may not (in the presence of credit constraints – see below) be able to obtain these inputs (to the extent required by efficiency). This will provide an incentive for these workers to sell or rent out their land. If these arrangements are prohibited, there is a loss in economic efficiency; if these arrangements are permitted, the effects of the land reform may not be sustained.

In any case, the observation that we made earlier – that efficiency and equity issues cannot be neatly separated, as is frequently done in traditional neo-classical analysis – holds for these models as well.

---

[61] In their model, all workers were identical; hence there were no reputation effects from being fired. With heterogeneous workers, being fired may have an adverse effect on the workers' reputation. It may be possible to sustain effort by those who have a reputation of being good workers by the threat of losing that reputation, without unemployment; but for low skilled workers, the threat of unemployment may still play an important role.

3.3.3. Adverse selection effects

The quality of the workers a landlord obtains depends on the attractiveness of the contract offered. A landlord who offered a less attractive contract than his neighbors would find that he only obtained the least productive workers. This is precisely the point made by Sismondi more than a hundred and fifty years ago:

> ...the landlord who attempted to exact more than his neighbor...would render himself so odious, he would be so sure of not obtaining a metayer who was an honest man, that the contract of all the metayer may be considered as identical, at least in each province, and never gives rise to any competition among peasants in search of employment, or any offer to cultivate the soil on cheaper terms than another [Simonde de Sismondi, *Political Economy* (1814)].

Of course, what is required is not only that the workers obtained at, say, a lower share be less productive, but be so much less productive that the expected income of the landlord is actually reduced. In a somewhat different context Stiglitz (1976b), Nalebuff and Stiglitz (1982), and Weiss (1980) have argued that this may indeed be the case.

Note that both the quality–efficiency wage model and the incentive–efficiency wage model are predicated on the impossibility of observing perfectly the actual actions of the individual, and therefore of having pay depend on those actions. In contrast, the nutritional–wage efficiency model can be viewed as a special case of the incentive–efficiency wage model (where the level of effort which a worker will provide, at a given level of monitoring, is a function of the wage); or, alternatively, it can be thought of as explaining why some individuals would remain unemployed, even if individuals could be compensated on a piece-rate basis. Either individuals get hired for, say, E^* efficiency units, at a cost of w^{**} per efficiency unit; or they do not get hired at all: they simply cannot supply (at the going wage per efficiency unit) less than E^* efficiency units.

3.3.4. Enforcement problems

In the preceding section we provided another set of explanations for why, even in the face of an excess supply of labor, the terms of the contract will not shift against workers: workers may have no incentive to comply with the terms of the contract.

Alternatively, we have noted that if the production of the farm cannot be monitored, then if the landlord offers a share less than that offered on neighboring farms, some of the output may be diverted to other farms, and the landlord will be worse off.

3.4. The rural sector as a whole: The interlinkage of markets

So far our discussion has focused on the landlord–tenant relationship, in effect, the market for labor and land. There are other markets as well: credit and product markets. It is widely believed that credit markets do not function well (perhaps because of the familiar adverse selection and incentive problems). These problems have only recently become the subject of systematic study [see Braverman and Guasch (1986) for a survey].

One aspect of the organization of the rural sector which has been the subject of some discussion is the fact that in many instances there is an important interlinkage among credit, land, and product markets. This interlinkage has been vilified as an attempt by landlords to extract more surplus out of the worker (and indeed, it has been contended that the interlinkage has strengthened the landlord's resolve to resist innovations which otherwise would have been adopted – see below). An immediate objection to this exploitation view is that it does not explain how interlinkage increases the power of the landlord. If the landlord chooses a contract to maximize his expected profit, subject to a subsistence utility constraint on the part of the worker, and if the landlord actually succeeds in driving the tenant down to that subsistence level, what more leverage is provided by the interlinking of markets? And if the landlord is in the monopsony position claimed by such exploitation theories, why can he not lower the utility level down to the subsistence level?

The view of the landlord as having only indirect control over his tenant provides an answer to this question. But at the same time, it shows that interlinkage may increase economic efficiency, and would occur in environments in which landlords had no monopsony power.

Whenever there are important incentive effects, there are important externalities extending across markets: the terms of the credit contract (and the amount of credit extended) affects the effort and choice of technique of the tenant, and this affects the expected income of the landlord; and the terms of the sharecropping contract affect the effort and the choice of technique of the tenant, and thus the likelihood of a default on a loan. These externalities exist regardless of what happens to a borrower who fails to repay a loan, i.e. whether he is put into bondage, or whether he can declare bankruptcy. Given the presence of these important externalities, it pays to internalize them; interlinkage does precisely that.

Indeed, our earlier discussion of cost sharing can be viewed as a form of interlinkage, between input markets and output markets. The argument there, that it would pay a landlord to subsidize an input which increases the value of the marginal product of effort (and hence which increases effort), extends to other input and product markets as well. Capital can be thought of as just another input. Similarly, it may pay the landlord to try to control the consumption bundle of his workers by controlling the prices at which they purchase various goods; he may want to discourage the consumption of alcohol, and encourage the consumption of protein.

Moreover, we have noted on several instances the importance of problems associated with the enforcement of contracts. Nowhere is this more important than in credit markets; the landlord may be in a better position to enforce the loan contract than others. (The landlord may also be in a better position than others for judging the likelihood that a loan will be repaid, i.e. adverse selection problems may be less important.)

4. The urban sector

The central point which we wish to discuss in this section is wage and employment determination in the urban sector. In many LDCs, the government employs a significant fraction – often a majority – of workers; and the government's wage and employment decisions are often determined more by political considerations than conventional "economic" considerations. In spite of its importance, we will not have anything to say about this; rather, we focus our attention on the private urban sector (whose wage policy, in turn, may affect that of the public sector).

The basic "stylized" fact is that firms in the urban sector pay more than the opportunity cost of labor; it appears that in most LDCs, firms could obtain workers at a lower wage. Though in some cases they may be prevented from lowering the wage by minimum wage legislation, there are many instances in which wages in excess of the minimum wage are paid, and yet there are queues of unemployed. How can we explain this?

Traditional explanations focused on institutional considerations or simply assumed wages to be fixed. Such "explanations" are inadequate, not only because they are incomplete, but even more importantly, because they provide little guidance for many of the central policy questions; though wages may be fixed in the short run, they may respond in the long run to prices; if so, the effect of the elimination of food subsidies may be drastically different from what it would be if wages remained unchanged.[62]

The wage productivity models which we discussed at length in the previous section provide an explanation for why firms might set wages at a level above market clearing. In their general form, they postulate that productivity is a function of the wage paid by the firm, w_i, other wages (both wages paid by other firms, denoted by w_{-i}, and wages paid in the rural sector, denoted by w_r), and

[62] Several papers have analyzed food subsidies and taxes, simply assuming that wages would remain unchanged. Such an assumption seems unpersuasive, at least in most contexts.

the unemployment rate, U:

$$\lambda = \lambda(w_i, w_{-i}, w_r, U).$$ (4.1)

Firms choose the wage to minimize their wage costs per efficiency unit,

$$\min_{w_i} w_i/\lambda_i,$$ (4.2)

taking the wages of others and the unemployment rate as given.[63] This yields the efficiency wage equation

$$\lambda_i' = \lambda_i/w_i.$$ (4.3)

Moreover, they hire labor to the point where the value of the marginal product equals the real wage, i.e.

$$w_i/\lambda_i = F_i'(L_i\lambda_i),$$ (4.4)

where F_i' is the marginal product of an additional efficiency unit of labor, and L_i is the number of workers in the ith firm. Inverting, we obtain the demand for labor as a function of the wage paid by this firm, by other firms, and the unemployment rate. Eqs. (4.3) and (4.4) can be solved simultaneously for the wage and employment of a given firm, as a function of the wages paid elsewhere in the economy and the unemployment rate.

The explanations for the dependence of productivity on wage rates in the urban sector are closely related to those in the rural sector: (i) nutritional; (ii) incentive effects; (iii) adverse selection; and (iv) morale.

A particular form of incentive effect, which we have not noted so far, has received particular attention in the context of urban employment: wages affect turnover, and there are real costs to labor turnover which the firm must bear. Firms do not lower their wages in part because to do so would increase their turnover costs [see Stiglitz (1974b)].

If, for simplicity, we postulate that all firms in the urban sector are identical, we can easily describe equilibrium in the urban sector. Let $w_u = w_i = w_{-i}$, and $L_u = ML_i$, where L_u is aggregate urban employment, M is the number of firms in the urban sector, and L_i is the employment of each firm. Note, moreover, that the unemployment rate $U = 1 - (L_u/N_u)$, where N_u is the total number of workers in the urban sector. By solving eqs. (4.3) and (4.4) we obtain:

---

[63] Firms are actually concerned with maximizing their profits. If output is a function of the number of efficiency units of labor, i.e. $Q_i = Q_i(L_i\lambda_i)$, then it can be shown that maximizing profits entails minimizing wage costs per efficiency unit. For a generalization, see Stiglitz (1982b).

$$w_{\mathrm{u}} = H(N_{\mathrm{u}}, w_{\mathrm{r}}), \tag{4.5}$$

$$L_{\mathrm{u}} = G(N_{\mathrm{u}}, w_{\mathrm{r}}). \tag{4.6}$$

From (3.5), urban wages and employment are a function of the number of workers in the urban sector and the rural wage. Increasing w_{r} will "normally" either increase urban wages or leave the urban wage unchanged (that is, $H_2 \geq 0$). In the nutritional–efficiency wage model, because the efficiency of workers depends solely on the absolute wage,[64] rather than the relative wage, the urban wage is unchanged. But when productivity depends on relative wages, when the rural wage increases, the wage which firms will wish to pay to minimize their labor costs will increase. More generally, total labor costs in the urban sector increase when the rural wage increases; and accordingly, employment will be reduced. (Hence, $G_2 \leq 0$.) Increasing the urban labor supply tends to lead to more employment (since at any given level of employment, unemployment is increased, and hence productivity is increased). (Thus, $G_1 \geq 0$.)

5. Market equilibrium

In the preceding section we described the equilibrium in the urban sector, a function of the rural wage and the number of individuals offering their services in the urban sector. The latter, in turn, is a function of the migration from the rural sector which, in turn, is a function of the urban wage (which, in turn, is an endogenous variable). We are thus in a position to fully determine the equilibrium in the economy.

We follow Sah and Stiglitz (1985c) in postulating that urban migration is a function of the rural and urban wages, and the number of jobs in the urban sector:

$$N_{\mathrm{u}} = N(w_{\mathrm{r}}, w_{\mathrm{u}}, L_{\mathrm{u}}).$$

A special form of this general migration equation is the Harris–Todaro model discussed earlier, in which migration continues to the point where expected urban wages equal the rural wage, i.e.

$$w_{\mathrm{r}} = w_{\mathrm{u}}^{\mathrm{e}} = w_{\mathrm{u}}(1 - U) = w_{\mathrm{u}}L_{\mathrm{u}}/N_{\mathrm{u}},$$

---

[64]Assuming there is no sharing of income between those employed by the firm and others.

or

$$N_u = w_u L_u / w_r.$$

A slight generalization of this is the case where the equilibrium unemployment rate is a function of the ratio of urban to rural wages, or

$$L_u / N_u = M(w_u / w_r).$$

A large number of variations on this basic model have been explored in the literature. (i) In one variant, workers are risk averse and equate the expected utility of a job in the urban sector with the expected utility of a job in the rural sector;[65] (ii) in another variant, workers queue for a job, with either those selected for a job being randomly chosen from the queue, or chosen on a first come basis (in either case, the higher the interest rate, the lower the expected present discounted value of migrating;[66] (iii) in several models, those who do not obtain a job in the urban formal sector nonetheless work in the urban informal sector;[67] and (iv) in other models, migration is limited by the availability of capital in the rural sector to finance the migration [Kanbur (1981)].[68]

We need one more relationship before we can complete the analysis: the rural wage, which we hypothesize is simply a function of the rural labor force. For most of the analysis we assume that it is equal to the value of the marginal product of labor, i.e. if we ignore wage–productivity considerations in the rural sector, then $Q_r = G(N_r)$, where Q_r and N_r are output and employment, respectively, in the rural sector, and

$$N_r = N - N_u,$$

where N is the total available labor force; and

$$w_r = G'(N - N_u).$$

The migration equation, the urban wage equation, and the urban employment equation then provide us with three equations in the three unknowns; the urban wage, the urban labor force, and urban employment.

---

[65] Most of this literature has emphasized the risk associated with obtaining an urban job; but at the same time, once the job is obtained, the riskiness of the wage is likely less than that associated with the rural sector.

Some variants in the literature emphasize the importance of price differences between the urban and rural sector; others emphasize the role of urban amenities ("bright lights"); while still others discuss the impediments presented by transportation costs.

[66] For a fuller discussion, see the appendix to Stiglitz (1974b).

[67] There is likely to be a distortion in that sector, arising from the excessive entry into that sector (with slight product differentiation).

[68] Still another variation on this general theme is provided by the utilitarian family migration functions, analyzed above.

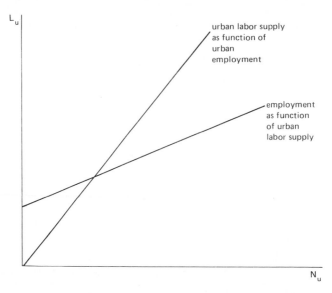

Figure 5.5. Determination of market equilibrium. The equilibrium level of employment may increase with the number of workers in the urban sector. And the number of workers in the urban sector may increase with the number of urban jobs.

One approach is to substitute the urban wage equation into the urban labor demand equation, to obtain a pseudo demand function, where the demand for labor is represented as a function of the supply; and similarly, substitute the urban wage equation into the urban labor supply equation, to obtain a pseudo supply function. Thus, the demand for labor is a function of the supply, and the supply is a function of the demand. The intersection of the two gives the market equilibrium. (See Figure 5.5.)

Some special cases

Rather than discuss at length this general case, it is easier if we focus on two special cases. In both cases, we employ the simple version of the migration hypothesis, where unemployment depends on the urban/rural wage ratio.

(a) *The absolute wage productivity hypothesis.* In the standard nutritional model, productivity depends only on the firm's own wage. Then there is an optimal wage, w^*; and we can then immediately solve for the level of urban employment. All that remains to be done is to solve for the equilibrium level of urban unemployment. This is immediate from the equation

$$G'(N - N_u) = w^* L_u^* / N_u.$$

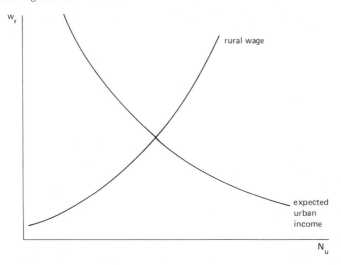

Figure 5.6. Determination of market equilibrium: Absolute wage hypothesis. As the number of individuals in the urban sector increases, the rural wage increases, and the expected urban wage decreases.

Since as N_u increases, the rural wage increases and the expected urban wage decreases, there is a unique equilibrium. See Figure 5.6.

   (b) *The relative wage hypothesis.* Assume, on the other hand, that productivity is homogeneous of degree zero in wages; then the productivity of the workers at the firm will be a function of the wage it pays, relative to the wage paid by all other firms, and relative to the wage paid in the rural sector, as well as the ratio of employment to the urban labor supply; focusing on equilibrium, in which all (other) firms in the urban sector pay the same wage, we can write:

$$\lambda_i = \tilde{\lambda}_i(w_i/w_{-i}; w_i/w_r; L_u/N_u).$$

Then the first-order condition for the optimal wage is (dropping the subscript i on the productivity equation, and denoting the derivative of the function with respect to its kth argument by $\tilde{\lambda}_k$)

$$\tilde{\lambda}_1/w_{-i} + \tilde{\lambda}_2/w_r = \tilde{\lambda}/w_i.$$

In the symmetric equilibrium, this can be rewritten as

$$\tilde{\lambda}_1 + \tilde{\lambda}_2 w_u/w_r = \tilde{\lambda},$$

where, in equilibrium, $\tilde{\lambda} = \tilde{\lambda}(1, w_u/w_r; L_u/N_u).$

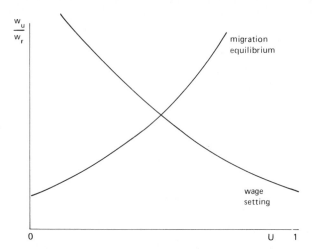

Figure 5.7. Determination of market equilibrium: Relative wage hypothesis. As the unemployment rate increases, the urban wage decreases relative to the rural wage. As the ratio of the urban to the rural wage increases, the equilibrium level of unemployment increases (from the migration equilibrium condition).

This equation can be solved for the equilibrium relative wage as a function of L_u/N_u; and this equation, together with the migration equilibrium equation (which gives L_u/N_u as a function of relative wage) can be solved for the market equilibrium. Normally, we would expect that higher unemployment results in firms in the urban sector setting lower relative wages; hence the higher L_u/N_u, the higher w_u/w_r; while the migration equilibrium equation is normally downward sloping (higher relative wages results in higher unemployment). There is thus a unique equilibrium (depicted in Figure 5.7).[69]

6. Government pricing policies, wage subsidies, and cost–benefit analysis

This general equilibrium model can now be easily employed to analyze the consequences of a variety of government policies. The objective of our discussion in this section is not to provide a thorough analysis of the appropriate government policy, but to emphasize the importance of taking into account the endogeneity of wages and the unemployment rate.

---

[69] It is an easy matter to proceed from here to solve for all the variables. If rural wages are fixed, then knowing w_u/w_r, one immediately solves for w_u; and knowing w_u and workers' productivity, one immediately solves for L_u, and hence N_u.

First, we note that if urban and rural wages (or more generally, the ratio of the two) were to remain constant, then, with a migration model of the Harris–Todaro form (or, more generally, any migration model where equilibrium unemployment is a function of relative wages), the urban unemployment *rate* will remain unchanged. Then increased urban employment will induce more migration; and if the rural wage correctly measures the opportunity cost of labor, the total opportunity cost of labor is just equal to the urban wage. (This should be contrasted with those models which assume that, because there is unemployment, the opportunity cost of labor is zero; or which assume that for every worker hired in the urban sector, only one rural worker migrates, in which case the opportunity cost is the rural wage.)

Second, taxes in the urban sector will, in general, result in a change in the wage rate. Studies which ignore this effect overestimate the increase in government revenue (investible surplus) resulting from such taxes. In particular, Sah and Stiglitz have shown that if productivity depends on the level of utility of the urban worker, then it is desirable to have that utility delivered efficiently, i.e. it is (Pareto) optimal not to have any distortionary commodity taxes in the urban sector.[70] (This contrasts markedly with the standard Ramsey analysis; but that analysis focused, implicitly, on the consequences of different tax structures on labor supply, a problem which is not central to most LDCs, who, on the contrary, face an unemployment problem; this illustrates the problems encountered in the unthinking application of results from developed countries to LDCs.) If productivity is more sensitive to food consumption than to the consumption of other commodities, then it can be shown that a food subsidy may be desirable.

Third, wage subsidies may be partly shifted; conventional discussions have simply assumed that all of the benefits are reflected in increased employment; in our analysis, some of the benefits accrue to existing workers, in the form of higher wages. At the same time, it should be noted that a combination of ad valorem and specific wage subsidies may be used to achieve the two goals of controlling both the level of employment and the wage rate.[71]

Finally, we noted that these models have markedly different implications for the effect of government policies (e.g. hiring an additional worker in the urban sector) on aggregate consumption, hence on the supply of investible funds, and hence on the shadow wage of labor. For instance, in the simple model where the rural wage is equal to the expected urban wage and in which the rural wage is

---

[70] The notion of Pareto optimality employed is the standard one, where there are certain (well-specified) constraints on the actions of the government. Here, we assume that lump-sum non-distortionary taxes are, for instance, not feasible. Similarly, if the efficiency wage relationship is informationally based (arising from incentive or selection effects), it is assumed that the government has no better, or worse, information than private producers.

[71] Pareto efficiency will, in general, entail there be some unemployment (if the government cannot directly control the level of migration). But in general, neither the market equilibrium level of employment nor the market equilibrium wage will be Pareto efficient.

fixed, as more workers are hired in the urban sector, aggregate consumption remains unchanged. We previously noted that the opportunity cost of hiring an additional worker was the urban wage. Hence, an increase in urban employment reduces the supply of investible funds by precisely the same amount that it reduces output; hence the shadow price of labor is the urban wage (regardless, indeed, of the relative valuation of consumption, since that is unaffected). [For a more general discussion, see Sah and Stiglitz (1985a).] These results should again be contrasted with the standard analyses, e.g. the OECD *Cost–Benefit Manual*.

7. The development process

The preceding discussion focused on the micro-economics of LDCs: on issues of resource allocation, and with the consequences of policies of limited government intervention, such as taxation, pricing policies pursued by marketing boards, and food and wage subsidies (though we have had a few remarks about the effects of more dramatic policies, such as land reforms). Our concern throughout has been primarily with what is referred to as static allocative efficiency. These consequences of government policy are of importance: when countries are very poor and resources are limited, it is imperative to use what resources are available efficiently. Yet there is a widespread feeling that even were these countries to pursue policies which ensured allocative efficiency, it would not enable them to reduce significantly the gap between their standard of living and that of the more developed. Something more fundamental is at stake, something which (some argue) requires more active government intervention.

Traditional neo-classical analysis has focused on differences in factor inputs. In this view, the differences between developed and less developed countries lie in the availability of capital and skilled labor. With less capital, and less skilled labor to use capital effectively, per capita incomes will inevitably be lower. Government action may be required to eliminate these shortages. In what follows we assess the evidence for this view, ask what the nature of the market failure might be, and enquire into the possible role for governments in alleviating these alleged market failures.

7.1. Factor supplies

7.1.1. Capital shortage

There is little doubt that poorer countries have less capital per capita. It is not obvious, however, whether this in itself is the "critical" factor. First, were it the critical factor, the marginal and average return to capital should be much higher in LDCs. For instance, with a Cobb–Douglas production function, if output per capita in some country is one-tenth that in the more developed countries, then the average and marginal product of capital should be *ten thousand times* greater, assuming a capital share of 0.2.[72] Even for a moderately poor country, with per capita income one-fourth that of the developed countries, the marginal and average product should be 64 times that of the developed countries. Thus, if the return to capital in the developed countries is 2 percent, the return in the moderately poor LDCs should be 128 percent. If the elasticity of substitution between capital and labor is less than unity – as most economists believe – then the returns to capital should be even higher. Though evidence on the exact value of the return to capital in LDCs may be lacking, it is clear that it is nowhere near as large as it should be if capital alone were the critical factor.

Secondly, one would expect much higher rates of capital utilization in LDCs; in fact, utilization rates often appear to be lower.

Those who believe that the central problems of LDCs arise from a general capital shortage face two problems: in a closed economy they must explain why savings are inadequate; in an open economy they must explain the barriers to the flow of funds. Whether one believes that capital is the critical element or not, so long as one believes that per capita capital levels are lower in LDCs, one must explain why the rates of return on capital in LDCs are not higher than they appear to be.

7.1.1.1. Undersaving. Economists have found it difficult to come up with a plausible explanation for why there is too little saving. One argument is that the utility of future generations enters as a public good into each individual's utility function. By standard arguments, there will be too little supply of this public good, i.e. too little saving. Though there is no easy way of assessing whether this assertion concerning individual's utility functions is correct (introspection only tells me that it is not true for me), if it were true, it would have strong implications for government policy: it would not imply that the government should actually save, for any saving by the government would be offset, on a dollar for dollar basis, by the private sector (ignoring non-negativity constraints). What is suggested is that the government should subsidize private saving.

It is equally plausible, however, to argue that if there is a market failure, it takes the form of excessive savings. Any individual who would like to save, to leave capital to his children, can do so; but any individual who would like to leave a negative bequest cannot. Thus, the presence of non-negativity constraints

---

[72] With a Cobb–Douglas production function, $\ln Q = \alpha \ln K + (1 - \alpha)\ln L + a$ constant, or $\ln Q/K = [(\alpha - 1)/\alpha]\ln q$, where q is output per capita.

implies that, relative to a world in which individuals could leave negative bequests, there may be excessive saving.

In some cases the social structure may serve to discourage saving. The absence of explicit insurance markets leads extended families to provide implicit insurance against a variety of risks; the individuals within the extended family who provide that insurance are those who have managed to accumulate savings. Thus, there is, implicitly, a high tax rate on savings. The establishment of formal insurance markets, while weakening some family ties, may thus have a beneficial effect on savings.

Of course, the issue of what is the appropriate savings rate is really equivalent to the question of what is the appropriate intertemporal distribution of welfare. There is no more a priori reason to believe that the intertemporal distribution of welfare is in accord with our views of equity than that the intratemporal distribution of welfare is. But again, it is not obvious that there is significant undersaving. Simulation exercises employing simple constant elasticity utility functions, with reasonable projections concerning future growth in per capita income, do not necessarily suggest that there is a significant undersaving.

7.1.1.2. Financial intermediaries. A rather different reason for undersaving is that there is an absence of institutions by which savings can be channeled to productive uses, to yield a return to the individual to compensate him for forgoing current consumption, an absence of financial intermediaries to screen potential borrowers, to differentiate good risks from bad risks, and to pool and spread risks. (McKinnon has emphasized this in his writings.) The problem is particularly acute in channeling savings from the rural sector to the urban sector.

Though general theoretical considerations make it ambiguous whether an increase in the rate of return on savings or in the riskiness of the rate of return would increase or decrease savings rates, there is a widespread presumption that developing better financial intermediaries would in fact increase savings rates.

Of course, even if they did not increase *aggregate* savings rates, they would improve the efficiency with which capital is allocated. Thus, the development of better financial intermediaries would enable an increase in aggregate output without any increase in aggregate savings rates.

Standard problems in asymmetric information (adverse selection, moral hazard) face the potential investor wishing to provide capital for the use of others: How can he discriminate between good investors and bad investors, i.e. those who are able to judge good investment projects and those who are not able to do so? And how can he be sure that those to whom he has entrusted his savings will not abscond with the funds?

These problems faced, of course, all countries in the early stages of their development: the scandals associated with early joint stock ventures are well known. It is sometimes suggested that the commercial success of certain closely knit groups was in part due to the advantages for economic transactions provided by the trust within these communities.

But in addition to these problems, investors in the urban sector face an additional problem: the ever present threat of nationalization or, equivalently, the imposition of taxes and restrictions which decrease the economic value of these assets. It is difficult for governments to commit themselves not to engage in these practices; and so long as they cannot or do not commit themselves, investors may be reluctant to invest, particularly in projects for which nationalization is easy. Investors may undertake actions which reduce the likelihood of nationalization, by, for instance, making sure that the gains from nationalization are lower. Foreign investors may, in this respect, be in an advantageous position: they may be able to ensure that certain supplies are not easily obtainable elsewhere (e.g. they may design machines with certain parts of low durability which cannot easily be manufactured by others).[73]

Recent work in the theory of credit markets in the presence of imperfect information has provided an·explanation for credit rationing, even under competitive conditions [Stiglitz and Weiss (1981, 1983, 1986)]; and it has also provided an explanation for why the marginal cost of raising funds through equity markets may be very high, sufficiently high that there will be little recourse to equity markets [Greenwald, Stiglitz and Weiss (1984)]. The problems of imperfect information which they argue are important in the capital markets of developed countries are all the more important in LDCs. Moreover, they have assumed that contracts are enforceable, through a well-functioning legal system. In quite separate work, Eaton and Gersovitz (1981a, 1981b) and Allen (1983) have shown how the presence of enforcement problems can give rise to credit rationing. [See also Eaton, Gersovitz and Stiglitz (1986).]

All of these arguments suggest that there are significant problems in making savings available to potential investors. It has, accordingly, frequently been suggested that the government take a more active role in credit markets. The central problems which this earlier literature noted facing the private sector also face the government: the government may not be in any better position to choose between good borrowers (projects) and bad borrowers (projects); and it is in no better position to control the actions of the borrower (e.g. to affect the degree of risk taking). The government does have one advantage, in principle, over private lenders: in the enforcement of contracts. But off-setting this are some important disadvantages: in the will to enforce contracts and, more generally, in the lack of incentives[74] to choose among borrowers and to design contracts to maximize the

---

[73] Foreign lending (as opposed to direct foreign investment) is in a disadvantageous position; in many cases, it is hard to understand why defaults on these loans have not occurred (or perhaps they have, in a somewhat disguised form?). See Eaton, Gersovitz and Stiglitz (1986).

[74] The ability of public lending institution to draw upon government funds may exacerbate these incentive problems.

expected returns from the available funds. Indeed, the government often claims that it is precisely because it wishes to maximize social returns in a broader perspective, rather than private returns, that it should have control of the credit market. But the power of allocating funds gives the bureaucrats enormous discretion to allocate funds using other criteria as well.

In a competitive market, potential borrowers would be placed into groups according to the actuarial value of the expected return (that is, groups with high bankruptcy probabilities would be charged correspondingly higher rates of inter-est than groups with low bankruptcy probabilities. Of course, the interest rates would also reflect the collateral that the borrower could put up.) Whenever funds are made available at terms that are more favorable than the interest rate that would have prevailed in the market for that borrower, there is an implicit subsidy; but since ascertaining the actuarial "correct" interest rate is no easy matter, it is difficult for outsiders to ascertain whether a subsidy has been granted, and if so, the extent of the implicit subsidy. Thus, giving bureaucrats the power to allocate funds gives them, in effect, the right to allocate subsidies at their own discretion, the consequences of which should be obvious.

7.1.1.3. Barriers to the flow of capital. Most of the arguments given above describing the difficulties in channeling savings from the rural sector to the urban sector apply with even greater force to channeling savings from developed to less developed countries. There are projects within LDCs which might yield high returns. The difficulty is in identifying them, and in monitoring them.

In addition, the problem of nationalization may be viewed to be more acute, though foreign firms can sometimes design their investments in such a way as to reduce the likelihood of nationalization (e.g. by ensuring that certain vital inputs to a manufacturing process cannot be obtained in the event of nationalization). When they cannot do so, the threat of nationalization may loom greater – the political and economic gains to the governments may appear greater from the nationalization of foreign firms than domestically owned firms. It should be apparent that there are a variety of instruments, short of direct nationalization, which effectively represent partial nationalization – including imposing high taxes on profits and imposing barriers and taxes on the return of capital abroad.

7.1.2. Shortage of skilled laborers

In many LDCs there are significant shortages of skilled laborers. But in others there often seems to be unemployment of skilled workers, or skilled workers are engaged in unskilled tasks.

Those who believed that the critical problem of LDCs was a shortage of skilled laborers emphasized the importance of the development of the education sector. They pointed to the high returns to education.

By contrast, some recent work has noted that some of the observed returns to education are not social returns but private returns. If the education system identifies who are the more able (the more productive) workers, then the higher wages received is not a result of an increase in productivity of these workers; the education system has simply enabled these workers to receive their ability rents. Indeed, in the extreme case the social return may be zero, though the apparent private returns may be significant. More generally, private returns will exceed social returns.[75]

The discrepancy between social and private returns may be even larger in the case where labor markets do not function well (as they often seem not to in LDCs). Thus, Fields (1983) has analyzed the situation where there is an excess of applicants for unskilled jobs as well as skilled jobs. Skilled workers who fail to obtain skilled jobs get priority in the unskilled jobs (even though their productivity may be no higher in these jobs). Employers have to have a way of deciding who to hire, and educational credentials provides one such way.[76] Thus, the skilled workers "bump" the unskilled workers. At the margin, there is again no social return to education (since there already is an excess supply of skilled people for the available skilled jobs). But there is a private return (the higher probability of obtaining an unskilled job, plus the chance of getting a skilled job). And indeed, as the number of individuals becoming educated increases, the private return may increase; though the probability of getting a skilled job decreases, the gain from the differential probability in obtaining an unskilled job increases (that is, the probability of unskilled workers getting an unskilled job decreases, since the trained workers have priority over these workers in the unskilled job).[77]

7.2. Technical change and entrepreneurship

The problem facing LDCs may thus not be so much as the available supply of inputs, but what is done with those inputs. It is apparent that, at least in many instances, resources are used less efficiently. This used to be represented formally by writing down a production function:

$$Q = F(K, L, A),$$

[75] For a discussion of this view of education as a screening device, see Spence (1973) and Stiglitz (1975).

[76] There may be some rationality in this: the employer may be able to obtain information concerning the potential abilities of the worker, so that when a vacancy occurs in a skilled job, he knows which worker to assign to which job.

[77] In this model, shadow wages may even exceed urban wages. See Stiglitz (1977).

where Q is output, K is input of capital, L is input of labor, and A is the "state of technology"; and asserting that A is different for LDCs than for developing countries. This begs the central questions: Why are resources used less efficiently, and what can be done about it?

7.2.1. Landlords' resistance of innovation

One hypothesis that has been put forward is that landlords have resisted innovations, particularly innovations which would have reduced the demand for credit because, it is contended, landlords earn "pure profits" on their loans to peasants [Bhaduri (1973)]. In this view, then, the interlinkage of land and credit markets has served to retard growth.

Braverman and Stiglitz (1986b) have attacked this view on two grounds. First, they point out that whether an innovation will be adopted, whether in a competitive environment[78] or in non-competitive environment, depends simply on whether it moves the utility possibilities schedule outward.

They make, however, an important distinction: some innovations, which increase output with any given input, may move the utilities possibilities schedule inward, because they exacerbate the incentive problems. Thus, an innovation which, at every level of input of effort, increased output, but which at the relevant levels of input of effort, decreased the marginal return to effort, might well not be adopted. There is, in this sense, a difference between innovations which are technologically superior, and innovations which are economically superior. Their analysis shows that economic structures can, in fact, have an important effect on the adoption of innovations: thus, an innovation which would not be adopted within a sharecropping economy, might well be adopted after a land reform, in which each individual worked on his own farm.

Interlinkage can, similarly, affect whether or not the utilities possibilities schedule moves outward. But they point out that in general, innovations may increase or decease the demand for credit. Moreover, to the extent that interlinkage internalizes the externalities associated with incentive problems, and thus reduces the importance of the residual incentives problem, it may lead to a closer link between technological innovations and "economic" innovations.

---

[78] In a competitive environment it is possible that some groups will, after the innovation, actually be worse off, even if the utilities possibilities schedule has moved outward.

A similar result obtains in the comparison of competitive equilibrium with free trade versus autarky. Free trade always moves the utilities possibilities schedule outward, but some groups may be disadvantaged.

If the utilities possibilities schedule moves outward, in competitive equilibrium, the innovation will be adopted, whether some group is disadvantaged or not. The monopolist, constrained to providing workers with a given level of utility, will also always adopt an innovation if (and only if) the utilities possibilities schedule moves outward.

(Differences between monopsony and competitive markets in the adoption of innovations may arise when the utilities possibilities schedules for the old and the new technology cross. Thus, if the monopsonist drives the expected utility of the worker down to the subsistence level, an innovation which lowers the utilities possibilities schedule at the subsistence wage but shifts it out at the competitive wage would not be adopted in the former situation, but would be adopted in the latter. Note that in the competitive situation, land saving innovations, which reduce the return to the landowners, will be adopted; it is possible that if the landowners in the village act collusively, they could restrict the adoption of such an innovation.[79])

7.2.2. Inappropriate technology

A concern often expressed is that the technologies which have developed in the developed countries are inappropriate for the LDCs; they do not take advantage of the particular set of factor supplies available in LDCs.

For instance, much of technical change is the result of learning by doing. If such learning is "localized",[80] then the production function shifts more at currently used input ratios than at other input ratios. The improvements in technology which have occurred may be markedly different from those which would have occurred, had the LDCs controlled the innovation process.[81]

This observation is, by itself, of little practical relevance. The question is: Given the currently available technologies does it pay to develop new technologies, or to adopt (and adapt) those of the currently available technologies which are best suited for the LDCs?

A full analysis of these issues would take me beyond the scope of this chapter; here I make only two observations. First, since machines embodying old technologies can often be acquired at low cost, what is relevant is not just a comparison between the capital and labor costs of using the best practices technologies, but the capital and labor costs of using technologies which are becoming obsolete within developed countries (given their factor prices). Secondly, there may be important public goods problems in the development of new "appropriate technologies"; these public goods problems inhibit not only entrepreneurs within a country from developing these technologies, but also inhibit the expenditures by any country for the development of these technologies. There is a potential role here for international agencies.

---

[79] We have described earlier how collusive outcomes can be maintained non-cooperatively in situations where there is repeated interaction.

[80] See Atkinson and Stiglitz (1969)

[81] Similar results would obtain if firms faced a trade-off in allocating research budgets between the search for, say, capital-augmenting and labor-augmenting innovations. Their search would be affected by the factor prices which they face.

7.3. Development strategies

7.3.1. Innovators and imitators

There is a widespread view that, if they are to be successful, the LDCs should follow the history of the developed countries. There are certain stages of economic growth that all countries must go through. This fallacy has been particularly prevalent in Marxian discussions of development, where emphasis has been placed on the necessity of first developing a capital goods sector, on heavy industrialization.

This view is, I think, fundamentally misguided. I agree with Schumpeter in emphasizing the fundamental role of technological change in understanding the evolution of modern developed countries. Whether the particular sequence of innovations which occurred was inevitable, or simply a happenstance, is of little concern to us here. What is crucial are the following two observations:

First, innovators are in a fundamentally different position from imitators. Innovators have to worry about how they are going to appropriate the returns to their innovation, how, in other words, can they be compensated for their expenditures on R&D and for the risks which are inevitably associated with the adoption of new technologies and the introduction of new products. Recent research in industrial organization has helped to clarify how it is that firms can capture some of these returns, and how attempts to appropriate returns, and limitations on appropriability, affect their behavior.

But imitators face a quite different problem: they are simply concerned with what technologies (products) they can profitably adopt and adapt. This distinction, though important, should not be overdrawn: there is an element of adaptation (a form of innovation) in most imitation. The circumstances in which most LDCs find themselves are sufficiently different from the circumstances facing the developed countries that some adaptation is required even to borrow a technology; and in any case, there are always risks associated with the attempt to borrow the more advanced technology. LDCs wishing to take advantage of the fruits of previous technological advances in the developed countries, may still well ask themselves: Are there adaptations of products and processes to the peculiar factor market conditions in which they (and possibly others) find themselves, which will give them a market niche which they can maintain? That is, they too may seek rents from adaptation; and to the extent that they can obtain such rents, they will be concerned about maintaining them, and therefore about imitation from other LDCs which will serve to dissipate those rents.

This brings us to our second observation: what is of concern, for imitating countries, for followers, is the adoption of technologies (products) which are appropriate for their current economic situation. During the past 20 years, there have been enormous technological improvements in agriculture, improvements which Marx did not, and probably could not, have foreseen. As a result, it may well be the case that for many LDCs, development should be directed at the improvement of the agricultural sector.

Learning to learn and learning by doing. The preceding analysis suggested that for many LDCs, development strategy should be determined by examining their current comparative advantages. We must qualify this, however, if there is learning by doing, in which case it will pay to adopt some technologies at a time when, on static considerations, it would not; and if the ability to learn is itself learned, in which case it may pay to adopt technologies neither for their current or prospective profitability, but for the benefits which will accrue in the adoption of future technologies.[82]

7.3.2. Further advantages of agricultural development

There are several further advantages of an agriculturally oriented development strategy, which we briefly note.

7.3.2.1. Relative immunity from nationalization. The argument for agricultural development is strengthened by two further considerations. First, we have noted that the threat of nationalization may serve as an impediment to the availability of (private) capital for industrialization. The limitations on government's ability, in many countries at least, to manage enterprises successfully (for good economic reasons) deters nationalization. The greater difficulties that governments have in managing agricultural enterprises suggests that the threat of nationalization within the rural sector may be less imminent than that within the urban sector,[83] and thus this threat may serve as a less serious barrier to the accumulation of capital and investment in the rural sector than in the industrial sector.

7.3.2.2. Managerial advantages. Moreover, the scale of organization, and the necessity of coordination, may be less in that sector than in the industrial sector.

7.3.2.3. Government policies discouraging entrepreneurship. There is a rather different set of concerns about the pursuit of a strategy of industrialization under the auspices of the government, versus agricultural development. The modes of behavior associated with government bureaucracies may, in fact, be inconsistent

---

[82] The question of whether learning by doing or learning to learn provide a basis of government subsidies remains debated. The question hinges on the extent to which a firm can appropriate the returns from the learning, and the extent to which it can borrow. Markets in which learning by doing is important are inherently imperfectly competitive. For further discussion on these issues, see Dasgupta and Stiglitz (1988).

[83] Though land expropriation remains a threat in many countries.

with the kinds of risk taking, innovative behavior associated with entrepreneurship. Thus, the government-sponsored industrialization strategy, rather than developing those attributes which may be essential for the long run success of the economy, may actually serve to stifle them.

7.3.3. Balanced growth of a sector versus balanced growth of LDCs as a group

One suspects, in fact, that were all LDCs to engage in a successful development program, there should be no single sector on which development should be focused; for were that the case, prices of those products would fall; though each country may well assume that it is small, and ignore these price effects, the LDCs as a group may be large enough that – were their development efforts even partially successful – there might be significant price effects.

The extent of these price effects depends, of course, on how diversified the LDCs as a group are. The share of LDCs in manufacturing as a whole is relatively small, perhaps less than 5 percent, sufficiently small that one might well argue they should ignore price effects. But the share of production in certain commodities, those for which they might have a comparative advantage, may be sufficiently great that they cannot ignore the price effects. What is then required is not balanced growth within any country, but balanced development among the entire set of countries, with those with a comparative advantage in agriculture developing that sector.

7.3.4. Externalities, capital market imperfections, and innovations

Market oriented economists begin with the presumption that there is a congruence between social and private returns; that if it is worthwhile for society to adopt some innovation, it is worthwhile for some private entrepreneur to do so. The theorem which provides the intellectual foundations for this belief which is so widespread among economists is the Fundamental Theorem of Welfare Economics; and that proposition explicitly assumes that there is no technological change. It does not (and the natural assumptions concerning technological change imply that it cannot) address the question of the efficiency of the economy in adapting and adopting new technologies.

Problems of appropriability are, of course, present in developed as well as LDCs.[84] But while new inventions may be protected by patents, the kinds of entrepreneurial efforts that predominate in LDCs cannot be so protected. Moreover, there are important externalities associated with successful entrepreneurship, not only in establishing an entrepreneurial climate and training labor, but also in providing a domestic source of inputs to other firms and a domestic

---

[84] The same is true for other problems presented by innovation for the competitive paradigm, e.g. the non-convexities which give rise to imperfectly competitive markets.

source of demand for the output of other firms. These interlinkages provide the basis of some of the traditional arguments for balanced growth.[85]

Finally, we note that the adoption of new technologies often requires significant capital expenditures; and in the presence of imperfect information, there may well be credit rationing [Stiglitz and Weiss (1981, 1983)]. The appropriate government response is a difficult question, on which we comment briefly in our concluding remarks.

8. Concluding remarks

8.1. Choice of managers

The preceding discussion focused on the importance of entrepreneurship and innovation in the development process, and the implications that this may have for development strategies. There is a more general issue, which is particularly important in the industrial sector: a central problem in any economy is how to decide to whom to entrust the management of its resources, particularly its capital resources. We all know that there are some enterprises in an industry which turn out to be very profitable, other enterprises within the same industry which are much less so. Intraindustry variability in profits may be as large as interindustry variability. Though there are a large number of factors which account for these differences, part of the difference lies in what we can refer to loosely as the quality of management. The allocation of resources among alternative management teams is a central information problem, which unfortunately has been ignored by most of the planning literature. Those attributes which engender success in being selected within a bureaucratic framework are not necessarily those attributes which engender success in running the enterprises which are entrusted to them.

8.2. Market failures and government failures

In preceding sections we have, on a number of occasions, touched on the potential role of the government. Here, we seek to put into a general perspective the role of the government in the development process. We have not sought here to develop a formal model of the government in LDCs, to explain the behavior of the government by a majority voting model, or the behavior of the bureaucrats in

---

[85] For those addicted to recasting all market failure problems into the language of Arrow and Debreu, some of these problems can be viewed as arising from missing markets; others from imperfect competition; and others as forms of externalities.

Some of these market failures can, in turn, be related to more fundamental problems with the Arrow–Debreu formulation, to which we have previously alluded: it assumes a given state of technology and that information, if not perfect, cannot be altered.

terms of a power maximization hypothesis. To do so would, again, take us beyond the scope of this chapter. But what we have tried to argue is that one simply cannot take the perspective of the government as purely benevolent and all-knowing. The distribution of income which emerges from market solutions may well not be in accord with one's view of a "just" distribution of income; it may well not maximize some appropriately chosen social welfare function. Governments can, and have, used their coercive power to redistribute income; but it is clear that the after-government-intervention income distribution is not always more in accord with an egalitarian social welfare function than the before-government-intervention income distribution. There are market failures. But there are also government failures. And assessing the proper role of the government requires paying careful attention to these as well. We have been particularly concerned here with the·problems posed by imperfect information, including the problems associated with incentives and the selection of managers. These are no less problems for the public sector than they are for the private sector; indeed, we have provided some reasons why they may be worse for the public sector than for the private sector.

8.2.1. Government as coordinator

The government, it used to be argued, had an advantage over private enterprises in resolving another information problem: in coordinating decision-making. But this view ignores the enormous amount of information exchange and coordination which occurs in decentralized market economies. Before U.S. Steel constructed its steel mills on the southern shore of Lake Michigan, it had to ensure that it had an assured source of supply for the necessary inputs (coal, limestone, iron ore) and it attempted to ascertain whether there would be a ready market for its output. An enormous amount of coordination, of information exchange, was required, but it occurred in a decentralized manner. Thus, the question is not whether there should be coordination, but how that coordination is to occur – where the locus of information exchange should be. If information transmission and processing were costless and if there were no incentive problems – so everyone transmitted all of his information accurately – clearly there would be everything to be gained, and nothing to be lost, from the centralization of information. But these assumptions are no more realistic than the assumption that goods are costlessly produced, and drop, freely from the sky, like manna from Heaven.

Note that the traditional competitive paradigm, as exemplified by the work of Arrow and Debreu, is no more realistic in this respect than the traditional planning literature: they assume that all information exchange occurs via prices, ignoring the importance of other signals and methods of information acquisition and dissemination.

8.2.2. Information problems and government

If the major source of market failure was one of the simple forms discussed in the early 1960s, e.g. externalities, the role of the government would be clear. It would need to intervene, either through fines/subsidies or regulations, to ensure that these externalities become effectively internalized. The government simply needs to change the incentives facing private firms, to ensure that they act in accord with what is socially desirable. But, if a major source of market failure is associated with the information problems with which we have been concerned here, there is no obvious prescription. The information problems, of selection, of incentives, of coordination and information exchange, are no different for the government than for the private sector, and indeed, in some dimensions, they may clearly be worse. One may argue that there are market forces which work to ensure that those who are entrusted to the management of capital and human resources are those who have a comparative advantage in doing so. There is no reason to believe that the electoral process (when it works) works to select public officials who have a comparative advantage in designing incentive structures which ensure that individuals work hard, and that their work is directed at pursuits which are or might be construed to be in the national interest. (Indeed, the fact that so many governments have devised regulatory systems and tax structures of such complexity and with so many distortions that much of the talented resources are devoted to dealing with, and making profits out of, them, suggests that governments may be particularly inept at solving these problems, for reasons which may be explained by the nature of the political process.)

Similarly, governments, noting the prevalence of credit rationing, have often intervened to improve the functioning of capital markets. They have simply assumed that the imperfection of the credit market is just another manifestation of the imperfection of market economies. A government, it was felt, could thus easily intervene to design a better functioning capital market, allocating capital on a more rational basis. The experience in many countries in which governments have attempted this is not entirely favorable: default rates have been high, real interest rates have been kept at low levels, access to credit has been based more on political considerations than on economic considerations, and overall, there has been little evidence that a greater degree of "rationality" in resource allocation has been achieved. Our analysis again provides some insight into this public failure: we have argued that credit rationing will occur in competitive markets characterized by imperfect information, where the lender is imperfectly informed concerning the characteristics of potential borrowers and cannot perfectly monitor their actions. These selection and incentive problems are no less important when the government takes over responsibility for allocating credit. Indeed, the problem becomes exacerbated, because political consideration may become paramount in the allocation of credit, in a way which they do not in a market economy.

I have attempted to argue here that the information problems which are central to private market economies are equally important in public enterprises; that they give rise to public (government) failures, just as they give rise to private (market) failures. I have not, however, had time to show more precisely how information analysis can provide some insight into the specific nature of public failures, into the widely observed phenomena of excessive red tape and rapid growth in the size of the administrative labor force in the public sector. A detailed analysis of the incentive structures within the public sector can, I believe, provide us with considerable insight into these phenomena.

In conclusion, let me reiterate: traditional economic theory has ignored the central problems associated with costly information. When due attention is paid to these information theoretic considerations, the basic propositions of neo-classical analysis no longer remain valid: market equilibrium may not exist, even when all the underlying preferences and production sets are "well behaved"; when equilibrium exists, it is, in general, not Pareto efficient; it may not be possible to decentralize efficient resource allocations; the separation between efficiency and equity considerations which characterizes traditional neo-classical theory no longer obtains; market equilibrium may be characterized by an excess demand for credit or an excess supply of labor (that is, the law of supply and demand no longer holds). The theory which has been developed explicitly incorporating information theoretic considerations provides an explanation of phenomena about which traditional theory simply had nothing to say.

I have been particularly concerned here with showing how this theory can provide insights into markets and market failures in less developed economies, to show how it can provide explanations for institutions which in neo-classical theory appear anomalous and/or inefficient. In some cases, it yields clear implications for policy, implications which are at variance with those emerging from traditional neo-classical analysis. In other cases, all we have obtained so far is a word of caution: information problems may give rise to public (governmental) failures just as they give rise to market failures. The analysis of the appropriate role of the government is far more complex than traditional analyses lead us to believe. But if we have learned this simple lesson, we have learned a lot.

References

Akerlof, G.A. (1970) 'The market for lemons: Qualitative uncertainty and the market mechanism', *Quarterly Journal of Economics*, 84:488–500.
Akerlof, G.A. (1980) 'A theory of social custom of which unemployment may be one consequence', *Quarterly Journal of Economics*, June.
Akerlof, G.A. (1984) 'Gift exchange and efficiency wage theory: Four views', *American Economic Review Proceedings*.
Allen, F. (1983) 'Credit rationing and payment incentives', *Review of Economic Studies*, 50:639–646.

Allen, F. (1985) 'On the fixed nature of sharecropping contracts', *Economic Journal*, March, 30–48.

Arnott, R. and Stiglitz, J.E. (1984) 'The welfare economics of moral hazard', Princeton University, mimeo.

Arnott, R. and Stiglitz, J.E. (1986) 'Moral hazard and optimal commodity taxation', *Journal of Public Economics*, 29:1–24.

Arrow, K.J. (1962) The economic implications of learning by doing, *Review of Economic Studies*, 29:155–193.

Atkinson, A. and Stiglitz, J.E. (1969) 'A new view of technological change', *Economic Journal*, LIX:46–49.

Bardhan, P.K. (1980) 'Interlocking factor markets and agrarian development: A review of issues', *Oxford Economic Papers*, March.

Bardhan, P.K. and Srinivasan, T.N. (1971) 'Cropsharing tenancy in agriculture: A theoretical and empirical analysis', *American Economic Review*, 51.

Baumol, W.J. (1986) 'Productivity growth, convergence, and welfare: What the long-run data show', *American Economic Review*, December:1072–1085.

Baumol, W.J., Panzer, J.C. and Willig, R.D. (1982) *Contestable markets and the theory of industry structure*. New York: Harcourt, Brace, Jovanovich.

Bell, C. and Zusman, P. (1976) 'A bargaining theoretic approach to cropsharing contracts', *American Economic Review*, 66.

Bhaduri, A. (1973) 'Agricultural backwardness under semi-feudalism', *Economic Journal*.

Bhaduri, A. (1980) 'Agricultural backwardness under semi-feudalism: A reply', *Economic Journal*.

Binswanger, H.P. (1978) 'Attitudes towards risk: Implications and psychological theories of an experiment in rural India', Yale University Economic Growth Center DP 286.

Binswanger, H.P. (1980) 'Attitudes towards risk: Experimental measurement evidence in rural India', *American Journal of Agricultural Economics*, 62:395–407.

Binswanger, H.P. and Rosenzweig, M.R. (1984) *Contractual arrangements, employment and wages in labor markets in Asia*. New Haven, CT: Yale University Press.

Bliss, C.J. and Stern, N.H. (1981a) 'Productivity wages and nutrition', *Journal of Development Economics*, 5.

Bliss, C.J. and Stern, N.H. (1981b) *Palanpur-studies in the economy of a north Indian village*. New Delhi: Oxford University Press.

Braverman, A. and Guasch, L. (1986) 'Rural credit markets and institutions in developing countries: Lessons for policy analysis from practice and modern theory', *World Development*.

Braverman, A. and Srinivasan, T.N. (1981) 'Credit and sharecropping in agrarian societies', *Journal of Development Economics*, 9:289–312.

Braverman, A. and Stiglitz, J.E. (1972) 'Sharecropping and the interlinking of agrarian markets', *American Economic Review*, 72:695–715.

Braverman, A. and Stiglitz, J.E. (1986a) 'Cost sharing arrangements under sharecropping – moral hazard, incentive flexibility and risk', *American Journal of Agricultural Economics*, 68:642–652.

Braverman, A. and Stiglitz, J.E. (1986b) 'Landlords, tenants, and technological innovations', *Journal of Development Economics*, 23:313–332.

Bulow, J.I. and Summers, L. (1985) 'A theory of dual labor markets with application to industrial policy, discrimination and Keynesian unemployment', NBER working paper no. 1666.

Calvo, G. (1979) 'Quasi-Walrasian theories of unemployment', *American Economic Review Proceedings*, 69:102–106.

Cheung, S.N. (1969) *The theory of tenancy*. Chicago: University of Chicago Press.

Coase, R.H. (1960) 'The problem of social cost', *Journal of Law and Economics*, 3:1–44.

Dasgupta, P. and Ray, D. (1986a) 'Inequality as a determinant of malnutrition and unemployment: Theory', *Economic Journal*, 96.

Dasgupta, P. and Ray, D. (1986b) 'Adapting to undernourishment: The clinical evidence and its implications', Cambridge University, mimeo.

Dasgupta, P. and Ray, D. (1987) 'Inequality as a determinant of malnutrition and unemployment: Policy', *Economic Journal*, 97.

Dasgupta, P. and Stiglitz, J.E. (1980a) 'Industrial structure and the nature of innovative activity', *Economic Journal*, 90:266–293.

Dasgupta, P. and Stiglitz, J.E. (1980b) 'Uncertainty, market structure and the speed of R&D', *Bell Journal of Economics*, 11:1–28.

Dasgupta, P. and Stiglitz, J.E. (1985) 'Sunk costs, competition and welfare', Princeton University, mimeo.

Dasgupta, P. and Stiglitz, J.E. (1988) 'Learning-by-doing, market structure, and industrial and trade policies', *Oxford Economic Papers*.

Debreu, G. (1959) *Theory of value*. New York: Wiley.

Eaton, J. and Gersovitz, M. (1980) 'LDC participation in international financial markets: Debt and reserves', *Journal of Development Economics*, 7:3–21.

Eaton, J. and Gersovitz, M. (1981a) 'Debt with potential repudiation: Theoretical and empirical analysis', *Review of Economic Studies*, 48:289–309.

Eaton, J. and Gersovitz, M. (1981b) 'Poor country borrowing and the repudiation issue', Princeton studies in international finance no. 47, Princeton, NJ.

Eaton, J., Gersovitz, M. and Stiglitz, J.E. (1986) 'The pure theory of country risk', *European Economic Review*, 30:481–513.

Farrell, J. (1987) 'The Coase theorem', *Journal of Economic Perspective*, Winter.

Fields, G. (1975) 'Rural–urban migration, urban unemployment and underemployment, and job-search activity in LDCs', *Journal of Development Economics*, 2:165–187.

Fields, G. (1983) 'Private and social returns to education in less developed countries', *Eastern Africa Economic Review*, June.

Greenwald, B. and Stiglitz, J.E. (1986) 'Externalities in economies with imperfect information and incomplete markets', *Quarterly Journal of Economics*, 101:229–264.

Greenwald, B., Stiglitz, J.E. and Weiss, A. (1984) 'Informational imperfections and macro-economic fluctuations', *American Economic Review*, 74:194–199.

Greenwald, B. and Stiglitz, J.E. (1988) 'Pareto inefficiency of market economies: Search and efficiency wage models', *American Economic Review*, 84 (May).

Harberger, A. (1971) 'On measuring the social opportunity cost of labor', *International Labor Review*, June.

Harris, J.R. and Todaro, M. (1970) 'Migration, unemployment, and development', *American Economic Review*, 60:126–42.

Hart, O. (1975) 'On the optimality of equilibrium when markets are incomplete', *Journal of Economic Theory*.

Heady, E. (1947) 'Economics of farm leasing systems', *Journal of Farm Economics*, 29:659–678.

Hurwicz, L. and Shapiro, L. (1978) 'Incentive structures maximizing residual gains under incomplete information', *Bell Journal of Economics*, 9:180–191.

Jaynes, D.J. (1984) 'Economic theory and land tenure', in: H. Binswanger and M. Rosenzweig, eds., *Rural labor markets in Asia: Contractual arrangements, employment and wages*. New Haven, CT: Yale University Press.

Johnson, D.G. (1950) 'Resource allocation under share contracts', *Journal of Public Economics*, April:111–123.

Kanbur, R. (1981) 'Short-run growth effects in a model of costly migration with borrowing con-straints: Will rural development work?', in D. Currie et al., eds., *Essays in microeconomics and economic development*. London: Croom Helm.

Leibenstein, H. (1957) *Economic backwardness and economic growth*. New York: Wiley.

Lucas, R. (1985) 'Learning by doing and development', mimeo.

Marshall, A. (1961) *Principles of economics*. Cambridge: Cambridge University Press.

Mirrlees, J. (1975) 'A pure theory of underdeveloped economies', in: L.A. Reynolds, ed., *Agriculture in development theory*. New Haven, CT: Yale University Press.

Nalebuff, B. and Stiglitz, J.E. (1982) *Prices and quality*. Princeton.

Nalebuff, G. and Stiglitz, J.E. (1983) 'Prizes and incentives: Towards a general theory of compensa-tion and competition', *Bell Journal of Economics*, Spring:21–43.

Nelson, R.R. and Winter, S.G. (1982) 'The Schumpeterian trade off revisited', *American Economic Review*, 72:114–132.

Newbery, D. and Stiglitz, J.E. (1979) 'Sharecropping, risk sharing, and the importance of imperfect information', paper presented to a conference in Mexico City, March 1976. Published in: J.A. Roumasset et al., eds., *Risk, uncertainty and development* (SEARCA, A/D/C, 311–341).

Reid, J.D. (1973) 'Sharecropping as an understandable market response: The post-bellum South', *Journal of Economic History*, 33.

Reid, J.D. (1976) 'Sharecropping and agricultural uncertainty', *Economic Development and Cultural Change*, 24.

Reid, J.D. (1979) 'Sharecropping and tenancy in American history', in: J.A. Roumasset, J.-M. Boussard and I. Singh, eds., *Risk, uncertainty, and agricultural development*. New York: Southeast Asian Regional Center for Graduate Study and Research in Agriculture and Agricultural Development Council.

Rotenberg, J. and Saloner, G. (1986) 'A supergame-theoretic model of price wars during booms', *American Economic Review*, June, 390–407.

Ross, S. (1973) 'The economic theory of agency: The principal's problem', *American Economic Review*, May, 134–139.

Roumasset, J.A. and James, W.T. (1979) 'Explaining variations in share contracts: Land quality, population pressure, and technicological change', *Australian Journal of Agricultural Economics*, 23.

Sah, R. and Stiglitz, J.E. (1984) 'The economics of price scissors', *American Economic Review*, 74:125–138.

Sah, R. and Stiglitz, J.E. (1985a) 'The social cost of labor, and project evaluation: A general approach', *Journal of Public Economics*, 28:135–163.

Sah, R. and Stiglitz, J.E. (1985b) 'Taxation and pricing of agricultural and industrial goods in developing economies', Economic Growth Center discussion paper no. 475, Yale University. Forthcoming in: D. Newbery and N. Stern, eds., *Modern tax theory for developing countries*.

Sah, R. and Stiglitz, J.E. (1985c) 'The social cost of labor, and project evaluation: A general approach', *Journal of Public Economics*, March:135–163.

Sah, R. and Stiglitz, J.E. (1986a) 'The economics of town-vs-country problems', *American Economic Review*, December.

Sah, R. and Stiglitz, J.E. (1986b) 'Technological change, economic and social structure and alternative development strategies', paper presented at the 8th International Economic Association Congress, New Delhi, India, forthcoming in Proceedings.

Sah, R. and Stiglitz, J.E. (1986c) 'Taxes, prices and the balance between industry and agriculture', presented at the 8th International Economic Congress, New Delhi, India, forthcoming in Proceedings.

Sah, R. and Stiglitz, J.E. (1986d) 'Price scissors and the structure of the economy', *Quarterly Journal of Economics*.

Sah, R. and Stiglitz, J.E. (1986e) 'Technological progress and socio-economic structure', presented at 'Debt, Stabilization, and Development', Conference in Memory of Carlos Diaz-Alejandro, Helsinki; to be published in Proceedings.

Sen, A.K. (1966) 'Peasants and dualism with or without surplus labor', *Journal of Political Economy*, 74.

Shapiro, C. and Stiglitz, J.E. (1984) 'Equilibrium unemployment as a worker discipline device', *American Economic Review*, 74:433–444.

Simonde de Sismondi, J.C.L. (1814/1966) *Political economy*. New York: Kelly.

Solow, R.M. (1956) 'A contribution to the theory of economic growth', *Quarterly Journal of Economics*, 1:65–94.

Spence, M. (1973) 'Job market signaling', *Quarterly Journal of Economics*, 87:355–374.

Spence, A.M. (1974) *Market signaling: Information transfer in hiring and related processes*. Cambridge, MA: Harvard University Press.

Srinivasan, T.N. (1979) 'Agricultural backwardness under semi-feudalism', Comment, *Economic Journal*.

Stiglitz, J.E. (1969) 'Rural-urban migration, surplus labor and the relationship between urban and rural wages', *East African Economic Review*, 1–2:1–27.

Stiglitz, J.E. (1973) 'Approaches to economics of discrimination', *American Economic Review*, 63:287–295.

Stiglitz, J.E. (1974a) 'Incentives and risk sharing in sharecropping', *Review of Economic Studies*, April:219–255.

Stiglitz, J.E.(1974b) 'Alternative theories of wage determination and unemployment in LDCs: The labor turnover model', *Quarterly Journal of Economics*, LXXXVII:194–227.

Stiglitz, J.E. (1974c) 'Theories of discrimination and economic policy', in: von Furstenberg, ed., *Patterns of racial discrimination*. Lexington, MA: Lexington, pp. 5–26.

Stiglitz, J.E. (1974d) 'Equilibrium wage distributions', IMSSS technical report no. 154, Stanford University; *Economics Journal*, 95:595–618.

Stiglitz, J.E. (1975) 'The theory of screening, education and the distribution of income', *American Economic Review*, 65:283–300.

Stiglitz, J.E. (1976a) 'The efficiency wage hypothesis, surplus labor and the distribution of income in LDCs', *Oxford Economic Papers*, 28:185–207.

Stiglitz, J.E. (1976b) 'Prices and queues as screening devices in competitive markets', IMSSS technical report no. 212, Stanford University.

Stiglitz, J.E. (1977) 'Some further remarks on cost–benefit analysis', in: H. Schwartz and R. Berney, eds., *Social and economic dimensions of project evaluation*, Proceedings of Symposium on Cost–Benefit Analysis. Washington: IDB, pp. 253–282.

Stiglitz, J.E. (1982a) 'Alternative theories of wage determination and unemployment: The efficiency wage model', in: M. Gersovitz, C.F. Diaz-Alejandro, G. Ranis and M. Rosenzweig, eds., *The Theory and Experience of Economic Development: Essays in Honor of Sir Arthur W. Lewis*. London: George Allen & Unwin, pp. 78–106.

Stiglitz, J.E. (1982b) 'The wage-productivity hypothesis: Its economic consequences and policy implications', paper presented to the American Economic Association, December 1982. Forthcoming in: M. Boskin, ed., *Essays in honor of A. Harberger*. London: Basil Blackwell.

Stiglitz, J.E. (1982c) 'Structure of labor markets and shadow prices in LDCs', in: R. Sabot, ed., *Migration and the labor market in developing countries*. Boulder: Westview Press, pp. 13–64.

Stiglitz, J.E. (1985a) 'Economics of information and the theory of economic development', *Revista De Econometria*, 1:5–32.

Stiglitz, J.E. (1985b) 'Labor turnover, wage structure & moral hazard: The inefficiency of competitive markets', *Journal of Labor Economics*, 3:434–462.

Stiglitz, J.E. (1986a) 'Theories of wage rigidity', in: J. Butkiewicz, K. Koford and J. Miller, eds., *Keynes' economic legacy*. New York: Praeger, pp. 153–221.

Stiglitz, J.E. (1986b) *Economics of public sector*. New York: W.W. Norton.

Stiglitz, J.E. (1986c) 'The new development economics', in: *World development*, 14:257–265. Forthcoming in: Charles K. Wilber, ed., *The political economy of development and underdevelopment*. New York: Random House.

Stiglitz, J.E. (1987a) 'Sharecropping', in: P. Newman, ed., *The new Palgrave*. New York: Stockton Press.

Stiglitz, J.E. (1987b) 'The causes and consequences of the dependence of quality on prices', *Journal of Economic Literature*, March:1–47.

Stiglitz, J.E. (1987c) 'Technological change and economic and social structure', in: P. Dasgupta and P. Stoneman, eds., *Economic policy and technological performance*. Cambridge: Cambridge University Press.

Stiglitz, J.E. and Weiss, A. (1981) 'Credit rationing in markets with imperfect information', *American Economic Review*, 71:393–410. (Presented at a meeting of the Western Economic Association.)

Stiglitz, J.E. and Weiss, A. (1983) 'Incentive effects of terminations: Applications to the credit and labor markets', *American Economic Review*, 73:912–927.

Stiglitz, J.E. and Weiss, A. (1986) 'Credit rationing and collateral', in: J. Edwards et al., eds., *Recent developments in corporate finance*. New York: Cambridge University Press, pp. 101–135.

Todaro, M. (1968) 'An analysis of industrialization. Employment and unemployment in less developed countries', *Yale Economic Essays*, 8:331–402.

Tversky, A. and Kalnemon, D. (1974) 'Judgment under uncertainty: Heuristics and biases', *Science*, 185:1124–1131.

Weiss, A. (1980) 'Job queues and layoffs in labor markets with flexible wages', *Journal of Political Economy*, 88:526–538.

Yellen, J. (1984) 'Efficiency wage models of unemployment', *American Economic Review*.

Chapter 6

LONG-RUN INCOME DISTRIBUTION AND GROWTH

LANCE TAYLOR

Massachusetts Institute of Technology

PERSIO ARIDA*

Pontifical Catholic University of Rio de Janeiro

Contents

1.	Introduction	162
2.	The heirs of Schumpeter	163
3.	Demand-driven models	165
4.	Resource limitations and reproduction	169
5.	Shades of Marx	174
6.	The neoclassical resurgence – trade	178
7.	Structuralists versus monetarists	184
8.	Patterns of growth	187
9.	Conclusions	189
	References	190

*Comments by T.N. Srinivasan and research support from the Ford Foundation are gratefully acknowledged.

Handbook of Development Economics, Volume I, Edited by H. Chenery and T.N. Srinivasan
© *Elsevier Science Publishers B.V., 1988*

1. Introduction

Development economics began macro. Though micro concerns have grown in importance – witness half of the chapters in this Handbook – the system-wide approach is still central to the field. It has to be. If the whole economy changes structure during the course of "development", then to understand the process one has to look at the economy as a whole.

Work before and during the Second World War laid the foundations for what is called development economics today, but it stems from the roots of the discipline. As Arthur Lewis discusses in Chapter 2 of this Handbook, classical economics was largely about development. Curiously, in industrial capitalism's vigorous spring, the classicals focused on the stationary state, or the end of the process. When classical themes were retaken by the new development economists forty years ago, the emphasis was on stagnation at the beginning. What were the forces that made poor countries poor, and how could the fetters be broken? Initial models were set up to characterize the growth process, to serve as a backdrop for medium-term plans. More recently, following a neoclassical reaction against the avowed classicism of the 1950s generation and a detour through models emphasizing income distribution (after academics publishing in North Atlantic journals belatedly realized that even with growth, poor people stubbornly remain poor), the focus shifted to short-run concerns. Increasing poverty and declining productive potential resulting from stabilization programs aimed at offsetting external shocks have been the rule for most developing countries in the 1980s. Small wonder that a great deal of thought has been devoted to making "stabilization" and "depression" non-synonomous words.

Chapter 17 of this Handbook is devoted to short-run issues, and should be read in connection with this one. However, as the founders of development economics emphasized, thinking about how to fight fires for the next few quarters is useless unless one has a notion about where the economy may go in the fullness of time. This chapter is devoted to their own and successors' secular theories. In Chapter 17, besides analyzing the economics of stabilization, we offer suggestions about how long- and short-run threads may be woven into whole cloth.

The long-run approach is presumably of interest because it tells something about how economies change in historical time, in particular over the century or two of what Kuznets (1966) calls modern economic growth. Evidently, formal models – our focus here – can never give a *complete* description of development, since it involves major institutional change. Indeed, it is foolish to specify models except in light of institutions, a methodological precept of which the first students of development were well aware. How their successors lost sight of institutions is one of the major themes of this chapter, which in the final analysis is an argument for a return to the classical approach. We begin the discussion with an economist whose fame is largely due to an attempt to re-establish classicism in his own time.

2. The heirs of Schumpeter

Schumpeter's *Theory of Economic Development* (German version 1912; English edition 1934) is infrequently read nowadays, but it is the true origin of the field. Schumpeter's theory of development is interesting in itself, because it emphasizes technical and institutional change. We also use the model (on our initiative, not his) as an organizing device for later contributions, most of which differ from the letter but not the spirit of his work.

Schumpeter begins with the kind of theory now considered long-run, and in a leap discards it for more interesting processes that have been dropped from the orthodox canon. He calls his initial point "circular flow", analyzed formally today as "steady growth". An economy in circular flow may be expanding, but it is not developing. Development occurs only when an entrepreneur makes an innovation – a new technique, product, or way of organizing things – and shifts coefficients or the rules of the game. He makes a monopoly profit until other people catch on and imitate, and the system moves to a new configuration of circular flow.

The invention or insight underlying the innovation need not be the enterpreneur's – Schumpeter's "new man" simply seizes it, puts it in action, makes his money and (more likely than not) passes into the aristocracy and retires. Ultimately, his innovation and fortune will be supplanted by others in the process of creative destruction that makes capitalist economies progress.

One key analytical question is how the entrepreneur obtains resources to innovate. To get his project going, he must invest – an extra demand imposed on the circular flow. He obtains loans from banks – credit and money are endogenously created in the process. The new credit is used to purchase goods in momentarily fixed supply. Their prices are driven up, and the real incomes of other economic actors decline. Obvious examples are workers receiving a fixed nominal wage or the cash flows of non-innovating firms. There is "forced saving" as workers consume less; at the same time, routine investment projects may be cut back. "Development" from one circular flow to another is demand driven from the investment side (though, of course, the innovation may involve production of new goods or changes in productivity) and short-run macro adjustment takes place through income redistribution via forced saving with an endogenously determined money supply. In a longer run, workers may regain income when the innovation hits the market. In later versions of the model, Schumpeter emphasized that bankruptcy of out-dated firms could also release resources for the innovators, but the essential process is much the same. However, it may be affected by socialization of bankruptcy risk, as discussed in section 4 of Chapter 17.

Another question is how to characterize circular flow. Here we go beyond Schumpeter in setting out five versions or model "closures" [Sen (1963)] that appear in the development literature. The first, closest to Schumpeter's own description of the process, is that of neoclassical growth models. There is one production input (conveniently called labor) which expands at a given rate of growth. Other means of production – fixed and circulating capital – are reproducible within the system. Their growth rates in steady state settle down to that of labor supply. In the short run, the capital/labor ratio follows from the economy's history of accumulation and an assumption that labor is fully employed. If one further postulates a neoclassical marginal productivity input demand story, the real wage and rate of profit will follow. But they could just as well be specified exogenously. What really makes the growth model work is the full employment assumption.

In the second version, the real wage of labor is fixed, in terms of a consumption basket when many goods are considered. A share of non-labor income is saved, and investment proportions adjust to exhaust saving and permit the system to grow at a steady pace.

The third form of circular flow has some sector's output growing steadily, e.g. capital goods production, food output, or capital inflows and/or exports which provide foreign exchange. The system converges to the key commodity's growth rate and its relative price, e.g. the agricultural terms of trade or the real exchange rate, may be the pivot of adjustment to macro equilibrium.

These first three steady states are all supply constrained in some sense. The first and third have given growth rates of a factor and a commodity respectively, while the second has a predetermined income distribution and (like the others) is built around the notion that saving determines investment in macro equilibrium.

The fourth variant supposes output free to vary in response to demand. If capital accumulation is considered, it comes from investment functions which are exogenous or else tie each sector's capital formation to other variables in the system. Sectoral rates of capacity utilization converge to a steady state configuration generating enough saving (a function of income) to meet investment demand.

Finally, generalizing the concept of steady state, there is the idea that development consists of continual introduction of new commodities as demand for old ones stagnates. Observed demand composition does not maintain constant budget shares, so proportionate expansion of all sectors cannot occur. However, if new commodities and associated production activities appear in regular fashion, a predetermined process underlying shorter-term fluctuations can play almost the same analytical role as a steady state.

Schumpeter, a good Walrasian, would have preferred to think of circular flow as something like our version one, perhaps with a bit of five thrown in to account for Engel's Law. He was not interested in limiting commodities or non-reproducible means of production (number three), and abhorred the under-consumptionist overtones of variant four. Curiously, his immediate followers, namely Rosenstein-Rodan and Nurkse – the founders of development economics as presently construed – went down the demand-determination (or fourth) route. Not long after, Kalecki and Mahalanobis proposed theories along the lines of our third characterization of circular flow, and Lewis and followers adopted the classical version two. All these writers followed the master in thinking of development as a process of transition from one steady state to another – they differed about how to characterize growth paths and how to get between them. Later, largely neoclassical economists dropped the method of transitions and sought "efficient" modes of growth directly. Schumpeter's (and the classicals') emphasis on studying how economies change over time in specific historical and institutional circumstances was abandoned during the 1960s, as development economics went out of step with the political trends of the time. It anticipated perfectly, however, the anti-statist, market-oriented politics that took over twenty years later on.

3. Demand-driven models

Rosenstein-Rodan's (1943) shoe factory is the epitome of demand-limited circular flow. The owner does not think it worthwhile to step up his operations because not all the income so generated will feed back into increased purchases of shoes. Nurkse's (1953) "vicious circle" follows the same lines, taking for granted Schumpeter's metaphor. Basu (1984) provides a formalization involving a fixed money wage and producers in two sectors who select production levels depending on wage costs and anticipated marginal revenues from expanding sales down kinked demand curves. They can easily arrive at an equilibrium in which not all available labor is employed. It might be possible to move toward fuller employment by increasing production in both sectors in line with consumers' tastes. Such an expansion is at the heart of "balanced growth".

This diagnosis was discussed roundly in the 1950s. A blow-by-blow recapitulation cannot be attempted here – see Dagnino-Pastore (1963) and Mathur (1966) for summaries of the debate. For later purposes, note the following points:

(1) Nurkse equilibrium is not Walrasian. Fleming (1955) said Nurkse was wrong flat out. Increased commodity demand, however arranged, will increase demand for labor, bid up wages and choke off incipient expansion from the side of costs. More subtly, Scitovsky (1954) emphasized externalities that prevent price signals from leading the economy to full employment. His main examples were economies of scale and monopoly power in trade. For the later debate

(Section 6) among Walrasians as to whether "getting the prices right" is the way to guarantee growth, Scitovsky is crucial. He matters less to those who do not lose sleep over whether or not the economy is tending toward Pareto optimality.

(2) Adherents of balanced growth stressed the virtues of investment planning. Critics like Hirschman (1958) and Streeten (1959) wanted "unbalanced growth" to shock the system from low level circular flow. In their view, the development process is characterized by the uneven advance of different sectors, disproportions and disequilibria, with inflationary and balance of payments tensions arising at different points. Under such conditions, policy should be oriented to the choice of investment strategy which shows the best chance of being self-propelling, i.e. of being able to induce further investments to correct imbalances created at previous stages. Myrdal (1957) and Perroux (1961) were largely in agreement with this diagnosis, and sought to clarify how unbalanced expansion might occur in a regional context. In Myrdal's view, cumulative processes – what we call transitions – were the essence of change, with final outcomes depending on a clash of forces between unequalizing "backwash effects" and "spread effects" which distribute prosperity. Perroux added the notion of "growth poles", around which development occurs. The authors in this school were simultaneously more Schumpeterian and (despite their penchant for evocative labels for ill-defined processes) more practical than advocates of balanced growth. The latter never really spelled out how their plans for expansion were to be formulated, let alone put into practice. Input–output models and shadow-pricing of investments were their chosen instruments to lead to balance, but neither could fulfill the detailed resource-allocation task.

(3) Even if we leave aside Fleming, a question of resource mobilization also is involved. Increasing output requires investment in working capital, perhaps fixed capital as well, and macro balance has to be maintained. Rosenstein-Rodan (1961) laid great emphasis on indivisibilities and economies of scale. The saving counterpart to his investment "big push" might come from decreasing costs. And as Rodan's London School mentor Allyn Young (1928) pointed out, expansion of output makes room not only for more, but more sophisticated capital equipment. The theme recurs in subsequent discussions of export-led growth.

Apart from the balanced/unbalanced growth debate, demand-driven models show up in other contexts. One example is the structuralist/stagnationist analysis of problems of industrialization in Latin America, reviewed by Lustig (1980). A second is more recent discussion in India about slow industrialization there.

To understand the issues, it is useful to begin with possible stagnation in a model with one sector, and then bring in multisectoral complications. Dutt (1984a), formalizing a literature beginning with Kalecki (1971) and Steindl (1952), points out that if investment responds to increased capacity utilization as in an accelerator, then a shift in the income distribution against high-consuming wage earners can lead to slower growth – the distributional change reduces consumption demand and capacity utilization, and capital formation slows down. A further feedback of capacity use to changes in distribution can lead to a steady state differing from the initial one, as discussed in more detail below.

Now suppose that in addition to changing the economy-wide marginal propensity to consume, income redistribution also shifts consumer demands by sector. The wealthy may prefer services and sophisticated manufactures, for example, and poor people simple industrial products and food. If redistribution occurs and sectoral demand patterns change, and *if* investment demand by sector responds, then the economy can go to a new steady state. The results need not be heartening for proponents of income redistribution. If profit income recipients preferentially consume labor-intensive services, by the Rybczynski (1955) theorem, a tax-cum-transfer aimed at shifting income toward labor will reduce the wage share in a two-sector system. Moreover, if investors respond more to demands for commodities preferred by rentiers, overall growth and capacity utilization can decline – for details see Taylor (1985b).

Latin American structuralists like Tavares (1972) and Furtado (1972) more or less viewed the world along such lines, but with causality reversed. If industrialization beyond production of simple goods like food and textiles is to occur, they said, then income concentration to sustain demand for more sophisticated commodities is unavoidable under present social conditions. Taylor and Bacha (1976) provide a formalization, in which investment responding to consumer demand for "luxuries" leads to forced saving, in turn creating more luxury sales and a further investment push. The economy undergoes a transition between steady states without and with luxury goods production. DeJanvry and Sadoulet (1983) set up a more complete model in which luxury goods output can either rise or fall.

The Indian debate centers around demand preferences by sector, induced investment response, and – especially – the role of investment demand and capacity creation by state enterprises. Demand composition may then underlie slow industrial growth, or else Ahluwalia (1986) argues that the cause may be limited capacity in infrastructural sectors, along lines discussed in Section 4. Chakravarty (1984) cautions like the Latins that unless steps are taken to preclude it, more rapid growth may benefit only the top segment of the income spectrum.

Attempts at empirical verification of these ideas have been incomplete at best. A spate of studies in the 1960s, partly surveyed by P.B. Clark (1975), found no great variation in *marginal* propensities to consume by sector – the relevant parameters – across income classes. Input–output computations thus showed that income redistribution would not change sectoral output composition very much. However, the feedback of changes in demand to investment has never been taken up in a developing country context – this is a promising area of research. It can be extended to examine the effects of policy interventions. For example, Buffie (1986) and Taylor (1987) show how currently modish "equal incentives" trade policy need not maximize output growth in investment-driven models. This finding is relevant to the criticism of gains-from-trade arguments in Section 6 below.

A final theme in models of circular flow which emphasize income distribution and demand is inflation. A common theory attributes inflation to conflicting income claims. In the capitalist/worker story – a favorite of theorists but not necessarily the most relevant in developing countries – let us assume prices are set by a mark-up over prime costs. The latter typically comprise the wage bill and (at a macro level) costs of imported raw materials and intermediates. If the mark-up rate or import cost rises, prices follow and the real wage declines. Workers counter by pushing up money wages – the instrument they control. But then prices go up further through the mark-up, wages follow, and so on. In Joan Robinson's (1962) phrase, there is an "inflation barrier" below which the real wage cannot fall before money wage inflation is set off.

The object of conflict may be the real wage, the labor share or some other distributional index. Suppose it is the profit share, a positive function of the mark-up rate. Let wage inflation rise with the mark-up and also the profit rate (the product of the profit share and the output–capital ratio) as an indicator of economic activity. If price inflation also goes up with wage pressure and activity, there may be a "natural" rate of profit at which both prices and wages grow at the same speed. Such a profit rate is the analog in radical growth models of the natural rate of unemployment in neoclassical ones [see Marglin (1984)]. The mark-up rate or capital share is constant at the natural rate of profit. At that point, its growth rate will be an increasing (decreasing) function of the profit rate if price inflation accelerates more (less) than wage inflation when activity rises.

Now recall that income concentration in the form of a higher capital share may depress economic activity (the Dutt linkage discussed above) or else could increase it if, for example, faster inflation reduces the real interest rate and stimulates investment demand. Taylor (1985a) describes a model with two long-run stable cases A and B. In case A, the growth rate of the mark-up is a positive function of the profit rate and a higher mark-up rate retards activity. A permanent fiscal expansion will initially raise activity, and give the mark-up a positive rate of growth. As income becomes more concentrated, demand falls and the system returns to the natural rate of profit with a permanently higher mark-up and capital share. The secular inflation rate is higher, and capacity utilization as measured by the output–capital ratio (the profit rate divided by the profit share) less. In contrast, in case B the growth rate of the mark-up declines with the profit rate and a higher mark-up stimulates activity. Expansionary policy leads to a lower mark-up in the new steady state and thus to higher capacity utilization. It also reduces core inflation. The transition to those pleasant results, however, is complicated. Fiscal expansion increases first both inflation and the profit rate; the positive effects come only in a later stage. Political courage is needed to implement expansionary fiscal policy in case B; but courage pays as rapid growth will ultimately slow inflation.

This last and other demand-driven models show that characteristics of the economy in circular flow (or steady state) need not be unique. Their traverses between steady states parallel Schumpeter's process of development, though along different paths. Whether the changes are plausible as historical processes is another question; in retrospect that was what the balanced vs. unbalanced growth debate was about. The query becomes even more relevant as we pass toward resource-constrained models.

4. Resource limitations and reproduction

The models discussed in the previous section implicitly assume that output can be increased without limit (at least in key sectors) in response to higher demand. The trick is to make the demand realize itself without unfavorable distributional or other consequences. In this section we assume that a specific sector's output cannot be increased in the short run. Its supply becomes a constraint limiting overall growth.

The economy can adjust to a supply constraint in various ways. One, important in practice, is through absolute price changes that affect patterns of income distribution and demand. Demand pressure against a sector with inelastic supply will swing prices in its direction. Models stressing this linkage have recently been worked out for agriculture and non-agriculture, for non-traded and traded goods, and (at the world economy level) for the "South" as a primary product exporter to an industrialized "North".

Terms of trade models date at least to the controversy between Ricardo and Malthus about whether the English Corn Laws limiting grain imports should or should not be repealed. A sketch of an agriculture-limited economy emphasizing the distributional role of food prices was Preobrazhenski's (1965) contribution to the Soviet debate about industrialization in the 1920s. Kalecki (1976) gave a version in lectures in Mexico City in 1953 which was adopted or reinvented by many others, e.g. Sylos-Labini (1984), Kaldor (1976), and Taylor (1983). In the recent versions, the "industrial" sector has prices formed by a mark-up over prime costs, while the price of "agricultural" goods varies in the short run to clear the market with supply fixed or not very responsive to price changes.

Output in the industrial sector is demand driven. It produces a commodity used both for consumption and capital formation. Agriculture produces food, and partly finances overall investment through savings flows. Urban forced saving is central to the workings of the model, since the urban wage is not fully indexed to the food price. On the other hand, agricultural savings need not play a major role. Empirically, Quisumbing and Taylor (1986) argue that the share is only a few percent of GDP except in countries where large agro-export flows can be easily tapped for investment finance.

Suppose that the terms of trade shift toward agriculture, say from a reduction in food imports. Manufactured goods output can either rise or fall. It will be pushed up by increased demand from higher rural income, but also held down by reduced real urban spending power (real wages decline). The implication is that if the farm sector is relatively small, a cheap food policy based on higher imports will increase industrial output. The urban sector is doubly benefited – food prices fall and production expands. Though he used a different model to argue his point, this outcome is consistent with Ricardo's advocacy of repeal of the Corn Laws.

The alternative view was espoused by Malthus who reasoned (more or less cogently) on aggregate demand lines. Agriculture is responsible for a large proportion of consumption demand. Farmers (or landlords for Malthus) hit by adverse terms of trade will cut spending enough to reduce overall economic activity. Which distributional configuration applies in developing countries today is highly relevant for policy. The answer seems to go either way in practice [McCarthy and Taylor (1980), Londono (1985)].

Besides import policy, other state interventions can affect the terms of trade. Fiscal expansion or increased investment, for example, will bid up the flexible price by injecting aggregate demand. As noted above, forced saving on the part of urban groups whose incomes are not fully indexed to food prices will occur. Ellman (1975) argues that food price-induced forced saving supported the Soviet investment push of the early 1930s, in contrast to Preobrazhenski's suggestion that the terms of trade be shifted *against* agriculture to extract an investable surplus. Along political economy lines, Mitra (1977) stresses distributional consequences of shifts in prices between two staples in India – rice and wheat – and industrial goods.

As is well known, distributional conflict over the terms of trade underlies the Latin American structuralist theory of inflation, set out by Noyola (1956) and Sunkel (1960) soon after Kalecki's lectures in Mexico City. As the agricultural terms of trade rise, the real wage declines. If workers bid up money wages in response, a conflicting claims inflationary process can be set off along the lines sketched in the previous section – Cardoso (1981) gives a formalization. As emphasized by Canavese (1982), the speed of the inflation depends on the size of the initial price shock and the degree and rapidity of indexation of wages to price changes. With extensive indexation, inertial inflation as discussed in Section 5 of Chapter 17 can arise.

The two-sector model has been used to deal with many issues besides the agrarian question. It is frequently stated with one sector producing traded goods (with prices determined by a mark-up and/or from the world market) and the other sector making non-traded goods with a variable internal price. Formalizations date back at least to Salter (1959) and Swan (1960), and another Australian, Cairns (1921), used the model to discuss the political economy of gold booms more than a century ago. The latest incarnation is the "Dutch disease", e.g. Corden (1984) and Chapter 28 in this Handbook.

The key relative price is between traded and non-traded goods – the "real exchange rate". When aggregate demand goes up – say from attempts to spend the proceeds of better external terms of trade for a primary export or capital inflows – part of the extra spending will be directed toward non-traded goods. If they are in relatively inelastic supply, their price will rise or the real exchange rate will fall. As a consequence, industrial exports (sensitive to the exchange rate) will decline, and demand for home products "similar" to importables may stagnate as well. In Boutros-Ghali's (1981) useful terminology, both internal and external diversification (of the production and export baskets) are reduced.

The familiar conflicting claims inflation appears in this set-up if money wages rise in response to higher non-traded goods prices. The inflation further worsens the real exchange rate unless aggressive nominal devaluation – itself a source of inflation as it drives up prime costs via higher intermediate import prices – is pursued. If it is not, persistent deterioration of the real exchange rate can stimulate capital flight on the part of wealth holders who anticipate a future "maxi-devaluation" to set right the current account. Typically, the capital flight creates conditions in which a maxi has to occur. Details of this and similar scenarios are set out in Chapter 17. They repeat with some frequency in the Third World.

A third application of the terms of trade model is in global macroeconomics built around the South as a primary product exporter and an industrialized North. The South is described as a Lewis-type economy while the North may be demand-driven or obey supply-limited circular flow. The South is triply dependent in that terms of trade for its exports depend on activity in the North, it imports a substantial fraction of its capital goods, and (barring unlimited capital flows) its investment is ultimately limited by its own saving plus whatever transfers come from the other party. Comparative static exercises can illustrate the implications of dependency. As in Houthakker's (1976) model discussed below, a productivity increase in the South will reduce its income and/or slow its rate of growth because its export commodity is sold in a flex-price market subject to low income elasticities of demand in the North. Also, patterns of convergence to steady state growth for the two regions can be complex, but the South is likely to suffer doubly (slower export sales and lower terms of trade) from adverse shocks to the system. Ocampo (1986) and Kanbur and McIntosh (1986) survey the growing literature.

A final point is that the terms of trade model, already a potted version of the agrarian question, is susceptible to simplistic optimization games. An example is treating Preobrazhenski's idea that the terms of trade should be shifted against agriculture as a problem in optimal taxation – the latest of two decades' worth of papers on the topic is by Sah and Stiglitz (1984). Manipulations of Lagrangian functions to find optimal tax rates for the peasantry are mildly illuminating so long as the results are not taken as serious policy advice. But if they are, then one has to ask if they make any sense in a given institutional context, e.g. Bukharin's (1971) observation that if Preobrazhenski's scheme were rigorously imposed in the 1920s Soviet economic system, the kulaks would simply abscond. (Neither author foresaw Stalin's drastic modifications of the system a few years later; both suffered greatly thereby.) Lines of policy also depend on the macro closures their proposers presuppose. Like all optimal taxationists, Sah and Stiglitz prefer a neoclassical closure – savings determines investment and full employment is maintained. With demand-driven circular flow, their distributional results can be shifted to those reported by Ellman – the Soviet state as the agent of accumulation benefits from forced saving induced by inflation acting on a working class whose numbers are increased and political leverage dramatically reduced by the de-kulakization campaign. The political implications cannot begin to be addressed by economic models but are crucial to those who seek to apply them. All "optimal" policy recommendations suffer such problems, as in the capital-constrained and foreign-exchange-constrained models we take up next.

When a relative price is fixed by state fiat, social convention, incomplete markets or other reasons, another set of models emphasizing quantity adjustments appears – the two-gap model set out by Chenery and Bruno (1962) is a famous example. Here, foreign exchange is a limiting factor – there is "external strangulation" in a Latin usage current at the time Chenery was beginning to formulate the model after visiting the Economic Commission for Latin America (ECLA) in Santiago, Chile.

The model's key assumption is that some proportion of gross capital formation must be imported – think of machines that cannot be produced within the country. With some capital (e.g. construction) produced at home, an additional unit of foreign exchange (from exports, import substitution, or capital flows) can support more than one unit of extra investment. At the same time, the extra foreign exchange raises the current account deficit by only one unit of "foreign saving". Following Bacha (1984), we can ask how these separate linkages between foreign resources and investment interact.

If saving determines investment, capital formation rises one-for-one with extra foreign resources. The part of the increased current account deficit not devoted to capital goods imports can go to extra purchases of consumer or intermediate goods. The gap between the saving and trade gaps is covered by trade, as Findlay (1971) observes in dismissing the two-gap dilemma. However, suppose foreign exchange is withdrawn. Then imports must fall or exports rise to maintain macro balance. Beyond a point, neither strategy is viable, and something else must adjust. Investment and the level of economic activity are the obvious candidates for reduction when external strangulation occurs.

In contrast, suppose that any extra foreign exchange is devoted to capital formation – because its import content is less than 100 percent, investment can rise more than one-for-one. A quantum of saving beyond that realized through extra machinery imports is required; it has to come from domestic sources. The obvious possibilities are distributional changes underlying forced saving, and capacity adjustment. Either may or may not be easily arranged. The potential gap between the gaps persists, whether investment is determined by available capital goods imports or by saving.

Longer-term growth in the two-gap model has traditionally been projected assuming one or the other gap is binding. If saving is scarce, the Harrod–Domar formula can be used to compute feasible growth; if the trade gap binds, formulas can be devised based on import propensities [Bacha (1984), Taylor (1983)]. In practice, how to interpret such calculations is not clear, since the realized gaps must be the same: investment less domestic saving must equal imports less exports in macro equilibrium. Critics were correct in emphasizing that the model is incomplete without a statement of the mechanisms which make discrepancies between the gaps disappear. But that does not mean that the problem it poses does not exist. In practice, it is often "solved" in the form of restrictions on government policy action (Sections 4 and 6 of Chapter 17).

One last commodity-limited model also focuses on capital goods. It was proposed by Mahalanobis (1953) in the era of the balanced growth, but its antecedents trace to the reproduction schemes in Volume II of Marx's *Capital*. The same model was used by Feldman in the Soviet industrialization debate; Domar (1957) gave a restatement and formalization.

The story is simple. One sector, like Marx's Department I, produces the means of production or capital goods; the other sector, like Department II, produces consumer goods. Both use capital goods as inputs, and once installed capital cannot be moved. Growth in the system is limited by the fraction of capital goods output devoted to new investment in that sector. It is easy to show [Taylor (1979)] that with a constant reinvestment proportion, the growth rate of the consumer goods sector will converge to that of capital goods.

The model is clearly incomplete. In his reproduction schemes, Marx worried about sectoral consistency and (implicitly) saving–investment balance. In his formal work, Mahalanobis did not go so far, though he kept a demand-driven "handicraft" consumer sector in the background to give macro equilibrium. Successors set up simple optimization exercises. They came up with the result that to maximize a discounted integral of utility from consumption, it is optimal initially to push the reinvestment rate in capital goods to the highest feasible level, and later switch to balanced growth. During the initial phase, the level of consumer goods output declines if capital in the sector depreciates rapidly enough. The analytically similar two-gap model was also subjected to the optimization treatment. The utility-maximizing solution there was to specialize initially in activities like export promotion and import substitution which generate foreign exchange (to import capital goods), and later relax into balanced growth.

Neither recommendation inspires confidence – putting all her eggs in some model's initial big push basket is something that no prudent planner would contemplate. Other difficulties are that the models (and their input–output cousins, for that matter) do not give enough detail for disaggregated resource allocation, and do not address the issue of reaching saving–investment balance.

What one learns from this section is that specific commodities – food, foreign exchange, or capital goods – may be in short supply, and that the system has to accommodate. Design of feasible policies in diverse institutional contexts becomes the interesting analytical question. A great deal of work remains to be done along such lines.

5. Shades of Marx

Since the education of most professional economists is devoid of reference to classical thought, it is not surprising that they had trouble dealing with the surplus labor notions of Lewis (1954, 1958). The story of how Lewis was absorbed into the neoclassical corpus is interesting to pursue, as are his similarities (conscious or not) with the other great proponent of surplus-based accumulation theories, Marx.

For our purposes, Marx's analytical scheme is best interpreted as it was absorbed by sympathetic non-Marxist economists – we are not interested in the notion of capital as the self-valorization of value, in capitalists as expressions of capital, and so on. Rather, we will work with a simple model built around pervasive unemployment (the reserve army) and technical progress or choice of technique (the organic composition of capital). In a capitalist upswing, employment rises and the real wage is bid up from the level consistent with social norms. A turning point is passed, beyond which capitalists undertake technical innovation or substitution of machines for labor. The organic composition rises, setting the stage for crisis. In Sylos-Labini's (1984) description, capitalists "...by substituting machines for workers... freeze a part of the wages into fixed capital, which therefore depresses the...rate of increase of workers' incomes". Demand does not grow rapidly enough to absorb a growing supply of commodities, and a realization crisis ensues. Long-term expansion of the capitalist system involves a sequence of such cycles, perhaps of increasing severity as time goes on.

The key assumptions in an economy not strongly open to trade are:

(1) There is a reserve army, from which labor can be drawn as necessary. As unemployment declines, the real wage may rise.

(2) Capitalists, the accumulating class, automatically transform their saving into capital formation. There are no realization problems from the side of

investment demand. The rising organic composition, or choice of technique, affects the mass of wages, and underlies cyclical collapse.

The Lewis story is much less dramatic, but shares common elements. He does not deal with cyclical growth, but rather assumes a gradual transition from a classical to neoclassical regime. The "reserve army" is called the "subsistence sector", but retains the function of providing labor at a socially determined wage until unemployment begins to dry up. Modern sector capitalists, meanwhile, accumulate and employ additional labor thereby. The overall share of saving in income is supposed to rise along with profits, so accumulation speeds up. Beyond a turning point, the labor supply curve slopes upward, wages are determined by conditions of labor demand and supply, and the world becomes neoclassical. Capital–labor substitution possibilities become important then.

Causality in both models comes from the supply side. The socially determined wage sets the income distribution, and there is no room in the specification for an independent function for investment demand. The causal story is only one step away from neoclassical determination of the rate of growth by forces of productivity and thrift.

Lewis's version was soon shorn of its starkness, as emphasized by Lluch (1977). The counterattack took .place on three fronts. First, Lewis's subsistence sector – made up of farmers, casual workers, petty traders, retainers, new entrants into the labor force from population growth, and women – was transformed by professional consensus into "agriculture". This reinterpretation led to a purely academic debate among proponents of different agriculture/industry models – Dixit (1973) presents a summary.

In the best-known contribution, Fei and Ranis (1964) set up a model with two turning points – when food supply begins to decline as labor is withdrawn from agriculture and when the marginal product of rural labor rises to the institutionally fixed urban wage. The parallels with Marx went unstated, as did the similarities of Fei and Ranis's landlords to Marx's capitalists. In Dixit's words, the landlord

> ...should be eager to save. He should sell his surplus to industry and should transfer his savings to industrial entrepreneurs. He should be eager to innovate, and thereby improve the technology in agriculture.

The social origins of this master manipulator do not flow naturally from the model. Jorgenson (1969) emphasized productivity in agriculture, and worked out a formula for the rate of technical progress that would have to occur in the sector for it to produce sufficient food to meet urban/industrial demand. Kelley, Williamson and Cheetham (1972) ran full employment simulations of two sectors with different patterns of demand on the part of income recipients in each. Turning points, surplus labor, and distinct social roles for landlords and capitalists had completely vanished from the scene.

The second line of attack was led by Schultz (1964). Already calling the subsistence sector agriculture, he challenged the existence of surplus labor. Another endless debate commenced, leading as a side-effect to an elegant paper by Sen (1966) recalling the emphasis of Chayanov and Lenin on the importance of the organization of production in agriculture. Attempts to dislodge the reserve army are recounted by Johnston (1970) and many others, while Rao (1986) reviews the more interesting micro literature stemming from Sen.

Schultz (1964, 1978) also led the third wave of attackers, that of the price mechanists. Their diagnosis was that agricultural prices have been held low in developing countries, in comparison to world market prices as a point of reference. Lewis is irrelevant to their prescription of higher prices as a way out of agricultural stagnation – he was interested in the terms of trade only insofar as they might affect industrial accumulation. In practice, Schultz's remedies lack potency, given the class relationships and institutional structure of many developing countries. For one thing, a rentier-dominated agriculture may respond "perversely" to improved terms of trade, as argued by Patnaik (1983) and Dutt (1984b). For another, the prescription to raise producers' prices fails to take account of the leading role that public investments often play in agricultural development. Econometric estimates rarely produce values of agricultural supply elasticities exceeding a few tenths; these numbers decline and the fit of the equation improves substantially when variables representing public inputs like irrigation are entered [Chhibber (1982)]. A favorable movement in the terms of trade, given political obstacles to taxation and public spending, may slow growth or lead to a distorted pattern of growth by accentuating structural dualism within agriculture. Finally, the Preobrazhenski/Kalecki model discussed in the previous section points to the fact that macroeconomic and distributive impacts of price adjustment may be unpleasant and politically unpalatable.

The intellectual time trend in these models went from class distinctions and saving growth mediated by distributional change to technical advance triggered by price policy – marginal conditions enveloped Lewis's mild radicalism. Both early and later models addressed issues of sectoral balance, but from divergent perspectives. This line of thought exhausted itself by the late 1960s, though the neoclassical synthesis has had major policy significance since.

Other work with supply-determined models has emphasized three themes – labor allocation across sectors, urban unemployment, and economic dualism. Sectoral migration models date at least to Simon (1947). He showed that if labor is the only production input with full employment and equal rates of productivity growth in two sectors, then workers will move toward the sector with income-elastic demand. Baumol (1967) argued that a non-progressive sector with low productivity growth will lose all its labor in the long run if its demand is sufficiently price elastic (or the recipient sector's demand price inelastic). Similarly, if agriculture faces price-inelastic demand, farmers' incomes will be hurt by rapid technical advance [Houthakker (1976)]. Kaneda (1986) generalizes these results – which all boil down to applying Slutsky demand decompositions to full employment income flows in a one-input model – to emphasize the importance of agricultural technical advance in liberating resources for industrial growth in Meiji Japan (the "Ohkawa thesis"). The moral resembles Jorgenson's discussed above, but focuses more on the market for labor than food.

The second issue is urban unemployment. Its characterization as the outcome of a search process by Todaro (1969) and Harris and Todaro (1970) spawned an enormous literature. Their closure is labor supply limited, with the twist that some people in urban areas are unemployed as they seek jobs with a less-than-unitary probability of success.

Two state variables describe dynamics in a general equilibrium version of this model – allocation of capital stock between the sectors and a migration function whereby people move according to the differential between the rural wage and the expected urban wage (actual wage times probability of finding a job). Following Bartlett (1983), Kanbur and McIntosh (1986) point out that equilibrium is only saddlepoint stable. If the initial rural population lies above a certain level,

> ... its rate of growth will dominate the change in the unemployment rate which provides the signal for the sectoral reallocation of labor... The share of population in agriculture will then *rise*, contrary to the stylized facts. However, if the share of agriculture and the unemployment rate are lower than certain critical values, then the population share of agriculture will go to zero, contrary to the observation that this share typically stabilizes around a low value.

As a theory of transition, the second path may make sense, though it is hard to believe that the economic growth process is driven solely by a search for urban jobs. The migration pattern is consistent with Kuznets's (1955) conjecture about a U-shaped relationship between income equality and development. The Kuznets story can also be rationalized in a full employment context by appropriate assumptions about technology in the two sectors (specifically, significantly lower capital–labor elasticities of substitution in industry than agriculture) as in Taylor (1979, ch. 11).

Finally, one can ask how asymmetry or "dualism" between agricultural and industrial sectors affects their mutual balance. Technological differences creating a "factor proportions problem" were stressed by Eckaus (1955). Chichilnisky (1981) elaborates the story in a model with a fixed-coefficients technology, assuming that labor supply is fully employed but elastic to the real wage, both sectors utilize labor and a given stock of shiftable capital, and agriculture is labor intensive. A movement in the terms of trade toward agriculture will bid up the real wage, by the Stolper–Samuelson (1941) theorem. Labor supply will increase, and the production mix will shift toward food by the Rybczynski (1955) theorem. All appears harmonious, except that consumption of food products by labor may rise enough to make the marketable or exportable surplus increase only slightly, or even decline.

This "perverse" price response of excess food supply is the consequence of simultaneous dualism in production structure, labor supply, and patterns of demand. It can be reproduced with fixed labor supply and substitution in production [Taylor (1979)], and helps rationalize econometric evidence that the macro response of marketed food surpluses to price is often small or negative. Lele and Mellor (1981) work through a similar model emphasizing technical change. If new agricultural technology raises the labor share, then the resulting increase in food demand may make marketed surplus problems worse. On the other hand, biased technical advance that increases food output can ease an urban wage constraint. Lele and Mellor do not ask how extra food sales are to be realized in an economy in which full employment is not presumed – state intervention to subsidize both consumption and stock accumulation may be required [McCarthy and Taylor (1980)]. The problem is likely to be important in practice, as the terms of trade models discussed above underline.

Distributional problems in dual economies can also be acute, as both Eckaus and Chichilnisky point out. Indeed, Roemer (1982) constructs a theory of exploitation based precisely on dualism in production technology, property ownership, and demand. The mathematics becomes ponderous, but as a sidelight does generate Lenin's and Mao's famous five-way classification of peasants – pure landlords who do not work, at the top; pure landless who hire out all their labor, at the bottom; and three intermediate classes (those who do some work on their land and hire in, those who hire neither in nor out, and those who hire out part of their labor) in between.

6. The neoclassical resurgence – trade

One function of neoclassical theory is to defuse radical economics by embellishment with optimizing agents and suppression of social content. A case in point is Schultz's redesign of Lewis's already mellow machine. In development literature, there are two other important examples – trade and financial liberalization.

Trade liberalization and "getting prices right" are the neoclassical responses to the questions raised by Nurkse and Rosenstein-Rodan. For an economy in a vicious circle, they proposed radical output expansion on a planned basis to get it out. Hirschman wanted the escape to be unbalanced, unplanned, and unguided in any direct fashion by market signals – even worse. An alternative strategy respecting the rules of the capitalist market was clearly required. It was not long in appearing in the form of a volume on *Industry and Trade in Some Developing Countries*, by Little, Scitovsky and Scott (1970), and a host of subsequent studies.

Before delving into the arguments, it makes sense to review trade patterns in the Third World [McCarthy, Taylor and Talati (1987)]. First and foremost, the commodities poor countries exchange internationally are noncompetitive – exports are not consumed in large quantities at home and imports are not produced. The implication is that trade theory's "Law of One Price" will play a minor role in determining resource allocation. First, the law itself will not apply insofar as large numbers of traders for the same commodity do not exist within and without the national borders. Second, even if arbitrage occurs, it will not enforce competition among domestic producers. To put the point succinctly, the share of effectively non-traded goods in the production basket of most developing countries is high. Chenery (1975) notes that development involves a secular shift from non-competitive toward competitive trade. His observation has strong implications for policy in the medium run.

Further points to be stressed include the fact that poor countries are strongly dependent on imports of capital goods. With few exceptions (South Korea, India, Brazil) they have had no success in penetrating export markets for such commodities. Finally, size and history strongly influence a country's trading role – bigger economies are more self-sufficient, and many small and poor ones suffer from their inherited dependence on primary commodity trade.

Trade theory disdains such empirical regularities. Rather, it starts from the opposite position – hypothetical open economy with tastes and technologies uncontaminated by history and a preponderance of traded goods subject to the Law of One Price. With such assumptions, orthodox arguments advance on two fronts. One stresses export-led growth, and is taken up below. The other, closer to the Paretian core of neoclassical thought, asserts that poor countries are inefficient because they suffer from "distortions" or gaps between observed prices and some optimal set. "Getting prices right" becomes the neoclassical slogan, with special emphasis on equating internal price ratios to those ruling in the markets of the world.

Two questions immediately arise. Does this argument make logical and institutional sense? Even if it did, would it be practical? Simple considerations suggest that the answer to both queries is no.

On its own terms, a neoclassical appeal to the welfare improvements that should result from relative price realignment does not look promising. Walrasian circular flow presupposes full employment and a near approach to Pareto efficiency. Removing distortions under such circumstances amounts to erasure of "little triangles" in the demand–supply diagram. The resulting welfare gains are trivial in magnitude, as Harberger (1959) noted to his chagrin in the days of balanced growth.

Faced with low estimates for the magnitude of an "effect", economists typically have two options for making the numbers bigger. One is to increase the proportional impact of the cause behind the result; the other is to increase the base to which the proportion is applied. Work following Harberger's has taken the latter option, by inventing "rents" which "agents" in developing countries are supposed to "seek" instead of devoting their efforts to productive activity. Following Krueger (1974), neoclassical trade theorists have been at the forefront of the quest for rent objects, though public choice theorists and economic historians are active as well – see Srinivasan (1985) for a review.

An import quota would be a typical source of a rent. If you own rights to it, you can buy goods in the world market cheaply and sell them to your fellow citizens more dearly. Since arbitrarily large rents can be postulated and then screened from view in the service items of the national accounts by enshrouding them in the "black economy", the field seems clear for massive welfare gains from liberalization to be obtained. However, the computations are still limited by fact. If quotas cover only a fraction of imports which, in turn, are a fraction of GNP, the corresponding rents cannot be huge. More fundamentally, rents are a form of exploitation, though with their naive political theory, neoclassical economists have a hard time making that explicit. Marxists, of course, have been in the business of estimating exploitation for a long time. Even with great ingenuity – as in Baran and Sweezy (1966) – they rarely raise their estimates of surplus values to a large fraction of GDP. Unfortunately for the neoclassicals, the same is bound to be true with regard to rents.

The implication of small calculable welfare losses from distortions is that neoclassicals are forced to a position like Schumpeter's. The economy can leap forward from one circular flow to another under appropriate incentive – specifically, those that result from getting prices right. The international marketplace has the right stuff, and internal price relatives should be steered toward external ones. Calculations of effective rates of protection and domestic resource costs can map the route. The propaganda for such policies is usually couched in terms of the gains to be realized from trade. But the Harberger problem of triviality remains.

A more important point is that gains from trade are not only small, but that the theory used in their calculation is irrelevant to trading relationships in the Third World. It ignores the non-competitive nature of most international transactions in poor countries, and relies on hypothetical autarkic conditions as the basis for its comparisons. It is debatable what this concept may mean, if factor availability, technologies, or even demand patterns are determined by export and import specializations imposed on countries by their historical role in world trade. Given the weakness of its visible foundation on the gains from trade, the true support of the neoclassical case can only be Schumpeterian.

Does that pillar hold? The purely neoclassical cautions raised by Scitovsky become relevant here. He showed that if economies of scale are important and if commodities are not perfectly tradable (in the sense of having ample import supplies and export demand at the same international prices), then even in a neoclassically closed model, price signals will not be adequate for *investment* decisions, though they might suffice for day-to-day market operations.

Common sense suggests that Scitovsky's conditions apply. Economies of scale are rife in industry, and we have already seen that most commodities are imperfectly tradable at best. In particular, as Pack and Westphal (1986) argue, mastery of technology is largely non-tradable as well as time- and resource-consuming in practice. Since technical innovation and transfer are required for productivity gains and are also closely tied to capital accumulation, price-guided investment decisions will neither maximize welfare in the standard neoclassical model, nor lead to jumps between circular flows.

In his investment-driven model, Schumpeter's entrepreneurs were supposed to choose their innovations on the basis of benefit–cost calculations based on market prices, but that turns out not to be advantageous on social grounds. Nor, as we have seen, need faster growth nor better income distribution result [Buffie (1986), Taylor (1987)]. These theories are not damaged if price signals for investors are replaced by "vision". But then, the question is whether an environment in which national prices are equated to international ones enhances clairvoyance in a non-convex, uncertain world. We come to an impasse, at least as far as theory is concerned. Can the ambiguities be resolved by an appeal to actual country experience?

One can try to answer such a question on the basis of retrospective studies or cross-country comparisons. We can briefly discuss findings from both approaches. Historically, there is no shortage of liberalization experiments. An early proponent [Krueger (1978, p. 277)] is circumspect about their effects: "...while there are numerous microeconomic changes that accompany devaluation, liberalization, and altered [trade policy] bias, it was not possible to detect significant effects of these changes on growth performance". Later experiments with extreme liberalization, as under the military regimes in the 1970s in South America's Southern Cone or in Mexico after the debt crisis, suggest that it cripples, at least in the short run. Models discussed in Section 1 of Chapter 17 help explain the reasons why.

Among cross-section studies, the best known is by Agarwala (1983), which was summarized with fanfare in the World Bank's (1983) *World Development Report* and the *Economist* magazine. Agarwala found a negative relationship between a "distortion index" based on seven indicators and growth in a sample of 31 developing countries in the 1970s.

The analysis can be criticized on several grounds. For example, Agarwala's choice of period makes slow-growing Argentina, China, and Uruguay appear highly distorted, even though all were undergoing major liberalization experiments in the latter half of the decade. Even if we accept his data, however, later work by Aghazadeh and Evans (1985) shows that only two of his index's indicators – real exchange rate appreciation and real wage growth in excess of productivity gains – bear a negative relationship with growth. The other indicators – tariff distortions for agricultural and industrial products included – are unrelated. Aghazadeh and Evans further show that institutional variables such as military spending and planning capacity do influence growth. Since strongly trending real wages and exchange rates also reflect institutional factors such as open distributional conflict or the onset of Dutch disease, one can conclude that an economy's historical circumstances affect its performance. But trade and other distortions do not play much of a role.

The practical conclusion is that the rationale for beneficial effects from liberalization is weak, and in some cases has been misguided. Finding the "right" prices, e.g. the correct ratio between traded and non-traded goods prices (or the real exchange rate), is a non-trivial task. Atempting to modify *nominal* prices to get to the right *real* levels can be even harder, because of the new price set's wide-ranging effects on financial markets, income distribution, inflationary expectations, and the level of economic activity. Major price revisions strongly influence flow income and asset market positions – unfavorably for at least some economic groups – and may easily be repulsed. By the same token, distributional conflict can easily lead to "wrong" prices which will not be righted until the underlying contradiction is resolved.

Is the case any stronger for export-led growth, the other component of the mainstream cure? A theoretical problem is why more rapid export expansion should stimulate output at all. If, as neoclassicals suppose, the economy is at full employment, faster growth of one component of demand can only lead to slower growth of another. If investment suffers, for example, overall capacity expansion may be slowed in the medium run. In demand-driven models, more exports may accelerate growth, as noted long ago by Hobson (1902) in his theory of imperialism. Moreover, export expansion does not run into a balance of payments restriction, as might other exogenous injections of demand (from investment or public expenditure).

However, simple demand expansion or the use of extra exports to break the trade constraint in the two-gap model does not seem to be what neoclassicals have in mind. Rather, they argue that by enhancing competition with the world, opening the economy through exports leads to greater enterprise efficiency and faster technical progress. The price mechanism is said to be involved, though the details are rarely made clear.

Given this lack of theoretical clarity, most arguments for export-led growth are presented along empirical lines. Indeed, showing a positive regression coefficient of output growth on export growth has become a thriving cottage industry in recent years, e.g. Balassa (1985). From the national accounts, the output growth rate can be expressed as a weighted average of growth rates of the components of final demand (consumption, investment, exports, etc.) with the weights being output shares. The export coefficient in regression studies often takes a value like an export share. It can be beefed up by making export growth "explain" the residual from the standard decomposition of the output growth rate into a weighted average of primary input growth rates [Feder (1983)], but the rationale is hardly convincing. McCarthy, Taylor and Talati (1986) run the regression the other way – export shares disaggregated by type on output growth, with per capita GNP, population, and other variables as controls – and find no strong relationships aside from a tendency of low-income countries to specialize more in primary exports than richer ones. One test of export-led growth might be *increasing* shares of total exports or some categories as per capita income rises in fast-growing countries, but this pattern also fails to occur in recent years. On a similar note, Jung and Marshall (1985) use Granger causality tests to show that export promotion leads output expansion in only four of their sample of 37 countries during the period 1950–81.

A more reasonable approach is to ask, along with Pack and Westphal (1986), whether a strong export orientation fits naturally into a planning framework. South Korean experience suggests that export targets are easy to verify, and ease communication between exporters and policy-makers who push exports. But the Korean system is highly *dirigiste* (as in most other countries that have favored export-led growth) and price signals do not play a central role in its process of taking investment decisions. Productivity growth, as a definitional matter, is high in Korea, but more as a result of a long history of industrialization, aggressive macro policy, and centralized pressures on exporters to perform than of getting prices "right".

The conclusions seem to be:

(1) The case for a positive association between trade liberalization and economic performance as measured by growth is prima facie difficult to make, and is not supported by the data. A few fast-growing countries have had rapid export expansion, but the correlation does not extend to the group of developing economies as a whole.

(2) In practical terms, finding "right" prices is a non-trivial exercise, let alone imposing them on a functioning economic system. For example, the exchange rate is not only a relative price between traded and non-traded goods, but has wide-ranging impacts on financial markets, expectations, and the inflationary process (Section 1 of Chapter 17). Finding a real rate which optimizes production decisions may be virtually impossible in light of its other effects.

(3) Perhaps in recognition of such difficulties, economic decision-making in the "success cases" is highly *dirigiste*; one can further argue that rapid growth is a major component of their process of political legitimation. Their planners have not used international prices as the keystone for investment decisions.

(4) A macroeconomic case can be made for rapid export growth in terms of the demand-limited models discussed in Section 3, but not in the full employ-

ment neoclassical set-up unless exports (and "correct" price signals) somehow stimulate Schumpeterian entrepreneurship on the part of the private sector or planners. On grounds of common sense, the demand-driven story might be preferred.

7. Structuralists versus monetarists

In the long run of economic thought since the eighteenth century, Kindleberger (1984) distinguishes two sets of opinions regarding directions of causation in the macro system and the sources of inflation. He calls the positions structuralist and monetarist, after a famous Latin American controversy in the 1950s. Other examples are the Banking and Currency Schools in nineteenth-century England, and Keynesians and Friedmanites or rational expectationists in North Atlantic macroeconomic debate. The Latin antagonists tried to sort out their differences at a conference in Rio de Janeiro with proceedings published in Baer and Kerstenetsky (1964). The book is still worth reading, but is not covered here since many of the same arguments crop up in the more recent discussions summarized in Chapter 17.

For our purposes the structuralist position can be summed up in the statements that inflation largely comes from conflicting claims or inertial processes, and that circular flow is demand driven. If resource limitations apply, they may take the form of external strangulation, a lagging sector, etc. When they want to emphasize forced saving processes, structuralists typically assume that the economy is at full use of capacity or available capital. (Other factors making investment demand exceed saving – such as the insensitivity of both to changes in capacity use – could be relevant as well.) Note that full capacity use is not the same thing as Walrasian full employment, which presupposes flexible real prices and enough substitution possibilities in the system for all inputs to end up with a remunerative use.

Regarding money, structuralists think that under most circumstances its supply is endogenously determined in the macro system. Indeed, they often prefer to focus on bank assets (credit) rather than liabilities (money) and think that credit expansion will stimulate trade. Contraction will have the opposite effect, inducing recession which generally weakens social resistance sufficiently to allow prices to fall from the side of costs.

As discussed in Taylor (1987), a simple structuralist short-run macro model (ignoring trade) has three equations:

(1) determination of prices from costs (a mark-up equation) with components incorporating inertial inflation;

(2) determination of output from aggregate demand;

(3) asset market equation(s) with sufficient endogenous variables such as interest rates or money supply to permit (1) and (2) to hold.

The monetarist vision of circular flow is full employment. If there is an independent source of demand – say investment or exports – it is incorporated into the system by a dual relative price – the interest or exchange rate. Money supply is exogenously determined by the authorities, and fixes the price level. With prices coming from asset markets, firms must either be off their cost or mark-up functions, or some component of costs (mark-ups?) varies to accommodate changes in prices. In open economy monetarism, prices come from the world market via trade arbitrage or the law of one price, and money supply becomes endogenous through changes in the economy's net foreign asset position.

The implications of these contrasting positions for short-run policy are set out in Taylor (1987) and Chapter 17. Recently, there has been debate about long-term financial strategy in which the two views partly coincide.

The initial salvos were books by Shaw (1973) and McKinnon (1973) who asserted that developing countries are handicapped by lack of financial depth or, more strongly, financial repression. Policies had been followed which limited intermediation by banks, and starved firms of funds for working capital or investment. Increased intermediation would ease these restrictions, and permit a jump to more active circular flow. The key policy change would be to increase the deposit rate of interest to bring more ample savings through the intermediaries. The leap to the larger activity level resembles the one that neoclassicals assert will come from trade liberalization. Structuralists countered that it is unlikely to occur.

The first round of models emphasized that working capital (advances for labor and raw materials) is an important component of costs. Shaw and McKinnon said the same thing, but disagreement came over the role of the interest rate. If loan rates rise with deposit rates (it is hard to imagine the contrary) then costs of working capital will be driven up. Firms will respond by raising prices and reducing activity – the outcome will be stagflation in an "effect" named after Cavallo (1977) by Latins and the easy-money Texas Congressman Wright Patman by Americans. Van Wijnbergen (1983a) provided econometric support for the model with data from South Korea, a favorite case study for the financial repressionists. Giovannini (1985) further showed that savings rates have a negligible elasticity with respect to interest rates in a sample of developing countries. With given investment, stagflation would also occur if saving propensities were to rise, as Dutt (1984c) pointed out.

Second round models emphasized alternative placement of assets, e.g. curb markets or rural moneylenders. If these markets (which function without reserve requirements, etc.) provide more intermediation than the banking system, then a policy aimed at shifting portfolio composition toward banks will be stagflationary [van Wijnbergen (1983b)].

The third round focused on hoarding, or hedge assets. Taylor (1983) argued that aggressive interest rate policy is useless if hoarded "gold" is not readily relinquished when deposit rates go up. In a rational expectations model which includes both curb market loans and inflation hedges, Park (1985) has shown again that raising interest rates is stagflationary. The novelty is that the initial stagflation is aggravated as speculators draw on time deposits and curb loan markets to earn a windfall gain on "gold" prices. Some recovery of the perverse effect of the aggressive interest rate policy may occur as speculative gains are later converted into working capital.

Given this background of criticism, one can hardly maintain that investigating the truth of the McKinnon–Shaw doctrine remains of policy interest today. Reality itself contributes to this judgement. As discussed in Chapter 17, attempts to implement the doctrine in the Southern Cone of South American and elsewhere failed; moreover, most LDCs can no longer be described as financially repressed. In fact, interest rates have risen higher than the external world rate. Instead of financial repression, it is the financial openness of processes of interest rate determination which is the pressing problem for LDCs in the 1980s.

Reverting to the closed economy, there are two other fields of debate about the effects of financial policy in the long run. First, it is easy to show that permanent tight money by raising interest rates can *increase* the steady state rate of inflation from the side of costs via the Cavallo or Wright Patman effect [Taylor (1983)]. In case B of Taylor (1985) discussed in Section 3, the same phenomenon occurs through an increased mark-up. In demand-driven circular flow, there is no reason why monetary contraction should slow inflation, unless (and until) the policy induces a recession deep enough to cut back on inflationary pressures from social groups who can no longer sustain their real income claims.

The second disagreement – more a matter of emphasis – is over the workings of an inflation tax. If the economy is at full capacity, additional investment or export sales can only be met through forced saving. If investors or exporters are given preferential access to credit, they have a prior claim on output which can be ratified by inflation-induced real income losses on the part of others. The inflation will be stronger insofar as indexation of wages and other payments is well entrenched – that is the structuralist angle. Monetarists stress that there may be flight from non-indexed assets, which makes the emission process more costly for the state. This effect has become crucial with dollarization or asset-indexation in many economies during the 1980s. Cardoso (1979) gives a formal synthesis of the two arguments in the traditional case in which money is not indexed and the state can collect seignorage or an inflation tax by issuing debt. Extensions of the analysis to deal with state liabilities whose interest is indexed to inflation should prove instructive. As faster inflation adds to total interest obligations, the public sector borrowing requirement will raise its ugly head.

8. Patterns of growth

Stylized facts about how sectors behave over the course of development amount to a catalog of phenomena without an integrating theory. Economists lack an analytical framework able to contain the demand, supply, and distributional shifts that underlie observed patterns of growth. The Walrasian system, with its dogged insistence that prices will adjust to bring overall full employment, is inappropriate. Can one do better? Several possibilities are open for theoretical and empirical work:

(1) Pasinetti (1981) uses a dynamic input–output model to ask when stable growth with differing sectoral demand patterns and rates of technical change may prove possible. One conclusion – first stated by Hawkins (1948) – is that conditions on sectoral rates of demand and productivity growth required to assure full employment of capacity and labor are very strong – so strong that they are virtually impossible to satisfy without institutional changes in labor force participation rates or the length of the working day.

(2) If Engel phenomena are restated in terms of initial increases, saturation and final decline of consumption of specific goods, then it is apparent that maintaining full employment requires the continual introduction of new commodities. In advanced economies, think of products in common use in the 1980s (Big Mac hamburgers, walkperson tape-players, video cassettes) that were unheard of a decade before. A role is naturally opened for entrepreneurs, and absorption of new production technologies could give rise to distributional problems.

(3) Another sort of demand shift that can be captured in an input–output framework stems from changes in social relationships and the role of the state. An old point raised by Kuznets (1966) is that much state activity – regulation and environmental protection, for example – is functional to the production process under prevailing political norms. The same applies to many consumer demands, e.g. for transport services. Institutional change during the development process would surely shift the magnitudes of the relevant commodity coefficients and flows.

(4) Changes in demand patterns and input–output coefficients as functions of per capita GDP can be fed into the usual Leontief balance equation to generate shifts in sectoral value-added shares [Chenery, Shishido and Watanabe (1962)]. Such decompositions reveal regularities of Engel phenomena and coefficient changes as development proceeds; they can be extended toward country typolo-

gies [Chenery and Syrquin (1986)]. Although it illuminates patterns of change in the past that may persist in the future, the open Leontief model used in these studies does not tie income generation back to demand in full circular flow. Analyses based on general equilibrium models under different closures are an obvious potential extension of this work.

(5) The input–output investigations could naturally be extended to deal with the secular relative price shifts against manufacturing observed by Gerschenkron (1951), but again a closure rule or explicit theory of price determination would have to be specific.

(6) Relative backwardness may determine both the sector-specific pattern of industrialization and the degree of state intervention required to support it – Gerschenkron's (1962) other famous hypothesis. Beyond historical studies for Europe and Japan, the notion has not been elaborated empirically. How well does it apply to the NICs?

(7) Finally, international trade becomes less complementary to the production structure as development proceeds [Chenery (1975)]. Primary exports fall off in importance, while imports shift from technically obligate purchases of capital and intermediate goods toward products more similar to those produced at home. At the industry level, a period of import substitution precedes export expansion [Urata (1986)]. Depending on policy, trade may become more competitive in the sense that the law of one price links imported and nationally produced goods. This observation is consistent with the rise in service prices that usually occurs in rich countries. Services are typically non-traded so that their prices cannot be held down by foreign competition [Balassa (1964)].

To these interindustry questions, one should add the problem of timing. Basing her theory on Marx's circuits of capital, Luxemburg (1968) pointed out that with lags in the system, realization of all potential labor power in the economy could prove impossible – an anticipation of Hawkin's more technology oriented point. Such difficulties underlie Marx's cyclical crises discussed in Section 5, and are formalized with specific lag structures for production, realization of demand, and recommitment of sales proceeds to production by Foley (1986). His accounting relies on integral equations, but for statistical application it would have to be restated in terms of lagged Leontief current and capital input matrices. The similarities with both the Pasinetti scheme and sectoral planning models like that of Eckaus and Parikh (1968) would then be more apparent.

A last area of investigation involves distribution and demand composition. On theoretical and empirical grounds respectively, Pasinetti (1981) and Burns (1934) argue that profit rates in "new" rapidly growing sectors are likely to be high – the firms need the cash flow for reinvestment. But if the fast-growing sectors do not generate all their own demand, how will sales for their products stay strong, e.g. how did Italy after the Second World War and Brazil in the 1960s sustain demand for rapid expansion of production of cars? The questions raised by the

Latin American structuralists and Rosenstein-Rodan have yet to be adequately addressed.

9. Conclusions

Maintained hypotheses about directions of macroeconomic causality are key to the results of most models discussed herein. Whether the models can incorporate empirical generalizations about the development process is another question. Sensible economics should be built upon both elements.

On the whole, the models that do best at reproducing the data are the input–output simulations discussed in the previous section. But since they do not fully close the income–expenditure nexus, they provide little insight into dynamics or distributional change. Thinking about these issues requires strong hypotheses about directions of macro causality. On the terms of trade in the agrarian question, for example, Preobrazhenski in the Soviet Union in the 1920s and Malthus when he defended the English Corn Laws 100 years before, used models based substantially on the same equilibrium relationships, but came to opposite conclusions on the basis of their politics and judgements about directions of causality. Malthus thought cheap food would reduce economic activity by curtailing landlords' spending; Preobrazhenski thought the state could direct their income loss toward increased capital formation. At a given time and place, both could not be right. Both could be wrong if the institutional rules were to change, as under Stalin.

Similar conclusions apply to other models. Agriculture/industry balance when savings drives investment may pivot on distributive shares (Lewis), technological progress (Okhawa), or intersectoral migration (Harris–Todaro). But if investment drives saving, the terms of trade and activity levels become central, as in structuralist theory. Incomes policies are likely to matter little in full employment neoclassical circular flow – redistribution at most affects growth by altering the savings supply. But depending on factor intensities, marginal propensities to consume by sector, and investment responses, redistribution could trigger either rapid or slow cumulative growth processes in investment-driven models. In the first case, foreign trade policies generating equal incentives across sectors will be near-optimal; they could brake expansion in the second.

There is no philosopher's stone to cull these theories – two centuries of economists' debate attest to that. In a particular circumstance, one causal structure may be more appropriate than another. However, the decision is mostly external to the models. Any description of circular flow can have enough epicycles added to fit the numbers. Criteria such as Occam's Razor, historical relevance, and political implications have to be used to select which one best fits the situation at hand. What *is* surprising is that some economists – principally neoclassicals at this juncture – really think that they can come up with a broadly applicable uniform model. One clear lesson from the history of economic change is that such a reductionist approach is bound to fail. What may serve better is a renewed classically based attempt to formulate development theories on the basis of institutions, macroeconomic power in the sense of being able to impose one's demands upon the system, and sectoral and class relationships that do (or are likely to) exist.

References

Agarwala, R. (1983) 'Price distortions and growth in developing countries', World Bank Staff working paper no. 575, Washington, DC.

Aghazadeh, I. and Evans, D. (1985) *Price distortions, efficiency, and growth*. University of Sussex: Institute of Development Studies.

Ahluwalia, I.J. (1986) 'Industrial growth: Performance and prospects', *Journal of Development Economics*, 23:1–18.

Bacha, E.L. (1984) 'Growth with limited supplies of foreign exchange: A reappraisal of the two-gap model', in: M. Syrquin, L. Taylor and L. Westphal, eds., *Economic structure and performance: Essays in honor of Hollis B. Chenery*. New York: Academic Press.

Baer, W. and Kerstenetsky, I., eds. (1964) *Inflation and growth in Latin America*. Homewood, IL: Richard D. Irwin.

Balassa, B. (1964) 'The purchasing-power parity doctrine: A reappraisal', *Journal of Political Economy*, 72:584–596.

Balassa, B. (1985) 'Exports, policy choices, and economic growth in the developing countries after the 1973 oil shock', *Journal of Development Economics*, 18:23–36.

Baran, P. and Sweezy, P. (1966) *Monopoly capital*. New York: Monthly Review Press.

Bartlett, W. (1983) 'On the dynamic instability of induced-migration unemployment in a dual economy', *Journal of Development Economics*, 13:85–95.

Basu, K. (1984) *The less developed economy*. Oxford: Basil Blackwell.

Baumol, W.J. (1967) 'Macroeconomics of unbalanced growth: The anatomy of the urban crisis', *American Economic Review*, 57:185–196.

Boutros-Ghali, Y. (1981) 'Essays on structuralism and development', unpublished Ph.D. dissertation, Department of Economics, Massachusetts Institute of Technology.

Buffie, E. (1986) 'Commercial policy, growth, and the distribution of income in a dynamic trade model', Department of Economics, University of Pennsylvania.

Bukharin, N.I. (1971) *Economics of the transformation period*. New York: Bergman Publishers.

Burns, A.F. (1934) *Production trends in the United States since 1870*. New York: National Bureau of Economic Research.

Cairns, J.E. (1921) 'The Australian episode', reprinted from an 1859 paper in: F.W. Taussig, ed., *Selected readings in international trade and tariff problems*. New York: Ginn and Co.

Canavese, A. (1982) 'The structuralist explanation in the theory of inflation', *World Development*, 10:523–529.

Cardoso, E. (1979) 'Inflation, growth, and the real exchange rate: Essays on economic history in Brazil', unpublished Ph.D. dissertation, Department of Economics, Massachusetts Institute of Technology.

Cardoso, E. (1981) 'Food supply and inflation', *Journal of Development Economics*, 8:269–284.

Cavallo, D. (1977) 'Stagflationary effects of monetarist stabilization policies', unpublished Ph.D. dissertation, Department of Economics, Harvard University.

Chakravarty, S. (1984) 'India's development strategy for the 1980s', *Economic and Political Weekly*, 21:845–852.

Chenery, H.B. (1960) 'Patterns of industrial growth', *American Economic Review*, 50:624–654.

Chenery, H.B. (1975) 'The structuralist approach to development policy', *American Economic Review* (*Papers and Proceedings*), 65, 310–316.

Chenery, H.B. and Bruno, M. (1962) 'Development alternatives in an open economy: The case of Israel', *Economic Journal*, 72:79–103.

Chenery, H.B., Shishido, S. and Watanabe, T. (1962) 'The pattern of Japanese growth', 1914–1954, *Econometrica*, 30:98–139.

Chenery, H.B. and Syrquin, M. (1986) 'Typical patterns of transformation', in: H. Chenery, S. Robinson and M. Syrquin, *Industrialization and growth*. New York: Oxford University Press.

Chhibber, A. (1982) 'Dynamics of price and non-price response of supply in agriculture', Department of Economics, Stanford University.

Chichilnisky, G. (1981) 'Terms of trade and domestic distribution: Export-led growth with abundant labor', *Journal of Development Economics*, 8:163–192.

Clark, C. (1957) *Conditions of economic progress*, 3rd ed. London: Macmillan.

Clark, P.B. (1975) 'Intersectoral consistency and macroeconomic planning', in: C. Blitzer, P. Clark and L. Taylor, eds., *Economy-wide models and development planning*. New York: Oxford University Press.

Corden, W.M. (1984) 'Booming sector and Dutch disease economics: Survey, and consolidation', *Oxford Economic Papers*, 36:359–380.

Dagnino-Pastore, J.M. (1963) 'Balanced growth: An interpretation', *Oxford Economic Papers*, 15:165–176.

DeJanvry, A. and Sadoulet, E. (1983) 'Social articulation as a condition for equitable growth', *Journal of Development Economics*, 13:275–303.

Dixit, A. (1973) 'Models of dual economies', in: J.A. Mirrlees and N.H. Stern, eds., *Models of economic growth*. New York: Wiley.

Domar, E. (1957) 'A Soviet model of growth', in: *Essays in the theory of economic growth*. New York: Oxford University Press.

Dutt, A. (1984a) 'Stagnation, income distribution, and monopoly power', *Cambridge Journal of Economics*, 8:25–40.

Dutt, A. (1984b) 'Rent, income distribution and growth in an under-developed agrarian economy', *Journal of Development Economics*, 15:185–211.

Dutt, A. (1984c) 'Interest rate policy, savings, and growth in LDC's: A note', Department of Economics, Florida International University, Miami.

Eckaus, R. (1955) 'The factor-proportions problem in underdeveloped areas,' *American Economic Review*, 45:539–565.

Eckaus, R. and Parikh, K. (1968) *Planning for growth: Multisectoral, intemporal models applied to India*. Cambridge, MA: MIT Press.

Ellman, M. (1975) 'Did the agricultural surplus provide the resources for the increase in investment in USSR during the first five year plan?', *Economic Journal*, 85:844–864.

Feder, G. (1983) 'On exports and economic growth', *Journal of Development Economics*, 12:59–73.

Fei, J.C.H. and Ranis, G. (1964) *Development of the labor surplus economy*. Homewood, IL: Irwin.

Findlay, R. (1971) "The 'foreign exchange gap' and growth in developing economics", in: J.N. Bhagwati, et al., eds., *Trade, balance of payments and growth: Papers in international economics in honor of Charles P. Kindleberger*. Amsterdam: North-Holland.

Fleming, J.M. (1955) 'External economies and the doctrine of balanced growth'. *Economic Journal*, 65:241–256.

Foley, D. (1986) *Money, accumulation and crisis*. New York: Harwood Academic Publishers.

Furtado, C. (1972) *Analise do "modelo" Brasileiro*. Rio de Janeiro: Civilizacão Brasileira.

Gerschenkron, A. (1951) *A dollar index of Soviet machinery output, 1927–28 to 1937*. Santa Monica, CA: Rand Corporation.

Gerschenkron, A. (1962) *Economic backwardness in historical perspective*. Cambridge, MA: Harvard University Press.

Giovannini, A. (1985) 'Saving and the real interest rate in LDCs', *Journal of Development Economics*, 18:197–217.

Harberger, A. (1959) 'Using the resources at hand more effectively', *American Economic Review* (*Papers and Proceedings*), 49:134–146.

Harris, J.R. and Todaro, M.P. (1970) 'Migration, unemployment, and development: A two-sector analysis', *American Economic Review*, 60:126–142.

Hawkins, D. (1948) 'Some conditions of macroeconomic stability', *Econometrica*, 16:309–322.

Hirschman, A.O. (1958) *The strategy of economic development*. New Haven, CT: Yale University Press.

Hobson, J.A. (1902) *Imperialism: A study*. London: J. Nisbet.

Hoffman, W.G. (1958) *The growth of industrial economies*. Machester: Manchester University Press.

Houthakker, H.S. (1976) 'Disproportional growth and the intersectoral distribution of income', in: J.S. Cramer, A. Heeertje and P. Venekamp, eds., *Relevance and preciston: Essays in honor of Pieter de Wolff*. Amsterdam: North-Holland.

Johnston, B.F. (1970) 'Agricultural and structural transformation in developing countries', *Journal of Economic Literature*, 8:369–404.

Jorgenson, D.W. (1969) 'The role of agriculture in economic development: Classical vs. neoclassical models of growth', in: C.R. Wharton, ed., *Subsistence agriculture and economic development*. Chicago: Aldine.

Jung, W.S. and Marshall, P.J. (1985) 'Exports, growth and causality in developing countries', *Journal of Development Economics*, 18:1–12.

Kaldor, N. (1976) 'Inflation and recession in the world economy', *Economic Journal*, 86:703–714.

Kalecki, M. (1971) *Selected essays on the dynamics of the capitalist economy*. New York: Cambridge University Press.

Kalecki, M. (1976) *Essays in developing economies*. London: Harvester Press.

Kanbur, S.M.R. and McIntosh, J. (1986) 'Dual economy models: Retrospect and prospect', Department of Economics, University of Essex.

Kaneda, H. (1986) 'Rural resource mobility and intersectoral balance in early modern growth', Department of Economics, University of California, Davis.

Kelley, A.C., Williamson, J.G. and Cheetham, R. (1972) *Dualistic economic development*. Chicago: University of Chicago Press.

Kindleberger, C.P. (1984) *A financial history of western Europe*. London: George Allen and Unwin.

Krueger, A.O. (1974) 'The political economy of the rent-seeking society', *American Economic Review*, 64:291–303.

Krueger, A.O. (1978) *Liberalization attempts and consequences*. New York: National Bureau of Economic Research.

Kuznets, S.S. (1955) 'Economic growth and income inequality', *American Economic Review*, 45:1–28.

Kuznets, S.S. (1966) *Modern economic growth*. New Haven, CT: Yale University Press.

Lele, U. and Mellor, J.W. (1981) 'Technical change, distributive bias, and labor transfer in a two-sector economy', *Oxford Economic Papers*, 33:426–441.

Lewis, W.A. (1954) 'Economic development with unlimited supplies of labor', *Manchester School of Economics and Social Studies*, 22:139–191.

Lewis, W.A. (1958) 'Unlimited labor: Further notes', *Manchester School of Economics and Social Studies*, 26:1–32.

Little, I.M.D., Scitovsky, T. and Scott, M. (1970) *Industry and trade in some developing countries: A comparative study*. London: Oxford University Press.

Lluch, C. (1977) *Theory of development in dual economies: A survey*, Washington, DC: World Bank.

Londono, J.L. (1985) *Ahorro y gasto en una economia heterogena: El rol macroeconomico del mercado de alimentos*. Bogota: Fedesarrollo Coyuntura Económica Dic. 1985.

Lustig, N. (1980) 'Underconsumption in Latin American economic thought: Some considerations', *Review of Radical Political Economics*, 12:35–43.

Luxemburg, R. (1968) *The accumulation of capital*. New York: Monthly Review Press.

Mahalanobis, P.C. (1953) 'Some observations on the process of growth of national income', *Sankhya*, 12:307–312.

Marglin, S.A. (1976) *Value and price in the labor surplus economy*. London: Oxford University Press.

Marglin, S.A. (1984) *Growth, distribution and prices*. Cambridge, MA: Harvard University Press.

Mathur, A. (1966) 'Balanced vs. unbalanced growth – A reconciliatory view', *Oxford Economic Papers*, 18:127–157.

McCarthy, F.D. and Taylor, L. (1980) 'Macro food policy planning: A general equilibrium model for Pakistan', *Review of Economics and Statistics*, 62:107–121.

McCarthy, F.D., Taylor, L. and Talati, C. (1987) 'Trade patterns in developing countries, 1964–82', *Journal of Development Economics*, 27:5–39.

McKinnon, R.I. (1973) *Money and capital in economic development*. Washington, DC: Brookings Institution.

Mitra, A. (1977) *Terms of trade and class relations*. London: Frank Cass.

Myrdal, G. (1957) *Economic theory and underdeveloped regions*: London: Duckworth.

Noyola Vasquez, J.F. (1956) 'El Desarrollo económico y la inflación en México y otros paises Latinamericanos', *Investigacion Economica*, 16:603–648.

Nurkse, R. (1953) *Problems of capital formation in underdeveloped countries*. Oxford: Basil Blackwell.

Ocampo, J.A. (1986) 'New developments in trade theory and LDC's', *Journal of Development Economics*, 22:129–170.

Pack, H. and Westphal, L.E. (1986) 'Industrial strategy and technological change: Theory vs. reality', *Journal of Development Economics*, 22:87–128.

Park, W.-A. (1985) 'Three essays on stabilization and speculation', unpublished Ph.D. dissertation, Department of Economics, Massachusetts Institute of Technology.

Pasinetti, L.L. (1981) *Structural change and economic growth*. New York: Cambridge University Press.

Patnaik, U. (1983) 'Classical theory of rent and its application to India: Some preliminary thoughts on sharecropping', in: T.J. Byres, ed., *Sharecropping and sharecroppers*. London: Frank Cass.

Perroux, F. (1961) *L'economie du XXe siècle*. Paris: Presses Universitaires de France.

Preobrazhenski, E. (1965) *The new economics*. Oxford: Clarendon Press.

Quisumbing, M.A.R. and Taylor, L. (1986) 'Resource transfers from agriculture', Department of Economics, Massachusetts Institute of Technology.

Rao, J.M. (1986) 'Agriculture in recent development theory', *Journal of Development Economics*, 22:41–86.

Robinson, J. (1962) *Essays in the theory of economic growth*. London: Macmillan.

Roemer, J. (1982) *A general theory of exploitation and class*. Cambridge, MA: Harvard University Press.

Rosenstein-Rodan, P.N. (1943) 'Problems of industrialization in Eastern and South-Eastern Europe', *Economic Journal*, 53:202–211.

Rosenstein-Rodan, P.N. (1961) 'Notes on the theory of the big push', in: H.S. Ellis and H.C. Wallich, eds., *Economic development for Latin America*. New York: St. Martin's Press.

Rothschild, E. (1985) 'A divergence hypothesis', *Journal of Development Economics*, 23:205–226.

Rybczynski, T.M. (1955) 'Factor endowment and relative commodity prices', *Economica*, 22:336–341.

Sah, R.K. and Stiglitz, J. (1984) 'The economics of price scissors', *American Economic Review*, 74:125–138.

Salter, W.E.G. (1959) 'Internal and external balance: The role of price and expenditure effects', *Economic Record*, 35:226–238.

Schultz, T.W. (1964) *Transforming traditional agriculture*. New Haven, CT: Yale University Press.

Schultz, T.W., ed. (1978) *Distortions of agricultural incentives*. Bloomington, IN: Indiana University Press.

Schumpeter, J.A. (1934) *The theory of economic development*. Cambridge, MA: Harvard University Press.

Scitovsky, T. (1954) 'Two concepts of external economies', *Journal of Political Economy*, 62:143–151.

Sen, A.K. (1963) 'Neo-classical and neo-Keynesian theories of distribution', *Economic Record*, 39:54–64.

Sen, A.K. (1966) 'Peasants and dualism with and without surplus labor', *Journal of Political Economy*, 74:425–450.

Simon, H. (1947) 'Effects of increased productivity upon the ratio of urban to rural population', *Econometrica*, 15:31–42.

Shaw, E.S. (1973) *Financial deepening in economic development*. New York: Oxford University Press.

Srinivasan, T.N. (1985) 'Neoclassical political economy, the state, and economic development', Department of Economics, Yale University.

Steindl, J. (1952) *Maturitry and stagnation in American capitalism*. Oxford: Basil Blackwell.

Stolper, W.F. and Samuelson, P.S. (1941) 'Protection and real wages', *Review of Economic Studies* 9, 58–73.

Streeten, P. (1959) 'Unbalanced growth', *Oxford Economic Papers*, 11:167–190.

Sunkel, O. (1960) 'Inflation in Chile: An unorthodox approach', *International Economic Papers*, 10:107–131.

Swan, T.W. (1960) 'Economic control in a dependent economy', *Economic Record*, 36:51–66.

Sylos-Labini, P. (1984) *The forces of economic growth and decline*. Cambridge, MA: MIT Press.

Tavares, M.C. (1972) *Da substituicao de importacoes ao capitalismo financeiro*. Rio de Janeiro: Zahar

Editores.

Taylor, L. (1979) *Macro models for developing countries*. New York: McGraw-Hill.

Taylor, L. (1983) *Structuralist macroeconomics*. New York: Basic Books.

Taylor, L. (1985a) 'A stagnationist model of economic growth', *Cambridge Journal of Economics*, 9:383–403.

Taylor, L. (1985b) 'Demand composition, income distribution, and growth', Department of Economics, Massachusetts Institute of Technology.

Taylor, L. (1986) 'Stabilization and growth in developing countries: How sensible people stand', Department of Economics, Massachusettsd Institute of Technology.

Taylor, L. (1987) 'Economic openness: Problems to century's end', Department of Economics, Massachusetts Institute of Technology.

Taylor, L. and Bacha, E.L. (1976) 'The unequalizing spiral: A first growth model for Belindia', *Quarterly Journal of Economics*, 90:197–218.

Todaro, M.P. (1969) 'A model of labor .migration and urban unemployment in less developed countries', *American Economic Review*, 59:138–148.

Urata, S. (1986) 'Sources of economic growth and structural change: An international comparison', Department of Economics, Waseda University, Shinjuku, Tokyo.

van Wijnbergen, S. (1983a) 'Interest rate management in LDC's', *Journal of Monetary Economics*, 12:433–452.

van Wijnbergen, S. (1983b) 'Credit policy, inflation and growth in a financially repressed economy', *Journal of Development Economics*, 13:45–65.

World Bank (1983) *World development report*. Washington, DC: World Bank.

Young, A. (1928) 'Increasing returns and economic progress', *Economic Journal*, 38:527–542.

PART 2

STRUCTURAL TRANSFORMATION

INTRODUCTION TO PART 2

HOLLIS CHENERY

Harvard University

Development economics has evolved through the interaction between theoretical inquiry and empirical studies. The principal theoretical approaches have been reviewed in Part 1. Some of them have led directly to models´that have been subject to econometric testing and refinement, but others are more abstract and have not been subjected to quantitative analysis, due in part to lack of appropriate data.

Two areas of interaction – one macro and the other micro – have proven quite fruitful, and have led to continuing programs of research. The first involves the study of changes in economic structure that typically accompany growth during a given period or within a particular set of countries. The central features of what has been termed "structural transformation" are such economywide phenomena as industrialization, agricultural transformation, migration and urbanization. All of these processes involve reciprocal interactions between rising income and changing proportions of demand and supply, and all are affected by macroeconomic and sectoral policies. These topics form the subject matter of Part 2.

The second empirical research program focuses more narrowly on behavior of individuals, households, and institutions as well as the various markets in which they are involved. In this "micro" or "household" approach, prices and markets play a central role and the neo-classical model provides a logical point of departure. Principal themes include human resource development and labor markets, which are treated in Part 3. Alternative ways of combining macro and micro analyses are taken up in Part 4.

The structural research program

Early studies of economic structure assessed the uniformity of shifts in resource allocation with rising income. Notable results include Engel's law of demand [Houthakker (1957)] and the universal reallocation of the labor force from

Handbook of Development Economics, Volume I, Edited by H. Chenery and T.N. Srinivasan
© *Elsevier Science Publishers B.V., 1988*

agriculture to manufacturing and services [Clark (1940)]. The postwar spread of national accounts to developing countries gave an added impetus to this type of research by making it possible to analyze related changes in the composition of demand, production, and factor use in a consistent statistical framework.

Kuznets (1957) achieved a substantial advance in the study of long-term growth by measuring the structural transformation as a whole rather than treating each component separately. This synthesis led to the identification of the uniform patterns of growth in demand, production, trade, and employment that are discussed by Syrquin in Chapter 7. Although they were originally estimated separately from historical data for developed countries and from cross-section data for less developed countries, Kuznets' main findings have proven to be quite robust in the light of more comprehensive econometric analyses.

Kuznets' work gave rise to a broader search for uniform features of develop-ment, which are commonly referred to as the "stylized facts". In an empirically oriented research program, the main function of stylized facts is to guide the choice of theoretical assumptions toward those that are particularly relevant in light of their known historical record. For example, recognition of the quantita-tive significance of international trade and capital flows led to an early shift of theoretical interest from closed to open models of development. To incorporate the effects of trade, it proved necessary to disaggregate tradable goods into several subcategories, a formulation that has set the style of development theorizing for several decades.

The analytical division of the economy into sectors is based on differences in demand and production functions. The most widely used categorization is Kuznets' division of production into agriculture, industry, and services, a variant of the primary–secondary–tertiary scheme of Clark (1940). Similar distinctions are now embedded in the United Nations' standard classifications of data on production and trade, which tend to be perpetuated in comparative studies of economic structure. The lack of comparable guidelines has handicapped research on employment and the size distribution of income, where the stylized facts are a matter of dispute.

Perhaps the most important result of the "structural research program" has been to establish the concept of the overall transformation of the structure of demand, trade, production, and employment as the central feature of develop-ment, in contrast to the steady-state conclusions of earlier "growth theory" for developed economies. How similar the patterns of structural change are across countries or over time have become questions for empirical research.

The next step in the structural research program has been to explore the connections among its main components. The results can be illustrated by contrasting the roles of agriculture and manufacturing in the transformation, which are discussed in Chapters 8 and 9. Along with mining, these two sectors constitute the main sources of foreign-exchange earning or saving and are therefore designated as tradables. In other respects – domestic demand, comparative advantage, technology – they are quite different.

Combining these sectors in a Walrasian framework brings out a more complex form of interdependence than that implied by the earlier concept of "balanced growth". In the early stages of development, agriculture constitutes a very large, but declining, share of production, exports, and employment, while manufacturing is small but usually expanding more rapidly. There is a corresponding movement of labor and capital from agriculture to manufacturing in response to higher returns. There is also a tendency towards accelerated growth in the economy as a whole through this reallocation.

This basic shift in the center of gravity of the economy from primary production to manufacturing – and later to services – is related to other types of structural change, of which the most notable are migration, urbanization, and shifts in comparative advantage. Thus, the term "structural transformation" will be used to describe the set of structural changes that are deemed essential to continued growth. These changes both contribute to and are affected by economic growth.

The chapters in Part 2 illustrate the usefulness of this way of organizing the results of research on development. Part 2 identifies common features of agricultural transformation, industrialization and trade, and migration and urbanization, as well as the nature of their interaction. In Volume II, Part 6 identifies four groups of countries having some common elements of development policy – due to a combination of resource endowments and policy choices – and discusses the relationship between these observed characteristics and the structural transformation. These empirical surveys shed light on the underlying questions of what structural changes are necessary for growth and how different combinations of endowments and policy choices affect the feasible patterns of development.

Balance among sectors

As Taylor and Arida showed in Chapter 6, development economics is largely concerned with the ways in which different sectors of the economy adapt over time to changes in demand, factor supplies, and technology. Correspondingly, its analytical apparatus consists of models designed to capture the differences among sectors that are most important for a particular problem. To evaluate the literature on the structural transformation, we therefore need to examine the rationale for disaggregating consumption, production, and trade.

It is notable that neoclassical economics makes little use of conceptual distinctions among sectors of production, such as agriculture and industry. In an open economy with competitive markets, all tradable goods are highly substitutable and the main sectoral distinction that needs to be made is that between tradables and non-tradables. So long as elasticities of substitution among commodities and factors are high enough to maintain full employment of labor and capital despite shifts in the composition of demand and trade, there is little analytic benefit from further disaggregation. Recent interest in "structural adjustment" arises from the observed limitations to these assumptions.

Development economists usually start by modifying some of the neoclassical assumptions; consequently, sectoral differences in demand or production functions assume greater importance. For example, recognition of "initial conditions", such as the stock of capital or natural resources used in each sector, reduces the feasible range of substitution in a subsequent period. Although changes in comparative advantage may indicate the desirability of a substantial shift from primary exports to light manufacturing, for example, it may take several decades for a given country to achieve this typical feature of the transformation. In such cases of resources with limited mobility, "sectors matter".

The stylized facts of productivity growth show that, early in the structural transformation, the level of labor productivity is relatively low in agriculture in comparison with other sectors but that this gap diminishes over time. The several explanations of this phenomenon, discussed by Timmer in Chapter 8 and Williamson in Chapter 11, require some disaggregation of production and labor markets. As more is learned about the sources of technological change, this too will affect the ways in which the transformation should be modelled.

These examples illustrate the results of efforts to incorporate the results of empirical research at a sectoral level into a broader view of the changing structure of developing economies. Each adds technological or behavioral assumptions to those that are standard in neoclassical models, but at the cost of differentiating among sectors of production. This approach is common to the chapters in Part 2 on agriculture, industry and trade, and urbanization, as well as to those in Part 6. "Dutch disease" and "structural adjustment," which are taken up in Part 5, are two other examples of this trend.

Interdependence of policies

Since its inception, development economics has been more concerned with the policy implications of its results than with the abstract elegance of its theory. Policy recommendations are traditionally formulated on a sectoral basis and labelled as such – agricultural policy, employment policy, trade policy, etc. Nevertheless, as will be shown in Part 4, each of these fields includes a mix of economywide (or macroeconomic) and sector-specific policy instruments.

Recent research has posed a challenge to this type of compartmentalization. Each sector has several roles in the development process, not only as a supplier of domestic demand, but also as a supplier (or user) of foreign exchange, investible resources, and labor. While in principle these complex relations can be formulated in a general equilibrium model (see Volume II, Chapter 18), the use of such models has so far been largely illustrative. Nevertheless, the state of the art in policy analysis has been moving towards recognition of the multiple roles of each sector.

Three variants of this problem are illustrated in the chapters on agriculture, industry and trade, and migration and urbanization contained in Part 2. These chapters start by identifying the principal functions of each sector in the structural transformation. In Chapter 8, Timmer specifies the role of agriculture as supplying the growing demand for foodstuffs, generating savings, earning (or saving) foreign exchange, and providing the main source of employment in the early stages of the transformation. In Chapter 9, Pack identifies the causes of the higher growth of industry, the corresponding shift of economic activities to cities, and the associated changes in comparative advantage. While the roles of industry and agriculture as producers of tradables are quite similar, as users of labor, capital, and natural resources they are very different.

The internal links between industry and agriculture are developed further in Williamson's chapter (Chapter 11) on migration and urbanization, which investigates urban and rural labor markets in a general equilibrium framework. This approach substantially revises the conclusions of partial analysis about the main sources of urban growth and the ways in which it can be influenced by policy. Migration and urbanization emerge as important equilibrating factors in the transformation, which are dependent on economywide variables such as the relative growth of productivity in industry and agriculture as well as the corresponding sectoral movements in wages and profits.

In sum, the concept of a structural transformation links together many of the policy problems of developing countries and suggests the need for a more integrated approach to their solution. This recognition has led to a progression from the broader analysis of interdependence to a reconsideration of the available policy instruments and their potential effects. For example, in the field of trade and industrialization there is a movement away from quotas and investment subsidies to greater reliance on exchange rates and tariffs to influence resource allocation. In urban development, attempts to impose limits on migration have been replaced by policies to redirect it to more productive activities.

Recognizing the interrelations among the principal elements of the structural transformation does not in itself constitute an argument for more government intervention or overall planning. It is only in situations where market forces may not lead to acceptable results – as in population growth, income distribution, or spatial policies – that there is an a priori case for selective intervention. Many of these cases stem from the initial structure of the economy and the technological or institutional limitations to rapid change.

References

Clark, C. (1940) *The conditions of economic progress*. London: Macmillan.

Houthakker, H.S. (1957) 'An international comparison of household expenditure patterns: Commemorating the centenary of Engel's law', *Econometrica*, 25: 532–551.

Kuznets, S. (1957) 'Quantitative aspects of the economic growth of nations: II. Industrial distribution of national product and labor force', *Economic Development and Cultural Change*, 5: supplement.

Kuznets, S. (1966) *Modern economic growth*. New Haven: Yale University Press.

Chapter 7

PATTERNS OF STRUCTURAL CHANGE

MOSHE SYRQUIN*

Bar-Ilan University

Contents

0. Introduction   205
1. The study of structural change   206
    1.1. Structural change in economic history   209
    1.2. Structural change in development economics   211
    1.3. The need for a typology   214
2. Empirical research on the structural transformation   216
    2.1. Bases for comparative analysis   216
    2.2. A unique path of development?   217
    2.3. The methodology of comparative analysis   218
    2.4. Time-series vs. cross-section studies   221
3. Patterns of growth and accumulation   223
    3.1. Growth patterns   223
    3.2. Accumulation   225
4. Changes in sector proportions   228
    4.1. The accounting framework   230
    4.2. Final demand   231
    4.3. Intermediate demand   231
    4.4. Trade   232
    4.5. Structure of production: Broad sectors   235
    4.6. Post-war patterns   239
    4.7. Manufacturing: Disaggregated results   242
5. Structure and growth   243
    5.1. Sectoral contributions to growth   244
    5.2. Typology of development patterns   248

*I am grateful to Hollis Chenery, James Ito-Adler, Howard Pack, T.N. Srinivasan, Lance Taylor, and Adrian Wood for their helpful comments and suggestions, and to Yosi Deutsch for help and advice on the empirical sections.

Handbook of Development Economics, Volume I, Edited by H. Chenery and T.N. Srinivasan
© *Elsevier Science Publishers B.V., 1988*

Contents (continued)

6. Accounting for the transformation   250
    6.1. Growth accounting: Demand side decomposition   250
    6.2. Growth accounting: Supply side   254
    6.3. Resource shifts and productivity growth   255
7. Relative prices and exchange rate conversions   258
    7.1. Relative prices   259
    7.2. Exchange-rate conversions   262
8. Approaches to policy   265
References   268

0. Introduction

Development economics can be characterized as dealing with issues of structure and growth in less developed countries.[1] Analysis of structure appears in two variants. The first, and more recent, is concerned with the functioning of economies, their markets, institutions, mechanisms for allocating resources, income generation and its distribution, etc. This is primarily a micro approach, solidly anchored in economic theory with little emphasis on economic history or long-run processes of structural change. In the second variant, economic development is seen as an interrelated set of long-run processes of structural transformation that accompany growth. The central features of this approach are economy-wide phenomena such as industrialization, urbanization, and agricultural transformation, regarded as elements of what Kuznets identified as "modern economic growth". This is essentially a comparative approach deriving its information from the historical evolution of the advanced economies and from intercountry associations of structural changes and growth.

Most of the early literature on development was "structural" in this sense. More recently, the supply shocks of the 1970s and stabilization programs shifted attention to shorter-run issues. However, even in this framework it is important to regard the long-run tendencies of the economy. This and the following chapters on structural transformation are mostly about such long-run processes.

This chapter deals with the patterns of structural transformation during the transition from a low income, agrarian rural economy to an industrial urban economy with substantially higher per capita income.[2] Section 1 reviews the basic concepts of the empirical research program[3] into the economic structure of developing countries during the transition process, which originated with the monumental work of Simon Kuznets. Section 2 deals with methodological issues of empirical research on structural transformation. A summary of the main stylized facts of development, with emphasis on growth, accumulation and sector proportions, is presented in Sections 3, 4 and 5. Attempts to model and explain the transformation are presented in Section 6. In Section 7 relative prices are considered, and Section 8 deals with the role of the state in facilitating, fostering, or at times hampering, an efficient transformation.

---

[1] Lewis (1984) defines the scope of development economics as dealing "with the structure and behavior of economies where output per head is less than 1980 US$ 2,000" (p. 1).

[2] Issues related to the adequacy of seeing the process of development as a transition (smooth or otherwise) and to the uniqueness of the path are discussed below.

[3] This follows Chenery's (1986a) characterization of the work on structural transformation as a research program.

1. The study of structural change

There are many uses of the concepts of structure and structural change in economics. Some of them have a clear meaning or are made clear by the context, while others are vague or worse.[4] This chapter deals with structural change in development economics and, therefore, employs the concepts and meanings prevalent in the field which, as explained below, differ from the concept in econometrics of the structure of a model. A brief discussion may be useful to clarify the main uses of the terms in this chapter.

The most common use of structure in development and in economic history refers to the relative importance of sectors in the economy in terms of production and factor use. Industrialization is then the central process of structural change. In this sense – structure as the composition of an aggregate – the term is also applied to other aggregates that have some bearing on the process of industrialization such as demand and trade.[5]

Following common use, structure also refers to some ratios derived from technological or behavioral relations. Input–output coefficients are an example of the former and the aggregate saving ratio of the latter. The principal changes in structure emphasized in the development literature are increases in the rates of accumulation (Rostow, Lewis); shifts in the sectoral composition of economic activity (industrialization) focusing initially on the allocation of employment (Fisher, Clark) and later on production and factor use in general (Kuznets, Chenery); and changes in the location of economic activity (urbanization) and other concomitant aspects of industrialization (demographic transition, income distribution).

The interrelated processes of structural change that accompany economic development are jointly referred to as the *structural transformation*.

The accumulation of physical and human capital and shifts in the composition of demand, trade, production, and employment are described [following Chenery (1986a)] as the economic core of the transformation, while the related socio-economic processes are identified as peripheral. It is in this sense that the term structure is used in this chapter. Its scope is restricted to those economic aspects deemed to be relevant for the analysis of growth although the process of modern economic growth is clearly more encompassing. In addition to the elements of transformation mentioned above, for example, it considers changes in institutions by which structural change is achieved. This wider framework is often acknowl-

---

[4] Machlup (1963) is still the best source for the various ways in which the terms have been used and abused in economics.

[5] Kuznets (1959, p. 162) defined structure as "...a relatively coherent framework of interrelated parts, each with a distinctive role but harnessed to a set of common goals".

edged, though seldom represented in empirical work [for notable exceptions see Kuznets (1971) and Adelman and Morris (1967)].[6]

The structure of a model in the econometric sense implies something else. A model is an abstraction, a simplified representation of an economy or of a certain aspect of it. When formally laid out, the postulated relations and the parameters of the equations represent the structure of the model. Clearly, structure in this sense is model-specific, and structural change reflects how general the model is. A better specified, more comprehensive model, captures endogenously what in a narrower model would appear as change in structure. At the risk of belaboring this point, two examples are presented, referring to accumulation and to sector proportions.

(1) Changes in structural parameters may reflect specification errors, or omitted variables. A doubling of the saving ratio may appear as a structural change in a model where the saving relation to income was assumed to be linear or in a model that omitted growth effects on saving. In alternative models the same rise in the saving ratio would be described as a movement along unchanged relations. In this paper, a long-term increase in the saving ratio is *always* regarded as an element of structural transformation.

(2) Changes in sector proportions are implied by a variety of models. In a small open economy producing two tradable goods, capital accumulation leads to a change in the relative weight of the two sectors in an unambiguous predictable way. In development economics, and in this Chapter, such a change in the relative importance of sectors is *defined* as a structural change.

A definition, when clear and used consistently, may or may not be useful but it is pointless to argue about its correctness.

Sections 2 and 3 present empirical results on patterns of structural change. The estimated relations can be interpreted as reduced forms from an underlying structural model. Reduced forms are most useful for studying structural change (as defined in this chapter) when the underlying model is stable, that is, when the structure (in the econometric sense) does not change.

The preceding discussion is also pertinent to the concept of equilibrium.[7] As with the structure of a model, equilibrium can only be defined in relation to a specific model and to the variables included. A position can be both, one of equilibrium for a certain model and one of disequilibrium for a different model.

---

[6] North (1981) gives an interpretation of structural change in economic history as institutional change, but almost completely omits shifts in the structure of production and factor use. The contribution of institutional change to economic growth is the subject of Matthews' presidential address to the Royal Economic Society (1986).

[7] I adopt Machlup's definition of equilibrium as "as constellation of selected interrelated variables so adjusted to one another that no inherent tendency to change prevails in the model which they constitute" [Machlup (1963, p. 54)].

In the cobweb model, for example, a position "will be both an equilibrium or a disequilibrium, depending on the length of time that is taken into account" [Machlup (1963, p. 52)].

The main instance where the issue appears in this chapter is the case of intersectoral differences in factor returns. They are here regarded as evidence of disequilibrium which is to say, a temporary situation "that cannot endure if left alone, that must give rise to further change" [Machlup (1963, p. 67)]. Change takes place in the form of migration for example. Though temporary, the disequilibrium could be of long duration if migration is slow, or if the initial shock that created the disequilibrium (differential productivity growth say) appeared as a recurrent phenomenon. It is always possible to build a wider model; one that considers migration, barriers to mobility, costs of adjustment and so on, for which the existence of gaps in marginal products among sectors would not be incompatible with equilibrium. The solution of the model would include an equilibrium rate of migration, etc.

Wage gaps among sectors could also be the result of an exogenously imposed constraint that prevents their disappearance. It is doubtful whether we want to refer to this situation as disequilibrium, unless we equate equilibrium with a standard of performance.

An obvious reason for studying structural change is that it is at the center of modern economic growth. It is, therefore, an essential ingredient for describing the process and for the construction of any comprehensive theory of development. More important is the hypothesis that growth and structural change are strongly interrelated. Most writers recognize their interdependence, and some emphasize the necessity of structural changes for growth. For Kuznets, "*some* structural changes, not only in economic but also in social institutions and beliefs, are required, without which modern economic growth would be impossible" [Kuznets (1971, p. 348, emphasis in the original)]. Chenery views economic development "as a set of interrelated changes in the structure of an economy that are required for its continued growth" [Chenery (1979, p. xvi)]. The interdependence also appears as a cumulative process: "Sectoral redistribution of output and employment is both a necessary condition and a concomitant of productivity growth" [Abramovitz (1983, p. 85)]; or more guardedly: "Neither structural change nor growth in GDP is an exogenous variable; both result from a complex of interacting causes on the supply side and the demand side" [Matthews, Feinstein and Odling-Smee (1982, p. 250)].

In the absence of a continuous equalization of factor returns across sectors, the reallocation of resources to sectors of higher productivity contributes to growth. In such disequilibrium situations, structural change becomes a potential source of growth if it leads to a fuller or better utilization of resources. The potential gains are likely to be more important for developing countries than for developed ones since the former exhibit more pronounced symptoms of disequilibrium and can achieve faster rates of structural change. In a dynamic context the gains can be far from negligible, accounting for as much as one-third of the measured growth in total factor productivity (see Section 6.3.2).

Much of the interest in the structural transformation derives from its possible implications for development policy. The range of policy analysis in the study of growth and transformation is vast. At the analytic end there are attempts to assess the effects of policies pursued on the observed, historical patterns of structural change. At the prescriptive end the roles assigned to policy have included that of facilitating change by, for example, removing barriers to mobility; coordinating the changes in demand, trade, production, and primary inputs to prevent bottlenecks from arising; and directing and stimulating change which otherwise might be defeated by inadequate or non-existent markets. All these approaches are represented in the policy sections in Chapters 8–11. A general discussion of economic policy and structural change appears in Section 8.

1.1. Structural change in economic history

The following sections present a selective review of the evolution of thought on structural change in economic history and in theories of development. They distinguish between structural change seen as an economy-wide phenomenon interacting with aggregate growth, and partial changes which may well be important elements in the overall framework but are analyzed as isolated phenomena. The most famous instance of the latter is Engel's study of consumption expenditures.

Economic historians have tended to concentrate on specific features, while paying less attention to more general or to economy-wide aspects of transformation. This assertion is based on the authority of a noted economic historian:

> The historians, however, have generally neglected structural change as an historical phenomenon, and, in particular, have usually ignored its role in economic growth. ...The main characteristic of the analyses of economic growth by the historians has been their almost unqualified belief in the prime importance of the industrial sector with its increasing physical capital formation embodying improved technology. Generally, there has been a comparative neglect of other factors, ...and almost complete neglect of structural change as a source of increasing productivity [Hartwell (1973, pp. 389, 391)].

One historical approach that emphasizes structural transformation is the "stages approach"[8] represented in the modern theories of growth and development by Rostow (1960). The central stage – the take-off – features two elements

---

[8] For a review of "stages" theories of growth see Hoselitz (1960).

of discontinuity that, in one way or another, appear in most discussions on structural change.[9] One is the sharp increase (doubling) of the rate of capital accumulation, the other is the concept of the leading sector, with its implied transformation of the productive structure. Although it made a great impact on contemporary theories of development, this approach fell into disrepute after it was severely criticized. Even today writers using the terms "phases" or "stages" invariably make sure to disassociate themselves from the original. The main criticisms focused on the notion of a unique path of development, on the absence of endogenous mechanisms of transition between stages, and on the concept of necessary "prerequisites" for the take-off.

The last point was dealt with by Gerschenkron in the title essay of his 1962 collection and in the postscript. He pointed out that processes of rapid industrialization started, in several European countries, from different levels of economic backwardness, and made the course and character of industrialization depend on the initial degree of such backwardness. The focus is then shifted from the set of prerequisites to a search for ways in which a missing prerequisite was substituted for and to an attempt to link the pattern of substitution with the degree of backwardness. This is illustrated, for example, in Gerschenkron's analysis of the sources of capital supply for industrialization; summarized in his propostion that "the more backward a country's economy [on the eve of its industrialization], the greater was the part played by special institutional factors [banks, the State] designed to increase supply of capital to the nascent industries" [Gerschenkron (1962, p. 354)]. The possibility of a variety of routes to reach a certain target is central to the notion of alternative paths of development. It can be formulated as a testable proposition: the variance of a certain process among countries is expected to be larger the more disaggregated the level of analysis.

A leading sector propagates growth through its "linkages" to other segments of the economy. This term, coined by Hirschman (1958), is at the core of the staples approach[10] derived in the context of the economic history of Canada and other regions of "recent settlement".[11] In this approach, growth and structural change are interpreted in terms of the production characteristics of the dominant natural resource (the staple) being exploited for external markets. The literature on the staple theory of growth contains examples of episodes of fast growth based on the exploitation of natural resources extending over long periods of time that, nevertheless, did not lead to continuous development when structural transfor-

---

[9] The "two theories" of take-off follows the interpretation of Fishlow (1965).

[10] In a later study, Hirschman (1977), generalized the linkage approach to development with special reference to the staples. Leading sectors and cumulative processes are also featured in Myrdal (1957) and Perroux (1955).

[11] See Baldwin (1956), Watkins (1963), and Caves (1965). In the more recent literature, shorter run impact of resource discoveries and price booms are discussed in relation to the Dutch disease [Corden and Neary, (1982), Roemer (1985)]. Stephen Lewis discusses the approach in Chapter 30, Volume II, of this Handbook.

mation (including the social and institutional structure) did not keep apace. Episodes of "growth without development" followed by stagnation are now common in dependency approaches that identify socio-economic structures as the root cause of underdevelopment.

In the staple approach there is surplus to be vented in response to external demand. This key role given to demand in igniting the process, is apparently the common view in economic history. Landes (1969, p. 77) sums up his discussion of demand and supply factors in the industrial revolution in Britain thus: "it was in large measure the pressure of demand on the mode of production that called forth the new techniques in Britain, and the abundant, responsive supply of the factors that made possible their rapid exploitation and diffusion".

1.2. Structural change in development economics

The emphasis on demand, reinforced by Keynesian theory, greatly influenced the early writings on development economics. The dynamic version of the Keynesian model (Harrod–Domar); dual-economy models (Lewis); demand complementarity, balanced growth, and "big-push"; these are among the central concepts of the 1950s. They all feature demand as the centerpiece of analysis and relegate trade to a minor position. In this vintage of development economics we recognize the two components of the economic core of the transformation: accumulation and sectoral composition. Both had policy implications, the former at the aggregate level and the latter, by its nature, at a disaggregated level but in an economy-wide framework. Accelerating and sustaining growth required increasing the rates of accumulation and maintaining sectoral balance to prevent disequilibrium in product markets, or to overcome disequilibrium prevailing in factor markets.

At about the same time neoclassical theory responded to the structuralist challenge posed by the Harrod–Domar model and came out with its own growth theory from the supply side [Solow (1956)]. Its implications were starkly different. In the aggregate version, there is no surplus labor and long-run growth is independent of the saving rate. In multisectoral versions of the von-Neumann type, growth, still independent of the saving rate, proceeds in a balanced fashion and no disequilibrium is allowed. These features may account for the initial limited impact of neoclassical growth theory on development economics. Together with steady-state theory, overboard went prices, incentives and market behavior, until the excesses of the policies pursued and the drastic change in the prices of fuels and other primary commodities in the early 1970s led to the neoclassical resurgence.

I return now to the two main components of the transformation in development economics: accumulation and sectoral composition. In the 1950s accumulation almost invariably referred to physical capital in commodity production and infrastructure. Capital appeared as the critical factor in the Harrod–Domar model. As mentioned above, Rostow (1960) emphasized the sharp increase in the rate of investment during the take-off stage. A doubling in the investment rate was also seen as indispensable by Arthur Lewis: "The central problem in the theory of economic development is to understand the process by which a community which was previously saving and investing 4 or 5 per cent of its national income or less, converts itself into an economy where voluntary saving is running at about 12 to 15 per cent of national income or more" [Lewis (1954, p. 155)].

In Lewis's model the shift of resources to the modern sector increased the profit share in income and thus raised the saving rate. "The central fact of economic development is that the distribution of incomes is altered in favour of the saving class" (p. 156). Two important early developments can be seen as attempts to specify the role of capital. For the closed economy, Mahalanobis (1953) argued that with non-shiftable capital the key planning problem is the allocation of investment between sectors producing consumption and production goods, or how many machines to use in making machines.[12] For the open economy Chenery and his collaborators introduced foreign-exchange require-ments as an additional constraint on growth besides the limitation imposed by savings [Chenery and Bruno (1962), Chenery and Strout (1966)]. These develop-ments were made an integral part of disaggregated dynamic input–output models and of optimizing multisector programming models.[13]

The main message of these studies and of the later emphasis on human resources is that a sustained increase in rates of accumulation, while not suffi-cient, is a necessary requirement for long-run growth and transformation.

Modern analyses of sectoral transformation originated with Fisher (1935, 1939) and Clark (1940), and dealt with sectoral shifts in the composition of the labor force. As in most areas in economics one can find precursors of their ideas in earlier writings.[14] However, they were probably the first to deal with the process of reallocation during the epoch of modern economic growth, and to use the form of sectoral division (primary–secondary–tertiary) which, in one way or another, is still with us today. The specific division into sectors was influenced by the conditions and debates in New Zealand. Its value was questioned in New Zealand[15] in particular and for low income countries in general. The latter primarily by Bauer and Yamey (1951), who argued that in the early stages of

---

[12] A similar model was developed in the mid-1920s by the Soviet economist Feldman. The modern reformulation is due to Domar (1957). See also Taylor (1979).

[13] These models and many more are surveyed in Taylor (1975).

[14] Sir William Petty and Friedrich List among others. See Clark (1940) and Hoselitz (1960).

[15] Fisher's 1939 paper was largely devoted to justifying and clarifying his definition of "tertiary production" first introduced in 1933 and popularized by his 1935 book.

development individuals are engaged in a variety of trades, and it is therefore difficult to assign them to any one occupation. With modern economic growth the size of the market increases and with it the degree of specialization and the differentiation of occupations. The difficulty – an empirical one – diminishes in importance as development proceeds.

Clark's approach was predominantly empirical, but he did relate the observed shifts to differential productivity growth and Engel effects, the two principal elements in subsequent attempts to account for the transformation in the structure of production. Clark and Fisher studied economy-wide phenomena. Hoffmann's (1958) attempt to derive a law of industrialization was similar in approach but restricted to industry only. In the early phases of industrialization, according to Hoffmann, the ratio of consumer goods to producer goods is as high as 4 to 1. The ratio declines steadily during the process and reaches a value of about 1 to 1 or less, in the more advanced stages. As with many such efforts, the main value of Hoffmann's analysis was probably in the careful compilation of historical data and in stimulating discussion.[16]

In addition to the need to increase the rate of capital formation, theories of development of the 1950s stressed sectoral differences. In Lewis's model sectoral differences appear as traditional versus modern sectors, and in Nurkse (1953) and Rosenstein–Rodan (1943, 1961) as a requirement for balanced growth. These approaches shared some views of the functioning of less developed economies: labor surplus in agriculture, low mobility of factors, price-inelastic demands, export pessimism, and a general distrust of the market. These are the hallmarks of what Little (1982) characterizes as the "structuralist view". They found a policy echo in the advocacy of inward-oriented strategies and planning primarily in Latin America and South Asia. Although this is a valid characterization of the prevailing views at the time, it remains necessary to recognize the diversity and evolution of ideas along a continuum.

On the empirical side, studies of long-run transformation are best represented by Kuznets' synthesis of modern economic growth in a series of seminal papers.[17] Kuznets established the stylized facts of structural transformation, but was reluctant to offer a theory of development. He saw his analysis as an essential building block towards such a theory. His approach, however, is quite different from the empiricism of earlier writers. Economic theory guided his choice of concepts and the all-encompassing interpretations that accompanied every statistical finding. His essays on modern economic growth are a compendium of ideas on growth, transformation, distribution, ideology, institutions, and their interrelations. General equilibrium modellers can find in these essays a rich source for

---

[16] For a critical evaluation see Kuznets (1966).

[17] "Quantitative Aspects of the Economic Growth of Nations" (1956–67). More compact statements are the 1966 monograph and the Nobel lecture (1973).

ideas, a guide to specification, and to the long-run relations against which to calibrate their models.

The amount of information assembled by Kuznets was enormous, but he did not use formal statistical techniques in its analysis. This task was later taken up by Chenery (1960). Before that, however, Chenery had contributed to the study of investment criteria in a multisectoral framework in a situation of disequilibrium, and to the development of input–output and programming models. For Chenery, the possibility of disequilibrium and differences among sectors implied the need for coordination to anticipate potential bottlenecks.[18] His 1960 "Patterns of Industrial Growth" fit well in this approach as an attempt to determine the "normal" transformation in the structure of production as income grows. In subsequent studies the "normal" pattern gives way to a standard or expected one devoid of normative connotations: "Probably the most that should be claimed for statistical comparisons of this sort is that they are helpful in diagnosing the structural problems of a given country and in suggesting feasible growth patterns" [Chenery and Syrquin (1975, p. 137)]. The patterns of production structure were initially derived from a general equilibrium system as reduced forms and, in later studies, were integrated with demand and trade in wider models.[19]

In the earlier models of Chenery, prices (accounting, shadow or otherwise) are explicitly considered, some (the exchange rate) playing an important allocative role. In the patterns approach they are silent bystanders. The reasons for not explicitly considering prices and the impact of this on the long-run patterns are discussed below.

1.3. The need for a typology

An additional feature of Chenery's approach, important for the links between growth and change, is the issue of typology. In the 1960 study only income and size were considered as explanatory variables. Shortly thereafter, natural resources were added to the analysis [Chenery (1964)], but they proved difficult to handle within the framework of a unique cross-country regression. The main problem was one of measuring economic resources. The various proxies of *available* resources missed the fact that in practice, the decision to exploit them and the extent to which the strategy of development was made dependent on

---

[18] Because of these contributions and his sojourn in 1957 at the Economic Commission for Latin America, Chenery appears as one of the originators of "structuralism" in Little (1982) and Arndt (1985). To this Chenery demurs, as he sees himself standing in the middle of the continuum rather than at one end of it. See Chenery (1975, 1986a).

[19] The wider approach was first presented in an historical study of Japan [Chenery, Shishido, and Watanabe (1962)] and later in cross-country models of industrialization [Chenery and Watanabe (1965), Taylor (1969), Chenery and Syrquin (1980, 1986a)].

them were policy decisions. In addition, the impact of resources appeared not to be additive to that of income growth.[20] The proposed solution was to determine alternative patterns for types of countries grouped according to characteristics such as size and degree of reliance on natural resources. Chenery and Taylor (1968) adopted a three-way classification: large, small-primary oriented, and small-industry oriented. This scheme was then expanded into a typology of development strategies in Chenery (1973) and Chenery and Syrquin (1975, 1986b).

The use of a typology in the analysis of long-run transformation was also advocated by Ranis (1984). Unlike Chenery, who began with a large sample of countries and then classified them, Ranis started with the historical experience of a single country and then progressively built up the typology by adding additional countries. The two approaches complement each other and some convergence appears to have been achieved [see Ranis (1984)]. One last example of the typology approach in long-run studies is the classification of agricultural paths of transformation in Hayami and Ruttan (1985), discussed by Timmer in Chapter 8 of this Handbook.[21]

Japan, as the one developed country not of European origin, has attracted a great deal of attention. Ohkawa has been a central figure in various collaborative enterprises to explain long-run growth and transformation in Japan, and the lessons to be derived from this experience for other developing economies.[22] Other studies of Japan that influenced research on patterns of structural change were Fei and Ranis (1964) on Japan as a surplus-labor economy and the general equilibrium model of Kelley, Williamson and Cheetham (1972).

A perennial issue in development economics is the relevance of the past (of today's developed economies) for the future (of LDCs). In research on long-run transformation in the Kuznets tradition, this issue, while not absent, is not on center stage. To assess the relevance of historical patterns, they have to be studied first. Some very useful research on long-run structural change refers to developed countries. Examples include Kuznets' work on modern economic growth, the long-run country studies in the SSRC project,[23] the comparative analyses of transformation in Europe by Svennilson (1954) and Kindleberger (1967), and the recent work of Maddison (1982) on phases of capitalist development.

---

[20] Interrelations of income effects and resources could be accounted for by interaction terms, but the simplicity of the original presentation would be lost.

[21] Lance Taylor informs me that Lenin had a similar classification in the form of alternative "roads" of agricultural development.

[22] Ohkawa and Rosovsky (1973); Ohkawa and Ranis (1985).

[23] The project was directed by Abramovitz and Kuznets. Publications have appeared on Japan by Ohkawa and Rosovsky (1973), the United States by Abramovitz and David (1973), France by Carre, Dubois and Malinvaud (1975) and, after a long gestation period, the United Kingdom by Matthews, Feinstein and Odling-Smee (1982).

2. Empirical research on the structural transformation

This section amplifies the discussion of structural change, focusing on the main recurring debates on the concepts and measurement of the transformation.

2.1. *Bases for comparative analysis*

The empirical research program on growth and transformation originating with Kuznets deals with *long-run* processes in a *comparative* framework. The long-run aspect, which would appear to be self-evident in studying development, is much de-emphasized in some recent research with a micro, neoclassical orientation.

Analysis of the comparative experience of nations varying in "size, location and historical heritage" is essential for establishing "common features and patterns" and for identifying "divergences from such patterns" [Kuznets (1959)]. The crucial question is why do we expect to find any uniform patterns? Kuznets addressed this question in various publications. Probably his best and most thorough answer appears in a little-known paper published in the proceedings of a conference on "The Comparative Study of Economic Growth and Structure" [Kuznets (1959)].[24] The rationale for the comparative study of structure and growth "is conditioned on the existence of common, transnational factors, and a mechanism of interaction among nations that will produce some systematic order in the way modern economic growth can be expected to spread around the world" (p. 170).

The principal *transnational* factors, "those potentially common to the world," are three:

(1) The industrial system, that is, the system of production based on the application of the technological potential afforded by modern science. Some of the requirements of the system are some minimum level of literacy, a non-familial, impersonal type of organization, and a high degree of urbanization.

(2) A community of human wants and aspirations. This is illustrated by the relatively weak resistance to the spread of modern technology in reduction in death rates, by the generality of Engel's law, and by the widespread desire for higher standards of economic performance and levels of living.

(3) Organization of the world into nation-states.

The way the transnational factors affect the pattern of growth is conditioned by *national* factors such as size, location, natural resources, and historical heritage. "The consideration of the national elements thus leads directly to an

---

[24] In this section I rely heavily on this paper, including the phrases in quotation marks in the previous paragraph. Chenery (1986a) derives from this study the core of the research program originating with Kuznets.

emphasis on the distinctive structure and on the differences in growth patterns" [Kuznets (1959, p. 166)]. Finally, there are the *international* factors relating to the various channels of interdependence among the different nations. The "complex of international relations can best be viewed, as a mechanism of transmission of the unequal impact of economic growth" (p. 167).

The "crucial point" stressed by Kuznets is that "if there were no substantial transnational factors, there would be no common features of significance in the economic growth of nations and comparative study would be hardly warranted" (p. 170).

The same idea appears in different form in Chenery (1960). *Universal* factors, of which he lists five,[25] lead us to expect uniform patterns of development, while *particular* factors and policy are behind divergences from a common path. In the analysis of development the sources of diversity are no less important than those leading to uniformity.

2.2. A unique path of development?

The presence of transnational (or universal) factors is the basis for expecting uniformities in the growth process. But national (or particular) factors recognized from the outset make clear the inevitability of differences at some level. The comparative approach thus suggests uniformities at a broad (macro) level of analysis or aggregation, but allows for variations at a lower (micro) level. This notion resembles Gerschenkron's (1962) concept of substitutability (among "pre-requisites") expanded to recognize that its nature depends not only on "relative backwardness", but also on other national particular factors.

The possibility of lower-level substitutability can be illustrated by the concept of a transition from an agricultural to an industrial economy. The transition may be likened to "something like a historical likelihood or near-necessity",[26] but one that allows for differences in many dimensions such as, industrial composition, timing or sequencing of changes during the process, and sources of financing of capital accumulation. For example, in resource-rich countries, the shift of resources away from primary production lags behind that in other countries at low income levels. At higher income levels, however, the difference in the degree of industrialization is much reduced. The availability of resources also affects the composition of industrial production. Resource-rich countries tend to emphasize more the capital-intensive branches of industry because of the relatively high

---

[25]"Among the universal factors are: (1) common technological knowledge; (2) similar human wants; (3) access to the same markets for imports and exports; (4) the accumulation of capital as the level of income increase [*sic*]; (5) the increase of skills, broadly defined, as income increases" [Chenery (1960, p. 626)].

[26]Solow (1977, p. 493).

price of labor in comparison to their degree of industrialization. At the other extreme, resource-poor countries have had to search for a substitute for primary exports as a source of foreign exchange. Early development of manufactured exports and a heavier reliance on foreign capital can thus be seen as largely a response to the absence of natural resources.

A different illustration comes from the field of economic history. The English model has sometimes been regarded as the one path for growth and, accordingly, "countries have been described as backward because their coal and iron and cotton production are relatively low".[27] O'Brien and Keyder (1978), however, reject this view. In a study on comparative long-run economic growth in France and Britain they argue that "[e]conomic theory lends no support to assumptions, that there is one definable and optimal path to higher per capita incomes and still less to the implicit notion that this path can be identified with British industrialization as it proceeded from 1780 to 1914" (p. 18). Instead, they argue, "there is more than one way of transition from an agricultural to an industrial economy and from rural to urban society" (p. 196). The notion of a broad transition is not questioned, but the view that the path of transition is unique is challenged.

A central thesis of the research program on transformation, therefore, goes beyond the question of whether or not countries need to industrialize; and focuses on the problem of when and in what manner it will take place.[28]

The presence of the transnational factors that clearly identify the epoch of modern economic growth, is the principal justification for expecting uniformities across countries in long-run patterns of transformation. But nowhere in such comparative analysis is it implied that there is a single unique path through which all economies have to pass.

2.3. The methodology of comparative analysis

It is neither feasible nor desirable to try to capture all the complexity of the transformation in one model. It is, therefore, pointless to search for one best approach for comparative analysis. Often alternative approaches, which are portrayed as competitive (if not mutually exclusive), are best seen as complementary. In this section two salient issues are elucidated: the level of analysis (micro–macro), and the contrast between modeling and description.[29]

---

[27] O'Brien and Keyder (1978, p. 16).

[28] Some advocates of an agriculture-based strategy of development such as Mellor (1986), aware of the natural limits to that strategy, nevertheless recognize that "[e]conomic development is a process by which an economy is transformed from one that is dominantly rural and agricultural to one that is dominantly urban, industrial and service in composition." (p. 67).

[29] Other issues related to the methodology of multisector comparative analysis are examined in Kubo, Robinson and Syrquin (1986).

2.3.1. The level of analysis

The appropriate level of analysis is closely related to the question of the unit of analysis in the study of modern economic growth; is it the individual, an industry, a region, or the nation?[30] In the process of development large numbers of households, firms, and other agents interact within a framework determined largely by the sovereign nation-state. Many long-term decisions that affect economic growth are made for the nation by its agencies of the nation-state. Any analysis dealing with policy aspects has to consider the decision-making units as well as the universe affected by such decisions.[31]

The nation-state can be distinguished from other regional aggregates by the presence of various discontinuities relating to political authority, language, religion, and institutions. These discontinuities are usually reinforced by trade policies.

A further consideration is that modern economic growth is a manifestation of the industrial system. Its inception requires significant social changes and is bound to encounter opposition and resistance. In this context the state is the key decision-maker.

Virtually all of the empirical work on structural change and much of that on development in general, has been conducted at the macro level. Disaggregation, essential for structural analysis, has usually proceeded to industries at a 2, 3 or higher digit level, but not beyond that. As with macroeconomics in developed countries, in the study of development, attempts have been made to provide a firmer micro foundation for macro theory. This has taken two forms. In economy-wide analysis, microtheory has guided the choice of relations and variables ranging from the centrality accorded to Engel effects to elaborate general equilibrium models: in the neoclassical tradition[32] or emphasizing structuralist features.[33]

A second approach deals directly with the behavior of individuals. It is represented in this Handbook by the chapters on human resource development and labor markets in Part 3 and to a large extent by Gersovitz's chapter on savings in this Part. These chapters attest to the progress made in understanding important features of the functioning of economies in less developed countries. However, for the analyses of economy-wide structural change, the micro approach faces a problem of aggregation. At a more aggregate level, results are

---

[30] The issue of the nation as the unit of analysis is addressed in Kuznets (1951, 1966) and Svennilson (1960). See also the discussion by Perkins and Syrquin in Chapter 33, Volume II, of this Handbook.

[31] A significant force at the national level nationalism has been interpreted as a public good explaining the universal drive to industrialize [Johnson (1965)].

[32] Kelley and Williamson (1984), for example.

[33] Taylor et al. (1984), for example.

sensitive to the distribution of micro characteristics among individuals. Few studies worry about the problem at all. When they do address the issue (as Gersovitz does) they mostly reach inconclusive results and yet, the corresponding macro relations are often quite robust. It appears that micro analysis has to be supplemented by macro research. Aggregation is not necessarily bad;[34] some effects can only be determined at a macro level. An example in the present context is the effect of country size on the level and composition of foreign trade, clearly an aggregate, cross-country effect.

2.3.2. Models vs. description

The distinction between a modelling approach and a purely descriptive one is largely a bogus issue. Statistical-descriptive analyses of modern economic growth are usually based on general models even if their structure is not always explicitly presented. Thus, Kuznets (1959) emphasized the need for, at least, a skeleton model that would give us some framework of the field; and Chenery (1960) began with a general model before estimating reduced-form equations.

A variety of approaches is demanded by the complexity of the topic and the paucity of information, in light of our inability to carry out controlled experiments. The historical, statistical, and theoretical work on transformation can be treated as a single research program, all involving some interaction between generalizations from comparative studies and elaborations from theoretical analysis [Chenery (1986a)].

The statistical approach focuses on the search for uniform features of development ("stylized facts") and on the main sources of growth and change. Its sources of information are long historical series from developed countries, shorter time series from developing countries, and cross-country comparisons. As is the case with other partial approaches, this approach is subject to limitations. Markets and prices are seldom studied directly; therefore, the links to policy are indirect. Uniform patterns reveal associations, but cannot determine causality. This is only partially remedied in the analysis of identity-based decompositions of observed changes into their proximate sources, as illustrated in Section 6.

Price endogenous models address some of the deficiencies of statistical analysis, usually focusing on a specific issue within a country. They rely on the historical experience of an economy, but have to do without the variation afforded by the comparative approach across countries. A computable general equilibrium model is better suited to confront issues of causality and to probe beyond "proximate" sources of growth by endogenizing effects regarded as exogenous in the statistical approach. The extent to which additional relations

---

[34] Paraphrasing the title of Grunfeld and Griliches (1960). See also Chapter 8 by Timmer in this Handbook.

can be incorporated into a model is basically limited by the available data. The main contribution of applied general equilibrium models has been the ability to go beyond partial effects to general equilibrium analysis. To date, however, such models have contributed little to unravel the threads between structural change and growth. Computable general equilibrium models are most useful for short- or medium-run studies. For long-term analysis their strength – the ability to model market behavior – becomes a weakness. Long-run transformation involves signifi-cant changes in the nature and working of markets and institutions. In this type of analysis a closer collaboration with the statistical approach has a potentially high pay-off. General equilibrium models can borrow some stylized facts and in return can act as a laboratory for assessing their robustness and their sensitivity to variables downplayed in the statistical approach (prices for example).[35]

2.4. Time-series vs. cross-section studies

Empirical research on the features of modern economic growth started with comparisons of long-term series in developed countries, and then turned to cross-country comparisons of less developed countries for a given year or for short periods. The reason for limiting the time horizon was of course, the absence of long-term records in LDCs. Cross-section relations, it was implied or hoped, were good substitutes for relations within countries over time: "cross-section analysis of national structures at a given point in time...add...an insight into current structural differences, viewed partly as points in the process of growth, caught, as it were, at different stages and phases" [Kuznets (1959, p. 174)].

This view, held by many analysts at the time, now seems unrealistic in its expectation of the congruence between cross-section and time-series patterns. After all, in the same paper, Kuznets stressed the sources of diversity among countries. Moreover, even if one huge dynamic model could perfectly capture the experience of every single country, we would still not expect a perfect fit in a simple relation between structure and level of per capita income. And indeed, Kuznets grew increasingly skeptical of the ability to identify long-term changes (past or future) in cross-section differentials.[36] His reasons were only in part statistical (sample coverage, short-term disturbances, non-linearities). A more fundamental reason was that cross-section analysis does not take into account technological innovations and changes in consumer tastes. Additional reasons for expecting differences between time-series and cross-section relations are the

---

[35] For a recent example of an eclectic approach that combines a variety of models to analyze long-term features of industrialization with a common framework, see Chenery, Robinson and Syrquin (1986).

[36] See, for example, Kuznets (1966, pp. 431–437) and (1971, pp. 182–198).

impact of varying policies, the omission of dynamic effects (besides those mentioned by Kuznets), and changes in the international environment.

For similar reasons, it is also unrealistic to expect identical time-series relations across countries.[37] At best we can expect a high degree of uniformity in the nature of the relations (not in specific coefficients) reflecting the operation of common universal factors; and discrepancies that can be interpreted.[38] Kuznets' skepticism was a case of looking at the half-empty glass. Other studies that compared long-term series of production structure to cross-section results, concluded that the degree of comparability between the two was high [Chenery and Taylor (1968)], especially at the aggregate level. At a more disaggregated industrial classification, results were mixed [Maizels (1963)].

As the time series of developing countries accumulated, the cross-country framework was expanded to include a comparison of short time series for a large number of countries. This allowed examination of the stability of cross-section results, and the estimation of uniform time shifts.

Instead of searching for a unique pattern, attention was turned to the determination of average patterns over time, and to an exploration of the relation between time-series and cross-section patterns.[39] As was the case in studies of saving and production, discrepancies between time-series and cross-section estimates have proved to be fruitful sources of ideas.

An important argument for joint estimation of cross-section and time-series estimates is that it may improve the efficiency of estimation, but this is not the only consideration. Some effects are primarily, if not solely, cross-sectional, either because some variables vary little over time, but differ widely among countries, or because the effect in question depends, in part, on the relative magnitude of a variable among countries. An example of the latter is the well-documented inverse association of country size and trade shares, examined at length by Perkins and Syrquin in Chapter 33 of this Handbook.

In contrasting cross-section and time-series results it is customary to interpret the former as reflecting long-term adjustments, and the latter as short-term or

---

[37] This is precisely what Eckaus (1978) seems to require from such analysis. In his review of the Chenery and Syrquin (1975) study on patterns of development he writes: "What has not been demonstrated is that the hypothesis can be rejected that the coefficients estimated separately from time series data for each country are different. Yet that is the crucial issue, and until it is settled it will require some faith to believe that development patterns common to all developing countries have been discovered" (p. 624). Now, it is true that "it cannot be concluded, with any conclusiveness that there is an *unique* pattern of development for each of the dependent variables" (p. 624, emphasis added) but, as emphasized repeatedly in the text, there is no reason to expect a unique pattern to begin with.

[38] "The discrepancies are, therefore, to be studied – not removed. To put is paradoxically, the value of the cross-section may lie *not* in its capacity to predict correctly the magnitude of changes over time; but rather in its revelation of the discrepancy between its implication and the observed historical change" [Kuznets (1971, p. 198)].

[39] See Chenery and Taylor (1968), Chenery and Syrquin (1975), and Syrquin and Chenery (1986).

partial adjustments to changes in exogenous variables. The cross-section approach was originally intended as a response to the limited data in developing countries. Comparisons of economic structure across countries are now regarded as useful in their own right. This is illustrated in recent studies of patterns of development applied to nineteenth-century Europe [Adelman and Morris (1984), Crafts (1984)].

3. Patterns of growth and accumulation

Empirical regularities accompanying development are commonly referred to as "stylized facts".[40] The term can be applied to the list of features taken by Kuznets to characterize modern economic growth. It is a more modest label than the "historical laws" of the past (Engel, Hoffmann, Sombart, Wagner), but more comprehensive in that they refer to system-wide phenomena. These "facts" are empirical regularities observed "in a sufficient number of cases to call for an explanation that would account for them...independently of whether they fit into the general framework of received theory or not" [Kaldor (1985, pp. 8–9)]

Various authors have published summary lists of the principal stylized facts of growth and transformation.[41] Some characteristics appear in all lists (e.g. the decline in the share of agriculture in output and employment), while others appear to reflect the idiosyncratic tastes of the selector. Some of the uniform features of development have held up quite well when confronted with new data and more countries, and have therefore acquired the status of stylized fact. Other apparent uniformities may not be so universally applicable and are still the subject of debate in the literature. In the presentation below both types are included, although I will try to point out those cases where the patterns are more conjectural than established.

This and the next two sections present a selection of patterns of growth and transformation derived from econometric studies, from multisectoral models within countries, and from a combination of both in the form of an open Leontief model of industrialization based on cross-country information, used to simulate patterns of structural change over the transition.

3.1. Growth patterns

The most obvious characteristic of modern economic growth in developed countries is the high rate of growth of total and per capita product; significantly

[40] The term was apparently coined by Kaldor (1961) in his summary of observations about the growth of industrial economies.
[41] Kuznets (1966, ch. 10; 1973), Perkins (1981), Taylor (1986).

higher than in previous periods. An acceleration of growth in middle-income countries and in the industrial economies, was also observed during the post-World War II period until the early 1970s. This acceleration was partly a response to the disruption of world trade and production in the preceding period and to the destruction of the war, but it also reflected the spread of modern economic growth to transitional countries, better known as semi-industrial countries or newly industrialized countries.

Indirect corroboration of growth acceleration at medium income levels comes from cross-country comparisons of growth over shorter periods of time. In every decade since 1950 middle-income countries have grown faster than the groups of countries with lower or higher income levels [Syrquin (1986a)]. The fast rate of growth of total output in developing countries has followed the even faster rate of manufacturing growth. One implication of growth acceleration in medium-income countries has been a substantial geographical redistribution of world manufacturing production. Between 1950 and 1973 developed countries saw their combined share of manufacturing decline from 72 percent to 56 percent, while the shares of transitional groups were rising by more than 50 percent [Chenery (1977)].

A common view in the 1930s, not totally extinct at the present, regarded the industrialization of primary-producing countries with some alarm. The argument was that the spread of technological advance would narrow the differences in relative costs and thereby eliminate the basis for international trade. Britain and other advanced countries would lose their export markets. This view, which goes back to Torrens, was represented in academic discussions by Keynes and Robertson.[42] The facts were not kind to it. After World War II, world trade in manufactures expanded enormously, largely in the form of intra-industry trade among industrial countries, but also through the significant participation of many semi-industrial economies. The proportion of foreign trade to output also rose significantly during the century preceding World War I. This increase in the share of foreign trade appears as one of the characteristics of modern economic growth in Kuznets' summary [Kuznets (1966, p. 498)].

The process of economic growth can be formally described as the result of the expansion in productive resources and the increase in the efficiency of their use. During the transition (or in the epoch of modern economic growth) the growth of inputs – labor and capital – also accelerates,[43] but the most important element accounting for output growth in developed countries by far, has been the growth of total factor productivity (TFP). However, it would be wrong to deduce from

---

[42] The same argument is sometimes known as Sombart's "law" of the declining importance of international trade. For an evaluation and references see Syrquin (1978). The policy debates are discussed in Maizels (1963).

[43] On the demographic transition, see World Bank (1984); on capital, see below the section on accumulation.

this result that capital accumulation is not an important factor for development. First, studies of productivity growth in developing countries, have shown that factor inputs account for a much higher proportion of growth than in advanced countries. This is due in part to the observation that the share of value added imputed to labor is higher in rich countries than in poor [one of Taylor's (1986) stylized facts]. Other reasons are the role of capital accumulation as a carrier of technological change, and its status as a necessary factor for intersectoral resource shifts. In addition to embodiment effects, a high rate of investment may be required to sustain aggregate demand and prevent idle capacity from arising. These observations point to a limitation of sources-of-growth analysis. The sources considered are (usually) assumed to act independently from each other, usually ignoring links and interactions among them. The missing link in this case, is the relation between measured productivity growth and capital accumulation.

Evidence from micro studies (see Chapter 9 by Pack in this Handbook) suggests another reason for the low measured growth of factor productivity in various developing countries: the resources deployed are used inefficiently relative to both international best practice and the best domestic firms.

The very large contribution of productivity growth to output expansion in developed countries is a relatively recent phenomenon. In most of the countries for which long-term records are available, factor productivity growth accelerated over time to a larger extent than output growth, thereby raising its relative contribution [see Syrquin (1986a) for references].

At the sectoral level most evidence indicates faster TFP growth in the industrial-modern sector than in agriculture. However, the high rate of productivity growth has been pervasive, encompassing all major production sectors. As Kuznets (1966, p. 491) pointed out in relation to the experience in developed countries, even "[i]f the rise in output per unit of input in agriculture was lower than that in industry, it was still so large compared with premodern levels that one can speak of an agricultural as well as of an industrial revolution". Recent studies have also identified strong "country" and "period" effects. Rates of labor and total factor productivity growth tend to be uniformly higher across sectors in countries with good average performance as well as within countries in periods of rapid growth of aggregate productivity. This finding suggests that the overall economic environment, which includes general macroeconomic and trade policies, is an important factor in explaining differences in productivity growth.

3.2. Accumulation

Accumulation refers to the use of resources to increase the productive capacity of an economy. Indicators of accumulation include rates of saving; investment in physical capital, in research and development, and in the development of human resources (health, education); and investment in other public services which augment productivity. This section focuses on aggregate saving and investment patterns. Most of the long-run results reported below apply to both savings and investment, even if their underlying determinants differ.

The importance accorded to rising rates of accumulation in development economics was mentioned before. Even if "capital fundamentalism" no longer enjoys wide currency, the critical role of saving and investment in income growth is still recognized.[44] During the epoch of modern economic growth, and over the transition range, there is a significant rise in the share of saving and investment in GDP.

Kuznets (1961, 1966) analyzed long-term trends in capital formation proportions[45] in ten countries. In most countries he found a significant secular rise in capital formation proportions. The two notable exceptions were the United Kingdom and the United States. In view of the subsequent impact of this finding for the United States on the study of consumption and saving, its exceptional nature is worth emphasizing.[46] Moreover, even in this case, according to Kuznets, a rising proportion would have been found if the records could be extended further back.

In a study on patterns of development in nineteenth century Europe, Crafts (1984) pooled time-series and cross-section data for 17 countries and found a significant income effect for the investment ratio. A dummy variable for Britain improved the fit, indicating Britain's low investment share after accounting for income.

Cross-country studies for the post-World War II period reveal significant income effects for saving and investment, both among countries and over time within countries. Syrquin and Chenery (1986) report estimates of development patterns for samples of over 100 countries during 1950–83.[47] The expected total

---

[44] On "capital fundamentalism" see, for example, Gillis et al. (1983).

[45] Kuznets dealt with four measures of capital formation proportions incorporating the distinctions between gross and net, and between domestic and national. The main findings apply to all four definitions. Gersovitz discusses other issues and problems of measurement.

[46] Gersovitz (in Chapter 10 of this Handbook) reviews studies on the aggregate saving proportion of national income, and finds support for the proposition that aggregate saving is affected by demographic variables and the rate of growth of per capita income, but not by the level of per capita income. This proposition is based on studies by Leff (on the aggregate domestic saving ratio) and by Modigliani (on the private saving ratio). In the present context, the former is more relevant. Leff (1969) argued that the effect of income in cross-section reflects demographic variables correlated with income. The regression results confirmed the importance of the demographic measures, although the coefficient of per capita income remained significant even in their presence. But even if the net effect of income had disappeared, the question about the existence of a long-run relation between the saving ratio and income would still remain.

[47] The study excludes centrally planned economies except Hungary and Yugoslavia. It updates and extends the earlier work of Chenery and Syrquin (1975).

change over the transition[48] derived from the pooled regression, is about 8 percentage points of GDP for the investment share and about 11 percentage points for the saving proportion. This difference between the changes in saving and investment, reflects the tendency for the inflow of foreign capital (measured by the current account deficit) to decline over the transition. A similar secular decline took place in advanced countries [Kuznets (1961)].

The accumulation of data in developing countries now makes it feasible to estimate time-series relations in a large number of countries. Average time-series effects can be obtained in a covariance framework by adding a set of country dummy variables. This assigns to each country its own intercept and yields slopes which are weighted averages of the within-country slopes [see Chenery and Syrquin (1975)]. The average income effects on investment and saving in the time series are positive and significantly larger than the implied effects across countries. That is, whatever the initial shares were, they tended to go up since 1950. The higher short-run propensities are in accord with predictions from theories of saving behavior and are similar to Houthakker's (1965) results for personal saving.

Are these average results representative of the experience in most countries? Simple regressions of the investment share on the log of per capita income were run for 106 countries. The distribution of the income coefficients (ignoring their statistical significance) is as follows: negative slopes were obtained in 20 cases, 7 of them in industrial countries; in 33 countries the slope came out positive but smaller than 0.10, and in the remainder 54 countries the coefficient exceeded $+0.10$.[49] A significant tendency was also found for the slope to decline with per capita income. This suggests a logistic-type pattern with a constant ratio at high income levels, but certainly not in the industrializing stage. Focusing on an alleged constant saving share seems a misplaced goal for developing countries. What we need is better understanding of the underlying sources of an increasing share for which per capita income may be only a proxy.

The previous discussion referred to both saving and investment. They were treated together since they are highly correlated among countries and over time. Feldstein and Horioka (1980) argue that such a correlation is critical in examin-

---

[48] In Chenery and Syrquin (1975) the transition was represented by the income interval $100 to $1000 in 1964 US dollars, based on the observation that about 75 – 80 percent of the transformation takes place within this range. In Syrquin and Chenery (1986) the interval in 1980 US dollars is $300 to $4000. The revised figures account for inflation since 1964, and reflect the observation that exchange rates in developing countries have tended to depreciate relative to the average for industrial economies [see Syrquin (1985) and Wood (1986)]. The figures and tables below refer to a slightly longer interval: $300 to $4500.

[49] This generalized rise in saving and investment proportions refutes Leff's contention (1969, p. 886) that "savings rates have generally not shown an upward trend" according to the time-series data in most countries.

ing the implications of the emergence of a world capital market in the last decades. If national savings go to a common pool from which they then flow to the various national centers according to differentials in return, as a perfect market would require, we should find a low correlation between domestic investment and saving. Even among industrial countries a high correlation was found.

So far the evidence reported referred mostly to current price shares. Changes in the relative price of investment goods are examined in Section 7.1.4 below. The main conclusion there is that the secular rise in the investment share is a real phenomenon and not due to a price effect.

The increase in overall accumulation rates[50] at a faster pace than population or employment, results in changes in factor proportions and in comparative advantage with implications for the sectoral allocation of economic activity.

4. Changes in sector proportions

Changes in the sectoral composition of production are the most prominent feature of structural transformation. Associated with income growth are shifts in demand, trade, and factor use. These interact with the pattern of productivity growth, the availability of natural resources, and government policies, to determine the pace and nature of industrialization. The development of the input–output approach stimulated analysis of individual aspects of transformation in a multisectoral, economy-wide framework. At the same time as Kuznets' work on modern economic growth, but using more formal statistical techniques, a series of cross-country comparative studies were published, mostly by researchers in or around Stanford University. Houthakker (1957) examined the universality of Engel's law, Chenery (1960) established uniform patterns of trade and industrialization, and together with Watanabe [Chenery and Watanabe (1958)] searched for similarities across countries in interindustry relations. These effects were integrated in multisectoral models following the spread of input–output analysis to developing countries. Multisectoral country models were used to analyze the effects of government policy, but usually covered only a small part of the transition range.

As a supplement to studies of individual countries, models were estimated from cross-country data to simulate the full range of the transformation, which typically involves at least a tenfold increase in per capita income. One such cross-country prototype model initially applied to Japan [Chenery, Shishido, and Watanabe (1962)], has proved useful for an integrated presentation of patterns of

---

[50]On the rising investment in human resources see the chapters in Part 3 of this Handbook. Studies with a longer-run focus include World Bank (1980).

structural change [Chenery and Syrquin (1980, 1986a)]. The cross-country model consists of two parts. The first is an open Leontief model in which growth rates of output and population are taken as given. Its solutions are estimates of structural change for a given income range. In the second part, growth of inputs, outputs, and productivity are considered in a multisectoral framework. Although weak on causality and market behavior, the model is a useful complement to direct estimates of patterns of structural change, whether econometric or Kuznets' type comparisons. If the latter are seen as reduced forms, the model presents a set of relations that might underlie the reduced forms. Its main virtue is that it incorporates into one system the various elements of growth and structure, from Engel effects to differential productivity growth. It illustrates in a simple and direct way the general equilibrium nature of the interrelations: changes in any one component imply variations throughout the system.

The stylized facts on sector proportions presented below are ·based on the cross-country model, on long-term comparisons for industrial countries of Kuznets and others, and on econometric estimates for a large number of countries since 1950, all within a common accounting framework.

In the comparisons of long-term historical trends of production structure to more recent information, there is an important data limitation (besides those in Section 2.4) that has to be emphasized, namely, the treatment of quality changes and of new products in particular.

The problem is not just one of aggregation. In addressing the issue, Kuznets found it "frustrating that the available sectoral classifications fail to separate new industries from old, and distinguish those affected by technological innovations" [Kuznets (1971, p. 315)]. This limitation constrains our analysis particularly if, following Kuznets, we identify science-based technological change as the prime mover of modern economic growth. An implication is that "both the true rate of shift in production structure and its connection with the high rate of aggregate growth are grossly underestimated" [Kuznets (1971, p. 315)].[51]

New products do not just substitute for old ones, but they tend to increase the variety of similar goods commonly grouped under the same classification. The income elasticity for variety is larger than one [Jackson (1984)]. The increase in variety of a generic good has various implications. To mention two: (1) The increase in intra-industry trade in manufacturing among industrial countries can be largely explained by product differentiation coupled with economies of scale [Helpman and Krugman (1985)]. (2) Behrman and Deolalikar, in Chapter 14 of this Handbook, point to the heterogeneity in nutrient quality among foods defined as "rice". Since consumers' demand for food variety increases with

---

[51]New commodities are central to the Schumpeterian analysis. They were also emphasized by Young (1928). On the input side, they often appear as embodied technical change.

income, estimated income elasticities derived from aggregate food demand equations overestimate the critical income elasticity for calories (nutrients).

4.1. The accounting framework

The accounting framework specifies a sectoral breakdown of the national income and product accounts in a simple interindustry system. The accounting unit is the productive sector defined in aggregate terms (primary, industry, services) or in the finer distinctions of standard international classifications of production and trade.[52] The elements of sectoral transformation are linked by the following accounting identities. First, total gross domestic product by use:

$$Y = (C + I + G) + (E - M) = D + T, \tag{4.1}$$

where Y is gross domestic product, C is private consumption, G is government consumption, I is gross investment, E is exports, M is imports,[53] D is domestic final demand, and T is net trade.

At the sectoral level we start with the material balance equation of the input–output accounts:

$$X_i = W_i + D_i + T_i, \tag{4.2}$$

where X_i is gross output of sector i, and W_i is intermediate demand for the output of sector i, (D and T are defined above).

Looking at a sector as a producing unit,

$$X_j = U_j + V_j, \tag{4.3}$$

$$V_j = v_j X_j, \tag{4.4}$$

where U_j is intermediate purchases by sector j, V_j is value added in sector j, and v_j is the value-added ratio in sector j.

Adding up GDP by source,

$$V = \sum V_j = Y. \tag{4.5}$$

Patterns of industrialization are chiefly concerned with changes in the distribution of the sectoral V_j's. It is clear from eqs. (4.2) and (4.3) that industrialization

---

[52] Sectors may be distinguished according to various criteria. The issue has recently been addressed in Taylor (1986) and Syrquin (1986b).

[53] All imports are treated as competitive. For alternative approaches see Kubo, Robinson and Syrquin (1986).

has to be analyzed in conjunction with changes in the structures of demand (final and intermediate) and trade. Since the stylized facts of the allocational aspect of the transformation have appeared in various places in the literature,[54] in this section only a brief account of the principal features will be presented.

4.2. Final demand

Among the most uniform changes in demand affecting industrialization, are the decline in the share of food in consumption and the rise in the share of resources allocated to investment. Thirty years ago Houthakker (1957) highlighted the universality of Engel's law in commemorating the centenary of the law, which additional cross-section and time-series studies have continued to confirm. At low income levels, food consumption accounts for as much as 40 percent of GDP and total private consumption for about 75 percent. Over the whole transition both shares decline; food consumption by more than 20 percentage points (of GDP) and total consumption by somewhat less. The rise in the shares of non-food consumption and investment imply a shift in demand away from agricultural goods and to industrial commodities and nontradables.

4.3. Intermediate demand

The largest element in the material balance equations (4.2), is the use of intermediate products, which in the aggregate accounts for over 40 percent of total gross output in most countries. Analysis of the evolution of interindustry relations has not received as much attention as other aspects of the transformation. This is surprising since, almost three decades ago, Chenery and Watanabe (1958), demonstrated the feasibility and the value of a comparative analysis of production structures. Chenery and Watanabe compared input–output tables of Italy, Japan, Norway, and the United States for years around 1950 and searched for similarities in patterns of interdependence among sectors. A recent study [Deutsch and Syrquin (1986)] generalized the approach and applied it to a much larger sample (83 tables from 30 countries). In addition to similarities in interindustry relations, the study also found some systematic changes associated with the level of development.

During the process of development, the total use of intermediates relative to total gross output, tends to rise, while varying its composition. The relative use of primary products as intermediates declines, while the uses of intermediates from heavy industry and services go up. Most of the overall rise in intermediate use is

---

[54] Kuznets (1966), Chenery and Syrquin (1975), Syrquin and Chenery (1986).

not due to changes in the composition of output but rather to increases in the density of the input–output matrices. These trends reflect the evolution to a more complex system with a higher degree of fabrication, and the shift from handicrafts to factory production.[55] The latter can also be observed in the change in the distribution of firms by size. The increase in the use of intermediate services is indicative of the dependence of industrial growth on a parallel expansion of modern services. This relation provides an additional explanation to those based on income elasticities, government expansion, and productivity growth, for the rising shares of services in employment and output.

The preceding results referred to the use of a sector's output as an intermediate input (a row measure). Looking at total intermediate purchases by a sector (a column measure) a systematic trend has been observed in agriculture. The share of intermediate inputs in the total value of output increases significantly with the level of income. Technical change in the sector and a rising relative price of labor, induce a more mechanized structure of production and a more intensive use of inputs from outside the sector – fuels, fertilizers and capital goods. During the course of the transformation the value-added ratio in agriculture (the counterpart of the ratio of intermediates purchased to gross output) typically goes down from close to 80 percent to less than 55 percent of the value of output [Chenery and Syrquin (1986a). See also Chapter 8 by Timmer in this Handbook.].

4.4. Trade

In a relatively closed economy the structure of production has to conform closely to the structure of demand, as stressed in the balanced-growth approach of the 1950s. In the open economy we also have to consider the level and composition of international trade. The extent of a country's participation in the international economy is only weakly related to the level of development across countries, in spite of the fact that over time the association has clearly been positive except for the period between the two wars. The principal determinant of the share of trade in income across countries is the size of the economy.[56] This relation, among the more robust of the empirical regularities in comparative analysis, cannot be found in traditional trade models. Furthermore, it is probably inconsistent with such models [Deardorff (1984)].

In small countries the shares of trade and capital inflows in GDP are relatively high, domestic markets relatively small, and the production structure, therefore, tends to be more specialized than in larger countries. The commodity composi-

---

[55] The trends also reflect substitution effects due to changes in relative prices. Unfortunately, there is almost no information on price structures by sector among countries to be able to make some general statements on substitution effects, let alone quantify them.

[56] Size is usually represented by population. For other measures and a general discussion of the effects of size, see Chapter 33, Volume II, by Perkins and Syrquin in this Handbook.

tion of trade and the type of specialization are largely determined by the availability of natural resources, by traditional factor proportions, and by policy. In practice, the evolution of comparative advantage and commercial policies have combined to create an export pattern that reinforces the shift from primary goods to industry, implicit in the pattern of domestic demand. The strength and timing of the reorientation of exports have not been the same across countries; small countries lacking a broad base of natural resources, had to develop manufactured exports at an earlier stage than resource-rich countries, where specialization in primary exports persists to a much later stage of development. Large countries have shifted away from the specialization in primary products through import substitution. These countries have been prone to adopt inward-oriented policies, which appear more feasible for them than for small countries.

Because of the diversity in trade patterns, it has proven useful to subdivide countries into more homogeneous categories, and to estimate separate patterns for each group. A two-way classification (further discussed in Section 5.2 below) based on population size and the relative specialization in primary or manufactured exports, yields four types: large-primary oriented (LP), large-manufactured oriented (LM), small-primary (SP), and small-manufacturing (SM). The diversity of trade levels and specialization is illustrated in Figure 7.1, which shows the average export patterns of the groups, including the predicted pattern for the combined sample. Large countries (those with populations of more than 15 million in 1970) are shown as a single group since – with few exceptions – they are considerably less specialized than small ones.

The large-country pattern has less than half the share of exports of the pooled regression, and the shift from primary to manufactured exports takes place at a lower income level. Among small countries, in the SM group manufactured exports overtake primary exports quite early in the transition. The typical SP economy, on the other hand, maintains a strong comparative advantage in primary exports throughout the transformation.

Natural resources and size influence the timing of the shift from primary to manufactured exports and the commodity composition of trade in manufactures. The expectation of the shift itself is based on predictions from trade theories as to the likely evolution of comparative advantage. The more rapid growth of all types of capital, relative to natural resources and unskilled labor, facilitates the development of manufactured exports and the replacement of manufactured imports by domestic production.[57] The shift is also supported by Linder's (1961) theory of representative demand, according to which comparative advantage is acquired through production for domestic markets. An increase in the relative importance of manufactures in total exports took place in the historical experience of the industrial countries [Maizels (1963)].

---

[57]Strictly speaking, the change in factor proportions has to be compared with the one taking place in trading partners.

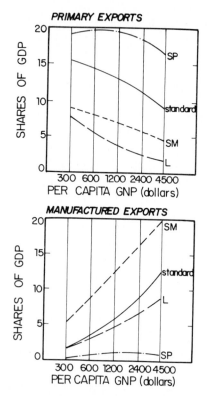

Figure 7.1. Trade patterns for three groups of countries. *Key*: L = large country pattern; SM = small, manufacturing-oriented country pattern; SP = small, primary-oriented country pattern. *Source:* Chenery and Syrquin (1986a).

Changes in the commodity composition of trade within manufacturing have also resulted in some regularities over time and across countries although it is important to stress the differences in the international environment. Today, industrialization takes place in the presence of countries already industrialized. The reliance on industrial imports in today's developing countries cannot help but differ from that in Britain and other industrial countries in the past. Still, some broad generalizations are possible.

Low income countries depend heavily on industrial imports. The common experience has been an early substitution of imports in light industry[58] in most countries. Large countries have then proceeded to institute import substitution in heavy industry and machinery to a greater extent than small countries.

---

[58] The classification of industries into light and heavy is partly arbitrary and follows conventional usage. The division in this Chapter is as in Chenery, Robinson and Syrquin (1986), and is based on the 1958 ISIC classification. Light industry includes food (20–22) and consumer goods (23–29, 39). Heavy industry includes producer goods (30–35) and machinery (36–38).

When a country begins to export manufactures these usually come from light industry, except for simple processed products based on natural resources (metals). At a later stage (often much later) exports of heavy industry become feasible, and then tend to rapidly increase their share in industrial exports. Japan is the best example of this pattern. In resource-poor countries (the SM pattern) light industry exports become important at an early stage. In resource-rich economies (the SP pattern) the need to develop manufactured exports is less apparent. When the shift to manufactured exports takes place at higher income levels, wages are relatively high and often preclude the fast growth of light industry exports. The preceding discussion was based on the premise that light and heavy industries differ in their factor intensities; there is some evidence that this is the case. Heavy industries on the whole tend to be more capital and skill intensive, enjoy faster productivity growth, and are more prone to exhibit increasing returns to scale [ECE (1977), Balassa (1979)].

The changing pattern of comparative advantage in the process of economic development was the subject of a study by Balassa (1979). Comparative advantage was defined in terms of relative export performance. By analyzing export performance in 30 countries; the factor intensity of 184 product categories, and such country characteristics as physical and human capital endowments, Balassa (1979, p. 141) showed that

> inter-country differences in the structure of exports are in large part explained by differences in physical and human capital endowments. The results lend support to the 'stages' approach to comparative advantage, according to which the structure of exports changes with the accumulation of physical and human capital. [See also Leamer (1984).]

Among industrial countries, trade in manufactures increased very rapidly in the postwar period. Simple factor-proportions theories cannot account for the high and increasing share of intra-industry trade during the period. Newer approaches emphasizing economies of scale and product differentiation have been developed for this task [Helpman and Krugman (1985)]. These approaches should prove useful for developing countries but, as shown by Balassa's study mentioned above, conventional explanations still go a long way in accounting for the evolution of comparative advantage in development. [Trade patterns in developing countries during the 1970s are examined in McCarthy, Taylor and Talati (1987).]

4.5. Structure of production: Broad sectors

The change in the commodity composition of trade reinforces the changes in final and intermediate demands to produce a more pronounced shift in production from primary activities to manufacturing and services. This shift is the centerpiece of the transformation and has been validated in the long-term experience in the industrial countries, and in virtually all countries in the postwar period.

Before proceeding to a more detailed analysis, I shall give an overview of the transformation in the production of commodities and how the various elements in eqs. (4.2) and (4.4) fit together. To focus on structural change, eqs. (4.2) and (4.4) are combined and each element is expressed as a share of GDP $(= V)$:

$$V_i/V = v_i(W_i/V + D_i/V + T_i/V).$$
(4.6)

Changes in sectoral shares in value added can be related to changes in the composition of demand (intermediate and final), changes in the composition of trade, and changes in the value-added coefficient:

$$\Delta(V_i/V) = \bar{v}_i[\Delta(W_i/V) + \Delta(D_i/V) + \Delta(T_i/V)] + (\overline{V_i/V})\Delta v_i/v_i$$
(4.7)

(a bar over a variable means that its value is set at the mean of the initial and terminal levels).

Both sides of eq. (4.7) are independently calculated for the whole transition range ($300 to $4000 in 1980 US$). The various components are derived from econometric estimates of cross-country patterns for the period 1950–83 [W and v from Deutsch and Syrquin (1986); all others from Syrquin and Chenery (1986)]. Table 7.1 shows predicted values at the end points, for the variables most relevant for computing eq. (4.7). In the computations I assume, as an approximation, that food consumption generates demands from the primary sector only, and that manufacturing supplies one-half of non-food consumption and investment (the other half represents construction and other non-tradables). With this assumption I can now present a concise summary of the dimensions of the transformation and a first approximation of its main determinants.

Over the course of the transition there is a significant shift in value-added from primary production to manufacturing and nontradables. The average patterns in Table 7.1 show a close correspondence between the directly estimated shift (the last row) and the one calculated by the right-hand side of eq. (4.7). Changes in domestic demand (Engel effects) directly account for less than one half of the change in structure, and changes in net trade for about 10 percent on the average.[59] The contribution of intermediates has two components. First, there is a significant increase in the demand for manufacturing products to be used as intermediates, and a decline in the relative use of intermediate inputs from the primary sectors. The second component refers to variations in the ratio of value-added to gross output in a sector. In agriculture this ratio tends to decline

---

[59] The decline in food consumption as a share of GDP equals 0.20. The assumption in the text is that the primary gross output falls by the same amount. Multiplying this value by the mean value-added ratio (0.71), yields 0.14 which is less than half of the total implied change in the primary share in GDP (0.30). The other results in the text are calculated in a similar way.

Table 7.1
Accounting for the transformation: A first approximation

	Predicted shares of GDP at			Contribution to change in share of:	
	$300	$4000	Change	Primary	Manufacturing
A. *Final demand*					
Food consumption	39	19	−20	−20	
Non-food consumption	34	42	8 ⎫ 1/2		8
Investment	18	26	8 ⎭		
B. *Intermediate demand*					
Primary	23	17	−6	−6	
Manufacturing	25	43	18		18
C. *Trade*					
Primary: exports	14	11	−3		
imports	6	8	2		
net trade	8	3	−5	−5	
Manuf.: exports	1	9	8		
imports	12	15	3		
net trade	−11	−6	5		5
Changes in gross output $\Delta(X_i/V)$				−31	31

D. *Value-added ratios*			Δv_i	Mean v_i	$\Delta v_i/v_i$
Primary	0.81	0.61	−0.20	0.71	−0.28
Manufacturing	0.33	0.36	0.03	0.35	0.09

Output				Mean V_i/V	
Primary	44	16	−28	0.30	
Manufacturing	12	24	12	0.18	

Implied changes in shares $= \bar{v}_i\Delta(X_i/V)$				−22	11
$+ (\overline{V_i/V}) \Delta v_i/v$				−8	2
				−30	13
Directly estimated change				−28	12

Source: Syrquin and Chenery (1986).

with the rise in income, or equivalently, the use of purchased intermediate inputs per unit of output tends to increase. As shown in the table, this factor accounts for about one-fourth of the decline in the share of primary production in total GDP. In an input–output model, the variation in intermediate uses can be further attributed to changes in final demand, trade and input–output coefficients. Such a decomposition is presented below in Section 6.1.

For a more complete picture of long-term changes in the structures of production and factor use, I now draw on the results from the cross-country model in Chenery and Syrquin (1986a). Changes in the composition of value added, labor, and capital that are generated by the model are shown in Figure 7.2. Although the same basic pattern can be detected in each, it is exaggerated in

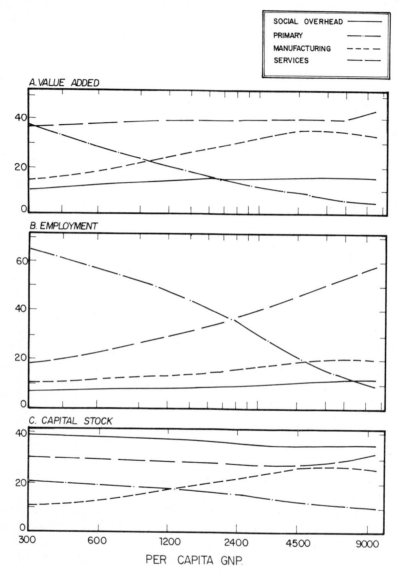

Figure 7.2. Simulation of value-added, employment, and capital (shares). *Source*: Chenery and Syrquin (1986a).

the case of employment and minimized in the case of capital. These differences are due to variations in rates of productivity growth and in factor proportions among sectors. The typical employment pattern reflects the lag in the movement of workers out of agriculture and the correspondingly lower growth in labor productivity in this sector during most of the transformation. The rise of employment in industry is much smaller than the decline in agriculture, and consequently most of the shift is from agriculture to services.

The pattern of capital use shows a much higher proportion in social overhead, which is larger than primary production and manufacturing combined. Because this difference in capital intensity persists at all income levels, the shift from primary production to manufacturing appears less pronounced. A more detailed breakdown would show a corresponding shift from infrastructure supporting primary production to infrastructure supporting industry.

Figure 7.2 illustrates the shift from primary activities to manufacturing during the transition. The figure also portrays the decline in the share of manufacturing in output and factor use at higher income levels. Such a decline has taken place in the last 20 years in virtually all industrial countries, and has become known as de-industrialization.

The cross-country relations on which the factor use patterns are based, are more erratic and less well documented than those for demand and output. Also, the country information available for analyzing those relations is scarcer and less reliable. The results, therefore, are mostly illustrative, and only broad trends and orders of magnitude are emphasized. Similar caveats appear in Kuznets (1966) particularly for the data on capital (reproducible wealth). The patterns in Figure 7.2 present a picture similar to the long-term patterns in advanced countries as described by Kuznets (1966, 1971), and to the estimated patterns for nineteenth-century Europe of Adelman and Morris (1984) and Crafts (1984).

4.6. Post-war patterns

With the accumulation of data in developing countries it has now become feasible to analyze individual time series for a large number of countries. To what extent have the post-war experiences been similar to the long-term patterns? To address this question, simple regressions for the structures of output and employment were estimated in about 100 countries with data for parts or whole of the period 1950–83. The equation estimated was:

$$x = a + b \ln y, \tag{4.8}$$

where x stands for a share in GDP or employment and y for per capita income. Output shares were defined in current and in constant prices. The estimates of b are measures of structural change with respect to income per capita, but not necessarily with respect to time, save for the case of a constant growth rate of per

Table 7.2
Time series relations averaged by income groups

Variable and sector	Low income	Lower middle income	Upper middle income	Industrial market economies
Value-added				
Current price shares				
No. of countries	28	30	21	18
Agriculture	−0.24	−0.17	−0.12	−0.09
No. with *b* > 0	3	4	0	0
Manufacturing	0.06	0.05	0.03	−0.05
No. with *b* < 0	6	5	7	13
Constant price shares				
No. of countries	18	27	16	16
Agriculture	−0.19	−0.14	−0.11	−0.05
No. with *b* > 0	2	4	0	1
Manufacturing	0.07	0.04	0.06	−0.03
No. with *b* < 0	3	4	1	6
Employment				
No. of countries	28	31	20	19
Agriculture	−0.10	−0.20	−0.22	−0.18
No. with *b* > 0	6	2	0	0
Industry	0.05	0.07	0.08	0.01
No. with *b* < 0	5	4	2	9

Source: Syrquin (1986b).

capita income. The results, summarized in Table 7.2, are presented as unweighted averages of the individual income slopes for groups of countries ranked by level of development.[60]

The most striking result is the almost universal inverse association of income and the share of agriculture in income and employment. Of the 97 countries for which adequate time series were available, the income coefficients for the share in value-added at current prices come out positive in only seven cases. In three of them (Liberia, Nicaragua, and Zambia), the estimated coefficient did not differ significantly from zero. In another three (Niger, Senegal, and Somalia), per capita income *fell* during the period; hence the positive coefficient signifies that the share of agriculture diminished in spite of the decline in income. The seventh, Burma, is the only true exception to this general phenomenon.

The average income slopes of the share of manufacturing at current prices is positive in developing countries, but diminishes with the level of income. There are many more exceptions in this case than was true with agriculture. In almost one-third of the cases recorded, the estimated slope is negative. It is instructive to identify the main cases with negative income elasticities. Among the very low

[60] The estimates by country are given in Syrquin (1986b). This section is based on that paper.

income countries we find some with negative growth (Niger, Somalia). In oil-exporting countries (Algeria, Congo, Egypt, Iraq, Iran, Libya, and Saudi Arabia), the decline in industry is the result of the oil boom – Dutch disease. In a third group there was a fall in the manufacturing share, but from extremely high initial values (Hungary, Israel, Yugoslavia). Finally, as mentioned above, in virtually every industrial country there was evidence of de-industrialization at some point during the period. For the period as a whole, negative slopes were estimated in 13 of the 18 countries defined as industrial and with the required data.

The decline in the share of employment in agriculture follows the decline in value-added but with a lag. Since initially the share of employment exceeds the share in output, labor productivity in agriculture declines. In the upper-middle income group, relative labor productivity in agriculture often improves. It is interesting to note the large size of the income slope of agriculture employment in industrial countries.

Comparing the results for value-added in current and constant prices we find that, in almost every case the prices of agriculture and manufacturing relative to the price of total GDP, declined in the period. At constant prices, the decline in agriculture's share was smaller and the increase in manufacturing larger than was true of the current price shares. Offsetting these changes in relative prices were the relative increases in the prices of mining and non-tradables. A significant part of the shift in industrial countries, from tradables to services, was, therefore, a price effect. The results in Table 7.2 suggest that the association of growth with a reallocation of economic activity away from agriculture is among the most robust of the stylized facts of development.

The post-war decline in the share of agriculture in the labor force has been as pronounced as the similar decline that took place in the historical experience of today's advanced countries. But, it is sometimes argued, today's migrating workers mostly go into services and not into manufacturing. The figures in Table 7.2 confirm that only between one-third and one-half of the decline in agriculture's share was taken up by industry (which includes mining, construction, and public utilities). Has this pattern really been that different from the experience of the industrial countries? Thanks to the efforts of Maddison (1980), we have information on the sectoral composition of employment in sixteen advanced countries at two distant dates: 1870 and 1950. The averages of the income slopes between the two points are − 0.27 for agriculture and 0.09 for industry. These values indicate a faster rate of transformation with respect to income (not necessarily per unit of time, since the growth rate of income per capita was much lower). The income slope for industry is slightly higher than the ones in Table 7.2 for middle income countries. As a proportion of the corresponding slope for agriculture it does not differ at all. Almost 30 years ago, Kuznets' analysis of long-term trends in the industrial distribution of the labor force led him to a similar conclusion: "In fact, in most countries the substantial decline in the share of the *A* sector is compensated by a substantial rise in the share of the *S* sector – not by a rise in the share of the *M* sector" (1957, p. 32).

Cross-country patterns are not always a reliable guide to variation over time. In the case of employment structure, however, the correspondence between the two has, on the average, been quite high.

4.7. Manufacturing: Disaggregated results

During the process of industrialization the composition of the manufacturing sector changes considerably. At a more disaggregated level, country-specific features and policies become more prominent in determining the pattern of specialization. Nevertheless, a high degree of uniformity still remains among countries and over long periods of time. Most disaggregated analyses have been done at the two-digit level of the international standard industrial classification (ISIC), and have usually included an attempt to group sectors into homogeneous categories, differing either in the demand for their products, their technology, or in their dynamism. Examples are Hoffmann's (1958) division into consumer and producer goods, and Chenery and Taylor (1968) grouping into early, middle, and late branches. This latter is done according to the stage at which they make their main contribution to the rise of industry.[61]

Table 7.3 shows the predicted change in the structure of manufacturing, derived from regression analysis of the pooled time series since 1950.[62] As income rises, the composition of manufacturing shifts from light to heavy industry. The early increase in light industry is generally the result of the expansion of domestic demand, and the opportunities for import substitution which are exhausted at an early stage. Heavy industry is composed of goods purchased by other sectors as intermediates or capital goods, and durable consumer goods with high income elasticities of demand.

Some indication on the changes in intermediate demands for the products of the two aggregate groups can be found in Deutsch and Syrquin (1986). In Table 7.1 it was reported that the increase in the ratio of manufacturing intermediates to GDP over the transition equals 18 percentage points. Of these, only 3 points originate in light industry, while the other 15 points come from heavy industry. A more detailed analysis of the sources of change appears below in Section 6.1.

In advanced countries, the long-term change in the structure of the industrial sector was generally in the same direction as the one found in cross-country

---

[61] Disaggregated industrial patterns also appear in Chenery (1960), Kuznets (1966, 1971), Maizels (1963), and UNIDO (1979, 1983).

[62] Based on Syrquin and Chenery (1986), where the early–middle–late classification is also presented. In this study we relied in part on an unpublished study by Prakash and Robinson (1979).

Table 7.3
Structure of manufacturing (percent)

Sector	ISIC code	Income per capita (1980 US $)		
		300	1000	4000
Food, beverages, tobacco	31	35	25	17
Textiles, clothing	32	22	18	13
Wood and products	33	3	3	4
Paper and printing	34	3	4	7
Other		1	1	2
Light industry		64	51	43
Chemicals and rubber	35	20	19	17
Non-metallic minerals	36	4	6	5
Basic metals	37	4	7	8
Metal products, machinery	38	8	17	27
Heavy industry		36	49	57
Share of manufacturing in GDP		12	19	24

Source: Syrquin and Chenery (1986).

comparisons in recent times. The most significant difference refers to chemicals, whose share in total manufacturing shows little association with income across countries, whereas in long time series it was the fastest growing component [Maizels (1963)]. The difference is largely due to the very heterogeneous make up of the sector. The relatively large share of chemicals observed in today's developing countries consists largely of "simply processed goods, such as soap, candles, matches and paint" [Maizels (1963, p. 53)].

5. Structure and growth

To this point the analysis of the transformation has been in static terms. The simulations of the cross-country model, on which the patterns in Figure 7.2 are based, can be seen as elements of a comparative-statics analysis. The next section is based on a dynamic extension of the cross-country model, designed to simulate typical changes in productivity growth and the effects of alternative patterns of specialization.

The static model is solved for various income benchmarks going from $300 to $4500 (in 1980 US$). In the dynamic version for each income interval (between adjacent benchmarks), the implied aggregate rate of growth is derived from the income-related investment rate and the incremental capital–output ratio. The latter is aggregated from the income-related sectoral capital–output ratios, with output weights obtained from the static solutions. Sectoral growth rates are then

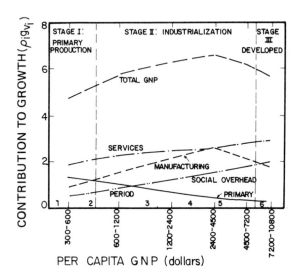

Figure 7.3. Sectoral sources of growth. *Source*: Chenery and Syrquin (1986a).

derived by combining outputs at various income levels with the aggregate growth rate [see Chenery and Syrquin (1986a), and Syrquin (1986a) for further details].

5.1. Sectoral contributions to growth

During the transformation, growth proceeds at an uneven rate from sector to sector. The relation between aggregate and sectoral growth can be derived by differentiating with respect to time the definition of total output, $V = \Sigma V_i$, and expressing the result in growth terms:

$$g_V = \sum \rho_i g_{Vi}, \tag{5.1}$$

where g_{Vi} and g_V are the growth rates of V_i and V, respectively, and the weights are sectoral output shares, $\rho_i = V_i/V$. The results of computing eq. (5.1) for the whole range of the transformation, are summarized in Figure 7.3. It shows the contribution of each of the major sectors to aggregate growth.[63]

The acceleration of growth until late in the transition is related to the rise in the rate of investment and to the acceleration of factor productivity growth. As

---

[63] The figure plots data for each period at the income level of the terminal years. This and the following section are based on Chenery and Syrquin (1986a).

shown below, the latter reflects the reallocation of resources to sectors with higher productivity.

Figure 7.3 can be regarded as the dynamic version of Figure 7.2(A). The contribution of each sector to growth is measured by its average share of total GDP, ρ_i, weighted by its growth rate, g_{V_i}. If all growth rates were identical in a given period, the relative contribution of each sector to aggregate growth would merely equal its share of GDP. The contribution of a rapidly growing sector, such as manufacturing in the early periods, is greater than its static share, whereas that of primary production is less.

In using these results for country comparisons, a further distinction should be made between outputs that are tradable, i.e. primary products and manufactures, and those that are essentially non-tradables such as social overhead and most services. Since imports and exports increase the range of choice of resource allocation, differences among countries are concentrated in the tradable sectors and in the non-tradables related to them.

Figure 7.3 distinguishes three stages of transformation: (1) primary production; (2) industrialization; and (3) the developed economy. Because there are no significant discontinuities in the processes that lead from one to the next, the dividing lines between them are somewhat arbitrary.[64] The extent to which different trade patterns influence this sequence is considered after summarizing the principal features of each stage. In the discussion I also refer to typical shifts in the sources of growth presented more extensively in Section 6.1.

Stage 1: Primary production. The first stage of the transformation is identified by the predominance of primary activities – principally agriculture – as the main source of the increasing output of tradable goods. Even though primary production typically grows more slowly than manufacturing, this difference is more than offset at low income levels by the limited demand for manufactured goods. The large weight of agriculture in value-added is also one of the main reasons for slower overall growth during this stage.

On the supply side, Stage 1 is characterized by low to moderate rates of capital accumulation, accelerating growth of the labor force, and very low growth in total factor productivity. As shown below, it is the absence of productivity growth more than low investment rates that causes the lower aggregate rates of growth in Stage 1. Although comprehensive studies of productivity growth in poor countries are few, this conclusion is consistent with the evidence cited in Chenery (1986b).

Stage 2: Industrialization. The second stage of the transformation is characterized by the shift of the center of gravity of the economy away from primary production and toward manufacturing. The main indicator of this shift is the

---

[64] The criteria used to distinguish the semi-industrial economies (Stage II) are discussed in Chenery and Syrquin (1986b).

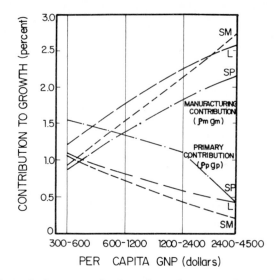

Figure 7.4. Sectoral contributions to growth: alternative trade patterns. *Source*: Chenery and Syrquin (1986a).

relative importance of the contribution of manufacturing to growth, as shown in Figure 7.3. In the standard pattern generated by the dynamic model, manufacturing makes a larger contribution to growth than primary production above an income level of about $1200. This shift occurs at lower or higher levels of income depending on the resource endowments and trade policies of different countries, as shown in Figure 7.4.

On the supply side, the contribution of capital accumulation remains high for most of Stage 2 because the rise in the rate of investment tends to offset the decline in the weight of capital in the sectoral production functions.

Stage 3: The developed economy. The transition from Stage 2 to Stage 3 can be identified in several ways. On the demand side, income elasticities for manufactured goods decline, and at some point their share in domestic demand starts to fall. Although this tendency is offset for a while by the continued growth of exports, it is ultimately reflected in a decline in the share of manufacturing in GDP and in the labor force. This turning point has occurred in virtually all the industrial market economies within the past twenty years.

On the supply side, the main difference between Stage 2 and Stage 3 is the decline in the combined contribution of factor inputs as conventionally measured. The contribution of capital falls because of both its slower growth and its declining weight. In addition, because of a slowdown in population growth, only a few developed countries still have significant increases in their labor force.

Table 7.4
Sectoral shares and contributions to growth: 1960–80 (percent)

Income group	No. of countries	Primary	Manufacturing	Social overhead	Services	GDP
A. *Shares in value-added:*						
Average for 1960–80						
Low *y*	13	45	13	11	31	100
Lower mid-*y*	24	32	14	14	40	100
Upper mid-*y*	16	23	22	15	40	100
Industrial	15	8	27	17	48	100
B. *Annual growth rates 1960–80*						
Low *y*		2.5	4.7	5.3	5.3	3.8
Lower mid-*y*		3.4	6.6	6.5	5.1	5.0
Upper mid-*y*		4.4	7.9	8.2	6.6	6.4
Industrial		1.6	4.8	4.2	4.2	4.2
C. *Sectoral contributions to growth*						
Low *y*		28	15	16	41	100
Lower mid-*y*		24	19	16	41	100
Upper mid-*y*		14	26	19	41	100
Industrial		3	30	17	50	100

Source: World Bank data.

In more developed countries, total factor productivity growth is less associated with industrialization and more widely diffused throughout the economy than in Stage 2. The most notable change is in agriculture, which has shifted from being a sector of low productivity growth to being the sector of highest growth of labor productivity in most of the developed countries. The underlying cause is the continued movement of labor out of agriculture and the closing of the wage gap between agriculture and other sectors, which has stimulated the substitution of capital for labor as well as technological improvements.

Table 7.4 summarizes the experience during 1960–80 of a large number of countries grouped by income level. In all the groups, growth in the primary sector was lower than aggregate growth, and the opposite was true of manufacturing. Consequently, the dynamic sectoral share (or sectoral contribution to growth) of primary production was lower than the mean static share over the period, while in manufacturing the incremental share exceeded the average one. Both the static and the incremental shares show a clear association with income across groups for the primary and manufacturing sectors. In industrial countries, services account for half of total GDP growth. The current price share of services in those countries has risen even more because of the rise in the relative price of services. By the middle of the period covered the manufacturing share started to decline in virtually all advanced countries.

The figures in Table 7.4 illustrate the acceleration of growth with the level of income among developing countries and the subsequent slowdown in the industrialized stage. This pattern encompasses all of the broad sectors distinguished in the table.

5.2. Typology of development patterns

Average patterns of development are a useful starting point. They provide an initial reference point stressing the uniformities of the transformation. Various other factors have a systematic effect on resource allocation, affecting the timing and sequence of structural change more than its overall nature.

The identification of systematic sources of diversity leads naturally to attempts to divide the sample into more homogeneous groups. In the literature on long-run comparative patterns of development, one finds two main approaches to constructing a typology. The first one lets a purely statistical method, such as clustering analysis, come up with the various types.[65] The second approach relies more on theoretical arguments and on a priori judgements. There are two variants of this latter approach, differing on whether they start from individual cases representative of ideal types, or from the whole sample and then proceed to subdivide it. Ranis (1984) refers to the first variant as the "comparative historical approach" and to the second as the "econometric comparative patterns approach".[66] The latter variant is now illustrated.

Differences in international specialization were identified above as the primary source of deviation from the average growth patterns described in the previous section. They include the effects of factor proportions on comparative advantage as well as policy decisions about the levels of trade and external capital inflows. The alternative trade patterns in Figure 7.1 lead to significant differences in the sectoral contributions to growth. These will now be presented assuming the same aggregate growth rates for all trade patterns, followed by some estimates of comparative performance during the period 1950–83.

The different trade patterns have a large impact on the timing of industrialization. These effects are brought out in Figure 7.4, which shows the growth contributions of primary production and manufacturing under each trade pattern. (Non-tradables are omitted since they show relatively little variation from the standard pattern of Figure 7.3.) The timing of industrialization is measured by the beginning of Stage 2, the income level at which the growth contribution of manufacturing begins to exceed that of primary production.

With this measure, large countries typically reach the semi-industrial stage at an income level of about $550, the standard pattern at about $850, and small

---

[65] See, for example, UNIDO (1979).
[66] The first is illustrated by Lewis (1954), Fei and Ranis (1964), and Kelley, Williamson and Cheetham (1972). The second by Chenery and Taylor (1968), Chenery and Syrquin (1975, 1986b) and by Adelman and Morris (1984).

Table 7.5
Annual growth rate of GDP 1950–83: Simple averages (percent)

Size	Trade orientation		Openness	No. of countries	g_v	S.D.
Large	Primary		In	10	4.94	1.35
			Out	5	5.12	2.13
		LP		15	5.00	
	Manufacturing		In	6	4.73	1.21
			Out	8	5.26	1.51
		LM		14	5.04	
	L			29	5.02	
Small	Primary		In	27	3.58	1.48
			Out	23	5.01	1.94
		SP		50	4.24	
	Manufacturing		In	17	4.74	1.85
			Out	10	5.73	2.43
		SM		27	5.11	
	S			77	4.54	
	All primary			65	4.42	
	All manufacturing			41	5.09	
	All inward			60	4.28	
	All outward			46	5.22	
		ALL		106	4.67	1.90

Note: Growth rates within countries are OLS estimates. The number of annual observations varies from 14 to 34.
Source: World Bank data.

primary exporters at \$1300. In the L pattern, early industrialization results from the widespread policy of import substitution in manufacturing. In the SP pattern, manufactured imports are replaced much more slowly. The SM pattern is more complex because it typically starts with a relatively high inflow of external capital, which is later replaced as a source of foreign exchange by the rapid growth of exports of light manufactures.

Table 7.5 presents a rough picture of comparative performance since 1950, based on unweighted averages of growth rates (estimated by OLS regressions). Three dimensions are considered in the typology.

Size: Economies are separated into small and large on the basis of their population size in 1965. The dividing line is 15 million.

Openness: Inward and outward orientations are distinguished according to the level of merchandise exports relative to the value predicted by regressions.

Trade orientation: To capture the combined effect of the abundance of resources and trade policy an index of trade orientation was defined. It compares the actual commodity composition of exports to the one predicted for a country of similar income and size. Countries are classified into primary or manufacturing oriented [see Chenery and Syrquin (1986b)].

The averages in Table 7.5 mask the variation within groups. Still, the differences are of interest, and quite suggestive. During the period 1950–83, large
countries seemed to have performed better than small ones [see Perkins and
Syrquin, Chapter 33, Volume II, in this Handbook); a manufacturing specialization outperformed the primary specialization, and an outward orientation exhibited faster growth than an inward orientation. The superiority of the outward
orientation is in evidence for all four types in the table (LP, LM, SP, and SM).

6. Accounting for the transformation

The transformation in the structure of production is part of the process of
economic development. To determine its basic sources, therefore, a general model
incorporating the interdependence between growth and structural change is
required. Some attempts at such general modelling are reviewed below, after
presenting results from simpler attempts to decompose growth and change into
their more proximate sources.

6.1. Growth accounting: Demand-side decomposition

The computation of sources of growth from the demand side starts from the
material balance equations (4.2), reproduced below in vector notation, with trade
separated into exports and imports:

$$X = W + D + E - M. \tag{6.1}$$

Assuming a linear input–output technology (A) for intermediate demands and
letting u_i represent the share of total domestic demand of sector i supplied from
domestic sources, we can substitute into (6.1) and solve for X:

$$X = R(\hat{u}D + E), \tag{6.2}$$

where $R = (I - A)^{-1}$ and the "hat" over u indicates a diagonal matrix.

From this accounting identity we derive a growth accounting system relating
output growth to its sources on the demand side,[67] by differentiating (6.2) with

---

[67] The "demand" label has become customary for this approach. Trade and comparative advantage
are more supply than demand driven.

respect to time ($\dot{x} = dx/dt$):

$$\dot{X} = R\hat{u}\dot{D} + R\dot{E} + R\dot{\hat{u}}(D + W) + R\hat{u}\dot{A}X. \tag{6.3}$$
$$\quad\text{(a)} \quad \text{(b)} \qquad \text{(c)} \qquad\qquad \text{(d)}$$

The four factors measure the total (direct and induced) effects of:

(a) domestic demand expansion (DD),

(b) export expansion (EE),

(c) import substitution (IS), and

(d) changes in input–output coefficients (IO).

This decomposition elaborates the formulation in eq. (4.7) by assigning the change in intermediates to the effects of demand, trade, and technology throughout the system. Eq. (4.7) computed changes in sector proportions, whereas eq. (6.3) refers to absolute changes in output. The latter can easily be adapted to consider changes in structure by comparing its results to a balanced growth case where all the right-hand elements in the equation expand at the same rate with unchanged import and input–output coefficients. This is an identity-based decomposition that provides logically consistent definitions of concepts such as import substitution and balanced growth.

I now present results based on eq. (6.3), for the transition range in the cross-country model and for a group of semi-industrial countries in the post-war period.

6.1.1. The shift from primary to manufacturing

Table 7.6 summarizes information on changes in shares in gross output, and the sources of those changes.[68] The results from the cross-country model suggest that the fall in the primary share is mostly due to demand (Engel effects) at low income levels, and to trade effects afterwards. Trade effects combine a lower than proportional expansion in primary exports, and, at higher income levels, import liberalization (defined as an increase in the sectoral import coefficient). Changes in input–output coefficients contribute to the decline in the primary share at all income levels. This effect captures the substitution of fabricated materials for natural resources induced by technology and relative prices.

The rise in manufacturing share, which best represents the process of industrialization, is due less to high income elasticities and more to trade and technology. Import substitution is quite significant at all income levels. A more disaggregated analysis would show early import substitution in consumer goods, shifting to

---

[68] The results in Table 7.6 refer to deviations from a balanced-growth path focusing, therefore, on changes in shares. In Table 7.7 the results pertain to absolute changes and refer only to manufacturing.

Table 7.6
Deviations from balanced growth: Gross output (percent)

	A. Decline in share of Primary				B. Increase in share of Manufacturing			
	Change in share	Source			Change in share	Source		
		Demand	Trade	I-O		Demand	Trade	I-O
Simulated results								
Income interval								
(1980 US $)								
I. $300 $600	−7	68	27	5	5	23	50	27
II. $600 $1200	−6	49	43	8	6	15	55	30
III. $1200 $2400	−5	30	59	11	6	10	62	28
IV. $2400 $4500	−4	13	76	11	6	7	63	30
Country results[a]								
Korea 1955–73	−22.3	68	4	28	27.6	17	82	1
Taiwan 1956–71	−12.2	55	16	29	23.5	2	84	14
Japan 1914–35	−10.4	92	19	−11	9.3	58	55	−13
Turkey 1953–73	−18.5	64	10	26	12.5	27	40	33
Mexico 1950–75	−7.6	40	48	12	9.4	35	40	25
Yugoslavia 1962–72	−12.7	58	12	31	12.6	64	4	32
Japan 1955–70	−11.7	42	27	31	12.2	40	13	47
Israel 1958–72	−3.9	123	−36	13	11.0	45	11	44
Norway 1953–69	−3.4	66	43	−9	1.3	−21	44	77

[a] Countries ranked by per capita income in the initial year.
Sources: Simulated results: Chenery and Syrquin (1980). Country results: Kubo et al. (1986).

producer and capital goods at higher levels of development. The increase in the overall density of the input–output matrix that accompanies development is especially important in heavy industry [Deutsch and Syrquin (1986)]. It shows here as large contributions of the IO term to the rise in the manufacturing share.

The country results show more variation than the smooth simulated patterns, but in general they conform to the generalizations based on the latter. A significant difference is the faster pace of industrialization in semi-industrial countries than in the typical case simulated by the cross-country model. This stands out particularly in the case of the East Asian super-exporters, Korea and Taiwan.

6.1.2. Manufacturing: A sequence of phases?

So far the contributions of export expansion and import substitution have been presented together as a general trade effect. They are now considered separately to assess their relative importance to the growth of manufacturing. Before discussing the results in Table 7.7, two conceptual points are worth noting. First,

Table 7.7
Trade sources of growth in manufacturing output (percent)

Income interval[a]			Contributions to output growth by type					
			Large (L)		Small-manufacturing (SM)		Small-primary (SP)	
			EE	IS	EE	IS	EE	IS
I			10	10	30	2	8	14
II			14	6	32	10	10	12
III			17	3	34	12	12	10
IV			21	2	35	12	13	8
					EE	IS		
Korea	1955–63				12	42		
	1963–73				48	−2		
Taiwan	1956–61				27	26		
	1961–71				57	4		
Japan	1914–35				34	5		
	1955–70				18	−2		
Turkey	1953–63				2	9		
	1963–73				8	3		
Mexico	1950–60				3	11		
	1970–75				8	3		
Israel	1958–65				27	12		
	1965–72				50	−37		
Norway	1953–69				50	−18		

[a]Intervals as in Table 7.6.
EE: contribution of export expansion.
IS: contribution of import substitution.
Sources: Background information for Chenery, Robinson and Syrquin (1986).

import substitution is defined as arising from changes in the ratio of imports to total demand for each sector. It is an approach with a long tradition in development, and it fits well with the view that imports are imperfect substitutes for domestic goods, so that the source of supply is an integral part of the economic structure.[69] In the present context the measure incorporates economy-wide effects through the interindustry relations. Different domestic supply ratios (u) are assumed for final and for intermediate demands, and for the latter, when the data are available, the input–output matrix is separated into domestic and imported components. In eq. (6.3) for simplicity, for each sector a unique u coefficient is presented. [The complete formulation appears in Syrquin (1976), where alternative approaches to the measurement of import substitution are discussed.]

[69]See de Melo and Robinson (1985) for a discussion of the implications of this treatment.

Second, this section deals with the sources of output growth rather than deviations from a balanced growth path as in Table 7.6. In this case there is an important asymmetry in the way we measure the effects of exports and of import substitution. Exports, in eq. (6.3), enter as a flow and their potential contribution is, in principle, unbounded; this is not the case for imports, which appear as ratios to final or intermediate demand. Typical u coefficients in semi-industrial economies in the 1950s were around 90 percent for light industry and 50 percent for heavy industry. The scope for further import substitution was ample in heavy industry but not in light industry.

Table 7.7 shows the relative contributions of export expansion (EE) and import substitution (IS) to the growth of manufacturing gross output. The long-term simulated patterns are shown by type. As expected, in large countries exports are less important especially at an early stage of industrialization. At such a stage import substitution is quite significant in large and SP economies. Most of the countries that vigorously pursued an import substitution strategy in the post-war period, were relatively large (Brazil, India) and/or primary oriented (Chile, Uruguay).

Country results are shown for two periods (except for Norway). Trade contributions appear to have followed a distinct sequence: periods of significant export expansion preceded by periods of strong import substitution. This sequence appears most clearly in Korea and Taiwan where it can be related to the changes in trade strategy in the early 1960s. Similar results were also found at a more disaggregated level [Kubo, de Melo and Robinson (1986)]. The results suggest than an economy may have to develop an industrial base and acquire a certain technological mastery before it can pursue manufactured exports on a significant scale.[70] The crucial question is then not one of export promotion versus import substitution, but rather one of designing the latter to avoid inefficient production and delays in shifting out of it.

6.2. Growth accounting: Supply side

The previous section presented sources of growth from the demand side. As with other growth-accounting exercises, it starts from an accounting identity and decomposes growth or structural change into its proximate sources without necessarily implying causality. An alternative growth-accounting approach, this time from the supply side, is the Abramovitz–Solow–Denison decomposition of

---

[70] For other analyses of sequencing and its relation to infant industry arguments, see Balassa (1979) and Westphal (1982). Along similar lines, it has been argued that in the large countries of Latin America import substitution provided "a preamble to the export stage" [Teitel and Thoumi (1986)]. See also Chapter 31, Volume II, by Bruton in this Handbook.

Table 7.8
Changes in sector proportions in the cross-country model:
Supply-side accounting (percent)

Income interval[a]	Differences between manufacturing and agriculture in the growth of:		
	Value added	Factor input	Factor productivity
I	1.8	1.0	0.8
II	2.9	1.5	1.4
III	4.1	2.9	1.2
IV	5.1	4.1	1.0

[a] Intervals as in Table 7.6.
Source: Syrquin (1986a).

the sources of growth into the effect of factor accumulation and productivity growth.

Changes in sector proportions, which clearly imply differential rates of sectoral growth, can be related in this approach to differential expansion of inputs and of total factor productivity. Some orders of magnitude for agriculture and manufacturing, based on the long-run model of industrialization, are presented in Table 7.8. The results indicate the importance of differential productivity growth in accounting for the shift in activity from agriculture to manufacturing. Only in the higher income interval, when labor is declining absolutely in agriculture and productivity has risen significantly, is the differential in factor input growth the dominant source of change.

6.3. Resource shifts and productivity growth

The supply-side analysis of sources of growth focuses on the growth of factor productivity. At the aggregate level, productivity growth cannot be analyzed independently of demand aspects. Formally, the measured rate of aggregate productivity growth (λ) equals a weighted average of the sectoral rates (λ_i) with output weights (ρ_i), plus a factor measuring the effect of intersectoral resource shifts (RE = reallocation effect):

$$\lambda = \sum \rho_i \lambda_i + RE. \tag{6.4}$$

The reallocation effect (RE), when positive, shows the increase in efficiency that results when resources (labor and capital) move from sectors with lower to sectors with higher marginal productivity, reducing the extent of disequilibrium.

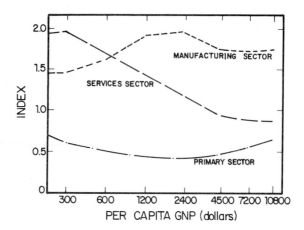

Figure 7.5. Relative labor productivity. *Note*: Index signifies labor productivity in a sector relative to labor productivity for the whole economy. *Source*: Syrquin (1986a).

The effect vanishes when resources are optimally allocated before and after the shift.

6.3.1. Relative labor productivity

A partial indicator of differential returns across sectors is the pattern of relative labor productivity, obtained by dividing a sector's share in value-added by its share in employment. It is partial because it refers to average and not marginal products and considers only one input (labor).[71] The pattern of relative productivity in the model simulations is illustrated in Figure 7.5.

If all sectors had the same production function and faced the same factor prices, and if resources were prefectly mobile, then labor productivity would follow the same pattern in all sectors. In the model simulations in Figure 7.5, labor productivity is significantly lower in agriculture than in the rest of the economy.[72] In the early stages of development the growth of productivity in agriculture lags behind that of other sectors, which further widens the productivity gap. These sectoral differences in the average product of labor reflect differences in the nature of the production function (which lead to different factor proportions) and in the rate of technological change. But they also stem

---

[71] See Syrquin (1984) for a comparison of approaches to measure the contribution of intersectoral resource shifts.

[72] Syrquin (1986a) presents data for various countries and compares them to the model simulations. In our earlier study [Chenery and Syrquin (1975)] we derived the patterns of relative productivity from regressions. The results for the primary sector were very similar, for manufacturing less so.

from the low mobility of resources, a condition that lies behind the persistence of disequilibrium phenomena such as surplus labor in agriculture and other low productivity activities, including handicrafts and services.

When the industrial sector accelerates its growth in response to domestic demand and to changes in comparative advantage (usually with some help from commercial policies), the productivity gap tends to increase. Labor starts to shift out of agriculture, at first in relative terms and eventually in absolute terms, but with a lag. Since productivity in agriculture rises even at this stage, a surplus of labor results.

The pattern of relative productivity in Figure 7.5 is related to and resembles the Kuznets curve of income inequality. The productivity gap between primary production on the one hand and industry and services on the other is greatest in the middle income range, which is typically the period of greatest inequality of income. It is also the period when, because of the productivity gap itself, resource shifts can make their largest contribution to aggregate growth.

In a second phase, once migration and capital accumulation have significantly reduced the surplus of labor, relative wages in agriculture increase and a catch-up process takes place. Capital intensity in this sector then increases faster than in other sectors. This is coupled with the continuing growth in factor productivity. As a result, agriculture begins to reduce the productivity gap.

Crafts (1984) estimated output and employment patterns in agriculture from data for nineteenth-century Europe, and calculated the implied productivity gap between the primary sector and the rest of the economy. He found that the gap narrowed substantially early in the transition, in contrast to "twentieth-century countries" [from Chenery and Syrquin (1975)] where the gap grows throughout. However, when comparing labor productivity in the primary sector to the economy-wide figure the results are quite similar. In both cases, relative productivity tends to decline within the range studied by Crafts ($300 to $900 in 1970 US$).

6.3.2. The effect of reallocation of resources

Illustrative estimates of the contribution of resource reallocation to growth are presented in Table 7.9. The results suggest that *RE* is a significant component of aggregate growth of output and TFP particularly in the industrializing stage. At its peak, it amounts to 11 percent of output growth and to almost 30 percent of aggregate TFP. Its pattern across periods resembles the initial acceleration and subsequent slowdown in the growth of output. In the last interval in the table – which corresponds roughly to Western Europe since the late 1960s – the effect of resource reallocation almost disappears. Part of the accompanying productivity slowdown reflects the exhaustion of the shift out of agriculture as a potential source of growth. If productivity gains continue to decline at income

Table 7.9
Contribution of resource shifts to productivity growth
for the cross-country model

Income interval[a]	Annual growth rate (percent)		
	GDP	Aggregate TFP (λ)	Reallocation effect (RE)
I	4.8	0.7	0.15
II	5.7	1.4	0.29
III	6.3	2.3	0.56
IV	6.6	2.9	0.75
Higher income	5.6	2.8	0.08

[a]Intervals as in Table 7.6. The higher income interval corresponds roughly to $8000 to $12000.
Source: Syrquin (1986a).

levels beyond those in the simulation, however, it will no longer be attributable, even partially, to the reduced shift out of agriculture. A different – and probably negative – allocation effect may become important as labor continues to shift into services.

In the presence of significant differences in factor returns across sectors, structural change becomes an essential element in accounting for the rate and pattern of growth. On the one hand, that change can retard growth if its pace is too slow or its direction inefficient. On the other hand, it can contribute to growth if it improves the allocation of resources. Market forces tend to move the economic system toward equilibrium, but they are blunted by inflexibility in the system and high adjustment costs, by shocks from external events and unbalanced productivity growth, and even by government policies (see Chapter 11 by Williamson in this Handbook).

7. Relative prices and exchange rate conversions

Previous sections presented patterns of structural change, namely, systematic associations of economic structure with the level of development. With few exceptions, prices have not appeared directly in the analysis. For comparative analysis of long-run transformation, the crucial question is not whether relative prices do not change (they do), but whether they change in a systematic way during the process of development. If such associations can be identified we may want to add them to our list of stylized facts and to examine their impact on the estimated patterns of change.

At a point in time, the internal structure of relative prices varies across countries. The estimated income effects in cross-country patterns incorporate price effects (and various other effects) correlated with per capita income. To the extent that the association is expected to continue to hold, the combined total income effects are of interest on their own, even if they no longer represent pure, real income effects.

This section examines some key relative prices and the issues of exchange-rate conversion of incomes.

7.1. Relative prices

There are various relative prices that can be expected to change in a regular fashion (the wage-rental, for example). Of these, some are particularly relevant for the study of structural change.

7.1.1. Consumer demand

The balanced-growth approach in the early literature on development [Rosenstein-Rodan (1943), Nurkse (1953)] is commonly associated with price-inelastic demands. In this context, it is instructive to quote from Nurkse's posthumous "Notes on 'Unbalanced Growth'" (1959, pp. 296–297):

> Shortages in specific factor supplies, among other possible causes, can and will naturally produce changes in relative prices, to which consumer demand will tend to adjust itself. To this extent the output expansion will deviate from the path of income elasticity, which assumes a constancy of relative prices. No one has denied that price-elasticities, too, help to determine a community's pattern of demand. *But changes in relative prices have no close or determinate relation to economic growth as such*, whereas changes in income are a direct reflection and measure of growth. Hence, the prominence given to income elasticities in a macro-economic approach to the problem of international growth economics (emphasis added).

7.1.2. Primary commodities

The internal and external terms of trade between primary commodities and manufacturing have figured prominently in the development literature. Central to the Prebisch–Singer advocacy of import-substitution industrialization was the alleged secular tendency for the (external) terms of trade to move against primary production. While a general tendency of deterioration in the terms of trade has not been supported by the evidence, the debate is still far from over. The prices of some primary products have fallen, but for other products sharp increases were recorded, especially after 1970.

Regarding the internal terms of trade two approaches can be distinguished. Work on the Soviet national income expected the prices of products based on natural resources to rise relative to industrial products because of diminishing returns in primary production and technological change in industry.[73] A negative association between relative prices of commodities and production levels implies that the measurement of real growth over long periods of time will differ according to whether we use initial or terminal year prices. This systematic difference became known as the "Gerschenkron effect".

The second approach does not predict a tendency, rather it advocates turning the internal terms of trade against agriculture to foster industrialization. It was one of Preobrazhensky's policy proposals in the 1920s and was widely followed by inward-oriented developing economies in the post-war period.[74]

If the "Gerschenkron effect" predominates, that is, if over the transition the relative price of primary commodities rises, then the extent of the real transformation in production, as estimated from current shares, is underestimated. The real shift in economic activity is partly offset by an opposite price trend. However, if the terms of trade are turned by policy against the primary sector, the observed reallocation can only partially be regarded as real. Little, Scitovsky and Scott (1970) analyzed the contributions of the primary and manufacturing sectors to the growth of GDP, in six countries that pursued an import substitution strategy during the 1950s. They compared the contributions as conventionally measured and as measured after allowing for the effects of protection. In every case the contribution of the primary sector was understated and that of manufacturing overstated when ignoring protection. The results from a much larger sample in Table 7.2, do not reveal any clear tendency in the terms of trade for the longer period examined.

7.1.3. The price of food

Food is a primary-based commodity and therefore the previous discussion applies to it, but since it is singled out by various analysts I shall add some further observations.

In Lewis's (1954) model of development in the dual economy, a rising price of food could choke off the process. Evidence on the importance of the relative price of food appears in the comparative study of consumption patterns by Lluch, Powell and Williams (1977). A decrease in the price of food was found to lead to an increase in the demand for food, to an increase in the aggregate demand for commodities other than food, and to a decrease in saving. The expected effects

---

[73] Perkins (1981).

[74] See Sah and Stiglitz (1984). In the USSR, however, the proposal was apparently not adopted [Ellman (1975)].

decline in importance at higher income levels. The various effects are quantitatively significant, but for them to affect the long-run patterns a systematic trend in the price of food needs to be established. A general association of the price of food with the level of income has neither been established over time nor across countries, except for some partial samples. An interesting example of the latter is Fishlow's (1973) comparison of American, British, and French expenditures of urban households around 1900. Fishlow documented smaller American expenditures on foodstuffs and related them to lower food prices. Since this took place at a time when income was relatively low and the share of food still high, it gave the low food prices more leverage, turning them into a significant factor in the rapid rate of industrialization in the nineteenth century.

7.1.4. Price of investment goods

It is not always the case that constant-price shares are the relevant measures for analysis. Saving behavior, for example, is more meaningful when expressed as shares in current prices, while for comparisons of the productivity of investment it is the constant share which is more relevant.

In the long-term records of developed countries analyzed by Kuznets (1961) there was a tendency for the relative price of capital goods to rise, thus reducing somewhat the secular increase in real capital formation proportions.[75] However, "an upward trend in the latter was still evident in most countries" (p. 54). The increase in the relative price of investment was due to construction and not to producers' durable equipment or inventories (p. 13). This implies a faster rate of productivity growth in the tradable component of investment than in the nontradable one – a key stylized fact of the "differential productivity model" used to account for the association of the national price level with the level of income [Kravis and Lipsey (1983), and Section 7.2 below].

For a more recent period we have the price comparisons of the International Comparisons Project (ICP) of Kravis and his associates. Summers and Heston (1984) use ICP data to derive price relatives of broad expenditure categories for a large number of countries during 1950–80. Regression results across countries show a negative relation between the relative price of investment and real per capita income, contrary to the long-term positive association found by Kuznets. The results imply that the difference among countries in the real share of investment is larger than the differential in nominal or current price shares. Within countries, however, the experience since 1950 shows no decline in the

---

[75] The experience in Japan was quite different. The impressive rise in the current share of capital formation was accompanied by a downward drift in the relative price of capital goods. The increase in capital formation and saving shares was therefore even more impressive in constant prices. For an endogenous explanation of accumulation and growth acceleration in Japan see Williamson and de Bever (1978).

relative price of investment. The relative overvaluation of investment in low and middle income countries has probably widened. Syrquin and Chenery (1986) also report regressions of investment shares at constant 1970 prices. The estimated income effects did not differ significantly from those at current prices.

7.1.5. Price of services – non-tradables

The relative price of non-tradables increases significantly with the level of income across countries and over time. Since this is the central element in the explanation of the systematic departure of exchange rates from purchasing power parities (PPPs) it is discussed in the next section on this topic.

7.2. Exchange-rate conversions

In the study of patterns of structural change the principal variable is the level of development. In this chapter it has usually been measured by income per capita in 1980 US dollars at official exchange rates.[76]

It is well known that exchange rates are an imperfect measure of the purchasing power of the various national currencies. Price structures vary across countries, and exchange rates at best reflect only the prices of internationally traded goods in the absence of impediments to trade. The alternative to using exchange rates as conversion factors for international comparisons is to reprice the local components of income in every country at a uniform set of prices. This is equivalent to the use of purchasing power parities (PPPs) as conversion factors, where PPPs, following Kravis (1984), refer to the number of currency units required to buy one US dollar's worth of output. PPPs are a weighted average of the ratios of domestic price (P_i) to the price of the same good i in the country chosen as numeraire (P_i^*) or to its price in some international units.

There have been various attempts to estimate real incomes for small samples of countries in which a high-income country was designated as numeraire. Until recently, similar estimates for a large number of developing countries were not available. This deficiency has begun to be remedied by the International Comparisons Project (ICP). In a series of studies, the ICP has estimated real incomes for an ever increasing number of countries [see, for example, Kravis (1984)]. Phase III of the project, which includes 34 countries, became available in 1982 [Kravis, Heston and Summers (1982)]. Results of phase IV, covering more than 60 countries, were published recently [United Nations (1986)].

The principal finding of the ICP and similar studies is that differences across countries in incomes converted at exchange rates tend to exaggerate the real differences in income.

---

[76] This section draws on the appendix to Chenery and Syrquin (1986a).

Let *YE* stand for GDP converted at exchange rate and *YR* for real income. If GDP is expressed in a country's own currency, the two income figures are obtained as:

$$YE = \text{GDP}/e, \qquad YR = \text{GDP}/\text{PPP},$$

where e is the exchange rate and PPP the purchasing power parity rate.

The systematic divergence between *YE* and *YR* per capita has been analyzed in two equivalent ways:

(1) The ratio *YR/YE*, labeled by Kravis and associates the "exchange rate deviation index" (*ERD*), declines steadily with the level of income per capita from levels close to 3 for very low income countries to a value of 1 for the United States.

(2) The reciprocal of the *ERD* is the national price level (PPP/e), which increases systematically with per capita income.[77]

Several explanations have been proposed to account for the systematic pattern of the *ERD* or of its inverse, the price level. The main one, which is most relevant for our purposes, is the "differential productivity model", of which there are various versions going back at least to Ricardo [see Kravis and Lipsey (1983)]. Its modern version [see Balassa (1964) and Samuelson (1964)], accepts the law of one price as approximately valid for traded goods but introduces a sector producing non-traded goods. Assuming that productivity differences among countries are larger for traded than for non-traded goods, that the production of the latter is relatively more labor-intensive, and that labor is relatively more abundant (relatively less expensive) in low income countries, the relative price of non-traded goods can be expected to be positively associated with per capita income. Since the prices of traded goods are similar across countries, the model also predicts that the national price level will be higher in high income countries.

The differential productivity model relies on real factors related to the structure of the economy. In addition to the level of per capita income, other such influences that have been suggested for examination include the industrial structure of output and employment and the degree of openness of the economy. These long-run factors determine the underlying price level, while short-run, mainly monetary, variables are the cause of deviations from that basic level [Kravis and Lipsey (1983, p. 10)].

The rise in the relative price of non-traded goods with the level of income across countries can also be derived from a model where differences in total factor productivity among sectors do not vary in a systematic way with income, Bhagwati (1984) has recently shown that the price effect is compatible with the traditional factor-proportion model in trade theory.

---

[77] The variation across countries in the national price level is analyzed in Kravis and Lipsey (1983) and Clague (1985).

Effects of using exchange rates

There are two types of international comparisons that could be affected by using exchange rates as conversion factors rather than purchasing power parities. The first one relates measures of economic structure to per capita income across countries and is essentially a static comparison. The second one refers to the dynamic simulation of an economy over time.

Static comparisons include studies of the structure of demand and production across countries as well as comparative static simulations of changes in structure with incomes.

The patterns using exchange rates show the average transformation in relation to income changes which incorporate a systematic variation in prices. If the price variation is not correlated with per capita income among countries, then the use of YE instead of YR may affect the precision of the estimates but will not necessarily bias the results. When the deviation of YE from YR is systematic, the results will be biased. However, a close relation between YE and YR per capita implies that there is a simple transformation between the results using YE and the ones that would obtain if YR were to be used.

When the bias in using exchange rates affects all components of GDP equally, the transformation in economic structure will take place over a narrower real income range than the one shown here. The pace of the transformation is therefore underestimated in our analysis.

A major component of the deviation between YE and YR is caused by differences in price structures. To correct for these differences, separate correction factors are needed for different components of GDP. Although the ICP examined expenditure categories, it does not provide information on the relative prices of goods by sector of origin.[78] For this a production approach to real income is necessary [see Maddison (1983) and Maddison and van Ark (1987)].

Once the time element comes in, the deviation of YE from YR becomes more significant. Growth rate calculations and comparisons, such as those in Figures 7.3 and 7.4, are intended to be in real terms, whereas the changes across benchmark levels of YE incorporate a price effect. The growth rates between benchmark levels of YE in Figures 7.3 and 7.4 give the time required to traverse the distance between the various levels of YE. The results are overestimates since they do not take into account the variation in the price level during the same interval. The quantitative results are sensitive to the use of exchange rates, but the important question is the extent to which the qualitative results about the transformation are also affected. As mentioned above, the use of exchange rates as conversion factors stretches the income range studied. A uniform stretching

---

[78] See, nevertheless, the attempt by Kravis, Heston and Summers (1983) to use expenditure data to examine the share of services in GDP. Ram (1985) compared estimates of production structure using "conventional" and "real" GDP per capita. Sectoral shares were not corrected since the required data are not available.

would be the least damaging to the nature of the results and the easiest to incorporate into the analysis. A uniform stretching implies a logarithmic relation between *YR* and *YE*, and most of the short-cut studies have postulated such a logarithmic relation and estimated it with quite good results. Based on the results of Phase III of the ICP, I estimated the following relation for 27 economies:

$$\ln YR = 2.81 + 0.68 \ln YE, \quad \bar{R}^2 = 0.97.$$
$$(16.7) \quad (28.19)$$

The implication of the results is that real growth amounts to 68 percent of growth in income converted at exchange rates at all income levels. The remaining 32 percent represents the systematic price effect.

The effect of switching to income converted at PPPs instead of exchange rates on the income intervals in Tables 7.8 and 7.9 would be to reduce all of them *uniformly* by 32 percent, but, most important, all the acceleration and deceleration effects on growth would still remain.

8. Approaches to policy

Policy analysis is most useful when applied to concrete situations as illustrated, for issues related to transformation, in the various chapters in Parts 2 and 6 of this Handbook. This concluding section draws on these chapters and offers some general observations on the role of the state in modern economic growth.

Structural change is a necessary corollary of economic growth but it is a disruptive process. By definition it implies that various segments of the economy grow at different rates. Groups of the population attached to slow growing segments lose out relatively to those in faster growing sectors. In addition, structural change requires the population to adapt itself to different working conditions and styles of life (factory production, impersonal firms, urbanization). As Kuznets noted, "policy action and institutional changes are required [to minimize] the costs of, and resistance to, the structural shifts implicit in, and required for, a high rate of growth" [Kuznets (1979, p. 130)]. For modern economic growth the sovereign state has to act "as a clearing house for necessary institutional innovations; as an agency for resolution of conflicts among group interests; and as a major entrepreneur for the socially required infrastructure" [Kuznets (1971, p. 346)].

The above describes what may be called the "minimal development state".[79] At the other extreme we find a state for which a certain pattern of structural change

---

[79] In the context of development it is a minimal state even if it goes well beyond the one in classical liberal theory "limited to the functions of protecting all its citizens against violence, theft, and fraud, and to the enforcement of contracts, and so on" [Nozick (1974, p. 26)].

becomes itself an objective, to be actively pursued or even imposed. This may take various forms: structural change may be fostered as the means to further growth and other aims as in ECLA's advocacy of import substitution or in the Stalinist approach to industrialization – or it could be dictated by ideology even at the expense of growth, as in the extreme case of Cambodia. A less extreme, and more positive case of determining structure exogenously is found in the early years of the Israeli state. Ideology (return to the land) and security considerations, called for an increase in agriculture's share in employment reversing the transformation which would otherwise have taken place [Syrquin (1986c)]. Adjustment between demand and supply was left to foreign capital inflows in the Israeli case and to coercion in Cambodia.

In between the two extremes there is a more pragmatic approach that tries to anticipate structural change, facilitating it or accelerating it, by removing obstacles and correcting for market failures. Following Pack and Westphal (1986), its representatives can be labeled "industrial strategists". Strategists worry about coordination of supply and demand and the design of adjustment mechanisms. These are "policy measures that are adopted to avoid disequilibrium and thus achieve more rapid development" [Chenery (1979, p. 62)].[80]

Issues tackled by strategists referred initially to factor accumulation (saving, labor surplus), and sectoral balance (agriculture vs. industry) with trade a minor consideration. At a later stage, trade strategy became the central issue.

Dissenters on the left regarded the approach as too narrow. Within mainstream economics the main challenge came from the neoclassicals who typically grew up in the tradition of international economics, in contrast to the strategists who came from a planning tradition.[81]

Comparative policy analyses relevant for the study of transformation have been dominated by trade issues. The main examples are the studies of the import substitution strategy of industrialization [Little, Scitovsky and Scott (1970), Balassa and associates (1971)]; the analysis of trade regimes by Krueger (1978) and Bhagwati (1978), and the studies of strategies in semi-industrial countries [Balassa and associates (1982)].

The typology of specialization patterns, used in previous sections, also emphasized trade aspects. The main reason is that trade policy has become the main instrument used by governments to influence resource allocation, and that differences in trade policy have led to substantial variation in economic structures and on performance [Chenery and Syrquin (1986b)]. The chapters in Part 6 of this Handbook look at country experience. The grouping of countries or the strategies analyzed are also trade determined. The other chapters in this part deal

---

[80] Disequilibrium has also been regarded as beneficial because it ellicits creative responses [Hirschman (1958)] and generates desirable forces such as innovation and competition [Kornai (1971)]. See also Hahn's (1973) review of Kornai's book.

[81] The following paragraphs owe much to Pack and Westphal (1986).

with external policy, but also emphasize internal aspects chiefly related to technological change.

The neoclassical approach focuses on the overall policy regime (it should be neutral not discriminatory) and, in one way or another, recommends "getting the prices right". This is important not just for the static gains of a more efficient allocation of resources, but more so for fostering technical change and dynamic efficiency.

Strategists have incorporated many of the neoclassical prescriptions, but remain convinced of the indispensability of selective intervention. They see industrialization as a process of technological change, with learning related to experience as a major source of externality. The generation of local technological capability becomes crucial and the consequence is to focus decisions about strategy and intervention on areas where technological capability either does not exist or exists in at least a rudimentary form but is not being deployed effectively. The neoclassical emphasis on choices among policy instruments is therefore regarded as incomplete. No less important are "the different ways of using the same policy instruments...whether they are used promotionally or restrictively" [Pack and Westphal (1986, p. 103)]. This distinction is related to a missing link stressed in various chapters, namely, the management factor. Selective intervention "works" only if its primary objective is a dynamically efficient process of industrialization. If it is not, then selective intervention may be counterproductive and the best advice is probably to adhere to the neoclassical prescription. "However, it should be noted that the factors responsible for a government's inability to intervene effectively may also preclude its following the neoclassical prescription" [Pack and Westphal (1986, p. 104)].

Managerial factors are brought out clearly in Mason's (1984) comparison of development policy and its implementation in Egypt and Korea. He considers differences in various managerial factors such as government objectives, the share of public enterprises in the public sector, managerial techniques in the public sector, implementation of policy, etc. The first one he regards as the most important factor: in Korea the primary purpose of government was to facilitate growth, while in Egypt it was not.[82] To this he adds one non-economic influence of "possibly overwhelming importance" – the cultural milieu. Cultural and social factors assume a similar conditioning role in the staple theory of growth. Exports of primary commodities (staples) can ignite a cumulative process of development only if no inhibiting traditions are present and if society and its institutions are favorably predisposed toward development [Roemer (1970)].

The importance of institutions and institutional change for modern economic growth is increasingly being recognized. Morris and Adelman (1988) go as far as

---

[82] This is similar to the argument in Adelman and Morris (1967), mentioned approvingly by Mason, that the single most important factor has been the leadership commitment to economic development.

identifying institutional change as the single most important differentiator of development performance among groups of countries.[83] The time may be ripe for trying to establish the stylized facts of institutional change and their role in the structural transformation.

References

Abramovitz, M. (1983) 'Notes on international differences in productivity growth rates', in: D.C. Mueller, ed., *The political economy of growth*. New Haven: Yale University Press.

Abramovitz, M. and David, P.A. (1973) 'Reinterpreting economic growth: Parables and realities', *American Economic Review*, 63:428–439.

Adelman, I. and Morris, C.T. (1967) *Economic growth and social equity in developing countries*. Stanford: Stanford University Press.

Adelman, I. and Morris, C.T. (1984) 'Patterns of economic growth, 1850–1914, or Chenery–Syrquin in perspective', in: M. Syrquin, L. Taylor and L.E. Westphal, eds., *Economic structure and performance: Essays in honor of Hollis B. Chenery*. New York: Academic Press.

Arndt, H.W. (1985) 'The origins of structuralism', *World Development*, 13:151–159.

Balassa, B. (1964) 'The purchasing power parity doctrine: A reappraisal', *Journal of Political Economy*, 72:584–596.

Balassa, B. (1979) "'A stages approach' to comparative advantage", in: I. Adelman, ed., *Economic growth and resources*, Vol. 4: *National and International Policies*. London: Macmillan.

Balassa, B., and Associates (1971) *The structure of protection in developing countries*. Baltimore, MD: Johns Hopkins University Press.

Balassa, B., and Associates (1982) *Development strategies in semi-industrial countries*. Baltimore, MD: Johns Hopkins University Press.

Baldwin, R.E. (1956) 'Patterns of development in newly settled regions', *Manchester School of Economic and Social Studies*, 24:161–179.

Bauer, P. and Yamey, B.S. (1951) 'Economic progress and occupational distribution', *Economic Journal*, 61:741–755.

Bhagwati, J.N. (1978) *Foreign trade regimes and economic development: Anatomy and consequences of exchange control regimes*. Cambridge, MA: Ballinger.

Bhagwati, J.N. (1984) 'Why are services cheaper in the poor countries?', *Economic Journal*, 94:279–286.

Carre, J.J., Dubois, P. and Malinvaud, E. (1975) *French economic growth*. Stanford, CA: Stanford University Press.

Caves, R.E. (1965) "'Vent for surplus' models of trade and growth", in: R.E. Baldwin et al. eds., *Trade, growth and the balance of payments*. Chicago: Rand McNally.

Chenery, H.B. (1960) 'Patterns of industrial growth', *American Economic Review*, 50:624–654.

Chenery, H.B. (1964) 'Land: The effects of resources on economic growth', in: K. Berrill, ed., *Economic development with special reference to East Asia*. New York: St. Martin's.

Chenery, H.B. (1973) 'Alternative strategies for development', IBRD working paper no. 165, World Bank, Washington, DC. Revised version published in: Y. Ramati, ed., *Economic growth in developing countries material and human resources*, Proceedings of the Seventh Rehovot Conference. New York: Praeger (1975).

Chenery, H.B. (1975) 'The structuralist approach to development policy', *American Economic Association Papers and Proceedings*, 65:310–316.

Chenery, H.B. (1977) 'Transitional growth and world industrialization', in: B. Ohlin, P.O. Hesselborn and P.M. Wijkman, eds., *The international allocation of economic activity*. London: Macmillan.

---

[83]See also Matthews (1986) and Olson (1982).

Chenery, H.B. (1979) *Structural change and development policy*. New York: Oxford University Press.

Chenery, H.B. (1986a) 'Structural transformation: A program of research', Harvard Institute for International Development, Discussion Paper no. 232, processed.

Chenery, H.B. (1986b) 'Growth and transformation', in: H. Chenery, S. Robinson and M. Syrquin, *Industrialization and growth*. New York: Oxford University Press.

Chenery, H.B. and Bruno, M. (1962) 'Development alternatives in an open economy: The case of Israel', *Economic Journal*, 72:79–103.

Chenery, H.B. and Strout, A. (1966) 'Foreign assistance and economic development', *American Economic Review*, 56:679–733.

Chenery, H.B. and Syrquin, M. (1975) *Patterns of development, 1950–1970*. London: Oxford University Press.

Chenery, H.B. and Syrquin, M. (1980) 'A comparative analysis of industrial growth', in: R.C.O. Matthews, ed., *Economic growth and resources*, Vol. 2: *Trends and Factors*. New York: Macmillan.

Chenery, H.B. and Syrquin, M. (1986a) 'Typical patterns of transformation', in: H. Chenery, S. Robinson and M. Syrquin, *Industrialization and growth*. New York: Oxford University Press.

Chenery, H.B. and Syrquin, M. (1986b) 'The semi-industrial countries', in: H. Chenery, S. Robinson and M. Syrquin, *Industrialization and growth*. New York: Oxford University Press.

Chenery, H.B. and Taylor, L. (1968) 'Development patterns among countries and over time', *Review of Economics and Statistics*, 50:391–416.

Chenery, H.B. and Watanabe, T. (1958) 'International comparisons of the structure of production', *Econometrica*, 26:487–521.

Chenery, H.B. and Watanabe, T. (1965) 'The process of industrialization', Paper read at the World Congress of the Econometric Society, Rome, Italy, September 9–14.

Chenery, H.B., Robinson, S. and Syrquin, M. (1986) *Industrialization and growth: A comparative study*. New York: Oxford University Press.

Chenery, H.B., Shishido, S. and Watanabe, T. (1962) 'The pattern of Japanese growth, 1914–1954', *Econometrica*, 30:98–139.

Clague, C.K. (1985) 'A model of real national price levels', *Southern Economic Journal*, 51:998–1017.

Clark, C. (1940) *The conditions of economic progress*. London: Macmillan.

Corden, W.M. and Neary, J.P. (1982) 'Booming sector and de-industrialization in a small open economy', *Economic Journal*, 92:825–848.

Crafts, N.F.R. (1984) 'Patterns of development in nineteenth century Europe', *Oxford Economic Papers*, 36:438–458.

Deardorff, A.V. (1984) 'Testing trade theories and predicting trade flows', in: R.W. Jones and P.B. Kenen, eds., *Handbook of international economics*, Vol. 1. Amsterdam: North-Holland.

Deutsch, J. and Syrquin, M. (1986) 'Economic development and the structure of production', processed.

Domar, E. (1957) 'A Soviet model of growth', in: *Essays in the theory of economic growth*. New York: Oxford University Press.

Eckaus, R. (1978) 'Review of Chenery and Syrquin, patterns of development, 1950–1970', *Economic Development and Cultural Change*, 26:621–625.

ECE (Economic Commission for Europe) (1977) *Structure and change in European industry*. New York: United Nations.

Ellman, M.J. (1975) 'Agricultural surplus and increase in investment: USSR 1928–32', *Economic Journal*, 85:844–863.

Fei, J.C.H. and Ranis, G. (1964) *Development of the labor surplus economy*. Homewood, IL: Irwin.

Feldstein, M. and Horioka, C. (1980) 'Domestic saving and international capital flows', *Economic Journal*, 90:314–329.

Fisher, A.G.B. (1935) *The clash of progress and security*. London: Macmillan.

Fisher, A.G.B. (1939) 'Production, primary, secondary and tertiary', *Economic Record*, 15:24–38.

Fishlow, A. (1965) 'Empty economic stages?', *Economic Journal*, 75:112–125.

Fishlow, A. (1973) 'Comparative consumption patterns, the extent of the market, and alternative development strategies', in: E.B. Ayal, ed., *Micro aspects of development*. New York: Praeger.

Gerschenkron, A. (1962) *Economic backwardness in historical perspective*. Cambridge, MA: Belknap.

Gillis, M., Perkins, D.H., Roemer, M.R. and Snodgrass, D.R. (1983) *Economics of development*. New York and London: Norton.

Grunfeld, Y. and Griliches, Z. (1960) 'Is aggregation necessarily bad?', *Review of Economics and Statistics*, 42:1–13.

Hahn, F.H. (1973) 'Review of Kornai, *Anti-equilibrium*', *Economica*, 40:323–330.

Hartwell, R.M. (1973) 'The service revolution: The growth of services in modern economy', in: C.M. Cipolla, ed., *The Fontana economic history of Europe: The industrial revolution*. Glasgow: Collins.

Hayami, Y. and Ruttan, V. (1985) *Agricultural development: An international perspective*. Baltimore, MD: Johns Hopkins University Press.

Helpman, E. and Krugman, P.R. (1985) *Market structure and foreign trade*. Cambridge, MA: MIT Press.

Hirschman, A.O. (1958) *The strategy of economic development*. New Haven, CT: Yale University Press.

Hirschman, A.O. (1977) 'A generalized linkage approach to development, with special reference to staples', *Economic Development and Cultural Change*, 25(supplement):67–98.

Hoffmann, W.G. (1958) *The growth of industrial economies*. Manchester: Manchester University Press.

Hoselitz, B.F. (1960) 'Theories of stages of economic growth', in: B.F. Hoselitz, ed., *Theories of economic growth*. New York: The Free Press.

Houthakker, H.S. (1957) 'An international comparison of household expenditure patterns: Commemorating the centenary of Engel's law', *Econometrica*, 25:532–551.

Houthakker, H.S. (1965) 'On some determinants of savings in the developed and underdeveloped countries', in: E.A.G. Robinson, ed., *Problems of economic development*. London: Macmillan.

Jackson, L.F. (1984) 'Hierarchic demand and the Engel curve for variety', *Review of Economics and Statistics*, 66:8–15.

Johnson, H.G. (1965) 'A theoretical model of economic nationalism in new and developing states', *Political Science Quarterly*, 80:169–185.

Kaldor, N. (1961) 'Capital accumulation and economic growth', in: F.A. Lutz and D.C. Hague, eds., *The theory of capital*. London: Macmillan.

Kaldor, N. (1985) *Economics without equilibrium*. New York: M.E. Sharpe, Inc.

Kelley, A.C. and Williamson, J.G. (1984) *What drives third world city growth? A dynamic general equilibrium approach*. Princeton, NJ: Princeton University Press.

Kelley, A.C., Williamson, J.G. and Cheetham, R. (1972) *Dualistic economic development*. Chicago: University of Chicago Press.

Kindleberger, C.P. (1967) *Europe's postwar growth: The role of labor supply*. Cambridge, MA: Harvard University Press.

Kornai, J. (1971) *Anti-equilibrium*. Amsterdam: North-Holland.

Kravis, I.B. (1984) 'Comparative studies of national incomes and prices', *Journal of Economic Literature*, 22:1–39.

Kravis, I.B. and Lipsey, R.E. (1983) *Towards an explanation of national price levels*. Special Studies in International Finance 52. Princeton, NJ: Princeton University Press.

Kravis, I.B., Heston, A.W. and Summers, R. (1982) *World product and income: International comparisons of real gross product*. Baltimore, MD: Johns Hopkins University Press.

Kravis, I.B, Heston, A.W. and Summers, R. (1983) 'The share of services in economic growth', in: F.G. Adams and B. Hickman, eds., *Global econometrics*. Cambridge, MA: MIT Press.

Krueger, A.O. (1978) *Foreign trade regimes and economic development: Liberalization attempts and consequences*. New York: National Bureau of Economic Research.

Kubo, Y., de Melo, J. and Robinson, S. (1986) 'Trade strategies and growth episodes', in: H.B. Chenery, S. Robinson and M. Syrquin, *Industrialization and growth*. New York: Oxford University Press.

Kubo, Y., Robinson, S. and Syrquin, M. (1986) 'The methodology of multisector comparative analysis', in: H.B. Chenery, S. Robinson and M. Syrquin, *Industrialization and growth*. New York: Oxford University Press.

Kuznets, S. (1951) 'The state as a unit in the study of economic growth', *Journal of Economic History*, 11:25–41.

Kuznets, S. (1956–1967) 'Quantitative aspects of the economic growth of nations', *Economic development and cultural change* (a series of 10 articles).

Kuznets, S. (1957) 'Quantitative aspects of the economic growth of nations: II. Industrial distribution of national product and labor force', *Economic Development and Cultural Change*, 5:supplement.

Kuznets, S. (1959) 'On comparative study of economic structure and growth of nations', in: National Bureau of Economic Research, *The comparative study of economic growth and structure*. New York: NBER.

Kuznets, S. (1961) 'Quantitative aspects of the economic growth of nations: IV. Long term trends in capital formation proportions', *Economic Development and Cultural Change*, 9:1–124.

Kuznets, S. (1966) *Modern economic growth*. New Haven, CT: Yale University Press.

Kuznets, S. (1971) *Economic growth of nations: Total output and production structure*. Cambridge, MA: Harvard University Press.

Kuznets, S. (1973) 'Modern economic growth: Findings and reflections', *American Economic Review*, 63:247–258.

Kuznets, S. (1979) 'Growth and structural shifts', in: W. Galenson, ed., *Economic growth and structural change in Taiwan: The postwar experience of the Republic of China*. Ithaca, NY: Cornell University Press.

Landes, D. (1969) *The unbound Prometheus: Technological change and industrial development in Western Europe from 1750 to the present*. Cambridge: Cambridge University Press.

Leamer, E.E. (1984) *Sources of international comparative advantage*. Cambridge, MA: MIT Press.

Leff, N.H. (1969) 'Dependency rates and savings rates', *American Economic Review*, 59:886–896.

Lewis, W.A. (1954) 'Economic development with unlimited supplies of labor', *Manchester School of Economic and Social Studies*, 22:139–191.

Lewis, W.A. (1984) 'The state of development theory', *American Economic Review*, 74:1–10.

Linder, S.B. (1961) *An essay on trade and transformation*. New York: Wiley.

Little, I.M.D. (1982) *Economic development: Theory, policy and international relations*. New York: Basic Books.

Little, I.M.D., Scitovsky, T. and Scott, M. (1970) *Industry and trade in some developing countries: A comparative study*. London: Oxford University Press.

Lluch, C.A., Powell, A. and Williams, R.A. (1977) *Patterns in household demand and savings*. New York: Oxford University Press.

Machlup, F. (1963) *Essays in economic semantics*. Englewood Cliffs, NJ: Prentice-Hall.

Maddison, A. (1980) 'Economic growth and structural change in the advanced countries', in: I. Leveson and J.W. Wheeler, eds., *Western economies in transition*. Boulder, CO: Westview Press.

Maddison, A. (1982) *Phases of capitalist development*. New York: Oxford University Press.

Maddison, A. (1983) 'A comparison of levels of GDP per capita in developed and developing countries, 1700–1980', *Journal of Economic History*, 43:27–41.

Maddison, A. and van Ark, B. (1987) 'International comparisons of purchasing power, real output, and productivity in manufacturing: A pilot study for Brazil, Mexico, and the U.S.A., 1975', Groningen, processed.

Mahalanobis, P.C. (1953) 'Some observations on the process of growth of national income', *Sankhyā*, 12:307–312.

Maizels, A. (1963) *Industrial growth and world trade*. Cambridge: Cambridge University Press.

Mason, E.S. (1984) 'The Chenery analysis and some other considerations', in: M. Syrquin, L. Taylor and L.E. Westphal, eds., *Economic structure and performance: Essays in honor of Hollis B. Chenery*. New York: Academic Press.

Matthews, R.C.O. (1986) 'The economics of institutions and the sources of growth,' *Economic Journal*, 96:903–918.

Matthews, R.C.O., Feinstein, C. and Odling-Smee, C. (1982) *British economic growth*. Oxford: Oxford University Press.

McCarthy, F.D., Taylor, L, and Talati, C. (1987) 'Trade patterns in developing countries, 1964–82', *Journal of Development Economics*, to appear.

Mellor, J.W. (1986) 'Agriculture on the road to industrialization', in: J.P. Lewis and V. Kallab, eds., *Development strategies reconsidered*. New Brunswick, NJ: Transaction Books for the Overseas Development Council.

Melo, J. de and Robinson, S. (1985) 'Product differentiation and trade dependence of the domestic price system in computable general equilibrium trade models', in: T. Peeters, P. Praet and P. Reding, eds., *International trade and exchange rates in the late eighties*. Amsterdam: North-Holland.

Morris, C.T. and Adelman, I. (1988) *Comparative patterns of economic development, 1850–1914*. Baltimore, MD: Johns Hopkins University Press.

Myrdal, G. (1957) *Economic theory and under-developed regions.* London: Duckworth.
National Bureau of Economic Research (1959) *The comparative study of economic growth and structure.* New York: NBER.
North, D.C. (1981) *Structure and change in economic history.* New York: Norton.
Nozick, R. (1974) *Anarchy, state, and utopia,* New York: Basic Books.
Nurkse, R. (1953) *Problems of capital formation in underdeveloped countries.* Oxford: Basil Blackwell.
Nurkse, R. (1959) "Notes on 'unbalanced growth'" *Oxford Economic Papers,* 7:295–297.
O'Brien, P.K. and Keyder, C. (1978) *Economic growth in Britain and France, 1780–1914.* London: Allen and Unwin.
Ohkawa, K. and Ranis, G., eds., (1985) *Japan and the developing countries: A comparative analysis.* Oxford: Basil Blackwell.
Ohkawa, K. and Rosovsky, H. (1973) *Japanese economic growth: Trend acceleration in the twentieth century.* Stanford, CA: Stanford University Press.
Olson, M. (1982) *The rise and decline of nations.* New Haven, CT: Yale University Press.
Pack, H. and Westphal, L.E. (1986) 'Industrial strategy and technological change: Theory vs. reality', *Journal of Development Economics,* 22:87–128.
Perkins, D.H. (1981) 'Three decades of international quantitative comparisons', Harvard Institute for International Development.
Perroux, F. (1955) "Note sur la notion de 'Pôle de croissance'", *Matériaux pour une analyse de la croissance economique.* Cahiers de l'Institute de Science Economique Applique, Serie D, No. 8.
Prakash, V. and Robinson, S. (1979) 'A cross-country analysis of patterns of industrial growth', Development Economics Department, The World Bank, Washington, DC.
Ram, R. (1985) "Conventional and 'real' GDP per capita in cross-country studies of production structure", *Journal of Development Economics,* 18:463–477.
Ranis, G. (1984) 'Typology in development theory: Retrospective and prospects', in: M. Syrquin, L. Taylor and L.E. Westphal, eds., *Economic structure and performance: Essays in honor of Hollis B. Chenery.* New York: Academic Press.
Roemer, M. (1970) *Fishing for growth: Export-led development in Peru, 1950–1967.* Cambridge, MA: Harvard University Press.
Roemer, M. (1985) 'Dutch disease in developing countries: Taking bitter medicine', in: M. Lundahl, ed., *The primary sector in economic development.* New York: St. Martin's.
Rosenstein-Rodan, P. (1943) 'Problems of industrialization in Eastern and South-Eastern Europe', *Economic Journal,* 53:202–211.
Rosenstein-Rodan, P. (1961) "Notes on the theory of the 'big push'", in: H.S. Ellis and H.C. Wallich, eds., *Economic development for Latin America.* London: Macmillan.
Rostow, W.W. (1960) *The stages of economic growth: A non-communist manifesto.* Cambridge: Cambridge University Press.
Sah, R.K. and Stiglitz, J.E. (1984) 'The economics of price scissors', *American Economic Review,* 74:124–138.
Samuelson, P.A. (1964) 'Theoretical notes on trade problems', *Review of Economics and Statistics,* 46:145–154.
Solow, R.M. (1956) 'A contribution to the theory of economic growth', *Quarterly Journal of Economics,* 70:65–94.
Solow, R.M. (1977) 'Comment of Chenery (1977)', in: B. Ohlin, P.O. Hesselborn and P.M. Wijkman, eds., *The international allocation of economic activity.* London: Macmillan.
Summers, R. and Heston, A.W. (1984) 'International comparisons of real product and its composition: 1950–80', *Review of Income and Wealth,* 30:207–262.
Svennilson, I. (1954) *Growth and stagnation in the European economy.* Geneva: United Nations Economic Commission for Europe.
Svennilson, I. (1960) 'The concept of the nation and its relevance to economic analysis', in: E.A.G. Robinson, ed., *Economic consequences of the size of nations.* London: Macmillan.
Syrquin, M. (1976) 'Sources of industrial growth and change: An alternative measure', paper presented at the European Meeting of the Econometric Society, Helsinki, Finland, August.
Syrquin, M. (1978) 'The share of trade and economic development', processed. Hebrew version in: N. Halevi and Y. Kop, eds., *Issues in economics 1977.* Jerusalem: Falk Institute.

Syrquin, M. (1984) 'Resource reallocation and productivity growth', in: M. Syrquin, L. Taylor and L.E. Westphal, eds., *Economic structure and performance: Essays in honor of Hollis B. Chenery*. New York: Academic Press.

Syrquin, M. (1985) 'Patterns of development since 1960: A comparison for China', processed.

Syrquin, M. (1986a) 'Productivity growth and factor reallocation', in: H.B. Chenery, S. Robinson and M. Syrquin, eds., *Industrialization and growth*, New York: Oxford.

Syrquin, M. (1986b) 'Sector proportions and economic development: The evidence since 1950', paper presented at the 8th World Congress of the International Economic Association, New Delhi, India.

Syrquin, M. (1986c) 'Economic growth and structural change in Israel: An international perspective', in: Y. Ben Porath, ed., *The Israeli economy: Maturing through crises*. Cambridge, MA: Harvard University Press.

Syrquin, M. and Chenery, H.B. (1986) 'Patterns of development: 1950 to 1983', processed, World Bank.

Taylor, L. (1969) 'Development patterns: A simulation study', *Quarterly Journal of Economics*, 83:220–241.

Taylor, L. (1975) 'Theoretical foundations and technical implications', in: C.R. Blitzer, P.B. Clark and L. Taylor, eds., *Economy-wide models and development planning*. London:Oxford University Press.

Taylor, L. (1979) *Macro models for developing countries*. New York: McGraw-Hill.

Taylor, L. (1986) 'Theories of sectoral change', paper presented at the 8th World Congress of the International Economic Association, New Delhi, India.

Taylor, L., Sarkar, H. and Rattso, J. (1984) 'Macroeconomic adjustment in a computable general equilibrium model for India', in: M. Syrquin, L. Taylor and L.E. Westphal, eds., *Economic structure and performance: Essays in honor of Hollis B. Chenery*. New York: Academic Press.

Teitel, S. and Thoumi, F.E. (1986) 'From import substitution to exports: The manufacturing exports experience of Argentina and Brazil', *Economic Development and Cultural Change*, 34:455–490.

UNIDO (1979) *World industry since 1960: Progress and prospects*, New York: United Nations.

UNIDO (1983) *Industry in a changing world*. New York: United Nations.

United Nations (1986) *World comparisons of purchasing power and real product for 1980, phase IV of the international comparison project*. New York: United Nations.

Watkins, M.H. (1963) 'A staple theory of economy growth', *Canadian Journal of Economics and Political Science*, 29:141–158.

Westphal, L.E. (1982) 'Fostering technological mastery by means of selective industry promotion', in: M. Syrquin and S. Teitel, eds., *Trade, stability, technology and equity in Latin America*. New York: Academic Press.

Williamson, J.G. and de Bever, L.J. (1978) 'Saving, accumulation and modern economic growth: The contemporary relevance of Japanese history', *Journal of Japanese Studies*, 4:125–167.

Wood, A. (1986) 'Puzzling trends in real exchange rates: A preliminary analysis', processed.

World Bank (1980) *World development report 1980*. New York: Oxford University Press.

World Bank (1984) *World development report 1984*. New York: Oxford University Press.

Young, A.A. (1928) 'Increasing returns and economic progress', *Economic Journal*, 38:117–132.

Chapter 8

THE AGRICULTURAL TRANSFORMATION

C. PETER TIMMER*

Harvard University

Contents

1. Introduction   276
2. The process of agricultural transformation   279
    2.1. Evolving stages   280
    2.2. Agriculture and economic development   283
    2.3. The role of the agricultural sector   288
3. Why agriculture is different   291
    3.1. Decision-making in agriculture   292
    3.2. Characteristics of agricultural production functions   294
    3.3. The farm household as both producer and consumer   299
    3.4. What difference does the difference make?   300
4. Transforming agriculture   302
    4.1. The sources and dynamics of technical change   302
    4.2. Unresolved issues   313
5. Agricultural development strategy   321
    5.1. Policies for "getting agriculture moving"   321
    5.2. Alternative strategies for maintaining the transformation process 323
    5.3. Agricultural policy and structural change   327
References   328

*I would like to thank the participants at the authors' workshop for helpful reactions to my initial ideas for this chapter. Particular thanks go to Larry Westphal, Pranab K. Bardhan, David Dapice, and Scott Pearson for serious and critical readings of the first draft. As always, my deepest debt is to my wife and editor, Carol, for her patience and persistence in helping me make my manuscripts readable and for her mastery of the wonderful new technology that permits me to lose half the manuscript with the push of a button and for her to get it back after considerable effort and anguish.

Handbook of Development Economics, Volume I, Edited by H. Chenery and T.N. Srinivasan
© *Elsevier Science Publishers B.V., 1988*

1. Introduction

The agricultural transformation has been a remarkably uniform process when viewed from outside the agricultural sector itself. As documented by Clark (1940), Kuznets (1966), Chenery and Syrquin (1975), and the patterns reported in the introductory chapter to Part II of the Handbook, the share of agriculture in a country's labor force and total output declines in both cross-section and time-series samples as incomes per capita increase. The declining importance of agriculture is uniform and pervasive, a tendency obviously driven by powerful forces inherent in the development process, whether in socialist or capitalist countries, Asian, Latin American, or African, currently developed or still poor.

It is at least slightly puzzling, then, that a second uniform and pervasive aspect of the development process also involves agriculture – the apparent requirement that rapid agricultural growth accompany or precede general economic growth. The logic of the classical model of economic growth requires it:

> Now if the capitalist sector produces no food, its expansion increases the demand for food, raises the price of food in terms of capitalist products, and so reduces profits. This is one of the senses in which industrialization is dependent upon agricultural improvement; it is not profitable to produce a growing volume of manufactures unless agricultural production is growing simultaneously. This is also why industrial and agrarian revolutions *always* go together, and why economies in which agriculture is stagnant do not show industrial development [Lewis (1954, p. 433, emphasis added)].

The historical record to which Lewis alludes supports the strong link between agricultural and industrial growth, at least in market-oriented economies. The English model is often held up as the case in point:

> Consider what happened in the original home of industrial development, in England in the eighteenth century. Everyone knows that the spectacular industrial revolution would not have been possible without the agricultural revolution that preceded it. And what was this agricultural revolution? It was based on the introduction of the turnip. The lowly turnip made possible a change in crop rotation which did not require much capital, but which brought about a tremendous rise in agricultural productivity. As a result, more food could be grown with much less manpower. Manpower was released for capital construction. The growth of industry would not have been possible without the turnip and other improvements in agriculture [Nurkse (1953, pp. 52–53)].

Despite a significantly different view in the current literature about the impact of the English agricultural revolution on labor productivity, the key importance of the increase in agricultural output has not been challenged [Timmer (1969), Hayami and Ruttan (1985)]. Nor is this importance restricted to the lessons from the currently developed countries. In surveying the statistical link between agricultural and overall economic growth in currently less-developed countries, the World Bank reached the following conclusions:

The continuing importance of agriculture in the economies of the developing countries is reflected in the association between the growth of agriculture and of the economy as a whole. Among countries where the agricultural share of GDP was greater than 20 percent in 1970, agricultural growth in the 1970s exceeded 3 percent a year in 17 of the 23 countries whose GDP growth was above 5 percent a year [see Table 8.1]. During the same period, 11 of the 17 countries with GDP growth below 3 percent a year managed agricultural growth of only 1 percent or less. Agricultural and GDP growth differed by less than two percentage points in 11 of 15 countries experiencing moderate growth. There have been exceptions, of course, but they prove the rule: fast GDP growth and sluggish agriculture was a feature of some of the oil- or mineral-based economies such as Algeria, Ecuador, Morocco, and Nigeria.

The parallels between agricultural and GDP growth suggest that the factors which affect agricultural performance may be linked to economy-wide social and economic policies.... Expanding agricultural production through technological change and trade creates important demands for the outputs of other sectors, notably fertilizer, transportation, commercial services, and construction. At the same time, agricultural households are often the basic market for a wide range of consumer goods that loom large in the early stages of industrial development – textiles and clothing, processed foods, kerosene and vegetable oils, aluminum holloware, radios, bicycles, and construction materials for home improvements [World Bank (1982, pp. 44–45)].

The need for rapid agricultural growth and for the decline in the agricultural sector's share of output and the labor force are not contradictory, of course, but the apparent paradox gave rise to a widespread misperception that agriculture is unimportant – that it does not require resources or a favorable policy environment – *because* its relative share of the economy declines.

So long as market forces provide the primary direction to the sectoral allocation of resources, how academics perceive this process is irrelevant to the process itself. When government planners intercede, however, they do so within a framework of objectives and constraints, and this framework is ultimately conditioned by the prevailing academic understanding of how economic growth proceeds. The mainstream paradigm of the 1950s suggested that agriculture could and should be squeezed on behalf of the more dynamic sectors of the economy. This strategy could be successful if agriculture was already growing rapidly (as in

Table 8.1
Growth of agriculture and GDP in the 1970s

Agricultural growth	GDP growth		
	Above 5 percent	3–5 percent	Below 3 percent
Above 3 percent	Cameroon Malawi[a] China[a] Malaysia Colombia Paraguay Dominican Rep. Philippines Guatemala Thailand Indonesia Tunisia Ivory Coast Turkey Kenya Yemen Arab Rep. Korea, Rep. of	Bolivia Burma[a] Mali[a] Somalia[a] Tanzania[a]	Liberia Nicaragua Senegal
1–3 percent	Costa Rica Ecuador Egypt Lesotho	Bangladesh[a] Central African Rep.[a] El Salvador Haiti[a] Honduras India[a] Pakistan[a] Sri Lanka[a] Sudan[a] Upper Volta[a]	Burundi[a] Sierra Leone[a] Zaire[a]
Below 1 percent	Morocco Nigeria	Togo[a]	Angola[a] Chad[a] Congo. Rep. Ethiopia[a] Ghana Madagascar[a] Mauritania[a] Mozambique[a] Nepal[a] Niger[a] Uganda[a]

[a] Low-income countries.
Source: World Bank (1982, p. 45).

Western Europe and Japan) or if it started with a large surplus relative to the subsistence needs of the rural population (as in the USSR). But if the agricultural sector started with traditional technology and yields and living standards near subsistence, the "squeeze agriculture" paradigm created economic stagnation, not growth. In those cases, major attention was needed to induce an agricultural transformation if the industrial revolution was to have any real hope of success.

Upon closer examination, it is not paradoxical that agricultural growth leads to agricultural decline. At least two mechanisms, now relatively well understood and documented, account for this process of structural transformation.[1] Engel's Law alone, in a closed economy with constant prices, explains a declining share for agriculture (and low farm incomes unless some farmers leave agriculture) no matter how fast the sector grows. Because growth is led by demand patterns in market economies, a less-than-unitary income elasticity for the products of the agricultural sector guarantees that gross value of sales by farmers will grow less rapidly than gross domestic product. As Lewis implies in the previous quotation, if agricultural output fails to grow rapidly enough, rising prices might actually garner farmers a higher share of consumers' expenditures. But this reflects *lower* real incomes, not the result of economic growth.

If the terms of trade are not to rise in favor of agriculture, farm productivity must rise – an agricultural revolution is needed. The second factor that explains the joint agricultural growth and relative decline is seen in the rapid growth in agricultural productivity, measured by output per laborer or output per hectare, in all the successfully developed countries. Technical change in agriculture in all of the OECD countries proceeded at such a pace that the long-run terms of trade declined for farm products. Lower prices thus exacerbated the sluggish demand growth due to low income elasticities; the combination put pressure on agricultural resources to move out of farming and into the more rapidly growing sectors of the economy. Such intersectoral movements of resources have been painful in all societies that have undergone successful structural transformation, and all societies have found mechanisms to cushion the adjustment process.

The paradox over the agricultural transformation occurs at this point. Just as countries learn how to institutionalize the process of rapid technical change in agriculture, its product no longer has high social value. The resulting low incomes for farmers create powerful political pressures to slow the process of structural change, and the seemingly inevitable result is massive distortion of the price structure [Johnson (1973), Anderson and Hayami (1986), World Bank (1986)]. Nearly all rich countries protect their agricultural sectors from international competition, and countries no farther along in the development process than Malaysia, Indonesia, Zimbabwe, and Mexico protect key food-producing sectors during periods of depressed world prices.

2. The process of agricultural transformation

From both historical and contemporary cross-section perspectives, the agricultural transformation seems to evolve through at least four phases that are roughly

---

[1] For a very useful summary of the literature that documents the agricultural transformation process itself and also attempts to explain it in terms of the prevailing models of economic development, see Johnston (1970).

definable. The process starts when agricultural productivity per worker rises. This increased productivity creates a surplus, which in the second phase can be tapped directly, through taxation and factor flows, or indirectly, through government intervention into the rural–urban terms of trade. This surplus can be utilized to develop the nonagricultural sector, and this phase has been the focus of most dual economy models of development. For resources to flow out of agriculture, rural factor and product markets must become better integrated with those in the rest of the economy. The progressive integration of the agricultural sector into the macro economy, via improved infrastructure and market-equilibrium linkages, represents a third phase in agricultural development. When this phase is successful, the fourth phase is barely noticeable; the role of agriculture in industrialized economies is little·different from the role of the steel, housing, or insurance sectors. But when the integration is not successfully accomplished – and most countries have found it extremely difficult for political reasons – governments encounter serious problems of resource allocation and even problems beyond their borders because of pervasive attempts by high-income countries to protect their farmers from foreign competition. Managing agricultural protection and its impact on world commodity markets thus provides a continuing focus for agricultural policy makers even when the agricultural transformation is "complete".

2.1. Evolving stages

The four phases in the agricultural transformation call for different policy approaches. In the earliest stage of development the concern must be for "getting agriculture moving", to use Arthur Mosher's vivid phrase [Mosher (1966)]. A significant share of a country's investable resources may well be extracted from agriculture at this stage, but this is because the rest of the economy is so small. Direct or indirect taxation of agriculture is the only significant source of government revenue.

Building a dynamic agriculture requires that some of these resources be devoted to the agricultural sector itself. As the section on agricultural development policy at the end of this chapter explains, these resources need to be allocated to public investment in research and infrastructure as well as to favorable price incentives to farmers to adopt new technology as it becomes available. As these investments *in* agriculture begin to pay off, the second phase emerges in which the agricultural sector becomes a key contributor to the overall growth process through a combination of factors outlined by Johnston and Mellor (1961).

As the empirical literature on structural patterns of growth emphasizes, there is a substantial disequilibrium between agriculture and industry at this early stage of the development process [Kuznets (1966), Chenery and Taylor (1968), Chenery and Syrquin (1975)]. Indeed, differences in labor productivity and measured income (as opposed to psychic income) between the rural and urban sectors persist to the present in rich countries, although the gap is narrowing and now depends on agricultural prices for any given year.[2]

The process of narrowing the gap gives rise to the third environment for agriculture, in which it is integrated into the rest of the economy through the development of more efficient labor and credit markets that link the urban and rural economies. This integration is a component of the contribution process; the improved functioning of factor markets merely speeds the process of extracting labor and capital from those uses in agriculture with low returns for those in industry or services with higher productivity. The improved markets have welfare consequences as well, because they lessen the burden on individuals trapped in low-income occupations. The gain has costs, however. As agriculture is integrated into the macro economy, it becomes much more vulnerable to fluctuations in macro prices and level of aggregate activity and trade [Schuh (1976)] and much less susceptible to management by traditional instruments for the agricultural sector, such as extension activities and specific programs for commodity development and marketing.

This vulnerability and complexity create the fourth phase in the agricultural transformation, the treatment of agriculture in industrialized economies. As the share of the labor force in agriculture falls below about 20 percent and the share of food expenditures in urban household budgets drops to about 30 percent, low-cost food is not as important to the overall economy nor is it as expensive in relative terms to increase in price [Anderson (1983)]. A host of political problems arise if low farm incomes, induced by rapid technical change and low farm-gate prices, are allowed to push resources out of agriculture. Farmers do not want to leave, especially if they must sell their farms under duress at low prices; and urban-based unions do not want to see them coming to the cities in search of industrial jobs. A nostalgic memory of farming as a "way of life" leads many second- and third-generation farm migrants living in cities to lend political support to higher incomes for agriculture, even at the expense of higher grocery bills (which may be barely noticeable). By this stage of the process, the share of the farm-gate price of the commodity in the consumer's market basket is small because of processing and marketing costs. Commodity price supports become

---

[2] The structural rigidities in the economy that give rise to this substantial disequilibrium obviously mean that neoclassical models based solely on perfect markets and rational actors will fail to predict accurately the impact of government interventions. However, purely structural models that assume an absence of market response might be equally far from the mark. A messy amalgam of structural rigidities, imperfect markets, and decision-makers interested in their own, but vaguely defined, welfare seems to characterize the actual starting point from which government interventions must be evaluated.

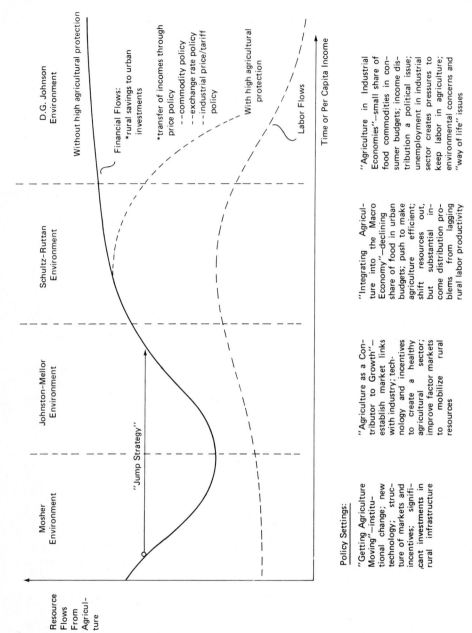

Figure 8.1. Changing environments for agriculture's contribution to economic growth.

the primary vehicle for supporting farm incomes, and the subsidies have devastating effects on resource allocation. Farmers invest heavily in land and machinery when farm prices are high, only to produce surpluses that are impossible to sell profitably [Johnson (1985), Cochrane (1979)]. Eventually, the budgetary and distortionary costs of this approach become so high that even the European Community, Japan, or the United States must face choices over how to rationalize agricultural returns with their social profitability.

The economic environments for agriculture created by these four phases are shown schematically in Figure 8.1. The financial and labor resource flows out of agriculture over time (or as incomes increase in a cross-section sample) are impressionistic. Whether the trough between the "Mosher environment" and the "Johnston–Mellor environment" in Figure 8.1 drops into negative ground or always remains positive presumably depends on alternative sources of financial resources at this stage in development. Urban or overseas remittances, petroleum revenues, or foreign assistance might temporarily fill the gap left by a declining relative contribution from agriculture.[3] But as agricultural productivity begins to rise, labor and financial flows to the rest of. the economy increase. The "Schultz–Ruttan environment" begins as the absolute population in agriculture starts to decline, and the "D.G. Johnson environment" begins as the agricultural labor force drops to a fairly small proportion of the overall labor force. Whether financial resources continue to flow out of agriculture at this stage in the process depends almost entirely on government price policy and its resulting impact on farm investment. Policies to cushion the impact on farmers of successful structural change need not inevitably rely on price interventions that impede the adjustment process, but price supports have been the most popular in the United States, Western Europe, and Japan for plausible political reasons [Anderson and Hayami (1986)].

2.2. Agriculture and economic development

This overview of the agricultural transformation raises two basic issues to be discussed in this chapter: the contribution or role of agriculture in economic development, and the conditions or factors that lead to the modernization of the agricultural sector itself. Obviously, many other important topics are not treated here. One is the changing control over resources in the rural sector, which determines who gains and loses during the agricultural transformation. Only the

---

[3] It is also important to distinguish subsectors within agriculture. An export crop subsector producing rubber or coffee might continue to provide financial resources to the rest of the economy, some of which could be returned to the foodcrop subsector in order to foster its development. Much of the discussion in this chapter is concerned with modernizing the foodcrop subsector while recognizing the important role played by the other agricultural subsectors.

structuralist and radical political economy literature deals directly with the distribution of income and power in rural areas as an integral component of agricultural development. A major theme of "neo-neoclassical analysis" since the mid-1970s, however, has been the incorporation of such issues into rational actor models of rural household decision-making [see Bardhan, Chapter 3 in this Handbook]. While much of the dynamic and macroeconomic perspective of the radical models is lost in the household models, much is gained in the form of testable hypotheses about the impact of new technology or pricing policies on the structure of rural markets and distribution of output in the short run.[4]

The historical record after the Second World War suggests that many countries saw an opportunity to pursue a "jump strategy" and move directly from the early stages of the Mosher environment in Figure 8.1 to the later stages of the Johnston–Mellor environment, thus bypassing the necessity to invest in agricultural development.

> ...the most significant comparison... is that between the levels of productivity in the under-developed countries and the western countries at the period when the latter began to industrialize.... [T]he present average level of agricultural productivity in African and Asian countries (between them representing four-fifths of the Third World population) is 45 percent below that reached by the developed countries at the start of the industrial revolution. In fact it is at the same level as that of the European countries before their agricultural revolution.
>
> Now, most under-developed countries wish, consciously or unconsciously, to by-pass this stage just when other structural conditions of development are making a "take off" more difficult than it was when most European countries and the United States were imitating England's example. What makes the failure to admit or even to recognize this problem all the more serious is that the problem itself is intractable. Leaving aside mental attitudes, landownership and political considerations, it cannot be stressed too forcibly that an increase in the area cultivated per agricultural worker is one of the essential conditions of an increase in productivity. But in view of the population explosion it is impossible to assume, even on most hopeful assumption, that the reduction in cultivated area per worker will be anything but slight [Bairoch (1975, p. 42)].

A jump strategy sees the extraction of resources from agriculture for economic development as being in conflict with the investment of public and private resources in its modernization. This has been especially true in countries with systems of planned resource allocations designed to force the pace of economic development. As more and more countries adopted the paradigm of central

---

[4]See Hart (forthcoming) for an eloquent complaint that such micro models effectively "gut" the Marxian analysis of its vision of class interactions providing the driving force to rural dynamics.

planning to direct these resource allocations, the separate issues of contribution and modernization became key analytical issues as well. Unfortunately, the economics profession was ill-equipped to address them because all previous examples of agricultural modernization had taken place within more or less market-oriented settings (except in the Soviet Union, where agricultural modernization remains quite incomplete). The behavior of backward agricultural systems under the new planning context became a topic of much theorizing and debate, but only in the 1960s and 1970s did the empirical record become both long and varied enough to draw reasonably firm conclusions.

It is worth summarizing briefly what the empirical record showed by 1960 when the results of Kuznets' decade-long study of the quantitative aspects of modern economic growth started to be widely available. The historical record began as early as the late eighteenth century in the United Kingdom and 1839 in the United States and as late as 1880 in Japan and 1925 in the USSR. For all countries for all time periods observed, the share of agriculture in the total labor force declined, sometimes sharply, as in Sweden, the United States, and Japan, and sometimes more gradually, as in the United Kingdom, Belgium, Italy, and Australia. The share of agriculture in national output showed slightly more mixed patterns than those of the labor force. The share was nearly stable or even rose slightly over some periods in the United Kingdom, France, the United States, and Australia. The more general tendency of the share in output to decline is clear, but the share of the labor force always declined more rapidly. The obvious result was that labor productivity in agriculture rose more rapidly than in the economy as a whole when measured over the long periods of time required for sustained economic growth to cause substantial changes in the structure of an economy. Although agricultural productivity per worker was nearly always less than the level of national productivity, its faster rise meant that the gap tended to narrow.

Three clear exceptions to this trend in Kuznets' data are Italy, Japan, and the USSR, all of which are latecomers to the process of sustained growth and are countries in which state intervention into the industrialization process was much more active than in the early developers. The failure of agricultural productivity per worker to rise as fast as national productivity in these three countries might thus be seen as an early signal that the patterns in the less-developed countries seeking to start down the path of modern economic growth might be significantly different from the historical path followed by the Western countries and documented by Kuznets. Table 8.2, drawn from a paper by Hayami (1986), shows that the recent productivity record for the rapidly growing East Asian economies confirms a strongly different pattern from that in North America and Western Europe. Even the more slowly growing developing countries (Philippines and India) have a mild reversal of the "traditional" pattern in which growth in labor productivity in agriculture exceeds that of labor productivity in manufacturing.

Table 8.2
International comparison in the growth rates of labor productivity
in agriculture and manufacturing, 1960 (1958–62 averages)
to 1980 (1978–82 averages)

	Labor productivity growth rate (%/year)[a]		
	Agriculture	Manufacturing	(1)–(2)
	(1)	(2)	= (3)
Developed countries:			
United States	6.3	3.2	3.1
United Kingdom	5.5	2.6	2.9
France	6.4	4.2	2.2
Germany (F.R.)	7.7	4.1	3.6
Japan	5.3	6.7	−1.4
Developing countries:			
Korea	4.0	7.5	−3.5
Philippines	3.2	3.5[b]	−0.3
India	1.3	2.1	−0.9

[a] Calculated from the ratios of the real output index to the employment index.
[b] Growth rate from 1960 to 1975.
Sources: FAO, *Production Yearbook*; UN, Yearbook of *Industrial Statistics*; ILO, Yearbook of *Labor Statistics*; OECD, *Labor Force Statistics*. Hayami (1986, p. 10).

This "premature" growth in manufacturing productivity (or, alternatively, the neglect of efforts needed to raise agricultural productivity) is especially troubling in historical perspective, as the quote from Bairoch previously indicated. Table 8.3 reproduces Bairoch's historical comparisons of "net agricultural production by male labor employed in agriculture expressed in 'direct' calories". Only Italy in 1840 had a lower productivity level than that of Africa and Asia in modern times. The gap in agricultural productivity on average between European countries beginning their industrial revolutions and Africa and Asia is, as Bairoch already noted, about 45 percent. "A gap of about 45 percent is sufficiently wide for us to be able to assert that agricultural conditions in the currently developed countries before the beginning of the industrial revolution must have been very different from those of the under-developed countries of Asia and Africa today" [Bairoch (1975, pp. 40–41)].

Based on data only up to the early 1970s, Bairoch's pessimism reflects the widespread neglect of agriculture in many development efforts in the 1950s and 1960s, as well as the shortfalls in food production that triggered the world food crisis in 1973–1974. A similar pessimism based on a quite different reading of the historical record is provided by scholars working in the Marxian tradition and following the insights of Lenin on the changing class structure of agriculture as it becomes more capitalistic under the pressures of modernization [Baran (1952),

Table 8.3
Comparisons between levels of agricultural productivity

Country and "stage" of development	Period	Index number of agricultural productivity
Developed countries:		
Recent position		
France	1968/72	100.0
United States	1968/72	330.0
Position before or during "take-off"		
France	1810	7.0
Great Britain	1810	14.0
Sweden	1810	6.5
Belgium	1840	10.0
Germany	1840	7.5
Italy	1840	4.0
Russia	1840	7.0
Switzerland	1840	8.0
United States	1840	21.5
Spain	1860	11.0
Less-developed countries:		
Recent position		
Africa	1960/64–1968/72	4.7
Latin America[a]	1960/64–1968/72	9.8
Asia	1960/64–1968/72	4.8
Middle East	1960/64–1968/72	8.6
Total for all less-developed countries:	1960/64–1968/72	5.5

[a] Excluding Argentina.
Source: Bairoch (1975, p. 40).

de Janvry (1981), Griffin (1979), Lenin (1899)]. The failure of the Marxist–Leninist prediction that peasant (family) agriculture disappears under the competitive pressures of modern corporate agriculture has led to a rethinking of the inevitability of all countries following a path through capitalism to socialism and eventually to communism. To explain the failure, the dependency school emphasizes relationships between the metropolitan (developed) center and the periphery (underdeveloped) countries in the third world. A single process of global economic growth occurs in a zero-sum context, in which the growth of the center is at the direct expense of the periphery. Class relationships in the urban-based governments of the periphery explain the perpetuation of economic policies that favor only a small urban elite (and possibly landlords). In Latin America, de Janvry (1981) and colleagues have extended the analysis to explain agricultural policy and performance on the basis of a process of marginalization. Their model argues that agricultural laborers and independent peasants gradually lose control of the resources needed to raise their living standards as large landowners invest in capital-intensive farming techniques and displace peasants from the market. The rural masses are too dispersed to mobilize effectively, and they suffer a process of gradual immiseration.

Hayami and Ruttan provide a useful summary of three theories of development and their implications for agriculture:

> The implications of dependency theory for agricultural development stand in sharp contrast to the growth-stage and dual-economy theories. The growth-stage theories attempt to explain the process of transformation from a primarily agrarian to an industrial economy. In the dynamic dual-economy models incorporation of peasants into the market results in the disappearance of dualism. The dependency perspective attempts to explain why the periphery remains trapped in a backward agrarian state. In the dependency view incorporation of rural areas into the market is the source of marginalization – it perpetuates rather than erodes dualism [Hayami and Ruttan (1985, p. 37)].

Although Hayami and Ruttan do not find the dependency theory very useful for designing policies that *foster* the process of agricultural development, one of the main questions asked by scholars of the dependency school remains unanswered: why has agricultural development played a strongly positive role in the overall development process in so few countries? Why have so many opportunities identified by agricultural scientists and economic planners been missed? Most neoclassical scholars will agree that they do not have answers to these questions.

√ *2.3. The role of the agricultural sector*

The debate over the role of agriculture in the process of economic development extends at least as far back as the Physiocrats in the eighteenth century. The biblical advice to store during seven good years to be ready for seven lean years certainly reflects a concern for agricultural planning. Clark (1940) and Kuznets (1966) provided the general facts about the role of agriculture during the growth process available to economists and planners at the beginning of the drive for economic growth in the less-developed countries. These facts formed the basis for the prevailing neoclassical view that agriculture was a declining sector, a "black box" in Little's phrase (1982), which contributed labor, food, and perhaps capital to the essential modernization efforts in industry. No policy efforts on behalf of agriculture's own modernization were needed because the sector declined naturally. Most interpretations of the Lewis model (1954), especially the Fei–Ranis versions (1964), which became the main teaching paradigms, ignored the factors needed to modernize traditional agricultural sectors so that they could play positive contributory roles in the development of the rest of the economy. The structuralist views of Prebisch (1950) about declining terms of trade for traditional products and the importance Hirschman (1958) attached to linkages to "modern" economic activities further diminished any apparent rationale for actively investing in the modernization of agriculture itself. As Hirschman wrote in 1958, "agriculture certainly stands convicted on the count of its lack of direct stimulus to the setting up of new activities through linkage effects – the superiority of manufacturing in this respect is crushing" [Hirschman (1958, pp. 109–110)].

A final reason for the neglect of agriculture has recently been clarified by Sah and Stiglitz (1984). The Soviet debate in the early 1920s over industrialization policy revolved around whether turning the terms of trade against agriculture (the "price scissors") would speed the rate of accumulation for investment by the state. Preobrazhensky (1965) argued successfully that it could. Sah and Stiglitz show the precise conditions under which he was right and the welfare consequences that flowed from implementing such a policy. Although the conditions that must hold for their analysis to be valid are very stringent, a robust result is that the agricultural terms of trade should be lowered only if the state has a low rate of time discount, that is, it favors investment over current consumption. Forced-pace industrialization campaigns in such circumstances then rely on the state's capacity to extract surpluses from agriculture even in the face of stagnant or falling agricultural production.

It is easy to see why agriculture was neglected as a source of growth in early strategies of economic development. The historical record shows that it always declines in relative importance in growing economies. It is the home of traditional people, ways, and living standards – the antithesis of what nation builders in developing countries envisioned for their societies. Moreover, agriculture was thought to provide the only source of productivity that could be tapped to fuel the drive for modernization. Surplus labor, surplus savings, and surplus expenditures to buy the products of urban industry, and even surplus foreign exchange to buy the machines to make them, could be had from an uncomplaining agricultural sector. Nothing more was needed to generate these resources than the promise of jobs in the cities and a shared nationalistic pride in the growing power of the state. Despite how simplistic these promises sound in the mid-1980s, the success of the Soviet approach caused them to be very appealing when first uttered by such charismatic leaders of the developing world as Sukarno, Nkrumah, Nasser, and Nehru. The unique features of agriculture as a sector were simply not widely understood in the 1950s. Nor was it accepted that the development of a modern agriculture was necessary as a concomitant to development of the rest of the economy.

Some of these factors began to be recognized by the 1960s, and a more positive emphasis was placed on "role" rather than the more forced concept of "contribution" of agriculture. The classic article by Johnston and Mellor (1961) listed five

roles for agriculture in economic development:
  (1) increase the supply of food for domestic consumption;
  (2) release labor for industrial employment;
  (3) enlarge the size of the market for industrial output;
  (4) increase the supply of domestic savings; and
  (5) earn foreign exchange.

Although the second, fourth, and fifth roles are certainly consistent with the earlier "extractive" views of agriculture, Johnston and Mellor insisted that all five roles are equally important. Agriculture in the process of development is to provide increased food supplies and higher rural incomes to enlarge markets for urban output, as well as to provide resources to expand that urban output.

> It is our contention that "balanced growth" is needed in the sense of simultaneous efforts to promote agricultural and industrial development. We recognize that there are severe limitations on the capacity of an underdeveloped country to do everything at once. But it is precisely this consideration which underscores the importance of developing agriculture in such a way as to both minimize its demand on resources most needed for industrial development and maximize its net contribution required for general growth [Johnston and Mellor (1961, pp. 590–591)].

Others, especially Nichols (1963), Schultz (1953), and Jorgenson (1961), also emphasized this interdependence between a country's agriculture and its industry. Myint (1975) stressed a curious inconsistency between the "closed economy" model implicit in this domestic interdependence and the fifth role, earning foreign exchange, which obviously implies the country is open to international trade. This trade perspective returns in the 1970s and 1980s to dominate thinking about appropriate development strategies, but it was largely ignored in the 1960s, perhaps because of the dominance of the "Indian model" in development thinking, in which sheer size keeps the importance of foreign trade quite small, even apart from the "inward looking" strategy being pursued.

Despite the early insistence by agricultural economists that the agricultural sector must be viewed as part of the overall economy and that the emphasis be placed on the sector's interdependence with the industrial and service sectors rather than on its forced contributions to them, the notion of agriculture as a resource reservoir has persisted in general development models. Reynolds emphasized an important but usually overlooked distinction between static and dynamic views of the resource transfers:

> In most development models, modern industry is the cutting edge of economic growth, while agriculture plays the role of a resource reservoir which can be drawn on for supplies of food, labor, and finance to fuel the growth of urban

activities. It is argued that this is both a logical necessity and a matter of historical experience, illustrated by the case of Japan.

In commenting on this view, I must emphasize a distinction that is often not clearly drawn: (1) It is one thing to assert that, in an economy where agricultural output is not rising, the agricultural sector contains potential surpluses of labor time, food output, and saving capacity requiring only appropriate public policies for their release. This we may term the static view of resource transfer. (2) It is quite a different thing to assert that, in an economy where agricultural output is being raised by a combination of investment and technical progress, part of the increment in farm output and income is available for transfer to non-agriculture. This we may term the dynamic view of resource transfer. The model-building implications of this approach are different, and its policy implications are decidedly different [Reynolds (1975, pp. 14–15)].

The welfare consequences of the two views are also sharply different. Forced extraction of resources from a stagnant agricultural sector almost always creates widespread rural poverty, sometimes famine. Market linkages that connect a dynamic agricultural sector to rapidly growing industrial and service sectors offer an opportunity for rural inhabitants to choose in which sector they wish to participate. There are certainly losers in this process: high-cost producers in unfavorable ecological settings who cannot compete with low-cost producers in favored locales who have access to new technology; or newly landless laborers who have lost their tenancy access to land when commercial relationships replace patron–client relationships. But new technology and market linkages create more opportunities than they destroy if both the agricultural and nonagricultural sectors are growing together. An emphasis on finding the policy environment that creates such mutual growth is needed. For agriculture, that environment must call forth rapid technical change. Experience since the mid-1960s has demonstrated how to do that, but the key has been to understand why the agricultural sector is different from the industrial and service sectors [Hayami and Ruttan (1985), Timmer et al. (1983)].

3. Why agriculture is different

The early purposeful neglect of agriculture can be partly attributed to development economists who were remote from any real understanding of what makes the agricultural sector quite different from either manufacturing or services [Little (1982)]. In developing countries, the agricultural sector is different from other productive sectors of an economy, particularly in its large contribution to national income and the large numbers of participants in the sector. Both the agricultural transformation itself and the contribution of agriculture to the rest of the economy depend on three important features discussed here: the peculiarities of the agricultural production function, the importance of home consumption of output for the sector, and the role of the agricultural sector as a resource reservoir. These features are more evident in traditional societies, and their distinctiveness erodes during the process of economic modernization. The design of agricultural policy, in both poor and rich countries, is complicated by these features, but a recognition of them is essential to a full understanding of the contribution agriculture might realistically be asked to make to a country's development effort.[5]

3.1. Decision-making in agriculture

The sheer size of agriculture in most poor countries' economies, with over 50 percent of national output and up to 80 percent of the labor force in agricultural activities, distinguishes the sector from all others in the early stages of development. When directly related input and output industries and marketing activities are included, "agribusiness" seldom declines to less than 20 percent of any country's economy. Hence the sector remains the largest single "industry" in absolute size even in rich countries.

In most countries, if the available arable land were divided equally among the farm population, the resulting average farm size would be "small" by comparison with United States or European standards. Farms of less than a hectare characterize China, Bangladesh, and Java; even in Japan average farm size is still only slightly greater than one hectare. The average in India is only about 1 to 2 hectares, and in Africa and Latin America farms tend to be less than 10 to 20 hectares in size. Average farm size in the United States is well over 100 hectares and over 50 hectares in the United Kingdom.

The available farmland, of course, is usually not equally divided among all the potential farmers. The conditions of land tenure and the size distribution of farms are important characteristics of a country's agricultural decision-making environment. A country with a unimodal distribution of farm sizes – a large number of small, family-operated farms capable of supporting the family members above a subsistence level, with only a fringe of smaller and larger farms around this modal norm – has the potential to use agricultural development strategy as a means of reducing rural poverty at the same time that it increases agricultural production. Countries with bimodal distributions of farm sizes – many

---

[5]An effort to formalize the impact of agriculture's distinct features, especially the behavioral and material determinants of production relations, is in Binswanger and Rosenzweig (1986).

very small farms on a minority of the land with a few very large, estate-like farms that occupy most of the arable land and produce most of the food surplus available for urban markets – face much more difficult dilemmas over how to reduce the impact of rural poverty while using traditional output-increasing strategies of agricultural development [Johnston and Kilby (1975)].

In both private and collective agricultures, decision-making is conditioned primarily by the nature of incentives to work rather than by the pace and design of the work itself, and these incentives are difficult to structure in an efficient manner unless the cultivator owns the land. In situations where ownership and operation are separate, a host of complicated contractual arrangements that strive for second-best efficiency outcomes have evolved in different settings [Bardhan, Chapter 3 in this Handbook, Binswanger and Rosenzweig (1981, 1986), Stiglitz, Chapter 5 in this Handbook].

Farming is an undertaking that involves many decisions. What crops to plant, what inputs to use, when to plow, to seed, to cultivate, to irrigate, to harvest, how much to keep for home consumption, how much to sell and how much to store for later sale are the farming decisions that occupy the daily routine of most agricultural producers. What is unique about agriculture is that literally millions of individuals and households are making these decisions themselves. Changing agricultural production decisions to increase food output is an entirely different process from changing decisions about how much steel or cement to produce. In most countries a dozen or so individuals could take direct action which would lead to a 10 percent increase in steel output in a year or so, and their decisions would be decisive.

Nowhere, not even in socialist countries, can a similar small group of individuals decide to raise food production by 10 percent. A small group of planners, or the president and the cabinet, can decide they *want* food production to rise by 10 percent. They can tell the food logistics agency, the ministry of agriculture, the newspapers, and agriculture extension agents that they want food production to rise by 10 percent. But they cannot increase food production 10 percent by themselves. They must also convince the millions of farmers in their country to want to increase food production by 10 percent and make it in their self-interest to do so.

The vast number of agricultural decision-makers implies that there are simply too many to reach directly with either pleas for cooperation or police power. Farmers must see the benefits of higher output for themselves because there are too many opportunities to let high yields slip beneath the hoe or in a late fertilizer application, even under the watchful eyes of a guardian. Farming is a subtle combination of skilled craft and brute force. The brute force alone will not achieve high yields.

In traditional agriculture with static technology, farmers learn these skills by repeated trial and error. The lessons of parents and grandparents remain relevant. But when new technology becomes available, farmers do not automatically acquire the requisite skills to deal with disequilibrium [Schultz (1964, 1975)]. Government interventions can have a high payoff, particularly investment in extension services, general education (especially rural primary education that includes instruction in farming skills), and rural infrastructure to lower the costs of exchanging inputs and outputs, which become essential ingredients in speeding the adoption of new agricultural technology.

The scope for effective government intervention is conditioned by the efficiency with which farms allocate the resources at their disposal to produce crops, relative to alternative uses of these resources, the technical ability of farmers to achieve the maximum output from a given set of inputs, and the impact of alternative forms of land tenure on both allocative and technical performance of farmers. Given the large number of farmers within a typical developing country, government extension agents cannot teach each individual farmer new agricultural techniques. Price policy for farm crops and agricultural inputs, on the other hand, is an intervention that reaches most farmers quite directly while being amenable to effective government control. Consequently, knowing the role of relative prices in influencing the behavior of farmers is extremely important. The effectiveness of prices in changing producer decisions also depends on farmers' allocative and technical efficiency and on the form of tenure contract for the land they farm [Streeten (1986), Krishna (1984)]. It is a mistake to think that farmer responsiveness to price is somehow immutable and is given exogenously to the agricultural sector. Even if all farmers were narrow-minded profit-maximizers of their available production functions, there would be substantial scope for altering both the production function and the economic environment in which the maximization takes place. In a world in which risk management involves the establishment of patron–client relations, in which substantial bargaining may go on within the farm household over task assignments, the division of income, and gender-specific access to nutrients, and in which the access of farm members to labor and credit markets may change radically over time even within fairly stable agricultural technology and prices, the decision-making process itself must also be treated as a variable.

3.2. Characteristics of agricultural production functions

One unusual feature of the agricultural production function is the efficiency cost of separating labor and management. Knowing what the right inputs are, how to combine them, and how to tend the process is the major function of management. In owner-operated farming, this management skill is combined with the farm household's own labor power, which is also an important ingredient in growing crops. Several unique features of agricultural production functions contribute to the decision-intensity of farming, to the productivity of the family farm, and to the search for reasonably efficient substitutes for direct land-ownership where the family farm is not prevalent. Seasonality, geographical dispersion, and the role of risk and uncertainty are the most important.

3.2.1. Seasonality

No agricultural region of the world has an absolutely constant year-round climate. Winter and summer create distinct growing seasons in the temperate zones. Wet and dry seasons, or the monsoon season, create conditions when planting is appropriate, when harvesting would be difficult, or simply when some crops will not thrive. Climatic variations cause agricultural production to follow distinct seasonal patterns even in most tropical areas, but seasonality is not a fixed and rigid constraint. Rice will grow in the dry season if irrigation water is provided, and tomatoes will grow in Siberia in January under artificial lights in a warm greenhouse. Seasonality is important to farmers because it is generally cheaper to let nature provide many of the essential inputs for agricultural production – solar energy, water, carbon dioxide, temperature control, and essential nutrients from natural soils. But it is not always economical to let nature dictate the agronomic environment. One of the major tasks of government policy is to invest in socially-profitable interventions, such as irrigation and drainage, that increase farmers' control over the crops that can be grown in particular regions and time periods.

Seasonality also tends to create high premiums to timely performance of such critical agricultural tasks as plowing, planting, cultivating, and harvesting. Even though the available labor pool might be more than adequate to provide the required number of workers per hectare over an entire year for all the crops being grown, if certain tasks must be performed very quickly at specific times to ensure maximum yields, important labor bottlenecks might occur in the midst of an average surplus labor pool. Such bottlenecks can meet with two responses. One is to work out long-term contracts with laborers that gives them preferential access to farm employment in the off-season (or access to land to operate as a tenant farmer, or to credit, etc.) in return for working on the landowner's farm during the peak seasons [Bardhan (1984)]. Alternatively, because such arrangements tend to impose high supervisory requirements on the owner's time, they frequently induce individual farmers to mechanize specific tasks – plowing or harvesting – even when much rural unemployment exists over the course of the year. In such circumstances, a tractor that pays for itself in both private and social terms by timely plowing also has a very low marginal cost of operation for other tasks as well, and labor displacement can be much more widespread than would be indicated by the removal of the plowing bottleneck alone.

Two features of seasonality are important in designing agricultural policy. First, seasonal aspects of agricultural production frequently constrain yields because of input bottlenecks. Labor (and its supervision) is most often the constraining factor, but fertilizer, seeds, credit, or irrigation water supplies must also be available in highly-specific time periods. When fertilizer reaches the village godown a month after the proper application time, it might as well not have arrived at all. Government authorities responsible for the management of agricultural input supply distribution are frequently unaware of or insensitive to the extreme importance of timely input availability. Suppliers whose incomes depend on providing inputs to farmers when and where needed are much more responsive to shifts in weather, cropping patterns, and new technologies than are agencies trying to allocate inputs within the guidelines of five-year plans and supplies available from a planned industrial sector. Modern agriculture that uses industrial inputs as the basis for high yields is a dynamic enterprise quite unlike factories. Input and output markets must function efficiently, reacting to weather changes, alterations in cropping patterns, and technical change if production is to grow rapidly. Centrally planned allocations of industrial products to the agricultural sector are almost never in the right place at the right time, or even the right product.

Second, there are often very high private economic returns to eliminating seasonal bottlenecks in production. When these private returns are at least partly generated by higher and more stable yields of agricultural products, society is also likely to gain. But if the private gains come from displacing hired labor that has few alternative production opportunities, the social gains might be small or even negative. The seasonal dimensions to agricultural production complicate the planning process considerably. Most agricultural data are published on an annual basis, and there is an inevitable tendency to think about the sector in terms of the same annual growth performance criteria that are used to evaluate the steel or cotton textile industries. Such an annual approach hides two important roles for government analysis and intervention: in the appropriate provision of inputs when and where they are needed, and in the full analysis of the social impact on agricultural production of private investments to reduce seasonal bottlenecks.

3.2.2. Geographical dispersion

Agriculture is the only major sector that uses the land surface as an essential input into its production function. Like seasonality, this widespread use of land is due to the largesse of nature. It is almost always cheaper to let farms capture the free solar energy and rain than it is to stack a hundred stories of hydroponic "fields" on top of each other and provide the light, nutrients, and water from industrial sources. This wide geographical dispersion of agricultural production has an important economic consequence. Transportation becomes essential if any output is going to leave the farm for consumption by others or if inputs, such as modern seeds, fertilizer, pesticides, or machinery, are to be used on the farm to raise output.

In combination, seasonality and geographical dispersion create the need for a marketing system that can store the product from a short harvest period to the much longer period of desired consumption and can move the commodity from the farm where it was grown to the many households where it will be consumed. Both of these functions require that the commodity change hands and that exchange of ownership take place. This transaction can happen only when both parties agree on the terms of the exchange or the price for the commodity at the point of sale. In socialist economies the terms of exchange are often set by the state. But all other marketing services must still be provided if the food grown by farmers is to be eaten by consumers.

The necessary growth of marketing services is an often overlooked component of the agricultural transformation. As Kuznets (1966) pointed out, farmers are caught in a double squeeze by Engel's Law. The income elasticity for overall food expenditures is less than one, implying a declining share of national income for agriculture if commodity prices are stable. But a rising share of the consumers' food expenditure is devoted to marketing costs, and so farmers receive a declining share of food expenditures, thus compounding the decline in their share of national income. As discussed below, technical change has proceeded so rapidly in agriculture in the past century that farm commodity prices have tended to fall relative to prices for other goods and services produced by growing economies. Technical change is also a major factor explaining the rapidly falling share of national income captured by agriculture directly.

3.2.3. Risk and uncertainty

Farmers the world over talk primarily about two topics: the weather and prices. On these two variables ride the rewards for the whole year's effort in farming. A failed monsoon, a flood, or a hailstorm can wipe out the crop. A bumper harvest can cause large losses if the price falls too low. No other industry, even construction or tourism, is so dependent on the whims of nature and volatile markets to bring in a profit on the investment of time and money that goes into farming. Farmers who repeatedly make good decisions in the context of rapid changes in their economic environment tend to survive and thrive. Those who do not frequently fail; they move to urban areas in search of jobs or become impoverished landless laborers dependent on the rural economy for their incomes and access to food. Socialist-managed agricultures can cushion much of the welfare shock to individuals by sharing risks, but the importance of rapid and effective decision-making remains as the key to dynamic efficiency in agricultural systems.

The fact that weather is uncertain causes farmers to behave differently than they would if weather were always known. This general uncertainty usually leads farmers to choose crops that will resist weather extremes, particular varieties of crops that are more tolerant of weather variations, and lower levels of inputs than would be optimal in a certain world due to the risk of losing the investment altogether. Equally important, farmers' reactions to weather variations as they actually occur also have aggregate consequences [Roumasset, Boussard and Singh (1979)]. A late monsoon might cause millet instead of wheat to be planted, good rains might permit a second or third rice crop, and high temperatures and humidity can lead to serious pest and disease problems that force farmers to change crop rotations. Each adjustment by farmers can spill over into rural labor markets, causing serious shortages if planting must be done suddenly when the weather breaks or the harvest brought in before a flood. A particularly "dry" dry season might mean the second crop is not planted or harvested, and an important, perhaps critical, source of wage income is eliminated for many rural workers. The reduced crop output might not be the most important consequence of such a crop failure. A famine could result because of the failed income opportunities [Sen (1981)].

Fluctuations in aggregate production are magnified at the level of marketings available for consumption by nonfarm households because farm-household consumption tends to vary somewhat less than production. In years of poor weather, net marketings decline proportionately more than production. Similarly, in good years the percentage increase in marketings is usually substantially larger than the production increases. These wide fluctuations simply add to the difficulty of stabilizing domestic food prices and provisioning urban areas.

Price uncertainty also adds to the farmer's difficulty in deciding what crops to grow and how many inputs to use in growing them. Unlike the handful of manufacturers in large-scale industries, farmers are unable to set their output prices and later adjust production and inventory levels to meet the price targets. Unlike consumers, who know with near certainty the price they must pay for a given quantity and quality of a commodity at the time they buy it, farmers must make major decisions about purchases of inputs well in advance of knowing what prices their resulting output will bring. At the time many key farming decisions are made – the allocation of land to various crops, fertilizer applications, hiring labor for weeding – the farmer can only guess at the prices for the output.

Reducing weather and price uncertainties is an important role for government interventions. Dams and drainage ditches can reduce the impact of rainfall variations, disaster insurance can provide a new start even if heavy investments are wiped out, and research on more adaptable but still high-yielding plant varieties can reduce the risks of new technology. Similarly, reducing price uncertainty is a major government role, which can be accomplished with better price forecasting information, the use of import and export policy to provide a band of prices within which domestic price formation can take place, or a more aggressive floor and ceiling price policy implemented with a government-operated buffer stock program. Of course, not all stabilizing efforts are worth their costs, and some fluctuations are necessary if changes in output are to be accommodated by changes in demand, even allowing for changes in stock levels. The relative costs and benefits of commodity price stabilization have been the subject of extensive theoretical analysis. Price stabilization schemes for *world* markets perform poorly in both theory and practice [see, especially, Newbery and Stiglitz (1981)], but the merits of domestic price stabilization programs that use trade as well as buffer stocks to achieve their goals depend very much on the local circumstances of dynamics of supply and demand [Streeten (1986), Timmer (1986)].

3.3. The farm household as both producer and consumer

Truly subsistence households produce to meet their own consumption needs and do not need the market for either buying or selling. To such households price signals are not only irrelevant, they are unseen. Few such households remain in today's world, not because farm families no longer consume produce from their own fields, but because most farm families now buy and sell inputs and output in rural markets. They are aware of and react to market prices in making a wide variety of household decisions. Most farm households still retain some or most of their farm production for home consumption, and this role of home consumption is a further distinguishing feature of the agricultural sector. Few steelworkers or even textile workers take their products home for household use.

Only under highly restrictive and unrealistic assumptions about the completeness of markets and access of all farm households to them can production and consumption decisions be analyzed separately [Singh, Squire and Strauss (1985)]. In rural areas of developing countries, the need to make connected production and consumption decisions within a single household obviously complicates life for the farm household; the value of additional time spent in food preparation or tending the children must be balanced against the productivity of an additional hour weeding the rice, driving the ducks, or tending the home garden. Where it exists, the opportunity to spend some of that time working for cash on a neighbor's farm or in a rural wage-labor market places a lower bound on the value of household-farm time, and the value of leisure ultimately places a limit on the willingness to work, especially at low-productivity tasks. For households with inadequate land to grow surplus crops for sale and with limited outside employment opportunities, however, the marginal value of leisure time might be low indeed, possibly near zero. Even tiny increments to output can be valuable for very poor households.

The importance of joint household-farm decision-making also raises complex questions for analysts in search of ways to organize data and research issues into manageable and comprehensible frameworks for analysis. These complex questions have recently become the focus of a revived interest in models of household economies. The "new household economics" provides a powerful perspective on joint decision-making about food production, food consumption, investment in human capital, and even fertility and other demographic decisions. By showing how all these decisions are related to each other because of the time constraint, and hence to the economic environment surrounding the household, the household economics models provide analysts with a conceptual understanding of the complicated lives that rural people live [see Schultz, Chapter 13, in this Handbook, Evenson (1981), Rosenzweig, Chapter 15 in this Handbook]. At the same time, most such models grossly simplify the actual complexity of rural household decision making. The key issue is nearly always the functioning of rural labor markets because it determines the *perception* of the opportunity cost of labor in each household. In a survey of the theoretical and empirical literature on the functioning of rural labor markets, Binswanger and Rosenzweig offer the following conclusions:

> Progress toward a richer, integrated theoretical framework that can deal with the complexities associated with market failures as well as the determination of wages and other contractual terms has been hampered by the evolution of theory along two, mutually inconsistent paths. The rural wage determination models developed so far assume the complete absence of a land rental or sales market; that is, they take land distribution as exogenously given. The contractual choice models, on the other hand, treat the wage rate as exogenously given, while concentrating on land and credit market transactions; thus they have little to say about the determination of earnings or employment. The strength of contractual choice models lies in their clarification of the efficiency and equity implications of contracts and in their identification of the underlying causes of the market imperfections that lead to the contracts. These models also suggest the difficulties associated with policy intervention in single-tenancy or credit markets that is aimed at curing symptoms or apparent deficiencies in such arrangements. Without this integration of all the major interrelated markets – land, labor, credit – into a single, coherent rural model, however, we will be severely handicapped in attempting to predict the consequences of economic development in the rural sector [Binswanger and Rosenzweig (1981, pp. 54–55)].

3.4. What difference does the difference make?

Two important implications flow from the distinctive characteristics of agriculture relative to industry, and both are treated extensively in sections that follow. First, if agricultural decision-making is in fact based on rational assessments of highly heterogeneous environments, substantial knowledge of micro environments is necessary to understand the impact of policy interventions or technical change on the agricultural sector. Designing new technology and fostering its widespread adoption is primarily a public sector activity because of the relatively small scale of individual farmers, but the success of any given technical innovation depends on the private decisions of those same multitudinous farmers. Understanding the source, dynamics, and impact of technical change in agriculture is thus a major part of understanding the agricultural transformation, a process vastly complicated by the smallness of scale, geographic dispersion, and heterogeneity of the environment, both economic and ecological, that is characteristic of agriculture in developing countries.

The second important implication of agriculture's distinctiveness is how it conditions the role of public policy, particularly that other than the design and implementation of research leading to technical change. The vision dies hard of agriculture as a resource reservoir to be tapped indiscriminately, without reinvestment or adverse consequences for growth, on behalf of the urban economy. Although a few countries have a record of sustained progress in agriculture and concomitant overall economic growth, the list is short. Only eight countries listed in the *World Development Report, 1986* have growth rates for agricultural GDP of 3 percent per year or greater for both the 1965–73 and 1973–84 periods, along with growth rates for total GDP of 4 percent per year or greater for the same two periods: Kenya, Pakistan, Indonesia, Ivory Coast, Philippines, Thailand, Brazil, and Mexico. Sri Lanka and Turkey came close; Malaysia would probably have been included had data been available for the earlier period. Because population growth in several of these countries is near or more than 3 percent per year, even these excellent aggregate performances leave the rate of growth per capita at levels that permit a doubling of incomes in a quarter of a century at best.

It has obviously been difficult to find the right mix of policies to sustain agricultural growth. Much of the reason traces to a failure of policy-makers to understand the characteristics of agriculture that make policy design so complicated. They face yet another paradox: the essentially private-sector nature of agricultural decision-making at the same time that the environment for that decision-making is heavily dependent on sound government interventions into agricultural research, rural infrastructure, and market relationships. The distinctive characteristics of agriculture argue that governments intervene into agricultural decision-making at great risk, for they can easily cause farmers to withdraw from making investments and producing for the market, which are essential to mobilizing resources for overall economic growth. And yet, intervene they must. The environment for transforming agriculture is a public good created by wise but active public intervention.

It is easy to get the mix wrong, even to have the elements backward. Some governments have tried to dictate farm-level decisions on inputs and outputs while totally ignoring both the investments in research and infrastructure needed to create a healthy agriculture and the pricing environment that will mobilize peasants on behalf of higher productivity. But enough success stories have been accumulated for some general lessons to be propounded. The dimensions of successful technical change are discussed next, followed by a review of overall policies for agricultural development.

4. Transforming agriculture

Agricultural output can increase along a given supply curve or with a shift in the supply curve to the right. The scope for increasing output along a fixed supply curve by continuing to raise prices is extremely limited even in fully commercial and technically advanced farming systems; nearly all long-term growth in crop and livestock production comes from investment that expands capacity and from technical change that increases output–input ratios. The importance of prices for transforming agriculture is not in triggering the short-run response of farmers, although this is sometimes quite dramatic in situations where severe distortions are eliminated, but in conditioning the investment climate and expectations of all decision-makers in the rural economy about the future profitability of activities in the sector. Positive expectations lead to rapid investment in technical change when it is available.

4.1. The sources and dynamics of technical change

Technical change is the source of most growth in productivity in the long run, since continued investment in capital that embodies traditional technology very quickly faces low marginal returns [Schultz (1964), Hayami and Ruttan (1985)]. As late as the 1920s, most of the agricultural innovations in Europe and the United States arose on the farm and were gradually diffused by word of mouth and by agricultural colleges. Such on-farm innovation continues, but the scientific revolution in agriculture has made the discovery of technical innovations much more dependent on knowledge and capital investment. Very few farmers even in the United States have the resources to carry out significant agricultural research programs, and most such research is conducted by publicly-funded centers for agricultural research and by a handful of large agribusiness concerns, which are involved primarily in developing hybrid seed technology, chemical technology (herbicides and insecticides), and agricultural machinery.[6] The small scale of operations and limited financial resources of most farms mean that little important agricultural research is conducted by farmers.

---

[6] The revolution in biotechnology might change the concentration of agricultural research in the near future. Numerous small companies, many associated with faculty members of universities, are engaged in genetic manipulation of important agricultural crops and animals, although the impact on farm productivity has not yet been significant.

Diffusion of new technology is also a matter of policy concern, especially because not all farm households have equal access either to the knowledge to use new technology or to the agricultural and financial resources needed to make it productive on their own farms. Some inputs are lumpy and cannot be used efficiently on farms of even average size in many parts of the world. Large-scale tube-wells and tractors might contribute significantly to higher productivity even on small farms if institutional arrangements could be found to separate the service flows that such inputs can provide from the ownership of the assets themselves.

The evidence suggests that truly profitable innovations spread quickly no matter what the government does. Wherever the entrepreneurship exists and the economic environment permits, rental arrangements and tractor-hire services frequently emerge spontaneously [Goldman and Squire (1982)]. However, the location-specific nature of much new agricultural technology, especially seed technology, means that large areas of a country might be bypassed by the diffusion process unless government research and extension workers are actively engaged in the on-farm testing and evaluation of new technology. Adapting a general agricultural technology to a specific seed strain or technique that fits individual farming environments is a major responsibility of local research and extension stations.

An important concern of government policy is the impact of technical change on agricultural employment and rural income distribution. Historical evidence shows enormous variation in both the short-run and long-run impacts of innovations. The issues cannot be addressed satisfactorily by looking only at an individual farm or even at the agricultural sector [Scobie and Posada (1978), Hart (forthcoming), Hayami (1984)]. The primary effect of higher-yielding varieties of wheat and rice, for example, has probably been on food intake of nonagricultural workers. In addition, agricultural innovations tend to be embodied in inputs that must be provided through markets. An increased role for market relationships might threaten the risk management aspects of established patron–client relationships and thus have complicated effects on the entire rural economy and eventually on the urban economy as well.

Most technical change in agriculture involves improvements in the biological processes by which plants and animals grow and yield output useful to society or in the mechanical functions that are necessary for the biological processes to carry on more efficiently than in a natural setting. Primitive agriculture uses natural biological materials and processes in combination with human labor and management to bring in a crop or livestock product. Modern agriculture uses scientific knowledge to reshape the biological materials so that each plant and animal is more productive, and it increasingly substitutes machines for human labor.

Biological–chemical innovations, such as hybrid seeds, fertilizers, and pesticides, all tend to be yield-increasing and thus save on land. Mechanical technology can also have a yield effect when it permits more timely cultivation and an extension of multiple cropping, cultivation of heavy soils, or the use of water pumps on dry lands, but most mechanical technology is designed to make agricultural work less physically burdensome and to save on the amount of labor needed to produce a unit of output.

4.1.1. A simple model of changing agricultural productivity

Productivity in agriculture traditionally is measured in one of two ways: in output per hectare, or output per agricultural worker. Despite the focus by agricultural scientists on the former measure, from a welfare perspective the latter measure is clearly the relevant one. Output per hectare is important only as a vehicle for raising output per worker. In land-scarce environments facing rapid population growth and limited absorption of labor by industry, of course, raising output per hectare might be the *only* way to raise labor productivity. Most analyses treat both measures, and the model here, derived from Hayami and Ruttan (1985), does as well.

Figure 8.2 plots agricultural output per unit of land area in logarithmic units on the vertical axis. Hayami and Ruttan convert agricultural output into wheat units, Bairoch (1975) uses "direct" calories, and the World Bank reports agricultural value-added and contribution to GDP in its annual *World Development Report*. For the purposes of this discussion, the vertical axis is simply crop yields per hectare.

The horizontal axis measures agricultural output per worker on a logarithmic scale. Most econometric analyses of changes in agricultural productivity use output per worker as the dependent variable, and the workforce is traditionally defined as male workers in agriculture for the reason, indeed a rather lame one, that women play very different roles in agricultural production in different parts of the world and national statistical offices are not very consistent in how they treat the matter. For the purposes here, the workforce is measured as the entire economically active agricultural population. Because both axes are measured in logarithms, 45° lines trace out constant ratios of land per worker. Productivity changes over time can be traced out by connecting the coordinates at the beginning and the end. Figure 8.2 illustrates a variety of possibilities.

From the point of view of improving the welfare of rural workers, only movements to the right – toward higher output per worker – can help. Even then, the distribution of output among workers, landowners, and owners of other factors of production will determine whether or not the higher productivity has widespread welfare effects. Straight movements to the right are likely to be relatively rare. As Figure 8.2 notes, such movements imply a declining agricultural workforce and no changes in yields, normally in conjunction with new

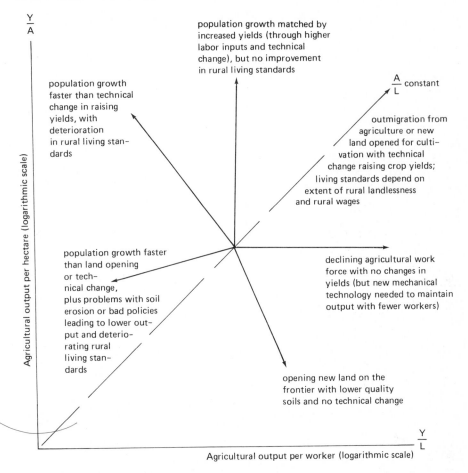

Figure 8.2. Various possibilities for changing land and labor productivities in agriculture.

mechanical technology to maintain levels of output with fewer workers per hectare.

What might have been a typical path while new continents were being colonized in the seventeenth and eighteenth centuries, but which is virtually unseen now, is rising labor productivity with falling land productivity. Lower-quality soils, distance from input and output markets, and low demand for technical innovations do not prevent extensification of agriculture at the frontier from raising living standards – and hence inducing migration – even while yields are falling.

The far more common pattern is a movement upward to the right, as the productivity of both land and labor increases. If the movement is exactly in a 45°

direction, agricultural land per worker remains constant, and yields must rise if labor productivity is to rise. A striking difference between currently developed countries and poor countries is their paths relative to this 45° line. As Bairoch (1975) noted, and evidence from Hayami and Ruttan (1985) to be presented shortly indicates, most developed countries increased land per worker even in the early stages of their development, whereas only a few less-developed countries are able to do so. The reasons are obvious. Either new lands must be opened faster than population growth, or out-migration from agriculture must proceed fast enough to cause an absolute reduction in the agricultural work force. Only a handful of countries can meet either of these conditions.

In countries with very limited agricultural land resources and rapid rates of growth in population, often the best that could be done since the early 1960s was to maintain constant labor productivity by increasing crop yields at the same pace as expansion of the rural workforce. This combination generates a vertical growth path, which might alternatively be described as running fast technologically to stand still economically. But some countries have not even done this well. Their populations have grown faster than the pace of technical change on farms, and their productivity path is an arrow up and to the left, reflecting lower standards of living in rural.areas.

The most dismal situation, however, is movement downward to the left, reflecting deterioration in *both* measures of agricultural productivity. Output per hectare and output per worker fall in such circumstances. The reasons might be extremely rapid growth in population with expansion into ecologically unstable agricultural areas, or such bad policies that farmers retreat from even the technology that they used previously. None of the countries in Hayami and Ruttan's analysis fits this last pattern, but no countries from sub-Saharan tropical Africa were in their sample.

4.1.2. The historical record

Hayami and Ruttan (1985) assembled evidence for changes in productivity of agricultural labor between 1960 and 1980 (see Figure 8.3). Three patterns are obvious. Nearly all countries in their sample showed improvement in *both* dimensions of productivity – only Bangladesh had a decline in labor productivity, and only Chile had a decline in land productivity. Most developed countries had faster increases in labor productivity than in land productivity, thus presenting patterns of change "flatter" than the 45° lines of constant area per worker – hence farm sizes had increased. Most developing countries had patterns of productivity change steeper than the 45° lines, implying decreased area per worker and smaller farm size.

Hayami and Ruttan see three basic patterns of agricultural development in this historical record (see Figure 8.4). The Asian path requires strongly rising land

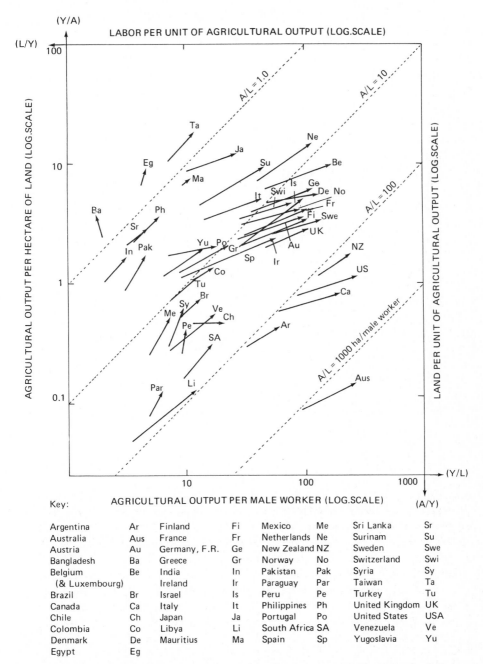

Figure 8.3. International comparison of labor and land productivities in agriculture, the 1960 data points connected to the 1980 points by arrows. *Source:* Hayami and Ruttan (1985, p. 121).

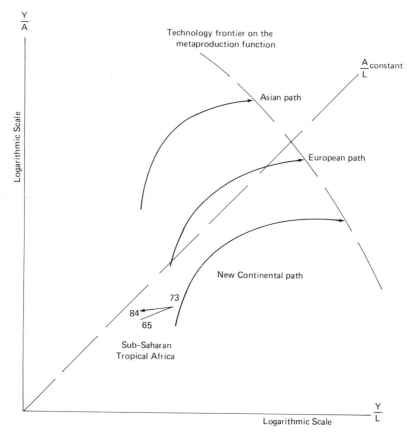

Figure 8.4. Patterns of change in agricultural productivity.

productivity in early stages to cope with small farm size and rapid growth in population, but eventually labor productivity grows rapidly as the rest of the economy absorbs rural workers and raises wages. This is the "Korea–Taiwan–Japan" model, but Pakistan, Philippines, Indonesia, Sri Lanka, and even Egypt might also have access to this path.

At the other extreme, the path of productivity change in the newly opened continents with surplus land is almost uniformly in the direction of higher labor productivity, and this has been true in the United States, Canada, and Australia since the mid-nineteenth century. It was only after the higher commodity prices caused by the world food crisis in 1973–74 that land productivity rose faster than labor productivity in the newly settled continental areas.

The European path falls nicely between the land-scarce and the land-surplus paths. In Figure 8.3, many countries are clustered here, and Hayami and Ruttan note that the paths for Denmark and the United Kingdom create an envelope that contains the entire European experience:

Denmark, which has remained relatively specialized in agricultural production among European countries, has attained a high labor productivity in agriculture by increasing output per unit of land. In contrast, the United Kingdom, which initiated the Industrial Revolution, has attained a relatively high level of agricultural efficiency mainly by enlarging agricultural land area per worker in response to the absorption of labor in nonagricultural occupations. France, which traditionally followed an agrarian policy designed to protect the peasant family farm (*la petite exploitation familiale*) from external competition and internal social change, achieved higher output per hectare than the United Kingdom but slower growth in output per worker than either the United Kingdom or Denmark until the formation of the European Economic Community (EEC). Since 1960, stimulated by increased demand for the protected EEC market, output and productivity of French agriculture have expanded at a very rapid rate [Hayami and Ruttan (1985, p. 130)].

Connecting the most advanced countries along each productivity path reveals the technology frontier (see Figure 8.4). Hayami and Ruttan describe this frontier as a metaproduction function, arguing that the underlying technologies that describe it are potentially available to all countries at a point in time. The technology actually developed and disseminated depends on relative factor scarcities. "Induced innovation" leads scientists to develop mechanical technologies to raise labor productivity in labor-scarce societies (for example, the new continents), whereas scientists in land-scarce societies, such as those in Asia, develop biological–chemical technologies to raise output per hectare. The potential of induced innovation to solve the agricultural problems of the currently developing countries will be discussed below. First, some special problems of the African experience must be placed in the context of productivity.

In addition to the three stylized productivity paths generated by the sample of countries in the analysis by Hayami and Ruttan, Figure 8.4 shows the growth path in agricultural productivity for Africa from 1965 to 1984, calculated from recent World Bank data. The definitions used are not identical to those used by Hayami and Ruttan, but the pattern shown is robust and perplexing. Between 1965 and 1973, Africa's productivity performance was very much like that of new continental areas: slow growth in land productivity and more rapid growth in labor productivity. Because of rapid growth in population, this increase in labor productivity reflected significant progress in increasing overall agricultural output.

Something quite unique in historical experience occurred in Africa between 1973 and 1984. For the entire continent between the Sahara and South Africa, the productivity of *both* land and labor declined. In Hayami and Ruttan's sample, only *one* country experienced a decline in each measure separately, and none declined in both. In Africa, an entire continent made up of more than thirty countries suffered a decline in both (although a few individual countries saw growth in both measures). The reasons for this startlingly poor performance are only beginning to be analyzed and understood, but it is virtually certain that a complex combination of bad weather, inadequate and inappropriate agricultural technology, and poor economic policies are to blame. The interplay between technology and agricultural development policy is the key issue here. Some analysts (but not Hayami and Ruttan) have seen induced innovation as an automatic market solution to a country's development problems. The African experience shows clearly that such is not the case.

4.1.3. Sources of productivity differences

Differences in agricultural productivity can stem from a variety of factors: different endowment of internal resources, such as land and livestock; different use of technical inputs, such as fertilizer and mechanical power; different investment in human capital through general and technical education; and different size of farms, which might generate economies or diseconomies of scale. Table 8.4 shows examples from the effort by Hayami and Ruttan (1985) to explain differences in productivity of agricultural labor according to differences in these factors' contributions to output. The contribution of each factor to productivity is based on econometric analysis of the same data set that generated Figure 8.3. Hayami and Ruttan estimated a production function by pooling their cross-section data for 44 countries for three time periods (1960, 1970, and 1980) and used the Cobb–Douglas output elasticities to account for differences in labor productivity. The results contradict Bairoch's pessimism about the potential of developing countries to raise their labor productivity in agriculture in the context of diminishing land per worker. In the three low-income countries in Table 8.4 – India, Philippines, and Peru – roughly half the difference in labor productivity relative to that of the United States was due to differential use of technical inputs and investment in human capital (general and technical education). Even the internal resource constraints are not completely binding because investment in livestock has an elasticity of output about double that of land. Scale economies are significant in Europe and newly opened continents but not on the small-scale farms characteristic of Asia and Africa.

Hayami and Ruttan conclude this part of their analysis on a positive note:

The perspective implied by the results of this analysis for agricultural development in the less developed countries is essentially encouraging. It is clear that

Table 8.4
Accounting for differences in labor productivity in agriculture of selected countries from the United States as percent of U.S. labor productivity

Country (per capita GNP in U.S. $ in 1980)		Output per worker (WU)	Difference in output per worker from U.S. as percent of U.S.	Percentage of difference explained by				
				Internal resources	Technical inputs	Human capital	Scale economies	Residual
Low-income countries:								
India (240)	1960	2.2	97.7	(100)[a]	28.0 (29)	25.0 (25)	29.0 (30)	26.4 (27)	-10.8 (-11)
	1980	3.1	98.9 (100)	29.2 (30)	24.9 (25)	24.7 (25)	27.3 (28)	-7.2 (-7)
Philippines (690)	1960	3.3	96.5 (100)	28.8 (30)	24.9 (26)	20.4 (21)	24.8 (26)	-2.4 (-3)
	1980	5.9	97.9 (100)	29.5 (30)	24.9 (25)	16.4 (17)	25.2 (26)	1.9 (2)
Peru (930)	1960	9.6	89.8 (100)	20.7 (23)	24.2 (27)	23.7 (26)	22.6 (25)	-1.5 (-2)
	1980	10.1	96.5 (100)	27.1 (28)	24.8 (26)	18.1 (19)	25.0 (26)	1.5 (2)
Middle-income countries:								
Argentina (2390)	1960	34.9	62.8 (100)	-3.1 (-5)	24.3 (39)	19.0 (30)	2.4 (4)	20.2 (32)
	1980	63.8	77.6 (100)	11.3 (15)	24.4 (31)	16.8 (22)	3.1 (4)	22.0 (28)
Greece (4380)	1960	9.1	90.3 (100)	27.2 (30)	23.9 (26)	20.3 (23)	23.4 (26)	-4.5 (-5)
	1980	25.8	91.0 (100)	28.4 (31)	23.6 (26)	16.5 (18)	23.5 (26)	-1.0 (-1)
Israel (4500)	1960	25.9	72.4 (100)	26.5 (37)	21.5 (30)	14.3 (20)	18.7 (26)	-8.6 (-12)
	1980	101.8	64.3 (100)	26.1 (41)	22.0 (34)	13.8 (21)	14.9 (23)	-12.5 (-19)
High-income countries:								
Japan (9890)	1960	10.3	89.0 (100)	29.2 (33)	22.4 (25)	8.3 (9)	25.8 (29)	3.3 (4)
	1980	27.8	90.2 (100)	28.9 (32)	22.6 (25)	9.8 (11)	26.2 (29)	2.7 (3)
France (11730)	1960	32.4	65.5 (100)	23.0 (35)	16.9 (26)	17.3 (26)	11.7 (18)	-3.4 (-5)
	1980	101.8	64.3 (100)	23.2 (36)	15.5 (24)	15.7 (25)	11.1 (17)	-1.2 (-2)
Denmark (12950)	1960	46.4	50.6 (100)	17.7 (35)	12.8 (25)	13.9 (28)	3.0 (6)	3.2 (6)
	1980	131.3	54.0 (100)	18.4 (34)	12.7 (24)	14.5 (27)	6.8 (12)	1.6 (3)

[a] Inside of parentheses are percentages with output per worker set equal to 100.
Note: Per capita GNP in 1980 and agricultural outputs per worker in 1960 and 1980 in the United States are $11 360 and 93.8 and 285.1 WU, respectively.
Source: Hayami and Ruttan (1985, p. 154).

agricultural output per worker in the LDCs, especially the poorest ones, can be increased by several multiples by adequate investments in education, research, and the supply of modern technical inputs, even if land area per worker continues to decline because of growing population pressure in the rural sector... It is especially encouraging to find that the agricultural production function of the LDCs is neutral with respect to scale. This implies that the low-income LDCs will not be too severely handicapped by the declines in the land-man ratio and farm size, relative to the older developed countries, at least over the next decade or two [Hayami and Ruttan (1985, p. 157)].

4.1.4. Problems with technical change

Biological–chemical innovations were discovered and introduced in land-scarce, labor-abundant societies, such as Japan and Western Europe, whereas mechanical innovations were developed and used in land-rich, labor-scarce societies, such as the United States, Canada, and Australia. Such induced innovation suggests that each society develops an agricultural technology appropriate to its resource endowments and agricultural needs. This process might not continue to yield appropriate results, however, in the context of a much more interdependent international agricultural system. Perhaps more troublesome, the examples Hayami and Ruttan used to illustrate the relevance of their induced innovation hypothesis are all large countries, which are easily able to justify the overhead expenses of a modern agricultural research and extension system. The means to develop appropriate technology for small poor countries, such as Chad, Haiti, or even Laos, remains to be seen.

Because most new agricultural technology is embodied in a physical input – a bag of fertilizer, a new seed, a tractor, or an irrigation pump – it can be effective in a farmer's field only if a purchase (or rental arrangement) is made. Several consequences flow from this simple fact. For small farmers to participate in the benefits of technical change, not only must it be workable on their small farms (combines, for instance, usually are not), but they must also be able to purchase the input that carries the new technology. If a new seed-fertilizer package has a 200 percent rate of return, even borrowing from a village moneylender at 10 percent per month might be profitable. But for the full benefits of modern technology to reach small farmers, it might be essential that formal rural credit systems be accessible to the farm household with only half a hectare or less.[7]

Equally important, if new technology is embodied in inputs, a marketing and distribution system is necessary for farmers actually to be able to purchase the inputs. Many traditional agricultural societies have a long history of small-scale

---

[7]The dangers of subsidizing this credit are now well recognized. See Adams and Graham (1981) and Gonzalez-Vega (1977).

marketing of surplus output to urban regions in exchange for consumer items, such as cloth, kerosene, or pots and pans, needed by farm households. There is no similar experience with large-scale movements of inputs, such as fertilizer or modern seeds, to those same dispersed farm households. The embodied nature of agricultural technology means that farmers cannot just be told about it. The marketing system must also deliver the inputs when needed.

A further characteristic of embodied agricultural technology is that complementary fixed capital investments are often required to achieve the maximum benefits from the innovation. Usually this investment takes the form of better water control, land-leveling, and drainage. Sometimes much better control of seed bed preparation or more sensitive and faster harvesting techniques to avoid shattering and other harvesting losses is also needed; these might require tractors with modern implements or, for harvesting, combines or threshers. Shorter-maturity cereal varieties often are ready to harvest while the rainy season is still under way and solar drying is difficult or impossible. In such cases mechanical dryers and added storage capacity are essential.

4.2. Unresolved issues

Many questions are unresolved or still contentious in the agricultural development profession. Most involve the relationship between technical change and the policy environment needed to make it effective. The problem in defining the relationship is partly due to the lack of understanding of household decision-making, especially in environments where linked contracts among labor, land, and credit complicate analytical models. Moreover, economists have had a difficult time modeling the interface between micro decisions and macro outcomes because neither micro competitive models nor macro policy models provide an adequate basis for analysis of decision-making in this grey area. Serious disputes over the long-run sustainability of modern, input-intensive agriculture are unresolved. The following discussion does not answer these questions but does frame them in the context of the previous discussion of technical change and the discussion yet to come of agricultural development strategies.

4.2.1. Evolution in thought

Research in the 1970s into the links between technical change and the decision-making environment at the farm level led to three quite significant changes in thinking about agriculture and development. First, and no doubt the most important for the long run, agricultural decision-makers – farmers and traders – began to be thought of as an integral part of the rest of the economy, connected to it by rational decision-making in the face of new technologies or income and price changes. Acceptance of this principle by economic modelers and policy-makers led to a fundamental shift in attitudes about how agriculture should be treated in the development process – not as an isolated appendage but as a key component essential to the health of the overall organism.

Second, new importance was given to developing and choosing appropriate technologies, whether in agriculture directly, in processing, or in the industrial sector. If millions of farmers, or thousands of traders and small industrialists, were making rational decisions about investment, the nature of the technology set facing them would be at least as critical as the set of prices in determining the consequences of economic growth for employment and income distribution. In addition, farm-level decision-making was obviously conditioned by farm-level constraints and opportunity costs for household resources, especially unskilled labor. Technical packages that were inappropriate in the face of those constraints – especially packages imported largely intact from Western agricultural systems – were not adopted, and agricultural development failed to take place. Sparked by the world food crisis in 1973–74, but guided by this earlier understanding of the importance of fitting technology to field-level conditions, nearly all the international centers for agricultural research devoted a significant share of their budgets to discovering the nature of farm-level constraints on the adoption of new technology and to developing specific crops as well as entire farming systems that dealt more effectively with these constraints [see IRRI (1978), CIMMYT (1984)].

The third major change in thinking in the 1970s also was sparked by the world food crisis, but it similarly had its roots in the new understanding of micro decision-making and the key role of technical change in agriculture. Early agricultural development strategies were aimed at providing resources for urban industry by helping "early adopters" of new farm technology. The consequences of this strategy for income distribution and rural welfare prompted the development of the "basic needs" movement and efforts to promote "growth with equity" [Chenery et al. (1974)]. In some sense this concern for equity was an almost inevitable consequence of renewed emphasis on improved technology, which better-off farmers tended to adopt earlier, and on better price incentives for higher output, which clearly benefited larger farmers with a higher proportion of marketed output. Indeed, the focus on price incentives to achieve production results often overlooked the potentially serious consequences for poor consumers who were net purchasers of food, many of whom were very small farmers or landless laborers in the countryside [Timmer (1979)]. Out of the concern for promoting equity and meeting basic needs came a major revival in interest in demand analysis. Although Indian planners had used income elasticities for staple foods disaggregated by income class in the earliest five-year plans, no one had attempted the empirical disaggregation of price elasticities by income class until after the world food crisis in the mid-1970s. Because food prices can change from year to year by much larger relative amounts than incomes per capita, knowing such disaggregated price elasticities became critical to judging the welfare impact of the wide price fluctuations characteristic of the 1970s.[8] As Eicher and Staatz (1984) summarized it, the 1970s were primarily a period when agricultural economists renewed their microeconomic roots, and the decade brought forth a rich, and often confusing, harvest of new empirical evidence. It remains for this evidence to be synthesized in the 1980s to provide better understanding of the development process and agriculture's role in it.

4.2.2. Farm decision-making

One of the difficulties in understanding decision-making in agriculture is that farmers face remarkably diverse ecological and economic settings. Corporate businessmen in California or Sao Paolo make their living from agriculture, but so too do near-subsistence peasants in India or Guatemala. Despite differences in scale of operation and location, however, private agriculture is a markedly homogeneous industry in the kinds of decisions that must be made day in and day out and in the uncertainties that surround those decisions. The corporate soybean farm in Sao Paolo or the rice farm in California has more in common with the wheat-growing peasant operation in the Punjab than with U.S. Steel or Volkswagen of Brazil. Much of the daily work done on these farms is at the initiative of the individual workers, and the incentives they face to perform this work in a timely and careful fashion strongly influence the quality and quantity of agricultural output.

Modeling farm decision-making is relatively simple under two extreme sets of assumptions: if the household is entirely self-sufficient and faces no markets, and if the household faces a complete set of perfect markets. Even these simple settings can be complicated by risk and uncertainty, by bargaining among members of the household over access to resources and output, and by non-pecuniary externalities in the welfare function as reflected by investment in the maintenance of a "moral economy" [Hart (forthcoming), Jones (1986), Scott (1976)]. As emphasized previously by Binswanger and Rosenzweig, however, it is the reality of interlocking land, labor, and credit markets and the explicitly limited access of some households to some markets that challenge model-builders who hope to capture the complexity of rural life and thereby be able to predict the outcome of changes in policy and technology or the commercialization of rural transactions. At a conference organized by Binswanger and Rosenzweig

---

[8]An attempt to generalize from early empirical results about the relationship between income level and the magnitude of the pure substitution term in the Slutsky matrix is in Timmer (1981); a review of the literature on disaggregated demand parameters is in Waterfield (1985) and Alderman (1986).

(1981) to examine the empirical record on these issues, what was striking was the sheer diversity of arrangements at the micro level. While this is not cause to reject model-building as an approach to understanding decision-making of rural households, it does caution against making general predictions without specific empirical foundation to the model. Building such empirical foundations to household decision-making models has occupied a substantial part of the agricultural economics profession since the early 1970s [Singh, Squire and Strauss (1985)]. The results show clearly the merits of treating the household as a combined producing and consuming unit, but, as Binswanger and Rosenzweig note, the dynamic aspects of the household's interactions with its environment are only beginning to be revealed:

> Explanations of the long-term changes associated with development must be found, ultimately, in models that explicitly treat the reproductive and techno-logical behavior that leads·to the long-term evolution of supply and demand. Attention has recently turned to the study of decisions that have long-term consequences – decisions about human capital investment, fertility, health, technical change, and agricultural intensification. Such decisions, however, are themselves conditioned by the outcomes and institutional arrangements in rural factor markets. The integration of market and household behavioral models within an explicit dynamic framework enveloping all sectors of an economy has yet to come [Binswanger and Rosenzweig (1981, pp. 55–56)].[9]

4.2.3. Micro–macro links and structural change

Trying to explain the declining share of agriculture during the process of structural transformation by analyzing the decision-making of farm households is a bit like trying to explain evolution by studying the molecular biology of plants and animals. The explanation for evolution, of course, must ultimately have its basis in molecular biology, and, likewise, structural transformation must be based on micro decision-makers. But our capacity to move from one level to the other is very limited. Aggregation of micro outcomes does not trace out macro growth paths very well, primarily because of the difficulty in specifying investment functions and the introduction of technical change. Even the reverse causation, where macro settings influence micro decision-makers, has only recently been incorporated into models of agricultural sector performance [Chilchilnisky and Taylor (1980), Schuh (1976), Taylor (1980), and Timmer, Falcon and Pearson (1983)].

---

[9]Such an integration obviously takes us outside the realm of this chapter into the other topics treated in this Handbook. In particular, see the chapters by Bardhan (Chapter 3), Behrman and Deolalikar (Chapter 14), Bell (Chapter 16), Birdsall (Chapter 12), Rosenzweig (Chapter 15), T. Paul Schultz (Chapter 13), Sen (Chapter 1), Stiglitz (Chapter 5), and Williamson (Chapter 11).

One specific attempt to measure the impact of macro prices on structural change in agriculture was reported in Timmer (1984). The share of agriculture in GDP was the dependent variable in the model, which used the same variables for income and population size as those used by Chenery and Syrquin (1975). However, the rural–urban terms of trade were also added as an explanatory variable. The terms of trade as well as the per capita income variable were explained by a simple four-equation, recursive structural model, with income per capita depending on lagged income per capita, lagged "real" foreign exchange rate, lagged investment, and the share of oil imports in GDP. The real exchange rate (in purchasing power parity) was then explained by lagged income per capita, the current account balance, real cereal prices in world markets, and the oil import share. In the next step, investment as a share of GDP was explained by current income per capita, the foreign exchange rate, the current account balance, and the oil import share. Finally, the rural–urban terms of trade were determined by the foreign exchange rate, real prices for noncereal agricultural products in world markets, real cereal prices in world markets, and the oil import share. It was then possible to estimate a Chenery–Syrquin equation with agricultural share of GDP as the dependent variable and predicted values of each of these dependent variables in the structural model as independent variables in the model of structural change.

The model was estimated for seven countries in the Asia–Pacific region for the years 1960 to 1980.[10] All variables in all equations were significant and of the right sign, confirming the logic of the structural model. More interesting was the separate importance of the foreign exchange rate and the oil import share in determining the rural–urban terms of trade in these countries, especially because the oil import share was also a highly important variable in explaining the foreign exchange rate itself. The two oil price shocks in the 1970s thus opened a window of opportunity to trace the effects of a major macro perturbation as it rippled through the economy, including the agricultural economy. The results of estimating the model and simulating changes in the oil price (holding import or export volumes constant in the short run) confirmed the notion that the agricultural sector is strongly influenced by variations in macro prices. The positive effect of currency devaluations on the rural–urban terms of trade was confirmation that rural goods and services tend to be more "tradable" than urban goods and services. No logic requires this result, of course, and many economists would tend to think the opposite – bulky, low-value agricultural commodities are naturally protected by high marketing costs and should therefore be less tradable than urban industrial goods. This view fails to reflect two considerations. First, strong

---

[10] The countries were Indonesia, South Korea, Malaysia, Mexico, Philippines, Sri Lanka, and Thailand. They were chosen to have a balance among oil importers, oil exporters, and a country approximately self-sufficient. An oil exporter naturally has a negative oil import share in the model.

substitutions are possible among agricultural commodities in both production and consumption. Sweet potatoes might not be tradable directly, but if they compete for resources and customers with rice that is tradable, the sweet potato economy will behave as if they were a tradable commodity. Second, extensive protection is provided to the urban industrial sector in most developing countries, protection that has the effect of converting the sector from tradable to nontradable. Consequently, these empirical results showed that the strong tendency of developing countries to maintain overvalued exchange rates (even for their existing degree of industrial protection) not only impedes efficient resource allocation and rapid growth (because of the importance of the foreign exchange rate in the per capita income equation), but also significantly biases income distribution against the rural sector.

Oil imports force countries to remove some of that bias. As pressures build to create incentives to export in order to pay for the oil imports, the rural sector receives improved terms of trade since it produces many of those exportable goods. The effect is symmetrical for oil exporters. As oil prices rise for exporting countries, the terms of trade deteriorate for their agricultural sectors. Since the oil share is also a significant factor in exchange rate determination, the ultimate impact of oil prices is even larger. Consequently, "Dutch Disease" – the decline in employment and output in labor-intensive export sectors in countries experiencing a boom in resource prices – is at least as much a rural problem as an urban industrial one. The agricultural difficulties of Nigeria, Venezuela, Mexico, and Indonesia (until 1978, when macroeconomic management changed in order to cope with the problems created by high oil prices) can be seen to have common macroeconomic roots. Likewise, the increased supplies of agricultural commodities in world markets and the reduced demand for them in the early 1980s must also have at least part of their explanation in sectoral responses to the oil price changes of the 1970s. As oil prices fall in the 1980s, some of the pressure to export agricultural commodities should be reduced (although servicing the debt incurred while oil prices were high attenuates this effect to some extent). As a consequence, agricultural commodity prices in world markets should recover somewhat relative to oil prices.

This type of analysis – conducted within a general-equilibrium perspective even if not within a formal, computable general-equilibrium model – reinforces the early and partial results obtained in the 1970s from analysis of choice of technique in production in developing countries: macroeconomic policies, especially with respect to macro prices – wage rates, interest rates, and foreign exchange rates – significantly influence these choices and consequent employment and output levels, as well as income distribution. The link from macro policy to agriculture is quite strong. In the other direction, the general-equilibrium consequences of agricultural adjustments to shifts in these policies seem to be quite significant, but these are not yet understood in other than the roughest theoretical and empirical way.

4.2.4. Resources for growth and sustainability

Parallel to the incorporation of agriculture into macroeconomic and general-equilibrium analysis has been the growing acceptance of what was a highly controversial and widely denied argument in the 1970s: that rapid economic growth with broad participation of the entire population for sustained periods of time was necessary for a country to deal successfully with widespread poverty and hunger. The desirability of such growth was seldom questioned; the controversy was over the adequacy of the world's resource base to sustain such rapid growth for more than a handful of special cases (the "Gang of Four": Singapore, Taiwan, South Korea, and Hong Kong). The more radical segment of the basic needs movement adopted a *small is beautiful* philosophy that called for substantial changes in the lifestyles of the rich in order that the poor could share more equitably in a limited standard of living for the entire world [Schumacher (1975), Lappe (1971)].

Although this perspective has certainly not disappeared, a decade-long decline since the mid-1970s in basic food prices on world markets, to historic lows in real terms, and the monthly efforts by OPEC in the mid-1980s to prop up oil prices against a seemingly inexorable market determined to lower them, have changed the nature of the debate. The issue is not whether the global resources are available for economic growth, but whether they can be managed appropriately to generate and sustain that growth. The record after the world food crisis in 1973–74 reveals that farmers and societies respond vigorously to apparent food shortages, whether in response to prices in world markets or to a perceived vulnerability to uncertain external market supplies. Technical change in agriculture, at least in the United States and Western Europe, has accelerated in the 1980s after stagnating in the 1970s, and it is difficult not to see this as a form of induced innovation in the Hayami–Ruttan sense.

The sustainability of this technical change has been repeatedly challenged, especially after the first oil shock in the early 1970s. Lester Brown has been one of the most articulate and influential of these challengers, and his *State of the World, 1984* contains a succinct statement of the concern:

> Although the economic crisis of the eighties is exacerbated by economic mismanagement, its roots lie in the depletion of resources, both nonrenewable and renewable. During the fifties and sixties the world economy steadily boosted its use of oil, a finite resource, putting it on a path that by definition was not sustainable over the long run. The depletion of oil reserves, and its effect on world oil prices, is the most immediate threat to world economic

stability, but the depletion of soil resources by erosion might be the most serious long-term threat. The unprecedented doubling of world food supplies over the last generation was achieved in part by adopting agricultural practices that led to excessive soil erosion, erosion that is draining the land of its productivity. After a point agriculture can no longer be sustained and the land is abandoned.

Sustainability is an ecological concept with economic implications. It recognizes that economic growth and human well-being depend on the natural resource base that supports all living systems. Technology has greatly expanded the earth's human carrying capacity, most obviously with advances in agriculture. But while the human ingenuity embodied in advancing technology can raise the natural limits on human activity, it cannot entirely remove them. A sustainable society is one that shapes its economic and social systems so that natural resources and life-support systems are maintained. Today, we study the archaeological sites of earlier civilizations that failed to do so, depleting their soils, mismanaging their irrigation systems, or otherwise embarking on an unsustainable development path [Brown (1984, pp. 1–2)].

Of course, none of these civilizations possessed the scientific capacity of modern societies to create new technologies specifically designed for the resource shortages that emerge over time. Unless this capacity suddenly erodes dramatically, it seems likely to provide solutions to future shortages of resources in similar fashion to those of the past.

4.2.5. Role of government

At the same time that planners have learned that resource management rather than resource constraints per se is the primary bottleneck to economic growth, they came to view prices generated in international markets as important signals about relative scarcity of various resources and to regard trade as the most efficient vehicle to alleviate significant imbalances of resources in a given country. The importance of market signals and trade has led to a growing consensus around a market orientation and the use of private incentives as the most effective way to achieve economic growth, at least in agriculture. Millions of decision-makers have turned out to be too many to reach from central planning offices, because agricultural diversity is too great for information to reach those offices effectively. Agriculture is itself changing too rapidly for planners to keep up. This rapid change is reflected primarily in international markets, and agricultural economies that are cut off from those markets miss key signals about the efficiency of domestic resource allocation.

An emphasis on the role of international markets and trade is easily caricatured into an argument for free trade and "getting prices right" by setting them at whatever the border price happens to be [Volrath (1985), for example]. The extent to which a country's internal decision-makers face international market signals is one of the key policy instruments available to a government to influence income distribution as well as efficiency of resource allocation. Because dynamic efficiency is more important for economic growth than static optimization, a concern for the long-run impact of prices on expectations, investment, and technical change is entirely legitimate. Free trade provides no guarantee that dynamic efficiency will be achieved, and the record of East Asia cannot be offered as evidence that free trade leads to rapid growth. That same record does suggest, however, the importance of an export orientation for industry in combination with growing incomes in the rural sector. For an agricultural development strategy to be relevant for the 1990s, it must incorporate the factors responsible for that record.

5. Agricultural development strategy

Several lessons have been learned since the mid-1960s about the functioning of the agricultural sector and its potential role in the development process. The agricultural sector has been seen in a general-equilibrium perspective, and the importance of macroeconomic policy for agricultural performance has been recognized. Rapid economic growth has been considered necessary to deal with the human welfare concerns that stem from poverty and hunger, and such growth is feasible because of the potential for technical change. Market-oriented systems with private incentives have shown superior performance in achieving this growth. Policy analysis has tended to concentrate on one of three dimensions of government intervention into the agricultural growth process: stimulating traditional agriculture into growth; maintaining agricultural growth to generate resources for the rest of the economy; and protecting the welfare of farmers from their own high productivity during the final and painful stages of structural change in industrialized societies.

5.1. Policies for "getting agriculture moving"

It has become increasingly recognized that in order for agriculture to play a multiplicity of positive roles, it needs resources and favorable development policies, not heavy taxation and neglect. By the 1970s, agreement was being reached on the nature of resources needed to develop agriculture, and some progress was being made in identifying the policies needed to make those resources effective. Heavily influenced by Schultz's book, *Transforming Traditional Agriculture*, and the increasingly widespread evidence that farmers responded rationally to economic incentives, strategists in the late 1960s and early 1970s focused on two complementary agendas: understanding the microeconomic setting of farm-level decision-makers in order to create incentives for investments in higher output, and generating the stream of technical innovations that would be profitable for individual farmers to adopt in order to produce that output.

With high food prices in world markets in the mid-1970s, providing better incentives to rural producers was a "simple" matter of liberalizing trade policy and permitting international price signals to be more freely transmitted to the domestic economy. Because rural economies had been discriminated against for so long by the industrialization strategies, rural incomes were very low relative to urban incomes. Goals in terms of both equity and efficiency were furthered by raising agricultural prices to their world levels, a point stressed by Schultz and his colleagues (1978) and now pursued by Western aid agencies.

The emphasis in the late 1970s and early 1980s on market liberalization as a means of providing adequate price incentives to agricultural producers has run into serious problems in the mid-1980s. Allowing domestic food and agricultural prices to be determined by world prices creates serious difficulties for both producers and consumers because commodity prices in world markets are much more variable than prices for industrial products. Since the mid-1970s when this strategy was articulated, many prices, especially for grains, have collapsed to historic lows, and there is relatively little prospect of recovery in the foreseeable future or at least within the vision of planning agencies and policy-makers. Once the painful decision is made to raise price incentives to farmers, it is not easily reversed, especially because the medium-term consequences for income distribution would be sharply negative.[11] To provide farmers with positive price incentives then requires agricultural price protection, which might possibly lead to the same type of high-cost, inefficient agricultural sector that presently exists for industrial sectors in these developing countries.

The appropriateness of an incentive-led strategy for agricultural development, as opposed to a market-liberalization strategy, depends on whether the argument for protection has any merit: that providing adequate price incentives to farmers through protection from international competition will encourage an infant industry to grow up and produce at low cost.[12] In the 1950s and 1960s, import substitution for industrial products was used to justify the use of price protection for domestic (infant) industry, through tariffs, quotas, or bans on cheaper foreign goods. As industries matured, their goods would be able to compete with foreign

---

[11] The very short-run consequences for poor consumers would be positive, just as they were negative when price incentives were adopted in the first place [Timmer (1979)].

[12] Protection has also been justified on the basis of price stabilization, i.e. that "low" prices in world markets would rise to "normal" or "trend" levels before long. But an analysis of alternative trends to be used to defend this proposition shows that the current price is a better predictor of future prices, for at least five years into the future, than estimated trends [see Schwartz (1987)].

goods in local markets and be exported, and trade barriers could come down. But for various reasons that had to do with "X-efficiency" and political economy, only a few countries were able to make this transition [see Pack, Chapter 9, and Westphal, Chapter 20, in this Handbook]. The industrial sectors in most developing countries are high cost and inefficient, and they remain heavily protected. The agricultural sectors in these countries have borne much of the burden imposed by the industrial and trade policies, in the form of high-cost inputs and overvalued exchange rates that (implicitly) subsidize imported foodstuffs and tax rural exports [see S. Lewis, Chapter 30 in this Handbook].

Protection for the rural sector carries clear benefits but equally clear costs and risks. Protection would maintain the momentum in agricultural production achieved through higher price incentives, and it would also support income levels in rural areas. But if the lessons from industrial protection in the 1960s are applicable to agriculture in the 1980s, planners should be cautious. If the agricultural sector is fundamentally different in its response to protection from that of the industrial sector, or if world markets for its output are sufficiently different because of price instability, then short-run protection might be appropriate. The answer is complicated by the realization that the economies most successful in translating import substitution into export-led growth – Japan, South Korea, and Taiwan – also have adopted the highest rates of agricultural protection [Anderson and Hayami (1986)].

5.2. Alternative strategies for maintaining the transformation process

The lessons from the Asian success stories do not define a single strategic approach to agricultural development. The agricultural sector is a means to an end – not an end in itself. Three sharply different paths for appropriate policies toward agriculture are open if the goal is to speed the overall process of development. The first path has parallels to the philosophy of the 1950s, in which benign neglect of agricultural policy was thought to be sufficient for stimulating the process of economic growth. This perspective grows out of the recognition of the role of well-functioning markets and decision-makers operating in a world of "rational expectations". In this view, most policy is irrelevant to farmers in more than a very transitory sense, and this is especially true of price policy:

> One lesson that we should be able to learn from observation of the world is that the absolute incomes earned by farm families in various countries have no relationship to farm prices. Even stronger, the relative incomes of farm families have no relationship to farm prices, except as benefits of higher prices have been capitalized into the value of land and land has been acquired by gift or inheritance [Johnson (1985, p. 43)].

In this world, agricultural incomes are determined by employment opportunities outside agriculture, the agricultural sector *must* decline in proportional output terms and absolutely in the labor force, and the long-run decline in basic agricultural commodity prices due to technical change simply emphasizes that society is best served by getting resources out of agriculture as rapidly as possible. Although the clearest case for this view of the world is in the OECD countries, a host of middle-income countries, and even some quite poor countries, are also facing the problem of declining real incomes in the agricultural sector under the impact of rapid technical change domestically and lower world prices for the resulting output. This perspective is obviously consistent with the view that open economies will show better performance than those with substantial trade barriers.

A sharply different path has been sketched by Mellor and Johnston (1984). Building on their earlier stress on balanced growth (1961), Mellor and Johnston call for an "interrelated rural development strategy" that improves nutrition in one dimension while it fosters the broader growth process in the other. The approach calls for a major role of government in strategic design and program implementation, a role that is in marked contrast with the free-market approach sketched out previously:

> We have, therefore, emphasized that improvements in nutrition [one of Mellor and Johnston's key objectives for agricultural development] require a *set of interacting forces*: accelerated growth in agriculture; wage goods production; a strategy of development that structures demand towards high employment content goods and services; increased employment; and increased effective demand for food on the part of the poor. Agricultural growth not only satisfies the need for food to meet nutritional requirements (which is the other side of the wage-goods coin), but fosters a favorable employment-oriented demand structure as well. Agriculture's role in generating a structure of demand, favorable to rapid growth in employment, is central [Mellor and Johnston (1984, pp. 567–568, emphasis added)].

Mellor and Johnston go on to summarize their earlier argument that agriculture can play this multiplicity of roles only if a unimodal development strategy is followed, that is, one in which a broad base of smallholders are the central focus of agricultural research and extension services and the recipient of the bulk of receipts from agricultural sales. The authors see the dualism inherent in bimodal strategies – those placing modernization efforts primarily on large, "progressive" farms while neglecting the "backward" smallholders – as the major obstacle to putting their set of interacting forces in motion:

> The most common barrier to the interrelated strategy indicated is pronounced dualism in capital allocations – too much to industry and the unproductive

elements of the private sector rather than to agriculture, and to capital-intensive elements within those, as well as to large-scale and therefore capital-intensive allocations within agriculture. The outcome of the strategy will depend upon national-level decisions about macroeconomic policies, exchange rates, interest rates, and investment allocations among sectors and regions, not just within agriculture itself. Indeed, the whole strategy fails if it is viewed simply as the responsibility of agriculture ministries [Mellor and Johnston (1984, p. 568)].

This interrelated strategy must be directed by government planners; there is relatively little concern or role for the private sector, other than small farmers. The analysis leading to the strategy remains heavily influenced by closed economy considerations, and little attention is given to either domestic marketing activities or their relationship to international markets. Three key elements are suggested as essential to meeting all objectives of agricultural development – massive investment in human capital through nutrition, health, and family planning services in the countryside, creation of the complex, rural organizational structures seen in Japan and Taiwan that provide services to small farmers while also serving as a voice for their interests, and investment in rapid technical change appropriate to these small farmers in order to raise agricultural output and rural incomes simultaneously.

Notably missing in this list of key elements is significant concern for the structure of incentives for agriculture relative to industry's or for the country's tradables relative to those of foreign competitors. Although it is realized that the macroeconomic setting is no doubt important to agriculture, it remains outside the scope of appropriate strategy for agricultural development. Not surprisingly, given the argument in Johnston and Clark (1982), the intellectual foundation for this strategy lies in rural development, not in a vision of agriculture linked to the macro economy and world markets by powerful market mechanisms. It is this latter vision which provides the third potential path for agricultural development strategy for the rest of the 1980s and into the 1990s.

The third approach contrasts with both the "free market" and "interrelated rural development strategy" approaches. It calls for government policy interventions into outcomes in domestic markets but uses markets and the private marketing sector as the vehicle for those policy interventions. This "price and marketing policy" approach recognizes widespread *market failures* in agriculture as well as extensive *government failures* in implementation of direct economic functions.[13] The strategic dilemma is how to cope with segmented rural capital and labor markets, poorly functioning land markets, the welfare consequences of sharp instability of prices in commodity markets, the pervasive lack of informa-

---

[13] This is a theme of both the Bardhan (Chapter 3) and Stiglitz (Chapter 5) in this Handbook.

tion about current and future events in most rural economies, and the sheer absence of many important markets, especially for future contingencies involving yield or price risks. One powerful lesson emerged from the postwar development record: direct government interventions through state-owned enterprises to correct market failures frequently make matters worse by inhibiting whatever market responses were possible in the initial circumstances, without providing greater output or more efficient utilization of resources. The agricultural sector in particular is vulnerable to well-intended but poorly conceived and managed parastatal organizations that attempt a wide array of direct economic activities, including monopoly control of input supplies, capital-intensive state farms, and mandated control over crop marketing and processing. As Bates (1981) has demonstrated, these direct controls and agencies have a strong political economy rationale for a government that tries to reward its supporters and centralize power and resources in the hands of the state [see also Lipton (1977)].

The answer to the dilemma over making matters worse, in the "price and market policy" approach, is to gain a much clearer understanding of the necessary interaction between the public and private sectors. Government intervention into agriculture for political reasons has an ancient history. One major claim of monarchs to the throne was their capacity to keep food prices cheap and stable, as Kaplan (1984) made clear and as several modern governments have discovered to their demise. Political objectives for the performance of agriculture – its capacity to feed the population regularly and cheaply, or its ability to provide fair incomes to farmers caught in the painful pressures of successful structural transformation – are inevitable and, in some long-run sense, highly desirable.

The "price and marketing policy" path argues that these objectives are best served by making carefully designed interventions into the prices determined in markets, not by leaving markets alone or by striving to reach the objectives through direct activities by the government [Timmer (1986)]. If the "free market" approach incurs heavy political costs as markets relentlessly redistribute incomes to the winners in the course of economic development, and the "interrelated rural development strategy" incurs heavy managerial and administrative costs as the government plays an active and direct economic role, the "price and marketing policy" approach incurs heavy analytical costs.

These analytical costs come from the need to understand each country's path of structural change, the workings of factor and commodity markets, and the potential impact of macro and commodity price interventions on these markets and ultimately on the structural path itself. It requires that government intervention be based on an empirical understanding of economic responses to a change in policy and the political repercussions from them. There is an important role for models in illuminating where to look for these responses, but the models themselves cannot provide the answers. This is especially true as attempts are made to build into the models the response of policy itself to changes in the economic environment [see Roe, Shane and Vo (1986)]. Such endogenous policy models might reveal some of the historical factors that accounted for policy shifts, but they seldom provide a sense of when the degrees of freedom for policy initiative are about to expand. Frequently, this is in times of crisis. Policy-makers often embark on bold experiments in such times, and the payoff would be very high if sufficient analytical understanding already existed in order for them to anticipate the response to a policy change.

All three strategic approaches recognize the importance of government investments in agricultural research and rural infrastructure. Even here, however, there are likely to be significant differences in emphasis. The free-market approach is likely to put a relatively greater share into research, the rural development strategy into human capital investments, and the price and marketing approach into rural infrastructure that lowers marketing costs. Investments in all three areas are obviously desirable. The issue is at the margin: where are scarce resources to be invested? In addition, different countries have different starting points and different needs, so no single strategic approach makes sense for all countries. But it is difficult to see how countries can develop their rural sectors without relatively efficient marketing systems and adequate financial incentives for their farmers. Accordingly, significant elements of the price and marketing approach seem destined to be incorporated into all successful agricultural development strategies, even if they emphasize the free market or rural development approaches in other dimensions.

5.3. Agricultural policy and structural change

Hayami and Ruttan have asked why agricultural growth has not been faster and more evenly spread around the world:

> We indicated that the basic factor underlying poor performance was neither the meager endowment of natural resources nor the lack of technological potential to increase output from the available resources at a sufficiently rapid pace to meet the growth of demand. The major constraint limiting agricultural development was identified as the policies that impeded rather than induced appropriate technical and institutional innovations. As a result, the gap widened between the potential and the actual productive capacities of LDC agriculture [Hayami and Ruttan (1985, p. 416)].

This emphasis on the relationship between policy and agriculture's role in structural change has provided the organizing theme for this chapter. A progression of topics has followed from understanding why the agricultural sector is different from the industrial and service sectors and how the differences condition the nature of effective policy interventions. The factors needed for inducing the agricultural transformation, to "get agriculture moving", involve a complex mix of appropriate new technology, flexible rural institutions, and a market orientation that offers farmers material rewards for the physical effort they expend in their fields and households and for the risks they face from both nature and markets.

The role of the government has been analyzed throughout this chapter, first, as it fosters the transformation process through its investments – in both budgetary and policy terms – in agricultural development, and, second, as it tries to cope with the problems of success. A recurrent theme of this chapter has been that a successful structural transformation is painful for the agricultural sector in all societies; nearly all rich countries protect their farmers at the expense of domestic consumers and taxpayers and of foreign producers. The rapidly growing economies of East and Southeast Asia are facing this issue in an acute fashion, well before their overall economies can bear the fiscal burden of heavy agricultural subsidies [Anderson and Hayami (1986)]. The experiences of the currently developed countries with respect to the social, political, and economic stresses caused by a declining role for agriculture have important lessons for latecomers about to encounter these same stresses [Reich, Endo and Timmer (1986)]. There is a world of difference, however, between those countries growing rapidly enough to be feeling the consequences for income distribution of the relative decline of the agricultural sector and those countries in which the agricultural transformation itself has yet to begin in a significant way. The contrast between Asia and Africa in this regard is striking. Many development specialists feel that reversing Africa's declining food production per capita and declining real incomes per capita is the most important challenge for the rest of the century. For the agricultural development profession, the difficult question is whether the lessons from Asia in stimulating the process of agricultural transformation can be transferred to the vastly different African setting. Many policy experiments are now under way; analysis of the record generated in the 1980s by these experiments will provide new insights in the 1990s into determining which models of development can best stimulate and explain the process of structural transformation.

References

Adams, D.W. and Graham, D.H. (1981) 'A critique of traditional agricultural credit projects and policies', *Journal of Development Economics*, 8:347–366.
Alderman, H. (1986) 'The effect of food price and income changes on the acquisition of food by low-income households', IFPRI Research Report. Washington, D.C.: International Food Policy Research Institute.
Anderson, K. (1983) 'Growth of agricultural protection in East Asia', *Food Policy*, 8:327–336.

Anderson, K. and Hayami, Y., with associates (1986) *The political economy of agricultural protection*: *East Asia in international perspective*. London: Allen and Unwin.

Baran, P.A. (1952) 'On the political economy of backwardness', *Manchester School of Economic and Social Studies*, 20:66–84.

Bairoch, P. (1975) *The economic development of the third world since* 1900. Berkeley: University of California Press.

Bardhan, P.K. (1984) *Land, labor, and rural poverty*. Cambridge: Cambridge University Press.

Bates, R.H. (1981) *Markets and states in tropical Africa: The political basis of agricultural policies*. Berkeley: University of California Press.

Binswanger, H.P. and Rosenzweig, M.R. (1981) *Contractual arrangements, employment and wages in rural labor markets: A critical review*. New York: Agricultural Development Council, and India: International Crops Research Institute for the Semi-Arid Tropics.

Binswanger, H.P. and Rosenzweig, M.R. (1986) 'Behavioral and material determinants of production relations in agriculture', *The Journal of Development Studies*, 22:503–539.

Brown, L.R. (1984) 'Overview', in: L.R. Brown, et al., eds., *State of the world, 1984*: A Worldwatch Institute report on progress toward a sustainable society. New York: W.W. Norton.

Chenery, H.B. and Syrquin, M. (1975) *Patterns of development, 1950–1970*. London: Oxford University Press.

Chenery, H.B. and Taylor, L. (1968) 'Development patterns among countries and over time', *Review of Economics and Statistics*, 50:391–416.

Chenery, H.B. et al. (1974) *Redistribution with growth*. London: Oxford University Press.

Chilchilnisky, G. and Taylor, L. (1980) 'Agriculture and the rest of the economy: Macro connections and policy restraints', *American Journal of Agricultural Economics*, 62:303–309.

CIMMYT Economic Staff (International Maize and Wheat Improvement Center) (1984) 'The farming systems perspective and farmers participation in the development of appropriate technology, in: C.K. Eicher and J.M. Staatz, eds., *Agricultural development in the third world*. Baltimore, MD: Johns Hopkins University Press.

Clark, C. (1940/1957) *The conditions of economic progress*, 3rd ed. London: Macmillan.

Cochrane, W.W. (1979) *The development of American agriculture: A historical analysis*. Minneapolis, MN: University of Minnesota Press.

de Janvry, A. (1981) *The agrarian question and reformism in Latin America*. Baltimore, MD: Johns Hopkins University Press.

Eicher, C.K. and Staatz, J.M., eds. (1984) *Agricultural development in the third world*. Baltimore, MD: Johns Hopkins University Press.

Evenson, R. (1981) 'Food policy and the new home economics', *Food Policy*, 6:180–193.

Fei, J.C.H. and Ranis, G. (1964) *Development of the labor surplus economy: theory and policy*. Homewood, IL: Irwin.

Goldman, R.H. and Squire, L. (1982) 'Technical change, labor use, and income distribution in the Muda irrigation project', *Economic Development and Cultural Change*, 30:753–775.

Gonzalez-Vega, C. (1977) 'Interest rate restrictions and income distribution', *American Journal of Agricultural Economics*, 59:973–976.

Griffin, K. (1979) *The political economy of agrarian change: An essay on the green revolution*, 2nd ed. London: Macmillan.

Hart, G. (forthcoming) 'Interlocking transactions: Obstacles, precursors or instruments of agrarian capitalism', *Journal of Development Economics*.

Hayami, Y. (1984) 'Assessment of the green revolution', in: C.K. Eicher and J.M. Staatz, eds., *Agricultural development in the third world*. Baltimore, MD: Johns Hopkins University Press.

Hayami, Y. (1986) 'Agricultural protectionism in the industrialized world: The case of Japan', prepared for a conference held at the East–West Center, Honolulu, February 17–21.

Hayami, Y. and Ruttan, V. (1985) *Agricultural development: An international perspective*, revised and expanded edition. Baltimore, MD: Johns Hopkins University Press.

Hirschman, A.O. (1958) *The strategy of economic development*. New Haven, CT: Yale University Press.

International Rice Research Institute (IRRI) (1978) *Economic consequences of the new rice technology*. Los Banos, Philippines: International Rice Research Institute.

Jones, C.W. (1986) 'Intra-household bargaining in response to the introduction of new crops: A case study from North Cameroon, in: J.L. Moock, ed., *Understanding Africa's rural households and farming systems*. Boulder, CO: Westview.

Johnson, D.G. (1973) *World agriculture in disarray*. New York: St. Martins Press.

Johnson, D.G. (1985) 'World commodity market situation and outlook', in: B.L. Gardner, ed., *U.S. agricultural policy: The 1985 farm legislation*. Washington, DC: American Enterprise Institute for Public Policy Research.

Johnston, B.F. (1970) 'Agriculture and structural transformation in development countries: A survey of research', *Journal of Economic Literature*, 3:369–404.

Johnston, B.F. and Clark, W.C. (1982) *Redesigning rural development: A strategic perspective*. Baltimore, MD: Johns Hopkins University Press.

Johnston, B.F. and Kilby, P. (1975) *Agriculture and structural transformation: Economic strategies in late developing countries*. New York: Oxford University Press.

Johnston, B.F. and Mellor, J.W. (1961) 'The role of agriculture in economic development', *American Economic Review*, 51:566–593.

Jorgenson, D.W. (1961) 'The development of a dual economy', *Economic Journal*, 71:309–334.

Krishna, R. (1984) 'Price and technology policies', in: C.K. Eicher and J.M. Staatz, eds., *Agricultural development in the third world*. Baltimore, MD: Johns Hopkins University Press.

Kaplan, S.L. (1984) *Provisioning Paris: Merchants and millers in the grain and flour trade during the eighteenth century*. Ithaca, NY: Cornell University Press.

Kuznets, S. (1966) *Modern economic growth*. New Haven, CT: Yale University Press.

Lappe, F.M. (1971) *Diet for a small planet*. New York: Ballantine.

Lenin, V.I. (1899, reprinted 1964) *The development of capitalism in Russia*. Moscow: Progress Publishers.

Lewis, W.A. (1954) 'Economic development with unlimited supplies of labor, *Manchester School of Economic and Social Studies*, 22:139–191.

Lipton, M. (1977) *Why poor people stay poor: Urban bias in world development*. Cambridge, MA: Harvard University Press.

Little, I.M.D. (1982) *Economic development: Theory, policy, and international relations*. New York: Basic Books.

Mellor, J.W. and Johnston, B.F. (1984) 'The world food equation: Interrelations among development, employment, and food consumption', *Journal of Economic Literature*, 22:531–574.

Mosher, A.T. (1966) *Getting agriculture moving: Essentials for development and modernization*. New York: Praeger.

Myint, H. (1975) 'Agriculture and economic development in the open economy', in: L.G. Reynolds, ed., *Agriculture in development theory*. New Haven, CT: Yale University Press.

Nichols, W.H. (1963) "An 'agricultural surplus' as a factor in economic development", *Journal of Political Economy*, 71:1–29.

Newbery, D.M.G. and Stiglitz, J.E. (1981) *The theory of commodity price stabilization: A study in the economics of risk*. Oxford: Clarendon Press.

Nurkse, R. (1953) *Problems of capital formation in underdeveloped countries*. New York: Oxford University Press.

Prebish, R. (1950) *The Economic Development of Latin America and Its Principal Problems*. Lake Success, NY: U.N. Dept. of Economic Affairs.

Preobazhensky, E. (1965) *The new economics*. Oxford: Clarendon Press.

Reich, M.R., Endo, Y. and Timmer, C.P. (1986) 'The political economy of structural change: Conflict between Japanese and United States agricultural policy', in: T.K. McCraw, ed., *America versus Japan*. Boston, MA: Harvard Business School Press.

Reynolds, L.G., ed. (1975) *Agriculture in development theory*. New Haven, CT: Yale University Press.

Roe, T., Shane, M. and De, H.V. (1986) 'Price responsiveness of world grain markets: The influence of government intervention on import price elasticity', Technical Bulletin no. 1720, Washington, DC: International Economics Division, Economic Research Service, U.S. Department of Agriculture.

Roumasset, J.A., Boussard, J.M. and Singh, I.J., eds. (1979) *Risk, uncertainty and agricultural development*. New York: Agricultural Development Council.

Sah, R.K. and Stiglitz, J.E. (1984) 'The economics of price scissors', *American Economic Review*, 74:125–138.

Schuh, G.E. (1976) 'The new macroeconomics of agriculture', *American Journal of Agricultural Economics*, 58:802–811.

Schultz, T.W. (1953) *The economic organization of agriculture*. New York: McGraw-Hill.

Schultz, T.W. (1964) *Transforming traditional agriculture*. New Haven, CT: Yale University Press.

Schultz, T.W. (1975) 'The value of the ability to deal with disequilibria', *Journal of Economic Literature*, 13:827–846.

Schultz, T.W. (1978) *Distortions of agricultural incentives*. Bloomington, IN: Indiana University Press.

Scobie, G.M. and Posada, R.T. (1978) 'The impact of technical change of income distribution: The case of rice in Colombia', *American Journal of Agricultural Economics*, 60:85–92.

Scott, J.C. (1976) *The moral economy of the peasant*. New Haven, CT: Yale University Press.

Schumacher, E.F. (1975) *Small is beautiful*. New York: Harper and Row.

Schwartz, R.J. (1987) 'Optimal trends for forecasting prices: An empirical assessment of three grains', unpublished Ph.D. thesis, Harvard University, Cambridge, MA.

Sen, A.K. (1981) *Poverty and famines* London: Oxford University Press.

Singh, I.J., Squire, L. and Strauss, J. (1985) 'Agricultural household models: A survey of recent findings and their policy implications', Yale University Economic Growth Center Discussion Paper.

Taylor, L. (1980) *Macro models for developing countries*. New York: McGraw-Hill.

Streeten, P. (1986) *What price food?* Washington, DC: Economic Development Institute of the World Bank.

Timmer, C.P. (1969) 'The turnip, the new husbandry, and the English agricultural revolution', *The Quarterly Journal of Economics* 83:375–395.

Timmer, C.P. (1979) 'Issues of production and consumption: A review of T.W. Schultz, ed., *Distortions of agricultural incentives*', *Science*, 205:385–386.

Timmer, C.P. (1981) "Is there 'curvature' in the Slutsky matrix?", *Review of Economics and Statistics*, 62:395–402.

Timmer, C.P. (1984) 'Energy and structural change in the Asia–Pacific region: The agricultural sector', in: R. Bautista and S. Naya, eds., *Energy and structural change in the Asia–Pacific region: Papers and proceedings of the thirteenth Pacific trade and development conference*. Manila: Philippine Institute for Development Studies and the Asian Development Bank.

Timmer, C.P. (1986) *Getting prices right: The scope and limits of agricultural price policy*. Ithaca, NY: Cornell University Press.

Timmer, C.P., Falcon, W.P. and Pearson, S.R. (1983) *Food policy analysis*. Baltimore, MD: Johns Hopkins University Press for the World Bank.

Volrath, T. (1985) 'Developmental consequences of unrestricted trade', Foreign agricultural economic report no. 213. Washington, DC: Economic Research Service, U.S. Department of Agriculture.

Waterfield, C. (1985) 'Disaggregating food consumption parameters', *Food Policy*, 10:337–351.

World Bank (1982) *World development report 1982*. New York: Oxford University Press.

World Bank (1986) *World development report 1986*. New York: Oxford University Press.

Chapter 9

INDUSTRIALIZATION AND TRADE

HOWARD PACK*

University of Pennsylvania

Contents

1.	Introduction	334
2.	A retrospective	336
	2.1. The compression of the industrialization process	336
	2.2. Initial conditions	337
	2.3. The elasticity of factor supplies	338
	2.4. The role of rationality	341
	2.5. The role of international trade	341
3.	The evolving structure of production	342
	3.1. Normal patterns	342
	3.2. The impact of policy intervention	344
	3.3. Import substitution, exports, and the patterns of growth	344
4.	The impact of trade on industrial performance	346
	4.1. Industrial productivity – a key variable	346
	4.2. The costs of protection	347
	4.3. Trade orientation and the growth of total factor productivity	348
	4.4. The empirical evidence	352
	4.5. Cross-country models	356
	4.6. The large country puzzle	357
5.	Micro studies of productivity	358
	5.1. Early intercountry comparisons of productivity levels	358
	5.2. The Hirschman hypothesis	359
	5.3. Firm-level productivity studies in less developed countries	360
6.	Employment creation in the manufacturing sector	365
	6.1. The choice of technology	366
	6.2. Factor market distortions and information costs	369
	6.3. The aggregate gains from improved technology choice	370
7.	Conclusions	371
	References	372

*I have received helpful comments on earlier drafts from Nathaniel Leff, Larry E. Westphal, and particularly Stephen E. Lewis.

Handbook of Development Economics, Volume I, Edited by H. Chenery and T.N. Srinivasan
© *Elsevier Science Publishers B.V., 1988*

1. Introduction

After four decades of intensive effort at industrialization in the LDCs, a high percentage of the literature evaluating that effort is critical of it. The growth of the manufacturing sector is viewed as having had largely negative effects, i.e. it was inefficient, inegalitarian, and the source of deleterious impacts on other productive sectors. Rarely does the critical literature refer back to the initial optimism about the industrial sector's potential role in fostering development and the reasons why almost all countries have pursued industrialization strategies with such determination.[1]

The initial attraction of manufacturing lay in a combination of perceived favorable characteristics: a chance to realize high (labor) productivity and its continued growth via the systematic application of science; a perception that the international price of industrial goods would secularly increase relative to that of primary products; the externalities generated in the form of skill accumulation and technology acquisition that would flow to other sectors as a result of labor mobility and "atmospheric" effects; and finally, the anti-colonial legacy, the belief that power stems from smokestacks.

Many of the anticipated benefits have failed to materialize and in some instances their realization has had perverse effects. High labor productivity has been achieved in small industrial enclaves, but rather than reflecting high total factor productivity (TFP), it has resulted from socially excessive capital–labor ratios and high rates of effective protection accorded to the sector. Those who are neither employers nor employees in the manufacturing sector have often been harmed by the high prices of its products and the disproportionate share of investment funds it has received [Little, Scitovsky and Scott (1970)]. The most important source of technology transfer to less developed countries (LDCs) has not been industrial, but agricultural technology from international agricultural research centers which has been locally adapted by institutes that are independent of the local industrial sector [Evenson (1981)]. The early emphasis on industry led many countries to miss the primary commodity boom of the 1950s and 1960s [Cohen and Sisler (1971)]. Rapid industrialization based on low cost sources of energy made many of the most industrialized LDCs vulnerable to an unanticipated form of weakness, high oil prices [World Bank (1982)]. Nevertheless, the subsequent falsification of some of the high and often romantic expectations about industrialization does not justify its summary dismissal as an important component of an overall development strategy. Rather, this constitutes an argument for a more realistic view of its potential role during the structural transformation.

---

[1] For an iconoclastic defense of the industrialization strategy, see Sen (1983).

The Lewis–Fei–Ranis two-sector model provides a useful guide to the role of manufacturing in the development process of a country without an international trade sector.[2] The growth of the industrial sector changes the sectoral center of gravity of the economy as a reallocation of low (marginal) productivity labor from agricultural to the more productive industrial sector occurs. Growing incomes in the sector provide a source of demand for increasing agricultural surpluses, these being paid for by the sale of manufactured inputs and consumer goods. Ideally, the growth of the two sectors is characterized by balance as measured by a constant intersectoral terms of trade, a changing ratio being likely to abort the process.

Among the implications of this model are the inevitable transformation in the sectoral structure of the economy, reflecting both Engel elasticities and changing factor supplies, and a concomitant growth in the share of primary factors in the industrial sector as its output expands. Inevitably, analysts of sectoral evolution have had to recognize that in almost all LDCs international trade affects the sectoral structure and external competition may affect the growth of productivity. The alterations in the structure of the economy implied by all of these simultaneous changes provide the theoretical basis for the empirical work of Chenery and others on the normal patterns of growth [see Chenery and Syrquin (1975), and Chapter 7 in this Handbook), and Chenery, Robinson and Syrquin (1987)].

Disasters being more newsworthy than the normal flow of everyday events, the focus of much of the literature has been on the inefficiency of the industrialization that has, in fact, taken place. Much of the remainder of this chapter thus, of necessity, covers these negative effects. The critical stance of much that follows may, however, suffer from an absence of balance. Though the reliance on externalities to justify a single industrial project is widely (and correctly) viewed with skepticism, it may be the case that the discipline learned in the manufacturing sector has had beneficial effects on other productive sectors and society as a whole. The growth in manufacturing may have had indirect beneficial effects on birth rates, public health measures, and the educational sector either through changes in workers' perspectives or via demands of firms on the government for the provision of social services.[3] In some cases the manufacturing sector has provided productive inputs or consumer goods with more appropriate attributes than would have been available on the world market. While it seems unlikely that such benefits, even if they could be measured, would equal in magnitude the excess social costs of the industrialization process followed by most import-substituting nations, it is also true that the latter costs, which rarely exceed 5 or 6 percent, are themselves not particularly large relative to GNP. Hence, even small

---

[2] Lewis (1954), Fei and Ranis (1965). The model is perhaps most usefully viewed as descriptive in a historical context – nineteenth-century England and pre-1950 Japan – and normative in the post-Second World War context of most LDCs.

[3] More precisely, the question is whether the growth of manufacturing has permitted a more efficient achievement of these objectives than other explicit policies that might have been employed.

beneficial externalities conferred on the much larger non-manufacturing sector could constitute a quantitatively significant offset to the better known and carefully documented costs.

This chapter concentrates on a few major recurring themes that have been prominent in the literature on industrialization. Section 2 discusses the initial conditions at the beginning of the post-colonial period and their relation to subsequent industrial development. Section 3 considers the determinants of the growing relative importance of the sector. Productivity growth and its relation to international trade orientation is considered in Section 4 at the sectoral level. Section 5 discusses studies of the efficiency of individual firms. The employment effects of industrialization are examined in Section 6 and conclusions are presented in Section 7.

2. A retrospective

2.1. The compression of the industrialization process

Looking back at the four decades since the end of the Second World War, the rapid growth of industrial output in LDCs is surprising. While much of it is inefficiently produced, this reflects economic policy as much as deficiencies in management and technology. Even those observers who were optimistic at the beginning of the period would be surprised at the extent and sophistication of physical production in the late 1980s. Cipolla (1976) and others have detailed the slow accumulation of relevant industrial skills over many centuries that were important preconditions of the industrial revolution. The attempt to compress centuries of skill accumulation into four decades while achieving rates of industrial growth exceeding those of the current developed countries in their early period of industrial development (Table 9.1) has resulted in slow rates of productivity growth (cf. Sections 4 and 5) and in current production that is highly inefficient.[4] Nevertheless, it is likely that trade liberalization combined with explicit efforts to improve technological capacity could result in a competitive industrial sector in many countries within a decade or less. Indeed, such a view is the basis for structural adjustment loans by the World Bank and other international aid agencies.

---

[4] The welfare implications of observed industrial growth must also be carefully assessed insofar as in some countries, such as China, it may have been achieved by the reallocation of primary factors from higher (agricultural) to lower (manufacturing) marginal productivity pursuits.

Table 9.1
Rates of growth of industrial and manufacturing output

| | Rate of growth of output | | | |
| | Industrial | | Manufacturing | |
	1960–70	1970–82	1960–70	1970–82
Low income countries other than China and India	6.6	4.0	6.3	3.2
India	5.4	4.3	4.7	4.5
China	11.2	8.3	na	na
Lower middle income	6.2	5.8	6.5	5.5
Middle income oil importers	7.0	5.5	7.5	5.3
Upper middle income	9.1	5.7	8.4	5.8

Country–Period	Rate of growth of industrial output
France (1872–1910)	2.1
Germany (1860–1914)	4.2
Sweden (1865–1914)	4.8
Italy (1863–1913)	1.6
United States (1874–1914)	5.0

Sources: Kuznets (1956, 1957); The World Bank (1984).
Note: "Industrial output" is defined by the World Bank (1984) to include the following sectors: Mining; Manufacturing; Construction; Electricity; Water; Gas.
Kuznets" definition of "Mining" includes Mining, Manufacturing, and Construction.

2.2. Initial conditions

In the immediate post-war period, the potential for industrial development varied considerably among LDCs. In Brazil, Egypt, and India, for example, relatively large manufacturing firms had 60 or 70 years of industrial experience,[5] primarily in food processing and textiles. Two countries, the Republic of Korea and Taiwan, which would later prove quite successful, possessed a considerable base of education and industrial experience.[6] In these and other countries there was also an extensive small-scale sector containing many skills useful to a modern industrial sector. Other nations, primarily in sub-Saharan Africa, had virtually no industrial base and few small-scale handicrafts that might permit the accumulation of the mechanical skills critical to large-scale industrial development [Duignan and Gann (1975)].[7]

---

[5] Fishlow (1972), Little (1982a), Morris (1965), Mabro and Radwan (1976), Stein (1957).
[6] Mason et al. (1980) and Ranis (1979). In Taiwan, for example, 20 percent of GNP originated in manufacturing in 1930, mostly in food processing; heavy industry was begun by the Japanese in the 1930s; and the country's industrialization benefited from the immigration of a large number of industrialists from the Chinese mainland in 1949.
[7] For a description and explanation for West Africa, see Hopkins (1973).

Surprisingly, there has been limited research relating the initial skill level in the early post-war period with subsequent industrial success. Casual empiricism suggests little, if any, relation between the initial endowment and the relative efficiency of later industrial growth, Korea and Taiwan being important exceptions.[8] Brazil, Egypt, and India have not achieved efficient growth, according to such conventional measures as domestic resource cost (DRC) or effective rates of protection (ERP).[9] India and Brazil, however, have realized somewhat broader production in intermediates and capital goods and more efficient growth than other import-substituting countries of large size, but shorter industrial history such as Indonesia and Nigeria.[10] In sum, greater industrial experience may have yielded somewhat higher productivity and greater ability to deepen the industrial structure though the desirability of the latter course would depend on its efficiency.

The major point of this brief survey is that initial endowment has had a tenuous relation to future industrial growth capable of producing goods that are competitive in international markets. Nor do variations in the colonial legacy provide systematic explanation of the pattern of industrialization in the post-war period. Countries with an extensive industrial heritage such as India have had poor records of industrial growth.[11] Policies pursued in the post-independence period appear to exert a significant impact which outweighs the inherited structure. Nevertheless, it is difficult to identify a country with a record of manufacturing growth which had not had substantial industrial experience before the Second World War. Korea and Taiwan certainly had such experience – policy is important but so is inheritance.

2.3. The elasticity of factor supplies

One surprise for an early post-war forecaster of industrial development would be the elastic supply of factors critical to industrial growth. Contrary to skeptics like Gerschenkron (1962), who based his views on the historical development process

---

[8]Ranis (1979) and Mason et al. (1980).

[9]Bergsman (1970), Bhagwati and Desai (1970), Bhagwati and Srinivasan (1975), Hansen and Nashashibi (1975). On the relation between effective protection rates and domestic resource costs, see Bruno (1972), Krueger (1972), Srinivasan and Bhagwati (1978), Lucas (1984), and Bliss, Chapter 24 in this Handbook.

[10]On Nigeria, see Kilby (1969). Recent research on the ability to generate local technology indicates that Indian and Brazilian firms have been relatively successful, although the precise welfare significance of this achievement has not been demonstrated. See the various articles in the special issue of *World Development*, May/June 1984, devoted to the evidence on local generation of technology. Also, see Lall (1985), Fransman and King (1984), and Chapter 20 by Westphal in this volume.

[11]A careful and thorough analysis of the sources of the poor Indian industrial performance is provided by Ahluwalia (1985).

in Western Europe,[12] in most countries the predicted multiplicity of obstacles never became constraining.[13] This can be seen most clearly in the case of the successful newly industrializing countries (NICs) whose experience is useful in highlighting some issues. In the absence of elastic factor supplies, even NICs which followed excellent economic policies (the standard explanation for their success), would have encountered constraints that would have led to rapidly increasing marginal costs. Contrary to early expectations, however, the accumulation of physical capital did not impose a constraint on growth given rapidly rising savings rates, the possibility of international borrowing, and the availability of direct foreign investment. A shortage of skilled operatives, managers, and technological knowledge also might have constrained development, but apparently did not.

The source of the growth of skills that were a necessary facilitating factor during industrialization has not been systematically explored even for the successful NICs. Two exceptions are the analyses of Saxonhouse (1978) and Izumi (1980), who analyze the generation of industrial skills, rather than formal education, in the early Japanese cotton textile industry. Similarly, Leff (1968) provides careful documentation of the source of skilled-labor growth in the Brazilian engineering sector. The two most comprehensive accounts of South Korean and Taiwanese development [Mason et al. (1980), and Galenson (1979)] neither include studies of the accumulation of industrial labor skills, nor of the acquisition of production technology. The Taiwan study does, however, contain an analysis of the role of general education, placing it within a "sources-of-growth" context.

Even though the East Asian growth pattern is usually viewed as being intensive in unskilled labor, this does not imply no skills; foremen and supervisors play an important role in most labor-intensive processes. Conversely, rapid Indian growth might, ex ante, have been viewed as likely, given its considerable absolute (though not necessarily per capita) endowments of highly educated labor. Presumably, the successful NICs had some combination of general and vocational education and on-the-job training in addition to good trade policies. Fields (1984) and Scitovsky (1985) argue that wage policies were also a critical determinant of overall performance. Without the necessary skill accumulation, the trade policies usually given credit for the success of the NICs would not have worked so spectacularly. Recent analyses of sub-Saharan Africa emphasize a paucity of

---

[12] On the process of socializing an industrial working class in England, see Thompson (1968) and Hammond and Hammond (1911, 1919).

[13] It is instructive to consult U.N. documents written in the early part of the period [United Nations (1955)], often written by academic consultants, which offered lists of the obstacles to successful industrialization, often claiming that all would have to be overcome simultaneously and that the prospect for this occurring was bleak.

"skills" as the dominant constraint on industrialization among the countries in this region [World Bank (1981), Acharya (1981)].

Technology, the other potentially scarce factor, may be obtained by licensing, informal accumulation of non-proprietary information, and from multinational firms. Proprietary technology may be subject to rapidly increasing marginal cost given the bilateral monopoly structure of the technology market [Arrow (1969)]; even non-proprietary technology can be expensive to obtain given the substantial search costs involved. Little systematic effort to examine the cost of technology acquisition in LDCs has been attempted though a useful beginning is that of Cortes and Bocock (1984). Important insights on the sources of Korean industrial competence are contained in the accounts of Westphal et al. (1981) and Rhee, Pursell and Ross-Larson (1984). After the fact, one can see that a technology constraint was not binding on the NICs. Relevant technology was often acquired cheaply on an informal basis and the emphasis on labor-intensive low-technology products not based on proprietary information made the issue moot for two decades of rapid growth among the Gang of Four (Hong Kong, Singapore, South Korea, and Taiwan).

Despite the lack of empirical confirmation, the growth of factors that might have acted as a serious constraint on development must have been quite fast in the NICs that experienced rapid growth. Otherwise, there would have been a more rapid change in relative factor prices and a widening in income inequality attributable to growing rents for the scarce factors of production. Such growth in inequality, however, did not occur [Mason et al. (1981), Fei, Ranis and Kuo (1980)]. A promising research area is the investigation of the types of infrastructure expenditures, broadly defined, that the market-oriented NICs have undertaken in support of their industrial growth objectives. There is some evidence that they devoted considerable resources to education as well as to the provision of inexpensive housing in order to hold down the cost of living and hence the nominal wage in the exporting sector.

In countries that have not grown as rapidly as the NICs it is possible that both skilled labor and technology acted as serious constraints on the growth process. The experience of the NICs, however, suggests that such limits are not an immutable feature of the LDC landscape, but are at least partly the outcome of public decisions such as expenditures on education and other infrastructure and the willingness to allow structural transformation to proceed rather than preserve the initial structure in deference to political interests of those who lose during the transformation.[14]

---

[14] Olson (1982) has a provocative discussion in which he argues that a major prerequisite for sustained growth is the ability of governments to override the objections to growth-augmenting changes by specific groups that would suffer losses.

2.4. The role of rationality

In the European context, Landes (1969) has argued that the accumulation of skills was widely spread among countries; the necessary conditions for its blossoming into sustained growth in industrial output were: (1) the prevalence of rationality, defined as an instrumental view of the world, and (2) the spread of the market system and its structure of incentives conducive to individual effort. Conventional wisdom, circa 1945, held that neither was typical of LDCs.[15] A prescient observer might also have forecast extensive public ownership. However, as the well-known and robust research on peasant price behavior and the newer literature on household economics in LDCs testify, there is considerable economic rationality even in the "traditional" sector and a fortiori in the modern sector. The rationality in many cases exercises itself against an often perverse set of incentives that may have done more to lead to inefficient industrialization than have insufficient rationality or skills. While it is difficult to separate the skill constraint, especially in the poorer countries, from the incentive structure as sources of inefficiency, recent empirical work discussed below suggests that inadequate operative skills are not the primary source of low industrial productivity. On the other hand, some studies (discussed in Section 5) have revealed considerable amounts of intrafirm allocative inefficiency which may be taken as an index of economic irrationality, although this view may have to be modified when information costs are explicitly recognized.

2.5. The role of international trade

In contrast to recent development research, an observer in 1950 might have predicted that few insights would be forthcoming from the theory of international trade. Differentials within developed countries, particularly between northern and southern Italy (the Mezzogiorno), implied that even without trade barriers, the flow of factors and goods was not sufficient to eliminate enormous differences among regions. While such differentials have received sporadic attention since the initial spurt of interest,[16] explanations of persisting regional disparities have not been convincing. These gaps suggest that important characteristics of economies exist apart from the international trade regime and may exert decisive effects on economic development, a truism often noted but occa-

---

[15] The same skepticism is present in many contemporary novelists such as V.S. Naipual and Salman Rushdie.

[16] For the earlier work see Chenery (1962). More recent research on regional problems includes, Leff (1972) on Brazil and Faini (1983, 1984). There is also a considerable literature in other social sciences, for example Banfield (1958) on the conundrum of southern Italy.

sionally lost sight of in the recent emphasis on the importance of trade policies.[17] More generally, early post-war concern with intrasectoral balance in industrial growth stemmed from a view that development would largely take place in relative autarchy, a view that reflected considerable export pessimism during this period [Little (1982b, ch. 4)].

3. The evolving structure of production

3.1. Normal patterns

As shown by Syrquin (Chapter 7 in this Handbook), distinctive patterns of change characterize economies as they move to successively greater levels of per capita income. In particular, the importance of industry, broadly defined to include construction and utilities, and more narrowly defined in terms of manufacturing, increases. The cross-country pattern of the relative size of individual manufacturing sectors is also well explained by per capita income and country size. These cross-section patterns conform to the historical evolution, systematically examined by Kuznets (1966), of the now developed economies.[18]

The typical equation estimated by Chenery and others is:

$$\log VA_i/V = B_1 \log(Y/P) + B_2 \log P, \tag{1}$$

where VA_i is value added in sector i, V is national income, Y is gross national product, and P is population. The regression coefficients are reduced form growth elasticities reflecting both supply and demand factors. The theoretical

---

[17]On the persistence and implications of regional differentials even in the United States, see J.R. Pack (1980).

[18]In both cross-country and intertemporal studies the interpretation of the value-added share of manufacturing and its components presents some problems. As the sector expands, its value-added increases as a share of national income partly as a result of the greater monopoly power that characterizes the sector, whether based on scale economies or other barriers to entry. In addition, value-added reflects the impact of high, but varying rates of effective protection. Thus, part of measured value-added contains an unknown component of economic rent as well economic waste. Observed cross-section and time-series patterns are thus better interpreted in terms of evolving claims on national income rather than contribution to it. The use of purchasing power parity measures as deflators [Kravis, Heston and Summers (1978)] would remove most of these problems. It is nevertheless the case that Chenery and Syrquin (1975) find that the allocation of primary factors also conforms to the structural transformation described by value added.

basis of the regressions is the Heckscher–Ohlin model, with per capita income serving as a proxy for the capital–labor ratio.[19]

Underlying the single equation is a complex set of supply and demand equations for each sector that reflects both structural features, such as comparative advantage, and economic policies such as the panopoly of interventions characterizing import-substitution programs.[20] In a large closed economy the structure of production reflects income elasticities, previous factor accumulation, and differences in production functions.[21] In open economies the sectoral production pattern also depends on the pattern of exports and import substitution which, in turn, depend on the policy environment. In general, government policy is likely to matter insofar as only 50 percent of the variation in manufacturing value added to total value added is explained by income per capita and population. To extrapolate the cross-section results to the evolution of economies requires an augmented framework that takes account of policy interventions and changing structural features such as factor productivity growth and its bias.[22]

Among the important issues raised a decade ago by Chenery and Syrquin several still have not been addressed in the literature. For example, they found that large countries typically have a greater share of their value-added concentrated in industries such as heavy metals, chemicals, and paper than do smaller nations. The simplest explanation is that the larger domestic market allows the earlier establishment of industries subject to significant static economies of scale. When export possibilities are recognized, a more complete explanation involving perceived asymmetries in risk between the domestic and foreign market, scale economies in marketing, or some market imperfection is required. While earlier discussions about the efficacy of balanced growth are generally recognized to be less salient in the face of trade opportunities, little attention has been given to the sector-specific implications of scale economies.[23] More generally, the role of scale economies in the industrial development process has not been the focus of sustained analysis in recent years[24] despite robust evidence that the minimum efficient scale of plant is quite large [Pratten (1971)].

---

[19]Chenery (1960). Krueger (1983, ch. 5) provides a comprehensive multi-country, multi-commodity analysis of trade patterns. Although not its primary objective, her analysis offers an amplification of the theoretical basis for normal patterns, expanding that suggested by Chenery.

[20]"From an empirical standpoint it is very difficult to separate the effects of development policies from the underlying structural characteristics that condition them" [Chenery and Syrquin (1975, p. 64)].

[21]Price elasticities of demand also become relevant when balanced growth does not occur. An interesting exercise incorporating purchasing power parity prices into international comparisons is that of Summers (1982).

[22]Chenery, Robinson and Syrquin (1987) address many of these issues.

[23]For important exceptions, see Manne (1967), Westphal (1975), Kendrick and Stoutjesdijk (1979), Choksi, Meeraus and Stoutjesdijk (1980), and Kendrick, Meeraus and Alatorre (1984).

[24]For exceptions, see Teitel (1975), Felix (1977), and Westphal and Cremer (1984).

3.2. *The impact of policy intervention*

The most thoroughly studied policies affecting the structure of production have been tariffs, quotas, and measures to encourage exports. Policies that usually fall within the province of public finance or monetary policy such as tax holidays, accelerated depreciation writeoffs, and selective credit intervention have been studied where their effects can conveniently be placed within the framework of effective protection of import substitutes or exports. Otherwise they have typically been neglected in discussions of the evolution of productive structure.[25] When countries attempt to utilize such policies to affect the composition of output in order to provide additional employment or generate greater regional balance, the sectoral impact of their efforts will not generally be apparent from the analysis of trade-related policy instruments. For example, tax holidays granted to textile firms as an inducement to locate in backward regions may lead to rapid growth of the sector. If the sector is fairly efficient and does not require unusually high levels of protection, trade-focused policy analysis will miss the important policy intervention that affects the structure of production.

3.3. *Import substitution, exports, and the patterns of growth*

There has been varied success in relating the impact of policy interventions to the structure of trade. For example, it has been very difficult to establish a systematic relation between various measures of the magnitude of protection, such as domestic resource cost and effective rates of protection (ERPs), and the growth of individual sectors. This initially surprising result has been addressed by Bhagwati and Srinivasan (1979). Among the reasons they offer as an explanation are the following:[26]

(1) A given ERP is compatible with many nominal tariff structures and hence with different effects on consumption and production.

(2) ERPs are measured in a static context with no growth in resources. As growth occurs, relative factor endowments change and the impact on output will be mediated, inter alia through effects described by the Rybczynski theorem.

(3) Where either tariffs or quantitative restrictions are anticipated by prospective investors as being granted automatically, the observed tariff structure will not capture this "guarantee effect" and its impact on investment decisions.

(4) The marginal returns to further expansion of a sector may be low even where high effective protection exists. Thus, if a sector has undergone consider-

---

[25]For an analysis of the impact of tax and subsidy policies on Israel's production structure, see Pack (1971). The effect of public finance measures have been utilized in examining the determinants of relative factor prices. See, for example, Krueger (1983).

[26]Also see Bhagwati (1978) and Deardorff (1979).

able import substitution, the local market may offer few opportunities for profitable introduction of new capacity.

Characteristics of an economy other than factor endowments and policies also affect both cross-country and intertemporal growth structures. Differential rates of productivity growth as well as biases in such growth may be important. Not only are national factor endowments changing, with different implications for the various sectors depending on their factor intensities, but as noted in an extensive literature beginning with Hicks' inaugural lecture (1953), productivity growth may have a variety of impacts on trade patterns in individual sectors [Findlay and Grubert (1959)]. The results of this literature and its potential insights into sectoral evolution have generally been ignored in the focus on the distorting effects of interventionist policies. Despite the difficult data and econometric problems attendant on estimating the factor biases in productivity growth,[27] the added insights about sectoral growth patterns from analysis of productivity performance may have greater value than further refinements in measurement of the impact of government intervention.

In some countries, a rapid growth in aggregate exports, largely concentrated in manufacturing, has resulted in rapid growth in manufacturing's share of value added. This growth can be ascribed to an outward looking policy, defined as the maintenance of the effective exchange rate (EER) for exports relatively close to that of imports though the ratio, even in export oriented countries, has typically been below unity.[28]

In contrast to the difficulties that have been encountered in relating sectoral growth rates to the pattern of import protection, Balassa and others have had considerable success, employing a slightly augmented (human and non-human capital) Heckscher–Ohlin framework in accounting for LDC sectoral export patterns.[29] While these recent studies of LDC exports have not explored systematically the usefulness of neotechnology, product cycle, or Linder models, the characteristics of typical, relatively simple, LDC exports suggest these would yield little additional explanatory power.[30] Presumably still better explanations would be obtained if the impact of policies were introduced. For example, tariffs and quantitative restrictions (QRs) on imported inputs discourage exports of goods using them, whether the intermediates are imported or domestically

---

[27]See Diamond and McFadden (1978) on the problems involved in estimating the bias of technical change. For a summary of the literature on biased technical change, see Nadiri [1970].

[28]The effective exchange rate is defined as the number of units of local currency actually paid or received for a one dollar international transaction [Bhagwati (1978)].

[29]The assumptions made in some of these studies are strong, for example Balassa (1979) assumes that U.S. capital–labor ratios characterize LDCs and that the elasticity of substitution in all sectors is the same. However, more realistic assumptions employed by Donges and Riedel (1976) and Balassa (1984) generate results that also confirm the Heckscher–Ohlin–Samuelson model. A careful survey of the predictions of the H–O–S model and relevant econometric evidence is provided by Leamer (1984).

[30]A survey of empirical tests of non-Heckscher–Ohlin models is given by Stern (1975).

produced. Differential effects on exports will occur depending on the input–output structure and the sectoral pattern of nominal tariffs.[31] Unless exporters face a free trade regime for their inputs, exports will be discouraged.[32]

4. The impact of trade on industrial performance

4.1. Industrial productivity – a key variable

While the preceding sections considered the trade-related determinants of structural transformation, purely domestic features are also important, particularly relative sectoral growth rates of productivity. The rate of growth of productivity in the industrial sector has been put forward as the key phenomenon in determining the sectoral evolution for the now industrialized economies [Kuznets (1966), Feinstein (1981)]. An extensive international trade literature [for example, Johnson (1955)] considers the implications of differential rates of growth of sectoral productivity while Fei and Ranis (1964) analyze the implications for the closed economy within a richer LDC specific structure. Both analyses can be used to trace the implications of differences in productivity growth between two sectors of an economy where intersectoral terms of trade are determined domestically. For many LDCs, including small ones, the closed economy model appears appropriate given the large number of government interventions that preclude world prices from being the major determinant of intersectoral prices.

Rapid growth in industrial productivity had major implications for the structural transformation of the now developed economies [Kuznets (1966)]. First, the increased economy-wide income from higher productivity accelerated the process insofar as the income elasticity of demand for industrial goods was greater than that for agricultural ones. Second, given relatively competitive pricing, the productivity increases were reflected in a decrease in the price of industrial goods relative to those of the dominant agricultural sector which had lower TFP growth rates. Such a decline in relative prices provided an incentive for the expansion of agriculture insofar as the cost of both consumer and producer goods purchased from the cities fell relative to the price of agricultural products.[33] Finally, the decline in the relative price of industrial products increased the quantity demanded of these goods via the high price elasticity of demand, helping to further

---

[31]Deardorff (1979) shows that the pattern of exports may bear little relation to relative factor intensities once tariffs on intermediates are introduced, making Balassa's results even more surprising.

[32]A good illustration of this point is provided by Chenery and Keesing (1979) who calculate that 90 percent of clothing exports from LDCs originate in the few countries that allow exporters access to inputs at international prices.

[33]Myint (1964) attaches particular importance to the changes in relative prices in explaining the process of growing specialization within agriculture. Balance of payment equilibrium between the sectors was maintained by transfers through taxes and voluntary saving from the agricultural sector.

accelerate the shift of both output and factor allocation towards the urban industrial sector.

Has productivity growth played an analogous role in the development of the LDCs of the past 40 years? While industrial sector incomes have grown rapidly, the literature on effective protection implies that much of the income growth represents an implicit tax on factors employed in other sectors rather than the gains from productivity growth. Indeed, the import substitution strategy can be viewed as one designed to accelerate the process of structural transformation by artificially augmenting the demand for domestically produced industrial goods, rather than relying on the slower process of factor movement among sectors in response to changing relative productivities and differential income elasticities.

A considerable literature suggests that internal terms of trade have moved *against* agriculture in contemporary LDCs, discouraging its growth. Several causes can be suggested for this phenomenon: a slow growth in industrial productivity; protection that precludes a drop in industrial prices even where industrial productivity grows;[34] and the fast growth of agricultural TFP due to the green revolution that acts to limit agricultural prices while adding to agriculture's demand for industrial products. While the rapid growth in industrial sector income made possible by high industrial investment has helped to catalyze the growing importance of LDC industry, the sources and results of this evolution in the last four decades appear to differ from those during the industrial revolution. The growth of industrial productivity plays a key role in the two experiences, and the following section considers the evidence on this critical question in contemporary LDCs.

4.2. The costs of protection

A considerable body of evidence has been accumulated demonstrating that significant inefficiency results from import-substituting industrialization (ISI). Calculations of both effective protection rates and domestic resource cost (DRCs) have been employed to establish the magnitude of these costs. Studies at the OECD, The World Bank, and the National Bureau of Economic Research[35] have carefully documented and analyzed the effects of both tariff and non-tariff interventions. The total costs of intervention range from close to zero (Malaysia) to 10 percent of GNP in Brazil.[36] The small reduction in GNP despite substantial

---

[34] There is an interesting question about the causality here, whether slow productivity growth encourages protection or vice versa.

[35] Little, Scitovsky and Scott (1970), Balassa (1971), Bhagwati (1978) and Kreuger (1978) summarize and integrate the results of the three projects.

[36] The low figure for Malaysia reflects the benefits from the restrictive trade regime on the terms of trade. See Bergsman (1974, table 1).

measured inefficiency within the manufacturing sector reflects the low share of industrial output in GNP; the costs relative to value-added in industry are much larger.

In an interesting variation on the conventional cost of protection argument, Stephen Lewis (1972) argues that the adverse effect of inefficient ISI goes beyond the losses usually calculated. If protection of manufacturing equals 5 percent of GNP, the sector is receiving that amount more than it produces in earning (or saving) foreign exchange. Another sector must earn a similar amount of foreign exchange in excess of the factor payments it receives. If not, a balance of payment problem will result. Hence, growth of the manufacturing sector not stemming from productivity growth implies the need for a subsidy that grows at a comparable rate. The implicitly taxed exporting sectors have to grow fast enough to provide the growing subsidy. If the export sectors account for 15 percent of GNP, a 5 percent deadweight loss implies a 33 percent tax must be placed on exporters. Unless the implicit tax falls entirely on rents, there will be a negative supply response as well as a deterioration in the incentive to invest. In Lewis's formulation the conventional calculation of deadweight loss significantly under-states the true costs of protection.

ERPs and DRCs are measures of allocative inefficiency as they indicate the loss from allocating factors to import-substituting sectors that cannot compete with imports when they are exposed to free trade. Technical inefficiency results when industries that could compete with imports under a free trade regime use more inputs per unit of output than is technically necessary.[37] Employing existing estimates of ERPs and informed guesses about which sectors in Brazil and other countries fall into the "hopeless" and "redeemable" categories, Bergsman (1974) finds that in five of the six countries he examines, technical inefficiency is considerably larger than allocative inefficiency, a finding consistent with Leibenstein's (1966) survey. While the specific numerical results depend on the categorization of sectors and on particular assumptions about the shape of industry supply curves, plausible variations on these assumptions would not reverse the relative importance of the two sources of inefficiency. A full assess-ment, however, awaits the application of computable general equilibrium models to this issue.[38]

4.3. Trade orientation and the growth of total factor productivity

Early proponents of import substitution based their policies partially on infant industry arguments and the rapid growth in productivity they expected during

---

[37] These concepts are discussed in detail in Section 5.3.

[38] For a survey of this literature, see Shoven and Whalley (1984). One important application addressing these issues is de Melo (1978).

the stage when industrial skills were created and modern technology mastered. Their main assumption was that the period of protection would be utilized to increase technical efficiency and move towards internationally competitive prices rather than simply to extract rents, whether in the form of leisure or excessive incomes. The high levels of protection remaining in force after two or three decades of intense industrialization suggest that in most nations such optimism was not warranted.

Nevertheless, even countries that initially pursued the import-substituting path could have realized significantly better performance with more flexible policies. For example, Korea and Taiwan began their industrialization efforts with high rates of protection and outright prohibition of the import of some products. They differ from other countries practising ISI in their insistence on a relatively quick transition to exports and the willingness to terminate protection when industries fail to meet international competition after a period of protection [Pack and Westphal (1986)]. The willingness and ability of the political system to cope with unsuccessful enterprises and their employees is an important and largely unexplored dimension of East Asian success [Olson (1982)]. With the prospect of international competition after an initial period of protection, firms in these countries had little choice but to undertake the investment in acquiring technological capability that is required for improved productivity in contrast to the implicit model underlying ISI that learning-by-doing is the most important mechanism fostering industrial progress.

While advocates of ISI expect higher rates of TFP growth in manufacturing from their policies, proponents of a neutral trade regime in which the effective exchange rate for exports relative to imports is close to unity, predict a higher rate of TFP growth from outward looking policies.[39] Exports are viewed as generating greater growth of productivity as a result of: greater capacity utilization in industries in which the minimum efficient size of plant (MES) is large relative to the domestic market; greater horizontal specialization as each firm concentrates on a narrower range of products;[40] increasing familiarity with and absorption of new technologies; greater learning-by-doing insofar as this is a function of cumulative output and exports permit greater output in an industry; and the stimulative effects of the need to achieve internationally competitive prices and quality. While some of these beneficial effects, for example greater capacity utilization and most plausible formulations of learning-by-doing, cannot yield greater steady-state growth of productivity, the others will do so. All will result in substantially higher intermediate-run growth rates.

---

[39] For good summaries of the expected benefits of a neutral trade regime, see Balassa (1980) and Krueger (1980).

[40] An analysis of intraindustry trade in Chamberlinian markets is given by Krugman (1979) and Lancaster (1980).

The impact of an external orientation may lie in its effect on allocative or technical inefficiency. As noted above, measured deleterious allocative effects are relatively small compared to GNP while technical inefficiency looms larger. Neither is particularly large, the combined effect being at the most one and a half years of GNP growth in countries where this has been investigated. On the other hand, the cumulative impact over two decades of the annual GNP forgone results in magnitudes that cannot be dismissed as "small". Proponents of a liberal trade regime argue that these purely reallocative estimates of the impact of ISI are static; in an intertemporal context, benefits from improved technical efficiency stemming from the effects noted in the preceding paragraph should occur when more neutral policies are followed. Advocates of ISI have a similar view about the technical efficiency gains from pursuing *their* policies although they tend to ignore allocative efficiency. Empirical testing of these competing hypotheses about the dynamic effects of ISI is possible, in principle, employing time-series analysis of the sources of growth.

A large number of studies have been carried out on the sources of growth of LDCs using one or another variant of the Denison–Kendrick–Solow methodology.[41] Before examining the results it is necessary to set out three issues that have not been explicitly discussed, namely (1) lag structures, (2) the inclusiveness of the sectors studied, and (3) domestic (as contrasted to trade-related) determinants of productivity growth.

4.3.1. Lag structures

Proponents of a neutral trade regime expect greater growth of TFP when a liberal trade policy is being followed than when ISI is actively pursued; presumably the opposite is true of ISI advocates. The specification of correct lag structures is critical but has received little attention. An observation of greater TFP growth after liberalization occurs can be interpreted as the lagged effect of the previous import-substituting regime. Or the failure of TFP growth to accelerate with liberalization might stem from the previous harmful effects of ISI operating with a lag. Econometric techniques suggested by Granger (1969) have not been introduced into the existing literature. Some of the ambiguity might be resolved with a sufficiently finely honed theory about the sources of improved performance in the short and long run, and by firm level information in addition to sectoral TFP growth rates. Nevertheless, it is unlikely that those with strong views will be convinced by such evidence. As Solow (1985) puts it: "few econometricians have ever been forced by the facts to abandon a firmly held belief."

---

[41] For a survey of LDC studies through the late 1960s, see Nadiri (1972). A more recent survey is presented in Chenery, Robinson and Syrquin (1986).

4.3.2. Sectoral inclusiveness

A second question involves the sectoral impact of different trade regimes. Assuming that a neutral trade orientation leads to greater productivity growth, is this manifested in the individual sectors that become exporters, in all of manufacturing, or indeed in all modern sectors including services? Some of the benefits enumerated above, for example greater horizontal specialization, are sector specific, whereas greater availability of imported inputs may reduce bottlenecks in other manufacturing sectors, and the discipline learned in the export sector may be carried by mobile workers to other manufacturing and non-manufacturing sectors.

4.3.3. Domestic determinants of productivity growth

While the forces of international competition are undoubtedly an important catalyst for improving economic performance, purely domestic factors have much to contribute. The developed country literature on the underlying determinants of productivity growth [Mansfield (1968), Nelson (1981), Scherer (1984)] emphasizes internal firm efforts including R&D and the creation of a harmonious work environment. The historical literature [Landes (1969) and Rosenberg (1976, 1982)] assigns an important role as well to informal tinkering within plants. Katz (1984) and others (see Chapter 20 by Westphal in this Handbook) have demonstrated that considerable effort of both types is seen in import-substituting countries. Other important determinants of disembodied productivity growth stem from characteristics of an economy that are not related to the trade regime. The impacts of education, health, nutrition, and industrial relations on labor productivity have all been shown to exert some effect on productivity.[42] Fields (1984) has suggested that a major source of the successful performance of the superexporters of East Asia has been labor market policies. And a large literature attests to the empirical importance of such purely domestic productivity depressants as inefficient public enterprises [Choksi (1979)] and regional allocation policies that direct investment towards areas exhibiting low productivity [Ahluwalia (1985)]. As noted above in Section 2, viewing all problems through the trade prism leaves unexplained severe regional backwardness in places as diverse as Italy's Mezzogiorno and Brazil's Northeast. Finally, purely domestic competition in large countries can play a major role in stimulating productivity

---

[42] For a thorough review of these issues, see Horton and King (1981). Scitovsky (1985), surveying the extensive literature on South Korea and Taiwan, also notes the important effects of non-traded related features of these two economies. For an effort to explain British–U.S. productivity differentials in which most of the several dozen explanatory variables are unrelated to international trade, see Caves (1980).

growth if it is not hampered by policies restricting interfirm rivalry. This is discussed further in Section 4.5.

4.4. The empirical evidence

4.4.1. Total factor productivity and trade regime

As yet there is no set of studies of productivity in individual countries in which the timing and scope questions have been approached on a consistent basis and no studies that systematically consider domestic determinants. Existing research concentrates on the task of obtaining accurate measures of output, input, and productivity and has not examined the issues suggested in the preceding sections; thus, they cannot be employed to resolve the questions on the trade–productivity nexus. Aggregative studies, examining either the national economy or broad sectors such as manufacturing, have found a residual, though typically one accounting for a relatively small percentage of total growth of output.[43] A major difference between the LDCs and DCs seems to be that growth in the former is largely accounted for by the accumulation of inputs rather than growing efficiency in their deployment. While for some periods in some LDCs the economy wide residual is fairly high [Chenery (1983)], the residual in manufacturing or more broadly defined industry is fairly close to zero.[44]

While the studies cited in footnote 43 were not concerned with the relation of productivity to trade regime as their core, a number of studies have had this focus. Some of the country studies in the National Bureau series on the effect of interventionist regimes attempted to estimate TFP growth. Bhagwati, in his summary volume,[45] reports no systematic evidence of an association between five trade regimes, defined in terms of reliance on quantitative restrictions, and TFP growth. Two recent studies on Turkey by Krueger and Tuncer (1982a, 1982b) are

---

[43] Examples include Behrman (1972) on Chile, Bruton (1967) on several Latin American countries, Gaathon (1971) and Pack (1971) on Israel, Williamson (1969) on the Philippines, and W. Kuo (1974) and S. Kuo (1983) on Taiwan. A survey of some of the studies through 1970 is provided by Nadiri (1972). Chenery (1983) discusses the relative importance of factor growth and the residual in explaining *economy wide* growth, noting it plays a major role in only a few of the LDCs, notably the Gang of Four. Recent studies of China [Tidrick (1986)] and India [Ahluwalia (1985)] find zero or negative TFP growth for all of manufacturing and many of its sub-sectors.

[44] It is possible that this result is an artifact of the underlying data-collection process though it seems implausible that the errors in all economies yield downward biased estimates of TFP growth. There is not enough information provided in the studies to evaluate the quality of the underlying national sources. The productivity analyses of well-defined industries and firms discussed in the next section are probably more reliable as the data were collected by individual researchers and there are fewer problems of aggregation and deflation given the relatively narrowly defined sectors examined. The issue is well worth additional research.

[45] Bhagwati (1978, ch. 5).

designed to explore hypotheses about infant industries and the relation between a more neutral regime and productivity growth. There is no confirmation of the infant industry argument given the lag structure and sectoral impact assumed by the authors. Also of interest is their calculation showing that in almost every sector, publicly owned enterprises exhibit lower *levels* of total factor productivity, suggesting that large potential gains exist from moving towards private ownership or more market discipline even where ownership is unchanged.

For individual two-digit manufacturing sectors Nishimizu and Robinson (1984) find support for the hypothesis that in Korea total factor productivity grew more rapidly than in internally oriented Turkey and Yugoslavia.[46] Kim and Kwon (1977), analyzing years that partly overlap those of Nishimizu and Robinson, find that almost all of the conventionally measured residual for the entire Korean manufacturing sector is eliminated by a correction for changes in capacity utilization.[47] While increased utilization is indeed one of the benefits stemming from export promotion, especially where plants with large minimum efficient scale are built, this is not equivalent to an inward shift in the unit isoquant arising from growing technical competence.[48] For Singapore, a country with extremely rapid growth of industrial exports, Tsao (1985) finds average TFP growth for two-digit branches of eight-tenths of one percent during the 1970s with many sectors exhibiting negative productivity growth.

Thus, to date there is no clear confirmation of the hypothesis that countries with an external orientation benefit from greater growth in technical efficiency in the component sectors of manufacturing. When combined with the relatively small static costs of protection, this finding leaves those with a predilection towards a neutral regime in a quandary. The rapid export growth of the Gang of Four and the improved performance of some other economies during periods of liberalization do not definitively manifest themselves in conventional measures of supply side success. While aggregate growth has been faster, there have been commensurate increases in productive inputs and the welfare implications of additional growth need to be analyzed quite carefully.

4.4.2. An interpretation

For the two great success stories, the Republic of South Korea and Taiwan, the stylized facts include a rapid growth of productive inputs, a fairly high economy wide residual, but a relatively low TFP growth in the manufacturing sector. Is the

---

[46] Christensen and Cummings (1981) also found a high economy wide residual for Korea.

[47] The differences in the two measures of productivity growth reflect the use by Nishimizu and Robinson of capital stock rather than the flow of services.

[48] Bruton (1967) and Williamson (1969) have also found, for five import-substituting Latin American countries and the Philippines, that most of the economy wide and measured residual is explicable in terms of growing capacity utilization.

success of these two countries not attributable to export orientation and the greater productivity it generated or has the question been incorrectly phrased?

Consider the Korean case. Over a period of 17 years its manufacturing sector realized average annual rates of growth of capital stock and labor of 13 percent and 5.3 percent, respectively.[49] Had the manufacturing sector been oriented towards the domestic market, the allocation of new factors inevitably would have been to products with lower marginal returns than were obtained by exporting to new markets, i.e. the domestic terms of trade would have been less favorable than the world terms of trade. Import-substituting countries have typically been unable to absorb much smaller additions to their stock of factors without running into severely diminishing returns due to the inability of the domestic market to absorb the additional output. Thus, the proper measure of the contribution of export orientation is the difference in realized TFP growth relative to that which would have occurred had the domestic market been the major destination of output.

While it is difficult to implement empirically, the counterfactual scenario provides a more appropriate framework for understanding the importance of export orientation. The absence of differences in measured TFP in manufacturing between import substituting and the export-oriented economies is not particularly relevant. It is the ability of the latter to maintain productivity in the face of a rapid absorption of factors from lower productivity uses in both agriculture and the urban informal sectors that is a major source of the success of the export strategy. The structural transformation measured by Chenery and Kuznets and predicted in the Lewis model occurs without the rapidly growing manufacturing sector facing a deteriorating terms of trade as may well occur in the closed economy. Viewed from this perspective, the advantage of export orientation is allocative – factors can be moved rapidly from low productivity to high productivity sectors without the latter encountering diminishing returns.[50] And given the size of the world market, the whole process can proceed much more quickly.

In addition, there is a macroeconomic gain from export orientation, namely the ability to avoid stop–go policies that frequently appear in the inward-oriented

---

[49] This chapter does not address the question of whether rates of factor growth, particularly capital, are greater in outward-oriented countries. It may be noted, however, that the export-oriented economies do not have higher measured rates of domestic saving than countries with an internal orientation [Bhagwati (1978)]. Nevertheless, even with similar savings rates, it is likely that their capital stock growth rates (sQ/K) are somewhat greater given their generally more labor-intensive pattern of sectoral expansion and choice of technology and the resultant lower initial capital–output ratio. Moreover, it is likely that the measured rates of saving in the inward-looking countries are overstated relative to those in the outward-looking countries and correct estimates would further increase the difference in the rate of growth of the respective capital stocks. See Pack (1971, pp. 213–214).

[50] Benefits from reallocation of factors among sectors implies a disequilibrium in which the marginal product of factors is not initially equal across sectors, a widely noted phenomenon in all LDCs.

countries. While the increasing average utilization rates that characterize export oriented economies do not, of themselves, lead to a more rapid growth rate of potential output, they do generate higher short- and medium-term growth rates. The greater output obtained in the short term allows some flexibility in dealing with the diverse problems encountered in rapidly changing economies. Workers may be more willing to accept changes in location, occupation, and industry and capitalists more willing to expand into new sectors in a more rapidly growing industrial sector than in one subject to "stop–go" policies.

The high level of education also played an important role in the rapid structural transformation of the East Asian superexporters [Scitovsky (1985)]. It is likely that the significant shift of factors among sectors would have led to a decline in the marginal productivity of factors in the industrial sector had it not been for the substantial technical and organizational abilities conferred by education. The typical adjustment to the natural labor force in Denison-type sources-of-growth-accounting is misleading. It is not the augmentation of natural units of labor that is critical, but the level of education that permits diminishing returns to be avoided through the greater adaptive ability of individual firms and better coordination of the entire economy. This may explain why labor force adjustments explain little of aggregate Korean growth [Kim and Park (1985)], although no studies have been done of the manufacturing sector alone using the Denison method for labor force adjustments. Purely domestic decisions, namely substantial public and private expenditure on education, constituted a necessary complement of the neutral trade policies. While export orientation would have avoided the adverse price impact on the manufacturing sector of a slowly growing non-industrial economy, at a lower level of education the effort to transform the sectoral structure rapidly via exports would have led to a decline in marginal productivities and hence a rise in costs, slowing or aborting the export expansion.

4.4.3. The contribution of sectoral reallocation to productivity growth – the evidence

The role of sector reallocation of factors has received some attention in the literature on the sources of growth in developed countries [Massell (1961)]. For the LDCs, however, only a few time-series studies have been done.[51] Pack (1971) found that relatively little of the aggregate growth of TFP in Israel could be accounted for by factor reallocation, a result largely attributable to the relative unimportance of dualism across sectors.[52] Syrquin (1986) finds relatively small gains from reallocation in South Korea with fairly large ones for Mexico and

---

[51] See Syrquin (1986) for references and a reconciliation of the various methods employed.
[52] This finding is confirmed by Syrquin (1984) for a longer period.

Taiwan. These results undoubtedly understate the true effect insofar as the impact of eliminating intrasector dualism, particularly that between the urban formal and informal sectors, is not included given data constraints. Moreover, Nelson (1986) argues that the typical elasticities employed to measure the impact of reallocation are incorrect.

4.5. Cross-country models

Given the difficulties of obtaining adequate time series to permit disentangling the many potential sources of differential productivity growth, a number of analysts have attempted cross-section analyses of the role of exports in explaining growth [Balassa (1978), Feder (1983), Michaely (1977), Michalopolous and Jay (1973)]. In these formulations the growth of output across countries is explained in terms of changes in the labor force, capital stock, and exports, with exports acting as a Hicks-neutral shift factor. Although the details of the various studies are not beyond cavil, particularly the proxy for the growth of the capital stock, there is no obvious reason to believe that the errors in measurement, if corrected, would eliminate the significance of exports.[53]

The coefficient of exports is usually positive and significant. However, its interpretation presents the same dilemmas as those involved in explaining the significance of trend terms in time series. Exports may be capturing the beneficial effects of such features as greater specialization. However, they may also reflect, given the typically short periods involved, increased utilization of capacity even in sectors not subject to increasing returns, as a result of greater availability of foreign exchange. Export proponents have argued that in exchange constrained economies, increased average utilization represents a major benefit from an export orientation. This and other plausible explanations of the coefficient of exports in cross-section studies do not imply that greater total factor productivity in the conventional sense of decreasing unit input requirements with a given production function are a result of exporting. Nevertheless higher short- and medium-term growth are beneficial.

Feder (1983) includes export growth as an independent variable explaining cross-country growth rates as well as sectoral reallocation of factors between

---

[53] The problem with the capital stock arises from the use in all of the studies of the investment/GNP ratio as a proxy for capital stock growth. Insofar as countries exhibiting more rapid export growth had lower capital–output ratios at the beginning of the period or chose less capital-intensive sectors, their capital stock growth rates are likely to be understated. Similarly, if education and other social overhead capital expenditures are induced by higher income, measured labor input growth may understate the correct quality adjusted measure. Undoubtedly, a diligent researcher could chip away at the existing results and obtain a coefficient of zero for exports. Nevertheless, given the explanation offered above of the possible sources of more rapid growth among exporters, it is likely that the result is not a statistical artifact.

exports and non-exported goods. This variable is found to be a significant determinant of overall growth, presumably reflecting discrepancies between marginal productivities between the two types of productive activities. This supports the argument set forth above about the role of sectoral reallocation in the growth process. Nevertheless, it is necessary to be cautious in relying on the evidence of cross-section research as it neither deals with the impact of fluctuations in aggregate demand, nor with the likelihood that production functions differ by sub-sector and in the aggregate across countries. A study by Jung and Marshall (1985), for example, which employed time-series analysis of individual country data, failed to confirm Feder's cross-section results.

Evidence recently obtained by Rhee, Ross-Larson and Pursell (1984) in Korea provides one plausible microeconomic explanation of the observed relation between productivity and export growth. Exporting firms are the beneficiaries of considerable informal transfers of technology, including advice on production engineering, as well as aid in product design and marketing. These injections of expertise raise productivity in existing operations and generate the flexibility to respond to new price signals, an ability that allows factors to move from activities with declining prices to more attractive areas. The South Korean experience confirms the studies of economic historians about the important technology transfer impact of foreign trade [Landes (1969), Jeremy (1981)].

4.6. The large country puzzle

One of the more puzzling development phenomena is the persistence of low productivity as evidenced by high domestic resource costs (DRCs) in large countries in which internal competition alone should be capable of enforcing considerable market discipline. Many of the countries for which detailed analyses of the impact of trade regimes have been carried out are large both demographically and in terms of the size of the domestic market. Brazil, India, Mexico, and the Philippines, for example, exhibit low concentration ratios in many industries such as textiles which are nevertheless quite inefficient.[54]

Even in sectors characterized by substantial concentration ratios, the monopoly position afforded by protection should not necessarily result in firms taking part of their profits in the form of a reduced effort to increase efficiency. As in other behavioral decisions there are income and substitution effects and a greater effort devoted to augmenting efficiency will improve profits [Corden (1974), Martin (1979), Martin and Page (1983)]. In large import-substituting countries, the cost of efforts to improve productivity can be allocated over a

---

[54] For relevant studies, see Stein (1957) on Brazil, Mazumdar (1984) on India, and Pack (1987) on the Philippines.

considerable domestic output and the absolute size of the potential benefits from cost reduction efforts will be substantial. Such considerations may account for significant R & D efforts in some of the larger import-substituting countries in Latin America [Katz (1984)] and India [Lall (1987)].

The most thorough discussion of these issues has been presented by Bhagwati and Desai (1970), Bhagwati and Srinivasan (1975), and Ahluwalia (1985) in the case of India. Protective trade policies have been accompanied by industrial licensing. With licenses allocated pro rata according to existing market shares or present productive capacity, a competitive environment is effectively precluded. Efficient firms cannot drive out less efficient ones, and over time, output will not be increasingly concentrated in firms with lower costs.[55] The failure of domestic competition to yield efficiency in other large countries with different policies has not been systematically explored.

5. Micro studies of productivity

The productivity studies discussed in the preceding section employed data from secondary sources available at the one- or two-digit level and were mainly concerned with estimates of the residual. Many issues of considerable importance cannot be addressed employing such methods nor can questions about the sources of differences in productivity among existing plants and sectors be answered. However, a new literature employing a different set of techniques and relying on primary data gathered at the firm level permits a number of insights into the industrial development process not previously obtainable. These new studies have antecedents in earlier productivity analyses which are briefly reviewed.

5.1. Early intercountry comparisons of productivity levels

It has long been assumed that total factor productivity in LDCs lies below that of comparable firms or sectors in developed countries. Early post-war research indicated that labor productivity in various sub-sectors of manufacturing was considerably lower in Western Europe and Japan than in the United States.[56] The labor productivity differentials were sufficiently large to make it unlikely that they could be explained simply by differential capital–labor ratios. Total factor

---

[55]A computable general equilibrium model estimated by Lucas (1986) shows that trade liberalization in the absence of removal of purely domestic interventions such as licensing will have a limited impact on the growth of Indian industrial output.

[56]See, for example, Rostas (1948). For a useful survey of this literature and more recent work as well see Kravis (1976).

productivity had to differ, although the precise reasons for the intercountry variation were given diverse weights by various scholars. Differences in labor quality, the age of the capital stock, and the size of the market and potential scale economies were emphasized, to one degree or another, by all authors. Surprisingly, in view of the relatively small, open nature of most of the economies analyzed, little attention was given to international competition as a determinant of productivity differentials.[57]

Rather than simply using labor productivity as an indicator of efficiency Arrow et al. (1961) calculated the neutral efficiency parameter for several two-digit sectors in India, Japan, and the United States and found that India and Japan achieved roughly 40–70 percent of U.S. total factor productivity. At the time of the comparison, Japan was an upper middle-income LDC. Daniels (1969) calculated efficiency parameters for two-digit manufacturing branches for a sample of eight countries and found that typical LDC branches exhibited low productivity relative to Spain, the most industrialized country in the sample. In contrast to the studies discussed later in this section neither Arrow et al. nor Daniels attempted to explain the observed productivity differentials. Moreover, to obtain estimates of the efficiency parameter, fairly strong assumptions were made about factor market competitiveness to permit estimation of the basic parameters such as the elasticity of substitution as well as the generation of the value of the capital stock.

5.2. The Hirschman hypothesis

One group of analysts attempted to account for *assumed* low LDC productivity in terms of lack of previous industrial experience and other features typically discussed in the post-war modernization literature [Moore (1951)]. Hirschman (1958) suggested a plausible hypothesis that productivity in LDCs relative to developed countries would be greater in those activities that were machine-paced and left relatively little latitude to managers and workers. In contrast, production that allows considerable scope in both the order of individual activities and the speed with which they must be carried out is more likely to exhibit relatively low total factor productivity. One implication of this view was that LDCs might enjoy a comparative advantage in capital-intensive industries. A number of researchers, including Clague (1970), Diaz-Alejandro (1965), and Teitel (1981) have attempted to test the "Hirschman hypothesis", and have obtained weak confirmation. A recent study [Pack (1984a)] found that sectoral differences in

[57]Even the prospect of a European Common Market did not significantly change the orientation. Most studies emphasized the potential allocative gains rather than increases in total factor productivity, a perspective that may explain the low potential benefits found by Johnson (1958) and Scitovsky (1958).

total factor productivity in a three-country comparison are best explained by differences in plant size and associated economies of scale, the Hirschman conjecture providing no explanatory power. Finally, a comparison [Pack (1984b)] of firms in the textile industry using different technologies showed that those employing the more labor-intensive ones are closer to international best practice than those using more capital-intensive technologies. One implication of these studies is that the expansion of highly capital-intensive industries or the choice of capital-intensive technology within a sector is not a route to high total factor productivity, a view implicitly held by many early proponents of industrialization.[58]

5.3. Firm-level productivity studies in LDCs

5.3.1. Static productivity levels

A number of studies since 1970 have attempted to estimate frontier production functions for a single homogeneous manufacturing sector instead of average production functions, a procedure originally suggested by Farrell (1957) and further developed by Aigner and Chu (1968). Rather than use all observations in estimating a production function, this technique eliminates those that are dominated by a combination of any two other observations. This yields an efficient unit isoquant of the standard textbook type which may be estimated using non-linear programming or statistical methods.[59]

In Figure 9.1, AA is the production frontier estimated from a sample of firms. All observations not on the isoquant lie to the northeast. Three factor price lines are shown. A firm observed to be producing at point m incurs higher costs, TC_3, than does the firm at p whose costs are TC_1. This differential may be decomposed into (a) the cost of technical inefficiency, $TC_3 - TC_2$, due to low TFP relative to firms at n on the efficient isoquant employing the same capital–labor ratio; and (b) the cost of allocative inefficiency, $TC_2 - TC_1$, due to the choice of the wrong technique at existing relative factor prices.

---

[58]Leibenstein (1960) and Atkinson and Stiglitz (1969) both suggest that localized technical progress is likely to improve productivity in the region of the technology actually employed. Technical progress is thus 'localized" rather than shifting the entire isoquant as most neoclassical growth models envisage. Although the argument has considerable a priori plausibility and important implications for the optimal choice of technology, the available evidence does not support this assumption.

[59]A survey of alternative estimation techniques is provided by Forsund, Knox-Lovell and Schmidt (1980). Early studies on developing countries employing the Farrell technique include Diaz-Alejandro (1973), Meller (1976), Pack (1974), and Timmer (1971).

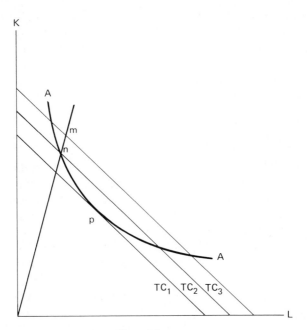

Figure 9.1.

This framework is also useful in interpreting the domestic resource cost (DRC) investment criterion [Page (1980)]. With w^* and r^* being the shadow wage and capital rental ratios underlying the isocost curves TC_i, social efficiency requires

$$\min(w^*L + r^*K)/Q. \tag{2}$$

If Q is defined as value-added at world prices, (2) becomes:

$$\min(w^*L + r^*K)\Big/\Big(QP_w - \sum_i a_{ij}P_{wi}\Big), \tag{3}$$

where P_w is the world price of a commodity and the a_{ij} are input–output coefficients. Expression (3) is the definition of the DRC [Bruno (1972), Krueger (1972)].

The percentage difference in the DRC between two firms in the same industry operating at two different points (m and p in Figure 9.1) can be shown to equal:[60]

$$D^* = \theta_K A_K^* + \theta_L A_L^* + \theta_K B_K^* + \theta_L B_L^*, \tag{4}$$

[60] Page (1980).

where θ_i is the share of each factor in value added at social prices, A^* is the percentage change in the unit factor input resulting from an alteration in the capital–labor ratio, and B^* the percentage change in primary input coefficients stemming from changes in technical efficiency. The decomposition of the sources of cost reduction shown in Figure 9.1 can provide an analysis of the differences in DRC among industries as well as firms.

A number of issues can be addressed employing this framework and slight variants of it:

(a) The potential increase in output from inefficient plants moving towards existing best practice within the country can be calculated. In contrast to studies relying on sector-wide measures of effective protection rates, the use of the production frontier approach allows a separation of the cost reduction based on greater technical efficiency from that resulting from an elimination of factor rents.

(b) The costs of allocative inefficiency within firms can be calculated, a cost included in but not explicitly calculated in DRC measures.

(c) Insofar as even the best practice domestic firms rarely match international productivity levels, the international efficiency frontier lies southwest of AA, the estimated domestic efficiency frontier. If the international frontier is also known, the additional output to be obtained by all firms approaching it, including those on the domestic best practice frontier, can be calculated.

(d) Measures at the firm level of technical and allocative inefficiency can be related to specific company characteristics such as entrepreneurial experience or technical knowledge.

(e) Intertemporal analysis of an industry permits the separation of calculated growth of total factor productivity into one component that measures the movement of the production frontier toward the origin and a second that measures the movement of technically inefficient firms towards the initial frontier.

None of the studies that have been done contains all of these calculations, but the magnitudes that have been obtained for the separate components suggest that substantial benefits can be obtained from using the resources at hand more effectively. Some of the potential gains from alternate sources are shown in Table 9.2.[61]

The results on actual versus best practice total factor productivity suggest a possible reconciliation of the relatively low level of TFP growth in the East Asian exporting countries with their superior industrial performance in comparison with import-substituting countries. Most of the estimates of frontier production

---

[61] Other recent studies containing similar orders of magnitude are Pitt and Lee (1981), Tyler (1979), and Cortes, Berry and Ishaq (1987).

Table 9.2
Increases in output from improved efficiency

Country	Percentage increase in output from:		
	Move to best practice	Improved allocative efficiency	Move to international best practice
Egypt	25		
Ghana	25	7	
India	60–100		
Kenya		15	45
Philippines		17	27

Sources: Egypt [Handoussa, Nishimizu and Page (1987)]; Ghana [Page (1981)]; India [Page (1984)]; Kenya and Philippines [Pack (1987)].

functions reveal very large intraindustry divergences within a given country in TFP among constituent firms as well as typically low average productivity relative to the best practice firms. All of the studies have been of industries in countries still pursuing import substitution. It may be conjectured that similar analyses of the firms in export-oriented countries would reveal a considerably smaller intraindustry variation in TFP as well as a better average *level* of TFP vis-à-vis best practice.[62] If the average *level* of TFP differs among countries with different trade regimes while the intracountry performance relative to best practice changes very slowly, the benefit from outward orientation will not manifest itself in productivity growth rates but in varying levels of TFP among countries.

The wide variation in realized productivity as compared to best practice also has important implications for social cost–benefit analysis. Most research on project evaluation has concentrated on refining shadow prices that are applied to the very weak productivity analysis contained in engineering feasiblity studies. Most of these refinements pale in significance when compared to the 30–70 percent discrepancies in productivity between actual operating parameters and those found in feasibility studies.

5.3.2. Intertemporal productivity

A study of Egypt by Handoussa, Nishimizu and Page (1986), employing the Farrell technique intertemporally, found that in most Egyptian industries a

---

[62]Assuming that intraindustry variation in domestic resource costs largely reflects differences among firms in technical rather than allocative efficiency, measures of the intraindustry variation in DRCs should confirm this hypothesis. Unfortunately, available studies of the impact of trade regimes present only industry wide measures of the DRC without providing measures for the constituent firms.

majority of the firms exhibited substantial technical inefficiency at the beginning of a period of trade liberalization around 1973. Over the next seven years a considerable amount of total factor productivity growth was realized, most of it resulting from inefficient firms moving towards the best practice frontier as a result of increasing capacity utilization made possible by the greater availability of foreign exchange.[63] Plants that were initially on this frontier were themselves improving their total factor productivity solely as a result of growing utilization rates. Thus, the recorded productivity growth was of a once-and-for-all type, the gains being exhausted as initially inefficient firms approached the existing efficiency frontier while those on the frontier did not improve their technical performance apart from higher utilization levels. In light of these results, we may conclude that liberalization may have a substantial initial impact but not yield any steady-state benefits. To realize the latter, specific policies are needed to increase technological absorptive capacity and reduce the marginal costs of relevant technology transfers.[64] In contrast to the Egyptian results, Nishimizu and Page (1982) found that in half of the Yugoslavian industries they analyzed, there was no change in the best practice performance over thirteen years, and that in many sectors there was a decline in efficiency relative to best practice.

5.3.3. Explanation of static productivity differentials

Several of the studies attempt to account for observed deviations from best practice. Page (1980) employs variables such as the experience of entrepreneurs, the age of the firm, and education of the labor force to explain the level of technical efficiency of firms. Except for education, none of these traditional variables is statistically significant. The significance of education is surprising given the nature of the industries such as saw milling that are not subject to rapidly changing technologies in which it is likely that education does confer an advantage.[65] Other attempts to find systematic explanations of technical efficiency employing measures of education and experience have had little success [Cortes, Berry and Ishaq (1987)]. All of these studies assume that the deviations are equilibrium phenomena. An alternative explanation in which deviations may be transitory is provided by Nelson and Winter (1982).

Pack (1987), employing both engineering and economic data, decomposes the deviation of Kenyan and Philippine textile plants from international best practice

---

[63] TFP is measured as total output divided by labor and capital stock rather than by a measure of the flow of capital services actually employed.

[64] For a more detailed discussion, see Pack and Westphal (1986), Pack (1987), and Westphal, Chapter 20 in this Handbook. Findlay (1978) has suggested that direct foreign investment and local emulation of management practices may be one method of achieving reduced costs of technology transfer.

[65] Nelson and Phelps (1966).

into three components, namely that due to the absence of product specialization, managerial ability (as measured by the realization of engineering norms), and worker skills. The major source of low total factor productivity in the Kenyan and Philippine factories stems from too large a diversification of products (partly reflecting tariff protection) and consequently short production runs.[66] In many plants inadequate managerial skills also decrease productivity by 10 percent compared to international best practice. In contrast, labor productivity in given tasks, after adjusting for the two preceding factors, is quite close to DC levels. These findings, if corroborated in other industries and countries, suggest a more nuanced view of the failure of import-substituting industrialization; firms and their workers may, in fact, have achieved the learning that was anticipated by early advocates of ISI, but this initial success may be offset by the subsequent failure to liberalize to obtain specialization and to permit firms to obtain inputs at international prices. In the least developed countries, however, it is likely that deficient technical ability of management is much more important than is the case in the more industrialized LDCs.

The data presented in the studies reviewed in this section indicate considerable variation in intrasector performance. The coefficient of variation of total factor productivity within sectors is not very different from variation in DRCs across sectors. If intrasector variation could be reduced and firms moved toward best practice, the gains in technical efficiency would be additional to those accruing from allocative gains stemming from the shifting of resources from sectors that cannot compete on the basis of comparative advantage. While trade liberalization is an important instrument to achieve both types of benefits, purely domestic policy measures are likely to also play an important role in achieving these gains.

6. Employment creation in the manufacturing sector

Among the major concerns of analysts of industrial sector performance has been the failure to create jobs for the burgeoning labor force. Given the rapid growth in population and limited availability of arable land, non-agricultural pursuits must provide a significant number of new jobs. The absolutely small size of the manufacturing sector in most countries militates against it being a major employer of new labor force entrants. Nevertheless, even where manufacturing accounts for only 10 percent of total national employment, it accounts for a considerably greater percentage of modern sector employment. A substantial increase in its labor intensity, therefore, could eliminate a large fraction of open

---

[66] The role of the length of production runs has received substantial attention in studies attempting to explain the performance of Canadian industrial firms. For references see Caves, Porter and Spence (1980). Also see Scherer et al. (1975).

unemployment and contribute to the absorption of labor from the ranks of the underemployed in the urban informal sector.

Much of the existing analysis has been framed in terms of the appropriate choice of technology, an issue directly related to the major questions of the efficiency of the sector and the equity impact of its growth. If firms choose capital-intensive techniques rather than cost-minimizing technology at prevailing factor prices, their cost of production will be raised. With a given level of national investment such choices reduce the potential level of output and compel workers not hired in the formal sector to seek employment in the informal sector. Both national income and equity can be increased by a proper choice of technology; where factor prices are distorted such that the market wage/rental ratio exceeds that at shadow prices, the potential benefits in both dimensions are still greater. These gains can be substantially augmented by improved intersectoral allocation, particularly via the latitude offered by the choice of products entering international trade.

6.1. The choice of technology

Eckaus's seminal article (1955) suggested the possibility that for some final bill of goods, full employment might not be achievable because of the low elasticity of substitution in some industrial sectors. The Eckaus view of the possibilities of factor substitution also undercuts the optimistic assumption of the Lewis model that the reallocation of labor from agriculture to industry could proceed smoothly. The level of reinvested industrial profits might be insufficient to insure the absorption of released agricultural workers if fixed proportions or a low elasticity of substitution prevailed. Little empirical basis existed for the assumed lack of substitutability except for the then regnant input–output model of production relations that ignored earlier research on the Cobb–Douglas function. Additional theoretical analysis of the problems of industrial sector employment absorption was provided by Fei and Ranis (1964) and Jorgenson (1961), the former emphasizing the important role played by the intensity and bias of technical innovation in the industrial sector. Simultaneously, a substantial literature arose on project evaluation and the choice of technology.[67]

Despite theoretical work, throughout most of the 1950s and early 1960s employment generation was not viewed as a pressing policy problem. An article by Baer and Herve (1966) crystallized the perception that growth in industrial output was having a very small impact on employment. The growth in average labor productivity in a large number of Latin American countries and industries considerably exceeded the magnitude found in developed countries. However, it was far from universally accepted that the observed discrepancy was attributable to inappropriate choice of technology.

---

[67]The issues are incisively reviewed by Sen (1968).

Most of the relevant issues can be set out within a simple algebraic framework. Assume a constant returns to scale production function:

$$Q = f[a(t)K(t), b(t)L(t)], \qquad (5)$$

where K and L indicate natural units of capital and labor and a and b reflect factor augmentation. The rate of growth of employment and output can be shown to equal:[68]

$$L^* = K^* + a^* - b^* + \sigma/S_K(b^* - w^*), \qquad (6)$$

$$Q^* = K^* + a^* + S_L/S_K \sigma(b^* - w^*), \qquad (7)$$

and

$$Q^* - L^* = (1 - \sigma)b^* + \sigma w^*, \qquad (8)$$

where an asterisk indicates the rate of growth, σ is the elasticity of substitution, w^* is the rate of growth of the real wage, and S_i indicates the factor share of output.

There are two issues of interest. First, (6) shows that the rate of growth of employment is positively related to the rate of growth of capital accumulation and capital-augmenting technical progress and negatively to the rate of labor augmentation and wage growth, assuming the elasticity of substitution is positive. Second, (8) shows that a high observed growth rate of labor productivity may stem from a high value of b^*, assuming $\sigma < 1$ or a high value of w^*, assuming $\sigma > 0$.[69]

Considering a value of $Q^* - L^*$ such as 7 or 8 percent per annum as the stylized fact which is often taken as the best indication of insufficient employment generation, it is clear from (8) that this can result from a high value of labor-augmenting technical progress, assuming σ is less than unity or the growth of capital intensity induced by growing wages.

Two views exist about the values of the magnitudes shown in (8). A prevailing neoclassical interpretation of the extensive empirical literature argues that the problem lies in factor price distortions, with growing wages, institutionally

---

[68] The formulation follows Bruton (1977). Although the discussion is expressed in terms of factor augmentation, this can be readily transformed to reflect the Hicksian definition of factor bias. A more complex formulation than (8) is required to take account of changes in the rates of wages to the user cost of capital. For the relationships among various definitions of technical change and its bias, see Nadiri (1970).

[69] Some studies, for example Baer and Herve (1966), focus on the high rate of growth of average labor product. Others refer to an employment lag or a low elasticity of employment with respect to output, L^*/Q^*. Since $Q^* - L^* = Q^*(1 - L^*/Q^*)$, a low output elasticity of employment implies a high growth rate of average productivity, the latter being greater the higher the growth rate of output.

determined, working via a positive σ leading to the substitution of capital for labor.[70] An alternative view contends that σ is close to zero, and that the major source of growing labor productivity arises from rapid labor-augmenting technical change embodied in new equipment that has been designed for use in high wage countries [Eckaus (1977)]. In the latter case the observed growth of wage/rental ratios does not play a significant role in slow employment expansion of individual manufacturing branches but intercommodity substitution within the manufacturing sector engendered by rising wages may still be a source of poor overall employment performance.

Existing evidence on the rate of growth of total factor productivity discussed in Section 4 does not support, at least in its simple form, the hypothesis that slow employment growth results from high rates of productivity growth combined with σ less than unity.[71] The alternative explanation, which posits a fairly high elasticity of substitution and growing real wages, has generated an extensive literature involving detailed case studies at the level of the firm or a particular industrial process such as fertilizer production as well as more conventional econometric work.[72] The general conclusion has been that the elasticity of substitution is positive for most industrial activities important in LDCs. The technical engineering alternatives giving rise to the observed factor substitutability include the choice afforded by selecting among international manufacturers of core processing equipment and the use of labor and simple devices in peripheral activities such as movement and storage of material within plants [Pack (1976), Ranis (1973)]. Additional flexibility can be obtained by the employment of used equipment.[73]

Finally, it is possible to argue that the static cost-minimizing choice of technology based solely on current relative factor prices is incorrect. More capital-intensive processes may yield higher non-wage income (assuming an elasticity of substitution exceeding unity), more saving and investment, and hence higher long-term growth rates [Galenson and Leibenstein (1955)]. Alternatively, if the opportunities for technical progress are greater with more capital-intensive technologies, then the choice of the latter may be justified in an intertemporal framework [Atkinson and Stiglitz (1969)]. National savings rates, however, are largely determined by a much broader range of variables than the factor shares of

---

[70]Surveys are found in Morawetz (1974), Stewart (1974), and White (1978). Econometric evidence, mainly relying on the CES function, has been surveyed by Gaude (1975) and Morawetz (1976). Behrman (1982), using more recent data, confirms the earlier econometric results of positive and significant elasticities of substitution.

[71]Relatively little empirical research has been done on the factor bias of productivity growth, partly reflecting the Diamond–McFadden impossibility theorem. See, however, Williamson (1971a, 1971b).

[72]See footnote 70 above.

[73]Among the most complete studies of this question are those of Cooper and Kaplinsky (1974) and Cortes and Escandon (1979).

new industrial projects. Although the localized technical progress assumed by Atkinson and Stiglitz is very plausible, firm-level evidence suggests that little productivity growth occurs in any new LDC enterprises, regardless of their capital intensity [Bell, Ross-Larson and Westphal (1984)].

6.2. Factor market distortions and information costs

Given the empirically convincing demonstration of factor substitutability, the blame for poor employment performance has typically focused on government-induced distortions in relative factor prices including minimum wage laws, high government sector wages inducing private sector emulation to retain employees, ceilings on lending rates, overvaluation of foreign exchange not compensated for by a tariff on imported capital goods, accelerated depreciation allowances, and tax holidays. These distortions have existed for three decades or more and there is little evidence to suggest they are worsening. They can thus account for an incorrect *level* of the wage/rental ratio, not its growth as required for the explanation of the growth of average labor productivity described in our expanded version of (8). Moreover, even the interpretation of the distorted level has been questioned. Stiglitz (1982, 1985) and others, expanding upon a suggestion of Leibenstein (1957), have argued that observed wage discrepancies between workers employed in modern sector firms and those outside it may reflect a cost-minimizing response by firms seeking to reduce turnover and to screen job applicants to obtain the most productive ones. In this view, the attribution of high wages to market imperfections may be incorrect.

Another line of research that reduces the force of the simple neoclassical reliance on factor price distortions as the sole source of poor employment performance has shown that frequently firms do not make private cost-minimizing decisions, i.e. they do not equate marginal rates of factor substitution to market wage–rental ratios [Amsalem (1983), Pickett, Forsyth and McBain (1974)]. The cost of searching for appropriate technological information may provide one component of a more complete model of actual technology choices. Evidence gathered on the choice of technology by multinational corporations (MNCs) provides indirect confirmation of the role of information costs. MNCs typically exhibit the same or lower capital intensity than domestically owned firms[74] despite the fact that they typically pay somewhat greater wages, borrow at lower interest rates either in the host country or internationally, and often are the beneficiaries of tax provisions such as accelerated depreciation denied to local companies. One reason for the better MNC performance is likely to be the

---

[74] Pack (1976), Forsyth and Solomon (1977), Lecraw (1977), and Ahiakpor (1986). A review of a number of studies is given in Pack (1979).

subsidiary's lower marginal cost of acquiring appropriate equipment given the economies of scale made possible by the sharing of the fixed search cost of the central purchasing office among numerous subsidiaries as well as the ability of this office to bargain for better prices in the imperfect international market for machinery.

Competition in product markets and the resulting pressure to minimize costs should be conducive to a cost-minimizing choice of technology. An intersectoral study in Pakistan by White (1976) confirms this hypothesis, as does research on the poor performance of public enterprises that are totally protected from competition [James (1984), Williams (1975)]. Trade liberalization and an altered environment for public sector firms can contribute to an improved employment performance, though the results may be limited unless search costs can be reduced.

Finally, there is a considerable literature on the paradox of low capacity utilization in economies characterized by a shortage of capital and the implications for employment policy [Betancourt and Clague (1981), Winston (1974)].

6.3. The aggregate gains from improved technology choice

What would be the aggregate effects if a typical poorer LDC were to systematically adopt the minimum cost technology, rather than a capital-intensive one in representative industries? Pack (1982) has calculated that annual value-added in manufacturing could be increased by 72 percent, employment by 311 percent, and non-wage income by 51 percent.[75] These figures assume that firms choose the correct technology at existing market prices, hence the potential benefits would be greater for still more labor-intensive technologies that become least-cost at shadow prices. The size of the potential benefits may justify the cost of a number of policy interventions designed to elicit improved technological choices [Pack (1982), Stewart (1979)].

Total employment that may be obtained from a given level of capital stock may also be increased by a change in the commodity composition of production. If policy-induced distortions were removed and countries specialized according to comparative advantage, a shift from the capital-intensive import-substitution industries to more unskilled labor-intensive exporting sectors should lead to an increase in total employment. This hypothesis is confirmed in a set of country studies directed by Krueger.[76] A shift in trade strategy with a fixed capital stock assumed to be fungible could increase total employment by an average of 47

[75] These are the gross benefits before subtracting the opportunity cost of labor in its current employment in the informal or rural sector.

[76] For a summary of the underlying country studies and an overview of the issues, see Krueger (1983). The summary figure given here excludes South Korea from her sample.

percent for eight sample countries, larger benefits accruing to countries that have engaged in extensive import-substitution programs.

One other potential source of increased employment, intensively investigated in the early 1970s, is the change in aggregate labor intensity stemming from a redistribution of income, the hypothesis being that the typical consumption basket of high income recipients in LDC is more capital intensive than that of lower income households. There is no empirical confirmation of the theory, the direct and indirect labor content (based on input–output tables) being the same in a number of countries.[77]

7. Conclusions

In the closing page of his Janeway lecture (1978) Lewis wrote: "the engine of growth should be technological change, with international trade serving as a lubricating oil and not as fuel. The gateway to technological change is through agricultural and industrial revolutions, which are mutually dependent."

The rapid industrial growth characteristic of the LDCs in the post-war period is extraordinary by historical standards, yet it is not clear that it constitutes a "revolution" in the sense that these countries were able to master the new technologies and achieve growing productivity that could serve as a basis for increasing standards of living. In a few countries swift export growth based on comparative advantage permitted an equally rapid transformation of the sectoral patterns of income generation and factor allocation. The industrial growth process in these nations was fairly equitable, reflecting the rapid growth of employment achieved by a reliance on labor-intensive exports and technology choices engendered by non-segmented factor markets. Equity, efficiency, and growth were complementary, precluding the need for explicit policy attention to income distribution or basic needs.

Yet in the long run, factor reallocation cannot supplant productivity as the engine of growth. By now, much of the factor market disequilibrium that allows gains from reallocation has been eliminated in the East Asian countries and further gains in real income must originate in growing productivity. While large potential benefits from an external orientation are still to be realized for the bulk of inward-oriented LDCs, the slow growth of the OECD countries suggests that even with a quick alteration in LDC policy regimes, the international economy will not be hospitable to a replication of the performance of the Gang of Four. Rapid growth will be more dependent, as Lewis suggested, on mutually reinforcing productivity growth in agriculture and industry.[78] The factors contrib-

---

[77]Soligo (1973).
[78] The importance of agriculture has been re-emphasized by Adelman (1984).

uting to growth in agricultural productivity are fairly well understood, as are the policies necessary to realize them.[79]

This chapter suggests, however, that productivity growth in manufacturing (and a fortiori in the rest of the industrial sector) is not equally well understood. Export orientation, whatever its other merits, does not appear to yield higher total factor productivity growth than does import substitution. Comparisons of total factor productivity growth among countries pursuing different international trade orientations do not reveal systematic differences in productivity growth in manufacturing, nor do the time-series studies of individual countries that have experienced alternating trade regimes allow strong conclusions in this dimension. Perhaps measurement problems are obscuring an outcome that to most economists seems inevitable. But given the weak comprehension of the determinants of productivity in the developed countries as revealed in the recent proliferation of explanations for their productivity slowdown, it seems unlikely that the absence of the expected pattern stems primarily from deficiencies in the data. Moreover, the firm-level data collected for estimation of production frontiers are quite reliable and confirm the pattern established at more aggregated levels.

It may be that the compression of industrialization noted in Section 2 is best viewed as a rapid transfer of factors to the manufacturing sector and that successful maturation and sustained productivity growth may require some historically "inevitable" minimum period. Short cuts to industrial proficiency may not exist. Nevertheless, further efforts to identify the determinants of productivity are important. Faster growth in industrial productivity provides part of the recipe for mutually reinforcing growth between agriculture and industry which may now become even more critical than when Lewis set forth his views in the mid-1970s. Despite a fall in oil prices in the 1980s, there is no hint of a reversal in the slow growth of the industrial economies. Even with slower growth in world trade, opportunities for exports will remain and should be exploited; but structural change in production patterns and the factor allocations underlying them is unlikely to be as fast as that in the quarter century preceding 1973. Productivity growth will perforce have to play a larger role than in the earlier period in improving standards of living in the LDCs.

References

Acharya, S.N. (1981) 'Perspectives and problems of development in Sub-Saharan Africa', *World Development*, 9:109–148.
Adelman, I. (1984) 'Beyond export-led growth', *World Development*, 12:937–950.

[79]See Chapter 8 by Timmer in this Handbook.

Ahiakpor, J.C.W. (1986) 'The capital-intensity of foreign, private local and state owned firms in a less developed country: Ghana', *Journal of Development Economics*, 20:145–162.

Ahluwalia, I.J. (1985) *Industrial growth in India*. Delhi: Oxford University Press.

Aigner, D. and Chu, S.F. (1968) 'On estimating the industry production function', *American Economic Review*, 58:826–839.

Amsalem, M.A. (1983) *Technology choice in developing countries: The textile and pulp and paper industries*. Cambridge, MA: MIT Press.

Arrow, K.J. (1969) 'Classificatory notes on the production and transmission of technological knowledge', *American Economic Review*, 59:29–35.

Arrow, K.J., Chenery, H.B., Minhas, B.S. and Solow, R.M. (1961) 'Capital–labor substitution and economic efficiency', *Review of Economics and Statistics*, 43:225–250.

Atkinson, A.B. and Stiglitz, J.E. (1969) 'A new view of technological change', *Economic Journal*, 79:573–578.

Baer, W. and Herve, M.E.A. (1966) 'Employment and industrialization in developing countries', *Quarterly Journal of Economics*, 80:88–107.

Balassa, B. (1971) *The structure of protection in developing countries*. Baltimore, MD: Johns Hopkins University Press.

Balassa, B. (1978) 'Exports and economic growth – further evidence', *Journal of Development Economics*, 5:181–190.

Balassa, B. (1979) 'A stages approach to comparative advantage', in: I. Adelman, ed., *Economic growth and resources*. London: Macmillan.

Balassa, B. (1980) 'The process of industrial development and alternative development strategies', World Bank Staff working paper no. 438. Washington, DC: The World Bank.

Balassa, B. (1984) 'Comparative advantage in manufactured goods: A reappraisal'. Washington, DC: The World Bank, processed.

Banfield, E. (1958) *The moral basis of a backward society*. Glencoe, IL: The Free Press.

Behrman, J.R. (1972) 'Sectoral elasticities of substitution between capital and labor in a developing economy: Time series analysis in the case of postwar Chile', *Econometrica*, 40:311–328.

Behrman, J.R. (1982) 'Country and sectoral variations in manufacturing elasticities of substitution between capital and labor', in: A.O. Krueger, ed., *Trade and employment in developing countries*. Chicago, IL: University of Chicago Press.

Bell, M., Ross-Larson, B. and Westphal, L.E. (1984) 'Assessing the performance of infant industries', *Journal of Development Economics*, 16:101–128.

Bergsman, J. (1970) *Brazil: Industrialization and trade policies*. London: Oxford University Press.

Bergsman, J. (1974) 'Commercial policy, allocative and x-inefficiency', *Quarterly Journal of Economics*, 88:409–433.

Betancourt, R. and Clague, C. (1981) *Capital utilization, a theoretical and empirical analysis*. Cambridge: Cambridge University Press.

Bhagwati, J. (1978) *Foreign trade regimes and economic development: Anatomy and consequences of exchange control regimes*. Cambridge: Ballinger.

Bhagwati, J. and Desai, P. (1970) *India: Planning for industrialization: Industrialization and trade policies since 1951*. London: Oxford University Press.

Bhagwati, J. and Srinivasan, T.N. (1975) *Foreign trade regimes and economic development: India*. New York: Columbia University Press.

Bhagwati, J. and Srinivasan, T.N. (1979) 'Trade policy and development', in: R. Dornbusch and J.A. Frankel, eds., *International economic policy*. Baltimore, MD: Johns Hopkins University Press.

Bhalla, A., ed. (1975) *Technology and employment in industry*. Geneva: International Labour Office.

Bruno, M. (1972) 'Domestic resource costs and effective protection: Clarification and synthesis', *Journal of Political Economy*, 80:16–33.

Bruton, H.J. (1967) 'Productivity growth in Latin America', *American Economic Review*, 57:1099–1116.

Bruton, H.J. (1977) 'A note on the transfer of technology', *Economic Development and Cultural Change*, 25(supplement):234–244.

Caves, R.E. (1980) 'Productivity differences among industries', in: R.E. Caves and L.B. Krause, eds., *Britain's economic performance*. Washington, D.C.: Brookings Institution.

Caves, R.E., Porter, M.E., Spence, A.M. and Scott, J.T. (1980) *Competition in the open economy.* Cambridge, MA: Harvard University Press.

Chenery, H.B. (1960) 'Patterns of industrial growth', *American Economic Review,* 50:624–654.

Chenery, H.B. (1962) 'Development policies for southern Italy', *Quarterly Journal of Economics,* 76:517–597.

Chenery, H.B. (1980) 'Interactions between industrialization and exports', *American Economic Review,* 70:281–287.

Chenery, H.B. (1983) 'Interactions between theory and observation in development', *World Development,* 11:853–861.

Chenery, H.B. and Keesing, D.B. (1979) 'The changing composition of developing country exports', World Bank Staff working paper no. 314. Washington, DC: The World Bank.

Chenery, H.B., Robinson, S. and Syrquin, M. (1986) *Industrialization and growth: A comparative study.* New York: Oxford University Press.

Chenery, H.B. and Syrquin, M. (1975) *Patterns of development, 1950–70.* New York: Oxford University Press.

Chenery, H.B. and Taylor, L. (1968) 'Development patterns: Among countries and overtime', *Review of Economics and Statistics,* 50:391–416.

Choksi, A.M. (1979) 'State intervention in the industrialization of developing countries: Selected issues', World Bank Staff working paper no. 341. Washington, DC: The World Bank.

Choksi, A.M., Meeraus, A. and Soutjesdijk, A. (1980) *The planning of industrial programs in the fertilizer industry.* Baltimore, MD: Johns Hopkins University Press.

Christensen, L. and Cummings, D. (1981) 'Real product, real factor input, and productivity in the Republic of Korea, 1960–73', *Journal of Development Economics,* 8:285–302.

Cipolla, C.M. (1976) *Before the industrial revolution: European society and economy 1000–1700.* New York: Norton.

Clague, C. (1970) 'The determinants of efficiency in manufacturing industries in an underdeveloped country', *Economic Development and Cultural Change,* 18:188–205.

Cohen, B.I. and Sisler, D.G. (1971) 'Exports of the developing countries in the 1960s', *Review of Economics and Statistics,* 53:354–361.

Cooper, C. and Kaplinsky R. (1974) *Second-hand equipment in a developing country.* Geneva: International Labour Office.

Corden, W.M. (1974) *Trade policy and economic welfare.* Oxford: Oxford University Press.

Cortes, M. and Escandon, J.F. (1979) 'The market for second-hand equipment in Colombia', mimeo. Washington, DC: The World Bank.

Cortes, M. and P. Bocock (1984) *North–South technology transfer – A case study of petrochemicals in Latin America.* Baltimore, MD: Johns Hopkins University Press.

Cortes, M., Berry, A. and Ishaq, A. (1987) *What makes for success in small and medium scale enterprises.* New York: Oxford University Press.

Daniels, M.R. (1969) 'Differences in efficiency among industries in developing countries', *American Economic Review,* 49:159–171.

Deardorff, A.V. (1979) 'Weak links in the chain of comparative advantage', *Journal of International Economics,* 9:197–209.

de Melo, J.A.P. (1978) 'Estimating the costs of protection: A general equilibrium approach', *Quarterly Journal of Economics,* 92:209–227.

Diamond, P.A. and McFadden, D. (1978) 'Identification of the elasticity of substitution and the bias of technical change: An impossibility theorem', in: M. Fuss and D. McFadden, eds., *Production economics: A dual approach to theory and application.* Amsterdam: North-Holland.

Diaz-Alejandro, C. (1965) 'Industrialization and labor productivity differentials', *Review of Economics and Statistics,* 47:207–214.

Diaz-Alejandro, C. (1973) 'Labor productivity and other characteristics of cement plants: An international comparison', in: J. Bhagwati and R. Eckaus, eds., *Development and planning.* Cambridge: MIT Press.

Donges, J.B. and Riedel, J. (1976) 'The expansion of manufacturing exports in developing countries: An empirical assessment of supply and demand issues', *Weltwirtschaftliches Archiv,* 113:58–87.

Duignan, P. and Gann, L.H., eds. (1975) *Colonialism in Africa, 1870–1960.* London: Cambridge University Press.

Eckaus, R.S. (1955) 'The factor proportions problem in underdeveloped areas', *American Economic Review*, 45:539–565.

Eckaus, R.S. (1977) *Appropriate technologies for developing countries.* Washington, DC: National Academy of Sciences.

Evenson, R.M. (1981) 'Benefits and obstacles to appropriate agricultural technology', *The Annals of the American Academy of Political and Social Science*, 458:54–67.

Faini, R. (1983) 'Cumulative processes of deindustrialization in an open region: The case of southern Italy, 1951–1973', *Journal of Development Economics*, 12:277–302.

Faini, R. (1984) 'Increasing returns, non-traded inputs and regional development', *The Economic Journal*, 94:308–323.

Farrell, M.J. (1957) 'The measurement of productive efficiency', *Journal of the Royal Statistical Society*, 120:253–281.

Feder, G. (1983) 'On exports and economic growth', *Journal of Development Economics*, 12:59–74.

Fei, J.C.H. and Ranis, G. (1964) *Development of the labor surplus economy: Theory and policy.* Homewood, IL: Richard D. Irwin.

Fei, J.C.H., Ranis, G. and Kuo, S.W.Y. (1980) *Growth with equity: The Taiwan case.* New York: Oxford University Press.

Feinstein, C.H. (1981) 'Capital accumulation and the industrial revolution', in: R.C. Flood and D.N McCloskey, eds., *The economic history of Britain since 1700.* Cambridge: Cambridge University Press.

Felix, D. (1977) 'The technological factor in socioeconomic dualism: Toward an economy-of-scale paridigm for development theory', *Economic Development and Cultural Change*, 25(supplement):180–211.

Fields, G.S. (1984) 'Employment, income distribution and economic growth in seven small open economies', *Economic Journal*, 94:74–83.

Findlay, R. (1978) 'Relative backwardness, direct foreign investment, and the transfer of technology: A simple dynamic model', *Quarterly Journal of Economics*, 92:1–16.

Findlay, R. and Grubert, H. (1959) 'Factor intensities, technological progress, and the terms of trade', *Oxford Economic Papers*, 11:111–121.

Fishlow, A. (1972) 'Origins and consequences of import substitution in Brazil', in: L.E. Di Marco, ed., *International Economics and Development.* New York: Academic Press.

Forsund, F.R., Knox-Lovell, C.A. and Schmidt, P. (1980) 'A survey of frontier production functions and of their relationship to efficiency measurement', *Journal of Econometrics*, 13:5–27.

Forsyth, D.J.C. and Solomon, R. (1977) 'Nationality of ownership and choice of technique in manufacturing in a less developed country', *Oxford Economic Papers*, 29:258–282.

Fransman, M. and King, K., eds., (1984) *Technological capability in the third world.* London: Macmillan.

Gaathon, A.L. (1971) *Economic productivity in Israel.* New York: Praeger.

Galenson, W. and Leibenstein, H. (1955) 'Investment criteria, productivity and economic development', *Quarterly Journal of Economics*, 69:343–370.

Galenson, W., ed. (1979) *Economic growth and structural change in Taiwan.* Ithaca NY: Cornell University Press.

Gaude, J. (1975) 'Capital–labor substitution possibilities: A review of empirical evidence', in: A. Bhalla, ed., *Technology and employment in industry.* Geneva: International Labour Office.

Gerschenkron, A. (1962) *Economic backwardness in historical perspective.* Cambridge, MA: Harvard University Press.

Granger, C.W.J. (1969) 'Investigating causal relationships by econometric models and cross spectral methods', *Econometrica*, 37:424–438.

Gulhati, R. and Sekhar, U. (1982) 'Industrial strategy for late starters: The experience of Kenya, Tanzania, and Zambia', *World Development*, 10:949–972.

Hammond, J.L. and Hammond, B. (1911) *The village labourer.* London: Longmans.

Hammond, J.L. and Hammond, B. (1919) *The skilled labourer.* London: Longmans.

Handoussa, H., Nishimizu, M. and Page, J.M., Jr. (1986) "Productivity change in Egyptian public sector industries after the 'opening', 1973–79", *Journal of Development Economics*, 20:53–74.

Hansen, B. and Nashashibi, K. (1975) *Foreign trade regimes and economic development: Egypt.* New York: Columbia University Press.

Hicks, J.R. (1953) 'An inaugural lecture', *Oxford Economic Papers*, 5:117–135.

Hirschman, A.O. (1958) *The strategy of economic development.* New Haven, CT: Yale University Press.

Hopkins, A.G. (1973) *An economic history of West Africa.* New York: Columbia University Press.

Horton, S. and King, T. (1981) 'Labour productivity: Un tour d'horizon', World Bank Staff working paper no. 497. Washington, DC: The World Bank.

Izumi, Y., (1980) 'Transformation and development of technology in the Japanese cotton industry', mimeo. Tokyo: The United Nations University.

James, J. (1984) 'Bureaucratic, economic and engineering man: Decision making for technology in Tanzania's state-owned enterprises', Boston University, mimeo.

Jeremy, D.J. (1981) *Transatlantic industrial revolution: The diffusion of textile technologies between Britain and America, 1790–1830s.* Cambridge, MA: MIT Press.

Johnson, H.G. (1955) 'Economic expansion and international trade', *Manchester School of Economic and Social Studies*, 23:95–112.

Johnson, H.G. (1958) 'The gains from trade with Europe: An estimate', *Manchester School of Economic and Social Studies*, 26:247–255.

Jorgenson, D.W. (1961) 'The development of a dual economy', *Economic Journal*, 71:309–334.

Jung, W.S. and Marshall, P.J. (1985) 'Exports, growth and causality in developing countries', *Journal of Development Economics*, 18:1–12.

Katz, J.M. (1984) 'Domestic technological innovation and dynamic comparative advantage: Further reflections on a comparative case study program', *Journal of Development Economics*, 16:13–38.

Keesing, D.B. (1979) 'Trade policy for developing countries', World Bank Staff working paper no. 353. Washington, DC: The World Bank.

Kendrick, D.A. and Stoutjesdijk, A.J. (1979) *The planning of industrial investment programs.* Baltimore, MD: Johns Hopkins University Press.

Kendrick, D.A., Meeraus, A. and Alatorre, J. (1984) *The planning of investment programs in the steel industry.* Baltimore, MD: Johns Hopkins University Press.

Kilby, P. (1969) *Industrialization in an open economy, Nigeria, 1945–66.* London: Cambridge University Press.

Kim, K. and Park, J.-K. (1985) *Sources of economic growth in Korea: 1963–82.* Seoul: Korea Development Institute.

Kim, Y.C. and Kwon, J.K. (1977) 'The utilization of capital and the growth of output in a developing economy: The case of South Korean manufacturing', *Journal of Development Economics*, 9:265–278.

Kuo, S. (1983) *The Taiwan economy in transition.* Boulder, CO: Westview Press.

Kuo, W. (1974) 'Technical change, foreign investment, and growth in Taiwan's manufacturing industries, 1952–70', *Industry of Free China*.

Kravis, I.B. (1976) 'A survey of international comparisons of productivity', *The Economic Journal*, 86:1–44.

Kravis, I.B., Heston, A. and Summers, R. (1978) *International comparisons of real product and purchasing power.* Baltimore, MD: Johns Hopkins University Press.

Krueger, A.O. (1972) 'Evaluating restrictionist trade regimes: Theory and measurement', *Journal of Political Economy*, 80:48–62.

Krueger, A.O. (1978) Liberalization attempts and consequences. Cambridge, MA: Ballinger.

Krueger, A.O. (1980) 'Trade policy as an input to development', *American Economic Review*, Papers and Proceedings, 70:288–292.

Krueger, A.O. (1983) *Trade and employment in developing countries: Synthesis and conclusions.* Chicago, IL: University of Chicago Press.

Krueger, A.O. and Tuncer, B. (1982a) 'Growth of factor productivity in Turkish manufacturing industries', *Journal of Development Economics*, 11:307–326.

Krueger, A.O. and Tuncer, B. (1982b) 'An empirical test of the infant industry argument', *American Economic Review*, 72:1142–1152.

Krugman, P. (1979) 'Increasing returns, monopolistic competition, and international trade', *Journal of International Economics*, 9:469–479.

Kuznets, S. (1956) 'Quantitative aspects of the economic growth of nations: 1. Levels and variability of growth rates', *Economic Development and Cultural Change*, 5:5–94.

Kuznets, S. (1957) 'Quantitative aspects of the economic growth of nations: 2. Industrial distribution of national product and labor force', *Economic Development and Cultural Change*, 5(supplement):3–111.

Kuznets, S. (1966) *Modern economic growth*. New Haven, CT: Yale University Press.

Lall, S. (1985) *Multinationals, technology and exports*. London: Macmillan.

Lall, S. (1987) *Learning to industrialise: The acquisition of technological capability by India*. London: Macmillan.

Lancaster, K. (1980) 'A theory of intra-industry trade under perfect monopolistic competition', *Journal of International Economics*, 10:151–175.

Landes, D. (1969) *The unbound prometheus*. London: Cambridge University Press.

Leamer, E. (1984) *Sources of international comparative advantage*. Cambridge, MA: MIT Press.

Lecraw, D. (1977) 'Direct investment by firms from less developed countries', *Oxford Economic Papers*, 23:442–457.

Leff, N.H. (1968) *The Brazilian capital goods industry 1929–1964*. Cambridge, MA: Harvard University Press.

Leff, N.H. (1972) 'Development and regional inequality in Brazil', *The Quarterly Journal of Economics*, 86:243–262.

Leibenstein, H. (1957) *Economic backwardness and economic growth*. New York: Wiley.

Leibenstein, H. (1960) 'Technological progress, the production function and dualism', *Banca Nazionale del Lavoro Quarterly Review*, 13:13–15.

Leibenstein, H. (1966) 'Allocative vs x-efficiency', *American Economic Review*, 56:382–415.

Lewis, S.R., Jr. (1972) 'The effects of protection on the growth rate and on the need for external assistance', Williams College, Williamstown, MA.

Lewis, W.A., (1954) 'Economic development with unlimited supplies of labour', *Manchester School of Economic and Social Studies*, 22:139–191.

Lewis, W.A. (1978) *The evolution of the international economic order*. Princeton, NJ: Princeton University Press.

Little, I.M.D. (1979) 'An economic reconnaissance', in: W. Galenson, ed., *Economic growth and structural change in Taiwan*. Ithaca, NY: Cornell University Press.

Little, I.M.D. (1982a) 'Indian industrialization before 1945' in: M. Gersovitz et al., eds., *The theory and experience of economic development*. London: George Allen and Unwin.

Little, I.M.D. (1982b) *Economic development*. New York: Basic Books.

Little, I.M.D., Scitovsky, T. and Scott, M. (1970) *Industry and trade in some developing countries*. New York: Oxford University Press.

Lucas, R.E.B. (1984) 'On the theory of DRC criteria', *Journal of Development Economics*, 14:407–418.

Lucas, R.E.B. (1986) 'Liberalization of Indian trade and industrial controls', mimeo.

Mabro, R. and Radwan, S. (1976) *The industrialization of Egypt 1939–73*. Oxford: Oxford University Press.

Manne, A.S., ed. (1967) *Investments for capacity expansion: Size, location, and time-phasing*. Cambridge, MA: MIT Press.

Mansfield, E. (1968) *The economics of technological change*. New York: Norton.

Martin, J.P. (1978) 'X-inefficiency, managerial effort, and protection', *Economica*, 45:273–286.

Martin, J.P. and Page, J.M., Jr. (1983) 'The impact of subsidies on LDC industry: Theory and empirical test', *Review of Economics and Statistics*, 65:608–617.

Mason, E.S., Kim, M.J., Perkins, D.H., Kim, K.S. and David C. Cole (1980) *The economic and social modernization of the Republic of Korea*. Cambridge, MA: Harvard University Press.

Massell, B.F. (1961) 'A disaggregated view of technical change', *Journal of Political Economy*, 69:547–557.

Mazumdar, D. (1984) 'The issue of small versus large in the Indian textile industry', World Bank Staff Working Paper no. 645. Washington, DC: The World Bank.

Meller, P. (1976) 'Efficiency frontiers for industrial establishments of different size', *Explorations in Economic Research*, 3:379–407.

Michaely, M. (1977) 'Exports and economic growth: An empirical investigation', *Journal of Development Economics*, 4:49–54.

Michalopolous, C. and Jay, K. (1973) 'Growth of exports and income in the developing world: A neoclassical view', Agency for International Development discussion paper no. 28. Washington, DC: Agency for International Development.

Moore, W.E. (1951) *Industrialization and labor*. Ithaca, NY: Cornell University Press.

Morawetz, D. (1974) 'Employment implications of industrialization in developing countries – a survey', *Economic Journal*, 84:491–542.

Morawetz, D. (1976a) 'Elasticities of substitution in industry: What do we learn from econometric estimates', *World Development*, 4:11–15.

Morawetz, D. (1976b) 'The electricity measure of capital utilization', *World Development*, 4:643–653.

Morris, M.D. (1965) *The emergence of an industrial labor force in India: A study of the Bombay cotton mills, 1854–1947*. Berkeley, CA: University of California Press.

Myint, H. (1964) *The economics of the developing countries*. London: Hutchinson.

Nadiri, M.I. (1970) 'Some approaches to the theory and measurement of total factor productivity: A survey', *Journal of Economic Literature*, 8:1137–1177.

Nadiri, M.I. (1972) 'International studies of factor inputs and total factor productivity: A brief survey', *Review of Income and Wealth*, 18:129–153.

Nelson, R.R. (1973) 'Recent exercises in growth accounting: New understanding or dead end', *American Economic Review*, 73:462–468.

Nelson, R.R. (1981) 'Research on productivity growth and productivity differences: Dead ends and new departures', *Journal of Economic Literature*, 19:1029–1064.

Nelson, R.R. (1986) 'Industry growth accounts and production functions when techniques are proprietary', Columbia University, mimeo.

Nelson, R.R. and Phelps, E.S. (1966) 'Investment in humans, technological diffusion and economic growth', *American Economic Review*, Papers and Proceedings, 56:69–75.

Nelson, R.R. and Winter, S. (1982) An evolutionary theory of economic change. Cambridge: Harvard University Press.

Nishimizu, M. and Page, J.M., Jr. (1982) 'Total factor productivity growth, technological progress, and technical efficiency changes: Dimensions of productivity change in Yugoslavia, 1965–78', *Economic Journal*, 92:920–936.

Nishimizu, M. and Robinson, S. (1984) 'Trade policies and productivity change in semi-industrialized countries', *Journal of Development Economics*, 16:177–206.

Olson, M. (1982) *The rise and decline of nations*. New Haven, CT: Yale University Press.

Pack, H. (1971) *Structural change and economic policy in Israel*. New Haven, CT: Yale University Press.

Pack, H. (1974) 'The employment-output tradeoff in ldcs – a microeconomic approach', *Oxford Economic Papers*, 26:388–404.

Pack, H. (1976) 'The substitution of labour for capital in Kenyan manufacturing', *Economic Journal*, 86:45–58.

Pack, H. (1979) 'Technology and employment: Constraints on optimal performance', in: S. Rosenblatt, ed., *Technology and economic development: A realistic appraisal*. Boulder, CO: Westview Press.

Pack, H. (1982) 'Aggregate implications of factor substitution in industrial processes', *Journal of Development Economics*, 11:1–38.

Pack, H. (1984a) 'Total factor productivity and its determinants', in: G. Ranis et al., eds., *Comparative development perspectives*. Boulder, CO: Westview Press.

Pack, H. (1984b) 'Productivity and technical choice: Applications to the textile industry', *Journal of Development Economics*, 16:153–176.

Pack, H. (1987) *Productivity, technology, and industrial development*. New York: Oxford University Press.

Pack, H. and Westphal, L.E. (1986) 'Industrial strategy and technological change: Theory vs. reality', *Journal of Development Economics*, 22:87–128.

Pack, J.R. (1980) Regional growth: Historic perspective. Washington, DC: Advisory Commission on Intergovernmental Relations.

Page, J.M. (1980) 'Technical efficiency and economic performance: Some evidence from Ghana', *Oxford Economic Papers*, 32:319–339.

Page, J.M. (1984) 'Firm size and technical efficiency: Applications of production frontiers to Indian survey data', *Journal of Development Economics*, 16:129–152.

Pickett, J., Forsyth, D.J.C. and McBain, N.S. (1974) 'The choice of technology, economic efficiency, and employment in developing countries', in: E.O. Edwards, ed., *Employment in developing nations*. New York: Columbia University Press.

Pitt, M. and Lee, L.F. (1981) 'The measurement and sources of technical inefficiency in the Indonesian weaving industry', *Journal of Development Economics*, 9:43–64.

Pratten, C.F. (1971) *Economies of scale in manufacturing industry*. London: Cambridge University Press.

Ranis, G. (1973) 'Industrial sector labor absorption', *Economic Development and Cultural Change*, 21:387–408.

Ranis, G. (1979) 'Industrial development', in: W. Galenson, ed., *Economic growth and structural change in Taiwan*. Ithaca, NY: Cornell University Press.

Rhee, Y.W. and Westphal, L.E. (1977) 'A micro-econometric investigation of choice of technique', *Journal of Development Economics*, 4:205–238.

Rhee, Y.W., Ross-Larson, B. and Pursell, G. (1984) Korea's competitive edge: Managing entry into world markets. Baltimore, MD: Johns Hopkins University Press.

Rosenberg, N. (1976) *Perspectives on technology*. London: Cambridge University Press.

Rosenberg, N. (1982) *Inside the black box: Technology and economics*. London: Cambridge University Press.

Rostas, L. (1948) *Comparative productivity in British and American industry*. Cambridge: Cambridge University Press.

Saxonhouse, G.R. (1978) 'The supply of quality workers and the demand for quality in jobs in Japan's early industrialization', *Explorations in Economic History*, 15:40–68.

Scherer, F.M. (1984) *Innovations and growth: Schumpeterian perspectives*. Cambridge, MA: MIT Press.

Scherer, F.M. et al. (1975) *The economics of multi-plant operation: An international comparisons study*. Cambridge, MA: Harvard University Press.

Scitovsky, T. (1958) *Economic theory and Western European integration*. Stanford, CA: Stanford University Press.

Scitovsky, T. (1985) 'Economic development in Taiwan and South Korea: 1965–81', *Food Research Institute Studies*, 19:215–264.

Sen, A.K. (1968) *Choice of techniques*, 3rd ed. New York: Augustus Kelley.

Sen, A.K. (1983) 'Development: Which way now?', *Economic Journal*, 93:745–762.

Shoven, J.B. and Whalley, J. (1984) 'Applied general equilibrium models of taxation and international trade', *Journal of Economic Literature*, 22:1007–1051.

Soligo, R. (1973) 'Factor intensity of consumption patterns, income distribution and employment growth in Pakistan', Rice University Program of Development Studies paper no. 44, Rice University, Houston, mimeo.

Solow, R.M. (1985) 'Economic history and economics', *American Economic Review*, Papers and Proceedings, 75:328–331.

Srinivasan, T.N. and Bhagwati, J. (1978) 'Shadow prices for project selection in the presence of distortions: effective rates of protection and domestic resource cost', *Journal of Political Economy*, 86:97–116.

Stein, S. (1957) *Brazilian cotton manufacture*. Cambridge, MA: Harvard University Press.

Stern, R.M. (1975) 'Testing trade theories', in P.B. Kenen, ed., *International trade and finance*. Cambridge: Cambridge University Press.

Stewart, F. (1974) 'Technology and employment in ldcs', in: E. Edwards, ed., *Employment in developing nations*. New York: Columbia University Press.

Stewart, F. (1977) *Technology and underdevelopment*. Boulder, CO: Westview Press.

Stewart, F. (1979) 'International mechanisms for appropriate technology', in: A. Bhalla, ed., *Towards global action for appropriate technology*. Oxford: Pergamon Press.

Stiglitz, J.E. (1982) 'The structure of labor markets and shadow prices in ldcs', in: R.H. Sabot, ed., *Migration and the labor market in developing countries*. Boulder, CO: Westview Press.

Stiglitz, J.E. (1985) 'The new development economics', Research Program in Development Studies discussion paper no. 121, Princeton University, mimeo.

Summers, R. (1982) 'Services in the international economy', University of Pennsylvania, mimeo.

Syrquin, M. (1984) 'Resource reallocation and productivity growth', in: M. Syrquin, L. Taylor and L.E. Westphal, eds., *Economic structure and performance*. Orlando: Academic Press.

Syrquin, M. (1986) 'Economic growth and structural change in Israel: An international perspective', in: Y. Ben Porath, ed., *The Israeli economy*. Cambridge, MA: Harvard University Press.

Teitel, S. (1975) 'Economies of scale and size of plant: The evidence and the implications for the developing countries', *Journal of Common Market Studies*, 13:92–115.

Teitel, S. (1981) 'Productivity, mechanization and skills: A test of the Hirschman hypothesis for Latin American industry', *World Development*, 9:855–871.

Thompson, E.P. (1963) *The making of the English working class*. New York: Random House.

Tidrick, G. (1986) 'Productivity growth and technological change in Chinese industry', World Bank Staff Working Paper 761. Washington DC: The World Bank.

Timmer, C.P. (1971) 'Using a probabilistic frontier production function to measure technical efficiency', *Journal of Political Economy*, 79:776–794.

Tsao, Y. (1985) 'Growth without productivity: Singapore manufacturing in the 1970s', *Journal of Development Economics*, 19:25–38.

Tyler, W.E. (1979) 'Technical efficiency in production in a developing country: An empirical examination of the Brazilian plastics and steel industries', *Oxford Economic Papers*, 31:477–495.

United Nations (1955) Processes and problems of industrialization in under-developed countries. New York: U.N. Department of Economic and Social Affairs.

Westphal, L.E. (1975) 'Planning with economies of scale', in: C.R. Blitzer, P.B. Clark and L. Taylor, eds., *Economy-wide models and development planning*. New York: Oxford University Press.

Westphal, L.E. and J. Cremer (1984) 'The "interdependence of investment decisions" revisited', in: M. Syrquin, L. Taylor and L. Westphal, eds., *Economic structure and performance*. New York: Academic Press.

Westphal, L.E., Rhee, Y.W. and Pursell, G. (1981) 'Korean industrial competence: Where it came from', World Bank Staff working paper no. 469. Washington DC: The World Bank.

White, L.J. (1976) 'Appropriate technology, x-efficiency, and a competitive environment', *Quarterly Journal of Economics*, 90:575–590.

White, L.J. (1978) 'The evidence on appropriate factor proportions for manufacturing in less developed countries: A survey', *Economic Development and Cultural Change*, 27:27–60.

Williams, D. (1975) 'National planning and the choice of technology: The case of textiles in Tanzania', unpublished Ph.D. dissertation, Harvard School of Business Administration.

Williamson, J.G. (1969) 'Dimensions of postwar Philippine economic progress', *Quarterly Journal of Economics*, 83:99–109.

Williamson, J.G. (1971a) 'Capital accumulation, labor saving, and labor absorption once more', *Quarterly Journal of Economics*, 85:40–65.

Williamson, J.G. (1971b) 'Relative price changes, adjustment dynamics, and productivity growth: The case of Philippine manufacturing', *Economic Development and Cultural Change*, 19:507–526.

Winston, G. (1974) 'The theory of capital utilization and idleness', *Journal of Economic Literature*, 12:1301–1320.

The World Bank (1980) *World tables*, 2nd ed. Baltimore, MD: Johns Hopkins University Press.

The World Bank (1981) *Accelerated development in sub-Saharan Africa*. Washington, DC: The World Bank.

The World Bank (1982) *World development report – 1982*. New York: Oxford University Press.

The World Bank (1984) *World development report – 1984*. New York: Oxford University Press.

Chapter 10

SAVING AND DEVELOPMENT

MARK GERSOVITZ*

Princeton University

Contents

1. Introduction   382
2. Personal savings   383
    2.1. A simple model of individual saving   384
    2.2. Evidence on the simple model   385
    2.3. Uncertainty and saving   390
    2.4. Borrowing constraints   392
    2.5. Education and asset choice   394
    2.6. Health, nutrition and savings   396
    2.7. Bequests and savings   400
    2.8. The family and savings   401
3. Savings at the national level   403
    3.1. Aggregation over cohorts   404
    3.2. Income distribution and aggregate savings   407
    3.3. Corporate savings   411
    3.4. The role of government   412
    3.5. Evidence at the aggregate level   413
4. Conclusions   418
    References   419

*I am especially grateful to Angus S. Deaton and Mark R. Rosenzweig for extensive discussion of these issues over a prolonged period and for comments on drafts of this chapter. I also thank Surjit S. Bhalla, T. Paul Schultz, T.N. Srinivasan, Arvind Virmani, and the other participants at the World Bank's workshop on savings of January 1986 for the opportunity to hear their opinions on many of the issues I discuss in this chapter. Anne C. Case, Hollis B. Chenery, S.M. Ravi Kanbur and Christina Paxson made valuable comments on an earlier draft.

Handbook of Development Economics, Volume I, Edited by H. Chenery and T.N. Srinivasan
© *Elsevier Science Publishers B.V., 1988*

1. Introduction

Saving, a sacrifice of current consumption, provides for the accumulation of capital which, in turn, produces additional output that can potentially be used for consumption in the future. The process is thus inherently intertemporal. Its presumed operation makes the saving behavior of citizens and their governments central to the development of poor countries. Moreover, threats of expropriation, repudiation and other hostile acts against foreign suppliers of capital, and donor resistance to significant increases in aid, mean that domestic savings is likely to remain the predominant source of capital accumulation in developing countries.[1]

In this chapter I focus on the determinants of the volume of savings. My motivation is that the transformation of domestic savings into additional income in the future via the accumulation of capital is not only operative, but is a significant factor in the growth of incomes in developing countries. In this sense, I follow Lewis (1954, p. 155) who stressed that the "central problem in the theory of economic development is to understand the process by which a community which was previously saving...4 or 5 per cent. of its national income or less, converts itself into an economy where voluntary saving is running at about 12 to 15 per cent. of national income or more". I do not, however, in any way document the linkages embodied in this hypothesis of the importance of saving; for the purposes of this chapter it is a matter of faith.

Savings not only allow for growth in income and increases in consumption, but also for the smoothing of consumption in the presence of various uncertainties. Saving behavior can only be understood fully after the sources of uncertainty facing decision-makers and their opportunities for responding to them are specified. In particular, the availability of insurance, the scope for borrowing and the role of the extended family can influence choices about saving in the uncertain environment of developing countries.

To the extent that there are theories of saving behavior supported by evidence, one can begin to judge the desirability of saving decisions and prescribe policies to improve saving performance. As with other normative discussions in economics, the optimality of saving behavior can only be discussed with reference to an explicit criterion of welfare, which for me is the value of individual's utilities over time. By contrast, much discussion of saving performance proceeds as though more saving, regardless of the way it comes about, is necessarily good. These two criteria are by no means the same thing; this chapter provides many instances in which (arguably) desirable policies may decrease savings. Thus, while the study of saving behavior is important to an understanding of which countries

---

[1] See Eaton and Gersovitz (1983) for a discussion of country risk and international capital mobility.

will develop and when, policy should not be directed to increasing saving for its effects on economic growth. Policy toward saving, like other policies, should be concerned with questions of efficiency and equity.

The development process is one of transition. While the proportion of income that is saved is a determinant of the level of income and not of its growth rate in the steady state [Solow (1956)], in the movement to the steady state a temporary increase in the saving rate temporarily increases the growth of income and shortens the time necessary to reach any given level of income. This distinction is worth keeping in mind, and is a specific instance of the fact that comparisons among steady states may be a poor guide to the evolution of an economy during development.

The plan of the chapter is as follows. In Section 2 I begin with a description of how individuals and households decide how much to save. This material is integrated with evidence on the posited relationships. In Section 3 I show how to add up savings from different sources in the economy, first by aggregating over individuals of different ages and incomes and then over the different sectors (household, corporate, and government). This section also summarizes the role of government policies in influencing the volume of saving, and reviews empirical studies of the determinants of aggregate savings. The conclusions comment on what is known and how more can be learned about savings.[2]

2. Personal savings

Choices by individuals and families about their savings are one set of fundamental determinants of national savings. These decision-makers divide the current increment to their resources between consumption, the satisfaction of current wants, and savings that in turn will influence their ability to satisfy wants in the future. Any model of rational decision-making by savers must, therefore, focus very explicitly on the trade-offs between satisfying wants now and later. Within this limitation, however, there is considerable latitude for different specifications of consumers' objectives and the constraints they face in attaining them. I start with a very simple model of intertemporal decision-making about saving, and proceed to discuss various complications in subsequent sections. Empirical findings on these topics are limited, and only sometimes narrow the range of plausible theoretical formulations.

---

[2] Two earlier surveys of saving in developing countries are Mikesell and Zinser (1973) and Snyder (1974). The theoretical and empirical literature devoted to understanding savings primarily in developed countries is vast, and is often highly relevant to the situation in the developing countries. I refer to individual studies as appropriate; recent surveys of aspects of this literature are King (1985), Sandmo (1985), and Modigliani (1986). Deaton (forthcoming) provides an overview of recent advances in the analysis of aggregate time series, results that have yet to be applied to developing countries.

2.1. A simple model of individual saving

In the simplest model of saving, a single individual who lives for T periods $(i = 0, \ldots, T-1)$, receives income (from labor or sources other than interest payments) of y_i and consumes c_i in the ith period; he neither receives nor leaves bequests. If an individual does not desire that $y_i = c_i$, he can and does borrow or lend at an interest rate r in the ith period. The only constraint on the individual's choices is that the present value of lifetime consumption, C, cannot exceed the present value of lifetime income, Y:

$$C \equiv \sum_{i=0}^{T-1} \left[\frac{c_i}{(1+r)^i} \right] \leq \sum_{i=0}^{T-1} \left[\frac{y_i}{(1+r)^i} \right] \equiv Y. \tag{1}$$

So much for the opportunities faced by the decision-maker. His goal is to maximize the sum, V, of the discounted utility of consumption in each period, $\delta^i U[c_i]$, $0 < \delta < 1$:

$$V \equiv \sum_{i=0}^{T-1} \delta^i U[c_i]. \tag{2}$$

The utility of consumption in each period is functionally the same, i.e. the function $U[\cdot]$ is time invariant.

The decision-maker's problem (for $T = 2$) is solved by the first-order condition:

$$U'[c_0] = (1+r)\delta U'[c_1] \tag{3}$$

which, along with condition (1) holding as an equality, yields optimal values of consumption, c_0^* and c_1^*. Current savings are then a residual, $y_0 - c_0$, dependent on eqs. (1) and (3) *and* the particular time profile of incomes, which is why most theories are formulated and tested in terms of consumption rather than saving functions. A model of this simplicity is only suitable for a first pass at a short list of questions about saving, but it does speak to some classic ones:

(1) Perhaps the central notion of this type of intertemporal, maximizing model is that current consumption depends on lifetime resources, Y, and not on current resources, y_0. The latter only affects consumption insofar as it affects the former. Furthermore, if future incomes change while current income remains constant, Y and therefore current consumption change. Various marginal propensities to consume are defined precisely by the effect on c_0 of different types of changes in income: (a) the marginal propensity to consume from a transitory increase in income, an increase in y_0 with y_1 fixed; and (b) the marginal propensity to consume from a permanent increase in (all) incomes, an equal increase in both y_0 and y_1 (when $T = 2$). The latter is larger than the former.

(2) The theoretical effect on saving ($y_0 - c_0$) of changes in the interest rate is ambiguous because the income and substitution effects work in opposite directions. On the one hand, when the interest rate rises the cost of consuming in the future falls, promoting saving. On the other hand, an individual who is a positive saver ($y_0 - c_0 > 0$) is better off, and tends to increase current consumption at the expense of savings.

Evidence on the interest elasticity of savings is difficult to obtain using micro data, because rates of interest are economy-wide variables that do not vary in cross-sections, while differential access to investment opportunities is difficult to measure (but see Section 2.5). There is no consensus from the research based on aggregate time series. In a recent study for developing countries, Giovannini (1985) estimates that this elasticity is essentially zero; see also Blinder and Deaton (1985) for the United States.

(3) The generalization of this model to many ($T > 2$) periods is straightforward. An increase in the horizon in this type of model can be used to analyze a change in life expectancy. Such an analysis corresponds to an increase in the expectation of life for adults since the model is of a decision-maker in full control of his initial consumption decisions (c_0). Much of the increase in life expectancy in the LDCs has been through decreases in infant mortality's raising the expectation of life at birth, and is therefore not well captured by this type of analysis. For instance, an understanding of how parents adjust the number of children they desire and their saving behavior in response to a change in the expectation of life at birth requires an explicit model of family decision-making; see Sections 2.8 and 3.1. Ram and Schultz (1979), however, present data that the expectation of additional years of life at age 20 for Indian males has increased from 33.0 to 41.1 between 1951 and 1971. This change has great potential significance for saving behavior, depending on the profile of income by age. For instance, if a large fraction of the additional years are spent in retirement, then the individualistic life-cycle model of this section suggests an increase in saving in the pre-retirement years to provide for consumption after retirement. (Section 2.7 provides further discussion of whether individuals do indeed dissave after retirement.)

To address additional issues in saving behavior as well as to re-assess the conclusions of this simple model requires the introduction of further considerations. Following sections take up such issues as: borrowing constraints and fragmented capital markets, human capital, uncertainty, nutritional effects, bequests, and the extended family. Before turning to these topics, however, I discuss some issues in the empirical analysis of saving behavior.

2.2. Evidence on the simple model

The model of Section 2.1 describes how an individual decides on the level of his savings. For many developing countries, household surveys would seem to provide information on the actual choices about savings that individuals and households make, because they typically report incomes and consumption expenditures of the respondents. These surveys are therefore the natural source of data for the investigation of issues raised by models of saving behavior. The prospective implementation of models of saving behavior using these surveys raises a large number of problems, however, because closer examination calls into question the correspondence between the measured variables and the theoretical constructs.

First, the accuracy and usefulness of these data are dependent on the period of observation. If respondents are asked to report on income and expenditures over a very short period, their answers may be reasonably accurate, but may be dominated by idiosyncratic events or seasonal influences. By contrast, data collected by asking respondents to recall their decisions over an extended period, say a year, may suffer from omissions. Visaria (1980, especially pp. 23–31) discusses these and related problems in more detail.

In practice, researchers using these household surveys have found grossly implausible values for the savings variable for some respondents, and have used various criteria to drop observations from the sample before proceeding to econometric estimation.[3] The criteria for exclusion tend to be somewhat arbitrary, may introduce selectivity bias because they are conditioned on the dependent variable, and in general are not a substitute for an (admittedly difficult) explicit integration of measurement error into the analysis. For instance, in their study of errors in panel data on the U.S. labor market, Duncan and Hill (1985) found that exclusion of outliers actually reduced the signal to noise ratio; in this case, error was not the predominant reason for atypical values. It could be a great help to have a similar study that cross-checked data on savings and identified the sources and nature of error.[4]

Visaria (1980, especially pp. 21–31) and Berry (1985, especially pp. 347–349) discuss checks for internal consistency in household surveys and for consistency with other data, and apply these tests to several surveys. Among the important findings are: (1) Household surveys underreport income relative to the national accounts. The most severe discrepancies arise for nonlabor income. (2) Units reporting negative savings are too numerous to reflect household responses to transitorily low incomes or high consumption needs. Income appears to be underreported relative to consumption. (3) There may be considerable differences in underreporting among surveys done in the same country with apparently similar methodologies, but at different dates.

---

[3] On the National Council of Applied Economic Research survey, see Bhalla (1980, p. 741) and Wolpin (1982, p. 588) as well as Bhalla (1979).

[4] Among Duncan and Hill's other important findings are that correlations between measurement errors in the dependent variable and the independent variables can bias parameter estimates to a serious degree.

Another issue in the empirical study of saving is the treatment of consumer durables. Expenditures for consumer durables are more appropriately considered to be a form of investment rather than consumption, because they are not purchased solely for immediate satisfaction. Instead, consumption expenditure should include an adjustment for the services (flow) from the stock of currently-owned consumer durables. Such adjustments are not easily made because they require: (1) a clear classification of current expenditure between durables and nondurables; (2) information on the current stock of durables; (3) information on the depreciation of this stock; and (4) assumptions about interest rates.

There may also be particular difficulties in valuing certain types of durables that are produced by the reporting unit rather than purchased, for example urban-squatter or rural housing. The problem of imputation is, of course, a general one, since elements of current consumption, such as food, will often be produced at home as well. The expectation is that these problems will be much more severe in poor countries where proportionately less production is monetized than in richer developing countries or the countries of the OECD; see Blades (1975) and Chandavarkar (1977). And, within developing countries. the importance of non-monetized consumption differs by occupation (being higher in agriculture than elsewhere); by commodity; and by income groups [Coondoo et al. (1979)]. The omission of non-monetized components from both income and consumption will overstate the saving ratio but not savings, while the omission of non-monetized investment from income will understate both the saving ratio and the level of savings. The relationship of these errors to income and occupation can then lead to mistaken inferences about the variables that determine saving, or the functional form of these behavioral relationships.

Furthermore, the income measure in household surveys typically excludes changes in the values of assets and liabilities carried into the period. An alternative approach to the income-minus-consumption calculation of savings relies on the identity that all savings must show up as changes in the values of assets and liabilities. Bhalla (1978, 1979, 1980) uses this approach; Wolpin (1982) compares results based on the two methods of calculating savings. Here again there are problems, including: incomplete enumeration of assets and liabilities; problems of valuing non-monetized investment; underreporting of asset stocks.

Despite these difficulties with data, a number of econometric studies do exist that analyze the saving behavior reported in household surveys. Ramanathan (1968) for India, Betancourt (1971) for Chile, Bhalla (1978, 1979, 1980) for India, Musgrove (1979) for Colombia, Ecuador and Peru, and Wolpin (1982) for India, all use variants of the permanent income hypothesis, while Kelley and Williamson (1968) for Indonesia look at some life-cycle features of saving behavior. The work by Bhalla and Wolpin has a particular strength in using three-year panel data [from the National Council of Applied Economic Research (NCAER) survey for India]. The Musgrove (1979) and Bhalla (1979) studies are notable for their explicit treatment of errors of measurement in the variables, including permanent income, although under the assumption that the means of the errors are zero.[5]

Friedman (1957) introduced the notion of permanent income as a determinant of consumption and saving behavior. The idea behind Friedman's approach is similar to the life-cycle model of Section 2.1; future resources as well as current resources affect saving. I will not present Friedman's approach as he originally did, partially because some of his assumptions, such as an infinitely lived consumer, are clearly untenable. The model of Section 2.1 can, however, be specialized to interpret the work of those analysts of saving and development who have used the permanent income approach:

A consumer with preferences such that $\delta(1 + r) = 1$ lives T periods and receives life-time income of Y. From first-order conditions like eq. (3) the consumer chooses

$$c_i = c^* = \frac{\left[(1 + r)^{T-1} - 1\right]}{r(1 + r)^{T-1}} Y \equiv y^{\mathrm{P}}, \tag{4}$$

in which y^{P} is termed permanent income. For purposes of estimation, this equation can be written (with an error term, u) as

$$c_i = \alpha + \beta y_i^p + \gamma(y_i - y_i^p) + u_i, \tag{4a}$$

with the permanent income hypothesis as formulated in eq. (4) implying that $\alpha = \gamma = 0$ and $\beta = 1$. Confirmation of these parameter values through econometric estimation is taken to support the notion that lifetime rather than current resources determines consumption, and implicitly that consumers do have the borrowing and lending opportunities hypothesized in Section 2.1.

The assumptions used to derive the preceding version of the permanent income hypothesis are rather special. Among the most important problems is that permanent income is not directly observed. One approach, used by many of the researchers on developing countries among others, is to assume that permanent income equals current income plus an intertemporally independent error term. If eq. (4a) is true with $\alpha = \gamma = 0$, a regression of consumption on current rather than permanent income would suffer from classic errors-in-variables bias. In turn, this problem could be corrected by using an instrumental-variables estimator.

There are, however, problems in finding suitable instruments. For instance, Musgrove's approach requires at least one variable that affects permanent income but not the propensity to consume. Bhalla assumes that average income over

---

[5] For a treatment of measurement error in a study on saving using U.S. data, see Altonji and Siow (1987).

three years or lagged income are valid instrumental variables, which is troublesome if the transitory component of income is serially correlated. Wolpin's use of a measure of long-run weather conditions as an instrument seems to solve these econometric problems. It is not entirely clear, however, why long-run weather conditions should be correlated with the permanent incomes of individuals; such favored regions may simply be more densely populated.

The general sense of the literature on developing countries is that a permanent, or lifetime, notion of income in line with eq. (1) is an appropriate determinant of consumption, rather than current income. These authors present estimates of the propensity to save from permanent income. The propensity to save out of transitory income $(1 - \gamma)$ is generally higher than that out of permanent income, as predicted by the theory, although it is not often estimated to be effectively one.

In addition to the difficulty of finding suitable instruments, however, a questionable assumption is that consumption is determined by permanent income which in turn equals current income plus an intertemporally independent error. First, the model of Section 2.1 is a certainty model. If, however, incomes are uncertain and consumers are risk averse, consumers' behavior in the face of uncertainty in income must be taken into account. (On the other hand, if consumers were risk neutral, the model of Section 2.1 with its emphasis on consumption smoothing would break down because marginal utility is constant.) With risk averse consumers, Y in eq. (4) cannot be replaced by its expected value so that eq. (4a) does not derive from optimizing behavior. The only assumption that is generally consistent with the permanent income formulation is that the discrepancy between current and permanent income is measurement error, perceived by the econometrician but not by the consumer.

Recent methodological advances avoid these problems by estimating directly the parameters of models similar to those of Section 2.1, or 2.3 that incorporate risk, without recourse to the permanent-income restrictions. These methods have yet to be applied to household survey data from developing countries. The essence of these approaches is to use the first-order conditions of the model, such as eq. (3), in the estimation. Estimation of the parameters of the utility function can be combined with an analysis of the parameters of the income-generating process, but need not be; see Hall (1978), Hall and Mishkin (1982), Flavin (1981), and Hansen and Singleton (1983), as well as Deaton (forthcoming) for an overview.

The studies of saving in developing countries also treat the income variable as exogenous, as in the theoretical model of the previous section. In particular, individuals do not choose their employment status or the hours they work. These assumptions may be more plausible in industrial economies that in the agricultural sectors of developing countries. In the latter case, owner-cultivators may have great flexibility in adjusting their work time and effort, and labor markets may be generally closer to a simple demand–supply model. Both income and savings are then the outcome of choices by individuals and households in response to the prices (including wages and interest rates) that they face currently, as well as those they will face in the future. It would seem worthwhile to investigate these questions in future research on saving in developing countries.[6]

2.3. Uncertainty and saving

Individuals and households face various uncertainties that affect their welfare. Because saving provides resources that are available in the future when these uncertainties are resolved and because the return on savings may be uncertain, the decision to save is intimately related to the nature and extent of uncertainty. The simple model of Section 2.1 suggests a typology of uncertainties. Savers may face randomness in: (1) future income, y_1; (2) the rate of return on savings, r; (3) the utility of consumption $U(\cdot)$, say because of health status; and (4) the length of life, T.

The theoretical effects on savings of all these types of uncertainty are quite indeterminate, depending in complicated ways on the parameters of the decision-maker's utility function. The model of Section 2.1 can be extended easily to analyze uncertainty in y_1, r and $U(\cdot)$; the fourth type of uncertainty, T, is analyzed by Levhari and Mirman (1977).[7] The first change is to substitute

$$V = U[c_0] + \mathrm{E}\, \delta U[c_1]. \tag{2a}$$

for eq. (2) in the two-period model, on the assumption that the decision-maker maximizes the sum of expected, discounted utilities. In conjunction with eq. (1), eq. (2a) leads to the modified first-order condition:

$$U'[c_0] - \mathrm{E}\{\delta U'[c_1](1+r)\} = 0, \tag{3a}$$

in which either y_1 or r may be random.[8]

Using the method of Rothschild and Stiglitz (1971), the effect of an increase in uncertainty in y_1 or in r on savings is determined by the sign of the second derivative of $\delta U'[c_1](1+r)$ with respect to the random variable. If savings are

---

[6]See Heckman (1974 and 1976) for some theoretical aspects of the problem. Browning et al. (1985) and Mankiw et al. (1985) empirically analyze saving and work decisions in an integrated fashion, and, provide references to the earlier literature.

[7]References on the first two sources of uncertainty are Levhari and Srinivasan (1969), Miller (1976), and Rothschild and Stiglitz (1971).

[8]The choice of savings ($y_0 - c_0$) must be consistent with $c_1 \geq 0$ regardless of the realization of the random variable.

initially positive, then savings increase with an increase in the riskiness of r if $2U'' - \alpha\{R'U' + (R + 1)U''\} > 0$, and decrease otherwise, in which $\alpha \equiv (1 + r)(y_0 - c_0)/\{(1 + r)(y_0 - c_0) + y_1\}$ and $R \equiv -U''c_1/U'$, the coefficient of relative risk aversion. In the special case of constant relative risk aversion ($R' = 0$), savings increase if and only if R exceeds one. Similarly, it can be shown that savings increase with an increase in the riskiness of y_1 if and only if $U'''[c_1] > 0$. If $R' = 0$, then $U''' > 0$. If utility is modified to depend on health status, H, a random variable, as well as consumption so that $U \equiv U[c_1, H]$ with $U_H > 0$, then savings increase with an increase in the riskiness of H if and only if $U_{c_1, H, H} > 0$.

A saver's exposure to these uncertainties depends not only on whether the variables are random, but also on the opportunities he has for insurance. Future agricultural income may be risky, but if these risks are insurable through crop insurance that is actuarially fair, then the individual can insure and need not take this uncertainty into account in choosing his savings. Other types of insurance that are relevant, if available, are: health insurance, life insurance, life annuities (which insure against long life), and social security.[9] These options are usually thought to be less available in developing than developed countries, although the extended family may substitute for various forms of insurance.

The availability of insurance is usually limited by adverse selection and moral hazard, but the extended family can acquire information about, and monitor and circumscribe the actions of, its members relatively costlessly. The extended family may consequently be better at insuring certain risks than insurance companies in the developed countries for whom their clientele is comparatively anonymous. If the extended family is to be good at insurance, however, the risks that its members face must be relatively uncorrelated, so that they can be diversified within the family. The extended family may have a comparative advantage in the implicit provision of health or life insurance including annuities [Kotlikoff and Spivak (1981)], but not in dealing with climatic effects on crops in an economy with few non-agricultural activities in which some family members may obtain employment.

Agriculturalists therefore are likely to face important and uninsurable climatological uncertainties in developing countries, and these can potentially be measured using parameters estimated from historical series on climatological variables. If a country with spatial variability in climatological uncertainty and good micro data on saving behavior can be identified, there is the opportunity to examine how savers respond to an important uncertainty. To date no one has

---

[9] With fair insurance the problem reverts to that of Section 2.1 with expected values replacing r or y_1. For uncertainty about health status, insurance cannot transform the problem back to that of Section 2.1 if health and income are not perfect substitutes in their effects on utility.

done such a study, but Wolpin (1982) provides a precedent in linking household survey data and information on rainfall to provide an instrument for permanent income. The next step is to see if the propensity to consume depends on agro-climatic variability.[10]

2.4. Borrowing constraints

An assumption of the simple model in Section 2.1 is that the individual can borrow (or lend) as much as he desires at a fixed rate of interest so long as the intertemporal budget constraint, condition (1), is satisfied. This assumption may not be valid, either with respect to borrowing or lending.

An individual is constrained in his borrowing in the simple model if he cannot borrow $y_0 - c_0^* < 0$. In this model, the most extreme case is a consumer without any opportunities to borrow and whose consumption is restricted to current income, $c_0 = y_0$. In this type of model, therefore, a borrowing constraint raises savings, but only from a negative value toward (or to) a zero level. The consumer is, nonetheless, worse off; higher savings and increased welfare are not the same thing.

In other formulations, a borrowing constraint can even convert a negative saver into a positive saver. For instance, a consumer who wants to take a trip (a consumption expenditure) as soon as possible, and can borrow for it, may report negative savings. But a consumer who cannot borrow and must save in advance of the trip will have positive savings until the target is met. An important assumption is that the particular consumption expenditure is indivisible, so that saving up for it makes sense, which is not true when choices are about a divisible good, the marginal utility of which declines in each period. The desire to purchase housing or other assets that are indivisible may also induce positive saving.[11] Furthermore, in a multiperiod model, an individual who would be a dissaver in one period if always unconstrained in his borrowing, may save positive amounts in the presence of constraints if these are expected to prevail in

---

[10] From an agricultural producer's point of view, uncertainty in yields may be offset by a negative correlation between price and output via the demand for output [Newbery and Stiglitz (1981)]. Indeed, if demand is inelastic, and most of their output is marketed, farmers will be better off in years of poor agricultural production. This possibility suggests another desirable characteristic of a data set, that it derive from a country where prices are exogenous to weather. This condition would hold for a country that is small in relation to world markets for an internationally traded crop or for one where markets within the country are sufficiently integrated for prices to be geographically uniform and where weather is spatially independent. In the absence of these conditions, the correlation between price and weather would have to be integrated explicitly into the analysis.

[11] For simulations based on this idea for the United States and Japan, see Hayashi et al. (1986).

the future as well.[12] Thus, positive saving is not per se evidence that a consumer's behavior is unaffected by borrowing constraints; see also Artle and Varaiya (1978).[13]

Are borrowing constraints likely to be prevalent in developing countries, and what kinds of consumers are likely to be subject to them? There are two considerations: (1) Will lenders establish credit ceilings, and at what levels for which type of borrower? (2) Which type of borrower will want to borrow amounts in excess of his assigned credit ceiling? A simple approach is to focus on the second question by implicitly assuming that the credit ceiling is exogenous, perhaps set at zero. The model of Section 2.1 can then be used to make predictions based on the size of $c_0^* - y_0$. For example, professions such as medicine that require an innate ability that is scarce and therefore provide high (discounted) lifetime earnings also seem to have steep age–income profiles. If this pattern is generally true, then individuals who are rich in a lifetime sense would also want to finance consumption in excess of current cash inflows (in their youth), and therefore would be potentially most susceptible to borrowing constraints. As Blinder (1976, p. 88) puts it: "The poor man with a flat age–income profile and no financial inheritance is constrained by many things but not by the inability to borrow against future receipts."

On the other hand, there are arguments that suggest that the (lifetime, i.e. low Y) poor may be more susceptible than the rich to borrowing constraints. For one thing, the poor may be more desirous of borrowing to offset various shocks than the rich because: (1) they experience shocks that are proportionately larger, say because there are economies of scale that discourage them from diversifying their income sources; or (2) the marginal utility of consumption is such as to place a premium on very stable consumption at low incomes, say because subsistence requirements must be met; or (3) the poor save proportionately less than the rich, and so have relatively less wealth to buffer consumption (see below on saving propensities of the poor versus the rich).

These factors are only part of a complete theory of credit constraints; neither asynchronous receipts and expenditures, nor risky receipts, nor risk aversion imply that credit relationships will be characterized by constraints on borrowing. When will lenders impose credit limits on borrowers? One set of considerations stems from the costs to a borrower relative to his lifetime income of not meeting his debt obligations. Presumably, lenders constrain borrowers because they fear that repayment is in doubt. In this case, a crucial determinant of the extent to which lenders constrain borrowers is the cost that can be imposed on a re-

---

[12] Consider a consumer with a moderate y_0, a very low y_1 and a very high y_2. With the option to borrow, it may be optimal to borrow in both periods 0 and 1. With a constraint on borrowing, it may be optimal to save in period 0 to consume in period 1.

[13] This observation casts doubt on the otherwise interesting econometric approach of Hayashi (1985) which relies on the assumption that high savers are unconstrained by borrowing opportunities.

calcitrant borrower to compel adherence to the debt contract. These penalties may be quite indirect, and it is not clear how they vary relative to income.[14]

An example of this approach is the contrast between the creditworthiness of a skilled artisan and a landless laborer. The village artisan may have a local reputation for reliable work that he would have to give up if he fled to another region in an effort to avoid his debt obligations.[15] On the other hand, a day laborer might not develop a reputation in any case and, being highly mobile as a consequence, might be a bad credit risk even relative to his low income.

In other cases, asymmetries in the information available to lenders and borrowers or moral hazard [Stiglitz and Weiss (1981)], or governmental regulation of credit markets especially through ceilings on interest rates [Paxson (1986)] may lead to the rationing of credit. Furthermore, credit constraints may lead to different choices of investments as well as different levels of investment, if assets differ in their suitability as collateral or in their association with problems of moral hazard or adverse selection. To the best of my knowledge, however, there are as yet no micro-econometric studies of borrowing constraints in LDCs. It is therefore not possible to turn to evidence that distinguishes among these hypotheses about the type of borrower that is constrained, or to look at the related issue of individuals who may be able to borrow at one rate but lend at a lower one, or to suggest additional hypotheses about how lending and borrowing opportunities differ from those assumed in the model of Section 2.1.

2.5. Education and asset choice

The inclusion of an expenditure in current consumption rather than in savings should depend on whether it contributes to the immediate satisfaction of consumers' wants. One important anomaly in this regard is the treatment of educational expenditures, which are classified as consumption. If these expenditures are made for their effects on future income, then they would qualify as an investment expenditure (human capital), and would respond to the same determinants as other types of savings. Even if consumers desire education solely for its effect on their enjoyment of life, this benefit is spread over a consumer's lifetime because it presumably is not restricted to the years in school, and therefore has the attributes of a consumer durable.

Ram and Schultz (1979) adjust the estimates of capital formation in India to include expenditures on educational institutions and the opportunity cost of students' time. The results are fairly dramatic; their estimates of human capital

---

[14] Eaton, Gersovitz and Stiglitz (1986) discuss models of willingness to pay in the context of international lending. Allen (1983) uses this approach in analyzing the agricultural loan market.

[15] A reputation for good work is not true collateral, however; if the artisan chooses to flee, it does not serve to indemnify the creditor.

formation account for between 5 percent (in 1950–51) and 11 percent (in 1970–71) of net national product, and from just over a third to just over half of gross domestic capital formation as traditionally defined. It is important to have a set of parallel calculations for other developing countries. There is no reason to expect constancy, at different stages of development, in the relative amounts of investment in human and physical capital necessary to keep the associated rates of return moving in step, as would be optimal. In particular, Ram and Schultz emphasize that the return to human capital rises with increases in the life expectancy of individuals who are old enough to be educated, suggesting that the appropriate allocation of investment between human and physical capital may move in favor of the former in response to decreases in adult mortality. The neglect of human capital could then easily lead to mistaken views of the ability and willingness of countries with different incomes to divert resources from current consumption.

While the distinction between human and physical capital is perhaps the most marked among all non-consumption uses of income, there are a whole range of investment opportunities in any economy. In an idealized situation, all individuals can choose among the same set of investments, each of which pays different investors identical rates of return. This situation may prevail approximately in developed countries. There, stock markets, mutual funds and other financial institutions repackage large, potentially risky investments in physical capital, each with their own special attributes, into financial instruments that are available in relatively small units at costs roughly independent of the total number of units purchased. As a consequence many savers have the option of participating in a large fraction of the economy's investment opportunities.

This view of relatively integrated capital markets and investment opportunities open to many savers is not the common view of the situation in many developing countries. In these economies, capital markets are thought to be fragmented with different investors choosing from very different menus of investment opportunities, see McKinnon (1973) and Shaw (1973). The closely-held or family firm is believed to be prevalent, in contrast to the public corporation of the developed countries. This picture is clearly correct in the predominant activity in most developing countries, i.e. agriculture, where production is often organized in small, family farms.

The introduction of more assets and rates of return does not result in any fundamental changes in concept. For instance, the economy may be composed of N individuals, each of whom solves the decision problem posed by the model of Section 2.1, but subject to a different r, say r_i for the ith individual. While a decrease in the dispersion of rates of return, if costless to achieve, may be expected to increase the efficiency of the allocation of savings among investments, it need not increase the volume of savings. A mean-preserving decrease in the dispersion in the rates of return available to different individuals has an ambiguous effect on total savings. This result follows from the ambiguity in the sign of dc_0/dr previously mentioned, and the ambiguity in the sign of d^2c_0/dr^2 even given the sign of dc_0/dr.

Bhalla (1978) investigates the effect of differences in investment opportunities on the saving behavior of rural Indian households. He argues that the option to adopt high yielding varieties (HYVs) was an opportunity available to these households in varying degree, depending on their geo-climatic location. Furthermore, the reaction of these households should differ depending on whether they were able to borrow to finance adoption, or not. Those households that could borrow freely and were suitably located to adopt, ought to have a decrease in current period savings, because their expectation of higher future incomes from the new investment opportunities would lead them to increase current consumption. By contrast, households that experience constraints in borrowing and have an opportunity to adopt would be more likely to increase their savings to self-finance the required investments, especially if adoption depends on a lumpy investment. Bhalla's empirical results support these predictions, although his distinctions between households that are constrained and those that are not (based on income level), and between households with good investment opportunities and those without (based on district-level adoption rates of HYVs), seem somewhat indirect.

2.6. Health, nutrition and savings

Health and nutrition expenditures share some attributes of educational ones; they affect welfare beyond the period when they are made. To a much greater extent than in the case of education, however, these expenditures also affect current well-being, and it would be impossible to devise a convincing allocation of these expenditures between current and future consumption. For instance, at low nutritional levels, food consumption has joint effects on current and future well-being and productivity. Despite these accounting difficulties, it seems both important and possible to introduce some notions about health and nutrition into an analysis of saving behavior at low incomes.

One way these factors enter is through their effects on life expectancy, as mentioned in Section 2.1. Modeling the effects of these expenditures as an exogenous (to the individual) change in life expectancy, T, is most suitable if these expenditures are beyond the control of individuals, for instance medical research or public health measures. In other cases, individuals may be able to take decisions that affect their life expectancies and physical conditions, and these situations need to be modeled explicitly.[16]

---

[16] See Gersovitz (1983) for a discussion of the effects on savings of public health improvements when individuals make related private health expenditures, and when they cannot.

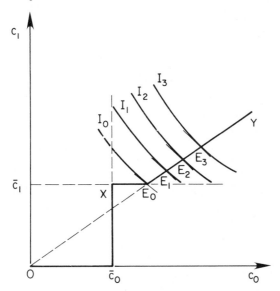

Figure 10.1(a). The income expansion path $O\bar{c}_0 X E_0 Y$ with survival constraints, after Zellner (1960). The I_j are (homothetic) indifference curves tangent to the (parallel) budget constraints at the points E_j.

One approach is to specify a subsistence consumption level, $\bar{c}$, that the individual must obtain. In the model of Section 2.1, this additional constraint can be represented by the requirement that $c_0 \geq \bar{c}_0$ and $c_1 \geq \bar{c}_1$. Following the analysis by Zellner (1960), the situation when $y_1 = 0$ and $\bar{c}_0 = \bar{c}_1 = \bar{c}$ is illustrated in Figures 10.1(a) and 10.1(b). Because an individual cannot survive to the second period with $c_0 < \bar{c}_0$, the individual will consume all first-period income up to $\bar{c}_0$ (along $O\bar{c}_0$). If the next priority is survival through the second period, then all first-period income above $\bar{c}_0$ will be saved until $(1 + r)(y_0 - \bar{c}_0) = \bar{c}_1$ (along $\bar{c}_0 X$). Beyond this point, the consumer will increase either c_0 or c_1 with either $c_1 = \bar{c}_1$ or $c_0 = \bar{c}_0$ until the first-order condition (3) prevails as before (along $X E_0$); the survival constraints are then infra-marginal under this specification (beyond E_0 along $E_0 Y$).[17] Because the individual must worry about second-period, as well as first-period, subsistence, the saving function [Figure 10.1(b)] is not well approximated by a linear one (familiar from elementary textbooks), with a negative intercept and a positive slope [Figure 10.1(c)]. On the other hand, once an individual finally has an income sufficiently high that eq. (3) holds, these

---

[17]With OE_0 above OX, the marginal propensity to save would be zero, one, one because XE_0 would be vertical, and then that given by eq. (3).

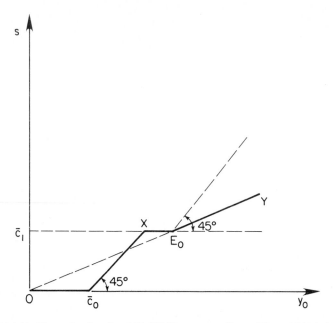

Figure 10.1(b). The saving function ($O\bar{c}_0 XE_0 Y$) corresponding to Figure 10.1(a), for $r = 0$.

thresholds play no role in saving decisions. (For instance, OE_0Y is a straight line through the origin if the indifference curves are homothetic.)

Nutritional and health factors may affects saving behavior in less extreme ways than indicated by an either–or survival threshold. In Gersovitz (1983), I investigated two formulations:

(1) The probability of survival, π, may depend on an individual's standard of living at very low incomes.[18] In this case the individual maximizes

$$V = U[c_0] + \pi[c_0]\delta U[c_1],\tag{2b}$$

with $\pi' \geq 0$ and $\pi'' < 0$, to yield the modified first-order condition:

$$U'[c_0] + \delta\pi'[c_0]U[c_1] - (1+r)\pi\delta U'[c_1] = 0.\tag{3b}$$

---

[18]An alternative formulation is that $\pi = \pi[Y]$, where Y is discounted lifetime resources. For instance, individuals with the same Y may live in the same neighborhoods and π may depend on public health externalities associated with the Y of all individuals in the community rather than with a single individual's own consumption. In this case, the term with π' disappears from the individual's first-order condition (3b), although the calculation of the comparative statics of a change in Y would require the differentiation of π.

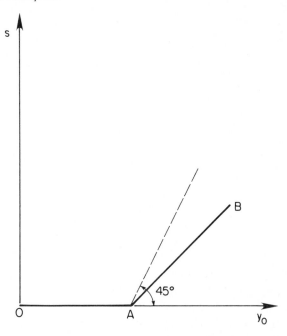

Figure 10.1(c). A Keynesian saving function OAB.

(2) A worker's productivity may depend on his own consumption. If the individual works only in the first period at wage w and has non-wage income of α, the budget constraint is

$$c_0 + s = y_0 = wh[c_0] + \alpha. \tag{1c}$$

The maximization of eq. (2) subject to (1c), for $T = 2$, yields the modified first-order condition:

$$U'[c_0] + (1 + r)\delta U'[c_1](wh' - 1) = 0. \tag{3c}$$

In both models, c_0 affects current welfare as well as future welfare via π or h, so that there is no way to assign c_0 expenditure between consumption and investment in an accounting sense; nonetheless the consequences for behavior can be examined. These formulations also suggest a distinction in their effects on saving between goods that do affect survival and efficiency-in-work and those that do not, thereby opening up a role for relative prices as a determinant of saving behavior.[19]

2.7. Bequests and savings

To this point I have focused on an individual who decides about saving with regard only to the consequences for his own well-being. The considerations that motivate this saver may loosely be termed: (1) *life cycle*, when they stem from the relationship between age and income, especially after retirement; (2) *precautionary*, if saving is to provide a reserve against bad outcomes of uncertain variables; and (3) *investment*, if the saver is motivated by rates of return and investment opportunities. That individuals leave bequests suggests another reason for their saving, one that raises the question of the relationships among individuals as a determinant of saving behavior. Indeed, much of the current debate about saving behavior in the developed countries is centered on the relative importance of life-cycle versus bequest motives.[20]

Individuals may leave estates for at least three reasons:[21]

(1) *Altruism*. They may save to provide their descendants with an inheritance. Alternative formulations of this notion are that the bequestor cares about (a) the size of the bequest or (b) the welfare (utility) of the heirs.

(2) *Control*. The bequestor may leave an estate to compensate the heirs for services or goods provided during his lifetime. By retaining assets until his death, the bequestor ensures his control over the actions of his heirs; for elaboration of this hypothesis and evidence, see Bernheim et al. (1985).

(3) *Accident*. When individuals do not know when they will die, they must provide for consumption if they survive but that they may not live to undertake. If life-contingent annuities are available, then individuals can buy the right to an income stream that continues as long as they live, at a level relative to the purchase price that is conditional on the probability distribution of life expectancy. In the two-period case, the budget constraint is

$$(1 + r)(y_0 - c_0) = p(c_1 - y_1),$$ (1d)

where $p = \pi$, the probability of survival, if the annuity is actuarially fair. These

[19] Lluch et al. (1977) discuss price effects on saving but use a restrictive functional form for consumer preferences.
[20] See Tobin (1967), Farrell (1970), Tobin and Dolde (1971), White (1978), Mirer (1979), Kotlikoff and Summers (1981), Soderstrom (1982), Blinder (1984), Modigliani (1984), Kotlikoff and Summers (1985) and Ando and Kennickell (1986). See Shorrocks (1975), King and Dicks-Mireaux (1982), Hurd (1987) and the references therein on the important question of whether wealth declines with age after retirement as is suggested by the simplest formulations of the life-cycle model.
[21] Data on bequests are not easily come by, see Menchik and David (1983).

contracts are not, however, generally entered into. In their absence, individuals will tend to maintain a reserve of wealth to finance possible future consumption. If they die before they exhaust this reserve, as must occur frequently if individuals plan for a negligible probability of living sufficiently long that their ability to consume is exhausted, they may be said to leave an unintended bequest [see Davies (1981)]. A similar pattern may arise if individuals plan for the possibility that they become ill toward the end of their lives in ways that can be mitigated by (or require) expensive health care.

Which motivation for bequests predominates is important. For instance, an estate tax will have no impact on behavior if bequests are accidental, but may be consequential in either of the other cases. Barro (1974) argues that operative intergenerational transfers motivated by altruism have important implications for government decisions on national debt versus taxes, and for the relation between social security and private savings; however, see Buiter (1979).

I know of no empirical studies of bequest behavior in developing countries. The prevalence of the family farm leads to the expectation that bequests may be an important phenomenon relative to the incomes of the bequestors and their heirs. Rosenzweig and Wolpin (1985) emphasize the transfer across generations of experience that is specific to particular landholdings as an important impediment to sales of land to outsiders, which would lead to a loss of this knowledge. Such a view is certainly not inconsistent with a control approach to the determination of bequests, as the older generation keeps the land within the family where its value is greatest in exchange for support in old age.

2.8. The family and savings

Family ties among individuals can have important implications for saving behavior, affecting preferences between consumption and saving or substituting for functions that markets might otherwise perform. The presumption is that family networks are much more pervasive in developing than in developed countries [Greenhalgh (1982, p. 86)]. Higher rates of population growth mean more relatives, and the economic relations among kin are thought to be more intensive and extensive. There are at least three approaches to conceptualizing the role of the family in the saving process: (1) as a veil concealing purely individualistic behavior; (2) as a substitute for absent or imperfect markets; or (3) as the fundamental and indecomposable decision unit.

Individuals may live in family units simply because they like each others' company, and may act entirely individualistically in their saving behavior, exactly as in the model of Section 2.1. As noted above, this view is not inconsistent with bequests, if bequests compensate younger family members for service to older ones. Under this first interpretation, the problem is an empirical one because data on income and especially consumption are reported on a household rather than on an individual basis, so one does not really know what choices individuals are making. This viewpoint suggests that in analyzing household saving behavior it is important to take into account the age composition of the household, because household savings is the aggregate of saving by the young and dissaving by the old. The aggregation of savings over individuals of different ages is discussed in more detail in Section 3, with respect to the national level of savings, but the issue is essentially the same. The country is just one big family, in this interpretation, and correspondingly, the family is just a small country.

A second interpretation of the family's role in the saving process is that it is an institution that helps to make behavior approximate the individualistic model. That is, in the absence of the family, various market imperfections would distort decision-making from the model of Section 2.1. One notable example of this is the role of the family in insuring risks when insurance markets are absent, in effect transforming the models of 2.3 back to that of 2.1. Another example might be the family's role in alleviating borrowing constraints if family members feel that repayment of intra-family loans is incumbent upon them when they would not otherwise repay outsiders. Alternatively, family members may have better knowledge about the characteristics of relatives and what they are doing with borrowed funds, negating problems of adverse selection and moral hazard. And, they may have more sanctions with which to enforce debt service. Note that in these cases the presumption is that the impact of the family is to increase the welfare of its members, although it may raise or lower the volume of savings. We need empirical information on these matters, but none exists that is based on household survey data about how individuals behave.

Third, the family can affect savings by providing for (part or all of) the consumption of its older members directly from the earnings of the economically active ones, without a transfer of assets. The incentive to accumulate assets while young is therefore attenuated or possibly removed entirely. This behavior presupposes a true altruism on the part of the young, i.e. a sense of obligation to care for the aged without recompense from them. It may be possible to formulate theories of preferences that are interdependent among family members, or that involve bargaining among family members, but there is as yet no work that has produced estimable models or econometric results about saving behavior based on these concepts.

If children support their elderly parents, individuals may adjust not only their savings but also their family size, the saving-through-children hypothesis [Neher (1971), Willis (1980) and Nerlove et al. (1985)]. These models have empirical, as well as theoretical and policy implications. For instance, if parents choose family size with a view to being supported in their old age, then family structure and savings are jointly determined. In this case, it would be inappropriate in econometric analysis to explain savings by demographic variables. An exception is the case of twins, an exogenous shock to the family's position that may prove fruitful in understanding saving, as it has in other areas of household behavior [Rosenzweig and Wolpin (1980)].

In all these cases it is important that data on savings and its determinants are collected so as to encompass the group of people whose saving behavior is interdependent. The relevant group may not be the household, the group of related or unrelated persons who live together and jointly supply basic living needs, or the narrower family household that excludes individuals who are not related by blood, marriage or adoption. For instance, Greenhalgh (1982) discusses the economic role of the Taiwanese *chia*, an economic family whose member need not be co-resident. She asserts (p. 73):

> Consumption in the chia is focused around maintenance of a common budget. In principle all income received by chia members goes directly into the chia coffer, whence it is redistributed by the "redistributor" in accordance with chia requirements for consumption, savings, and investment in human and physical capital. In practice dispersed workers usually pay for their own living expenses, and they may remit all, a portion, or none of their earnings back to the primary household.

In principle, there is no problem if the saving unit differs from the household. Analysis can be focused at the former level, although the theory needs to be developed beyond that of Sections 2.1–2.7. In practice, the household is the unit of data collection for most surveys that provide information on saving. There will usually be no way to link households that share in saving decisions, most of which will have been omitted by the survey rather than census design of the data collection.

3. Savings at the national level

The sum of savings of all individuals and households is the national level of personal savings. If all individuals were identical as regards their saving behavior, then aggregate saving would simply be the product of a single (representative) individual's saving and the size of the population. To the extent, however, that individuals do differ in characteristics that impact on their saving behavior, the distribution of these characteristics in the population is a determinant of national savings. In fact, there is at least one characteristic that is both a potential important influence on individual saving behavior *and* that certainly varies among individuals, namely age. Another important determinant of saving over which aggregation may be undertaken is the level of lifetime resources, Y, available to individuals. Finally, the savings of individuals can be added to that of the corporate sector and the government.

3.1. Aggregation over cohorts

As individuals age, their saving behavior may change, as suggested by the life-cycle model (Section 2.1). In this model, active workers save for retirement, while the retired dissave to pay for consumption. The aggregate amount of saving, S, therefore, depends on the relative number of active, n_0, and retired, n_1, people in the population, which, in turn, depends on the population growth rate:

$$S = \sum_{i=0}^{1} n_i (y_i - c_i). \tag{5}$$

If individuals do not leave bequests, then they consume all the resources available to them over their life cycle. As a consequence, if the population is not growing so that there are equal numbers of individuals at each age, aggregate saving is zero; the amount of saving done by workers is exactly offset by the dissaving done by the retired.[22] In the two-period model, an increase in the population growth rate caused by an increase in age-specific fertility rates that have persisted for some time increases the number of active workers (savers) relative to the number of the retired (who are dissaving), and therefore increases the total amount of saving.

The two-period model ignores the period of childhood dependency. Like the aged, the young consume more than they earn, if they earn anything at all. On the assumption that what each age group consumes and earns is independent of the population growth rate, there are two (equivalent) ways to account for the period of childhood dependency in analyzing the relationship between aggregate personal savings and the population growth rate.

(1) The model can be extended to incorporate three age groups (young, active, and retired). An increase in the population growth rate increases the number of active individuals relative to the retired, but decreases their number relative to the young. Because both the young and the retired (the dependent generations) consume more than they earn, the net effect on aggregate saving is theoretically ambiguous.

(2) Alternatively, the two-period structure of the model can be retained. Population growth has the following effects: (a) a change in the relative numbers of active and retired (adult) individuals; and (b) the consumption of active workers inclusive of that of their (more numerous) children rises.[23]

---

[22] In this case, eq. (5) coincides with the budget constraint of eq. (1) holding as an equality.

[23] Arthur and McNicoll (1978) and Lee (1980) provide an elegant analysis of the continuous age case, but the principles are the same.

The second way just mentioned of incorporating the young into the life cycle highlights the fact that the young do not consume independently of the family. This perspective on dependency suggests that saving need not be adjusted in response to additional children in the way that a model with fixed income per earner and consumption per child would predict: (1) With economies of scale in family consumption, children in large families can be provided with the same welfare as children in smaller families with a less than proportionate increase in expenditure. (2) Parents may choose to decrease the consumption and welfare of children or themselves when they choose larger families. (3) Parents or children or both may increase their work time (or effort). On the other hand, the time involved in child care may decrease the labor force participation of women. (4) Parents may increase their saving in advance of births. Finally, some of the relationships between lifetime income and savings discussed in Section 3.2 may also come into play if changes in the population growth rate alter income per capita via changes in the economy-wide availability of capital and land relative to labor. Hammer (1986) discusses the evidence on these questions addressed by such authors as Epenshade (1975), Kelley (1976, 1980), Bilsborrow (1979a) and Smith and Ward (1980). None of these studies, however, incorporates a fully adequate treatment of the income variable along transitory–permanent, expected–unexpected lines, and some ignore this important issue entirely. Furthermore, there is neglect of the possibility that choices about children and savings are joint decisions that should respond to a set of common *exogenous* determinants.

The effects of changes in mortality on savings can be quite different from the corresponding effects of changes in fertility. In the short run, a drop in adult mortality increases population growth and changes the dependency rate in a direction dependent on the nature of the shift in age-specific mortality schedules. In the long run, the population growth rate is unaffected, but the dependency rate is. Furthermore, there may be changes in individual age-specific saving rates as incentives to save for old age change. Thus, the source of changes in population growth rates as well as how long they have been ongoing affects the aggregate saving rate.

The life-cycle model can also account for the effect of technological change that increases the lifetime incomes of each successive cohort. As with population growth, technological change has an ambiguous effect on savings. On the one hand, each young worker, expecting to be richer during his own lifetime than his parents, wishes to provide for retirement consumption that is higher than what the currently retired are each consuming. Aggregate savings will tend to rise with increased technological change for this reason even if population is not growing. For example, if individuals earn the same wage in each period of their lives but each successive cohort's wage is higher, so that technological change is embodied in labor, this effect is the only one. If technological change is unembodied, however, so that every worker's wage rises in each period, there is another effect. Because a disproportionate amount of a worker's income is received toward the end of his working life, when young he may wish to save less or even to borrow against higher future incomes. In this case, increases in technological change can decrease aggregate savings.

The recognition that aggregate savings is the outcome of the saving behavior of cohorts of different ages that are contemporaneous raises issues of the optimality of aggregate savings, of the role for intergenerational transfers, and of the interaction between saving decisions and fertility decisions. The overlapping generations models of Samuelson (1958) and Diamond (1965) provide a framework for analyzing savings and intergenerational transfers. Without intergenerational transfers, saving to provide for retirement through the accumulation of capital can lead to steady-state welfare that is lower than it need be [Diamond (1965)]. Either too much or too little capital may be accumulated relative to the Golden Rule steady state in which the lifetime utility of individuals is at a maximum and the rate of return on capital equals the rate of population growth.

Consider two economies with the same preferences, technologies and rates of population growth. Both are in the steady state. Individuals follow a two-period life cycle, as in Section 2.1. One economy has no intergenerational transfers, and there is too much saving relative to the Golden Rule. Another has intergenerational transfers, from the young to the old. If these transfers are of the right magnitude, the second economy can be in the Golden Rule steady state. Indeed, the adoption by the first economy of an altruistic ethic mandating the right level of transfers can make all generations better off; in particular the generation gains that is old when the change is made.

The situation is quite different when the economy is saving too little relative to the Golden Rule level of saving. Developing countries are likely to be in this situation because their rates of return to capital probably exceed their population growth rates. In this case, the appropriate alteration necessary to attain the Golden Rule steady state is to an ethic embodying reduced transfers from the young to the old, or possibly requiring transfers from the old to the young, to induce more savings. Those individuals who are old when such a change is first introduced will be net losers; they cannot be compensated by more consumption in their youth, which is past. The policy of transition is consequently not a Pareto improvement. At levels of capital below the Golden Rule level, therefore, unambiguous welfare comparisons can only be made between economies already in the steady state that are otherwise identical except for the level of intergenerational transfers. In such comparisons across steady states, the economy with lower transfers from the young to the old would have a capital–labor ratio closer to that of the Golden Rule, and a higher present value of lifetime utility for each of its members.

As in the case of capital accumulation, individuals who depend only on their children for old-age support may over or under invest, i.e. have too few or too many children [Willis (1980)]. Giving these individuals the opportunity to save in the form of other assets will likely lower their fertility. Nerlove et al. (1985) argue, however, that income effects or the existence of individuals who wish to borrow to have more children but could not prior to the improvement in financial markets may work in the opposite direction.

If individuals can save through physical capital accumulation as well as children, the question of the optimal rate of population growth arises. It has not yet been fully resolved; see Samuelson (1975, 1976) and Deardorff (1976) for some of the problems and references to earlier literature. Eckstein and Wolpin (1985) suggest one solution when the utility of parents has the number of their children as an argument. Furthermore, these models of endogenous population do not incorporate the possibility of altruistically motivated bequests, another fundamental determinant of whether the saving decisions of individuals are socially optimal [Barro (1974), Drazen (1978), Buiter (1979), Carmichael (1982), Burbidge (1983, 1984), and Buiter and Carmichael (1984)]. Finally, and perhaps most importantly, the bulk of the results in these papers are derived by comparing different economies that are in the steady state; for an exception, see Laitner (1984). The concern about many of the questions from a developmental perspective, however, is motivated by situations of transition, say as the result of the actual diffusion of the ability to save through financial assets or because mortality and fertility rates are changing.

3.2. Income distribution and aggregate savings

Individuals differ in their lifetime access to resources (income plus transfers received, including inheritances). If differences in lifetime resources affect individuals' saving behavior, then the distribution of income becomes a determinant of the fraction of aggregate income that is saved. For instance, in an economy in which individuals behave as in Section 2.1 with $s_0 = y_0 - c_0 > 0$, and in which the number of savers with a given level of lifetime resources exceeds the number of dissavers (in the second period of their lives) with the same lifetime resources, saving aggregated over all individuals with the same lifetime resources is positive. If the marginal propensity to save, m, in the first period rises with lifetime resources ($m' > 0$), then policies that equalize the distribution of lifetime incomes will decrease the aggregate level of savings [using the method of Rothschild and Stiglitz (1971)]. Or, if there is an income threshold below which savings are a low fraction of income (or zero) and above which they are a higher fraction, then transfers of income from those below the threshold to those above increase aggregate savings. While models based on thresholds and those based on a smoother specification of behavior often incorporate similar notions about factors that motivate saving, there can be important qualitative differences in their implications; I give an example below.

A belief that a decrease in the dispersion of incomes lowers aggregate saving is one potentially important underpinning for purported trade-offs between growth and equity.[24] The hypothesis deserves further scrutiny, and is by no means established, either theoretically or empirically. Indeed, the opposite view that the rich indulge in (conspicuous) consumption to the neglect of saving also has its adherents. Of course, even if the poor do save relatively less of their incomes, it may not reflect any market failure, and so this fact in itself need not suggest the desirability of a policy intervention.[25]

The hypothesis that the marginal propensity to save rises with the level of lifetime resources can be addressed using the various theoretical models of saving presented in Section 2. To simplify the exposition, I assume that all income is received in the first period. In the simple model of Section 2.1, the lifetime utility of consumption, V, is additive in the utility of consumption in each period, the U's. In this case, the marginal propensity to save is independent of lifetime resources if *either*: (1) one plus the interest rate $(1 + r)$ is equal to the inverse of the discount rate $(1/\delta)$ *and* the form of the utility of consumption in each period, U, is age invariant, so that $c_0 = c_1$ [from eq. (3) of Section 2.1], *or* (2) the utility function is age invariant *and* (a) belongs to the generalized Bergson family (of which constant relative risk aversion functions are special cases), or (b) belongs to the family of constant absolute risk aversion utility functions [Pollak (1971, p. 405)].[26] If V is not additive, the condition for a constant marginal propensity to consume out of lifetime resources is the general one that $V(c_0, \ldots, c_T)$ have linear Engel curves.

Because these are rather special conditions, there is no theoretical presumption that the marginal propensity to consume is constant. A suitable parameterization of preferences, the $U(\cdot)$, is all that is necessary to show that saving behavior need not be characterized by a constant marginal propensity to save. Obviously, such a parameterization could make utility in any period depend on age, but clearly need not.

---

[24] For instance, Kuznets (1962, pp. 7–8) appears to adhere unequivocally to the view that reductions in inequality of incomes decrease savings.

[25] The shape of the relation between income and saving also plays an important role in the big-push or low-level-equilibrium-trap theories of development; see Nelson (1956).

[26] To calculate the marginal propensity to save, m, simply totally differentiate the equilibrium equations of the saver, say eqs. (1) and (3), with respect to y_0. Then totally differentiate the expression for m with respect to y_0 to get m', substituting from the equations of the saver's equilibrium to simplify. Because the resultant expressions for m' for the several variant models that I present are quite complicated and relatively uninformative, I have not reproduced them.

On the other hand, there is no particular reason suggested by the simple model to expect that the marginal propensity rises rather than falls with lifetime resources. Intuitively, there needs to be a reason why a poor man would wish to split his (meagre) lifetime resources between current and future consumption in a way that is proportionately different from what a rich man chooses. A belief that the marginal propensity to save rises with lifetime income suggests that the poor prefer that consumption in their youth more closely approximate that of the rich than does their consumption in their old age. Is this a theoretical or psychological law? To see if there is a theoretical presumption about how the marginal propensity might vary with lifetime resources, I turn to the models of Sections 2.3 through 2.8.

3.2.1. Bequests

Blinder (1976) presents a model in which individuals choose consumption and bequests to maximize the present discounted value of their utility, inclusive of the utility, ϕ, of bequests, B:

$$V = \sum_{i=0}^{T-1} \delta^i U[c_i] + \phi[B], \tag{2e}$$

where $U = c_i^\alpha$ and $\phi = B^\beta$ subject to

$$\sum_{i=0}^{T-1} \left[\frac{c_i}{(1+r)^i} \right] + \frac{B}{(1+r)^T} \le Y. \tag{1e}$$

If $\alpha < \beta$, so that bequests are a luxury, aggregate savings increase when income is transferred from the poor to the rich.

3.2.2. Education

Blinder (1976) also reviews the argument that individuals will not allocate income to uses conventionally defined as savings to provide for bequests until the (marginal) return to educating their children (or other prospective heirs) is driven down to the return on savings. Lump-sum redistribution of income from individuals below this threshold to those above it would then increase aggregate savings, as conventionally defined.[27]

---

[27]On the other hand, individuals may finance their own education. The more able, having higher marginal returns to education and higher lifetime incomes, would then be low savers, as conventionally measured, in their youth when they are being educated. If the age distribution were such that these cohorts were important in aggregate savings, transfers from the lifetime rich to the lifetime poor might increase aggregate savings. See also the discussion in Section 2.4.

3.2.3. Investment opportunities

Lewis (1954) argues that saving is predominantly undertaken from profits by entrepreneurs in a modern, industrial sector. The national capital market is segmented, in that investment is limited to individuals who are directly involved in organizing production in this sector. These rich entrepreneurs save a high (and constant) fraction of their incomes while other groups save a lower fraction. Redistribution from low saving groups to entrepreneurs via a change in the distribution of aggregate income between profits and other categories would then increase aggregate savings.

3.2.4. Physiological influences

The health and nutrition models of Section 2.6 also provide for possible structural explanations for a relationship between lifetime resources and the marginal propensity to save. Because current consumption is more likely to influence survival and efficiency-at-work at low levels of consumption, these factors suggest that the poor will be more concerned than the rich to consume in the present. Despite this promise, I have been unable to obtain readily interpretable expressions for m' in these models. By contrast, in threshold models such as that embodied in Figure 10.1(b) there are quite unambiguous predictions about the effects of redistribution among individuals in the different zones $O\bar{c}_0$, $\bar{c}_0 X$, XE_0 and $E_0 Y$. On the other hand, there can be few economies in which individuals are typically in the first two zones. The smoother models of eqs. (3b), (3c) and footnote 18 therefore seem inherently more attractive, although less tractable, descriptions of the circumstances of the poor.

3.2.5. Uncertainty

The presence of uncertainties of the types discussed in Section 2.3 can also affect the relation between the marginal propensity to save and lifetime resources. To the best of my knowledge, no one has derived and interpreted general results on the relation between lifetime resources and the marginal propensity to save in the presence of these different types of uncertainty.

3.2.6. Borrowing constraints

Following the discussion of Section 2.4, transfers of income between constrained and unconstrained individuals may increase or decrease savings because the constrained may be low or high savers, and the constrained may be either relatively rich or poor.

At the micro level, a number of authors find that consumption is not proportional to their measures of permanent income. Musgrove (1979) estimates a log-linear relation between consumption, c, and permanent income, y^P, $c = \beta(y^P)^\alpha$ and concludes that the elasticity, α, is less than one, so that the marginal propensity to consume out of permanent income falls with increases in permanent income. Bhalla (1980) is the only author to have estimated a relation between savings and permanent income that provides for a marginal propensity to save from permanent income that can reach an asymptote (of less than one). He finds that the marginal propensity does rise with permanent income, although the structure of his model does not suggest any particular source for the nonlinearity [among explanations (1) to (6) or any others]. In this sense the approach of these authors is inherently somewhat ad hoc because it does not explicitly model the factors in an individual's dynamic optimization problem that lead to a non-linear relation between lifetime resources and savings.

By contrast, Wolpin (1982) shows that using a measure of long-run weather conditions as an instrument produces an estimate of the permanent income elasticity of consumption in a log-linear model that is much higher than those produced with instruments used in earlier studies. In some cases his estimates are statistically indistinguishable from one. Wolpin argues that his choice of an instrument is likely to be closer to exogenous than those used by previous researchers, and that for this reason it is both more appropriate, and more likely in theory to produce the results that he obtains.

It is also important to recall the general issue of the potential for biases in the measurement of saving that may be related to the level of permanent income (Section 2.2). As well, the NCAER data used by Bhalla and Wolpin have particular weaknesses; the measurement of consumption expenditures was peripheral to the design of the survey and the calculated change in assets omit gold, jewelry and currency, as well as revaluations [NCAER (1975, ch 6)]. It may be that the data used so far in the analysis of savings cannot disentangle hypotheses about behavioral non-linearities in savings from problems in measuring the variables.

3.3. Corporate savings

The difference between private savings and personal savings is retained earnings, the savings of the corporate sector. The corporation is termed a veil if individuals and households consider earnings that are retained to be part of their current incomes in the same way as income that corporations distribute to them via dividends. If this is so, individuals will choose their savings based on income inclusive of corporate retained earnings. Because retained earnings are a form of savings, individuals will act to choose their savings recognizing this component.

Other things equal, if corporations increase their retained earnings, individuals will decrease their own savings to maintain a constant relationship between total (private) savings and their incomes (inclusive of retained earnings). In this case the discussion of Section 2.1 can be viewed as determining private rather than personal savings, based on this comprehensive definition of income.

The view that the corporation is a veil is not consistent with all the models presented in Section 2. For instance, an individual may own part of a corporation that is not widely traded and therefore cannot be sold easily. If this person is constrained in his borrowing, he may find that a decision by the corporation to retain earnings forces him to decrease his consumption if he is saving nothing or if he is saving to meet a future expenditure target, as in Section 2.4.

These issues have so far not received attention in the literature on savings and development. Contributions by David and Scadding (1974), Feldstein (1973), Feldstein and Fane (1973) and Bhatia (1979) have produced conflicting results on whether savers in the developed countries view the corporation as a veil.

3.4. The role of government

Government affects the level of national savings in two ways. First, it chooses the level of one of the three components of national savings, government savings, by raising income for itself through taxation and spending it on government consumption. Second, government indirectly affects the other two components through its influence on the incentives to save faced by households and corporations.

While the government can choose the level of its own savings directly, a change in this variable need not imply a one-for-one change in national savings. The other sectors may respond in such a way as to offset the goverment's actions, at least to some extent. In the extreme, such as in Barro (1974), a government issue of bonds to finance its dissaving results in an equal increase in private saving, because the private sector saves in anticipation of a future increase in taxes to service the bonds. This view presupposes, among other things, that government consumption is a perfect substitute for private consumption. The assumption of close substitutibility may be a reasonable approximation in some cases, such as the provision of retirement pensions through pay-as-you-go financing, which at least some developing countries have introduced. On the other hand, when governments shift funds from consumption to particular types of investment, such as infrastructure, that the private sector is unlikely to undertake, the return to, and volume of, private savings may increase.

Governments also affect private savings without necessarily altering the volume of government savings. Administrative regulation of credit markets affects the rates of return that savers earn in developing countries. Choices between the taxation of income (including income from past savings) and taxation of consumption (via indirect taxes) also have implications for the after-tax rate of return that savers earn.[28] Governments may provide insurance programs that reduce uncertainties when the private sector would not otherwise do so, say because there are problems of adverse selection. It may be able to do so by making membership in such programs universal. Finally, governments provide the legal and administrative framework that enforces contracts and proscribes various types of activities, such as insider trading in stock markets. Presumably, financial markets, more than others, need government involvement of this type if they are to emerge and to function efficiently.

Other government activities that are not directly related to saving behavior of individuals may be at least as important as policies that are conventionally targeted at savings. Examples are policies that affect population, health, nutrition and education, as suggested by the models of Sections 2 and 3.

3.5. Evidence at the aggregate level

A comparison of the proportion of national income that is devoted to saving in different countries reveals a striking dispersion. For instance, Modigliani (1970) analyzes the ratio of private saving to private income, averaged over periods of mostly seven to nine years, for each of 36 countries. The mean of this (averaged) ratio over all countries is 11.2 percent, but ranges from −2.1 to 21.0 percent. There is thus a lot to be explained, and the potential for learning much about the determinants of saving behavior. On the other hand, there are considerable obstacles to arriving at a convincing analysis of these data. First, there are marked problems of measurement that confound the way the data are constructed with the behavioral determinants of saving, and that might contribute significantly to the apparent cross-country differences in this variable. Second, problems of exogeneity and simultaneity are at their most extreme when the unit of analysis is the country. I have already raised variants of these concerns in connection with the analysis of micro data from household surveys, and some of the specific issues are the same, but there are new ones as well.

In most developing countries, savings at the national level are calculated via the identity aggregate savings equals aggregate investment, $S = I$, where S is defined inclusive of foreign savings. In the commonly used commodity flow

[28] King (1980), Kotlikoff (1984) and Sandmo (1985) discuss aspects of taxation and savings. As for the choice between income and expenditure taxes, it is important to allow for a labor–leisure tradeoff as well as a present-versus-future-consumption tradeoff. If revenue is to be constant, exemption of interest income (the expenditure tax) must be compensated by greater taxation of labor income, so that one distortion is removed at the cost of changing another.

approach for estimating I, goods are assigned between investment and consumption based on their supposed end use; saving is then calculated as a by-product.[29]

Investment has two components, inventories and fixed investment, $I = I_i + I_f$. Hooley (1967) gives examples of developing countries where inventories are estimated on the basis of the holdings of a few primary commodities. In countries where manufacturing is expanding relative to primary industry, this method can impart a downward bias to estimates of investment in inventories. This problem is exacerbated by the tendency of manufacturing in developing countries to operate with a high ratio of inventories to fixed capital in comparison to practice in developed countries [Hooley (1967)]. Furthermore, changes in inventories held by households are not included in the definition of inventory investment, and these may be large in the rural sector of developing countries. On the other hand, Rakshit (1982) argues that recent Indian saving rates may be overstated by as much as 3.3 percent by the way the procurement of grain stocks enters the estimates of saving. Because there has been a recent step-up in government acquisition of grain, it (arguably) accounts for a spurious jump in the Indian saving rate.

As for fixed investments, these are often estimated by referring to the imports· of capital goods and making an allowance for construction. Perhaps the bulk of investment in agriculture, which is not included in these categories, may simply be ignored [Hooley (1967, p. 202)]. Furthermore, official exchange rates are often overvalued, making imports artificially cheap; tariffs and exchange controls promote smuggling; and tariffs lead to underdeclaration of the value of imports. Because investment is often import intensive relative to consumption, these factors lead to a relative underestimate of investment and an underestimate of the saving rate. On the other hand, the desire to keep funds overseas may lead importers to overinvoice imports, working against the effects just mentioned. Hooley's (1967, p. 204) evidence on the value of imports recorded by developing countries relative to their value as given in the trade statistics of the exporting countries suggests a net positive relation between the overvaluation of the exchange rate and the degree of understatement of imports, and therefore investment and savings. Mamalakis (1976) argues that extreme trade regimes that make it very difficult to import capital goods induce levels of equipment maintenance that go beyond usual practice, and that should be included in investment. He speaks (1976, p. 326) of a "quasi capital goods sector that uses secondhand capital goods as inputs for the production of new ones" in Chile.

Once an estimate of total savings is obtained from the estimate of investment, national income accountants use various methods to break the total down into its

---

[29] Mamalakis (1976, ch. 13) and Rakshit (1982) discuss the measurement of savings in some detail in the cases of Chile and India, respectively. I refer to their findings only when they seem to be of potential applicability to developing countries as a whole, but their review of seemingly idiosyncratic practice in each of these countries is also an important caution about the potential variation in procedures across countries.

components, foreign savings, government savings, and private savings, the latter decomposable into corporate and personal savings, $S = S_f + S_g + S_c + S_p$. Mamalakis (1976) argues that government savings are overestimated in Chile by the transfer of current expenditures to the capital account. This, in turn, affects the estimate of private saving, which is calculated as a residual. On the other hand, Rakshit (1982) suggests that national income is underestimated, and the saving *ratio* overestimated, by the convention of accounting for government's contribution to value-added by its expenditure on wages and salaries, neglecting any imputation for the services of government capital.

There is finally the problem of inflation accounting in the treatment of the components of saving. In a closed economy, saving at the national level must ultimately take the form of an increase in tangible capital; there are no outside financial assets. In the case of an open economy, or when it is desired to distinguish the components of national saving, say government versus private, the situation is different. There are then outside financial assets; the sum of a sector's financial assets and liabilities need not be zero. In an inflationary context, part of the net interest paid by a sector or the residents of a country is actually amortization of the principal, which is declining in real terms. Thus, foreign saving might be viewed as zero if the real value of foreign debt, rather than its nominal value, is constant and similarly with government savings.[30]

On balance, these factors seem to suggest that savings, and especially private savings which are calculated as a residual, may be understated, possibly to an extent that varies inversely with the level of development.[31] No econometric study attempts to correct its data base for these problems, however. Nor is there much analysis of whether the appropriate dependent variable is personal, private or domestic savings based on questions of substitutability as raised in Sections 3.3 and 3.4. Different authors use different definitions of the dependent variable.[32] Econometric analyses of cross-national data on the saving ratio have focused largely on the effect on the saving ratio of: (1) the growth rate and age structure (as in Section 3.1) and (2) the level of income and the distribution of income (as in Section 3.2).

Leff (1969) and Modigliani (1970) are the primary studies using cross-country aggregate data to provide support for the propositions that:[33]

(1) Aggregate saving is affected by demographic variables, either the population growth rate or the proportion of the population that is economically dependent (the dependency rate). The theory of Section 3.1 is based on the latter

---

[30]See Eisner and Pieper (1984), Eisner (1984), and Buiter (1985) for a discussion of alternative measures of the government deficit.

[31]Kuznets (1960, pp. 24–25) seems to agree with this presumption.

[32]On the appropriate definition of the dependent variable, see Modigliani (1970, pp. 219–221), Bilsborrow (1979b, pp. 189–190), and Leff (1979, pp. 206–208).

[33]Leff (1969) uses the aggregate domestic saving ratio while Modigliani (1970) gives primary attention to the ratio of private saving to private income, with a secondary analysis of the distinction between the private and personal saving ratios.

variable. There is not a one-to-one relationship between the two variables because economies need not be in the steady state, and even when they are, different age-specific mortality rates can imply different dependency rates but the same population growth rates.

(2) The rate of growth of per capita income affects the saving rate.

(3) The level of per capita income does not have an independent effect on the saving rate if the growth of per capita income and/or the dependency variables are also included in the estimated equations. This result is most marked in the Modigliani paper. Leff finds that per capita income is a marginally to moderately significant additional variable, but he uses annual rather than averaged data. Modigliani's results are therefore more indicative of the effect of permanent income on saving rates. This evidence suggests that the non-linear effects discussed in Section 3.2 may not be operative. By contrast, regressions of the saving rate on per capita income as the sole explanatory variable do exhibit a strongly significant relationship between the two, a relationship emphasized by Kuznets (1960, 1961, 1962) based on his tabular examination of national saving rates and per capita incomes.

These conclusions are elaborated and sometimes qualified by the papers of Adams (1971), Gupta (1971, 1975), Leff (1971, 1973, 1979), Goldberger (1973), Singh (1975), Bilsborrow (1979b), and Ram (1982). Ram's study provides the strongest evidence that per capita income has a significant effect on the saving rate, and that the dependency variables are insignificant, although his growth variable is the growth in total rather than per capita income and so implicitly includes demographic influences. Fry and Mason (1982) argue that the effect of population growth on the saving rate may be non-linear, and present a specification to incorporate this effect. On balance, these papers seem to point to some instability in the statistical significance of the dependency rate as an explanatory variable, depending especially on the definition of the sample.

A particular problem with these studies is the potential for simultaneous-equations bias in the estimates, because the rate of population growth, and certainly the rate of growth in per capita income, may depend on, or be jointly determined with, the saving ratio. The problem of bias may easily degenerate into the more serious one of identification, if there are not any convincingly exogenous variables that can be introduced into the analysis.

Modigliani (1970) and Gupta (1975) do use a simultaneous equations estimation technique, but their specification depends crucially on the doubtful assumption that movements of foreign capital are exogenous. Foreign capital inflow can be divided into two components, private flows and aid, but both seem to be potentially endogenous. Donors may provide aid in response to low savings or other economic conditions in the recipient country. Private flows are even less likely to be exogenous. One set of considerations arises from an analogy between the position of an individual and that of a country: an individual chooses to consume, to accumulate some assets, and to issue some liabilities; the accumulation of assets net of liabilities is savings. It is incorrect to explain an individual's net addition to assets by his issuance of liabilities; these decisions are taken jointly. At least part of what happens at the aggregate level probably reflects this type of mechanism, with foreign capital flows analogous to the individual's borrowing or lending. Even if the inflow of foreign private capital is sometimes constrained by country risk [Eaton and Gersovitz (1983)], the constraint itself may depend on the attributes of countries. For these reasons, foreign capital inflow does not seem to be exogenous. Nor can it confidently be postulated as an independent explanatory variable in the saving equation, as has been done by some authors; see Papanek (1972) for a discussion and references.

Della Valle and Oguchi (1976) and Musgrove (1980) investigate the relationship between savings and the distribution of income using cross-country data.[34] Their findings are largely negative; the distribution of income seems to have no statistically significant effect on savings. The exception is when the sample is restricted to higher income countries; there is then some support for the hypothesis that increases in inequality increase savings. Measures of the distribution of income in developing countries are notoriously error ridden [Berry (1985)], and the results of these studies may derive from this problem. Presumably, there is some improvement in the accuracy of statistics in the richer countries, most particularly for Della Valle and Oguchi's sample of OECD countries, and this may explain the latter results.

A problem in interpreting regression results of the type presented by these authors is that they refer to changes in the distribution of income that arise for any reason [Blinder (1975)]. For instance, an increase in the proportion who are young as a result of increased population growth may increase or decrease measures of the distribution of income such as the Gini coefficient, as well as the saving rate (as indicated in Section 3.1). Such changes in the distribution of income are not, however, equivalent to shifts in lifetime income among otherwise identical individuals, as posited in Section 3.2. In fact, these studies ignore the growth rate and age structure variables so much emphasized by Modigliani and Leff, and an integration of these two types of aggregation (over age groups and income groups) might be valuable.

One set of issues that could be, but has not yet been, explored using cross-country data is the effect of fluctuations in variables such as the terms of trade and climatic conditions on aggregate saving rates.[35] Data from the last two decades, when the terms of trade were particularly volatile, provide the potential

---

[34] Van Doorn (1975) and Musgrove (1980) show how to build up aggregate consumption functions that depend on the distribution of income from the behavior of individual consuming units.

[35] A number of the cross-country studies referred to above define their variable as averages of annual observations over about ten years, so that they are attempts in a rough way to estimate relationships among permanent variables.

for a fruitful analysis. A first step would be to distinguish transitory from permanent changes in these variables, as well as expected from unexpected changes. This information could then be used to understand how saving behavior adjusts to shocks, the ex post realizations of random variables. It would also be useful to examine the behavior of countries in response to differences in the extent of uncertainties that they face by looking at the impact of ex ante measures of variability in random variables. A particular focus could be the behavior of oil-exporting countries.

A further factor that influences the aggregate saving of many developing countries is remittances by short-term emigrant workers. Examples include southern Africa, Turkish workers in Europe, and the substantial flows of manpower to oil-exporting countries after 1973. These episodes have yet to be studied.

4. Conclusions

What do economists know and what should they try to find out about savings in developing countries?

On the theoretical side there is a considerable body of hypotheses, part of which derives from work done to explain savings in the developed countries. Notions deserving special emphasis in the context of developing countries include: family structures; the prominence of agriculture; the self-financing of investment; borrowing constraints; uncertainties; the roles of education, health and nutrition; and non-linearities in the saving function and the relationship between the distribution of income and the aggregate level of savings. One significant gap in the theory is the definition and role of the group of individuals whose saving decisions are interdependent and the associated problem of the motivation behind bequests.

Empirical knowledge about saving seems to lag considerably behind the theory, so that most of the implications of the theories remain untested. Evidence is not yet available on the effects on savings of exogenous factors that influence nutrition, health, life expectancy, education, the availability of other investment opportunities and their returns, family structure, and bequests. One reason is the relatively severe problems of measurement that make it difficult to investigate hypotheses about savings. Very simply put, savings is a difficult variable to measure.

In this context it may be useful to think about hypotheses that are robust in the face of errors in the measurement of savings and those that are fragile. In the former category is the hypothesis that consumption depends on lifetime or permanent, in addition to (or even rather than) current, resources available to the consuming unit. Here, one can point to evidence that suggests the importance of lifetime factors; there is little reason to think that the systematic problems of measurement that I have catalogued would overturn this conclusion. On the other hand, hypotheses about a non-linear behavioral relation between lifetime resources and saving could easily be confounded with errors in measuring saving that are themselves a non-linear function of lifetime resources. For this reason, I believe that we just do not know much about the relation between the distribution of (lifetime) income and the aggregate saving ratio.

Another difficulty in empirical work is that the intertemporal nature of saving means that data on the behavior of individuals over time is required, if the lifetime behavior of individuals is not to be inferred from the behavior of contemporaneous cohorts of different ages. Also, if responses of individuals to uncertainties are to be studied, time series on various variables, such as rainfall, are necessary to estimate the uncertainties from repeated realizations of the random variables; some of these data can be obtained, and suggest one practicable and potentially fruitful area for research. Furthermore, while information on saving behavior is widely available from household surveys, their very household focus means that the surveys are silent on relationships among households embodied in extended families.

All in all, then, it seems that a lot of effort is needed to improve the data base on saving, so that further progress can be made through econometric analysis.

References

Adams, N.A. (1971) 'Dependency rates and savings rates: Comment', *American Economic Review*, 61:472–475.

Allen, F. (1983) 'Credit rationing and payment incentives', *Review of Economic Studies*, 50:639–646.

Altonji, J.G. and Siow, A. (1987) 'Testing the response of consumption to income changes with (noisy) panel data', *Quarterly Journal of Economics*, 102:293–328.

Ando, A. and Kennickell, A.B. (1986) 'How much (or little) life cycle is there in micro data? Cases of U.S. and Japan', mimeo.

Arthur, W.B. and McNicoll, G. (1978) 'Samuelson, population and intergenerational transfers', *International Economic Review*, 19:241–246.

Artle, R. and Varaiya, P. (1978) 'Life cycle consumption and homeownership', *Journal of Economic Theory*, 18:38–58.

Barro, R.J. (1974) 'Are government bonds net wealth?', *Journal of Political Economy*, 82:1095–1117.

Bernheim, B.D., Shleifer, A. and Summers, L.H. (1985) 'The strategic bequest motive', *Journal of Political Economy*, 93:1045–1076.

Berry, A. (1985) 'On trends in the gap between rich and poor in less developed countries: Why we know so little', *Review of Income and Wealth*, 31:337–354.

Betancourt, R.R. (1971) 'The normal income hypothesis in Chile', *Journal of the American Statistical Association*, 66:258–263.

Bhalla, S.S. (1978) 'The role of sources of income and investment opportunities in rural savings', *Journal of Development Economics*, 5:259–281.

Bhalla, S.S. (1979) 'Measurement errors and the permanent income hypothesis: Evidence from rural India', *American Economic Review*, 63:295–307.

Bhalla, S.S. (1980) 'The measurement of permanent income and its application to savings behavior', *Journal of Political Economy*, 88:722–744.

Bhatia, K.B. (1979) 'Corporate taxation, retained earnings, and capital formation', *Journal of Public Economics*, 11:123–134.

Bilsborrow, R.E. (1979a) 'Age distribution and savings rates in less developed countries', *Economic Development and Cultural Change*, 28:23–45.

Bilsborrow, R.E. (1979b) 'Dependency rates and aggregate savings rates revisited: Corrections, further analysis, and recommendations for the future', *Research in Population Economics*, 2:183–204.

Blades, D.W. (1975) *Non-monetary (subsistance) activities in the national accounts of developing countries*. Paris: OECD.

Blinder, A.S. (1975) 'Distribution effects and the aggregate consumption function', *Journal of Political Economy*, 83:447–475.

Blinder, A.S. (1976) 'Intergenerational transfers and life cycle consumption', *American Economic Review*, 66:87–93.

Blinder, A.S. (1984) 'Discussion of Modigliani', mimeo.

Blinder, A.S. and Deaton, A. (1985) 'The time series consumption function revisited', *Brookings Papers on Economic Activity*, 2:465–511.

Browning, M., Deaton, A. and Irish, M. (1985) 'A profitable approach to labor supply and commodity demands over the life-cycle', *Econometrica*, 53:503–543.

Buiter, W.H. (1979) 'Government finance in an overlapping generations model with gifts and bequests', in: G.M. von Furstenberg, ed., *Social security versus private saving*. Cambridge, MA: Ballinger.

Buiter, W.H. (1985) 'A guide to public sector debt and deficits', *Economic Policy*, 1:13–79.

Buiter, W.H. and Carmichael, J. (1984) 'Government debt: Comment', *American Economic Review*, 74:762–765.

Burbidge, J.B. (1983) 'Government debt in an overlapping-generations model with bequests and gifts', *American Economic Review*, 73:222–227.

Burbidge, J.B. (1984) 'Government debt: Reply', *American Economic Review*, 74:766–767.

Carmichael, J. (1982) 'On Barro's theorem of debt neutrality: The irrelevance of net wealth', *American Economic Review*, 72:202–213.

Chandavarkar, A.G. (1977) 'Monetization of developing countries', *International Monetary Fund Staff Papers*, 24:665–721.

Coondoo, D., Mukherjee, R. and Rao, D.S.P. (1979) 'Interoccupation differences in the pattern of monetized and non-monetized consumer expenditure in rural India', *Review of Income and Wealth*, 25:105–124.

David, P.A. and Scadding, J.L. (1974) "Private savings: Ultrarationality, aggregation and 'Denison's law'", *Journal of Political Economy*, 82:225–249.

Davies, J.B. (1981) 'Uncertain lifetime, consumption, and dissaving in retirement', *Journal of Political Economy*, 89:561–577.

Deardorff, A.V. (1976) 'The optimum growth rate for population: Comment', *International Economic Review*, 17:510–515.

Deaton, A.S. (forthcoming) 'Consumers' expenditures', in: J. Eatwell et al., eds., *The new Palgrave*. New York: Stockton.

Della Valle, P.A. and Oguchi, N. (1976) 'Distribution, the aggregate consumption function, and the level of economic development: Some cross-country results', *Journal of Political Economy*, 84:1325–1334.

Diamond, P. (1965) 'National debt in a neoclassical growth model', *American Economic Review*, 55:1126–1150.

van Doorn, J. (1975) 'Aggregate consumption and the distribution of incomes', *European Economic Review*, 6:417–423.

Drazen, A. (1978) 'Government debt, human capital, and bequests in a life-cycle model', *Journal of Political Economy*, 86:505–516.

Duncan, G.J. and Hill, D.H. (1985) 'An investigation of the extent and consequences of measurement error in labor economic survey data', *Journal of Labor Economics*, 3:508–532.

Eaton, J. and Gersovitz, M. (1983) 'Country risk: Economic aspects', in: R.J. Herring, ed., *Managing international risk*. Cambridge: Cambridge University Press.

Eaton, J., Gersovitz, M. and Stiglitz, J.E. (1986) 'The pure theory of country risk', *European Economic Review*, 30:481–513.

Eckstein, Z. and Wolpin, K.I. (1985) 'Endogenous fertility and optimal population size', *Journal of Public Economics*, 27:93–106.

Eisner, R. (1984) 'Which budget deficit? Some issues of measurement and their implications', *American Economic Review*, 74:138–143.

Eisner, R. and Pieper, P.J. (1984) 'A new view of the federal debt and budget deficits', *American Economic Review*, 74:11–29.

Epenshade, T.J. (1975) 'The impact of children on household savings: Age effects versus family size', *Population Studies*, 29:123–125.

Farrell, M.J. (1970) 'The magnitude of "rate-of-growth" effects on aggregate savings', *Economic Journal*, 80:873–894.

Feldstein, M.S. (1973) 'Tax incentives, corporate saving, and capital accumulation in the United States', *Journal of Public Economics*, 2:159–171.

Feldstein, M. and Fane, G. (1973) 'Taxes, corporate dividend policy and personal savings: The British postwar experience', *Review of Economics and Statistics*, 55:399–411.

Flavin, M.A. (1981) 'The adjustment of consumption to changing expectations about future income', *Journal of Political Economy*, 89:974–1009.

Friedman, M. (1957) *A theory of the consumption function.* New York: NBER.

Fry, M.J. and Mason, A. (1982) 'The variable rate-of-growth effect in the life-cycle saving model', *Economic Inquiry*, 20:426–441.

Gersovitz, M. (1983) 'Savings and nutrition at low incomes', *Journal of Political Economy*, 91:841–855.

Giovannini, A. (1985) 'Saving and the real interest rate in LDCs', *Journal of Development Economics*, 18:197–217.

Goldberger, A.S. (1973) 'Dependency rates and savings rates: Further comment', *American Economic Review*, 63:232–233.

Greenhalgh, S. (1982) 'Income units: The ethnographic alternative to standardization', *Population and Development Review*, 8:70–91.

Gupta, K.L. (1971) 'Dependency rates and savings rates: Comment', *American Economic Review*, 61:469–471.

Gupta, K.L. (1975) 'Foreign capital inflows, dependency burden, and saving rates in developing countries: A simultaneous equation model', *Kyklos*, 28:358–374.

Hall, R.E. (1978) 'Stochastic implications of the life cycle-permanent income hypothesis: Theory and evidence', *Journal of Political Economy*, 86:971–987.

Hall, R.E. and Mishkin, F.S. (1982) 'The sensitivity of consumption to transitory income: Estimates from panel data on households', *Econometrica*, 50:461–481.

Hammer, J.S. (1986) 'Population growth and savings in LDCs: A survey article', *World Development*, 14:579–591.

Hansen, L.P. and Singleton, K.J. (1983) 'Stochastic consumption, risk aversion, and the temporal behavior of asset returns', *Journal of Political Economy*, 91:249–265.

Hayashi, F. (1985) 'The effect of liquidity constraints on consumption: A cross-sectional analysis', *Quarterly Journal of Economics*, 100:183–206.

Hayashi, F., Ito, T. and Slemrod, J. (1986) 'Housing finance imperfections and national saving: A comparative simulation of the US and Japan', mimeo.

Heckman, J. (1974) 'Life cycle consumption and labor supply: An explanation of the relationship between income and consumption over the life cycle', *American Economic Review*, 64:188–194.

Heckman, J.J. (1976) 'A life-cycle model of earnings, learning, and consumption', *Journal of Political Economy*, 84:S11–S44.

Hooley, R.W. (1967) 'The measurement of capital formation in underdeveloped countries', *Review of Economics and Statistics*, 49:199–208.

Hurd, M.D. (1987) 'Savings of the elderly and desired bequests', *American Economic Review*, 77:298–312.

Kelley, A.C. (1976) 'Savings, demographic change, and economic development', *Economic Development and Cultural Change*, 24:683–693.

Kelley, A.C. (1980) 'Interactions of economic and demographic household behavior', in: R.A. Easterlin, ed., *Population and economic change in developing countries.* Chicago, IL: University of Chicago.

Kelley, A.C. and Williamson, J.G. (1968) 'Household saving behavior in the developing economies: The Indonesian case', *Economic Development and Cultural Change*, 16:385–403.

King, M.A. (1980) 'Savings and taxation', in: G.A. Hughes and G.M. Heal, eds., *Public policy and the tax system*. London: George Allen & Unwin.

King, M. (1985) 'The economics of saving: A survey of recent contributions', in K. Arrow and S. Hankapohja, eds., *Frontiers of Economics*. Oxford: Basil Blackwell.

King, M.A. and Dicks-Mireaux, L.-D.L. (1982) 'Asset holdings and the life-cycle', *Economic Journal*, 92:247–267.

Kotlikoff, L.J. (1984) 'Taxation and savings: A neoclassical perspective', *Journal of Economic Literature*, 22:1576–1629.

Kotlikoff, L.J. and Spivak, A. (1981) 'The family as an incomplete annuities market', *Journal of Political Economy*, 89:372–391.

Kotlikoff, L.J. and Summers, L.H. (1981) 'The role of intergenerational transfer in aggregate capital accumulation', *Journal of Political Economy*, 89:706–732.

Kotlikoff, L.J. and Summers, L.H. (1985) 'The contribution of intergenerational transfers to total wealth: A reply', mimeo.

Kuznets, S. (1960) 'Quantitative aspects of the economic growth of nations. V. Capital formation proportions: International comparisons for recent years', *Economic Development and Cultural Change*, 8:1–96.

Kuznets, S. (1961) 'Quantitative aspects of the economic growth of nations. VI. Long-term trends in capital formation proportions', *Economic Development and Cultural Change*, 9:1–124.

Kuznets, S. (1962) 'Quantitative aspects of the economic growth of nations. VII. The share and structure of consumption', *Economic Development and Cultural Change*, 10:1–92.

Laitner, J. (1984) 'Transition time paths for overlapping-generations models', *Journal of Economic Dynamics and Control*, 7:111–129.

Lee, R. (1980) 'Age structure, intergenerational transfers and economic growth: An overview', *Revue Economique*, 31:1129–1156.

Leff, N.H. (1969) 'Dependency rates and savings rates', *American Economic Review*, 59:886–896.

Leff, N.H. (1971) 'Dependency rates and savings rates: Reply', *American Economic Review*, 61:476–480.

Leff, N.H. (1973) 'Dependency rates and savings rates: Reply', *American Economic Review*, 63:234.

Leff, N.H. (1979) 'Dependency rates and savings rates: A new look', *Research in Population Economics*, 2:205–214.

Levhari, D. and Mirman, L.J. (1977) 'Savings and consumption with an uncertain horizon', *Journal of Political Economy*, 85:265–281.

Levhari, D. and Srinivasan, T.N. (1969) 'Optimal savings under uncertainty', *Review of Economic Studies*, 36:153–163.

Lewis, W.A. (1954) 'Economic development with unlimited supplies of labour', *The Manchester School*, 22:139–191.

Lluch, C., Powell, A.A. and Williams, R.A. (1977) *Patterns in household demand and saving*. Washington, DC: World Bank.

Mamalakis, M. (1976) *The growth and structure of the Chilean economy: From independence to Allende*. New Haven, CT: Yale University Press.

Mankiw, N.G., Rotemberg, J.T. and Summers, L.H. (1985) 'Intertemporal substitution in macroeconomics', *Quarterly Journal of Economics*, 100:224–251.

McKinnon, R.I. (1973) *Money and capital in economic development*. Washington, DC: Brookings.

Menchik, P.L. and David, M. (1983) 'Income distribution, lifetime savings, and bequests', *American Economic Review*, 73:672–690.

Mikesell, R.F. and Zinser, J.E. (1973) 'The nature of the savings function in developing countries: A survey of the theoretical and empirical literature', *Journal of Economic Literature*, 11:1–26.

Miller, B.L. (1976) 'The effect on optimal consumption of increased uncertainty in labor income in the multiperiod case', *Journal of Economic Theory*, 13:154–167.

Mirer, T.W. (1979) 'The wealth-age relation among the aged', *American Economic Review*, 69:435–443.

Modigliani, F. (1970) 'The life cycle hypothesis of saving and intercountry differences in the saving ratio', in: W.A. Eltis, M.F.G. Scott and J.N. Wolfe, eds., *Induction, growth and trade*. Oxford: Oxford University Press.

Modigliani, F. (1984) 'Measuring the contribution of intergenerational transfers to total wealth: Conceptual issues and empirical findings', mimeo.

Modigliani, F. (1986) 'Life cycle, individual thrift and the wealth of nations', *American Economic Review*, 76:297–313.

Musgrove, P. (1979) 'Permanent household income and consumption in urban South America', *American Economic Review*, 69:355–368.

Musgrove, P. (1980) 'Income distribution and the aggregate consumption function', *Journal of Political Economy*, 88:504–525.

NCAER (National Council of Applied Economic Research) (1975) *Changes in rural income in India*. New Delhi: NCAER.

Neher, P.A. (1971) 'Peasants, procreation, and pensions', *American Economic Review*, 61:380–389.

Nelson, R.R. (1956) 'A theory of the low-level equilibrium trap in underdeveloped economies', *American Economic Review*, 46:894–908.

Nerlove, M., Razin, A. and Sadka, E. (1985) 'The "old age security hypothesis" reconsidered', *Journal of Development Economics*, 18:243–252.

Newbery, D.M.G. and Stiglitz, J.E. (1981) *The theory of commodity price stabilization: A study in the economics of risk*. Oxford: Oxford University Press.

Papanek, G.F. (1972) 'The effect of aid and other resource transfers on savings ànd growth in less developed countries', *Economic Journal*, 82:934–950.

Paxson, C. (1986) 'Portfolio choice with endogenous borrowing constraints', mimeo.

Pollak, R.A. (1971) 'Additive utility functions and linear Engel curves', *Review of Economic Studies*, 38:401–414.

Rakshit, M. (1982) 'Income, saving and capital formation in India: A step towards a solution of the saving-investment puzzle', *Economic and Political Weekly*, 17:561–572.

Ram, R. (1982) 'Dependency rates and aggregate savings: A new international cross-section study', *American Economic Review*, 72:537–544.

Ram, R. and Schultz, T.W. (1979) 'Life span, health, savings, and productivity', *Economic Development and Cultural Change*, 27:399–421.

Ramanathan, R. (1968) 'Estimating the permanent income of a household: An application to Indian data', *Review of Economics and Statistics*, 50:383–388.

Rosenzweig, M.R. and Wolpin, K.I. (1980) 'Testing the quantity–quality fertility model: The use of twins as a natural experiment', *Econometrica*, 48:227–240.

Rosenzweig, M.R. and Wolpin, K.I. (1985) 'Specific experience, household structure, and intergenerational transfers: Farm family land and labor arrangements in developing countries', *Quarterly Journal of Economics*, 100:961–987.

Rothschild, M. and Stiglitz, J.E. (1971) 'Increasing risk II: Its economic consequences', *Journal of Economic Theory*, 3:66–84.

Samuelson, P.A. (1958) 'An exact consumption-loan model of interest with or without the social contrivance of money', *Journal of Political Economy*, 64:467–482.

Samuelson, P.A. (1975) 'The optimum growth rate for population', *International Economic Review*, 16:531–538.

Samuelson, P.A. (1976) 'The optimum growth rate for population: Agreement and evaluations', *International Economic Review*, 17:516–525.

Sandmo, A. (1985) 'The effects of taxation on savings and risk taking', in: A.J. Auerbach and M. Feldstein, eds., *Handbook of public economics*. Amsterdam: North-Holland.

Shaw, E.S. (1973) *Financial deepening in economic development*. New York: Oxford University Press.

Shorrocks, A.F. (1975) 'The age–wealth relationship: A cross-section and cohort analysis', *Review of Economics and Statistics*, 57:155–163.

Singh, S.K. (1975) *Development economics: Some findings*. Lexington: Heath.

Smith, J. and Ward, M. (1980) 'Asset accumulation and family size', *Demography*, 17:243–260.

Snyder, D.W. (1974) 'Econometric studies of household saving behaviour in developing countries: A survey', *Journal of Development Studies*, 10:139–153.

Soderstrom, L. (1982) 'The life cycle hypothesis and aggregate household saving', *American Economic Review*, 72:590–596.

Solow, R.M. (1956) 'A contribution to the theory of economic growth', *Quarterly Journal of Economics*, 70:65–94.

Stiglitz, J.E. and Weiss, A. (1981) 'Credit rationing in markets with imperfect information', *American Economic Review*, 71:393–410.

Tobin, J. (1967) 'Life cycle saving and balanced growth', in: W. Fellner, ed., *Ten economic studies in the tradition of Irving Fisher*. New York: Wiley.

Tobin, J. and Dolde, W. (1971) 'Wealth, liquidity and consumption', in *Consumer spending and monetary policy: The linkages*. Boston: Federal Reserve Bank of Boston.

Visaria, P. (1980) *Poverty and living standards in Asia: An overview of the main results and lessons of selected household surveys*, Living Standards Measurement Study working paper no. 2. Washington, DC: World Bank.

White, B.B. (1978) 'Empirical tests of the life cycle hypothesis', *American Economic Review*, 68:547–560.

Willis, R.J. (1980) 'The old age security hypothesis and population growth', in: T.K. Burch, ed., *Demographic behavior: Interdisciplinary perspectives on decision making*. Boulder, CO: Westview.

Wolpin, K.I. (1982) 'A new test of the permanent income hypothesis: The impact of weather on the income and consumption of farm households in India', *International Economic Review*, 23:583–594.

Zellner, A. (1960) 'Tests of some basic propositions in the theory of consumption', *American Economic Review*, 50:565–573.

Chapter 11

MIGRATION AND URBANIZATION

JEFFREY G. WILLIAMSON*

Harvard University

Contents

1.	The problem	426
2.	The urban transition	427
	2.1. Quantifying the urban transition	427
	2.2. Migrant selectivity bias	430
	2.3. Selectivity bias, the brain drain, and remittances	431
	2.4. City growth, migration, and labor absorption	433
3.	Disequilibrating labor market shocks and equilibrating migrant responses	433
	3.1. Disequilibrium and wage gaps	433
	3.2. Are migrants rational?	435
	3.3. Are there too many city immigrants?	437
4.	What does "overurbanization" mean?	439
	4.1. Push, pull, and the engines of city growth	439
	4.2. The urban bias	441
5.	How do urban labor markets work?	442
	5.1. The evolution of conventional wisdom	442
	5.2. The Todaro model	443
	5.3. Critique: How do urban labor markets really work?	445
	5.4. Some evidence	446
6.	Migration and city growth in general equilibrium: What are the driving forces?	449
	6.1. What drives Third World migration and city growth?	449
	6.2. Modeling migration and city growth	453
	6.3. Understanding the past and projecting the future	455
7.	Where do we go from here?	459
	References	461

*The research underlying this paper has been financed by NSF Grant No. SES-84-08210. The helpful comments of Charles Becker, Jere Behrman, Barry Eichengreen, Peter Lindert, Mark Montgomery, Richard Sabot, Oded Stark, Rick Steckel, Moshe Syrquin, Michael Todaro, and the participants in the Handbook of Development Economics project are greatly appreciated.

Handbook of Development Economics, Volume I, Edited by H. Chenery and T.N. Srinivasan
© *Elsevier Science Publishers B.V., 1988*

1. The problem

What explains the timing and the extent of the transition from a traditional rural to a modern urban society? Why does city growth speed up in early development and slow down in later stages? What role does migration play in the process, and do migrants make rational location decisions? Do urban labor markets serve to absorb urban immigrants quickly? Are rural emigrants driven by "push" conditions in the countryside or by "pull" conditions in the cities? Is the Third World "overurbanized"?

Speculation on these issues has never been in short supply. Friedrich Engels (1845, 1974) thought that Manchester's booming growth in the early nineteenth century – and the urban decay associated with overcrowding – could easily be explained by the rapid development of Britain's manufacturing. Ravenstein (1885, 1889) and Redford (1926, 1968) thought that rural–urban migration, and thus city growth, was conditioned by Malthusian forces, agricultural land scarcity, and enclosure. In short, Engels favored "pull", whereas Ravenstein and Redford favored "push". Meanwhile, Mayhew (1861) documented low-wage ("informal sector") labor in London, viewing these urban poor as a reserve army driven there as an employment of last resort.

Despite a century and a half of debate, social scientists are still uncertain about the quantitative sources of the urban transition, how it can be influenced by policy, and if so whether it should be influenced by policy. While successful industrialization clearly fosters urbanization, what accounts for the "explosive" city growth in the Third World since the 1950s? The two principal hypotheses advanced in the literature are that rapid city growth and urbanization can be explained primarily by (1) unusually rapid rates of population growth pressing on limited farm acreage, pushing landless labor into the cities; and (2) economic forces pulling migrants into the cities. In the contemporary developing world these latter forces include: domestic policies that distort prices to favor cities (e.g. the domestic terms of trade have been twisted to "squeeze" agriculture); cheap energy prior to the first OPEC shock favoring the growth of energy-intensive urban sectors, thus creating urban jobs; the diffusion of technology from the developed world, which favors modern, large-scale urban industries; foreign capital flows into urban infrastructure, housing, power, transportation, and large-scale manufacturing – further augmenting the growth of cities in the Third World; and the liberalization of world trade since the late 1950s, which has stimulated demand for manufacturing exports produced in Third World cities.

Most demographers favor the first hypothesis. Exploding numbers of people must be employed, and a marginal agriculture with quasi-fixed arable land stocks cannot offer sufficient employment for the Malthusian glut created by the demographic transition. Marginal survival by hawking urban services may be the only way a social system can absorb the population glut, and squalid urban living conditions have been an attribute of early stages of industrialization since Engels wrote of Manchester in the 1840s. The demographer, writing in the shadow of Malthus, is likely, therefore, to favor a causal sequence running from a population boom, to labor pushed off the land, to city immigration, and thus to rapid urban growth under squalid living conditions. This view has also had a profound influence on economists' thinking about development. It is central to Lewis's (1954) labor surplus model – a model that also worked well for the classical economists developing their paradigms of growth during the British industrial revolution. It is also central to the Todaro (1969) thesis that rising immigration to the city is associated with high and even rising rates of urban unemployment. On the other hand, most economists now tend to favor the second hypothesis; that is, an emphasis on those economic forces which contribute to urban pull.

The literature on Third World migration and urbanization is enormous and growing. Development analysts have learned much since we began to worry about such issues in the 1950s. A comprehensive review of that literature is beyond the scope of this chapter; nevertheless an assessment of the most important components is possible. Section 2 begins with the demographics of the urban transition. Economists should know these "stylized facts", but, as it turns out, their perception of the facts is often in error. Section 3 examines the labor markets which link city with countryside. The size and persistence of rural–urban wage gaps and their implications for national income allocative losses are explored. This is followed by an assessment of the extent to which migrants actually respond to the gaps. From private rationality we then turn to social optimality including the questions of whether there are "too many" city immigrants in the Third World and the desirability of suppressing migration through government policy. Section 4 dwells on the sources of city growth and the so-called Hoselitz thesis: Is manufacturing an engine of growth in the Third World and, if so, to what extent is that growth fueled by an "urban bias" in government policy? Section 5 raises the question of how urban labor markets work. Here, the main debate since 1969 has been over the Todaro thesis. This section explores the evidence and contrasting policies which have emerged from the debate. Section 6 returns to the central issue raised at the beginning of this chapter: What drives Third World city growth? It turns out that computable general equilibrium models of city growth offer an excellent device for organizing an answer to that question.

2. The urban transition

2.1. Quantifying the urban transition

The sixteen large Third World cities surveyed by Sinclair (1978, p. 15) had growth rates over the quarter century 1950–1975 ranging between 2.4 (Calcutta) and 8.3 (Seoul) percent per annum. The average growth rate was 5.4 percent – a very high rate of growth indeed. Furthermore, by the end of the 1960s, slums and uncontrolled settlements housed a large share of most urban populations, almost 43 percent on average, ranging from a low of 14 percent in Amman to 90 percent in Addis Ababa. Such rapid growth implies rising density, congestion and urban land scarcity. Not surprisingly, rents have risen, living conditions have often deteriorated, and the delivery of public services has been minimal at best. Immigration, of course, played a key role in the process throughout the 1950s and 1960s, accounting for about 58 percent of population growth in eleven major cities reported by Sinclair. The range was from a low of 33 percent in Bogota to a high of 76 percent in Abidjan.

While such detailed demographic accounts are useful, there are 837 cities in the Third World with populations in excess of 100 000, so aggregation is necessary if analysis is to move from anecdote to "stylized fact". Furthermore, the Third World performance ought to be compared with earlier industrial revolutions if we are to isolate conventional from unusual city growth experience. Given the common alarmist view that Third World societies have "overurbanized", a brief look at the past might be a useful antidote. The most careful quantitative assessment can be found in a United Nations' publication, *Patterns of Urban and Rural Population Growth* (1980), written by Samuel Preston, as well as his own summary [Preston (1979)] of the volume.

In the first place, Third World city growth is not a new problem, but rather seems to have followed a relatively smooth "urban transition" since the late nineteenth century. While the urban share of the Third World's population rose sharply between 1925 and 1950 (from 9.3 to 16.7 percent), it had been on the rise since 1850. And while the share rose even more sharply between 1950 and 1975 (from 16.7 to 28 percent), Third World urbanization over the past century seems to obey the usual rules of logistic curves tracing the diffusion of new technologies. The point of inflexion in this case appears to have been in the quarter century terminating just after the first OPEC shock. City growth rates trace out a similar pattern, although, as reported in Table 11.1, there is considerable variety by level of development: Latin America reached a peak rate of city growth in the 1950s, East Asia (excluding China and Japan) in the 1960s, Africa in the late 1970s, and South Asia (according to projections) in the 1980s.

In contrast with earlier assertions by Hoselitz (1955, 1957) and Bairoch (1975), we now know that Third World urbanization experience has been fairly conventional by historical standards. Between 1875 and 1900, currently developed countries' urban share rose from 17.2 to 26.1 percent, about the same increase which took place in the Third World between 1950 and 1975, 16.7 to 28 percent [Preston (1979, p. 196)]. While the rate of urbanization in the Third World has not been exceptional, the rate of city growth has. Between 1875 and 1900, city populations in the currently developed countries rose by about 100 percent;

Table 11.1
City growth rates in the Third World, 1950–2000 (percent per annum)

Region	1950–1960	1960–1970	1970–1975	1975–1980	1980–1990	1990–2000
	City growth rate					
Africa	4.42	4.85	4.97	5.10	5.00	4.56
Latin America	4.57	4.21	4.01	3.86	3.56	3.06
East Asia (exc. China and Japan)	4.16	5.20	4.52	4.00	3.33	2.36
South Asia	3.37	3.91	4.01	4.33	4.47	4.27
	City minus rural growth rate					
Africa	2.65	2.90	3.08	3.20	3.14	2.86
Latin America	3.34	3.19	3.19	3.03	2.74	2.29
East Asia (exc. China and Japan)	3.53	4.60	4.78	4.41	3.73	2.65
South Asia	1.55	1.72	1.88	2.18	2.65	3.20

Source: United Nations (1980, pp. 13–15).

between 1950 and 1975, city populations in the Third World increased by 188 percent. City growth was faster in the Third World in part simply because overall rates of population growth were faster, in both city and countryside. Given the far higher rates of overall population growth in the Third World compared with nineteenth-century developing countries, it should come as no surprise that immigration accounts for a smaller share of Third World city growth. On average, immigration accounted for 39.3 percent of city growth in the 1960s [Preston (1979, p. 198)], while, as we shall see below, it was far higher during the First Industrial Revolution in England.

Table 11.2 summarizes English experience with the urban transition. Consistent with Preston's figures in Table 11.1, Todaro (1984, p. 13) estimates the rate of city growth in the Third World in the 1960s and 1970s to have been 4.32 percent per annum. While these city growth rates are double the English rates in Table 11.2, we must remember that everything was growing more rapidly in the Third World. Indeed, the overall population growth in the Third World [2.33 percent per annum: Todaro (1984, pp. 10–11)] was almost double that of England over the century 1776–1871 [1.23 percent per annum: Wrigley and Schofield (1981, p. 529)]. In any case, the English city immigration rates were not so much lower in the three decades 1776–1806, ranging between 1.10 and 1.91 percent per annum, than they were in the Third World, averaging 1.79 percent per annum. Thus, while England's growth was more gradual, recorded city immigration rates were on par with the so-called "exploding" Third World.

Now consider rural emigration. With the exception of the war-induced good times for English agriculture between 1801 and 1806, rural emigration took place at every point over the century. Furthermore, the rate of emigration about doubled over the century. From 1816 to 1871, the rural emigration rate from the English countryside ranged from 0.87 to 2.10 percent per annum. The rates estimated for the Third World in the 1960s and the 1970s range between 0.97 and 1.37 [Preston (1979, p. 197), Kelley and Williamson (1984a, p. 93)]. In summary, judged by the standards of the First Industrial Revolution, the urban transition associated with ongoing industrial revolution in the Third World hardly seems exceptional.

2.2. Migrant selectivity bias

Cities are dynamic, but how much of that dynamism is attributable specifically to urban behavior, and how much to the fact that cities are simply full of young adults? Are cities different largely because of selectivity bias, young adults favoring the cities and shunning the countryside? Table 11.3 summarizes the evidence for both the Third World in 1970 and England in 1861. The rural–urban differences are significant although not spectacular; in both cases the cities tend to be full of young adults. The source of the rural–urban age differences is also

Table 11.2
The urban transition in England, 1776–1871

Years	Urban share (%)	Annual percentage rate			Percent of city growth due to immigration
		City growth	City immigration	Rural emigration	
1776–1781	25.9	2.08	1.26	0.86	59.5
1781–1786	27.5	1.81	1.62	0.50	89.0
1786–1791	29.1	2.20	1.37	0.56	61.1
1791–1796	30.6	2.17	1.20	0.79	53.7
1796–1801	32.2	2.08	1.10	0.83	51.9
1801–1806	33.8	2.15	1.91	−0.18	88.2
1806–1811	35.2	2.07	0.59	1.07	27.5
1811–1816	36.6	2.40	1.37	0.59	55.6
1816–1821	38.3	2.39	1.06	0.87	42.8
1821–1826	40.0	2.61	1.12	1.19	41.4
1826–1831	42.2	2.33	1.06	1.14	44.0
1831–1836	44.3	2.08	1.04	1.01	48.7
1836–1841	46.3	2.04	0.83	1.20	39.5
1841–1846	48.3	2.41	1.23	1.57	49.7
1846–1851	51.2	2.05	0.97	1.73	45.9
1851–1856	54.0	2.06	0.77	1.54	36.4
1856–1861	56.4	2.08	0.60	1.60	27.9
1861–1866	58.7	2.35	1.06	2.10	43.7
1866–1871	62.0	2.29	1.15	2.05	48.6

Source: Williamson (1985a, Tables 4 and 5).

Table 11.3
Age distributions in the contemporary Third World (1970)
and in England (1861): Rural versus urban (%)

Age class	Third World		England	
	Urban	Rural	Urban	Rural
0–4	14.4	16.5	13.2	13.6
5–14	24.3	26.4	20.7	23.0
15–19	11.1	10.1	9.6	9.7
20–29	17.0	14.5	18.7	15.9
30–39	12.4	11.5	14.2	12.3
40–49	9.0	8.7	10.7	10.1
50–59	6.0	6.2	6.7	7.3
60 +	5.8	6.0	6.0	8.2
Dependency rate	42.4	46.7	40.0	44.8

Source: Williamson (1985a, Tables 7–10).

clear: migration tends to select young adults. Indeed, Rogers (1984) has constructed a "basic standard schedule" – reproduced in Figure 11.1 – which clearly reveals the clustering of migrants ranging from their late teens to their early thirties. Figure 11.1 also shows that immigrants to England's cities in the 1850s had an even more pronounced age-selectivity bias than is the case now.

The economic implications of the young adult selectivity bias appears to be straightforward, although there has been little research devoted to an assessment of their quantitative importance. The higher urban activity rates would imply higher per capita incomes. The lower dependency rates would imply lower relief burdens in the city. Lower dependency rates also imply higher saving rates in the cities [Leff (1969), Coale and Hoover (1958)]. In addition, the young adult bias implies that the cities, ceteris paribus, should have higher crude birth rates, lower crude death rates, and thus eventually higher rates of growth in the natural labor supply as the urban transition unfolds. The moral of this demographic tale is that cities should increasingly find it easier to satisfy their growing labor requirements without the need for additional immigrants. And we do indeed find that over time the share of immigration in total urban population increase declines [Rogers (1984), Keyfitz (1980)].

2.3. Selectivity bias, the brain drain, and remittances

Concern with the rural "brain drain" is at least as old as the First Industrial Revolution in England [Graham (1892)]. Even taking into account only the rural rearing costs of children, the rural–urban transfer embodied in England's rural

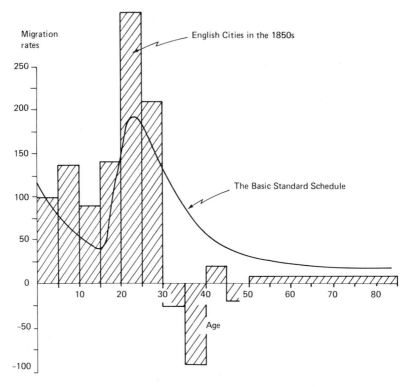

Figure 11.1. Migrant age-selectivity: English cities in the 1850s and the "standard" schedule according to Rogers (outmigration rates, where age 0–5 = 100, and the rural age-specific population is taken as a base). *Source:* Williamson (1985a, p. 51).

emigration in 1850 cost the rural sector the equivalent of 56 percent of its investment in that year [Williamson (1985b)]. While I am unaware of any similar data for Third World countries, if they are even close to the estimated value for the English case, then the brain drain certainly does take on an important dimension. The above estimate is, if anything, a lower bound, due to the presence of the migrant selectivity bias: rural emigrants are young adults whose present value is positive and large; and rural emigrants may also be drawn from the best and the brightest.

Unfortunately, we have little evidence on the economic importance of the brain drain. Equally important, we have very little evidence about rural returns on that investment flow, although the recent literature on the rural consequences of outmigration contains some evidence on urban–rural remittance flows [Johnson and Whitelaw (1974), Knowles and Anker (1981), Lucas and Stark (1985)]. Rempel and Lobdell (1978) undertook a comprehensive survey of this literature almost a decade ago and, based on some fifty studies, concluded the following: (i) urban–rural remittances are very large in Africa, ranging from 10 to 13 percent of urban incomes; (ii) while there is some limited evidence supporting similar conclusions for Asia [Papola (1981, pp. 84 and 93)], there is almost none for Latin America; and (iii), remittances associated with international migration tend to be far higher. As Rempel and Lobdell point out, however, none of these studies controls for the funds emigrants bring with them, especially for those youths going to urban areas for additional education. When these emigrant funds are subtracted from immigrant remittances, the net remittances turn out to be small even for Africa, although this conclusion is disputed by Stark (1980a) and Lucas and Stark (1985).

The stakes in the debate on urban–rural remittances seem to be large. If remittances are indeed small, then rural emigration has important welfare and distributional implications. Furthermore, low remittances would imply high child "default rates" on rural parental investment, thus suggesting a force which might serve to lower fertility in the countryside. [See Caldwell (1982), Cain (1981), Williamson (1985c), Sundstrom and David (1986), Ransom and Sutch (1986). In contrast, see Stark (1981), Katz and Stark (1985).]

2.4. City growth, migration, and labor absorption

The remainder of this chapter will deal with the labor market forces which condition the stylized demographic facts presented above. Throughout, we need to view the migration and urbanization process in terms of a system of five equations: (1) rural and (2) urban labor supply conditions, (3) rural and (4) urban labor demand conditions, and (5) a migrant-clearing equation. While the literature tends to dwell most heavily on the last two of these – urban labor absorption and migration – the problem should be posed in general equilibrium. We shall try to do so wherever possible.

3. Disequilibrating labor market shocks and equilibrating migrant responses

3.1. Disequilibrium and wage gaps

The simplest multi-sectoral models assume long-run wage equalization. But even in such simple models, unbalanced output growth and derived labor demand can imply labor market disequilibrium and wage gaps in the short run. Migration, after all, responds only with a lag to wage differentials. Furthermore, when such models are consistently shocked by disequilibrating economic and demographic events, wage gaps can persist and even increase. Since such shocks are precisely the ingredients of industrial revolutions, development economists have come to expect the appearance of wage gaps in Third World countries, especially between rural agriculture and urban manufacturing.

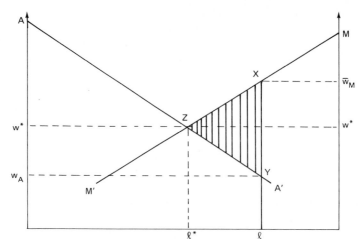

Figure 11.2. Wage gaps and employment distribution in two-sectors.

Figure 11.2 describes the familiar two-sector example of labor market disequilibrium with wage gaps between agriculture (A) and manufacturing (M). The derived labor demand functions, AA' and MM', intersect at Z where the distribution of labor is optimal, and the prevailing wage is w^*. In the presence of a wage gap like XY, however, the distribution of labor is sub-optimal: here there are too many farm laborers and not enough manufacturing operatives. I have also shaded in the Harberger Triangle XYZ, representing the allocative losses associated with this labor market failure. The economic significance of the market failure is conditioned by two forces, the size of the wage gap and the share of the labor force misallocated, $\ell - \ell^*$.

How big are rural–urban wage gaps? Lewis (1954) thought the gap was about 30 percent when he was writing in the early 1950s, but a recent review suggests they are about 41 percent [Squire (1981, Table 30, p. 102)]. Real wage gaps for relatively homogeneous unskilled male labor were somewhat smaller in England at the end of the First Industrial Revolution, about 33 percent [Williamson (1986)].

There has always been considerable disagreement about the magnitude of these gaps. As Kannappan (1985, pp. 708–711) points out, the measurement problems are often overwhelming [see also Knight (1972), Taira (1973)]. Indeed, Behrman and Birdsall (1983) have argued that the addition of differences in schooling quality to the more conventional list of explanatory variables causes urban–rural earnings differentials to evaporate for Brazilian males.

There has also been considerable debate over trends in the real wage gap, in part motivated by the fact that rising wage gaps are a central premise of the Todaro model. As it turns out, there is little evidence confirming a rise in the wage gap in the Third World [Kannappan (1985, pp. 712–713), Gregory (1975), Glytsos (1977)], but there is abundant evidence coming from the First Industrial Revolution. It appears that the nominal wage gap in England rose from about 16 percent in 1815 to a peak of 64 percent in 1851 [Williamson (1985d, p. 49)]. All of this evidence on wage gap trends, however, should be treated with caution since nominal, not real, wages are almost always employed in the analysis.

Based on evidence from Brazil [Fishlow (1972), Thomas (1982)], Peru [Thomas (1980)], the American South [Bellante (1979)], and nineteenth-century England [Williamson (1986)], I suspect nominal wage gaps are poor proxies for real wage differentials. Not only do rural areas have a lower cost-of-living, but it appears to be the non-food component that explains most of the differentials [Thomas (1980, p. 89), Williamson (1986)]. On the other hand, urban amenities associated with government services may well serve as a partial offset to the higher cost-of-living in the cities, since these amenities may be capitalized into rents.

Given an initial wage gap, what would the national income gains be if migration to the cities drove the wage gap to zero? This calculation has in fact been made for England in the midst of the First Industrial Revolution [Williamson (1986)], where the deadweight loss embodied in that Harberger Triangle turns out to have been only 0.5 percent of GNP. As is so often the case in such calculations [Leibenstein (1957), Dougherty and Selowsky (1973), Shoven and Whalley (1984)], the figure is trivial. One would have thought it would have been bigger given that an outmigration of about 20 percent of the labor force would have been necessary to achieve wage equalization. The 0.5 percent estimate may seem small for another reason. Figure 11.2 and the calculation for England assume that the derived labor demands in the two sectors remain stable in the face of massive outmigration to the cities. It seems far more likely that AA' would shift upwards while MM' would shift downwards in response to the migration since the ensuing agricultural output contraction and the urban output expansion would serve to improve agriculture's terms of trade (depending, of course, on the price elasticities underlying the demands for A and M). On the other hand, this "partial" general equilibrium calculation does not allow capital to chase after labor. When a full general equilibrium assessment is made of the British case, the deadweight loss is considerably larger, some 3.3 percent of GNP.

3.2. Are migrants rational?

Wage gaps imply some labor market disequilibrium, and the migration necessary to eliminate that disequilibrium is quite large in typical developing countries, like England in the first half of the nineteenth century. Do migrants in fact respond to wage gaps?

Since Sjaastad's (1962) seminal work, an enormous amount of empirical evidence has accumulated on the determinants of individual migration. Most studies confirm that migrants are motivated by earnings differentials, although it is hard to imagine that we would find otherwise. By far the best survey of this research can be found in Yap (1977) whose summary of the available data shows quite clearly that migrants are rational and do indeed respond to earnings differentials. For example, a recent study of Ahmedabad [Papola (1981, pp. 82–83)] reports informal sector workers at least doubled their earnings upon immigration to the city. Yet, and as Todaro insists, the chance of obtaining employment matters, and the *expected* wage often (but not always) yields better results in regression analysis than the wage alone. But the critical issue is not so much whether migrants respond to earnings differentials, but whether the rate of return to migration is "high" (implying insufficient migration), and whether the elasticity of migrants to wage differentials is "large" (implying low costs of migration). On this score, the literature is much too quiet.

As Yap (1977, pp. 253–254) points out, even though migrants improve their incomes by city immigration, they may have been limited to marginal employment. The evidence, such as it is, does not appear to support this view. While we shall have more to say about the issue below in Section 5 where the Todaro thesis is confronted, "income comparisons between migrants and natives suggest that the incomes of urban dwellers are more a function of education and skill levels than of migration status" [Yap (1977, p. 254)]. The same was true of urban immigrants in England's cities in 1851 [Williamson (1985e)].

As noted above, Thomas (1980) has shown for Peru that the non-food component of the cost-of-living index explains most of the cost-of-living differential between city and countryside. To the extent that rents are the central ingredient of the cost-of-living differential, and they seem to have been in England in the 1830s [Williamson (1986)], that fact implies, ceteris paribus, that the nominal wage gap should increase over time as land scarcity in the city rises with urbanization. Furthermore, it suggests that government policy towards urban housing should be critical to the migration decision and to the cost of labor facing firms in the city. In addition, the availability and cost of public services should also matter to the migration decision, suggesting that government policy regarding urban social overhead (including schooling and health) should be an important determinant of city immigration rates [Linn (1983)]. To quote Yap (1977, p. 245):

> When the destinations are cities, better living conditions, better educational opportunities...may...be important motivating factors. Since anti-poverty programs are apt to include improvements in urban services, it is useful to know whether programs to upgrade housing, sanitation, health, and public education facilities will also stimulate in-migration....

Unfortunately, econometric studies have only been able to confirm the general attraction of cities. They have not been able thus far to isolate the impact of non-wage components of the migration decision, primarily because effective measures of urban services and quality-adjusted rents are hard to get. This surely should be a key goal of future research on Third World migration.

3.3. Are there too many city immigrants?

Given wage gaps favoring Third World cities, it would appear that the rate of outmigration from the countryside is too low. In the face of such evidence, how could anyone argue that there are too many city immigrants, that cities are too large and too many? The only way that both statements can be correct is, of course, if the social cost of the migrants exceeds their private cost, in which case Third World cities would represent another example of the "tragedy of the commons".

There are only two ways that the too-many-city-immigrants argument can be accommodated. First, it may be argued that the marginal cost of urban public goods is far above the user price charged, and that the subsidy fails to get capitalized into rents. While this argument certainly sounds plausible, as far as I know there has been no attempt to assess its quantitative relevance. Furthermore, if the problem is underpricing urban public services, then the solution is not to close the cities down, but rather to get the prices right. Second, it may be argued that immigration generates important negative externalities. One such negative externality might be that the relative poverty of the urban migrants tends to create social and political tensions. Of course, it could be argued just as plausibly that the presence of external agglomeration economies implies that cities are too small and that the observed level of urban immigration is too little [Shukla and Stark (1985)]. In any case, it is never quite clear whose objective function is being considered in the too-many-city-immigrants argument. One can appreciate the planners' dilemma of dealing with what appears to be an overwhelming rush to the cities, or their complaints that the quality of urban services newly created rapidly deteriorates as they get stretched across an ever increasing set of users, but what about the urban and, indeed, the national residents who the planning bureaucracy serve?

Oddly enough, there is almost no attention in the development literature to the issue of who gains and who loses from an influx of unskilled labor to the city. The relative silence in this literature on the distributional impact of urban immigration is especially odd given the attention which economists have lavished on the distributional impact of *international* migrations.

In the simplest general equilibrium model, who gains and who loses from city immigration of unskilled labor seems clear enough. In the countryside, unskilled labor that stays behind should gain, to the extent that increased labor scarcity tends to raise their earnings [although the empirical evidence is mixed: Johnson

(1960), Gardner (1974), Greenwood (1978), and Schuh (1982)], and land rents should fall (in the absence of offsetting terms of trade effects). In the cities the immigrants gain, as we have seen. Unskilled city-born laborers and previous immigrants who are crowded-out by the competition from the new immigrants surely lose as the urban labor market becomes glutted with more unskilled labor. In contrast, skilled labor will gain as the increase in unskilled labor supplies augments output and drives up the demand for skills. Certainly capitalists gain for identical cheap labor reasons. And finally, to the extent that middle class and rich tend to consume heavily the personal services offered by the urban unskilled, they get an additional cost-of-living gain. Thus, while planners may push for restrictions on immigration – making their job of coping with city growth easier – one can hardly imagine any other class of city residents pushing for restrictions, especially given that the previous unskilled immigrants have very little political power. It is hardly surprising, therefore, that immigration restrictions have hardly been tried, and have often failed when tried.

A reduction of city immigration was one of the first policy options suggested for reducing *urban* poverty and unemployment in the Third World [Frank (1968), Yap (1976, p. 227)]. The policy makes some sense if the focus is solely on the welfare burden of the urban poor. However, the policy makes no sense at all if the focus is on *national* poverty and welfare burdens. After all, outmigration to the city is one of the best ways to escape rural poverty. Yet, it is quite apparent that some development analysts and many governments think there are too many city immigrants, and that policies should be devised to reduce their number. Preston's summary [Preston (1979, p. 195), U.N. (1980, p. 3)] indicates the popularity of this view:

> Among the 116 developing countries that responded to the United Nations' "Fourth Population Inquiry Among Governments" conducted in 1978, only six declared the spatial distribution of their population to be "acceptable". Forty-two replied that it was "unacceptable to some extent", and 68 declared it to be "highly unacceptable". To another question addressed specifically to the desirability of current rates of rural-urban migration, only three countries expressed a desire to accelerate such migration. Twenty-three wished to maintain it at present levels, 76 to slow it down, and 14 to reverse it.

As Shukla and Stark (1985, p. 297) point out, things had not changed when a similar U.N. survey was taken in 1983.

Simmons (1979) documents Asian experience with slowing down metropolitan city growth, and Shaw (1978) focuses on housing as one key policy instrument to effect the same goal [see also Laquian (1981)]. In spite of such policies, however, governments have generally been ineffective in substantially reducing city immigration in the Third World. Their failure seems to stem from two sources: the evidence in support of the too-many-city-immigrants view is much too weak to motivate policy-makers to do more; and the urban political forces that matter come from classes who clearly gain from city immigration.

4. What does "overurbanization" mean?

Much of the previous section dealt with what city immigration ought to be, but a parallel debate exists over the forces which have actually driven migration and city growth in the Third World. Part of this debate deals with "push" versus "pull" forces, and part of it deals with what has come to be called the "urban bias". This debate was important in motivating the Todaro model and what might be called the new urban pessimism.

4.1. Push, pull, and the engines of city growth

One of the central arguments used to support the view of overurbanization is that Third World populations are supported by an unusually small industrial labor force [Preston (1979, p. 207)]. The evidence on this point was first marshalled by Hoselitz (1953, 1955, 1957) who found that Third World ratios of industrial employment to urban population were small in contemporary developing nations (Asia in particular) compared with currently developed countries in the late nineteenth and early twentieth centuries. Not too long ago, Bairoch (1975, p. 150) replicated Hoselitz's finding:

> The degree of urbanization in under-developed countries was the same in 1960 as it had been in Europe in 1880–85 when the latter's percentage of working population engaged in manufacturing was twice that of the less-developed countries.

Using World Bank data from the 1960s, Berry and Sabot (1984, p. 106) have made the same point:

> Whereas at the turn of the century the industrializing European nations absorbed almost half of their incremental labor force into industry each year, today the developing countries absorb less than 30% of their additional workers into industry.

However, given the more sophisticated level of social services now offered in major cities everywhere, and given the far more rapid rate of city population growth augmenting employment in the formal and informal construction sector, it is not at all clear that contemporary Third World cities *should* replicate the employment patterns which prevailed almost a century ago.

Nonetheless, Hoselitz's thesis has encouraged the view that Third World city growth is being driven by somewhat different forces than has been true historically. According to this view, sometime after 1930, "urbanization without industrialization" began to appear in the Third World [Bairoch (1975, p. 144)], and the problem took on alarmist dimensions in the 1960s when urban unemployment and underemployment captured our attention.

Since so much seems to ride on the issue, fresh new tests of the Hoselitz thesis have gained high research priority with the appearance of more employment data during the last two decades of Third World city growth. Based on an exhaustive assessment of industrial employment trends in the Third World between 1950 and 1970, Preston has been unable to find any evidence of deterioration in industry/urban ratios for the Third World as a whole [Preston (1979, pp. 207–209), U.N. (1980, pp. 17–19)]. Indeed, in the largest of the developing regions – Middle South Asia (including India) – the industry/urban ratio has risen. Latin America, on the other hand, seems to be an exception. Furthermore, where the urban service sector has been rising, "it is typically a result of rising fractions of professional, technical, and administrative personnel" [Preston (1979, p. 209)]. A more recent study by Gregory (1980) has offered an even sounder rejection of the Hoselitz thesis: employment in the tertiary sector has not grown at an explosive rate in the Third World, but rather has matched that of the secondary sector (p. 682); employment in sales and services has in fact grown at a slower rate than employment in production (p. 686); furthermore, there is no evidence to support the view that informal sector urban employment has grown at an exceptionally rapid rate (p. 696). Generally, urbanization does not seem to have outpaced industrialization in the Third World since 1950, although it is still true that cities in the developing world have lower industry/urban ratios than was the case at the turn of the century for currently developed countries.

While urbanization has not outpaced industrialization in the Third World, the higher service/urban ratios have still suggested to some that there are over-urbanization forces at work. Hoselitz's original findings encouraged the view that the urban service sector must be too large. Rather than viewing the growth of urban services as a response to buoyant demand, Hoselitz viewed that growth mainly as a response to immigrant-swollen labor supplies. He believed that migrants were pushed to the city by unfavorable employment conditions in the countryside, that glutted labor markets in the city could not be cleared by employment in high-wage modern sectors, and thus that city service sectors were simply offering employment of the last resort. Low-wage employment in the "unproductive" service sector boomed, thus assuring the finding of relatively low industry/urban ratios in the Third World by historical standards.

If Hoselitz is right, then urban service sectors – the informal sector in particular – should exhibit relatively low wages and be dominated by migrants. If he is wrong, then we should find no such evidence. And if he is wrong, then we should be able to offer explanations for buoyant labor demand in urban services. How much of that demand might stem from government final demand? How much from employment multipliers emanating from the manufacturing export base? How much from the construction of social overhead and housing, the latter including squatter housing? The literature has yet to supply an effective accounting of these potential sources of labor demand for urban services, and it matters to our understanding of the city growth process.

The literature does offer answers to the following questions: Do urban service sectors in the Third World exhibit relatively low-wage employment? Are they dominated by migrants? Apparently migrants do not dominate urban service employment [Yap (1977, p. 255)]. Nor can it be argued that wages are relatively low in urban service sectors, including the informal sector [Yap (1977), Papola (1981), Kannappan (1985)]. Indeed, Mazumdar (1976) and others have questioned the view that urban informal service sectors are a point of entry for the immigrant any more than they are for the city-born. Furthermore, Udall (1976) has shown that when rural disturbances led to a dramatic labor migration into Bogota, the influx failed to increase the relative size of the service sector, a result in complete contradiction with the Hoselitz thesis. While we shall have more to say about the issue below when we examine urban labor markets in greater detail, it appears that the evidence is not consistent with Third World "overurbanization".

4.2. The urban bias

Of course, the Third World may be overurbanized for another reason. Lipton (1976) and Keyfitz (1982, pp. 662–667) have both reminded us that an "urban bias" favors city growth [see also Mamalakis (1969), Mitra (1977), Bates (1981), Moore (1984)]. There is no shortage of policies which have that effect: the domestic terms of trade is twisted against agriculture, thus encouraging more rapid rural emigration to the city than would have been true in the absence of such policies; tariff and exchange-rate management also serve to protect urban industry, fostering its expansion at agriculture's expense (although the higher capital intensities thus encouraged may offset urban employment effects); financial markets are manipulated by government policy to create cheap capital for favored urban industries (although, once again, the higher capital intensities thus encouraged may offset urban employment effects); and social overhead is allocated disproportionately to the cities (schools, health facilities, roads, water supplies, and electricity), all offered at less than user cost, and all financed from general tax revenues rather than from urban land taxes. While it is easy enough to list the sources of urban bias [and its magnitude: e.g. Little, Scitovsky and Scott (1970), Bale and Lutz (1981), Agarwala (1983)], it is quite another matter to establish the impact of this bias on Third World city growth. I know of no study which has performed this exercise, and it is central to policy debate. While Montgomery (1985) has explored the correlations between Agarwala's (1983) indices of price distortions and urbanization among 31 developing countries, he finds it difficult to control for other forces driving city growth. It seems to me that this issue deserves high research priority, and I suspect it will require a full computable general equilibrium model to attack it properly.

5. How do urban labor markets work?

5.1. The evolution of conventional wisdom

Development economists in the 1950s viewed rural–urban migration and city growth with optimism. City immigration was seen as a favorable process whereby "surplus rural labor was withdrawn from traditional agriculture to provide cheap manpower to fuel a growing modern industrial complex" [Todaro (1980, p. 361)]. Demand pull was central to such development models [Lewis (1954), Fei and Ranis (1961)], and in the absence of labor-saving technological change in urban industry, city job creation insured a steady decline in low-productivity employment nation-wide as per capita incomes rose. Accumulation was the key constraint on economic transformation in such models, but with an elastic immigration response to favorable employment conditions, real wages tended to remain stable, profit shares in GNP rose, the domestic saving rate increased, and the accumulation constraint was released.

Things began to change in the 1960s. The appearance of large-scale household surveys documented for the first time what appeared to be high rates of unemployment throughout the Third World. By the end of the decade, "the dominant impression was that rates of urban unemployment were increasing and that urban unemployment in LDCs was a chronic problem" [Berry and Sabot (1984, p. 105)]. Furthermore, many economists were persuaded that underemployment touched even greater numbers than did open unemployment – the ILO suggesting that there were three or four underemployed for every person unemployed [Berry and Sabot (1984, p. 114, fn. 20)], and an urban informal service sector was viewed as the main holding area of low-wage underemployed. Indeed, informal service sector employment in the cities began to be viewed as a "mere manifestation of an impoverished rural 'surplus'" [Kannappan (1985, p. 702)].

The optimism of the 1950s was slowly being replaced by a neo-Malthusian pessimism, and urbanization debates shifted to gloomy accounts of unemployment, poverty and inequality. Demographers and labor economists began to construct an "excess supply-limited demand" paradigm [Fry (1979), Kannappan (1985, p. 699)]. Not only did this gloomy neo-Malthusian perspective discount the role of demand-pull in the cities, but it even viewed immigration to the city with alarm.

5.2. *The Todaro model*

This neo-Malthusian pessimism was given theoretical rationalization in 1969 with the appearance of Michael Todaro's model of labor migration and urban unemployment. Not surprisingly, the Todaro model took the profession by storm. After all, it had very attractive ingredients:

> The idea that migrants compare expected gains with the current costs of being unemployed represented rather standard theory. The model's appeal lay rather in the fact that it fitted well with three prevalent stereotypes: high wages in the modern sector; presumptions of mass unemployment; permissive or overly generous policies and/or articulate, militant labor movements [Kannappan (1985, p. 703)].

The Todaro model and its extensions [Harris and Todaro (1970), Zarembka (1972), Stiglitz (1974), Corden and Findlay (1975), Cole and Sanders (1985)] has enjoyed considerable popularity since 1969.[1] The hypothesis is simple and elegant. Perhaps the most effective illustration can be found in Corden and Findlay (1975), reproduced in Figure 11.3. There are only two sectors analyzed in the figure, and labor is the only mobile factor there, but it is sufficient to illustrate the point. Under the extreme assumption of wage equalization through migration, and in the absence of wage rigidities, equilibrium is achieved at E (the point of intersection of the two labor demand curves, AA' and MM'). Here wages are equalized at $w_A^* = w_M^*$, the urbanization level is $O_M L_M^*/L$ (the share of the total labor force, L, employed in urban jobs, $O_M L_M^*$), where M denotes urban manufacturing and A denotes agriculture. Wages are never equalized in the real world, of course, and so the model incorporates the widely-held belief that the wage in Third World manufacturing is pegged at artificially high levels, say at $\bar{w}_M$. If for the moment we assume unemployment away, then all of those who fail to secure the favored jobs in manufacturing would accept low-wage jobs in agriculture at w_A^{**}. The model now allows for a wage gap between the two sectors, a feature of developing economies explored at length in Section 3.

Figure 11.3 makes it clear that the level of city employment would be choked off by the high wage in manufacturing, but would city immigration also fall off? Not necessarily. Indeed, the model was originally motivated by concerns with urban unemployment, as well as by the coexistence of dramatic city growth,

---

[1] The Todaro model is also strikingly similar to Mincer's (1976) two-sector framework used to assess the impact of minimum wage legislation in "covered" and "uncovered" sectors.

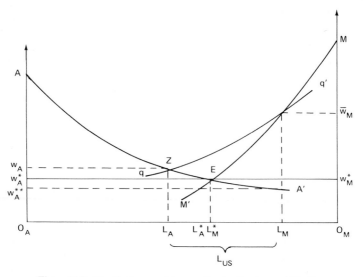

Figure 11.3. The Todaro model according to Corden and Findlay.

unemployment, *and* the expansion of the informal urban service sector where, it was alleged, low-wage underemployment prevailed. Todaro explains this apparent conflict (e.g. immigration in the face of urban unemployment and underemployment at very low wages) by developing an expectations hypothesis which, in its simplest form, states that the favored jobs are allocated by lottery, that the potential risk-neutral migrant calculates the expected value of that lottery ticket, and then compares it with the certain employment in the rural sector. Migration then takes place until the expected urban wage is equated to the rural wage. Given $\bar{w}_M$, and a wage in informal urban services so low that it can be taken as zero, at what rural wage would the migrant be indifferent between city and countryside? If the probability of getting the favored job is simply the ratio of employment in manufacturing, L_M, to the total urban labor pool, L_U, then the expression

$$w_A = (L_M/L_U)\bar{w}_M$$

indicates the agricultural wage at which the potential migrant is indifferent about employment location. This is in fact the qq' curve in Figure 11.3. The equilibrium agricultural wage is given by w_A, and those unemployed or underemployed in the city (e.g. the size of the informal service sector plus those without any work at all) is thus given by L_{US}.[2]

---

[2] The qq' curve is a rectangular hyperbola with unitary elasticity. The elasticity of the labor demand curve MM' is assumed to be less than unity in Figure 11.3, an assumption motivated by empirical evidence available for the Third World.

The new equilibrium at Z in Figure 11.3 seems to offer an attractive explanation for some of the stylized facts of Third World labor markets. It yields a wage gap, $\overline{w}_M - w_A$, and urban low-wage employment or unemployment, L_{US}. Moreover, when the dynamic implications of the model are explored, it turns out that an increase in the rate of manufacturing job creation need not cause any diminution in the size of the low-wage informal service sector. Indeed,

> as long as the urban–rural [wage gap] continues to rise sufficiently fast to offset any sustained increase in the rate of job creation, then...the lure of relatively high permanent incomes will continue to attract a steady stream of rural migrants into the ever more congested urban slums [Todaro (1969, p. 147)].

Nor has Todaro changed his view since 1969. A decade later he stated that city immigration in the Third World is

> the major contributing factor to the ubiquitous phenomenon of urban surplus labor and as a force that continues to exacerbate already serious urban unemployment problems caused by growing economic and structural imbalances between urban and rural areas [Todaro, (1980, p. 362)].

Furthermore, the model makes some firm assertions about how urban labor markets work and how immigrants are absorbed into that labor market. First, it asserts that immigrants earn lower incomes than non-immigrants, the latter having first claim to the favored jobs. Second, it asserts that immigrants have a higher incidence of unemployment. Third, it implies that wages are lower in informal service sector employment than in industrial employment. Fourth, it implies that immigrants earn less in the cities when they first arrive, than they earned in the rural areas they left.

5.3. Critique: How do urban labor markets really work?

There are five critical assumptions of the Todaro model which lead to its dramatic results. Each of these seems restrictive, or at the very least deserve far more research.

First, as Willis (1980, p. 396) points out, job allocation rules are not likely to obey the simple lottery mechanism embedded in the Todaro model. The literature on job search has grown considerably since 1969, and it all emphasizes the role of investment in the search. In contrast, there is no such explicit investment in the Todaro model, except for the actual decision to migrate. In fact, recent evidence from the Third World suggests that unskilled immigrants do not engage in long job searches, and that overt urban unemployment is an attribute of the skilled rather than the unskilled [Yap (1976, 1977), Papola (1981)]. Indeed, this fact has encouraged the development of two-stream migration models and explicit attention to labor heterogeneity [Fields (1975), Fallon (1983), Cole and Sanders (1985)].

Second, there is no attention to informal sector labor market behavior in the Todaro model. In particular, we need to know far more about the sources of labor demand. After all, wages do clear that labor market, they are responsive to demand and supply, and they certainly do not settle to zero.

Third, there has been little evidence marshalled in support of the modern sector rigid-wage assumption [Montgomery (1985)]. This statement holds true for trade union pressure and minimum wage legislation. After all, wage differentials between urban formal and informal sectors could be explained just as well by appealing to firm-specific training costs [Mazumdar (1973, 1976), Stiglitz (1974)].

Fourth, there is the issue of discount rates and rational migrants. What matters to Todaro's migrants is the present value of expected urban earnings compared with the present value of expected rural earnings. Given modern sector wages double those of rural wages, given some unemployment duration before a migrant secures the modern sector job, and given some discount rate, how long a time horizon would a potential migrant have to have before present values were equated? Cole and Sanders (1985, p. 485) have made that calculation where discount rates are allowed to vary between 5 and 15 percent. They conclude: "If one must assume very long time horizons, in some cases greater than 50 years, an alternative explanation of migration may be in order" [Cole and Sanders (1985, p. 485)].

Fifth, and perhaps most important, the model abstracts from many additional influences on the potential migrant's decision. This is the thrust of much of Stark's recent work on risk aversion [Stark and Levhari (1982), Katz and Stark (1986)], relative deprivation [Stark (1984)], and cooperative family games.

This debate is not merely academic nit-picking, since conflicting policy morals may emerge from the Todaro model and an alternative model which relaxes these critical assumptions. One of the first morals likely to be reversed is that "underemployment" in the informal service sector is socially unproductive. A second moral likely to be reversed is that rapid job creation in the modern sector fosters increasing urban unemployment. However, an important third moral is likely to remain unchanged: namely, development strategies should continue their recent emphasis on rural growth [Fields (1980, p. 390)].

5.4. Some evidence

To assess the empirical relevance of the Todaro model, we need answers to five key questions. First, are earnings in the urban informal sector less than those in the modern sector? Indeed, are they less than those in rural areas? Second, do city migrants suffer relatively protracted unemployment during job searches? Third, do migrants earn less than non-migrants? Fourth, do "new" immigrants to the city earn less than their rural counterparts? Fifth, are migrants slow to assimilate into city labor markets?

Are earnings in the urban informal sector less than those in the modern sector? To begin with, labor force data do not support the proposition that urban economies can be cleanly separated into "capitalistic" and "traditional" sectors along dualistic lines [Kannappan (1985, pp. 705–708)]. Nor does the evidence support the view that wages in the modern sector are well above those in the informal sector, especially for manual workers [Kannappan (1985, pp. 708–712)]. Nor is there much evidence to support the view that manufacturing wages have outpaced agricultural wages in the Third World [Gregory (1975), Glytsos (1977), Bose (1978)]. The available data do not, therefore, support Todaro's premise of rising wage gaps, a necessary premise to get his result that unemployment increases over time even in the face of modern sector job creation.

Is there high and rising urban unemployment in the Third World? Apparently not, at least based on 14 countries with adequate data across the 1960s and 1970s [Gregory (1980, p. 697), Berry and Sabot (1984, p. 109 and p. 115, fn. 32)]. Most of the early assertions which reached the opposite conclusion were based on poor data, a warning raised long ago by Turnham (1971) and more recently by Kannappan (1985, pp. 718–719). And who's unemployed? Is it the urban immigrant? Not in Ahmedabad, where unemployment rates among the migrants were low and labor participation rates high [Papola (1981, p. 99)]. Nor in Colombia, Tanzania, and Malaysia where:

> the pool of unemployed comprises predominantly non-heads of household, the young, and married women who typically do not bear main economic responsibility for others and who have access to transfer payments from parents or husbands. They can and frequently do remain unemployed for long periods... Most of the unemployed are relatively educated... [Berry and Sabot (1984, p. 111)].

In fact, the duration of job search seems to be low for city immigrants, especially among the unskilled. Based on a World Bank survey completed in 1975 [Sinclair (1978, pp. 50–51)], two-thirds of migrant job-seekers had found a job after one month, and a significant share of these had arranged for employment prior to the move. In Ahmedabad, the duration of job search was 1.5 months for the average migrant, and 53 percent of these were "sponsored" in some form or another [Papola (1981, pp. 83–84)]. Similar findings of short duration of job search are also reported in Yap's survey [Yap (1977, p. 251)]. Todaro's job-lottery and high-unemployment view of urban labor markets in the Third World simply fails to pass the test of evidence.

Do migrants earn less than non-migrants? Perhaps before we try to answer that question, we might first determine whether migrants dominate the informal service sector in Third World cities. The evidence appears to be mixed. While Papola (1981) can find no evidence to support the Todaro prediction in Ahmedabad, Yap (1976, p. 238) has found the opposite for Brazil, and others have found the same elsewhere in Latin America [Yap (1977, p. 255)]. The explanation, however, has less to do with their migrant status than with their age and skills [Yap (1976, p. 238)]. This emphasis on the heterogeneity of the immigrants to Third World cities has, in fact, motivated the recent development of models of two-stream migration. In any case, the evidence does not support the view that migrants earn less than non-migrants [Yap (1977), Nelson (1979), Mohan (1980)], leading Yap to her important conclusion that:

> Income levels...seem to be more a function of an individual's human capital endowments than of his migration status. Accordingly, strategies to alleviate poverty should place more emphasis on raising the skill levels of the urban population than on restricting migration to the cities [Yap (1976, p. 241)].

Are the earnings of "new" city immigrants less than their rural counterparts? Are immigrants slow to assimilate into city labor markets? The answer to both questions is no. Yap (1977) and others have shown conclusively that city immigrants improve their income over their rural options immediately upon finding an urban job. Furthermore, the rate of assimilation and income improvement is very fast [Yap (1977, pp. 253–256)].

Most economic historians would have been surprised that the debate over Third World city immigrants' economic progress lasted so long, since the historical literature seems to be consistent with the view that migrants improved their earnings with the move, that they assimilated quickly into city labor markets, that duration of job-search was short and unemployment low, and that immigrants and native-born had similar earnings experience (after controlling for age, education and other components of human capital). This is certainly what the literature on nineteenth-century foreign migration into American cities suggests [Higgs (1971), Chiswick (1979), Hannon (1982), Williamson (1982b)]. It is also what the evidence from British cities in 1851 suggests [Williamson (1985e)]. It is hardly surprising, therefore, that the Third World evidence suggests the same.

In short, while there is some evidence which confirms the role of expectation in migration behavior [Todaro (1980, pp. 380–382)], other evidence refutes their importance [cited in Katz and Stark (1986, p. 134)]. In any case, the evidence appears to reject all the remaining premises in the Todaro model on how urban labor markets work.

6. Migration and city growth in general equilibrium: What are the driving forces?[3]

6.1. What drives Third World migration and city growth?

This question brings us full circle back to the issues raised at the beginning of this chapter. Regardless of the model of migration preferred and one's view as to how urban labor markets work, the central question lurking behind all Third World urban debates is the quantitative importance of the underlying forces pushing and pulling migrants to the city. Oddly enough, while the debate has been intense, until recently the literature has provided little guidance as to which of the contending forces is doing most of the work.

As this chapter has already implied, there is certainly no shortage of hypotheses as to what drives Third World migration and city growth. Each of these hypotheses can be classified under one of three headings: first, the endogenous "limits" to city growth; second, exogenous external events; and third, exogenous internal events.

Based on the firmly-held belief that the current structure of an economy – including urbanization levels – can influence subsequent economic performance, macro models of Third World countries have stressed sectoral detail from the start. The classic examples are offered by the dual economy models pioneered by Lewis (1954), Fei and Ranis (1964), and Jorgenson (1961), the latter extended by Kelley, Williamson and Cheetham (1972). Central to these models and their more elaborate extensions are the output gains associated with resource transfers from traditional low-productivity sectors to modern high-productivity sectors. Such resource transfers – labor migration in particular – have obvious spatial implications, the most notable example being urbanization.

In the classic labor surplus version, urbanization augments aggregate output both through short-run efficiency gains and long-run growth effects. In the short run, labor is shifted from low to high marginal productivity employment. In the long run, accumulation rates are raised since saving rates are higher in the modern urban sectors – indeed, in the extreme version only capitalists save, and capital is an argument in the modern, urban-based production functions only. Hence, city immigration leads to higher savings, investment, and output growth [Stark (1980b, p. 97)]. Rising urban accumulation rates imply increased rates of modern-sector job vacancies, a rural–urban migration response, and further urbanization. Thus, output growth, trend acceleration, and increased urbaniza-

---

[3] This section draws heavily on previous collaborative work in Kelley and Williamson (1984a, especially pp. 7–10), Kelley and Williamson (1984b), Becker, Mills and Williamson (1986), and Becker, Williamson and Mills (in progress).

tion are the likely outcomes of the labor surplus model. The neoclassical dual economy model makes the same prediction, at least in the long run.

What forces tend to inhibit the rate of urbanization in these dual economy models? Obviously the share in urban areas cannot exceed 100 percent. Thus, in the very long run, urbanization rates must slow down as this limit is approached and city growth rates decline to the national population growth rate. In the medium term, however, increasing labor scarcity is typically the only source of retardation in the rate of urbanization, even when such models are expanded for demoeconomic simulation [see Sanderson (1980)]. The rise in the real wage serves to choke off the rise in the saving rate, to reduce the rate of urban capital accumulation, to retard the rate of increase in new urban job vacancies, and thus to limit urban growth. The ultimate source of the limits to urban growth in models of this sort is agriculture, either through the disappearance of a rural labor surplus and/or through the rise in the relative price of agricultural products – the key wage good in such models.

Nowhere in this account are competing, and potentially voracious, urban "unproductive" investment demands on the national savings pool considered. In addition, while inelastic agricultural land supply insures an eventual constraint on city growth through rising food costs and real wage increases (at least in relatively closed economies), nowhere is the impact of inelastic *urban* land supply on city rents – another key wage good – and urban cost-of-living considered. Nor, for that matter, is there any concern with inelastic urban land supply on density, crowding, and urban disamenities. Such models say nothing about the costs of urbanization, and are equally silent on the possible limits to urban growth generated within the growing urban sector itself.

It seems likely that more insight into the limits of urban growth might be gained by examining various urban costs that influence the migration decision, on the one hand, and rising urban investment requirements that compete with "productive" capital accumulation, on the other. As we pointed out above, first among these influences are inelastic urban land supplies. Urban land constraints serve to raise rents, augment urban relative to rural living costs, and inhibit city immigration. (At least in the long run immigration would be inhibited. In the short run, higher rents may induce residential construction, a booming demand for unskilled labor used there, and thus more immigration.) To the extent that rising rents and urban disamenities are both caused by density, crowding, and other manifestations of inelastic urban land supplies, then city rents reflect more than living costs alone, but the quality of urban life as well.

The housing-cum-social overhead investment requirements of city growth must also matter. "Unproductive" urban investments of this type, which do not create capacity for future urban employment, may well take priority over those forms of accumulation that do create capacity for future urban employment [Coale and Hoover (1958)]. In any case, unproductive urban investment requirements compete directly with productive capital accumulation. Any model of urban growth must deal with these competing requirements since new urban housing-cum-social overhead investment requirements may serve to check urban growth. Of course, if the housing-cum-social overhead investment is forgone, then housing costs will rise and the quality of urban services fall, further discouraging city immigration. In short, the rise in city cost of living (and of doing business) may impose a limit to urban growth and/or the rise of urban unproductive investment requirements may diminish the rate of productive urban capital accumulation and new urban job vacancies, thus limiting urban growth.

Another set of forces driving migration and city growth are external events over which the economy has little control. Three of these have attracted special attention in the literature. First, in view of the relative capital intensity of city economies, Lewis (1977) has suggested that urban growth breeds foreign capital dependency and that a relative abundance of foreign capital must therefore be a significant determinant of urban growth. This hypothesis encourages the view that foreign capital inflows to the Third World must have played a critical role in accounting for the rapid urban growth up to 1973–74. After all, the Third World was a heavy recipient of foreign capital during the 1960s and early 1970s, reaching an average of about 3 percent of gross domestic product. It follows that the greater austerity in world capital markets since must have played a role in contributing to a city growth slow-down. Second, the relative price of traded goods in world markets should matter. While the relative price of urban manufactures has drifted downwards throughout the past quarter century, the decline was far less dramatic in the 1960s and early 1970s when Third World city growth was especially rapid. Surely we would like to get a clearer understanding of the influence of these world market conditions on migration and city growth. Third, since cities are energy intensive, the rise in the relative price of energy across the 1970s should have contributed to a city growth slow-down. Indeed, can part of the rapid city growth in the Third World in the 1960s and early 1970s be explained by cheap oil?

Another set of forces driving migration and city growth are exogenous internal events. Five of these are most important, and they lie at the heart of the debate. First, has agricultural land scarcity played an important role in pushing labor to the cities? Hoselitz (1955, 1957) thought that arable land shortages generated a powerful rural push, accounting for heavy rural emigration to the cities as well as for "overurbanization" compared with the nineteenth-century developing economies. If the price of agricultural products remains unchanged, then the economics is obvious: land scarcity breeds redundant labor, and the rural emigrants flee to the city. Even though the qualitative result is obvious, it is not at all clear how important agricultural land scarcity has been in accounting for Third World city growth. Furthermore, suppose the price of agricultural products rises in response to the land-scarcity-induced supply contraction? If the demand for agricultural products is price inelastic, land scarcity may induce a decline in farm labor's marginal physical product, but the greater rise in price will serve to increase the value of farm labor's marginal product. Thus, land scarcity can, at least in theory, create rural pull not push. Second, there are Engel effects to consider. The conventional wisdom has it that "the income elasticity of demand for goods provides clues as to why cities and economic growth invariably seem to accompany each other" [Mohan (1979, pp. 6–7)]. As an economy grows, the proportion spent on food declines, increasing the relative demand for urban-based non-food products. Presumably, the faster the growth, the more rapid the demand shifts toward urban-based activities. While this conventional argument certainly makes sense, one can still doubt its empirical relevance for open economies where world demands and domestic supplies are far more critical in determining structural transformation and urbanization. Third, what about the urban bias? How much of the measured city growth in the Third World is due to price distortions (including commercial and exchange rate policy) which favor urban activities? Fourth, what about government manipulation of capital markets and, fifth, the distribution of public investment between rural and urban areas? While the literature is full of assertions about the magnitude of such policy forces, I am not aware of a single systematic effort to measure the quantitative impact of the urban bias.

However, among these internal events driving migration and city growth, two are especially important: unbalanced total factor productivity advance and Malthusian pressures. By unbalanced total factor productivity advance I mean simply that technological change is usually much more rapid in the modern, urban-based manufacturing sectors than in the traditional, rural-based primary product sectors. Traditional service sectors, of course, also tend to lag behind [Baumol (1967), Baumol, Blackman and Wolff (1985)]. The size of the bias and the magnitude of the unbalancedness vary across countries and over time, but they have been a technological fact of life since Britain's First Industrial Revolution, and in spite of past agricultural revolutions and the contemporary Green Revolution [for Britain, see Floud and McCloskey (1981, vol. 1, ch. 6) and Williamson (1985d, ch. 6); for America, see Williamson and Lindert (1980, ch. 7)].

While such supply-side forces are likely to be at the heart of city growth experience, demand is hardly irrelevant, although it is price elasticities that matter, not income elasticities and Engel effects. After all, if output demand is relatively price elastic, then sectoral total factor productivity growth tends to generate an elastic supply response rather than a relative price decline. This distinction is important since cost-reducing innovations will be passed on to users by falling prices in the inelastic demand case. Thus, the rise in the marginal physical product of factors used in a technologically dynamic sector will be partially offset by price declines, so that marginal value products rise by less, and resource shifts to the technologically dynamic sector may therefore be minimal, and this includes labor. If, on average, urban sectors tend to have relatively high rates of total factor productivity growth, and if the demand for urban output is relatively price elastic, then final demand shifts towards the dynamic sectors, the derived demand for urban employment is augmented, urban job vacancies are created, migration responds, and city growth takes place. The higher are price elasticities of demand for urban output, the greater is the city growth impact of unbalanced productivity advance favoring the modern sectors. The more open is the economy to foreign trade, the more likely will those conditions be satisfied.

Finally, we have Malthusian forces to consider. Popular accounts of Third World urbanization and city growth often suggest that high rates of population growth lie at the core of the problem. Indeed, not too long ago a World Bank team asserted that "the increase in population growth of the 20th century is the single most important factor distinguishing present and past urbanization" [Beier et al. (1976, p. 365)]. While the assertion sounds plausible, this conventional wisdom has never been adequately tested. Certainly rapid population growth fosters rapid city growth, but it is not clear by how much. In addition, rapid population growth does not offer an explanation for Third World urbanization experience. On the contrary, classical trade theory has shown that a decline in the price of a factor due to an expansion of its supply (in this case the labor force, swollen by population pressure) will result in the relative expansion of the sector in which it is used most intensively. Since we believe that cities tend on average to contain the more capital-intensive activities, rapid population growth should lead to slower urbanization rates, not faster.

How are we to assess the quantitative importance of these forces driving Third World migration and city growth? If economic forces play a critical role in determining rural–urban migration, then urbanization and city growth are surely determined by those same forces. It follows that urbanization and city growth cannot be analyzed without explicit attention given to the interaction between rural and urban labor markets. Furthermore, those labor markets cannot be fully understood without explicit modeling of labor supply and demand forces in both the sending and receiving regions. In short, urbanization and city growth can only be understood by embedding the process in a general equilibrium model.

6.2. Modeling migration and city growth

Two computable general equilibrium (CGE) models have been used recently to address these topics, one constructed to confront the "typical" city growth experience of a group of 40 developing countries [Kelley and Williamson (1984a, 1984b)], and the other constructed to confront city growth experience in India [Becker, Mills and Williamson (1986)]. These two CGEs join a rapidly growing family of such models applied to developing countries [e.g. Adelman and Robinson (1978), Dervis, deMelo and Robinson (1982)], and to public finance and trade problems [Shoven and Whalley (1984)]. These two multisectoral models are predominantly neoclassical and contain considerable price endogeneity: households maximize utility and producers maximize profits. Optimizing behavior, however, faces constraints: households have limited endowments, migrants incur costs when they move, firms face capital scarcity, mortgage markets are absent, and so on. Furthermore, factor markets are imperfect and governments obey rules that often conflict with optimal resource allocation. Much of the novelty of the two models, however, lies with the inclusion of spatial variables likely to influence city growth, variables that have been omitted from all previous CGEs. These additional variables include squatter housing as well as more formal urban housing, as well as other non-tradables. In addition, the Indian model develops a two-stream view of migration, a view which is consistent with the critical response to the Todaro model discussed above in Section 5.

This chapter is not the place to elaborate and defend these models, but it does seem appropriate to summarize how they are used as well as the findings that have emerged from their application. I will focus on the Kelley and Williamson (KW) model in what follows.

The KW model was given empirical content by relying on the fictional construct of a "representative developing country". This is simply the average experience of a large group of developing countries that satisfy the conditions that underlie the model's theoretical structure. These conditions are: low per capita income in 1960; some per capita income growth over the past 25 years; primary reliance on domestic saving for accumulation; and that the country be a price taken in world markets. The last condition required exclusion of a number of countries (most notably, the OPEC countries) that have an impact on world prices of key resource-intensive products. Fairly extensive historical documentation on economic and demographic variables back to 1960 was necessary for a country to be included in the sample. The 40 countries that met these requirements accounted for about 80 percent of the Third World's population (excluding China).

Using this data base, the model was used to simulate the urbanization process over the period 1960–80. Five groups of variables are taken as exogenous, each one central to debates regarding the sources of city growth listed above. The first group contains the prices of three main types of commodities that enter world trade – imported fuels and raw materials; manufactured goods; and primary products. By comparing simulations based on pre-OPEC fuel price trends with those based on post-OPEC fuel price trends, for example, we can assess the influence of fuel scarcity on migration and city growth. The second exogenous variable is agricultural land stock growth, making it possible to assess the role of arable land scarcity as a source of push to the cities. Third, the level of foreign capital inflow is exogenous, permitting us to explore the hypothesis that foreign capital has been an essential ingredient to migration and city growth. Fourth, rates of total factor productivity growth by sector are determined exogenously and are held to be "unbalanced" in favor of the modern sectors. Finally, the aggregate rates of population and labor force growth are exogenous, making it possible to vary the Malthusian burden so as to assess its importance in contributing to Third World migration and city growth.

Given historical trends in these five sets of exogenous variables, the KW model determines the rate of capital accumulation, investment in dwellings and training and skill development; the patterns of resource allocation and income distribution; the rate of industrialization; and, of course, trends in rural to urban migration and city growth. Although historical documentation is not available for many of these variables, the historical data base is adequate to test the model's ability to track Third World experience across the 1960s and 1970s. It performs quite well overall, and especially well for the migration and city growth experience which motivated the model in the first place. Growth rates of the city population average 4.6 percent per annum in the 40-country sample, and the model prediction is almost exactly the same, 4.7 percent per annum. The model also predicts an acceleration in city growth across the 1960s and early 1970s, conforming to the pre-inflexion point phase along logistic urbanization curves found so commonly in time series. Migration experience is also closely replicated by the model. The rural outmigration rate is predicted at 1.1 percent per annum, while Preston (1979) has estimated the outmigration rate to have been about 1 percent. Similarly, the per annum urban immigration rates are 2.0 in the model and 1.8 percent in Preston's estimates. Finally, the model predicts that 45 percent of the urban population increase can be attributed to immigration, a prediction that lies approximately midway between Preston's estimate of 39.3 percent and Keyfitz's (1980) estimate of 49 percent.

6.3. Understanding the past and projecting the future

There are many ways the KW model can be used, but I will illustrate with one example. First, the model is simulated under the actual exogenous conditions which prevailed up to 1980 as well as the most likely conditions that will prevail up to the year 2000 (the latter based on World Bank projections). This simulation is called BASELINE. Second, the model is simulated under the assumption that the exogenous conditions prior to 1973–74 and the OPEC oil price increase, continued up to 2000. This simulation is called STABLE. The results are reported in Table 11.4.

Whether we focus on BASELINE or STABLE, the model produces the conventional logistic curve with rising then falling city growth and immigration

Table 11.4
Urbanization, urban growth, and inmigration in the Third World:
BASELINE and STABLE projections, 1960–2000

Year	Population urban (%)	Ratio of percent labor force in mfg. to percent urban	Urban population growth rate (%)	Net rural outmigration rate (%)	Net urban inmigration rate (%)	Net inmigrant share of urban population increase (%)
BASELINE						
1960	32.6	0.374	5.56	1.41	2.91	
1965	35.8	0.394	4.11	0.82	1.50	45.1
1970	39.9	0.406	5.15	1.60	2.51	
1975	45.2	0.420	4.48	1.38	1.72	48.1
1980	49.2	0.435	4.10	1.28	1.35	
1985	54.3	0.450	4.84	2.23	1.96	44.7
1990	59.7	0.466	4.67	2.53	1.79	
1995	64.4	0.478	4.33	2.45	1.41	35.6
2000	68.4	0.486	3.97	2.21	1.05	
STABLE						
1960	32.6	0.374	5.56	1.41	2.91	
1965	35.8	0.394	4.11	0.82	1.50	45.1
1970	39.9	0.406	5.15	1.60	2.51	
1975	46.2	0.427	5.94	2.67	3.29	60.6
1980	54.8	0.454	5.97	3.74	3.31	
1985	62.9	0.480	4.98	3.75	2.35	53.0
1990	69.3	0.493	4.32	3.64	1.70	
1995	74.2	0.499	3.79	3.26	1.18	34.7
2000	77.9	0.501	3.43	2.85	0.84	

Source: Kelley and Williamson (1984b, Table 3, p. 430).

rates. Based on these simulations, it certainly appears that urban growth problems will be far less severe by the end of the century, even though there will be no serious diminution in Malthusian population pressures in the Third World over the remainder of this century. Presumably, we will hear fewer complaints from the urban planners, the much-abused term "overurbanization" may disappear from our lexicon, and pessimists' stress on urban environmental decay might lose some of its urgency. Far slower urban growth rates by the year 2000 will make it easier to cope with the accumulated problems associated with decades of rapid urban expansion.

Table 11.4 offers more information of interest to the urban analyst. Consider, for example, the debate on overurbanization that was initiated by Hoselitz in the 1950s. To repeat, his thesis was that urbanization was outpacing industrialization in developing countries in the sense that urban population shares were large in relation to industrial employment shares, at least when compared with the historical performance of currently developed countries. This statistic is also produced by the model in the second column of Table 11.4, although "industry" is limited to manufacturing. While Hoselitz found support for his thesis in data fro the early 1950s, a United Nations study (1980, p. 13) which compared the 1970 with the 1950 statistics, concluded that "urban growth is no longer outpacing industrial growth: if anything, a slight reversal of the over-urbanization tendency has appeared". The model's predictions are consistent with the U.N. finding since the statistic rises, although at a declining rate, throughout the four decades. According to the United Nations, manufacturing has served as the "engine of urbanization" over the past two decades in the Third World, and according to both the BASELINE and the STABLE projections, it will continue to do so in the future.

What happens when the "representative developing country" experiences abrupt changes in the macroeconomic/demographic environment? It turns out that the urban transition can be sharply retarded, halted, or accelerated by changes in the economic/demographic environment over which most Third World countries have little control. This can be seen most clearly in Figure 11.4 where the STABLE and BASELINE predictions are plotted. Note the period from OPEC to the early 1980s. The BASELINE plot tells us what actually happened to Third World city growth in response to changing economic/demographic conditions after 1973–74, while STABLE tells us what would have happened had the pre-OPEC conditions persisted. It appears that the city growth slowdown in the late 1970s was attributable entirely to changes in the economic/demographic environment. Thus, conditions prior to 1973–74 were unusually favorable to rapid city growth. While urban immigration and city growth would have been high and rising in the absence of these favorable conditions, they were even higher due to their presence. Furthermore, the modest urban growth slow-down in the Third World during the remainder of the 1970s was initiated entirely by the appearance of unfavorable exogenous conditions. Had the favorable pre-OPEC conditions persisted after 1973, urban growth rates would have risen still further, making Third World urban problems even more "severe" than in fact was the case.

Which exogenous shocks mattered most? Population pressure? Unbalanced productivity advance? Adverse terms of trade between manufactures and primary products? The relative scarcity of imported fuels and raw materials? Increasing scarcity of arable land? Relative austerity in international capital markets and limits on the availability of foreign capital? Our technique for identifying the impact of various exogenous events on Third World city growth has been to employ historical counterfactuals – what if conditions had been different from those which actually prevailed after 1973–74?

Has arable land scarcity been an important quantitative ingredient of Third World city growth? The answer coming from counterfactual analysis is an unambiguous no. Is a relative abundance of foreign capital a significant determinant of urban growth? Apparently not. Is the increase in population growth in

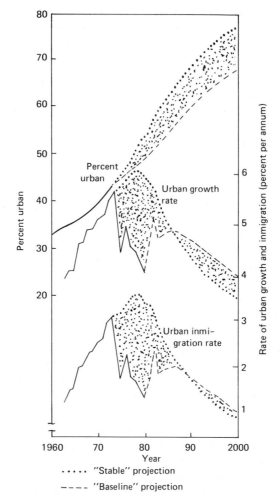

Figure 11.4. Urbanization, urban growth, and inmigration in the Third World: BASELINE and
   STABLE projections, 1960–2000. *Source:* Kelley and Williamson (1984b, Figure 1, p. 427).

the twentieth century the "single most important factor" distinguishing present
from past urbanization? Once again, the answer is no. Had the Third World
experienced the much lower population growth rates that prevailed in the
industrial countries in the 1960s, the rate of immigration and urban growth
would have still been very high, much higher, for example, than in Britain during
the First Industrial Revolution. Furthermore, the forces of "demographic transition" over the next two decades are unlikely to play a major role in city growth in

the future. Finally, what about the pace and character of technological progress? In spite of conventional appeal to Engel effects and overall rates of productivity and income growth to get those effects, it turns out that it is the unbalanced character of that productivity growth which has done most of the work in the past and is likely to do so in the future. The unbalanced rate of technological progress in the Third World was the key condition accounting for the unusually rapid rates of urban growth in the 1960s and 1970s. It follows that if the productivity slow-down currently characterizing the industrial nations spills over into the industrializing Third World during the next two decades, Third World city growth rates will slow down as well.

7. Where do we go from here?

In spite of the attention which Third World migration and city growth has received since the late 1960s, a good share of the questions which really matter have yet to be adequately confronted.

Who gains and who loses from city immigration? While there has been a long-standing interest in the growth–distribution trade-off, and while urbanization has always played a role in such trade-off debates, nowhere in the literature can we find an adequate quantitative assessment of the distributional impact of city immigration itself. This is a rather puzzling state of affairs given the large and growing literature on the distributional implications of international migrations, especially so given that rural–urban migrations in the Third World far exceed in numbers contemporary international migrations, including Latin illegals over American borders today and guestworkers over European borders in the 1960s and 1970s. Who gains and who loses from these rural–urban migrations? The development literature has focused almost entirely on the migrants themselves, who, of course, gain from the move. But what about urban residents with whom they compete as substitutes in production and employment? What about skilled urban labor and capital with whom they are complements? And what about those left behind in rural areas? While it is likely that landlords lose, what about the landless and small owner-occupiers left behind? Here, the net impact may be more complex and subtle. And when we have finally assessed the impact of emigration on factor productivity of those rural resources left behind, what about urban–rural remittances from cityward movers to rural stayers? The size of those (net) remittances and their function has still to be properly documented, and distributional assessment of the impact of migration is likely to hinge on their magnitude.

Economic–demographic interactions need more serious empirical attention. Rural emigration is selective, especially of the young adult. What does this selectivity bias do to the stock of females at fertility risk in the countryside, and thus to rural fertility rates and the demographic transition? And if high rural fertility is driven in part by parental "pension motives", how do parents respond to the high and rising emigration of their children? Does the emigration of children imply a default on parental investment in old age? Do parents respond by having fewer children? And what does the migrant selectivity bias do to the spatial distribution of the welfare burden? If the very old, the very young, and the disabled are left behind in rural area, what social systems can and should be devised to maintain their support to replace the income of the emigrants? And who should be targeted in any transfer to the rural poor left behind? The young (via more education, better health facilities and improved nutrition), who are themselves encouraged to migrate after such transfers have been made? Or the old and disabled?

What role does the "informal service vector" serve in the cities? The literature has always contained a persistent bias against services, viewing them as a parasitic activity with little social value. It is certainly hard to understand how such a view could persist given that services have accounted for 40 or 50 percent of national income since Britain began the First Industrial Revolution in 1780. Yet, Marx gave it little attention when writing in the midst of the First Industrial Revolution, and contemporary development economists tend to do the same. The best example of this is the so-called "informal service sector", labeled the "residuum" in Victorian England. The Todaro model views that sector as a holding area for the reserve army, where the employed are at the subsistence margin, and the unemployed are supported by transfers. Research over the past decade has shown this view to be totally inappropriate, but we still need to learn far more about how this sector works, the demands that it satisfies, and its link via the employment multiplier to the city's export base, namely manufacturing.

While the development literature has devoted an enormous amount of attention to empirical work on migration in the Third World, almost all of that work has had a micro focus. We have, as a result, learned a great deal about who migrates and about which components of the total quality of life induce the move – cheap housing, the quality of public services, current job vacancies, good wages, and good chances for higher paying jobs. We have also learned much about the elasticity of migration to such incentives by type of migrant. Yet, there has been almost no work done on the macro forces determining the magnitude of the flows, the rural–urban wage gap, and the intra-urban wage structure Computable general equilibrium models offer one way to attack these problems, but we need alternative approaches to improve our understanding of the macroeconomic and macroedemographic forces driving city migration and the structure of wages.

The literature is full of anecdote and assertion regarding the impact of policy on Third World migration and city growth. Yet, there has been almost no effort to quantify the impact of various policies, including any overall "urban bias".

Which policies are most effective in achieving which targets? What are the trade-offs between city migration and city size targets, on the one hand, and distribution and growth goals, on the other? Once again, computable general equilibrium models offer one useful way to attack these questions.

Finally, development economists would be well advised to take another careful look at history. There is very little that is unique about Third World migration and city growth. The overall quantitative patterns appear to replicate those of Britain during the First Industrial Revolution and, I suspect, most of the other nineteenth-century industrial revolutions which followed. Many of the debates over how urban labor markets operate, whether there is overurbanization, whether migration is driven by rural push or urban pull, who gains from migration, the determinants of wage gaps, and optimal investment in city social overhead were raised as early as the 1830s in Britain. It is folly for economists interested in Third World migration and city growth to remain ignorant of those debates and to treat the contemporary Third World experience as unique.

References

Adelman, I. and Robinson, S. (1978) *Income distribution policy in developing countries: A case study of Korea*. Stanford, CA: Stanford University Press.

Agarwala, R. (1983) 'Price distortions and growth in developing countries', World Bank Staff working paper no. 575. Washington, DC: The World Bank.

Bairoch, P. (1975) *The economic development of the third world since 1900*. Berkeley, CA: University of California Press.

Bale, M.D. and Lutz, E. (1981) 'Price distortions in agriculture and their effects: An international comparison', *American Journal of Agricultural Economics*, 63:8–22.

Bates, R.H. (1981) *Markets and states in tropical Africa*. Berkeley, CA: University of California Press.

Baumol, W.J. (1967) 'Macroeconomics of unbalanced growth: The anatomy of urban crisis', *American Economic Review*, 57:415–426.

Baumol, W.J., Blackman, S. and Wolff, E.N. (1985) 'Unbalanced growth revisited: Asymptotic stagnancy and new evidence', *American Economic Review*, 75:806–817.

Becker, C.M., Mill, E.S. and Williamson, J.G. (1986) 'Modeling Indian migration and city growth 1960–2000', *Economic Development and Cultural Change*, 35:1–33.

Becker, C.M., Williamson, J.G. and Mills, E.S. (in progress) *Indian urbanization and economic growth: Modeling the past, the present and the future*.

Behrman, J.R. and Birdsall, N. (1983) 'The quality of schooling: Quantity alone is misleading', *American Economic Review*, 73:928–946.

Beier, G.J., Churchill, A., Cohen, M. and Renaud, B. (1976) 'The task ahead for the cities of the developing countries', *World Development*, 4:363–409.

Bellante, D. (1979) 'The north-south differential and migration of heterogeneous labor', *American Economic Review*, 69:166–175.

Berry, A. and Sabot, R.H. (1984) 'Unemployment and economic development', *Economic Development and Cultural Change*, 33:99–116.

Bose, S.R. (1978) 'Wage behavior in selected developing countries', background paper for *World development report*. Washington, DC: World Bank.

Boyer, G. (1985) 'The poor law, migration, and economic growth in England, 1795–1850', paper read to the Economic History Association, New York, September 20–22.

Cain, M. (1981) 'Risk and insurance: Perspectives on fertility and agrarian change in India and Bangladesh', *Population and Development Review*, 7:435–474.

Caldwell, J.C. (1982) *Theory of fertility decline*. New York: Academic Press.

Chiswick, B. (1979) 'The economic progress of immigrants: Some apparently universal patterns', in: W. Fellner, ed., *Contemporary American issues*. Washington, DC: American Enterprise Institute.

Coale, A.J. and Hoover, E.M. (1958) *Population growth and economic growth in low-income countries*. Princeton, NJ: Princeton University Press.

Cole, W.E. and Sanders, R.D. (1985) 'Internal migration and urban employment in the third world', *American Economic Review*, 75:481–494.

Corden, W. and Findlay, R. (1975) 'Urban unemployment, intersectoral capital mobility and development policy', *Economica*, 42:59–78.

Dervis, K., de Melo, J. and Robinson, S. (1982) *General equilibrium models for development policy*. Cambridge: Cambridge University Press.

Dougherty, C. and Selowsky, M. (1973) 'Measuring the effects of the misallocation of labor', *Review of Economics and Statistics*, 55:386–390.

Engels, F. (1974) *The condition of the working class in England*. Translated from the 1845 edition, with an introduction by J. Hobsbawm. St. Albans, England: Panther Press.

Fallon, P.R. (1983) 'Education and the duration of job search and unemployment in urban India', *Journal of Development Economics*, 12:327–340.

Fei, J.C.H. and Ranis, G. (1961) 'A theory of economic development', *American Economic Review*, 51:533–565.

Fields, G. (1975) 'Rural–urban migration, urban unemployment and underemployment, and job-search activity LDCs', *Journal of Development Economics*, 2:165–187.

Fields, G.S. (1980) 'Comment', in: R. Easterlin, ed., *Population and economic change in developing countries*. Chicago: University of Chicago Press.

Fishlow, A. (1972) 'Brazilian size distribution of income', *American Economic Review*, 62:391–402.

Floud, R. and McCloskey, D. (1981) *The economic history of Britain since 1700, volume I: 1700–1860*. Cambridge: Cambridge University Press.

Frank, C. (1968) 'Urban unemployment and economic growth in Africa', *Oxford Economic Papers*, 20:250–274.

Fry, J. (1979) 'A labour turnover model of wage determination in developing countries', *Economic Journal*, 89:353–369.

Gardner, B. (1974) 'Farm population decline and the income of rural families', *American Journal of Agricultural Economics*, 56:600–606.

Glytsos, N.P. (1977) 'Determinants of wage and price changes in less developed countries', *Journal of Development Economics*, 4:315–342.

Graham, P.A. (1892) *The rural exodus*. London: Methuen.

Greenwood, M. (1978) 'An econometric model of internal migration and regional economic growth in Mexico', *Journal of Regional Studies*, 18:17–31.

Gregory, P. (1975) 'The impact of institutional factors on urban labor markets', World Bank Studies in Employment and Rural Development no. 27. Washington, DC: The World Bank.

Gregory, P. (1980) 'An assessment of changes in employment conditions in less developed countries', *Economic Development and Cultural Change*, 28:673–700.

Hannon, J. (1982) 'Ethnic discrimination in a 19th century mining district', *Explorations in Economic History*, 19:28–50.

Harris, J.R. and Todaro, M. (1970) 'Mining, unemployment, and development: A two-sector analysis', *American Economic Review*, 60:126–142.

Higgs, R. (1971) *The transformation of the American economy, 1865–1914*. New York: Wiley.

Hoselitz, B.F. (1953) 'The role of cities in the economic growth of underdeveloped countries', *Journal of Political Economy*, 61:195–208.

Hoselitz, B.F. (1955) 'Generative and parasitic cities', *Economic Development and Cultural Change*, 3:278–294.

Hoselitz, B.F. (1957) 'Urbanization and economic growth in Asia', *Economic Development and Cultural Change*, 5:42–54.

Johnson, D.G. (1960) 'Output and income effects of reducing the farm labor force', *Journal of Farm Economics*, 42:779–796.

Johnson, G.E. and Whitelaw, W.E. (1974) 'Urban–rural transfers in Kenya: An estimated remittances function', *Economic Development and Cultural Change*, 22:473–479.

Jorgenson, D.W. (1961) 'The development of a dual economy', *Economic Journal*, 71:309–334.

Kannappan, S. (1985) 'Urban employment and the labor market in developing nations', *Economic Development and Cultural Change*, 33:669–730.

Katz, E. and Stark, O. (1985) 'Desired fertility and migration in LDCs: Signing the connection', Migration and Development Program discussion paper no. 15, Harvard University.

Katz, E. and Stark, O. (1986) 'Labor migration and risk aversion in less-developed countries', *Journal of Labor Economics*, 4:134–149.

Kelley, A.C. and Williamson, J.G. (1984a) *What drives third world city growth?* Princeton, NJ: Princeton University Press.

Kelley, A.C. and Williamson, J.G. (1984b) 'Population growth, industrial revolutions, and the urban transition', *Population and Development Review*, 10:419–441.

Kelley, A.C., Williamson, J.G. and Cheetham, R.J. (1972) *Dualistic economic development: Theory and history*. Chicago: University of Chicago Press.

Keyfitz, N. (1980) 'Do cities grow by natural increase or by migration?', *Geographic Analysis*, 12:142–156.

Keyfitz, N. (1982) 'Development and the elimination of poverty', *Economic Development and Cultural Change*, 30:649–670.

Knight, J.B. (1972) 'Rural–urban income comparisons and migration in Ghana', *Oxford Bulletin of Economics and Statistics*, 34:199–228.

Knowles, J. and Anker, R. (1981) 'An analysis of income transfers in a developing country: The case of Kenya', *Journal of Development Economics*, 8:205–226.

Laquian, A. (1981) 'Review and evaluation of urban accommodationist policies in population redistribution', in: *Population distribution policies in development planning*. New York: United Nations, Department of International Economic and Social Affairs.

Leff, N. (1969) 'Dependency rates and savings rates', *American Economic Review*, 69:886–895.

Leibenstein, H. (1957) 'The theory of underemployment in backward economics', *Journal of Political Economy* 65:91–103.

Lewis, W.A. (1954) 'Development with unlimited supplies of labor', *Manchester School of Economics and Social Studies*, 20:139–192.

Lewis, W.A. (1977) *The evolution of the international economic order*. Princeton, NJ: Princeton University Press.

Linn, J. (1983) *Cities in the developing world: Policies for their efficient and equitable growth*. New York: Oxford University Press.

Lipton, M. (1976) *Why poor people stay poor: Urban bias in world development*. Cambridge, MA: Harvard University Press.

Little, I.M.D., Scitovsky, T. and Scott, M. (1970) *Industry and trade in some developing countries*. London: Oxford University Press.

Lucas, R.E.B. and Stark O. (1985) 'Motivations to remit: Evidence from Botswana', *Journal of Political Economy*, 93:901–918.

Mamalakis, M.J. (1969) 'The theory of sectoral clashes', *Latin American Research Review*, 4.

Mayhew, H. (1861) *London labor and the London poor*, Vols. 1 and 2. London: Griffin Bohn.

Mazumdar, D. (1973) 'Labor supply in early industrialization: The case of the Bombay textile industry', *Economic History Review*, 26:477–496.

Mazumdar, D. (1976) 'The urban informal sector', *World Development*, 655–679.

Mincer, J. (1976) 'Unemployment effects of minimum wages', *Journal of Political Economy*, 84:587–604.

Mitra, A. (1977) *Terms of trade and class relations*. London: Frank Cass.

Mohan, R. (1979) *Urban economic and planning models*. Baltimore, MD: Johns Hopkins University Press.

Mohan, R. (1980) 'The people of Bogata: Who they are, what they earn, where they live', World Bank Staff working paper no. 390. Washington, DC: World Bank.

Montgomery, M. (1985) 'The impacts of urban population growth on urban labor markets and the costs of urban service delivery: A review', Office of Population Research, Princeton University.

Moore, M. (1984) 'Political economy and the rural–urban divide', *Journal of Development Studies*, 20:5–27.

Nelson, J.M. (1979) *Access to power: Politics and the urban poor in developing nations.* Princeton, NJ: Princeton University Press.

Papola, T.S. (1981) *Urban informal sector in a developing economy.* New Delhi: Vikas Publishing House.

Preston, S.H. (1979) 'Urban growth in developing countries: A demographic reappraisal', *Population and Development Review*, 5:195–215.

Ransom, R. and Sutch, R. (1986) 'Did rising out-migration cause fertility to decline in ante bellum New England?', Social Science working paper no. 610, California Institute of Technology.

Ravenstein, E.G. (1889) 'The laws of migration', *Journal of the Statistical Society*, 52:214–301.

Ravenstein, E.G. (1885) 'The laws of migration', *Journal of the Royal Statistical Society*, 48:167–227.

Redford, A. (1968) *Labor migration in England 1800–1850.* Revised by W.H. Chaloner from the 1926 edition. New York: Augustus Kelley.

Remple, H. and Lobdell, R.A. (1978) 'The role of urban-to-rural remittances in rural development', *Journal of Development Studies*, 14:324–341.

Rogers, A. (1984) *Migration, urbanization and spatial population dynamics.* Boulder, CO: Westview Press.

Sanderson, W.C. (1980) 'Economic–demographic simulation models: A review of their usefulness for policy analysis', International Institute for Applied Systems Analysis, report no. RM-80-14. Laxenburg, Austria.

Schuh, G.E. (1982) 'Outmigration, rural productivity, and the distribution of income', in: R. Sabot, ed., *Migration and the labor market in developing countries.* Boulder, CO: Westview Press.

Shaw, P.R. (1978) 'On modifying metropolitan migration', *Economic Development and Cultural Change*, 26:677–692.

Shoven, J.B. and Whalley, J. (1984) 'Applied general-equilibrium models of taxation and international trade: An introduction and survey', *Journal of Economic Literature*, 22:1007–1051.

Shukla, V. and Stark, O. (1985) 'On agglomeration economies and optimal migration', *Economic Letters*, 18:297–300.

Simmons, A.B. (1979) 'Slowing metropolitan city growth in Asia: Policies, programs and results', *Population and Development Review*, 5:87–104.

Sinclair, S.W. (1978) *Urbanisation and labor markets in developing countries.* London: Croom Helm.

Sjaastad, L.A. (1962) 'The costs and returns of human migration', *Journal of Political Economy*, 70:80–93.

Squire, L. (1981) *Employment policy in developing countries.* Oxford: Oxford University Press.

Stark, O. (1981a) 'On the role of urban-to-rural remittances in rural development', *Journal of Development Studies*, 16:369–374.

Stark, O. (1980b) 'On slowing metropolitan city growth', *Population and Development Review*, 6:95–102.

Stark, O. (1981) 'The asset demand for children during agricultural modernization', *Population and Development Review*, 7:671–675.

Stark, O. (1984) 'Rural-to-urban migration in LDCs: A relative deprivation approach', *Economic Development and Cultural Change*, 32:475–486.

Stark, O. and Levhari, D. (1982) 'On migration and risk in LDCs', *Economic Development and Cultural Change*, 31:191–196.

Stiglitz, J. (1974) 'Wage determination and unemployment in LDCs', *Quarterly Journal of Economics*, 88:194–227.

Sundstrom, W. and David, P. (1986) 'Old age security motives, labor markets, and farm family fertility in ante bellum America'. Paper given to the Tenth Conference of the University of California Intercampus Group in Economic History, Laguna Beach, May 2–4.

Taira, K. (1973) 'Unemployment, labor markets and wage differentials in Asian countries', in *Industrialization and manpower policy in Asian Countries*, proceedings of the 1973 Asian Regional Conference on Industrial Relations. Tokyo: Japan Institute of Labor.

Thomas, V. (1980) 'Spatial differences in the cost of living', *Journal of Urban Economics*, 8:108–122.

Thomas, V. (1982) 'Differences in income, nutrition and poverty within Brazil', World Bank, South Asia Programs Department, mimeo.

Todaro, M. (1969) 'A model of labor, migation and urban unemployment in less developed countries', *American Economic Review*, 59:138-148.

Todaro, M. (1980) 'Internal migration in developing countries: A survey', in: R.A. Easterlin, ed., *Population and economic change in developing countries*. Chicago, IL: University of Chicago Press.

Todaro, M. (1984) 'Urbanization in developing nations: Trends, prospects, and policies', in: P.K. Ghosh, ed., *Urban development in the third world*. Westport, CT: Greenwood.

Turnham, D. (1971) *The employment problem in less developed countries: A review of evidence*. Paris: OECD.

Udall, A.T. (1976) 'The effect of rapid increase in labor supply on service employment in developing countries', *Economic Development and Cultural Change*, 24:765-785.

United Nations (1980) *Patterns of urban and rural population growth*. New York: United Nations, Department of International and Social Affairs.

Williamson, J.G. (1982a) 'Was the industrial revolution worth it? Disamenities and death in 19th century British towns', *Explorations in Economic History*, 19:221-245.

Williamson, J.G. (1982b) 'Immigrant-inequality trade-offs in the promised land', in: B. Chiswick, ed., *The gateway: U.S. immigration issues and policies*. Washington, DC: American Enterprise Institute.

Williamson, J.G. (1985a) 'The urban transition during the first industrial revolution: England, 1776-1871', Harvard Institute of Economic Research paper no. 1146, Harvard University.

Williamson, J.G. (1985b) 'City immigration, selectivity bias and human capital transfers during the British industrial revolution', Harvard Institute of Economic Research paper no. 1171, Harvard University.

Williamson, J.G. (1985c) 'Did rising emigration cause fertility to decline in 19th century rural England? Child costs, old-age pensions and child default', Harvard Institute of Economic Research paper no. 1172, Harvard University.

Williamson, J.G. (1985d) *Did British capitalism breed inequality?* Boston: Allen and Unwin.

Williamson, J.G. (1985e) 'Migrant earnings in Britain's cities in 1851: Testing competing views of urban labor market absorption', Harvard Institute of Economic Research paper no. 1176, Harvard University.

Williamson, J.G. (1986) 'Did British labor markets fail during the industrial revolution?', Harvard Institute of Economic Research paper no. 1209, Harvard University.

Williamson, J.G. and Lindert, P.H. (1980) *American inequality: A macroeconomic history*. New York: Academic Press.

Willis, R.J. (1980) 'Comment', in: R.A. Easterlin, ed., *Population and economic change in developing countries*. Chicago, IL: University of Chicago Press.

Wrigley, E.A. and Schofield, R.S. (1981) *The population history of England, 1541-1871: A reconstruction*. Cambridge: Cambridge University Press.

Yap, L. (1976) 'Rural–urban migration and urban underemployment in Brazil', *Journal of Development Economics*, 3:227-243.

Yap, L. (1977) 'The attraction of cities: A review of the migration literature', *Journal of Development Economics*, 4:239-264.

Zarembka, P. (1972) *Toward a theory of economic development*. San Francisco: Holden-Day.

PART 3

HUMAN RESOURCES AND LABOR MARKETS

INTRODUCTION TO PART 3

T.N. SRINIVASAN

Yale University

In most societies a family or a household is the basic decision-making unit, although in some of the developed countries (and even some developing countries in Latin America) the cohesion of the family seems to be weakening.[1] It is no exaggeration to say that the decisions made by the households in a society significantly influence the course of its economic and social development. For example, the fertility decisions of households determine the growth (or lack thereof) of a nation's population. The decisions of households regarding which of its members will work and for how many days in a year (or hours in a day) and where to work are crucial for the evolution of the size of the labor force, the supply of days (or hours) of work, and for the location of workers across space. The decisions as to which members of the family are to be educated or to acquire various skills determine the skill composition and the endowment of human capital in an economy. Of course, household consumption provides the demand for goods and services and household savings and investment influence the accumulation of physical capital and its allocation across sectors and areas. To be sure, household decisions are affected by the institutional framework (markets, laws and regulations, and the extent to which the laws are enforced) of the society; the institutions, in turn, may be influenced by household decisions in the political arena as well as by technical change.

The unifying analytical focus of the five chapters of Part 3 (and Chapter 10 on household savings in Part 2) is modeling the behavior of the households. Most of these authors assume that the household can consistently rank the actions of its members according to its preferences and then choose its preferred set of actions given the constraints it faces, although in a few models a household welfare ranking is not presumed and conflict (rather than cooperation) among its members is allowed.

---

[1] A household, as defined in surveys as a set of individuals eating from a common kitchen, is distinct from a family, that is, a set of individuals connected by blood, and marriage (consanguinity and affinity). This important distinction is discussed by anthropologists and sociologists. However, it will be ignored here. Indeed, the authors of Part 3 have also ignored it.

Handbook of Development Economics, Volume I, Edited by H. Chenery and T.N. Srinivasan
© *Elsevier Science Publishers B.V., 1988*

In the celebrated model of Malthus, fertility of a household was not an endogenous-decision variable but depended in a mechanical way on its consumption relative to its subsistence needs. Any excess of consumption over subsistence led to an increase in fertility, while any shortfall led not only to a reduction in fertility but an increase in mortality. This process led to increases (or decreases) in population size depending on whether aggregate consumption exceeded or fell short of subsistence needs. This fertility process in a model of production with no technical progress and diminishing marginal returns to labor on a fixed amount of land, led inexorably to a stationary equilibrium in which consumption was maintained at subsistence levels. Of course this extremely simple model did not turn out to be very helpful in explaining the historical trends in population growth and levels of consumption in the developed countries of the contemporary world. Nevertheless, this specter of disaster in which population outstrips resources and in turn brings about a reduction in levels of living, still haunts many. Increasingly complex, if not sophisticated, models have been built, among the most debated being the early model associated with Meadows and Meadows in their study *Limits to Growth* [see Meadows et al. (1972)]. Most of these essentially mechanistic models either underestimate or ignore the responses of households, institutions, and technology to actual and anticipated scarcities of specific goods or services.

In contrast, contemporary analyses of household behavior under the rubric of the "new home economics" start from the presumption that a household which is concerned with the welfare of its members (and the welfare of all their progeny in the indefinite future) would choose its fertility and make other decisions so as to maximize its welfare subject to whatever constraints it faces in the market and elsewhere. These privately optimal decisions will also be socially optimal provided there are no externalities that are not internalized in household decision-making. Thus, any concern about population growth adversely affecting the economic development of a society, for example, must arise from such factors as: (1) the presence of the externalities that are not internalized, (2) the preferences of households not reflecting sufficiently (from a social point of view) the welfare of their future progeny, or (3) households not being well informed about the consequences of their own decisions, and therefore of the means by which they can control their fertility. An informed case for societal intervention in household fertility decisions can best be made only after an examination of the possible externalities, particularly their likely quantitative significance, and whether the observed behavior of households in any way suggests that concern for future generations is inadequately reflected.

Nancy Birdsall (Chapter 12) discusses issues involved in the debate on the consequences of rapid population growth on development. Her review of the analytical models and empirical studies arrives at the judgment that, while there is room for some concern about the extraordinarily rapid population growth in some developing countries, excessive gloom and doom are not warranted.

Ever since the work of Solow, Kendrick, and others showed that only a portion of the growth in output in today's developed countries over the last several decades can be explained by the growth in the quantity of conventionally measured inputs such as labor and capital, there has been an extensive literature on the determinants of the unexplained residual. One of the major explanatory factors is the growth in the quality of the inputs, both of labor and capital. Improvements in the quality of the labor force are brought about by schooling and acquisition of skills. Returns to schooling have been estimated for a number of countries and these are substantial, particularly in developing countries. However, as Paul Schultz (Chapter 13) argues, there are reasons to believe that the available estimates in the literature on the returns to education may be biased. Simply put, whether to educate one of its members or not is a decision that is made by a household. In so far as this decision is influenced by a set of attributes of households and their children which influence the subsequent earnings of the educated child, but which are not part of the data, any methodology which does not take into account this self-selection feature of educational decisions may lead to biased estimates of the contribution of education to earnings. Thus, a model for household schooling decisions and schools' policies regarding promotion from one class to the next has to be estimated jointly with a model of the determinants of earnings conditional on schooling. This objective has seldom been realized in empirical analyses of returns to schooling.

In addition to the productivity-based view of schooling, there are two other common perspectives. One is the so-called "signaling" hypothesis in which the role of schooling is simply to signal to potential employers the innate ability of the individual who has acquired school credentials. In this view schooling in and of itself has no productivity-enhancing value, but since success in acquiring schooling proxies individual abilities which are related to productivity in work, the acquisition of schooling signals this aspect of the individual to the employer. Thus, schooling has *private* value. But whether it has any *social* value depends on whether other more efficient ways exist for matching workers and jobs so that productivity rises with better matches.

The other perspective attributes to education a socializing role rather than productivity per se, the socializing essentially implying that educated individuals adhere to certain norms of conduct which might have positive implications for their productivity in work.

The analytical aspects of screening and signaling theories are discussed by Stiglitz (Chapter 5 of Part 1). However, it is difficult to formulate empirically testable models that can distinguish between these alternative paradigms from observations on years of schooling, subsequent labor market experience, and other relevant variables. Having drawn attention to this almost insoluble problem, Paul Schultz discusses the available studies, both cross-section and time series, micro as well as economy-wide, to assess the implications of schooling and education for economic development. Indeed, schooling enters as a significant variable in many of the relationships reported in other chapters of Part 3. For instance, Nancy Birdsall notes that a mother's schooling influences the fertility decisions of her household and the health of her children. Behrman and Deolalikar also find that a mother's schooling positively influences the nutritional status of her children.

The health status of individuals not only contributes to their well-being but has an impact on productivity, similar to that for schooling. The attained health status of an individual depends in part on the decisions (including past decisions) of the household relating to its consumption, particularly of nutrients and also to its allocation of resources for health maintenance. In addition, the environment, both in the sense of the disease vectors that may be present and the available public facilities, has its effects on health. Thus, the resource allocation within households for activities that promote and maintain health, as well as the public expenditures on the sectors providing services relating to health and sanitation, are important both from a welfare point of view and from the point of view of productivity of workers.

Behrman and Deolalikar (Chapter 14) set up a formal analytical framework to model household decisions regarding the allocation of material resources and of time, for health-promotion and other activities. Just as in assessing productivity of schooling, in attempting to evaluate the productivity effect of better nutrition through enhanced intakes of nutrients, a selection bias problem raises its head. It is likely that a set of unobserved characteristics of a household may lead it to choose to consume more nutrients and also for its members to be more productive. If this is ignored in the estimation procedure, one is likely to get a biased estimate of the productivity-enhancing effect of nutrients. According to Behrman and Deolalikar, with very few exceptions the available empirical studies which claim the presence or absence of a nutrient–productivity relationship are subject to this caveat.

The fact that individuals often prefer foods with better taste, appearance, or higher status associated with their consumption, compared to other foods with better nutrient contents, suggests that nutrient intakes may not be very sensitive to increases in income, even in relatively poor societies. Behrman and Deolalikar find that nutrient intakes are quite price responsive and with high substitutability among foods and positive income effects. Because of the income effects, food price increases often result in increased intakes of some critical nutrients. They find that the response of health status to changes in nutritional intakes and prices is limited, possibly because of the difficulties in capturing the truly dynamic process of health status by an essentially static empirical model. Although mother's schooling seems to be an important determinant of health and nutrition, the former relation is not robust. In the schooling–health relationship, estimated without controlling for mother's background, schooling appears to be merely a proxy for the uncontrolled variables.

From a policy perspective, the efficiency of the markets for health services, nutrients, and inputs for fertility control is an important issue. To the extent market failure occurs because of economies of scale in the production of these goods or because some are in the nature of public goods, policy intervention to correct the market failure would be necessary.

The realization of the productive potential embodied in the health and schooling of the members of a household depends on the household's decisions regarding the labor force participation and labor supply of each of its members. These two decisions are influenced by the expectation of earnings that might accrue to each of its members through work and also the nature of the contractual arrangements under which such work will be undertaken. Rosenzweig (Chapter 15) looks in detail at the functioning of the labor markets in developing countries. In particular, he examines models of wage determination in the rural and urban sectors of the economy and how the differentials, if any, between rural and urban wages might influence the migration decisions of workers, an issue discussed also by Williamson (Chapter 11 of Part 2).

In the development literature, particularly in models that emphasize the dualism between rural and urban sectors, it is assumed that the labor market functions in different ways in the two sectors. A central proposition of the dual economy models is that the real wage rates in rural areas have a floor and as a consequence unemployment is substantial in rural labor markets. Several theoretical models have been proposed in the literature for rationalizing an inflexible (at least in the downward direction) real rural wage. In one theory a positive relationship is assumed between the nutritional status of workers and their work efforts. It is further assumed that the consumption of a worker is determined by his wage income and, up to a point the greater the consumption the greater the work effort per unit of consumption. An employer wanting to minimize the cost per unit of work effort would pay a wage which achieves just that. Any lower wage (or higher wage, for that matter) will imply a higher cost per unit of work effort. In this model in equilibrium every worker is paid the same wage, namely the wage that minimizes the cost to the employer of a unit of work effort. If there are more workers willing to work than could be employed at that wage, there is unemployment. Rosenzweig finds that few empirical studies of the nutrition–productivity relationship are satisfactory from an econometric perspective and of those available none supports the assumptions or implications of the theory, such as inflexible wages and high unemployment.

Another model of the agricultural sector is based on an extreme form of dualism which postulates the coexistence of autarkic small landowners who produce for their own consumption and do not participate in the labor market and large landowners who produce for the market and hire labor at the market wage. With land not traded among households, equilibrium in such a situation is characterized by inefficiency, i.e reallocation of resources (land and labor) across the two groups of households would increase output. Another implication of this equilibrium is that small farmers apply labor beyond the point where the marginal returns from labor would equal the going wage rate. Rosenzweig points out that the empirical evidence strongly rejects this extreme form of dualism. He then examines the models that realistically assume that agricultural activity is risky or assume that the cost of monitoring the work effort of laborers is high so that the problem of moral hazard is serious. These models that explicitly take risk-sharing and incentives into account are of a recent origin. They attempt to explain the bewildering variety of contractual forms that characterize land tenure and labor markets in developing countries. Most of this literature is still theoretical, and econometrically tractable models of farm households embodying risk behavior and contractual choice await further development.

Sectoral or spatial disparities in the returns to labor are common in many developing countries. Reallocation of labor from less to more productive activities improves efficiency and indeed this reallocation plays a central role in the development process. A household-based approach as contrasted with an individual-based one for analyzing the temporary migration of some members of a household is a feature of a number of studies discussed by Rosenzweig. Such temporary migration can arise from an insurance consideration if the returns to farm activity and the remittances from the members who migrate are less than perfectly correlated. In addition to insurance and earnings gains, there may be other motives for migration as well which depend upon differences in publicly provided amenities between rural and urban areas. To the extent the members of the household who choose to migrate have superior earning abilities in cities, the urban–rural wage gap that is observed may overestimate the return to migration for those who have not migrated. Indeed, there is some empirical support for the hypothesis that the returns to migration are significantly overestimated if the selectivity is not taken into account.

Analogous to rural–urban dualism, some analysts take the coexistence of informal and organized sectors in urban areas as evidence of urban dualism. Empirical studies based on or derived from this view attribute differences in earnings among workers who share the same measured characteristics across different types of firms as confirming this dualism. However, as Rosenzweig argues, other differences among firms and among individuals may be just as important in explaining wage differences as the posited formal–informal sector dualism.

Clive Bell (Chapter 16) analyzes credit markets in developing countries. He starts from the premise that a complete set of contingent markets in the

Arrow–Debreu sense in unlikely to be present in any economy, let alone that of a developing country. Important markets may be absent, such as insurance markets and capital markets, for intertemporal allocation of resources. Individuals, nevertheless, attempt to achieve similar goals in the absence of such markets through transactions in the existing set of markets. This might lead them, for example, to link transactions across markets.

Bell considers the linkage between land, labor, product, and credit markets in rural areas with formal analysis confined to land and credit market linkages. Stiglitz (Chapter 5, Part 1) also discusses the analytics of interlinkages. One popular view of interlinkage has been that the more powerful in rural areas exploit the less powerful through interlinked contracts. The literature on incomplete markets and interlinkage, on the other hand, views such interlinkage not as a reflection of the exercise of market power per se, but as an optimal response to absent markets. Given that such interlinkages are present, public policy intervention may have consequences which are different from the consequences the same policies would have had, in the absence of such interlinkage. Bell considers a number of policy reforms, ranging from tenancy reform which sets a floor on tenants' crop share to a more extreme land reform that redistributes land from landlords to the tillers. Subsidized credit to different agents in the rural economy is also considered by Bell. In theory, depending upon the nature of the interlinkage, reforms other than the redistribution of land may have little or no effect in raising tenants' welfare and may even have perverse output effects. In spite of this policy relevance, very few empirical studies testing these models with data from developing countries are available.

The chapters in Part 3 point to the relevance of several microeconomic factors that influence development: fertility decisions, schooling, risk-bearing, monitoring and control of labor processes, incompleteness of markets, etc. However, what we have are a number of partial models of some aspects and an even smaller number of empirically tested and verified models. A comprehensive framework is yet to be developed. Policy advice based on partial models without strong empirical support may be hazardous. On the other hand, policy making cannot wait for such a framework to be enunciated and tested. In the meantime, the more robust of the conclusions of partial analysis can be usefully employed in policy formulation. Each of the chapters in Part 3 does contain a number of such robust results.

Reference

Meadows, D.H., Meadows, D.L., Randers, J. and Behrens, W.W., III (1972) *Limits to growth*. New York: Universe Books.

Chapter 12

ECONOMIC APPROACHES TO POPULATION GROWTH

NANCY BIRDSALL*

The World Bank

Contents

1. Introduction and overview   478
2. Recent demographic change in the developing world   479
3. Macroeconomic analyses of the economic consequences
   of population growth   483
   3.1. Malthus and successor pessimists   486
   3.2. The optimists   490
   3.3. The revisionists   493
4. Microeconomic foundations: The determinants of fertility   501
   4.1. Economic models of fertility behavior   503
   4.2. Fertility models: Differences, conceptual limitations   509
   4.3. Empirical studies of fertility behavior   512
   4.4. Endogenous fertility, optimal population size, and social welfare   522
5. The welfare economics of public policies to reduce fertility   523
   5.1. Externalities   523
   5.2. Fertility control and market failure   525
   5.3. Specific policies   526
6. Summary and conclusions   529
References   535

*The World Bank does not accept responsibility for the views expressed herein, which are those of the author and should not be attributed to the World Bank or to its affiliated organizations. I am grateful to Jere R. Behrman, T. Paul Schultz and T.N. Srinivasan for useful comments on earlier drafts; I remain fully responsible for any errors of fact or interpretation.

Handbook of Development Economics, Volume I, Edited by H. Chenery and T.N. Srinivasan
© *Elsevier Science Publishers B.V., 1988*

1. Introduction and overview

The economic growth of Western Europe and North America during the eighteenth and nineteenth centuries was accompanied by the first steady and sustained increase of population the world had ever known. Malthus's gloomy prediction, made in 1801, that population growth would run up against the fixity of the earth's resources and condemn most of humankind to poverty and recurring high death rates, was proved wrong. Indeed, Kuznets defined modern economic growth in 1966 as a sustained increase in population attained without any lowering of per capita product, and viewed population growth as a positive contributor to economic growth.[1]

But population growth in industrializing Europe was slow, seldom exceeding 1 percent a year, compared to the rapid growth of developing countries in the period after the Second World War. In the postwar period, as mortality rates declined dramatically in most developing countries, and fertility rates remained high, or even rose, population growth rose to between 2 and 4 percent a year. Economists in the 1950s and 1960s began to consider systematically whether and under what circumstances this rapid population growth was contributing to economic growth and development. By the 1970s economists were developing tools to analyze not only the consequences but also the causes of the high fertility underlying rapid population growth in developing countries.

This chapter reviews the principal analytical approaches of the last several decades to the study of the relationship between population growth and economic development. Migration and urbanization, dealt with extensively elsewhere in this Handbook, are treated only insofar as necessary for a coherent treatment of population growth itself. The chapter as a whole (1) describes briefly demographic change in developing countries over the last three decades; (2) reviews the macroeconomic literature on the consequences of high population growth rates in developing countries, covering both partial and general equilibrium approaches; (3) reviews the microeconomic literature on the determinants of family fertility decisions, including theory and empirical work (the microeconomic literature on determinants of mortality is discussed in the chapter on health and nutrition); and (4) discusses the welfare economics of arguments for and against various public policies to reduce fertility, covering such policies as public subsidies for family planning, entitlement and tax policies (incentives and disincentives), and quantity rationing of children.

---

[1] Kuznets (1966, p. 20). For other views of the positive effects of population growth on economic growth see United Nations (1973, pp. 41–44), where the views of Adam Smith, Marshall and others are discussed.

2. Recent demographic change in the developing world[2]

In the year 1 A.D., the population of the world was probably about 300 million. It then took more than 1500 years to double. Though the general trend was rising, population growth was not steady; the balance of births over death was tenuous, and crises such as wars or plague periodically reduced populations in parts of the world. Only in the eighteenth century did the number of people start to rise steadily. From 1750 until well into the twentieth century, the world's population grew at the then unprecedented rate of about 0.5 percent a year, faster in today's developed countries, slower elsewhere. World population size doubled again, this time in about 150 years; it had reached about 1.7 billion by 1900. In the twentieth century, growth continued to accelerate, from 0.5 to 1 percent until about 1950 and then to a remarkable 2 percent a year. In less than forty years, between 1950 and 1987, world population nearly doubled again – growing from 2.5 billion to almost 5 billion.[3]

Since 1950 population growth has been concentrated largely in the developing countries. In the industrial countries, though a postwar baby boom combined with falling mortality, the population growth rate has not exceeded 1 percent in Europe since 1950 and exceeded 1.5 percent only briefly in North America. At its postwar peak, fertility in the United States meant that families had on average little more than three children; in Europe and Japan postwar families were even smaller. By the 1970s, fertility had fallen in most developed countries to a level near or even below "replacement", that is about two children per couple, the level which over the long run holds population constant. The "demographic transition", that is the shift from a period in which population grows because birth rates exceed death rates, to a period of low death and birth rates and thus little or no population growth, was thus complete in the developed world.[4]

In the same postwar period, population growth in the developing world reached historically unprecedented rates. Driven by falling mortality and continued high or even rising fertility, the population growth rate for developing countries as a group rose above 2 percent a year, peaking at 2.4 percent in the 1960s. It is now around 2 percent a year, because of a slightly greater decline in birth rates than in death rates (see Table 12.1).

Demographers assume the demographic transition will eventually run its course in developing countries as well. The population growth rate in developing countries (and so for the world as a whole), is predicted to decline toward a zero

---

[2] This section is largely adapted from World Bank, *World Development Report 1984*, and Birdsall (1980b).

[3] For a history of world population growth, see Wrigley (1969). The long-run figures for world population growth are from Durand (1977).

[4] See Notestein (1945) for a statement by a demographer of the theory of the demographic transition.

Table 12.1
Birth and death rates and rates of natural increase, by region, 1950–55 to 1980–85

	Crude birth rate			Crude death rate			Natural increase		
	1950–55	1960–65	1980–85	1950–55	1960–65	1980–85	1950–55	1960–65	1980–85
Developed countries	22.7	20.3	15.5	10.1	9.0	9.6	1.3	1.1	0.6
Developing countries	44.4	41.9	31.0	24.2	18.3	10.8	2.0	2.4	2.0
Africa	48.3	48.2	45.9	27.1	23.2	16.6	2.1	2.5	2.9
Latin America	42.5	41.0	31.6	15.4	12.2	8.2	2.7	2.9	2.3
East Asia[a]	43.4	39.0	22.5	25.0	17.3	7.7	1.8	2.2	1.5
Other Asia	41.8	40.1	32.8	22.7	18.2	12.3	1.9	2.2	2.1

[a] China, Hong Kong, Democratic People's Republic of Korea, Republic of Korea, Mongolia, Burma, Democratic Kampuchea, East Timor, Indonesia, Lao People's Democratic Republic, Malaysia, Philippines, Singapore, Socialist Republic of Vietnam, Thailand.
Source: United Nations, Department of International Economic and Social Affairs. *World Population Prospects as Assessed in 1984* (printout).

rate, bringing population stabilization in the twenty-second century.[5] If demographers are correct, the latter part of the twentieth century would thus mark a demographic watershed, the high point of several centuries of accelerating growth, and the beginning of a subsequent monotonic decline in rates of world population growth.

Even with declining growth rates, absolute population size would continue to increase, with world population likely to double to almost 10 billion by 2050.[6] Developing countries could more than double in population size by 2050, while industrial countries increase in population size by perhaps 20 percent.[7]

[5] Based on population projections of the World Bank. Projections of the United Nations and the United States Bureau of the Census differ little at the global level.

[6] See footnote 5.

[7] How certain are demographers' projections of future population growth? For the next three to four decades, the range of error is small. Apart from the unpredictable possibility of catastrophic mortality increases, due to a world war or massive political disintegration, greater or lesser change in mortality than predicted would have minor effects on projected population size – shifting total population size in the developing world up or down by perhaps 5 to 10 percent by the year 2020. One reason is that for most of the developing world, the time when declining mortality produced surges in population growth has passed, because mortality, though still high compared with developed countries, has already fallen considerably. On the fertility side, the range of error is small for several decades because most people who will bear children over that period are already born; population size will differ from that projected only within the range of variation associated with their average number of children. For example, much of the large absolute increases in population projected for developing countries is virtually inevitable; it would occur even were the average fertility of couples to fall immediately to the level typical of industrial societies – about two children per couple. In developing countries, the high fertility and falling mortality of the last three decades mean women now entering childbearing age constitute a large proportion of the total population, and as a group will outnumber greatly the previous cohort of women of childbearing age. Brazil's current population of 138 million is projected to increase to 226 million by the year 2020, while fertility falls gradually to

The rapid population growth of developing countries in the postwar period is partly due to rapid falls in mortality to relatively low levels, given income levels. Since the 1920s, and especially since the end of the Second World War, the main reasons for rising life expectancy in developing countries have been better public health systems, including immunization and pest control, as well as curative health services, educational advances, and the greater political stability that permitted these. Rising incomes and associated improvements in nutrition and sanitation, important to the earlier mortality declines in Europe, have in general played a lesser role in bringing mortality decline in developing countries. For example, a quarter of Sri Lanka's decline in mortality after 1945 is attributable solely to the control of malaria.[8] As a result, the same income today is associated with much lower mortality than has been the case historically. Life expectancy is higher in developing countries today than it was in developed countries at the turn of the century, despite income and education levels that in many countries are still lower.[9] One analyst suggests, on the basis of cross-country regressions of changes in life expectancy from 1960 to 1970 on changes in income and education in the same period, that life expectancy in the developing countries in 1970 would have been about eight years lower had it not been for factors not included in the regression, for example improvements in public health.[10]

In somewhat analogous fashion, fertility has been declining in many developing countries faster than it did historically in today's developed countries (though from higher levels). For Austria, England, and the United States it took about fifty years to go from birth rates of thirty-five to twenty per thousand, an average decline of 0.3 points per year. Postwar birth rate declines in China, Colombia, and Costa Rica have exceeded one point per year. There are plausible explanations, discussed below: education and income growth have been rapid; modern communication has increased the speed with which the idea and legitimacy of fertility control can spread; and modern contraceptives have lowered the costs and increased the effectiveness of individual fertility control. Fertility is also declining at lower levels of income. Marital fertility started falling in most European provinces between 1880 and 1930, when average per capita income already exceeded $1000 (in 1982 dollars), compared with perhaps half that figure when fertility decline began in Latin America and much of Asia.

---

about two children per couple by 2010. Were fertility instead to fall instantaneously to two children per couple (in 1985), the population in 2020 would still increase – to 200 rather than 226 million, a 13 percent difference.

[8] Newman (1965).

[9] Life expectancy in India was fifty-five in 1982, yet India's per capita income is still probably below $300 a year and its literacy rate below 40 percent. Life expectancy in England, Sweden, and the United States was still below fifty in 1900, although average income (in 1982 dollars) was more than $1000 and the literacy rate exceeded 80 percent in all three countries.

[10] Preston (1976).

Has this rapid population growth prevented any rise in income in developing countries? No. Regarding the effect of population growth on economic growth, Malthus appears to have been as wrong about developing countries in this postwar era of demographic transition as he was about nineteenth- and twentieth-century industrializing economies. Except in sub-Saharan Africa in the last decade, growth in total income since 1950 has exceeded growth in population in developing countries, so income per capita has been increasing. Improvements in other measures of living standards have also been marked (other chapters in this Handbook describe improvements in education and health). Indeed, the declines in mortality which contributed to population growth have been in themselves a major achievement. Even in today's poorer developing countries, life expectancy is above the level achieved by richer countries eighty years ago (as are primary school enrollment rates, though income per person and adult literacy are not). Whether countries might have been better off still with slower population growth is a question dealt with in Section 3.

The idea that rapid population growth may have slowed development arises in part from the casual observation that across countries, current fertility and mortality rates tend to be inversely related to per capita income. Figure 12.1 shows the relationship between fertility and country per capita income, based on

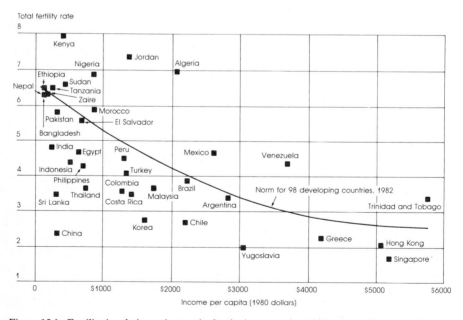

Figure 12.1. Fertility in relation to income in developing countries, 1982. *Source:* World Bank (1984).

a regression including 98 developing countries. Sub-Saharan Africa and the Indian subcontinent (Bangladesh, India, and Pakistan) have the highest levels of fertility and mortality and the lowest incomes; fertility averages five to eight children per woman, and life expectancy is as low as fifty years. Countries of East Asia and Latin America have lower fertility (three to five children), higher life expectancy (about sixty years), and higher incomes. This association across countries also tends to hold within countries. Within countries, individuals with higher income tend to have lower fertility and mortality.

However, there are important exceptions to the general rule. Countries with significantly lower fertility than the norm for those with their income level include China, Colombia, India, Indonesia, Korea, Thailand, and Sri Lanka (Figure 12.1). Countries with high fertility, given their income, include Algeria, Jordan, and Morocco, most countries of sub-Saharan Africa, Venezuela, the Arab oil-rich countries such as Kuwait and Libya (the latter not shown), and even with its recent decline in fertility, Mexico. China, Costa Rica, and Sri Lanka also have relatively high life expectancy. High per capita income (and the industrialization and high rates of urbanization associated with high income) are apparently not necessary for low fertility and high life expectancy. The exceptions suggest the importance of factors other than average income which affect demographic variables – factors that operate at the individual and family level: education, availability and distribution of health services, women's status, access to family planning, prevailing religious views, a country's population policy, and so on. The theory and evidence regarding determinants of fertility at the micro, or family level, are discussed in Section 4.

3. Macroeconomic analyses of the economic consequences of population growth

No consensus has emerged on the effects of the rapid population growth of developing countries on their economic growth. The assumption that rapid population growth was detrimental prevailed in the 1950s and 1960s – when the emphasis in the general development literature was on lack of capital (and savings) coupled with surplus labor in agriculture as the major constraints to economic growth. By the late 1970s, with attention shifting to the efficiency with which capital and other factors of production were utilized, and to the roles of policy in creating (or distorting) positive incentives for efficiency, challenges arose to the conventional view that the apparent abundance of labor in poor countries compared with capital and land was hindering economic growth. Recent analyses have been characterized as "revisionist" Malthusian, in that population growth is viewed as only one among a number of factors that slow development, and the population problem is not seen as a problem of global food scarcity or other natural resource scarcities.[11] Mainstream debate now centers on the quantitative importance of rapid population growth – whether its negative effects are minimal, and in any event so interlinked with more central problems such as poor macroeconomic policies, weak political and social institutions and so on, as to hardly merit direct attention; or greater than minimal, and in effect contributory to other problems.

The argument is not likely to be easily resolved. The amount of solid empirical work on the subject is limited, especially for developing countries, partly because the problem is not for the most part a tractable one for quantitative analysis. In the real world, population change is not only a cause but a consequence of economic change; it cannot be shifted up or down as an exogenous variable in a simple counterfactual experiment. The only natural experiment available for analysis is human history – cross-section analyses are a poor substitute. But long time series of demographic and economic data are rare.[12] Moreover, because population change is a consequence as well as a cause of economic change, the effects of population change are hard to trace. Any effects of population growth on the economy as a whole, positive or negative, are likely to be obscured as families adjust their own economic behavior in response to the economic changes in their environment initially brought on by the population change. For example, an increase in fertility that raises population density in an agricultural area, lowering potential per capita income in the short run, is likely to lead quickly to outmigration, new agricultural techniques, or other adjustments – including a subsequent decline in fertility.[13] And it is not only families that can adjust their own demographic behavior quickly in response to the economic forces arising from population change. Societal institutions and government-designed policy can also play a role in mediating any effects of population change – for example through investment in a search for new technologies (the Green Revolution) to raise agricultural production.

Much of the work on consequences has been in the form of macroeconomic–demographic models. Whether analytic or simulation models, such models, to be tractable, require adoption of some simplifying assumptions, for example regard-

---

[11] See, for example, the report of the National Academy of Sciences [cited as National Research Council (1986)] and World Bank (1984, ch. 5). Kelley, in King and Kelley (1985) has characterized both reports as revisionist.

[12] See Kelley and Williamson (1974) for one of the few cases of a general equilibrium model of economic and demographic change built and tested using historical series – of industrializing Japan. Of course these difficulties apply to other subjects as well – for example, to studies of the effect of education on development.

[13] Indeed, the fundamental behavior is at the micro or family level, and many of the difficulties of the "macro" literature arise because the latter is not grounded in any behavioral formulation. An obvious example is a tendency in much of the literature on macroeconomic consequences not to distinguish between the consequences of a population increase due to declining mortality vs. rising fertility – though the economic conditions producing and resulting from one vs. the other have tended to be very different.

Table 12.2

Rates of growth of population, GNP and GNP per capita, selected countries, 1973–83

	GNP per capita 1983 U.S. ($)	Population growth rate (%) 1973–83	GNP growth rate (%) real 1973–83	GNP per capita growth rate (%) real 1973–83
Low income countries				
Bangladesh	130	2.4	5.5	2.9
India	260	2.3	4.2	1.9
Sri Lanka	330	1.7	5.2	3.4
Kenya	340	4.0	4.7	0.6
Pakistan	390	3.0	6.2	3.1
Middle income countries				
Indonesia	560	2.3	6.8	4.4
Egypt	690	2.5	9.1	6.4
Philippines	750	2.7	5.3	2.5
Nigeria	770	2.7	1.5	−1.1
Thailand	820	2.3	6.3	4.0
Peru	1040	2.4	1.3	−1.1
Costa Rica	1070	2.4	2.4	−0.1
Colombia	1410	1.9	4.1	2.1
Brazil	1870	2.3	4.4	2.0
Korea, Rep. of	2010	1.6	7.0	5.4
Mexico	2180	2.9	5.0	2.0
Venezuela	3830	3.5	2.4	−1.1
Industrialized countries				
United Kingdom	9180	0.0	1.0	1.0
Japan	10110	0.9	4.2	3.3
France	10480	0.4	2.4	2.0
Germany, Fed. Rep.	11400	−0.1	2.1	2.1
Sweden	12440	0.2	1.0	0.8
United States	14080	1.0	2.4	1.3

Source: World Bank (1986b).

ing the substitutability of labor for capital in production, or the rate and sources of technological change. The assumptions themselves often drive the particular results regarding population effects. Even the few large macro models that employ econometrically-estimated empirical results as a way to quantify the direct and indirect effects and the countervailing adjustments, e.g. of the effects of population change on savings or on capital accumulation, cannot mirror the complexity of the real world, and have had little influence on the debate.[14] Empirical work on partial effects – the effect of rapid population growth on natural resources, educational expansion, income distribution, for example – has been more successful in yielding insights into particular links between population

[14] For useful critical reviews of large interactive economic-demographic models, see Sanderson (1980) and Arthur and McNicoll (1975).

growth and economic change, but by its nature has been far from definitive on the net effects of rapid population growth on economies as a whole.

A simple bivariate comparison of countries' rates of growth of gross national product (GNP) with growth rates of population during the 1970s and 1980s illustrates the problem (Table 12.2). There is no clear association between the two rates. In the 1970s, population growth was high in both the low-income countries and in better-off middle-income countries; in the middle-income countries, GNP growth was much higher. In the industrialized countries, both rates were relatively low. Insofar as the two rates are independent of each other, slower overall population growth would raise per capita income faster (or prevent its decline, as in much of Africa in the 1980s). But in at least one sense the two rates are probably not independent; economic growth is likely to contribute to lower death rates and thus faster population growth.

The following discussion is organized according to the concluding points of view of analysts of the macroeconomic consequences of rapid population growth: pessimists, optimists, and what might be called revisionists. For more detailed discussions, the reader is referred to a recent review of the economic literature [McNicoll (1984)], and to two recent assessments of the consequences of rapid population growth: the World Bank's 1984 report on population and development and the National Academy of Science's 1986 report.[15]

3.1. Malthus and successor pessimists

Malthus gave to economics a simple model[16] in which aggregate economic and demographic change were tied together by reproductive behavior at the family level. His model incorporated the classical wage theory, that the supply of labor was completely elastic at the subsistence wage level. In good times, i.e. when average product rose above the subsistence level, marriage occurred more often and earlier and couples had more children; thus higher income per capita led to an increase in population and in the supply of labor. A population increase, however, eventually brought falling wages and rising food prices as an increasing supply of labor ran up against the fixity of land and, given diminishing returns, labor productivity fell. With falling consumption, marriage and fertility rates fell and mortality rose, completing the cycle. In this classical system, total economic output could increase, but the standard of living for most families would not permanently rise; the long-run equilibrium standard of living was at the subsistence level.

Malthus assumed that people would not exercise "preventive checks" to reduce births (his axiomatic "fixity of passion"). That, combined with the assumption of

---

[15] See footnote 11.
[16] Malthus, *Essay on Population*, 1st edition.

diminishing returns in agriculture, made his gloomy predicted outcome a logical necessity.

As a description of trends in the several centuries preceding his 1801 essay, Malthus was largely correct. Data pieced together by demographers and economic historians, on wages, rents, food prices, and fertility and mortality in England from the fourteenth century through the eighteenth century, fit well portions of the Malthusian model.[17] For example, in the fourteenth century the Black Death brought a largely exogenous increase in mortality; as total population fell, wages rose. By the mid-sixteenth century mortality was lower and total population size was recovering; land rents and the relative price of food were rising and wages were falling. Late in the seventeenth century, population growth slowed again; wages again rose and food prices fell.[18]

But as a predictor of the future, Malthus turned out to be wrong,[19] both about diminishing returns and about human reproductive behavior. Even as he wrote, the Industrial Revolution in England was ushering in a period of sustained improvements in technology, yielding gains in labor productivity that outstripped any effect of diminishing returns and assured per capita income gains. And by the end of the nineteenth century, couples were practising conscious control of fertility within marriage, leading to smaller family size. By the beginning of the twentieth century, the economic and demographic characteristics of modern industrial economies were set: steady but slow population growth, with low fertility consciously controlled, sustained productivity increases, and improving consumption standards for the majority.

Malthus and the classical economists were writing at a time when in England population growth was accelerating. With the new burst of population growth in developing countries after the Second World War, economists returned to the Malthusian tradition. The analytic models of Leibenstein (1954) and Nelson (1956) reintroduced population as an endogenous variable influenced by income. In these models, small increases in income in populations at the subsistence level lead to increases in labor supply that swamp small increases in capital or other small "displacements" or stimuli to the economy. The result: a low-level equilibrium trap. Only massive capital formation or a major stimulus can overcome the trap.

Early one-sector neoclassical growth models [Solow (1956)] were similarly Malthusian in that the faster the rate of population growth, and thus the more rapid the increase in labor supply compared with capital formation, the lower the

---

[17] The data provide support for the Ricardian idea of diminishing returns to labor embedded in Malthus's model, but do not actually support Malthus's idea that mortality responds to changes in wages. See Lee (1980) for analysis of a time series of real wage and population figures for England.
[18] See World Bank (1984, Box 4.2, p. 57). The data for that box were assembled by Peter Lindert.
[19] Malthus actually revised his views in a subsequent essay. See Birdsall et al. (1979) for a discussion and citations to Malthus's subsequent essay.

level of per capita consumption. With constant returns to scale and a constant rate of saving, a faster growth rate of the labor force decreases the capital–labor ratio and the productivity of labor. More resources must be used to maintain capital per head, preventing immediate higher consumption and preventing increases in capital per head that would bring higher consumption in future periods. Thus, rapid population growth is harmful even in the absence of diminishing returns. In steady-state growth (with a constant population growth rate as well as a constant savings rate), the steady-state level of consumption is higher the lower the constant rate of population growth. Population growth in these neoclassical steady-state models, however, was treated as exogenous, with no effort to incorporate the determination of population growth via the effects of economic change on mortality, fertility, or marriage rates.

Population growth is also treated as exogenous, and has similar negative effects, in two-sector growth models [Lewis, (1954), Fei and Ranis(1964)]. In these models surplus labor in the agricultural sector is absorbed into manufacturing only if savings and thus capital grow faster than population, or if technological change in the dynamic manufacturing sector offsets the combined effects of diminishing returns in agriculture and population growth. All other things the same, the transfer of labor into manufacturing occurs more rapidly and the share of labor in manufacturing thus grows more rapidly the slower the growth of population. Slower population growth thus speeds the elimination of dualism (the different production and wage determination relations in the two sectors) and hastens the time when neoclassical processes of growth and wage determination permeate the economy as a whole.

These early growth models treated population growth and labor force growth as equivalent, and ignored age structure. In his overlapping generations model, Samuelson (1958) introduced a crude approximation of age structure. He posited two age groups: a younger working population and an older retired population. The younger generation transfers consumption "loans" to the older generation, the "loans" to be repaid by the subsequent generation of younger workers. A sustained increase in population growth raises the proportion of the younger group, causing higher consumption transfers to the old. If a higher population growth rate persists, each generation benefits. Thus, Samuelson came to the opposite conclusion from that reached in the neoclassical growth models: a sustained higher population growth rate leads to higher lifetime economic welfare.

Samuelson ignored dependent children, in effect assuming they pose no costs to parents nor to the economy external to the household.[20] In fact, however, higher population growth that results from higher fertility will increase the proportion of children in a population (and not increase labor supply for about

---

[20] For a steady-state analytic model in which production and consumption are spread more realistically over the life cycle, see Arthur and McNicoll (1978). They find that under typical demographic structures, the net intergenerational transfer effect of higher population growth is likely to be negative.

15 years). To the extent children consume more than they produce, their existence must reduce the consumption and/or the savings of workers or retirees. In a tradition wholly different from the above analytic and deductive models, Coale and Hoover (1958) developed a model highlighting the fact that children are costly, and that high fertility increases the proportion of children in the population. Maintaining that in high fertility societies children's proportionately greater consumption needs (including for education and health, which Coale and Hoover in effect treated as consumption rather than investment) will reduce average savings, Coale and Hoover built into their simulation model of the economy of India the assumption that savings per capita and thus investment per capita fall as the proportion of non-working dependents in the economy rises. Using this model, they made projections of per capita income for India under low, medium and high (exogenous) fertility assumptions, and concluded that over a 30-year period, per capita income could be as much as 40 percent lower under the high compared with the low fertility assumption.

In the Coale and Hoover model, as well as in the standard neoclassical growth models, as long as there is little room for adjustment in the capital–labor ratio and constant or increasing capital–output ratios, the impact on total income of higher fertility and, with a 15-year lag, of faster labor force growth, is bound to be close to zero; thus the impact on per capita income is negative – even without taking into account any negative effect of higher fertility on the savings rate and thus on capital formation. Even if a production function allowing adjustment in the capital–labor ratio is used, the contribution of additional labor to per capita income will still be negative as long as there is a negative effect of population growth on savings and thus insufficient growth of the capital stock. In these models, the only escape is technological progress. If there is sufficient technological progress, and it is responsive to factor scarcities and thus labor-using, additional labor can lead to increases in per capita income even without equivalent capital growth.

The 1958 Coale and Hoover study was followed by a series of related studies in the 1960s and 1970s, simulating the effects of alternative future paths of fertility (and thus changing age structure regimes) on public sector costs associated with provision of education and health services, job opportunities and so forth in different countries.[21] Generally, as in Coale and Hoover, changes in mortality and fertility were treated as exogenous to the economic system, although potentially affected by government policy regarding family planning. Analysts would then compare the costs of a family planning program to reduce fertility to the projected savings in health or education costs associated with lower fertility. In an influential study, Enke (1966) applied this general idea in a cost–benefit analysis of family planning programs. Using estimates of the cost of family planning programs, and his own estimate of the benefit of an "averted birth"

---

[21] Such studies are cited in Birdsall (1977).

achieved by family planning, he compared the return from spending on family planning programs to the return from other forms of development spending, and concluded that spending on family planning was 100 to 500 times more effective.

This conclusion, however, is undoubtedly exaggerated (or surely public spending on family planning programs in developing countries would be much greater than it is – even allowing for political and religious barriers). First, the real costs of family planning programs are not easy to estimate (particularly where family planning is delivered as part of a health program) and are extremely sensitive to the chosen discount rate.[22] Enke probably understated the true costs. Second, estimates of the benefits of an averted birth are sensitive to assumptions about future costs in health, education and other areas. Third, and most important, estimates of the benefits of an averted birth are conceptually problematical, given that most societies value children per se in addition to consumption of goods and services.[23]

Similarly, the Coale and Hoover model and successor macro models designed to illustrate the negative consequences of population growth[24] have been consistently criticized on the grounds that their assumptions – e.g. regarding limited substitutability of capital and labor, the negative effect of a high dependency rate on savings, and the limits of technological change – are incorrect, and on the grounds that fertility is not, as assumed in most of these studies, exogenous. Despite criticism, however, these models did influence thinking substantially in the 1960s and 1970s. In the international development community, they reawakened interest in population growth as a potential policy variable; they alerted those concerned with development to the importance of growth rates and age structure as well as size of populations, making population an issue for Latin America and Africa as well as the densely-populated countries of Asia; and they undoubtedly contributed to the view, especially in the rich countries of the West, that, other things being equal, rapid population growth rates were exacerbating development problems in the world's poor countries.[25]

3.2. The optimists

The pessimists' models have not gone unchallenged. Optimists about the effects of population growth have tended to emphasize as the critical contributors to

---

[22] Estimates of the cost of averting a birth through provision of family planning services ranged, for example, from $1 to $400 in the mid-1970s.

[23] Estimates of the benefits of averting a birth ranged from $100 to $900 in the mid-1970s.

[24] See also *Limits to Growth* [Meadows et al. (1972)], an elaborate but essentially mechanical modelling exercise, in which fixed factors of production and fixed absorptive capacity of the environment were assumed.

[25] That view was reflected, for example, in the 1971 publication of the U.S. National Academy of Sciences, *Rapid Population Growth: Consequences and Policy Implications*.

economic growth such factors as innovation, efficiency in use of productive factors, human as opposed to physical capital, and technological change (in contrast to the neoclassical emphasis on the critical role of physical capital formation). Optimists proffer a growing population as a net contributor to economic growth for two principal reasons: (a) because a larger population brings economies of scale in production and consumption (note the neoclassical models are all scale-neutral); (b) because population pressure and the scale economies population growth brings are likely to encourage technological innovation and organizational and institutional change, particularly in agriculture. In addition, optimists argue that a growing population can stimulate demand and thus reduce investment risk, and permits constant improvement of the labor force with better-trained workers.[26]

In the classical period, Adam Smith invoked scale and resultant induced innovation not only to explain economic growth itself (as is well known) but also as arguments for a positive effect of population growth on economic growth. He noted that a growing population, by widening the market and fostering creativity and innovation, facilitates the division of labor, leading to higher productivity.[27] Later, Marshall also emphasized scale and innovation, noting that "while the part which nature plays in production shows a tendency to diminishing returns, the part which man plays shows a tendency to increasing returns".[28] Economies arise out of increased knowledge, greater specialization, better communications and other organizational changes – all associated with increasing scale of production, which might result from population growth (as well as other factors).

In the modern era, Kuznets, Hirschman and others have also emphasized the potential contribution of a growing population to scale economies and to innovation.[29] But there has been only limited effort to test the expected effects empirically, and that effort has focused solely on the scale effect. Glover and Simon report a strongly positive elasticity of roads per unit area with respect to population density in a cross-national analysis controlling for income.[30] Simon has also estimated positive, though small, elasticities of economic growth with respect to population size (not population growth) using Denison's data on the sources of postwar economic growth in industrial countries.[31] It does seem likely that transport and other infrastructure investments, and public services such as health and education, will have scale economies up to a certain population size:

---

[26] Leibenstein (1967) provides the arithmetic for the latter argument.

[27] See United Nations (1973, p. 41).

[28] See United Nations (1973, p. 44).

[29] Kuznets (1966), Hirschman (1958), Hansen (1939).

[30] Glover and Simon (1975).

[31] See Simon (1977, p. 69). See also Chenery (1960) who reports a small partial elasticity of manufacturing output with respect to population. McNicoll (1984) discusses some possible disadvantages of demographic scale economies and notes that there are other routes to expansion of market size, including of course, higher per capita income (p. 39).

these scale economies mean greater population density could improve economic growth potential in thinly populated rural areas, for example in parts of Africa.

The most effective argument that population growth may encourage innovation has been made by Boserup (1965, 1981) for the agricultural sector. She suggests that increasing population density induces a shift to more labor-intensive farming systems; the shift from long fallow to more frequent cropping then confronts farmers with new innovation possibilities. The shift initially requires greater labor input per workers and results in diminishing returns to labor; therefore it will not occur unless rising population pressure necessitates it. Once such a shift does occur, however, the use of new tools and techniques (for example, the plow) permits large increases in productivity.[32]

On the other hand, there are not only historical but some contemporary examples that appear to refute the Boserup argument; there are cases – nineteenth-century China, twentieth-century Bangladesh and parts of Africa in the last few decades – in which population growth has probably contributed to declining returns. For Bangladesh, a country where high population density in rural areas means labor is already used very intensively, it is difficult to envision what new technologies or tools could be both more labor-intensive and allow higher labor productivity.[33] Finally, outside of agriculture, it is difficult to show that population pressure, rather than other factors, has been the major impetus to innovation.[34]

In his influential 1981 book, *The Ultimate Resource*, Julian Simon also ties innovation to population size, maintaining that a larger population, and thus more people available to use their minds, implies a larger amount of knowledge, all else being equal. Simon constructs a simulation model in which technological innovation is a function of population size. He finds "moderate" population growth (less than 2 percent) to have a positive effect on welfare in the "medium run", that is after a "short-run" period of thirty to eighty years.[35] As with the

---

[32] See also Clark (1967). For formal modelling of the Boserup approach, see Robinson and Schutjer (1984). Note that Robinson and Schutjer, however, fail to distinguish between the shift in farming systems and the introduction of new tools and techniques, lumping both together as "technological change" that shifts the production function outward. For Boserup, only the latter implies the outward shift in production function.

[33] As is pointed out by Ghatak and Ingersent (1984), cited in National Research Council (1986, p. 22). Cassen (1978, pp. 226–227) makes a related point – that rapid population growth leads countries like India to a quicker shift to capital-intensive production, which is less "appropriate" given the greater availability of labor compared to capital but more efficient in terms of total cost. Agriculture in India has become more capital intensive in order to maintain per capita output, as efficient labor-intensive means have been exhausted.

[34] The modern economic theory of induced technological change ties the rate and factor-bias of innovation to factor prices and research investments; but research investment strategies are driven not only by factor prices but by policy views. See Binswanger and Ruttan (1978).

[35] See Simon (1977) for a more technical presentation than in the popularized *The Ultimate Resource*. See Sanderson (1980) for a useful critique of Simon's model and of new Malthusian simulation models.

neo-Malthusian simulation models discussed above, however, it is the assumption built into the model which drives the particular result.

In short, the arguments of the optimists, with the possible exception of the advantages of greater population density in rural areas, though of intuitive appeal, are as poorly supported empirically (and as intrinsically difficult to support) as are the arguments of the pessimists. The arguments rest largely on theory. Yet in theory, the technological and other innovations and scale economies population growth (and greater size and density) may encourage, can also be encouraged independent of rapid population growth – especially through economic policy in the modern era of conscious policy effort to encourage economic growth.

Yet, as with the pessimists in the 1960s and 1970s, the optimists have made their mark on the policy debate. In the 1980s, at least in the United States, optimists' views have caused considerable questioning by the policy community of the earlier consensus that rapid population growth slows development.[36]

3.3. The revisionists

The revisionists view population change as the aggregate outcome of many individual decisions at the micro or family level, and thus one aspect of a larger complex system. The micro or family-level decisions are made in response to signals provided by the larger system; under the Smithian logic of an invisible hand, these family decisions should be presumed to maximize not only individual welfare, but also social welfare, unless there are clear market failures. Among revisionists, differences in the quantitative importance of the negative effects of rapid population growth depend on differences in views of the pervasiveness and relevance of market failures, with for example the World Bank (1984) and Demeny (1986) emphasizing market (and institutional) failures, and the National Research Council of the National Academy of Sciences (1986) emphasizing the ability of the market and institutions to adjust.

The revisionist emphasis on micro-level decisions leads to two related ideas regarding the consequences of population growth for development. First, rapid population growth is not a primary impediment to economic development, but under certain conditions interacts with and exacerbates the effects of failings in economic and social policy. Second, the negative effects of rapid population

---

[36] For a sense of the debate, see the American Enterprise Institute publication [Wattenberg and Zinsmeister (1985)] and the reviews of the National Research Council study (see footnote 11) in *Population and Development Review*, 12:3 (September 1986). The views of the optimists were embodied in the official position taken by the United States at the international conference on population sponsored by the United Nations in Mexico City in August 1984.

growth are likely to be mitigated, especially in the long run, by family and societal adjustments; indeed, insofar as families choose to have many children, certain short-term adjustments, for example a decline a family consumption per capita, are not necessarily a sign of welfare loss.

Revisionists thus refuse to admit to any generalization; the effects of population growth vary by time, place, and circumstances, and must be studied empirically. Most empirical work has been done at the sector level, in contrast to the largely theory-bound economy-wide models of the optimists and pessimists. The sector studies tend to illustrate the limitations of extreme optimist or pessimist views.

3.3.1. Savings and physical investment

Neoclassical growth theory and intergenerational transfer models point to a negative effect of rapid population growth on aggregate savings and investment. In the case of savings, there is little empirical evidence to support the idea. Cross-country studies of the effects of a high dependency burden on aggregate savings have generally found little or negative effect, except in high-income industrial economies, where the high dependency burden is associated with a large proportion of elderly, not with the youthful population due to high fertility.[37] This is not really surprising. For one thing, business savings are not likely to be related systematically to population growth. In addition, governments can, within limits, use fiscal and monetary measures to change a country's savings rate, irrespective of demographic conditions. At the household level, savings in poor countries are probably confined to a small proportion of relatively rich households among whom fertility is already low. For the majority of poorer households, with limited or costly access to banking and credit systems, accumulation of land, tools or other assets is a more likely form of "savings" than financial savings. In poor households in which savings are low or zero to begin with, it is likely that additional children come at the cost of lower per capita consumption rather than lower savings. In less poor households, the anticipated needs of children, especially for schooling, could induce parents to work harder and save more rather than less [Kelley (1980)].[38] Indeed, children may themselves provide a relatively riskless form of savings (e.g. for old age) in environments in which poor capital markets mean other mechanisms to insure future consumption

---

[37]Leff (1969) reports a negative effect of the dependency ratio on savings but the effect disappears if a few East European countries (with high savings and low dependency ratios) are excluded from the regression [see Bilsborrow (1973)]. Mason (1985) finds a negative effect of the old-age dependency burden on savings in industrial countries, but among developing countries, a negative effect only under certain conditions of rapid economic growth.

[38]Kelley uses household data from Kenya.

are unavailable or highly risky [Cain (1983)]. Finally, the association between household savings and fertility at the household level, even where in the expected direction, is probably not a causal one. Rather, both presumably are influenced as development proceeds by improvements in financial markets, increasing access of women to employment in the modern sector, and so on [Hammer (1986)]. Families choose both savings and fertility (as well as labor supply and education for children); savings and fertility are less likely to depend on each other than to be jointly determined by other forces exogenous to the household.

Regarding the effect of rapid population growth on investment, Coale and Hoover (1958) argued that high fertility would deflect public investment resources from "productive" investment to spending on the education and health of the young. But education and health are themselves investments, and may well have higher returns than physical investments,[39] even if governments are more aware of the short-term benefits of physical investments. The argument from neoclassical growth models is that investment per worker will be lower with a higher rate of labor force growth (assuming a savings rate independent of population growth). But the net effect on output depends on the substitutibility of labor for capital and the capital–output ratio, and can be shown to be small under realistic assumptions about the capital–labor ratio and capital–output ratio.[40] Of course it can be argued that developing economies are unlikely to "choose" the labor-intensive technologies that are appropriate for their plentiful labor factor endowment. The revisionist counterargument is that to the extent that poor choice is due to government subsidies to the urban, capital-intensive sector, the fundamental problem is not rapid population growth but poor economic policies.[41] A more straightforward counterargument comes from the simple arithmetic of investment rates in relation to gross domestic product. Comparing poor and rich countries, the effect of differential rates of population growth on capital accumulation is small compared with the effect of the initial level of gross domestic production; in 1980, Kenya, with an investment ratio (gross domestic investment as a percentage of gross domestic product) of 22 percent, could spend only about $5 per potential new worker, while the United States with a lower investment ratio of 18 percent, could spend almost $200, because of its much higher GDP.

---

[39] Wheeler (1985) concludes, for example, that a "social investment" package of education and family planning has much higher returns, on the basis of an econometrically based simulation model.

[40] See National Research Council (1986, p. 42): "Per capita income in a population growing at 3 percent a year would be only 13 percent lower than in one growing at 1 percent a year".

[41] This counterargument fails to note that low capital–labor ratios using existing technology do not necessarily coincide with (efficient) low capital–output ratios, if only technologies appropriate for industrial economy factor endowments are available. As Sen (1975, p. 47) notes, early vintage labor-intensive methods of presently industrialized countries may be inefficient and non-competitive in today's international markets. See footnote 33 for the same point applied to agriculture.

3.3.2. *Natural resources and environment*

The revisionist view is straightforward: for non-renewable resources, such as minerals and oil, over which property rights are generally well established, the market works. The price mechanism assures that any change in their scarcity value will reduce consumption and impel a search for substitutes. More rapid population growth may shorten the period during which humans consume a particular commodity, but will not reduce the number of humans who consume it.[42] Indeed, greater use in one period may be economically justified given the immediate needs of a rapidly growing population and the likelihood that a rising price will speed the discovery of technological substitutes. The only counterargument (and a weak one) is that a longer period might allow more time for serendipitous technological advances – but there is no evidence that such advances are serendipitous as opposed to scarcity-induced.

For renewable resources, however, such as land, forests and fisheries, the problem is more complicated. In contrast to non-renewable resources, greater use in one period need not reduce use in the future – unless use exceeds the rate of regeneration. If use is "excessive", there may be irreversible loss of both the stock and the potential stream of future replenishments. With a large and rapidly growing population, the risk of excessive use and thus permanent degradation is high. Though some borrowing of the stock may be economically sensible in a period of rapid population growth, the benefits of irreversible overuse of the stock in one period must be great indeed to justify the loss of the stream of resources that would otherwise be available in perpetuity.

If renewable resources are also held in common, the risks of rapid population growth are greater. Where property rights are well defined, private landowners or public managers will resist degradation of their property in order to protect its long-run value. But where resources are held in common, and traditional rules have broken down – as when long-established production systems are subject to new economic and social pressures, including a surge in population growth – there can occur a "tragedy of commons".[43] Individual users have no incentive to restrict their own use knowing others will not; and all abuse the commons. This is the classic prisoner's dilemma, or negative externality.

The situation in the African Sahel provides an example where the combination of rapid population growth and poorly-defined property rights may be contributing to overgrazing of cattle during periods of drought (and some say to permanent desertification). There, as elsewhere in Africa, low population density has historically mitigated any need for definition of individual property rights

---

[42] Indeed, application of any positive discount rate would imply more rapid population growth is welfare-enhancing. See National Research Council (1986, pp 15–16).

[43] See Hardin (1968).

and creation of the legal and organizational mechanisms to protect such rights. The revisionist argument would be that the fundamental problem is not rising population but the absence of well-defined property rights; the rapid development of such rights once population density reaches a certain point, e.g. in the agriculturally-rich Kenyan Highlands, would be viewed as a natural and timely institutional response. A sophisticated version of the pessimists' argument is that under some not uncommon conditions, rapid population growth contributes to permanent degradation faster than institutional mechanisms to define rights and control access can be developed.[44] In either case, the role of population growth is seen as one of interaction with and exacerbation of a more fundamental problem rooted in a market failure. However, an empirical measure of the relative contribution of population growth to the overall problem is difficult to conceive.

3.3.3. Health and education

The pessimists' concern that a high dependency burden will reduce the volume of public resources devoted to health and education is only weakly borne out. For education, Schultz (1985) reports no effect of higher population growth on enrollment rates, based on a cross-country regression, though some negative effect on spending per student.[45] There is no comparable analysis of the effect of population growth on government health spending, and in any event those expenditures appear to have little relationship to health conditions, probably because they are often absorbed by urban-based curative services that reach only a small minority. Reforms in health care delivery might easily provide as much improved health as reduction in demand due to lower population growth.[46]

But on this issue, the revisionist emphasis on the need to examine family-level decisions does lead to concern about the potential negative effects of high fertility – not through effects on government budgets, but through effects on family budgets. There is substantial evidence that children from large families have lower educational attainment and reduced levels of health, in developed as well as developing countries.[47] Though many studies have inadequate controls for parents' income and education, there is some evidence that the negative association is greater at lower levels of family income, and pertains especially after four children.[48] Since families in poor countries have on average lower

---

[44] See World Bank (1986a). The unsophisticated version, at least from an economist's point of view, is the standard argument of ecologists that more people implies more rapid resource depletion.

[45] In an earlier study Simon and Pilarski (1979) find a negative effect of higher population growth on secondary enrollment and a positive effect on primary enrollment.

[46] Birdsall (1977, p. 69).

[47] Work on the consequences of high fertility for child health and development has been largely the domain of psychologists, public health specialists and demographers. See Blake (1983) and Maine and McNamara (1985). For an economic view, see Birdsall and Griffin (1988).

[48] Birdsall (1980a). See also studies cited in Birdsall (1977).

income and higher family size than families in rich countries, in poor countries the negative association of large family size and reduced health and education of children will have greater weight in the population as a whole.

However, the strong cross-section association should not be interpreted necessarily as a causal one – of family size on health and education. It is possible that parents decide jointly and simultaneously on both the number of children to have and the size of their parental investment in child health and education. Low income, low returns to education and health investments, and reasonable concern about their own long-term security could lead parents to choose simultaneously both large numbers of children and low investments per child. Thus, an exogenous shock which reduced the number of children – for example the unexpected death of a child – would not necessarily raise parental investments in the health and education of remaining children, in the absence of other changes in the family's environment.

The question thus arises whether parents consciously trade off more children against higher inputs per child, deciding jointly on the quantity and "quality" of children and viewing these as substitutes (a model of fertility which is discussed further in Section 4 below), or whether they invest in children taking the number as given. The question is an important one for policy. If there is a quantity–quality tradeoff, and parents are not "altruistic" toward their children, that is they do not incorporate into their own utility that of their children, then the negative relation of large families with children's health and education may signal a negative intertemporal externality (arising perhaps because parents do not believe they can capture the returns on investing in their children's health and education) – a market failure which could justify public intervention to discourage high fertility. But if parents are altruistic, then efforts to force parents into higher investments in child health and education through certain kinds of interventions, such as quantitative restrictions on numbers of children or imposition of mandatory school attendance, could simply reduce overall family welfare.[49] From a welfare point of view it is reasonable to assume, except in the case of "unwanted" children, that parents have another child only when they feel that the benefits of an additional child to the family as a whole, including to the children already born, exceed the costs.

Governments have generally taken the view that parents are altruistic (or at least that if they are not, they still retain total rights over their own reproductive lives), and that the decision regarding family size should be left to parents. The most widespread form of population policy is public support for family planning programs, justified as a means to assist parents avoid unwanted children for whom the private costs would add to any social costs of additional births. If some

---

[49]A whole range of pricing policies could distort parental demand for the number and "quality" of children; these are discussed in Section 4 below.

children are unwanted, then even altruistic parents must in effect take the number of children as given, and are forced into sequential decision-making and possibly lower investments in child health and education than they would otherwise have made. In a few countries, especially in Asia (where governments view the social costs of high fertility as substantially above the private costs), government spending on family planning is also justified to provide information and "education" to parents about the likely effects of their own high fertility on the health and education of their own children.

The best evidence that unwanted births do reduce parental investments in children is from a study of the effects of twins on children's school enrollment in India. Rosenzweig and Wolpin (1980a) posit that the birth of twins is likely in at least some cases to constitute the exogenous imposition of an "unwanted" child; they report that children from families in which the most recent birth was of twins were significantly less likely to be in school. Here the causal link – from an exogeneously-imposed extra birth to less child schooling – can easily be inferred. The implication is that the elimination of unwanted births, through for example a reduction in the cost of family planning, would raise average education levels among children.

How might the apparent adverse consequences of high fertility for individual families slow a country's overall development? Kuznets, T.W. Schultz and others have argued that the effects of the quality of human effort on aggregate economic growth are substantial;[50] the loss of individual potential due to poor health or lack of education can be translated into lower aggregate labor productivity and lower stocks of entrepreneurial ability and technological innovativeness. The effects of high fertility on parental investments in children may also have bearing on income distribution, as discussed in the next section.

3.3.4. Income distribution

Does high fertility among the poor in all countries, and in poor countries relative to rich, make it more difficult to reduce income inequality?[51] Analysts that have included measures of population growth in cross-national empirical studies of inequality generally do report a positive effect, both in single-equation studies [e.g. Adelman and Morris (1973)] and using simultaneous equations [Repetto (1979)] – but not always [Rodgers (1984)]. However, the single equation studies

---

[50] Kuznets (1966, pp. 80–81); Denison (1962, p. 270), T.W. Schultz (1971). See also the chapters in this Handbook on education and on health and nutrition.

[51] The effects of population growth on the distribution of income (i.e. on income of units relative to each other), must be carefully distinguished from effects on absolute poverty. The latter is closer to effects on "development" broadly defined. For a review of concepts and evidence, see Rodgers (1984). For reviews of the relationship between population growth and income distribution, see Rodgers (1984), Boulier (1977), and Lam (1985).

can be faulted for failure to take into account the possible (also positive) effect of an unequal income distribution on fertility, and the simultaneous equation studies can be faulted for arbitrary use of identifying restrictions. Moreover, all cross-national studies on this subject are reportedly sensitive to the sample of countries chosen [according to Lam (1985)]. Macro-level studies are thus far from definitive; and micro-level studies cannot address this essentially macro question.

The theory, however, linking high population growth to greater income inequality, is straightforward. At least in the short run, increases in the supply of labor relative to capital and land will reduce the return to labor and increase the returns to the other factors, all other things equal, unless there is perfect substitutability between labor and other factors in production. This would imply a period of increasing income inequality since generally a high-income minority owns a disproportionate share of capital and land, and assuming less than proportional substitution of labor for other factors. As discussed above, this Malthusian scenario apparently applied in pre-industrial Europe; and in modern agriculture, though returns to labor have not fallen absolutely, they may have fallen relative to returns to other factors, at least in densely-populated areas of Asia such as Bangladesh.

A more relevant indicator of inequality may now be changes in shares of different types of labor – educated and uneducated, skilled and unskilled, since in today's economies, such a large share of income accrues to labor. There is some empirical evidence that higher fertility rates reduce the share of less-educated workers, presumably increasing income inequality. Apparently workers of different types are not substitutes for each other. Williamson and Lindert (1980) report that increases in the wages of skilled relative to unskilled workers have been a positive function of the rate of population growth in the United States. For Brazil, Behrman and Birdsall (1988) report that wages of uneducated, but not educated, workers, are lower if they belong to a large cohort.

The effects of high fertility on inequality will be heightened or reduced depending on the distribution of fertility levels and of any fertility change across income classes.[52] Suppose aggregate high fertility actually reflects an average of high fertility among the poor majority and low fertility among the rich minority – because, as has tended to be the case in the early stages of a fertility transition, fertility decline has occurred disproportionately among the rich. Then the effect of high fertility on inequality will be heightened since on a per capita basis poor households will have even lower income. On the other hand, the

---

[52] See National Research Council (1986, p. 63). Effects are difficult to establish in any case because measures of inequality such as the Gini coefficient are sensitive to the definition of income – whether on a household or per capita basis [Kuznets (1976)] – and are often ambiguous, indicating greater inequality in some cases even though the income of the non-rich is increasing. Lam (1985) shows why almost no definitive conclusion can be drawn about the effects of fertility change on income distribution using cross-section and time-series data.

opposite will occur if, in the later stages of the transition, fertility decline occurs disproportionately among the poor. Furthermore, if the fertility change is induced by a subsidized family planning service, itself a form of income to households, the above effects will be exaggerated.[53] Insofar as the non-rich are in most countries the beneficiaries of such subsidies (the rich obtaining services through private physicians), family planning subsidies can be said to reduce inequality.

Finally, it is worth noting the long-run effect on income distribution that would result if the adverse effects of high fertility on children's health and education are greater in poor families, as implied by evidence discussed above. If an association between low parental income and high fertility persists over a long period, and high fertility is also associated with lower parental spending on children's human capital, then it is possible to imagine a syndrome of poverty and large family size extending from one generation to the next, producing a kind of permanent underclass which would, barring any change, become ever-larger and poorer.[54] There is, however, no evidence that this has occurred in any society.

4. Microeconomic foundations: The determinants of fertility

As is clear from the discussion in Section 3, much of the work on the macroeconomic consequences of population growth abstracts completely from the causes of the individual and family demographic behavior which in aggregate account for population growth. (An important exception is the literature on the consequences of high fertility for children's health and education.) Fertility behavior is generally ignored or treated as an exogenous policy variable – affected by government through family planning, but independent of the economic events modelled.[55] Malthus is an exception; in his model demographic behavior adjusts in response to economic change. Marriage and fertility rates rise in good times and fall in bad times. But Malthus's model is unsatisfactory in explaining the fertility decline associated with rising incomes in industrializing economies, first in Europe, Japan and America, and more recently in most developing countries

---

[53] National Research Council (1986, p. 63).

[54] Assortative mating, in which the sons of rich parents are more likely to marry the daughters of rich parents and also are likely to have fewer children, would further exaggerate this effort. See Meade (1964, pp. 46–48). For an exploration of the effects of the combination of high fertility, low human capital expenditures and assortative mating on intergenerational mobility using empirically derived estimates, see Birdsall and Meesook (1986).

[55] The behavior at the individual and family level that affects mortality is similarly ignored in the macro-consequences literature. Microlevel analyses of the determinants of mortality are not treated here, but are dealt with in the health and nutrition chapter of this Handbook.

outside Africa. Nor does it explain the generally higher fertility in poor compared with rich countries and households.

This section discusses the relatively recent and rapidly growing microeconomic literature on the determinants of fertility in developing countries. As a body of work, this literature is barely more than a decade old. First, two approaches to the modelling of fertility behavior are described; their conceptual advantages and limitations for analysis of fertility behavior in developing countries are discussed. Second, empirical work on the determinants of fertility in developing countries is reviewed. The review of empirical work is preceded by a discussion of the difficult methodological issues that arise in the estimation of fertility models, focusing on the potential of poor specification and methodologically induced bias to lead to incorrect understanding of fertility behavior.

Several closely related topics are only cursorily dealt with – a necessity given on the one hand the breadth of the literature and on the other the need to provide some coherent focus in this chapter. A relatively new literature (even new compared to the decade life referred to above) on the spacing and timing of births is virtually ignored,[56] at least partly on the grounds that it has to date shed relatively little new light on fertility patterns and trends in developing countries. The literature on intrahousehold allocation of resources[57] – especially of parental resources among children – is not explicitly discussed, though it provides market explanations for phenomena such as the higher infant mortality of girls than boys in India[58] and has bearing on empirical representations of the concept of child "quality" discussed below. Finally, analyses of the determinants of marriage and of household size and structure, including the phenomenon of extended families, are discussed only briefly below.[59] Economic theories of marriage have hardly been tested using developing country data, though the prevalence and average age of marriage are important in accounting for fertility variation across societies.[60] Economic analyses of household structure could shed substantial light on the workings of labor and other factor markets in rural areas of developing countries; an important question is whether having many children and/or a large extended household is an optimizing strategy allowing households to derive benefits otherwise lost due to poorly functioning markets, as suggested for example by Cain (1977, 1983), or whether poorly functioning capital and land

---

[56] But see Newman (1983).

[57] For example, Behrman, Pollak and Taubman (1982). See also Becker and Tomes (1976) and Behrman (1987b).

[58] See Rosenzweig and Schultz (1982b).

[59] For useful discussions of the economics of household structure, see Ben-Porath (1980) and Pollak (1985).

[60] For a theory, see Becker (1973). The study of Boulier and Rosenzweig (1984) is an exception; they provide a careful test using Philippine data. They report that virtually all the variation in fertility across households can be explained by variation in marriage age (itself a positive function of education) and in unobserved (to the econometrician) "marital attractiveness".

markets are not needed to explain large (extended family) households, as suggested by Rosenzweig and Wolpin (1985). But in this field, relatively little has been done to date by economists. (Anthropologists have of course long been interested in characterizing family and kin relations, and in explaining variation across societies in the nucleation or extendedness of households.)

Finally, the discussion below gives short shift to the enormous and rich literature on determinants of fertility in developing countries by other social scientists,[61] except in a few specific instances.

4.1. Economic models of fertility behavior

4.1.1. The household "demand" model

Modern economists' modelling of fertility behavior began with two related insights: that "production" – of meals, healthy children and so on, i.e. of the whole range of goods and services not normally traded in the market – occurs in the household as well as the factory; and that an important input to the production (and consumption) of household-produced commodities is the scarce time of household members. This approach, by explicitly treating non-market activities of households as optimizing decisions representing economic choices, made fertility, an apparently non-economic area of human behavior, a valid subject for study by economists.

In the "household demand" model of fertility [Becker (1960), Willis (1973)],[62] the household maximizes a utility function which includes both the number and quality of children, as well as other consumption:

$$U = U(N, Q, Z), \tag{1}$$

where N is the number of children, Q is per child quality or the household investment in each, and Z represents the rate of consumption of all other commodities.

Parents maximize utility subject to a linearly homogeneous production function constraint in which production of children (and of Z) requires inputs not only of money but of parents' time:

$$C = NQ = f(t_c, x_c), \tag{2}$$

---

[61] Of particular note are Caldwell (1976, 1978), to which economists have reacted; Freedman (1979), discussed below; and various essays in Bulatao and Lee (1983), a volume sponsored by the U.S. National Academy of Sciences. A paper by Davis and Blake (1956) was critical in establishing a framework for analyzing fertility, one which has stood very well the test of time.

[62] See also Reid (1934) for an earlier less formal explication of the same ideas.

where t_c and x_c are vectors of the total amount of time and goods parents devote to children during the parents' lifetime. N and Q enter as separate arguments in the utility function, but in the production function it is child services, C, set equal to NQ, which is produced.

The family faces a "full-income" budget constraint, i.e. a budget constraint defined in terms of non-labor income and total value of parents' time. The budget constraint can be written

$$I = NQ\pi_c + N_{P_N} + Q_{P_Q} + Z\pi_Z, \tag{3}$$

where I is the family's full income; the π_i are the cost-minimizing shadow prices; P_N is a fixed price applying to that component of total child costs that is independent of the level of Q chosen; and P_Q is a fixed price applying to that component of total child costs that is independent of the level of N chosen. The budget constraint reflects the fact that the time and other parental resources devoted to child production represent resources that could have been allocated to market work or to leisure.

Solving the resultant first-order conditions yields a system of demand equations that can be estimated using ordinary least squares:

$$N = N(I, \pi_c, \pi_Z, P_N, P_Q), \tag{4}$$

$$Q = Q(I, \pi_c, \pi_Z, P_N, P_Q), \tag{5}$$

$$Z = Z(I, \pi_c, \pi_Z, P_N, P_Q). \tag{6}$$

In this system of "reduced-form" equations, each of the demands for child numbers and quality, as well as for other goods, is a function of all prices and of income. Child "quality" and child "quantity" are jointly determined dependent variables; neither can be assumed to be an independent determinant of the other. So, for example, the number of children in a family cannot be assumed to be an exogenous influence on the schooling of the children.

In this household model, children, or more correctly child services, are a normal good; with rising income parents will, all other things the same, want more child services. How then does the model explain the association of high and rising income with low and falling fertility? In two possible ways. First is a price effect. A principal component of the cost of children is the time parents devote to childbearing and childrearing [embedded in π_c in eqs. (1) and (2)]. In higher-income societies, wages and thus parents' opportunity cost of time are relatively higher. Insofar as children are more time intensive than other consumption commodities, their relative price rises with rising wages. This price effect may swamp the positive income effect associated with higher wages.[63] Insofar as childbearing and childrearing are women's activities, an increase in women's education, and thus in the opportunity cost of women remaining out of the labor force, should be associated with a decline in fertility – to a larger extent than an increase in men's education (at least as long as women's opportunity cost of time is lower on average than men's, if only because of labor market discrimination). That this appears to be the case (as will be discussed more below) is seen as validation of the household model.

A second explanation for the association of rising income levels with falling fertility is the possibility that parents will substitute "quality" of children for high numbers of "quantity" in the production (rearing) and consumption (enjoying) of children – for example, preferring a few well-educated children to many who are not educated. What might induce such substitution? First, it may be that demand for child quality is more responsive to income gains than demand for child quantity – this is an empirical question. Second, because of the peculiar nature of the production function for child services, a decline in the shadow price of child quality, e.g. an exogenous (to the family) decline in the price of schooling or health care, is likely to cause a decline in the equilibrium quantity of children desired. In the production function for child services, quantity and quality interact – because one must have some children to invest in their quality, one cannot be produced independent of the other. As a result, in the budget constraint the shadow price of child quantity rises with the level of child quality chosen. Similarly, the shadow price of child quality rises with child quantity, or the number of children chosen.[64]

In short, insofar as modern economies are characterized by secular increases in the price of time (indeed the case with rising labor productivity), secular declines in the price of child quality (indeed the case given rising life expectancy and rapidly expanding schooling opportunities), and secular increases in the price of child quantity (indeed the case insofar as modern contraceptives make reduction of child quantity easier), a decline in fertility is not surprising. In the household

---

[63]Of course, among households in which income is not from labor, increases in income are likely to be associated with increases in the demand for children. Given children are more time intensive than most other sources of utility, the price effect can also be stated in these terms: the opportunity cost of parents' time rises in modern societies with rising wages and as the number of non-work alternative uses of time rises (and the relative price of alternative uses of time falls) – consider books, movies, and other entertainment; travel; sports; and so on.

[64]This is true without any special assumption about the substitution between quantity and quality of children in the parents' utility function or in household production. The budget constraint thus includes three types of expenditures on child services: expenditures on child quality that are independent of the quantity of children chosen (such as for household sanitation), expenditures on child quantity that are independent of the level of child quality chosen (here the sole example is probably expenditures on contraceptives, which restrict child quantity), and expenditures on child quality that depend on the number of children chosen (such as for the education of children).

model, the combined price effects swamp any income effect, and in rich countries and households, fertility is lower than in poor countries and households.

4.1.2. The synthesis model

A second approach of economists is the so-called "synthesis" model of fertility [Easterlin, (1978), Easterlin, Pollak and Wachter (1980)]. Like the household demand model, the synthesis model posits a utility maximizing household which faces a set of market and shadow prices, a particular household production function and so on. However, the synthesis model combines this economists' demand-oriented analysis with demographers' modelling of the supply of children, thus "synthesizing" economic and demographic approaches. It also incorporates some aspects of sociologists' emphasis on the endogeneity of tastes (as opposed to the economists' emphasis on utility maximization constrained only by prices and income), thus "synthesizing" economic and sociological approaches.

The synthesis model posits a utility function,

$$U = U(Z, N, d, \alpha, l, \theta, \tau; Z^*, N^*), \tag{7}$$

which includes not only commodities (Z) and completed family size (N), but the utility associated with the frequency of intercourse (α), and the disutility associated with the length of time over which contraception is practiced (θ) and its intensity (τ), and with infant mortality (d). Z^* and N^* denote "normal" levels of consumption and family size in a particular society; the semicolon indicates that the preference ordering over the variables (Z, N, d, etc.) depends on the value of Z^* and N^*. The disutility of infant deaths and the utility of intercourse rule out infanticide and abstinence as means to limit family size. Preferences play a role in determining use of contraception; societal norms play a role in determining preference orderings. The variable (l) denotes a vector of "practices" or societal norms, such as lactation or breastfeeding, appropriate age at marriage, appropriate period of postpartum abstinence and so forth.

Utility is maximized subject to a budget constraint which includes the cost of fertility regulation:

$$f(\theta, \tau),$$

and two production constraints – a birth and a death function:

$$b = \beta(\alpha, Z, X, l, \theta, \tau, \Delta),$$

$$d = D(b, Z, l),$$

$$(N = b - d),$$

where X denotes goods that are purchased and Δ is the length of the reproductive span.

The household takes as given not only goods prices, wage rates and non-labor income (as in the previous model), but the birth and death functions, the cost function for contraception, and the family's reproductive span (thus age at marriage is taken as given).

Regarding demographers' concern with the supply of children, the synthesis model makes two useful and closely related contributions. First is its incorporation of explicit attention to the "supply" of births in the form of the birth production function. Second is its more explicit attention (than in the household model) to the determinants of contraceptive use for a particular couple, given the supply of births, the costs of fertility regulation, and the couple's demand for children.

The production or supply function for child births depends in part on the health and nutritional status of individual parents (incorporated via Z and X),[65] and in part on a set of societal norms which affect fertility (incorporated via l) – for example regarding the appropriate duration of breastfeeding. The set of norms, which may differ across societies, leads to a societal level of "natural fertility" – defined by demographers as the number of children a couple would have if it made no conscious effort to control its fertility.[66] In the long run, these norms may change in response to economic factors, but they are viewed as changing slowly enough so that for individual couples within a given society they can be considered as exogenous to fertility and contraceptive decisions.[67] The birth production function also implicitly assumes couples lack perfect information about the effects of their own behavior on their fertility ("unperceived jointness") – for example they may be unaware (in the short run) that improvements in their own health status will increase their fertility, or that behavior taken for granted, such as breastfeeding, has fertility implications.

Incorporation of a birth production function means the synthesis model is able to account for a widespread empirical reality: that fertility levels in many societies have risen temporarily before beginning a secular decline. The explanation is simple: the "supply" of births increases with improvements in health and

---

[65] Except under famine conditions, there is little empirical evidence that malnutrition reduces fecundity [see Bongaarts (1980)]. However, poor health and disease may reduce the frequency of intercourse, and may lead to fetal loss, and are certainly associated with infant and child mortality; higher infant and child mortality would not reduce fertility per se but would reduce average completed family size.

[66] Henry (1953). See Coale and Trussell (1974) for the presentation of a summary measure of the extent of conscious control of fertility in a society, a measure which relies on the assumption that parity-specific control, if it exists, increases with parity (and age) of the mother.

[67] This effect may be viewed as an effect of "tastes" which in the short run may not be consistent with relative prices, i.e. the marginal rate of substitution along an indifference curve is not equal to the relevant relative prices. However, this is not the "endogenous tastes" with which the proponents of the synthesis model are also concerned.

nutrition, or changes in natural fertility behavior such as reduced breastfeeding or the abandonment of postpartum taboos on intercourse. As long as populations do not perceive the link between changes in behavior and fertility, or have a level of desired fertility that had exceeded "natural" fertility before the changes, the supply function alone will determine overall fertility.

The concern with supply leads logically to explicit modelling of the decision to use contraception to control fertility. Only when the supply of births exceeds demand will deliberate fertility control be considered. (Some would argue that it is only then that the household "demand" model becomes a useful tool for analyzing fertility behavior.) Deliberate fertility control will not occur automatically, however, but only when the benefits of control exceed the costs. The costs of fertility control are explicitly incorporated in the model via inclusion of the disutility of contraception in the parents' utility function. A distinction is made between "optimal" fertility, which results from maximization of the utility function subject to all constraints, including the costs of fertility control, and "desired" fertility, which is the number of children a couple would have were contraception costless. As long as optimal fertility exceeds desired fertility (implying "unwanted" or "excess" births), exogenous (to the couple) declines in the cost of fertility control will lead to lower fertility. Such declines can occur because family planning services become cheaper in money terms; more accessible, reducing time costs; more convenient and easier to use with improvements in technology; and so on.[68]

The synthesis model is also distinguished from the household demand model by its incorporation of endogenous tastes, that is of the possibility, long asserted by sociologists, that one family's fertility behavior is influenced by the fertility behavior and average consumption of other families (via N^* and Z^*).[69] A particular form of endogenous tastes, explored by Easterlin as an explanation for the decline and then postwar rise of fertility in the United States [Easterlin (1973)], is that in which a couple's preferences depend on the consumption and family size of the families in which the husband and wife grew up. However, empirical studies of fertility in developing countries, using the synthesis model [e.g. Easterlin and Crimmins (1985)], have not included any effort to specify and test the formation of tastes, either across generations (as in Easterlin's U.S. study) or across households (for example, of the same socioeconomic class) at one point in time. It would be difficult to do so, though potentially rewarding, since a substantial amount of fertility decline in developing countries is not explained by observed price and income changes.[70] Empirical specification in a one-period

---

[68] See also Bulatao and Lee (1983) for a useful discussion of this aspect of the synthesis model.

[69] For a sociological statement, see Freedman (1979).

[70] Boulier (1985), for example, in a cross-national study explains 77 percent of fertility change between 1965 and 1975, using such variables as changes in income per capita, in education, in availability of family planning and in percent of population in urban areas. Wheeler (1985) explains 80 percent, using a similar model.

model would require use of a simultaneous equations model (in which each couple's tastes, or preferences, depend on other couples' current behavior) or a recursive model (in which each couple's preferences depend on the behavior of previous cohorts), and the data demands are substantial.[71]

4.2. Fertility models: Differences, conceptual limitations

The differences between the household and synthesis model arise much more in the approach to empirical work and the interpretation of empirical results of their respective proponents than in conceptual distinctions. The synthesis model essentially raises additional but not contradictory issues for interpretation and testing. For example, the household demand model easily accommodates the emphasis of the synthesis model on contraceptive use; a decline in the cost of fertility regulation through a decline in the price of contraception is simply modelled as an increase in the price of child quantity. In fact, the importance of the supply of births, the possibility of incomplete information about fecundity, and the resultant effects on contraceptive use and choice have been incorporated into recent household demand model studies, for example by Rosenzweig and Schultz (1985a) in a study of U.S. fertility. An effective specification of the formation of tastes could undoubtedly be similarly incorporated into household demand models.

The synthesis model does suggest an alternative interpretation of empirical results viewed as price and income effects in the household demand model. Wolfe and Behrman (1986) note, for example, that the negative effect of female schooling on fertility may arise due not to a price effect but because female schooling picks up a taste effect. In a study of fertility in Nicaragua they control for family background (their "taste" variable) by looking at fertility differences between siblings; when they do so, the negative effect of female schooling on fertility is eliminated. (Note that this approach assumes an effect of tastes through family background, but does not test any model of how tastes are formed.)

Similarly, what is interpreted in the household demand model as a price effect may be viewed as the effect of a change in taste for children, with that change a function of income. Suppose, for example, that increases in income simply shift parents into a higher socioeconomic reference group, where a higher expenditure

---

[71]An alternative more tractable approach used by sociologists is to test the effect of contemporaneous non-economic variables, which have been purged of "economic" influence. Lestaeghe and Wilson (1986), for example, examine the effect of "secularization" of fertility in Western Europe, 1870–1930, using a variable which is the residual of a measure of secularization regressed on a measure of occupational structure (labor force outside of familial production).

level per child is the norm. Then the price or "cost" of children cannot be viewed as an exogenous variable independent of income.[72]

The major difference between the models, however, is in the manner of their adaptation for empirical work. Proponents of the synthesis model generally view the supply of births and the cost of regulating births as separable from demand for purposes of empirical representation, and as exogenous. Thus, breastfeeding, age at marriage, and previous child mortality experience are treated as exogenous variables in fertility estimations. However, Schultz (1986), in a critique of Easterlin and Crimmins, maintains that these variables should be treated as endogenous in a fertility equation, since they may well reflect the household's fertility preferences and are also likely to be correlated with unobserved fecundity (e.g. more fecund women breastfeed longer, to reduce fecundity). Similarly, he argues that in a contraceptive-use equation, use of such variables as the couple's subjective statement of their desired fertility and the number of methods they know are likely to lead to bias, since such variables are probably not independent of the truly exogenous costs of fertility control. [Easterlin (1986) responds to this criticism by citing demographic evidence that suggests some portion of fertility is exogenous in non-contracepting societies, and evidence from consistency studies indicating that stated attitudes regarding desired fertility are a good predictor of actual subsequent fertility.]

The similarities between these two economic models are greater, however, than the differences. Together, the two models do provide useful insights linking fertility change to the process of economic development.

First, they highlight that fertility behavior in poor economies is (at least largely) rational – the result of an implicit weighing up by parents of the costs and benefits of children. High fertility occurs not because poor families are ignorant or myopic; it occurs because the time costs of raising children are low (indeed there may be little difference between women's and children's wage rates, so that any loss of mother's time in raising young children is quickly made up), and the costs of regulating fertility are high.[73]

Second, the economic models clarify that fertility is one among a number of other household economic decisions, all of which are interdependent, including decisions regarding parental investments in children's health and education and regarding the labor supply of the wife. The household demand model, because of

---

[72] Duesenberry (1960, p. 233), who analyzed the relative income hypothesis (my income relative to my reference group), in explaining aggregate consumption, believes the same approach should explain fertility behavior.

[73] In addition, children provide not only consumption but investment returns – since they can work on the family farm or in the family business and may eventually contribute to the support of parents. This is a point not formally incorporated in the original simpler forms of the household demand or synthesis models, but implicit in the idea that children entail benefits to parents – investment as well as consumption benefits. The point is emphasized in much empirical work on fertility in developing countries.

its emphasis on exogenous price and income changes as the driving force behind the set of household decisions, makes clear that a number of public interventions (not just family planning, but interventions altering time costs or the costs of schooling) are likely to alter fertility. The synthesis model draws attention to the importance of mortality decline and other changes such as declines in breastfeeding in raising the "supply" of children and eventually triggering a demand for a means to limit births; it also underlines the importance, once that point is reached, of the "price" or disutility of using contraception to its actual use.

At the same time, both models have their limits, generally well recognized by their designers, both conceptually and as tools for empirical work. To a large extent, these limits reflect the fact that fertility behavior is itself complex (and these limits are germane for many other economic models – e.g. those explaining education decisions). Among the conceptual limitations of the models are:

(1) The assumption of utility maximization. As is true in the larger field of economics, this assumption has been challenged. The critique is that an increasing degree of rationality in society as a whole is ignored as a possible explanator of fertility decline. For example, a decline in the influence of religion could reduce fertility even in the absence of price changes.

(2) The fact that these are˙ one-period, static models, requiring near perfect information and full certainty. Neither model deals with the likelihood that fertility decisions are not made all at once but are sequential. The collapsing of what is actually a series of decisions, some but not all simultaneously determined, into one decision, in effect requires additional assumptions – including full information and perfect foresight. Parents are assumed to have good information on their lifetime stream of income, on future relative prices of schooling and contraceptives, and on their own fecundity. They are assumed to have full information about characteristics of their children such as innate ability, sex, congenital health problems and so on, which could affect subsequent fertility decisions as well as returns to quality investments. The more educated are expected to be more efficient in use of contraception, in part because they are better processors of new information.[74] But the sociologists' idea that diffusion of information about fertility regulation (absent any price changes) could lower fertility is not incorporated into the models. (The diffusion of the idea and methods of fertility control within linguistic areas is highlighted in the Princeton studies of European fertility decline as critical in explaining the pattern of that decline.[75]) Finally, parents are assumed to face no uncertainty about their own emotional response to future children.

(3) The "family" utility function. In these models, a single utility function is assumed to embody the preferences of husband and wife for number (and

---

[74] For a careful exposition and test of this view, see Rosenzweig and Schultz (1985b).
[75] Coale and Watkins (1986).

quality) of children. Yet there is evidence that husband and wife do not always agree; statistically significant differences are reported in many studies in developing countries [Mason (1986)]. Bargaining models have been proposed, and Folbre (1986) discusses feminist analyses of the household decision-making process – but these have not been incorporated into the standard economic models of fertility.

(4) The issue of marginality. These economic micro models of fertility appear more effective in explaining changes at the margin than in explaining the broad sweep of fertility change over time. Unless the price and income changes on which they focus are very broadly conceived – to include institutional and historical factors (political change, the decline of religion, the rise and fall of "communities") – the contribution of economic models to understanding the broad sweep of fertility change could be limited.

4.3. Empirical studies of fertility behavior

Early empirical studies by economists of the determinants of fertility generally relied on cross-national data. In the typical study, some national measure of fertility is estimated as a function of such indicators of a nation's development as literacy, urbanization, the proportion of labor in agriculture, per capita gross national product, enrollment rates, life expectancy and so on.[76] These studies generally find, not surprisingly, that indicators of advanced development are consistently correlated with low fertility, a point made in Section 2. As is always the case with such regressions, correlations cannot be interpreted as causal. For one thing, a low level of development may be a consequence as well as a cause of high fertility. (This proposition is in fact the subject of Section 3.) Similarly, government support for family planning, included as a variable in more recent single-equation regressions of fertility, is likely to be a consequence as well as a cause of low fertility. Nor can the relative impact of particular variables be interpreted from such regressions since variables missing from the typical specification may be the critical ones affecting fertility. If the Moslem religion causes high fertility, for example, and is negatively correlated with school enrollment (as it is), then the coefficient on enrollment will be upwardly biased in a specification excluding religion.

More recent cross-national studies have resolved these problems to some extent. Wheeler (1985) uses a simultaneous equations framework in which change in per capita income is endogenous to changes in life expectancy and fertility, and public support for family planning is endogenous to earlier fertility change. He and Boulier (1985), who also uses simultaneous equations, specify their fertility equations in terms of changes over various time periods to eliminate bias induced by unobserved country effects.

---

[76]See, for example, Adelman (1963) and other studies tabulated in Birdsall (1977).

Such macro studies have been valuable in establishing broad patterns – especially, for example, that female education above a certain level has a negative effect on fertility and that family planning programs do reduce fertility over and above reductions due to socioeconomic change (a subject discussed further below). However, they cannot elucidate the specific mechanisms through which changes in gross indicators over time, or differences in gross indicators across countries, influence the fertility behavior of individuals. A richer analysis requires studies at the individual and household level.

4.3.1. Methodological issues in micro studies

Adaptation of the economic models outlined above to empirical work is far from straightforward. The most careful studies have dealt with three types of problems:

(1) Some variables and processes central in the models are intrinsically unobservable. "Optimal" and "desired" fertility are not observed at all. Among the "economic" variables, full income and the shadow prices of time of household members who are not employed in the market are not observed. Child quality and fecundity are difficult to measure[77] – fecundity may not even be known with any certainty to the couple. The household production function cannot be specified – time inputs are hard to measure, and production technology is not observed. (How does one measure a mother's efficiency in child care and food preparation?)

(2) Data on variables that could be measured are lacking in most data sets; this is especially the case for the exogenous price variables [eqs. (4), (5), and (6) above]. With a few exceptions, census and household surveys collect no information on the exogenous "prices" critical to the models: e.g. the price of child quality (i.e. price of schooling, health care, child care providers other than parents, food); the price of child quantity or cost of fertility regulation (i.e. access to and cost of contraceptive methods); the price of parental time (i.e. expected wage rates for men and women).[78]

---

[77]On child quality, see Behrman (1987a).

[78]In addition, other variables are often measured with error in developing country settings. For example, data on income and sources of income are difficult to collect in rural settings where own farm production and other self-employment is common. [In a fully specified fertility model, family income is endogenous, since children produce income and labor supply of parents may change as more children are born (the wife's is likely to decline, the husband's to increase). Since income must be treated as a dependent variable, thus measurement error is a real problem.] Even the dependent fertility variable raises problems; completed fertility is only available for older households whose economic situation may be different from what was anticipated when the fertility decisions were made. Panel data on households over several decades would solve the problem (and permit sequential modelling), but are virtually non-existent in developing countries. Statistical techniques such as use of hazard rates and corrections for truncated samples can help, but raise other problems (especially if "natural fertility" is itself changing).

(3) In microanalysis of fertility, the simultaneity problem is a difficult one – at the household level, fertility is likely to be simultaneously determined along with age at marriage, mother's labor supply (and thus household income), savings, infant and child mortality, investment in children, and so on. The rarely available exogenous price data mentioned above are critical to avoiding this problem (and, in fact, allow straightforward reduced-form analysis, avoiding use of a simultaneous equations approach altogether).[79]

Other specification problems are unmeasured and sometimes unobservable fixed effects at the family level – analogous to the problem discussed above in nation-level data; and sample selectivity problems – exclusively rural samples may capture, for example, only couples with a taste for many children, other couples having migrated to urban areas. These specification problems are common to other areas of study besides fertility.

The discussion of results of empirical work on fertility by economists below focuses on a few issues, and illustrates the issues by reference to studies which have dealt effectively with the difficulties cited above.

4.3.2. Female education, labor force participation, and wages

There is some evidence that at low levels of education (e.g. between zero and three or four years), education's effect on fertility is positive [Cochrane (1979)]. This may be due to an increase in fecundity (supply of children) as education increases from very low levels in populations in which fertility is initially below desired fertility, as posited in the synthesis model. It may be that more education is associated with higher income (a variable often missing from studies Cochrane cites), and that the higher income is having a positive effect on fertility (by increasing fecundity or increasing the demand for children), without any offsetting change in a woman's shadow price of time (especially in the largely illiterate populations where this positive effect tends to obtain).

Female education above about four years, however, bears one of the strongest and most consistent negative relationships to fertility. Its negative effect is consistent with the price of time effect postulated in the household model, with a "taste" effect of education on a desire for fewer, more educated children postulated in the synthesis model, and with an efficiency effect, operating through a woman's improved efficiency in the use of contraception. Female education is also associated with a higher age at marriage, and may well have some intangible effect on a woman's ability to plan and on her taste for non-familial activities.

Distinguishing empirically among the postulated mechanisms by which education reduces fertility is difficult. For women who work, the wage rate in theory

---

[79] In some cases it may be difficult to interpret the reduced form coefficients without an underlying structural model; in others, the underlying model may be obvious – e.g. when a decline in the price of contraception leads to lower fertility, an increase in the use of contraception is a reasonable inference.

represents the price of time; but labor supply is endogenous to the fertility decision, and high labor supply and low fertility could result from the taste effect as well as the price of time effect of education. Using U.S. data, Rosenzweig and Seiver (1982) and Rosenzweig and Schultz (1985b) have shown that at least part of the education effect operates through greater efficiency in contraceptive use. Rosenzweig and Schultz demonstrate that the efficiency effect operates through more effective use by educated women of relatively ineffective methods (and their greater ability to decipher information about their own fecundity). Since education's effect is partly one of information-processing, schooling and birth control information programs are substitutes as public programs to encourage low fertility (and both are substitutes for birth control services). (No comparable studies using developing country data are known to this author. Insofar as birth control information is less available in developing countries, the efficiency effect of education may well be critical.)

Female education is also associated with entry by women into the formal market, especially into jobs in the modern sector. Participation in the labor market is negatively associated with fertility only for women in relatively high-wage modern sector jobs. Though there may be a causal effect of work in the formal labor market on fertility, virtually no studies in developing countries have allowed for the simultaneity of the fertility and labor supply decisions – for example, the possibility that women who have few children due to low fecundity decide to work more.[80] The identification problem in a simultaneous model is severe, since most factors that influence labor supply would also influence fertility.[81] Jobs outside the modern sector – in agriculture, cottage industry and so on – which do not take women far from the household and allow flexible hours, do not increase the time cost of raising children and are not associated with low fertility.[82]

As female education and female wages rise, the differential between female and child wages widens. This in itself tends to reduce fertility, since it means that the family's loss of the mother's income when children are young is not easily and quickly made up by children's work.

4.3.3. Child schooling (the "quality" of children)

Though the effect of changing prices for child quality on quantity of children is a fundamental idea in the household demand model, only a few studies have

---

[80] But see McCabe and Rosenzweig (1976).

[81] Fertility but not labor supply would be affected by the price of contraceptives. As Rosenzweig and Wolpin (1980a) point out, in estimating a labor supply equation, if the only source of variation in fertility not due to preferences is the price of contraceptives, two-stage least squares in a simultaneous equations model is redundant. The contraceptive price variable should simply be included in a reduced-form labor supply equation.

[82] See Standing (1983) for a review of the literature on fertility and female labor force participation.

rigorously explored this cross-price effect, i.e. the hypothesis that a decline in the price of child schooling (or child health) will reduce fertility. (The converse effect of a decline in the price of child quantity, and thus in fertility, on child schooling, was discussed in Section 3.) Rosenzweig and Wolpin (1982) show that in India, households in villages with a school have, all other things the same, lower fertility than households in villages without a school. (They also confirm the converse cross-price effect.) Their study is a classic in its demonstration of the use of simple reduced-form ordinary least squares regressions to test the effects of various governmental interventions (more schools, more family planning) on various outcomes – direct own-price effects and indirect cross-price effects. In a subsequent study using the same Indian data, Rosenzweig (1982) shows that farm households more intensively exposed to (exogenous) new agricultural technologies have lower fertility and higher child schooling, similarly implying an alteration in the household's allocation of resources between child quantity and quality in the face of exogenous price changes.

4.3.4. Family income and income distribution

In studies controlling for parents' education and taking into account the endogeneity of family income [e.g. Kelley (1980)], income has a positive effect on fertility.[83] This positive effect is consistent with the pure income effect of the household demand model,[84] and with the increased fecundity or supply of births postulated when income rises in low income households in the synthesis model. Within the same socioeconomic group, e.g. among small farmers, higher income parents also tend to have more children;[85] and in industrial countries, income growth in the short run is associated with higher fertility (e.g. in the United States in the 1950s). In the long run, however, income growth tends to be offset by social changes that reduce fertility – such as rising education, so that people with more income want and have fewer children.

As a result, the association of income and fertility tends to vary according to absolute levels of income. Below some minimum income, increases in income are associated with higher fertility. In the poorest countries of Africa and South Asia, many families are below that threshold. Above that threshold, further increases in income are associated with lower fertility – for a given increase in income, the reduction is greater for low-income groups. Raising the incomes of the rich (be it of rich countries or of rich groups within countries) reduces fertility less than does raising the incomes of the poor. There is, however, no good evidence that the distribution of income has an independent effect on fertility; it is influential

---

[83] Kelley shows that use of ordinary least squares, rather than two-stage least squares with income endogenous, produces a non-significant coefficient on income in a fertility regression.
[84] For a full discussion see Simon (1977).
[85] World Bank (1984, p. 108).

only to the extent that poor households usually have higher absolute incomes if their share of the total is higher.

4.3.5. Markets and old-age security

An important feature of development is that markets enlarge and diversify. Contacts and kin begin to matter less as guarantors of jobs and help with the harvest; children begin to matter less as a form of old-age security. Children's greater geographical mobility in an expanding labor market makes them less dependable as a form of old-age support; at the same time, an expanding capital market means other instruments for old-age security, including private savings and social insurance, emerge.

The household and synthesis models of fertility emphasize the importance to fertility decline of increases in the relative costs of children, especially the time costs as women's education and wages increase and as the market for women's labor expands [see also Lindert (1980, 1983)]. Cain (1981, 1983), however, has criticized the failure of empirical studies based on these models to take into account the pension value of children as security in old age in societies where land and capital markets are poor and means of accumulation other than children are limited.[86] He examines, for example, the near-total reliance of women in societies such as Bangladesh on their sons' support should they be widowed, as an explanation of persistent high fertility that pertains irrespective of the rearing costs of children.

Williamson (1985) incorporates the effect of a poor capital market and an expanding labor market in a study of fertility decline in nineteenth-century England. He notes the importance of "default risk", i.e. the probability that adult children will emigrate from rural areas, and thus leave the parents' household just as they become a net economic benefit at the margin, both to the net cost of a child and to a child's pension value.[87] Using data from nineteenth-century England on rural emigration rates, he shows that rising rates throughout the period reduced the present value of rural male children to parents (but not female children) by about 18 percent of farm wages (using a 5 percent discount rate).[88]

---

[86] Rosenzweig and Wolpin (1985) argue that Cain's approach requires an assumption of a poor capital and land market, but that in fact, the apparent absence of such markets (e.g. of land sales) may itself be simply a manifestation of an optimal implicit contract across generations which maximizes the gains from farm-specific knowledge; older people in effect trade information they have on own-farm characteristics, for support from children.

[87] Caldwell's (1976, 1978) restatement of demographic transition theory emphasizes the shift from child-to-parent "wealth" transfers to parent-to-child transfers in explaining fertility decline, but does not refer explicitly to the "default risk" issue.

[88] The lower the discount rate the greater the relative effect of the default (or emigration rate) on the present value of children. Cain's view that the pension motive affects fertility in effect favors a low discount rate.

The emigration rate matters only if remittances from absent children to parents were small; Williamson notes there is little evidence of remittances, and that capital markets that might have eased transfers were poor. His emphasis on the importance of rural emigration in explaining fertility decline thus relies on the combined assumptions of an increasingly integrated labor market and a poor capital market – a combination of assumptions that has not been explored in developing country settings.

Hammer (1986) has proposed that improvements in capital markets should lower fertility (and increase savings; he argues that increased savings per se are not the cause of lower fertility), and Nugent et al. (1983), using household data from India, show in a fully specified structural model that a weak local capital market is positively associated with higher fertility in nuclear households (and not in extended households, which presumably have greater access to capital through family networks).

4.3.6. Infant mortality and fertility

The demographic transition idea posits that a decline in infant mortality brings about a compensating decline in fertility. The exact nature of any causal link is not well understood, however. At the aggregate level, declines in fertility have tended to lag behind declines in mortality, producing in the 1950s through the early 1970s the rapid rates of population growth outlined in Section 2. The real issue, however, is the effect of declining mortality at the individual and family level. At this level, several problems complicate empirical analyses of the effect of infant mortality on fertility behavior. First, at the family level, high mortality and high fertility may be jointly determined, so that ordinary least squares estimates will be biased. Only recently have analysts attempted to isolate the family-specific exogenous component of life expectancy, in order to analyze the effect on fertility of exogenous changes in mortality; these effects appear much smaller than the endogenous mortality component [Olsen and Wolpin (1983)]. The problem of bias due to simultaneity can also occur because high fertility may cause high mortality, rather than vice versa, for example when the birth of a new child leads to rapid weaning (and poor nutritional status, diarrhea and death) of the preceding child.

Second, there is a biological as well as a behavioral effect of mortality on fertility, for example when with the death of a child a woman ceases breastfeeding, and is then more likely to become pregnant. To predict the long-run effects of declines in mortality on fertility, isolation of the behavioral effect is critical.

Schultz (1981, pp. 131–132) notes that knowledge that some fraction of children is likely to die has two offsetting effects on parents: it increases the cost per surviving child, and increases the number of births required to obtain a survivor. The effect on fertility of declines in the probability that children will die depends on the price elasticity of parental demand for surviving children; if demand is elastic, a reduction in the cost or "price" of births with a decline in (exogenous) mortality should increase the demand for children and raise fertility. If demand is inelastic, mortality decline should reduce fertility. The latter is likely if an exogenous reduction in mortality, by lowering the price of child "quality", encourages investment in child quality, i.e. in schooling and health, as allowed for in the quantity–quality model outlined above.

Finally, once a behavioral response to mortality decline is established, an additional question arises: whether the effect represents a reduction in "replacement" behavior (individual couples replacing lost children) or in "insurance" or "hoarding" behavior (couples having more births than they might otherwise have in order to insure against the possibility of loss). Replacement behavior is purported to be more prominent in populations at the highest and lowest levels of development, such as the industrial economies on the one hand, Bangladesh on the other [Preston (1975)]; for a country like Malaysia, replacement effects appear small [Wolpin (1984), Olsen (1983)].

On average, the evidence is that families do not completely replace a lost child, so that in the short run infant mortality reduces overall population growth, all other things the same. However, the indirect and long-run effect of reduced mortality is probably to reduce fertility in a more than compensating amount – as, with greater certainty about child survival, parents reduce "insurance" births and shift toward child "quality" investments. The need for hoarding or insurance births would appear limited, given the sequential nature of childbearing (which allows replacement); however, it is likely that in high mortality environments, couples begin childbearing earlier (which increases aggregate population growth), and have children more rapidly. Thus, hoarding effects appear to be greater than replacement effects [e.g. Olsen (1983)]. However, the likely root of the apparent long-run response of lower fertility to declining mortality is in the shift toward an entirely new pattern of child investment, as parents adjust their behavior in response to a new environment of costs and benefits of children, of which reduced mortality may be only one component.

4.3.7. Family planning programs and fertility

Whether organized family planning programs, privately or publicly subsidized, contribute to fertility decline is of obvious policy interest; governments of many developing countries, especially in Asia, have subsidized family planning in an effort to reduce fertility, and donors, especially the United States, have supported such efforts financially.

Measuring the impact of family planning programs on fertility decline requires controlling for other possible causes of fertility decline discussed above – such as increases in education or declines in mortality. It also requires data on some exogenous change in the availability or quality of family planning to a household, community or nation. Any such exogenous change would correspond to a change (increase) in the price of child quantity in the household demand model or change (reduction) in the cost of fertility control in the synthesis model. Information on change in the use of services is generally more widely available than information on availability, but does not suffice, since use is endogenous to people's fertility goals.

Lack of good information on change of the "price" of family planning (i.e. in the availability and quality of information or services) meant that until about a decade ago it was difficult to resolve the debate about the relative importance to fertility decline of the supply of family planning services vs. the "demand" factors – increasing education, falling infant mortality and so on. Early family planning programs in Korea, Hong Kong, and other areas of East Asia had been established in countries where a marked fall in fertility was already in progress; some of the continued decline might have occurred even without official programs. In other countries (such as India and Pakistan), where programs were also established in the 1950s and 1960s, fertility was changing little during the 1960s.

More recently, however, such information has accumulated, especially at the national level, e.g. the nation-level measures of family planning program effort of Mauldin and Lapham (1985), and at the community level; and though this and other such measures remain controversial due to measurement problems, they have permitted analyses of fertility change taking into account both supply and demand factors.

In general, the evidence from these analyses is that family planning programs do matter, having some negative effect on fertility independent of demand factors. The negative effect is relatively weak where other factors do not encourage low fertility, but powerful where other factors do. Boulier (1985), for example, estimates a variant of the household demand model for a sample of developing countries, using the Mauldin and Lapham 1972 index of family planning as one variable explaining fertility change over the period 1965–75. Other variables include the change during the same period in life expectancy, in adult literacy, in income per capita, in the proportion of the population in cities of 100000 or more, and in fertility change 1960–65. The 1972 index is treated as an endogenous variable, statistically identified using pre-1965 socioeconomic data. (Boulier himself notes that this is rather arbitrary.) Fertility decline in the period 1960–65 turns out to be an important predictor of the 1972 index; it is plausible that fertility decline itself induces government officials to augment resources for encouraging more fertility decline, particularly if it represents real demand for more services. However, even taking into account that a stronger family planning program in 1972 is associated with prior fertility decline (in 1960–65), the effect of the program on fertility decline in the concurrent period (1965–75) is still positive.

In a similar analysis, Wheeler (1985) estimates the effect of change in the Mauldin–Lapham index between 1972 and 1982 on fertility change from 1970 to 1980. He experiments with various functional forms in a simultaneous equations model, and concludes that in explaining fertility change over this period in developing countries, it is the combination of family planning availability with female education which must be stressed, since specifications including the interaction of these two are the most powerful.

Studies within countries tend to complement these nation-level studies. Not surprisingly, cross-section studies of households, summarized by Boulier (1985), find that people are more likely to know about and use contraception the closer they live to a reliable source. Use of contraception does not necessarily reduce aggregate fertility, of course. However, Schultz (1973a) in a study of administrative regions of Taiwan, found that fertility over the period 1964–69 declined more rapidly where health and family planning workers were more plentiful. Consistent with Wheeler's findings, the impact of workers was greater where child school enrollment rates were greater and infant mortality had declined more.

In another study, Rosenzweig and Wolpin (1982) examined the determinants of recent fertility among women in India in 1968–71, measuring family planning inputs by the fraction of villages having a family planning clinic in the district in which a woman resides. Holding constant wife's and husband's education, wife's age, farm and non-farm residence, and district level health, schooling, and sanitation characteristics, they reported that doubling the number of villages in a district with a family planning clinic (from 2 to 4 percent) would reduce fertility by 13 percent, as well as reducing child mortality and raising school attendance. In a later study [Rosenzweig and Wolpin (1986)], they examined the possibility that the availability of public services such as family planning and health to households cannot be treated as exogenous, given that governments may locate such services in specific places in an effort to compensate for or to complement "demand" factors. For the particular case they study, of the Philippines, they conclude that family planning services do reduce fertility; they also show that conventional tests could understate the true price effect of public programs in reducing fertility and improving health, since government appears to be following a compensatory strategy, locating services where other factors would mitigate against lower fertility and better health.

Finally, recent experimental studies testing the impact of family planning, summarized in World Bank (1984, pp. 119–121) suggest sustained programs can reduce fertility even in rural relatively uneducated populations; the most widely noted of these is that in Matlab, Bangladesh.

Greater availability or improved quality of family planning services, usually at no charge, reduces the overall price to potential users most obviously by reducing the cost of information or of travel. The economic models predict such a price reduction will reduce fertility (except where demand for births still falls short of biological supply); the empirical evidence is consistent with the prediction.

4.4. Endogenous fertility, optimal population size, and social welfare

The discussion in Section 4 underlines the increasing recognition among economists that fertility is endogenous, i.e. that parents determine the number of children they have (and what they bequeath to them) in response to the economic constraints they face and in such a way as to maximize their own utility (which is likely to be in part a function of the welfare of their children). This recognition has in turn led to interest in and analyses of the implications of various potential policies – such as imposition of particular taxes designed to redistribute income – for intra and intergenerational welfare, given that fertility is endogenous. The issue is whether individual or household fertility decisions will bring about a socially optimal size and growth rate of population (in the absence of any purposeful intervention).

A central difficulty in this literature is that, with fertility endogenous, the definition of the population whose welfare is at issue is unclear. How should claims of different people at different times be valued? In particular, should the social welfare function be Benthamite utilitarian, maximizing the total sum of human happiness; Millian, maximizing average human happiness (even if over fewer people); be defined taking both average happiness and its distribution into account, etc. [see Dasgupta (1985)]? The Benthamite criterion will generally lead to a larger optimum population than the Millian.

Nerlove, Razin and Sadka (1984a, 1984b, 1987) [see also Eckstein and Wolpin (1985)], have explored the consequences for optimal population size and for intergenerational social welfare of various individual utility functions, given that fertility is endogenous. The approach, among other things, allows exploration of the consequences of certain market failures. For example, they point out that through marriage, families derive utility from bequests and human capital investments of other families; however, in a world in which parents have virtually no property rights in their children (as they once did through arranged marriages), Pareto optimality cannot be obtained. The result is that parental bequests and investments in children's human capital will be suboptimal; and under certain additional assumptions, the number of children in each family will be too large [Nerlove, Razin and Sadka (1984a)]. In a similar analysis, Batina (1985) shows that policy changes in social security benefits or costs to individuals will affect fertility, in turn affecting retirement savings, future labor stock and possibly the long-run ability of government to finance social security; in short the endogeneity of fertility has implications far beyond the household. [In a similar vein, see Becker and Barro (1985).]

The endogeneity of fertility has been the theme of Section 4; the endogeneity of fertility in turn has welfare theoretic implications for optimal population size. Analyses of these implications is still relatively new, but is likely to be central in closing the loop between the literature on consequences of population growth, and the literature on its determinants.

5. The welfare economics of public policies to reduce fertility

Two rationales have generally been proposed to justify a public policy to influence private fertility behavior: externalities – that the social costs of children may exceed their private costs; and an imperfect market for information about the means of fertility control [e.g. National Research Council (1986)].

5.1. Externalities

A difference between the private and social costs of children could in principle justify public intervention. If parents do not fully internalize the costs of children, they are likely to have higher fertility than is optimal from society's point of view. The opposite case can also apply: if private benefits fall below social benefits (as is argued to be the case in parts of Europe where fertility is now below replacement), parents will not have enough children from society's point of view. There is no consensus on the existence, let alone the size, of negative externalities in developing countries, as demonstrated by the ongoing debate on the macroeconomic consequences of population growth, discussed in Section 3.

There are three situations where externalities may arise.[89] The first is the classic "tragedy of the commons" [Hardin (1968) and see in Section 3 the discussion of natural resources and the environment], applying where a renewable resource is commonly owned and property rights to the resource are not defined.[90] Examples include common agricultural land (for grazing or crops), fisheries, forests, and water for irrigation and sanitation. The fundamental problem is not an externality created by population growth but a market failure – the lack of definable property rights in the common resource. The market failure may be exacerbated by population growth. (Indeed, it is sometimes argued that where resources are held in common, families have a positive incentive for high fertility, as a strategy to increase access to the common resource, while passing most of the cost of higher use to others [see World Bank (1984, p. 55)].) The question in any event is whether or not it is more technically feasible and culturally acceptable to introduce property rights or population limitation; and whether population limitation, in and of itself, could compensate fully for lack of property rights.

---

[89] The following discussion relies heavily on Chomitz and Birdsall (1987).

[90] With a renewable resource, such as land or fisheries, there is the potential of "overexploitation", i.e. use which erodes the base, permanently reducing the otherwise infinitely sustainable productivity of the resource. Rapid population growth may, under some circumstances, increase the likelihood of "overexploitation"; indeed, it may make overexploitation reasonable from an efficiency point of view. Ironically, rapid population growth does not pose the same problem vis-à-vis finite resources. It may accelerate the time period before which the resource is used up, but it will not reduce the absolute numbers of people that benefit from the resource [National Research Council (1986)].

A formally identical situation arises if government spending on social welfare is viewed as a common resource. For a number of reasons (including the existence of external benefits and of natural monopolies), governments provide subsidies for such services as education, health, urban transit, and sanitation. In many countries it is reasonable to suppose that the present value of the cost of these services to a newly born citizen will exceed the present value of that citizen's lifetime tax contributions (or, perhaps, that capital markets do not permit the government to borrow for current educational expenses against a birth cohort's future earnings). In that case, government services are subject to congestion, so that each additional child dilutes the educational and health services available to his classmates. Evidence for the resultant capital dilution with respect to education is presented in Schultz (1985).

In principle, the congestion problem could be eliminated were the subsidy set at the socially optimal level. In fact, however, such subsidies are seldom designed to take into account the potential congestion problem; they are more likely to be a response to external benefits and natural monopolies, as noted above, or to capital market failures. Government efforts to compensate for poor access to capital markets in developing countries may similarly contribute to capital dilution in agriculture and industry [World Bank (1984)]. Again this is a situation not caused by population growth, but probably exacerbated by such growth. The argument then is that rapid population growth dilutes the amount of physical as well as human capital available per worker; this is a version of the "capital-widening" argument of Coale and Hoover (who emphasized dilution of investments in physical capital) discussed in Section 3.

The third situation arises in the labor market, and creates a so-called pecuniary externality, rather than a true externality. As population and thus labor supply increase, especially in rural areas, wages of labor go down, and rents (or returns to physical capital investments) increase. Individually, it is rational for landless or land-poor laborers to have many children as a strategy for maximizing current family labor income as well as their own security in old age. When all pursue this strategy, however, wages are depressed, and both the living standards of parents and of their children are reduced below their expectations. Hence, one poor family's decision to have children can impose costs on its peers.

Such a decline in returns to labor relative to other factors is generally classified as a pecuniary, rather than a true externality, since its consequences are fully reflected in the market. Although wages are depressed by population growth, rents are boosted, so landowners or owners of capital gain (as noted in the discussion of the effects of population growth on income distribution in Section 3). Only if one views a reduction in poverty incidence as a public good can the effect of population growth on wages be construed as a true (non-pecuniary) externality. In any case, decreasing the proportion of the population living in poverty via slowed population growth, though low-cost, and (perhaps) politically feasible, is a slow-acting alternative to such alternative measures as land reform.

5.2. Fertility control and market failure

The second rationale for public policy in the arena of fertility control is the proposition that the market for contraceptive information is poor, and that therefore people have more children than they want, or would want had they more information about easier fertility control.[91] The argument is that there is no opportunity for profit, and thus no private market for the dissemination of information about such means of contraception as rhythm and withdrawal, which involve no sale of a product. In industrial countries, even the market for information about contraceptives that are sold appears to be distorted; for example, magazine and television advertising regarding contraceptives continues to be frowned upon in the United States, even in the face of the rising social costs of adolescent fertility and of AIDS (acquired immune deficiency syndrome, a sexually transmitted disease against which condoms can provide protection).

The argument that the market for contraceptive information is poor, justifying public intervention, is sometimes extended to the idea that the market for certain contraceptive services is poor [World Bank (1984)]. Here the argument is that such contraceptive methods as the pill and the intrauterine device (IUD) require medical backup; they are in effect jointly produced along with health care. Where the demand for private health care is limited, e.g. in poor rural areas of developing countries, the demand for these modern contraceptives per se is therefore unlikely to be met in the private sector.[92]

The result of poor markets, for information and services, can be "unmet need" for family planning, a concept developed by demographers; it denotes a specific empirical measure – i.e. the number (or usually proportion) of eligible (of reproductive age, not pregnant, etc.) women in a sample who say that they want no more children or want to delay childbirth, but are not using contraception. It is not equivalent to the economic concept of unmet demand, as it does not take into account any cost constraint, monetary or otherwise, to the use of contraception [World Bank (1984)]. Unmet need is estimated to be in the range of 10 percent (in Africa) to 30 percent (in such countries as Peru and Bangladesh) of married women aged 15 to 49 [World Bank (1984)]. These figures provide crude indicators of the maximum extent of market failure across countries – maximum since they

---

[91] Other kinds of information that would reduce fertility may also be unavailable, or available at too high a cost for individuals, e.g. information about declining infant mortality (reducing the need for additional births to assure a particular number of surviving children), and information about possible negative health effects for the infant of stopping breastfeeding (breastfeeding inhibits conception).

[92] It could be argued that jointness arises not in production but in consumption, i.e. that to be effective the pill and IUD must be used along with medical care, and that therefore demand for the pill and IUD are reduced (shifted to the left). In fact, however, in the case of the pill, there is evidence of demand independent of medical backup; for example, more than one-half of all purchases of the pill in Brazil are from pharmacists without prescription. The absence of a comparable private market outside Latin America may be due either to heavier government regulation or, in fact, to insufficient demand.

measure "need" (assuming contraception were costless), not demand at a given price or cost.

5.3. Specific policies

Four types of policies to reduce fertility can be distinguished in terms of their potential social welfare effects.

5.3.1. Family planning information and services

Assuming public subsidies are financed appropriately (e.g. the tax system is not highly regressive), and programs are fully voluntary, public involvement in family planning as a means to reduce fertility is likely to improve individual welfare, and is generally endorsed in the economics literature, even when the evidence on the size and importance of externalities is questioned [see, for example, Srinivasan (1987); Bauer (1985), worries, however, that in many countries of Asia and Africa, advice, education and persuasion "in practice shade into coercion"[93]].

5.3.2. Entitlements[94]

Entitlements or "incentives" are specified rewards for specified fertility-related behavior. Chomitz and Birdsall (1987) distinguish two types of incentives for individuals: incentives that reduce barriers to contraceptive use, such as time and travel costs, lack of information, and psychic costs; and incentives that change the relative costs of children and thus directly reduce the demand for children.

In the first category would be payments to individuals who agree to attend a session providing information on contraception, or who are compensated for their time and travel costs when they attend a family planning clinic. These "entitlements" are relatively easy to justify, particularly if they are merely for receipt of information, on the grounds that they help correct for the market failures noted above. The most common form of entitlement in this category, however, is a payment designed to compensate for time and travel costs of clients undergoing sterilization, an irreversible contraceptive procedure; such payments take up as much as 20 percent of total public spending on family planning programs in India and Sri Lanka. These payments do raise a danger. If the desperately poor have difficulty borrowing, as they often do, such payments may be coercive. Such payments also raise the problem of "entrapment" of the

---

[93] Bauer (1985, p. 24).
[94] This and the following section rely heavily on Chomitz and Birdsall (1987).

myopic, who may be induced to forgo long-term benefits of additional children to capture a short-term monetary payment.

In the second category would be payments to individuals (immediate or deferred) associated with maintaining a limit on their number of children. Entitlements to Chinese couples who have only one child – for better housing, higher wages, education privileges for their one child – are a classic example. This second category of entitlements, designed to alter the demand for children, is justified from an efficiency standpoint only where there are externalities; given external costs to private decisions to have children, incentive payments can be used to transfer to parents the savings society receives when the parents forgo a birth. The optimal entitlement or incentive payment (in the sense of maximizing social welfare gains) is the amount at which the gain to society of the last birth averted just offsets the forgone benefits to parents of that birth. The net social gain is equivalent to the difference between the sum of marginal private valuations of births forgone, and their social costs.

The welfare-economic approach to population policy implicit in this argument is very different from the standard outlook. Population policies commonly set a quantitative target for a reduction of the birth rate; how that reduction is allocated among families is treated as a secondary consideration, subordinated to logistical and managerial constraints in meeting the quantity goal. The welfare-economic approach is principally concerned not with the total reduction in births, but with assuring that the private and social value of each birth is identical and that the distribution of any births averted due to entitlement (or tax) policies reflects optimizing decisions by individuals given those policies. The number of averted births is irrelevant.

5.3.3. Taxes and disincentives

A child tax (or any outright payment or loss associated with children, such as reduction of maternity benefits beyond a certain parity) is a disincentive with potential efficiency gains analogous to incentives – but only under perfect market conditions. Disincentives have been used in China and in Singapore (including, for example, restricted education opportunities for higher order children).

Disincentives, particularly in the form of outright payments, pose an obvious distributional problem. Child taxes are likely to affect the poor most severely. Disincentives such as rising costs of education for higher-order children are likely to penalize the wrong generation, i.e. the children who under many circumstances are the generation whose welfare a population policy is intended to improve.

In addition, unless capital markets are perfect, disincentives can become coercive, with substantial welfare losses. For the poor much more than the rich, children are likely to be an important source of old-age income and security. Yet in no society, developed or developing, is it easy to borrow against the future earnings of one's children. Because of this failure of capital markets, a small tax (if non-optimal from a social point of view) could force a poor couple to forgo the birth of a child whose financial security value alone would be greater than the tax.

The potential coercive effect of disincentives contrasts to the overall improvement in welfare with incentives. Compared to a laissez-faire choice set (for example to have two children at income Y, or three children at income Y), an incentive payment clearly improves the choice set (to have two children at income Y plus the payment, or to have three children at income Y). In contrast, a disincentive degrades the choice set (to have two children at income Y or three children at income Y minus the payment), making the family worse off. As the disincentive becomes larger, the effective area of choice becomes smaller; the line between the disincentive and coercion then becomes merely one of degree.

Obviously the system of financing incentives or disincentives can affect the family's true choice set, and thus modify the simple conclusions above.[95] If incentives are financed by taxes, or disincentives are distributed as rebates, the overall effects on social welfare are less clear. Finally, at least in principle, if there are large negative externalities of childbearing, the immediate impact of a disincentive could be offset by a family's share in the social gains of slower population growth.

5.3.4. Quotas

On the face of things, a quota on the number of children any couple can have may appear more "fair" than incentives, since rich and poor alike would be equally constrained. (In China the system of incentives and disincentives to encourage one-child families has amounted to a quota on individual couples in some local areas where officials have been overambitious in meeting local targets.) In contrast to incentives, however, a quota is less fair. A quota in developing countries would deprive the poor of the benefits of additional children – and without any compensation; the rich are less reliant on having many children for economic reasons (and are likely to have more consumption options as well).

In addition, quotas are far less efficient than incentives, imposing potentially heavy welfare costs on many couples and thus on society as a whole. Quotas, to be efficient, would require that the shadow cost of the quota were identical across individuals, and that the marginal benefits of the additional child or children were identical. Yet this is unlikely to be the case. With a quota, some individuals will in effect be rationed; others might choose the number of children permitted,

---

[95]Another argument is that incentive payments in poor societies pose a "tragic choice" – a morally unacceptable choice, for example, between food for the desperately poor, and childbearing. The framing of such choices raises ethical issues beyond the scope of welfare economics.

or fewer children anyway. In short, quotas eliminate any use of the market, with the typical associated losses in consumer welfare.

6. Summary and conclusions

The last four decades have been a period of historically unprecedented rates of population growth in the developing countries, rates that are likely to remain high (though declining) into the next century. Future students of economic development are likely to view these high rates of population growth as a central characteristic of the developing countries in the latter half of the twentieth century – along with the extraordinary increases in education, the modernization of agriculture, the advance of urbanization and so on.

Economists have been the main contributors to the rich literature on the relation between this rapid population growth and the development process itself. The assumption that rapid population growth slowed development prevailed in the 1950s and 1960s – when the emphasis in the economic development literature was on lack of physical capital and surplus labor in agriculture as the major impediments to economic growth. (Even then, however, views on the effects of population growth were not uniform, as the work of Kuznets and others attests.) In early one-sector neoclassical growth models [Solow (1956)] and in the dualistic models with an agricultural and an urban sector [Lewis (1954)], population growth was treated as exogenous. A higher rate of population and thus labor force growth implied a lower rate of capital formation per worker and slower absorption of surplus agricultural labor into the high productivity urban sector, resulting in lower per capita consumption. Later models [Coale and Hoover (1958)] emphasized the possible negative effects of rapid population growth on savings and thus on physical capital formation.

By the 1970s, with attention shifting to the efficiency with which capital and other factors of production are used, and to the role of the state in creating an environment encouraging (or discouraging) efficiency, challenges arose to the then conventional view that the apparent abundance of labor in poor countries compared with capital and land was a factor inhibiting growth and development. Optimists about the effects of population growth began emphasizing and modelling several reasons why rapid population growth might actually encourage economic growth: economies of scale in production and consumption [Glover and Simon (1975)]; technological innovation induced by population pressure [Boserup (1965, 1981)]; and the likelihood that with more births there will be more great minds to produce new ideas and show human ingenuity [Simon (1981)].

Recent critical overviews [World Bank (1984); National Research Council (1986)] conclude that rapid population growth can slow development, but only under specific circumstances and generally with limited or weak effects. In these assessments, the population problem, to the extent it exists, is seen not at all as one of global food scarcity or other natural resource scarcities. These reviews emphasize that rapid population growth is only one among several factors that may slow development, and see rapid population growth as exacerbating (rather than causing) development problems caused fundamentally by other factors, especially government-induced market distortions (such as subsidies to capital that discourage labor-intensive production). Reflecting the influence of the micro-economic literature on the determinants of fertility, these "revisionist" assessments emphasize population change as the aggregate outcome of many individual decisions at the micro or family level, and thus as only one aspect of a larger complex system. The micro or family-level decisions are made in response to signals provided by the larger system. Under the Smithian logic of an invisible hand, these family decisions should be presumed to maximize not only individual welfare, but also social welfare, unless there are clear market failures. Among revisionists, differences in the quantitative importance of the negative effects of rapid population growth depend on differences in views on the pervasiveness and relevance of market failures, with for example the World Bank (1984) and Demeny (1986) emphasizing market (and institutional) failures, and the National Research Council of the National Academy of Sciences (1986) emphasizing the ability of the market and institutions to adjust.

The revisionist emphasis on micro-level decisions leads to two related ideas regarding the consequences of population growth for development. First, rapid population growth is not a primary impediment to economic development, but under certain conditions interacts with and exacerbates the effects of failings in economic and social policy. Second, the negative effects of rapid population growth are likely to be mitigated, especially in the long run, by family and societal adjustments; indeed, insofar as families choose to have many children, certain short-term adjustments, for example a decline in family consumption per capita, are not necessarily a sign of welfare loss.

Revisionists thus refuse to admit to any generalization; the effects of population growth vary by time, place and circumstance, and must be studied empirically. Mainstream debate is now likely to center on the quantitative importance of rapid population growth in particular settings over particular time periods (historical as well as current) – whether any negative effects are minimal, and in any event so interlinked with more central problems such as poor macroeconomic policies or weak political institutions as to hardly merit specific attention; or are large enough to warrant some kind of policy intervention to reduce fertility.

The issue warrants new empirical research for economies with two characteristics: in which there is some likelihood that the social costs of high fertility exceed the private costs, as signalled, for example, by societal and parental difficulties in educating children (e.g. in Bangladesh and in parts of sub-Saharan Africa, where population growth rates remain high and per capita income is low); and in economies in which particular market failures, such as lack of property rights or policy induced market distortions that discourage labor-using technology, are likely to heighten any negative effect of rapid population growth.

In terms of methodology, at least three avenues for new work appear promising. First is the analysis of long (at least 70 years) time series of aggregate economic and demographic data, in which exogenous and endogenous components of population change can be distinguished, and the effects of any exogenous changes (in mortality, for example), thus studied. Such long series should allow a general equilibrium analysis covering indirect (and often compensating) effects as well as direct effects of population growth. Though simulation models of this type have not been particularly useful or convincing, they have tended to rely on cross-section data and intelligent guesses as a basis for parameter estimates; long time series would permit development of more reliable estimates as a quantitative basis for the models. Second is the analysis of family or household data in which any component of exogenous mortality or fertility can be isolated, and its effects examined. Studies of the consequences over several decades for parents and children of large or small family size – in terms of parents' old-age security, children's education, and so on – are surprisingly rare. Studies in a variety of settings – where technology is changing, and where property rights are poorly defined – could contribute significantly. Finally, the development of models linking population growth to the growth and development of social and political institutions and to the creation and adaptation of new technology would enrich considerably the current debate. Since rapid population growth seems most likely to slow development in settings where social and political institutions fail to adapt to the resultant pressures and where market failures or policy-induced market distortions restrict technological change, an interesting question is whether rapid population growth itself contributes to the institutional failures which make such population growth problematic.

Compared with work on the consequences of population growth, which economists have dominated, economists have played a smaller role in work on the determinants of fertility, traditionally the domain of sociologists and demographers. However, the influence of economic thinking on the field has been much greater, if controversial, then the volume of work alone would suggest.

Modern economists' modelling of fertility behavior is based on two related insights: first, that an important range of goods and services not traded in the market – such as meals, healthy children, and so on – are in fact "produced" in the household; and second, that an important input to the production (and consumption) of household-produced commodities is the scarce time of household members. This approach, developed by Mincer (1962) and Becker (1960), explicitly treats non-market activities of households, including childbearing and childrearing as optimizing decisions representing economic choices.

The "household demand" model of fertility [Becker (1960), Willis (1973)], treats the number and "quality" of children as the outcome of parents' utility-maximizing decisions, constrained by shadow prices of the time of household members, by prices of other goods, unearned income and so on. The decline in fertility associated at the societal level with rising income is predicted as the outcome of the increasing cost of children as the shadow price of parents' time rises with overall increases in productivity in developed economies; the fact that children are relatively time intensive is important in raising their costs. This price effect outweighs a positive income effect. The opportunity cost of women's time is particularly important, given women's traditionally dominant role in child care. Falling fertility may also be the result of the decline in the relative price of child quality compared with quantity, which may induce substitution of the former for the latter.

In short, insofar as modern economies have been characterized by secular increases in the price of time (with rising labor productivity), secular declines in the price of child quality (with rising life expectancy, expanding schooling opportunities and high returns to schooling), and secular increases in the price of child quantity (with declines in the cost of fertility control), the decline in fertility is entirely consistent with the household demand model.

The "synthesis" model [Easterlin (1978), Easterlin, Pollak and Wachter (1980)] combines this demand-oriented analysis with demographers' modelling of the supply of children, and incorporates some aspects of sociologists' emphasis on the endogeneity of tastes (thus synthesizing the approaches of different social sciences).

The synthesis model directs explicit attention to the issue of the biological supply of births in traditional societies, through a birth production function which depends on the health status of parents and on societal norms that affect fertility such as breastfeeding practices. Attention to the possibly-constrained supply of births means the synthesis model is able to account for a widespread empirical regularity: that fertility levels in many societies have risen temporarily before beginning a secular decline. One explanation for this is the possibility that populations have an initial level of desired fertility that exceeds the supply of births. As the supply increases with improvements in health or reductions in breastfeeding, aggregate birth rates increase. Only when desired fertility becomes biologically attainable do demand factors play a role in determining overall fertility.

The synthesis model also incorporates explicit attention to the determinants of contraceptive use for a couple, given the supply of births, the costs of fertility regulation, and the couple's demand for children. When the potential supply of births exceeds the couple's demand, deliberate fertility control will be considered. Fertility control will be adopted, however, only if the benefits of control exceed the costs. "Optimal" fertility (taking into account the disutility of contraceptive use) may exceed "desired" fertility (the fertility level a couple would have were contraception costless); as long as it does, declines in the cost of fertility control will lead to lower fertility. Such declines can occur because family planning services become, for example, more accessible, more convenient to use as technology improves, or cheaper in money terms.

These models have provided a basis for a considerable body of empirical work using household level data to test the fundamentally behavioral models. This work has grown both in volume and in sophistication; much of it is highly technical, with considerable effort going to resolving, through improved econometrics, problems of unobservable variables (such as the shadow price of a mother's time); of poor data, particularly on exogenous prices of child quality and fertility control; and of simultaneity among many household decisions. In contrast to early empirical studies which primarily established overall patterns using more aggregated data, these efforts have borne fruit in the form of increasing confidence in certain results, and increasing ability to focus on critical policy questions.

For example, such work has strongly confirmed the hypothesis that parents' education, especially a mother's education above primary level, will be associated with lower fertility. The effect of education may be due to the shadow price of time effect, to a "taste" effect on a desire for more educated higher quality children, or to an efficiency effect associated with more efficient use of contraception; empirical work has rarely succeeded in distinguishing among these, or in formally excluding any one explanation (or model).

Improved access to child schooling and to health facilities (lowering the relative price of child quality) has also been established as a factor reducing fertility. There is some evidence that increasing access to capital markets, which improves opportunities for saving in old age, reduces fertility (at least in nuclear households) although this idea has been much less widely tested.

Extensive work on the relationship between fertility and infant mortality shows convincingly that reductions in infant mortality induce lower fertility over and above any strictly biological effect. Recent analyses suggest, for example, that families in high-mortality environments "hoard" births, i.e. have extra births to insure against the possibility of child deaths; part of fertility decline in societies with falling mortality is probably due to a reduction in this hoarding. In the short run, however, fertility declines are not offsetting, so population growth rates rise (as in much of the postwar period in developing countries).

Finally, increasing work on the question of whether organized family planning programs reduce fertility indicates they do, over and above the effects of other factors such as increasing education.

The economic models guiding this empirical work have provided useful insights linking fertility change to the process of economic development and useful insights regarding appropriate policies to reduce fertility. First, they highlight that fertility behavior in poor economies is largely rational – the result of an implicit weighing up by parents of the costs and benefits of children. High fertility occurs not because poor families are poor or myopic, but because the time costs of raising children are low, the relative price of child quality is high, and the costs of regulating fertility are high. Because fertility outcomes reflect parental choices, policies to reduce fertility must be aimed at altering the prices that affect those choices, not at quantitative controls, if such policies are to be welfare enhancing. At the same time, as noted above, an increase in the number of children in a family must be considered as welfare enhancing from the parents' point of view, even if it reduces per capita consumption of the family (and, of course, the same principle applies at the societal level).

Second, the models clarify that fertility is one among a wide range of other interrelated household decisions, including decisions regarding parental investments in children's health and education and regarding the labor supply of the wife. Thus, a number of interventions (not just family planning, but interventions altering women's shadow price of time, the costs of schooling, the costs of child health) are likely to alter fertility.

A high priority for new research on fertility determinants is more explicit modelling of how changes in capital and labor markets affect fertility. Changes in these markets are a central part of the overall development process, tend to be interlinked, and are closely affected by government policies. Two obvious examples are the effects on fertility of changing labor markets for women and of financial markets for old age savings. A second area where economists' work has been limited is the cost effectiveness and welfare effects of family planning and entitlement and tax policies designed to reduce (and sometimes to increase) fertility.

The above-summarized work of economists on macroeconomic consequences of population growth and on microeconomic determinants of fertility behavior have each contributed to an increasingly coherent view on the part of economists of the merits of various approaches to population policy. This view has played a key role in shaping recent debate on policy in the development community, as seen most obviously in the approach taken in National Research Council (1986).

Economists have proferred two rationales for a public policy to influence private fertility behavior [World Bank (1984), National Research Council (1986)]. The first is externalities – that the social costs of children may exceed their private costs. From this point of view, negative consequences of population growth, if those negative consequences are narrowly defined as slower growth of per capita income, should not be a public concern as long as the costs of such growth are internalized completely by those who have children. If those costs are fully internalized, parents are clearly accepting some loss of consumption in return for other benefits children provide. The need for public policy arises only if some such costs are passed on to society as a whole. An example is the possibility that a larger population will exacerbate abuse of common property (the environmental issue). Here the fundamental problem is in externality caused by lack of definable property rights in the common resource. Population growth is not the cause of the externality, but could exacerbate the resultant abuses.

The second rationale is the proposition that the market for contraceptive information, and possibly for certain contraceptive services, is poor, especially in developing countries. This would justify some public subsidies for contraceptive information and services, to relieve the otherwise "unmet need" for such information and services. This second rationale is important in justifying family planning programs, irrespective of any consensus on the economic consequences of population growth. It also justifies outright payments to individuals (incentives) who spend time acquiring information about contraception. (Other incentive programs, however, that are tied to irreversible sterilization, do raise the danger of entrapment of the myopic, or entrapment of the desperately poor wherever imperfect, capital markets prevent borrowing by the poor – which is virtually everywhere.)

In contrast, payments or entitlements and taxes designed to alter the demand for children are justified from an efficiency standpoint only where there are externalities. Such payments are difficult to design and administer even where externalities can be shown. From a welfare-theoretic point of view, such payments (or such taxes), taking into account their financing, should assure that births averted are precisely those for which the social costs would have exceeded the private costs – implying extraordinarily difficult design of policy to assure targetting to the right couples and prevent welfare losses. Taxes are more problematic than outright payments since they restrict choice wherever borrowing is difficult. Finally, quotas on the number of children per family are still worse. They are likely to impose substantial welfare costs since the shadow cost of any quota and the marginal benefits of additional children are bound to vary across households.

References

Adelman, I. (1963) 'An econometric analysis of population growth', *American Economic Review*, 53:314–338.

Adelman, I. and Morris, C.T. (1973) *Economic growth and social equity in developing countries*. Palo Alto, CA: Stanford University Press.

Ananta, A. (1985) 'Observable variables in Easterlin's synthesis fertility model: The case of Indonesia', *Economic Development and Cultural Change*, 33.

Arthur, W.B. and McNicoll, G. (1975) 'Large-scale simulation models in population and development: What use to planners?' *Population and Development Review*, 1:251–265.

Arthur, W.B. and McNicoll, G. (1978) 'Samuelson, population and intergenerational transfers', *International Economic Review*, 19:241–246.

Batina, G. (1985) 'Social security in an overlapping generations model with endogenous fertility decision-making', Washington State University, mimeo.

Bauer, P.T. (1985) paper (no title), in: B. Wattenberg and K. Zinsmeister, eds., *Are world population trends a problem*? Washington, DC: American Enterprise Institute for Public Policy Research.

Becker, G.S. (1960) 'An economic analysis of fertility', in: Universities–National Bureau Committee for Economic Research, ed., *Demographic and economic change in developed countries*. Princeton, NJ: Princeton University Press.

Becker, G.S. (1965) 'A theory of the allocation of time', *The Economic Journal*, 76:493–517.

Becker, G.S. (1973) 'A theory of marriage, part I', *Journal of Political Economy*, 81:813–846.

Becker, G.S. (1984) *A treatise on the family*. Cambridge, MA: Harvard University Press.

Becker, G.S. and Barro, R.J. (1985) 'A reformulation of the economic theory of fertility', University of Chicago, mimeo.

Becker, G.S. and Lewis, H.G. (1973) 'Interaction between quantity and quality in children', *Journal of Political Economy*, 81:S279–S288.

Becker, G.S. and Tomes, N. (1976) 'Child endowments and the quantity and quality of children', *Journal of Political Economy*, August (supplement):S143–162.

Behrman, J.R. (1987a) 'Is child schooling a poor proxy for child quality?', *Demography*, 24:341–359.

Behrman, J.R. (1987b) 'Nutrition, health, birth order and seasonality: Intrahousehold allocation in rural India', *Journal of Development Economics*.

Behrman, J.R. and Birdsall, N. (1988) 'The reward for choosing well the timing of one's birth: Cohort effects and earnings functions for Brazilian males', *Review of Economics and Statistics*, forthcoming.

Behrman, J.R., Pollak, R.A. and Taubman, P. (1982) 'Parental preference and provision for progeny', *Journal of Political Economy*, February:52–73.

Ben-Porath, Y. (1980) 'The F. connection: Families, friends and firms and the organization of exchange', *Population and Development Review*, 6:1–30.

Berelson, B. and Lieberson, J. (1979) 'Government efforts to influence fertility: The ethical issues', *Population Bulletin*, 5:581–613.

Bilsborrow, R.E. (1973) 'Dependency rates and aggregate savings rates: Corrections and further analyses', University of North Carolina, mimeo.

Binswanger, H. and Ruttan, V.W. (1978) *Induced innovation: Technology institutions and development*. Baltimore MD: Johns Hopkins University Press.

Birdsall, N. (1977) 'Analytical approaches to the relationship of population growth and development', *Population and Development Review*, 3:63–102.

Birdsall, N. (1980a) 'A cost of siblings: Child schooling in urban Colombia', in: J. Simon and J. DaVanzo, eds., *Research in population economics*, Vol. 2. Greenwich, CT: JAI Press.

Birdsall, N. (1980b) 'Population growth and poverty in the developing world', *Population Bulletin*, 35.

Birdsall, N. and Griffin, C.C. (1988) 'Fertility and poverty in developing countries', *Journal of Policy Modeling*, forthcoming.

Birdsall, N. and Meesook, O. (1986) 'Children's education and the intergenerational transmission of inequality: A simulation', *Economics of Education Review*, 5:239–256.

Birdsall, N., Fei, J., Kuznets, S., Ranis, G. and Schultz, T.P. (1979) 'Demography and development in the 1980s', in: P. Hansen, ed., *World population and development – Challenges and prospects*. Syracuse, NY: Syracuse University Press.

Blake, J. (1983) 'Family size and the quality of children', *Demography*, 18:421–442.

Bongaarts, J. 'Does malnutrition affect fecundity? A summary of evidence', *Science*, 208:564–569.

Boserup, E. (1965) *The conditions of agricultural growth*. London: Allen and Unwin.

Boserup, E. (1981) *Population growth and technological change: A study of long-term trends*. Chicago, IL: University of Chicago Press.

Boulier, B.L. (1977) 'Population policy and income distribution', in: C.R. Frank and R.C. Webb, eds., *Income distribution and growth in the less developed countries*. Washington, DC: Brookings Institution.

Boulier, B.L. (1985) 'Family planning programs and contraceptive availability: Their effects on contraceptive use and fertility', in: N. Birdsall, ed., *The effects of family planning programs on fertility in the developing world*. World Bank Staff working paper no. 677, Washington, DC.

Boulier, B.L. and Rosenzweig, M.R. (1984) 'Schooling, search and spouse selection: Testing the economic theory of marriage', *Journal of Political Economy*, 92:712–732.

Bulatao, R.A. (1984) 'Reducing fertility in developing countries: A review of determinants and policy levers', World Bank Staff working paper no. 680, Washington, DC.

Bulatao, R.A. and Lee, R.D., eds. (1983) *Determinants of fertility in developing countries*, Vols. I & II. New York: Academic Press.

Cain, M.T. (1977) 'The economic activities of children in a village in Bangladesh', *Population and Development Review*, 3:201–228.

Cain, M.T. (1981) 'Risk and insurance perspectives on fertility and agrarian change in India and Bangladesh', *Population and Development Review*, 7:435–474.

Cain, M.T. (1983) 'Fertility as an adjustment to risk', *Population and Development Review*, 9:688–702.

Caldwell, J.C. (1976) 'Toward a restatement of demographic theory', *Population and Development Review*, 2:321–366.

Caldwell, J.C. (1978) 'A theory of fertility: From high plateau to destabilization', *Population and Development Review*, 4:553–577.

Cassen, R.H. (1978) *India: Population, economy and society*. New York: Holmes and Meir Publishers, Inc.

Chenery, H. (1960) 'Patterns of industrial growth', *American Economic Review*, 50:624–654.

Chomitz, K.M. and Birdsall, N. (1987) 'Incentives for reducing fertility: Concepts and issues', World Bank, Population, Health and Nutrition Department discussion paper.

Clark, C. (1967) *Population growth and land use*. New York: St. Martin's Press.

Coale, A.J. and Hoover, E.M. (1958) *Population growth and economic development in low-income countries*. Princeton, NJ: Princeton University Press.

Coale, A.J. and Trussell, J.T. (1974) 'Model fertility schedules: Variations in the age structure of childbearing in human populations', *Population Index*, 40:185–258.

Coale, A.J. and Watkins, S.C., eds. (1986) *The decline of fertility in Europe*. Princeton, NJ: Princeton University Press.

Cochrane, S.H. (1979) *Fertility and education: What do we really know?* World Bank Staff occasional paper, no. 26. Baltimore, MD: Johns Hopkins University Press.

Cochrane, S.H. and Zachariah, K.C. (1983) 'Infant and child mortality as a determinant of fertility: The policy implications', World Bank Staff working paper no. 556, Washington, DC.

Crimmins, E.M., Easterlin, R.A., Jejeebhoy, S.J. and Srinivasan, K. (1984) 'New perspectives on the demographic transition: A theoretical and empirical analysis of an Indian state, 1951–1975', *Economic Development and Cultural Change*, 32:227–253.

Dasgupta, P. (1985) 'The ethical foundations of population policy', Background paper prepared for the Working Groups on Population and Economic Development, Committee on Population, National Research Council, Washington, DC.

Davis, K. and Blake, J. (1956) 'Social structure and fertility', *Economic Development and Cultural Change*, 4:211–235.

Demeny, P. (1971) 'The economics of population control', in: *Rapid population growth*, Vol. 2. Baltimore, MD: Johns Hopkins University Press.

Demeny, P. (1986) 'Population and the invisible hand', *Demography*, 23:473–487.

Denison, E.F. (1962) *The sources of economic growth and the alternatives before us*. New York: Committee for Economic Development.

Duesenberry, J. (1969) "Comment on 'An economic analysis of fertility' by Gary Becker", in: *Demographic and economic change in developed countries*. National Bureau of Economic Research Conference Series. Princeton, NJ: Princeton University Press.

Durand, J.D. (1977) 'Historical estimates of world population: An evaluation', *Population and Development Review*, 3:253–296.

Easterlin, R.A. (1973) 'Relative economic status and the American fertility swing', in: E.B. Sheldon, ed., *Family economic behavior: Problems and prospects*. Philadelphia, PA: J.B. Lippincott.

Easterlin, R.A. (1975) 'An economic framework for fertility analysis', *Studies in Family Planning*, 6:54–63.

Easterlin, R.A. (1978) 'The economics and sociology of fertility: A synthesis', in: C. Tilley, ed., *Historical studies of changing fertility*. Princeton, NJ: Princeton University Press.

Easterlin, R.A., ed. (1980) *Population and economic change in developing countries*. Chicago, IL: University of Chicago Press.

Easterlin, R.A. (1986) 'Economic preconceptions and demographic research – A comment', *Population and Development Review*, 12:517–528.

Easterlin, R.A. and Crimmins, E. (1985) *The fertility revolution: A supply–demand analysis*. Chicago, IL: University of Chicago Press.

Easterlin, R.A., Pollak, R.A. and Wachter, M.C. (1980) 'Toward a more general economic model of fertility determination: Endogenous preferences and natural fertility', in: R.A. Easterlin, ed., *Population and economic change in developing countries*. Chicago, IL: University of Chicago Press.

Eckstein, Z. and Wolpin, K.I. (1985) 'Endogenous fertility and optimal population size', *Journal of Public Economics*, 27:93–106.

Enke, S. (1966) 'The economic aspects of slowing population growth', *The Economic Journal*, 76:44–56.

Fei, J.C.H. and Ranis, G. (1964) *Development of the labor surplus economy: Theory and practice*. Homewood, IL: R.D. Irwin.

Folbre, N. (1986) 'Cleaning house – new perspectives on household and economic development', *Journal of Development Economics*, 22:5–40.

Freedman, R. (1979) 'Theories of fertility decline: A reappraisal', in: P. Hauser, ed., *World population and development: Challenges and prospects*. Syracuse, NY: Syracuse University Press.

Ghatak, S. and Ingersent, K. (1984) *Agriculture and economic development*. Baltimore, MD: Johns Hopkins University Press.

Glover, D.R. and Simon, J. (1975) 'The effect of population density on infrastructure: The case of road building', *Economic Development and Cultural Change*, 23:453–468.

Hajnal, J. (1965) 'European marriage patterns in perspective', in: D.V. Glass and D.E.C. Eversley, eds., *Population in history: Essays in historical demography*. Chicago, IL: Aldine.

Hammer, J. (1986) 'Population growth and savings in LDCs: A survey article', *World Development*, 14:579–591.

Hansen, A.H. (1939) 'Economic progress and declining population growth', *American Economic Review*, 29:1–15.

Hardin, G. (1968) 'The tragedy of the commons', *Science*, 162:1243–1248.

Heer, D.M. (1983) 'Infant and child mortality and the demand for children', in: R.A. Bulatao and R.D. Lee, eds., *Determinants of fertility in developing countries*, Vol. 1. New York: Academic Press.

Henry, L. (1953) 'Fondements theoriques des mesures de la fecondite naturelle', *Review de l'Institut Internationale de Statistique*, 21:135–151. Translated in: M. Sheps and E. Lapierre, eds., *On the measurement of human fertility*. Amsterdam: Elsevier, 1972.

Hirschman, A.O. (1958) *The strategy of economic development*. New Haven, CT: Yale University Press.

Keeley, M.C. (1977) 'The economics of family formation', *Economic Inquiry*, 15:238–249.

Kelley, A.C. (1974) 'The role of population models in models of economic growth', *American Economic Review, Papers and Proceedings*, 64:39–44.

Kelley, A.C. (1980) 'Interactions of economic and demographic household behavior', in: R.A. Easterlin, ed., *Population and economic change in developing countries*. Chicago, IL: University of Chicago Press.

Kelley, A.C. and Williamson, J. (1974) *Lessons from Japanese development: An analytical economic history*. Chicago, IL: University of Chicago Press.

King, T. and Kelley, A.C. (1985) 'The new population debate: Two views on population growth and economic development', Public Trends and Public Policy Series No. 7, Population Reference Bureau, Washington, DC.

King, T. et al. (1976) *Population policies and economic development*. Baltimore, MD: Johns Hopkins University Press.

Knodel, J. and van de Walle, E. (1979) 'Lessons from the past: Policy implications of historical fertility studies', *Population and Development Review*, 5:217–245.

Kotlikoff, L.J. and Spivak, A. (1982) 'The family as an incomplete annuities market', *Journal of Political Economy*, April:372–391.

Kuznets, S. (1966) *Modern economic growth*. New Haven, CT: Yale University Press.

Kuznets, S. (1967) 'Population and economic growth', *Proceedings of the American Philosophical Society*, June.

Kuznets, S. (1976) 'Demographic aspects of the size distribution of income: An exploratory essay', *Economic Development and Cultural Change*, 25:1-94.

Lam, D. (1985) 'Distribution issues in the relationship between population growth and economic development', background paper for Working Group on Population Growth and Economic Development, Committee on Population, National Research Council, Washington, DC.

Lee, R.D. (1980) 'An historical perspective on economic aspects of the population explosion: The case of pre-industrial England', in: R.A. Easterlin, ed., *Population and economic change in developing countries*. Chicago, IL: University of Chicago Press.

Lee, R.D. and Bulatao, R.A. (1983) 'The demand for children: A critical essay', in: R.A. Bulatao and R.D. Lee, eds., *Determinants of fertility in developing countries*, Vols. 1 and 11, New York: Academic Press.

Leff, N. (1969) 'Dependence rates and savings rates', *American Economic Review*, 59:886-896.

Leibenstein, H. (1954) *A theory of economic-demographic development*. Princeton, NJ: Princeton University Press.

Leibenstein, H. (1967) "The impact of population growth on 'non-economic determinants of economic growth", in: *Proceedings of the world population conference, Belgrade, 1965*, Vol. 4, pp. 8-11.

Leibenstein, H. (1974) 'An interpretation of the economic theory of fertility: Promising path or blind alley?', *Journal of Economic Literature*, 12:457-479.

Leibowitz, A. (1974) 'Education and home production', *American Economic Review*, 64:243-250.

Lestaeghe, R. and Wilson, C. (1986) 'Modes of production, secularization, and the pace of the fertility decline in Western Europe, 1870-1930', in: A.J. Coale and S.C. Watkins, eds., *The decline of fertility in Europe*. Princeton, NJ: Princeton University Press.

Lewis, W.A. (1954) 'Economic development with unlimited supplies of labour', *Manchester School*, 22:139-191.

Lindert, P.H. (1978) *Fertility and scarcity in America*. Princeton, NJ: Princeton University Press.

Lindert, P.H. (1980) 'Child costs and economic development', in: R.A. Easterlin, ed., *Population and economic change in developing countries*. Chicago, IL: University of Chicago Press.

Lindert, P.H. (1983) 'The changing economic costs and benefits of having children', in: R.A. Bulatao and R.D. Lee, eds., *Determinants of fertility in developing countries*. New York: Academic Press.

Maine, D. and McNamara, R. (1985) *Birth spacing and child survival*. New York: Columbia University.

Mason, A. (1985) 'National savings rates and population growth: A new model and new evidence', Background paper prepared for the Working Group on Population Growth and Economic Development, Committee on Population, National Research Council, Washington, DC.

Mason, K.O. and Taj, A.M. (1986) 'Gender differences in reproductive orientation: A review of existing knowledge in developing countries', paper prepared for Conference of Population Association of America, April.

Mauldin, W.P. and Lapham, R.J. (1985) 'Measuring family planning effort in LDCs: 1972 and 1982', in: N. Birdsall, ed., *The effects of family planning programs on fertility in the developing world*, World Bank Staff working paper no. 677. Washington, DC: World Bank.

McCabe, J. and Rosenzweig, M.R. (1976) 'Female labor force participation, occupational choice and fertility in developing countries', in: R.G. Ridker, ed., *Population and development: The search for selective interventions*. Baltimore, MD: Johns Hopkins University Press.

Meade, J.E. (1964) *Efficiency, equality and ownership of property*. London: Allen and Unwin.

Meadows, D.H., Meadows, D.L., Randers, J. and Behrens, W.W., III (1972) *The limits to growth*. New York: University Books.

McGreevey, W.P. and Birdsall, N. (1974) *The policy relevance of recent research on fertility*. Washington, DC: The Smithsonian Institution.

McNicoll, G. (1984) 'Consequences of population growth: An overview', World Bank Staff working paper no. 691, Washington, DC. See also *Population and Development Review*, 10:177-240.

Mincer, J. (1962) 'Market prices, opportunity costs and income effects', in: C. Christ et al., eds., *Measurement in economics: Studies in mathematical economics and econometrics in memory of Yehuda Grenfeld*. Stanford, CA: Stanford University Press.

Mueller, E. (1976) 'The economic value of children in peasant agriculture', in: R.G. Ridker, ed., *Population and development: The search for selective interventions*. Baltimore, MD: Johns Hopkins University Press.

National Academy of Sciences (1971) *Rapid population growth: Consequences and policy implications*. Baltimore, MD: Johns Hopkins University Press.

National Research Council (1986) *Population growth and economic development: Policy questions*. Washington, DC: National Academy Press.

Nelson, R. (1956) 'A theory of the low-level equilibrium trap in underdeveloped economies', *American Economic Review*, 46:894–908.

Nerlove, M., Razin, A. and Sadka, E. (1984a) 'Bequests and the size of the population when population is endogenous', *Journal of Political Economy*, 92:527–531.

Nerlove, M., Razin, A. and Sadka, E. (1984b) 'Investment in human and non-human capital, transfers among siblings, and the role of government', *Econometrica*, 52:1191–1198.

Nerlove, M., Razin, A. and Sadka, E. (1986) 'Some welfare theoretic implications of endogenous fertility', *International Economic Review*, February.

Nerlove, M., Razin, A. and Sadka, E. (1987) *Household and economy: Welfare economics of endogenous fertility*. New York: Academic Press.

Newman, J.L. (1983) 'Economic analyses of the spacing of births', *American Economic Review*, 73: 33–37.

Newman, P. (1965) 'Malaria eradication and population growth with special reference to Ceylon and British Guiana', Research Series no. 10. Ann Arbor, MI: University of Michigan, Bureau of Public Health Economics, School of Public Health.

Notestein, F. (1945) 'Population: The long view', in: T.W. Schultz, ed., *Food for the world*. Chicago IL: University of Chicago Press.

Notestein, F. (1953) 'Economic problems of population change'.

Nugent, J., Kan, K. and Walther, R.J. (1983) 'The effects of old-age pensions on household structure, marriage, fertility and resource allocation in rural areas of developing countries', University of Southern California, mimeo.

Olsen, R.J. (1983) 'Mortality rates, mortality events and the number of births', *American Economic Review*, 73:29–32.

Olsen, R.J. and Wolpin, K.I. (1983) 'The impact of exogenous child mortality on fertility: A waiting time regression with dynamic regressors', *Econometrica*, 51:731–749.

Pollak, R.A. (1985) 'A transaction cost approach to families and households', *Journal of Economic Literature*, 13:581–608.

Preston, H. (1975) 'Health programs and population growth', *Population and Development Review*, 1:189–199.

Preston, S.H. (1976) 'Causes and consequences of mortality declines in less developed countries during the 20th century', Conference on Population and Economic Change in Less Developed Countries, September 30–October 2, 1986, Sponsored by Universities–National Bureau Committee for Economic Research, New York (draft), p. 20.

Preston, S.H., ed. (1978) *The effects of infant and child mortality on fertility*, New York: Academic Press.

Reid, M.G. (1934) *Economics of household production*. New York: Wiley.

Repetto, R. (1979) *Economic equality and fertility in developing countries*. Baltimore, MD: Johns Hopkins University Press for Resources for the Future.

Robinson, W. and Horlacher, D. (1971) 'Population growth and economic welfare', *Reports on Population / Family Planning*, 6.

Robinson, W. and Schutjer, W. (1984) 'Agricultural development and demographic change: A generalization of the Boserup model', *Economic Development and Cultural Change*, 32:355–366.

Rodgers, G. (1984) *Poverty and population: Approaches and evidence*. Geneva: International Labour Organization.

Rosenzweig, M.R. (1982) 'Educational subsidy, agricultural development and fertility change', *Quarterly Journal of Economics*, February:67–88.

Rosenzweig, M.R. and Evenson, R. (1977) 'Fertility, schooling and the economic value of children in rural India: An econometric analysis', *Econometrica*, 45:1065–1078.

Rosenzweig, M.R. and Schultz, T.P. (1982a) 'Child mortality and fertility in Colombia: Individual and community effects', *Health Policy and Education*, 2:305–348.

Rosenzweig, M.R. and Schultz, T.P. (1982b) 'Market opportunities, genetic endowments and the intrafamily allocation of resources: Child survival in rural India', *American Economic Review*, 72:803–815.

Rosenzweig, M.R. and Schultz, T.P. (1983) 'Consumer demand and household production: The relationship between fertility and child mortality', *American Economic Review*, 73:38–42.

Rosenzweig, M.R. and Schultz, T.P. (1985a) 'The demand for and supply of births: Fertility and its life-cycle consequences', *American Economic Review*, 75:992–1015.

Rosenzweig, M.R. and Schultz, T.P. (1985b) 'Schooling, information and non-market productivity: Contraceptive use and its effectiveness', Yale University, mimeo.

Rosenzweig, M.R. and Seiver, D. (1982) 'Education and contraceptive choice: A conditional demand framework', *International Economic Review*, 23:171–198.

Rosenzweig, M.R. and Wolpin, K. (1980a) 'Testing the quantity–quality fertility model: The use of twins as a natural experiment', *Econometrica*, 48:227–240.

Rosenzweig, M.R. and Wolpin, K. (1980b) 'Life-cycle labor supply and fertility', *Journal of Political Economy*, 88:328–348.

Rosenzweig, M.R. and Wolpin, K. (1982) 'Governmental interventions and household behavior in a developing country', *Journal of Development Economics*, 209–225.

Rosenzweig, M.R. and Wolpin, K. (1985) 'Specific experience, household structure and intergenerational transfers: Farm family land and labor arrangements in developing countries', *Quarterly Journal of Economics*, C (supplement):961–988.

Rosenzweig, M.R. and Wolpin, K. (1986) 'Evaluating the effects of optimally distributed public programs: Child health and family planning interventions', *American Economic Review*, 76:470–482.

Samuelson, P. (1958) 'An exact consumption-loan model of interest with or without the social contrivance of money', *Journal of Political Economy*, 66:467–482.

Sanderson, W. (1980) *Economic–demographic simulation models: A review of their usefulness for policy analysis*. Laxenberg, Austria: International Institute for Applied Systems Analysis.

Schultz, T.P. (1969a) 'An economic model of family planning and fertility', *Journal of Political Economy*, 77:175.

Schultz, T.P. (1969b) 'Effectiveness of family planning in Taiwan: A methodology for program evaluation', P-4253. Santa Monica, CA: Rand Corporation.

Schultz, T.P. (1971) 'An economic perspective on population growth', in: *Rapid Population Growth*, Vol. 2. Baltimore, MD: Johns Hopkins University Press.

Schultz, T.P. (1973a) 'Explanation of birth rate changes over time: A study of Taiwan', *Journal of Political Economy*, 31 (supplement):238–274.

Schultz, T.P. (1973b) 'A preliminary survey of economic analyses of fertility', *American Economic Review*, 53:71–78.

Schultz, T.P. (1978) 'Fertility and child mortality over the life cycle: Aggregate and individual evidence', *American Economic Review*, 68:208–215.

Schultz, T.P. (1981) *Economics of population*. Reading, MA: Addison-Wesley Publishing Company.

Schultz, T.P. (1985) 'School expenditures and enrollment, 1960–1980: The effects of income, prices and population growth', background paper for the Working Group on Population and Economic Development, Committee on Population, National Research Council, Washington, DC.

Schultz, T.P. (1986) 'The fertility revolution: A review essay', *Population and Development Review*, 12:127–138.

Schultz, T.W., ed. (1974) *Economics of the family: Marriage, children and human capital*. Chicago, IL: University of Chicago Press for the National Bureau of Economic Research.

Sen, A. (1975) *Employment technology and development*. Oxford: Clarendon Press.

Simon, J.L. (1977) *The economics of population growth*. Princeton, NJ: Princeton University Press.

Simon, J.L. (1981) *The ultimate resource*. Princeton, NJ: Princeton University Press.

Simon, J.L. and Pilarski, A.M. (1979) 'The effect of population growth upon the quantity of education children receive', *Review of Economics and Statistics*, 61:572–584.

Solow, R.M. (1956) 'A contribution to the theory of economic growth', *Quarterly Journal of Economics*, 70:65–94.

Srinivasan, T.N. (1988) 'Population growth and economic development', *Journal of Policy Modeling*, forthcoming.

Standing, G. (1983) 'Women's work activity and fertility', in: R.A. Bulatao and R.D. Lee, eds., *Determinants of fertility in developing countries*, Vols. 1 and 2. New York: Academic Press.

United Nations (1973) *The determinants and consequences of population trends*, Vol. 1. New York: United Nations.

Wattenberg, B. and Zinsmeister, K., eds. (1985) *Are world population trends a problem?* Washington, DC: American Enterprise Institute for Public Policy Research.

Welch, F. (1979) 'Effects of cohort size on earnings: The baby boom babies' financial bust', *Journal of Political Economy*, 87:565–597.

Wheeler, D. (1980) 'Human resource development and economic growth in LDC's: A simulation model', World Bank Staff working paper no. 407, Washington, DC.

Wheeler, D. (1985) 'Female education, family planning, income and population: A long-run econometric simulation model', in: N. Birdsall, ed., *The effects of family planning programs on fertility in the developing world*, World Bank Staff working paper no. 677. Washington, DC: World Bank.

Williamson, J.G. (1985) 'Did rising emigration cause fertility to decline in 19th century rural England? Child costs, old-age pensions and child default', Harvard Institute for Economic Research, Harvard University, Cambridge, MA.

Williamson, J.G. and Lindert, P.H. (1980) *American inequality: A macroeconomic history*. New York: Academic Press.

Willis, R. (1973) 'A new approach to the economic theory of fertility', *Journal of Political Economy*, March/April (supplement):S14–S64.

Wolfe, B.L. and Behrman, J.R. (1986) 'Child quantity and quality in a developing country: Family background, endogenous tastes and biological supply factors', *Economic Development and Cultural Change*, 34:703–730.

Wolpin, K. (1984) 'An estimable dynamic stochastic model of fertility and child mortality', *Journal of Political Economy*, 92:852–874.

World Bank (1984) *World development report 1984*. New York: Oxford University Press. Also available as *Population change and economic development*. New York: Oxford University Press (1985).

World Bank (1986a) *Population growth and policies in sub-Saharan Africa*. Washington, DC: World Bank.

World Bank (1986b) *World bank atlas*. Washington, DC: World Bank.

Wrigley, E.A. (1969) *Population and history*. New York: McGraw-Hill.

Chapter 13

EDUCATION INVESTMENTS AND RETURNS

T. PAUL SCHULTZ*

Yale University

Contents

1. Introduction and preview   544
   1.1. An overview   545
   1.2. Problems: Conceptual and empirical   547
2. National educational systems: Interpretation of aggregate patterns   550
   2.1. World trends   551
   2.2. Adjustment of the educational system to demand and supply   557
   2.3. A model of the educational system   562
   2.4. An empirical decomposition of educational expenditures   564
   2.5. Estimates of school expenditure equations   568
   2.6. Sex differences in school enrollment rates   571
   2.7. Regional patterns in residuals   573
   2.8. Cross-sectional findings and time-series forecasts   575
3. Alternative models of education and earnings, data,
   and policy implications   577
4. Rates of return to schooling in market activities   585
   4.1. Student ability, parent background, and school quality   587
   4.2. Labor supply and unemployment   591
   4.3. Occupational choice   593
   4.4. The education and productivity of farmers   597
   4.5. Migration   599
   4.6. Male–female comparisons of returns   602
   4.7. Interactions with educational returns   605
   4.8. Efficiency and equity   606
5. Nonmarket production and schooling   607
6. Policy   610
7. Conclusions   615
Appendix   618
References   621

*I greatly appreciate the comments on an earlier draft by J. Behrman, N. Birdsall, H. Chenery, C. Griffin, W.E. Huffman, J.L. Moock, T.W. Schultz, T.N. Srinivasan, J. Strauss and the research assistance of Paul McGuire and Andrew Yuengert.

Handbook of Development Economics, Volume I, Edited by H. Chenery and T.N. Srinivasan
© *Elsevier Science Publishers B.V., 1988*

1. Introduction and preview

The record of sustained modern growth in real per capita income cannot be
accounted for by the accumulation of conventional units of physical capital or by
the increased application of hours of labor per capita [Kuznets (1966)].[1] The
sources of modern economic growth are sought instead in the changing quality of
labor and capital, in the more comprehensive accounting of other inputs, and in
change of organization, policy environment, or technology [Denison (1962), T.W.
Schultz (1963), Kuznets (1966)]. While the issues surrounding the accounting of
aggregate economic growth are unresolved and research strategies in this field
remain controversial [Griliches (1970), Nelson (1981)], research on various aspects
of the microeconomic relationship between education and development has
expanded rapidly, forging a consensus on questions for study and appropriate
methodologies to address these questions. Studies across persons, households,
farms, and firms have documented, first generally in the United States and then
in many low income countries, strong empirical regularities between educational
attainment of populations and their productivity and performance in both
market and nonmarket (home) production activities. Microeconomic empirical
studies have refined and extended this base of evidence, showing that more
educated men and women receive more earnings and produce more output than
do the less educated in a wide range of activities [Psacharopoulos (1985), Jamison
and Lau (1982)]. If these relationships are causal, and education enhances the
productivity and earnings of labor, it is not surprising that governments have
been willing to expend a substantial fraction of national income on public
education; neither is it hard to understand why parents have set aside an
increasing amount of their private disposable income to school their children,
foregoing the productive contribution the children would have made to family
income had they not attended school. This microeconomic perspective helps to
explain the motivation of public groups and private individuals to supply
resources to produce schooling services on the expectation that the rate of return
warrants the investment. The rapid expansion in world demand for education

---

[1]As Kuznets (1966, p. 81) observed: "the inescapable conclusion is that the direct contribution of
man-hours and capital accumulation would hardly account for more than a tenth of the rate of
growth in per capita product – and probably less". Since man-hours per capita tended to decline by
2–3 percent per decade, relatively rapid accumulation of capital could not provide a satisfactory
explanation for sustained periods of modern economic growth. The labor share of national income
was increasing from the nineteenth to the twentieth centuries from somewhat more than half to about
three quarters in the 14 industrially developed countries for which Kuznets had long-term economic
series.

that we have witnessed in the last three decades is, thus, broadly consistent with apparent high social and private rates of return to schooling investments. Moreover, education is widely viewed as a public good (with positive externalities), which increases the efficiency of economic and political institutions while hastening the pace of scientific advance on which modern economic growth depends. Finally, education has always been valued by individuals and society as a consumption good and as a means to preserve and transfer cultural values to subsequent generations. The focus of this chapter on schooling as an investment with market returns is not intended to detract from the importance of education as a public good and as a source of consumption benefits, but rather to review how economic concepts and statistical methods have recently progressed in quantifying the roles of education in economic development.

If the value of education is seen as primarily determined in the marketplace, and the recent expansion of education is attributed to an increase in returns to schooling, then the challenge remains to explain why the returns to schooling have recently been bid up. What accounts in the aggregate for the shift outward in the derived demand for educated labor? What particular recent developments have boosted the payoff to investing the education, not only for an elite, but increasingly for the rank and file of the population? Education is highly valued not only for males entering the labor force, but for females whether or not they are likely to work outside the home. Hypotheses have been advanced to explain this phenomenon, relating it to dynamic economic conditions that create opportunities in the form of disequilibria that are exploited more effectively by an educated population [T.W. Schultz (1975)]. But testing such hypotheses that identify a specific initial cause for the spread of education is intrinsically difficult. Mass education may be at the very origins of modern economic growth, a process that has only in the last fifty years spread notably beyond Europe, areas of European settlement, and Japan. This chapter surveys a small part of the extensive literature on the linkages among education, productivity, and development, and assesses several areas where concerted research might clarify important issues and potentially change policies.[2]

1.1. An overview

The expansion of public educational systems worldwide has provided the average child in every country with increased years of schooling during the period 1960 to

---

[2] The literature on economics of education is vast, and much of it is relevant to low income countries. For different perspectives on this field, consult the surveys by T.W. Schultz (1963), Blaug (1973, 1976, 1985), Psacharopoulos (1973, 1981, 1985), Rosen (1977, 1985), Griliches (1977), Psacharopoulos and Woodhall (1985), and Willis (1987).

1983.[3] The gap between high and low income countries in educational opportunities has narrowed, relatively and absolutely; the wide gap between the educational attainment of women and men has also narrowed, on average. This chapter presents an economic interpretation of this educational explosion and what has governed the process. Most of the growth in public expenditures on education is attributed to increases in growth of real income per adult. The income elasticity of public expenditures on primary and secondary education is quite high, 1.4 and 1.5, respectively. The declining price of teacher salaries relative to average incomes is the second major engine of education growth, which lowers the unit cost of providing schooling to a growing fraction of the child population. These tendencies appear to have been partially frustrated by rapid population growth which increases the proportion of the population in school ages. This population growth effect does not appear to have restrained enrollments at the primary level but has eroded the resources available per student at both the secondary and primary levels.

Certain regions have increased public expenditures on education more rapidly or slowly than would have been expected, based on incomes, cost of teachers, and population distribution. East Asia and Africa are, in this regard, overachievers while South and West Asia and Latin America are investing less in education than is expected on the basis of this framework.

At the individual level the positive relationship between the education of a worker and his or her earnings helps to account for the noted expansion of national educational systems. Under certain conditions, the proportionate increase in average lifetime wages associated with a year's education approximates an internal private rate of return to investing a year's time in that form of schooling. Many empirical studies confirm the nature of this relationship, and proceed to estimate the private returns to education in developing countries. They show that basic primary and secondary schooling yields private returns between 10 and 40 percent, and generally somewhat lower at university or college levels. No pronounced differences are noted between men and women. Much of the returns to schooling for women arise from their increased productivity in nonmarket production, as evidenced in their ability to improve the health of family members, produce a more nutritious diet for the same outlays, and control more effectively their reproduction.

Needless to say, this empirical regularity between schooling and wages can be approached using a variety of more complicated econometric methods. Although additional controls and the choice of model structure influence estimates of the

---

[3] I appreciate that J. Behrman drew my attention to the fact that in the period 1960–81 one country did indeed report a decline in expected years of schooling. In El Salvador this figure declined from 5.63 to 5.06 years according to the *1984 World Development Report* (table 25). *The 1986 World Development Report* (table 29), however, reports even in El Salvadore an increase in expected schooling from 1965 to 1983 from 6.04 to 6.18 years.

partial association between schooling and wages, the evidence evaluated below supports the view that private returns to basic education are substantial.

Few countries charge fees to students for the full cost of providing them with educational services. Social returns to schooling after deducting the unreimbursed public expenditures on schools are, therefore, lower than the private rates of return. Particularly for higher education, where the public cost of providing a student with instruction may be 50 times larger than at the primary level, the social rates of return in some developing countries may be insufficient to warrant further expansion of subsidized public higher education. This is rarely the case at the primary and secondary level.

Management of the educational sector seeks to promote an efficient and equitable use of public and private resources. Beyond the broader generalizations that can be applied to the financing and expansion of the education sector, there are many country-specific issues that are not pursued here. Most of these issues can be analyzed with econometric methods where labor force survey and census data are availabe for estimating the relative benefits of various types of education, and school input and output data are available to evaluate the efficiency of school systems to produce what the labor market demands in the way of skills.

1.2. Problems: Conceptual and empirical

The empirical evidence supporting education's effect on factor productivity must be approached critically, however. At one level, there is innate skepticism born of casual empiricism and nurtured on the richness of alternative theoretical models; economists can propose many models to accommodate the stylized fact that elites are often relatively well educated and relatively well paid. At another level, the statistical evidence on education's productive roles is never ideal, because data on the "consequences" of education are obtained from populations in which educational attainment is not randomized but is itself an economic choice variable. The social sciences are rarely able to perform social experiments. Therefore, statistical studies of how education affects individual behavior and performance can be biased or misleading because of the nonrandom selection of comparison groups; the omission of other factors; the simultaneity among outcome variables, such as wages, and potential determinants of these outcomes, such as job tenure; and, of course, measurement error and flaws of functional form approximations that are assumed in statistically estimating group differences associated with education.

There are also palpable differences between the formation of concrete physical capital and the accumulation of productive skills in schools. In the former case, land is improved by drainage or irrigation, railways are built, and factories are constructed, from which productive services are derived that can usually be priced in a competitive marketplace. In the latter case, people of different ability attend schools of varied quality, and then they perform diverse and often incomparable tasks. It is frequently difficult to infer the marginal productivity of workers, and the selection of those that report a wage may subtly bias comparisons. Other workers may be employed in production teams or families, or within large integrated firms where the productivity of the individual is not readily monitored. Markets for the services of labor may not be competitive in the sense of spot markets that clear in the short run; labor markets may be further linked to other imperfect factor markets, such as those for land and credit, in the case of agriculture. (See Chapter 15 by Bell and Chapter 16 by Rosenzweig in this Handbook.) Although similar problems exist in the evaluation of the services of heterogeneous physical capital, many comparisons of labor market behavior and outcomes can be misleading unless care is used to explicitly deal with the heterogeneity of labor. Four distinctive features of human capital warrant brief discussion here.

Differences in property rights between human and physical capital imply that empirical studies must rely largely on rental market transactions in the case of human capital, i.e. wage rates, rather than on both rental and asset prices in the case of physical capital [Rosen (1985)]. Given the durable lifetime nature of human capital, this constraint on available data is a serious limitation for testing theory, particularly when market lifetime equilibrium theories of investment are the basis for several influential frameworks for analyzing human capital [Becker (1964), Mincer (1962, 1974)]. Long-term contracts between firms and workers, or between landlords and laborers, may add additional dynamic incentive problems to the labor market when information regarding the effort and productivity of labor is notably imperfect and costly to monitor. How do these convenient micro equilibrium investment approaches of the human capital tradition mislead researchers in a world where disequilibrium rents are the rule and not the exception?

Preferences of workers are likely to intrude on human capital models of individual behavior, while they are conveniently set aside by economists in their analyses of the production of market goods and services. An individual's decision on how much time to work in the labor market is dependent on his or her preferences for nonmarket time or leisure versus preferences for the goods that can be purchased with market income. Consequently, preferences may influence human capital investment decisions, unless human capital is assumed to be specifically neutral in its productive effect on market and nonmarket activities, including the formation of additional human capital [Ben-Porath (1967), Michael (1982)].

Commodities that are produced for consumption within the household and are not readily traded across households will be produced in response to variations in consumer preferences of household members [Rosenzweig and Schultz (1985)]. To avoid these complications, it is common to assume that farm-households produce for the marketplace as well as for their own consumption, and view the labor of family members as equivalent to labor hired from or supplied to the market; this homogeneity of output and labor input permits production and consumption decisions within the household to be sequentially optimized, and greatly simplifies empirical analysis of the behavior of farm-households [Singh, Squire and Strauss (1986)]. Hired and family labor may not be perfect substitutes for each other in all tasks, because the ease of monitoring and therefore decentralizing work may differ for these two types of labor [Deolalikar and Vijverberg (1983)]. While the family production–consumption model is attractive for the study of farm production of food staples, it seems less appropriate for the study of the production of untraded goods, such as children, the schooling of those children, and the health of family members [Rosenzweig and Schultz (1983)].

Any attempt to measure nonmarket benefits of schooling that accrue within the domestic spheres of household production is subject to worrisome error, because of the "social and emotional factors involved" [Kuznets (1954, p. 432)]. This is one among many reasons that led Kuznets and those who followed him to exclude household nonmarket production and the housewife's nonmarket contribution to welfare from their reckoning of national income, valued, to the extent possible, at market prices. However, an important feature of development is the tendency for the market to take over progressively more of the productive activities carried out initially within the household. Thus, to ignore nonmarket production and human capital's contribution to these forms of production is perhaps a more serious omission in the study of low-income countries, and in the characterization of the process of economic development in general, than it is in the analysis of growth in today's industrially advanced countries.

These several differences between physical and human capital, and the different context of household and market production are real, and are responsible for some of the indirect estimation methods used in this field that rely on difficult to test assumptions of functional form and other identification restrictions. In situations where many economic and demographic choices of the household are viewed as jointly and simultaneously determined over a lifetime, including possibly the human capital investments of both the parents and children, it is difficult to specify exogenous constraints on which to base consistent estimates of behavioral relationships or household production functions. Community programs, local prices, and regional characteristics derived from outside of the household decisionmaking unit are, therefore, increasingly used to identify household choice models [T.P. Schultz (1984)]. This estimation strategy depends critically, however, on the assumption that migration does not sort persons according to their preferences for these regional services, activities, and amenities [Tiebout (1965), T.P. Schultz (1983), Rosenzweig and Wolpin (1984)]. This assumption concerning the independence of migration may not always be defensible in developing countries, where local health and education programs may differ greatly today, particularly between rural and urban areas. Alternatively, the location of the public sector programs may also represent a calculated response to unobserved local environmental conditions or average population characteristics that the programs are themselves designed to change. Examples might be public health facilities and specific disease control programs that are established to serve communities with particularly severe health problems. Yet turning to community level constraints to help identify the determinants of household behavior is an attractive means to escape the vicious circle of simultaneity among closely related forms of household economic and demographic behavior.

In sum, the problems of measurement or productivity are serious in the nonmarket sector. Relevant statistical comparisons across persons or households tend to be subject to many sources of selection bias that cannot always be persuasively corrected by available econometric techniques, theory, and data. Consequently, the evidence of education's market and nonmarket productive roles is sometimes fragile, and the working assumptions and statistical procedures that underlie this evidence need to be closely scrutinized and affirmed from a variety of methodological perspectives.

The outline of the chapter is as follows. Section 2 describes the expansion of the world's educational system both in terms of its inputs of public and private resources and its output of students, and then estimates how income, price, and population constraints appear to govern this process. Section 3 contrasts causal frameworks proposed to explain the relationship between education and productivity, and discusses sources of data to measure the relationship and discriminate among causal interpretations. Section 4 reviews evidence on the market returns to schooling measured for both entrepreneurs and employees, men and women, and migrants and nonmigrants. Section 5 considers the evidence of schooling's effects on nonmarket production. Section 6 considers the policy issues for development that arise from the apparent effects of education on economic productivity and the mechanisms used to finance and manage the educational system. In the concluding section, Section 7, questions for further research are reiterated.

2. National educational systems: Interpretation of aggregate patterns[4]

A distinctive development of the last 25 years is the rapid expansion of school systems in all parts of the world. Despite the unprecedented rate of growth in the population reaching school age, enrollment rates at these ages have increased in

---

[4] Section 2 draws on Schultz (1985).

virtually every country. These developments are examined in this section to understand their origins and how economic and demographic factors may be governing this rapidly growing dimension of world investment. Incomes, relative factor prices, production technology, and demographic structure are interrelated in a production–demand framework as constraints and conditions affecting the costs of, and demands for, educational services. Data for 89 countries from 1960 to 1980 are then used to test quantitatively hypotheses within this framework. Differences in school enrollment between males and females are also analyzed. Finally, regional deviations in educational expenditures and achievements are calculated, based on the fitted model, to document departures from international patterns.

2.1. World trends

Figure 13.1 summarizes the level and increase in enrollment ratios at the primary, secondary, and higher education level for countries grouped by income level, market/nonmarket economy, and oil exporter status. For summary comparison of overall levels of schooling, a synthetic cohort measure is constructed and called hereafter the "expected years of schooling". It is defined as the sum of six times the primary, six times the secondary, and five times the higher education enrollment ratios; where these weights, i.e. 6, 6, and 5, correspond to the average number of single-year age groups combined in the denominators of these three standardized enrollment ratios. This new synthetic cross-age measure of expected years of exposure to the educational system should not be confused with a cohort measure of completed years of schooling, which also excludes years that are repeated or not accredited.

Expected years of schooling increased 32 percent from 1960 to 1981 in the low income class of countries; 46 percent gains were achieved in the middle income countries who imported oil, and 50 percent gains occurred in the upper middle income class. The East European nonmarket countries increased their expected years of schooling by 35 percent, while the industrial market high income countries advanced 16 percent. Oil exporters in the middle income class achieved a doubling of expected schooling levels, while nearly a fourfold increase was reported in the high income oil exporters.

In general, the percentage gains in schooling were greater for those countries that started from a lower income level in 1960. *The gap in expected years of schooling between the low and high income countries is therefore closing, on average, whether expressed in relative terms or even as an absolute difference in years, which more adequately reflects the economic value of education. This closure in the absolute gap in education appears to be at least as rapid as that achieved in health,*

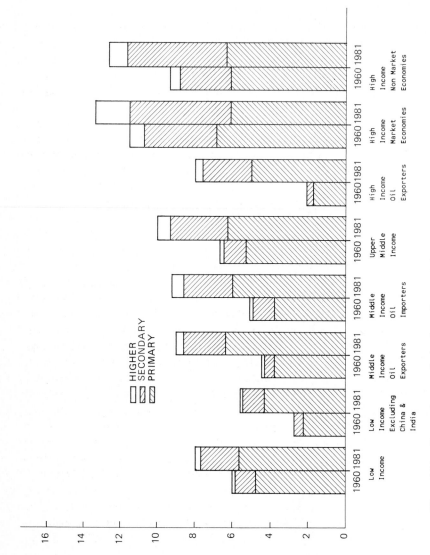

Figure 13.1. Expected years of school enrollments, by school level for groups of countries: 1960 and 1981. *Source*: Derived from *World Development Report (1984)*. Definitions and data reported in Schultz (1985).

analogously summarized by life expectation at birth.[5] Figure 13.2 shows the corresponding figures for expected years of enrollments for males and females, summarized by cultural–regional areas; differences between enrollments of males and females have also decreased markedly and this trend also warrants an explanation.

The salient fact is that all classes of countries, and indeed every country for which overall comparisons can be drawn from 1960 to 1983, increased over these years the expected schooling that it provided to the "average" child, despite the extraordinarily rapid growth in the number of school-aged children in many of the poorest countries.[6] The number of children between the ages of 6 and 17 more than doubled in the less developed regions from 1950 to 1980. The proportion of the population in these ages increased from 24.5 percent in 1950 to 29.1 percent in 1980. That the poorest countries and those that have suffered actual declines in their real income in this period were nonetheless able to expand their schooling systems rapidly enough to accommodate an increasing fraction of their children is remarkable.

However, a less sanguine picture of recent educational progress emerges from expenditure data assembled in Table 13.1 from World Bank sources. Central governmental expenditures on education, when expressed in constant GNP prices, have declined in many countries in the past decade. Resources allocated to education per capita by central governments appear to have declined markedly in real terms in the lowest income countries (including or excluding India and China) and increased by only 22 percent in the middle income oil-importing countries. In contrast, oil-exporting middle income and upper middle income countries were able to more than double their per capita real public expenditures for education, while the high income industrial countries raised their real outlays on education by 88 percent.

---

[5] The gap in expected education and life at birth between the lowest income countries (excluding India and China in the World Bank categories) and the high income industrial market economies decreased markedly in the last two decades. Life expectation stood at about 43 and 71 years in 1960, and had increased to roughly 51 and 75 years by 1982 in these two groups of countries, respectively. Expected years of schooling, on the other hand, increased for these two groups of countries from almost 3 and 11.5 years in 1960, to almost 6 and 13.3 years in 1982, or from one-to-four to one-to-two. These achievements were recorded despite the fact that income (GNP) per capita in constant prices grew in the same period three times faster in the high income countries than it did in this lowest income group of countries. These illustrative figures are drawn from *World Development Report 1984*, World Bank Staff, Oxford University Press, 1984, Tables 1, 23, and 25. See also Preston's (1980) comparisons of life expectation across more uniform and reliable data from a smaller number of countries. There are differences between and limitations of such synthetic summary measures of health and education. The schooling in high and low income countries (as suggested in Tables 13.1 and 13.2) may be of increasingly disparate quality, so the gap in quality-adjusted years may not be decreasing though the gap in years is. Analogously, the gap between the quality of life (however that is measured) in high and low income countries may be widening, undermining consideration of the expectation of life as an overall indicator of health and vitality. There is also the bounded nature of both life expectation and years of education which may imply a narrowing gap as many countries approach that boundary.

[6] See explanatory footnotes to Table A.1.

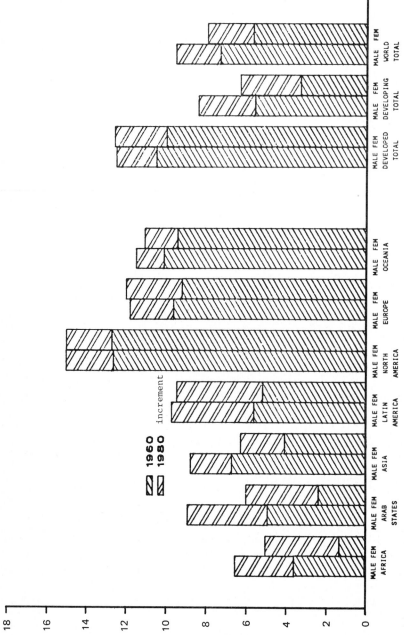

Figure 13.2.   Expected years of school enrollment for males and females by region: 1960 and 1980.
Source: Derived from *UNESCO Yearbook.* Definitions and data reported in Schultz (1985).

Table 13.1
Central government expenditures: 1972, 1981

World bank country class[a] (Number)	Percent of government expenditures on education		Total government expenditures as percent of GNP		Percent of growth in real per capita GNP	Percent of growth in per capita real expenditure on education
	1972	1981	1972	1981	1972–1981[b]	1972–1981
	(1)	(2)	(3)	(4)	(5)	(6)
Low income (34)[c]	16.4	5.9	21.0	15.4	26	−67
Excluding China and India[c]	16.4	11.5	21.0	17.6	7	−37
Middle income (38)						
Oil exporters	15.4	16.6	17.2	27.8	34	+133
Oil importers	11.0	10.0	20.7	21.8	28	+22
Upper middle income (22)	10.8	14.3	15.0	20.6	32	+140
High income						
Oil exporters (5)	13.5	9.2	36.6	26.3	0	−51
Industrial market (18)	4.3	5.1	21.7	28.3	21	+87
East European nonmarket (8)	NR	NR	NR	NR	NR	NR

[a] The low income class has an annual GNP per capita of less than U.S. $410 in 1982 prices. The middle income class includes countries with GNP per capita between $410 and $1650, while the upper middle income class ranges from $1650 to about $6000.
[b] Annual growth. Rate on per capita real GNP derived for 1970 to 1982 from Bank Tables, and interpolated for the nine years corresponding to expenditure data, 1972–81.
[c] The lack of data for China or for India throughout this period makes the overall "Low Income" country class comparisons of limited value.
Source: 1984 World Development Report, appendix, table 2, page 220; table 19, page 254; and table 26, page 268.

How have the poorer countries sustained increases in enrollments despite the evidence that central government outlays have not kept pace with population growth? One explanation for these divergent trends might be that local, state, and private expenditures on schooling expanded to replace central government outlays. Table 13.2 reports UNESCO estimates of public school expenditures at all governmental levels, confirming a decline in real public outlays on schools in Africa, Asia, and Latin America after 1980. I cannot assess how the data underlying Tables 13.1 and 13.2 might differ beyond the inclusion in Table 13.2 of noncentral government educational expenditures. Private school expenditures are not well documented, but the share of private school enrollments is generally modest and declining in most low income countries [World Bank (1986a)]. Tuition and fees at public schools have also been eroded by inflation and public policy changes during the 1970s [Jimenez (1984)], though this trend may have reversed recently.

Another explanation could be that unit costs of producing educational services declined, as might occur if the school system realized economies of scale or

Table 13.2

Public expenditures on education per child of school age, 1970–82

Region	Percent of world's population age 6–17 in 1970	Public expenditures on education (billions of current U.S. dollars)				Public expenditures per child 6–17 (Constant 1970 U.S. Dollars)				Percentage growth in real public expenditures per child on education 1970–80
		1970	1975	1980	1982	1970	1975	1980	1982	
Africa, excluding Arab states	8.0	1.89	5.05	12.1	11.7	23.7	39.5	57.3	44.8	142
Arab states	3.8	1.80	8.44	17.7	22.1	49.0	144.	187.	187.	282
Asia, excluding Arab states	59.4	12.0	38.3	85.6	89.7	20.2	42.1	60.9	54.2	201
Latin America	8.5	5.54	14.3	32.8	36.5	65.3	108.	158.	147.	142
Northern America	5.3	71.8	113.	200.	232.	1350.	1570.	2170.	2280.	61
Europe, including U.S.S.R.	14.7	64.5	146.	252.	224.	436.	714.	909.	703.	108
Oceania	0.5	1.98	6.99	10.4	11.4	418.	996.	1010.	931.	142
Developed[a] Total	22.5	147.	295.	529.	536.	654.	956.	1260.	1120.	93
Developing Total	77.5	12.6	37.4	81.9	92.0	16.2	31.3	43.7	41.2	170
World Total	100.	160.	332.	611.	628.	160.	220.	266.	232.	66

[a]Europe, Oceania, North America, Japan, Israel and South Africa.

Sources: UNESCO Statistical Yearbook 1984, table 2.12. GNP deflator for U.S. used to express current dollars (1975: 1.375; 1980: 1.950; 1982: 2.261): Statistical Abstract of the United States 1985, table No. 715. Population age 6–17 from U.N. Demographic Indicators of Countries, Estimates and Projections Assessed in 1980, for 1975, 1980 and interpolated to 1982 and extrapolated to 1970. For Arab States and Africa and Asia excluding Arab States, UNESCO Statistical Yearbook 1984, table 1.2, uniformly interpolated from 5–19 age groups to 6–17.

incurred a decline in the price of educational inputs relative to the GNP deflator used here. Alternatively, the quality (or resource intensity) of schooling services may have deteriorated.

In sum, alternative factors could be behind the decline in government expenditures on education in some low income countries: (1) the actual quality of schooling per student may have declined; (2) the unit costs of production of educational services of a constant quality may have declined relative to the general price level (GNP deflator); and (3) the underlying data may be in error. The subsequent cross-country empirical analysis of public educational systems is restricted to countries for which there are data on enrollments, teachers, expenditures on current and capital account, estimates of GNP in constant prices, urbanization, total fertility rates, and the population's age composition. The data from this restricted sample of countries are believed to be more reliable than the comprehensive figures reported above, but possibly less representative. Before considering intercountry patterns in these data, it is useful to have a framework within which to account for variation in the provision of educational services. The framework involves three parts: an interpretation of the political economy translating private demands into public expenditures, a production technology linking educational inputs to outputs, and the determinants of household demand for public educational services.

2.2. Adjustment of the educational system to demand and supply

Education is demanded both as a consumer good that yields direct utility and as a producer good that is expected to enhance the future productivity of the educated individual [T.W. Schultz (1961)]. Private demand for consumer goods depends on consumer income, relative prices, and tastes. As a produced means of production, economists have reasoned that the private and social demand for education should be an increasing function of its private and social rates of return [Becker (1964)]. However, the relationship across countries between the level of returns and the average quantity of schooling represents intersections of the presumably upward sloping private/public supply function of investment in education and the downward sloping aggregate derived demand function for more educated workers. Unless variables can be specified a priori that shift one and not the other side of this market for more educated labor, it is not generally possible to identify statistically the individual's investment supply response function from the aggregate derived demand function for educated labor. Most empirical analysis based on consumer demand theory or the human capital framework studies the behavioral response of individuals or families to aggregate market-determined wage rates, prices, initial endowments, etc. The latter are exogenous constraints that are expected to partially explain the individual response. At the aggregate level, derived demands for labor of various types and the aggregated responses of individuals to invest in human capital and supply labor to the market cannot be as readily disentangled or statistically identified. In the course of economic development both the aggregate demand and supply schedules are likely to shift. It would be useful for our purposes if we could specify exogenous endowments to the economy, such as original natural resource stocks, or exogenous technological dimensions to the development process that differ over time and across countries, that affect the derived demands for relatively better educated labor and hence raise (or lower) the producer returns to education. However, there is as yet no agreement on what these identifying variables might be.

In the subsequent empirical analysis of aggregate school systems, national income per adult, relative prices, and other technological and demographic constraints are tentatively interpreted as influencing the individual and family's investment supply function of education, or, in other words, the private and public sector demand for schooling services. But the same income, price, and technology factors may also shift aggregate derived demands for educated labor and thereby vary the rate of return to education as a producer good.[7] The relationships estimated below to explain school expenditures and outputs are consequently reduced-form equations that may embody the underlying investment supply and aggregate demand parameters. Identifying these underlying structural supply and demand parameters is not attempted here.

Actual estimates of the social rates of return for secondary schooling for some 40 countries are plotted in Figure 13.3 against lagged secondary school enrollment ratios. The downward sloping scatter of observations suggests that the private/public supply of schooling is shifting to the right over time with development to trace out, approximately, the downward sloped (and probably also shifting) demand schedule. Some countries for which there are available repeated estimates of social returns confirm the same pattern within a country of falling social returns as the expansion of school systems overtakes expanding aggregate demands for more educated labor. But demand schedules may also shift more (or less) rapidly than supplies of educated labor, and this might explain the period of rising returns in South Korea from 1967 to 1971. The extreme drop in returns in Peru from 1972 to 1980 may signal the added impact of a cyclical decline in demand for better educated labor.

A second unusual feature of the educational system is that it produces its own main input, teachers. It thereby affects by its past production the current wage required to retain the services of teachers and consequently the unit cost of

---

[7] The most comprehensive comparison of rate of return studies is that by Psacharopoulos (1973, 1981, 1985). Differences in methodology across these summarized country studies limit the precise comparability of the return calculations.

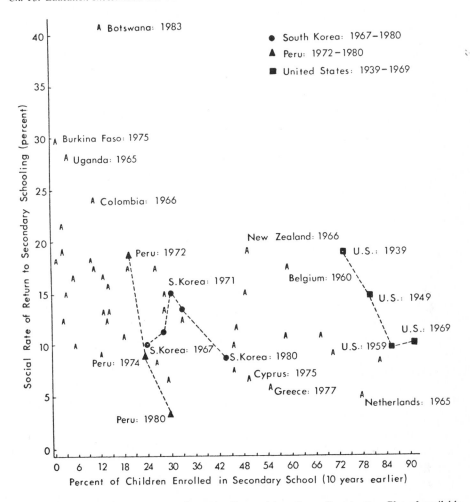

Figure 13.3. Social returns to secondary schooling and lagged enrollment rates: Plot of available country observations. *Source:* Single most recent observation on secondary schools from each country available in Psacharopoulos (1981, 1985). Repeated observations added for the United States, South Korea, and Peru to indicate within-country variation.

producing further education, other things being equal. This feedback effect of output on future unit costs suggests that choosing the best expansion path for education involves additional issues of intertemporal optimization and intergenerational equity, topics that implicitly arise in the educational planning literature, but which remain to be explicitly incorporated into many empirical analyses [Bowles (1969), Freeman (1971)]. For example, to expand a school system rapidly from a very limited national educational base involves inevitably bidding up temporarily the cost of teachers and may even require the costly importation of trained personnel. These high initial costs of expansion tend to decline as the pool of domestically trained secondary school graduates increases and these new graduates compete for available teacher posts. This decline in the relative price of teachers then encourages, along with rising incomes, more private demand for public education as both a consumption and investment good. Figures 13.4 and 13.5 illustrate this downtrend in the relative price of primary and secondary

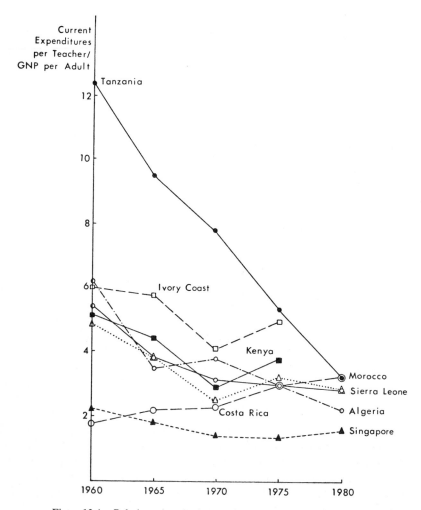

Figure 13.4.   Relative price of primary school teachers to GNP per adult.

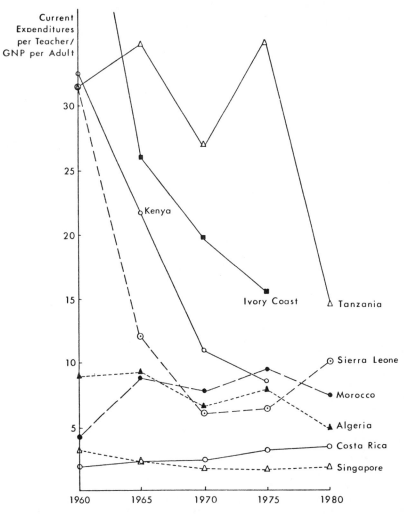

Figure 13.5. Relative price of secondary school teachers to GNP per adult.

school teachers, most clearly evident in a number of African countries which have recently expanded their national educational systems. In middle income countries, such as Latin America, the downtrend in wages of at least primary school teachers relative to that of the average worker is more irregular. Some part of this decline in the relative price of teachers may reflect a substitution of women for men in teaching.

Although there is no established framework for dealing with these dynamic and recursive features of national educational systems, the current wage of teachers clearly depends on the current level of demand for schooling. Consequently, the price of teachers is endogenous to a model determining the demand for educational services. To estimate without simultaneous equation bias the effect of this price on current demand, instrumental variable methods are later adopted.

2.3. A model of the educational system

The technological possibilities for producing educational services are assumed to be identical across countries. This production function for educational services is also assumed in the long run to exhibit constant returns. This does not seem to be an unrealistic assumption for primary and secondary school systems. If the elasticity of substitution between labor and capital is one, the production function may be expressed in standard Cobb–Douglas form:

$$X = ZL^{\alpha}K^{1-\alpha}, \tag{1}$$

where X is the output of educational services, L is the labor input, K is the physical capital input, α is the share of wages in output, and $1 - \alpha$ is the capital share, while Z is a set of exogenous technological shifters that affect the unit costs of producing schooling in different environments, but are neutral with respect to labor and capital productivity and use. One such technological factor might be the distribution of the population. Dispersed populations may incur greater private and public transportation costs, in terms of both time and money, to provide the same effective schooling services. It is also frequently assumed that rapid population growth, which increases the school age fraction of the population, strains the capacity of the government to provide desired school services.

Analyses of the private demand for public goods have generally assumed that citizens know about the costs of production and the benefits of government spending [e.g. Borcherding and Deacon (1972)]. The political process is assumed to be more or less democratic, in the sense that entrepreneur-politicians seek "election" to deliver efficiently the public goods and services and the associated tax burden that taken together command the support of a majority of voters.[8] The essential idea is that public, as well as private, institutions tend to optimize

---

[8]The political process may not assign everyone's vote an equal weight, however. For example, urban populations in many low income countries appear to exercise greater influence on public sector decisions than do dispersed rural populations [Lipton (1977)]. Without data on the distribution of income, public services, or taxes across subgroups within countries, it is not fruitful to speculate further here on the distributional implications of how this political process works.

their input allocation and production decisions as constrained by consumer incomes and perceived benefits of outputs, on the one hand, and technological possibilities and relative input prices, on the other.

If the educational sector thus minimizes its unit costs, that is, produces efficiently, the marginal cost or price of schooling services, P_x, can be expressed as a multiplicative function of the wage paid labor in the educational sector, W, and the return, r, required on public capital [e.g. Borcherding and Deacon (1972)]:

$$P_x = \left(\frac{1}{Z}\right)\left(\frac{W}{\alpha}\right)^\alpha \left(\frac{r}{1-\alpha}\right)^{1-\alpha}. \tag{2}$$

World capital markets are probably more effective than international labor markets in equalizing factor returns. If rates of return on educational physical capital were equalized, the only remaining constraints that would influence the marginal cost of education across countries and over time are the real wage paid to teachers, W, and the exogenous technological conditions denoted by Z. Teacher salaries are most of the recurrent expenses for most school systems. In recent years about 95 percent of current expenses in the primary school systems of low income countries were teacher salaries, whereas in high income countries the proportion is about 75 percent [World Bank (1983, p. 99)]. Current expenditures in a school system divided by the number of teachers is the rough measure used here of labor costs for the educational system and is the principal factor determining the relative price of educational services in a country. The price equation can be rewritten as the following, if the rental rate on capital does not vary:

$$P_x = e^{\beta_0} Z^{\beta_1} W^\alpha e^{u_1}, \tag{3}$$

where β_0 is a constant, $\beta_1 = -1$, and u_1 is a multiplicative error in the production technology affecting unit costs. Because labor's share of educational expenditures, α, can be observed, the effect of price variation can be estimated from data on teacher wages [Gramlich and Rubinfeld (1982)]. For simplicity, educational services are assumed to flow equally to all citizens who have equal numbers of eligible children to benefit.

Finally, the quantity of schooling demanded by the median voter, q, is assumed to be log-linear in the tax, t (or price), in the taxpayers' income, Y, and possibly in technological factors, Z,

$$q = Dt^\eta Y^\delta Z^\varepsilon e^{u_2}, \tag{4}$$

where u_2 is a multiplicative error in the demand relationship.

Expenditures per school aged child (E/P) are then obtained by multiplying quantity demanded by price, where the general tax rate is equal to the marginal price of school services:

$$E/P = DY^\delta P_x^{(\eta+1)} Z^\varepsilon e^{u_2}. \tag{5}$$

Substituting from the production technology (3) in for the price of educational services, logarithms are taken of (5) and the partial effects of income per adult, relative prices (teacher wage), and technological shifters on public educational expenditures per child are expressed as a combination of underlying household demand and production technology parameters:

$$\ln(E/P) = b_0 + b_1 \ln Y + b_2 \ln W + b_3 \ln Z + v, \tag{6}$$

where

$b_0 = (\eta + 1)(\beta_0) + \ln D,$
$b_1 = \delta,$
$b_2 = \alpha(\eta + 1),$
$b_3 = \beta(\eta + 1) + \varepsilon.$

The errors from the production technology and household demand relationships are combined in v, and are assumed independent of Y and Z. Knowledge of the labor share of inputs, α, permits the identification of the price elasticity, η. The net effect of incomes, δ, and the Z factors – cohort size and urbanization – on educational inputs and outputs can also be inferred from estimates of the reduced-form equation (6). Cohort size is closely associated with lagged fertility and family size, and these demographic outcomes are inversely correlated with investments in child schooling at the family level. To distinguish between these factors, the total fertility rate is also included in the vector of control variables denoted by Z [T.P. Schultz (1985)].

2.4. An empirical decomposition of educational expenditures

The composition of educational expenditures may also vary with price, income, and demographic factors, in addition to the overall level of educational expenditures. To evaluate these compositional effects, it is convenient to divide school expenditures per school-age child into a multiplicative function of four observable components:

$$\frac{E}{P} = \left(\frac{S}{P}\right)\left(\frac{T}{S}\right)\left(\frac{C}{T}\right)\left(\frac{E}{C}\right). \tag{7}$$

The first term on the right-hand side is the ratio of students enrolled to the number of children of school age, the enrollment ratio, which can be computed in most countries for boys and girls separately. The second term is the teacher to student ratio, that is treated as one possible indicator of the human capital "quality" of schooling [Pryor (1968), Bowles (1969), Fuller (1986)], which may be contrasted with the "quantity" response in terms of enrollments. The third term is the current expenditures per teacher. The fourth and final term is the ratio of total expenditures to current expenditures, or an index of the physical capital intensity of the educational system. Logarithms of the four component ratios in eq. (7) are regressed on the same income, price, technology, and population composition variables used to explain expenditures per child. The sum of the log-linear regression coefficients for each conditioning variable in these four component regressions is equal to that variable's coefficient in the overall expenditure per child function. In this way, the effect of income, price, and other factors on overall educational expenditures estimated from eq. (6) may be decomposed into the additive effects of each conditioning variable operating on quantity, quality, capital intensity, and teacher salaries.[9]

[9]Eq. (11) may be rewritten in logarithms:

$$\ln(E/P) = \ln(S/P) + \ln(T/S) + \ln(C/T) + \ln(E/C),$$

and regressions would be calculated in the following form at each level of schooling:

$$\ln(E/P) = \beta_{11} + \beta_{12}\ln Y + \beta_{13}\ln P_x + \beta_{14}Z,$$

$$\ln(S/P) = \beta_{21} + \beta_{22}\ln Y + \beta_{23}\ln P_x + \beta_{24}Z,$$

$$\ln(T/S) = \beta_{31} + \beta_{32}\ln Y + \beta_{33}\ln P_x + \beta_{34}Z,$$

$$\ln(C/T) = \beta_{41} + \beta_{42}\ln Y + \beta_{43}\ln P_x + \beta_{44}Z,$$

$$\ln(E/C) = \beta_{51} + \beta_{52}\ln Y + \beta_{53}\ln P_x + \beta_{54}Z.$$

The adding up of component effects implies that

$$\beta_{1i} = \sum_{j=2}^{5} \beta_{ji}, \quad \text{for } i = 1,\dots,4.$$

Educational expenditures are deflated to constant local prices using the GNP deflator and converted to 1970 U.S. dollars according to the prevailing average foreign exchange rate in 1969–71.[10] The "average" teacher salary is the public current expenditures per primary and secondary school teachers, which is then deflated by national productivity or GNP per working age adult. This relative price of educational services is determined simultaneously with production costs and consumer demands for schooling. Unexplained variation in either production costs, u_1, or consumer demands, u_2, will thus be correlated with relative prices. Consequently, instrumental variable (IV) techniques are employed in estimating eq. (6) under the assumption that the price variable is endogenous; the instrumental variables are specifically secondary school enrollment rates, incomes, and urbanization, all lagged ten years.[11] The IV estimates have the additional attraction of being consistent despite the systematic errors-in-variable problem that arises because the logarithmic transformation of relative prices, incomes, and teacher wages are linearly dependent.[12] Although the auxiliary instrumental variable equations for wages undoubtedly simplify the structural process underlying time series of educational systems, the relative price of teachers today is, as

[10] It may be argued that the use of foreign exchange (FX) rates in 1969–71 to translate GNP from local currencies into the common unit of dollars gives insufficient weight to nontraded commodities. The tendency is to exaggerate differences across countries in real consumer income per adult. Recent work to construct a purchasing power parity (PPP) basis for comparing incomes across countries by Kravis, Heston and Summers (1982) is built on a sample of countries for which price indexes were constructed and then generalized and revised to apply to other countries by Summers and Heston (1984). For example, FX translated GNP per adult is forty-three times larger in the United States than in India in 1970, whereas the PPP real income per adult difference is only thirteen to one. Consumer welfare may be better approximated by the PPP income deflator and therefore the PPP deflated figures were used in reestimating the schooling equations reported in this chapter. In general, PPP income elasticities of school expenditures increased by as much as a quarter, as would have been expected since the sample variance in log PPP incomes is markedly less than the variance in log FX incomes. Price elasticities were reduced somewhat, suggesting that some of the differences in the relative price of teacher salaries are captured in the PPP adjustment procedure. No systematic changes occurred in the coefficients on relative size of school aged cohorts, nor were the estimated effects of urbanization noticeably changed by this substitution of one measure of real GNP for the other. Substantive conclusions were not particularly sensitive, therefore, to this choice of procedure for translating GNP across countries into common welfare units.

[11] The disturbances in the equation determining current demand for schooling that would affect today's wages of teachers might also be correlated with the unexplained disturbances in the equation determining enrollment rates ten years earlier, such as might arise from a persistent country-specific unobserved effect. This form of error structure would imply that the lagged enrollment variable was not actually exogenous to the wage equation. The two-stage estimates based on the lagged enrollment instrument would then be subject to the classical simultaneous equation bias and also would be inconsistent. Estimates were calculated without the lagged enrollment as an instrument and the coefficient estimates of the price elasticities did not change appreciably, though their standard errors tended to increase. See also footnote 13 below.

[12] An analogous errors-in-variable bias occurs in the study of labor supply, where earnings are divided by hours worked to obtain a wage rate that is specified by theory as a determinant of hours.

expected, inversely associated with the supply of potential teachers trained in the country in previous decades.[13]

Income is measured as GNP in local constant prices converted, as are educational expenditures, to 1970 dollars, and divided by the population of working age, 15–65.[14] Population density is measured as the proportion of the population living in an urban area. The relative size of the school-aged cohort is the proportion of the population age 6–11 for primary school, and the proportion age 12–17 for secondary school, following UNESCO conventions. Period fertility is measured by the total fertility rate, which is equivalent to the sum of age-specific birth rates for women age 15–49.

Data were first collected for 155 countries with populations greater than one million in 1983, for each five years from 1950 to 1980. Data on all required series were obtained for at least one year in 89 countries, of which 30 were in Africa, 19 Latin America, 21 Asia, 2 Oceania, 1 North America, and 16 Europe. The maximum number of country–year observations was 321 for primary schools and 258 for secondary schools. In pooling of time-series observations from a cross-section, it is clear that all observations are not independent; neglect of error covariation across observations on a particular country undoubtedly biases reported tests of statistical significance and may bias estimates as well.

---

[13] The implicit primary and secondary school logarithmic wage equations for teachers were estimates as conditioned on the secondary school enrollment rate, income per adult and proportion of the population urban, all of which explanatory variables were evaluated ten years earlier:

$$\ln W_{p_t} = -1.84 - 0.349 \ln E_{s_{t-10}} + 0.355 \ln GNP/A_{t-10} - 0.808 U_{t-10}, \quad n = 186, \ R^2 = -0.264,$$
$$\quad (3.38) \quad (6.22) \qquad\qquad (4.30) \qquad\qquad\quad (2.67)$$

$$\ln W_{s_t} = -0.931 - 0.646 \ln E_{s_{t-10}} + 0.305 \ln GNP/A_{t-10} - 1.25 U_{t-10}, \quad n = 139, \ R^2 = 0.601,$$
$$\quad (1.18) \quad (8.25) \qquad\qquad (2.61) \qquad\qquad\quad (3.22)$$

where $E_{s_{t-10}}$ refers to the secondary school enrollment proportion ten years ago, GNP/A_{t-10} indicates GNP per adult (age 15–65) measured ten years earlier, U_{t-10} is the urban proportion of the population ten years ago, and W_{pt} or W_{st} are the school current expenditures per primary or secondary school teacher divided by GNP per adult today.

[14] Wealthier countries may have lower labor force participation rates in ages 15–24, in part because the returns to schooling are relatively attractive for these youth. Thus, this available productive resource of the time of students is being saved and invested, though it is not fully counted in national income accounts. At the other end of the life cycle, wealthier countries tend to report lower participation rates, at least for males after age 55. In other words, earlier retirement from the market labor force occurs at higher income levels. The time of the elderly is also a productive resource available to the society, but it is used increasingly for direct consumption (e.g. leisure) as per capita incomes rise. The bias in my measure of GNP per adult arises because the market value of leisure in retirement and the time of students is not included in GNP and thus differentially understates the real value of national factor income in wealthier societies that invest in more schooling and consume more of their life cycle budget of time in retirement activities.

There are substantial differences across regions in the size and resource intensity of primary and secondary school systems, which may stem as much from differences in relative prices as they do from the more widely recognized differences in incomes. For example, primary enrollment ratios are 59 percent in Africa and 95 percent in Latin America, while the teacher student ratios and capital intensity are similar, 0.024 and 0.030, and 1.22 and 1.15, respectively. Primary school teachers are paid about the same in the two regions, but because GNP per adult is one-third as large in Africa, the relative price of teachers is fully twice as high in Africa as it is in Latin America. Expenditure per primary school aged child is $20 in Africa compared with $51 in Latin America. The potential explanatory role of income and relative prices in determining school expenditures and achievements is suggested from even such gross regional comparisons. The large differences between enrollment ratios for boys and girls in Africa compared with Latin America may also stem from economic differences between regions. The next section summarizes the fit of the multivariate production/demand relationships across country observations and discusses the estimated magnitude of price and income effects, as well as the effects of urbanization and population growth.

2.5. Estimates of school expenditure equations

Total expenditure elasticities are reported in row 5 of Table 13.3, separately for the primary and secondary school systems. Rows 1 through 4 in Table 13.3 report the elasticity of the expenditure components designated in eq. (7). The income elasticity of total expenditures, δ, exceed unity; they are 1.35 and 1.47 at the primary and secondary school level, respectively (row 5, first column). The share of income expended on each level of schooling thus tends to increase with real GNP per adult. The elasticity of total educational expenditures with respect to the relative price of teachers is 0.16 and 0.24 at the two school levels (second column). This implies that the elasticity of the quantity of school services demanded, approximately enrollment, with respect to the price of labor, or η in eq. (4), is equal to -0.80 and -0.70 at the primary and secondary school levels.[15]

The components underlying these income and price effects on total public expenditures per school-aged child differ by school levels. In the primary schools (top panel Table 13.3) the income elasticity is about twice as large for enrollments as for teacher–student ratios: 0.31 for quantity and 0.17 for quality (rows

---

[15] From eq. (6) the coefficient on the relative price or teacher wage variable in the expenditure function is $b_2 = \alpha(\eta + 1)$, and thus the estimated price elasticity, $\eta = (b_2/\alpha) - 1$. The sample mean of α is 0.82.

Table 13.3
Estimated elasticity of school system enrollments and inputs,
with respect to changes in explanatory variables

| Level of school system | Explanatory variables | | | |
	Real income per adult	Relative price of teachers	Relative size of school-aged population	Proportion of population urban
Primary school level:				
1. Enrollment ratio (quantity: S/P)	0.31^b	-0.70^b	0.54^a	0.16
2. Teacher–student ratio (quality: T/S)	0.17^b	-0.18^b	-0.46^b	-0.14^b
3. Teacher salaries (C/T)	0.87^b	1.05^b	-1.08^b	0.08^a
4. Capital intensity (E/C)	0.00	-0.01	-0.12	-0.03
5. Total expenditures per school-aged child (6–11) (E/P)	1.35^b	0.16	-1.12^b	-0.25^b
Secondary school level:				
1. Enrollment ratio (quantity: S/P)	0.43^b	-0.96^b	0.08	-0.38^b
2. Teacher–student ratio (quality: T/S)	0.11	0.19^b	-0.81^b	0.09
3. Teacher salaries (C/T)	0.94^b	1.02^b	-0.69^b	0.05^b
4. Capital intensity (E/C)	-0.01	-0.01	-0.23	-0.03
5. Total expenditures per school-aged child (12–17) (E/P)	1.47^b	0.24^b	-1.68^b	-0.26^b

[a] Underlying regression coefficient is statistically significantly different from zero at the 5 percent level.
[b] Underlying regression coefficient is statistically significantly different from zero at the 1 percent level.
Source: T.P. Schultz (1985, tables 7 and 8).

1 and 2). The physical capital intensity index is not well explained by any of the economic or demographic variables (row 4), and may contain largely transitory variations in capital appropriations or measurement error. Teacher salaries increase 87 percent as fast as do incomes per adult (row 3), contributing to the large elasticity of the income–expenditure relationship (row 5). Conversely, the relative salary position of primary school teachers declines by about 13 percent with a doubling of average income in a country, a pattern noted over time in Figure 13.4.

At the secondary school level (bottom panel Table 13.3), the income elasticity is four times larger for quantity (0.43) than for quality (0.11). The price elasticity is larger in absolute value for secondary schools than for primary, -0.97 versus -0.70. A decline in the price of school teachers relative to national productivity is associated with a substantial increase in enrollment but with only a modest increase in the ratio of primary school teachers to students and a puzzling decrease in secondary school teacher–student ratios.

Urbanization exhibits a relatively weak, but consistent, relationship with public expenditures on schooling. A country which has 10 percent more of its population in urban areas, with 50 versus 40 percent urban, tends to expend 5 percent less on schooling per child, at both the primary and secondary school levels. These data do not indicate precisely how urban school systems reduce the public costs of education. Consolidation of schools into more efficient sized units to exploit specialized teaching functions in more densely populated areas is often cited as an important source of economies of scale in public schools.[16] Higher population densities could also reduce the private opportunity cost or travel time for students. But the lack of large effects of urbanization reducing teacher–student ratios in secondary schools, or increasing enrollments, suggests that economies of scale or reductions in private student time costs may not lie behind this pattern in school expenditures.

The relative size of the school-aged cohort, which is highly correlated with recent levels of population growth, is significantly associated with lower expenditures per student on primary and secondary schools. An increase in the proportion of the population of primary school age by 10 percent, from 0.153 to 0.168, is associated with an 11 percent decline in primary school expenditures per child. In other words, primary school expenditures do not increase in response to an increase in the size of the school-aged cohort. There are offsetting tendencies for primary school enrollment rates to increase for the larger cohorts, whereas teacher–student ratios fall. Teacher salaries, in addition, are substantially lower (10 percent) for the larger school-aged cohort, and this appears to be the main factor accounting for the lower expenditures per child.

A 10 percent larger cohort is associated with an even larger decline in expenditure per secondary school aged child, of about 17 percent. Secondary enrollments are little affected, but teacher salaries and teacher–student ratios are notably lower. Thus, larger birth cohorts do not seem to receive fewer years of

---

[16] Economies of scale in producing school services might be distinguished at three levels: (1) with the size of the national educational system; (2) with the size of the school measured in terms of its number of full time teachers; and (3) with the size of the teacher's span of control or student–teacher ratio. The importance of (1) in primary and secondary school systems was assumed at the outset to be negligible. The number of primary schools is reported in the 1984 UNESCO Yearbook. If the system's average school size (i.e. log of teachers per school) is added to eq. (6), one might expect this added scale variable to diminish the coefficient on urbanization, if larger urban schools realized economies that reduced unit costs. In a sample of 60 countries for which these data are recently available, school size is associated with *greater* expenditures per child due to higher teacher–student ratios and higher current outlays per teacher. The coefficients on urbanization are not reduced in magnitude by the addition of school size. Consolidation economies, however, could remain important at the secondary level, but no data were found to test this conjecture.

A plausible interpretation of this pattern would presume that there are economies in using teachers in the larger scale urban schools and perhaps compensating amenities in urban areas that teachers value, such as attractive employment opportunities for teachers when schools are not in session. In fact, urban teachers are probably better trained than rural ones in most countries, so qualitatively one would expect to otherwise see higher teacher costs in urban school systems.

schooling, as attested to by the pattern of enrollment ratios, but they do appear to receive schooling of lower human and physical capital intensity.

This pattern of adjustment in the factor intensity in schools is a plausible economic response to the relative scarcity of both human and physical capital in many poor countries recently experiencing rapid population growth. Much thought has been given to how health care delivery systems might be encouraged to use less human- and physical-capital intensive technologies in low income countries, rather than borrow directly the highly capital intensive (hospital based) procedures used in the industrially advanced high income countries. The tendency for low income countries to substitute away from human- and physical-capital intensive educational production technologies appears, therefore, to be a reasonable innovation on economic grounds to different relative factor scarcities [e.g. Binswanger and Ruttan (1978), Hayami and Ruttan (1971)].[17]

Fertility, as anticipated, is inversely associated with school expenditures per child, and this partial correlation (not reported) stems primarily from the inverse association between enrollment and fertility, particularly at the secondary level [T.P. Schultz (1985)]. Such a pattern could be expected if parents substitute more schooling resources per child for not having as many children. But the estimated relationship between fertility and school enrollments or expenditures is not statistically different from zero at the 5 percent level, except for primary enrollments of girls. The deletion of fertility from eq. (6) leads to slightly larger (more negative) estimates of the effect of cohort size on schooling inputs, but the changes are relatively small (less than 10 percent).

2.6. Sex differences in school enrollment rates

Differences in the school enrollment rates of boys and girls may have much to do with the level of child mortality and fertility, the rate at which women migrate from rural to urban areas, leave family and domestic productive activities for employments in the market labor force, and in particular with women's increased participation in the nonagricultural sector, as discussed below in Section 5. The future economic status of women relative to men appears to depend heavily on their enrollment in school and their ability to benefit directly from the increased productive opportunities created by modern economic growth.

---

[17]Standardized test comparisons do confirm that spending far less per student in low income countries is associated with lower standardized test scores [Heyneman and Loxley (1983)]. What is not clear is whether marginal gains from additions to school quality and quantity that can be purchased with marginal increments in educational expenditures raise the market wages of existing students by more than the amount those resources would accomplish if they extended education to a larger number of students as discussed in the next section of the chapter. One suggestive study that draws this conclusion for Brazil is Behrman and Birdsall (1983).

Table 13.4
Elasticity of enrollment ratios of females and males
with respect to changes in explanatory variables

	Explanatory variables			
Enrollment ratio by school level	Real income per adult	Relative price of teachers	Relative size of school-aged population	Proportion of population urban
Primary level:				
Females	0.43[b]	−0.76[b]	0.98[b]	−0.21
Males	0.24[b]	−0.63[b]	0.30	−0.12
Secondary level:				
Females	0.65[b]	−1.07[b]	0.75	−0.49[b]
Males	0.30[b]	−0.91[b]	−0.34	−0.30[a]

[a] Statistically significantly different from zero at the 5 percent level.
[b] Statistically significantly different from zero at the 1 percent level.
Source: T.P. Schultz (1985, tables 7 and 8).

First, the estimates summarized in Table 13.4 imply that the income elasticity is larger for female enrollment rates than for male enrollment rates: the point estimates for female and male enrollment rates are 0.43 and 0.24 at the primary level, and 0.65 and 0.30 at the secondary level. These differences in income elasticity are statistically significant at the 10 percent level. Second, the price enrollment elasticities are greater in absolute value for female than for male enrollments: −0.76 and −0.63 for primary, and −1.07 and −0.91 for secondary. A 50 percent increase in incomes per adult from the sample mean of $721 (1970 U.S.) would raise primary enrollment rates for girls from 69 to 83 percent, while the rate for boys would increase from 88 to 97 percent. The girls would improve their school achievement relative to boys from 0.78 to 0.85. The "gender gap" in secondary schools would also in this scenario close by a quarter, with girls increasing their enrollment rates from 17 to 22 percent, while the rate for boys would increase from 26 to 30 percent. Reducing the relative price of schooling has a further effect of improving female enrollments relative to males. According to these cross-sectional estimates of income and price elasticities, economic development with its effects on adult incomes and relative wages of teachers is associated with an equalizing of schooling opportunities between boys and girls; these tendencies are also evident in the restricted sample of less developed countries. Here may be a potent dimension of the development process that unleashes demands for the schooling of girls and young women that in turn play a pivotal role in governing the timing and pace of the demographic transition.

Religion is often cited as a traditional cultural force that influences the status of women and their educational opportunities relative to men. Muslim culture, in particular, is often singled out for its distinctive attitudes toward women's status, education, employment and, consequently, fertility. Adding to our framework percentage of the population that is Muslim and the percent that is Catholic, for example, does not change the above noted patterns [T.P. Schultz (1985)].

2.7. Regional patterns in residuals

Variation across countries and overtime in five variables – income per adult, teacher relative prices, urbanization, size of school cohort, and total fertility – account for 92–94 percent of the variation in expenditures per child at the primary and secondary school levels. Somewhat less of the variation is explained in enrollment ratios, 38–72 percent, respectively. Half of the wide variation in teacher–student ratios is explained by the model at the primary level, but only one-fifth of the more limited variation in this qualitative indicator is explained at the secondary school level. Holding these five explanatory variables constant, the residuals from the model are averaged across countries by region and by development status and reported in Table 13.5. Since the educational input and enrollment variables are expressed in logarithms, the average residuals

Table 13.5
Regional average deviation of primary and second school
expenditures and outputs from those predicted

Region: Primary sample size:	Africa (62)	Latin America (e3)	East Asia (21)	South and West Asia (24)	Europe, Oceania & Canada (36)
Total expenditures per child (log)	0.135	−0.0492	0.0941	−0.244	−0.0664
Male enrollment ratio (log)	0.151	−0.164	0.110	−0.276	0.0558
Female enrollment ratio (log)	0.227	−0.106	0.202	−0.663	0.0601
Teacher–student ratio (log)	−0.0002	−0.0256	−0.0599	0.0633	0.0234
Teacher relative wage (log)	−0.0303	0.155	−0.0058	0.0385	−0.155
Secondary sample size:	(49)	(35)	(18)	(18)	(21)
Total expenditures per child (log)	0.155	−0.177	0.0258	−0.0383	−0.0596
Male enrollment ratio (log)	0.292	−0.502	0.170	−0.0742	0.0671
Female enrollment ratio (log)	0.356	−0.355	0.235	−0.615	0.0289
Teacher–student ratio (log)	−0.129	0.227	−0.188	0.0707	0.0295
Teacher relative wage (log)	−0.0123	0.0753	0.0104	0.0338	−0.132

can be interpreted as the proportion by which the region exceeds or falls short of that predicted by the model.

Expenditures per primary school aged child are 9–14 percent above average in East Asia and Africa, but 24 percent below average in South and West Asia. Enrollment rates at the primary level are also above average in Africa and East Asia, but 28 percent below average in South and West Asia and 16 percent below in Latin America. Secondary school expenditures per child are about 16 percent above average in Africa, and some 18 percent below average in Latin America. Enrollment rates at the secondary level show more variation, with Latin America and South and West Asia again reporting rates below that which is expected. In contrast, Africa and East Asia again exhibit enrollment rates well above expectations. The teacher–student ratio is above average in Latin America, but below in East Asia and Africa. Teacher wages are higher in regions such as South and West Asia and Latin America which have invested less than the predicted amount in secondary schooling in the past.

The primary and secondary school regressions identify similar regional patterns in residuals. They suggest an unexplained underinvestment in primary and secondary schooling in the South and West Asian region and in Latin America. Enrollment rates, in particular, are below the expected levels in these regions. The high level of teacher wages in Latin America and South and West Asia may be traced in part to the failure to enroll more children at the secondary level in earlier years. The higher current wage paid for teachers contributes to the higher price of educational services which deters these regions from expending more resources on their school systems.

Deviations from the pattern predicted by the model based on income, price, and demographic characteristics of the population may signal a disequilibrium that might encourage the private sector to provide schooling. There do not appear to be sufficient data to test this conjecture, but private schools in Latin America and portions of Asia and Africa are not increasing their share of enrollments in response to the sluggish public sector provision of schooling services [World Bank (1986a)]. Another hypothesis might be that stagnant economic conditions have reduced the rewards for education in the work force, and thereby depressed social and private rates of returns to education lowering investment in schooling.[18] At least in the case of Latin America, studies do not support the view that the underinvestment in secondary schooling is due to a low

---

[18]Returns to education may not increase with modern economic growth because of limited regional and occupational mobility rewarding individuals on the basis of their skills and education. Public policies may also have failed to encourage technological change through adaptive research and development. Finally, the absence of competitive domestic factor and product markets, or distorting trade and foreign exchange regimes, may have eroded the incentives to invest in education or skewed the distribution of income so as to discourage broadly based educational programs. These possibilities cannot be explored here.

Table 13.6
Average social and private rates of returns to education by school level
(number of countries reported in parentheses below mean)

Region	Social			Private		
	Primary	Secondary	Higher	Primary	Secondary	Higher
Africa	27	19	14	45	28	33
	(12)	(12)	(12)	(9)	(9)	(9)
Asia	18	14	12	34	15	18
	(9)	(11)	(11)	(5)	(8)	(8)
Latin America	35	19	16	61	28	26
	(8)	(8)	(8)	(5)	(5)	(5)
High income countries[a]	13[b]	10	8	19[b]	12	11
	(6)	(15)	(15)	(7)	(14)	(15)

[a] Europe, United States, New Zealand, Israel.
[b] Not calculable in the majority of high income countries where the comparison group without a primary education is small and highly unrepresentative at younger ages.
Source: Calculated by the author for most recent years when social returns were available at all levels or all but primary level for high income countries. Original studies summarized by Psacharopoulos (1973, table 14) and (1985, table A-1).

return. Indeed, the private returns that accrue to those in Latin America who manage to get a secondary education are substantial (see Table 13.6). If the overall framework proposed in this section is tenable, then further study of country-level educational outlays and achievements is warranted, both to discover why expenditures on schooling deviate from the pattern estimated here and to determine if these deviations help to account for the rate and structure of modern economic growth occurring in these countries.

2.8. Cross-sectional findings and time-series forecasts

One method for evaluating the overall framework proposed above is to calculate how well the educational changes in the last decade are explained by the actual changes in the conditioning variables that occurred in this period, weighted by the cross-section estimates of the model.[19] For this purpose only about half of the countries in the cross-section sample report sufficient data for the decade of

[19] There are several possible reasons for divergence. First, the model is fit to a pooled combination of cross section data from several time periods, and not to just the 1965–75 time-series changes within countries. Second, the sample of countries for which the 1965–75 comparisons can be performed is more restricted than the sample used in estimating the model. A third reason is, of course, the omission or misspecification of explanatory factors. On the other hand, this test is less strong than it might appear, because it is based on overlapping samples. Though the *within*-country changes are not the basis for the reported estimates, repeated observations on these same countries do represent about a fifth of the pooled cross-section sample used for the estimation of the original model.

1965–75 and time-series forecasts are described only for this subsample [T.P. Schultz (1985)].

The estimated model simulates the changes in expenditures and enrollments reasonably well for the average of 65 observed primary school systems, that is, 93 and 94 percent of the growth is explained from 1965 to 1975 in expenditures and enrollments, respectively. Increases in incomes per adult of about a quarter in this decade would have contributed by itself to an even larger increase in expenditures than the one-third increase actually observed. The relative decline in primary school teacher salaries and urbanization moderated slightly the predicted growth in expenditures. Enrollment rates at the primary level responded predominantly to the decline in relative prices (of teachers), but also increased with incomes, particularly for females.

At the secondary school level the model underpredicts the increases of a third in expenditures and a half in enrollments that actually occurred across the sample of 48 countries. Again, income growth alone would have suggested a more rapid increase in expenditures than actually occurred, whereas the decline in prices, urbanization, and a small increase in cohort size restrained the growth in secondary school expenditures per child. Enrollments at the secondary level respond strongly to the decline in relative price of teacher salaries; these price effects are larger at the secondary level than they are at the primary level. Demographic characteristics of the sampled population did not change appreciably in this period and therefore had little effect on predicted school resources or enrollments.

The main finding of this analysis of international aggregate data from educational systems is that public expenditures on schools have conformed to anticipated patterns with respect to consumer incomes, relative factor prices, and demographic constraints. At the secondary level, and probably also at the primary level, rapid population growth has depressed levels of expenditures per child of school age. This has occurred by increasing class size and lowering teacher salaries, but not by restricting notably enrollment. In the future, as the percentage of the population of school age declines markedly in Latin America and East Asia, an increase in teacher–student ratios may be expected, whereas in Africa where the share of school-aged children will continue to increase for some time, average classroom size may continue to increase. Future research may help assess whether the decline in public school expenditures per student that is associated with rapid population growth is an inefficient bureaucratic distortion in the allocation of social resources or an efficient adjustment in factor proportions to local relative factor prices and returns to the quantity and quality of school services. Since Africa still confronts relatively high prices for teachers, given the described dynamics of expanding their school systems, the continued decline in teachers relative prices should help this continent increase enrollments without necessarily increasing outlays per student. A critical policy question is:

How can the public sector facilitate this efficient downward adjustment in the relative level of teacher salaries? Teachers will tend to lobby in their own self-interest to postpone this adjustment, and if they succeed it will slow the continuing expansion in enrollments.

3. Alternative models of education and earnings, data, and policy implications

A positive relationship between the schooling of workers and their earnings is observed in household surveys and censuses in many countries [Psacharopoulos (1985), Blaug (1976)]. This empirical regularity was first examined in high income countries, such as the United States, and then described in many other countries. The conventional economic interpretation is to assume wages measure labor's marginal product and that persons acquire education as they do vocational training at a cost in terms of forgone opportunities that is repaid by future streams of enhanced earnings. The emphasis given to monetary returns to education in the market labor force does not preclude the private and social importance of nonmarket production returns to schooling or, for that matter, the pure consumption benefits of schooling. The early focus on labor market returns reflected the availability of data and the historic reliance of economists on the marketplace to adjudicate issues of value as codified in national income accounts.

The treatment of education as a form of capital investment embodied in the human agent can be traced back at least as far as Adam Smith, though it enters into the mainstream of economic thinking in the 1950s and 1960s in the work of T.W. Schultz (1961) and Becker (1964). The empirical relationship of wages and schooling is conceptualized as a life cycle regularity or age–wage profile, with the wage increasing first in the cross-section with the age of the worker and then decreasing beyond some age, when depreciation of productive skills outweighs new investments in human capital. Mincer (1962) proposed human capital investments on-the-job after the completion of schooling as an explanation for the age–earnings profile. By assuming that post-schooling human capital investment declined regularly with the worker's accumulation of labor market experience, and that human capital investment eventually ceased as retirement approached, Mincer (1974) was able to account for many interrelated aspects of U.S. earnings for males, by schooling and by post-schooling experience.

These basic empirical regularities are summarized in the earnings function. This relationship has many interpretations, however, depending on what factors generate the relationship [Rosen (1977)]. Assume that the real wage, w, of a worker is a function of the individual's years of schooling, s, and other productive characteristics, z, such as ability:

$$w = f(s, z), \tag{8}$$

where z is assumed exogenously given to the individual, while hours of work, school quality, and nonschool investments in productive marketable skills are initially ignored. If the private cost of schooling to the student or family is approximated by the full-time opportunity cost of the student's time not spent working in the labor market, then the present value, V, of the individual's future earnings can be evaluated at the age of entering school:

$$V(s, z) = \int_s^n w(s, z)^{-rt}\, dt = w(s, z)(1/r)(e^{-rs} - e^{-rn}), \tag{9}$$

where n is the number of years after entering school when the individual retires from the labor force and ceases to benefit from education. If the internal rate of return to additional schooling falls with increased schooling, and the discount rate or financial constraint, r, does not vary across schooling levels, then the family or individual continues to invest in schooling until the present value of the individual's earnings is maximized. The optimal level of schooling is that which equates the opportunity cost of attending school (i.e. not working) to the discounted value of the lifetime gain obtained from the increment to schooling, adjusted for the finiteness of the working life:

$$w_s = wr(1 - e^{-r(n-s)}), \tag{10}$$

where w_s is the partial derivative of the wage with respect to schooling. If retirement is viewed as infinitely distant, permitting one to neglect e^{-rn}, an expression for the logarithmic wage equation is obtained:

$$\ln w = \ln rV(s, z) + rs. \tag{11}$$

Interpersonal differences in s shift the wealth intercept and slope of the wage with respect to the discount rate, while differences in z affect the intercept. Thus, observations on $\ln w$ and s do not generally identify the wage function (8) or the optimal schooling attendance rule, $s = D(r, z)$. Observations on ability, z, and the financial constraint, r, may permit one to describe empirically the wage and schooling functions. If capital markets are perfect, and r is the same for everyone, differences in z may allow one to estimate r from a regression of the logarithm of the wage on years of schooling. This estimate does not describe how schooling affects the earnings of any particular person, because z may still influence how much schooling is optimal for each individual. This interpretation of the wage equation (11) is consequently called a reduced-form hedonic wage equation, embodying both a school attendance equation conditional on r and z, and a wage function conditional on s and z [Rosen (1974, 1977)]. This hedonic wage function does not presume to identify how individuals vary their school enrollment in response to human capital returns, or how the derived demand for labor depends on the educational attainment of the worker. This hedonic interpretation of the wage function, however, admits more readily to the existence of market imperfections and unanticipated developments contributing to substantial disequilibrium rents in the implicit valuation of different types of inelastically supplied skills [Rosen (1977), Lucas (1977), Heckman and Sedlachek (1985)].

The more common interpretation of the wage function is that developed by Mincer (1974) in which everyone is equally well off from a lifetime perspective; long-run equilibrium compensating differences in costs and gains leave individuals indifferent among alternative levels of investment in schooling. In this case, $\ln rV(s, z)$ is identical for all persons, or at least unrelated to schooling. Consequently, eq. (11) is an identified structural relationship. Regressions of $\ln w$ on s provide estimates of r that can be interpreted as the average private internal rate of return on the opportunity costs of schooling for a representative individual.[20]

To accommodate a monotonically declining rate of on-the-job human capital investment by workers after finishing schooling, Mincer (1962, 1974) illustrates how a quadratic in post-schooling labor market experience, x, could describe proportionate changes in wages, net of on-the-job training costs:

$$\ln w_i = \ln w_0 + rs_i + a_1 x_i + a_2 x_i^2 + e_i, \tag{12}$$

where the i's now refer to the variables that are observed to differ across individuals, and e_i is the residual error that is assumed uncorrelated with all right-hand variables. When x is unobserved, Mincer (1974) approximated it by age minus age of entry into the school system, minus years of schooling completed. In other words, it is assumed for males at least that they are attached full time to the market labor force after completing their schooling. Hanushek and Quigley (1985) incorporate information on actual employment experience for males, assuming that on-the-job training should be curtailed during spells of unemployment. For women the above empirical approximation that all post-schooling experience is equally relevant to market earnings may seem particularly misleading and Mincer and Polachek (1974) demonstrate the differential effects

---

[20] If there are additional private costs of schooling, these are assumed to be offset by part-time employment by the student. Obviously, where students incur large direct costs, private returns are overstated by r and conversely where private stipends are available for all students, such as in Francophone Africa for higher education, the private returns are understated in this Mincerian earnings function. Clearly, this specification is a simple approximation, which fits reasonably well many sources of data. Tests of functional form specification are rarely performed, but some that have been reported do not reject this semi-log form [Heckman and Polachek (1974)].

of spells of market and nonmarket work experience on women's market earnings in the United States. However, the post-schooling experience variable originally proposed by Mincer has the attraction of being fixed for the individual, once schooling has been determined and is, therefore, not a choice variable or one that is likely to be particularly correlated with unobserved market-oriented abilities or preferences. Women's actual entry into and exit from the labor force and even unemployment are endogenous choice variables that must be jointly modeled with training investment, if the effect of labor market histories on wages are to be suitably estimated.

Four broad overlapping problems with this human capital approach will be taken up in the next section. First, there are variables that may determine wages, such as ability, but which are omitted from the above simplified specification of the earnings function, and their omission may lead to biased estimates of the partial association between schooling and wages that is the basis for benefit–cost calculations or internal rate of return estimation.[21] Moreover, some variables used as explanatory variables in the earnings function are to some degree adult lifetime choice variables, such as labor supply or tenure on current job, and treating these as exogenous conditioning variables to explain the wage may also bias the estimated coefficient on schooling. Finally, even education can be viewed as endogenous to the wage determination process, when the focus of analysis is to estimate how parents trade off various human capital investments in their children and other bequests conditional on their children's exogenous endowments, such as sex and innate ability. But the simplifying convention in most studies of wage determinants is to treat education as parentally determined and thus exogenous to the child's lifetime choices as an adult that affect her or his life cycle productive opportunities in both market and nonmarket activities.

Second, the profile of post schooling on-the-job training investment cannot generally be observed, and alternative proxies for Mincer's post-schooling investment profile have been proposed. An analogous tendency may exist for employers to adopt a life cycle incentive scheme that drives a wedge between wages and labor's short-run marginal product, with the goal of reducing shirking by employees whose output is costly to monitor [Lazear (1979)]. In either scheme the present value of the workers' profile of wages is equivalent to the present value of marginal productivity.

---

[21] If z had a proportionate effect, a_3, on wages in eq. (11), its omission would bias the OLS estimate of r to the extent that z and s were partially correlated in the sample, i.e. $\text{cov}(z, s)/\text{var}(s) > 0$. Thus, if z were height and $\text{cov}(z, s)$ were zero, the bias due to omitting a factor affecting wages would not affect estimates of educational returns. Alternatively, if more able individuals in each birth cohort were selected to obtain more schooling, $\text{cov}(z, s) > 0$, and more able workers received higher wages given schooling, the omission of ability from the wage equation (11) would bias upward the OLS estimate of r due to the misspecification of the wage equation by $\alpha_3 \text{cov}(z, s)/\text{var}(s)$ [Griliches (1957, 1977)].

Third is the absence of suitable comparison groups. It is never possible to observe what particular persons would have earned, if they had obtained more or less schooling than they did. Comparisons are needed across schooling groups to estimate benefits and they therefore depend on restrictive assumptions, of which the most convenient is that parents choose the schooling of their children, according to the parents' endowments and preferences, but that these parent attributes do not affect their children's earnings, except to the extent that they influence the children's schooling [see alternative specifications estimated by Leibowitz (1974)]. Holding constant in the wage function for parent economic attributes (status) is then one strategy for developing better schooling comparisons [Carnoy (1967a), Bowles (1972)], but other strategies exist and they can yield divergent conclusions [Griliches (1977), Chamberlain and Griliches (1977), Behrman and Wolfe (1984a)]. Another approach is to specify explicitly the decision rule for schooling and then correct for the implicit selection bias of schooling in the estimation of the wage function [Willis and Rosen (1979)]. In this quasi-structural equation approach to self-selection of education and the determination of earnings, the researcher must still specify variables that influence the education decision, but do not have a persisting effect on wages, conditional on schooling. This identification restriction has not yet been motivated by an economic theory and, therefore, has some of the arbitrariness associated with the earlier approach that assigns the decision to prior parent attributes. The empirical importance of these alternative comparison methods are reviewed in Section 4.

Fourth is a discontinuity between the conceptual framework and observations. Theory pertains to individuals investing in their productive capacity over a life cycle, but most data relate to different individuals of different ages, which are then combined to describe a "synthetic" life cycle profile of earnings by age. The different aged individuals in the cross-section have matriculated through different quality schools, lived through different historical conditions, such as depressions and spells of unemployment, and were born into different sized birth cohorts which may influence their schooling and earnings opportunities [Freeman (1979), Welch (1979), Falaris and Peters (1985), T.P. Schultz (1985), Freeman and Bloom (1986)]. Moreover, the standard interpretation of the coefficient on schooling in the wage function is that of a private rate of return in an equilibrium investment setting [Mincer (1974)]. The applicability of the equilibrium investment theory to a country where modern economic growth has only established itself recently, and then occurred sporadically over time, may be misleading. Older cohorts were probably educated without the expectation of their current realized returns. The effects of economic growth on life cycle returns to schooling in low income countries have rarely been analyzed with appropriate longitudinal data, an exception being that of Malaysia by Smith (1983). Lacking the required panel or retrospective data in most countries, short- and medium-run fluctuations in the aggregate economy can perturb the apparent levels of educational returns as estimated from "synthetic" age cross-sections, particularly at younger ages.[22]

All of the above problems in the human capital interpretation of the relationship between schooling and earnings could be viewed as "revisionist" in spirit. This is because they attempt to revise and reformulate the human capital concepts, to modify its empirical specification, to use better estimating techniques for the wage equation, and to collect more appropriate data to bring the evidence closer to the core of the theory. Other critiques of the human capital interpretation of the education–wage regularity seek to find a fundamentally different way to explain how education influences labor market outcomes.

The primary alternative hypothesis is that of signaling or screening [Spence (1973), Arrow (1973)]. According to this view, education does not act to train or to socialize a worker to perform more productive tasks individually or in a team. Rather, education filters or screens on the native ability or productivity of the worker, without enhancing it. Information on ability is signaled to the employer by the worker investing his time and resources in the acquisition of schooling. A private gain from schooling may still be inferred from the schooling–wage relationship, but the social return to schooling is more complex. The production of information needed to assign more able workers to jobs where these abilities are more productive yields a social product, but what is not clear is whether education is an efficient mechanism to accomplish this matching of workers and jobs? To many observers, education would seem to be a time-consuming and costly device to screen for the ability of workers, if schools do not also augment their skills. If it could be shown that an alternative screen worked as well as education, but had lower social costs, then the alternative scheme would be socially preferable to education.

The simple fact that no society, capitalist or socialist, has pursued an alternative scheme to education to produce the information needed to match workers to jobs casts doubt on the validity of this extreme form of the signaling hypothesis.

---

[22] Cases have been described in the literature, such as Brazil in the 1960s and 1970s, where rapid modern economic growth created large rents for well-educated workers. Before the rapidly expanding educational system of Brazil could catch up to these demands for higher educated workers, the private returns to secondary and higher education reached high levels [Langoni (1973), Fishlow (1973)]. But these rents were reduced among the younger birth cohorts whose relative supplies of schooling increased. High returns persisted, however, for some older educated workers for whom the more plentiful young educated workers were apparently poor substitutes. Conversely, foreign exchange crises in Colombia were associated with depressed wage premia for younger university graduates in Bogota in 1965 [Schultz (1968)]. As the import dependent modern sectors of Colombia revived in the late 1960s and 1970s, private returns to university training rebounded [Psacharopoulos (1981), Fields and Schultz (1982)]. The point is that the business cycle may perturb substantially the apparent cross-sectional returns to schooling in the short run [Kniesner et al. (1978)], while the appropriate criteria for a long-run human capital investment should be returns averaged over short-run business cycles and not confounded with other short-run changes that occur cyclically, such as changes in the relative size of birth cohorts entering the labor force [Freeman and Bloom (1985)].

But a more moderate interpretation would hypothesize that school credentials provide an important source of information in the labor market that employers can access at low cost. Educational attainment is a means to "discriminate statistically" among workers in hiring; it is, moreover, a means that is accepted by some as fair [Blaug (1985)], whereas many other groupings of individuals that might be used to discriminate statistically are challenged by some as socially unfair, such as by race, sex, age, marital status, and ethnic group.

Within an undistorted general equilibrium framework, both the human capital and the screening hypotheses provide alternative explanations for the schooling–wage relationship. It remains to be demonstrated whether the screening theory "can be made to yield interesting and testable implications in the absence of direct measurement of ability" [Arrow (1973, p. 215)]. Empirical tests of the importance of the screening hypothesis have followed several directions. The first identifies situations where labor market institutions appear more or less likely to depend on the screening information of schooling in determining labor's payment. Private returns to schooling according to the screening hypothesis should be greater in those situations where the hiring mechanism could readily rely on schooling as a screen. Many studies have contrasted the private returns to schooling in wage employment and in self-employment. Self-employed, and in particular small farmers, are a class of workers producing within a reasonably well understood technology, where outputs and inputs are competitively sold and bought, respectively. Higher earnings associated with a farmer's schooling, net of inputs, cannot be readily explained by screening but can by human capital. Analogous reasoning suggests that public sector employment might be most prone to emphasize educational credentials as a screen, but this does not emerge clearly from empirical studies [Psacharopoulos (1985), Van der Gaag and Vijverberg (1986b)]. Educational differentials in wages might be exaggerated at the time of hiring by screening, but should diminish with job tenure as the employer learns more about the worker's productivity. But they do not appear to [Layard and Psacharopoulos (1974)]. Since none of these testable implications of the screening hypothesis receives strong support from data in high or low income countries, are we to conclude that screening by education does not occur? Self-selection of occupation could explain the first results, if the ablest educated workers choose to be self-employed and the ablest uneducated seek to be wage earners, widening the observed education–wage differentials for self-employed compared with wage earners. Analogously, job tenure is not exogenous, and employers may selectively fire the educated worker who does not produce at the anticipated level, leading to the persistence in wage differentials by educational level with increasing job tenure. Self-employment may be more risky than wage employment and a risk premium to the self-employed complicates comparisons of earnings across these types of jobs. The more educated worker may be less prone to quit or turn over at his or her initiative, and this tendency may explain part of the wage premium received by the more educated [Weiss (1984), Kiefer (1985), Donohue (1986)]. The intrinsic difficulty in discriminating between the human capital and screening interpretation leaves in doubt whether for most practical purposes it matters which mixture of these stories best describes reality.

A third approach views education as an instrument for job competition in a distorted labor market [Bhagwati and Srinivasan (1977)]. If wages are not flexible downward and an excess supply of educated labor exists for the available jobs requiring a specified level of education, the employer is assumed in this model to clear the market by raising the educational standards for the job until the supply of educationally qualified job applicants no longer exceeds the respective demand for labor. This "job ladder" model is similar to the Harris and Todaro (1970) model where urban unemployment, a form of queuing, clears the labor market that is also distorted by an excessive and rigid wage in urban employment. The rationing of jobs by education, if wages are sticky downward, provides a second-best economic outcome in the presence of labor market distortions, and leads to the employment of overqualified workers. An inefficient match of workers and jobs occurs in this formulation. A similar "bumping" model is proposed by Fields (1974a) in a partial equilibrium context. I have not found empirical tests of this third approach to modeling the effects of education in a distorted labor market.

Measurements of distortions in labor markets are rarely conclusive, even though many influential theories of economic development are built on specific sectoral distortions and distinctions in the labor market. The intrinsic problem with estimating the magnitude of distortions is the expectation that variation in unobserved productive characteristics of workers provides an alternative explanation for wage differences between workers in distorted and undistorted sectors. For example, the empirical tendency for union wages to exceed nonunion wages, given the worker's observed skills, suggests that an economic distortion may be created by unions [Lewis (1963, 1985)]. But if unionized sectors attract more productive workers or the union as an institution raises the productivity of its membership, no loss in efficiency may result [Freeman and Medoff (1984)]. A challenge to labor economics is to document situations where there appear to be wage differences between otherwise similarly endowed and situated groups of workers. If explanations for these regularities, or group wage differences, cannot be confirmed, the empirical weight of the evidence may grow and a consensus for policy might follow, as in the case of the effect of minimum wage policies on employment opportunities for the least experienced and skilled workers in high income countries [Welch (1978)]. One conclusion of this survey is that *studies that ignore the human capital heterogeneity of labor in low income countries may be seriously misleading.* The large wage differentials observed by worker education (as well as by sex and often region) realistically preclude interpretation of aggregate sectoral wage variation as compelling evidence of distortions, particularly in low income countries. Refining the evidence of labor market distortions within and across low income countries at the disaggregate level of workers and firms is an important research frontier in development economics. The theories of wage variation that were recapitulated in this section may provide a basis for these microeconomic studies of wage structures. The next section reviews in more detail the empirical problems of inferring the returns to education from micro-econometric studies.

4. Rates of return to schooling in market activities

Estimates of the rates of return to education can be calculated on two bases. The *private* rate of return is the internal rate of return that equalizes the present discounted private opportunity and direct cost of schooling with the discounted value of the private after-tax gains. The *social* rate of return adds to private costs the public and private subsidies that the individual student and family do not bear, and augments the private gains to include taxes and any net positive social externalities that are not captured by the private individual and family. In reality, it is rare for studies to assign monetary values to social externalities of education, or to private nonmarket benefits of schooling. Relatively few private return calculations even deduct for the marginal income taxes paid the state by the more educated worker. This latter task is not conceptually difficult, but would not make any difference if taxes were proportional to wages. Consequently, the distinction between private and social returns is, in practice, the inclusion of the social cost of public expenditures per pupil in addition to private family costs of schooling. Social returns are, therefore, always lower than private returns to the extent that the educational system is publicly subsidized.

Private returns provide one incentive for individuals and families to invest in education, while the consumption value of schooling provides the second (unobserved) motivation for private decisions regarding education. For social resources to be efficiently allocated, they should be invested in each level and type of education to the point where the marginal social returns are driven down to levels that social and private investments receive in other sectors of the economy.

Private individuals are attracted to higher private return activities, but the efficiency rationale for public subsidies in education is no different than elsewhere, as Becker (1964) observed many years ago. Neglecting distributional issues, public subsidies for education should vary in proportion to the positive social externalities generated by the specific type and level of education. It is commonly believed that externalities from education are more substantial at the basic primary level, and eventually peter out at the higher technical specialized levels of university training, where persons capture most of the social benefits (minus taxes) from their education [Weisbrod (1964)]. Research activities that are often combined with higher education may, however, be responsible for substantial social externalities, to the extent that their services are nonappropriable by the research university and hence freely available to firms and households.

Estimates of rates of return to education for 46 market economies are summarized in Table 13.6 (p. 575), by region and school level [data drawn from Psacharopoulos (1973, 1985) based on the most recent year reported]. As noted earlier, social returns decrease at more advanced levels of development across countries and they decrease, as a rule, at higher levels of schooling within countries. Social returns tend to be about twice as large in Africa and Latin America (15–30 percent) as they are in high income countries (8–13 percent). Moreover, private returns are often twice social returns in low income regions. The exception is Asia, where social returns in secondary and higher education for the same countries (not reported) are only moderately higher than private returns, because public subsidies at these levels are a moderate share of private costs. Africa, and to a lesser degree Latin America, has provided large public subsidies for secondary and higher education. These relative differences in rates of return are generally replicated by estimates of Mincerian earnings or wage functions based on household survey data, as illustrated by eq. (12) in Section 3. The average proportionate shifts of these earnings functions with respect to years of schooling are smaller, however, ranging from 13–20 percent for Latin America and Africa to 6–9 percent for high income countries [e.g. Psacharopoulos (1985, table 3)].

Within a country the pattern of diminishing social marginal efficiency of human capital investments gives support to the view that public subsidies should focus first on the expansion of primary and then secondary school systems. The overall picture suggests that returns are highest in Africa where large educational investments began only recently. The high returns in Latin America may be due to the sluggish expansion of public schools (Section 2), whereas East Asia and high income countries have achieved a level of human capital investments such that social returns to schooling are roughly on a par with private returns after taxes from physical capital. All of these calculations of returns to education neglect the consumption gains associated with schooling and any externalities or "public good" attributes of education, because there is no consensus on how to measure these benefits.

There are, however, issues surrounding the empirical measurement of the returns to schooling outlined in Section 3, that need to be discussed further. The first class of problems involves estimation bias introduced by inadequate specification of student ability, parent background, and school quality. Ideally, these could be corrected by agreement on specification and availability of better data. Short of that ultimate goal, most studies must build on imperfect specifications and data. My own judgments are offered below as to what are the more serious problems and the direction of bias to be anticipated. The second class of problems arises because only a portion of the population reports the information sought on wages and related productive characteristics. If selection into the sample is related to the schooling–wage relationship, a bias may be expected. Selection problems are likely to be more important when the criteria for inclusion in the sample involve the choice of occupation, labor force participation, or migration, all of which can be plausibly linked to the educational qualifications of the worker. In these cases, the sample selection problem is essentially one of the estimating by simultaneous equations methods some form of labor market behavior and the wage equation. There is no consensus, however, on how to choose the identifying restrictions needed to estimate the returns to education while correcting for this source of sample selection.

4.1. Student ability, parent background, and school quality

The foremost source of bias embodied in estimated education–wage relationships occurs because of the role of student ability and parental status in a more completely specified model of the wage determination process. As illustrated earlier, it is likely that more able students obtain more schooling, and wage payments for native ability are then being incorrectly attributed to schooling. Even when ability is observed before schooling occurs, a rich variety of alternative methods have been proposed to disentangle education's independent effect on wages. This large literature cannot be adequately summarized here [e.g. Griliches and Mason (1972), Hause (1972), Welch (1975), Taubman (1976), Behrman et al. (1980), Willis (1987)]. If ability is simply omitted from the wage function, estimates of the rate of return to schooling may be upward biased, but in most cases by no more than 5–15 percent. Indeed, when ability and schooling are symmetrically treated as variables which are measured with error and potentially affected by common unobservables, Griliches (1977) illustrates with U.S. panel data how the "true" effect of schooling is actually underestimated by omitting ability and covariant unobservables from the analysis. Boissiere, Knight and Sabot (1985) examine data from Tanzania and Kenya to assess how cognitive achievement is influenced by schooling and native ability, and how all three factors affect later earnings in the labor force. Not only can ex ante ability be held constant, it is also possible to evaluate whether education's effect on wages operates through test scores or by other means such as credentialism or screening. They conclude from their data that "literate and numerate workers are more productive, and education is valuable to workers because it can give them skills that increase their productivity" (p. 1029). Their analysis of contemporary East Africa "provides strong support for the human capital interpretation of the educational structure of wages" (p. 1029).

Another important and often omitted variable is parent background or social status. If wealthy and powerful parents secure for their offspring both education and a well-paying job, the correlation between their children's education and wages may overstate the "true" effect of education on wages or labor productivity. Carnoy (1967a) examines this hypothesis with intergenerational data from Mexico and others have replicated this approach elsewhere, conditioning wages on various characteristics of the parents as well as on the worker's education, age, etc. Most studies have found, as did Carnoy, that father's occupation is strongly related to the child's wages, but, contrary to expectations, that much of this "effect" of parent background is intermediated through the child's educational attainment. Thus, "increasing the average skill level of the father has only a small effect on the son's incomes" given the son's schooling [Carnoy (1967a, p. 418)]. In other words, the substantial private rates of return to education that Carnoy found in Mexico "show little sensitivity to changes in average occupational level" of the father. Heckman and Hotz (1986) found a greater sensitivity of schooling returns to their inclusion of both mother's and father's education in a recent analysis of a 1983 survey from Panama. Their results suggest that the role of the mother's education may exceed that of the father's, just as Leibowitz (1974) found in a U.S. sample from the 1950s. The estimated average private rate of return to schooling in Panama was reduced from 13.0 to 8.6 percent with the inclusion of both parents' education variables [Heckman and Hotz (1986)].

Various interpretations are given to the explanatory role of parent education or background in the child's wage function. The one proposed at the outset is nepotism and social stratification that allow influential parents to place their child in a favorable job, frustrating, efficient market mechanisms [Bowles (1972)]. Alternatively, more educated parents may provide the child with a more favorable learning environment at home, thereby lowering the cost of learning or increasing the market productivity of attending school for a given number of years [Leibowitz (1974), Murnane et al. (1981)]. The genetic transmission of ability from parent, proxied by education, to child is another possible mechanism behind this relationship. Parents may also vary their market investment in their children, given the number of years that their children attend school, through the "quality" or resource intensity of the schooling they provide their children. Adopting this final interpretation of the source of the parent background effects on the child's future wages, social scientists have proceeded to specify and measure how home learning environments differ, and how the level and mix of resources internally allocated by the school system to the pupil's education varies, and, finally, what are the effects of these different mixes of investment inputs on the child's subsequent earnings in the labor force.

Originally the addition of parent education or other indicators of parent socioeconomic status to the earnings function of a child was designed to purge the returns to education of the effects of parent wealth and influences that were not operating through the child's education. But Griliches (1977) and others have shown that inclusion of parent education or background can also over-correct for this possibility and bias downward the educational returns or merely increase the erratic performance of the earnings function. To the extent that more educated parents tend to invest more in the education of their children, it is not clear why this component of education should not be examined to infer returns to schooling. To understand how educational decisions are made intergenerationally should provide a structural foundation for explaining who gets educated, as well as eventually estimating how the observed returns to education are affected by who receives the education [Willis and Rosen (1979)]. It may then be possible to estimate additionally how parent education also influences their children's earnings by providing them with home investments, social connections, and physical wealth.

Unfortunately, relatively few bodies of data measure the home and school environment in such detail and also follow over time the child's subsequent wage profile in the labor market. Nonetheless, imperfect data have been used widely since the 1960s to appraise the returns to the quality as well as quantity of schooling, culminating in the estimation of education production functions [Kiesling (1971), Averch et al. (1974), Hanushek (1979, 1986)]. Welch (1966) first analyzed public expenditures per pupil, length of school year, teacher salaries, and classroom size, among other variables, to account for market wage returns to expenditures on schooling across U.S. states (assuming people did not move). Where parallel school systems serve distinct segments of the population, the consequences for wage differences between these populations can be decomposed into those attributable to different years of schooling and to the different resource intensities of their segregated school systems [Welch (1975), Orazem (1983)].

Others have employed micro data on the earnings of individual workers, their schooling, and the characteristics of the schools they attended [e.g. Johnson and Stafford (1973), Link and Ratledge (1975), Rizzuto and Wachtel (1980)]. The analogous analytical process has been pursued in low income countries with proxies devised to measure the "quality" of schools and teachers [Birdsall (1985)]. These studies address the policy choice of extending more schooling to more people by pushing out the extensive margin, or investing those resources in more intensive schooling activities, such as improving the training and salaries of teachers. Clearly, a tradeoff of efficiency and equality of opportunity may have to be faced when in practice public funds may either be used to expand the quantity or quality of schooling [Behrman and Birdsall (1983)]. Even if it could be assumed that the benefits flow in either case to the same person, and thus there were no distributional effects, it is difficult to infer whether the future market productivity of a worker who is offered more years of existing quality schooling will be larger or smaller than if those same educational resources had been used to provide the worker with better quality schooling.

One empirical conclusion should be expected: when "qualitative" measures of schooling are added to the earnings function, the estimated private returns to "years of schooling" will undoubtedly decrease. This follows from the general underlying positive covariance between quantity and quality of schooling. Regions spending more on schooling will attract more students to enroll and stay in school longer, because for the same private opportunity cost of the student's time, a more concentrated and presumably more valuable investment is accumulated. It is also a common empirical regularity to observe a positive regional association between parent private home investments (that are generally unobserved in data used to study wages) and public school quality investments. Thus, unless the home environment is held constant, variables that measure school quality will also proxy these reinforcing background private investments and bias upward estimates of the wage returns to school quality and quantity. Regardless, the simple estimate of returns to school quantity should always be interpreted as capturing the effect of increased quantity plus the uncontrolled background association in the sample between school quality and levels of schooling.

While we cannot confidently generalize about the relative returns of school quality and quantity on market wages, international comparative studies of education's effects on standardized school achievement tests do suggest several regularities that might guide future research to measure how the economic returns to schooling differ across these extensive and intensive margins. Generally, "the potency of a pupil's home background or social status is significantly less (important) than it is in the industrialized countries in determining pupil achievements" [Heyneman (1984, p. 299)]. Conversely, "the variation in academic achievement attributable to factors internal to school classrooms, such as the quality of the teacher and physical facilities" is significantly more important in explaining test performance in low income countries than in the more developed countries [Heyneman (1984, p. 299)]. Although the reason for these differences in the roles of family background and school quality in determining pupil achievement is not well established, some have concluded that the leverage of public policy on pupil performance through improvements in school quality is greater in low income countries than it is in high income countries [Heyneman and Loxley (1983)]. Unfortunately, the relationship between test achievement scores and subsequent wage rates is not always strong, raising the question whether test achievement is a satisfactory indicator of schooling output, particularly across countries where the derived demands for educated skills differ greatly. Indeed, it has been a frustrating finding of many of the more thorough studies of educational production functions in the United States and in other countries that well-accepted dimensions of school quality, such as teacher–student ratios, exhibit little systematic relationship to student performance [Averch (1974), Simmons and Alexander (1978), Hanushek (1979, 1986)]. More research is required to generalize about how changes in the mix of school inputs and management incentives affect school outputs. Moreover, economic evaluation studies of schools must go beyond assessing the impact of schools on student test achievements and follow up the differential economic success of students in the labor market by measuring their subsequent earnings. As with estimates of the returns to years of schooling, estimates of the benefits from using a more efficient mix of inputs in the school may be biased if the sample variation in input mix is not randomized, and thus potentially correlated with unmeasured variables determining earnings or who is educated, either at the level of the individual or school.

Reallocations of inputs internal to school systems may improve the efficiency of schools, but inputs other than teachers absorb only a small fraction of public school expenditures in poor countries. Policies that attempt to raise the quality of educational services, when public sector educational budgets are already strained, may retard the growth of enrollments. The last to enroll or to be allowed to advance to the next class, when rationing of school places occurs, is likely to be a child from a relatively poor family. Hence, improvement in the quality of schooling may, in practice, be purchased at the cost of a less equitable distribution of schooling opportunities. Given the pattern of social returns by level of schooling (Table 13.6), both efficiency and equity would dictate expansion of basic primary and secondary education. When it comes to reorienting educational policy to improve school quality in low income countries, achieving this goal will probably entail a sacrifice in terms of moderating growth in enrollments. Any gain in returns associated with increasing school quality will come at a cost in terms of equity or the personal distribution of those returns.

4.2. Labor supply and unemployment

Individuals with different levels of education may choose to work different numbers of hours. Rates of return to education will then differ depending on whether returns are based on comparisons of hourly wage rates or on an annual rate of earnings [T.P. Schultz (1968)]. Appropriate methods for dealing with adjustments in labor supply in constructing the benefit stream from education have received little attention, but may be more important in low income countries than they are in the industrially advanced countries.

The first source of such a change in labor supply behavior might be attributed to the investment resources used to acquire the education. This reduction in the more educated individual's or family's physical wealth would reduce the demand for leisure and induce him or her to work longer hours [Lindsay (1971)]. The negative sign of the physical wealth effect on labor supply is based on the standard assumption that the demand for leisure and time in nonmarket production is a positive function of wealth. But according to Mincer's (1974) equilibrium investment framework, the present value of the *sum* of human and physical capital is not affected by investments in schooling. In this case, the total wealth effect of schooling should be unimportant.

The voluntary labor supply response to the increased wage rate offered to more educated workers can be decomposed in the Slutsky equation into an income effect and an income-compensated price (wage) effect. Again the Mincerian framework would lead us to expect relatively small income effects associated with schooling, if individuals face a common financial constraint and can borrow at the same interest rate. This assumption may be less realistic in countries with less developed loan markets for investment in human capital and greater inequality in family wealth. In these countries one should expect to observe a greater tendency for the more educated to work *fewer* hours. This tendency would lead to underestimating the private return to schooling based on annual earnings, because the more educated receive part of their return from schooling in the form of increased time for nonmarket activities, including leisure. Conversely, this argument would lead one to expect a greater tendency for the more educated to work longer hours in societies where family wealth is more equally distributed and loan instruments for investments in human capital are widely available. The income compensated price (wage) effect would encourage the more educated to work longer hours. If this were the only effect of education on labor supply, annual earnings comparisons would overstate the private returns to schooling.

For youth and married women, the partial association of education and hours of market work tends to be positive, if other sources of income, such as family or husband income, are held constant. If hours in the labor market increase with education, then the change in "annual earnings" associated with schooling probably overstates private returns, because the offsetting loss of nonmarket production and leisure is not deducted from the gains in market earnings. Changes in "wage rates" (e.g. annual earnings divided by hours) attributable to education is thus a more suitable approximation of the welfare benefits from schooling than changes in weekly, monthly, or annual earnings, particularly for women.[23] The preferred dependent variable in the earnings function is, thus, the logarithm of the *hourly* wage rate, deflated of course by local prices. To introduce measures of labor supply among the right-hand-side explanatory variables in the wage function is also inappropriate, unless they are treated as endogenous.[24]

---

[23] If the labor supply equation is jointly estimated with the wage equation, the gain in earnings associated with education can be decomposed into direct wage effects plus income and compensated wage effects on labor supply. The case could be made for focusing analysis on the direct wage and indirect income effects of wages on hours as the benefits to education, holding constant for the loss of leisure induced by the compensated change in relative wage. If the income effect of the wage change is close to zero, as is commonly estimated for at least prime age males, then the gross effect of schooling on wage rates is a satisfactory approximation for the total private market benefits to schooling.

[24] Mincer introduced the logarithm of weeks worked to explain the logarithm of annual earnings [Mincer (1974, table 5.1, p. 92)]. This specification should be avoided except where weeks worked is treated as endogenous and estimated suitably.

Unemployment can represent a productive period of search for an appropriate match of workers' skills and job opportunities. If unemployment is greater among more educated youth during a relatively short period after they complete their schooling, the opportunity cost of this search should be reckoned along with the other costs of schooling to be paid back by enhanced earnings in later employments [Turnham (1971), Blaug (1973), Berry (1975), Gregory (1980), Berry and Sabot (1984)]. A decade or longer after entry into the labor market, unemployment is generally lower among the more educated [Ashenfelter and Ham (1979), Nickell (1979)]. If this pattern does not reflect a current choice of the worker between nonmarket activities and market work, then unemployment may be called "involuntary". One of the private gains from increased schooling is presumably the enhanced access to regular work opportunities in the market labor force, and hence a lower incidence of such involuntary unemployment. While individuals may reduce their own unemployment by investing in schooling, it has not been empirically shown that a more educated labor force experiences in the aggregate less unemployment. Private returns to education may, thus, exceed social returns from this source.[25] In many studies that construct estimates of the returns to education, the unemployed appear to be excluded and variation in labor supply is neglected. One explanation for the omission of the unemployed from the working samples from which rates of return to education are estimated by regression methods is simply the lack of an appropriate wage for the currently unemployed. Unemployment is probably also more difficult to measure reliably in low income than in high income countries, because of the greater ambiguity in classifying activity as nonmarket or market. Nonetheless, returns to schooling should be estimated for all persons, to avoid potential sources of selectivity bias. Simultaneous analysis should, therefore, evaluate how education affects market labor supply behavior, unemployment, and the wage rate of those employed.

4.3. Occupational choice

Returns to education are, for a variety of reasons, sometimes calculated within subpopulations. If these subpopulations are defined by exogenous characteristics, such as race, caste or sex, interpretation is relatively straightforward, though differential participation in the labor force may remain a source of bias in intergroup comparisons. But when the subpopulations are not closed, as in the

---

[25] Job turnover and quit behavior is also a decreasing function of education for men and women [Weiss (1984), Kiefer (1985), Donohue (1985)]. These aspects of job search and mobility might be interpreted as increasing the private returns to schooling. Social returns might also be realized if the labor market in the aggregate sustained a lower level of turnover as schooling levels increased. Private returns may thus differ systematically over the business cycle with the changing distribution and level of unemployment [Kniesner et al. (1978)].

case of regions, because interregional migration is substantial, or in the case of occupations, because education may be an important qualification for entry into an occupation, a complex problem of selection bias may be present, and its empirical valuation may be difficult. In an extreme instance, Eckaus (1973b) calculated for the United States returns to education within a large number of narrow occupations, and drew the conclusion that educational returns (within occupations) were lower than other studies would have led us to expect. With hindsight, it is obvious that what Eckaus had shown was that much of the returns to education accrue through the changes in occupation that education facilitates. University education might not increase substantially the productivity of a plumber, for example, and consequently persons with university degrees who remained plumbers would be a highly unrepresentative sample of university graduates. Both the technology of plumbing and the self-selection of persons into that occupation could contribute to the observed unrepresentative returns within this single occupation.

The same criticism is relevant to the careful studies by Wolpin (1977) and Riley (1979), that sought to determine whether the wage–education relationship would differ across subsamples of occupations, for which the informational screening role of schooling might be more or less important. Their evidence in support or against the screening hypothesis is ambiguous, therefore, because of the possible self-selection of different types of persons into different occupations. The problem is posed and solved under specific assumptions by Hay (1984), where he models the decision of U.S. physicians of their specialization, for example surgery, and the later earnings they receive within such a medical specialty. A selection correction term [see Heckman (1979)] is introduced for all of the occupational choices in all of the occupation-specific earnings equations. Hay's method then permits one to estimate the returns to each specialized educational path for a representative individual, rather than the biased-by-selection returns for those who actually opted for each specialization. Vijverberg (1986) has also developed a method for analyzing jointly the occupational choice and wage equation, conditional on being a wage earner. *Much further empirical study of occupational choice and earnings will be needed before it can be confidently concluded that returns to education are distinct in different occupations, or that these differences in returns are those prescribed by any form of the screening hypothesis.*

It is still tempting to decompose the effects of such exogenous traits as education, race or gender on earnings, and appraise what portion of the effect occurs because of occupational sorting and what portion occurs within occupations [Polachek (1979)]. Since the stochastic processes determining occupation and earnings are undoubtedly affected jointly by unobserved factors, this form of decomposition of a simultaneous equation system is feasible only when identifying restrictions are known a priori, that is, a factor is known that influences occupation but not earnings, which can therefore be used to explain occupational sorting but can be justifiably omitted from the structural earnings equation. Studies nonetheless assume, without a clear justification, that occupational choice and earnings are block recursive and hence stochastically independent [Birdsall and Sabot (forthcoming)]. How well these single-equation estimation methods approximate reality is not yet known.

Possibly the most important occupational distinction is between wage and salary earners, on the one hand, and self-employed workers, on the other hand. Most research on the returns to schooling focuses on the former class of employees, because labor earnings are more directly observed for them, without first deducting inputs from gross income.[26] When wage earners are a large fraction of the labor force, as in high income countries, omitting the self-employed has become a standard, if indefensible, practice in empirical studies. When employees are a small but growing fraction of the labor force, there is reason to suspect that the synthetic age–wage profile across education groups of employees may not be a satisfactory basis for estimating lifetime returns to schooling in the overall economy.[27] Yet there are relatively few studies that analyze how selection into the employee subsample could bias estimated returns to education [e.g. Anderson (1982), Griffin (1985)].

If one ignores the probable covariance between the choice of whether to be a wage earner or a self-employed worker and the worker's potential earnings, it is possible to estimate without selection correction the wage functions for self-employed and wage earners separately, and simply compare the coefficients on the worker's years of schooling within the two strata. The proportionate upward shifts in wage rates or earnings with schooling are of a similar magnitude within these strata in Thailand [C. Chiswick (1979)], Colombia [Fields and Schultz (1982)], and Israel [Ben-Porath (1986)]. The greater role of transitory income variation in the earnings of self-employed has been frequently emphasized in the economics literature, but its relevance to the returns realized from education is unclear. There are, nonetheless, two salient weaknesses with such comparisons. First, they assume that the self-employed are able and willing to report their labor earnings, net of the value of purchased and owned inputs (e.g. rental value

---

[26]Another serious problem is the treatment of unpaid family workers. This group should be imputed wages for their labors in family enterprise. Kuznets (1959, 1966) made various working assumptions to estimate factor shares. C. Chiswick (1977) has proposed a method that uses the survey detail available at the household level. Other studies examine income distributions and impute an opportunity value to the time of unpaid family workers [Fishlow (1972, 1973)]. However, even if a satisfactory wage could be imputed to unpaid family workers, few data sets report the number of hours these workers contribute to family enterprise. See, for example, C. Chiswick (1978).

[27]For example, Armitage and Sabot (1986) report an interesting analysis of wage relationships in the manufacturing sector of Tanzania for men and women. In that country in 1967 this elite sector employs 1 percent of the male labor force and 0.05 percent of the female labor force. Can one assume the same type and magnitude of selection bias would be present for men and women, so that the evidence of wage differences in manufacturing between men and women could be accepted as indicative of broader patterns in sex differences in wages.

of owned land and business capital). In fact we know from developed countries such as the United States that farmers and unincorporated business persons report incomes to surveys and tax authorities that are much less than the income imputed to them by trustworthy national accounts. How this understatement of self-employed income would bias comparisons by education is unclear. To reduce this potential source of reporting bias, Teilhet and Waldorf (1983) followed a small sample of self-employed in the informal sector of Bangkok to derive estimates of their net return to labor. The returns to schooling appeared to be no less for these self-employed than for wage earners, though obtaining more education predisposed men in their sample to obtain a job for wages.

Second, the fraction of the labor force that is self-employed tends to increase across age groups in the cross-section. It would appear then that the life-cycle process of accumulating skills, experience, contacts, and physical capital increases the likelihood that the individual chooses to become self-employed [Fields and Schultz (1982), Ben-Porath (1986)]. In approaching retirement, self-employment may also afford a worker more opportunity than does wage employment to adjust labor supply downward and is thus more attractive as a means to smooth the labor supply path at older ages [Fuchs (1980)]. However, the tendency for the share of self-employed workers in the labor force to decline with development has been long noted [Kuznets (1966)] and it could also explain the below average fraction of young workers in self-employment and the rising fraction before retirement. There is little empirical evidence to disentangle the life cycle and the development process as they both influence who chooses wage versus self-employment and how this choice interacts with returns on education. The null hypothesis remains to be rejected, namely that education increases equally the productive possibilities of workers in both wage and self-employments.

A study by Behrman and Wolfe (1984b) of Nicaragua in 1977 presents estimates of earnings functions for men and women corrected for two aspects of sample selection: participation in the labor market, and reporting of labor earnings. This second restriction of the sample may exclude many self-employed workers, whose gross income includes undetermined amounts of returns to capital and land and unpaid family workers. How to treat missing variables in microeconometrics is a largely unresolved problem; to treat missing data as a potential source of selection bias is appealing in its generality. However, this corrective strategy can be effective only to the extent that the structure of the selection decision rule is well understood. Observed variables must be singled out that reasonably enter that decision rule but do not belong directly in the earnings equation. In the Behrman and Wolfe study of Nicaragua, the self-employed may find it particularly hard to reckon net earnings exclusive of the value of intermediate inputs and the rental value of land and owned productive assets. In their sample, only 68 percent of Nicaraguan male members of the rural labor force report earnings, while 91 percent of the male labor force in the capital city of Managua report earnings. Reporting earnings may thus be a proxy for the individual's occupation or sector of employment. The variables that Behrman and Wolfe specify to identify who reports earnings are the participant's "other income" and "own-farm other income" and the female respondent's "participation in the formal or informal sector". As anticipated, farmers and participants in the informal self-employed sector report their earnings less often than do those working in the formal sector, particularly those in Managua. Selection correction procedures that introduce occupational effects into the earnings function may introduce their own bias, as discussed above, and these might be more serious than ignoring the original selection problem associated with nonresponse. This would seem a danger when the variables identifying the selection correction are themselves endogenous and correlated with the earnings outcome, as would appear to be true here (i.e. owned land or informal sector attachment). But the perennial problem of missing data and nonresponse bias is important and must continue to be studied from many perspectives in the hopes that eventually we will learn how to live with this limitation of microeconomic household survey data.

Anderson (1982) corrected for the selection bias in her sample of Guatemalan husbands, where only about half of her sample reported a wage and the others were mainly self-employed. The slope of her estimated market wage offer curve (identified by the exclusion of wealth) with respect to schooling was slightly larger than the slope of the nonmarket (reservation) wage curve (identified by the exclusion of experience) with respect to schooling, 0.094 versus 0.074, based on Heckman's (1979) assumption that the errors were normally distributed [Anderson (1982, table 3)]. Her selection correction was statistically significant but her data do not appear consistent with the normality assumption. In this case, husband's weeks of participation as a wage laborer are positively related to his education, and negatively to his wealth.

4.4. The education and productivity of farmers

Many studies have specifically analyzed the education of farmers as a factor in agricultural productivity. Griliches (1964) in the United States, and Hayami and Ruttan (1970) across countries, found that the education of farmers was an important determinant of agricultural productivity. Sixteen studies of the relationship between farmer education and productivity in low income countries were recently surveyed by Lockheed et al. (1980) and extended in Jamison and Lau (1982). These studies analyzed 37 sets of farm level data that allowed estimation of the effect of farmer education on profits or output, controlling for other variables. Averaging the varied effects of education obtained in these studies, the productivity of farmers was on average 8.7 percent higher if they had completed four years of primary schooling (a threshold level) compared with none. More refined calculations are also developed by Jamison and Lau (1982) for three countries where they could further analyze the primary data. From their samples from Malaysia, Thailand, and South Korea they estimate a year of schooling is on average associated with a net increment to farm product of 5.1, 2.8, and 2.3 percent. Social returns to rural schooling are then calculated for the 1970s under various working assumptions; the social returns are between 25–40 percent, 14–25 percent, and 7–11 percent in Malaysia, Thailand, and South Korea, respectively.

How education influences production has been scrutinized most closely in the case of farmers, where researchers can build on a long tradition of econometric production and management studies. The organizing hypothesis first advanced by Welch (1970) was that education could have three distinct effects on production. First, education might enhance the productivity of measured inputs including that of an hour of labor. Second, education might lower the cost of deciphering information about the production technology that thereby increases productive efficiency by changing the selected mix of outputs and inputs. This is a static allocative efficiency effect. Third, education might facilitate more rapid entrepreneurial responses to disequilibria created by changes in output and input prices, and by the introduction of new inputs and production technologies. Huffman (1974, 1976, 1977), Fane (1975), Khaldi (1975), Wu (1977), and Pudassini (1983) proceeded to decompose the productivity gains of more educated farmers into efficiency and allocative gains. Huffman (1974) illustrates how the decline in fertilizer prices led more educated farmers to use more fertilizer and thereby increase their net farm income. Aggregate and individual data are also used to document how more educated farmers are more likely to adopt new productive innovations and accelerate the diffusion of such innovations [Jamison and Lau (1982), Rosenzweig (1982b)].

A final dimension of the adaptive response of the more educated farmer is his supply of family labor off-farm. In other words, the occupational mobility that education facilitates is also linked to dual employments, on-farm and off-farm. In the United States and in low income countries, a growing share of the income of farm families is from nonfarm activities [Huffman (1980), Rosenzweig (1980)] and education increases these income flows as well as adding to agricultural production. When returns to education are larger elsewhere in the economy [Gisser (1965), Moock (1976)], the more educated farmer and his family are the first to leave agriculture, and when returns in agriculture boom, it is the more educated managers who are the first to re-enter agriculture, at least in the United States [Tolley (1970)]. The measurement of returns to education from migration can, thus, as with occupational choice, not be readily separated from the returns to education within a particular segment of an open economy.

4.5. Migration

It is generally observed that the better educated are more likely to migrate, unconditionally and when conditioned on other motivating factors [Greenwood (1975), Schwartz (1976), T.P. Schultz (1982b)]. Several of the working assumptions that permit one to interpret the proportionate shift in the earnings function associated with a year of schooling as a private rate of return may be in error when migration occurs. Real wages are generally higher in urban than in rural areas of low income countries,[28] and net migration therefore tends to occur from the rural to the urban sector. Individuals who incur their opportunity costs of education (forgone earnings as a student) in the low wage rural sector and then enter the high wage urban labor force stand to gain from education, from migration, and from a combined effect of arbitrage in the investment process. Because more educated men and women are more likely to migrate in their youth shortly after finishing school, it can be misleading to estimate a return to schooling within the rural sector and thus exclude the gains from the increased probability of outmigration from the rural to the urban sector. Conversely, estimating a wage function for only the urban labor market residents may also be misleading, because it does not incorporate the additional educational returns realized by rural–urban migrants who "paid" less to attend school in rural areas (i.e. lower wage opportunities) than did the urban born.

The problem is illustrated empirically in Table 13.7 with data from the 1973 Census of Colombia. Estimates of monthly earnings functions in the upper panel for men and women are reported separately for the subpopulations resident in urban and rural areas. Estimated private returns to schooling for men who reside in rural areas appear to be about one-half as large as for men in urban areas, 10 percent as contrasted with 18 percent. This pattern of lower returns to schooling in the rural sector is frequently noted and often attributed to the lesser quality of rural schools [Behrman and Birdsall (1983)] or to the less dynamic technology of traditional agriculture that creates fewer opportunities for the educated worker to recoup his investment [Jamison and Lau (1982)]. Correspondingly, the slope of the earnings profile with respect to post-schooling experience, that is interpreted by Mincer (1962, 1974) as a return to on-the-job training, is substantially lower within rural than within urban residential strata of Colombia. These differences are equally evident among employees and the self-employed male workers in Colombia [Fields and Schultz (1982, table 6)]. Smith (1983) finds similar rural–urban differences in returns to post-schooling experience in Malaysia based on longitudinal data. The explanation may be fewer opportunities to accumulate

---

[28] Price levels tend to be higher in urban than rural areas primarily because of housing and food prices. Health and educational services that are publicly provided may be an exception to this pattern. There are few countries where regional price indices are readily available over time.

Table 13.7

Monthly income equations for rural and urban workers by current residence and birthplace: Colombia 1973
(beneath regression coefficients in parentheses are the absolute values of the *t* ratios)

	Intercept	Schooling in years	Post-school experience in years	Experience squared (10^{-2})	Sample size	R^2
A. By current residence						
Men:						
Urban	5.029	0.181	0.0827	−0.118	77 320	0.4130
	(447.)	(227.)	(100.)	(75.)		
Rural	5.320	0.103	0.0389	−0.0539	42 130	0.0638
	(294.)	(48.)	(29.)	(23.)		
Women:						
Urban	4.742	0.208	0.0547	−0.0813	38 144	0.4656
	(332.)	(181.)	(48.)	(36.)		
Rural	4.624	0.201	0.0246	−0.0270	4734	0.2279
	(0.77)	(36.)	(5.53)	(3.43)		
B. By region of birthplace						
Men:						
Urban	4.972	0.191	0.0831	−0.121	37 330	0.4858
	(340.)	(185.)	(73.)	(53.)		
Rural	4.924	0.190	0.0699	−0.0969	82 120	0.3191
	(386.)	(192.)	(73.)	(57.)		
Women:						
Urban	4.798	0.205	0.0589	−0.0892	15 451	0.4719
	(218.)	(118.)	(34.)	(24.)		
Rural	4.666	0.213	0.0487	−0.0706	27 429	0.4050
	(251.)	(135.)	(33.)	(25.)		

Source: Data are from the four percent public use sample of the Colombian 1973 Census of Population.
The dependent variable is the natural logarithm of monthly earnings of individuals in pesos. Urban areas of
residence are Cabeceras or county seats in the 900 municipalities and other urban areas. Birthplaces are only
identified by municipality. Thus, it is not known whether a person was born in an urban or a rural area or
whether the location of the birth was the family's usual residence. Here it is assumed that persons born in
municipalities with a Cabecera larger than 35 000 inhabitants in 1973 were born in an "urban area", and
otherwise they are attributed to a rural birthplace category. See Schultz (1983) and Fields and Schultz (1982)
for further description of data.

on-the-job training and work experience that raise the workers' subsequent
earnings in traditional agriculture compared with those experiences available in
the urban economy.

But about half of the men born in rural areas of Colombia had migrated to
urban areas by 1973, and half of those residing in urban areas in 1973 were born
in rural areas. Categorizing the workers by whether they were born in a municipality with an urban center (i.e. a town over 35 000 in 1973) or otherwise in a
rural area, leads to the second panel of stratified income equation estimates.
Ignoring the relocation costs of migration, the private returns to a year of
schooling for the rural born are virtually identical to those earned by the urban
born, namely 19.0 and 19.1 percent, respectively. The slope of the income
experience profile is also much more similar between rural and urban birth

cohorts than it was between rural and urban resident populations. Thus, almost half of the gains to rural schooling is obtained through migration to urban areas of Colombia.

Other studies of earnings in Colombia document that rural migrants are not disproportionately among the unemployed upon arrival in the cities. Indeed, the immigrants overtake the earnings of the native city-born workers within five years of their arrival, holding constant for their education, age, and sex [Ribe (1979)]. Yap (1977) found a similar tendency for rural–urban migrants in Brazil, where they achieve income parity with city natives in less than a decade. These studies are parallel to the extensive evidence that immigrants to the United States progressively close the earnings gap they initially confront in competition with U.S. natives, and reach income parity after about a decade [B. Chiswick (1978)]. Estimates of the private return to rural schooling for men are seriously biased downward in Colombia when analysis is restricted to persons remaining in the rural sector. Analyses focused on regional or rural populations subject to large net outflows of migration may contain similar biases, as in Colombia. The magnitude of this bias in educational returns within the rural sector in developing countries warrants more study.[29]

Alternatively, if many local markets are aggregated to include possible migratory destinations, and thereby approximate a closed population, returns to schooling can also be biased by the omission of regionally relevant factors [Birdsall and Behrman (1984)]. For example, geographical variation in the cost of living, the quality and private cost of schooling, migration costs, and region-specific income reporting problems may all deserve explicit attention in the aggregate, but may be more easily neglected in some stratified samples. Because the perfect single capital and labor market underlying Mincer's (1974) equilibrium model for the earnings function is not entirely realistic, modifications may be made in the list of conditioning variables, while the levels of aggregation should correspond as closely as possible with the birth cohort which proceeds to obtain specific amounts and qualities of schooling.

Since the rate of rural–urban migration and its educational selectivity differs substantially from Latin America to South Asia and Africa, to East Asia and the Middle East, there is no reason for the rural–urban migration effects evident in Colombia to be universally replicated. Some areas of traditional agriculture may not have off-farm opportunities open to the educated. For the same reason that

---

[29] The average private returns to schooling of Colombian women summarized in Table 13.7 are much less sensitive than were those for men to the migration bias. This is probably due to the much greater female market labor force participation in urban than rural areas of Colombia (i.e. 25 versus 10 percent of the women over age 25–54), whereas for men at these ages the difference in labor force participation is negligible between urban and rural areas [Schultz (1981, table 7.5)]. Birdsall and Behrman (1984) control for origin and destination effects on earnings in Brazil and find different results. It is difficult for me to interpret their findings, although Brazil is different from many countries in having large differences between rural and urban areas in the northeast and elsewhere in the country.

Eckaus (1973a) found private returns to education low within a sufficiently narrow U.S. occupation, private returns to schooling among day labor in rural India for relatively unskilled agricultural tasks may also be low, unless mobility is allowed for. The private returns to schooling for the landless in these circumstances may reside in the ability of the more educated to gain access to other forms of employment and possibly exit the rural sector altogether. Care must be exercised in constructing comparison groups, therefore, to evaluate the returns to education including the full range of economic opportunities open to the more and less educated. Following a birth cohort or school–class cohort provides one way to minimize the sample selection bias that mobility may otherwise introduce. Stratifications of samples along the lines of regions, rural–urban areas, or occupations can all lead to selection bias in estimating returns to schooling. These sources of bias may be particularly serious in the study of educational returns in low income countries, as illustrated above with reference to Colombia.

4.6. Male–female comparisons of returns

If all men and women work the same time for wages, private market returns to schooling could be calculated for each sex separately and readily compared. An efficient allocation of investment resources to the schooling of women and men would then tend to equalize these sex-specific market returns, to the extent that returns to schooling in nonmarket production within households were of a similar magnitude for women and men. But women generally participate less often and when they do participate they may work fewer hours in the market labor force than do men [Durand (1975), Standing (1978), Layard and Mincer (1985)]. Thus, the potential for a sample selection bias on this account would appear more obvious in the case of computing returns to women's education than in the case of men and add to our uncertainty in comparing rates by sex. But the nature of this bias, if any exists, remains to be empirically documented in the various cultural and economic regions of the world.

It is incorrect to assume that women gain less from schooling merely because they spend fewer years after school working in the market labor force. As shown in Section 5 below, schooling also increases the productivity of women's time in nonmarket production. Demands for nonmarket production, however, are limited by the extent of the household market, because the final commodities produced in the household are largely untradable.[30] The tendency for more educated women to allocate more of their time to market labor force activities can be

---

[30] "The extent of the market" limits the amount of human capital individuals invest in themselves, according to Becker (1964, p. 52). Because women often prepare to work both in the home and market, they are less likely to invest as do men in specialized market skills. The limitations of the

explained by both the relatively inelastic demand for nonmarket output and the likelihood that education enhances specialized market production skills more than education increases the value of the marginal product of women's time in nonmarket production. The family labor supply model suggests that it is also appropriate to control in such comparisons for the wage rate of the woman's husband or other family members and the nonearned income of the family.[31] Because the value of other members' time and nonearned income is likely to reduce the woman's market labor supply and be positively correlated with her education, these controls specified by the family labor supply framework are likely to increase the estimated positive partial effect of women's education on her market labor supply. Moreover, this empirical regularity may be strengthened further if unpaid family work that is conventionally counted as being in the labor force is excluded from our measure of market labor supply. Unpaid family worker status for women is the least satisfactorily measured aspect of labor supply across societies [Durand (1975), C. Chiswick (1978), Hill (1983)] and it is precisely a labor market transaction within the family rather than in the labor market for which a shadow wage cannot be directly observed.

Thus, given the sensitivity of women's market allocation of time to their educational attainment, direct estimates of market returns to schooling inferred from only women working for wages may well be unrepresentative of the potential returns received by a representative woman in the population.[32] Here is an important issue for public policy that has received surprisingly little empirical study.

Griffin's (1985) analysis in the Philippines is an exception. He considers the earnings of married women in the Bicol region in 1980 to appraise how robust estimates of schooling returns are to alternative methods for dealing with this pervasive source of sample selection bias. He estimates jointly for women outside

---

household market circumscribe the opportunities for specialized investments open to women, and help to account, in Becker's view, for fewer U.S. women than men graduating from college (p. 101).

[31] The family labor supply model is based on the household demand framework where the wife's labor supply is conditioned on the wage rate of her husband or other family members, the family's nonearned income, and an exogenous proxy for her permanent wage opportunities (e.g. education and age). Ashenfelter and Heckman (1974) examine only couples for whom the wife and husband work for a wage, and they simply treat her actual wage as though it were exogenous. The papers edited by Smith (1980) explore other procedures for dealing with sample selection for wage earners and wage imputation for nonworking women.

[32] The direction of such a bias is not prescribed by the selection model and empirical evidence is scarce. Suppose an unobserved trait, called taste for market production, influenced positively the likelihood that a woman is observed to work for a wage and to get an education. Then the direct correlation of education and wages among working women will be upward biased even if this taste has no independent effect on labor productivity. But if women's education increases the likelihood that they will retire from the labor market when their children are of preschool age [Leibowitz (1975)], then the bias could change direction at different stages in the life cycle.

the market labor force a nonmarket (reservation) wage function and a market wage function for wage offers to those working. The selection-corrected model of Heckman's is plausibly identified within the context of the family labor supply model. Based on the conventional log-linear specification of the earnings function where returns to schooling are constant across schooling levels, the selection-corrected estimate of schooling returns is 18 percent, compared with the conventional estimate of 14 percent, based on only the quarter of the sample which is working in the market labor force and reporting the requisite wage. The selection correction is highly significant statistically and certain features of earnings function change. But based on a single regional sample from a single country, it is not reasonable to draw any general conclusions regarding the magnitude or even direction of this selection bias on women's returns to schooling.

Conventional earnings function estimates of the private returns to schooling for males and females that ignore the selected nature of the female samples are summarized in several papers [Woodhall (1973), Psacharopoulos (1973)]. The average of 16 country studies recently cited by Psacharopoulos (1985, table 5) suggests that the uncorrected returns to women may be somewhat higher than to men at the secondary level and overall, but marginally lower at the primary and higher educational levels. Because there is no a priori basis to conclude that sample selection bias would necessarily alter these estimates upward or downward, they must stand as the best evidence currently available. In that light, there may exist an underinvestment in women's schooling relative to men's on efficiency grounds, which is not inconsistent with the cross-country comparisons of enrollments analyzed in Section 2. This is an area that needs further empirical research. The family labor supply model provides some guidance as to how corrections for the self-selection of women into the market labor force can be reasonably identified by family wealth or husband wage variables.

Traditional labor market institutions may segregate different groups of workers by industry, occupation, or activity. Though such arrangements may have had at one time relatively little effect on the efficient allocation of labor, they may become increasingly inefficient as economic opportunities for individuals change more rapidly with modern economic growth [Birdsall and Sabot (forthcoming)]. Women in particular may be caught in family enterprises and household production functions that are displaced by firms that exploit new technological economies of large scale in the organization of production. Until women can acquire the requisite schooling and transferable skills to find suitable employment in firms in expanding sectors of the modern economy, the opportunity value of women's time relative to men's time may decline. Fragmentary historical and anthropological evidence supports the view that early industrialization reduced the relative value of women's contribution to the household. During later stages of industrialization the economic contribution of women relative to men has increased [Boserup (1970), Shorter (1975), Goldin (1980, 1983), T.P. Schultz

(1987b)]. This cycle may be associated with a change in the returns to schooling for women, but historical evidence to test this hypothesis is not yet in hand.

4.7. Interactions with educational returns

If returns to education reflect in part the acquired general ability of workers to profit from new opportunities, as emphasized by Welch (1970) and T.W. Schultz (1975), then investments in enlarging the pool of locally relevant technological options and other profitable resource reallocations should spur the private returns to education. This pattern of complementarity between local research and development activity and the returns to schooling in agriculture is a widely noted empirical regularity [Griliches (1964), Huffman (1974), Jamison and Lau (1982), Evenson (1986)].

By the same reasoning, it is expected that agricultural extension activity, while it raises productivity in specific agricultural functions, would also substitute for farmer schooling, diminishing the productive advantages enjoyed by the more educated farmer in exploiting new specific opportunities. Schooling's effect on nonmarket production may also be sensitive to the rate of growth of knowledge in that specific area of nonmarket production. As effort is expended to diffuse that specific knowledge, the differential advantage enjoyed by the educated worker would eventually diminish. The generalized knowledge obtained by schooling substitutes (imperfectly) for the specific body of functional knowledge disseminated by vocational extension programs. Rosenzweig and Schultz (1982) found that the effect of mother's education in reducing child mortality and fertility in Colombia was diminished with improvements in local health infrastructure. Barrera (1986) examined child height and height-for-weight as measures of child health and nutritional status in the Bicol region of the Philippines. He found that gains associated with mother's education were larger in communities that lacked health infrastructure. In contrast, Strauss (1987) found evidence in a rural Ivory Coast survey of complementarity of mother's education and local health infrastructure, as they interactively affected child height and height-for-weight. T.P. Schultz (1971) and Rosenzweig and Schultz (1985) found in Taiwan and the United States that schooling of couples and local family planning extension activity are substitutes in their effect on fertility reduction. Consequently, the least educated gain the most from some types of information-extending programs, whether they provide farmers with new agricultural inputs or provide housewives with knowledge of health practices or family planning techniques. There would seem to be a basis, therefore, for analyzing other research and development and information diffusion and extension programs to refine our understanding of which activities increase or decrease the private nonmarket and market returns to schooling. It may be noted that although extension activity may depress private returns to schooling, they may still be an efficient or cost-effective method to increase average productivity and to redistribute income more equally. Here again, more empirical documentation of these patterns of substitution and complementarity of activities with schooling in low income countries could clarify the distributive implications of policy options that focus on educational endowments and family welfare.[33] The pattern of productive interactions between education and the family's environment and endowments can be estimated from reduced-form equations, and consequently do not depend on controversial structure assumptions.

There appears to be an inverse empirical association between fertility and the resources parents provide each of their children, proxied generally by the child's schooling. An interaction between the quality (i.e. schooling) and quantity (i.e. number) of children in the parents' budget constraint is a widely accepted rationalization for this tradeoff between "quality" and quantity of children [Becker and Lewis (1974)]. Alternatively, the empirical relationship can be interpreted, without imposing a specific structure on the budget constraint and family choice process, as indicating parents view child quality and quantity as substitutes [Rosenzweig and Wolpin (1980)]. In either case, estimating without bias the magnitude of this cross-substitution effect is difficult, because both outcomes are endogenous to the family's lifetime allocation problem. What exogenous factor can be specified that shifts either fertility or the amount of schooling children receive, allowing the other factor to then behaviorally adjust, but not be directly affected by the identifying constraint? Only in the natural experiment of "twins" are we presented with a clear situation for evaluating the magnitude of this quantity–quality substitution effect, and for rural India the data support the economists' conjecture [Rosenzweig and Wolpin (1980)]. This would imply that family planning programs that lower the cost of averting unwanted births should encourage parents to invest more in the schooling of each of their children. Conversely, extending effective compulsory schooling should be expected to contribute to a fertility reduction. Here then is another area in which public policy, i.e. family planning, may induce greater investments in schooling, presumably by raising the privately perceived rate of return to educating children.

4.8. Efficiency and equity

A recurrent theme in the literature on economics of education is a discussion of who benefits from the public subsidies extended to education [T.W. Schultz

---

[33] Caldwell (1979), for example, believes that in Africa the provision of health facilities widens differentials in health status by education class, for only the educated mothers know how to use effectively the over burdened public health facilities.

(1972)]. This policy objective is more salient in low income countries where the public subsidy to secondary and higher education can be relatively large and these educational levels are filled by the children of the upper class [Bhagwati (1973)]. For example, in 1962, the Colombian government's operating expenses per public school student was five times greater at the secondary than at the primary level, and fifty times greater at the higher education level than at the primary level [T.P. Schultz, (1968, table 8)]. These differentials tend to be smaller in South Asia and perhaps even larger in Africa, because cost-of-living stipends are often provided to university students. The disproportionate size of public subsidies for higher education may have begun to decrease in some low income countries, but the inequities of the current schemes for financing higher education remain clear in economic terms [Minget and Tan (1985)]. The distribution of public educational subsidies is an area of increasingly active debate. This concern with public financing of education and its implications for equity as well as efficiency is outlined later in Section 6; it is reviewed extensively in several recent studies [Psacharopoulos and Woodhall (1985), World Bank (1986a)].

5. Nonmarket production and schooling

While the effects of schooling on market earnings are relatively well documented, though sometimes subject to uncertainty due to problems of measurement and estimation, the evidence is more recent and fragmentary on the returns to schooling in nonmarket production within the household [Michael (1982), Haveman and Wolfe (1984)]. In low income countries these benefits are particularly important. This review only surveys the evidence in this field. Two other chapters in this Handbook also address health and fertility consequences of education (Behrman and Deolalikar, Chapter 14, and Birdsall, Chapter 12).

More educated workers tend to work more in the market labor force, holding constant for other sources of family income and capital that may combine to enhance their productivity in nonmarket production. As noted earlier, a married woman is likely to work less time in home production the greater is her education, given her husband's education and business capital. This pattern prevails in most low income surveys of urban areas and in rural areas where off-farm employment opportunities for educated women are reasonably developed. Thus, nonmarket production activities must be curtailed or at least substitutes found for the educated woman's nonmarket time. Nonetheless, most studies confirm increased home output in several quantifiable dimensions with a woman's schooling, despite the fact that she may actually spend less time in the home.

Child mortality, for example, is lower for more educated mothers whether or not family income or husband's wages and education are also held constant

[Cochrane et al. (1980), T.P. Schultz (1980)]. An additional year of mother's schooling in either rural or urban subpopulations, is associated in many low income countries with a 5–10 percent reduction in child mortality, regardless of the tendency for these more educated women to reallocate their home time toward market activities [Cochrane et al. (1980)]. By neglecting education's effect on rural–urban migration and its consequences on child health, these studies understate the child health returns to rural schooling of girls [T.P. Schultz (1983)].

Is this empirical association of schooling and child mortality due to (1) the benefit of the purchased health inputs obtained from the mother's added market earnings, or (2) the enhanced productivity of her remaining time at home, or (3) her improved allocative efficiency in using various health inputs, given their prices? Because the household's nonmarket output – child health in this case – is consumed directly by the couple, tastes or preferences of the couple are relevant to production decisions, unlike the market sector where profit maximization alone determines production decisions. Consequently, education might modify child health (and fertility) investments by inducing a change in tastes, holding constant prices, income and household technology [Easterlin, Pollak and Wachter (1980)]. To disentangle efficiency, input allocation, and taste effects of education on household production, the household production technology must be separately identified and estimated [Rosenzweig and Schultz (1983)]. Lack of sufficient information on this technology has slowed progress toward understanding precisely how education affects nonmarket outcomes. The total effect of schooling on the outcomes can, nonetheless, be estimated by reduced-form-like equations that embody both the parameters of the utility/demand system and that of the household production technology.

The association between female education and fertility and contraceptive behavior is analogous, but more complicated. Education may permit a couple to achieve more precisely their desired target level of fertility, given uncontrolled biological reproductive capacity (i.e. fecundity) and other random events. A simple association is noted between schooling levels of women and their contraceptive knowledge or use, recent marital fertility rate, and cumulative number of births in recent sample surveys from 22 low-income countries [United Nations (1983)]. Schooling of the women is positively correlated with contraceptive knowledge and use in every country and between every pair of (five) schooling levels, controlling for the woman's age and age at marriage. This descriptive regression study by the United Nations does not control, however, for the household demand determinants, such as husband's income, earnings, assets or land, which often exhibit a positive partial correlation with fertility [T.P. Schultz (1973), Mueller (1984)]. Since these income variables tend to be positively correlated with a wife's schooling, their omission as controls for wealth from the above fertility regressions is likely to weaken the reported inverse mother schooling–fertility association. Regardless of this lapse in specification, the association was inverse in 20 of the 22 countries. Cochrane (1979), in an earlier review of the evidence, reached similar conclusions, but stressed the nonmonotonic simple association between women's schooling and their fertility. She noted the tendency for fertility, particularly in a few of the poorest rural populations, to increase with basic primary schooling and only thereafter fall. The unanswered question is: If controls were included for husband's wealth or land, would the early rising phase of fertility with the woman's education have been mitigated or eliminated, leaving a monotonic negative partial relationship of women's education on fertility?

But to proceed further and assess how education affects nonmarket production and thereby influences fertility requires the estimation of contraceptive use and contraceptive efficiency equations, conditional on the woman's schooling, the couple's endogenous demand for further births, and the couple's biological fecundity inferred from past reproductive behavior and performance. Better educated wives in Malaysia and the United States appear to know more about contraception, and are able to use contraceptive methods more efficiently. The more educated couple is better able than a less educated one to perceive their reproductive propensities and effectively compensate by means of birth control for these differences in fecundity [Rosenzweig and Schultz (1985, 1987)].

The investments of parents in the "quality" of children are difficult to measure, but two outcomes of this nonmarket production process are the health and schooling of the children. Child mortality, discussed above, is the least ambiguous indicator of child health investments by parents. Schooling of the children is frequently studied as another nonmarket outcome of the family, and one in which the education of the mother often appears more important than that of the father. Evidence on these issues has been reported for the United States [Swift and Weisbrod, (1965), Leibowitz (1974, 1975), Hill and Stafford (1974), Murnane et al. (1981)], Philippines [King and Lillard (1983)], Malaysia [DeTray (1987)], and India at the aggregate district level [Rosenzweig and Evenson (1977)]. The empirical basis to generalize about the family-level determinants of child schooling investments may depend on different regional configurations of the family and the distribution of child-rearing responsibilities between mother, father, and extended family. It would be surprising, nonetheless, if parent education did not help to explain offspring educational attainment, when controls are included for local school facilities, parent assets, and wages opportunities.[34]

---

[34] This intergenerational effect of education could be interpreted as arising from at least three distinct mechanisms: a genetic component of ability proxied by education, a disproportionate productivity in educating one's child, and an acquired taste for having children become like oneself.

The significance of nonmarket production effects of schooling, particularly those associated with the education of women, should not be underrated as factors shaping the development process.[35] A major research challenge is to measure these effects of schooling on nonmarket production with greater precision and to begin to develop methods for measuring the value of these effects in a way that is more or less commensurate with the estimates of private market returns to schooling derived from wage functions.

Nonmarket returns to schooling are not generally an additional benefit from education over and above the market returns described earlier. Nonmarket production is usually obtained by forgoing market income and reallocating time from market to nonmarket production. Just as it is inappropriate to conclude that women receive a low return on their schooling because they allocate only a small fraction of their time after school to market work, it is incorrect to attribute the market rate of return to their schooling and then additionally credit their schooling with the noted nonmarket production gains, such as in child health, child schooling, and birth control.[36]

To the extent that reductions in disease, decreases in fertility, and increases in child schooling embody social externalities that benefit other members of the society beyond the private family, then an externalities case can be made for public subsidization of education that contributes to these types of nonmarket production activities. Current research on household production suggests that female schooling may, according to this reasoning, warrant a larger subsidy than male schooling. But most of the benefits of family health improvements, fertility control, and child schooling that are associated with female education are privately captured by families.

6. Policy

Public expenditures on education absorb between 2 and 8 percent of the GNP of most countries [World Bank (1986a, p. 46)]. The share of school-aged children is substantially larger in low than in high income countries, because the less

---

[35] Other nonmarket benefits not considered here are in spouse selection and subsequent marital stability [Becker et al. (1977), Boulier and Rosenzweig (1984), Montgomery (1985)]. Reduced marital dissolution might also influence child investments. The reduction in crime [Ehrlich (1975)] is often cited as a source of private and social gains. Political behavior and the functioning of democracy are also often linked to schooling as are the social benefits of a more equal personal distribution of income. These issues were beyond the scope of this chapter.

[36] This would appear to be the implication of Woodhall (1973) and Psacharopoulos and Woodhall (1985) where the nonmarket effects are cited as added support for the very high returns to women's schooling.

developed countries have recently experienced rapid population growth. This age composition may increase the GNP share of educational budgets in low income countries, while the income elastic demand for schooling operates in the opposite direction. In reality, the share of GNP devoted to education is on balance positively related to per capita income, but the relationship explains little of the variance across countries [T.P. Schultz (1985)]. Many poor Sub-Saharan African countries, for example, spend more than 5 percent of their GNP on public education, whereas this is also the figure reported on average for both the Western and Eastern European industrial countries. Education is frequently the largest or second largest share of the public budget, after defense, claiming between 10 and 20 percent of the total [World Bank (1986a)]. The efficient and equitable allocation of this relatively large budget warrants careful scrutiny by economists.

The educational system influences the long-run evolution of an economy and society in complex and subtle ways; some of these channels of influence are as yet poorly understood. The interdependence among the levels and parts of the educational system indicates the need to evaluate the long-run implications of expansion or change in priorities, for they will have ramifications at many points in the public and private sectors [Hicks (1965)]. Enrollment levels at primary, secondary, and higher educational levels must mesh with each other, and, as discussed in Section 2, the educational system is one of the largest employers of educated workers in the economy. If the demand for teachers outruns the domestic supply, the rising cost of expanding the school system hinders the achievement of long-run goals.

Confronted by the complexity of the educational system, models to forecast manpower requirements of the economy were developed in the 1960s as a guide to setting education policy in developing countries [Harbison and Myers (1964), Bowles (1969), Pyatt et al. (1977)]. But forecasts of the derived demands for educated labor have not always proven reliable, particularly at the level of specific occupations and technical specialities which educational administrators find most useful. Even projecting the overall distribution of enrollment demands among primary, secondary, vocational, and higher education has proven difficult [Psacharopoulos and Woodhall (1985)]. Accumulating empirical evidence has directed increasing attention to the task of estimating the actual scarcity of different groups of workers in a country's labor market. Private returns to schooling that reflect this scarcity are one means for monitoring imbalances between the supply of and demand for educated workers in an economy, but forecasting them conditional on educational policy is not yet a practical tool. Moreover, these estimates of returns are subject to all the difficulties of measurement discussed in Section 4. Nonetheless, they provide a means for objectively describing the economic scarcity of many specific levels of skills that the educational system contributes to producing, and thus translate much of the available information on the costs and benefits of education into a form where priorities can be set with a view to maximizing returns on public (and private) resources and improving the distribution of those returns among persons.

Although models of manpower requirements have lost favor among economists, they remain in use for setting long-term quantitative targets for educational systems in many parts of the world. These models assume that there exists a fixed (often indeed linear) relationship between output, occupation, and education at the aggregate level or disaggregated to the sectoral level. As with input–output models, the technological parameters that drive these forecasting models are often borrowed from other countries, where descriptive tabulations of the labor force are available and in no way imply optimality in other settings. The relative prices of inputs and relative wages are not permitted to influence the optimal, or least cost, labor force mix for producers. This forecasting strategy must assume that it is highly inefficient to deviate from the fixed-coefficient technology, now or in the future. In other words, this Leontief planning technology neglects entirely substitution among types of labor in production or underlying substitution in consumption among goods according to the scarcity of the skill content of the goods. Evidence to the contrary has accumulated in the last decade that the input mix of producers in developing countries adjusts substantially to variations in relative factor prices, including relative wages. Consequently, in the education sector itself, Section 2 illustrated how the ratio of students to teachers (i.e. classroom size) varies across countries, particularly at the primary school level, apparently in response to per capita income and the relative price of teachers. Linear programming and input–output analyses are useful analytic tools for the study of many well-specified engineering problems, but in educational forecasting they have not proven very satisfactory when pursued without reference to costs and benefits or relative returns in the labor market [Blaug (1973, 1985), Hollister (1983)].

Imbalances between the educational system and the needs of developing economies have often been noted by policy advisors, but careful empirical analysis has not always confirmed the view of these casual empiricists. As public expenditures on education increased in the 1960s and 1970s, overinvestment in education was attributed a role in creating unemployment among the educated and encouraging the inefficient allocation of relatively unskilled jobs to over-educated workers [Lewis (1962), Edwards (1974), Edwards and Todaro (1974)]. But these subjective interpretations of labor market conditions found little support from labor market surveys, where lifetime unemployment was generally observed to be relatively low among the better educated workers [Gregory (1980), Berry and Sabot (1984)], and wage differentials by education continued to imply substantial market returns to basic primary and general secondary education (Table 13.6 p. 575). Where imbalances have occurred, the means of financing higher education (i.e. the size of scholarships or fees) may be a factor contributing to the imbalance as well as the mechanisms used for rationing any excess private demands for schooling.

In some countries higher education overexpanded and a "brain drain" emerged, as in Colombia in the 1960s [T.P. Schultz (1968)]. To deal with the international "brain drain", a variety of tax-transfer schemes were proposed [Scott (1970), Bhagwati and Partington (1976)], but the welfare implications of labor mobility between nations are unclear because individual and state objectives may conflict, and thus a coordinated international response never materialized. The methods of financing higher education may often account for the instances of apparent excess demand for and overexpansion of higher education. Tuition fees are often minimal and student living stipends are awarded only on the basis of merit or examination. The resulting public subsidies per student enrolled in higher education have become sufficiently large that there is little likelihood that the private sector will evolve complementary higher educational services, even in the form of a low-cost–low-quality system. Private returns to the student admitted to the public higher educational system may, as a consequence, be substantial, while the social returns are unjustifiably low. When domestic university graduates can obtain employment abroad, as may be the case in engineering, medicine, and technical sciences, these job opportunities can augment further the *private* returns to higher education. Depending on the level of remittances of the emigrants to their families and the likelihood that they return home and bring with them enhanced productive skills and capital, this form of publicly subsidized "brain drain" may erode further the realized *social* returns to public expenditures on higher education. The obvious economic solution is to reduce the size of the public subsidy and allow student fees to cover a larger share of the costs of higher education. Scholarships and educational loans awarded on the basis of family means can still achieve redistributive objectives [Hansen and Weisbrod (1969), T.W. Schultz (1972), Blaug (1973), Fields (1974a, 1974b), Psacharopoulos and Woodhall (1985), Tan (1985), World Bank (1986a)].

In other countries, such as Brazil, the rapid pace and structure of economic growth sustained unusually large returns to higher education in the 1970s. Public and private university enrollments increased accordingly [Langoni (1973)]. Other countries, such as Taiwan, were reluctant to expand general university education as rapidly as the private demand for enrollment increased for fear of creating unemployment among its educated youth. To deal with the excess demand for higher education, college entrance examinations were increasingly relied upon to ration access to the high-quality publicly subsidized universities. But in contrast to other Asian countries, lower quality private schools were not allowed to expand and fill the gap. Secondary school graduates in Taiwan retake repeatedly the college entrance examinations and their failure to enter the labor force in the interim suggests that rationing can be an inefficient mechanism for dealing with excess demands for schooling [Academic Sinica (1983)].

Kenya and Tanzania illustrate the consequences of following quite different educational expansion policies combined with alternative mechanisms for the selection of students. Starting from a similar base in the 1960s, both countries achieved nearly universal primary school attendance by the 1980s, but public and private secondary schools expanded more rapidly in Kenya than in Tanzania with the introduction of substantial schools fees in Kenya to finance the secondary school systems. Tanzania alternatively employed a "meritocratic" examination system to ration the excess demand for places in the secondary school system. These different responses to growing private demand for secondary education allowed a larger share of the children of less educated parents to advance into secondary schools in Kenya than in Tanzania [Armitage and Sabot (1986)]. In other words, the meritocratic examination system screened on characteristics that the educated parents were willing and able to produce in their offspring, either through greater investments of own time and market goods (including higher quality primary schooling), or because of inherited ability. Including the secondary school fees in Kenya, the private rate of return to secondary schooling was only marginally lower in Kenya than in Tanzania [Knight and Sabot (1985)]. Consequently, the increased rate of investment in secondary educations in Kenya compared with Tanzania may have contributed importantly to the more rapid growth enjoyed by Kenya in the 1970s, though other misguided economic policies in Tanzania probably played a more important role in that country's slower growth. The egalitarian intentions of the Tanzanian meritocratic rationed educational policy frustrated rather than facilitated intergenerational mobility and deterred an efficient level of schooling investment [Armitage and Sabot (1986)]. The market-clearing expansion of secondary schools in Kenya also contributed to a more equal distribution of income among educational classes, as the relative wage premia for secondary school graduates has slowly diminished over time among younger Kenyan workers [Knight and Sabot (1981)], analogous to Figure 13.3 (above). There are clear advantages in terms of efficiency when some of the costs of secondary and higher education are borne by students who will thereby gain higher lifetime incomes. Special means-tested financial aids can then be designed to achieve a wide distribution of subsidized educational opportunities. If these financial aids can be used by students in either public or private schools, pluralism might be maintained and desirable competitive pressure exerted on public (and private) schools to improve their quality and efficiency.

Schools in low income countries are often observed to be inefficient [World Bank (1986a)]. Unfortunately, the task of defining and then measuring productive efficiency is complex, and requires agreement on (1) the valuation of outputs and (2) on the opportunity cost of inputs, as well as (3) knowledge of the production technology that defines how the inputs are transformed at the margin into outputs. Evidence cited in the education literature to demonstrate school inefficiency is not yet rigorous, and includes characteristics such as high dropout rates and low advancement rates [Fuller (1986)]. To interpret such evidence on efficiency requires a measure of student productivity associated with exposure to various training regimes. If returns to education fall at the margin after completing four or five years, it may not pay all students to continue in school to obtain a primary or secondary certificate. It could be an efficient use of educational resources to train partially many students, but graduate few. The efficiency of a training regime depends on the gains in labor market productivity produced in a birth cohort passing through the schools, and on how much more public and private resources are required to effect a change in the relevant retention and advancement rates without altering the standards of the graduates that matter for the labor market. Clearly, collecting the necessary figures to measure efficiency in schools is difficult. I have not seen an analysis that defines, in this sense, the optimal schedule of retention and advancement rates for any country's school system. This is not to say, however, that current regimes with low attendance rates and frequent repetitions represent an efficient use of either the student's or teacher's time.

Decentralized management of school systems could have advantages in setting local enrollment goals and fixing programs priorities. An orderly flow of information to the central government would nonetheless be needed to rationalize centralized educational subsidies and evaluate national progress. Monitoring labor market returns to schooling may also be a function that is best performed by the central government. Student fees might be retained to fund local school initiatives, while centrally administered financial aids would reduce differential access to schools across economic classes and regions of a country. Recommendations to increase sharply school quality in low income countries [World Bank (1986a)] need to be evaluated thoroughly [Zymelman (1982, 1985)]. Local communities may be better positioned than the central government to evaluate the tradeoffs between expanding enrollments and increasing the quality of school offerings. Nonetheless, there is an urgent need for more quantitative analysis of how effective schools are in producing valuable skills in low income countries.

7. Conclusions

This chapter has reviewed several themes in the economic literature on education and development: (1) intercountry evidence of how income, price, and demographic constraints govern public expenditures on schools; (2) alternative conceptual interpretations of the relationship between education and income; (3) uncertainties underlying the micro statistical evidence on the private and social returns to schooling in the labor market; and finally (4) indications of the returns to schooling in nonmarket production of child health and education, and fertility control.

Integration of these four themes has not yet occurred. It would entail a firm idea of the factors that initiated the modern disequilibrium in education. What change in the institutional or technological environment created the derived demands for more educated labor? How did these conditions increase the private returns to schooling, encouraging the increased investment of private resources in schooling and public expenditures on education throughout the world? As these resources in schooling increased, they enlarged the pool of educated workers which operates, other things equal, to reduce returns to schooling, until a new equilibrium rate of return is established that more or less equals the opportunity cost of diverting public and private investment from the formation of further physical capital. It cannot be said, with any precision, how far the expansion of education can expect to proceed in any particular country before demands for educated labor are satisfied and returns decrease to "normal" levels. A dynamic model of both the demand for and supply of educated workers is needed to answer these questions. Given the time lags between production of students, their entry into the labor force, and the determination of their lifetime wage levels, it may be possible in the future to use the historical record to form estimates of a recursive model of education and development than could answer questions such as these. The challenge of the field is to clarify the origins and dynamic structure of such a model of education and development, and though speculatory theory is beginning to emerge [Lucas (1985)], we have a long way to go.

This chapter surveys several limited empirical regularities and provides economic frameworks to help interpret the meaning of these patterns, and to focus attention on many unresolved problems in model specification and empirical implementation. It will prove impossible in practice to deal with many of these complicating issues simultaneously, and hence assigning priority to questions for further research reveals my intuition on which issues are most important to advance our understanding of education in the process of modern economic growth.

The wage function is a powerful device for summarizing data on individual wages or earnings. Even the most simplified semi-logarithmic wage function, conditioned on years of schooling and a quadratic in postschooling years of experience, accounts for a remarkable one-quarter to one-half of the log variance in male wages across most national labor markets. There are few internationally replicated regularities in the social sciences that have this descriptive power at the individual level, and also have the intuitive appeal of providing a rough approximation of the market pecuniary rate of returns earned from schooling, viewed as an economic investment in human capital.

Once economists had developed a conceptual framework for inferring the private rate of return to schooling, estimates of returns were derived for different types and levels of schooling and for different racial groups. Returns to qualitative improvements in the educational system are also estimated frequently, but findings as to the returns to various dimensions of school quality differ markedly across studies. Returns to school quality are approximated by measuring variation in schooling inputs per student across schools in a single labor market. Variation in input use is then related to the earnings of pupils across regions, holding constant years of schooling [e.g. Welch (1966)]. Since observed variation in years of schooling is generally positively associated with the quality of schooling across schools, the estimates of returns to school years tend to decrease as controls are added to the wage function for the qualitative dimensions of the schools. When rates of return to schooling are computed based on variation in only "years" of schooling completed, it is reasonable to interpret the measured returns as summarizing the gains from both length of study and the prevailing association with the quality of that schooling. When the single proxy for educational inputs (i.e. years) is supplemented by other measures of input mixes, there is a basis for predicting how changes in years of schooling and the input mix will subsequently influence the earnings capacity of educated workers.

Wage and earnings functions stratified by sex reveal that relative wage differentials by schooling are of about the same magnitude for women in the labor force as they are for men. Because the sample of women reporting wages is not representative of all women in the population, a sample selection bias could affect these estimates of schooling returns for women. Too few studies have addressed this important empirical issue to draw any firm conclusions. Nor have many studies collected reliable data on the net earnings of self-employed workers and analyzed them appropriately to clarify whether returns to schooling in this self-selected segment of the labor force are the same as among employees. Clearly, farmers recoup substantial income from their education, and there is no obvious reason why the self-employed in nonagricultural activities should fare differently. But appropriate statistical evidence is not yet in hand.

Finally, schooling raises the productivity of individuals in nonmarket production. The schooling of parents affects the level of home production of health, nutrition, mobility, fertility control, and child schooling. Decomposing the sources of these changes requires the identification and structural estimation of household production functions and input demand equations. The gains in household production attributable to a mother's schooling are important for social welfare and should not continue to be neglected by economists. The topic of this chapter will remain incomplete until it is possible to clarify the origins and trace through the consequences of these nonmarket returns to women's schooling. A microeconometric framework for such studies of household production and behavior has been proposed [Rosenzweig and Schultz (1983)]. Current progress in implementing such analyses is limited by the scarcity of suitably detailed longitudinal or retrospective household survey data for low income countries.

Appendix

Table A.1
Growth in educational enrollments by school level and countries by income classes, 1960–81[a]

World bank country (number)	Primary (6–11) education		Secondary (12–17) education		Higher (20–24) education		Expected years of enrollment[b]		Percent of increase in enrollment ratios (1960–81) from cols. (1)–(8)			
	1960 (1)	1981 (2)	1960 (3)	1981 (4)	1960 (5)	1981 (6)	1960 (7)	1981 (8)	Primary (9)	Secondary (10)	Higher (11)	Expected (12)
Low income (34) excluding China[c] and India	0.80	0.94	0.18	0.34	0.02	0.04	5.98	7.88	18	89	100	32
Middle income (38)	0.38	0.72	0.07	0.19	0.01	0.02	2.75	5.56	89	171	100	102
Oil exporters	0.64	1.06	0.09	0.37	0.02	0.08	4.48	8.98	66	311	300	100
Oil importers	0.84	0.99	0.18	0.44	0.04	0.13	6.32	9.23	18	144	225	46
Upper middle income (22)	0.88	1.04	0.20	0.51	0.04	0.14	6.68	10.0	18	155	250	50
High income												
Oil exporters (5)	0.29	0.83	0.05	0.43	0.01	0.08	2.09	7.96	186	760	700	281
Industrial market (18)	1.14	1.01	0.64	0.90	0.16	0.37	11.5	13.3	−11	41	131	16
East European non-market (8)	1.01	1.05	0.45	0.88	0.11	0.20	9.31	12.6	4	96	82	35

[a] The low income class has an annual GNP per capita of less than U.S. $410 in 1982 prices. The middle income class includes countries with GNP per capita between $410 and $1650, while the upper middle income class ranges from $1650 to about $6000.

[b] Synthetic cohort concept defined as six (years) times the sum of primary and secondary enrollment ratios plus five (years) times higher educational enrollment ratio. Discrepancies may occur due to rounding.

[c] The lack of expenditure data for China and India in Table 13.2 justifies our consideration of the "low income" class of countries excluding these two large states.

Source: World Bank (1984, table 25).

Table A.2

Educational enrollment ratios by school level and region for males and females, 1960–80

	Primary education (approx. 6–11)		Secondary education (approx. 12–17)		Higher education (approx. 20–24)		Expected years of enrollment[b] (weighted sum)		Percentage increase in enrollment ratios, 1960–80			Total experience[b]
	1960	1980	1960	1980	1960	1980	1960	1980	Primary	Secondary	Higher	
Africa, excluding Arab states												
Male	0.540	0.864	0.050	0.203	0.005	0.027	3.57	6.54	60	306	440	83
Female	0.309	0.704	0.022	0.131	0.001	0.008	1.99	5.05	128	495	700	154
Total	0.424	0.784	0.036	0.167	0.003	0.017	2.78	5.79	85	364	467	108
Arab states												
Male	0.641	0.936	0.148	0.454	0.031	0.112	4.89	8.90	46	207	261	82
Female	0.339	0.680	0.052	0.279	0.007	0.051	2.38	6.01	101	437	628.6	153
Total	0.493	0.810	0.101	0.368	0.019	0.082	3.66	7.48	64	264	331.6	104
Asia, excluding Arab states												
Male	0.809	0.952	0.269	0.417	0.044	0.109	6.69	8.76	18	55	148	30.9
Female	0.527	0.734	0.139	0.270	0.013	0.052	4.06	6.28	39	94	300	54.7
Total	0.670	0.846	0.205	0.346	0.029	0.081	5.40	7.56	26	69	179	40.0
Latin America												
Male	0.750	1.052	0.149	0.435	0.042	0.160	5.60	9.72	40	192	281	73.6
Female	0.712	1.025	0.136	0.448	0.018	0.126	5.18	9.47	44	229	600	82.8
Total	0.731	1.039	0.143	0.442	0.030	0.143	5.39	9.60	42	209	377	78.1
Northern America												
Males	1.174	1.221	0.694	0.828	0.348	0.537	13.0	15.0	9.4	19	54	15.4
Females	1.164	1.227	0.714	0.833	0.208	0.531	12.3	15.0	5.3	17	155	22.0
Total	1.169	1.224	0.704	0.831	0.279	0.534	12.6	15.0	4.7	18	91.4	19.0
Europe, including U.S.S.R.												
Male	1.034	1.041	0.465	0.738	0.123	0.234	9.61	11.8	0.7	59	90.2	22.8
Female	1.027	1.032	0.446	0.791	0.072	0.210	9.20	12.0	0.5	77	192	30.4
Totals	1.030	1.036	0.456	0.764	0.097	0.222	9.40	11.9	0.6	68	129	26.6

Table A.2 Continued

	Primary education (approx. 6–11)		Secondary education (approx. 12–17)		Higher education (approx. 20–24)		Expected years of enrollment[b] (weighted sum)		Percentage increase in enrollment ratios, 1960–80			
	1960	1980	1960	1980	1960	1980	1960	1980	Primary	Secondary	Higher	Total experience[b]
Oceania												
Male	1.022	1.022	0.538	0.702	0.140	0.231	10.1	11.5	0	30.5	65	13.9
Female	1.007	0.986	0.518	0.711	0.056	0.189	9.43	11.1	−2.1	37.3	238	17.7
Total	1.015	1.005	0.528	0.706	0.099	0.211	9.75	11.3	−1.0	33.7	113	15.9
Developed[a] *Total*												
Male	1.064	1.069	0.553	0.766	0.165	0.317	10.5	12.6	0.5	38.5	92.1	20
Female	1.054	1.064	0.544	0.801	0.091	0.282	10.0	12.6	0.9	47.2	210	26
Total	1.059	1.066	0.548	0.783	0.128	0.300	10.3	12.6	0.7	42.9	134	22
Developing *Total*												
Male	0.726	0.951	0.180	0.373	0.031	0.095	5.59	8.42	31	107	206	51
Female	0.476	0.765	0.073	0.249	0.010	0.052	3.34	6.34	61	241	420	90
Total	0.602	0.859	0.127	0.312	0.020	0.074	4.47	7.40	43	146	270	66
World *Total*												
Male	0.850	0.981	0.304	0.471	0.080	0.163	7.32	9.53	15	54.9	104	30
Female	0.687	0.842	0.228	0.386	0.040	0.122	5.69	7.98	23	69.3	205	40
Total	0.770	0.913	0.267	0.430	0.060	0.143	6.52	8.77	19	61.0	138	35

[a] Europe, Oceania, North America, Japan, Israel and South Africa.

[b] The Expected Years of Schooling is derived by multiplying the sum of the primary and secondary enrollment ratios by six (approximate duration of school levels) and adding the higher education enrollment ratio multiplied by five (assumed five year age group in denominator).

Source: UNESCO, *Statistical Yearbook 1984*, Table 2.10. Adjusted gross enrollment ratios divide enrollment for level by age group that according to national regulations should be enrolled at this level. Note these are UNESCO estimates and projections as assessed in 1982.

References

Academia Sinica (1983) *Experiences and lessons of economic development in Taiwan*. Taiwan: Institute of Economics, Taipei.

Anderson, K.H. (1982) 'The sensitivity of wage elasticities to selection bias and the assumption of normality', *Journal of Human Resources*, 17:594–605.

Armitage, J. and Sabot, R. (1986) 'Educational policy and intergenerational mobility: Analysis of a natural experiment', paper presented at Northeast Universities' Consortia in Development Economics, Yale University.

Arrow, K.J. (1973) 'Higher education as a filter', *Journal of Public Economics*, 2:193–316.

Ashenfelter, O. and Ham, J. (1979) 'Education, unemployment and earnings', *Journal of Political Economy*, 87:S99–S116.

Ashenfelter, O. and Heckman, J.J. (1974) 'The estimation of income and substitution effects in a model of family labor supply', *Econometrica*, 42:73–85.

Averch, H.A., et al. (1974) *How effective is schooling?* Englewood Cliffs, NJ: Educational Technology Publications.

Barnum, H.N. and Sabot, R.H. (1976) *Migration, education, and urban surplus labour*. Paris: OECD.

Barrera, A. (1986) 'Maternal schooling and child health', Department of Economics, Yale University.

Becker, G.S. (1964) *Human capital*. New York: NBER, Columbia University Press. (2nd ed. 1975.)

Becker, G.S. and Lewis, H.G. (1974) 'Interactions between quantity and quality of children', T.W. Schultz, ed., *Economics of the family*. Chicago, IL: University of Chicago Press.

Becker, G.S., Landes, E.M. and Michael, R.T. (1977) 'An economic analysis of marital instability', *Journal of Political Economy*, 85:1141–1188.

Behrman, J.R. (1986) 'Schooling in developing countries', University of Pennsylvania, mimeo.

Behrman, J.R. and Birdsall, N. (1983) 'The quality of schooling', *American Economic Review*, 73:928–946.

Behrman, J.R. and Wolfe, B.L. (1984a) 'The socioeconomic impact of schooling in a developing country', *Review of Economics and Statistics*, 66:296–303.

Behrman, J.R. and Wolfe, B.L. (1984b) 'Labor force participation and earnings determinants for women in the special conditions of developing countries', *Journal of Development Economics*, 15:259–288.

Behrman, J.R. and Wolfe, B.L. (1986a) 'How does mother's schooling affect family health?', University of Pennsylvania, mimeo.

Behrman, J.R. and Wolfe, B.L. (1986b) 'Does more schooling make women better nourished, but less healthy?', University of Pennsylvania, mimeo.

Behrman, J.R., Wolfe, B.L. and Blau, D.M. (1985) 'Human capital and earnings distribution in a developing country', *Economic Development and Cultural Change*, 34:1–30.

Behrman, J.R., Hrubec, Z., Taubman, P., and Wales, T.J. (1980) *Socioeconomic success*. Amsterdam: North-Holland.

Bell, C. and Srinivasan, T.N. (1985) 'The demand for attached farm servants in Andhra Pradesh, Bihar and Punjab', working paper no. 11, The World Bank, Washington, DC.

Ben-Porath, Y. (1967) 'The production of human capital and the life cycle of earnings', *Journal of Political Economy*, 75:4.

Ben-Porath, Y. (1986) 'Self employment and wage earners in Israel', in: U.O. Schmelz, ed., *Studies in the population of Israel*, Vol. 30. Jerusalem: Hebrew University, Magres Press.

Berger, M.C. (1985) 'The effect of cohort size on earnings growth', *Journal of Political Economy*, 93:561–573.

Bergstrom, T.C. and Goodman, R.P. (1973) 'Private demand for public goods', *American Economic Review*, 63:280–296.

Berry, A. (1975) 'Open unemployment as a social problem in urban Colombia', *Economic Development and Cultural Change*, 23:276–291.

Berry, A. and Sabot, R.H. (1978) 'Labour market performance in developing countries: A survey', *World Development*, 6:1199–1242.

Berry, A. and Sabot, R.H. (1984) 'Unemployment and economic development', *Economic Development and Cultural Change*, 33:199–116.

Bhagwati, J. (1973) 'Education, class structure, and income equality', *World Development*, 1:21–36.

Bhagwati, J. and Partington, M. (1976) *Taxing the brain drain: A proposal.* Amsterdam: North-Holland.

Bhagwati, J. and Srinivasan, T.N. (1977) "Education in a 'job ladder' model and the fairness-in-hiring role", *Journal of Public Economics*, 7:1–22.

Binswanger, H. and Ruttan, V.W. (1978) *Induced innovation: Technology: institutions and development.* Baltimore, MD: Johns Hopkins University Press.

Birdsall, N. (1985) 'Public inputs and child schooling in Brazil', *Journal of Development Economics*, 18:67–86.

Birdsall, N. and Behrman, J. (1984) 'Does geographical aggregation cause overestimates of the returns to schooling', *Oxford Bulletin of Economics and Statistics*, 46:55–72.

Birdsall, N. and Sabot, R., eds. (forthcoming) *Labor markets discrimination in developing economies.* Washington, DC: World Bank.

Blau, P.M. and Duncan, O.D. (1970) *The American occupational structure.* New York: Wiley.

Blaug, M. (1973) *Education and the employment problem in developing countries.* Geneva: International Labour Office.

Blaug, M. (1976) 'Human capital theory: A slightly jaundiced view', *Journal of Economic Literature*, 14:3.

Blaug, M. (1985) 'Where are we now in the economics of education', *Economics of Education Review*, 4:17–28.

Boissiere, M., Knight, J.B. and Sabot, R.H. (1985) 'Earnings, schooling, ability and cognitive skills', *American Economic Review*, 75:1016–1030.

Borcherding, T.E. and Deacon, R.T. (1972) 'The demand for the services of non-federal governments', *American Economic Review*, 62:891–901.

Boserup, E. (1970) *Women's role in economic development.* New York: St. Martin's Press.

Boulier, B.L. and Rosenzweig, M.R. (1984) 'Schooling, search, and spouse selection', *Journal of Political Economy*, 42:712–732.

Bowles, S. (1969) *Planning educational systems for economic growth.* Cambridge, MA: Harvard University Press.

Bowles, S. (1972) 'Schooling and inequality from generation to generation', *Journal of Political Economy*, May/June:219–251.

Cain, G. (1976) 'The challenge of segmented labor market theories to orthodox theory', *Journal of Economic Literature*, 14:1215.

Caldwell, J.C. (1979) 'Education as a factor in mortality decline', *Population Studies*, 33:395–413.

Carnoy, M. (1967a) 'Earnings and schoolings in Mexico', *Economic Development and Cultural Change*, July.

Carnoy, M. (1967b) 'Rates of return to schooling in Latin America', *Journal of Human Resources* 2:3.

Chamberlain, G. and Griliches, Z. (1977) 'More on brothers', in: P. Taubman, ed., *Kinometrics.* Amsterdam: North-Holland, pp. 97–124.

Chiswick, B.R. (1971) 'Earnings inequality and economic development', *Quarterly Journal of Economics*, 85:21–39.

Chiswick, B.R. (1978) 'The effect of Americanization on the earnings of foreign born men', *Journal of Political Economy*, 86:897–921.

Chiswick, C.U. (1977) 'On estimating earnings functions for LDC's', *Journal of Development Economics*, 4:67–78.

Chiswick, C.U. (1978) 'A procedure for estimating earnings of unpaid family workers', *Proceedings of American Statistical Association.* Washington, DC: American Statistical Association, Business and Economics Statistics Section.

Chiswick, C.U. (1979) 'The determinants of earnings in Thailand', Research Project 671-36. Washington, DC: World Bank.

Cochrane, S.H. (1979) *Fertility and education.* Baltimore, MD: Johns Hopkins University Press.

Cochrane, S.H., O'Hara, D.J. and Leslie, J. (1980) 'The effects of education on health', World Bank Staff working paper no. 405, Washington, DC.

Colclough, C. (1982) 'The impact of primary schooling on economic development', *World Development*, 10:167–185.

Correa, H. (1962) *The economics of human resources.* The Netherlands: Den Haag.

Dean, E. (1984) *Education and productivity.* Cambridge, MA: Ballinger.

Denison, E. (1962) *The sources of economic growth in the United States*. New York: Committee on Economic Development.

Denison E. (1967) *Why growth rates differ*. Washington, DC: Brookings Institution.

Deolalikar, A. and Vijverberg, W. (1983) 'The heterogeneity of family and hired labor in agricultural production', *Journal of Economic Development*, 8:45–69.

DeTray, D. (1987) 'Government policy, household behavior and the distribution of schooling', in: T.P. Schultz, ed., *Research in population economics*, Vol. 6. Greenwich, CT: JAI Press.

Donohue, J. (1985) 'A continuous time stochastic model of job mobility: A comparison of male–female hazard rates', Yale University, mimeo.

Dooley, M.D. (1985) 'Changes in the relationship among earnings, education, and age for Canadian men: 1971–1981', working paper 85-17, Department of Economics, McMaster University.

Durand, J.D. (1975) *The labor force in economic development*. Princeton, NJ: Princeton University Press.

Easterlin, R.A., Pollak, R.A., and Wachter, M.L. (1980) 'Toward a more general economic model of fertility determination' in: R.A. Easterlin, ed., *Population and economic change in developing countries*. Chicago, IL: NBER, University of Chicago Press.

Eckaus, R.S. (1973a) 'Estimation of returns to education with hourly standardized incomes', *Quarterly Journal of Economics*, 87:121–131.

Eckaus, R.S. (1973b) 'Estimating the returns to education: A disaggregated approach', technical report, Carnegie Commission on Higher Education, Berkeley, CA.

Edding, F. (1958) *Internationale tendenzen in der entwicklungen der ausgaben fur schulen und hochschulen*, Kieler Studien 47. Kiel, Germany: Weltwirtschaftliches Archiv.

Edwards, E.O., ed. (1974) *Employment in developing countries*. New York: Ford Foundation.

Edwards, E.O. and Todaro, M.P. (1974) 'Education, society, and employment', *World Development*, 2:25–30.

Ehrlich, I. (1975) 'On the relation between education and crime', in: F.T. Juster, ed. *Education income and human behavior*. New York: McGraw-Hill.

Evenson, R.E. (1986) 'The IARCs: Evidence of impact on national research and on productivity', Yale University, mimeo.

Falaris, E.M. and Peters, H.E. (1985) 'The effect of the demographic cycle on schooling and entry wages', working paper no. 85-4, Department of Economics, Ohio State University.

Fane, G. (1975) 'Education and the managerial efficiency of farmers', *Review of Economics and Statistics*, 57:452–461.

Fase, M.M.G. (1969) 'An econometric model of age–income profiles: A statistical study of Dutch income data 1958–1967', Rotterdam, Netherlands: University of Rotterdam.

Fields, G. (1974a) 'The private demand for education in relation to labor market conditions in less-developed countries', *Economic Journal*, 84:906–925.

Fields, G. (1974b) 'Private returns and social equity in the financing of higher education', in: D. Court and D.P. Ghai, eds., *Education, society and development: New perspectives from Kenya*. Nairobi: Oxford University Press, pp. 187–197.

Fields, G. and Schultz, T.P. (1982) 'Income generating functions in a low income country: Colombia', *Review of Income and Wealth*, 28:71–87.

Fishlow, A. (1972) 'Brazilian size distribution of income', *American Economic Review*, 62:391–402.

Fishlow, A. (1973) 'Distribuicao de renda do Brasil', *Dados*, 11.

Freeman, R.B. (1971) *The market for college-trained manpower*. Cambridge, MA: Harvard University Press.

Freeman, R.B. (1979) 'The effect of demographic factors on age-earnings profiles', *Journal of Human Resources*, 14:289–318.

Freeman, R.B. and Bloom, D.E. (1986) "The 'youth problem': Age or generational crowding", in: *Employment outlook*. Paris: OECD.

Freeman, R.B. and Medoff, J.L. (1984) *What unions do*. New York: Basic Books.

Fuchs, V.R. (1974) 'Some economic aspects of mortality in developed countries', in: M. Perlman, ed., *The economics of health and medical care*, Conference of International Economics Association, Tokyo. London: Macmillan.

Fuchs, V.R. (1980) 'Self employment and labor force participation of older males', NBER working paper no. 584.

Fuller, B. (1986) 'Is primary school quality eroding in the third world?', *Comparative Education Review*, 30:491–507.

Gisser, M. (1965) 'Schooling and the farm problem', *Econometrica*, 33:582–592.

Goldin, C. (1980) 'The historical evolution of female earnings functions and occupations', NBER working paper 529.

Goldin, C. (1983) 'The changing economic role of women', *Journal of Interdisciplinary History*, 13:707–733.

Gramlich, E.M. and Rubinfeld, D.L. (1982) 'Microestimates of public spending demand functions and tests of the tiebout and median voter hypothesis', *Journal of Political Economy*, 90:536–560.

Greenwood, M.J. (1975) 'Research on internal migration in the U.S.', *Journal of Economic Literature*, 3:397–433.

Gregory, P. (1980) 'An assessment of changes in employment conditions in less developed countries', *Economic Development and Cultural Change*, 28:673–700.

Griffin, C. (1985) 'Methods for estimating value of time in low-income countries with an application to the Philippines', Yale University, mimeo.

Griliches, Z. (1957) 'Specification bias in estimates of production functions', *Journal of Farm Economics*, 39:8–20.

Griliches, Z. (1964) 'Research expenditure, education and the aggregate agricultural production function', *American Economic Review*, 54:961–974.

Griliches, Z. (1970) 'Notes on the role of education in production functions and growth accounting', in: W.L. Hansen, ed., *Education, Income, and Human Capital*, Studies in Income and Wealth, No. 35. New York: Columbia University Press.

Griliches, Z. (1977) 'Estimating the returns to schooling: Some econometric problems', *Econometrica*, 45:1–22.

Griliches, Z. and Mason W.M. (1972) 'Education, income and ability', *Journal of Political Economy*, 80:S74–S103.

Grossman, M. (1976) 'The correlation between health and schooling', in: N.E. Terleckyj, ed., *Household production and consumption*, National Bureau of Economic Research, Vol. 40, Studies in Income and Wealth. New York: Columbia University Press.

Grubel, H.G. and Scott, A. (1977) *The brain drain*. Waterloo, Canada: Wilfred Laurier University Press.

Guisinger, S.E., Henderson, J.W. and Scully, G.W. (1984) 'Earnings, rates of return to education and the earnings distribution in Pakistan', *Economics of Education Review*, 3:257–267.

Hansen, W.L. and Weisbrod, B.A. (1969) 'The distribution of the costs and benefits of public higher education', *Journal of Human Resources*, 4:176–191.

Hanushek, E.A. (1979) 'Conceptual and empirical issues in the estimation of educational production functions', *Journal of Human Resources*, 14:351–388.

Hanushek, E.A. (1986) 'The economics of schooling', *Journal of Economic Literature*, 24:1141–1177.

Hanushek, E.A. and Quigley, J.M. (1985) 'Life-cycle learnings capacity and the OJT investment model', *International Economic Review*, 26:365–385.

Harbison, F. and Myers, C.A. (1964) *Education, manpower and economic growth*. New York: McGraw-Hill.

Harris, J. and Todaro, M. (1970) 'Migration, unemployment, and development: A two sector analysis', *American Economic Review*, 58:1.

Hause, J.C. (1972) 'Earnings profile: Ability and schooling', *Journal of Political Economy*, 80:S108–S138.

Haveman, R. and Wolfe, B. (1984) 'Education and economic well being: The role of nonmarket effects', *Journal of Human Resources*, 19:377–407.

Hay, J.M. (1984) 'Occupational choice and occupational earnings: A method for dealing with selection bias among economic activities', in: T.P. Schultz and K.I. Wolpin, eds., *Research in population economics*. Greenwich, CT: JAI Press.

Hayami, Y. and Ruttan, V. (1970) 'Agricultural productivity differences among countries', *American Economic Review*, 60:895–911.

Hayami, Y. and Ruttan, V. (1971) *Agricultural development: An international perspective*. Baltimore, MD: Johns Hopkins University Press.

Heckman, J.J. (1979) 'Sample selection bias as a specification error', *Econometrica*, 47:153–161.

Heckman, J.J. and Hotz, V.J. (1986) 'An investigation of the labor market earnings of Panamanian males: Evaluating sources of inequality', *Journal of Human Resources*, 21:507–542.

Heckman, J.J. and Polachek, S. (1974) 'Empirical evidence on the function form of the earnings–schooling relationship', *Journal of the American Statistical Association*, 69:346.

Heckman, J.J. and Sedlachek, G. (1985) 'Heterogeneity, aggregation and market wage functions: An empirical model of self selection in the labor market', *Journal of Political Economy*, 93:1077–1125.

Heller, P.S. (1979) 'The underfinancing of recurrent development costs', *Finance and Development*.

Heller, P.S. (1985) 'Analyzing and adjusting government expenditures in LDCs', *Finance and Development*, 22:2–5.

Heyneman, S. (1984) 'Research on education in the developing countries', *International Journal of Educational Development*, 4:293–304.

Heyneman, S. and Loxley, W. (1983) 'The effects of primary school quality on academic achievement across 29 high and low income countries', *American Journal of Sociology*, 88:1162–1194.

Heyneman, S., Farrell, J.P. and Sepulveda-Stuardo, M. (1981) 'Textbooks and achievement in developing countries: What do we know', *Journal of Curriculum Studies*, 13:227–246.

Hicks, U.K. (1965) *Development finance: Planning and control*. New York: Oxford University Press.

Hill, C.R. and Stafford, F.P. (1974) 'Allocation of time to preschool children and educational opportunity', *Journal of Human Resources*, 9:323–343.

Hill, M.A. (1983) 'Female labor force participation in developing and developed countries: Consideration of the informal sector', *Review of Economics and Statistics*, 65:459–468.

Hollister, R. (1983) 'A perspective on the role of manpower analysis and planning in developing countries', in: G. Psacharopoulos, ed., *Manpower issues in educational investment*, World Bank Staff working paper no. 624. Washington, DC: World Bank.

Huffman, W.E. (1974) 'Decison-making: The role of education', *American Journal of Agricultural Economics*, 56:85–97.

Huffman, W.E. (1976) 'Productive value of human time in U.S. agriculture', *American Journal of Agricultural Economics*, 58:672–683.

Huffman, W.E. (1977) 'Allocative efficiency: The role of human capital', *Quarterly Journal of Economics*, 91:59–77.

Huffman, W.E. (1980) 'Farm and off farm work decisions: The role of human capital', *Review of Economics and Statistics*, 62:14–23.

Huffman, W.E. (1985) 'Human capital for agriculture', Iowa State University, mimeo.

Inkeles, A. and Smith, D. (1974) *Becoming modern*. Cambridge, MA: Harvard University Press.

Jamison, D.T. and Lau, L.J. (1982) *Farmer education and farm efficiency*. Baltimore, MD: Johns Hopkins University Press.

Jimenez, E. (1984) 'Pricing policy in the social sectors: Cost recovery for education and health in developing countries', University of Western Ontario and the World Bank, Washington, DC, mimeo.

Johnson, G. (1984) 'Subsidies for higher education', *Journal of Labor Economics*, 2:303–318.

Johnson, G. (1985) 'Investment in and returns to education', in: P.H. Hendershott, ed., *The level and composition of household savings*. Cambridge, MA: Ballinger.

Johnson, G. and Stafford, F. (1973) 'Social returns to quantity and quality of schooling', *Journal of Human Resources*, 8:139–155.

Joshi, P.C. and Rao, M.R. (1984) 'Social and economic factors in literacy and education in rural India', *Economic Weekly*, January.

Juster, F.T. (1975) *Education, income and human behavior*. New York: McGraw-Hill.

Khaldi, N. (1975) 'Education and allocative efficiency in U.S. agriculture', *American Journal of Agricultural Economics*, 57:650–657.

Kiefer, N.M. (1985) 'Evidence on the role of education in labor turnover', *Journal of Human Resources*, 20:445–452.

Kiesling, H.J. (1971) *Multivariate analysis of schools and educational policy*. Santa Monica, CA: The Rand Corporation.

King, E.M. and Lillard, L.A. (1983) 'Determinants of schooling attainment and enrollment rates in the Philippines', report no. 1962-AID. Santa Monica, CA: The Rand Corporation.

Klevmarken, A. (1972) *Statistical methods for analysis of earnings data*. Stockholm, Sweden: Industrial Institute for Economic and Social Research, Almquist & Wiksell.

Kniesner, T.J., Padilla, A.H. and Polachek, S.W. (1978) 'The rate of return to schooling and the business cycle', *Journal of Human Resources*, 13:264–277.

Knight, J.B. and Sabot, R.H. (1981) 'The returns to education: Increasing with experience or decreasing with expansion', *Oxford Bulletin of Economics and Statistics*, 43:51–71.

Knight, J.B. and Sabot, R.H. (1985) 'Educational policy and labor productivity: An output accounting exercise', World Bank, Washington, DC, mimeo.

Kravis, I.B., Heston, A. and Summers, R. (1982) *World product and income*. Baltimore, MD: Johns Hopkins University Press.

Krueger, A.O. (1968) 'Factor endowments and per capita income differences', *Economic Journal*, 78:641–659.

Kuznets, S. (1954) *National income and its composition 1919–1938*, New York: National Bureau of Economic Research.

Kuznets, S. (1959) 'Quantitative aspects of the economic growth of nations: IV. Distribution of national income by factor shares', *Economic Development and Cultural Change*, 7:1–100.

Kuznets, S. (1966) *Modern economic growth: Rate, structure, and spread*. New Haven, CT: Yale University Press.

Kuznets, S. (1971) *Economic growth of nations*. Cambridge, MA: Harvard University Press.

Langoni, C.G. (1973) *Distribuicao da renda e desenvolvimento economico do Brasil*. Rio de Janeiro: Expressao e Cultura. Also in *Estudios Economicos*, October (1972).

Layard, R. and Mincer, J. (1985) 'Trends in women's work, education, and family building', *Journal of Labor Economics*, 3:1.

Layard, R. and Psacharopoulos, G. (1974) 'The screening hypothesis and the returns to education', *Journal of Political Economy*, 82:5.

Lazear, E. (1979) 'Why is there mandatory retirement?', *Journal of Political Economy*, 87:1261–1284.

Lee, K.H. (1984) 'Universal primary education: An African dilemma', The World Bank, Washington, DC, mimeo.

Leibowitz, A. (1974) 'Home investment in children', in: T.W. Schultz, ed., *Economics of the family*. Chicago, IL: University of Chicago Press.

Leibowitz, A. (1975) 'Education and the allocation of women's time', in: F.T. Juster, ed., *Education income and human behavior*. New York: McGraw-Hill.

Lewis, A. (1962) 'Education and economic development', *International Social Science Journal*, 14:685–699.

Lewis, A. (1963) *Unionism and relative wages in the United States*. Chicago, IL: University of Chicago Press.

Lewis, A. (1985) *Union relative wage effects: A survey*. Chicago, IL: University of Chicago Press.

Lindauer, D.L. and Sabot, R. (1983) 'The public/private wage differential in a poor urban economy', *Journal of Development Economics*, 12:137–152.

Lindsay, C.M. (1971) 'Measuring human capital returns', *Journal of Political Economy*, 79:1195–1215.

Link, C. and Ratledge, E.C. (1975) 'Social returns to quantity and quality of education', *Journal of Human Resources*, 10:78–79.

Lipton, M. (1977) *Why poor people stay poor: Urban bias in world development*. Cambridge, MA: Harvard University Press.

Lockheed, M., Jamison, D. and Lau, L. (1980) 'Farmer education and farm efficiency: A survey', *Economic Development and Cultural Change*, 29:1.

Lucas, R. (1977) 'Hedonic wage equations and psychic wages in the returns to schooling', *American Economic Review*, 76:549–558.

Lucas, R.E., Jr. (1985) 'On the mechanics of economic development', Marshall Lectures, Cambridge University. London: Basil Blackwell, forthcoming.

Meerman, J. (1979) *Public expenditure in Malaysia: Who benefits and why*. New York: Oxford University Press.

Michael, R.T. (1973) 'Education and the derived demand for children', *Journal of Political Economy*, 81:S128–S164.

Michael, R.T. (1982) 'Measuring non-monetary benefits of education: A survey', in W.W. McMahon and T.G. Geske, eds., *Financing education*. Urbana, IL: University of Illinois Press.

Mincer, J. (1962) 'On-the-job training', *Journal of Political Economy*, 70:50–79.

Mincer, J. (1974) *Schooling experience and earnings*. New York: NBER, Columbia University Press.

Mincer, J. and Polachek, S. (1974) 'Family investments in human capital: Earnings of women', *Journal of Political Economy*, 82:S76–S108.

Minget, A. and Tan, J.P. (1985) 'On equity in education again: An international comparison', *Journal of Human Resources*, 20:2 (Springer) 298–308.

Montgomery, M.R. (1985), 'Female education and first marriage in Malaysia: An application of the theory of search', Princeton University, mimeo.

Moock, P.R. (1976) 'The efficiency of women as farm managers: Kenya', *American Journal of Agricultural Economics*, 58:831–835.

Moock, P.R. (1981) 'Education and technical efficiency in small scale production', *Economic Development and Cultural Change*, 29:723–739.

Mueller, E. (1984) 'Income aspirations and fertility in rural areas of less developed countries', in: W.A. Schutjer and C.S. Stokes, eds., *Rural development and human fertility*. New York: Macmillan.

Murname, R.J., Maynard, R.A. and Ohls, J.C. (1981) 'Home resources and children's achievement', *Review of Economics and Statistics*, 63:369–377.

Nelson, R.R. (1981) 'Research on productivity growth and differences', *Journal of Economic Literature*, 19:1029–1064.

Nickell, S. (1979) 'Education and lifetime patterns of unemployment', *Journal of Political Economy*, 87:S117–S132.

Orazem, P. (1983) 'Two models of school achievement and attendance with application to segregated schools', unpublished dissertation, Yale University.

Polachek, S.W. (1979) 'Occupational segregation among women' in: C.B. Lloyd, E.S. Andrews and C.L. Gilroy, eds., *Women in the labor market*. New York: Columbia University Press.

Preston, S.H. (1980) 'Causes and consequences of mortality declines in LDCs during the twentieth century', in: R.A. Easterlin, ed., *Population and economic changes in developing countries*. Chicago, IL: University of Chicago Press.

Pryor, F.L. (1968) *Public expenditures in communist and capitalist nations*. Homewood, IL: Irwin.

Psacharopoulos, G. (1973) *Returns to education*. San Francisco, CA: Jossy Bass–Elsevier.

Psacharopoulos, G. (1981) 'Returns to education: An updated international comparison', *Comparative Education Review*, 17:321–341.

Psacharopoulos, G. (1984) 'The contribution of education to economic growth', in: J.W. Kendrick, ed., *International comparisons of productivity and causes of the slowdown*. Cambridge, MA: Ballinger, pp. 325–360.

Psacharopoulos, G. (1985) 'Returns to education: A further international update and implication', *Journal of Human Resources*, 20:4, 583–604.

Psacharopoulos, G. and Woodhall, M. (1985) *Education for development*. New York: Oxford University Press.

Pudassini, S.P. (1983) 'The effects of education in agriculture: Evidence from Nepal', *American Journal of Agricultural Economics*, 65:509–515.

Pyatt, G., Roe, A.R. and associates (1977) *Social accounting for development planning with special reference to Sri Lanka*. Cambridge: Cambridge University Press.

Ram, R. (1980) 'Education in production: A slightly new approach', *Quarterly Journal of Economics*, 95:365–373.

Ram, R. and Schultz, T.W. (1979) 'Life span, health, savings and productivity', *Economic Development and Cultural Change*, 27:399–421.

Ribe, H. (1979) 'Income of migrants relative to nonmigrants in Colombia', unpublished dissertation, Yale University.

Riley, J.G. (1975) 'Information screening and human capital', *American Economic Review*, 66:254–260.

Riley, J.G. (1979) 'Testing the educational screening hypothesis', *Journal of Political Economy*, 87:S227–S252.

Rizzuto, R. and Wachtel, P. (1980) 'Further evidence on the returns to school quality', *Journal of Human Resources*, 15:240–254.

Rosen, S. (1974) 'Hedonic functions and implicit markets', *Journal of Political Economy*, 82:34–55.

Rosen, S. (1977) 'Human capital: A survey of empirical research', in: R.G. Ehrenberg, ed., *Research in labor economics*, Vol. 1, Greenwich, CT: JAI Press.

Rosen, S. (1985) 'Human capital', University of Chicago, mimeo.

Rosenzweig, M.R. (1980) 'Neoclassical theory and the optimizing peasant', *Quarterly Journal of Economics*, 94:31–56.

Rosenzweig, M.R. (1982a) 'Educational subsidy, agricultural development and fertility change', *Quarterly Journal of Economics*, 97:67–88.

Rosenzweig, M.R. (1982b) 'Agricultural development, education and innovation', in: M. Gervsovitz, et al., eds., *The theory and experience of economic development*. London: George Allen Unwin.

Rosenzweig, M.R. and Evenson, R.E. (1977) 'Fertility, schooling and the economic contribution of children in rural India', *Econometrica*, 45:1065–1079.

Rosenzweig, M.R. and Schultz, T.P. (1982) 'Child mortality and fertility in Colombia: Individual and community effects', *Health Policy and Education*, 2:305–348.

Rosenzweig, M.R. and Schultz, T.P. (1983) 'Estimating a household production function', *Journal of Political Economy*, 91:723–746.

Rosenzweig, M.R. and Schultz, T.P. (1985) 'Schooling, information, and nonmarket productivity: Contraceptive use and its effectiveness', discussion paper no. 490, Yale University Economic Growth Center.

Rosenzweig, M.R. and Schultz, T.P. (1987) 'Fertility and investment in human capital: Estimates of the consequences of imperfect fertility control in Malaysia', discussion paper, Economic Growth Center, Yale University.

Rosenzweig, M.R. and Seiver, D. (1982) 'Education and contraceptive choice: A conditional demand framework', *International Economic Review*, 70.

Rosenzweig, M.R. and Wolpin, K.I. (1980) 'Testing the quantity quality model of fertility: The use of twins as a natural experiment', *Econometrica*, 48:227–240.

Rosenzweig, M.R. and Wolpin, K.I. (1982) 'Governmental interventions and household behavior in a development country', *Journal of Development Economics*, 10:209–226.

Rosenzweig, M.R. and Wolpin, K.I. (1984) 'Migrant selectivity and the effects of government programs', discussion paper no. 464, Yale Economic Growth Center.

Sai, F.T. (1984) 'The population factor in Africa's development dilemma', *Science*, 226:801–805.

Saxonhouse, G.R. (1977) 'Productivity change and labor absorption in Japanese cotton spinning, 1931–1935', *Quarterly Journal of Economics*, 91:195–200.

Schultz, T.P. (1968) *Returns to education in Bogota, Colombia*, report no. RM-5645. Santa Monica, CA: The Rand Corporation.

Schultz, T.P. (1971) *Evaluation of population policies: A framework for analysis and its application to Taiwan's family planning program*, report no. R-643-AID. Santa Monica, CA: The Rand Corporation.

Schultz, T.P. (1973) 'A preliminary survey of economic analyses of fertility', *American Economic Review*, 63:2.

Schultz, T.P. (1980) 'Interpretation of relations among mortality economics of the household and the health environment', *Socioeconomic Determinants and Consequences of Mortality Differentials*. Geneva: WHO.

Schultz, T.P. (1981) *Economics of population*. Reading, MA: Addison-Wesley.

Schultz, T.P. (1982a) 'Notes on the estimation of migration decision functions', in: R. Sabot, ed., *Migration and the labor market in developing countries*. Boulder, CO: Westview Press.

Schultz, T.P. (1982b) 'Lifetime migration within educational strata', *Economic Development and Cultural Change*, 30:559–593.

Schultz, T.P. (1983) 'Migrant behavior and the effects of regional prices: Aspects of migrant selection in Colombia', discussion paper no. 443, Yale Economic Growth Center.

Schultz, T.P. (1984) 'Studying the impact of household economic and community variables on child mortality', *Population and Development Review*, 10:215–235.

Schultz, T.P. (1985) 'School expenditures and enrollments, 1960–1980: The effects of income, prices and population', discussion paper no. 487, Yale Economic Growth Center. Forthcoming in: D. G. Johnson and R. Lee, eds., *Population growth and economic development*. Madison WI: University of Wisconsin Press.

Schultz, T.P. (1987a) 'Economic demography and development: New directions in an old field', in: G. Ranis and T.P. Schultz, eds., *State of development economics: Progress and perspective*. London: Basil Blackwell, forthcoming.

Schultz, T.P. (1987b) 'The value and allocation of time in high income countries', *Population and Development Review*, 13: supplement.

Schultz, T.P. and Vijverberg, W. (1983) 'Education and informal sector employment and migration', Yale University, mimeo.

Schultz, T.W. (1953) *Economic organization of agriculture*. New York: McGraw-Hill.

Schultz, T.W. (1961) 'Investments in human capital', *American Economic Review*, 51:1.

Schultz, T.W. (1963) *The economic value of education*. New York: Columbia University Press.

Schultz, T.W., ed. (1972) 'Investment in education: The equity–efficiency quandary', *Journal of Political Economy*, 80:3, Part II.

Schultz, T.W. (1974) 'Fertility and economic values', in: T.W. Schultz, ed., *The economics of the family*. Chicago, IL: University of Chicago Press.

Schultz, T.W. (1975) 'The ability to deal with disequilibria', *Journal of Economic Literature*, 13:827–846.

Schwartz, A. (1971) 'On efficiency of migration', *Journal of Human Resources*, 6:193–205.

Schwartz, A. (1976) 'Migration, age and education', *Journal of Political Economy*, 84:701–720.

Scott, A.D. (1970) 'The brain drain – Is a human capital approach justified?', in: W.L. Hansen, ed., *Education, income and human capital*. New York: National Bureau of Economic Research.

Selowsky, M. (1971) 'Labor input substitution in the study of sources of growth and educational planning', in: H.B. Chenery, ed., *Studies in development planning*. Cambridge, MA: Harvard University Press.

Selowsky, M. (1976) 'A note on preschool-age investment in human capital in developing countries', *Economic Development and Cultural Change*, 24:707–720.

Selowsky, M. (1979) *Who benefits from government expenditures?* New York: Oxford University Press.

Sewell, W.H. and Hauser, R.M. (1975) *Education, occupation, and earnings*. New York: Academic Press.

Shorter, F. (1975) *The making of the modern family*. New York: Basic Books.

Simmons, J. and Alexander, L. (1978) 'The determinants of school achievement in developing countries', *Economic Development and Cultural Change*, 26:341–358.

Simon, J.L. and Pilarski, A.M. (1979) 'The effect of population growth upon the quantity of education children receive', *Review of Economics and Statistics*, 61:572–584.

Singh, I., Squire, L. and Strauss, J. (1986) *Agricultural household models: Extensions, applications and policy*. Baltimore, MD: Johns Hopkins University Press.

Smith, J.P., ed. (1980) *Female labor supply*. Princeton, NJ: Princeton University Press.

Smith, J.P., (1983) *Income and growth in Malaysia*, report no. R-2941. Santa Monica, CA: Rand Corporation.

Soloman, L.C. and Taubman, P.J., eds. (1973) *Does college matter*. New York: Academic Press.

Spence, A.M. (1973) 'Job market signalling', *Quarterly Journal of Economics*, 87:355–374.

Spence, A.M. (1974) *Market signalling: Information transfer in hiring and related screening processes*. Cambridge, MA: Harvard University Press.

Standing, G. (1978) *Labour force participation and development*. Geneva: International Labour Organization.

Stiglitz, J. (1975) "The theory of 'screening', education and the distribution of income", *American Economic Review*, 65:283–300.

Strauss, J. (1987) 'Households, communities and preschool children's nutrition outcomes: Evidence form rural Cote d'Ivoire', Economic Growth Center, Yale University.

Summers, R. and Heston, A. (1984) 'Improved international comparisons of real product and its composition, 1950–80', *Review of Income and Wealth*, 30:207–262.

Sumner, D. and Frazao, E. (1986) 'Wage rates in a poor rural area with an emphasis on industry specific experience', working paper no. 94, Department of Economics and Statistics, North Carolina State University.

Swift, W.J. and Weisbrod, B.A. (1965) 'On the monetary value of education: Intergenerational effects', *Journal of Political Economy*, 73:643–649.

Tan, J-P. (1985) 'Private enrollments and expenditure on education: Some macro trends', *International Review of Education*, 31:103–117.

Taubman, P. (1976) 'The determinants of earnings: Genetics, family, and other environments', *American Economic Review*, 66(5).

Taubman, P. and Wales, T. (1973) 'Higher education, mental ability and screening', *Journal of Political Economy*, 81:28–36.

Taubman, P. and Wales, T. (1974) *Higher education: An investment and a screening device*. New York: NBER and Carnegie Commission on Higher Education.

Teilhet-Waldorf, S. and Waldorf, W.H. (1983) 'Earnings of self employed in the informal sector: A case study of Bangkok', *Economic and Development and Cultural Change*, 31:587–607.

Thias, H. and Carnoy, M. (1973) *Cost-benefit analysis of education: A case study on Kenya*. Baltimore, MD: Johns Hopkins University Press.

Tiebout, C.M. (1965) 'A pure theory of local expenditures', *Journal of Political Economy*, 65:416–424.

Tolley, G.S. (1970) 'Management entry into US agriculture', *American Journal of Agricultural Economics*, 52:485–493.

Turnham, D. (1971) *The employment problem in less developed countries*. Paris, OECD.

United Nations (various years) *Demographic yearbook*. New York: United Nations.

United Nations Education and Social Commission (various years) *UNESCO statistical yearbook*. New York: United Nations.

United Nations Population Division (1983) *Relationship between fertility and education: A comparative analysis of world fertility survey data for 22 developing countries*, report no. ST/ESA/SER.R/48. New York: United Nations.

Van der Gaag, J. and Vijverberg, W.P.M. (1986a) 'Wage determinants in Cote d'Ivoire: Experience, credentials and human capital', World Bank, mimeo.

Van der Gaag, J. and Vijverberg, W.P.M. (1986b) 'A switching regression model for wage determinants in the public and private sector of a developing economy', World Bank, mimeo.

Vijverberg, W.P.M. (1986) 'Consistent estimates of the wage equation when individuals choose among income earning activities', *Southern Economic Journal*, 52:1028–1042.

Weisbrod, B. (1964) *External benefits of public education*. Princeton, NJ: Industrial Relations Section, Princeton University.

Weiss, A. (1984) 'Determinants of quit behavior', *Journal of Labor Economics*, 2:371–387.

Welch, F. (1966) 'Measurement of the quality of schooling', *American Economic Review*, 56:379–392.

Welch, F. (1970) 'Education in production', *Journal of Political Economy*, 38:35–59.

Welch, F. (1975) 'Human capital theory: Education, discrimination and life cycles', *American Economic Review*, 65:63–73.

Welch, F. (1978) *Minimum wages: Issues and evidence*. Washington, DC: American Enterprise Institute.

Welch, F. (1979) 'The baby boom babies' financial bust', *Journal of Political Economy*, 87:S65–S97.

Willis, R.J. (1987) 'Wage determinants', in: O. Ashenfelter and R. Layard, eds., *Handbook of labor economics*. Amsterdam: North-Holland (forthcoming).

Willis, R.J. and Rosen, S. (1979) 'Education and self selection', *Journal of Political Economy*, 87:S7–S36.

Wise, D. (1975) 'Academic achievement and job performance', *American Economic Review*, 65:350–366.

Wolfe, B.L. and Behrman, J.R. (1982) 'Determinants of child mortality, health and nutrition in a developing country', *Journal of Development Economics*, 11:163–194.

Wolfe, B.L. and Behrman, J.R. (1986) 'Women's schooling and children's health', University of Pennsylvania, mimeo.

Wolpin, K. (1977) 'Education and screening', *American Economic Review*, 67:949–958.

Woodhall, M. (1973) 'Investment in women', *International Review of Education*, 19:9–28.

World Bank Staff (1980) *Education sector policy paper*, 3rd. ed. Washington, DC: World Bank.

World Bank Staff (1983) *World development report 1983*. New York: Oxford University Press.

World Bank Staff (1984) *World development report 1984*. New York: Oxford University Press.

World Bank Staff (1986a) *Financing education in developing countries: An exploration of policy options*. Washington, DC: Education and Training Department, World Bank.

World Bank Staff (1986b) *World development report 1986*. Oxford University Press: New York.

Wu, C.C. (1977) 'Education in farm production', *American Journal of Agriculture Economics*, 59:699–709.

Yap, L. (1977) 'The attraction of cities: A review of the migration literature', *Journal of Development Economics*, 4:239–264.

Zymelman, M. (1982) 'Educational expenditures in the 1970s', World Bank.

Zymelman, M. (1985) 'Educational budgets and quality of instruction: Are they unequivocally related?', Washington, DC: World Bank.

Chapter 14

HEALTH AND NUTRITION

JERE R. BEHRMAN

University of Pennsylvania

ANIL B. DEOLALIKAR*

Harvard University

Contents

1. Introduction   633
2. Theoretical framework   637
   2.1. Micro considerations: Household production functions and reduced-form demands for health and nutrients   637
   2.2. Supply considerations   649
   2.3. Macro or aggregate considerations   649
3. Measurement and estimation problems in health and nutrition relations   650
   3.1. Measurement of health status   650
   3.2. Measurement of nutrient intakes and nutritional status   653
   3.3. Measurement of non-nutrient health-related inputs   656
   3.4. Measurement of prices, health-related inputs, and assets   657
   3.5. Estimation problems   658
4. Empirical studies of determinants of health and nutrition in developing countries   660
   4.1. Determinants of health   660
   4.2. Determinants of nutrients   674
5. Empirical studies of the impact of health and nutrition in developing countries   683
   5.1. Impact on labor productivity   683
   5.2. Impact on schooling productivity   688
   5.3. Impact of female nutrition on fertility   689
   5.4. Impact of infant mortality on fertility   690

*We thank NIH for support for this study and Nancy Birdsall, Christopher Bliss, Hollis B. Chenery, Judith S. McGuire, Sam Preston, Per Pinstrup-Andersen, Mark Rosenzweig, T. Paul Schultz, T.N. Srinivasan, John Strauss, Lance Taylor, and Peter Timmer, for useful comments on earlier drafts, but we assume all responsibility for any errors remaining in this chapter.

Handbook of Development Economics, Volume I, Edited by H. Chenery and T.N. Srinivasan
© *Elsevier Science Publishers B.V., 1988*

Contents (continued)

6.   Empirical studies on supply considerations and related policies   692
     6.1.   Food subsidies   692
     6.2.   Other health goods and services subsidies   696
     6.3.   Impact of macro adjustment policies on health and nutrition   697
7.   Summary and conclusions   698
     7.1.   Summary of available studies   698
     7.2.   Directions for future research   702
References   704

1. Introduction

Health and nutrition are important as ends in themselves and often are emphasized as critical components of basic needs in developing countries. In addition they may be channels through which productivity and distributional goals of developing societies may be pursued effectively if, as is often hypothesized, the productivity of low-income persons in work and in human–capital formation is positively affected by health and nutrition status.

Cross-country comparisons of standard data suggest that on the average health and nutrition in the developing world falls considerably short of that in the developed world (Table 14.1).[1] The differences in means across countries in 1983 were considerable: in the other low-income countries (i.e. excluding China and India) life expectancies at birth were 50 and 52 years for males and females, as compared with 72 and 79 in industrial market economies; for the same two country groups infant mortality rates were 115 versus 10 per 1000 inhabitants; per physician were 17,990 versus 554, and daily calorie supplies were 2118 versus 3400. The proportion of the population with access to safe water in 1975, moreover, was less than a third for the low-income countries.

On the other hand, the changes in such indices in recent decades in the developing countries have been enormous, and in many cases the absolute gaps between the developing countries and developed countries have been reduced. Between 1960 and 1983, for example, life expectancies at birth for males increased by 16 years for low-income countries, 10 years for middle-income countries and 14 years for high-income oil exporters, as compared with only four years for industrial market economies and one year for East European nonmarket economies. Thus, while significant gaps remain in health and nutritional status across country groups defined by their level of development, by a number of indices such gaps have been reduced more rapidly in recent decades than has been the reduction in gaps, for example, in per capita income.[2]

---

[1] Of course the interpretation of averages must be qualified since health and nutrition attainment may depend critically on the shapes of the distributions of key variables; we return to distributional questions below. There also are some critical measurement issues which we discuss below in Section 3.

[2] However, one should be careful about extrapolating the past relative gains into the future for at least two reasons. First, for some such measures, there has been an advantage to being a relative latecomer. But closing the last 10 percent of the gap may be much more difficult than closing the first 10 percent since the transfer to latecomers of new techniques (e.g. public health measures) typically focuses on higher productivity techniques initially. Second, the last columns of Table 14.1 suggest a decline in relative shares of health and nutrition-related expenditures at least in central government budgets. The declines in the shares of health expenditures are large enough so that absolute health expenditures also have declined despite growth in overall governmental budgets, though private health expenditures may have increased and other related government expenditures (e.g. housing, community amenities, social security and welfare) increased.

Table 14.1
Indicators of recent levels and changes in health and nutrition
and in related percentage shares of government expenditures[a]

| | Life expectancy in years at birth | | | | Mortality rates per 1000 | | | | Population per | | | | Daily caloric supply per capita (1982) | |
| | Male | | Female | | Infant (age < 1) | | Child (1–4) | | Physician | | Nursing person | | | |
	1960	1983	1960	1983	1960	1983	1960	1983	1960	1980	1960	1980	Total	% of requirement
Low-income economies	42	58	41	60	165	75	27	9	12088	5556	7226	4564	2408	105
China and India	42	61	41	63	165	61	26	6	7019	1858	6734	3279	2503	109
Other low-income	42	50	43	52	163	115	31	18	37092	17990	9759	8697	2118	93
Middle-income economies	49	59	52	63	126	75	23	9	17257	5995	3838	1945	2661	114
Lower middle income	44	55	47	59	144	87	29	11	28478	7555	4697	2292	2495	109
Upper middle income	55	63	58	68	101	59	15	5	2532	2018	2752	995	2880	119
High-income oil exporters	43	57	45	60	175	90	44	11	14738	1360	4996	836	3271	…
Industrial market economies	68	72	73	79	29	10	2	(·)	816	554	470	180	3400	133
East European nonmarket Economies	65	66	72	74	38	30	3	1	683	345	358	130	3419	133

| Percentage of population with access to safe water | % of central government expenditure | | | |
| | Health | | Housing, community amenities, social security, welfare[b] | |
1975	1972	1982	1972	1982
31	6.1	3.0	3.8	5.0
...	...	...	...	...
29	6.1	4.0	3.8	6.0
52	6.5	4.7	20.2	17.7
...	4.5	3.7	4.9	6.8
...	7.0	5.1	24.2	21.0
88	5.6	5.5	12.5	9.1
...	9.9	11.7	36.8	40.4

[a]*Source*: World Bank (1982, Table 22; 1984, Tables 23, 24, 26; 1985; Tables 23, 24, 26).

[b]According to the World Bank (1985, p. 241): "Housing and community amenities and social security and welfare covers (1) public expenditure on housing, such as income-related schemes; on provision and support of housing and slum clearance activities; on community development; and on sanitary services; and (2) public expenditure for compensation to the sick and temporarily disabled for loss of income; payments to the elderly, the permanently disabled, and the unemployed; and for family maternity, and child allowances. The second category also includes the cost of welfare services such as care of the aged, the disabled, and children, as well as the cost of general administration, regulation, and research associated with social security and welfare services."

In recent years economists have directed increasing attention towards exploring the determinants of and the impact of health and nutrition in the development process. Some progress has been made in our understanding of a number of important issues, but substantial lacunae remain in our knowledge about health and nutrition and development. Important issues concern the extent of health and nutrition problems, the determinants of health and nutrient status, the impact of health and nutrition on incomes and other outcomes, and appropriate policy design.

The measurements issues about the extent of health and nutrition problems in some cases precede and in some are intertwined with the economic analysis. To what extent are the standard indices (such as in Table 14.1) useful for characterizing health and nutrition well-being? To what extent are these misleading because of confusion between inputs and outputs, ambiguity between curative and preventive health measures, failure to recognize the endogeneity of health status and health inputs, intra- and interpersonal variability in health and nutrient standards, and individual economic and psychological adaptability?

The determination of health status and nutrition is largely by individuals and the households in which they reside given their resources and the prices that they face, both broadly defined. Important questions about this process include: What is the production process that determines health status? What are the lags? How do biology, behavior, and environment interact? What is the nature of complementarities and substitution in this production process? How important are nutrient and other purchased (or produced) inputs? How important is education (especially of women) and, if it is important, what is it representing? How critical are various dimensions of the household and community environment? How responsive are nutrition and health status to changes in prices that households face and in resources that households have? To what extent are there interhousehold variations in these responses depending on relative or absolute income? Will income increases associated with development result in substantial increases in health and nutrition? To what extent are there intrahousehold variations in such responses depending on age and gender? Are seasonal variations critical? How well do the relevant prices reflect the true social costs of resources used for nutrition and health inputs? In what cases are there significant externalities with respect to the production of these inputs? What are the expected returns to private versus social and to preventive versus curvature health inputs?

The possible impact of nutrition and health status on other outcomes also raises a number of questions. To what extent is improved nutrition reflected in greater metabolism, greater energy expenditure or better ongoing health? Are there important own-farm, labor market and schooling productivity effects of nutrition and health? What is the impact of nutrition and health of adults and of their children on fertility?

Finally, based on as good answers to these questions as possible given information and research costs, what are the implications for policies? To what extent do externalities or distributional concerns warrant governmental subsidies to certain health and nutrition inputs? What do the patterns of price and income demand elasticities across different health and nutrition inputs and among various population groups imply about policy design? To what types of governmental health and nutrition investments are the social returns likely to be highest?

In this chapter we review a number of these issues regarding health and nutrition in developing countries and available studies on the determinants of health and nutrition and on their impact on productivity in developing countries. We consider first a theoretical framework and some issues pertaining to the empirical representation of health and nutrition. We then survey existing studies on both health and nutrition determinants and on their productivity impact and conclude with some discussion of policy issues and directions for future research.

2. Theoretical framework

A theoretical framework for the determinants of health and nutrition and their possible productivity impacts is essential in order to analyze these variables in an organized manner and to be able to interpret empirical studies. Since most of the studies that we review below in Section 4 focus on demand determinants and since most macro studies appeal to micro rationales for their specifications, we begin with micro production function and demand considerations. We then more briefly consider the supply side and macro relations.

2.1. Micro considerations: Household production functions and reduced-form demands for health and nutrients

The proximate determinants of an individual's health and nutrition usually are decisions made by the individual or by the household in which he or she lives – given assets, prices, and community endowments (some of which may be determined in part by governmental actions). Therefore a natural starting point is the determination of individual health and nutrition at the household level (some individuals, of course, live in single-person households). Since many individuals in developing countries live in consumption units for which the production–consumption separability conditions (which are required to permit consideration of income generation and demand for consumption goods and services as a two-stage process as in most studies) are not satisfied because of incomplete markets or because of productivity effects of health and nutrition input consumption, we consider the case of a household-firm decision-making unit. The most analyzed such unit is the household-farm model considered by Lau, Lin and Yotopoulos (1978), Barnum and Squire (1979), Singh, Squire and Strauss (1986) and others, but similar considerations may be important for nonagricultural family enterprises in services and industry, particularly in the informal sector. The situation in which separability is an appropriate assumption can be considered to be a special case of this model in which the prices, assets, and endowments that affect the income-generation side alone can be replaced by predetermined income in the health and nutrient demand relations. If the nature of one's occupation and one's productivity directly interact with one's health and nutrition, however, the separable case may not be as common as often is assumed.

We structure our presentation of this model "as if" the household maximizes a single preference function subject to a set of constraints.[3] For simplicity, we also consider a one-period model under certainty. Of course the period may be long, so long lags such as the impact of some occupational choices on health [say, such as analyzed by Bartel and Taubman (1979) for the United States] can fit within this framework. Uncertainty is pervasive in the real world with regard to many long-run health effects of a myriad of choices, from diet to occupation to residential location. Within a simple neoclassical household model the impact of the introduction of uncertainty given risk aversion, ceteris paribus, would be that people would tend to shy away from more uncertain outcomes as compared with

---

[3]This assumption bothers some who think it is a misleading abstraction of the bargaining and negotiations that actually occur in the household [e.g. Folbre (1983, 1986), Jones (1983)] and that instead bargaining models should be used, such as developed by Manser and Brown (1980) and McElroy and Horney (1981). For most purposes given generally available data (though not including questions of household formation and dissolution) and for virtually all purposes of this review, the alternative bargaining model has no different implications for empirical specification since the same structural and reduced-form relations for health and nutrition result [e.g. Rosenzweig and Schultz (1984)]. The interpretation of some variables, however, might differ to the extent that such variables reflect the bargaining power of different household members instead of the productivity of their human capital. One potential contribution to our understanding would be to collect data that permitted the empirical distinction between maximization of a joint utility function and a bargaining framework and to test empirically how important the difference is. For example, one could explore if it made a difference in the reduced-form demand relations to (from) whom in the household extra income were given (taken away). However, such income would have to be distributed randomly and *not* be associated with human capital directly or indirectly (e.g. through the number of children) in order to be able to identify from cross-sectional data between bargaining models with their emphasis on bargaining strength emanating from the income controlled by an individual and the shadow prices associated with human capital that are emphasized in neoclassical household models with an unified utility function. Therefore, for instance, analysis that assumes that women with higher wages have more bargaining power as in some of the studies reviewed by Folbre (1986) does *not* provide support for the bargaining models relative to the unified utility function model since higher wages change the opportunity cost of women's time. Jones' (1983) study is another example of the identification difficulty. She argues that evidence of allocative inefficiency within households supports the bargaining model interpretation since such inefficiency might reflect bargaining strategies by household members. But there also is considerable evidence that is consistent with the possibility that allocative inefficiencies reflect human capital inadequacies, as is reviewed in Schultz (1975).

more certain ones – the more so the greater their risk aversion. The impact of uncertainty on decisions pertaining to health and nutrition indeed might be an interesting one to explore. But we are unaware of any efforts to do so to date in the economic development literature on health and nutrition, so we abstract from uncertainty in what follows.

We turn now to an algebraic statement of the one-period, household-firm model with constrained maximization of a joint utility function. We emphasize, however, that the objective of the general form of the model that we present is not necessarily to derive a priori testable predictions of household responses to exogenous shocks. The model is far too complicated for such exercises. Testable predictions can be derived only if one is willing to simplify the assumptions in the model considerably and probably unrealistically. Instead, our objective in presenting the general model is to distinguish the endogenous variables from the exogenous ones under our assumptions, to guide the choice of right-side variables in estimated production and demand relations, to indicate what instruments should be used for endogenous variables in estimating structural relations, and to suggest what variables may be missing from estimated relations in the literature. In other words, our basic purpose is to indicate how the available empirical estimates of health, nutrition, mortality and health-care determinants and of the impact of health, mortality and nutrition on labor productivity and on fertility fit into a household decision-making framework.

2.1.1. Household preference functions

Assume that the household has a preference function:

$$U = U\left(H^i, C^{\mathrm{p}}, C^i, T_{\mathrm{L}}^i, E^{i|c}, S; \xi\right), \quad i = 1, \dots, I, \tag{1}$$

where

H^i	is the health of household member i,
C^i	is the consumption of household member i, with the superscript p referring to household pure public goods,
T_{L}^i	is the leisure time of household member i,
$E^{i|c}$	is the education of household child i,
S	is the number of surviving children,
ξ	are taste norms, and
I	is the number of individuals in the household.

(All of these variables and others defined below may be vectors with multiple dimensions.)

Utility is presumed to depend on the health of each of the household individuals, with a negative impact of poor health and mortality.[4] Pure public goods consumption and private consumption and leisure[5] of each household member have positive impact. An individual's health may affect critically the extent of enjoyment of both consumption and leisure, so sensible explicit forms of the utility function include interactions of health with consumption and with leisure. The education of each child is included because of possible altrustic interests of the parents, concern about the child's expected prospects as an adult which may affect the parents' material well-being in their old age, or as a proxy for the child's future consumption or utility in a multiperiod model.[6] The number of surviving children is presumed to improve parental welfare (perhaps with diminishing returns) whether for altrustic, insurance, or other reasons. The utility function, finally, is conditional on norms. Most economists assume that these norms are exogenous, though some have considered the implications of intergenerational or intragenerational endogenous norms [e.g. Easterlin, Pollak and Wachter (1980)]. If norms are endogenous, empirical identification of structural effects and private welfare analysis both are much more difficult than if norms are exogenous. If parental schooling affects these norms, for example, it becomes very difficult to identify possible productivity effects of parental schooling on health and nutrition in reduced-form health and nutrition demand functions (see below). And whether schooling has a productivity or a norm impact may make a great deal of difference in making positive or normative conclusions about policy impacts.

The preference function in (1) is maximized subject to two sets of constraints, given assets and prices.

The first set of constraints is a set of production functions. These production functions, in turn, can be subdivided into three categories: ones that produce health and nutrition, ones in which health and nutrition affect other outcomes, and ones in which health and nutrition do not enter. We discuss the first two of these categories.

2.1.2. Production functions determining health, mortality and nutrient intakes

The *health* of the *i*th individual is produced by a number of choices relating to the consumption and time use of that individual, the education of that individual

---

[4] The utility function generally has arguments of living household members, but mortality may enter because, for example, infant and child mortality may reduce the utility of surviving household members. Also see footnote 9 below.

[5] We make the standard assumptions that nonleisure time (i.e. time working) is not differentiated with respect to its impact on utility. A more complicated formulation with the nature of work time having a direct impact on utility would not add to the analysis of existing studies.

[6] Though schooling may not be a very good proxy if parents also transfer assets to their children or if endowments (genetic and otherwise) are important in determining child quality. See Behrman (1987a).

health-related inputs, the failure to control for simultaneously determined health inputs in the estimation of the health production function may bias downward the estimated health impact of such inputs.[10] Exogenous variables, such as the market prices discussed below, should be used with simultaneous estimation techniques to avoid simultaneity biases. Second, there are a number of variables on the right-hand-side of these relations that often are not observed, e.g. time use and endowments. If these variables are correlated with the included variables, omitted variable bias may be widespread. If households with better unobserved endowments tend to have more-educated mothers, for example, the estimated impact of mother's education in health and mortality is upward biased.[11] Third, the relations may differ for different types of individuals in the same household and the distribution of inputs among and individuals may not be uniform. Therefore estimates based on household averages may be misleading. If, for example, marginal nutrient increases are consumed primarily by prime-age adult males (either because of power relations within the household or because of high productivity returns), then average household nutrient demand relations are not very informative about what happens to nutrient intakes, say, for prime-age males or infant girls if household income increases. Fourth, the above productions functions are presented for simplicity in a one-period framework. But in empirical applications the nature of lagged responses may be critical for understanding long gestations and expectational formation. If lagged responses in health to nutrients, to illustrate, are not well represented, empirical estimates may understate the health impact of better nutrition.

There are not many econometric studies of the nutrient production function in relation (4). Instead, in most empirical work this relation is reduced to a weighted average of food intakes by using standard nutrient/food conversion factors, thus supressing all but the food components of C^i. This procedure means that nutrient intakes are measured with error that is systematically associated with the last three variables in (4). To the extent that this error is randomly associated with nutrient intakes, if nutrients are right-hand-side variables as in the estimation of health production functions, the impact of nutrients is likely to be underestimated, and the direct health impact of variables such as the mother's education, her time spent in health-related activities, and the household endowment over-estimated.

---

[10] There also may be biases in the estimates of other parameters, but it is difficult to make any general statement about the magnitude and direction of such biases. See any standard econometrics text.

[11] Any correlation between the omitted variables and included predetermined variables (e.g. schooling in many studies) also means that the variations in the residuals are biased estimates of the variations in the unobserved variables. Thus, unobserved exogenous impacts of, say, endowments *cannot* be identified with the estimated structural residuals, as proposed in various studies [e.g. Rosenzweig and Schultz (1983b)], unless the unobserved variables *truly* are uncorrelated with right-hand-side variables.

2.1.3. Production functions with health and nutrients as inputs

Health and nutrient effects on labor productivity and on fertility are frequently postulated. Two types of relevant labor market or income-generation production functions are particularly important. The *wage* (P_L^i) of the ith individual reflects a maximizing choice given the individual's characteristics and the labor market characteristics (or community endowments):

$$P_L^i = P_L\left(H^i, N^i, E^i, \eta, \theta\right), \tag{5}$$

where

θ refers to community characteristics, including – but not limited to – labor market conditions,

P_L^i is the wage of the ith individual, and all other variables are defined above.

The *household firm/farm production function* depends upon the characteristics of all individuals in the household who work on these activities, capital stock (K, including land), intermediate inputs (A), hired labor (L^*) used in the production process and the household/firm environment (Ω):

$$Y^h = Y\left(H^i, N^i, E^i, T_F^i, \eta^i, K, A, L^*, \Omega\right), \quad i = 1, \ldots, I, \tag{6}$$

where

Y^h is the household firm/farm product,

K is the capital stock (including land) used in the firm/farm production process, part of which may be owned by the household (K^h) and the rest of which may be rented (K^*),

T_F^i is the time of the ith household member spent on household firm/farm production,

A are the intermediate inputs used in firm/farm production,

L^* is the effective hired labor used in firm/farm production, and all other variables have been defined above.

Health and nutrition enter into both of these relations in the hypothesis of Leibenstein (1957), Mazumdar (1959), Stiglitz (1976), Bliss and Stern (1978) and others that better health and nutrition may increase labor productivity. Better nutrition may work indirectly through improving health status, but also may permit greater productivity through greater energy expenditure without altering on-going health status, so it is included as a separate variable.

Health and nutrition also may enter into the production function for *births* (B):

$$B^{mf} = B\left(H^m, H^f, N^m, N^f, \eta^m, \eta^f, C_C, E^m, E^f, \xi\right), \tag{7}$$

where C_C is contraceptive use or other birth control efforts, and the superscripts m and f refer to the mother and to the father.

Births are determined by the health, nutrition, and endowments of the parents because such characteristics may affect both fecundity and frequency of intercourse. Taste norms also may affect the latter. For a given frequency of intercourse, the extent of conscious birth-control efforts affects the probability of conception, though the success of such birth-control efforts may depend on the education of the users. Births, like mortalities, affect household utility by changing family size.

For the estimation of the impact of health and nutrition in these production functions, the implications are similar to those above: health and nutrition and other endogenous variables should be treated as simultaneously determined to avoid simultaneity bias since health and nutrition well may be greater due to higher income if productivity is greater. Omitted variable bias due to unobserved endowments may be a problem with the result, for example, that greater productivity wrongly may be attributed to better health if better health is associated with unobserved endowments such as abilities that increase productivity.[12] Aggregation of the household level may be misleading if, for example, marginal nutrients are concentrated among workers (or vice versa). Lags may be critical for understading real-world relations.

2.1.4. Full-income constraint

The second set of constraints are the time and income constraints that can be combined into a full-income constraint:[13]

$$\sum P_L^i T_W^i + R + P_Y Y^h - PA - P_L^* L^* - \sum P_L^i T_F^i - dK^h - rK^* + \sum T^i P_L^i$$

$$= P_C C + P_F C_F + \sum_{i=1}^{I_C} P_E E^i$$

$$+ \sum P_L^i \left(T^i - T_F^i - T_W^i - T_H^i - T_E^i \right), \tag{8}$$

where

r is the rental rate on hired capital,
d is the depreciation rate on capital,
T^i is total time of the ith individual,
T_W^i is the labor-market work time of the ith individual,
T_E^i is the school time of the ith child,
R is transfers minus taxes (assumed to be lump-sum for simplicity), and
P_j refers to different prices.

---

[12]And once again, structural residuals may not be good representations of unobserved endowments if such endowments are correlated with observed variables such as schooling as often would seem plausible.

[13]Since the model is a one-period model, for simplicity we ignore savings and investment.

2.1.5. Reduced-form demand relations

Under the assumption that the underlying functions have desirable properties so that an internal maximum is obtained,[14] the constrained maximization of preferences leads to a set of reduced-form demand functions. The left-hand-side variables are all of the endogenous variables in the system for the household. The right-hand-side variables are all of the exogenous (to the household) prices, endowments, transfers minus taxes, and predetermined wealth:[15]

$$Z = f(V), \tag{9}$$

where

$$Z = \left(H^i, N^i, C^i, C^i_{\mathrm{B}}, C_{\mathrm{F}}, P^i_{\mathrm{L}}, T_{\mathrm{H}}, Y^h, T^i_{\mathrm{L}}, T^i_{\mathrm{W}}, T^{i|c}_{\mathrm{E}}, L^*, A, E^{i|c}, B, M \right),$$

and

$$V = \left(P_{\mathrm{C}}, P_{\mathrm{F}}, P_{\mathrm{E}}, P^*_{\mathrm{L}}, P_{\mathrm{A}}, P_{\mathrm{Y}}, r, P_K, E^{i|a}, \eta^i, \Omega, \theta, \xi, R, K^h, \Sigma, d \right).$$

Estimation of the reduced-form relations usually does not provide much information about the structural coefficients in (2)–(7), but it does provide a consistent framework within which to examine the impact of changes in market prices, endowments, and policies on the health- and nutrition-related consumption of different types of individuals. Estimates of such reduced-form demand relations for health, nutrition and other health-related inputs are fairly common (see Sections 4.1 and 4.2).

Several characteristics of these reduced forms merit emphasis. First, all of the exogenous prices – for all consumption goods, birth control, education, hired labor and capital, intermediate inputs and the firm/farm product – enter into the determination of each of the endogenous variables. Thus, health, for example, depends inter alia on the prices of all consumption goods and services and of all farm/firm products and inputs, not just on food and direct health-related input prices. Only if markets are sufficiently complete and if household members' firm/farm labor productivities and wages are independent of household consumption choices can the separability between production and consumption be invoked to obtain standard demand functions; in this case net income can replace all the production-related prices and assets, though of course all of the

---

[14] In some cases this may be a strong assumption since corner solutions with, say, zero values of certain health-related inputs may occur, which complicates estimation.

[15] We write the reduced-form relations as being dependent on predetermined tastes as is standard practice among most economists. If tastes are endogenous [e.g. Easterlin, Pollak and Wachter (1980)], identification of productivity versus taste effects becomes difficult.

consumption prices and household production related assets remain. Empirically, of course, it is difficult, if not impossible, to include the full range of relevant prices. Omitted variable biases possibly result. For example, if farm/firm product prices are high and are positively associated with food prices but excluded from the estimation, the estimated impact of food prices on nutrient intake and on health may be biased towards zero. Second, if wages are endogenous as is posited in (5), they do *not* enter into the reduced forms as right-hand-side variables. In such a case individual wages *cannot* be used to represent the predetermined opportunity cost of time as Rosenzweig (1985) and others have suggested.[16] Third, *all* of the predetermined assets enter into *all* of the reduced-form relations. The endowments of the adults and the production assets of the firm/farm, for example, have an effect on the health and nutrient intakes of children in the household. Moreover, a number of the components of the endowments – for instance genetic dimensions of η^i and some environmental dimensions of Ω and θ – usually are not observed in socioeconomic data sets. Their exclusion may cause omitted variable bias in microestimates of health and nutrition reduced-form determinants if they are correlated with observed variables, which often may be the case, for example, for education of adults. Note that tastes may be just another form of endowments in this regard. Fourth, governmental policies affect health and nutrition primarily through prices, community endowments, and income transfers. Policies acting through prices include free or subsidized provision of health services, but also any other policies that affect *any* of the prices on the right-hand-side of (9), such as fertilizer subsidies or import tariffs and quotas. Policies may alter community endowments through public work programs and malaria and other disease control; to the extent that individuals can change the relevant community endowments through migration, however, these endowments are endogenous. Income transfer policies, of course, work through changing the budget constraint. Fifth, private firms and farms also alter the environment in which the household operates, most notably through the labor market, but also through other markets and through the community endowments. Technical choices made by such entities affect the wage and occupational choices of households and the environment in which the household members live and work, all with feedback on the health and nutrition of individuals in the household. The impact of Union Carbide on Bhopal, both before and after the 1984 disaster, provides a vivid example. Sixth, different individuals in the same household may be affected differently by an exogenous change in prices or endowments. Therefore analysis at the household level of

---

[16] If wages are endogenous, moreover, their reduced-form determinants include *all* prices and *all* predetermined assets (i.e. everything in V), which means that these variables *cannot* be used to identify labor force participation determinants and possible selectivity as in the widely used Heckman (1976) procedure (except for functional form differences, which seems a weak reed on which to base identification).

aggregation may not be very informative about what happens, for example, to infant girls. On the other hand, successful targeting of nutrients or other health-related inputs to particular individuals may be very difficult if resources are fungible within the household. Seventh, in empirical applications, once again, correct specification of lag structures may be important both because of gestation periods and because of expectational formation. For an example of the latter, investment in children's health may be of interest in part because of expected labor market returns when the children become adults. If so, some representation of the expected returns needs to be included among the right-hand-side variables in the reduced-form relations. Eighth, different groups of households may have different reduced-form relations because the constraints are not well represented in the reduced forms. For example, consider the situation in which all households receive a subsidized food ration that they *cannot* resell in the open market.[17] Then the households can be classified into three groups: those who buy their entire food ration and more in the open market, those who buy just the rationed amount, and those who buy only a part of their ration. If there is a small increase in the rationed commodity, the first household type has just an income effect, the second buys just the extra ration, and the third is unaffected. Thus, the same change in the exogenous ration produces different responses in these three household groups because of the preclusion against resale of the rationed food. Either the resale preclusion need be included in the reduced-form relations explicitly, or relations of the three household groups need to be estimated separately. Ninth, if enough structure is imposed on the underlying structural relations, there may be restrictions on the reduced-form coefficients.

2.1.6. Quasi-reduced forms

In addition to empirical estimates of production functions which determine health and nutrition and in which health and nutrition are determinants of other outcomes and of reduced-form demand relations for health and nutrition, there are many estimates of quasi-reduced forms in which health or nutrition is posited to be determined by some inputs from the structural production function (e.g. health-related inputs like innoculations or good water) and some variables from reduced-form demand relations (e.g. income). Such quasi-reduced forms would seem to be of limited interest because they generally neither reveal all of the structural parameters nor the total impact of exogenous changes. If they are to be estimated, however, the simultaneity of right-hand-side endogenous variables should be controlled in the estimation. Also, as in the estimates of production function and of reduced-form demand relations, omitted variable bias, aggregation and correct specification of lags may be problems.

---

[17]We thank T.N. Srinivasan for this example.

2.2. Supply considerations

Household or individual demand for health, nutrients and other health-related inputs are aggregated to obtain total market demand. On the other side of markets for health-related inputs are supplies. There are not special considerations on the supply side except that certain market failures may be more common for health-related inputs than for many other goods and services and there may be more of a tendency to attempt to use governmental policies in such markets to pursue distributional goals than in many other markets. Market failures may be more common because of the extensive public good element in some health inputs (e.g. control of contagious diseases) and the difficulty in privatizing the returns to information about health practices (e.g. about oral rehydration techniques). Internal efficiencies may be relatively difficult to obtain in the production of certain health-related inputs because of information problems (e.g. about the quality of drugs), and because of governmental regulations adopted ostensibly to maintain quality or for distributional purposes. Distributional concerns are reflected in the subsidization of health-related inputs such as food or noncontagious curative medicine for which there are not obvious market failures. The provision of many drugs may be affected by patients, limited information about technology, the behavior of multinational companies, and developing country policies regarding such companies. Only recently has there been almost any effort to clarify systematically to what extent a particular health-related input has purely private returns and the efficiency versus distributional motives for various policies [e.g. de Ferranti (1985), Jimenez (1984, 1986)].

2.3. Macro or aggregate considerations

At a very general level, most the macro demand or production function considerations are obtained basically by aggregating over the micro factors considered for individuals and households. Four important observations, however, need to be made about this aggregation.

First, distribution of income or wealth may make a great deal of difference for health and nutrition. Sen (1981a, 1981b), for instance, highlights this point in his discussion of nutrition and real purchasing power (or what he calls entitlements). Given the concentration of inadequate health and nutrition in the left-hand tail of the income distribution, analysis of averages over large groups may be misleading. In such analysis, in fact, some variables such as literacy rates may in part be proxies for distribution rather than only representing their purported effects.

Second, some variables that are exogenous to households may be endogenous at a more aggregate level. An example may be the nature of community endowments and prices in so far as they are affected by governmental policies, which in turn depend on total income of the society.

Third, the more aggregate analysis has at least one advantage in that random errors tend to average out. However, systematic errors which the micro discussion suggests may be important (e.g. due to unobserved endowments) still may cause problems.

Fourth, some aggregate relations appear to be aggregate representations of production functions or reduced-form demand relations, but others appear to be market reduced forms in which both demand and supply factors are combined. Satisfactory interpretation of such relations is difficult.

3. Measurement and estimation problems in health and nutrition relations

There are basic definition and related measurement problems regarding health and nutrition that underlie some of the ambiguities and controversies in the literature and in policy formation. There also are problems with empirical representations of the relevant prices, health-related inputs, and assets for the relations discussed in the previous section. Finally, several major econometric problems are ubiquitous in empirical studies attempting to relate health, nutrition, and socioeconomic variables. We now review some of these issues.

3.1. Measurement of health status

Health status in relations (2), (3), (5), (6), (7), and (9) above is not directly observed. Representation of health status in micro empirical studies generally is by: (i) clinical measures of bodily attributes; (ii) anthropometric measures of height, weight, triceps skinfold thickness, arm circumference, etc.; (iii) respondent-reported disease symptoms, mortality histories, and general health evaluation; and (iv) reports on incapacity for undertaking normal respondent activities. These measures differ significantly in regard to their costs and the extent of measurement error. They also may refer to different dimensions of health status, rather than a unidimensional construct; if so, measurement errors may be dependent on the dimension of health status that is relevant for a particular study.

The four categories of health status measurement indicated above are in order of decreasing data collection costs for most developing countries. Rarely do socioeconomic data sets of any size have health-status measures of the first type due in part to the collection costs. Anthropometric measures are somewhat more common, but still relatively rare due in part to collection costs. More common are the self-reports (or reports on other individuals, such as children) in the last two categories, for which the collection costs are about the same as for other respondent-reported socioeconomic census or survey data. Though collecting some sort of measures of health status seems to be increasingly common in socioeconomic data collection efforts, in many – probably the majority of existing socioeconomic data sets – no, or virtually no representation of health status is included. Conversely in many health-oriented data sets, information on socioeconomic variables that is needed to estimated reduced-form demand or structural production function relations usually is not present. Tradeoffs obviously exist among sample size, data completeness, sample variance and accuracy, but many existing data sets do not seem to have a good balance from the point of view of analyzing health and nutrition and development.

Measurement errors in some narrow sense probably tend to be less for the first two categories in which outsiders take "scientific-objective" readings. However, social scientists, out of ignorance or out of naive admiration for "more scientific" disciplines, quite possibly overstate the accuracy of such measurements. Measurement error is unavoidable even for clinical readings and anthropometric measurements. Moreover, the relation between accurately measured bodily attributes and health status of the sort that affects an individual's welfare [i.e. enters into the utility function in relation (1)] probably is less tight than often presumed, and may be culturally determined [e.g. Low (1984)]. Furthermore, the anthropometric measures and some of the other measures of bodily attributes often are interpretable as indicators of health status only with comparison to some reference group, though this is not the case for exploring some productivity effects of health. But such comparisons raise basic questions about the appropriate standards that are akin to those discussed below with regard to nutritional status. Some studies use gender–age standards defined from the sample data themselves, which permits relative comparisons within the sample, but not an indication of absolute health status relative to other populations. Other studies use as standards the sample statistics from supposedly healthy populations, such as healthy individuals in United States, though there has been a tendency in recent years to develop standards for populations more similar to those under study. But the use of standards such as those based on U.S. samples raises the question of whether people may not be, in Seckler's (1982) terms, "small but healthy".[18] Why should, for example, North American or Northern European height and weight distributions indicate desirable standards for Africans, South Asians, or Latin Americans? Of course, the use of such reference standards may overstate health problems in the developing countries, which practice may or may not be misleading regarding the analysis of the determinants of health status as in

---

[18] Which raises another question about the possible detrimental effects of the situation which led (at least the survivors) to be small, even if perhaps healthy. For a critical survey of the "small but healthy" hypothesis, see McGuire and Austin (1986).

relation (2) or the impact of health status on various outcomes as in relations (5) and (6). If, for example, the reference used were always exactly 130 percent of the appropriate standard, this would not cause biases in estimates of elasticities from relations such as (2), (5), and (6). On the other hand, if the difference between the standards used and the appropriate standards varies systematically with gender or age and if other observed characteristics in relations such as (2), (5), and (7) are associated systematically with gender or age, the coefficients of such characteristics could be biased by the standardization procedure. Moreover, for relations exploring the impact of health such as (6), even if the standardization error is random across gender and age categories, it tends to bias the estimated impact of health towards zero as in the classical errors-in-variable model. Finally, independent of what standards are used, there is a question for multivariate regression analysis (as opposed to simple characterizations of health status) of whether the marginal relations between such indicators and true health status is constant over the range of observations as is assumed in much such analysis. That is to say, is someone at 150 percent of the weight standard twice as well off as someone at 75 percent of the standard? Often – such as with respect to weight – the answer to this question would seem to be negative.

Respondents' reports are subject to better known (among social scientists, at least) measurement errors due to incorrect self-diagnosis of health status and to recall error. Such diagnoses may be conditioned, for example, by education, as is suggested by the results presented by Wolfe and Behrman (1984). They also are in part culturally determined as emphasized by Low (1984). What is "normal" or "good" health in the Sahael might not be normal or good in Korea. Moreover, within a given culture, some of these responses are likely to be conditioned by socioeconomic status. Whether one is healthy enough to perform normal duties, for example, is likely to be endogenous, so that an individual with a given objective health status is more likely to try to perform his or her normal activities if he or she is from a poorer household than if he or she is from a richer household due to diminishing marginal utility of consumption goods in the utility function of relation (1). If so, such respondent reports understate the extent of health problems among the poor, understate the health improvements that occur with income gains, and probably cause biases in estimates of both the determinants and impact of health.

The existence of all of these problems with the micro representations of health status leads to caution for the researcher and for the user of the research results. Since such health status measures are inherently imperfect, it also suggests the advantages of using a multiplicity of them to represent health status in empirical analysis. Wolfe and Behrman (1984, 1986b), Behrman and Wolfe (1987), and Behrman and Deolalikar (1987d) are recent examples in which this strategy has been followed in analysis of health in developing economies by using a latent variable representation of health status with a number of imperfect indicators.

Their results suggest that the latent variable representation of health status may lead to a different understanding of the determinants of, and role of, health than do many of the frequently used anthropometric and respondent-reported health indicators of health status in isolation. Their results, of course, are conditional on their overall model specifications and the health indicators available to them, so further explorations along these lines with different health indicators for different populations might be valuable.

For aggregate studies the basic indicators of health status that have been used are life expectancies (particularly at birth) and mortality rates (particularly for infants and children). These data are constructed from census and survey micro data and standard demographic procedures. While the health status that enters into relations such as (1), (2), (5), (6), and (9) above is likely to be related positively with life expectancy and negatively with mortality rates, the relationships are hardly likely to be perfect. For given life expectancies it is easy to conceive of very different health statuses prevailing due to very different morbidity experiences. It would be of value to explore the associations between these aggregate indicators of health status utilized for aggregate analysis and micro indicators such as those discussed above. We are unaware of such explorations.

3.2. Measurement of nutrient intakes and nutritional status

There are issues and ambiguity on several levels about what is meant by nutritional status.

On one level there seems to be confusion between using nutritional status on one hand to refer to nutrient intakes as we have done in relations (2), (4), and (9) and as do Reutlinger and Selowsky (1976), Srinivasan (1981), and many others and – on the other hand – to refer to health outcomes that are thought to be related closely to nutrient intakes, particularly anthropometric measures, as do Horton (1984) and many nutritionists. If indeed there are many non-nutrient determinants of health status as we posit in relation (2) – such as water supply, individual and household endowments, community endowments, time devoted to health-related activities, health-care inputs related to preventative and curative medicine, education – then the latter usage seems misleading to us. Why should some of a multitude of inputs in the production of health status be characterized as representing such health status? Though it is simply a matter of definition, therefore, we think it clearer to use nutritional status in the former way to refer to nutrient inputs and we use the term in this way in what follows. To attempt to increase clarity, however, we use "nutrient intake" or "nutrients" instead of "nutritional status".

A second possible measurement problem has to do with the use of fixed conversion factors for food with heterogeneous nutrient qualities. If there is substantial heterogeneity in nutrient quality among foods defined as narrowly as "rice", as appears to be the case, then the use of fixed nutrient to food conversion factors may lead to substantial misrepresentation of the impact of changed income on nutrient intakes. Shah (1983) and Behrman and Wolfe (1984a), for example, conjecture that nutrient elasticities with respect to income calculated by applying fixed conversion factors to food elasticities may overstate substantially true nutrient elasticities since, for marginal food expenditures, other food attributes – taste, appearance, status value, degree of processing – may be much more important than nutrients.[19] Behrman and Deolalikar (1987c, 1987e) provide estimates consistent with this conjecture for a relatively poor sample from rural south India and for an international cross-section sample (see Section 4.2 below).

A third possible nutrient measurement problem is that certain critical data are available only on, or at least used only on, an aggregate level. Most striking in this regard are the studies such as those by Reutlinger and Selowsky (1976) and Berg (1981) that characterize malnutrition for large groups of people based on a comparison of their *average* nutrient intakes with *average* nutrient requirements. Such studies ignore the fact that there are distributions of nutrient intakes and requirements so that when the mean intake meets (or falls short of) the nutrient standard, there are likely to be substantial numbers of individuals above and below that standard. Clearly, such a procedure misrepresents whether or not many members of a given developing country group meet the nutrient requirements. While there obviously is such a problem with aggregate data for nations, regions, or other large groups, it also may be a problem for many microdata sets. Such data often are based on total household intakes of nutrients, but there appears to be substantial intrahousehold variations in nutrient intakes in the relatively few data sets that have such measures [see Behrman and Deolalikar (1987d), Behrman (1987a, 1987c, 1988), Horton (1984) and the references therein]. Of course the data on individual nutrient intakes probably is subject to considerable measurement error, which may be systematically associated with characteristics such as age or the education of the respondent. If so, such data may not reflect true nutrient distribution patterns within households.

More contentious are problems in defining nutritional "norms", "requirements" or "standards", and therefore "malnutrition". Such definitions are important in assessing the nature and extent of malnutrition in the developing world and in analyzing the determinants of, and the impact of, nutrition. Payne and Culter (1984) distinguish between two paradigms for nutrient requirements.

The first is the "establishment" or the "genetic potential model" in which the body is self-regulating and self-optimizing, the optimal diet depends on inherent

---

[19] Which is one reason that the foods consumed, and not the nutrients consumed, are included in the preference function in relation (1).

genetic characteristics that differ among individuals, the "optimal" diet for given genetic characteristics can be determined from the diet of those whose food choices effectively are unconstrained in well-fed populations, and malnutrition can be measured in a straightforward manner by shortcomings in comparison with such "optimal" diets. Estimates of calorie deficiencies based on this approach have suggested massive malnourishment in the developing world.

The second paradigm is the "individual adaptability model" emphasized by Payne (1975), Sukhatme (1977, 1982), Sukhatme and Margen (1978), Srinivasan (1981, 1985) and Seckler (1980, 1982) in which individuals adapt to their environment, with differences among individuals in the extent to which they are able to adjust in response to environmental stresses and in the efficiency with which they convert nutrient intakes to energy (partly due to genetic differences, but also due to the accumulative effects of past adjustments), with substantial interpersonal and intrapersonal variations, with productivity dependent on nutrition as well as vice versa, and with no fixed optimal levels. Adaptation includes shorter-run adjustment to variations over time in energy intakes and expenditures around unchanging means (homeostatis) and longer-run adjustments to changes in the means through changes in body weight.[20] Within this paradigm, the term "nutrient requirements" has a much less precise meaning than with the genetic potential paradigm since there is no true optimal. Certainly the nutrient intakes of healthy whites in industrialized countries, the standard used in many studies, do not provide an obvious reference standard. Moreover, there is the implication that malnutrition estimates based on the genetic potential paradigm are likely to be substantially overstated because of their failure to recognize individual adaptability.

Empirical evidence to discriminate between the two paradigms is very limited. Increasingly those such as Sukhatme, Srinivasan, Payne, and Seckler interpret the evidence to point to individual adaptations to the nutritional situation, though in many cases sample sizes are quite small, not obviously representative, and the evidence seems limited. If such adaptations do occur within limits, they raise questions about the use of international standards for characterizing the extent of malnutrition and, as Srinivasan has emphasized, the identification of what segments in a population are malnourished. They also raise questions about the extent of malnutrition in developing countries. Sukhatme (1977), for example, estimates that the estimated incidence of poverty in India declines from 50 to 25 percent in urban areas and from 40 to 15 percent in rural areas if allowance is made for variations in individual calorie requirements instead of using a poverty line based on average calorie requirements, but his estimates are not unchal-

---

[20] Sometimes there also appears to be an even longer-run genetic adaptation to environmental changes in this literature, but this possibility is emphasized less and seems to be relatively speculative.

lenged.[21] Parallel to the discussion above about standardizing health status indicators for age and gender, such standardization may or may not cause biases in our understanding of the impact of nutrients in relations such as (2) and in the determinants of nutrient intakes in relations such as (4) and (9).

3.3. Measurement of non-nutrient health-related inputs

We include in the health production function of relation (2) a number of non-nutrient health determinants. These may range from individual preventative and curvative inputs, such as innoculations and formal medical care, to household public goods inputs, such as shelter and water supply, to the community environment regarding matters such as control of contagious diseases and parasites and availability of formal medical care facilities. Empirical representations of these inputs also range broadly. Two points seem useful to emphasize about these measures.

First, like nutrient intakes, these are *inputs* into the health production process in relation (2), not measures of health status itself, though sometimes they are interpreted to represent health status. Care should be taken not to misidentify such inputs as indicators of health outputs. Examples exist in which factors such as education increase the use of such inputs, but do not measurably improve health status [e.g. Wolfe and Behrman (1984)].

---

[21] There is a large literature which seeks to establish poverty lines and measure the incidence of poverty on the basis of minimum cost diets that satisfy calorie requirements [Dandekar and Rath (1971), Bardhan and Srinivasan (1974)]. Greer and Thorbecke (1986) have proposed a new way of establishing a food poverty line which takes into account regional food preferences and prices, and have applied this methodology to study the incidence of poverty in Kenya. In a paper that we received as we were completing the final version of this chapter, Kakwani (1986a) reviews much of the literature on measuring undernutrition, develops a new class of undernutrition measures that incorporates the extent of undernourishment (and not just whether an individual is undernourished), explores what can be said about the ranking of populations according to the degree of undernutrition if the distribution of calorie requirement is completely unknown, develops upper and lower bounds on the head-count measure of undernutrition if only the mean requirement is known and the distribution of requirements is assumed to be uniform or normal, criticizes the Sukhatme procedure for defining undernutrition to be nutrition intakes less than two standard deviations below the mean requirements, and presents empirical estimates for India that suggest much broader malnutrition than do Sukhatme's estimates primarily because Sukhatme ranked households by expenditures rather than by calories, Sukhatme focuses on households rather than on individuals (even though the more poorly nourished households tend to be larger), and Sukhatme uses an arbitrary threshold for undernourishment. Neither Kakwani nor Sukhatme, however, deal satisfactory with the empirical difficulty of ascertaining undernourishment or malnutrition from cross-sectional data if there is considerable intrapersonal variability, as Sukhatme and Srinivasan, among others, maintain. In such a case, just because an individual has low nutritional intakes during the sample period does not mean that he or she is poorly nourished due to persistent nutrient shortages.

Second, such inputs are in part culturally and economically determined [e.g. see Low (1984)]. Within a particular society, care must be taken in empirical analysis to consider an appropriate range of such inputs, and not just those that are identified with public health measures or curative medicine in industrialized countries.

3.4. Measurement of prices, health-related inputs, and assets

For the most part, the conceptual bases for the measurement of the prices, health-related inputs and assets that are included on the right-hand side of relations such as (2)–(7) and (9) are fairly clear, and probably clearer than the conceptual bases for health and nutrient measures. However, problems of empirical representation still often are severe for these variables. As a result, measurement error (both random and systematic) and omitted variable biases abound.

The empirical problems for prices are of several types. First, samples with interesting health and nutrition data generally do not include empirical representations of the full range of consumption and firm/farm production prices in relation (9). As a result, the impact of unobserved prices may be picked up in the estimated coefficients of observed variables, prices and otherwise. Second, usually if there are observations on prices, the observations are limited to market prices, and do not include important time costs that have to be incurred in travel and in waiting for relevant goods and services. This may be a particularly severe problem for emergency health services because such services must be obtained at the time of health emergencies. In contrast, for more routinized health inputs and other goods and services, trips for purchases may be combined with other market (and nonmarket) activities so the marginal nonmarket costs may not be so large, though queuing costs for formal nonemergency medical services often seem to be considerable. Third, available frequently used proxies for prices may be quite imperfect. For example, hospital beds and formal medical care personnel per capita may be very poor proxies for the prices of preventative and minor aliment curative care that may be critical in the health production process, though such variables may serve adequately for prices for curative care for more severe illnesses.

For health-related inputs and assets, the problems are similar. For health-related inputs, for example, time inputs often are not observed well. The difficulties in measuring or controlling for some assets – in particular individual genetic endowments, moreover, are quite severe with most data sets. Sibling data, particularly on twins, may be attractive for this purpose for use as in Behrman, Hrubec, Taubman and Wales (1980), Behrman and Wolfe (1986, 1987) and Wolfe and Behrman (1987).

3.5. Estimation problems

Our catalog of possible estimation problems is *not* meant to lead to despair about the possibility of learning anything systematic about health, nutrition, and development. These problems are hardly unique to the study of health and nutrition. Applied work in the social sciences almost always has such problems to various degrees. The art of undertaking good applied studies is to control for the most probable difficulties, see what difference they make, and to replicate studies to see how robust they are. In considering any particular study, however, it is important to be aware of the range of possible problems and to try to judge how important is each. It is for this reason that we have reviewed these problems before turning to reviews of specific studies.

First, simultaneity occurs quite often in health and nutrition studies. For example, while estimating health production functions which relate, say, anthropometric measures to nutrient intake, many studies do not recognize that the latter is subject to individual choice and likely to be endogenous. Since individuals presumably decide on nutrient intake to improve health outcomes, the disturbance term in the health production function (which might include the effects of unanticipated shocks, omitted variables, or heterogeneity) is transmitted to the nutrient demand relation. The correlation between nutrient intake and the disturbance term means that OLS estimates of the health production function are biased. Unfortunately, it is not always easy to identify the direction of the bias [Maddala (1977)].

Unfortunately, many studies propose solutions for simultaneity that are purely empirical and not guided by economic theory. Theory suggests, for example, that the reduced-form nutrient demand equation in the above example has prices and certain (exogenous) individual/household characteristics as its arguments. These should be used as instruments since they are likely to be correlated with nutrient demand, yet uncorrelated with the disturbance term in the health production function. If more than one right-hand-side variable is endogenous, then all of the appropriate reduced-form exogenous variables should be used as instruments for each such variable. Instead, many investigators make what appear to be arbitrary restrictions by precluding from the relevant set of instruments different exogenous variables for each endogenous variable.

A second econometric problem that is endemic in empirical studies on health and nutrition is the classical errors-in-variables problem. Data on health and nutrition are typically collected over short reference periods (24 hours to a week), and are often based on self-reported rather than clinically-observed symptoms. For example, one rarely has data on effective nutrient intake, which is the correct variable to include in a health production function. What most consumption surveys manage to obtain are data on food availability. Only if the cooked food is weighed as it is about to be eaten could one obtain a measure of intake, and the intervention of such measurements itself may cause data distortions. Thus, there is likely to be substantial measurement error in health and nutrition-related variables. If health/nutrition variables are right-hand-side variables, this causes bias (towards zero if the measurement errors are random) in the estimates of the effect of health/nutrition on other variables, such as productivity or wages. If these variables are dependent variables, random measurement error leads to imprecise parameter estimates. To make matters worse, the measurement error is not always random. For instance, the accuracy of reporting illness symptoms or food intake is likely to be positively related to the education of the household head or the food preparer.

One solution, used in very few empirical studies, is to explicitly model true health and nutrient consumption status as latent (or unobserved) variables, for which are observed imperfect indicators like anthropometric measures, self-reported illnesses, and nutrient availability.

A third common problem has to do with omitted variables. The genetic endowments of an individual are unobserved but important factors in most health and nutrition relations. The exclusion can cause widespread omitted variables bias in parameter estimates. Consider the case of a health production function that does not control for such unobserved effects. Since genetically better-endowed individuals are likely to utilize more nutrients, the unobserved excluded variable in this case is positively correlated with the included nutrient intake variables. As a result, the estimated elasticities of health outcomes with respect to nutrient intakes are likely to be overstated if unobserved genetic effects are not controlled.

A fourth common problem is related to sample selectivity. This arises because there may be selection rules which determine the presence of healthy or un-healthy persons in a sample. The extremely unhealthy – those for whom nutrient intake produced no positive health outcome – do not live to be enumerated in a sample. Consequently, in a health production function, for example, the esti-mated effect of nutrient intake on health outcomes is upward biased since those individuals for whom the estimated effect was too low to insure survival are not in the sample.

A fifth problem pertains to the specification of appropriate lags for adjust-ments and for expectation formation. Most theory is static and provides no guidance regarding such lags. Yet in the real world they may be critical. Estimation of the impact of nutrition on health with current data on each, for example, may miss most of the effects if in fact they are lagged considerably.

A sixth problem is that aggregation to the household level may produce misleading results for individual welfare. A small nutrition response of the household to food price increases may hide widely different responses of individ-ual members; for instance, children or women in the household may face the brunt of price increases, while adult males might be relatively protected. It is, therefore, important, wherever possible, to disaggregate the analysis beyond the level of the household.

Finally, most of the micro empirical studies reviewed below account for a limited proportion of the observed variance in the variables of interest. This is particularly the case for the studies on individual and household health determinants. Few of these studies are consistent with more than 10 percent of the interindividual or interhousehold variation in health status even after including individual and family background variables and health-care related prices. The limited explanatory power of such studies, highlights once more the problems involved in measuring and modeling health status; it is a variable which is very imperfectly observed and whose dependence on food and nutrient intake as well as on family background variables is too complicated and dynamic to be estimated well with cross-sectional data. The studies on nutrient and food consumption demand have somewhat greater explanatory power, with typical R^2's of 0.3–0.4. The studies on health/nutritional consequences have a range of explanatory powers; when multi-input agricultural production functions are estimated, a large portion of the cross-sectional variation in farm output or productivity is explained, but those studies that attempt to explain variations in economic outcomes only with health and/or nutrition variables have very low explanatory power.

However, it should be emphasized that important information *may* be obtainable about the magnitudes of critical responses, such as to prices or to policies, from relations that may be consistent with a limited portion of the variance in the outcome of interest. The critical question is not what is the proportion of explained variance, but whether there are biases in the relevant estimates due to specification errors, simultaneity or omitted variables.

4. Empirical studies of determinants of health and nutrition in developing countries

4.1. Determinants of health

Two broad categories of studies of health determinants are of particular interest: those attempting to estimate the reduced-form demand for health outcomes [H^i in eq. (9)] and health-care goods [C_H^i in eq. (9)] and those attempting to estimate the underlying health production function [eq. (2)]. Unfortunately, few researchers maintain clearly the distinction between the two. Most studies estimate hybrid demand–production functions or quasi-reduced forms for health. Not surprisingly, interpretation of the results from such studies is difficult.

4.1.1. Demand functions for health outcomes and health-care utilization

There are relatively few studies on health and health-care demand, at least compared to the number of health production function studies. Moreover, since most of the demand studies are based on cross-sectional data, few of them explicitly include market prices as explanatory variables. For the most part, they include household characteristics, income, and availability of health care, the latter, of course, being interpretable as the price of health services.

Among the micro studies, Blau (1984) estimates a demand function for age-standardized height using 1977–78 data on children under five years of age in Nicaragua. He includes the mother's age, education, urban origin, other income, and predicted formal and informal sector wage rates (corrected for selection bias) as independent variables. Blau's rationale for separating the two types of wage rates is that female informal-sector jobs in developing countries may be consistent with own childcare in a way that formal-sector jobs are not, since childcare often can be combined with informal-sector jobs. If this is indeed the case, the substitution effect of the mother's formal-sector wage rate on child health should be negative and that of the informal-sector wage rate should be zero. After allowing for a positive income effect, the gross impact on child health of the informal-sector wage rate should be greater in magnitude than that of the formal-sector wage rate. Blau's results, however, indicate the opposite: he finds the mother's (predicted) formal-sector wage rate to have a significant *positive* effect on child health and the informal-sector wage rate not to have any significant effect.

Akin et al. (1985) study the determinants of a household's decision to use medical services and its choice of a medical practitioner (i.e. whether public, private, or traditional), applying multiple-choice logit models for adults and children to data on 1903 households from 100 barangays in the Philippines. An extensive set of price variables for each of the four types of medical facilities, including the cash price of using the facility, the transport time and cost in reaching the facility, and the drug costs involved, are included as explanatory variables in the demand functions for health services. In addition, variables such as whether the sickness is covered by insurance; the value of household assets; gender, education, and urban location of the patient; and the severity of the illness are included in the demand equations. The authors obtain an almost total lack of statistical significance of any of the economic (price, time) variables. Since the pecuniary and nonpecuniary costs of consuming medical care are not trivial in the sample, results which show that these costs are not significant determinants of practitioner choice are very surprising.

Unfortunately, Akin et al. include the demand for health outcomes (namely, the severity of illness) as an explanatory variable in their demand for health-care utilization, without treating it as an endogenous variable. Indeed, they find that it is the most important (and only significant) determinant of practitioner choice. While this result is perfectly logical (since there is likely to be a segmentation in the facilities available for treating particular types of illnesses, with severe illnesses being treated in large public facilities and minor complaints by traditional medicine men), the fact that individuals have a choice' of allowing their illnesses to become severe introduces a bias in the price effects estimated by Akin et al. Indeed, it could well be the case that health-care prices do matter in determining the demand for health-care utilization and practitioner choice by influencing the degree to which individuals ignore their initial symptoms and allow their illnesses to become severe.

Birdsall and Chuhan (1986) also estimate a multiple logit system for the demand for type of curative health services in Mali. Unlike Akin et al., they find significant effects of a number of dimensions of prices – i.e. distance and quality measures. They do not explore, however, whether there are price effects on health status as opposed to the demand for health inputs.

Merrick (1985) uses infant mortality as a proxy for health outcomes in his analysis of the effect of piped water supply in Brazil on the demand for health outcomes. Although he formulates the mortality determination process in a multi-equation framework (with husband's education influencing household income; husband's and wife's education, household income, and community water *availability* influencing the household *utilization* of piped water; and husband's and wife's education, household income, and piped water utilization affecting child mortality), he estimates the system by OLS methods, arguing for recursivity among the three relations. However, he also presents reduced-form estimates of mortality (which are preferable to the OLS-estimated structural estimates); these suggest that, while piped water supply has a negative impact on infant mortality, the effect of parental education on mortality is much greater.

One study that includes a very comprehensive list of community-level infrastructural variables, most of which can be interpreted as health-care price variables, in explaining the household demand for health outcomes is that by Rosenzweig and Schultz (1982a). They use a 4 percent sample of the 1973 population census for Colombia to study the joint determinants of fertility and child mortality. Among the independent variables included in their mortality equation are the woman's age and schooling and the per capita number of hospital beds and clinics, family planning expenditures per capita, transportation time to the capital city, average daily temperature and temperature squared, price of food, and the average schooling of women aged 15 and above in the region of residence. Additionally, all the community-level variables, with the exception of the price of food and the regional schooling variable, are interacted with the woman's schooling. Separate equations are estimated for each five-year age group of women residing in rural and urban areas.

Rosenzweig and Schultz find that, in the urban areas, child mortality in families with less-educated mothers is strongly affected by public health and family planning programs. They thus conclude that "...urban public health institutions are substitutes for the health care knowledge and the management capacity that an educated mother brings to her family" [Rosenzweig and Schultz (1982a, pp. 58–59)]. They also find that, in the urban areas, clinics are a more cost-effective means of lowering child mortality than are hospitals. For the rural sector, however, they find little effect of health and family planning programs on child mortality. They attribute the lack of these effects to the greater dispersion of health and family planning programs in rural areas. In both urban and rural areas, finally, Rosenzweig and Schultz observe a strong negative effect of maternal education on child mortality.

The Rosenzweig and Schultz study is an example of a study that is relatively consistent with the model we have presented in Section 2.1. They treat health outcomes and fertility as jointly determined choice variables by households, and do not include any endogenous variables in their reduced-form demand relations. However, while the health infrastructure variables they include are exogenous to an individual household's fertility and mortality decisions, they may be endogenous with respect to the fertility and mortality experiences of a community. It is possible, and indeed very often the case, that governments choose to locate hospitals and family planning clinics in communities that have high mortality and fertility rates. In such a situation it would not be surprising to find no, or even negative, cross-sectional association between household mortality patterns and the presence of health programs, as Rosenzweig and Schultz do. It would be incorrect, however, to interpret this result as reflecting the inefficacy of governmental health programs. Moreover, they do not control for unobserved household and individual endowments, which might cause a substantial upward bias in the estimated health input of maternal education (see below).

Most of the above studies are not sensitive to intrahousehold variations in health and the differential response of the health of different members within a household to prices and income. Most studies also are not sensitive to the fact that a large proportion of households in many less-developed countries are farm households, and, as such, the omission of farm input prices and farm assets from the health demand functions is tantamount to making very restrictive assumptions about product and labor markets and about the lack of links between health and nutrient inputs on one hand and productivity on the other (see Section 2). Two recent studies that incorporate both these concerns are Pitt and Rosenzweig (1985) and Behrman and Deolalikar (1987d).

Using data on 2347 farm households from Indonesia, Pitt and Rosenzweig have estimated separate health outcome demand (or, as they call it, "illness demand") functions for husbands and wives. These functions have as arguments prices of thirteen consumption goods (foods and nonfoods); source of drinking water; availability of hospitals, family-planning clinics, public lavatories, and clinics; owned land; farm profits; and the age and education of the husband and the wife.[22] Using ordered probit equations, the authors find relatively few significant determinants of health. The authors attribute the lack of precise estimates to the definition of illness in the survey: it was self-reported (and hence subject to differences in subjective sensitivity to illness symptoms and in propensities to report them, see Section 3.1) and it was recorded over a short reference period of only one week.

Using panel data on rural south Indian households and utilizing a much wider and probably more reliable (than used by Pitt and Rosenzweig) set of health status indicators, Behrman and Deolalikar (1987d) estimate joint reduced-form health and nutrient consumption status relations which allow for differing price and income responses by different household members (namely, adult males, adult females, male children, and female children) and which control for individual-specific fixed effects. Like Behrman and Wolfe (1987) and Wolfe and Behrman (1984, 1986b), they use a latent variable representation of unobserved health status, for which they have three observed (but imperfect) indicators: (age–gender) standardized arm circumference, triceps fatfold, and weight-for-height. They find three of the six prices (namely, of rice, milk, and male labor) to have significant positive effects on health status, even with a control for income. However, they find neither a significant income effect nor significant differences in price or income responses across household members.

The positive (income constant) price effects on health status may be surprising prima facie. However, they are consistent with strong cross-price substitution effects in the underlying food demand equations toward foods with high nutrient-to-food conversion factors (see the discussion on price impacts in Section 4.2). This means that if the price of, say, milk increases, a sufficiently large increase in the demand for other foods and thereby in nutrient intake and health status is induced so that the direct deterioration in health status resulting from reduced milk consumption is more than offset by the induced increases in nutrient consumption of other high-nutrient foods.

Horton (1984) also analyzes the demand for individual health outcomes by using data on approximately 2000 predominantly rural children aged 15 or less from the Philippines. To correct for heterogeneous tastes (particularly with respect to child quality and quantity) across households, Horton explores the differences in weight-for-height and height-for-age among children *within a single family* in terms of differences in their age, gender, and birth order. She also allows some household-specific variables to enter her health demand function indirectly by specifying that the coefficient on birth order depends on maternal

---

[22] The authors treat farm profits as an exogenous variables since a Wu–Hausman specification test could not reject the production/consumption separability hypothesis.

education and total household expenditure per capita. Her results suggest that birth order has a significant adverse effect on both height-for-age and weight-for-height (such that later-born children have poorer health than earlier-born children), but that maternal education significantly weakens these adverse effects of birth order.

While differencing across individuals within a family is an attractive method for resolving the twin problems of heterogeneity across households and endogeneity of right-hand-side variables (which Horton has in her birth order variable), it purges observed household-specific and community variables such as prices and wealth as well from the health demand function. This is unfortunate since the impact of such variables on health is of policy interest. Behrman and Wolfe (1986) and Wolfe and Behrman (1987) also estimate intrafamilial deviation estimates for health and nutrition demand relations for a Nicaraguan sample, but, since their sample includes adult sisters (including half siblings), many of whom live apart from each other, they are able, unlike Horton, to retain crude price (proxied by population size of the community of residence) and income variables in their demand equations and are able to control for common unobserved childhood background characteristics of the mothers in estimates of the impact of maternal schooling. They find that, without the deviation control, mother's schooling apparently has widespread positive health and nutrition effects. But once there is a control for unobserved family-origin endowments, the impact of female schooling on female health (proxied by the number of days ill and the presence of parasitic diseases), child health (proxied by standardized height, weight, and biceps circumference), and infant mortality is not significant, although the impact on calorie and protein intake is. Their results, thus, raise doubts about standard estimates without control for unobserved mother's childhood–family background characteristics that claim to find strong positive health effects of women's schooling. They also find that mother's schooling has a significant negative effect on length of breastfeeding. Income effects are not significant in any equation, while population size (proxying food prices) has a significant negative effect on nutrition and on breastfeeding.

A somewhat different approach to intrahousehold allocation is taken by Behrman (1987c, 1988). He adopts a specific form of the preference function in relation (1) and estimates two critical parameters of these preferences from data on the distribution of individual nutrient intakes and of individual health outcomes for sibling children in rural south India. The estimation is from first-order conditions which have the advantage, conditional on the functional forms specified, that unobserved child endowments (such as inherent robustness) do not appear explicitly. The first parameter is the extent of parental inequality aversion, which indicates to what extent there is a tradeoff between distribution and productivity in the allocation of nutrients. The estimates suggest that there is a tradeoff, with significant concern about inequality, but parents act as if they are closer to pure investors in the lean season when food is relatively scarce than when food is more available. The second parameter is the extent of unequal concern, that is the extent that the preference function weights equal health outcomes differently for different children. The estimates suggest that larger weights are placed on health outcomes for boys and for older children, particularly by lower caste households, in the lean season. Thus, when food is scarcest, intrahousehold allocation of nutrients more closely follows a pure investment strategy and leaves the more vulnerable children in the household, particularly younger girls, more at risk.

The final study we review which analyzes intrahousehold variations in health outcomes is the Rosenzweig and Schultz (1982b) analysis of the determinants of male–female differentials in child survival rates in rural India using both household and district level data. They argue that the male–female survival differential depends upon the relative returns to male and female labor, since· the latter determines parental investments in male and female children. They use predicted employment rates of men and women as proxies for the economic returns to male and female labor, arguing that wage rates may not accurately reflect the shadow value of time because cultural factors such as religion and caste may prevent women from equalizing market and household marginal products. Their results are interesting: in both the household as well as the district-level samples, they find predicted female employment rates to be a significant (and negative) determinant of the male–female child survival differential. Predicted male employment rates are not significant in either sample. They thus conclude that children who are likely to be more economically productive adults receive a greater share of family resources and therefore have a greater propensity to survive.

The health demand studies reviewed above that incorporate prices have found few significant price effects in the demand for health outcomes and, in some cases, health-care utilization. This either means that prices are in fact largely irrelevant in explaining interhousehold variations in health status or that prices may matter but empirical studies have not been able to find significant price effects owing to the use of faulty methodologies or improper data. We tend to be drawn to the latter view because evidence of price responsiveness seems pervasive in other contexts and because of the limitation in the existing studies of health determination. The results of many of the studies can be discounted because they ignore probable simultaneity in right-hand-side choice variables. Almost all studies use poor proxies for health status, use inappropriate prices, and ignore the long lag with which prices may influence health in the real world. True health status may be poorly measured by reported illness or by anthropometric measures used in these empirical studies, though very limited effects are found even in the studies which try to account for the measurement problems regarding health status with multiple indicators in a latent variable framework. However, the Rosenzweig–Schultz (1982b) results for India suggest that prices different from those usually considered by most studies, namely, those related to expected labor market returns rather than food or other direct health related input prices, may be more important in determining health.[23] Finally, since health status, especially of adults, is a *cumulative* outcome of events over a long period of time, it may be poorly explained by *current* prices and income/wealth, which most studies use as explanatory variables. This suggests the need for collecting historical/retrospective data on individuals and households, confining studies on the demand for health outcomes to infants and young children for whom the lag between current and cumulative factors may not be large, or devising methods using limited lags from which the impact of longer lags can be deduced.[24]

4.1.2. Health and mortality production functions

Health production functions are much more susceptible to simultaneous-equations bias than are health demand functions because many right-hand-side variables (namely, variable inputs) are subject to individual/household choice. Unfortunately, a large majority of studies do not treat such inputs as endogenous.

There are two types of production functions that have been estimated widely: the first is the mortality production function M^i [eq. (3)], which has as its input the discrepancy between the health status, H^i, of an individual and the critical (minimum) level of health H^* (with the latter generally not represented directly). The second is the morbidity/anthropometric production function H^i [eq. (2)], which has as its inputs nutrient intakes and health-related consumption goods, among other variables. Studies of the mortality production function have been largely clinical in nature, while health production function studies have been based on social survey data.

There is a large scientific literature on the relationship between clinical measures of malnutrition (e.g. stunting and wasting) and morbidity on the one hand and mortality on the other. A few of the large number of studies that establish a link between anthropometric measures and mortality are Bairagi (1981), Chen et al. (1980), Kielmann and McCord (1978), Sommer and Lowenstein (1975), and Trowbridge and Sommer (1981). Martorell and Ho (1984)

---

[23] However Behrman (1988) reports that the addition of Rosenzweig and Schultz-type expected labor market returns to health to his preference model does not swamp nor dominate the role of preferences in exploring intrahousehold allocations of nutrients between boys and girls in rural south India.

[24] For example, conditional on particular functional forms for adjustment processes and price expectational formation, long-run responses might be deduced without long lags in the data by formulations parallel to those used for stock/flow considerations in tree crop and other capital investments [e.g. Bateman (1965), Behrman (1968)].

provide a good survey of this literature. They conclude (p. 61) that

> ...the studies reviewed here all show that severely malnourished children (i.e., those with very low anthropometric readings) have greatly increased mortality risks relative to normal children. Children with mild and moderate malnutrition (i.e., those with lower-than-average anthropometric readings) also showed increased mortality risks... Arm circumference was found to be an excellent predictor of mortality by all authors who included this measure.

Black (1984), Bradley and Keymer (1984), and Foster (1984), among others, show that morbidity, particularly in the form of parasitic and immunizable diseases (such as diarrhea, tetanus, and measles), significantly increases the risk of mortality among children and infants.

The link between nutrient and other health-related intakes and anthropometry or morbidity has been explored by two distinct types of studies. On the one hand, there are experimental studies, such as those based on the INCAP project in Guatemala (conducted between 1969 and 1971) and the Narangwal project in Punjab, India (conducted between 1968 and 1973), which have attempted to analyze the effect of nutritional supplementation programs by comparing the morbidity of individuals in villages benefiting from such programs to those in control villages not having such programs (Martorell and Ho). Using the INCAP data, Clark (1981), for example, found that the physical growth of infants (weight gain up to 12 months) was associated significantly ceteris paribus with the number of calories of atole (a high-protein–high-calorie supplementary diet introduced in one of the villages) consumed and length of breastfeeding. Using the Narangwal project data, Taylor et al. (1978) found that (controlling for factors such as age, gender, caste, season, and number and composition of siblings) children in villages receiving nutritional care, whether alone or in combination with medical care, had the highest weights and heights, those in medical care villages the next highest, and those in control villages the lowest. Chernichovsky and Kielmann (1977) used two-stage least squares with the same data as Taylor et al. to measure the impact of calorie intake on the weight of children aged 6–36 months. They found a significant positive effect of calories on weight after controlling for age and gender.

Another set of studies try to relate nutrient intakes, including breastfeeding, to anthropometric measures of physical growth and to infant mortality, using nonexperimental household survey data. Magnani et al. (1985), for example, analyze the determinants of child weight (treated as a dichotomous variable, with a value of one if the child weighs 75 percent or more of the age–gender standardized weight and zero otherwise) with a sample of 1500 children aged 1–59 months in the Philippines. Using OLS (and not logit or probit, which would be more appropriate given the dichotomous nature of the dependent variable), they find that breastfeeding ceteris paribus reduces significantly the probability of the child weighing less than 75 percent of the standardized weight. However, since breastfeeding is not treated as a choice variable in their analysis, their results are likely to be biased. Indeed, their results may simply reflect the fact that underweight children may receive priority in breastfeeding from their mothers or that the sickest children or mothers may be least able to breastfeed.

DaVanzo and Habicht (1984) exploit the panel nature of their Malaysian data by estimating a fixed-effects logit model for infant mortality. They find that decreases in the durations of both supplemented and unsupplemented breastfeeding led to an increase in infant mortality between 1956–60 and 1971–75. However, increases in maternal education and in piped water availability (particularly for women who did not breastfeed) resulted in large (and offsetting) declines in infant mortality over the same period. By estimating the model in first differences, DaVanzo and Habicht purge their estimates of unobserved household-specific health management and taste effects. However, they do not treat duration of breastfeeding as a choice variable, thus making their estimates susceptible to simultaneous-equations bias.

Similarly, Wolfe and Behrman (1987) control for unobserved family endowments by estimating child health (proxied by standardized weight, height, and arm circumference) and infant mortality production functions in intrafamily deviations for the Nicaraguan adult sister sample mentioned in the previous section. Their standard estimates (i.e. using individual data in the standard manner) suggest a strong positive impact of women's schooling on child health, though not a significant effect of calories and breastfeeding.[25] When they control for unobserved childhood–background related characteristics of the mothers through adult sister deviation estimates, however, the impact of mother's schooling no longer is significant. This suggests that in the standard estimates mother's schooling is only a proxy for her unobserved characteristics. Only the negative effect of duration of breastfeeding on child weight is significant at the 15 percent level in the deviation estimates.

In contrast, Khan (1983) attempts to correct for simultaneity in estimating the impact of *average* household per-capita calorie intake on individual standardized height and of height on the number of sickdays for a sample of Bangladeshi individuals. However, his bases for identification seem to make so little sense that it is not clear whether his simultaneous equations estimates are any better than OLS. He finds calorie intake to be a statistically significant determinant of height for three demographic groups, and height to be an important negative determinant of the number of sickdays for males and females over 19 and females aged 5–14. Blau (1984), on the other hand, develops his estimation model, including

---

[25] Their standard estimates use ordinary least squares procedures. However, they report that when they use simultaneous estimates for calories and length of breastfeeding, women's schooling has even less estimated impact on child health than in the ordinary least squares estimates, apparently because it is highly correlated with the instrumented estimates for calories and length of breastfeeding.

his choice of instruments and identification restrictions, from a well-specified theoretical framework for a sample of Nicaraguan children under 5 years of age. He uses food prices and the woman's characteristics as instruments (with arbitrary exclusions to identify the effects of breastfeeding duration (which he finds to be significantly positive) and *average* food expenditure per adult equivalent (which he observes to be insignificant) on the standardized height of children.

Pitt and Rosezweig (1985) estimate a health production function with the same Indonesian data used to estimate health demand functions reviewed earlier. Since only aggregate household nutrient (but individual illness) data are available to them, they regress the average incidence of illness in a household on the average per capita household consumption of nine nutrients (treated endogenously) as well as on the exogenous) source of drinking water and the age and schooling of the husband and the wife. Prices of food and nonfood items and access to infrastructural facilities (such as hospitals, drinking water, etc.) serve as instruments, though the identifying restrictions are arbitrary. In their instrumental-variable Tobit equation, five of the nine nutrients have statistically significant coefficients, whereas in the single-equation Tobit equation (which they also present) none of the coefficients is significant at the 5 percent level. Furthermore, in the former, the consumption of several nutrients, including protein, fat, and carbohydrates, is observed to have a negative (and significant) impact on health.

One problem with all the above studies is that they use average nutrient intakes based on aggregate household nutrition data. If the intrafamily distribution of food is unequal [as suggested by the studies by Behrman (1987c, 1988), Behrman and Deolalikar (1987d), and Horton (1984) reviewed above], the health or illness of a family member may be poorly related to the average level of nutrient intake in the household even in the presence of a strong positive association between nutrient intakes and health for each individual member. Wolfe and Behrman (1987) avoid this problem by utilizing information on different individuals within a family. They estimate a latent variable simultaneous equations system including health production functions for women and their children, using Nicaraguan data. Standardized height, weight, and biceps circumference are used as the observed indicators for child health, while the number of days too ill to work and the presence of parasitic diseases, medically preventable diseases, and therapeutically treatable diseases are used as the observed indicators for female health. Medical-care usage (which is represented by the age–standardized number of injections received by the child, the term of the mother's first pregnancy-related medical examination, and coverage in social security schemes), household nutrition (represented by standardized intakes of calories and protein by the family and by household ownership of a refrigerator), and water and sanitation facilities (represented by the absence of indoor toilets and baths) are included as endogenous inputs. Household income, the mother's initial endowments (represented by her own mother's schooling, her urban upbringing, mother present in adolescence, father present in adolescence, and number of siblings), and community endowments (represented by population, population density, number of hospital beds per 1000 inhabitants, and the literacy rate) are some of the instruments used to identify the parameters of the production function. Wolfe and Behrman's results are somewhat discouraging for standard analyses: they find that medical-care usage, nutrition and mother's schooling appear to have significant positive effects on child health and community endowments appear to have significant positive effects on mother's health *if* mother's childhood–family related endowments are excluded a priori, but that all of these coefficients become insignificant if mother's childhood–family related endowments are included. Similar results are presented in Behrman and Wolfe (1987) for child health with adult sibling deviation control for mother's unobserved endowments. They interpret such endowments to include health-related abilities, knowledge and habits and prior health status all of which relate to usually unobserved (and therefore uncontrolled) dimensions of childhood–family environment. Thus, the standard results about the positive health impact of nutrition, water and sanitation, maternal schooling and community endowments may be misleading due to the failure to control for maternal endowments.

The lack of a strong association between nutrient intakes and health outcomes may not be very surprising, especially in the case of adults. In most surveys, data on nutrient intakes are collected over a short reference period. Health, on the other hand, is a cumulative outcome of nutrient intakes ingested over a much longer period of time. Moreover, as discussed above in Section 3.2, intraperson variations in nutrient intakes apparently are considerable. Only in the case of infants and young children is the lag between the nutrient intakes and health outcomes likely to be short and the cross-sectional mapping between them significant. No wonder then that studies by Clark (1981), Taylor et al. (1978), Chernichovsky and Kielmann (1977), Magnani et al. (1985), DaVanzo and Habicht (1984), and Blau (1984), which estimate health production functions for infants and young children, find significant positive associations between nutrient intakes/breastfeeding and health outcomes. Even for infants and small children, however, the relation between nutrient intakes and health is not always robust with control for unobserved characteristics [e.g. Behrman and Wolfe (1987), Wolfe and Behrman (1987)].

There is perhaps another reason for the poor association between nutrient intakes and health outcomes for older children and adults. Increased nutrient intakes may be reflected in increased metabolism or work effort rather than in the types of health outcomes commonly observed and reported in surveys (see Sections 3.2 and 5.1).

Yet another important factor is that these studies generally omit the time usage or work effort of individuals in the health production function. In so far as part of the nutrients consumed contribute to increased work effort and that effort is not controlled in the health production function estimate, the coefficient of the impact of the remaining nutrients (i.e. those not absorbed by the work effort) is biased downwards. To the extent that individual metabolic responds to nutrient intakes as Sukhatme (1982) and others have argued (see Section 3.2), the failure to control for endogenous metabolic adjustments also causes a downward bias in the estimated impact of nutrition on health.

At any rate, the true human health production function is a complex relationship that cannot be captured easily by regression analysis based on single-period, cross-sectional nutrient intake, anthropometric, morbidity and endowments data. Individual-specific immunity, either acquired or inherited, may have an important bearing on the conversion of nutrients into health. The lag between ingestion of nutrients and the production of health also is likely to be complex and probably needs to be modeled as a dynamic process. In addition, while diseases (health outcomes) are determined by the level of nutrient intakes, they also influence the utilization of .nutrients. For instance, episodes of severe diarrhea during infancy can affect adversely the production of a child's height from given levels of nutrients [Heller and Drake (1979), Barlow (1979)]. Most health production function studies have not been sufficiently sensitive to these problems.

4.1.3. Cross-country studies of health demand

Some studies, namely Preston (1980, 1983), Wheeler (1980), and Horton et al. (1985), have analyzed the determinants of health at the cross-country level. Preston (1980), for instance, explores the determinants of life expectancy using cross-country data for 1940 and 1970. He finds that per capita income and adult literacy are highly significant determinants of life expectancy for both periods. Furthermore, the coefficients of the life expectancy equations are very similar for the two periods. However, an additional variable that he includes to measure the extent of malnutrition in a country – namely, the excess of average daily calorie availability per capita over 1500 – is not significant for either period.

To assess the contribution of increases in per capita GDP, literacy, and calorie availability to the increase in life expectancy between 1940 and 1970, Preston calculates what life expectancy would have been for individual less-developed countries if no structural changes had occurred in the relationship between life expectancy and socioeconomic development. The difference between actual life expectancy in 1970 and that predicted if 1940 relations had continued to prevail in 1970 indicates the amount of change in life expectancy attributable to structural shifts in the life expectancy equation. He finds that approximately half of the total gain in life expectancy during the 30 years was unrelated to changes in per capita income, literacy, and calorie availability.

A problem with Preston's study is that prices and endowments are not included in the relation; if they are associated with income or literacy (as a priori seems plausible), the coefficient estimates for the included variables are biased because they are representing in part the excluded ones. Quite possibly, for example, the coefficient estimates for both income and literacy are biased upwards because they capture in part the effect of excluded endowments that also increase in the development process. However, when, for a smaller sample of countries for which data are available for both 1940 and 1970, Preston estimates the life expectancy equation in first differences, his results are largely unchanged. Since first differencing purges his estimates of unobserved country-specific fixed effects (including at least some cross-country differences in the measurement and definition of life expectancy), it means that the omitted variables problem was not severe for such fixed effects (though no insight is provided regarding variables that change over time) even in Preston's levels equation for life expectancy.

Since the measures of per capita GDP used above are based on international exchange rates, which are subject to many distortions, Preston (1983) re-estimates the relationship between life expectancy and income using the International Comparisons Project (ICP) measures of per capita GDP, which are based on purchasing power parities of various currencies. Estimating the life expectancy equation (in levels) for 1965–69 and 1975–79 with both measures of income (and with literacy rate and excess calories availability as control variables), he finds that the coefficient of income in the ICP-based regressions is 50 percent larger than that in the other regressions.

Using a sample of 54 countries, Wheeler (1980) estimates a simultaneous-equations model of the relationship between percentage changes in life expectancy between 1960 and 1970 and percentage changes over the same period in per capita GDP, adult literacy, per capita calorie availability, population per doctor, and population per nurse. The first three (namely, changes in GDP, literacy, and calorie availability) are treated as endogenous variables in the model, with the 1960 levels of per capita calorie availability and literacy, the 1960–70 percentage change in primary school enrollment, and the 1960–70 percentage changes in (physical) capital and labor input serving as instruments. All explanatory variables also are interacted with the level of life expectancy in 1960 (which is assumed to be exogenous). The fit of the model is generally poor and all coefficients are estimated imprecisely. Only the percentage change in the adult literacy rate has a significant positive (but declining with the initial level of life expectancy) impact on percentage changes in life expectancy. The intercept term is statistically significant and indicates an exogenous increase in life expectancy of 9.6 percent between 1960 and 1970.

Wheeler's analysis suffers from arbitrariness – in the specification of equations, in the choice of which variables are endogenous and which exogenous, and in his identification restrictions. Unlike Preston, Wheeler claims to estimate a full model of income, health, and nutrition determination. Yet none of his equations is derived from an economic model of health or nutrition behavior. For example, there is no price of food in his calorie availability or life expectancy equation. Change in the *quantity* of labor input in the production function is treated as exogenous at the same time as changes in the *quality* of that input (namely, life expectancy, calorie availability, and literacy) are treated as endogenous. Similarly, per capita GDP is treated as an endogenous variable, but infrastructural variables like population per nurse and doctor are treated as exogenous, though it is not clear why it is more important to treat GDP as endogenous than to treat health expenditures and infrastructure as endogenous.

Horton et al. (1985) estimate a demand relation for infant mortality from pooled cross-country (34 LDCs) and time-series (1966–81) data. The innovation of this study is the inclusion of the "price of cheap calories", namely, the average of ICP-adjusted, open-market/controlled retail prices of rice, maize, wheat, millet, and sorghum from FAO series. Estimating separate demand equations for each country, the authors find that nine of the 34 countries have negative and significant income elasticities of infant mortality, while six have positive and significant price elasticities. Seven countries have the "wrong" signs (positive and significant) for income elasticities and eight have the "wrong" signs (negative and significant) for price elasticities (but see the discussion on price effects in Section 4.2). The country-by-country results thus are ambiguous and permit no broad generalizations.

This brings us to a general discussion about the merits and demerits of estimating health demand relations derived from household and individual behavior with cross-country data. The assumption that is maintained in such analysis is that a country corresponds to a "representative consumer". Even if one is willing to avoid attaching any behavioral interpretations to cross-country analysis, there are still serious estimation problems. The use of average data, however, may be misleading if distribution is important and differs across countries. Few variables, furthermore, are exogenous at a national level. Those that are (such as international prices) have limited cross-country variability, and therefore are not very useful in single cross-section regression analysis. The variables that most cross-country studies on health demand have treated as exogenous – viz. infrastructure facilities, per capita GDP, food prices – very often reflect choices of national health (and other) policy makers. Finally, the per capita GDP of a country may serve as a proxy for a much larger number of variables than the average income of its residents; it is highly collinear with urbanization, literacy, health (and other) infrastructure, and many other variables. A positive association between health and per capita GDP thus tells us very little about the specific determinants of health.

4.2. Determinants of nutrients

As in the case of health, there are two ways of looking at the determinants of nutrient consumption: the demand for nutrients [N^i in eq. (9) in Section 2.1] and the production of nutrients [N^i in eq. (4)]. In the first, prices, income, and given endowments are presumed to determine the nutrient intakes of an individual, while in the second, better nutrient intakes are determined by the food consumption of the individual and the education and time of the household food preparer. In both functions, individual-specific unobserved variables, e.g. metabolism rates in the former case, may play an important role.

4.2.1. Nutrient demand

Virtually all the studies that have analyzed the determination of nutrient intakes are demand relations. Most have either followed the approach of (i) estimating food demand/expenditure systems and then converting the price and income elasticities obtained from these to nutrient elasticities using fixed food–nutrient conversion facts [Strauss (1984), Pitt (1983), Pinstrup-Andersen et al. (1975), Pinstrup-Andersen and Caicedo (1978), Murty and Radhakrishna (1981)], or (ii) estimating directly the demand for nutrients as a function of food prices, household size, and income/expenditure [Wolfe and Behrman (1983, 1986b), Behrman and Wolfe (1984a, 1986), Ward and Sanders (1980), Timmer and Alderman (1979), Williamson-Gray (1982), Pitt and Rosenzweig (1985), Mateus (1985), Behrman and Deolalikar (1987a, 1987c, 1987d)].[26]

Estimates of the income/expenditure elasticities (hereafter referred to as income elasticities) for calories, which is included in most of the above studies, vary widely, from a low of 0.0–0.1 for Managua, Nicaragua [Wolfe and Behrman (1983)], rural south India [Behrman and Deolalikar (1987c)] and Indonesia [Pitt and Rosenzweig (1985)] to a high of 0.9 for rural Sierra Leone (Strauss). Estimates of the income elasticity of proteins, which are far fewer in number than calorie income elasticity estimates, also range from 0.0–0.1 for small children and infants in rural India [Levinson (1974)] and households in Indonesia (Pitt and Rosenzweig) to 0.6–0.8 for rural Bangladesh (Pitt).

Furthermore, most studies that analyze the relationship between the income elasticity of nutrient demand and income have found it to be negative [Timmer and Alderman, Pinstrup-Andersen and Caicedo, Williamson-Gray, Mateus, Behrman and Wolfe (1984), but not Behrman and Deolalikar (1987c) nor Strauss]; such an inverse association between the income elasticity of nutrients and the level of income is consistent with the possibility that income changes play an important role in the marginal determination of nutrients at very low incomes but not at high ones. The most dramatic evidence of this is provided by Mateus (1985), who estimates income elasticities of both calories and protein of 1.2 for

---

[26] Pitt suggests that the expenditure system route is superior, but does not explain why he thinks this. But to us his apparent reasoning suggests the characterization that we give below in the text.

low-income Moroccan households, of 0.5 for average-income households, and of −0.15 for high-income households.

Behrman and Deolalikar (1987c) argue that calorie (more generally, nutrient) income elasticities which are derived from aggregate food demand equations tend to be overestimates, since households switch purchases among disaggregated foods to higher priced, but nutritionally not necessarily much better, foods with increasing income. Since foods are typically aggregated into broad groups in the estimation of demand/expenditure systems, the problem is one of the commodity aggregation and the possible dependence of group price indices on income levels. Using 1970–71 data from the Indian National Sample Survey, Radhakrishna (1984) calculates that the average cost of calories from each of six broadly-defined food groups increases consistently with total expenditure for both rural and urban households. Pitt also observes this in his sample for Bangladesh. He reports that the 25th percentile household spent 22 percent more per gram of protein, 15 percent more per calorie, and as much as 44 percent more per milligram of iron than did the 90th percentile household. Finally, Williamson-Gray estimates the income elasticity of the average price paid per calorie (which she treats as a proxy for food quality) to be 0.288 even for relatively malnourished households in her Brazilian sample.[27]

If the income elasticity of the average cost of a nutrient is indeed positive, the income elasticities of food demand tend to overstate the income elasticity of nutrients. Behrman and Deolalikar (1987c) show this by estimating expenditure elasticities of demand for six foods (namely, grains, sugar, pulses, vegetables, milk, and meat) and nine nutrients (namely, calories, protein, calcium, iron, carotene, thiamine, riboflavin, niacin, and ascorbic acid) for rural south India with OLS, OLS-IV, and fixed-effects estimation techniques. They find large and statistically significant expenditure elasticities of food demand for all foods (ranging from 0.4 to 3.5), but small (and sometimes even negative) and often not significant expenditure elasticities of nutrient demand (ranging from −0.3 to 0.8 but less than 0.4 for calories and proteins) across all model specifications.

The other determinants of nutrient demand explored by empirical studies include food prices. Strauss obtains negative food price effects on calories demand when he controls for farm profits in his sample of Sierra Leonean farm households. However, the majority of the food price elasticities turn positive when farm profits are allowed to vary (i.e. when it is recognized that food prices have a positive impact on farm profits and thereby on consumption). On the other hand, Pitt finds that, even after controlling for income, calorie demand in

---

[27]Of course, the difference in the *effective* price of a calorie obtained from low-priced grains and that obtained from high-priced grains may not be as large as we have emphasized, if the latter types of grains contain fewer stones and impurities (which need to be removed before consumption) than the former types. However, we believe that even the effective nutrient prices are likely to vary substantially because of taste, odor, status, and quality variations.

Bangladesh has positive elasticities with respect to the prices of five of the nine foods he considers – pulses, fish, mustard oil, onions, and spices. In their latent variable study, Behrman and Deolalikar (1987d) also find a large number of positive food price effects on the unobserved nutrient consumption status of all household members, even after controlling for income and individual-specific fixed effects. In fact, only the price of sorghum seems to affect nutrient consumption inversely in their study. Finally, Pitt and Rosenzweig also find a large number of positive price effects on nutrient demand for this sample of Indonesian farm households even with farm profits held constant. The only food price which has a consistently negative (profits-constant) effect on *all* nutrients is the price of milk.

There is thus a great deal of evidence on positive income-compensated food price effects on nutrient consumption. This reflects strong cross-price substitution effects among foods together with variations in nutrient-to-food conversion factors. Thus, when the price of, say, rice increases, a sufficiently large increase in the demand for other relatively nutritious foods and thereby in nutrient consumption may be induced to more than offset the direct decrease in nutrition resulting from reduced rice consumption.

The finding of frequent positive price elasticities for nutrients has important implications for policy. It suggests that certain food subsidies may not only fail in improving the nutritional status of the poor, but that they may actually worsen it.

A survey by Alderman (1984) of 15 nutrient demand studies notes that the majority of these, including the studies by Pitt and Strauss reviewed above, find that own-price elasticities of food demand decline in absolute values with income or expenditure. Sometimes the trend is pronounced, as in Williamson-Gray who observes a compensated own-price elasticity of cereals demand of -0.74 for the poor, -0.16 for the middle, and not significantly different from zero for the rich in Brazil. A few studies, namely Williamson-Gray and Timmer and Alderman, also observe an inverse relationship between the absolute value of *cross*-price elasticities and the level of income or expenditure. There is thus compelling evidence that the poor are more responsive – to income, own-prices, and cross-prices – than are the rich. This has important distributional implications for food subsidy and price policies.

By estimating nutrient demand equations at the household level, most studies lose the intrafamily distributional consequences of price and income changes. The study by Behrman and Deolalikar (1987d) is an exception, since it addresses the issue of differing price and income responses by different members within a household. They find that price-induced adjustments in nutrient consumption are not uniform across different household members. Female children are made to accept the greater nutritional burden of adjustment to unfavorable price movements (and, by the same token, receive the greater nutritional bonus in response to favorable price changes), while the other members' nutrient consumption is allowed to fluctuate much less. Their findings are consistent with other evidence from South Asia, such as that reported by Rosenzweig and Schultz (1982), Sen and Sengupta (1983), Behrman (1988), and Kakwani (1986b), showing sex bias in favor of boys and against girls in intrahousehold resource allocation.

Household size often is entered as a determinant of nutrient demand. Behrman and Wolfe (1984a) argue that not only the sign but the magnitude of the household size elasticity relative to the household income elasticity is important, since it reflects the extent of returns to scale with respect to household size. They as well as Ward and Sanders and Wolfe and Behrman (1983) obtain statistically significant negative effects of household size on nutrient demand. The estimates presented by all three studies imply considerable increasing returns to scale. A study by Iyengar et al. (1968) obtains economies of scale in the consumption of "necessities" like cereals and fuel-lighting but not in the consumption of "luxuries" like milk and clothing. However, all the above estimates are likely to be biased since fertility and hence household size are endogenous variables that are jointly determined along with nutritional status choices, but not treated as such in these studies. Therefore the estimated household size variable coefficients are likely to represent in part unobserved profertility determinants (e.g. tastes), which may be associated with less investment in nutrition – and this understates the returns to scale. Pitt and Rosenzweig do not include household size as a determinant of per capita nutrient intakes, but do include household composition (treated as an endogenous variable) and find it to be a significant determinant of per capita nutrient intakes. In particular, per capita consumption of calories, protein, carbohydrates, and phosphorous are all observed to increase with mean household age.

The model in Section 2.1 also suggests the inclusion of the education of the food preparer in the household in the nutrient demand equation. Ward and Sanders, and Pitt and Rosenzweig find no significant effect of women's schooling on household nutrient consumption, but Wolfe and Behrman (1983, 1986b, 1987) and Behrman and Wolfe (1984a, 1986, 1987) do. The latter group of studies find that Nicaraguan households in which women have more schooling tend to be significantly and substantially better nourished, ceteris paribus, particularly in regard to vitamin A, proteins, and calcium. Furthermore, they find that this effect persists even if there is adult sibling deviation control for unobserved childhood–background related characteristics of the woman, in sharp contrast to the estimated impact of women's schooling on health (Section 4.1).

One other determinant of nutritional status, which is not explicitly included in the household model sketched in Section 2.1 but which, according to authors in Chambers et al. (1981) is important in the rural areas of LDCs, is seasonality. In particular, the wet season in these countries is often the most difficult time of the year when shortages of food are coincident with high energy demand for agricultural activities. Food is at its scarcest and most expensive at this time of the year. Unfortunately, it is precisely at this time that exposure to infections and diseases, like diarrhea, malaria, cholera, and dengue fever, is also most common. The result is that morbidity and mortality, particularly infant mortality, are at their highest levels during the wet season.

There have been few attempts to systematically incorporate seasonality in the determination of nutrient demand. The only study we are aware of which attempts this is Behrman and Deolalikar (1987a). They estimate separate nutrient and health demand equations for individuals for the lean and the surplus seasons of the year in rural south India. They obtain significantly negative food price elasticities of calorie and protein demand for the lean season, but elasticities that are close to zero or even slightly positive in the surplus season. On the other hand, the wage elasticities of calorie and protein demand they estimate are significantly positive for the lean season, but much smaller for the surplus season. They conjecture that this pattern of estimates occurs because the farm households are net suppliers of food but net buyers of labor in the surplus season and net buyers of food but net sellers of labor in the lean season. As a result, an increase in food prices in the surplus season exerts a positive (negative) income effect on nutrient demand which mitigates or overwhelms the negative substitution effect.

Behrman and Deolalikar's explanation of these results rests on the assumption that farmers cannot store sufficiently food or food purchasing power from one season to another. Given that most of the foods they consider are cereals – rice, sorghum, millet – this assumption seems strong. If valid, there may be important implications in their results for seasonal price stabilization or storage policies. If not, there is a puzzle as to why they obtain such strong seasonal differences. One possibility that they do not discuss is that the parameters in the reduced-form relations change because of unobserved seasonal changes in the environment or because of seasonal changes in time usage that affect health through the health production function.

4.2.2. Household nutrient production functions

There is only one study of which we are aware that attempts to estimate the nutrient production function in eq. (4) of Section 2.1. This is a study by Ybañez-Gonzalo and Evenson (1978) for the Philippines. Most other empirical exercises reduce the household nutrient production function to a weighted average of food intakes by using standard nutrient/food conversion factors.[28]

---

[28] In a different sense some other studies estimate nutrient production functions which relate effective nutrient intakes to the indicators of individual nutrients. Behrman and Wolfe (1984a), for example, report estimates for a range of elasticities of substitution (from zero to infinity) among different nutrients; they find that their results are not very sensitive to a wide range of elasticities of substitution, though very low elasticities seem less empirically relevant. Behrman and Deolalikar (1987d) use a latent variable representation of nutrition and estimate the relative association of various observed nutrients with that latent variable, as is discussed above.

Ybañez-Gonzalo and Evenson estimate a Cobb–Douglas production function for household nutrient intakes, using calories, protein, vitamin A, and a weighted sum of the three nutrients as alternative measures of nutrient intake. The inputs in the production process are the value of raw food prepared and served to the household (valued at constant market prices), the time elapsing from the beginning to the end of meal preparation, an index of home capital (namely, the value of refrigerators, stoves, and cooking utensils), the work status of the mother, and the number of adult equivalents in the household.

The (OLS) estimated production function reveals a large production elasticity with respect to household size (0.54), a very small elasticity with respect to home capital (0.008), and medium-sized elasticities with respect to value of food and time inputs (0.26 and 0.23, respectively). The sum of all the output elasticities is not significantly different from one, indicating constant returns to scale in nutrient production. The authors explain the relatively large impact of household size on nutrient production by arguing that larger households have lower food wastage, a result which is consistent with the estimates of the impact of household size on nutrient demands discussed above.

While the Ybañez-Gonzalo and Evenson study is an interesting and innovative study, to us the point estimates – especially the high one for household size – seem puzzling. The estimation of the nutrient production function by OLS techniques, moreover, is a definite shortcoming. Since all the explanatory variables used in the study are subject to household choice, an estimation procedure that treats them as exogenous or predetermined may produce biased estimates. It is not clear why the authors do not use simultaneous estimation techniques since they appear to have data on prices which could serve as exogenous instruments. Another problem with their estimation of the nutrient production function is that the true dependent variable that should be used in the function – namely, the level of nutrients actually ingested given the amount and type of cooking done – is not observed. What is observed instead is the amount of nutrients *purchased* given standard food/nutrient conversions. The use of the latter as a proxy for the former is likely to exaggerate the responsiveness of nutrient production to food expenditures and to underestimate its responsiveness to cooking time and cooking methods.

4.2.3. Cross-country studies on nutrient demands

All of the problems we discussed earlier about using cross-country data to estimate health demand functions hold in the estimation of cross-country nutrient demand functions as well. However, the data problem may be even more serious for nutrients. Most cross-country studies of nutrient demand use as their dependent variable the average daily calorie availability per capita constructed from FAO food balance sheets. Since large components of the balance sheets are not known with any degree of precision (particularly, food wastage, change in stocks, and subsistence production), there are likely to be large errors in the per capita calorie availability variable. What is even more worrisome is that these errors are likely to be systematically related to the level of per capita GDP of a country. This probably results in exaggerated income elasticities of nutrient demand from cross-country estimates.

Wheeler (1980), Reutlinger (1984) and Horton et al. (1985) are among the studies that have analyzed the determinants of nutrient demand at the cross-country level. In the same simultaneous-equations model discussed in Section 4.1, Wheeler estimates percentage growth (over 1960–70) of per capita calorie availability as a function of per capita GDP growth (treated as an endogenous variable) and the interaction of percentage GDP growth and the level of per capita calorie availability in 1960. He finds a significant positive (but declining with the initial level of per capita calorie availability) effect of per capita GDP growth on the growth of per capita calories availability. The implied income elasticities of calorie availability are 0.27 at 70 percent average calorie adequacy (according to WHO standards) and almost zero at the 100 percent level.

Reutlinger has used annual data from 1970 to 1980 for a larger sample of 84 countries to estimate a similar equation. He estimates a log-linear equation in which the annual rate of growth of average calorie availability between 1970 and 1980 is a function of the annual growth rate of per capita real income, a food production index, a real food price index, and the urban share of the population. The elasticity of average calorie availability with respect to income is allowed to vary with the initial (1970) level of per capita income and average calorie availability as a percentage of the WHO-recommended calorie intake. Reutlinger's results suggest a significant positive food production, but an insignificant food price effect on average energy availability. The effect of real income on average energy availability is very strong, and the income elasticity is observed to decrease with the initial energy adequacy of the national diet and, surprisingly, to increase with initial per capita income. For a country with a per capita real income in 1970 of $1250, the estimated income elasticity of average energy intake is 0.22 with 90 percent initial energy adequacy of diet, 0.14 with 110 percent initial energy adequacy, and 0.06 with 110 percent initial energy adequacy.

Unlike Wheeler, Reutlinger does not treat per capita GDP as an endogenous variable in his analysis. It is also not clear why he includes the index of food production along with the index of real food prices in his demand function. The two variables are most likely strongly correlated, which may explain the nonsignificance of the price effect.

In the study cited in Section 4.1, Horton et al. also estimate a calorie demand equation using pooled cross-country and time-series data for 34 LDCs from 1966 to 1981. They include as arguments ICP-adjusted real per capita GDP and an index of the real cereal price. The income elasticity of calorie availability they obtain is not too dissimilar to Wheeler's and Reutlinger's estimates (0.16). However, unlike Reutlinger, they do find a significant but small (elasticity of 0.03) effect of cereal price on calorie availability. It is interesting to note that they obtain a positive effect of real cereal prices on calorie availability a la many of the microeconomic studies (Strauss, Pitt and Rosenzweig, and Behrman and Deolalikar).

When the calorie demand equation is estimated separately for each country (which is what an *F*-test for the equivalence of parameters across countries suggests), the cereal price elasticity of calories availability is negative and significant for six countries and positive and significant for eight countries. In virtually all cases, however, the magnitude of the elasticity is relatively small. What is surprising, however, is that the income elasticity of calorie demand is observed to be negative and significant in six countries (five of which are relatively well-off countries in Latin America). With the exception of Bangladesh, all the Asian countries they include have positive income elasticities of calorie demand (ranging from 0.2 to 0.6).

Despite their problems, there seems to be a consensus emerging out of the cross-country studies, namely, that the elasticity of calorie demand with respect to GDP is relatively small even for the poor countries. A cross-country study of a different nature by Behrman and Deolalikar (1987e) sheds light on one reason why this may be so; they find that consumers' demand for food variety increases rapidly with incomes. Using ICP and FAO data on 34 developed and developing countries, they estimate a system of demand equations for average calorie consumption, for the average price paid for calories and for variety in the food basket, which they proxy by the share in total real food consumption of the three, five, and eight largest items (out of a total of 37 detailed food groups in their data set) in the food budget and by the Hirschman–Herfindahl index of concentration (namely, the sum of squared food shares of 37 food groups). The independent variables in the demand equations include ICP-adjusted per capita GDP, per capita GDP-squared, and the relative prices of nine aggregated food groups. Only one price – that of breads and cereals – turns out to be significant (with a negative sign) across all variety equations. Both GDP and GDP-squared have significant effects on variety such that increased income levels are associated with greater, but at a diminishing rate, demand for variety in food consumption.

With the same data, Behrman and Deolalikar then proceed to estimate the curvature of the underlying preference function (which they assume to be CES in the quantities of the nine aggregated food groups). They find the elasticity of substitution between food groups to be significantly and inversely dependent on the level of per capita GDP; the estimated elasticity has a value of 0.10 at a per capita GDP level of $500, of -0.43 at a level of $2800, and of -0.83 at a level of $4500. These results suggest that the indifference curves across food groups become significantly more curved as income increases – moving from a curvature between the linear and Cobb–Douglas cases to one between the Cobb–Douglas and the L-shaped cases within the sample. The increased curvature of the indifference curves in turn suggests that consumers demand more variety with increased incomes, and purchase more variety instead of just more calories.

Another cross-country analysis of dietary quality by Chandhri and Timmer (1986) uses the starchy staple ratio and the proportion of total proteins derived from animal protein as indicators of diet quality. They find that the (per capita) income elasticity of the starchy staple ratio is -0.39 (-0.64 for developed countries and -0.23 for less-developed countries) and that of the animal-total protein ratio is 0.52 (0.43 for DCs and 0.50 for LDCs).

5. Empirical studies of the impact of health and nutrition in developing countries

The model developed in Section 2.1 suggests that individual health and nutrition may have impacts on several outcomes. First, they may enter the wage (P_L^i) relation, as shown in eq. (5). Second, they may enter as inputs in the household firm/farm production function [Y^h in eq. (6)]. In a parallel way they may affect productivity in other activities, such as in schooling. Third, the health and nutritional status of parents also may enter into the production function for *births* [B in eq. (7)]. Finally, although the model treats the infant mortality and birth (fertility) decisions of households as jointly determined, there is a literature which attempts to analyze the impact of infant mortality on parental fertility.

5.1. Impact on labor productivity

5.1.1. Micro studies

The idea that, at low levels of income, there is a technically determined relationship between nutritional status or health and labor effort or productivity is not a new one. This hypothesis – often called the Efficiency Wage Hypothesis – has been discussed by Leibenstein (1957), Mazumdar (1959), Stiglitz (1976), and Bliss and Stern (1978), among others. Although the hypothesis has important implications for developing country labor markets and for the possibility of separability between production and consumption (which usually is assumed a priori), it has been subjected to little systematic empirical testing. We review only the major studies in this area, referring the reader interested in other studies to surveys by Gwatkin (1983), Barlow (1979), Strauss (1985), Srinivasan (1985), and Martorell and Arrayave (1984).

Using experimental data from the INCAP nutrition supplementation project, Immink and Viteri (1981) compare the gains in productivity (daily cane harvest) between two groups of otherwise similar Guatemalan sugar-cane workers: one receiving a high-energy supplementation and the other receiving a low-energy supplementation. They find that the productivity of both groups rose during the supplementation period, but that there is hardly any difference between the productivity gains of the two groups. Their results suggest that whatever additional energy expenditure that the supplementation permitted (energy supplementation was found to successfully raise the energy intake and expenditure of workers) was dissipated in heat or spent on activities other than enhancement of work productivity.

Immink and Viteri include in their regression of change in sugar-cane cut per day the daily energy intake of the worker as well as whether he was in the high-supplementation group. Since daily energy intake includes calories from the supplementation diet (which is exogenous) as well as from the worker's diet at home (which is endogenous), it is an inappropriate variable to include as an explanatory variable. In this case, the lack of significance they obtain for the total energy intake variable may simply reflect the fact that workers with high productivity (and thereby greater earnings, if they were paid on a piece rate) do not spend their additional earnings on food with high calorie content – a result consistent with the evidence presented in Section 4.2 above.

In the same vein, Wolgemuth et al. (1982) regress gains in labor productivity in road construction on total calorie intake from a supplementation diet and the number of days worked. Unlike Immink and Viteri, they randomly assign workers to treatment groups. Their results indicate a large positive (but only marginally significant) effect of calories (a calorie output elasticity of 0.5), but a negative and significant effect of labor supply. As Strauss (1985) has pointed out, since labor supply is subject to individual choice, their alleged negative effect of labor supply on productivity may simply reflect an income effect on labor supply – whereby workers with increased productivity (due to the diet supplementation) and therefore increased earnings (if the work was paid by piece rate) cut back on their labor supply. Wolgemuth et al. also present their productivity results without including labor supply. In this case, they still obtain a marginally significant effect of calorie intake on average productivity, which casts doubt on Strauss' conjecture.

Popkin (1978), Baldwin and Weisbrod (1974), and Weisbrod and Helminiak (1977) have attempted to link productivity to health indicators. Popkin regresses daily productivity of road construction workers in Bicol, Philippines, on their hemoglobin levels, while Baldwin and Weisbrod and Weisbrod and Helminiak regress daily and weekly earnings of plantation workers in St. Lucia on dichotomous variables indicating the presence of schistosomiasis (a parasitic infection endemic to the island). However, since health may be as much of a choice variable as nutrition (see Section 2.1 above), and is a cumulative outcome of past investments in nutrition and health, which presumably would be influenced by higher productivity and earnings, it is also inappropriate as an exogenous explanatory variable.

There are other studies that have attempted to correlate productivity with anthropometric indicators. Surveying such studies, Martorell and Arroyave (1984) conclude that body size (namely, weight, height, or weight-for-height) is an important determinant of productivity. Since most of the cited studies are based on simple correlations between simultaneously-determined variables, none of them offers definitive evidence of a productivity effect of body size. Ryan and Wallace (1986) estimate wage equations (corrected for selectivity bias) having height and weight as arguments, using the ICRISAT data from rural south India for a sample of rural labor participants. They find that weight-for-age has a significant positive effect on male but not on female wage rates. However, what is disturbing is the significant negative sign that they obtain on the coefficient of height-for-age in the male wage equation. No explanation is offered for this puzzling result. Indeed, it is very likely that their wage equation estimates are contaminated by simultaneous equations bias which arises because of the endogenous nature of the weight (and, to a smaller extent, height) variable.

The only studies of which we are aware that are sensitive to the endogeneity of the nutrition and health variables and which estimate technical production functions to relate labor productivity to nutrition and health are two studies by Strauss (1986) and Deolalikar (1988). Deolalikar analyzes the impact of individual health and nutritional status (namely, weight-for-height and energy intake) on individual market wage rates and on-farm labor productivity for a sample of agricultural households in semi-arid south India. Strauss estimates the effect of average (over the household) per adult consumer equivalent calorie intake on the productivity of on-farm family labor in Sierra Leonean agriculture. Both studies estimate agricultural production functions having hired labor and nonlabor inputs in addition to family labor inputs.

Strauss estimates a Cobb–Douglas production function for a sample of farm households practicing hoe agriculture in Sierra Leone. One of his inputs is "effective family labor", which is a nonlinear function of the number of actual on-farm family labor hours and the average availability of calories per consumer equivalent in the household. He finds effective family labor to be a statistically significant input in the agricultural production function, and effective family labor to increase significantly, albeit at a diminishing rate, with per consumer equivalent calorie availability within the household. He estimates the output elasticity of per consumer equivalent calorie availability to be 0.33 at the sample mean level of family calorie availability, 0.49 at a calorie availability of 1500 calories a day, and 0.12 at a calorie availability of 4500 calories a day. Beyond a daily per consumer equivalent intake of 5200 calories, calories have a negative impact on effective labor. The other results of interest are the estimated increase in the relative efficiency of an hour of labor with calorie intake (namely, labor consuming 1500 calories a day is 40 percent less and labor consuming 4500 calories a day is 20 percent more efficient than labor consuming 3000 calories a day). Since Strauss' results hold across a wide range of specifications, including dropping several variables (such as family size and farm assets) from the instrumental variable set, Strauss' finding of a link between agricultural labor productivity and calorie availability per consumer equivalent appears to be robust.

Since Deolalikar has data on the same farms for two years, he estimates a fixed-effects instrumental variable-estimated Cobb–Douglas farm production function in which effective family labor is a Cobb–Douglas function of the number of actual on-farm family labor hours and the weighted averages of calorie intake and weight-for-height of family farm workers. The weights used in averaging over family farm workers are the shares of total hours of on-farm family labor contributed by each family member. All inputs, including average energy intake and weight-for-height (but not cropped area, which is treated as a fixed factor of production), are treated as household choice variables, for which food prices are used as instruments. Although the relationship between productivity and the health/nutrition variables may be nonmonotonic, Deolalikar assumes a monotonic relationship by adopting a Cobb–Douglas functional form, since for the range of values of calorie intake and weight-for-height observed in his sample, he finds no evidence of nonmonotonicity.

Deolalikar argues that it is important to include both energy intake and weight-for-height in the agricultural production function since the two fulfill qualitatively different needs in agricultural operations. Weight-for-height is associated with endurance and innate strength (or horsepower), while calorie intake is associated with energy expenditure. Some agricultural tasks like harvesting or weeding require sustained periods of energy expenditure but relatively little strength, while others like ploughing require peak horsepower. His results show a significant positive effect of weight-for-height but not calorie intake on farm output. The output elasticity of weight-for-height is estimated to be as large as four, while that of calorie intake is not significantly different from zero.

Using the same data as Ryan and Wallace, Deolalikar also tests whether the greater marginal productivity of healthy and well-nourished workers holds in casual agricultural labor performed outside the family farm. He estimates a wage equation for workers participating in causal agricultural labor market in first differences, treating individual calorie intake and weight-for-height as endogenous variables (instrumented by food prices and the value of farm assets). The results show significant effects of both weight-for-height and calorie intake on wages, although the effect of calorie intake is barely significant at the 5 percent level. (Deolalikar pools observations on male and female participants in his estimation, since an F-test for the equality of parameters across separate male and female wage equations reveals no significant differences.)

Deolalikar's results appear to be convincing for two reasons. First, differencing does not reduce the coefficients of weight-for-height and calorie intake towards zero, as might be the case if there were substantial random measurement errors in these variables.[29] This attests to the good quality of the data, particularly on weight-for-height and calorie intake. Second, he obtains quite similar estimates of the effect of weight-for-height and calorie intake on *both* market wage rates and family farm output. Calorie intake has a small and marginally significant effect, while weight-for-height has a large significant effect, on both wages and farm output.

Deolalikar speculates that the strong observed effect of weight-for-height and the weak effect of calorie intake on agricultural productivity may be the result of greater adaptability of the human body to low energy intakes but lack of such adaptability to low levels of strength and endurance in performing strenuous tasks.

Behrman and Deolalikar (1987a) further explore the labor market effects of health and nutrition in the ICRISAT sample for rural south India by focusing on seasonality, within a simultaneous framework. They find that there are nutrient and health (weight-for-height) effects only for males, with the former more important in the peak season (when greater sustained energy expenditure is required for tasks like harvesting) and the latter more important in the slack season (when innate strength may be relatively important).

In a different type of analysis, Pitt and Rosenzweig (1986) relate farm profits and adult male labor supply to morbidity for a sample of farm households in Indonesia. They find no statistically significant effects of number of sickdays (which is treated as an endogenous choice variable) on farm profits, but do find a significant adverse effect on adult male labor supply. As the authors themselves point out, however, their results cannot be used to test the efficiency wage hypothesis, since the absence of an effect of illness on profits may reflect availability of an active labor market through which sick family labor can be replaced by healthy hired workers at a constant wage rate, not necessarily the absence of an effect of morbidity on labor productivity.

5.1.2. Cross-country studies

There have been several attempts to estimate the impact of health and nutrition on GDP at the cross-country level [see the survey by Gwatkin (1983)]. Among the better known studies is an early one by Malenbaum (1970) which uses data from 22 LDCs to estimate the impact of infant mortality and per capita availability of

---

[29]However if measurement errors are systematic and sufficiently correlated across observations on the right-hand-side variables being differenced, the downward bias in the estimated coefficients may be greater in estimates from the nondifferenced data than in those based on the differenced data [see Behrman (1984)].

physicians on the post-war change in agricultural output, holding constant the share of labor in agriculture, the use of commercial fertilizer, and the extent of illiteracy. Almost 80 percent of the variation in output change is consistent with the variation in the two health variables. However, because of serious problems of simultaneity, the study's results only reflect association, and cannot be interpreted comfortably to reflect causality.

In the same cross-country study reviewed in Sections 4.1 and 4.2, Wheeler (1980) estimates a GDP production function in which percentage change in GDP is a function of percentage changes in calorie availability, adult literacy, and life expectancy – all treated as endogenous variables – and percentage changes in labor and capital stock. Identification is achieved with variables like the initial (1960) levels of literacy, life expectancy, and calorie availability; primary school enrollment; population per nurse; and population per physician. Wheeler finds a significant positive effect of life expectancy and calorie availability on output, with elasticities of output for the two inputs of 1.7 and 2.7, respectively (compared to output elasticities of 0.2 for labor and capital). He thus concludes that better health and nutrition in a country significantly increase the growth of income.

Wheeler's results are somewhat dramatic and almost suspiciously large. One does not know if they are the consequence of using inappropriate and possibly endogenous instruments such as 1960 levels of literacy, life expectancy, and calorie availability, or whether they reflect true large effects of health and nutrition on income growth.

5.2. Impact on schooling productivity

Among children, health and nutrition may influence schooling productivity in much the same way as it affects labor productivity among adults. There are at least two studies that have tried to estimate this productivity effect and found it to be significant.

Moock and Leslie (1986) estimate schooling enrollment (demand) and grade attainment (productivity) equations for a sample of approximately 350 children from the terai (plains) region of Nepal. The former is estimated by the probit maximum likelihood method and the latter by OLS. Besides control variables such as sex, age, father's schooling, family land ownership and caste affiliation, they include the child's weight-for-age, height-for-age, and weight-for-height as explanatory variables in both equations. They find that a child's height-for-age significantly and positively influences not only the probability of his/her enrollment in school but also how far ahead he/she is in school (in terms of compiled grade) relative to other children of the same age.

Another study of over 3000 children from urban and rural areas in China by Jamison (1986) also finds a strong effect of height-for-age on grade attainment. Like Moock and Leslie, Jamison also finds height-for-age to be a much better predictor of schooling performance than weight-for-age or weight-for-height. Since height is a cumulative outcome of malnutrition over a period of time, the results˘suggest that chronic nutritional abuse – but not transitory fluctuations in nutrient intake – adversely affects schooling performance among children. Unfortunately, since both the studies use OLS methods to estimate their schooling productivity equations, one cannot rule out bias in their estimated schooling productivity impacts of health/nutrition. Better endowed children might do better in schooling and be better by health indicators, with no causal impact of the latter on the former. There is also likely to be selectivity bias in their estimates which will tend to exaggerate the productivity effects. The selectivity bias arises from the fact that schooling performance is observed only for those children who did not drop out of school. Since children who drop out are likely to be those that perform poorly, estimates that exclude such children will show an exaggerated effect of health/nutrition on performance. It is impossible to know from the material presented in these studies whether the Moock and Leslie and Jamison estimates would be rendered insignificant were they to control for health endogeneity and sample selection.

5.3. Impact of female nutrition on fertility

It has been argued by some researchers that nutrition is related to fertility through ovulation [Frisch (1978)]. According to Frisch, a critical minimum weight-for-height is required to maintain regular ovulation and menstruation; hence, ovulation ceases among women who are subject to chronic malnourishment and whose fat level falls below the critical level. Frisch maintains that this level is well above the starvation level. Hence, not only severe nutritional deprivation, but also any weight loss which reduces body fat reserves below the critical minimum, cause anovulatory cycles during which conception cannot occur.

Bongaarts (1980) and Menken et al. (1981) have systematically reviewed the evidence for a nutrition–fertility link and concluded that "... little support is provided for the existence of a significant link between food intake and childbearing in situations of chronic or endemic malnutrition" [Menken et al. (1981, p. 425)]. They find that, although there is evidence suggesting that the length of the childbearing span is reduced by chronic malnourishment (mainly through a postponement in menarche), in few societies is the age of marriage determined by menarche. Nutrition thus has little effect on fertility through this link.

Menken et al. also review the evidence and conclude that the length of postpartum amenorrhea, which is a proxy for the duration of postpartum anovulation – the period after a birth when there is no ovulation, is affected very slightly, if at all, by chronic malnourishment among women. Lunn et al. (1980) do report evidence that supplementing lactating women's diets decreases post partum fertility in the Gambia. However, the total evidence to date suggests that this effect, although perhaps significant in some cases, is miniscule on overall fertility.

Finally, the waiting time from the resumption of ovulation after a birth to the next live birth is even less variable than the duration of postpartum amenorrhea. No significant association between nutritional indicators and the waiting time to conception have been found by Bongaarts and Delgado (1979) for Guatemala and by Chowdhury (1978) for Bangladesh.

Menken et al., therefore, conclude that while "... when food supplies are so short as to cause starvation, there is little doubt that fertility is lowered [,] ... when malnourishment is chronic and nutritional intake is above starvation levels, it is not clear that fertility is affected by any physiological mechanism determined by nutritional status" [Menken et al. (1981, p. 439)]. They do not consider behavioral mechanisms, such as frequency of intercourse, that may affect fertility through the birth production function.

There, however, have been few attempts to estimate empirically the birth production function [eq. (7) of the model developed in Section 2.1]. Efforts to estimate such a function are likely to run into some of the same problems encountered by studies testing the nutrition–productivity link. The problems of reverse causality (whereby high fertility and very short birth intervals pose a health risk for the mother), endogeneity of nutrient intake and health status, and heterogeneity across individuals are likely to be serious in birth production function estimation. Wolfe and Behrman (1986b), however, present a set of reduced-form estimates for fertility, nutrition, and contraceptive use that are consistent with a possible nutrition–fertility link in that increased income causes increases in nutrition, fertility, and contraceptive use.

5.4. Impact of infant mortality on fertility

Improvements in health can influence fertility in another way, namely through a reduction in infant and child mortality. Historically, declines in birth rates have followed periods of mortality decline. This phenomenon, called the Demographic Transition, took place in Europe during the eighteenth and nineteenth centuries, and is evident in several countries of Latin America and Asia, where crude and age-standardized fertility rates have been falling since the mid-1960s – some two to three decades after the onset of large mortality declines.[30]

There are two mechanisms through which fertility is influenced by mortality: a *replacement* effect whereby a dead infant is replaced ex post by another birth, and a *hoarding* effect whereby parents respond ex ante to anticipated deaths by bearing more children. There is in addition a biological response of fertility to mortality as well. The survival of infants who need to be breastfed can lengthen the duration of postpartum amenorrhea and thereby delay subsequent births. However, according to Schultz (1978), if empirical estimates of the derivative of births with respect to deaths exceed 0.1 or at most 0.2, the excess is likely to reflect voluntary response of parents rather than biological factors.

Using four samples, three based on urban household surveys in 1964 in Rio de Janeiro, San Jose, and Mexico City, and one on a survey of rural households in India in 1970, Schultz regresses cumulative fertility of a woman on the number of deceased children (normalized for the number of births, the age pattern of fertility, and an appropriate life table) and a set of control variables (age, education, income, and urban origin). He finds that in all samples the level of fertility is positively associated with child mortality, although the derivative of births with respect to deaths varies widely from 0.8–1.4 in Rio de Janeiro, to 0.4–0.8 in San Jose, to 0.2–0.3 in Mexico City, and to 0.3–0.5 in rural India. To explain this wide variation in fertility responses to child mortality across populations, Schultz proposes a hypothesis, namely that

> ... couples react to their child mortalilty experience by changing their reproductive performance, to the extent that they are aware of a general downtrend in mortality in their segment of society.... Thus, individual reproductive responses to child mortality increase to fully compensating levels (i.e., the derivative of births to deaths is one) only in those populations where child survival has markedly improved [Schultz (1978, pp. 212–214)].

Studies by Williams (1977), Mauskopf and Wallace (1984) and Olsen (1983) have shown, however, that a strong effect of mortality on fertility cannot be inferred from a regression of household fertility data on child deaths because of a spurious correlation between micro mortality and fertility data. This occurs because families with more births tend to have more deaths simply because they have more children at risk. Furthermore, since infant mortality is a variable subject to household choice (and influenced by inputs such as breastfeeding, nutritional supplementation, and utilization of health-care services), the alleged strong effect of mortality on fertility simply may reflect the fact that higher

---

[30] Though recent studies suggest that neither in some European countries (e.g. France) nor in some developing countries has the Demographic Transition always followed the stereotypic pattern. See Birdsall, Chapter 12 in this Handbook, for an extensive discussion of fertility determinants and experience in the developing world.

fertility resulting in shorter birth intervals significantly increases the probability of infant deaths.

Using merged data on Colombian households and communities, Rosenzweig and Schultz (1982c) estimate fertility and child mortality demand functions conditional on each other. To identify the effect of child mortality on fertility, they use per captia community expenditure on family planning, arguing that these proxy contraceptive prices and can be excluded from the child mortality (but not the fertility) equation; since all of the exogenous variables enter into all the reduced-form relations for all of the endogenous variables, however, this identification appears arbitrary. Their results indicate a positive effect of child mortality on fertility among mothers at all ages. The implied response derivatives of births with respect to deaths results range from 0.14 to 0.44 for different age groups of women.

Olsen (1983) estimates the impact of infant mortality on fertility, using Malaysian household data and controlling for the spurious correlation between the two variables and for family-specific fixed effects. The Olsen paper is the most thorough attempt to distinguish between the replacement, hoarding, and biological effects of child deaths on births. Olsen finds that, when the biases of simple regression procedures are eliminated, one is still left with a sizeable replacement response of fertility to mortality of some 30–40 percent. Replacement due to hoarding accounts for 14 percent; the biological impact of a death via lactation adds another 12 percent to the rate of replacement; and direct behavioral replacement is between 5 and 15 percent.

Interval regressions performed by Olsen suggest that the behavioral response to a death is fairly immediate. Thus, children who die soon after birth are replaced to a greater extent than older children who die, which implies that "...apparently replacement is more complex than just a simple attempt to achieve a goal for live children" [Olsen (1983, p. 25)].

6. Empirical studies on supply considerations and related policies

There have been a number of studies that have attempted to analyze the impact of governmental programs and policies seeking to supply health and nutritional goods to target households. We now review such studies on food subsidies, subsidies for other health related inputs, and on the impact of macro adjustment programs on health and nutrition in developing countries.

6.1. Food subsidies

Food subsidies have been used widely in developing economies, and a number of major programs persist to date. Numerous studies of the impact of these programs have been considered over the years, with the earlier studies focusing relatively on the extent of disincentives created for domestic food productions. We review some of the more recent studies that have substantial focus on the nutritional impact of such programs.

Alderman and von Braun (1984) study the impact of the Egyptian food ration and subsidy system at the micro level using household survey data. Egypt has had a long history of implicity of explicitly subsidizing food, with the food subsidy bill accounting for 10–15 percent of the government's total expenditures since the mid-1970s. They find that over 90 percent of the households in urban and rural areas have ration cards and frequently buy rationed commodities. The sum of all income transfers[31] from all outlets directly controlled by the government (rations, cooperatives, bakeries, and governmental flour shops) is $36 per capita for urban consumers and $24 per capita for rural consumers (in 1981–82). Thus, the subsidies transferred through the government outlets favor the urban population. In fact, the urban bias of the subsidy system is even greater, since food pricing (although not directly linked to food subsidy) adversely affects rural residents who are producers of food. Taking this into account (as well as the fact that input subsidies and livestock protection are transfers *to* producers), the authors estimate that the average net production transfer to rural areas is actually negative (approximately − $4 per capita), indicating an implicit tax on the rural sector.

The authors also note that the use that consumers make of the rationing system depends inversely on the time required to acquire food at the governmental outlets. Urban consumers are willing to pay higher prices for open market goods when lines at cooperatives increase. Interestingly, there is not much difference in the willingness of low- and high-income consumers to wait in line, indicating the similar opportunity costs of time for all consumers and that queing may not be a very effective redistribution mechanism.

To increase the effectiveness of the food subsidy system while reducing its cost, Alderman and von Braun suggest elimination of subsidies in such products as frozen meat and chicken and refined (fine) flour and its products, which contribute little to the amount of protein and calories that households consume and which have high income and price elasticities of demand. Since these subsidies are regressive, their elimination would also have distributionally appealing effects.

Williamson-Gray's (1982) study of food subsidization policies in Brazil finds these to be inefficient in helping the poor improve their nutritional status. This is because the commodities whose prices are generally subsidized, namely wheat, liquid milk, beef, and vegetable oils, are consumed primarily by high-income and well-nourished households. Williamson-Gray argues that rice and cassava flour are the best commodities to subsidize from the point of view of increasing calorie

---

[31] Defined as {(border or world price − local transport costs) − reported purchase price} × quantity purchased.

consumption by calorie-deficit groups. A subsidy on wheat bread may in fact reduce the calorie consumption of the poor and malnourished as they might shift from high-calorie, low-status goods like rice and cassava flour to what bread. The study uses demand system parameters along with an analysis of the demand for food quality (proxied by the average price of a calorie consumed) to draw its conclusion. Williamson-Gray observes a high income elasticity of quality even among the poor and the malnourished. This implies that these (food subsidy) target groups would be quick to shift to high calorie-cost foods with the smallest increases in real income, a result consistent with the discussion in Section 4.2.

Trairatvorakul's (1984) investigation of alternative rice price policies in Thailand finds that, contrary to widely held beliefs, the net gains to the rural poor from *increases* in the price of rice are likely to be minimal, since many small farmers are subsistence oriented and one-fourth are actually net purchasers of rice. A rice price increase would create short-run hardships for many of the rural poor, while most of the gains would accrue instead to large commercial farms.

Thailand long used export controls to regulate the domestic price of rice. In effect, this meant a subsidy on domestic rice, since the domestic price of rice was lower than the international price. Using partial equilibrium models of paddy supply, labor demand and supply, and food consumption behavior, Trairatvorakul analyzes the effect of rice price changes on the calorie intake of consumers and paddy farmers, among other things. He finds that, while a rice price increase of 50 percent would reduce the percentage of rice growers living under a fixed poverty line from 33.7 to 26.5, it would *increase* the percentage of other (consumer) households in poverty from 16.4 to 19.9. The national average rate of poverty therefore would fall only slightly, from 26.0 percent to 23.6 percent. Disaggregating his analysis by expenditure deciles and by rural/urban origin, he finds that 37 percent of the net gains to the rural sector from a rice price increase of 10 percent are acquired by the richest three deciles, while the largest net relative losses to the urban sector are borne by the lower expenditure groups.

Edirisinghe's (1985) study of the food stamps scheme in Sri Lanka finds that it has primarily benefited the poor. The percentage of total calories derived from food stamps is 11 percent for the poorest quintile of households (in 1981–82) and 6 percent for the next poorest quintile. However, the average cost of supplying 100 calories via food stamps is estimated to be around 53 cents, while the cost of supplying that number of calories to the poorest 20 percent of the households is 38 cents. Since the average cost of providing a calorie increases with income, this implies that the cost of the food stamp scheme in Sri Lanka could be almost 30 percent lower if recipients were restricted to the poorest 20 percent of the population. Edirisinghe thus concludes that, while the food stamp scheme in Sri Lanka has been successful in helping the poor, its cost effectiveness can be increased with better targeting and lower leakage to households who do not need nutritional supplementation assistance from the state.

The issue of targeting and cost effectiveness in food subsidies is discussed in detail in two surveys by Pinstrup-Andersen (1985) and Mateus (1983). The cost effectiveness of food subsidies depends directly on the degree of targeting. Pinstrup-Andersen suggests that subsidies may be either limited to certain times of the year, e.g. the lean months when malnutrition is severe, or targeted to specific individuals or households on the basis of criteria such as income, residence (e.g. rural areas and urban slums), and extent of malnutrition. In reviewing various food subsidy projects, Mateus argues that the most efficient programs are the special intervention programs designed for the malnourished and most vulnerable groups: children and pregnant–lactating mothers. Targeting also can be achieved by requiring customers who desire to purchase subsidized foods to wait in long lines (since this would seem to discourage participation by higher income households having a high opportunity cost of time, though the Alderman and von Braun results just reviewed raise questions about this assumption for Egypt) and by offering lower quality foods that are generally undesirable to high-income groups. The success of targeting certain types of individuals within households, however, is quite limited by the fungibility of resources among household members. Food programs for children and pregnant and lactating women, for example, tend to result in considerable offsets in the food available to such individuals from the household.

According to Pinstrup-Andersen, the "best" commodities to be subsidized can be chosen on a number of criteria, including their availability, own-price elasticity, share in the budget of poor households, and the price per calorie supplied. Additionally, since many studies have shown large production disincentive effects of nutrition programs and food procurement policies [Mateus (1983, pp. 40–41)], the ideal candidates for subsidies might be commodities with low supply responses. Many so-called inferior cereals in developing countries – namely sorghum, millet, cassava – might qualify for subsidization based on the above criteria. However, as we noted earlier in this section, many countries subsidize such inappropriate commodities as frozen meat and fine flour (Egypt), beef, liquid milk, wheat, and vegetable oils (Brazil).

Finally, of the various systems via which food subsidy programs can be implemented, Mateus regards the food coupon system as less demanding as long as it uses the traditional wholesale and retail trade systems. Colombia and Sri Lanka are two of several countries that have had highly successful and cost-effective food coupon schemes.

Mateus also notes that there is a dramatic improvement in the benefit/cost ratio of nutrition programs combined with health delivery systems. The integration of health and nutrition programs often has resulted in 40–50 percent declines in infant mortality, at the same time allowing a reduction in costs since joint use of facilities capitalizes on fixed-cost investment, personnel, and management.

According to Pinstrup-Andersen, foreign food aid is an attractive source of obtaining food for subsidy programs, since it greatly reduces governmental costs of the program. Procurement schemes that obtain food from producers at below-market prices are difficult to enforce and impose large economic costs on the agricultural sector. Of course, foreign food aid programs also can result in local production disincentives if the market in which the recipients participate is not segmented from the market for local producers.

Mateus and Pinstrup-Andersen argue somewhat convincingly that targeting of food subsidies can be used to shift income to poorer members of society who purchase their food (i.e. not for poor subsistence farmers). However, they do not consider whether other policies might be more effective in redistributing income, nor that income increases may not have much impact on nutrition (see Section 4.2).

All of the above studies on food subsidies are based on partial equilibrium models. In particular, they do not address the macroeconomic impacts of food subsidies, which, for many countries (e.g. Sri Lanka, Egypt, Morocco, and Sudan), have been considerable and probably quite negative. Studies addressing the non-nutrition impacts of food subsidies are reviewed in an excellent survey of the food subsidy literature by Horton and Taylor (1986). In general, however, studies focusing on the macroeconomic and general equilibrium dimensions of food subsidies are very few [with a few exceptions such as Taylor (1979) and Narayana et al. (1985)]. Because pressures have increased substantially in recent years to cut food and other health-related subsidies as part of overall macro stabilization programs, further macro work seems warranted.

6.2. Other health goods and services subsidies

De Ferranti (1985) discusses the policy options of providing and financing health goods and services in developing countries. Most such countries finance health care to a very large extent from public revenues. de Ferranti argues for a reorientation of such policies, with greater focus on having users bear a larger share of health-care costs through a combination of fees for services and fees for coverage. This should particularly be followed for nonreferred curative care, which accounts for the bulk of public health expenditures in developing countries. For preventive services, however, de Ferranti suggests zero or even negative fees, since "... for many of the major preventive services currently feasible on a large scale in developing countries – including immunization, oral rehydration therapy, antenatal and perinatal care, promotion of breast-feeding and improved weaning practices, and hypertension control – the facts and concepts that users need to know are simple and can be communicated to the target population easily and at reasonable cost" [de Ferranti (1985, p. 61)]. The real issue would not seem to be, however, whether costs are "reasonable", but whether there are externalities, large increasing returns to scale, or distributional reasons for such subsidies.

In a survey of pricing policy for health and education in developing countries, Jimenez (1986a) also concludes that the efficiency gains from user charges for selected types of health and education (i.e. those for which the benefits accrue primarily to the individuals concerned, such as hospital care) could be substantial, and that the impact of increased user charges need not be inequitable since

> the present distribution of subsidies tends to be highly skewed towards higher income groups who obtain greater access to more costly social services... even if they are uniformly free for all. Under these circumstances, the expansionary effect of fee increases for selected services (and, if possible, for selected individuals) may actually improve equity in the distribution of public resources [Jimenez (1986a, abstract)].

While both of these studies are suggestive of general guidelines for deciding to what extent, if any, health inputs should be subsidized due to externalities or returns to scale, they do not provide concrete estimates of the gains to be reaped in different specific situations.

6.3. Impact of macro adjustment policies on health and nutrition

Several studies associated with UNICEF [Jolly and Cornia (1984), UNICEF (1984)] have attempted to evaluate the impact of macroeconomic adjustment policies specifically on health and nutrition. These studies do not formalize explicitly the links between recession and/or economic adjustment and the health and nutrition of children. But they attempt to use secondary data to characterize some of the links relating to factors such as unemployment, the composition of governmental expenditures, and direct indicators of health and nutrition. They conclude that the negative impact of recessions and adjustment policies on health and nutrition are multiplied for the most vulnerable members of society. In a review of these studies, however, Preston (1986, p. 375) suggests that the appropriate conclusion from surveying these studies would seem to be – subject to conceptual and data difficulties – that the available evidence from these studies indicates "how much can be achieved even in the face of unusual economic adversity – surely good news for social policy...". Instead of such emphasis, however, the editors have a "penchant for stressing the negative trends... (a distinct minority) [which] receive the lion's share of the editors' attention in the introduction and summary". Thus, a set of studies that seem to lead to the conclusion of little, or at least unproven, systematic impact of recession and economic adjustment on health and nutrition, is summarized as finding that adjustment policy usually multiples negative recessionary impact on the poor and vulnerable.

Hicks and Kubisch (1983, 1984) analyze the impact of economic adjustment programs on social sector spending on less-developed country governments by examining the pattern of cuts in expenditure induced by such adjustment programs for all 37 LDCs that reported cuts in real government annual expenditures during 1972–80. They find that, contrary to popularly-held beliefs, on the average social expenditures were the *most* protected of social, defense and administration, production, infrastructure, and miscellaneous expenditures (somewhat more so in low- than in middle-income countries). Thus, the frequent assumption that social sectors are particularly vulnerable to cuts in governmental expenditures may be wrong – in fact, the opposite may be the case.

Behrman (1976b) reviews evidence from a number of macro and micro studies. He concludes that "...the effects [of economic adjustment policies on health and nutrition] *may* be very limited because of the limited effectiveness of macroeconomic policies, the lack of impact of policies on some of the poorest, and the adjustment and substitution capabilities of those of the poor whose real income and prices broadly-defined are altered negatively" [Behrman (1987b, pp. 32–33)].

7. Summary and conclusions

The studies on health and nutrition in developing economies to date have provided some insights, but they also raise a number of important questions and point to great lacunae in our knowledge. In this concluding section we first summarize the insights and then consider directions for future research.

7.1. Summary of available studies

Although there is substantial variation in the estimates, the extent of malnutrition and poor health in the developing world as measured by conventional standards is considerable. Consideration of the adaptability of the human body to its environment and the extent of inter- and intraperson variations leads to a less pessimistic characterization of the current situation and somewhat different identification of who is at risk. Nevertheless, large numbers of individuals in the developing world have lower nutritional input and health status than many would think desirable. Such inadequacies are likely to be exacerbated at times of unfavorable relative price movements for the poorer members of societies, such as during famines. Such a characterization is appropriate for the late 1980s despite very considerable absolute and relative gains in indicators of average nutrition and health status in developing countries – such as life expectancy – in recent decades. These gains have been larger in fact than the gains indicated by narrowly defined economic indicators. Of course the national averages hide a wide range of variances and, since the situation for the poorer may be particularly critical in determining average health and nutrition, countries that appear similar according to the per capita income averages have had widely different average nutrition and health status. The life expectancy at birth in 1983 of 69 years in Sri Lanka as compared to 38 years in Sierra Leone, though both have per capita income estimates of $330 for that year, provides a vivid example.[32]

Efforts to investigate the micro level determinants of health status or of health-care utilization, whether by estimating health production functions or reduced-form demand equations, have met with some, but fairly limited success. Some micro health production function estimates suggest that direct nutritional supplements improve child, but not adult, health. This contrast between the health production function results for children versus those for adults may not be surprising given the apparent relatively greater importance of nutrients in the child development stage and strong intraperson serial correlation in health status. For adults, nutrient increases seem to result in increased energy expenditures, in some cases associated with increased productivity. Reduced-form micro demand relations for both child and adult health find little evidence of responses to relative market prices, income, or wealth. The micro estimates, however, contrast sharply with the aggregate estimates of fairly strong associations between measures such as life expectancy and per capita real income or product. This contrast raises the question of whether the micro results are misleading because of measurement errors for health and/or income and specification errors regarding lags and time use, or whether in the macro estimates per capita income or product is representing not the purchasing power of individuals so much as the general level of development and associated public health measures that are not well represented in micro estimates. For a number of both the micro and the macro estimates, furthermore, standard estimates often indicate a substantial role for women's schooling, in some cases substituting for other inputs. In the one sample for which adult sibling deviations permit extensive control for the women's unobserved childhood background characteristics, however, the impact of women's schooling on health vanishes with such a control.

Studies of the reduced-form demand relations for nutrient intakes suggest some substantial price responses, not only for foods consumed, but also for agricultural products and inputs in the case of farm households. The substantial price responses mean that many policies and market developments may affect nutrition whether or not that is their intent. Policy-makers need to be sensitive to such possibilities in their policy design and implementation. The food price responses, moreover, are not always negative; in some cases, particularly for farm

---

[32] Bhalla (1984) and Bhalla and Glewwe (1986) discusses in some detail the Sri Lankan experience.

or rural labor households, the price elasticities for locally produced foods may be positive and considerable in magnitude. For such households, food price floors may improve nutrition more than the price subsidies that often are rationalized on such grounds. Of course, the same result is not likely to be true for the nonrural poor, but many of the poorest and most malnourished are in the rural areas. Another interesting characteristic of the price elasticities is a tendency for them to be larger for poorer households. Differential price elasticities across the income distribution presents some possibilities of price policies that favor the poor for distributional reasons without too great leakages to those who are better off. Allocation of nutrients within households, finally, seems to favor males and older children in absolute terms, but there is some interesting evidence for rural south India that adjustments to price changes are relatively smaller for girls than for other household members – suggesting that in this sense nutrients for girls are treated less as luxuries than are those for others.

Estimates of nutrient determinants indicate a wide range of income or expenditure elasticities. However, in a number of cases large expenditure elasticities result from aggregate (with respect to foods) estimates based on a priori assumptions that nutrient elasticities are identical to a weighted average of food elasticities at a high level of aggregation. But this assumption may be very misleading if the prices paid for nutrients vary positively with income, as appears to be the case. Comparison of directly estimated nutrient elasticities with food elasticities for rural south India, in fact, suggest that the former are much smaller than the latter. Apparently other food characteristics – taste, appearance, status value, degree of processing – are valued much more than nutrition at the margin even among individuals in this relatively poor population. Cross-country estimates also suggest that in part the low income elasticities of nutrients (as compared with those for food expenditures) reflect an increasing taste for food variety as income increases. If non-nutritive food characteristics are favored highly at the margin, then income increases and the general development process will not alleviate malnutrition nearly as much as the World Bank (1980), Srinivasan (1985), and others have claimed. On the other hand, the limited importance placed by individuals in such populations on increasing nutrient consumption at the margin (if they are making informed choices) raises doubts about whether they are so malnourished as conventional estimates suggest, and thus provides a different type of evidence consistent with the Sukhatme–Srinivasan–Seckler–Payne hypothesis about individual adaptability to nutrient availabilities and "small but healthy" people. Of course such evidence does not speak to the question, why are many people in some populations so small, nor does it allay the suspicion that the malnutrition experienced by many children in such populations is associated not only with small adults, but also with high infant and child mortality.

Beyond relative prices and perhaps income, some – but far from all – studies point to the possible importance of women's schooling, nutritional knowledge, and public health measures in improving nutrient consumption (particularly for children). The impact of women's schooling and nutrient knowledge may reflect that better-educated consumers make more nutritious food choices, ceteris paribus. The impact of women's schooling on nutrient consumption, in contrast to that on health, is robust to control for unobserved background characteristics in the one sample that permits such adult sibling control. Better public health services such as safer water may reflect the greater value of nutrients when such factors are present because of their complementarity with nutrients in the health production function. Of course women's schooling also may be playing such a role in addition to or instead of working only by improving information about nutrient qualities of different foods.

Nutrient intakes and health status both appear to affect positively agricultural productivity and labor market wages and possibly schooling productivity for some poor populations. Nutrient intakes might affect productivity without altering indicators of health status because nutrient changes may be transferred largely to energy expenditure changes, including some that are productivity related. Except in extreme cases, malnourishment does not seem to alter fertility. However, declines in infant mortality do seem broadly to reduce fertility. Therefore health and nutrition are not only important ends in themselves, but also may be important means through which productivity and population goals are affected.

Investigations on the supply side have focused on the impact of subsidy policies for food and, to a lesser extent, other health-related inputs. Such studies suggest that general food subsidies are not very effective in redistributing income to the poor, but that targeted food programs can be used to shift income to some segments of the poor that depend on market purchases for food. However, the small nutrient elasticities with respect to income imply that nutrient intakes do not improve substantially as a result of such subsidies. Recent studies of actual nutrition and other health-related input pricing policies suggest that in fact they often redistribute income *from* the poor and are not justified on the grounds of externalities, though subsidies for preventive measures for contagious diseases may be justifiable on the latter grounds.

Strong claims have been made by UNICEF and others about very negative multiplied effects of macroeconomic adjustment policies on health and nutrition. Careful examination of the relevant studies, however, suggests that the empirical basis for such a claim currently is quite weak. In fact the underlying studies seem to be characterized better as reflecting how well societies and people have adapted to minimize negative health and nutrition effects rather than the more negative interpretation given by UNICEF.

7.2. Directions for future research

Despite the growing number of studies of health and nutrition in developing countries, the lacunae in our knowledge remain substantial. Many of the questions raised in our introduction remain unanswered.

Major questions pertain to the measurement of nutrient input and health status, and thus the extent, incidence and determinants of nutrient and health inadequacies. The adaptability hypothesis discussed in Section 3.2, for instance, raises difficult questions about how can policy-makers or other analysts identify at a reasonable cost who is malnourished in a population. The failure to find much in the way of positive results regarding the determinants of health (particularly for adults), for another example, may be due to substantial measurement errors in representing health status. Frequently, respondent-reported disease data are used as indicators, though such reports are likely to be determined endogenously by characteristics like wealth. The gains of obtaining clinical-based health indicators, therefore, may be worth the added costs. Perhaps it would be cost effective to obtain such information not so much by expanding socioeconomic surveys to include clinical information on health, but by working with health professionals like epidemiologists and expanding their data collection efforts to include broader samples and more socioeconomic data, with sample designs to assure sufficient variance in critical price and asset variables. In the meantime, conclusions based on the types of data available to date have to be qualified because of their conditionality on quite imperfect health and nutrition indicators. More studies might explore fruitfully how robust are their results to alternatives such as latent variable specifications of health and nutrition as have been undertaken in several recent studies.

With respect to the determination of health, major questions remain. To what extent does the very limited success in estimating micro health production functions and reduced-form demand relations reflect data inadequacies regarding health measures, inappropriate lag structures, energy expenditure adaptations, or the failure to specify the influence of individual, household and community endowments? What are the nature of the biological processes involved, the extent of substitutabilities and complementarities in health production processes, the nature of lags, and the role of nutrition? How important is women's education in determining health? Is its often significant role in standard estimates reflective of increased productivity in using given health-related inputs, or is it primarily proxying for unobserved individual and household endowments as suggested by the one available adult–sibling deviation study? Are education and public health measures substituted broadly, as Rosenzweig and Schultz suggest for their Colombian study? More generally, what is the nature of substitution and complementarities in health production functions? How important are seasonal variations, particularly in rural areas? How can the very limited success in estimating micro health relations be reconciled with the fairly strong association between health and development across societies? What role does uncertainty play in the determination of health?

With respect to the determination of nutrient intakes, progress apparently has been greater, but questions remain. To what extent would more extensive specification of prices, assets and endowments change our current understanding? What is the nature of the intrahousehold allocation process? Is it better represented by a bargaining framework? If so, what difference does it make? How fungible are resources within the household? For instance, how much do school children benefit from food provided at school and to what extent is such food received at school offset by receiving less food at home? Likewise, there are questions about to what extent food subsidies, food stamps, or food rationing improve the nutrition of recipients, or only result in the increased purchase of other food characteristics or of nonfood goods and services? How fungible are resources across seasons? How much is nutrition likely to improve with income increases associated with the process of development? Do the Behrman–Deolalikar results about the relatively limited nutrient income elasticities hold for other societies? If so, what explains the international nutrient differences that are associated with development?

Recent systematic estimates suggest that in some low-income contexts, the impact of health and nutrition on farm and labor market productivity may be substantial. How can such results be reconciled with the a priori scepticism such as summarized in Rosenzweig (Chapter 15 in this Handbook)? Do the Deolalikar–Strauss results carry over to other societies? If so, what are the implications for productivity growth, understanding labor market structure, and for health and nutrition policy?

Of course, one major reason for being concerned with the determinants of health and nutrition is to provide a better basis for policy formation. What are the implications of the growing corpus of empirical work on health and nutrition for policy? Can the apparent greater price and income responsiveness of poorer members of society (at least for nutrients) be utilized in more effective policies? Is the relative optimism of Mateus (1983) and Pinstrup-Andersen (1985) about targeting food subsidies warranted? If income increases have little nutritional impact, might direct income transfers for distributional reasons be preferable to food subsidies? What is the nature and extent of externalities, returns to scale, imperfect information or distributional concerns that warrant nutrition and other health-related price subsidies? Are the de Ferranti (1985) and Jimenez (1986a) type distinctions between nonreferred curative care versus preventive care useful in making operational policy decisions about health subsidies? What would be the distributional and health impact of increasing user charges or of new insurance schemes on different types of health inputs in specific contexts? How is dissemination of new inputs and knowledge affected by governmental pricing and subsidy policies, information problems, and industrial structure? To what extent are such policies justified in particular circumstances by externalities, public-good characteristics, returns to scale and other types of market failures or by distributional objectives? To what extent do governmental policies cause inefficiencies in the provision of health-related inputs? Do macro adjustment policies have multiplied or mitigated health and nutrition consequences? Could better policy design and monitoring lessen the negative effects?

References

Akin, J.S., Griffin, C.C., Guilkey, D.K., and Popkin, B.M. (1985) *The demand for primary health services in the Third World*. Rowman and Allanheld Publishers.

Alderman, H. (1984) 'The effects of income and food price changes on the acquisition of food by low-income households', International Food Policy Research Institute, Washington, DC, mimeo.

Alderman, H. and Von Braun, J. (1984) 'The effects of the Egyptian food ration and subsidy system on income distribution and consumption', International Food Policy Research Institute, Research Report 45.

Anderson, K.H. (1984) 'The effect of health programs on breastfeeding and child mortality in Peninsular Malaysia', in: T.P. Schultz and K.I. Wolpin, eds., *Research in Population Economics*, 5.

Bairagi, R. (1981) 'On validity of some anthropometric indicators as predictors of mortality' (letter to the editor), *American Journal of Clinical Nutrition*, 34:2592–2594.

Baldwin, R. and Weisbrod, B. (1974) 'Disease and labor productivity', *Economic Development and Cultural Change*, 22:414–435.

Bardhan, P. and Srinivasan, T.N. eds. (1974) *Poverty and income distribution in India*. New Delhi: Statistical Publishing Society.

Barlow, R. (1979) 'Health and economic development: A theoretical and empirical review', *Human Capital and Development*, 1:45–75.

Barnum, H.N. and Squire, L. (1979) 'An econometric application of the theory of farm-household', *Journal of Development Economics*, 6:79–102.

Bartel, A. and Taubman, P. (1979) 'The impact of specific diseases on earnings', *Review of Economics and Statistics*, February.

Bateman, M.J. (1965) 'Aggregate and regional supply functions for Ghanaian case, 1946–1962', *Journal of Farm Economics*, 47:384–481.

Battad, J.R. (1978) 'Nutritional status of preschoolers', *The Philippine Economic Journal*, 17:1,2.

Behrman, J.R. (1968) 'Monopolistic cocoa pricing', *American Journal of Agricultural Economics*, 50:702–719.

Behrman, J.R. (1981) 'Review of Lance Taylor, "Macro Models for Developing Countries"', *Journal of Development Economics*, 81:134–141.

Behrman, J.R. (1984) 'Sibling deviation estimates, measurement error and biases in estimated returns to schooling', University of Pennsylvania, mimeo.

Behrman, J.R. (1987a) 'Is child schooling a poor proxy for child quality?', *Demography*.

Behrman, J.R. (1987b) 'The impact of economic adjustment programs on health and nutrition in developing countries', in: D.E. Bell and M.R. Riech, eds. *Health, nutrition and economic crises: Approaches to policy in the third world*. Boston, MA: Oelgeschlager, Gunn and Hain Publishers, Inc.

Behrman, J.R. (1987c) 'Nutrition, health, birth order and seasonality: Intrahousehold allocation in rural India', *Journal of Development Economics*, September.

Behrman, J.R. (1988) 'Intrahousehold allocation of nutrients in rural India: Are boys favored? Do parents exhibit inequality aversion?' *Oxford Economic Papers*.

Behrman, J.R. and Deolalikar, A.B. (1987a) 'Seasonal demands for nutrient intakes and health status in rural south India', in: D.E. Sahn, ed., *Causes and implications of seasonal variability in household food security*. Washington, DC: International Food Policy Research Institute.

Behrman, J.R. and Deolalikar, A.B. (1987b) 'Wages and labor supply in rural India: The role of health, nutrition and seasonality', in: D.E. Sahn, ed., *Causes and implications of seasonal variability in household food security*. Washington, DC: International Food Policy Research Institute.

Behrman, J.R. and Deolalikar, A.B. (1987c) 'Will developing country nutrition improve with income? A case study for rural south India', *Journal of Political Economy*, 95:108–138.

Behrman, J.R. and Deolalikar, A.B. (1987d) 'Determinants of health and nutritional status of individual family members in rural India: A latent variable approach', University of Pennsylvania, mimeo.

Behrman, J.R. and Deolalikar, A.B. (1987e) 'Is variety the spice of life? Implications for nutrient responses to income', University of Pennsylvania, mimeo.

Behrman, J.R. and Wolfe, B.L. (1984a) 'More evidence on nutrition demand: Income seems overrated and women's schooling underemphasized', *Journal of Development Economics*, 14:105–128.

Behrman, J.R. and Wolfe, B.L. (1984b) 'The socioeconomic impact of schooling in a developing country', *Review of Economics and Statistics*, 66:296–303.

Behrman, J.R. and Wolfe, B.L. (1986) 'Does more schooling make women better nourished, but less healthy? Adult sibling estimates for Nicaragua', University of Pennsylvania, mimeo.

Behrman, J.R. and Wolfe, B.L. (1987) 'How does mother's schooling affect the family's health, nutrition, medical care usage, and household sanitation?,' *Journal of Econometrics*.

Behrman, J.R., Hrubec, Z., Taubman, P. and Wales, T.J. (1980) *Socioeconomic success: A study of the effects of genetic endowments, family environment, and schooling*. Amsterdam: North-Holland.

Berg, A.D. (1981) 'Malnourished people: A policy view', World Bank, mimeo.

Bhalla, S.S. (1984) 'Is Sri Lanka an exception? A comparative study of living standards', mimeo.

Bhalla, S.S. and Glewwe, P. (1986) 'Growth and equity in developing countries: A reinterpretation of the Sri Lankan experience', *World Bank Economic Review*, 1:35–64.

Birdsall, N. (1988) 'Economic approaches to population growth', chapter 12 in this volume.

Birdsall, N., et al. (1983a) 'Willingness to pay for health and water in rural Mali: Do WTP questions work?', World Bank, mimeo.

Birdsall, N., et al. (1983b) 'The demand for health and schooling in Mali: Results of the community and service provider survey', World Bank, mimeo.

Birdsall, N. and Chuhan, P. (1986) 'Client choice of health care treatment in Mali', World Bank, mimeo.

Black, R.E. (1984) 'Diarrheal diseases and child morbidity and mortality', in: W.H. Mosley and L.C. Chen, eds., *Child survival strategies for research*, Cambridge: Cambridge University Press.

Blau, D.M. (1984) 'A model of child nutrition, fertility, and women's time allocation: The case of Nicaragua', in: T.P. Schultz and K.I. Wolpin, eds., *Research in population economics*, 5. Greenwich, CT: JAI Press.

Bliss, C. and Stern, N. (1978) 'Productivity, wages and nutrition; Parts I and II: The theory', *Journal of Development Economics*, 5:331–398.

Bongaarts, J. (1980) 'Does malnutrition affect fecundity? A summary of the evidence', *Science*, 208:564–569.

Bongaarts, J. and Delgado, H. (1979) 'Effects of nutritional status on fertility in rural Guatemala', in: H. Leridon and J. Menken, eds., *Natural fertility*. Liege, pp. 107–133.

Bradley, D.J. and Keymer, A. (1984) 'Parasitic diseases: Measurement and mortality impact', in W.H. Mosely and L.C. Chen, eds., *Child survival: Strategies for research*. Cambridge: Cambridge University Press.

Chambers, R., Longhurst, R. and Pacey, A. eds. (1981) *Seasonal dimensions to rural poverty*. London: Frances Pinter.

Chandhri, R. and Timmer, C.P. (1986) 'The impact of affluence on diet and demand patterns for agricultural commodities', World Bank Staff working paper no. 785.

Chen, L.C. Chowdhury, A.K.M., and Huffman, S.L. (1980) 'Anthropometric assessment of energy–protein malnutrition and subsequence risk of mortality among preschool-aged children', *American Journal of Clinical Nutrition*, 33:1836–1845.

Chernichovsky, D. and Kielmann, A.A. (1977) 'Correlates of preschool child growth in rural Punjab', in: A.A. Kielmann et al., eds., 'The Narangwal nutrition study' mimeo.

Chowdhury, A.K.M.A. (1978) 'Effects of maternal nutrition on fertility in rural Bangladesh', in: W.H. Mosley, ed., *Nutrition and human reproduction*. New York, pp. 123–145.

Clark, C.A.M. (1981) 'Demographic and socioeconomic correlates of infant growth in Guatemala', Rand Corporation report no. N-1702-AID/RF.

Cochrane, S.H., O'Hara, D., and Leslie, J. (1980) 'The effects of education on health', World Bank Staff working paper no. 405, mimeo.

Correa, H. (1975) *Population, health, nutrition, and development*. Lexington, MA: Heath.

Dandekar, V.M. and Rath, N. (1971) 'Poverty in India', *Economic and Political Weekly*, 6: Nos. 1 and 2.

DaVanzo, J. and Habicht, J.P. (1984) 'What accounts for the decline in infant mortality in peninsular Malaysia, 1946–1975?', in: J. DaVanzo, J.P. Habicht, K. Hill and S. Preston, eds., *Quantitative studies of mortality decline in the developing world*. Washington: DC: World Bank.

de Ferranti, D. (1985) 'Paying for health services in developing countries: An overview', World Bank Staff working paper no. 721.

Deolalikar, A.B. (1988) 'Do health and nutrition influence labor productivity in agriculture? Econometric estimates for rural south India', *Review of Economics and Statistics*, 70:2, May.

Durnin, J.V.G.A. et al. (1974) 'A cross-sectional nutritional and anthropometric study, with an internal of 7 years, on 611 young adolescent school children', *British Journal of Nutrition*, 32:169–179.

Easterlin, R.A., Pollak, R.A., and Wachter, M.L. (1980) 'Towards a more general model of fertility determination', in: R.A. Easterlin, ed., *Population and economic change in developing countries*. Chicago: University of Chicago Press, pp. 81–150.

Edirisinghe, N. (1985) 'Preliminary report on the food stamp scheme in Sri Lanka: Distribution of benefits and impact on nutrition', Washington, DC: International Food Policy Research Institute.

Folbre, N. (1983) 'Household production in the Philippines: A non-neoclassical approach', *Economic Development and Cultural Change*.

Folbre, N. (1986) 'Cleaning house: New perspectives on households and economic development', *Journal of Development Economics*, 22:5–40.

Food and Agricultural Organization (FAO) (1977) *The fourth world food survey*. Rome: FAO.

Foster, S.O. (1984) 'Immunizable and respiratory diseases and child mortality', in: W.H. Mosley and L.C. Chen, eds., *Child survival strategies for research*. Cambridge: Cambridge University Press.

Frisch, R.E. (1978) 'Population, food intake, and fertility', *Science*, CIC: 22–30.

Greer, J. and Thorbecke, E. (1986) 'A methodology for measuring food poverty applied to Kenya', *Journal of Development Economics*, 24:59–74.

Gwatkin, D.R. (1983) 'Does better health produce greater wealth: A review of the evidence concerning health, nutrition, and output', Overseas Development Council.

Heckman, J.J. (1976) 'The common structure of statistical models of truncation, sample selection, and limited dependent variables and a simple estimator for such models', *Annals of Economic and Social Measurement*, 475–492.

Heller, P.S. and Drake, W.D. (1979) 'Malnutrition: Child morbidity and the family decision process', *Journal of Development Economics*, 6:203–236.

Hicks, N. and Kubisch, A. (1983) 'The effects of expenditures reductions in developing countries', The World Bank, mimeo.

Hicks, N. and Kubisch, A. (1984) 'Cutting government expenditures in LDCs', *Finance and Development*, September.

Hicks, N. and Streeton, P. (1979) 'Indicators of development: The search for a basic needs yardstick', *World Development*, 7.

Horton, S. (1984) 'Birth order and child nutritional status: Evidence on the intrahousehold allocation of resources in the Philippines', University of Toronto, mimeo.

Horton, S. and Taylor, L. (1986) 'Food subsidies in developing countries: Theory, practice and policy lessons', MIT, mimeo.

Horton S., Kerr, T. and Diakosavvas, D. (1985) 'Effects of the real cereal price on consumers: Some cross country evidence', mimeo.

Immink, M. and Viteri, F. (1981) 'Energy, intake and productivity of Guatemalan sugarcane cutters: An empirical test of the efficiency wages hypothesis, parts I and II', *Journal of Development Economics*, 92:251–287.

Iyengar, N.S., Jain, L.R. and Srinivasan, T.N. (1968) 'Economies of scale in household consumption: A case study', Econometric Annual of *Indian Economic Journal*, 15:465–477.

Jamison, D.T. (1986) 'Child malnutrition and school performance in China', *Journal of Development Economics*, 20:299–310.

Jimenez, E. (1986a) *Pricing policy in the social sectors: Cost recovery for education and health in developing countries*. The World Bank.

Jimenez, E. (1986b) 'The public subsidization of education and health in developing countries: A review of equity and efficiency', *The World Bank Research Observer*, 1:111–129.

Jolly, R. and Cornia, G.A. (1984) *The impact of world recession on children: A study prepared for UNICEF*. Oxford: Pergamon Press.

Jones, C. (1983) 'The mobilization of women's labor for cash crop production: A game theoretic approach', *American Journal of Agricultural Economics*, 65:1049–1054.

Kakwani, N. (1986a) 'On measuring undernutrition', World Institute for Development Economics Research, Helsinki, mimeo.

Kakwani, N. (1986b) 'Is sex bias significant', World Institute of Development Economics Research, Helsinki, mimeo.

Khan, Q.M. (1983) 'The impact of household endowment constraints on nutrition and health: A simultaneous equation test of human capital divestment', *Journal of Development Economics*, 15:313–328.

Kielmann, A.A. and McCord, C. (1978) 'Weight for age as an index of risk of death in children', *Lancet*, 1:1247–1250.

Knudsen, O.K. and Scandizzo, P.L. (1982) 'The demand for calories in developing countries', *American Journal of Agricultural Economics*, February: 80–86.

Krishnan, P. (1975) 'Mortalilty decline in India, 1951–1961: Development vs. public health program hypothesis', *Social Science and Medicine*, 9:475–479.

Lau, L.J., Lin, W. and Yotopoulos, P.A. (1978) 'The linear logarithmic expenditure system', *Econometrica*, 46:840–868.

Leibenstein, H.A. (1957) *Economic backwardness and economic growth*. New York: Wiley.

Levinson, F.J. (1974) *Morinda: An economic analysis of malnutrition among young children in rural India*. Cambridge, MA: Cornall/MIT International nutrition policy series.

Low, S.M. (1984) 'The cultural basis of health, illness and disease', *Social Work in Health Care*, 9:3.

Lunn, P.G., et al. (1980) 'Influence of maternal diet on plasma prolactin levels during lactation', *Lancet*, 1:623–625.

Maddala, G.S. (1977) *Econometrics*. New York: McGraw-Hill.

Magnani, R.J., Clay, D.C., Adlakha, A.L. and Tourkin, S.C. (1985) 'Breastfeeding, water/sanitation, and childhood nutrition in the Philippines', mimeo.

Malenbaum, W. (1970) 'Health and productivity in poor areas', in: H.E. Klarman, ed., *Empirical studies in health economics*. Baltimore: Johns Hopkins University Press.

Manser, M. and Brown, M. (1980) 'Marriage and household decision-making: A bargaining analysis', *International Economic Review*, 21:31–44.

Margen, S. (1981) 'Retrospective reactions', in: Maharashtra Association for Cultivation of Science, eds. *Report on the summer institute on newer concepts in nutrition and health and their implications for social policy*. India: Pune.

Martorell, R. and Arroyave, G. (1984) 'Malnutrition, work output, and energy need', paper presented at the International Union of Biological Sciences Symposium on Variation in Working Capacity in Tropical Populations, mimeo.

Martorell, R. and Ho, T.J. (1984) 'Malnutrition, morbidity, and mortality', in: W.H. Mosely and L.C. Chen, eds., *Child survival strategies for research*. Cambridge: Cambridge University Press.

Mateus, A. (1983) 'Targeting food subsidies for the Needy: The use of cost-benefit analysis and institutional design', World Bank Staff working paper no. 617, World Bank.

Mateus, A. (1985) 'Morocco: Compensatory programs for reducing food subsidies', World Bank, mimeo.

Mauskopf, J. and Wallace T. (1984) 'Fertility and replacement: Some alternative stochastic models and results', *Demography*, 21:519–536.

Mazumdar, D. (1959) 'The marginal productivity theory of wages and disguised unemployment', *Review of Economic Studies*, 26, 190–197.

McElroy, M.B. and Horney, M.J. (1981) 'Nash-bargained household decisions: Toward a generalization of the theory of demand', *International Economic Review*, 22:333–350.

McGuire, J.S. and Austin, J.E. (1986) 'Beyond survival: Children's growth for national development', James E. Austin Associates, Cambridge, MA, mimeo.

Menken, J., Trussell, J. and Watkins, S. (1981) 'The nutrition fertility link: An evaluation of the evidence', *Journal of Interdisciplinary History*, 11:425–441.

Merrick, T.W. (1985) 'The effect of piped water on early childhood mortality in urban Brazil, 1970 to 1976', *Demography*, 22:1–24.

Moock, P.R. and Leslie, J. (1986) 'Childhood malnutrition and schooling in the Terai region of Nepal', *Journal of Development Economics*, 20:33–52.

Murty, K.N. and Radhakrishna, R. (1981) 'Agricultural prices, income distribution and demand patterns in a low-income country', in: R.E. Kalman and J. Martinez, eds., *Computer applications in food production and agricultural engineering*. Amsterdam: North-Holland.

Narayana, N.S.S., Parikh, K.S. and Srinivasan, T.N. (1985) 'Indian Agricultural Policy: An applied general equilibrium analysis', Economic Growth Center, Yale University, mimeo.

O'Connell, S.A. and Mwabu, G.N. (1986) 'Health maintenance by workers in rural and urban production structures', University of Pennsylvania, mimeo.

Olsen, R.J. (1983) 'Cross-sectional methods for estimating the replacement of infant deaths', Ohio State University, mimeo.

Olsen, R.J. and Wolpin, K.I. (1983) 'The impact of exogenous child mortality on fertility: A waiting time regression with dynamic regressors', *Econometrica* 51:731–749.

Payne, P.R. (1975) 'Safe protein-calorie ratios in diets: The relative importance of protein and energy as causal factors of malnutrition', *American Journal of Clinical Nutrition*, 28:281.

Payne, P. and Cutler, P. (1984) 'Measuring malnutrition: Technical problems and ideological perspectives', *Economic and Political Weekly*, 25:1485–1491.

Pinstrup-Andersen, P. (1985) 'Food prices and the poor in developing countries', *European Review of Agricultural Economics*, 12:1/2.

Pinstrup-Andersen, P. and Caicedo, E. (1978) 'The potential impact of changes in income distribution on food demand and human nutrition', *American Journal of Agricultural Economics*, 60:402–415.

Pinstrup-Andersen, P., Ruiz de deLondõno, N. and Hoover, E. (1975) 'The impact of increasing food supply on human nutrition: Implications for commodity priorities in agricultural research and policy', *American Journal of Agricultural Economics*, 58:131–142.

Pitt, M.M. (1983) 'Food preferences and nutrition in rural Bangladesh', *Review of Economics and Statistics*, 65:105–114.

Pitt, M.M. and Rosenzweig, M.R. (1986) 'Agricultural prices, food consumption and the health and productivity of farmers,' in: I.J. Singh, L. Squire and J. Strauss, eds., *Agricultural household models: Extensions, applications and policy*. Washington: World Bank.

Pitt, M.M. and Rosenzweig, M.R. (1985) 'Health and nutrient consumption across and within farm households', *Review of Economics and Statistics*, 67:212–223.

Poleman, T.T. (1981) 'Quantifying the nutrition situation in developing countries', *Food Research Institute Studies*, 18:1–58.

Poleman, T.T. (1983) 'World hunger: Extent, causes, and cures', in: D.G. Johnson and G. E. Schuh, eds., *The role of markets in the world food economy*. Boulder, CO: Westview Press.

Popkin, B. (1978) 'Nutrition and labor productivity', *Social Science and Medicine*, 12C:117–125.

Preston, S.H. (1980) 'Causes and consequences of mortality declines in less developed countries during the twentieth century', in: R.A. Easterlin, ed., *Population and economic change in developing countries*. Chicago: University of Chicago Press.

Preston, S.H. (1983) 'Mortality and development revisited', University of Pennsylvania, mimeo.

Preston, S.H. (1986) 'Review of Richard Jolly and Giovanni Andrea Cornia, eds., 'The Impact of World Recession on Children', *Journal of Development Economics*, 21:374–376.

Radhakrishna, R. (1984) 'Distributional aspects of caloric consumption: Implications for food policy', in: K. T. Achaya, ed., *Interfaces between agriculture, nutrition and food science*. Tokyo, Japan: The United Nations University, pp. 231–240.

Reutlinger, S. (1984) 'Changes in the energy content of national diets and in the energy deficient diets of the poor: 1970–80', World Bank, mimeo.

Reutlinger, S. and Selowsky, M. (1976) *Malnutrition and poverty: Magnitude and policy options*. Baltimore, MD, and London: Johns Hopkins University Press.

Rosenzweig, M.R. (1985) 'Program interventions, intrahousehold allocation and the welfare of individuals: Economic models of the household', Minneapolis: University of Minnesota.

Rosenzweig, M.R. (1988) 'Labor markets in low-income countries', chapter 15 in this volume.

Rosenzweig, M.R. and Schultz, T.P. (1982a) 'Child mortality and fertility in Colombia: Individual and community effects', *Health Policy and Education*, 2. Amsterdam: Elsevier Scientific Publishing Co., pp. 305–348.

Rosenzweig, M.R. and Schultz, T.P. (1982b) 'Market opportunities, genetic endowments, and intrafamily resource distribution: Child survival in rural India', *American Economic Review*, 72:803–815.

Rosenzweig, M.R. and Schultz, T.P. (1982c) 'Determinants of fertility and child mortality in Colombia: Interactions between mother's education and health and family planning programs', draft final report for USAID, mimeo.

Rosenzweig, M.R. and Schultz, T.P. (1983a) 'Consumer demand and household production: The relationship between fertility and child mortality', *American Economic Review*, May:38–42.

Rosenzweig, M.R. and Schultz, T.P. (1983b) 'Estimating a household production function: Heterogeneity, the demand for health inputs, and their effects on birth weight', *Journal of Political Economy*, 91:723–746.

Rosenzweig, M.R. and Schultz, T.P. (1984) 'Market opportunities and intrafamily resource distribution: Reply', *American Economic Review*, 74.

Rozenzweig, M.R. and Wolpin, K.J. (1982) 'Governmental interventions and household behavior in a developing country: Anticipating the unanticipated consequences of social programs', *Journal of Development Economics*, April.

Ryan, J.G. (1982) 'Wage functions for daily labor market participants in rural south India', Progress Report no. 38, Economics Program, ICRISAT, Patancheru, Andhra Pradesh, India.

Ryan, J.G. and Wallace, D. (1986) 'Determinants of labor market wages, participation, and supply in rural south India', mimeo.

Schultz, T.W. (1975) 'The value of the ability to deal with disequilibria', *Economic Literature*, 13:827–846.

Schultz, T.P. (1978) 'Fertility and child mortality over the life cycle: Aggregate and individual evidence', *American Economic Review*, 68:208–215.

Schultz, T.P. (1984) 'Studying the impact of household economic and community variables on child mortality', *Population and Development Review*, 10 (suppl.):215–235.

Seckler, D. (1980) 'Malnutrition: An intellectual odyssey', *Western Journal of Agricultural Economics*, December:219–227.

Seckler, D. (1982) 'Small but healthy: A basic hypothesis in the theory, measurement and policy of malnutrition', in: P.V. Sukhatme, ed., *Newer concepts in nutrition and their implications for policy*. India: Maharashtra Association for the Cultivation of Science Research Institute.

Selowsky, M. (1978) 'The economic dimensions of malnutrition in young children', World Bank.

Selowsky, M. (1979) 'Target group-oriented food programs: Cost effectiveness comparisons', *American Journal of Agricultural Economics*, December.

Selowsky, M. (1981) 'Nutrition, health and education: The economic significance of complementarities at an early age', *Journal of Development Economics*, 9:331–346.

Selowsky, M. and Taylor, L. (1973) 'The economics of malnourished children: An example of disinvestment in human capital', *Economic Development and Cultural Change*, 22:17–30.

Sen, A.K. (1981a) *Poverty and famines: An essay on entitlement and deprivation*. Oxford: Clarendon Press.

Sen, A.K. (1981b) 'Public action and the quality of life in developing countries', *Oxford Bulletin of Economics and Statistics*, 43.

Sen, A.K. and Sengupta, S. (1983) 'Malnutrition of rural children and the sex bias', *Economic and Political Weekly*, Annual Number, May:855–864.

Shah, C.H. (1983) 'Food preference, poverty, and the nutrition gap', *Economic Development and Cultural Change*, 32:121–148.

Singh, I., Squire, L. and Strauss, J., eds. (1986) *Agricultural household models: Extensions, applications and policy*. Washington, DC: World Bank.

Sommer, A. and Lowenstein, M.S. (1975) 'Nutritional status and mortality: A prospective validation of the QUAC stick', *American Journal of Clinical Nutrition*, 28:287–282.

Srinivasan, T.N. (1977) 'Development, poverty, and basic human needs: Some issues', *Food Research Institute Studies*, 16:11–28.

Srinivasan, T.N. (1981) 'Malnutrition: Some measurement and policy issues', *Journal of Development Economics*, 8:3–19.

Srinivasan, T.N. (1983) 'Hunger: Defining it, estimating its global incidence, and alleviating it', in: D.G. Johnson and G.E. Schuh, eds., *The Role of Markets in the World Food Economy*. Boulder, CO: Westview Press.

Srinivasan, T.N. (1985) 'Malnutrition in developing countries: The state of knowledge of the extent of its prevalence, its causes and its consequences', mimeo.

Stiglitz, J. (1976) 'The efficiency wage hypothesis, surplus labour, and the distribution of income in LDC's', *Oxford Economic Papers, New Series*, 28:185–207.

Strauss, J. (1984) 'Joint determination of food consumption and production in rural Sierra Leone: Estimates of a household-firm model', *Journal of Development Economics*, 14:77–104.

Strauss, J. (1985) 'The impact of improved nutrition in labor productivity and human resource development: An economic perspective', Economic Growth Center discussion paper no. 494, Yale University.

Strauss, J. (1986) 'Does better nutrition raise farm productivity?' *Journal of Political Economy*, April.

Sukhatme, P.V. (1977) 'Malnutrition and poverty, ninth Lal Bhaduri Shastri memorial lecture', Indian Agricultural Research Institute, New Delhi.

Sukhatme, P.V., ed (1982a) *Newer concepts in nutrition and their implications for policy*. India: Maharashtra Association for the Cultivation of Science Research Institute.

Sukhatme, P.V. (1982b) 'Poverty and malnutrition', in: P.V. Sukhatme, ed., *Newer concepts in nutrition and their implications for poverty*. India: Maharashtra Association for the Cultivation of Science Research Institute.

Sukhatme, P.V. and Margen, S. (1978) 'Models for protein deficiency', *American Journal of Clinical Nutrition*, 31:1237–1256.

Tanner, J.M. (1978a) *Education and physical growth*. New York: International Universities Press.

Tanner, J.M. (1978b) *Foetus into man – physical growth from conception to maturity*. London: Open Books.

Taylor, C., et al. (1978) 'The Narangwal experiment on interaction of nutrition and infections: I, Project design and effects upon growth', *Indian Journal of Medical Research*, 68(suppl.):1–20.

Taylor, L. (1979) *Macro models for developing countries*. New York: McGraw-Hill.

Timmer, C.P. and Alderman, H. (1979) 'Estimating consumption parameters for food policy analysis', *American Journal of Agricultural Economics*, 61:982–987.

Trairatvorakul, P. (1984) 'The effects on income distribution and nutrition of alternative rice price policies in Thailand,' International Food Policy Research Institute, Washington, DC.

Trowbridge, F.L. and Sommer, A. (1981) 'Nutritional anthropometry and mortality risk', letter to the editor, *American Journal of Clinical Nutrition*, 34:2591–2259.

UNICEF (1984) 'The impact of world recession on children: A UNICEF special study', *The state of the world's children 1984*. Oxford: Oxford University Press.

von Braun, J. and de Haen, H. (1983) 'The effects of food price and subsidy policies on Egyptian agriculture', International Food Policy Research Institute, Washington, DC.

Ward, J.O. and Sanders, J.H. (1980) 'Nutritional determinants and migration in the Brazilian northeast: A case study of rural and urban areas', *Economic Development and Cultural Change*, 29:141–163.

Weisbrod, B. and Helminiak, T. (1977) 'Parasitic diseases and agricultural labor productivity', *Economic Development and Cultural Change*, 25:505–522.

Wheeler, D. (1980) 'Basic needs fulfillment and economic growth: A simultaneous model', *Journal of Development Economics*, 7:435–451.

Williams, A.D. (1977) 'Measuring the impact of child mortality on fertility: A methodological note', *Demography*, 14:581–590.

Williamson-Gray, C. (1982) 'Food consumption parameters for Brazil and their application to food policy', International Food Policy Research Institute, Washington, DC.

Wolfe, B.L. and Behrman, J.R. (1982) 'Determinants of child mortality, health and nutrition in a developing country', *Journal of Development Economics*, 11:163–194.

Wolfe, B.L. and Behrman, J.R. (1983) 'Is income overrated in determining adequate nutrition?' *Economic Development and Cultural Change*, 31:525–550.

Wolfe, B.L. and Behrman, J.R. (1984) 'Determinants of women's health status and health-care utilization in a developing country: A latent variable approach', *Review of Economics and Statistics*, 56:696–703.

Wolfe, B.L. and Behrman, J.R. (1986a) 'Child quantity and quality in a developing country: Family background, endogenous tastes and biological supply factors', *Economic Development and Cultural Change*, 34:703–720.

Wolfe, B.L. and Behrman, J.R. (1986b) 'Fertility, infant and child mortality, contraception, nutrition and breastfeeding: Latent variable system estimation of the impact of income, women's schooling and tastes', University of Pennsylvania, mimeo.

Wolfe, B.L. and Behrman, J.R. (1987) 'Women's schooling and children's health: Are the effects robust with adult sibling control for the women's childhood background?', *Journal of Health Economics*.

Wolgemuth, J.C., Latham, M., Hall, A., Chesher, A. and Crompton, D. (1982) 'Worker productivity and the nutritional status of Kenyan road construction laborers', *American Journal of Clinical Nutrition*, 36:68–78.

World Bank (1980) *World development report, 1980.* Washington: World Bank.

World Bank (1982) *World development report, 1982.* Washington: World Bank.

World Bank (1985) *World development report, 1985.* Washington: World Bank.

Ybañez-Gonzalo and Evenson, R.E. (1978) 'Production and consumption of nutrients in Laguna', *The Philippine Economic Journal*, 17:1,2.

Chapter 15

LABOR MARKETS IN LOW-INCOME COUNTRIES

MARK R. ROSENZWEIG*

University of Minnesota

Contents

1.	Introduction	714
2.	Employment and wage determination in rural labor markets	715
	2.1. Surplus labor, disguised employment and unemployment	715
	2.2. The family enterprise model and agricultural dualism	728
3.	Rural labor contracts: Risk, information and incentives problems	733
	3.1. Casual and permanent laborers: Spot and future markets for labor	736
	3.2. Tenancy contracts	738
4.	Geographic mobility	743
	4.1. The basic human capital model of migration	744
	4.2. Information and capital market constraints on mobility	745
	4.3. Two-sector unemployment equilibrium models	746
	4.4. Risk, remittances and family behavior	751
	4.5. Heterogeneity and selective migration	753
5.	Urban labor markets	754
	5.1. Diversity and unemployment	754
	5.2. Urban dualism and dual labor markets	756
6.	Conclusion	757
	References	759

*I am grateful to T.N. Srinivasan, Hollis Chenery, Jere Behrman, Mark Gersovitz, T. Paul Schultz, and John Strauss for careful readings of earlier drafts of this chapter.

Handbook of Development Economics, Volume I, Edited by H. Chenery and T.N. Srinivasan
© *Elsevier Science Publishers B.V., 1988*

1. Introduction

Labor being by far the most abundant resource in low-income countries, the determination of the returns to labor plays a central role in models of development. Any barriers to the reallocation of labor resources accompanying economic development are potentially critical impediments to further income growth. In the last 25 years, a great deal of knowledge has accumulated about labor markets in low-income countries. Extreme views on labor market processes that had influenced thought for many years have been moderated by the accumulation of empirical knowledge into a more eclectic and empirically grounded approach. This transformation has been influenced by both new developments in microeconomic theory concerned with information and risk problems, critical realities of low-income countries, and the increased availability of good data, which have disciplined theoretical exercises and helped weed out the merely clever models from those that inform.

One polar view of labor markets in developing countries was that such markets are riddled with imperfections and/or operate quite distinctly from those in high-income countries; with low income sometimes being taken to mean that labor was not a scarce resource in some sectors. The alternative view was that labor markets in low-income countries conform more closely to textbook Marshallian markets than do such markets in high-income countries, as the principally rural-based technology in such settings is relatively homogeneous, direct governmental interventions in the *labor* market are rare, relatively little of the labor force is unionized, and contractual arrangements are relatively uncomplex. There now appears to be important elements of truth in both views, although the influence of problems in other markets, principally intertemporal markets, on labor arrangements is understated in both perspectives.

Are there features of low-income countries that require special attention in modeling the operation of labor markets? Certainly one important and pervasive characteristic of low-income countries is the large proportion of the labor force in agriculture. To the extent that agricultural production requires different organizations than and/or confronts problems different from those in industrialized sectors, labor market analysis in such countries will differ from those in other settings. A second salient feature of low-income countries is the low proportion of workers who earn income wholly or chiefly in the wage labor market compared to the labor force in high-income countries. Workers in family enterprises or unpaid family laborers (the alternative employment modes) not only dominate the labor force in agriculture, but make up a significantly larger proportion of the work force in the non-agriculture sector as well, compared to that sector in high-income countries. The behavior of the family enterprise and its members, particularly in the context of agricultural production, thus forms the core of many labor market models depicting low-income labor markets.

In this chapter I discuss the operation of low-income labor markets with reference to the models that have been and continue to be influential in shaping the study of such markets. These models are evaluated in terms of their ability to shed light on the realities of the allocation, pricing and employment of labor in low-income countries. In Section 2, I discuss models directly concerned with and evidence on the employment and pricing of labor in the rural (agricultural) sector. I begin with those models concerned with the shadow value of labor in agriculture that were motivated by the highly influential "surplus labor" development models positing the redundancy of a large proportion of the rural labor force [Lewis (1954), Ranis and Fei (1961)]. Section 2 is also concerned with how rural wages are determined and their rigidity, the social and private costs of reallocating labor from agriculture to other activities, labor supply behavior, labor market dualism and unemployment determination. Section 3 is concerned with risk-mitigating and effort-eliciting contractual arrangements involving rural labor and the organization of the agricultural enterprise in an environment characterized by incomplete markets.

In Section 4, I consider the issue of whether labor is efficiently allocated across sectors and across geographical areas and problems of barriers to mobility. Models of migration incorporating human capital investments, information and capital constraints, uncertainty with respect to employment, riskiness in annual incomes, temporary migration, remittances, and heterogeneity in preferences and abilities among workers are discussed. Section 5 is concerned with urban labor markets, and addresses issues concerning the duality of urban labor markets and unemployment determination. In the final section, I highlight issues about which there has been little research but which appear to be of importance to the study of developing economies, in particular, life-cycle and intergenerational labor market mobility.

2. Employment and wage determination in rural labor markets

2.1. Surplus labor, disguised employment and unemployment

Since the majority of the population of low-income countries reside in rural areas and agriculture constitutes the largest industry in terms of employment, it is not surprising that most of the literature concerned with low-income-country labor markets is concerned with rural labor markets. A central question addressed is the determination of the opportunity cost of removing a laborer from the agricultural sector. The macro development models of Lewis (1954) and Ranis and Fei (1961), as noted, presumed that in the early stages of development, agricultural laborers would be shifted to the industrial sector without any reduction in total agricultural output. Such economies are characterized as *surplus labor* economies, i.e. the shadow wage of an agricultural laborer is nil. These models also assumed that the private costs of moving out of agriculture for an agricultural agent was his/her consumption, approximated by the average product in agriculture. Thus, private and social costs of reallocating labor are presumed also to be different, the discrepancy implying the immobility of agricultural labor vis-à-vis the industrial sector and representing a source of inefficiency.

In this section I review the combined models of household behavior and the operation of the rural labor market that yield the surplus labor presumptions of these macro development models, as in Sen (1966). Three basic extreme approaches have been taken in the literature concerned with the opportunity cost or surplus labor issue. In the first, no labor market is presumed to exist at all. In the second, labor markets are assumed to operate perfectly, and in the third, agriculture is assumed to be characterized by rigid wages and unemployment, i.e. agents seeking employment but unable to find it.

In considering these basic models, I will employ for the most part the same prototype model of the agricultural household. I will assume that the household has multiple members, that some members (dependents) do not provide resources to the family (do not work), that household size and its composition are exogenous, that there is a single family welfare function in which the consumption and leisure time of each member is given equal weight, and that the household obtains returns from the land its members work, with the land area being fixed in size. Specifically, I assume that a household with n members and N workers owns or has assigned to it a piece of land on which it produces output X which it also consumes (or sells). The technology of production is given by:

$$X = F(L, A), \quad F_L, F_A \geq 0; \; F_{LL} < 0, \tag{1}$$

where $L = Nh$, $h =$ hours of work and X is total output.

The family welfare function is:

$$U = U(c, l), \tag{2}$$

where $c = X/n$ and $l = \Omega - h$, i.e. c is average family consumption and l is the leisure of each of the N family workers, where Ω is the total time available to each worker. Each rural household maximizes (2) subject to (1) and other constraints discussed below.

2.1.1. Absent labor markets: The autarkic household

The simplest route to surplus labor is to assume that there is no labor market and that, contrary to (2), the leisure of household members is not valued. In that case, the only choice variable for the household is the number of hours each member will work and the first-order condition for that choice is:

$$U_c F_L = 0, \tag{3}$$

where U_c and F_L are the marginal utility of consumption and the marginal product of family labor, respectively. If U_c is positive, that is, low-income households have not reached satiety with respect to consumption, expression (3) indicates that work time is allocated such that the marginal product of an additional time unit of work (hour) by any family member is zero. Since this is optimal, expression (3) shows that the total output of families with the same amount of land A is invariant to the number of family laborers as long as the work time of family workers never reaches the full extent of Ω hours. Moreover, if a family workers leaves and is not provided any resources by the family (does not become a new dependent), the loss to him/her of moving out is c^*, average family consumption at $F_L = 0$. The discrepancy between the social and private costs of moving are due here both to (i) the absence of a labor market and (ii) the family sharing rule, for if the migrant family members still received c^* when working outside the household, then c^* would not enter into the decision to leave.

Sen (1966) considered an autarkic model in which the family welfare function included leisure, as in (2). In that case the first-order condition is:

$$(N/n)U_c/U_l = F_L, \tag{4}$$

and the marginal product of an extra hour of work by the family worker is no longer zero. Here, labor is in surplus only if the removal of a family member leaves the marginal rate of substitution between consumption and leisure unchanged, since in that case F_L and total output is unaltered. Thus, the existence of labor surplus depends importantly on the characteristics of the family welfare function; specifically, on family members fully compensating for the lost hours of work associated with the loss of a family worker by increasing their labor supply. Sen characterizes this situation as one in which there is *disguised unemployment*, since hours of work have a non-zero marginal product but laborers can be removed from the household (agriculture) without any loss in output.

2.1.2. Perfect labor markets

The possibility of compensatory family labor supply leading to disguised unemployment and surplus labor is independent of Sen's assumption of absent labor markets. Consider the perfect labor market model in which each family member can work as many hours as he/she wants at a given wage per hour and in which labor hours can be hired at a constant wage per hour. Assume, initially, for simplicity, that hired laborers are perfect substitutes in production for family laborers. Thus, the wage rate of a worker is the same whether he is working on his or her own farm or outside. What is "perfect" about this setup is that there is full information about the work of all individuals and no uncertainty about (labor) costs or returns, features that will be addressed below.

It will be demonstrated below that in such a model, the allocation of labor to production is independent of the family's welfare function; consumption and production decisions are separable and the household will, in maximizing its utility, always maximize farm profits. Letting the maximized profit level be given by Π^*, per capita family consumption is given by:

$$c = \Pi^*/n + Wh(N/n), \tag{5}$$

and the first-order condition for the allocation of family work time is:

$$U_l/U_c = W(N/n). \tag{6}$$

Note that the shadow value of leisure for family workers is less than the wage rate, since as long as there are dependents, per capita consumption increases by less than the (hourly) wage rate when work increases by one hour.

To ascertain if the removal of one worker from the family leads to an increase in the work by other family members when labor markets are perfect we can treat N and n as variables (ignoring, for simplicity, the discrete nature of family membership). In the case in which a migratory family member does not retain his/her rights to farm profits, this can be expressed as a (small) decrease in N compensated by an equal decrease in n. In that case, it can be readily shown that the elasticity of leisure l per remaining family worker with respect to a change in the number of family workers N is given by:

$$\eta_{l,N} = \frac{N-n}{n} \eta_{l,w}^c - N(Wh - c)\varepsilon_{l,\Pi^*} \tag{7}$$

where $\eta_{l,w}^c$ is the compensated own price elasticity of leisure and ε_{l,Π^*} is the income elasticity of leisure.

Expression (6) contains two terms. The first corresponds to the compensated price effect: a *reduction* in the number of family workers increases the dependency ratio $(N-n)/N$, lowers the shadow wage of leisure [remaining family workers must give up a larger share of their earnings (Wh)], and thus *decreases* family labor supply per remaining worker. The sign of the income effect, the second term in (6), will depend on (i) whether a reduction in the number of family workers lowers or raises per capita consumption, whether earnings per worker Wh exceeds c, and (ii) on whether leisure is a normal good, $\varepsilon_{l,\Pi^*} > 0$.

If we assume the normality of leisure, then (7) indicates that when the earnings of a family worker is less (more) than per capita consumption, so that there is a gain to (loss of) per capita consumption when a worker leaves the family, the demand for leisure rises (declines). Thus, for example, if absent family members lose their rights to family income and lose their obligations to pool their incomes, leisure is a normal good, and consumption from non-earnings income is sufficiently high (so that $Wh < c$), the labor supply of each remaining family worker unambiguously *decreases* when a laborer is removed from the household. In that case, output declines by *more* than the earnings contribution of the shifted laborer. Note that in the special case in which there are no dependents and no non-earnings income (e.g. a landless household), the loss of a family worker leaves the labor supply of remaining workers unaltered – there is neither an income effect (since $Wh = c$) nor a substitution effect. The loss in total output is thus equal to the contribution of the laborer.

The elasticity of total family labor supply Nh with respect to the number of workers N, η, is $1 - \eta_{hN}$, where $\eta_{hN} = -\eta_{lN}$. The labor surplus hypothesis of fully compensating family labor supply is thus $\eta = 0$; when $\eta_{hN} > 1$, family workers decrease their labor supply when a worker leaves, and when $0 < \eta_{hN} < 1$, remaining family workers increase their labor supply but by less than the loss in total family labor supply induced by the loss of the worker.

Estimates of the family worker labor supply elasticity have been obtained by Lau, Lin and Yotoupolos (1978) for Taiwan, by Adulavidhya et al. (1979) for Thailand, by Barnum and Squire (1978) for Malaysia, and by Strauss (1983) for Sierra Leone based on the perfect labor market model. In all of these studies, in which absent members are assumed neither to receive nor contribute to family income, total family labor supply is estimated to decline when a household worker is removed. The Lau et al. studies impose a unitary income–leisure elasticity and estimated η to be 1.3 in Taiwan and 0.94 in Thailand; the Barnum and Squire, and Strauss studies used a somewhat more flexible form for the household expenditure system. In both of these studies, estimates of the income–leisure elasticity are far below 1, with η being 0.62 in (Malaysia) and 0.55 in Sierra Leone, although it was assumed that removal of a family worker has only an income effect. All of these estimates thus reject the behaviorally based labor surplus hypothesis in the countries studied. Note, of course, that given the same behavioral rules embodied in the household model, differences across the Malaysian and Sierra Leone samples in either the mean proportions of agricultural earnings in total household agricultural income or in dependency ratios, from (7), imply that there will be cross-sample differences in η.

Both η and a family member's opportunity cost of outmigration depend on the family-sharing rule. If the migrant worker retains all familial rights and obligations, then the relative private gain (or loss) from migrating depends only on the ratio of market wage rates at home to those in the new area, implicitly assumed to be the same in eq. (5). The sign of $\eta_{l, N}$ will then depend only on whether the migrant worker's earnings are higher or lower in the new setting or in the rural market. The evidence on migrant-family income pooling is discussed below in the context of the migration literature.

2.1.3. Unemployment, underemployment and rigid wages: The nutrition-based efficiency model

The third theoretical route to surplus or redundant labor is to hypothesize that there are agricultural agents willing to, or seeking, work but unable to find employment, unable to contribute to production. If wages do not decline in the face of this excess supply of laborers, the removal of workers from agriculture presumably leaves the number of employed people and thus agricultural output unchanged. The question of theoretical interest in this approach is why wage rates are downwardly rigid.

The most important explanation for the downward rigidity of rural wages is the nutrition-based efficiency wage model [Leibenstein (1957), Mirrlees (1975), Stiglitz (1976)]. In this framework, labor effort (or labor power) is distinguished from labor time worked. While time worked is (or may be) a family decision variable, as above, individual labor effort per unit of time is hypothesized to be a technological (i.e. non-behavioral) and particular function of individual nutritional intake or consumption at low consumption levels. The appeal of the nutrition–efficiency wage model is that it provides a reason why low-income labor markets might be different from high-income labor markets. In this model, low income per se is the cause of a labor market problem (unemployment), not the reverse. Like the labor surplus hypothesis, however, as will be discussed below, it is unclear if the model has any relevance to any known population on this planet.

The central element of the nutrition-based efficiency wage theory is a hypothesized technical association between a worker's consumption c and his work effort λ per unit of time. Thus, the production function (1) is modified such that output is a function of total labor effort, rather than just labor time:

$$X = F(Nh\lambda(c)), \quad \lambda' > 0, \ F' > 0. \tag{8}$$

In Mirrlees (1975) and Stiglitz (1976), the work effort λ-function is given by Figure 15.1. Alternatively, as used in Bliss and Stern (1978) and Dasgupta and Ray (1984), the functional relationship between c and λ is given by Figure 15.2.

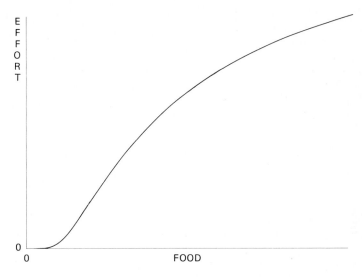

Figure 15.1

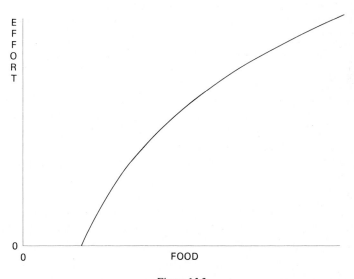

Figure 15.2

The non-convexity in the Mirrlees–Stiglitz function gives rise to a number of theoretical oddities, including the implication that an unequal distribution of consumption among family members may be optimal even when the family welfare function is additive in family members' utilities. Both forms provide the same explanation for the possible coexistence of unemployment and downwardly rigid wages.

In its simplest form, the efficiency wage theory assumes that the consumption of all workers is provided solely out of wage income, there are no lags between productivity and consumption, and employers can appropriate all of the additional effort induced by the wage increase. The latter two assumptions imply that the theory, if it is relevant at all, may be most appropriately applied to *longer-term* contractual relationships between the worker and employer, i.e. when the contractual period exceeds the likely lag between consumption and productivity, and in situations where the employer can monitor the consumption of the worker (by providing, for example, meals at the work site). While the latter is not uncommon, the predominant contractual period in many rural areas of low-income countries does not exceed one day (see Section 3 below).

The efficiency wage model also assumes that laborers are in infinitely elastic supply at some time wage W. It is easy to show that, given (8), profit-maximizing firms may pay a time wage higher than W if W is sufficiently low. The firm or employer's problem is to select the amount of labor and the time wage that maximizes profits. Assuming for simplicity that each worker works some standard amount of time, then the farm or firm chooses optimally the number of employees N and the wage paid each worker (= his or her consumption), i.e.

$$\max_{N, W} F(N\lambda (W)) - NW. \tag{9}$$

The necessary first-order conditions for (9) yield an equation which can be solved for the *efficiency* wage, that time wage which minimizes the cost per level of effort, given by:

$$\frac{W}{\lambda} = \frac{1}{\lambda'}, \tag{10}$$

where it is assumed that $c = W$. This efficiency wage ω is chosen such that the average cost per level of effort just equals marginal cost $(\lambda')^{-1}$, or the tangent from the origins in Figures 15.1 and 15.2 to the respective λ curves. Expression (10) indicates that firms paying time wages below ω will experience diminished profits; an excess supply of workers cannot therefore bid down the time wage below ω. The efficiency wage sets a floor to wages.

Some immediate difficulties with this simplest form of the theory are that, as long as wages are the only source of consumption, the optimal level of savings is zero and there would be no dependents [Gersovitz (1983)]. Moreover, all unemployed workers would disappear (starve). Leibenstein (1957) attempts to resolve this latter problem by hypothesizing that employers altruistically conspire to lower wages below ω (and thus their profits and total output) so that all workers are employed. In that case, removal of a worker from the rural area allows this "institutional" wage to rise. More interestingly, outmigration increases total output, since all workers, now consuming more, supply more effort until the institutional wage rises to just equal the efficiency wage – the marginal product of a laborer in this full employment equilibrium is *less* than zero. Leibenstein labels the maximum quantity of workers who, if removed from the agricultural sector, would increase agricultural output, as the *underemployed*. This definition of underemployment, while precise, differs from others in the literature, discussed below.

An alternative to the employer altruism–conspiracy scenario is one in which jobs are rationed randomly on a daily basis among potential workers. Those workers who are hired on a given day receive the efficiency wage and put in the "full" level of effort dictated by the efficiency wage function. On those days workers are not hired, they do not eat. In this case the workers receive a wage lower than the efficiency wage in the expected value sense; a "wage" that rises and falls inversely with the number (supply) of workers willing to work. Here, since workers eat on some days, they need not disappear as long as there are biological "savings". However, this story requires that the efficiency – consumption relationship is strictly contemporaneous – a day's work effort is a function only of that day's wage (consumption).

If the efficiency wage model is modified to include alternative sources of consumption other than wage income for some workers, the model predicts diversity in time wages among workers, as long as employers have information about individual workers' circumstances (a likely scenario in the village economy). In particular, the model would imply that the time wage rates received by workers will vary with the number of workers and dependents in their family and with their income from land (land ownership holdings) to the extent that employers are informed about workers' alternative income sources and family composition. To see this, assume that there are excess supplies of landless laborers so that the equilibrium wage per unit of labor effort λ is $\omega/\lambda(\omega)$, where $c = \omega$ for workers from landless households. Two polar cases have been discussed in detail. In one, the employment decision is made by a monopsonistic employer [Bliss and Stern (1978)]; in the other, employers are competitive [Dasgupta and Ray (1984)].

Consider a monopsonist who can employ the landless laborers ν_0 at time wage ω and ν_1 "landed" laborers from households in which some non-earnings income V is shared among N members (all of whom work); the monopsonist maximizes profits by choosing the time wage ω_1 to be paid to the ν_1 landed laborers and optimal quantities of ν_0 and ν_1. The problem is:

$$\max F(\lambda_0(\omega)\nu_0 + \lambda_1(\omega_1)\nu_1) - \nu_0\omega - \nu_1\omega_1 \tag{11}$$

subject to a landed laborer availability constraint $\nu_1 \leq \bar{\nu}_1$ from which it can be shown that:

$$\lambda'(\omega) = \lambda'(\omega_1 + V/N) \tag{12}$$

and $\nu_1 = \bar{\nu}_1$; that is, the monopsonist pays out wage rates such that the consumption of both landless and landed laborers is equalized. Since this means that the monopsonist pays a lower time wage to landed workers, $\omega_1 < \omega$, to achieve the same efficiency per worker-hour, such workers are preferred to landless workers and landed workers will always be hired before the landless. Landless workers are only hired if not enough landed laborers are available for work. Among the landed, moreover, those with higher non-earnings income receive lower wages and those with more family members (or dependents) receive higher wages. The monopsonistic–efficiency wage model thus implies that (i) no landed workers are unemployed (if any landless workers are employed) or, conversely, only landless workers are unemployed, (ii) landless workers receive higher time wages than landed workers, and (iii) time wage rates are inversely related to sources of non-wage income and positively associated with family size or the number of dependents (for those with alternative income sources).

In the competitive equilibrium case considered in detail in Dasgupta and Ray (1984), wage rates also differ across worker types. Here, because of competition, each worker receives the same payment per unit of work effort. Thus, those workers with higher levels of alternative consumption sources, and who supply more effort per time unit, command a higher time wage in the market, in contrast to the monopsonist case. Thus, if the landless are employed, they receive time wages *lower* than workers with alternative consumption sources. In this case, (i) those (landed) workers with the highest consumption prior to their wage employment both command the highest time wage and are the least likely to be unemployed (note that such workers may choose not to seek work if their non-employment income is sufficiently high), (ii) time wage rates are lower for those (landed) workers with more dependents, and (iii) if the competitively set effort wage implies a time wage for the landless at or below the efficiency wage, then at least some and possibly all landless workers are unemployed. An interesting and serendipitous distributional implication of this model is that there may exist an equalizing redistribution of landholdings, if there is unemployment under the regime of unequal landholdings, that will increase total output. The reason is that the redistribution increases the amount of efficiency units employed by reducing the number of individuals too poor to gain employment. However, in this model the problem of the appropriability by competitive employers of wage-induced efficiency gains is not discussed, a problem that is naturally circumvented in the monopsony model.

It is clear that a nice feature of the nutrition-based efficiency wage model is its large number of testable implications. Despite this, there have been few direct tests of the predictions of the theory. Bliss and Stern (1978) review some evidence both from the nutrition and economics literatures (but perform no rigorous tests of their own). There are a number of different tests possible. The most basic would be to test if productivity is positively related to food consumption. Another would be to test if wage rates are related to workers' consumption or to the determinants of per capita consumption, such as the number of dependents or the amount of income-producing assets. Before considering these, however, it is important to examine empirically the central proposition that wage rates have a floor and unemployment is substantial in rural labor markets, for these are the phenomena that motivate the theory.

India would appear to be a good country in which to test the applicability of the nutrition–wage efficiency theory, as it is a low-income country with reasonably good data on employment and wages. Inspection of the 1961 Indian Census reveals rural unemployment rates for males and females of less than 1 percent. However, as noted by Sen (1975), the Census criteria for rural unemployment are very restrictive. A person is unemployed only if he or she did not work at least one hour per day on a regular basis during the "working" season and is "seeking" work, where work is inclusive of activities in family businesses that provide no direct compensation. The National Sample Survey (NSS) of 1960–61, and subsequent rounds of that survey through the latest (1982–83), have constructed alternative measures of unemployment based on different definitions. In 1960–67, for example, rural unemployment rates according to the NSS were 2.6 percent for males and 6.5 percent for females, where the unemployed were defined as persons who did not work at least one day in a reference week and were seeking work, criteria more like those of employment surveys in developed countries. While the concept of unemployment is difficult to measure, whether current or usual employment status is used, measured rates do not suggest that unemployment, as more or less conventionally defined, is any more a salient feature of rural labor markets in the second most populous country in the world than it is in developed countries. Moreover, wage rates are quite flexible over the crop season in India, as they are in Egypt [Hansen (1969)] and Indonesia [White and Makali (1975)]. It is not clear, therefore, why a *special* theory of unemployment is required for rural labor markets. However, the seasonality of agricultural production implies some special employment problems, discussed below, some of which may uniquely lead to unemployment.

The lack of an overly conspicuous unemployment rate according to the only data sources available providing information on this phenomenon may not be

Table 15.1
Distribution of female–male agricultural wage ratios in India:
159 districts in 1960/61 (all India) and six villages,
1974/75–1982/83, in the semi-arid tropics

Percent of men's wages	District distribution 1960/61[a]	Villages distribution 1974/75–1982/83[b]
< 40	3.1	1.9
40–45	1.9	9.3
45–50	3.8	11.1
50–55	3.1	16.7
55–60	8.2	16.7
60–65	8.8	14.8
65–70	9.4	11.1
70–75	23.9	9.3
75–80	15.1	7.4
80–85	9.4	1.9
85–90	5.0	–
90–95	4.4	–
95–100	3.8	–
Mean	79.6	58.7

[a]*Source*: *Agricultural Wages in India 1960–61.*
[b]*Source*: ICRISAT Village Studies, 1984.

sufficient to convince those who understand the difficulties of measuring unemployment of the absence of important wage rigidities. Thus, it may also be useful to examine whether the distribution of (time) wage rates in India exhibits a floor. In particular, if the nutrition–productivity relationship is stable, based as it is on presumably biological grounds, one would expect that the minimum of real wages across the year would be similar across areas. The difficulty is that computation of area-specific real wages, at least in a country such as India, is problematic, given quite different sets of relative prices and consumption patterns across regions. Moreover, the model implies, as we have seen, that wages will differ by the characteristics of workers. Thus, inter-area differences in family structure and in landholding patterns will result in variations in the distributions of time wages paid across areas. However, the *ratio* of male to female wage rates should exhibit stability across areas if the consumption–productivity association is stable since (i) this ratio is unaffected by inter-area variability in relative food prices and (ii) males and females may not be distributed too differentially across households characterized by their landholdings. Table 15.1 displays the distributions of the male–female agricultural wage ratios across Indian districts in 1960–61, from Rosenzweig (1984), and for six Indian villages in the semi-arid tropics of that country in 1974–75 through 1983–84. As can be seen, there is considerable variability exhibited. Such variation, unexplained by the nutrition–wage theory, of course, requires an explanation. One possibility is that the relative number of male and female *workers* varies by wealth holdings. Geographical variability in wage rates and labor supply behavior are discussed below.

What of wage diversity, called an "odd implication" of the nutrition–efficiency wage theory by one of its authors [Mirrlees (1975)]? Do individuals by dint of their relationship to land receive different wage rates for the same work? Rosenzweig (1980), using data on 700 male and 522 female rural agricultural workers from a national probability sample of rural Indian households, tested this proposition. He found that, controlling for age, weather, schooling and some local industry variables, a worker's wage rate in a agriculture was not statistically significantly related to the amount of land owned by the worker or his/her family. He did not test whether the number of dependents affected the wage rate received, since this would have involved the difficult task of taking into account the possibility, implied by fertility models [e.g. Willis (1973)] and evidence [e.g. Rosenzweig and Evenson (1977)], that family size is itself a function of wage rates. The uniformity of sex-specific daily wages paid adult workers is also noted by Bardhan and Rudra (1981) in West Bengal and by White and Makali (1979) in West Java.

There does not appear to be support for any of the wage diversity predictions of the nutrition-based efficiency model nor any obvious evidence of the phenomenon the theory was originally designed to explain, namely the coexistence of high unemployment rates and rigid wages in rural areas of low-income countries. What of the hypothesis that productivity is significantly affected by food consumption, of the relationships depicted in Figures 15.1 and 15.2? Bliss and Stern (1978) and Strauss (1986) review the evidence from both experimental and non-experimental studies. Both studies do not find much, if any, rigorous supporting evidence. One fundamental problem with the evidence is that food consumption is obviously dependent on a worker's earnings as well as (possibly) a determinant of earnings. None of the studies prior to Strauss' work has treated this problem econometrically – that is, it is not clear whether Figures 15.1. and 15.2 merely trace out a consumption function.

Strauss (1986) estimated a production function similar to that in expression (8) based on Sierra Leone survey data, with per capita calorie consumption of family workers employed as a production input. He employed simultaneous equations methods to circumvent the problem that unobserved factors influencing output, such as land quality, farmer ability, etc. will also increase consumption (and influence other input allocations). His estimates indicate that output does increase at a decreasing rate with per capita calorie consumption (the effects are statistically significant). Strauss does not attempt, however, to test whether the relationship has a non-convex segment, as in Figure 15.1. Of course, the model implies that no one would be observed to be on this segment of the effort–consumption curve in equilibrium. Experimental data may be needed.

Despite the evidence for the nutrition–productivity association, Strauss reports that daily wage rates in Sierra Leone vary by season, by sex, and by region, but not by the caloric demands of the task performed. It is curious why wage payments do not appear to reflect the nutrition-based differences in productivity found by Strauss. Agents might be ignorant of the relationship (or know it not to be important!), but more likely what bars the use of such information, if true, is the difficulty of ascertaining or monitoring the food consumption of individual workers. The income-sharing egalitarian household may "tax away" any additional earnings of individual members by reducing their food allocation and workers have incentives to "appear" well fed. Only the food consumption of family members or attached servants (longer-term contract labor) could be monitored and/or controlled; but the latter form of employment is relatively scarce; most workers do not work even from day to day for the same employer [Strauss (1986), Bardhan and Rudra (1979)]. The difficulties of ascertaining the intra-household allocation of food are well known to survey researchers; measuring and monitoring an individual's contributions to output may be no less difficult than ascertaining his/her inherent productivity through the monitoring of food intake. Such issues of moral hazard and information constraints are not discussed in the literature on the nutrition-based efficiency wage theory; these considerations are discussed more fully below.

The nutrition-based efficiency wage model is only one of a set of models developed to explain the (second-best) optimality of downwardly rigid wages and an excess-applicant equilibrium. Other models include the labor recruitment model of Bardhan (1979), the screening model of Weiss (1980), and the turnover model of Stiglitz (1974). These models have no particular relevance to low-income rural labor markets; since the pervasiveness of daily labor markets in such settings implies that turnover or recruitment costs are probably quite low. The prevalence of such spot labor markets vis-à-vis other contractual arrangements in rural areas has not received a satisfactory explanation, however. I discuss alternative equilibrium models in the context of urban labor markets, where their applicability appears more obvious.

2.2. The family enterprise model and agricultural dualism

The conventional model of labor markets distinguishes between the institutions that determine the supply of labor to the market – households – and the institutions that utilize and demand labor for production purposes – firms. For an important segment of the rural economy of low-income countries, both the demand for and supply of market labor are determined within the same organization, the family enterprise. The majority of households in agriculture, and a large proportion of households in the non-agricultural sector, integrate production and consumption decisions.

The modeling of the family enterprise in the context of "peasant" agriculture has a long tradition beginning with Chayanov (1925 [1966]). Singh et al. (1986) provide an excellent overview and summation of the relevant work concerned with modeling and econometrically estimating the family enterprise model in agriculture, what they call the agricultural household model. A prototypical model is analogous to the standard international trade model of a small, price-taking economy and is similar to the perfect labor model described in the previous sections in which households (i) are price-takers for all production inputs and consumption goods (including leisure) and (ii) family and hired labor are perfectly substitutable in production. In this static one-period, perfect certainty model in which all markets exist and are competitive, as noted, consumption and production allocations are *separable*; the allocation of production inputs are independent of the household's preference orderings, and thus of (i) the relative prices of goods that are consumed but not produced and (ii) the household's wealth. Thus all households in maximizing their utility also maximize profits.

The separability property of the perfect markets family enterprise model has important implications. To see this, consider a one-person variant of the model. Preference orderings are described by the utility function (13):

$$U(X^c, l), \quad U_i > 0, U_{ii} < 0, \quad i = X^c, l, \tag{13}$$

where X^c = good consumed, l = leisure time. Given a market wage rate W and a price p for the good produced according to the technology embodied in (1), the income constraint of the "household", is:

$$V + pF(L, A) - WL + Wh - pX^c = V + \Pi - Wh - pX^c = 0, \tag{14}$$

where V = income from sources other than wages and profits, and $h = \Omega - l$. The household maximizes (13) subject to (14), choosing optimal quantities of labor in production L, leisure time l, and consumption X^c. The necessary first-order condition for the labor input in production is:

$$pF_L = W, \tag{15}$$

which is the profit-maximizing condition.

The optimal leisure–consumption good combination is given by (6), with $N = n$ and $p = 1$. Condition (6) is identical to that for landless households not engaged in production activities, that merely sell labor in the market, since their full income constraint is identical to that in (14), except that $\Pi = 0$. Thus, labor supply behavior would appear to be similar across producer–consumer and pure consumer households facing identical prices and having equal endowments of *wealth* $(V + \Pi)$. However, that is not the case. Consider the effect of a wage change on labor supply. The appropriate expression, in elasticity terms, is:

$$\eta_{h,w} = -\eta_{l,w}^{c} - \frac{W(h - L^*)}{F}\varepsilon_{l,F}, \tag{16}$$

where F = full income = $pX^* - WL^* + \Omega W + V$, and X^* is the profit-maximizing output level. The first term is the negative of the conventional Hicks–Slutsky compensated own price (wage) elasticity, and must be positive. The second term is the income elasticity weighted by the share of *net* labor supply in full income, where net labor supply is the difference between the (optimal) amount of labor used in production L^* and the (optimal) amount of labor supplied by the family worker.

Net labor supply can be positive or negative. On "large" (small) farms, where total labor demand exceeds (is less than) the amount of labor supplied by the family, net labor supply is negative (positive); that is, labor is "imported" (exported). Increases in the market wage rate thus reduce full income for importers of labor and increase full income for net exporters of labor. Consequently, if utility functions are approximately homothetic and leisure is normal, households without land (exporters of labor to the market) will, on average, exhibit lower labor supply elasticities than will households with land. Rosenzweig (1980) tests and confirms these implications of the complete markets, static agricultural household model using Indian household data.

Households will also differ with respect to the responsiveness of their labor supply to changes in the price of goods that are both consumed and produced. The relevant elasticity expression is:

$$\eta_{h,p} = -\eta_{l,p}^{c} - \frac{p(X^* - X^c)}{F}\varepsilon_{l,F}. \tag{17}$$

Again, the income elasticity of leisure is weighted by a term that differs across households with different levels of *productive* assets but the same exogenous wealth, in this case according to whether the household is a net consumer or supplier of the X good. A rise in the price of the agricultural good increases the income of net suppliers of the X good to the market ($X^* > X^c$) and reduces their labor supply if leisure is a normal good and leisure and goods are not strong complements. For landless and small-farm net purchasers, however, the price rise could increase labor supply.

Despite these differentials in the responsiveness of labor supply to exogenously induced alterations in wages that are associated with land ownership in the complete markets model, a reallocation of land holdings does not affect the efficiency with which inputs are used or total output (net of demand effects) in the absence of technological scale economies. The absence of a land market implicit in these models (land holdings are usually assumed exogenously given and identical to operational holdings) thus is not a barrier to efficiency because of the free movement of labor (and all other production inputs) across farms.

In contrast to the complete markets model is the model of the family enterprise in which no markets exist [Sen (1966)], or, equivalently, in which there is a separate market for each household. In this autarkic or perfectly segmented markets model, labor in production is always (and can only be) supplied to a plot of land by the household that owns (or is assigned to) that land, i.e. $h = L$. From the first-order condition for labor allocation in this model, given by (4), it can be seen that a family's preference orderings affect production. Hence, the allocation of inputs will be dissimilar among farmers heterogeneous in wealth (financial assets) even among farmers with identical-sized plots of land, and, given hetero-geneity in preferences or household demographic structure, even among farmers with identical sets of assets.

The "subjective equilibria" of the absent or segmented markets model are inconsistent with the achievement of productive efficiency, as the shadow or virtual prices of productive inputs will differ across farms; that is, a reallocation of labor across "markets" can increase total output. Moreover, unlike in the complete markets model, a rise in the product price, which has both income and substitution effects on family labor supply, can induce a reduction in output. A "backward-bending" output supply schedule is likely when what is provided is also consumed and leisure and the consumer-produced good are substitutes in consumption. The "backward-bending" supply curve of family labor, a possibil-ity in both models, can only be reflected in the output supply response of autarkic households, since neither income nor substitution effects in consumption are relevant to the allocation of farm labor or other production inputs when no markets are absent.

Dualistic models of agriculture posit the coexistence of households char-acterized by the two models. In particular, "small" landholders do not participate in the labor market and are characterized by autarky, while "large" landowners purchase labor at the market wage and profit maximize. The implication of this framework stressed by its proponents is that the poorer, small landowners in their subjective equilibria will supply more labor per acre than will the large landowners, since the cost of labor to the larger farmers is likely to exceed the subjective marginal rate of substitution between leisure and goods among small farmers. Note that absent labor markets are not sufficient for this inefficiency result, since there would be incentives for larger farmers to rent out their land to smaller landowners in order to take advantage of their lower labor costs. Given barriers to both the movement of labor *and* land across farms, the obvious prescription for the achievement of increased efficiency and output, as in the nutrition-based efficiency wage model, is an egalitarian redistribution of land-holdings.

Empirical evidence appears to strongly reject this extreme form of dualism. Evidence from Egypt [Hansen (1969)] and from India [Paglin (1965), Rosenzweig (1978, 1984)], for example, indicates that small farm households participate substantially in the labor market; indeed, as both buyers and sellers of labor. Dichotomization of family enterprises according to their objective functions (profits or utility) or by their isolation from markets thus appears less empirically relevant than distinguishing among households by their status as net consumers or producers of specific agricultural goods or net importers or exporters of wage labor. These latter distinctions are relevant to the distributional impact of policies altering wage rates (labor demand) or commodity prices, since we have seen that they determine the direction and magnitude of income gains from such price changes. Discrepancies across farms in the prices of production inputs might exist, however, for other reasons than posed in the traditional, extreme dualism models. These are discussed in the next section.

There have been a number of econometric studies of the complete markets, family enterprise model; these are reviewed in Singh et al. (1986). All of these studies maintain but do not test the assumption of separability; thus estimates of the technology are obtained separately from and independently of estimates of the parameters describing household preferences and consumer demand, some-times with different samples (from the same country) for each household sector. One additional pervasive feature of these econometric studies is the aggregation of family labor supply and labor demand across sex and age groups and the specification of one labor price (a "unisex" wage). While the Hicks composite goods theorem justifies aggregation of consumption goods over individual family members, since each member faces the same goods price vector, as displayed in Table 15.1, for example, relative wage rates for male and female (and child) labor vary significantly across areas and over time.

In Rosenzweig's (1980) study of Indian household data, it is shown that not only do male and female labor supply elasticities differ substantially, with female labor supply being substantially more elastic than male labor supply (as in developed countries), but there are important cross-wage effects. For example, increases in relative male wage rates significantly reduce the amount of labor supplied to the market by women (wives), while increases in female wage rates relative to male wage rates raise female labor supplied to the market and slightly reduce the amount of male market time. The marked differentiation in agricul-tural tasks by gender [K. Bardhan (1984)] also suggests that sex-specific labor inputs are not perfectly substitutable in production, as also assumed in most econometric studies.

Lopez (1986) is the first econometric study to test (and reject) the separability (complete markets) assumption; however, the model formulated assumes a specific source of non-separability – that the time spent in on-farm and in off-farm activities are different consumption commodities. Aside from this, the Lopez study, as in all other applications of consumer demand models, embeds the test in a particular specification of household preferences (in this case, a specification implying linear Engel curves). In addition, Lopez employs geographically aggregated data (Canadian census divisions) and ignores labor heterogeneity associated with sex. Pitt and Rosenzweig (1986), in a more loosely structured econometric analysis of household data from Indonesia (with, however, sex-specific disaggregated labor), performed an indirect test of separability. They found that while a farmer's illness significantly reduced his labor supply, farm profits net of actual and imputed family labor costs were not affected. These results imply that those farm households afflicted by illness were able to substitute hired for the lost family labor time with no sacrifice in factor returns. The econometric evidence on separability is, at this stage, inconclusive.

The perfect markets (separable) and segmented, household-specific markets (autarkic) models represent polar opposites. A more general framework for modeling rural markets would incorporate the possibility that the household faces two prices in each market: a purchase price, paid by the household when it buys the commodity, and a sale price, received when it sells the commodity. The separable model assumes that in all markets purchase and sale prices are equal. When a wedge exists between these two prices, however, some households may optimally choose not to participate in one or the other side of the market or not to transact at all. The existence of distinct transaction prices in particular markets thus may provide implications for observed behavior in rural economies, but themselves require explanation.

3. Rural labor contracts: Risk, information and incentives problems

The complete markets and autarkic household models, as noted, are extreme caricatures of rural labor markets. While the latter appears to be of little relevance to at least Asian and Latin American low-income countries and the former may be a reasonably good approximation of the behavior of agents in rural labor markets, with the important advantage of econometric tractability, a number of non-trivial problems are ignored. First, even the daily labor market does not operate perfectly smoothly. Not all seekers of wage work can find employment at any time and not all employers can find workers at the market wage when they need them. When small-farm household members on a given day seek but cannot find work, they are likely to work their own land, supplying labor on that day up to the point where their marginal rate of substitution between goods and leisure equals the marginal value product of their labor time rather than the market wage. Similarly, on larger farms, when insufficient labor time can be purchased on the market, i.e. the notional demand for labor at the going wage exceeds the amount of labor that is hired, the marginal value of labor will exceed the market wage. Such frictions in the labor market could yield the result that the marginal product of labor on small farms is less than that on large farms ("weak" dualism), although, again, such discrepancies could be minimized if there were no barriers to the land rental or sales market. Note that in this model, if the probability distribution of these frictions is common knowledge (and appropriately specified), the expected marginal product of labor may not differ between small and large farms.

Ryan and Ghodake (1984) compared unemployment probabilities for men and women in the daily agricultural labor market in six villages in the semi-arid tropics of India. They found that in 13–14 percent of the total number of days male laborers were willing to work, they could not find employment. Their results did not support, however, the additional hypothesis that small farmers behave as if the opportunity cost of male labor is the male market wage multiplied by the probability of finding employment, although they did find evidence of such behavior with respect to the opportunity cost of female labor. Bardhan (1979) also concluded from his study of Indian survey data that male labor supply behavior is not importantly affected by unemployment prospects, although that of females is. No empirical studies appear to exist which document the uncertainties surrounding the hiring of labor. This is peculiar, since employers and employees are often the same people and there do not appear to be any obvious asymmetries in the market. Indeed, Bell and Srinivasan (1985a) emphasize the employee–employer symmetry of employment uncertainties in their study of the demand for and supply of farm servants, discussed below.

More fundamental aspects of low-income, rural labor markets are also not reflected in the complete markets model. These include the inherent riskiness and seasonality of agricultural production, the absence of an insurance market, and information-cum-incentives problems. As a consequence, the model cannot account for such contractual arrangements as sharecropping, the prevalence of daily (*casual*) or spot markets relative to longer-term implicit or explicit labor contracts, or even why the family enterprise is the dominant agricultural organization.

A principal theme of the rapidly expanding literature concerned with contractual arrangement in rural economies is how the incompleteness of markets (the existence of unmarketable inputs) combined with some of the special attributes of agricultural technology shape labor arrangements. Two classes of models, each emphasizing different market problems, are predominant in the literature. The first class of models emphasizes the riskiness of agriculture due principally to the unpredictability of an important agricultural production input, weather, and the absence of a market for output insurance. These two characteristics of the rural economy imply that contractual arrangements in the labor market might contain elements that in part substitute for the absent insurance contracts, given risk-averse agents.

A second problem highlighted in this literature rests on the assumption that "labor" is composed of two bundled factors – time and effort – as in the efficiency wage models, except that effort in this context is a choice variable and effort cannot be costlessly monitored. While work time and work effort both affect the utility (negatively) of their suppliers and contribute to output, there is no distinct market for each. The time wage-rate alone insufficiently rewards effort, which must be elicited by other means. Thus, in this class of models, the utility function (2) becomes:

$$U = U(c, l, e), \tag{18}$$

where e = effort, $U_e < 0$, and labor is expressed in terms of effort units in the technology, as in (8).

The prevalence of the family enterprise in agriculture can at least in part be explained on the basis of the problems of production risk inherent in agriculture and on effort incentives or "moral hazard" problems [Binswanger and Rosenzweig (1986)]. For example, family members may be more able than others to enter into risk-sharing and consumption smoothing arrangements, as discussed in Section 4.4 below.

The tendency for workers to withhold effort, to shrirk, without supervision when paid only according to their time worked is viewed as the principal reason why production costs rise after a certain point with the scale of agricultural operations. While payments according to tasks performed or output produced (piece rates) provide superior incentives to time wages, since they directly reward effort, such arrangements are not feasible where haste can cause damage (weeding or apple picking). Thus, farm operations cannot be performed exclusively with workers paid by piece rates. Family labor is seen as superior to hired labor, since family laborers are residual claimants on the profits of the family enterprise, as in the model described by eqs. (1), (2) and (5); their consumption levels are thus directly tied to their work effort. As the number of family members increases, however, the share each individual family member receives from family profits is diluted. Thus, there is a natural upper bound to the optimal size of the family labor force and to the size of agricultural operations. Large landowners can avoid hiring (time) wage laborers by renting their land out in smaller parcels to other families, since land tenancy transforms non-family workers into residual claimants with the accompanying incentive efficiencies.

Binswanger and Rosenzweig also claim that the salient exception to the income-sharing, family-run farm enterprise, the plantation system, with its large-scale use of hired labor, can be explained by the inherent technological features of the crops grown. The plantation system is only advantageous when (i) there are important scale economies in processing *and* coordination problems between harvesting and processing, as in sugar cane, and/or (ii) the crops require sustained care across the usual crop cycles, which bars the use of annual tenancy contracts.

3.1. Casual and permanent laborers: Spot and future markets for labor

The two classes of models, one emphasizing risk and the other incentives problems, characterize the literature concerned with explaining an important feature of the rural labor market – the coexistence of "casual" laborers, hired on a daily basis in the spot market, with "permanent" laborers, also called attached farm servants, who are hired in advance for multiple time periods at a fixed wage. All models purporting to describe the "two-tiered" rural labor market highlight the two-stage nature of agricultural technology. The production process is described by (19) and (20), instead of (1):

$$x = f(L_1, A), \tag{19}$$

$$X = F(L_2, A, x, \theta), \tag{20}$$

where x is intermediate output, a function of first-period inputs, and θ represents exogenous and stochastic inputs beyond the control of the farmer (state of nature, weather). The work force in period i is composed of casual and permanent workers, the latter being hired in both production periods. Thus, $L_i = L_p + L_{ci}$; $i = 1, 2$.

Bell and Srinivasan (1985a) and Bardhan (1983) emphasize that the demand for labor in the second stage of production cannot be known in advance because of weather uncertainty. As a consequence, both (net) buyers and sellers of labor each year face riskiness in the wages to be paid or received at the end of the crop cycle. A risk-averse landless household, the model predicts, would find it optimal for at least some members to enter into an annual (futures) contract that sets the second-stage wage in advance (the attached servant contract). With some sellers of labor in the household using only the daily spot market and others engaged as attached farm servants, family income is hedged against wage (and employment) risk; for net purchasers of labor, use of both types of labor contracts also reduces exposure to risk. Since the attached servant contract serves as an insurance substitute, if agents are risk-averse the (certain) income from the annual contract will be less than the expected income over the year obtained from participation in the casual labor market, spot (casual) wages W_c exceed permanent labor wages (W_p) in an equilibrium characterized by fully compensatory wages differentials. These models thus imply that the choice of wage contract will depend on both the levels and sources (riskiness) of household non-labor income.

Despite the apparent advantages of annual or crop-cycle wage contracts, they do not appear to be important in all environments. Bell and Srinivasan in fact report that in their sample from 20 Indian villages "... most households do not have such contracts" (p. 3), although Bardhan finds them to be prevalent in the Indian state of West Bengal, from which his data are taken. These particular risk-shedding models can explain the apparent lack of interest in such contracts in some areas and not in others on the basis of differences in endowed (wage and output) risk, but this central implication of these models has not been tested. One alternative possibility, not considered, is that other contractual arrangements may be superior; as discussed below, output-sharing arrangements also diminish risk. Moreover, participation by some household members in non-agricultural activities also diminishes the household's exposure to agricultural wage uncertainty, and such opportunities may vary across environments. Another possibility is that second-stage wages co-vary positively with gross income from production [final-stage wages are high (low) when there is a lot of (little) production to harvest]; wage risk does not independently increase income risk for net purchasers of labor in all environments.

Eswaran and Kotwal's (1985a) model of permanent wage contracts, in contrast to the stochastic price and output models, assumes away risk aversion and instead emphasizes incentives problems attendant to eliciting unmonitorable effort. They assume that (i) agents maximize utility function (18), (ii) first-period tasks in (19) are distinct from second-period tasks in that effort cannot be easily monitored in that period (tasks require discretion in period one), and (iii) landlords can discern worker effort in period 1 at the completion of period 2. A permanent wage contract serves to elicit first-period effort; thus, only permanent laborers are hired in the first period, i.e. $L_1 = L_p$, $L_2 = L_p + L_c$ and $L_j = e^* N_j$, where e^* is the appropriate effort and $N_j = $ number of workers of type j ($j = $ p, c).

What induces (permanent) workers to supply effort at level e^*, despite its disutility and unobservability, is the prospect of being fired (becoming a casual laborer) when their shirking is discovered at the end of the harvest cycle. Of course, the termination threat is only credible if the utility from not shirking exceeds the utility from shirking and being relegated to the casual labor market. This must imply that permanent worker contracts are superior (in terms of worker welfare, inclusive of effort) to a series of casual or spot contracts. To see this, consider a time horizon of four periods (two seasons). The (indirect) utility for an honest permanent worker, supplying e^* of effort in the first period, is

$V(W_p, e^*)$. If the per-period discount rate is δ, then it must be true that a shirking worker, who supplies no effort in the first period and then is fired at the end of the season, is not better-off than an honest worker, i.e.

$$V(W_p, e^*)(1 + \delta + \delta^2 + \delta^3) > V(W_p, 0) + \delta V(W_p, e^*) + \delta^2 V(0,0)$$

$$+ \delta^3 V(W_c, e^*), \tag{21}$$

so that, since $V(0,0) < V(W_p, e^*) < V(W_p, 0)$,

$$V(W_p, e^*)(1 + \delta) > \delta V(W_c, e^*), \tag{22}$$

where W_c is the casual worker wage rate. Note that workers can be monitored in the second period of each season so that e^* of effort is always supplied then.

Expression (22) suggests that there will be an excess supply of permanent workers, since W_p will not be bid down to equate the per-season utilities of the two types of workers, as this would result in shirking and lower output. No unemployment must ensue, however, since, in the absence of any other restrictions on the technology and preferences, all workers can be employed as casual laborers. In contrast to the wage-insurance models, the Eswaran–Kotwal model thus consists of two classes of workers, one of which (the permanent worker class) is better off than the other. Moreover, unlike the former models, this model implies little (or no) turnover among the privileged permanent workers; permanence pertains both to intra-season and inter-year employment.

A shortcoming of the Eswaran–Kotwal wage-contract model is that it does not provide the assignment rules characterizing which workers are in each class nor does it predict whether the *daily* wage rates of permanent workers W_p will exceed or not those of daily laborers W_c. As in the literature concerned with wage risk models, moreover, alternative contractual arrangements, in particular, tenancy, that elicit effort under the same set of technological assumptions, are not considered, although the assumption that workers cannot validate the landlord's assessment of their performance effectively rules out worker's posting a performance bond. And, of course, the existence of wage heterogeneity across individuals performing different tasks could be explained by worker heterogeneity in innate or acquired skills.

3.2. Tenancy contracts

There has been considerable attention to the contractual terms associated with the rental of land in the development literature, and no complete discussion of this literature will be attempted here [see Chapter 16 in this Handbook, and

Otsuka and Hayami (1985)]. The relevance of the tenancy contract in this context is that such contracts also influence the allocation and returns to labor. Tenancy contracts are an important rural institution in many low-income countries – in Egypt, Iran and Pakistan, for example, about 40 percent of cultivated land is under tenancy; in Taiwan, over half of cultivated land was cultivated by tenants in the 1930s.

The theoretical literature concerned with tenancy is characterized by the same two themes as the pure labor contract literature – leasing of land provides landowners access to unmarketable inputs, such as labor effort, and/or the land rental terms serve to mitigate risk in production. As noted, if there are difficulties monitoring the effort of non-family workers, the renting of land to tenants for a fixed fee (rent) transforms the workforce to residual claimants and solves the effort problem. This one problem of eliciting labor effort (worker's moral hazard), however, is insufficient to explain the existence (or coexistence) of land tenancy contracts in which owner and tenant share the proceeds of cultivation (sharecropping), since such a contract may lead to an inefficient allocation of resources (inputs) compared to fixed rent tenancy.

Consider the budget equation for a tenant who leases in land, self-cultivates and works the labor market at a fixed wage w. Consumption of this tenant farmer, C_T, is given by:

$$c_T = \alpha X_T - R + X_o + wL, \qquad (23)$$

where α = share rent, R = fixed rent, X_T = output from tenanted land, X_o = output from self-cultivated land, and L = time in wage labor market. With the utility function and technology described by (1) and (2) as before, the equilibrium conditions for the allocation of the tenant's labor time is

$$w = \alpha \frac{\partial X_T}{\partial L_T} = \frac{\partial X_o}{\partial L_o}. \qquad (24)$$

Thus, returns to labor time are not equated across all activities when α is less than one. In particular, in the absence of other contractual stipulations, the marginal product of labor (and other inputs) will be higher on sharecropped land than on own-cultivated land and higher there than the market price of labor. It has been argued [e.g. Cheung (1968)] that landlords would, as part of the contract, stipulate input levels, such that labor and other inputs would be allocated efficiently. However, this leaves open the question of the enforceability of labor effort, which was a rationale for land rental to begin with: Why does the landowner not just charge a fixed fee [let $R > 0$, $\alpha = 1$ in (23)], which results in efficient allocations without monitoring? There are two answers – avoidance of risk and the existence of unmarketable inputs owned by the *leasor*.

If tenants are risk averse and output risk is uninsurable, then lessees may be unwilling to accept all of the risk of production, leaving the landowner exposed only to the risk of non-payment of the fixed fee that a fixed rental entails. By sharing output, landlords and tenants share production risk, and share it optimally when the optimal allocation of inputs on tenanted land is enforceable. As Newbery (1975) has pointed out, however, risk reduction to the same degree can be accomplished by the tenant (without inefficiency) by his allocating a *share* of his time to risky activities (self-cultivation) and a share to a non-risky activity, such as afforded by an attached-servant labor contract. While it may be argued that it is difficult for one individual to divide up his time among activities (transaction costs, market frictions), the existence of the multi-member household, ignored in almost all tenancy models, means that a family can allocate each or some of its members to different activities. Risk diversification and/or risk reduction may thus be achieved without incurring transaction costs or sacrificing the returns to specialization. The choice or prevalence of fixed rent and share tenancy contracts will then depend on the availability of alternative risk-reducing opportunities.

Eswaran and Kotwal (1985b) have set out a framework that focuses directly on the issue of why certain forms of labor-cum-land arrangements are chosen over others. In the model, riskiness is ignored and the problem of obtaining unmarketable inputs plays a central role. They posit the existence of *two* productive factors that cannot be bought or sold directly – managerial skill and labor effort. The prevalence of share, fixed rent or pure wage contracts then depends on both the importance of these two inputs in production (the technology) and the ownership *distribution* of the inputs across landowners and tenants. When owners of land have a monopoly on managerial knowledge and only tenancy can elicit unmonitorable labor effort from workers, owners and tenants find it in their interest to share their inputs through share tenancy. A fixed-rent tenancy is inferior in this case since it provides no incentives for the landowner to supply his skills to production. It is the *double* coincidence of moral hazard (two, not one, market failures) that makes share tenancy potentially superior to fixed rate tenancy, even though neither tenant nor landowner supplies the full level of his own input that would be forthcoming under self-cultivation. This model thus suggests that as landowners lose their managerial advantage relative to tenants, due to the introduction of new technologies or through the acquisition of cultivation experience by tenants, fixed rental becomes more likely; as labor tasks become more routinized, through mechanization or other technological changes, the use of wage labor as opposed to tenancy contracts becomes more prevalent.

Empirical studies pertinent to tenancy models have chiefly been devoted to the narrowly defined efficiency issue concerning whether share tenancy induces the withholding of inputs, as implied in (24), and less to the question of the determination of the choice of contractual forms. The conceptual experiment needed to resolve the input allocation question is straightforward – compare the input allocations (or marginal products) for the same farmer, on the same plot of land, under the same weather conditions but under different contracts. However, no survey has as yet produced information on such an experiment; indeed, the probability of weather conditions being identical in different years is zero! Most of the empirical studies compare input intensities across different farmers with different plots of land and different contracts; the possibility that there is heterogeneity in farmer's characteristics or land which may importantly affect the *choice* of contract and input allocations makes such studies inconclusive. For example, Eswaran and Kotwal's model implies that less competent tenant farmers sharecrop rather than rent (and possibly so do less competent landowners); sharecropping tenants may thus appear to be less productive, but not necessarily because of insufficient incentives. Studies by Bell (1977) and Shaban (1986) of the efficiency question exploit data that come closest to the best experiment; they were able to compare the same farmer under different contracts, but on different plots of land. Although there are controls for several different measured land characteristics, heterogeneity in unobserved characteristics of land may bias the results, which appear consistent with the input misallocation hypothesis in that input intensities appear to be lower on sharecropped land compared to self-cultivated land or to land leased under fixed rent. No attempt was made in either of these studies to measure or compare marginal products of inputs across contracts, however, which would have required estimation of the technology parameters.

The more fundamental issue of contract choice has received far less empirical study. As for permanent labor contracts, specific forms of tenancy contracts are prevalent in some areas and not in others, even within the same country. For example, in the Philippines 84 percent of rented land is sharecropped, while in Egypt only 12 percent of rented land is leased on a share basis. In India, 90 percent of rented landholdings are sharecropped in the state of West Bengal (where, it will be recalled, attached-servant contracts were also prevalent), while in the Indian state of Madras, 78 percent of tenancy contracts were fixed-rent (National Sample Survey, Eighth Round).

The risk-based tenancy models imply that differences in the riskiness of the environment and the availability of less risky income opportunities can explain tenancy contract choice. The conceptual experiment is again straight-forward – provide, *randomly*, different amounts of fixed payments across poten-tial tenants; those receiving greater assured levels of income should be more likely to select fixed rent contracts (as long as risk aversion is non-increasing with wealth). Such an experiment, of course, has not been performed.

Bell and Sussangkarn (1985) in an important study in a sense have attempted to simulate the riskless income experiment, but based on information on tenants from cross-section data. They tested if tenants with greater levels of transfer income, greater numbers of non-agricultural family workers, and greater land-holdings were more willing to engage in riskier tenant contracts. The difficulty with this exercise is that sources of income and the occupational composition of the family labor force are also attempts by the household to cope with risk. Indeed (non-governmental) net transfer income is in part the manifestation of an implicit contract with non-household agents that presumably is designed to smooth consumption under risk [Rosenzweig (1988)]. The estimated associations between different means of risk-coping (contracts) and the outcomes of risk-sharing arrangements do not shed much light on how *opportunities* for risk reduction and environmental (exogenous) risk in production influence the portfolio of explicit and implicit contracts. Attached farm servant and share-tenancy contracts are in part substitutes for each other as risk-mitigating mechanisms but are also more likely to be observed in riskier environments or among households who are risk averse; the sign of the association between different contractual forms is not obvious from the theory, nor therefore can it represent a test of the insurance-based tenancy model.

The Eswaran–Kotwal tenancy model, which focuses on the distribution of managerial knowledge and the technology of supervision, suggests, as noted, that owners and tenants are more likely to share in allocation decisions under a share contract than under a fixed-rent tenancy agreement. Bell and Srinivasan (1985), based on data from 10 villages in the Punjab in India, did, indeed, find this to be true. This model also implies that as tenants acquire more experience in farming, they will be less dependent on the managerial input of the landowner and will thus be more likely to become fixed-rent tenants. There is as yet little information on this "tenancy ladder" implication or on how technical change, which may obsolesce land-specific experience, influences contractual arrangements. Longitudinal information on the life-cycle land relationships of rural agents would be useful in this regard. Such data could also be helpful in testing the risk-insurance tenancy model in that it might allow better methods for dealing with the problem that observationally identical tenants are heterogeneous in their aversion to risk, which jointly influences all of their contractual choices, and thus the sources, variability and levels of their incomes.

As noted, the complete markets models, since they ignore incentives problems and do not incorporate risk, cannot account for sharecropping or explain the mixture of contractual arrangements engaged in by farmers. The alternative models that do accommodate these considerations, however, have tended to concentrate on one or another part of the farm or household allocation problem (choosing farm servants or daily laborers, choosing fixed or share rent tenancy contracts) to the neglect of other important decisions (labor supply, land rental, consumption choices) and narrowly define the range of formal and informal contractual alternatives. The complete markets model has thus seen the most direct econometric applications; econometrically tractable models of the farm-household model embodying risk behavior and contractual choice await development.

4. Geographic mobility

Whatever the absolute level of the marginal contribution to output of the rural labor force, the reallocation of labor from less to more productive activities or sectors is a central element in development models. Moreover, sectoral or spatial disparities in the returns to *homogeneous* labor, i.e. controlling for skill differences, are evidence of market imperfections, although not necessarily of imperfections in the labor market. While, as noted, mobility of labor across farms within small localities in rural areas appears high, there appears to be evidence of important spatial barriers to mobility in low-income countries. Wage rates for seemingly comparable tasks in agriculture appear to differ *persistently* across geographical areas [Rosenzweig (1978)] and even between adjacent villages, and "unskilled" manufacturing wage rates in urban areas have remained, over long periods of time, from 1.5 to 2 times agricultural wage rates [Squire (1981)], although careful analyses of real wage differentials by skill group remain to be performed. Indeed, a large part of disparities in wage rates can be explained by differentials in skill-related attributes across workers (e.g. schooling and work experience).

In his econometric analysis of the determination of rural wage rates across districts in India, Rosenzweig (1978) assumes inter-district immobility and finds that, consistent with this assumption, within each district relative supplies of male, female and child labor influence the district's absolute and relative wage levels in accordance with classical supply–demand models. Thus, the spatial variation in relative male–female wage rates appears at least in part to be determined by differentials in the relative supplies of female labor associated with caste and religious restrictions, and to demand factors associated with locality-specific weather conditions, given stratification by sex in agriculture tasks. In Rosenzweig's (1980) econometric analysis of labor supply and wage rate determination based on household data, the findings suggest that women are less mobile than men [as found also by Bardhan (1979) and Ryan and Ghodake (1984)] and that landless laborers are more geographically mobile than owners of land.

There is also substantial evidence, however, of large population movements in low-income countries, particularly from rural to higher-wage urban areas. Yap (1977) reports that migration typically accounts for from 30 to 60 percent of urban population growth rates in such countries. There thus appears to be both large spatial population flows as well as persistent spatial disparities in labor returns. Are there particular barriers to mobility in low-income countries? Do standard models of migration not pertain to such settings? A large proportion of the development economics literature is concerned with these questions of the mobility of labor.

4.1. The basic human capital model of migration

The beginning point in modeling the migration decision of agents is the human capital model. In this framework, migration is viewed as an income-augmenting investment in which costs are incurred initially and returns accrue over time. An individual compares the direct costs of migrating with the discounted present value of income gains, if any, from each potential destination; he or she thus finds the maximum of a set of potential migration gains across all possible destinations, where the gain G_j for any destination j is:

$$G_j = \int_0^T e^{(g-r)t} \left(Y_{Dj} - Y_o \right) dt - c_j, \tag{25}$$

c_j is the cost of migration (transportation costs) to destination j, Y_{Dj} is the per-period income the individual would receive by migrating to j, Y_o is per-period origin income, and r is the discount rate. Y_o, Y_D and c may also have time subscripts, may vary with age, although direct migration costs are incurred all at once. If $\max\{G_j\}$ is positive, then the potential migrant will choose to move to that destination with the highest gain.

The human capital migration model in (25) yields the following predictions, aside from the implication that agents' migration choices will tend to erase income differentials: (i) the young, who will reap returns over a longer period, will have larger values of G and will be more mobile than the old, (ii) *neutral* productivity growth across areas or sectors [given by g in (18)] will increase mobility; that is, accelerating along a balanced growth path, say in urban and rural areas, will induce a greater *absolute* differential in favor of the high-income (urban) area, increase G, and thus raise the level of rural–urban migration flows, and (iii) a greater distance (higher c) between two areas reduces migration flows between them. As Yap (1977) reports in her survey of econometric studies of internal migration in low-income countries, there is substantial evidence that, indeed, the vast majority of migrants are young, high-growth economies are characterized by high levels of migrant flows, and migration rates between any two areas i and j are positively related to the size of the differential in real earnings or wages across i and j and are negatively related to the distance between them. Kuznets (1982) also concludes, based on ILO data pertaining to 181 countries from 1950 to 1970, that those countries that had greater rates of growth of per capita product also were marked by more rapid shifts out of the agricultural sector, although it is unclear whether the growth rates were "balanced".

Like the perfect markets model, the simple human capital approach to migration yields a number of empirically verified implications but abstracts from a number of problems, some particularly relevant to low-income countries. These include capital market and information constraints, uncertainty with respect to both employment prospects and intertemporal income fluctuation, joint household decision-making, and the existence of heterogeneity among agents and in area-specific non-income attributes (relative prices of goods and services).

The model thus seeks to explain permanent rather than seasonal migration and ignores multiple moves, assuming perfect foresight. Additionally, without introducing worker heterogeneity into the model, it is difficult to reconcile the model with the observation that migration streams often flow simultaneously from place i to place j and from place j to place i. Nevertheless, the major implication of this framework, namely that wage differences across regions explain interregional migration for comparably skilled workers, appears to have received strong support.

4.2. Information and capital market constraints on mobility

The importance of information flows is used to explain why it is usually found that the more educated are likely than the less educated to be migrants, and why distance between origin and destination is less of a migration deterrent for the more educated [e.g. Schwartz (1976), Levy and Wadycki (1974)], since the more educated are presumed to be better informed about spatially separated alternative earnings opportunities. Similarly, the existence of information sources in destination areas is presumed important and is also consistent with pervasive findings that the stock of prior immigrants to an area j from a destination i is positively correlated with current immigration flows from origin i to j [e.g. Greenwood (1971)]. Such findings, however, may merely reflect the persistence of unmeasured factors influencing migration from i to j. Indeed, the interpretation of the estimated effects of wage differentials on migration flows based on specifications including lagged migration (the stock of immigrants) is not obvious, particularly when such variables are treated inappropriately as exogenous. There is, however, more direct evidence of the positive influence of destination–area contacts on migration flows [Nelson (1976)].

The findings that the more educated are likely to be migrants and that migrants, at least to cities, tend not to be from the poorest families in the origin area, suggest that migration may be income-constrained. Capital market constraints may thus influence the degree to which returns to labor remain geographically diverse. Basu (1983) develops an alternative model in which geographic wage diversity coexists with frictionless geographic mobility as a result of capital market imperfections. The risk of default is assumed to induce landlords in rural areas to confine their lending to laborers under longer-term contract to them; that is, to borrowers over whom they have more "control" or information. Basu then explains spatial wage diversity as reflecting differentials in interest costs to moneylenders (landlords) across areas – the contractual *interlocking* of loans and wage payments implies that laborers choose among alternative wage–interest cost contracts. With complete labor mobility, the utility value of the different combined wage–interest contracts must be equal (for homogeneous laborers) across areas. Thus, where interest costs are high (for landlords), wage rates offered by landlords to laborer-borrowers must also be high. Basu thus views capital immobility, combined with incentives problems, as the principal cause of spatial wage diversity. Of course, the reasons why capital costs are not arbitraged spatially is not indicated, nor is there any evidence presented or cited on flows of capital. Moreover, as noted above, labor contracts of more than one day are not prevalent in many rural labor markets; the interlinked credit–pure wage labor contract is thus not adequate to explain the pervasiveness of spatial rural wage differentials.

A more direct capital-market-cum-information constraint on labor mobility in *rural* areas is suggested by the findings that (i) laborers with land are less mobile than the landless [Rosenzweig (1980)] and (ii) migrants to urban areas from households owning land in rural areas are more likely to be temporary migrants [e.g. Balan et al. (1973), Nabi (1984)]. If households owning land are unable, or find it difficult, to sell their holdings, then movement out of the rural area by the household entails a capital loss. Indeed, Rosenzweig and Wolpin (1985) show that in India less than 2 percent of landowners sell any of their land in a given year, and almost all who do, do so because of severe cash constraints induced by at least two consecutive years of poor weather. However, they also provide evidence consistent with the hypothesis that variability in land qualities across plots combined with weather risk leads to *specificities* in plot-specific experience (information) returns. Thus, even when land markets operate perfectly, farmers incur a capital loss upon the sale of land they and their family have farmed. Mobility is reduced because part of the capital accumulated by farmers is not transportable.

4.3. Two-sector unemployment equilibrium models

Another way to reconcile persistent disparities between unskilled urban and rural wages with unfettered labor mobility is to assume that the risk of finding a higher wage urban job is not negligible and that potential migrants take employment risk into account. In Todaro (1969), the basic human capital model of migration is modified so that the per-period income flow in the urban sector is weighted by the probability of obtaining a job in that sector; G_j becomes G_j'.

$$G_j' = \int_0^T e^{(g-r)t}\big(p(t)Y_{Dj} - Y_0\big)\,dt - c_j, \tag{26}$$

where $p(t)$ is the destination (urban) employment probability. G_j' is now the expected net return from migration, and is clearly lower than G_j as long as $p(t) < 1$.

Harris and Todaro (1970), based on the model of Todaro (1969), embed the notion of employment risk into a two-sector general equilibrium model of migration, employment and wage determination. In this model, wages are determined competitively (by supply and demand) in the rural sector, but the wage rate in the urban sector is an institutionally set ("politically determined") rigid minimum wage set above the initial rural wage. Employment is a Bernoulli process in which the probability of employment in the urban sector is equal to the number of urban jobs (E_U) divided by the size of the urban labor force or number of job-seekers (N_U). Since all agents are assumed to maximize G' (are risk neutral), and are perfectly mobile, and the rural wage ($=$ marginal product in agriculture) is origin income, the unemployment equilibrium condition is:

$$W_R = W_U(E_U/N_U), \tag{27}$$

i.e. the rural wage is equal to the expected urban wage. Thus, in this model the only labor market distortion is in the urban sector (and is unexplained; see below); the institutionally set urban wage leads to a misallocation of labor resources across areas and to wasted resources (unemployed workers).

Given the technology of production in the urban and rural sectors (described in Harris and Todaro by standard, neoclassical functions with fixed capital stocks and mobile labor as inputs) and a fixed total endowment of labor in the economy, eq. (27) describes how rural wages, urban unemployment, and rural and urban employment change when the exogenously determined institutional wage is altered. In the case in which labor demand in the urban sector is inelastic (demand elasticity < 1), a rise in the minimum wage reduces employment and output in *both* the rural and urban sectors and increases urban unemployment. In that case, when the minimum wage increases, employment decreases proportionally less than the urban wage increase, leading to an increase in the expected urban wage and increased migration from the rural to the urban sector. However, if urban demand is elastic, a rise in the urban minimum wage increases rural output and lowers the wage in the agricultural sector; in that case, migration flows from the urban sector to the rural sector. In either case, an exogenous increase in urban employment brought on by, say, an urban wage subsidy induces migration from the rural to the urban sector and increases the number of urban unemployed, since the urban (minimum) wage is unaffected.

It is the seemingly paradoxical result that urban wage subsidies increase the size of the urban unemployment pool that apparently has made the Harris–Todaro version of the two-sector unemployment equilibrium model of interest. Moreover, the basic idea that migrants pay attention to destination employment prospects as well as wage levels appears consistent with the evidence obtained in many econometric migration studies [e.g. Levy and Wadycki (1974)]. However, if nominal urban manufacturing wages are taken as representative of the urban wage, then the magnitude of actual urban unemployment rates does not reconcile the observed rural–urban wage differential, does not balance (27) – nominal urban manufacturing wages are allegedly from 50 to 100 percent higher than nominal rural agricultural wages, while urban unemployment rates are typically less than 10 percent.

One way to solve the problem that the Harris–Todaro framework appears to overpredict unemployment rates is to carefully measure sectoral wage differences for comparable classes of workers and to appropriately allow for sectoral cost of living differentials. Careful empirical studies of the alleged wage gap have been absent. Instead, researchers have modified the model, adding, for example, an additional sector to the urban area – workers are assumed to queue for the high-wage urban jobs, not in the unemployment line, but in an urban informal, subsistence, or "murky" sector (where the minimum wage presumably does not pertain), as in Fields (1975) and Cole and Sanders (1985). Presumably, the weighted average of urban high (minimum) wages, weighted by the urban unemployment rate, and lower murky-sector wages is approximately equal to the rural wage. However, it is difficult to measure the return to labor in the informal urban sector (see below) and, again, little empirical evidence exists on this component of this modified, three-sector balance equation. In addition, despite the critical role that the magnitude of the urban demand elasticity plays in the Harris–Todaro model [see also Mincer (1976)], there is little or no evidence to support the assumption that the urban aggregate demand elasticity is less than one.

An unsatisfying feature of the Harris–Todaro model itself is that the source of the labor market imperfection, the urban minimum wage, is determined outside the model in an ad hoc manner. While governments do impose binding minimum wages, it is difficult to believe that the fixed wages would be set independently of unemployment or migration rates. The evidence on how constraining governmentally imposed minimum wages are in urban areas is not clear in any event [Squire (1981)]. Stiglitz (1974) and Calvo (1978) have attempted to rectify this shortcoming of the Harris–Todaro framework. Calvo assumes monopolistic behavior by urban labor unions to obtain an equilibrium wage differential. Stiglitz formulates a two-sector unemployment equilibrium model in which urban unemployment results from the behavior of competitive urban firms; urban wages and urban unemployment along with rural wages are thus endogenously determined in these models. As in the Harris–Todaro model, moreover, there is no rural unemployment, and rural wages are competitively set (the nutrition–efficiency wage model is not employed).

In the Stiglitz model, monopolistically competitive firms in the urban sector incur hiring and training costs associated with labor turnover and set wages to minimize the cost per worker. The total labor costs C_L of the firm are assumed to be given by:

$$C_L = WL + qtL, \tag{28}$$

where L = firm's labor force, t = training or hiring costs per worker, and q = probability that an employee leaves the firm (quit rate). As in the efficiency wage model, labor costs are both directly and indirectly a function of the wage rate paid by the firm, here because it is assumed that the quit rate declines as the firm's wage increases. Unlike in the efficiency wage model, however, worker costs (turnover) are a function of *relative*, not absolute, wage rates and are influenced by the unemployment rate. In particular, Stiglitz assumes that

$$q = q(W_U/W_U^e, W_U/W_R, U), \tag{29}$$

where W_U^e = mean wage of all other urban firms, U = urban unemployment rate, and $q_i < 0$, $i = 1, 2, 3$. That is to say, workers are less likely to quit if the rewards in the firm in which they are employed are high relative to those of their alternatives, namely migrating to the rural sector or becoming unemployed. The firm can only use its own wage as an instrument to minimize (28); moreover, in equilibrium all wages in the urban sector will be equal ($W_U = W_U^e$). The wage paid by urban firms will thus be a function of the unemployment rate and the rural wage, and in eq. (27) all components of the equilibrium equation are endogenously determined.

The consequences of a wage subsidy (financed by a profit tax) differ between the Harris–Todaro and Stiglitz "turnover" models of unemployment equilibrium. In the former, wage subsidies, up to a certain point, increase the economy's total output. In the turnover model, however, wage subsidies lower output. This is because part of the wage subsidy is partially shifted to workers (which cannot happen in the rigid wage model). The rise in employment and the urban wage leads unambiguously to a rise in the urban unemployment rate, from (28).

An important feature of Stiglitz's turnover model is that urban unemployment is not only endogenous but is optimal, in the sense that if the government chose the urban wage and urban employment levels so as to maximize total output in the economy (allowing free migration), it would set the urban wage above the rural wage and allow a non-zero level of unemployment. The lost output due to (optimal) unemployment is less than the gain to output from the lower turnover costs – unemployment prospects and the urban–rural wage gap "discipline" workers and lower labor costs. This unemployment result, and all of the welfare-theoretic implications of the model, rest on the assumption that a firm (government) can only influence turnover via the wage it pays. Indeed, none of the costs of turnover is borne by workers. The optimality of unemployment comes about because of the artificial restriction placed on the types of contractual arrangements the firm can engage in with its labor force. As has been well established in the human capital literature [Becker (1975)], for example, when workers are free to leave firms and training is specific to a firm, as assumed in the Stiglitz model where trained workers receive no higher wages than untrained workers, sharing of the costs of training with workers is optimal. When workers incur part of the costs of their training and thus share in the returns from that training, they incur a capital loss when they leave the firm, as the training is not valued elsewhere in the economy. The sharing of training costs and the wage wedge between the firm where the specific training was undertaken the other firms eliminates the need for the pool of unemployed or the rural–urban wage gap to serve as turnover deterrents.

The firm behavior embedded in the Stiglitz turnover model, its essential ingredient, implies that workers' wage rates do not rise over time, as employees neither pay for nor obtain the rewards from training costs. However, pervasive evidence from a large number of countries suggests that urban workers' wages rise over their life cycle, consistent with such workers financing at least some investment costs and reaping returns. There is no evidence supporting the training arrangements assumed in, and fundamental to, the Stiglitz turnover model.

Fry (1979) tests a turnover model similar to that of Stiglitz, by ascertaining if workers who are less likely to remain with a firm are also less likely to receive training. Again, all costs are assumed to be borne by firms. He finds that among urban workers in Zambia, those from the poorest backgrounds were more likely to be trained as a consequence of their being less likely to return home. This finding, however, is perfectly consistent with a model in which *workers*, anticipating how long they intend to remain with a firm, choose to incur training costs. The data do not indicate who finances the training; moreover, Fry does not attempt to test whether wage rates rise with tenure in the firm in order to test the assumption that workers do not invest in training.

Finally, Stiglitz (1982) also develops unemployment equilibrium models incorporating equilibrium condition (27) in which (i) the absolute magnitude of the wage paid by a firm raises worker effort (the efficiency wage model *without* nutritional underpinnings) and (ii) the wage paid by the firm relative to wages paid by other firms determines the firm's ability to recruit high quality workers (the "efficiency wage–quality" model). In these models, unemployment persists, even when the government sets urban wages and employment to maximize total output. No evidence appears to exist to support the critical behavioral assumptions that are the basis of the effort–wage or quality–wage relationships, and no consideration is given in these models to the possible superiority of alternative contractual arrangements that minimize shirking or optimally sort workers and do not entail unemployment.

4.4. Risk, remittances and family behavior

The two-sector unemployment equilibrium (UE) models do not contain features special to low-income countries. Indeed, a similar model to that of Harris and Todaro has been applied to describe the employment effects of minimum wages across covered and uncovered sectors in the United States [Mincer (1976)], and turnover costs and problems of worker effort and recruitment are not especially confined to low-income urban areas. More importantly, neither the basic human capital model nor the UE models can readily explain temporary migration – planned return migration – or the directions and magnitudes of cross-area resource transfers associated with migration. Yet in the African setting that the UE model was designed to describe, the vast majority of urban migrants state that they intend to return to their rural home, had left their wives and children in their origin area, and/or owned land in the rural area [e.g. Kenya, Rempel (1974), Harris and Todaro (1970)]. Moreover, flows of funds – remittances – from urban migrants to family members in home areas in both Africa and South Asia account for 10–25 percent of urban migrants' incomes [Rempel and Lobdell (1978)]. The negative impact of migration on incomes in rural areas is thus overestimated by the UE model.

Temporary migrants might be considered members of a geographically extended family described by the income-sharing household model of (1), (2) and (5). In such a model, when the consumption of each member enters an additively separable household utility function, it is easy to show that family members (temporary migrants) with wages above the mean consumption level of the family will transfer funds to other members (origin members) until consumption levels of all members are equalized. Thus, remittances will be greater the higher is the income of the migrant member and lower the higher are the pre-remittance incomes of the origin family members.

The geographically extended joint household model is not entirely an adequate explanation of temporary migration. First, it does not explain why, if incomes are higher where the temporary migrant resides, the entire family does not move to the high-income area. Second, it does not explain, without resort to arbitrary assumptions about preferences, why higher-income migrants remit funds to their lower-income parents or other relatives at origin. Third, the available evidence from national probability samples from Kenya [Knowles and Anker (1981)] and Botswana [Lucas and Stark (1985)] suggests that while the migrant's income is positively related to the size of transfer made to the origin family, in accordance with the model, remittances are not negatively related to the pre-transfer income or wealth of the origin household members, as the joint household model also predicts. Finally, the model does not explain why geographically extended families should be prevalent in low-income but not in high-income countries.

As noted, an important feature of low-income countries is the inability of farmers to insure against production risk. Since farming is by far the principal occupation in low-income settings compared to high-income countries, attention to risk-induced behavior may illuminate spatial labor mobility in such areas. Note that the rural household, by diversifying its *spatial* portfolio of income sources, reduces total income risk in a context (agriculture) in which the principal source of risk is locational. Even occupational diversification among co-resident family members may not be adequate in rural areas where incomes from agriculture significantly influence non-agricultural activity levels. Thus, temporary migration of rural household members may be a manifestation of a familial, risk-sharing insurance contract, with remittances reflecting both insurance payoffs and compensation for the family's investment costs incurred in sending the migrant away or in financing his/her schooling, The migrant's income *net* of his (temporary migrants are predominantly male) transfers may be higher than that of his rural kin, reflecting compensation for the disutility of being away from home. Finally, incentives for remitting may be provided by prospects of inheritance, as in the bequest model of Kotlikoff and Spivak (1982).

Lucas and Stark (1985) is the first study to attempt to test the household-theoretic approach to temporary migration and remittances. Based on a national survey of households in Botswana, they find evidence consistent with the hypotheses that (i) temporary migration is in part a co-insurance arrangement, as remittances are higher when family incomes are *temporarily* low, (ii) prospects of bequests influence remittance flows positively as well as who migrates, as (male) migrants from wealthier (larger cattle herd) families send more remittances and sons are more likely to inherit in Botswana, and (iii) remittances rise with the migrant's (predicted) earnings and schooling. The latter finding is interpreted as indicating that remittances reflect in part the repayment of investment costs undertaken by the family on behalf of the migrant.

Lucas and Stark's findings are suggestive of the complexity of household arrangements. They do not, however, derive their hypotheses within the context of a rigorously formulated, integrated model of the household incorporating risk-sharing via formal labor or tenancy contracts, inter-generational and spatial transfers, wealth accumulation and/or bargaining. Moreover, their finding that family wealth and remittances are positively associated could merely reflect the greater ability of households receiving remittances to accumulate wealth, rather than the bequest motive or the absence of altruistic income-sharing (which implies a negative wealth–remittance correlation). Longitudinal data may be required to distinguish among hypotheses. As in the case of contractual arrangements involving labor, richer models of the family enterprise appear needed to understand fully the complex nature of the spatial mobility of labor.

4.5. Heterogeneity and selective migration

All of the models of migration discussed assume that potential migrants are concerned only with income. However, areas are also differentiated by or are heterogeneous in other attributes that utility-maximizing agents may value (and may value differentially). Thus, wage disparities across urban and rural areas may be consistent with a hedonic equilibrium in which the higher wages of the city compensate new city dwellers for the lost amenities of rural life. The utility associated with the high-wage, urban squalor bundle may be no greater than the utility associated with low-wage rural life for the representative agent.

Schultz (1983) and Rosenzweig and Wolpin (1984), based on separate household data sets from Colombia, found that migration behavior is influenced by characteristics of areas other than income prospects (i.e. relative prices). Moreover, their results suggest that households are heterogeneous in their preferences. Households appeared to differentially sort themselves across localities differing in relative prices. In particular, households who migrated exhibited different fertility and health investment behavior prior to their migration compared to observationally identical households at both origin and destination. Such differences appeared consistent with households, characterized by differing demands for human capital investments, being differentially influenced by spatial diversity in the relative prices of such investments. The selective migration of households heterogeneous in preferences may thus bias estimates based upon cross-sectional associations between the average behavior of populations containing residents and migrants and locality-specific program subsidies and/or relative prices.

Heterogeneity among individuals in earnings ability may also account for the urban–rural wage gap, even when such measured characteristics as schooling and age are taken into account. To the extent that a proportion of the population in urban areas in low-income countries consists of relatively recent migrants, and (self-selected) migrants have superior earnings abilities in cities compared to rural residents, the observed urban–rural wage group may overestimate the return to migration for the non-mobile. Indeed, the human capital migration model implies that those individuals with the highest returns from migration would be the most likely to migrate. Comparison of the wages of (origin) individuals who choose not to migrate with those (destination) individuals who migrate may thus lead to the false conclusion that there is underinvestment in migration.

Robinson and Tomes (1983) were the first to test the earnings–ability–migration selectivity hypothesis. Applying standard, two-stage selection correction procedures [Heckman (1976)] to household data from Canada, they found that returns to migration were significantly overestimated when such selectivity was not taken into account – persons who moved to an area *j* from area *i* earned more in *j* than those who did not move from *i* *would have* earned in *j*. Almost all samples from low-income countries provide earnings information only for migrants at destination and for non-migrants at origin; few estimates of migration behavior or the returns to migration in such settings have taken into account this selectivity problem.

5. Urban labor markets

5.1. Diversity and unemployment

The environment in which labor markets operate in urban areas is different in three important respects from that in rural areas. First, there is substantially more heterogeneity in the products produced; technologies are thus diverse, requiring a wide variety of worker activities and skills. Second, production in urban areas is not so highly seasonal or as highly sensitive to weather variations. Third, production activities are, definitionally, not so geographically dispersed as in rural agriculture.

These technological features of the urban environment have important implications for the operation of the urban labor market. Production diversity is likely to be manifested in heterogeneity in the rewards to labor to the extent that (i) individuals differ in innate talents and these are *differentially* productive across technologies (products) and/or (ii) there are cross-sector differences in the productivity of acquired skills (through schooling or via job training). Whether this technological complexity translates into differences in payments to labor services among people with the same skills depends on the extent of labor mobility. The high density of urban areas suggests that mobility costs – inclusive of the cost of information flows – are lower in urban than in rural areas; "natural" barriers to mobility are less. The existence of technological differentials in rewards to different worker characteristics, however, implies that the payoffs to search, to finding the right match, are high. Thus, periods of search, particularly for new entrants to the labor force for whom the payoffs are received over the longest period and/or for persons with specialized skills, may be long. Indeed,

Table 15.2
Ratios of urban to rural and young male to total male unemployment rates
in selected low-income countries

Country	Ratio		
	Urban to rural	Males aged 15–24 to male total	Year
Chile	3.1	n.a.	1968
Colombia	n.a.	2.1	1968
India	1.7	1.4	1972–73
Republic of Korea	4.1	1.8	1965
Malaysia	1.6	2.4	1971
Philippines	1.9	2.2	1967
Trinidad	1.9	1.9	1971

Source: Squire (1981).

unemployment rates in urban areas are significantly higher than they are in rural areas of low-income countries and are predominantly concentrated among the young and the more educated, far more so than in rural areas. Table 15.2 provides the ratios of urban to rural unemployment rates and urban youth to overall urban unemployment rates for a number of diverse countries that display these characteristics.

Urban areas of low-income countries, in contrast to rural, are also characterized by more intensively regulated labor markets. Unlike in agriculture, many urban industries are subject to minimum wage restrictions and to laws governing employment conditions and worker layoffs, although there is typically as well a largely unregulated service sector. Workers may, in addition, participate in formal, publicly administered unemployment insurance schemes. Moreover, again unlike in most rural agricultural environments, trade unions may play a large role in determining the pricing and allocation of labor and, in some areas, the government is one of the most important employers. Unemployment differentials between the urban and rural areas thus may in part be due to publicly enforced labor market restrictions, as assumed in the Harris–Todaro model, but also may reflect the inherent differences between the two environments.

An informed reader will see that most of the features of the low-income-country urban environments described also characterize urban areas of high-income countries. And the issues of the impact of governmental labor market interventions and trade unions and the determinants and consequences of job search strategies, which appear to be particularly pertinent to such settings, form an important part of the core of modern labor economics. Few distinct analytical models specifically targeted in any meaningful way to problems of low-income country urban labor markets have emerged in the literature.

5.2. Urban dualism and dual labor markets

There are some distinct features of *low-income* urban settings. Chief among them is the importance of family-based enterprises, as in agriculture. And, presumably, the consumption–production household models, applied principally to rural settings, are of use in understanding urban-based labor market phenomena. A problem in studying such enterprises is that even in this sector of the urban economy, product diversity (e.g. food shops, automobile shops, pharmacies) almost precludes estimation of "the" technology that is importantly influencing production and consumption decisions in such households.

The contrast between the organization of small-scale family enterprises and the large industrial firms that coexist in urban settings has led to the emergence of a literature characterizing the urban sector as dualistic [Fields (1975), Mazumdar (1977), Sabot (1977)]. This approach emphasizes differences between the urban "informal" sector, characterized by small, family-based firms, and the urban "formal" sector, characterized by large enterprises subject to legal restrictions, i.e. characterized by more institutionalized (rigid) wage setting procedures. Such a characterization is purely descriptive, having no predictive content. The vast empirical literature on urban labor markets in low-income countries, influenced by this framework, however, focuses on testing the hypothesis that there are barriers to mobility across these sectors, that there are two distinct labor markets with workers on average better off in one sector than in the other.

In these empirical studies, wages or earnings of workers of given measured human capital characteristics (schooling, age) are compared across different types of firms as indicated by firm size or firm ownership type, e.g. public, private, multinational, family-based. Findings of wage differences by firm size for workers of given schooling and some measure of potential labor market experience are common [e.g. Mazumdar (1981)] – workers in larger firms earning more than workers of smaller firms. How are such findings to be interpreted? Do they suggest barriers to mobility – non-competing groups – or do they merely reflect compensatory differentials, rewards for unmeasured skills or compensation for unmeasured differences in the disutility of the workplace?

First, technological differences in production across industries, sectors and products may entail different organizations, inclusive of operational scale, and possibly different contractual wage payments. Thus, some sectors (firms) may "require" specific job skills and others may need to reward productivity by delayed incentives arrangements when the outcomes of effort are not immediately observed [Lazear (1979)]. In that case life-cycle wage *schedules* may differ across firms and cross-sectional differences in wages among workers of the same age or years in the labor market may not reflect any differences in lifetime earnings. Second, if workers are heterogeneous in unmeasured skills and such skills have greater payoffs in large enterprises (the consequences of errors in judgment may be greater, for example), then seemingly identical employees of firms of different size may have different lifetime earnings [Rosen (1981)].

A third reason that such studies may find inter-sectoral wage differences is that the earnings of family workers in family-based enterprises reflect the contribution of other production factors, since such workers are residual claimants; their earnings are not comparable to those of salaried employees or wage workers. The relevant comparison is the marginal product of labor in family enterprises with the wage rates of employees in other sectors (among "comparable" workers). This requires the estimation of the family enterprise technology, not an "earnings" function, and is made problematical by the heterogeneity of technology in the urban sector.

A second class of empirical studies in the "dualistic" tradition tests if the structure of the relationship between earnings and worker characteristics differs across two sectors or earnings groups. A difficulty with this "dual labor market" approach [Cain (1976)], in addition to some of those measurement and interpretation problems mentioned, is the seeming arbitrariness of (i) there being only *two* non-competing groups, (ii) the qualitative criterion for grouping (firm size, earnings level, etc.) and/or (iii) the quantitative cutoff points. Moreover, as discussed in Heckman and Hotz (1986), such tests require that the selectivity bias associated with workers allocating themselves across sectors (income groups) according to unmeasured earnings characteristics be taken into account and that the assumed functional form of the earnings relationship (whose parameters are hypothesized to differ across groups) be correct. Misspecification of the earnings function and/or the process sorting workers across groups may lead to highly misleading inferences. This problem, in its generality, is not unique to these hypothesis tests, however. It is the lack of a precise behavioral interpretation of the results that is the principal shortcoming of the dualistic labor market empirical studies.

6. Conclusion

The starting point for most studies concerned with labor markets in low-income countries is the assumption of some market distortion. Solid empirical research documenting many alleged distortions, however, has been relatively scarce. Where careful work has been carried out, e.g. econometric estimation of farm household behavior and wage determination, rural unemployment measurement, many of the pre-suppositions of development theorists have been shown to be wrong or overemphasized. Moreover, the most important of the alleged distortions characterizing labor markets, the persistence of spatial differentials in real wages for workers within homogeneous skill classes, has received relatively little documentation, despite the multiplicity of models designed to explain such phenomena. As many policies carried out or promoted are supported by reference to the inefficiencies associated with the "natural" distortions existing in labor markets, the accumulation of evidence on the magnitudes of distortions as well as empirical evidence relevant to the implications of models incorporating market problems remains a high priority.

The growth rate of empirical evidence pertinent to markets' and agents' behavior in low-income environments, particularly in rural areas, has increased rapidly in recent years. In part as a result, the development economics literature concerned with the allocation of labor in low-income countries has moved from its emphasis on rigidities and distortions to focusing on the range of alternative arrangements and mechanisms employed by agents in such countries. Characterizations of low-income settings as composed of capitalist farms and family farms, of formal and informal sectors and even as agricultural and non-agricultural or rural and urban significantly understate the mobility of agents in such environments and overlook some essential features of these areas. We have seen that in many settings almost all farming households import (hire) labor from and export (supply) labor to the market, a substantial fraction of income in rural farm households has its source in the non-agricultural sector (30 percent in India [Rosenzweig and Wolpin (1985)]), considerable resources flow between family members located in rural and urban areas, and many workers in urban areas have immediate family members and own land in rural areas to which they eventually return.

There has also been increased recognition that an important aspect of low-income labor markets is the variety of arrangements used to cope with risk and information problems, from formal futures contracts to informal intra-family transfer arrangements, and the spatial variability of these important institutions. Yet models developed to describe rural behavior have generally focused on only one type of arrangement, ignoring alternative arrangements and thus the important question of contractual choice. Little is thus known about how flexible both prices and contractual arrangements are to change. The choice-theoretic models imply that prices, contractual terms and the mix of institutions presumably respond importantly to technological changes, particularly if they reduce or mitigate problems such institutions are designed to alleviate. New substitute arrangements such as governmental efforts to increase the availability of credit or to improve water control may also influence the mix of "traditional" institutions, inclusive of traditional family living arrangements. But there is little detailed, micro time-series information on and few integrative models pertinent to these important changes that accompany the transformation of agriculture (see Timmer, Chapter 8 in this Handbook). The literature is not yet ready to predict the full range of consequences of interventions in the rural sector designed to encourage productivity growth, reduce disparities in incomes, or reduce apparent inefficiencies and distortions.

Even less is understood about the degree of life-cycle and intergenerational mobility experienced by agents in low-income countries. How rigid is the distinction between types of workers? Do wage earners remain as wage workers all their lives? How open are opportunities for using allocative or entrepreneurial skills, e.g. is tenancy a route to land ownership? Longitudinal and/or retrospective life-history data, now scarce, may provide an essential base for examining such issues and for model formulation aimed at integrating capital accumulation with labor allocation. In addition, more focus on the family as the central allocating mechanism may be warranted [see, for example, Pollak (1985), Rosenzweig (1988)]. Understanding the causes and consequences of the transformation of institutional arrangements, formal and informal; the processes by which skills are accumulated; and the mobility of households and individuals lies at the core of development economics. Only what appears to be a promising foundation for an enquiry into these issues appears to have been established.

References

Adulavidhya, K., Kurida, Y., Lau, L., Lerttamrab, P. and Yolopoulos, P. (1979) 'A microeconomic analysis of the agriculture of Thailand', *Food Research Institute Studies*, 17:79–86.

Balan, J., Browning, H. and Jelin, E. (1973) *Man in a developing society.* Austin TX: University of Texas Press.

Bardhan, K. (1984) 'Work patterns and social differentiation: Rural women of West Bengal', in: H.P. Binswanger and M.R. Rosenzweig, eds., *Contractual arrangements, employment and wages in rural South Asia.* New Haven, CT: Yale University Press.

Bardhan, P.K. (1979) 'Labor supply functions in a poor agrarian economy', *American Economic Review*, 69:479–500.

Bardhan, P.K. (1983) 'Labor tying in a poor agrarian economy: A theoretical and empirical analysis', *Quarterly Journal of Economics*, 98:501–514.

Bardhan, P.K. and Rudra, A. (1981) 'Terms and conditions of labor contracts in agriculture', *Oxford Bulletin of Economics and Statistics*, 43:89–111.

Barnum, H.N. and Squire, L. (1978) 'An econometric application of the theory of the farm household', *Journal of Development Economics*, 6:79–102.

Basu, K. (1983) 'The emergence of isolation and interlinkage in rural markets', *Oxford Economic Papers*, 35:262–280.

Becker, G.S. (1975) *Human capital*, 2nd ed. New York: Columbia University Press.

Bell, C. (1977) 'Alternative theories of sharecropping: Some tests using evidence from northeast India', *Journal of Development Studies*, 13:317–346.

Bell, C. and Srinivasan, T.N. (1985a) 'The demand for attached farm servants in Andhra Pradesh, Bihar and Punjab', mimeo.

Bell, C. and Srinivasan, T.N. (1985b) 'Some salient features of tenancy contracts, commodity prices and wages: A comparison of Andhra Pradesh, Bihar and Punjab', mimeo.

Bell, C. and Sussangkarn, C. (1985) 'The choice of tenancy contract', mimeo.

Binswanger, H.P. and Rosenzweig, M.R. (1986) 'Behavioral and material determinants of production relations in agriculture', *Journal of Development Studies*, 22: 503–539.

Bliss, C. and Stern, N.H. (1978) 'Productivity, wages and nutrition', Parts I and II, *Journal of Development Economics*, 5:331–398.

Cain, G. (1976) 'The challenge of segmented labor market theories to orthodox theory: A survey', *Journal of Economic Literature*, 14:1215–1257.

Calvo, G.A. (1978) 'Urban development and wage determination in LDC's: Trade unions in the Harris–Tadaro model', *International Economic Review*, 19:65–81.

Chayanov, A.K. (1925, 1966) *The theory of the peasant economy*. Homewood, IL: Irwin Press.

Cheung, S.N.S. (1968) 'Private property rights and sharecropping', *Journal of Political Economy*, 76:1107–1122.

Cole, W.C. and Sanders, R.D. (1985) 'Internal migration and urbanization in the third world', *American Economic Review*, 75:481–494.

Dasgupta, P. and Ray, D. (1984) 'Inequality, malnutrition and unemployment: A critique of the market mechanism', mimeo.

Eswaran, M. and Kotwal, A. (1985a) 'A theory of two-tier labor markets in agrarian economies', *American Economic Review*, 75:162–177.

Eswaran, M. and Kotwal, A. (1985b) 'A theory of contractual structure in agriculture', *American Economic Review*, 75:352–367.

√ Fields, G.S. (1975) 'Rural–urban migration, urban unemployment and underemployment, and job search activity in LDCs', *Journal of Development Economics*, 2:165–187.

Fry, J. (1979) 'A labor turnover model of wage determination in developing economies', *Economic Journal*, 89:353–369.

Gersovitz, M. (1983) 'Savings and nutrition at low incomes', *Journal of Political Economy*, 91:841–855.

Greenwood, M. (1971) 'A regression analysis of migration to urban areas of a less-developed country: The case of India', *Journal of Regional Science*, 11:253–262.

Hanson, B. (1969) 'Employment and wages in rural Egypt', *American Economic Review*, 59.

Harris, R. and Todaro, M.P. (1970) 'Migration, unemployment and development: A two-sector analysis', *American Economic Review*, 60:126–142.

Heckman, J.J. (1976) 'The common structure of statistical models of transaction and censoring', *Annals of Economic and Social Measurement*, 415:493–504.

Heckman, J.J. and Hotz, V.J. (1986) 'The sources of inequality for males in Panama's labor market', *Journal of Human Resources*, 21:507–542.

Knowles, J.C. and Anker, R. (1981) 'An analysis of income transfers in a developing country', *Journal of Development Economics*, 8:205–226.

Kotlikoff, J. and Spivak, A. (1982) 'The family as an incomplete annuities market', *Journal of Political Economy*, 90:272–291.

Kuznets, S. (1982) 'The pattern of shift of labor force from agriculture, 1950–70', in: M. Gersovitz, C.F. Diaz-Alejandro, G. Ranis and M.R. Rosenzweig, eds., *The theory and experience of economic development*. London: George Allen and Unwin.

Lau, L., Lin, W.-L. and Yotopoulos, P. (1978) 'The linear logarithmic expenditure system: An application to consumption–leisure choice', *Econometrica*, 46:843–868.

Lazear, E.P. (1979) 'Why is there mandatory retirement?', *Journal of Political Economy*, 87:1261–1284.

Leibenstein, H. (1957) *Economic backwardness and economic growth*. New York: Wiley.

Levy, M. and Wadycki, W. (1974) 'Education and the decision to migrate: An econometric analysis of migration in Venezuela', *Econometrica*, 46:377–388.

Lewis, W.A. (1954) 'Economic development with unlimited supplies of labor', *Manchester School of Economic and Social Studies*, 22:139–191.

Lopez, R. (1986) 'Structural models of the farm household that allow for interdependent utility and profit-maximization decisions', in: I. Singh, L. Squire and J. Strauss, eds., *Agricultural household models: Extensions and applications*. Baltimore, MD: Johns Hopkins University Press.

Lucas, R.E.B. and Stark, O. (1985) 'Motivations to remit: Evidence from Botswana', *Journal of Political Economy*, 93:901–918.

Mazumdar, D. (1977) 'Analysis of the dual labor market in LDC's', in: S. Kannappan, ed., *Studies of urban labor market behavior in developing areas*. Geneva: International Institute for Labor Studies.

Mazumdar, D. (1981) *The urban labor market and income distribution, a study of Malaysia*. Oxford: Oxford University Press.

Mincer, J. (1976) 'Unemployment effects of minimum wages', *Journal of Political Economy*, 84:S87–S104.

Mirrlees, J. (1975) 'A pure theory of underdeveloped economies', in: L. Reynolds, ed., *Agriculture in development theory*. New Haven, CT: Yale University Press.

Nabi, I. (1984) 'Village and considerations in rural–urban migration', *Journal of Development Economics*, 14:129–145.

Nelson, J. (1976) 'Sojourners versus new urbanites: Causes and consequences of temporary versus permanent cityward migration in developing countries', *Economic Development and Cultural Change*, 24:721–757.

Newbery, D. (1975) 'The choice of rental contracts in peasant agriculture', in: L. Reynolds, ed., *Agriculture in development theory*. New Haven, CT: Yale University Press.

Otsuka, K. and Hayami, Y. (1985) 'Theories of share tenancy: A survey', mimeo.

Paglin, M. (1965) '"Surplus" agricultural labor and development: Facts and theories', *American Economic Review*, 55:815–834.

Pitt, M.M. and Rosenzweig, M.R. (1986) 'Agricultural prices, food consumption and the health and productivity of farmers', in: I. Singh, L. Squire and J. Strauss, eds., *Agriculture household models: Extensions and applications*. Baltimore, MD: Johns Hopkins University Press.

Pollak, R.A. (1985) 'A transaction cost approach to families and households', *Journal of Economic Literature*, 23:581–608.

Ranis, G. and Fei, J. (1961) 'A theory of economic development', *American Economic Review*, 56:533–558.

Rempel, H. (1974) 'The role of urban-to-rural remittances in rural development', *Journal of Development Studies*, 14:189–210.

Rempel, H. and Lobdell, R. (1978) 'The role of urban-to-rural remittances in rural development', *Journal of Development Studies*, 14:324–341.

Robinson, C. and Tomes, N. (1983) 'Self-selection and interprovincial migration in Canada', The Canadian Journal of Economics, 15:474–502.

Rosen, S. (1981) 'The economics of superstars', *American Economic Review*, 71:845–858.

Rosenzweig, M.R. (1978) 'Rural wages, labor supply and land reform: A theoretical and empirical analysis', *American Economic Review*, 68:847–861.

Rosenzweig, M.R. (1980) 'Neoclassical theory and the optimizing peasant: An econometric analysis of market family labor supply in a developing country', *Quarterly Journal of Economics*, 95:31–55.

Rosenzweig, M.R. (1984) 'Determinants of wage rates and labor supply behavior in the rural sector of a developing country', in: H.P. Binswanger and M.R. Rosenzweig, eds., *Contractual arrangements, employment and wages in rural labor markets in Asia*. New Haven, CT: Yale University Press.

Rosenzweig, M.R. (1988) 'Risk, private information and the family', *American Economic Review*, 78:837–844.

Rosenzweig, M.R. and Evenson, R.E. (1977) 'Fertility, schooling and the economic contribution of children in rural India', *Econometrica*, 45:1065–1080.

Rosenzweig, M.R. and Wolpin, K.I. (1984) 'Migration selectivity and the effects of public programs', mimeo.

Rosenzweig, M.R. and Wolpin, K.I. (1985) 'Specific experience, household structure and the intergenerational transfers: Farm family land and labor arrangements in developing countries', *Quarterly Journal of Economics*, 100:961–988.

Ryan, J.G. and Ghodake, R.D. (1984) 'Labor market behavior in rural villages in South India: Effects of season, sex and socioeconomic status', in: H.P. Binswanger and M.R. Rosenzweig, eds., *Contractual arrangements, employment and wages in rural South Asia*. New Haven, CT: Yale University Press.

Sabot, R.H. (1977) 'The meaning and measurement of urban surplus labor', *Oxford Economic Papers*, 29:389–411.

Schultz, T.P. (1983) 'Migrant behavior and the effects of regional prices: Aspects of migrant selection in Colombia', mimeo. Forthcoming in: *Research in Population Economics*.

Schwartz, A. (1976) 'Migration, age and education', *Journal of Political Economy*, 84:701–720.

Sen, A.K. (1966) 'Peasants and dualism with or without surplus labor', *Journal of Political Economy*, 74:425–450.

Sen, A.K. (1975) *Employment, technology, and development*. Geneva: International Institute for Labor Studies.

Shaban, R.A. (1986) 'Testing between competing models of sharecropping', mimeo.

Singh, I., Squire, L. and Strauss, J. (1986) *Agricultural household models: Extensions and applications*. Baltimore, MD: Johns Hopkins University Press.

✓ Stiglitz, J.E. (1974) 'Alternative theories of wage determination and unemployment in LDC's: The labor turnover model', *Quarterly Journal of Economics*, 88:194–227.

Stiglitz, J.E. (1976) 'The efficiency wage hypothesis, surplus labor and the distribution of income in LDCs', *Oxford Economic Papers*, 28:185–207.

Stiglitz, J.E. (1982) 'Alternative theories of wage determination and unemployment: The efficiency wage model', in: M. Gersovitz, E. Diaz-Alejandro, G. Ranis and M. Rosenzweig, eds., *The theory and experience of economic development*. London: George Allen and Unwin.

Strauss, J. (1983) 'Determinants of food consumption in rural Sierra Leone: Application of the quadratic expenditure system to the consumption–leisure component of the household–farm model', *Journal of Development Economics*, 10:327–354.

Strauss, J. (1986) 'Does better nutrition raise farm productivity', *Journal of Political Economy*, 94:235–238.

Squire, L. (1981) *Employment policy in developing countries: A survey of issues and evidence*. Oxford: Oxford University Press.

Todaro, M.P. (1969) 'A model of labor migration and urban employment in less developed countries', *American Economic Review*, 59:138–148.

Weiss, A. (1980) 'Job queues and layoffs in labor markets with flexible wages', *Journal of Political Economy*, 88:526–538.

White, B. and Makali (1975) 'Wage labor and wage relations in Japanese agriculture: Some preliminary notes from the agro-economic survey', mimeo.

Willis, R.J. (1973) 'A new approach to the economic theory of fertility behavior', *Journal of Political Economy*, 81:S14–S64.

Yap, L. (1977) 'The attraction of cities: A review of the migration literature', *Journal of Development Economics*, 4:105–127.

Chapter 16

CREDIT MARKETS AND INTERLINKED TRANSACTIONS

CLIVE BELL*

Vanderbilt University

Contents

1. Introduction   764
2. Credit markets   766
   2.1. The credit contract   769
   2.2. Innovation and the rate of interest   782
   2.3. Public policy   783
   2.4. Some evidence   791
3. Interlinked transactions   797
   3.1. The causes of interlinking   798
   3.2. The interlinking of tenancy with credit: The principal–agent approach   803
   3.3. An alternative to contract-taking equilibrium: The Nash bargaining solution   810
   3.4. Interlinking and innovation   813
   3.5. Welfare and income distribution   816
   3.6. Policy reforms   823
4. Concluding remarks   826
References   828

*I am grateful to Pranab Bardhan, Hans Binswanger, Nicholas Stern, Christopher Udry and John Von Pischke for valuable comments on an earlier draft. I am especially indebted to T.N. Srinivasan for unstinting discussions, comments and encouragement throughout the writing of this chapter. Surviving errors of analysis, opinion and emphasis are mine alone.

Handbook of Development Economics, Volume I, Edited by H. Chenery and T.N. Srinivasan
© *Elsevier Science Publishers B.V., 1988*

1. Introduction

When output follows inputs with an appreciable lag, the agents organizing production will usually be involved in credit transactions, in the sense of exchanging future claims on resources for present ones. The impulse toward such exchange will be all the stronger if output is also uncertain; for then there are compelling reasons to smooth consumption in the face of fluctuating income. This applies equally well to the peasant farmer who commits labor, draft power, seed and fertilizer in order to harvest a crop some months later; to the landless laborer who borrows in the slack season against harvest wages; and to the firm which decides to build a new plant to produce widgets. Moreover, as economic development involves the accumulation of physical and human capital, it follows that once the limitations of self-finance are reached, credit transactions occupy a central place in that process.

Now uncertainty is an inherent element in this picture, and its presence introduces a number of difficulties. In particular, in the absence of a complete set of markets for contingent commodities, creditors cannot be sure that debtors will settle their accounts when they are due. Thus, there are problems both of information: What sort of person is the borrower, and what sort of use will he or she make of the loan? And of enforcement: What can be done to ensure that principal and interest are paid whatever be the borrower's inclination?

Faced with these problems, it is natural that creditors certainly, and perhaps borrowers also, will hunt about for ways to alleviate them. One such method, which has attracted a good deal of attention in the recent theoretical literature and whose pervasiveness in rural economies has been revealed in recent empirical work, is to "interlink", or "bundle", transactions in the credit market with those in related markets. For example, a landlord may insist on being his tenants' sole creditor, if such interlinking promises better control over what sort of tenants offer their services and what they will do with a tenancy. In this view, therefore, interlinked transactions are the responses of rational economic agents to incomplete and/or imperfect market structures, perhaps with an undertone of exploitation through superior contractual control over the weaker party.

These considerations involve important departures from the standard competitive framework, in which agents might as well be anonymous, since prices then convey all relevant information costlessly to buyers and sellers alike. It is quite possible, of course, that a particular pair of agents will trade with each other in more than one market, though in an anonymous setting they will be quite unaware of so doing. In any event, a multiplicity of transactions between two agents has no significance, since it does not – indeed, cannot – affect anyone's decisions. This is far removed from the case discussed above, in which the deliberate intertwining of several transactions between two agents springs directly from the necessity of close control when information is costly to obtain and asymmetrically held.

Two themes identified above recur throughout this chapter and exert considerable influence over its analytical approach and emphasis. First, where information is concerned, there is the distinction between not knowing what sort of person one is dealing with, which may result in adverse selection, and not knowing what actions that person will take if a contract is sealed, which may result in moral hazard. [Alternatively, one can employ Arrow's (1985) more precise terminology of "hidden information" and "hidden action".] When there is a good deal of repeat business, as is certainly the case in village life, few personal attributes of any economic significance are hidden. Thus, I have chosen to put far more emphasis on moral hazard than adverse selection. (For a somewhat different view, see Chapter 5 in this Handbook by Joseph Stiglitz). Secondly, the problems of contractual enforcement and willful, or strategic, default by borrowers are given a prominent place in the analysis.

A third theme stems from these departures from the framework of complete and competitive markets, namely, how the scope for strategic behavior is resolved in equilibrium. Here, the overwhelming choice in the literature has fallen on the principal–agent formulation, in which one party faces a perfectly elastic supply of prospective contractual partners who have some alternative form of employment yielding a parametric level of utility. This is sometimes referred to as a contract-taking equilibrium, to distinguish it from the price-taking equilibrium of pure perfect competition. The principal–agent formulation appears in a number of guises throughout the chapter, and in Section 3, which deals with interlinked transactions, it is contrasted with an alternative approach to the determination of contractual equilibrium. When there are gains from cooperation between two parties and the number of potential players is finite, though not necessarily small, there will be scope for bargaining. It turns out that the solutions provided by these two approaches differ qualitatively in various important respects.

The main positive questions to be addressed are: First, how is the rate of interest determined and to what extent is rationing an inherent feature of credit markets? This question involves costs, the nature of uncertainty, information and market structure. Not surprisingly, different models give different answers. Secondly, how does the introduction of innovations affect the rate of interest and other terms of loans? Thirdly, what are the reasons for interlinking and how does its introduction affect the allocation of resources and welfare? Fourthly, there are important empirical questions. How high are rates of interest, and do they appear to contain a significant element of supernormal profit? How extensive is participation in the regulated and unregulated segments of the credit market? How important is tangible collateral in securing loans? What is the nature and extent of interlinked transactions, and does interlinking wax or wane with commercialization? What are the forms of intervention which governments have chosen and with what effects?

The normative questions follow naturally. Where credit markets are concerned, intervention can seek to lower private lender's costs if there is free entry into lending, or sharpen competition if there is not. The latter may take the form either of encouraging private entry or of direct competition from state-owned or closely regulated commercial banks. This, of course, raises further questions about how the institutions in question should be regulated. Where interlinking is concerned, two questions arise. First, under what circumstances will such arrangements defeat piecemeal reforms? Secondly, should interlinking be banned, to the extent that this step is enforceable, or indirectly discouraged?

The structure of the chapter has been already laid out. The only elaboration needed here is that Section 2 begins with a general specification of a credit contract, which is then specialized to yield the three main models to have appeared in the literature. In so doing, most of the important themes and ideas are introduced. The section closes with a discussion of some of the relevant evidence, which establishes the empirical importance of interlinking and so motivates Section 3. Following a discussion of the reasons for interlinking, the principal–agent and bargaining theoretic approaches are compared and contrasted in the context of resource allocation, innovation and welfare.

In closing, it should be remarked that the exposition refers to rural life and its principal actors: farmers, laborers, landlords, tenants, moneylenders and traders. Much of the analysis, however, can be applied fairly readily to urban life, though the balance of emphasis between the problems of "hidden information" and "hidden actions" must then be shifted in favor of the former.

2. Credit markets

The salient feature of a credit transaction arises from the fact that current claims over resources are exchanged for future ones, and the delivery of future claims may not be fully assured. There are two forms of uncertainty. First, the borrower may be unable to repay, whether through bad luck, poor judgment or lack of diligence. Secondly, the borrower may be *unwilling* to meet his obligations when they fall due, which introduces strategic considerations. Together, they give dealings in the credit market their peculiarly "contractual" character.

Lenders attempt to protect their interests by closely scrutinizing would-be clients and attaching a variety of provisions, both explicit and implicit, to the contracts they offer. In particular, they may demand collateral, which necessarily implies a transaction in more than one (contingent) market. For example, if a farmer does not repay a loan, he will lose the land or other assests pledged against it. Furthermore, the borrower's ability to make timely repayments depends on, inter alia, his activities and dealings in other markets. Thus, there will be a tendency for borrower and lender to deal with each other in other markets as a matter of deliberate policy if such dealings give the lender greater assurance that he will be able to recover his loan without imposing unduly burdensome transactions costs. For example, an employer may give a substantial advance of salary to an attached farm servant; a landlord may finance his tenants' needs for working capital and family consumption if rents are paid in arrears; and a trader or commission agent may do likewise for cultivators who normally produce a marketable surplus. These so-called interlinked transactions will be taken up in detail in Section 3; but they will keep on intruding into our discussion of the credit market alone.

It follows that the rate of interest is a very incomplete description of the terms of a loan, even if the maturity is specified. Yet the rate of interest, as the "price" of funds, is usually the center of attention, so that is where we will begin. Some readings of the evidence have it that the rate of interest in rural areas is both high, on average, and highly variable across individuals. To the extent that it is high, opinions differ sharply as to the cause. There are those, like Bottomley (1971, 1975) and Von Pischke, Adams and Donald (1983), who see the money-lender as an efficient fellow who provides a valuable service to his clients, albeit in an environment that is often far removed from the textbook ideal. If his rates are high, that is mainly because his costs are high, due to a high opportunity cost of his funds and a substantial risk of partial or total default on his loans. At the other extreme, Bhaduri (1973, 1977), Basu (1984) and Rudra (1984) and others see instead a predator, who relentlessly wields his monopoly power over a pauperized peasantry and rural proletariat. In another, earlier tradition, Darling (1925) sees enough redeeming virtues to accept the moneylender's presence in rural life as a regrettable necessity.

In any event, the fact that different prices are charged to different customers is neither necessary nor sufficient for the inference that someone is exercising market power. There may be offsetting differences in other terms of the contract, which make the real cost of funds much more uniform than appears to be the case from the rate of interest alone. For example, the market value of the collateral required of the borrower may exceed the principal and interest on the loan thus secured by more than the cost of seizure and liquidation. Hence, if the borrower defaults, the lender is more than compensated. Similarly, a trader who gives a "soft" loan to a cultivator may stiffen the terms by paying the latter less than the ruling spot price for the crop when it is put up for sale. Yet even allowing for such offsetting adjustments in the terms of contracts, there appear to be no particularly compelling grounds for presuming that the real cost of funds will be uniform unless lenders and borrowers are, respectively, homogeneous. On the contrary, the modern theory of contracts suggests that the terms of each contract will usually reflect those characteristics of the parties to it which are mutually observable. Thus, in general, one cannot seize upon variations in the terms of contracts as decisive evidence that someone is wielding market power, any more than one can point to uniformity as evidence that there is perfect competition. What can be said is that a credit market cannot be perfect in the sense that an individual of a recognizable type can borrow as much as he pleases at the going rate for his type: by borrowing more, he becomes a different "type", since the level of indebtedness is a significant personal characteristic.

Cross-cutting these views of the social value of the moneylender's role are equally diverse views about the role of information and how it affects the way in which the moneylender goes about his business. Inspired by eastern India, writers like Basu, Bhaduri and Rudra assume that people stay put in their villages, so that local borrowers and lenders acquire an intimate knowledge of one another's resources and character. As a consequence, so the argument runs, rural credit markets tend to be highly fragmented, with formidable barriers to entry. Binswanger et al. (1985) describe surviving examples of the traditional system of moneylending in two Deccan villages.

In an extreme version of this story, even the lender's risk is banished, through the provision of acceptable collateral to cover the loan in full. It is then immaterial to the lender whether the borrower defaults on his obligations, since recovery is effected by taking possession of his collateral. Indeed, if the collateral is sufficiently valuable, lenders may even induce their clients to take out impru- dently large loans precisely to improve their chances of getting hold of the collateral on favorable terms. In this connection, Darling (1925) gives a vivid account of the large-scale acquisition of land by lenders in Punjab towards the end of the nineteenth century, when land had become a commercial commodity. Jodha (1978) documents a recent, but much more modest, replay in a Deccan district.

An implicit assumption in the above account is that lenders experience no difficulty in taking possession of collateral, whether by due legal process or extra-legal coercion. Bottomley (1971), while also laying much emphasis on the value of the moneylender's "insider's knowledge", is not persuaded that his operations are risk-free. Even where the law permits the alienation or sale of land to settle debts, legal process is costly and its outcome by no means certain. Moreover, when the assets are in his hands, disposing of them may be difficult in the face of fellow villagers' moral scruples against bidding for the possessions of a neighbor who is down on his luck. This consideration is likely to be particularly important in the case of land and other immoveable assets if the lender has no taste for cultivation or the management of tenancies. Finally, loans are often given without formal security, presumably because lenders are aware of these difficulties. Thus, while "inside knowledge" remains as a barrier to entry, the risk of default re-emerges as a consideration in the moneylender's calculations.

Inside knowledge of this sort is, of course, a particular form of asymmetric information: within each fragment of the market, information is complete or substantially so; outside, it is seriously wanting, perhaps to the point of being virtually non-existent. Another, extreme form of asymmetry is that in which the qualities of borrowers are not known to lenders. In this case, lenders may face the problems of adverse selection, and their policies will be shaped, in part, by the potential gains from getting borrowers to reveal their qualities through their choice of contract. Stiglitz and Weiss (1981) provide a detailed analysis of just such a case. It should be noted, however, that if a borrower were to offer collateral whose value exceeded principal, interest and transactions costs in all states of nature and whatever the borrower's performance, there would be no value in the information we have been discussing.

In the absence of inside information and adverse selection, the credit market would be unified and operate more smoothly. Even then, it would not be perfectly competitive in the standard sense, unless borrowers possessed indefinitely large amounts of what might be called "perfect" collateral. That this ideal is not attained in practice must, therefore, stem from some residual uncertainty as to whether the value of collateral will suffice in the case of default, whether from legal challenge, an adverse state of nature or imperfect knowledge of its value on the lender's part. Without such uncertainty, we should be back in a world devoid of lender's risk, and without such risk, credit transactions would lose their peculiar character.

2.1. The credit contract

Let the borrower obtain an amount B bearing a rate of interest r with a maturity of one period. In return, he pledges certain physical assets, K, as collateral. Suppose the lender has first claim on the returns, R, from the borrower's projects. If these returns are insufficient to cover interest and principal in full, the lender takes possession of as much of the collateral as is needed to make up the shortfall, up to the limit K.[1] The collateral itself is valued at a price v, which may be agreed on in advance, or the ruling spot price at the time of default or upon disposal by the lender.

The borrower may use the loan to finance a number of "projects", for example changing his intertemporal pattern of consumption, intensifying current cultivation and acquiring new assets. Given the terms of the credit contract, including

---

[1] Other arrangements are possible. For example, the lender may take possession of the entire collateral whenever the borrower defaults, while the borrower would then keep the returns R. The arrangement in the text makes for simpler exposition.

the collateral pledged to the lender, and his prior distribution of the states of nature, let there be a particular portfolio of projects that the borrower most prefers. Thus, the borrower may be thought of as choosing a particular distribution function of payoffs.

When the time comes to repay, the borrower's position is summarized by his return (net of any repayment) and his assets (net of any loss of collateral). Denoting this pair of variables by Y, the borrower's position at the time of repayment is

$$Y = \begin{cases} [X, \bar{A}], & \text{if } X \geq 0, \\ [0, \bar{A} + X/v], & \text{if } -vK \leq X < 0, \\ [0, \bar{A} - K], & \text{otherwise,} \end{cases} \tag{1}$$

where $X = R - (1 + r)B$ is the borrower's net return and $\bar{A}$ denotes his initial assets. If the value placed on the collateral by the borrower when repayment falls due is indeed vK and all of his assets are fully marketable, there will be no need to distinguish between the cash flow and closing assets elements of Y. Otherwise, the distinction is important. Let the borrower's preferences over Y be represented by

$$U^b = U^b(Y). \tag{2}$$

Turning to the moneylender, we begin by setting out the various elements that make up his costs. Bottomley (1971) gives a clear account, which is followed here.
- The opportunity cost of the principal.
- The costs of administering the loan.
- A premium to cover the possibility that the borrower may be unable, or even if able, unwilling to repay.

To these, we add an element to the lender's total return which is not a cost, but a reflection of his market power (if any), namely,
- Monopoly profit.

In making the loan, the lender foregoes the next best opportunity for his funds, which, for simplicity, is assumed to be a perfectly safe placement yielding r_0, and incurs some administrative costs (a_0). When the loan matures, further costs are incurred: either those of recovering principal and interest in full from the borrower's returns (a_1); or those of taking possession and disposing of the borrower's collateral, in addition to collecting the borrower's returns (a_2). Each of a_0, a_1 and a_2 contains a substantial fixed element, while the remainder varies with the size of the loan. If the latter is linear in B, it can be subsumed under r_0. For simplicity, that will be assumed here; so that a_0, a_1 and a_2 are all fixed costs.

In the absence of a first claim by the lender on the borrower's returns, the distinction between the borrower's unwillingness and inability to repay is clearly important. If the borrower values his collateral, including his good reputation and access to credit in the future, more highly than principal and interest on the loan, he will default only if he is unable to repay out of current income. Even when the lender has such a claim, however, wilful default cannot be ruled out. For although the lender can then seize the returns whatever be the borrower's attitude, if the returns are insufficient to cover principal and interest in full, the borrower may still have options which affect the lender. For example, a farmer who has pledged land against a loan will weigh the value of the land against his reputation if there is a fair chance that he could successfully contest seizure. In this case, the lender's cost of recovery will depend on the borrower's attitude. Moreover, possessing a claim on the borrower's returns will be of no avail if the borrower can make off with the loan beyond the lender's reach. A borrower who places little value on his collateral and has the good fortune to secure a sizeable loan, may choose *strategic* default, that is, he may intend to withhold repayment from the outset. Here, a plausible example is that of a young, unmarried landless worker lacking family connections in the village, who gets a loan against future labor services. If $(1 + r)B$ is large enough, his best policy will be literally to take the money and run.

Astute moneylenders will, of course, be quite aware of these strategic possibilities, and the terms of their loans will be chosen accordingly. Clearly $(1 + r)B$ must not be too large, though it can still exceed the value of the borrower's collateral without inducing default, provided the borrower has access to sufficiently attractive projects while staying put. For his part, the lender faces a certain loss if there is a strategic default, unless the collateral can be seized and happens to be especially valuable to him. Thus, if lenders are fully informed about would-be borrowers' preferences and opportunities, strategic default should occur only when a lender has suffered a failure of judgment; for if the terms of the contract are suitably chosen, strategic default will be unprofitable to borrowers. More generally, if a lender is imperfectly informed on these matters, his optimal policy will imply some positive probability of strategic default. The ensuing complications will not be tackled here.

In the absence of strategic default, the lender's closing position with respect to the loan in question is made up of the repayment less the opportunity cost of his capital and the costs of administration, and the collateral (if any) that has come into his hands:

$$
\Pi = \begin{cases} [(r - r_0)B - (a_0 + a_1), 0], & \text{if } X \geq 0, \\ [R - (1 + r_0)B - (a_0 + a_2), -X/v], & \text{if } 0 > X \geq -vK, \\ [R - (1 + r_0)B - (a_0 + a_2), K], & \text{otherwise.} \end{cases} \tag{3}
$$

If, as is plausible, $a_2 > a_1$, the first component of Π will jump discontinuously at

$X = 0$. Again, let the lender have preferences over Π represented by

$$U^l = U^l(\Pi), \tag{4}$$

where the remarks about $U^b(Y)$ also apply, mutatis mutandis, in this case.

Three specializations of the above system have appeared in the literature.

2.1.1. Pure screening

Suppose each project is characterized by a particular distribution function of returns, $D(R)$, which the borrower is unable to alter. For simplicity, suppose further that the only feature of $D(\cdot)$ that lenders are able to discern is the expected value of R, so that prospective borrowers seeking to finance projects that yield the same mean return appear identical to lenders. Finally, suppose that projects are indivisible and require a fixed amount of investment, and that borrowers have insufficient equity to undertake a project without a loan. If lenders can observe how much equity the borrower possesses, this last set of assumptions implies that each borrower can undertake only one project. Thus, while moral hazard has been excluded, adverse selection may occur if borrowers are not, in fact, homogeneous and the terms of the credit contract affect the mix of applicants seeking loans. This is the basic model of Stiglitz and Weiss (1981).

In order to facilitate comparisons with the models of Sections 2.1.2 and 2.1.3, the accompanying assumptions about the treatment of collateral and the money-lender's costs must be specified precisely. Stiglitz and Weiss implicitly assume that: (i) both parties put the same cash value on the collateral; (ii) this valuation is, in turn, the spot value of the collateral when the state of nature has been revealed; and (iii) the spot price is known in advance and is equal to the "contractual" price, v. As noted above, these assumptions permit us to do away with the distinction between cash flow and assets, so that the parties' closing positions can be represented as the cash value of their sum. The lender's risk remains, however, since it is further assumed that the value of the borrower's assets, all of which are pledged as collateral, is insufficient to cover $(1 + r)B$ in full. Hence, as $K = \bar{A}$, the closing positions of the borrower and lender are, respectively,

$$y = \begin{cases} X + vK, & \text{if } X \geq -vK, \\ 0, & \text{otherwise,} \end{cases} \tag{1a}$$

and

$$\pi = \begin{cases} (r - r_0)B - (a_0 + a_1), & \text{if } X \geq 0, \\ (r - r_0)B - (a_0 + a_2), & \text{if } 0 > X \geq -vK, \\ R + vK - (1 + r_0)B - (a_0 + a_2), & \text{otherwise.} \end{cases} \tag{3a}$$

Borrowers and lenders alike are assumed to be risk-neutral.

Stiglitz and Weiss ignore administrative costs altogether, which, as we shall see, is a further specialization with significant consequences. They also assume that all projects yielding the same mean return cost the same and that all borrowers have the same amount of equity. Hence, all borrowers will seek loans of the same size. In that case, a lender's expected profit from a loan of size B is:

$$E\pi = \int_0^{(1+r)B-vK} [R + vK - (1+r_0)B]\, dD(R)$$

$$+ \int_{(1+r)B-vK}^{\infty} (r - r_0)B\, dD(R)$$

$$= \int_0^{(1+r)B-vK} [R - (1+r)B + vK]\, dD(R) + (r - r_0)B, \tag{5}$$

provided, of course, that the borrower wants a loan. As the borrower is risk-neutral, that condition is $Ey \geq vK$.

Now suppose there are diverse types of borrowers, all of them proposing projects yielding the same expected return, $\bar{R}$. At any rate of interest (r), the lender's overall expected profit will be a weighted average of the expected profit from a loan given to each type of borrower who wishes to borrow at r, where the weights are simply the relative frequencies of the types of borrowers seeking loans at that rate. For as lenders cannot tell borrowers apart, these relative frequencies determine the composition of lenders' portfolios of loans. Differentiating (5), we have:

$$\frac{\partial E\pi}{\partial r} = B[1 - D((1+r)B - vK)] > 0. \tag{6}$$

Hence, the lender's expected profit will rise with r, so long as the pool of applicants for loans does not change. Ey, however, falls as r increases, so that one after another, various groups of borrowers will drop out. As each does so, there is a discontinuous change in the lender's expected profit.

Stiglitz and Weiss prove that if borrowers can be characterized by a parameter implying greater risk in the sense of Rothschild and Stiglitz (1970), then increases in the rate of interest (i) leave the lender with a riskier portfolio of borrowers and (ii) reduce the lender's expected profit each time a marginal, i.e. comparatively "safe", group of applicants for loans drops out. Hence, as the lender's expected profit is increasing with r with an unchanged pool of applicants, it will not be monotonic in the rate of interest.

An important consequence of such non-monotonicity, whatever be its origins, is that there may be rationing in equilibrium. Consider the case in which all lenders have identical cost functions. It is plausible that if r_0 is taken as parametric, there will exist a symmetric Nash equilibrium, in which all lenders charge the same rate of interest, r^* say. Suppose there is also free entry, so that each lender will make zero expected profits at r^*. Inspection of (5) reveals that for a sufficiently large collateral and favorable distribution of returns, $D(R)$, there exists a positive r_0^* ($< r^*$) such that expected profits will be zero. Now if the demand for funds at r^* exceeds the supply lenders can obtain at r_0^*, lenders will ration credit. For by raising r to eliminate excess demand, a lender would lower his expected profits – indeed, he would no longer break even, since expected profits attain a maximum of zero at r^* when the cost of funds is r_0^*. Hence, some would-be borrowers will be turned away, and as all borrowers look alike to lenders, random exclusion will be the only good rule.

The above example is of a pooling equilibrium in which there is free entry and each lender sets the rate of interest to his clients, while making Nash conjectures about the actions of his competitors. It is not a competitive equilibrium as the term is usually defined, and it is misleading to refer to it as such. At the other extreme, if there were a single, price-setting lender, it is clear that his optimal policy might entail rationing, regardless of whether he has any influence over r_0.

Finally, a remark on the absence of administrative costs is in order. Their neglect looks innocuous enough; but if it be granted that loan collection is more expensive when there is a default ($a_2 > a_1$), then the lender's payoff jumps discontinuously at $R = (1 + r)B$, from $(r - r_0)B - (a_0 + a_2)$ to $(r - r_0)B - (a_0 + a_1)$. Hence, the lender's return is not concave in R, so that the proof of Theorem 3 in Stiglitz and Weiss – that the lender's expected profit on a loan is a decreasing function of the riskiness of the loan – is no longer valid. This is troubling, as the said theorem yields the result that the lender's expected profit is non-monotonic in r, which is a necessary condition for the existence of credit rationing. The theorem may still be true, of course, but stronger assumptions may be needed.

2.1.2. Moral hazard and incentives

At the opposite extreme, consider a situation in which lenders know a great deal about individual clients, but the expense of monitoring their actions is prohibitive and projects are divisible, so that lenders do not attempt to control directly how their clients make use of loans. For their part, borrowers choose a course of action in the light of, inter alia, the contractual terms facing them. In an uncertain world, this entails each borrower choosing a particular distribution of payoffs.

Now unless the collateral tendered under the contract covers principal, interest and administrative expenses in all states of nature, the lender's expected return will depend on the borrower's choice of $D(R)$. As the latter depends on the terms of the credit contract, the lender is in a position to influence the borrower's choice indirectly. Thus, there is a principal–agent relationship. This, in essence, is the formulation pursued by Bottomley (1964, 1971, 1975) and, more recently and formally, by Bell and Zusman (1980) and Stiglitz and Weiss (1981).[2]

It turns out that the derivation of $D(R)$ from the borrower's choice of projects is, in general, quite messy and complicated, since it is a mapping from the distribution function of the states of nature, $D(\theta)$. In the following discussion, therefore, we shall eschew the technical details in favor of more heuristic arguments.

Excluding, for the present, the possibility of strategic default, let the borrower have a well-behaved demand function for credit and associated with it, a well-behaved map of iso-utility contours in the space of (B, r). In keeping with Bottomley's pessimism about the lender's chances of seizing the borrower's collateral in the event of a default, no collateral is offered, other than the returns from the borrower's projects. In order to protect his claims thereon, however, a lender will insist upon an *exclusive* contract, i.e. one in which the borrower will deal with no other lenders. If the moneylender is risk-neutral, attention can be confined to his expected profit, which is given by

$$\text{E}\pi = \int_0^{(1+r)B} [R - (1+r)B] \, \mathrm{d}D(R) + (r - r_0)B - [a_0 + a_1], \qquad (7)$$

where $D(R)$ is chosen by the borrower.[3]

Starting with the case in which there is free entry for moneylenders, with no inside knowledge, we must have $\text{E}\pi = 0$ in equilibrium. Hence, the borrower's choice of $D(R)$ and (7) yield a particular contour in the space of (B, r). If there is no mass point at $R = 0$, then for sufficiently small B,

$$\text{E}\pi = [g(0) + (1 + g(0))r - r_0]B - [a_0 + a_1],$$

where $g(0)$ is the density of R at $R = 0$. Hence, as B falls, r must increase to

---

[2]Although their paper is mainly concerned with screening, Stiglitz and Weiss deal with a simple model in which there is a role for incentives.

[3]If collateral K is involved, (7) becomes:

$$\text{E}\pi = \int_0^{(1+r)B - vK} [R - (1+r)B + vK] \, \mathrm{d}D(R) + (r - r_0)B - [a_0 + (1 - \delta)a_1 + \delta a_2],$$

where

$$\delta = \int_0^{(1+r)B} \mathrm{d}D(R)$$

is the probability of default. In this case, the lender's cost of recovering the loan is stochastic and dependent on the borrower's actions. The argument in the text does not depend in any essential way on the assumption that $K = 0$.

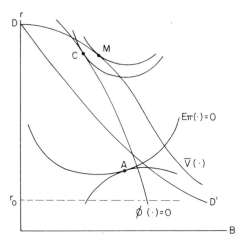

Figure 16.1.   The credit contract under free entry and monopoly.

cover the moneylender's (fixed) cost of administering the loan. For sufficiently large B, a rise in B will lead to a decrease in the first term on the RHS of (7). It follows that r must increase with B to preserve $E\pi = 0$. As increases in r arguably produce the same effects as increases in B, it is plausible that r is convexly increasing with B along the contour $E\pi(B, r) = 0$ for B sufficiently large. For intermediate values of B, the contour will be fairly flat, at a rate of interest exceeding r_0 (to cover the costs of administering the loan). The contour is thus drawn in Figure 16.1.

By the same reasoning, all iso-expected profit contours will have a similar shape. As expected profit increases, inspection of (7) suggests that the value of B at which r attains a minimum also increases. The locus of such pairs of (B, r) can be viewed as a pseudo-supply curve: with the rate of interest treated parametrically, the corresponding value of B is the amount the lender would like to advance; for his expected profit takes a maximum there.

Now, with free entry for moneylenders, all points along the contour $E\pi(B, r) = 0$ are available to the borrower. If the borrower's iso-expected utility contours are strictly concave to the left of the demand curve, he will choose a point such as A on $E\pi(B, r) = 0$, where an iso-utility contour is tangent to it. Thus, with free entry for moneylenders, borrowers will choose contracts (B, r) to the left of their respective demand curves.[4] Moreover, if the characteristics of borrowers vary, so too will their choice of contract.

---

[4] The strict convexity of $E\pi(B, r) = 0$ and the strict concavity of the borrower's indifference map to the left of the demand curve ensure that the borrower's choice of contract is unique.

On the face of it, this case looks much like that in Stiglitz and Weiss' screening equilibrium when there is rationing. The mechanisms and allocative consequences are, however, quite different. Here, any would-be borrower whose demand curve intersects $E\pi(B, r) = 0$ and who desires a loan will get one. His choices are constrained by the requirement that the lender break even on average, so that in the presence of lender's risk and administrative costs, the borrower does not face an elastic supply of credit at r_0. His best choice, which is also constrained efficient for the economy, is to choose a point on $E\pi(B, r) = 0$ such that he would demand more credit if it were available at the rate of interest in question; but no lender will satisfy his notional demand at that rate.

In the screening equilibrium, there is a uniform contract for all borrowers, whatever their characteristics, since lenders cannot tell them apart. Also, lenders, not borrowers, set the terms. With the exception of the safest borrowers, all those who are successful in getting a loan earn a surplus, the size of which increases with the riskiness of the project that will be undertaken. Unsuccessful applicants get nothing, however, even though their projects might yield an expected profit for both parties; they are frustrated in their plans by the fact that there is no way in which they can convey this information to lenders.

In contrast to free entry, we now consider the case in which inside knowledge is vital and there is but one local moneylender who has it. In this setting, it is plausible that he can choose both quantity and price (B, r) freely, subject only to the requirement that the borrower obtain at least his reservation level of expected utility, $\bar{V}$, which is that afforded by not taking a loan at all. By definition, the iso-expected utility contour $\bar{V}(B, r)$ passes through D, the point at which the demand curve, DD', intersects the r-axis,[5] where the slope of $\bar{V}(\cdot)$ is also zero. If the moneylender's expected profit is increasing in both B and r in a sufficiently large neighborhood of D,[6] then he will choose a point such as M, where an iso-expected profit contour is tangent to the borrower's reservation frontier. (M may not, of course, be unique, although it is so depicted in Figure 16.1.) It is at once apparent that the borrower is now being force-fed with credit, since he is to the right of his demand curve. Thus, rather paradoxically, the borrower voluntarily limits his appetite for credit (relative to his notional demand for it) when there is free entry for moneylenders, whereas he finds himself force-fed when confronted by a monopolist who offers an all-or-nothing deal. It does not necessarily follow, of course, that he borrows more in the latter case than in the former, though it is certain that he pays a higher rate of interest.

We must now re-introduce the matter of strategic default, for there is nothing in the above analysis that ensures that this is not the borrower's best option at

---

[5] The borrower is indifferent among all points on the r-axis. It would be more accurate, therefore, to define the point D as $\lim_{B \to 0} r$, where (B, r) satisfy $\bar{V}(B, r)$.

[6] This cannot be assumed in general. If not, the moneylender will attain an interior maximum, that is, it will not be profitable for him to drive the borrower down to the reservation utility level of $\bar{V}$.

M, or even A for that matter. Let $\phi(B, r) = 0$ denote the set of all (B, r) such that the borrower is indifferent between strategic default and choosing a portfolio of projects with the intention of repaying the loan if at all possible. Clearly, in the absence of collateral, $\phi(\cdot)$ lies to the NE of D, since there must be some money to abscond with, if absconding is to be profitable. Furthermore, r must decrease as B increases along $\phi(\cdot)$, since the attractiveness of absconding increases with r given B. Whether $\phi(\cdot)$ passes to the NE of both A and M, or to the NE of A and SW of M, or to the SW of them both is difficult to determine. Whatever the case, however, it may act as a binding constraint on the moneylender's policy. As drawn in Figure 16.1, the possibility of strategic default does not affect the outcome under free entry for moneylenders; but it does constrain the monopolist to what is, from his point of view, the inferior, but self-enforcing, policy represented by point C. Thus, the active threat of strategic default enables the borrower to do better than his reservation utility in this case.

The above account shares a good deal in common with that in Bottomley (1971), both placing much emphasis on risk and incomplete coverage of principal and interest by collateral. It is somewhat more general, however, in that the role of strategic default as a constraint on the lender's policies emerges from the analysis rather than appearing as an exogenously random event for which a given risk premium must be charged. Also, equilibrium under free entry and monopoly is more precisely characterized.

2.1.3. Usury and alienation of collateral in the absence of lender's risk

In the third model, too, the lender has an intimate knowledge of the borrower and is the only lender to possess it. Where it departs radically from both the screening and moral hazard models is that the lender's risk is banished entirely by the assumption that the collateral tendered by the borrower suffices to cover any randomness in the lender's return arising from the borrower's inability to repay in full when the loan falls due. These are the key features of Bhaduri (1977), Borooah (1980) and Rao (1980), with subsequent formalization and generalization by Basu (1984). Although the lender's costs of administering loans are not considered, it is consistent with their view that such costs are covered just like principal and interest, whatever be the outcome.

Accepting this for the moment, consider Figure 16.2, which is a specialization of Figure 16.1, with the additional restriction that borrowers do not have access to the riskless placement yielding r_0, so that the demand curve intersects the horizontal line $r = r_0$. In the absence of lender's risk, the marginal cost of funds to the moneylender is constant at r_0. Basu, in a lucid piece of exposition, shows that Bhaduri's monopolistic lender is implicitly confined to price strategies; he therefore chooses a rate of interest $\hat{r}$ such that MR equals MC in traditional style. The borrower chooses a loan of size $\hat{B}$, and obtains a surplus over his

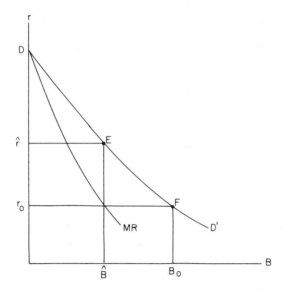

Figure 16.2. Monopoly in the absence of lender's risk.

reservation utility in the amount $DE\hat{r}$, while the monopolist obtains a pure profit of $(\hat{r} - r_0)\hat{B}$, less his costs of administering the loan. As Basu points out, however, the lender can certainly do better if he is not restricted to price strategies alone, a result which is well known [see, for example, Oi (1971)]. Under perfect competition, the borrower would choose a loan of size B_0,[7] and obtain a surplus DFr_0. In a setting of personal dealings and full knowledge, the monopolistic lender could offer an all-or-nothing contract for a loan of size B_0 at a rate of interest r^* such that $(r^* - r_0)B_0$ equals DFr_0, thereby appropriating the entire surplus himself and leaving the borrower at the latter's reservation utility level, at a point to the right of DD'. Alternatively, the lender could charge the borrower a lump-sum fee in the same amount as the surplus, together with a uniform rate of interest r_0 on each dollar borrowed. In effect, the borrower is then confronted by a two-part tariff.

It is of interest to compare these results with those illustrated in Figure 16.1. Excluding strategic default, which has no place in the schema just discussed, the monopolist who inhabits Figure 16.1 is also not confined to price strategies alone, and he usually finds it profitable to drive the borrower down to $\bar{V}$, unless strategic default is then an active threat. However, the presence of lender's risk arising from strategic default, together with the borrower's possible risk aversion, rule

---

[7] The costs of administering the loan are ignored in the interest of tidy exposition.

out the two-part tariff scheme with r_0 as the marginal charge. For in the presence of uncertainty, these contractual instruments will not suffice, in general, to effect one-for-one transfers between the two agents of the sort depicted in Figure 16.2.

To this it may be objected that the risks associated with default can be ruled out by an increase in the value of the collateral, which is held constant (at zero) in Figure 16.1. This is readily granted; but as a borrower has only a certain amount of acceptable collateral, it must be shown that it is never profitable for a lender to extend a loan exceeding that value if lender's risk is not to reappear. Consider first the case of free entry for moneylenders. If the borrower's demand curve intersects the flat segment of the contour $E\pi(B, r) = 0$, there will be no such risk and the borrower will choose a point on his notional demand curve. If, however, the borrower tenders all of his acceptable collateral while choosing a point such as A, where the contour $E\pi(\cdot) = 0$ slopes upwards, that is still perfectly acceptable to a risk-neutral moneylender, even though lender's risk has reappeared (see footnote 3). Turning to the case of monopoly, there is similarly nothing in the analysis which suggests that expected profit maximization implies that the probability of default is zero; if anything, the contrary is the case. In general, therefore, risk-neutral lenders can eliminate lender's risk entirely only by eschewing expected profit maximization, whether there be free entry or monopoly.

Implicit in the above account is the assumption that when title to the collateral passes to the moneylender it is valued at the ruling spot price and this is also the valuation that he places on it. As noted in Section 2.1.1, this is a special case of (3) and (4). It would be closer to the spirit of the writings of Bhaduri and his school, however, to open up the possibility that collateral is systematically undervalued, so that the moneylender will be able to acquire the borrower's collateral on the cheap in the event of default. The formulation of (3) and (4) accommodates this possibility as follows.

We begin by noting that the spot price, p, of the collateral at the time of repayment is itself a random variable, which may not be independent of the state of nature. In a drought, for example, not only will the borrower's projects yield low returns, but the market value of his livestock will be small, if not actually zero. Thus, if livestock are pledged as collateral, the lender may not be fully assured of a bargain, however low the contractual value the parties agree on in advance. Be that as it may, suppose the borrower's returns are insufficient to cover interest and principal in full, i.e. $X < 0$. Then the moneylender will acquire some assets whose value to him, in terms of the numeraire, is at least as great as $p \cdot [\min(-X/v, K)]$, since he always has the option of keeping some or all of the assets so acquired. In particular, if $(1 + r)B \leq pK$ and $v < p$ for all θ, default begins to look potentially profitable to the lender. To be precise, let the lender value each unit of the collateral at p, however much of the collateral he acquires.

Then his expected profit from the loan is:

$$\mathrm{E}\pi = \int_{-(1+r)B}^{0} \int_{0}^{\infty} \left\{ X + p \cdot \left[\min(-X/v, K) \right] \right\} g(X, p) \, \mathrm{d}p \, \mathrm{d}X$$

$$+ (r - r_0)B - \left[a_0 + (1 - \delta)a_1 + \delta a_2 \right], \tag{8}$$

where $g(\cdot)$ is the joint density of X and p and $\delta = D[(1 + r)B]$ is the probability of default. The value of the integrand is negative for sufficiently small p, and the region in which it is negative can be made small by increasing K and/or decreasing v. Note, however, that $g(\cdot)$ is also affected by changes in the terms of the contract. In any event, if the moneylender's choice is such that the value of the integral on the RHS of (8) is positive, then he will welcome a default. It does not follow, however, that this is his best policy. It may be better to set r so high as to make the expected profits from disposing of collateral negative, if the improvement in interest income, $(r - r_0)B$, is sufficiently large. In any event, while this formulation seems to respect the spirit of Bhaduri's school, the lender's payoff is still, in general, uncertain.

What about the borrower? He, too, will place a cash value on the assets given up at least as large as $p \cdot [\min(-X/v, K)]$, and perhaps considerably greater if they have some features that are especially valuable to him, but not fully reflected in their prevailing market price (assuming there is a market for them). Hence, if $X < 0$, he may incur substantial losses, the prospect of which will induce him to select projects that will lessen the chances of his suffering them. Thus, these arrangements are, to a degree, incentive-compatible, provided both parties wish to avoid default.

That default may involve the borrower in large losses relative to principal and interest on the loan prompts the obvious question: Why does he take the chance instead of not borrowing? The conventional answer is that the need for liquidity is often very pressing, and in a system of thin and poorly developed markets, the borrower may not be able to sell his assets when and as he desires. This is persuasive, but it is surely not the whole explanation. It is quite possible, for example, that borrower and lender do not share the same prior beliefs about the distribution of outcomes. What the former dismisses as a possibility too remote to warrant anxiety, the latter may savour as a tangible prospect of another profitable foreclosure. Even if they do share the same beliefs, they may place different valuations on a given outcome.

One important conclusion to emerge from this discussion is that collateral demands more careful treatment than it is often accorded. Binswanger and Rosenzweig (1986) provide a valuable discussion which addresses the fact that, in general, collateral is itself risky; but while it contains many insights, their account is too informal as it stands to tackle the difficulties identified above. Nevertheless, their recognition that risk is pervasive goes to the heart of the matter.

2.2. Innovation and the rate of interest

The adoption of new crops, varieties, or methods of cultivation often involves the use of extra working and fixed capital, and thus might be expected to put some upward pressure on the rate of interest. Against this, however, is the possibility that increases in borrowers' average returns may lower lenders' risks. Bottomley (1971), in particular, stresses the importance of improvements in agricultural productivity in lowering interest rates, with the caveat that the variance of the borrower's returns should not increase "too rapidly".

We start by examining this claim in the light of Section 2.1.2. Without confining ourselves to risk-neutral borrowers – Bottomley deals with expected net returns – suppose borrowers adopt an innovation which raises expected total returns. By inspection of (7), it is clear that with given collateral, the changes induced in the menu of options offered by lenders under free entry will depend on those induced in $D(R)$. That borrowers adopt the innovation leads one to infer that they are better off thereby (in partial equilibrium, at least); but an increase in mean total returns is perfectly compatible with greater riskiness, so that the chances of default may increase, especially if the amount borrowed rises. Thus, the rate of interest and the amount borrowed could move in the same or opposite directions, depending on the nature of the shifts in the zero-expected profit frontier and the iso-expected utility map of the borrower.

In the case of monopoly, so long as borrowers are free to choose whether to adopt an innovation, they will not be worse off if that is what they choose to do. If, initially, strategic default is not an active threat, so that equilibrium is established at M in Figure 16.1, this implies that borrowers would be better off with the innovation even if they were not to borrow. (Since the lender finds it profitable to force them down to their reservation utility in this case, adoption on some scale must be feasible without borrowing.) Suppose, furthermore, that the innovation shifts the demand schedule to the right, so that the borrower's reservation frontier shifts to the NE. Then it does not necessarily follow that the rate of interest will fall, nor even that the amount lent will rise; for the map of iso-expected profit contours will also shift.

In the screening equilibrium of Stiglitz and Weiss, the effects of a rise in productivity are also ambiguous. Suppose, to start with, that the innovation increases the mean return of all projects by the same amount, but leaves their spreads unchanged. Let the amount of debt finance needed by all projects increase equally, too, but not by so much as to make adoption of the innovation unprofitable. Then the demand for loans will increase at each rate of interest; for at each rate of interest the innovation will permit some borrowers who were unable to do so before to break even, while yielding larger expected returns to those who were breaking even or better in the absence of the innovation. Hence, the lender's expected net return, viewed as a function of the rate of interest, will also shift upwards and to the right. For a sufficiently small increase in the rate of interest will leave the mix of applicants unchanged, and the lender's expected net return will certainly increase. Thus, if there is free entry, competition among lenders will bid up the cost of loanable funds, r_0, until expected profits are squeezed back to zero. The amount lenders can obtain will also increase – provided the supply schedule of loable funds is at all elastic and does not shift adversely as a result of the innovation. However, since borrowers' demand for funds has increased, there can be rationing in the new equilibrium. Indeed, rationing may be intensified, with the rate of interest, the total amount lent and the degree of excess demand all greater following the innovation.

If the innovation is associated with greater risk, in the sense of Rothschild–Stiglitz, the demand for loans may fall, and the lender's expected net return function may shift in the opposite direction to that just discussed. Hence, the final result may be a fall not only in the rate of interest, but also in loan activity.

The relation between innovation and the rate of interest in the model of Section 2.1.3 is usually discussed in the context of interlinked markets. We shall follow tradition here, and this matter will be taken up in Section 3.4 below.

To sum up, it appears that the claim that improvements in agricultural productivity will lower the rate of interest is not secure in either of the theoretical frameworks considered above. In the moral hazard setting adopted by Bottomley himself, it is quite possible that innovations entailing a modest increase in risk will raise the rate of interest. When adverse selection is the problem, as in Stiglitz and Weiss, it is even possible that rather risky innovations will lower the rate of interest, while less risky ones will increase it. In all this, it has been assumed that the supply schedule of loanable funds does change. If agricultural improvements lead to greater prosperity and thrift, the supply price of such funds may fall sufficiently to bring about a fall in the rate charged to borrowers despite the effects discussed above; but that is another story.

2.3. Public policy

What is the scope for public policy, in the light of the preceding discussion? The answer depends on both market structure and the nature of the informational problems confronting lenders. While there may be room for improvements in efficiency and distribution in the settings analyzed above, it may be difficult, if at all possible, for the government to effect them.

In the case of free entry into moneylending, expected profits will be zero; but it does not then follow that there is no scope for intervention. For the welfare of borrowers still depends on lenders' costs, which can be influenced by public policy. The inside knowledge possessed by moneylenders will not be directly available to regulated or state-owned banks, and when there are adverse selection problems, it is implausible that the banks will do a better job of screening applicants. Thus, unless the banks enjoy advantages in other costs, direct competition prompted by the state is not the right form of intervention here, though the case for laissez-faire is not sealed either.

If private lenders have significant market power, the case for intervention may look stronger; but in a setting of incomplete markets, second-best considerations intrude. There is also the related point that the instruments available to the government may not suffice to bring about full efficiency.

With this preamble, let us now examine the forms of intervention systematically. First, where lender's costs are concerned, it is plausible that the moneylender's inside knowledge and informal style of operation will keep his administrative costs low. That leaves the opportunity cost of his principal and the premium to cover risk as the remaining elements of his costs that might be the object of intervention.

In the above discussion, the former has been treated as a perfectly safe placement yielding r_0, which may be interpreted as the rate on government bonds. Leaving aside reductions in r_0 effected through changes in monetary policy – to the extent that such policies are effective nowadays – it may be the case in practice that bond markets are so poorly developed that local lenders do not have much access to such placements. More extensive open market operations would lower lender's costs in these circumstances. It is also argued that the maturities of these instruments, when available, are not always well attuned to the cycle of the moneylender's operations. If his loans are used to finance working capital for cultivation, he will normally receive repayment about six months later. Thus, in the absence of a secondary market, if bonds have a minimum maturity of one year, his funds will be idle for half the year, unless there is double-cropping or a conveniently located bank offering deposit accounts. At worst, the effective rate for arriving at the opportunity cost of his principal would not be r_0, but twice that rate. Here, the creation of new instruments with appropriately short maturities, or a well-organized secondary market, would lower a significant element in the lender's total costs. Recalling Section 2.2, it is worth noting that double-cropping is one agricultural improvement which produces the same effect.

While there may be some scope for the monetary authorities to effect improvements of this sort, the distribution of the gains therefrom will depend on market structure. In the case of free entry for lenders, all the gains will go to borrowers, although the rate of interest they pay may not fall pari passu with the reduction in lenders' opportunity cost of funds. In the case of monopoly, all the gains will accrue to the lender if the borrower is on his reservation frontier. If, however, the borrower is on the "absconding frontier" $\phi(B, r) = 0$, his welfare will improve if the reduction in costs induces the moneylender to increase B. The best that can be said here is that the general improvements in financial intermediation brought about by the monetary authorities or innovations in private instruments may induce more entry into the private segment of the local market. That seems a rather frail and speculative argument to set against a presumptive transfer to local lenders, especially if the borrower remains on his reservation frontier.

Turning to lender's risk, where strategic default is concerned, we have already seen that with complete information, this should happen only through a failure of judgment on the lender's part. The risk arising from the borrowers' inability to pay is affected by the riskiness of the projects that they undertake. Improvements here lie more in the province of the ministries of agriculture and irrigation than in that of the central bank, though the latter is certainly capable of affecting the volatility of prices. There is, however, one respect in which such risk could be affected by legal and administrative action. For example, cadastral surveys and registration of land titles together with well-defined and formal procedures for the registration of loans could improve the acceptability of land and other assets as collateral to moneylenders.[8] As argued above, this would not necessarily eliminate lender's risk entirely; but when there is free entry for moneylenders, it would improve the terms obtained by borrowers whose collateral was previously constraining. Under monopoly, of course, all the gains thereof would once more accrue to the lender.

This discussion suggests that indirect intervention – to lower the moneylender's costs – will bring little, if any, benefit to borrowers if lenders are able to exercise considerable market power. That leaves direct intervention, and here there are two options. First, the government can attempt to regulate the private market, in particular by setting a ceiling on the rate of interest the moneylender may charge. Secondly, the government can attempt to introduce some competition, in the form of state-owned or regulated commercial banks.

Taking them in order, the first, if enforceable, removes one of the lender's control variables (r). Given the regulated rate, $\bar{r}$, he can then offer the borrower an all-or-nothing deal, choosing the size of the loan to maximize his expected profits. In Figure 16.3, this will be the value $B(\bar{r})$ on his pseudo-supply curve, SS', unless the amount in question would induce strategic default, in which case the loan would be scaled back to a value satisfying $\phi(B, r) = 0$ at the regulated rate or less. If, in the absence of a ceiling on r, equilibrium is established at a

---

[8] More ambitiously still, the state could declare that in the event of natural disasters which would otherwise precipitate a collapse of the prices of assets used as collateral, it would step in as a buyer of last resort, thereby staving off the collapse in question. In view of the administrative difficulties confronting such a policy, it is rather doubtful that it would be credible.

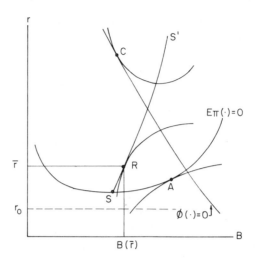

Figure 16.3. An optimal ceiling on the rate of interest.

point such as C on the absconding frontier $\phi(\cdot) = 0$, then regulation will usually improve the borrower's welfare regardless of whether equilibrium in the presence of the ceiling gets established on $\phi(\cdot) = 0$ or to the SW of that frontier. For in the former case, the borrower's welfare increases as r decreases along $\phi(\cdot) = 0$. In the latter case, the lender will be at a point on SS' to the SW of its intersection with the frontier $\phi(\cdot) = 0$, and since the latter is an improvement over point C for the borrower, it is plausible that the new offer is also superior to C. If strategic default is not an active threat either before or after the imposition of a ceiling on the rate of interest, so that equilibrium is established at a point such as M in Figure 16.1, the intervention will improve the borrower's welfare if, and only if, the ceiling is set below the level at which SS' intersects the reservation frontier, $\overline{V}(B, r)$. Otherwise, equilibrium will be established on the latter frontier at the regulated rate.

In the light of this discussion, what is the ceiling that should be imposed so as to make the borrower as well off as possible? There are two cases. First, there is the minimum rate of interest on the zero expected profit contour, so that the lender would choose point S. This will be optimal for the borrower, provided the borrower's indifference curve passing through S has a smaller slope than the lender's pseudo-supply curve, SS', at S itself. In that case, no monopoly profit will be earned, but the borrower will still be worse off than under free entry for moneylenders, when he would choose point A. Secondly, there may exist a point of tangency between SS' and one of the borrower's indifference curves, which is illustrated by point R in Figure 16.3, where the borrower is better off than at S.

In this case, the moneylender obtains some pure profit, and the regulated rate of interest exceeds the rate at S, and even that at A. This residual profit is, of course, a consequence of the fact that one instrument of intervention is unlikely to suffice if the goal is efficiency in a second-best world of the sort discussed here.

Finally, we note that the indirect interventions discussed above have a useful role to play if the rate of interest can be effectively regulated. For the former will shift SS' to the right, and thereby benefit the borrower. Of course, the prospects of enforcing such regulation when lenders are socially and politically powerful, and borrowers and lenders are widely dispersed over a wide and rather inaccessible hinterland, may seem rather bleak. In that case, there is nothing for it but to resort to direct competition, to which we now turn.

Banks will usually have an advantage over the traditional moneylender to the extent that they can turn to the central bank for funds. That is, the opportunity cost of their funds will normally be lower. They will not, however, possess the moneylender's inside knowledge of rural life and prospective clients, and they will be burdened with overheads and a salary bill that looks profligate beside his. Except for borrowers seeking very large loans, therefore, it seems that the bank's administrative costs will far exceed those of the moneylender. Moreover, in the absence of "inside knowledge", there may be numerous instances of strategic default, thereby necessitating a risk premium for this eventuality. (Naturally, if collateral is pledged, but not seized in such cases, the problem of strategic default will be greatly exacerbated.) Thus, supposing for the present that the bank aims simply to cover its costs, it appears that the schedule of contracts it must offer will lie above that for private lenders when there is free entry. It is thus drawn as $\psi(B, r) = 0$ in Figure 16.4, in which the free entry equilibrium at A is retained for reference.

It is implicitly assumed that the bank is not so utterly inefficient as to be incapable of offering a contract that is superior to a monopolistic lender's when he is doing his best or, as borrowers would see it, his worst. It is also important that the bank have some way of enforcing exclusive contracts; for if borrowers can get loans from the moneylender too, it is very likely that the latter will be able to lay first claim to the borrower's returns, thereby increasing the bank's risks arising from the borrower's inability to repay his loan. Such exclusivity is hard to enforce, though a pledge of immoveables as collateral will help.

The borrower, when confronted with this opportunity, can escape from the clutches of the lender by moving from point M to an appropriate position on $\psi(\cdot) = 0$, at point A', say. With exclusive contracts, the moneylender will be forced to offer terms as attractive as those represented by A'. His best policy will be to move a point such as M', say, where an iso-expected profit contour is tangent to the borrower's indifference curve passing through A'. He continues to earn a pure expected profit by virtue of his cost advantages over the bank, but his clients are now better off.

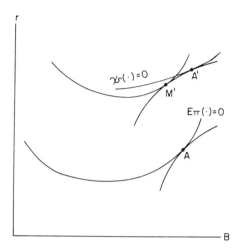

Figure 16.4. Competition between a bank and a single moneylender.

The case depicted in Figure 16.4 is perhaps the best that can be hoped for. In practice, banks are unlikely to possess the intimate knowledge of borrowers that is needed to formulate a schedule like $\psi(B, r) = 0$, which must be tailored to each individual's characteristics. Thus, they will surely resort to cruder procedures, of which the most common is to charge a uniform rate of interest on each dollar borrowed, with an upper limit on how much each borrower can have, which is based on information that is easily obtainable, such as land holdings. Faced with such a schedule, the borrower will wind up with either his notional demand or his credit limit (ration), whichever is less. Once again, the moneylender's competing offer cannot be less attractive if he is to continue in business. Figure 16.5 illustrates the essentials, with the borrower rationed by the bank, this being the usual outcome. The competing offer from the moneylender is M'. If the credit limit point A' lies on the schedule $\psi(B, r) = 0$ in Figure 16.4, the outcome for the borrower will be inferior to that depicted in Figure 16.4, except by fluke. If, however, the rate of interest and the rule for determining individual credit limits are chosen so the bank just breaks even over all prospective borrowers, some borrowers may get larger loans than their true characteristics warrant, perhaps so large as to do better than they would under the arrangements depicted in Figure 16.4. Most borrowers would do worse, however, since the cruder rule is based on a sort of representative borrower with the object of the bank just breaking even.

Unfortunately, this is not the end of the bank's potential failings. With little incentive to keep costs low and knowing that there are rents to be had from the system, the officers of the bank may pay themselves better salaries financed by

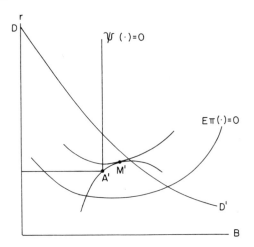

Figure 16.5.   The bank lends at a uniform rate of interest up to a credit limit.

suitable adjustments to their offer schedule $\psi(\cdot) = 0$. In other words, the existence of the moneylender's pure expected profits may induce the people who
run the bank to move in the direction of M, rather than conversely, as assumed
above. If a gap remains, while borrowers will do better than they would at point
M, that very fact gives individual officers of the bank an incentive to solicit
bribes, and borrowers an incentive to pay them. For example, bribes may be
tendered when there is excess demand for funds at the announced rate of interest
or the borrower, claiming inability to repay, wishes to roll-over a loan. The
moneylender will accommodate himself quite happily to such moves, for they will
cut into his profits less by limiting the effectiveness of the bank's challenge to his
market power. Despite the absence of a careful analysis of the strategic game
between these duopolists, it still seems prudent to avoid the claim that the bank's
entry will do borrowers no good at all. Casual observation of backward areas
where commercialization is limited suggests, however, that when traditional
moneylenders continue to exercise a good deal of market power, the banks settle
for a quiet, even a venal, life.

As this direct form of intervention has been paramount, it is desirable to go
beyond casual observation to more definite knowledge of how the institutions
have operated and the effects thereof. First, they very commonly insist on land as
collateral, which remedies to some extent their lack of inside information and
imposes a degree of exclusivity in their contracts with clients. As a result, those
with little or no land get little or no institutional credit, while those with large
holdings do well. Where, as in parts of Africa, individual titles to land are not
well established, this policy of the credit institutions generates pressures to

register titles, often when land policy is itself not fully resolved. One, possibly unintended, consequence is a transfer of wealth from women to men [see, for example, Collier and Lal (1985)].

Secondly, the institutions are usually required to charge the same rate of interest to all borrowers, so that the only decision left to them is how much to lend to each client, as in Figure 16.5. In the presence of fixed transactions costs for processing loans, that gives them an incentive to lend to clients who seek large loans and have the collateral to make them credit-worthy [Gonzalez-Vega (1976)].

Thirdly, the formal and lengthy processing procedures adopted by institutions impose heavier transactions costs on borrowers than does the traditional lender's style of doing business. This was ignored in the preceding analysis; but just how powerfully this can affect the borrower's effective cost of funds is brought home by Adams and Nehman (1979), who draw on studies of farmers in Bangladesh, Brazil and Colombia in the early 1960s and 1970s. In Bangladesh, the nominal rate of interest charged by the Agricultural Development bank was 7 percent a year; yet even for the largest category of loans, interest charges comprised just over one-half of the total costs of borrowing on a 12-month loan. The effective annual rates on a 6-month loan ranged from 74 percent on a loan of Rs.50, to 18 percent on one of Rs.1300. In the Brazilian sample, the effective rate varied from 44 to 18 percent, against an average nominal rate of about 13 percent a year. In the Colombian one, the average effective rate was 42 percent, also against a nominal rate of about 13 percent.

It is no great wonder, therefore, that the rural poor saw little of the great expansion of formal agricultural lending which occurred in the 1970s [Ladman and Adams (1978), Lipton (1976)]. But does this mean that institutional lenders must always serve the interests of the well-to-do and the well-connected? The main counter-example is provided by the *Grameen* Bank of Bangladesh, which has been studied by Hossain (1985). This started as a project in November of 1979, with the object of making loans without collateral to the rural poor, who were defined to be individuals belonging to households owning up to half an acre of land. Borrowers formed groups of five, unrelated persons. If any defaulted, the entire group become ineligible for new loans. Additional enforcement was provided by weekly collection of dues (2 percent of the loan) at the group's meeting place by the local employee of the Bank, and compulsory contributions to insurance and savings funds against default, death, illness and acute need. Five years later, the Bank had grown from two to 108 branches covering about 2000 villages, with outstanding loans of over Tk. 200 million to 110 000 clients. A very modest 2.5 percent of loans were overdue at the end of 1982. The effective annual rate of interest was 20 percent, excluding transactions costs. Borrowing at the rate of 8.5 percent from the Bangladesh bank, the *Grameen* Bank was just able to cover its costs. The unanswered question is whether further expansion will be possible without a deterioration in the quality of management and supervision provided by the Bank's staff of pioneers.

To sum up, experience suggests that traditional moneylenders have valuable inside knowledge that formal banks are unlikely to acquire, so that using the latter to challenge the market power of the former may be an expensive and inefficient form of intervention. In view of the difficulties of regulating the rate of interest in dealings between private parties, one alternative is to induce private lenders to act as agents for the banks, always provided entry into such agency arrangements can be encouraged sufficiently to limit the expected profits that stem from inside information. Inasmuch as the banks finance traders, who in turn finance cultivators, this happens anyway, although the authorities frown on such practices. Where the banks have a clear advantage is in building an extensive network of deposit banking, since there are economies of scale; though traditional lenders do appear to take deposits from richer clients. Unless the *Grameen* Bank can be widely replicated, therefore, the establishment of rural banks should be motivated by the desire to encourage thrift and mobilize rural savings rather than challenge traditional lenders directly at the outset. That should await the time when the banks have acquired sufficient experience, starting with relatively large and long-term loans, in which they should have some advantages over traditional lenders.

2.4. Some evidence

Most people, whether borrowers or lenders, regard indebtedness as a rather delicate matter, and show some reluctance to discuss it. Investigating dealings in the credit market is not, therefore, an easy job, as the patchy coverage and quality of the evidence bear out. Moreover, much extant empirical work is not fully informed by the theories examined in this chapter – though that is not to say that it lacks valuable insights. Thus, the available evidence is rarely able to settle decisively whether one theory is more closely tethered to reality than another, or whether a particular form of intervention produces superior results to the alternatives. With this caution in mind, we shall examine: (i) the relative importance of sources of funds; (ii) the terms on which credit is secured; (iii) market structure; and (iv) the extent to which dealings in the credit market are tied to those in other markets.

In a landmark study of 9000 families in 1951/52, the Reserve Bank of India (1954) found that during the year surveyed, 93 percent of the total amount borrowed by cultivators was supplied by private parties, excluding the commercial banks, which accounted for about 1 percent. The residual came from government and cooperatives in roughly equal amounts. Among private parties, the professional moneylender and the agriculturist moneylender accounted for 45 and 25 percent, respectively, of the whole. Relatives (14 percent), landlords (2 percent) and traders and commission agents (6 percent) made up the rest. Twenty years later, the professional moneylender had fallen from his pre-eminent position, to a share of just 13 percent, while agriculturist moneylenders, landlords and traders and commission agents had raised their combined share to 40 percent [Reserve Bank of India (1977)]. It is important to note, however, that lending is rarely the moneylender's only line of business. In the early 1950s, a very high proportion of lenders were cultivators and/or traders of some kind. Thus, the decline of the professional moneylender may be more apparent than real. In any event, there has been a great expansion of lending by the cooperatives and the banks, which reflected the government's aim of competing with the moneylender, ultimately to drive him out of business.

Another decade later, a study of 34 villages in three diverse States – Andhra Pradesh (transitional), Bihar (backward) and Punjab (commercialized) – revealed that institutions were still gaining at the expense of private parties, the shares of the former in total lending being 33, 34 and 51 percent, respectively [Bell and Srinivasan (1985)]. It seems that where commercialization is greatest, so is the relative importance of institutional sources of credit, a conclusion which is further supported by the fact that the institutions' share in the irrigated tracts of Andhra Pradesh was 46 percent. Moreover, the specialist village moneylender had all but vanished, there being only 9 such households in the 34 villages, and none at all in Punjab. In some places, private lenders have been more strongly pressed. Bliss and Stern (1982), in a careful study of a village in Western Uttar Pradesh, report that in 1974/75 institutions accounted for 75 percent of all households' outstanding debt and that there were no specialist moneylenders doing business there. Similar findings are reported by Binswanger et al. (1985) for some villages in Maharashtra, but traditional lenders were still holding their own in a semi-arid tract of Andhra Pradesh.

In Kenya, there were few professional moneylenders to displace, traditional lending being confined to tribal and kinship groups, within which social sanction provides some repayment discipline [Collier and Lal (1985)]. The same applies to Malawi and Tanzania; but in Nigeria and Ghana, informal credit markets are active [Jones, (1980), Collier (1985)].

An important related question is the extent to which households participate in the institutional and informal segments of the credit market. From Table 16.1 it appears that access to institutional credit in the more backward areas of India is very limited indeed. However, as the institutions' share of total lending is about one-third of the whole, those who do obtain institutional credit get far larger loans on average than those who borrow from private sources. Similar findings emerge from Binswanger et al. (1985). We note also that exclusive institutional contracts are hardly the rule in Punjab – on the contrary, households borrowing from both segments of the market heavily outnumber those borrowing from institutions alone. Bliss and Stern (1982) report that 66 and 49 percent of all households were free of private and institutional debt, respectively, so that some households had both kinds.

Table 16.1
Participation in the credit market (proportion of all households)

State \ Source	Informal only	institutional only	Both	Neither	Total
Andhra Pradesh	30	5	2	63	100
Bihar	40	6	2	52	100
Punjab	28	12	19	41	100

Source: Bell and Srinivasan (1985).

Where the terms of credit are concerned, there seems to be some uniformity. In the period before Independence, the annual rate on loans secured against land was commonly 12 percent, but somewhat higher in the eastern States [Darling (1925)]. The rate on unsecured loans was naturally higher, but also somewhat more variable. Owners usually paid 15–18 percent, while tenants paid 18–37.5 percent. The (own) rates on grain loans ranged between 25 and 50 percent, though when the seasonal movements in grain prices are taken into account, the corresponding nominal rates were much lower for a loan taken at sowing and repaid at harvest, as is the usual practice. The Reserve Bank of India (1954, pp. 173–176) reported that rates above 25 percent were charged on a substantial fraction of total credit in some states, especially the eastern ones, but it does not say what part of this fraction was made up of grain loans. With legal maximum rates on unsecured loans ranging from 5.5 to 24 percent, the most common being 12 percent, it is also unsurprising that the law was honored mainly in the breach: two-thirds or more of all borrowings were at rates above the legal limit in more than half the States. A wide range of practices that increase the effective rate of interest was also described and deplored.

Turning to more recent evidence, a study of rice and input markets in North Arcot District, Tamil Nadu, in 1973/74 found that the rate of interest was highly uniform just above the legal ceiling of 12 percent a year [Harriss (1982)] – though other charges associated with marketing may have raised the effective rate. Bliss and Stern (1982, p. 108) found that most private loans were at rates of 24 or 36 percent, but say nothing about the associated collateral, if any. Bell and Srinivasan (1985) found that the rate on loans from commission agents or traders in Punjab and the commercialized areas of Andhra Pradesh was commonly 24 percent, the only security being the borrower's pledge to sell the crop through or to the lender after harvest. Large cultivators with long-standing relations with their lenders often did somewhat better. The surviving professional moneylenders studied by Binswanger et al. (1985) charged between 18 and 30 percent to their established clients.

In a study of 200 farmers in the Central Provinces of Chile in the mid-1960s, Nisbet (1967) found that relatives, friends and *patrones* lent in cash at negative real rates in that inflationary setting, whereas stores, traders and moneylenders lent in kind at high rates, ranging from 27 to 360 percent with a mode of 60–75 percent. It appears, however, that the latter were own rates, so that if commodity prices fluctuated seasonally around an inflationary trend, the corresponding nominal rates were lower. Here, too, loans were made against just a verbal pledge to repay, moneylending being illegal. In a more moderate inflationary environment, Adams and Nehman (1979) cite evidence that the nominal rates charged to Colombian farmers in the early 1970s averaged 50 percent.

While a certain degree of uniformity can be discerned in the above data, one needs evidence on market structure before asserting that rates are influenced by lenders' market power. In some of the literature, there is a tendency to view the lender as possessing a natural monopoly stemming from his intimate knowledge of his clients, their ignorance and poor communications with the rest of the economy, all of which isolate the area in which he operates. This view is embraced by Wharton (1962), Nisbet (1967) and Bottomley (1971), who draws on Reserve Bank of India (1954). Nisbet provides perhaps the clearest evidence in support of the contention that lenders have significant market power. Moneylenders, who were all agriculturists, were active in 18 of the 34 *communas* studied. Each had a small, well-defined geographical base, with no instances in which such areas were adjacent to one another. Stores that made loans were more widespread (29 of 34 *communas*) and more numerous (2 to 5 each) in central locations; they also accounted for most private credit. This suggests that with rather limited access to institutional finance, conditions ranged from monopoly to oligopoly in the credit markets of rural Central Chile. To clinch the argument, however, it is necessary to demonstrate that the barriers to entry were sufficiently formidable to deter other potential lenders from going into business if expected profits were supernormal. Nisbet did not do this directly, but the general tone of his exposition suggests that this is what he had in mind.

In the commercialized tracts of India, traders and commission agents are numerous, and many of them are engaged in lending to cultivators. For example, Harriss (1982) reports that traders made loans to about one-half of their customers, and the loans were not small. As an estimated 2300 traders were doing business, it is hard to make a strong case that barriers to entry were high. Poorer farmers resorted to village moneylenders and, increasingly, pawnbrokers, whose numbers expanded greatly between 1965 and 1975. Thus, Harriss offers us a picture of a "competitive" market, though she notes that as lenders need personal knowledge of clients, there is a limit to the number of clients each lender can maintain. As argued in Section 2.1, it would be more accurate, therefore, to regard this market as a set of contestable monopolies in which the only barrier to entry is inside knowledge. Bell and Srinivasan (1985) arrived at similar conclusions for Punjab and Andhra Pradesh, where it is common for several commission agents to do business in each village. Hence, inside knowledge is shared, to some extent at least. In predominantly semi-arid states, Raju and von Oppen (1980) note that some 30 marketing centres had at least a score of commission agents and/or wholesale traders, and most of them at least a hundred thereof. While such lenders may possess some market power, it strains belief that it could be very large, except perhaps in the remoter tracts, where geographical isolation and small marketable surpluses reinforce inside knowledge to keep the terms of credit onerous.

The demise of the specialist moneylender is clear enough from the above account. In his place, there is the state institution, commercial bank or, in the informal segment of the market, the lender who is also engaged in some other line of business, cultivation or trade. This brings us to interlinked trans-actions – the landlord who finances his tenants' working capital or his workers' consumption, or the trader who finances the cultivator in exchange for exclusive rights to purchase his crop. This observation is certainly not new – it appears, for example, in Darling (1925) – and there is some evidence of its importance. Wharton (1962), who is concerned with the role of middlemen in Malaysia's rubber trade, cites Bevan (1956) to the effect that a sample of 145 primary dealers reported that about 13 percent of their small-holder clients producing rubber were indebted to them. It is only in recent years, however, that more systematic measurements of the nature and incidence of interlinking have been undertaken.

In a series of notable papers, Bardhan and Rudra (1978, 1980, 1981) examine the prevalence of various forms of interlinking in eastern India in the period 1975 through 1979. Overall, about two-thirds of all landlords were reported to have cultivation as their principal occupation; trade and then moneylending managed barely 10 percent between them. In this respect, the divergence between "ad-vanced" and "backward" villages was sharper still. Nevertheless, the landlord was an important source of credit to his tenants. Consumption loans were made in about one-half of tenancy contracts, and production loans in almost 45 percent, the latter being much more prevalent in advanced than backward areas. Where labor services are concerned, only 10–15 percent of landed tenants reported rendering them to landlords, but the proportion among landless tenants was one-half or more, and by no means confined to backward areas. In any event, a majority of those who did work for their landlords claimed to have been "properly" paid. Turning to labor contracts proper, Bardhan and Rudra found rather few instances of debt-peonage, which was reported in 7 percent of the villages surveyed. Aside from bonded labor, the great majority of attached farm servants took consumption loans from their employers, while about one-third of casual laborers did so (the proportion rose in the east). All in all, Bardhan and Rudra deal some heavy blows against the theorists of "semi-feudalism", with its emphasis on usury and debt bondage as the main forms of exploitation.

Bliss and Stern (1982) reported that only 2 of 40 tenants in Palanpur were indebted to their landlords, and that tenants financed landlords inasmuch as the

Table 16.2
The extent of tying between credit and other markets[a]

	No tie	Tenancy alone	Output	Labor alone	Combinations	Total
Andhra Pradesh	62.0	[b]	20.0	16.9	1.1	100
	1355	463	1387	230	264	1188
Bihar	63.8	10.6	1.2	8.3	16.1	100
	494	121	1166	296	72	434
Punjab	56.9	3.8	30.6	3.9	4.8	100
	1155	551	5000	662	829	1838

[a] The upper number in each cell is the proportion of all borrowing households falling into the category in question; the lower is the average amount borrowed in Rs.
[b] Smaller than 0.1 percent.
Source: Bell and Srinivasan (1985).

latter often made their contractual contributions to variable costs out of rental payments at harvest. In a recent re-survey of the same village, Drèze and Mukherjee (1987) found that of the 67 households supplying some casual labor in the course of the season, 19 were free of debt and 16 of those in debt worked for their creditors. Similarly, of the 110 households involved in tenancy, 23 reported credit dealings with the other party to the tenancy contract.

Investigating the same matter, Bell and Srinivasan found that links between credit and marketing were far more prevalent and significant, in terms of the volume of credit, than those between credit and tenancy or labor. A summary of their findings is presented in Table 16.2, from which it is also clear that households borrowing from commission agents or traders obtained, on average, much larger loans than did workers from employers or tenants from landlords, or even those who had no other dealings with their creditors. Moreover, links between credit and output were strongest in the more commercialized areas. On reflection, this is hardly surprising, since traders and commission agents will seek out business – and seal it with finance – where there is a substantial marketable surplus. Hence, finance follows trade to commercialized areas and, in particular, to the door of the big farmer. Backward areas and the poor farmer are neglected. Taken together, these studies suggest that interlinking is not, as some would argue, a remnant of a semi-feudal mode of production, but rather a flexible market response to growing commercialization.

Interestingly, there is some evidence that the same forces are at work in West Africa. For example, Jones (1980) reports that of a sample of 404 farmers in a rice-growing district of Ghana, 112 borrowed from traders against the crop (with the price to be negotiated at the time of purchase) and 110 borrowed from the

Agricultural Development Bank. (The extent of any overlap is not indicated.) Moreover, traders were beginning to borrow from the Bank, so a modest degree of intermediation was underway. This striking contrast with East Africa leads one to speculate that West Africa's historically extensive networks of trade may have been the basis for its relatively well-developed credit markets. It also suggests that the creation of tangible collateral through land registration may not be enough in East Africa [see also Collier (1985)].

One final remark is in order. Many of those who have done careful fieldwork emphasize the necessity for the lender to have an intimate knowledge of the borrower's character and circumstances. Writers as diverse as Darling, the Reserve Bank of India, Nisbet and Harriss put such knowledge at the centre of the moneylender's system of operation. This is unwelcome news for those who would appeal mainly to theories of screening to explain what is happening in rural credit and related markets.

3. Interlinked transactions

In a rural economy, people know a good deal about the business of others, and when prices do not reveal all relevant information, it is usually in their interests to do so. Thus, if two people from the same locality trade with each other in two or more markets, it is pertinent to ask whether they do so deliberately rather than purely by chance, and if deliberately, for what reasons and with what consequences. We offer a general definition of interlinking and then pursue the analysis in the light of the presumed rationale for it.

Definition

An *interlinked* transaction is one in which the two parties trade in at least two markets on the condition that the terms of all such trades are jointly determined.

Loosely speaking, there is a "package" or "bundled" deal, in which each element in the deal is connected to every other in an essential way. As we saw in Section 2.4, far from being theoretical curiosa, such arrangements are quite common in South Asia and elsewhere.

While such trades are occasionally contemporaneous, they normally involve an exchange of current for future claims, and hence an element of credit, if only an implicit one. This emerges clearly from empirical studies of the main arrangements: the landlord who finances his tenants' consumption and working capital [Bardhan and Rudra (1978), Jodha (1984)]; the employer (sometimes the landlord in another guise) who gives advances to laborers in return for a claim on their time when he needs them or as part of a contract to employ them for a continuous, extended period [Bardhan and Rudra (1981), Binswanger et al. (1984)]; and the trader or commission agent who finances cultivators on the condition that they sell to, or through, him when the crops go to market [Wharton (1962), Rao and Subrahmanyam (1985)].

We begin with a discussion of the reasons which have been advanced to explain the existence of interlinking, and then proceed to analyze some formal models. These yield results bearing on equity and efficiency, the adoption of innovations and the effects of public policies.

3.1. The causes of interlinking

The following example is open to several interpretations. In India, it is common for agricultural laborers to take loans from a farmer during the slack season in exchange for a promise to work for him during the peak periods, when otherwise he may have no assurance of getting enough workers just when he needs them. (These workers may receive a wage which is lower than the spot wage ruling in the peak season, but that is not relevant to the argument here.) Leaving aside risk-sharing, Bardhan (1984) states that the simplest interpretation of this arrangement is that it is a barter transaction in which credit changes hands at one point and the same parties trade in the labor market later on. If, as Bardhan argues, the only collateral possessed by the workers were their future earnings from labor and this collateral were unacceptable to any potential creditors but farmers, then one source of the gains from the arrangement is clear. It is important to emphasize, however, that there would be gains to be had even in the presence of a well-functioning credit market. For by concluding a deal early in the season, the farmer spares himself the trouble of getting workers in the peak period and the workers avoid the extra costs of searching for, and negotiating with, other creditors. Questions of enforcement also arise in both cases; for the exchange is not contemporaneous, and the workers have the option of strategic default at harvest. They are taken up further in Section 3.1.4.

This is not to dismiss Bardhan's argument. As his example makes clear, imperfect and incomplete market structures provide a powerful motive for interlinked contracts. It is not, however, the only one.

3.1.1. Transactions costs

Interlinked arrangements may arise when there are significant transactions costs, which depend on the number of separate occasions an individual attempts a transaction and, whenever there is negotiation over terms, the number of other parties with whom he deals. Thus, when two people trade with each other in two or more markets, at least one of them should profit thereby. These gains can be realized as well in monetary as in barter economies: the shopper who uses a credit card to buy a dishwasher and perfume on the same trip to the department store is a vivid case in point. Nevertheless, although a double coincidence of wants between the two parties is not strictly necessary, it commonly underlies the examples which appear in the literature on rural economies.

Compared with the pattern of trading in anonymous markets, deliberate pairing off should produce savings in transactions costs and will therefore lead to a somewhat different structure of relative prices and resource allocation in equilibrium, although how, precisely, the two will differ on this account is hard to say.

There is, however, another more subtle reason why the two equilibria will differ. The savings in transactions costs through deliberate pairwise dealings over several markets constitute a "surplus". As an alternative, each of the two agents has the option of trading separately with other parties, thereby "unbundling" the deal. Thus, there is a system of bilateral bargains in which the agents' fall-back positions are their opportunities in separate deals. Their payoffs in the latter are called disagreement payoffs, which, with complete and symmetric information, determine their relative bargaining strengths and hence have a strong influence over the cooperative outcome. If the division of the surplus is not accomplished by lump-sum transfers, it will affect resource allocation quite independently of the savings in transactions costs themselves. For otherwise prices will be neither uniform over separate and coordinated deals, nor, probably, within the latter as a group.

To pursue the above example of credit and labor transactions, suppose the farmer offers workers the full spot wage in the peak season and credit on the terms available from other creditors. In accepting, the workers are certainly no worse off than they would be with separate deals; indeed, their overall transactions costs are likely to be lower. As for the farmer, if he is competitive in the credit market, so that his costs of, inter alia, finding clients and administering the loans advanced to them are fully covered by his returns, then he, too, is better off under this arrangement. For his marginal cost of labor in the peak season is simply the ruling spot wage, his recruitment costs at that time being zero provided he has engaged enough laborers under this form of contract. The farmer who relies on the spot market, however, faces a marginal cost of labor which is higher by at least the marginal cost of recruitment. When the possibility of rationing in the labor market in the peak season is also introduced, it is clear that the marginal cost of labor in the peak season is likely to vary across employers who have chosen different contractual arrangements.

3.1.2. Moral hazard and incentives

The second reason for a pair of agents to "bundle" their transactions arises in settings in which there is asymmetric information and the terms of their dealings involve, or introduce, moral hazard. In short, "bundling" may permit one agent to exercise a greater degree of profitable control over the doings of the other.

Once again, it is illuminating to examine the dealings between India's farmers and laborers. In the above example, there are two sources of uncertainty: the spot wage in the peak season, which is determined in the market for labor after the state of nature has been revealed; and the future delivery of workers' labor, the probability of which depends, inter alia, on the costs they would incur by reneging on their contracts. Implicitly, the latter possibility was ignored, so that the marginal cost of labor to the employer was simply the ruling spot wage. Let us consider, then, the case in which the input of labor early on cannot be closely monitored at the time except at very high cost; for example, the transplanting and weeding of paddy requires care and attention if yields are to be good. One way of inducing workers to pay due care and attention while transplanting and weeding is to offer them *exclusive* rights to harvest the crop on a share basis: higher real labor inputs early on, which are imperfectly monitorable, are then rewarded by higher payments to the same workers later on.[9] Also, the workers now have an incentive to turn up for the harvest, an incentive that can be sharpened further by paying them a lower wage early on than that ruling in the spot market at that time. Thus, the crucial difference from the foregoing example is that the form of the contingent trade in the peak season induces greater effort from workers in the early stages of the cultivation cycle. Where future delivery is concerned, the boot is now on the other foot in that it is the employer who must make good on a promise to engage the same workers in the peak season. He will have an incentive to keep his word if he has also lent to the workers in question; for if he does not, they could refuse to repay what they owe him. In the absence of loans, such arrangements boil down to interlinked transactions in the markets for slack and peak season labor alone that are not fully incentive-compatible.

Turning to other examples of "bundled" deals, the one that has received the most attention is that in which a landlord grants a tenancy only if the would-be tenant also borrows exclusively from him [Bhaduri (1973), Braverman and Srinivasan (1981), Braverman and Stiglitz (1982), Mitra (1982)]. If the amount and terms of credit available to the tenant affect his performance as a cultivator and this, in turn, affects the landlord's income, the landlord may do better by playing the moneylender too, bundling the tenant's transactions in the two markets to his own advantage. Many authors have approached the relationship between landlord and tenant in this way, which amounts to treating it as a principal–agent problem.[10] A relationship that has received much less attention in the theoretical literature but, as we saw in Section 2.4, is probably more

---

[9]Such contractual arrangements are common in Northern India; see, for example, Bliss and Stern (1982).

[10]For general treatments of the principal–agent problem, see Shavell (1979), Holmstrom (1983) and Hart and Holmstrom (1985).

prevalent and important in practice, is the one between a commission agent (or trader) and a cultivator. Here, the commission agent may lend to the cultivator on condition that the latter use the former's services when selling his crop. As before, this arrangement may be fruitfully analyzed as a principal–agent problem.

These relationships will be examined in detail below. For the present, we note that viewed as principal–agent relationships, each of the above arrangements must give the principal some additional measure of influence over the agent's actions beyond that afforded by separate deals, since "unbundling" is always an option open to the principal in his quest for the best (indirect) methods of controlling what the agent does. Also, there is often some uncertainty about future delivery, since the trades involved are rarely all contemporaneous. Usually, the source of uncertainty about future delivery is output, the level of which is subject to both moral hazard affecting inputs and variations in the state of nature. If delivery in full is not possible and collateral is inadequate or not contractually provided for, the consequences can range from rolling over the obligation to the next season, through an injured reputation, as far as bankruptcy or even indentured servitude. Thus, the question of enforcement remains.

3.1.3. Screening

Enforcement has a prominent place in Basu (1983, 1984) and Allen (1985). Although these authors have quite different views of what a rural economy is like, both are concerned with the possibility that the borrower may default. In the face of such "potential risk", as Basu calls it, the "market [in question] has an innate tendency to seek another market with which to get interlocked" (1984, p. 150). Landlords reduce potential risk to zero, so Basu argues, by offering loans only to those borrowers over whom they have control, by virtue of a tenancy or labor contract. While the idea clearly has merit, the contractual mechanism that ensures future delivery is not precisely specified, his elegant analysis being confined to a principal–agent problem in which there is no real time. Thus, if the borrower promptly absconds with the loan, perhaps to the employ of another landlord, nothing is said about how his creditor obtains redress. One would expect the "Eastern India" school to emphasize enforcement through the action of a coalition of landlords or, at the very least, the consequences of an irreparably damaged reputation when there is little mobility. There is also the darker threat of physical violence. As it stands, however, Basu's formulation implicitly appeals to a costless *deus ex machina*.

Allen, in contrast, assumes that direct enforcement is prohibitively costly and people are highly mobile. The problem is, therefore, to devise a schedule of contracts that will induce newcomers to reveal their abilities and make it unprofitable for both newcomers and those with established reputations to abscond to distant places, where they would be, once more, newcomers. (It is assumed that rents are paid in arrears from share and fixed rental arrangements alike, so that there is an implicit element of credit and the landlord must guard against the possibility that the tenant will make off with the crop.) With labor supplied inelastically and no uncertainty in production, Allen proves that new-comers will face the choice of a wage or a sufficiently small parcel of land on a fixed rent basis, with the incompetent choosing the former at once. The results of one season's cultivation suffice to reveal the abilities of the rest, who then join the ranks of those already having established reputations. They, in turn, are divided into those of high ability, who choose fixed rents and would not find it profitable to abscond, and those of modest ability, who sharecrop on terms that just induce them to stay put. The difficulty with Allen's model, like the pure screening models discussed above, is that its assumptions do not square very well with the basic features of rural economies. For example, most tenants, including sharecroppers, possess some land and other immoveable property. The notion that all sharecroppers are within an ace of absconding strains belief; for getting rid of such property in a hurry is difficult and costly, and if a tenant attempted to do so, the landlord would surely get wind of the fact. Moreover, it is well known that fields are closely watched by all interested parties up to and including the harvest itself. Hence, the argument that sharecropping arrangements arise to ensure that contracts are honored is unconvincing, though this is not to say that contractual enforcement is a minor problem.

Writers in the so-called "Marxisant" tradition are also concerned with en-forcement, as this is central to "control over the labor process". Among those who have addressed the phenomenon of interlinking from this perspective are Hart (1986, 1986a) and Rao (1986). While such writings appeal, implicitly or explicitly, to the notion of indirect control that the principal exercises in an agency relationship, they emphasize that the strong often resort to the instru-ments of extra-economic coercion to ensure compliance by the weak.

To close this discussion of the reasons for interlinking – savings in transactions costs; more effective contractual control in the face of moral hazard; the construction of finer screening devices; and enhanced enforcement – it is worth noting that while these categories are taxonomically convenient, it is usually the case that more than one of them is at work in the interlinked arrangements found in practice. Consider, for example, the moneylender-commission agent. By lend-ing to cultivators, he secures business in advance of the harvest, when his time is particularly scarce. By negotiating the terms of the loan, he can influence the cultivator's actions in a manner advantageous to his expected profits from moneylending and marketing *combined*. In particular, by providing a fairly generous amount of credit, he can induce the cultivator to use inputs more intensively; so that the expected volume of output for sale will increase. And by acting as the channel for sale of the marketable surplus, he is in a position to exercise first claim on the proceeds to settle what is owed him.

The incorporation of all of the above considerations in a single framework constitutes a tall order indeed. In particular, the existence of transactions costs introduces non-convexities, and the ensuing complications are considerable. These will, therefore, be skirted by assuming them away. Turning to screening, it has been argued above that the forms of asymmetric information relevant in this case are not very plausible in economies in which people are fairly settled and know one another quite well. That leaves moral hazard and enforcement in the context of agency relationships, which will provide the main theme for the remainder of this chapter.

In the light of the foregoing discussion, several features seem especially desirable in a model. First, time should appear in an essential way, the simplest form being a distinction between "today" and "tomorrow". In the presence of uncertainty (the second requirement), this permits actions to be taken before the state of nature and future trading conditions are known. Similarly, future delivery is no longer assured, because one party can abscond today or fail to meet his obligations tomorrow out of either wilfulness or inability to pay. Thirdly, although a general treatment of enforcement tomorrow is too demanding, there should be room for this difficulty to appear.

3.2. The interlinking of tenancy with credit: The principal–agent approach

A general model is very difficult to work with. Accordingly, we examine a specific arrangement, in the hope that this will yield a flavor of the principles involved and the sort of results to be expected. We bow to the theoretical literature in choosing for this purpose interlinkages between credit and tenancy. Other arrangements have received less attention.

The model employed here is essentially that of Braverman and Stiglitz (1982) and Mitra (1983), with some minor modifications.

Starting with the tenant, suppose he can lease a plot of area h by paying a share $(1 - \alpha)$ of the output to the landlord. Production takes two periods, with inputs of land and labor effort, e, being applied in the first and nature playing its part in the second to produce a crop. It will simplify exposition without, in this context, sacrificing much substance to assume that there is multiplicative risk in production. Thus, let output from the tenancy be given by:

$$Q = \theta \cdot F(e, h), \tag{9}$$

where the random variable θ represents the state of nature and $E\theta = 1$. The tenancy contract is *exclusive*, in the sense that the tenant may not work elsewhere.

Let the tenant's preferences over realized outcomes be represented by:

$$U = U(c_1, c_2, e),$$ (10)

where c_i $(i = 1, 2)$ is his consumption in period i. If he chooses not to enter a tenancy contract, let him have other economic opportunities, such as wage labor, which yield a reservation level of utility $\overline{V}$. Apart from his labor, the tenant owns no assets, so that his share of the crop is the only collateral he can offer. To carry himself through the first, or "lean", season, he borrows an amount B, which he consumes at once, so that $c_1 = B$. Both principal and interest thereon at a rate r are to be repaid out of his share of the crop at harvest time. Hence, consumption in the second period is given by

$$c_2 = \max[\alpha Q - (1 + r)B, 0].$$ (11)

The tenant's problem is to

$$\max EU(\cdot)$$

by choice of the variables under his control, which may include B, subject to (9) and (11). If

$$\overline{V} \le V^0,$$ (12)

where V^0 is the value of $EU(\cdot)$ at the optimum, the tenancy will be at least as attractive as alternative employment.

Two related difficulties now arise. First, if there is some chance that the crop will fail completely, however hard the tenant works, i.e. $D(0) > 0$, then there is nothing he can do to ensure that $c_2 > 0$ in all states of nature. If zero consumption in the second period is a sufficiently severe or catastrophic outcome, then a tenancy contract will be less attractive than forms of alternative employment that do not entail this risk. Braverman and Stiglitz avoid this difficulty by implicitly assuming away complete crop failures; so that if $D(\theta) = 0$ $\forall \theta \in [0, \underline{\theta})$, the tenant is assured of producing at least $\underline{\theta}F(e, h)$ with effort e. Mitra, however, addresses the problem directly. He deals with it by introducing a linear sharing rule, in which the tenant may also receive a fixed side-payment in period 2. If this is to ensure that $c_2 > 0$, the side-payment must be greater than $(1 + r)B$.

A second difficulty still remains, namely the threat of strategic bankruptcy. If the tenant can abscond with the loan in period 1, he can enjoy a level of utility at least as great as $U(B, 0, 0)$, since he may be able to work or even lend in the place to which he has fled. The larger the loan and the higher the rate of interest, the more attractive this option becomes. If effort is not monitorable and the landlord guarantees the tenant at least $\hat{c}_2$ (> 0), literally making off with the money will not be necessary; for the tenant can then idle away his time in leisure ($e = 0$) and then blame the absence of any output on the weather or pestilence. His utility would be at least $U(B, \hat{c}_2, 0)$ in this case; and he could clearly do better still if storage or lending at interest were options open to him. Indeed, it will now be shown that this may be his best policy, even when he cannot choose B.

The guarantee comes into play whenever $\theta < \hat{\theta}$, where

$$\hat{\theta} = \left[(1 + r)B + \hat{c}_2\right] / \alpha F(\cdot).$$ (13)

The tenant's problem is to

$$\max_{\{e\}} EU.$$

The first-order condition (FOC) is:

$$\left. \int_0^{\hat{\theta}} U_3 \, \mathrm{d}D(\theta) + \int_{\hat{\theta}}^\infty (U_2 \cdot \alpha\theta F_e + U_3) \, \mathrm{d}D(\theta) \leq 0 \atop e \geq 0 \right\} \text{ complementarily.}$$ (14)

Now, as $e \to 0$, $\hat{\theta} \to \infty$. Hence, if the distribution function of θ has a compact support, i.e. $D(\theta) = 1 \; \forall \theta \geq \bar{\theta}$,

$$\left. \frac{\partial EU}{\partial e} \right|_{e=0} = U_3(B, \hat{c}_2, 0) < 0.$$ (15)

Thus, the corner solution $e = 0$ cannot be ruled out as an optimal policy for the tenant.

If the tenant can also choose the size of the loan (with $B = c_1$), the problem is further exacerbated, perhaps to the point of becoming insuperable. By choosing a sufficiently large sum, the tenant can ensure that, with probability one, he will receive the guaranteed payment in period 2, since $D(\theta)$ has a compact support. Hence, he can assure himself the consumption vector $(c_1, \hat{c}_2)$ without the drudgery of cultivation. It follows that if $U(c_1, \hat{c}_2, 0)$ becomes sufficiently large as c_1 increases without bound, then not only is $e = 0$ the tenant's best policy, but his demand for loans will also be insatiable.

The non-convexity arising from bankruptcy is clearly recognized by Braverman and Stiglitz, but they ignore its possible ramifications by explicitly confining their attention to interior solutions. Mitra ignores the problem of strategic bankruptcy altogether, although his introduction of a positive side-payment in period 2 makes such an option more attractive. How, then, is the matter to be remedied?

The alert landlord must obviously ensure that, however B is determined, strategic bankruptcy is not attractive, that is,

$$U(B, \hat{c}_2, 0) \leq V^0, \tag{16}$$

where V^0 is the tenant's (expected) utility at the interior optimum.[11] Under suitable regularity conditions, V^0 will be a function of the contract parameters (α, h, r, B), with $V_\alpha^0 > 0$, $V_h^0 > 0$ and $V_r^0 < 0$. It should be noted that conditions (12) and (16) have exact counterparts in the discussion of the monopolistic moneylender in Section 2.1.2. They are evidently distinct and must be retained separately. It is immediately clear that while the landlord can influence V through his choice of α and h, control over the terms of the credit contract is also highly desirable, if not essential, especially if the tenant would otherwise be in a position to choose the size of the loan. Hence, there is a strong motive for contractual interlinking to ensure enforcement, as well as indirect control over the tenant's choice of projects in the usual sense.

In this connection, it should be noted that the tenant's optimal choice of effort, e^0, is not continuous everywhere in (α, h, r, B). For if (16) holds with strict equality and the terms of his contracts are then moved slightly against him, the tenant will promptly abscond, metaphorically if not literally.

With this cautionary introduction, consider the landlord's problem as a whole. Despite the attractions of interlinking as a means of reducing the potential costs of strategic bankruptcy, suppose first of all that he shuns work and moneylending as unbecoming professions, so that the would-be tenant must approach other creditors, who are not landlords, tendering his prospective share of the crop as collateral. Suppose also that the landlord is wealthy enough to be risk-neutral, so that he maximizes the expected value of his rental income.

In order to proceed further, it is necessary to specify the control variables at his disposal; but that cannot be done without specifying how equilibrium is established. As emerges clearly from the exchange between Newbery (1974) and Bardhan and Srinivasan (1971, 1974), the share parameter, α, is only a price-like variable, which cannot, in general, adjust to force excess demand for tenancies to zero unless landlords stipulate and enforce labor–land ratios. [As Bliss and Stern (1982) have reminded us, this point was also clearly recognized by Marshall (1920).] The above assumption of exclusivity will normally be adequate to eliminate excess demand, however, even though the level of the tenant's effort may not be monitorable. In any event, while α may be regarded as given by both parties, the landlord will certainly be able to choose the size of the tenancy.

---

[11] This exists and is unique by virtue of the strict concavity of $U(\cdot)$ and $F(e; h)$.

What constrains his choices? If the relationship is viewed as a principal–agent one and there is a perfectly elastic supply of identical would-be tenants, then the landlord cannot offer a contract which yields tenants a level of (expected) utility which is inferior to their reservation level and still attract takers. In a competitive setting, the reservation level is given by alternative employment on terms which are parametric to both landlords and tenants. If the landlord is a monopolist, he must still ensure that tenants obtain bare "subsistence". In both cases, the tenant's reservation utility is parametrically given in the landlord's calculations.

For the sake of generality, let the landlord be in a position to choose both α and h. All his land is cultivated by identical tenants, who experience the same state of nature (θ). Hence, his choice of h implies the number of tenants, n, he takes on. His problem is to

$$\max_{[\alpha, h]} E\pi,$$

where

$$E\pi = n(1 - \alpha)F, \tag{17}$$

subject to (12), (16) and the tenant's response functions $c_1^0(\cdot)$ and $e^0(\cdot)$ in the case of each tenancy, as well as the land constraint $nh = \bar{H}$, where $\bar{H}$ is the landlord's endowment. Recall that as the tenant consumes the loan in period 1, $c_1 = B$. The FOC for an interior maximum are

$$E\pi_\alpha = n\left[-F + (1 - \alpha)F_e \frac{\partial e^0}{\partial \alpha}\right] + \lambda V_\alpha + \mu\left(V_\alpha - U_1 \cdot \frac{\partial c_1^0}{\partial \alpha}\right) = 0 \tag{18}$$

and

$$E\pi_h = n(1 - \alpha)\left[F_h + F_e \frac{\partial e^0}{\partial h} - \frac{F}{h}\right] + \lambda V_h + \mu\left(V_h - U_1 \cdot \frac{\partial c_1^0}{\partial h}\right) = 0, \tag{19}$$

where λ and μ are the dual variables associated with the constraints (12) and (16), respectively. The derivatives $\partial c_1^0/\partial \alpha$ and $\partial c_1^0/\partial h$ will be zero if the tenant cannot choose B. Otherwise, it must be assumed that the tenant's preferences, $D(\theta)$ and $\hat{c}_2$, are such that cultivation with a finite B is the tenant's best policy, or the landlord will be faced with the certainty of strategic bankruptcy whatever he does.

As the landlord does not choose B, (12) and (16) will both bind at the optimum only by fluke. In general, however, it will still be profitable for the landlord to drive the tenant down to whichever of $\bar{V}$ and $U(B, \hat{c}_2, 0)$ is the greater, so that either $\lambda > 0$ or $\mu > 0$. Taking these cases in turn, if $\lambda > 0$, inspection of (19) reveals that by virtue of constant returns to scale, the landlord's optimum must lie in a region where the elasticity of the tenant's effort with respect to the size of the tenancy is less than unity. Whether effort is also increasing with the tenant's share is unclear, however. If, instead, strategic default is the binding constraint, i.e. $\mu > 0$, this characterization of the landlord's optimum also holds – provided the tenant cannot choose the size of the loan. Otherwise, it is plausible that $\partial c_1^0 / \partial h > 0$, if consumption in period 1 is a normal good, so that the term $(V_h - U_1 \cdot \partial c_1^0 / \partial h)$ may take either sign.

Now suppose the landlord loses his disdain for moneylending. He can borrow at the (parametric) rate of interest r_0 and he considers the profitability of offering tenancies on the condition that he be the *sole* creditor. With exclusivity in both credit and tenancy transactions, the new contract on offer is thoroughly inter-linked. In this case, the possibility of default through inability to repay must enter the landlord's calculations. Suppose, for simplicity, that no guarantee is offered ($\hat{c}_2 = 0$) and there exist contracts that make strategic default unattractive to the tenant. With such a contract, the landlord's income is given by:

$$\pi = \begin{cases} n[(1-\alpha)\theta F(e, h) + (r - r_0)B], & \text{if } \alpha\theta F(\cdot) > (1+r)B, \\ n[\theta F - (1 + r_0)B], & \text{otherwise,} \end{cases} \tag{20}$$

so that his expected income from renting and moneylending combined is

$$E\pi = n\left\{ \int_0^{\hat{\theta}} [\theta F - (1 + r_0)B] \, dD(\theta) + \int_{\hat{\theta}}^{\infty} [(1-\alpha)\theta F + (r - r_0)B] \, dD(\theta) \right\}$$

$$= n\left\{ [(1-\alpha)F + (r - r_0)B] + \int_0^{\hat{\theta}} [\alpha\theta F - (1+r)B] \, dD(\theta) \right\}, \tag{21}$$

where the landlord's control variables are (α, h, B, r) and $n = \overline{H}/h$.

One advantage of controlling how much the tenant borrows is immediately apparent. If, in the absence of interlinking, the strategic default constraint is binding, the landlord has no way of reducing $U(B, \hat{c}_2, 0)$ to $\overline{V}$ – or even further – by reducing B, thereby making strategic default unattractive to the tenant. Not only is this a profitable move in itself, but it also opens up additional possibilities of putting a profitable squeeze on the tenant through reductions in α and h and/or increases in r, subject to the tenant's reservation level, $\overline{V}$. Even if strategic default is not an active threat in the absence of interlinking, with more instruments (B, r) at his disposal, the landlord cannot do worse with an interlinked contract.

The associated FOC are:

$$E\pi_\alpha = n\left[-F + (1-\alpha)F_e\frac{\partial e^0}{\partial \alpha} + \int_0^{\hat{\theta}}\left(F + F_e\frac{\partial e^0}{\partial \alpha}\right)\theta\,\mathrm{d}D(\theta)\right] + (\lambda+\mu)V_\alpha = 0,$$

(22)

$$E\pi_h = n\left\{(1-\alpha)\left[F_h + F_e\frac{\partial e^0}{\partial h}\right] - \frac{(1-\alpha)F + (r-r_0)B}{h}\right.$$

$$\left. + \int_0^{\hat{\theta}}\alpha F_e\frac{\partial e^0}{\partial h}\theta\,\mathrm{d}D(\theta)\right\} + (\lambda+\mu)V_h = 0,$$

(23)

$$E\pi_r = n\left\{(1-\alpha)F_e\frac{\partial e^0}{\partial r} + B[1 - D(\hat{\theta})]\right\} + (\lambda+\mu)V_r = 0,$$ (24)

$$E\pi_B = n\left\{(1-\alpha)F_e\frac{\partial e^0}{\partial B} + (r-r_0) - (1+r)D(\hat{\theta})\right\} + (\lambda+\mu)V_B - \mu U_1 = 0.$$

(25)

It remains to be shown that interlinking is strictly profitable. Suppose it were not so. Then the landlord would lose nothing by unbundling the deal and offering the tenant loans at the rate of interest charged by other creditors. In that case, (22) and (23) would specialize to (18) and (19), respectively, only under highly implausible conditions. Even if they were met, (24) and (25) must be satisfied at the solution values to the landlord's unbundled problem, as defined by (17)–(19), which is quite improbable. Thus, interlinking will usually be strictly profitable.

Comparing (23) with (19), we see also that if the landlord chooses to subsidize credit $(r < r_0)$, the elasticity of the tenant's effort with respect to h must be strictly less than unity, as before. If, however, the landlord's optimal policy entails income from moneylending $(r > r_0)$, that elasticity may be greater than unity without violating (23) and $(\lambda+\mu) > 0$.

Comparatively simple though it is, the structure of the above system affords the principal a number of opportunities for influencing the agent's choices. With preferences defined over dated consumption and effort, variations in the terms of the tenancy contract alone will not usually suffice to exploit these to the full, and control over at least some of the terms of credit transactions will be advantageous to the principal.

3.3. An alternative to contract-taking equilibrium: The Nash bargaining solution

Instead of a perfectly elastic supply of would-be tenants, let there be a finite, but not necessarily small, pool of identical, qualified tenants, who are distinguished from the general mass of agricultural laborers by their possession of a non-tradable factor or skill which is essential to production, for example draft animals or husbandry and managerial skills. Suppose this pool is parcelled out among landlords, so that there will be exclusive contracts in the sense that each tenant will deal with only one landlord. How this allocation of tenants among landlords is brought about need not concern us here. We simply note that if landlords are risk-neutral, it is plausible that each will deal with the same proportion of all tenants as his total landholding comprises in all land, an allocation which is necessary for efficiency. In any event, the number of tenants with whom each landlord deals is assumed to be exogenous.

When the pool of qualified tenants has been thus parcelled out, each landlord is a party to a bilateral arrangement with each of a particular subset of tenants.[12] The terms of the contract between a landlord and each of his tenants will depend not only on their preferences and the technology, but also on their respective bargaining strengths. The latter depend on the payoff each would receive in the event of a disagreement over terms. Since both stand to gain from agreement – the landlord from the tenant's skills and the tenant from putting them to work on the landlord's land – the game is a cooperative one. Following Bell and Zusman (1976), it will be assumed that the outcome of each such game is the Nash solution to the two-person bargaining problem.

Suppose, without loss of generality, that a landlord possessing one unit of land will draw n tenants from the overall pool of those who qualify. Let the disagreement payoffs of a landlord and any of his tenants be denoted by $\bar{\pi}$ and $\bar{V}$, respectively. We note that the landlord has the option to leave one-nth of his land idle, which does not affect any of his remaining tenants, while the tenant in question can fall back on wage labor, for example, even though his special skills would then be of no account. These are certainly feasible strategies in the event of a disagreement. What should be emphasized, however, is that the assumption that $\bar{V}$ is parametric implicitly entails the absence of strategic default.[13] This should be borne in mind when comparing the results that follow with those derived above.

As before, let us start with the case in which there is no interlinking, so that the tenant is free to seek loans from other sources. In the cooperative outcome, all

---

[12] In view of exclusivity, each landlord can disregard what other landlords are up to when bargaining over terms with his pool of tenants. Thus, contractual externalities among landlords are avoided [see Zusman and Bell (1985)].

[13] Variable threats based on $U(B, \hat{c}_2, 0)$ would introduce considerable difficulties, and are omitted here.

qualified tenants in the subpool of a particular landlord will have a tenancy, and by symmetry, each will operate an area equal to $1/n$. That leaves the tenant's share of the crop to be determined by bargaining. If the outcome is given by Nash's solution to the bargaining problem, then α^0 is the solution to

$$\max_{\alpha} \left\{ \left[n(1-\alpha)F(e^0, 1/n) - \bar{\pi} \right] \cdot \left[V(\alpha, 1/n, r) - \bar{V} \right] \right\},$$

where $e^0 = e^0(\alpha, 1/n, r)$. Treating the remaining $(n-1)$ contracts as given, the FOC for the bargain with a particular tenant is:

$$\left[-F + (1-\alpha)F_e \frac{\partial e^0}{\partial \alpha} \right] \Delta V + V_\alpha \Delta E\pi = 0, \tag{26}$$

where $\Delta V = [V - \bar{V}]$ and $\Delta E\pi = [n(1-\alpha)F(e^0, 1/n) - \bar{\pi}]$ are the tenant's and landlord's gains from cooperation, respectively. It should be noted that the assumptions used here ensure that both parties realize strictly positive gains over their alternatives. In particular, the presence of the tenant's non-tradable resource entails that $F(\cdot)$ is strictly concave in land and effort alone.

Next, suppose there is interlinking. Then not only α, but also the rate of interest and even the amount borrowed will be the object of bargaining. The outcome (α^0, r^0, B^0), is the solution to

$$\max_{\{\alpha, r, B\}} \left\{ n \left[(1-\alpha)F(e^0, 1/n) + (r - r_0)B \right. \right.$$

$$\left. \left. + \int_0^{\hat{\theta}} [\alpha\theta F - (1+r)B] \, dD(\theta) \right] - \bar{\pi} \right\}$$

$$\times \left\{ V(\alpha, 1/n, r, B) - \bar{V} \right\},$$

where $e_0 = e^0(\alpha, 1/n, r, B)$. The FOC are

$$\left[-F + (1-\alpha)F_e \frac{\partial e^0}{\partial \alpha} + \int_0^{\hat{\theta}} \left(F + F_e \frac{\partial e^0}{\partial \alpha} \right) \theta \, dD(\theta) \right] \Delta V + V_\alpha \Delta E\pi = 0, \tag{27}$$

$$\left[(1-\alpha)F_e \frac{\partial e^0}{\partial r} + B(1 - D(\hat{\theta})) \right] \Delta V + V_r \Delta E\pi = 0, \tag{28}$$

$$\left[(1-\alpha)F_e \frac{\partial e^0}{\partial B} + (r - r_0) - (1+r)D(\hat{\theta}) \right] \Delta V + V_B \Delta E\pi = 0. \tag{29}$$

Dividing throughout by ΔV and comparing the FOC (26) and (27)–(29) with their counterparts in the principal–agent formulation, it is apparent that the two sets of conditions are formally identical if $\mu = 0$, with the ratio $\Delta E\pi/\Delta V$ having the role played by λ, the dual variable associated with the constraint $\bar{V} \leq V$ in the principal–agent formulation. This is as is should be, since λ/n represents the marginal cost, in terms of the landlord's expected profits, of raising one tenant's expected utility by one util.

The question that arises at once is whether there will be interlinking or not. There was a ready answer in the principal–agent setting: the choice is the landlord's, and, in general, it will be profitable for him to insist on interlinking. Here, the matter seems to be left hanging. On reflection, however, it is clear that the discrete choice of whether or not to have an interlinked contract will be bargained over just like the continuous contractual parameters α, r and B. As the Nash solution is (constrained) efficient, the outcome must be sought over all feasible arrangements.

Consider, therefore, the principal–agent problem, in which the tenant's expected utility in alternative employment is parametrically given. If, in equilibrium, his contract with the landlord is barely attractive and interlinking is profitable to the landlord, as will usually be the case with the structure examined here, then the utility possibility frontier (UPF) in the presence of interlinking will lie wholly to the northeast of that in its absence. Hence, if the disagreement payoffs $\bar{V}$ and $\bar{\pi}$ are independent of the contractual parameters (α^0, r^0, B^0) in the cooperative equilibrium, there will be interlinking in the system of bilateral bargains if there is interlinking in an otherwise identical economy of

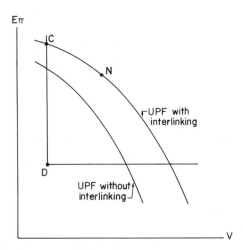

Figure 16.6.   The principal–agent and bargaining solutions when interlinking is Pareto improving.

principal–agent arrangements. For then it is always possible to find an inter-linked contract which yields a higher value of the Nash product $\Delta V \cdot \Delta E\pi$ than the maximal value of that product under the restriction that no interlinking take place. Figure 16.6 depicts the relevant details, D being the disagreement point $(\overline{V}, \overline{\pi})$ for the two parties, point C being the principal–agent solution, and point N being the (Nash) bargaining solution.

3.4. Interlinking and innovation

Bhaduri (1973) has advanced the rather startling proposition that a landlord who is also the sole source of credit to his tenants may prevent them from adopting an innovation that raises output. The argument runs as follows. If the tenant's (absolute) share of the crop rises, his income will rise and that may cause him to reduce his borrowing. Thus, although the landlord's rental income may increase as a result of the innovation, his income from usury may also fall, so that the possibility that he will be worse off, on balance, cannot be ruled out.

This proposition provoked a stormy exchange [Griffin (1974), Newbery (1975), Ghose and Saith (1976), Srinivasan (1979), Bhaduri (1979)], from which it emerged that, as originally formulated, the argument is not wholly satisfactory. First, as Srinivasan points out, it requires that for the tenant, borrowing be an inferior good, which is not particularly appealing. Second, and more tellingly in the setting considered by Bhaduri, not only would a monopolistic landlord always find it profitable to drive the tenant down to his reservation utility, but he would also always gain from an increase in output.

This second point is easily shown. Suppose, following Bhaduri, that the tenant borrows and consumes an amount c_1 in the first period, to be repaid with interest out of his income from cultivation in the second period. There is no uncertainty, natural or strategic, and output is independent of the tenant's effort, presumably because the landlord can monitor and enforce its level costlessly. Suppose, furthermore, that innovations demand no extra effort. Then, if the second period is sufficiently short, in steady state equilibrium,

$$(1 + r)c_1 = \alpha Q, \tag{30}$$

since there is no consumption in the second period and the tenant must enter the next cycle in the same condition as he did the last. The landlord's total income is, trivially,

$$\pi = (1 - \alpha)Q + rc_1,$$

$$= Q - c_1. \tag{31}$$

Hence, if the landlord can keep the tenant at his reservation utility level, which in this case entails setting the amount the tenant borrows by choice of α and r, the landlord will always profit from an increase in output. The point to note here is that for any level of output, there is a set of (α, r) yielding the reservation level of c_1. Indeed, provided $Q > c_1$ (a reasonable requirement), a restriction on either α or r will be of no account if the other can be chosen freely. With such a redundancy among instruments,[14] it does not matter to the landlord that his income from either usury or tenancy may fall, because he can always obtain more than full compensation from the other. As originally formulated, therefore, Bhaduri's argument is not persuasive: as an exploiter who does not vary α or r, his landlord is not trying hard enough.

A little reflection on the findings of the previous sections suggests, however, that with the introduction of uncertainty and costly monitoring, which subject the tenant's effort to moral hazard, Bhaduri's claim cannot be ruled out entirely. For under these circumstances the landlord will find control over both α and r profitable, so that a binding restriction on either could render certain innovations unprofitable even if they promised higher expected output for each level of effort. In fact, it is possible to go further. Consider the case in which an innovation reduces the riskiness of cultivation while preserving the mean value of output. As tenants are risk-averse and landlords (by hypothesis) are risk-neutral, it seems plausible that such an innovation would shift the UPF outwards. Mitra (1983), however, shows that if (i) α is fixed, (ii) the tenant's absolute risk aversion is declining in income and (iii) certain other conditions are satisfied, then the amount the tenant chooses to borrow may rise or fall following the innovation, as may the landlord's expected profit. With incomplete control over the tenant's actions, the landlord's choice of values for the instruments must balance the need to share risks and the need to provide incentives to effort, and the fewer the instruments, the harder it is to strike such a balance in an efficient way.

Even if α and r were free of public regulation or long-established custom, there remains a possibility that landlords will block certain innovations. Here, a useful clue is provided by Braverman and Srinivasan (1981), who prove that if there is no uncertainty and the production function is Cobb–Douglas, a Hicks-neutral technical improvement will always be welcomed by landlords. This suggests that for landlords to resist an innovation, the UPF must shift in a non-neutral way. Consider, therefore, an innovation which enhances both mean output and riskiness, but requires no extra effort. If the tenant's absolute risk aversion is decreasing with income and his mean income does not increase too much, he will increase his risk-taking if the amount that he must repay, $(1 + r)B$, decreases. Hence, in order to induce the tenant to adopt the innovation, the landlord must reduce $(1 + r)B$, which entails a fall in usury income if either

---

[14] Bhaduri's formulation is obviously a special case of Braverman and Srinivasan (1981).

$r > r_0$, or B rises and $r < r_0$. The reduction in $(1 + r)B$ will make the tenant better off, ceteris paribus, if $B(= c_1)$ does not fall; but the spread in second-period consumption may also rise along with the mean, even if α stays constant. Thus, it may not be feasible for the landlord to reduce α sufficiently to compensate for the loss in usury income while still keeping the terms of the contract attractive to the tenant.[15] The likelihood of this occurring is obviously greater if the landlord cuts $(1 + r)B$ by cutting B, since this cuts the tenant's consumption in the first period pari pasu.

To pursue our earlier comparison of the principal–agent and bilateral bargaining settings, it is important to emphasize at the outset that whether an innovation is adopted in the latter is an outcome of the cooperative game between both parties, just as is the choice of whether to have an interlinked or untied tenancy contract (see Section 3.3). Thus, the decision to adopt the innovation is not the landlord's alone. In principle, the answer is supplied by the analysis of Section 3.3, though settling the practical details is almost certainly a very complicated task. Provided the UPF with the innovation lies wholly to the northeast of the UPF without it, the innovation will be adopted, even though one party may be worse off as a result. Now we have just argued that in the case of certain innovations, the UPF with the innovation may lie to the southwest of the UPF without the innovation, at least in the neighborhood where the tenant obtains just his reservation utility level. In a system of bilateral bargains, however, the Nash solution may lie far way from that neighborhood of the UPF. Thus, if the two UPFs in question cross each other, it is quite possible that an innovation that would be rejected by the landlord in a principal–agent setting would be agreed to without hesitation in a bilateral bargain. This possibility is depicted in Figure 16.7, in which the landlord, left to himself, chooses point C on the UPF with the tried and true methods, while the Nash solution, N, is planted firmly on the UPF with the innovation. It should be noted that the converse case may also arise. For by switching the labels on the two UPFs, it is immediately clear that an innovation that is warmly welcomed by the landlord in a principal–agent setting may not be chosen when there is bilateral bargaining.

The above discussion has been confined to the case in which there are no instruments to effect non-distortionary transfers of utility. Without such transfers, those who stand to gain from innovation may be unable to compensate those who stand to lose, while still retaining some gains. The outcome in the principal–agent case depicted in Figure 16.7 exemplifies this result, since the landlord has the power to block outcomes that are inferior, from his point of

---

[15] Braverman and Stiglitz (1982) proceed more formally, using the Rothschild–Stiglitz (1970) notion of a mean-preserving spread to characterize the innovation in order to prove that a risk-averse tenant will reject some innovations of the kind considered here. They do not, however, consider the landlord's options over (B, r, α). They also refer to the quantity $(1 + r)B$ as "borrowing", which is not only confusing, but also inaccurate when B and r are independent.

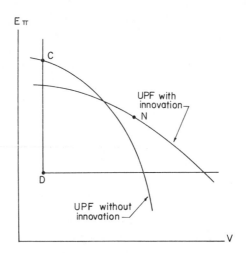

Figure 16.7.   An innovation whose acceptance depends on the solution concept.

view. The outcome in the bargaining game is different because neither party possesses unilateral powers.

While the theoretical possibilities are richer and more interesting than some of the early exchanges on this subject might suggest, two remarks are in order. First, the possibility that changes in technology, markets and institutional arrangements which would yield improvements in efficiency may be blocked is not new, as the analogous case in trade theory of a movement from autarky to trade makes clear. Secondly, whether the required conditions for landlords to resist innovations are commonly encountered in practice is very much open to question. The work of Bardhan and Rudra (1978, 1980) suggests that even in eastern India, these conditions are not present.

3.5. *Welfare and income distribution*

When agents are averse to risk and effort, utility and income may move in opposite directions. However, although welfare is based on utility, there are two reasons to examine output and income. First, they are measurable. Secondly, changes in the output of the subeconomy considered here may result in changes in prices, and hence welfare, in the rest of the economy.

We begin by considering the effects of interlinking on welfare in a partial equilibrium setting. In the principal–agent case, interlinking is chosen only if profitable, and if chosen, it will skew the distribution of utilities in favor of the landlord, since the tenant's utility will remain at the parametric reservation level.

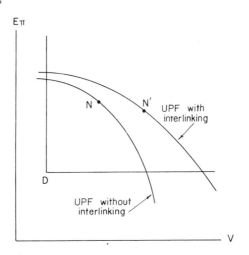

Figure 16.8.   Landlord may be worse off with interlinking in the bargaining outcome.

In a system of bilateral bargains, however, the effect of a switch from unlinked to interlinked contracts on the distribution of utilities depends on the way in which the utility possibility frontier shifts outwards and the position of the disagreement point relative to the origin. Indeed, a sufficiently strong departure from an equiproportional shift may bring about a reduction in utility for the disadvantaged party. This possibility is illustrated in Figure 16.8, in which interlinking is so favorable to the tenant relative to the disagreement point that the landlord is absolutely worse off with interlinking. If interlinking induces a fairly neutral shift of the frontier relative to the disagreement point, both parties will gain.

One circumstance in which it is possible to be definite about the effects of interlinking on the distribution of utilities in a system of bilateral bargains is that in which there is transferable utility. It is then easy to show that both parties gain equally in the cooperative outcome, relative to their disagreement payoffs, whether there is interlinking or not. As the landlord's expected profit is his utility index, a lump-sum transfer out of, or to, profits will result in a one-for-one transfer of utility if the tenant's expected utility rises or falls by the same amount. Let P be the point on the UPF in the absence of side payments which maximizes $(\Delta V + \Delta E\pi)$. Hence, with transferable utility, all points on the line with slope -1 that passes through P (which is also tangential to the UPF at P) become available to the two parties through lump-sum transfers. It follows at once that $\Delta V \cdot \Delta E\pi$ attains a maximum at the intersection of this availability locus with the ray through D having a slope of unity, which establishes the claim that both parties gain equally in the cooperative outcome. This solution is depicted in Figure 16.9.

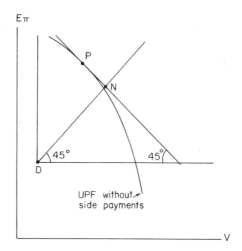

Figure 16.9.   Bargaining outcome with transferable utility.

The beauty of such lump-sum transfers is that they leave the remaining contractual parameters free to accomplish an efficient outcome, in the sense of maximizing the sum of the landlord's and tenant's expected utilities. The gains from cooperation are then distributed without affecting efficiency. This result yields an important conclusion for the discussion of innovations in Section 3.4: with transferable utility and side payments, innovations which are potentially Pareto superior will never be blocked. Once again, there is a clear parallel with a well-known result concerning a shift from autarky to free trade.

By hypothesis, the tenant's utility depends on consumption in each of the two periods and effort, so it would appear that strong assumptions are needed to yield transferable utility. For example, if $U(\cdot)$ were additively separable and the contribution of (random) consumption in the second period to expected utility were linear in its mean and some function of its higher order moments, then lump-sum transfers in the second period would effect one-for-one transfer. This is not, of course, a necessary condition, but its stringency suggests that instruments for the lump-sum transfer of utility, as opposed to income, may be hard to come by.

While it is difficult, if at all possible, to measure utility, income and output can be measured. In the principal–agent setting, the tenant's expected utility will remain at his reservation level in any shift to an interlinked contract, though "prices" α and r will generally change. It does not follow, however, that his expected income will be unchanged, too; for changes in the terms of his contracts will, in general, affect his effort. The tenant's expected income is given by:

$$Ey = \alpha F(e^0, h), \tag{32}$$

where e^0 depends on the values of (α, r, h, B) in each case. In general, these will differ, so that it is not clear whether Ey will rise or fall with a shift to interlinking (recall that $E\pi$ certainly rises if interlinking is chosen). The expected output from the landlord's tenancies is:

$$n \cdot EQ = nF\left(e^0, \overline{H}/n\right)$$

$$= \overline{H} \cdot F\left(e^0/h, 1\right) \tag{33}$$

by virtue of constant returns to scale, with $nh = \overline{H}$. Hence, a necessary and sufficient condition for expected output to be higher under interlinking is that effort per acre be higher.

While there is insufficient space to lay out a full taxonomy of cases, the following [Braverman and Stiglitz (1982)] illustrates what is involved in a shift to interlinking. Suppose borrowing (c_1) were unchanged but the rate of interest were to rise. Then α would have to rise by way of compensation. Moreover, an increase in $(1 + r)c_1$ will increase the tenant's effort with α unchanged if $U_{2e} \leq 0$, which is a reasonable condition [Mitra (1983)]. Hence, the tenant's effort will rise on both counts – an increase in α and an increase in r. Thus, if the size of the tenancy is unchanged, too, both expected income and output will rise: greater drudgery is offset by just enough extra income to leave the tenant's expected utility unchanged. How much his expected income rises in this case depends on the whole gamut of preferences, technology and the terms of credit offered by third parties. Not much more can be said, except that a worsening of the distribution of utilities between landlords and tenants following interlinking could be accompanied by an improvement in the distribution of incomes, and it is only the latter that we can measure.

Two further points should be made in this connection. First, in the traditional models of household behavior, the wage rate is parametrically given to the household. Hence, barring uncertainty and rationing, consumption and leisure will be chosen so that the marginal value of leisure is equal to the wage rate. Thus, the wage rate anchors the whole system, and if nothing disturbs it, the real cost of labor (effort) to the household stays constant. In the principal–agent setting with exclusive contracts, while a parametric expected utility level for the tenant will come about through offsetting changes in expected income and leisure, there is nothing that guarantees that the marginal value of leisure will be unchanged after interlinking is introduced. To put it somewhat differently, the marginal rewards in terms of income from working an extra day are constant everywhere when there is access to a perfect labor market, whereas the marginal rewards are endogenous within the terms of an exclusive contract.

Secondly, some care is needed when discussing the effects of interlinking on expected output. If the number of tenants does not change, the effort of each tenant must increase if expected output is to rise. If, however, the number of tenants changes, there are two relevant effects. As noted above, in the sharecropping subeconomy, an increase in effort per acre, which will usually entail a rise in the number of tenants, is both necessary and sufficient to raise expected output. However, a rise in the number of tenants implies that workers are drawn out of their alternative lines of employment, in which their marginal products are presumably positive. In any event, an increase in both national income (excluding the value placed on leisure) and expected output in the sharecropping subeconomy will attend the introduction of interlinking only if the value of the output foregone in alternative employment is less than the rise in the expected value of output in the sharecropping subeconomy. As the alternative in most LDCs is wage employment, which must be monitored to elicit effort, while tenancy gives incentives to effort, then if a shift to interlinking results in more tenants, it is plausible that national income as well as the expected value of output in the sharecropping subeconomy will rise.

It is also hard to be definite about the effects of a shift to interlinking on expected output and income in a system of bilateral bargains, especially since it is quite possible for one party to be worse off (in utility terms) as a result. Here, matters are slightly simplified by the fact that the number of tenants is exogenously given, so that everything hinges on whether interlinking results in a tenant putting out more effort. In the case of transferable utility, the landlord's expected profits must increase with interlinking if the UPF shifts outwards everywhere, so that if the bargain calls for credit to be subsidized ($r < r_0$), expected output will also increase. Otherwise, the direction of expected output is unclear.

Thus far, nothing has been said about the case in which tenants are not identical. Differences in preferences, especially towards risk-bearing are obviously important. More pertinent here, however, are differences in ability or endowments of some tangible non-tradable resource which is needed in production. Suppose that differences in such attributes do not affect the tenant's parametric utility level in alternative employment (presumably, they are of no value there) and the landlord knows all about each tenant possessing them. Then in the principal–agent setting, the landlord derives the full benefit of their contribution to production. Among tenants, the able and mediocre alike are driven down to a common level of expected utility by the landlord's judicious choice of contractual variables in each case. This will not, however, happen in a system of bilateral bargains if, as is plausible, the UPF for a landlord with a more able tenant is a roughly equiproportional shift of the UPF with a less competent one. For under the Nash axioms, with a common disagreement payoff, the more able tenant will bargain successfully for a somewhat higher level of expected utility and so keep some of the "rents" from his ability to himself.

The assumption that the tenant has no traits that are especially valuable in alternative employment is not, however, very appealing. A skillful and diligent tenant will often be a skillful and diligent worker, and hence command a premium in wage employment. In that case, he will also obtain more attractive terms from a contract-setting landlord.

It is interesting to note that the able also do better than the incompetent when the landlord knows nothing about each individual's ability, so that contracts are formulated for the purposes of screening. Braverman and Guasch (1984) show that in a world with riskless production, the landlord can devise a schedule of interlinked contracts, a tenant's choice from which will reveal his ability. In monopolistic competition, they show that the only possible equilibrium is a sorting one, there being a tenant of marginal ability who is just indifferent between an interlinked tenancy-cum-credit contract and alternative employment. All other tenants are more able, and earn a surplus over their common reservation utility.

So much for partial equilibrium. In general equilibrium, things may turn out quite differently. At one extreme, the sharecropping subeconomy could be a relatively small part of the whole, so that changes in the former would leave unchanged the utility available to tenants from working in the latter. In that case, of course, the above partial equilibrium analysis would hold. At the other extreme, the subeconomy could face a perfectly inelastic supply of tenants lacking any opportunities elsewhere, in which case the utility they would obtain from working as tenants would be endogenously determined.[16] In this setting, the fact that each landlord finds it profitable to insist on interlinked contracts does not imply that landlords as a group will be better off than they would have been had they confined themselves to tenancy contracts alone. For if the switch to interlinking bids up the demand for tenants, a less than perfectly elastic supply will result in a higher level of expected utility for tenants, perhaps so much higher that landlords will wind up being worse off. This possibility is analyzed by Braverman and Stiglitz (1982), which is drawn upon here (Figure 16.10).

As before, the landlord takes the tenant's utility as parametrically given. For each such level, the landlord's optimal choice of contract includes the size of each tenancy – or, equivalently, the number of tenants to work his land. Summation over all landlords yields the total demand for tenants at the parametric level of their expected utility. Hence, by varying the latter, we obtain what Braverman and Stiglitz call the pseudo-demand curve for labor. It is at once apparent that tenants gain or lose from interlinking according as the landlord's optimal choice of plotsize falls or rises, respectively. Braverman and Stiglitz (1982) go on to show that in the case of a Cobb–Douglas production function, tenants will be worse off with interlinked contracts if their borrowing is also restricted (relative to their free choice of borrowing from third parties), but better off if the contract calls for

---

[16]Clearly, this is true whenever the supply of tenants is at all inelastic. The extreme case is chosen for ease of exposition and analysis.

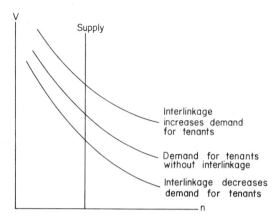

Figure 16.10.   The tenant's welfare in general equilibrium.

them to borrow more. In the former, the partial and general equilibrium effects are quantitatively the same; in the latter, they run in opposite directions.

Once again, it must be emphasized that the above discussion is concerned with changes in utility. Where changes in expected output and income are concerned, the story may be different. If the supply of tenants is perfectly inelastic, the size of each tenancy in equilibrium will not change with a switch to interlinking, so that its effects on expected output depend on what happens to each tenant's effort. Suppose tenants are worse off, in utility terms, as a result. If leisure is a normal good and income effects are strong, effort may rise. If, furthermore, the tenant's share of output does not fall too much, his expected income, $\alpha F(e, h)$, may actually rise, too. Recalling that a landlord's utility index is expected profit, it is clear that the distribution of incomes will worsen less acutely, if at all, than will the distribution of utilities.

Turning to a setting in which there is a system of bilateral bargains, two questions arise in general equilibrium. First, is the parcelling out of the fixed pool of qualified tenants among landlords immune to "poaching"? Or, to put it differently, is exclusivity sustainable? Secondly, are the disagreement payoffs of landlords and tenants independent of the set of contractual parameters ruling in equilibrium? These questions are examined in some detail by Zusman and Bell (1985). Suffice it to say on the second question that if both parties' disagreement payoffs do increase as a result of the introduction of interlinking, then it is more likely that both will gain in the cooperative outcome, even if utility is not transferable.

In all this, we have been concerned with the effects of a switch to interlinking. Whether interlinking will be chosen is another matter. While theory gives us guidance in both cases, it should be recalled from Section 2.4 that there is fairly solid evidence that interlinking has intensified in the presence of output-enhancing innovations in Indian agriculture.

3.6. Policy reforms

It is now natural to ask what effects various interventions will have on welfare and output. The reforms considered here are: (i) putting a ceiling on the landlord's cropshare; (ii) providing subsidized credit to tenants but not landlords; and (iii) a program of "land to the tiller", discussion of which is deferred until later.

The simplest case is that in which tenants obtain just their expected utility from alternative employment, which is independent of what happens in the sharecropping subeconomy. Provided it is profitable for the landlord to keep the tenant's expected utility from their contract at the latter's reservation level and it is possible for him to accomplish this by varying the size of the tenancy alone, then any intervention short of "land to the tiller" will have no effect on the tenant's welfare. Braverman and Srinivasan (1981), who deal with steady states in which the loan is used to finance consumption through the entire season, prove that these two conditions are met in the special case where there is no uncertainty, by showing that effort per acre rises as the size of each tenancy declines, even if the effort put out by each tenant falls. It seems likely that this result will continue to hold for the more general specification considered here.

Whether the landlord will be adversely affected by either of the first two reforms depends solely on whether the cropshare and rate of interest he charges the tenant are imperfectly collinear in their influence over the tenant's actions. If they are, any binding restriction on his choice of their levels will reduce expected profits. In general, unrestricted control over both variables is advantageous to the landlord, although in the special case analyzed by Braverman and Srinivasan, one of them turns out to be redundant, so that either reform undertaken alone will then have no effect on the system whatever.

Suppose the tenant now has access to subsidized credit, which is denied the landlord. Then interlinking may lose some of its attractiveness to the landlord if, with the cropshare given, the tenant's effort increases as a result of the lower rate of interest he would face in an untied deal. For if the landlord were charging above the subsidized rate in his interlinked contract, and then decided to match it, his moneylending operations would show a smaller profit. As a result, he would have to raise his cropshare to stay even, and that would discourage the tenant from making as strong an effort. Hence, the provision of subsidized credit by public agencies could induce the landlord to give up interlinking; but were it to do so, he, not the tenant, would be the beneficiary.[17]

---

[17] In the special case considered by Braverman and Srinivasan (1981), the landlord always directs the tenant to the cheaper source of credit if there is no restriction on the cropshare.

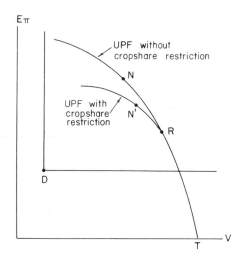

Figure 16.11.   A binding restriction on the landlord's cropshare.

It would appear that in those circumstances, a program of "land to the tiller" is the only reform that offers any hope of improving the tenant's lot, provided he has access to credit from other sources at the same rate of interest as that charged to the landlord. If, however, the tenant faces an appreciably higher rate than does the landlord, ownership of his erstwhile tenancy may be a worthless gift; for although his expected utility is increasing in α, it is decreasing in r. At worst, he could leave the land fallow and fall back on alternative employment. Whether matters reach such a pass depends on whether owning the land improves his creditworthiness sufficiently for his cost of funds to be not much greater than his former landlord's. In practice, it appears likely that tenants would indeed benefit from a program of land to the tiller; but this discussion suggests that what happens in the credit market may also exert a strong influence on how much they would gain.

As before, it is instructive to compare the findings from the principal–agent case with those for the system of bilateral bargains. As any binding restriction affects the UPF in a non-neutral way relative to that in the absence of restrictions, it will affect both the level and distribution of utilities. Figure 16.11 illustrates such a case when a ceiling, $(1 - \underline{\alpha})$, on the landlord's cropshare is binding. In the absence of a restriction on α, the solution (α^0, r^0, B^0) would be the point N. At $\alpha = \underline{\alpha}$, suppose there is a point, R say, on the UPF. In the presence of the floor on α, points on the UPF more favorable to the landlord than R are no longer available. Instead, there is a UPF with α fixed at $\underline{\alpha}$, which lies to the southwest of the original UPF except at R. As depicted in Figure 16.11, the restriction on α is so damaging to the landlord for any given level of expected utility obtained by the tenant that at the new cooperative outcome N', not only is the landlord worse off (as expected), but the tenant is actually better off. Thus, the distribution of utilities may be much more sensitive to public intervention in a system of bilateral bargains than in a principal–agent setting.

The effects of "land to the tiller" are subject to the same caveat about the tenant's cost of credit as that discussed above, the point T being attainable if, and only if, that cost is no greater than the landlord's.

In general equilibrium, some or all of the above findings may be overturned in the principal–agent setting, as will be clear from the discussion in Section 3.5. Suppose, as before, that the supply of tenants to the sharecropping subeconomy is perfectly inelastic. Then, as we have seen, a reform will improve the tenant's lot if, and only if, the landlord chooses a smaller tenancy with the tenant's utility held constant. Again, let the ceiling on the landlord's cropshare bind, so that if nothing else changes, the tenant will be better off as a result of the reform. His effort will increase, too, α having risen. Now with the tenant's plotsize held constant, the only point to be settled is whether it is profitable for the landlord to raise the rate of interest to a level at which the tenant is no better off than he was before the floor on α was imposed. In general, it is not clear that this will be the landlord's optimal policy. Thus, reforms short of "land to the tiller" may benefit tenants when the supply of tenants is at all inelastic.

To complete this discussion, we consider the effects of reforms on output. In the setting considered by Braverman and Srinivasan (1981), the imposition of a binding ceiling on the landlord's cropshare will induce the landlord to increase the rate of interest to a level that will nullify any additional incentives to effort, without changing the number of tenants. Hence, this reform will have no effect on output. If interlinking is banned, however, while the landlord will lose, he will also find it profitable to reduce the size of each tenancy. The net result is an increase in effort per acre, and hence total output, even though the tenant remains at his parametric reservation level. Selective, subsidized credit to tenants yields similar results.

That a program of "land to the tiller" will make the tenant better off is clear. Whether it will induce him to produce more output is not. Such a reform will increase the tenant's share (to unity) without a change in the size of the tenancy; so that, if the tenant does not reduce his effort, his consumption (income) will increase. Moreover, as the tenant's marginal returns to effort are now greater, there is a substitution as well as an income effect. Braverman and Srinivasan prove that effort (and hence output) will increase (decrease) if the elasticity of the marginal rate of substitution between consumption and leisure with respect to consumption is less (greater) than unity. If $U(\cdot)$ is separable in consumption and effort, the critical condition takes a form that is more easily grasped, namely that the elasticity of the marginal utility of consumption be unity.

It must be emphasized that these results may not survive the introduction of uncertainty. A good reason for this caution is that the redundancy between α and r would then vanish.

To close, it is worth noting that while governments often deplore interlinking as an instrument of exploitation in the hands of landlords or traders, they tacitly acknowledge its virtues where the operation of state agencies is concerned. The Reserve Bank of India (1954), for example, makes considerable play of the fact that cooperative societies would be more profitable if they were engaged in business related to lending, such as the provision of inputs and the marketing of outputs, which is interlinking by any other name.

4. Concluding remarks

Experience has made some of us less confident than we were that cheap and plentiful institutional credit is a completely satisfactory solution to the problems of households (firms) whose outlays and incomes are lumpy and uncertain. If private credit is dear and scarce, the first step is to establish why it is so; only then, is sensible prescription possible. There are several ways in which the government can reduce the lender's cost of doing business; and if market power keeps private credit dear, the government can attempt to encourage entry. In both cases, indirect intervention may be best. For example, public investments in rural infrastructure and policies which promote agricultural output may reduce lenders' costs and encourage entry far more powerfully and efficaciously than a volume or two of regulation. Thus, it is quite possible that well-functioning rural credit markets are a consequence rather than a cause of general development. In any event, it should now be clear that the extension of highly regulated, institutional banking services, which has been so vigorously prosecuted by governments, is not the sole means of realizing economic efficiency and distributive justice where dealings in credit markets are concerned.

Governments are unlikely to forsake this path entirely, however, so it is important that the associated policy be pursued in the right way. It is sometimes argued, for example, that the ills of the regulated institutions can be cured by the simple expedient of raising the rate of interest on their loans, as if credit were a commodity like wheat or milk. Theory warns against such a view and, in particular, the notion that excess demand for loans should necessarily be eliminated. That higher rates of interest may be beneficial for other reasons, for example, by reducing the subsidies received by the well-connected, by permitting regulated institutions to pay higher rates on their deposits and by improving their credit-worthiness in the eyes of their creditors, the central banks, is not in dispute. But as the rate of interest is not a sufficient statistic of the "price" of funds, one should not expect too much of it. What is needed is more work on the nature and consequences of competition between the regulated and unregulated sources of credit, with special attention to the kind of regulation that is employed.

Strategic default has had a prominent place in the analysis of this chapter. The closely related matter of tangible collateral has received less attention, and that of reputation scarcely none. While the literature provides a useful start in some respects, much remains to be done, especially in integrating the three. As for the role of asymmetries in information, I would place great importance on moral hazard, but rather little, in this context, an adverse selection. A rather different view emerges from Chapter 5 in this Handbook by Joseph Stiglitz.

Where interlinking is concerned, the available evidence suggests that far from being an exotic element of contract theory, it is a prominent feature of some rural economies and may be gaining in importance where commercialization is proceeding. Yet current evidence is so fragmented that the gathering of simple facts on the nature and incidence of interlinking in different regions would make a valuable contribution. The crucial evidence, however, will be much harder to win. To judge the effects of an interlinked contract, the full details of both its provisions and those of the unbundled alternatives are needed.'This is no mean task. Consider, for example, transactions in the credit and output markets. In an interlinked deal, the farmer may lose the option of when to sell. This is certainly costly; but then so too is trading in the spot market when there are no storage facilities in the marketing center. Establishing the net cost of the interlinked arrangement in this single respect alone demands painstaking and minutely detailed fieldwork by skilled investigators.

Where theory is concerned, the interlinking of credit and output needs more specific attention than it has received so far. First, price risks are of the essence here, so that the contingent possibilities are larger than in the case of credit-cum-tenancy. Secondly, the unbundled alternatives are complicated, for they involve the same sort of contingencies and must, therefore, be investigated thoroughly before some reservation level of utility is assigned to them. The extant evidence on the importance of this form of interlinking and its apparent tendency to grow stronger with commercialization warrants a careful theoretical appraisal.

We should be spared all this effort, of course, if we were to embrace the position that the existence of interlinking suffices to establish its efficiency; or, at the other extreme, that it provides a more efficient apparatus for the exploitation of the weaker party and should, therefore, be banned. The former should not be taken too seriously in a second-best world which is undergoing changes in market structure and economic organization. The latter, as a general prescription, is also misguided – to the extent that it is enforceable. Once again, the nexus between credit and output markets provides a telling example. A successful attempt to drive private traders and commission agents out of business through the operations of a state trading organization would almost certainly lead to a substantial contraction, if not collapse, of private credit to cultivators producing a marketed surplus. It is just possible, of course, that the cultivators would be better off dealing with a state monopoly. But before a government embarks on such an enterprise, one hopes for the cultivators' sakes that someone has investigated the relevant interlinked arrangements carefully – and then put the findings before the Cabinet. Here lie rich possibilities of unintended consequences of public policy, as well as important questions for empirical and theoretical research.

References

Adams, D.W. and Nehman, G.I. (1979) 'Borrowing costs and the demand for rural credit', *Journal of Development Studies*, 15:165–176.

Allen, F. (1985) 'On the fixed nature of sharecropping contracts', *Economic Journal*, 95:30–48.

Arrow, K.J. (1985) 'The economics of agency', Discussion Paper 451, IMSSS, Stanford University.

Bardhan, P.K. (1980) 'Interlocking factor markets and agrarian development: A review of issues', *Oxford Economic Papers*, 32:82–98.

Bardhan, P.K. (1984) *Land, labour and rural poverty: Essays in development economics*. New York: Columbia University Press.

Bardhan, P.K. and Rudra, A. (1978) 'Interlinkage of land, labour and credit relations: An analysis of village survey data in East India', *Economic and Political Weekly*, 13:367–384.

Bardhan, P.K. and Rudra, A. (1980) 'Terms and conditions of sharecropping contracts: An analysis of village survey data in India', *Journal of Development Studies*, 16:287–302.

Bardhan, P.K. and Rudra, A. (1981) 'Terms and conditions of labour contracts in agriculture: Results of a survey in West Bengal 1979', *Oxford Bulletin of Economics and Statistics*, 43:89–111.

Bardhan, P.K. and Srinivasan, T.N. (1971) 'Cropsharing tenancy in agriculture: A theoretical and empirical analysis', *American Economic Review*, 61:48–64.

Bardhan, P.K. and Srinivasan, T.N. (1974) 'Cropsharing tenancy in agriculture: A reply', *American Economic Review*, 64:1067–1070.

Basu, K. (1983) 'The emergence of isolation and interlinkage in rural markets', *Oxford Economic Papers*, 35:262–280.

Basu, K. (1984) *The less developed economy*. Oxford: Blackwell.

Bell, C. and Srinivasan, T.N. (1985) 'An anatomy of transactions in rural credit markets in Andhra Pradesh, Bihar and Punjab', World Bank, mimeo.

Bell, C. and Zusman, P. (1976) 'A bargaining theoretic approach to cropsharing contracts', *American Economic Review*, 66:578–588.

Bell, C. and Zusman, P. (1980) 'On the interrelationship of credit and tenancy contracts', World Bank, mimeo.

Bevan, J.W.L. (1956) 'A report on the marketing of smallholder's rubber with special reference to the first buyer level', Rubber Research Institute, Kuala Lumpur.

Bhaduri, A. (1973) 'Agricultural backwardness under semi-feudalism', *Economic Journal*, 83:120–137.

Bhaduri, A. (1977) 'On the formation of usurious interest rates in backward agriculture', *Cambridge Journal of Economics*, 1:341–352.

Bhaduri, A. (1979) 'Agricultural backwardness under semi-feudalism: A rejoinder to Srinivasan's comment', *Economic Journal*, 89:420–421.

Binswanger, H. and Rosenzweig, M. (1984) *Contractual arrangements, employment and wages in rural labor markets in Asia*. New Haven: Yale University Press.

Binswanger, H. and Rosenzweig, M. (1986) 'Behavioral and material determinants of production relations in agriculture', *Journal of Development Studies*, 22:503–539.

Binswanger, H., et al. (1984) 'Common features and contrasts in labor relations in the semi-arid tropics of India', in: Binswanger and Rosenzweig.

Binswanger, H., et al. (1985) 'Credit markets in rural South India: Theoretical issues and empirical analysis', World Bank, mimeo.

Bliss, C.J. and Stern, N.H. (1982) *Palanpur: The economy of an Indian village*. New Delhi: Oxford University Press.

Borooah, V. (1980) 'High interest rates in backward agricultural communities: An examination of the default hypothesis', *Cambridge Journal of Economics*, 4:265–269.

Bottomley, A. (1964) 'Monopoly profit as a determinant of interest rates in underdeveloped rural areas', *Oxford Economic Papers*, 16:431–437.

Bottomley, A. (1971). *Factor pricing and economic growth in underdeveloped rural areas*. London: Crosby Lockwood.

Bottomley, A. (1975) 'Interest rate determination in underdeveloped rural areas', *American Journal of Agricultural Economics*, 57:279–291.

Braverman, A. and Guasch, J.L. (1984) 'Capital requirements, screening and interlinked sharecropping and credit contracts', *Journal of Development Economics*, 14:359–374.

Braverman, A. and Srinivasan, T.N. (1981) 'Credit and sharecropping in agrarian societies', *Journal of Development Economics*, 9:289–312.

Braverman, A. and Stiglitz, J. (1982) 'Sharecropping and the interlinking of agrarian markets', *American Economic Review*, 72:695–715.

Cheung, S.N.S. (1969) *The theory of share tenancy*. Chicago: University of Chicago Press.

Collier, P. (1985) 'The allocation of factors in African peasant agriculture', mimeo.

Collier, P. and Lal, D. (1985) *Labour and poverty in Kenya: 1900–1980*. London: Oxford University Press.

Darling, M. (1925) *The Punjab peasant in prosperity and debt*. London: Oxford University Press.

Drèze, J. and Mukherjee, A. (1987) 'Labour contracts in rural India: Theories and evidence', Discussion Paper 7, Development Research Programme, London School of Economics.

Ghose, A.K. and Saith, A. (1976) 'Indebtedness, tenancy and the adoption of new technology in semi-feudal agriculture', *World Development*, 4:305–320.

Gonzalez-Vega, C. (1976) 'On the iron law of interest rate restrictions: Agricultural credit policies in Costa Rica and other less developed countries', Ph.D. dissertation, Department of Economics, Stanford University.

Griffin, K. (1974) *The political economy of agrarian change*. London: Macmillan.

Hallagan, W. (1978) 'Self selection by contractual choice and the theory of sharecropping', *Bell Journal of Economics*, 9:344–354.

Hart, G. (1986a) *Power, labor, and livelihood*. Berkeley: University of California Press.

Hart, G. (1986b) 'Interlocking transactions: Obstacles, precursors or instruments of agrarian capitalism?', *Journal of Development Economics*, 23:177–203.

Hart, O. and Holmstrom, B. (1985) 'The theory of contracts', presented at the Fifth World Conference of the Econometric Society, Boston.

Harriss, B. (1982) 'Money and commodities: Their interaction in a rural Indian setting', *Development Digest*, 20:16–23.

Holmstrom, B. (1979) 'Moral hazard and observability', *Bell Journal of Economics*, 10:74–91.

Holmstrom, B. (1983) 'Equilibrium long-term labor contracts', *Quarterly Journal of Economics*, 98(suppl.):23–54.

Hossain, M. (1985) *Credit for the rural poor: The Grameen Bank in Bangladesh*, Research Monograph 4. Dhaka: Bangladesh Institute of Development Studies.

Jodha, N.S. (1978) 'The role of credit in farmer's adjustment against risk in arid and semi-arid tropical areas in India', Occasional Paper 20, ICRISAT, Andhra Pradesh.

Jodha, N.S. (1984) 'Agricultural tenancy in semi-arid tropical India', in: Binswanger and Rosenzweig.

Jones, W.O. (1980) 'Agricultural trade within tropical Africa: Achievements and difficulties', in: R.H. Bates and M.F. Lofchie, eds., *Agricultural development in Africa: Issues of public policy*. New York: Praeger.

Ladman, J.R. and Adams, D.W. (1978) 'The rural poor and the recent performance of formal financial markets in the Dominican Republic', *Canadian Journal of Agricultural Economics*, 26.

Lipton, M. (1976) 'Agricultural finance and rural credit in poor countries', *World Development*, 4:543–554.

Marshall, A. (1920) *Principles of economics*. London: Macmillan.

Mitra, P. (1983) 'A theory of interlinked rural transactions', *Journal of Public Economics*, 20:169–191.

Newbery, D.M.G. (1974) 'Cropsharing tenancy in agriculture: A comment', *American Economic Review*, 64:1060–1066.

Newbery, D.M.G. (1975) 'Tenurial obstacles to innovation', *Journal of Development Studies*, 11:263–277.

Newbery, D.M.G. (1977) 'Risk sharing, sharecropping and uncertain labor markets', *Review of Economic Studies*, 44:585–594.

Newbery, D.M.G. and Stiglitz, J.E. (1979) 'Sharecropping, risk sharing and the importance of imperfect information', in: J.A. Roumasset, et al., eds., *Risk, uncertainty and agricultural development*. SEARCA: A.D.C. Publication.

Nisbet, C.T. (1967) 'Interest rates and imperfect competition in the informal credit markets of rural Chile', *Economic Development and Cultural Change*, 16:73–90.

Oi, W.Y. (1971) 'A Disneyland dilemma: Two-part tariffs for a Mickey Mouse monopoly', *Quarterly Journal of Economics*, 85:77–96.

Raju, P.T. and von Oppen, M. (1980) 'Market channels for selected crops in semi-arid tropical India', Economics Program, Progress Report 16, ICRISAT, Andhra Pradesh.

Rao, J.M. (1980) 'Interest rates in backward agriculture', *Cambridge Journal of Economics*, 4:159–168.

Rao, J.M. (1986) 'Agriculture in recent development theory', *Journal of Development Economics*, 22:41–86.

Rao, T.V.S. and Subrahmanyam, E.V.R.S. (1985) 'Interlocking of credit and product markets and its impact on agricultural productivity', World Bank, mimeo.

Reserve Bank of India (1954) *All-India rural credit survey*, Vols. I–III. Bombay: Reserve Bank of India.

Reserve Bank of India (1977) *Indebtedness of rural households and availability of institutional finance*. Bombay: Reserve Bank of India.

Rothschild, M. and Stiglitz, J.E. (1970) 'Increasing risk I: A definition', *Journal of Economic Theory*, 2:225–243.

Rudra, A. (1984) 'Local power and farm-level decision-making', in: M. Desai, S.H. Rudolph and A. Rudra, eds., *Agrarian power and agrarian productivity in South Asia*. Berkeley: University of California Press.

Shavell, S. (1979) 'Risk sharing and incentives in the principal and agent relationship', *Bell Journal of Economics*, 10(1):55–73.

Srinivasan, T.N. (1979) 'Bonded labour contracts and incentives to adopt yield-raising innovations in semi-feudal agriculture', *Economic Journal*, 89:416–419.

Stiglitz, J.E. and Weiss, A. (1981) 'Credit rationing in markets with imperfect information', *American Economic Review*, 71:393–410.

Von Pischke, J., et al. (1983) *Rural financial markets in developing countries*. Baltimore: Johns Hopkins University Press.

Wharton, C.R. (1962) 'Marketing, merchandising, and moneylending: A note on middlemen monopsony in Malaya', *Malayan Economic Review*, 7:24–44.

Zusman, P. and Bell, C. (1985) 'The equilibrium set of pairwise-bargained agency contracts with diverse actors and principals owing a fixed resource', Giannini Foundation, University of California, mimeo.

INDEX

Abidjan (Ivory Coast), 428
Ability: factor in earnings function, 580; and returns on education, 587; and screening, 582–584
Abramovitz, M., 254
Abramovitz–Solow–Denison effect, 254
Accumulation, 225–228; defined, 225
Adams, D.W., 767, 794
Addis Ababa (Ethiopia), 428
Adelman, I., 239
Africa, 492; agriculture in, 286, 292, 309–310, 328; city growth in, 428; education in, 546, 568, 574, 576, 607; income and fertility rate in, 516, 525; population growth in, 496–497; social returns on education in, 586; sub-Saharan region, 337, 339–340, 483, 531; urban migration in, 751; urban–rural remittances in, 433. *See also* East Africa; South Africa, West Africa
Agarwala, R., 181, 442
Age: and migrant selectivity bias, 430–431; in population growth models. 489; and the self-employed, 596
Aghazadeh, I., 181
Agricultural dualism, and family enterprise model, 728–733
Agricultural transformation, 276–328; decision-making in, 292–294; development strategy, 321–328; and economic development, 283–288; evolving stages, 280–283; farm household of, 299–300; growth and decline of, 276–279; micro–macro links in, 316–319; process of, 279–291; production functions, 294–299; resources for, 319–320; role of agriculture section, 288–291; sources and dynamics of, 302–313; unresolved issues of, 313–321; why agriculture is different, 291–302
Agriculture: advantages of development in, 151–152; alternative strategies for, 323–327; and balanced growth, 83–86; and concept of dualism, 75, 76; education and productivity of farmers, 597–598, 617; effect of institutions on, 45; household in, 299–300, 395; implications of distinctiveness, 300–302; and individual incomes, 240; and industry, 201, 276–277; labor market in, 714; as limit to urban growth, 450; Marx and critics on, 174–178; moves against growth of, 347;

nationalization of, 151; nutrition and labor productivity, 683; and organizational dualism, 80–82; place of in economy, 313–314; and population growth, 492; products of closed dualism, 76–80; risks in, 297–299; seasonality in, 295–296; share of employment in, 241, 257; wage gaps in, 434
Ahluwalia, I.J., 167, 358
Ahmedabad, 436, 447, 448
Aigner, D., 360
Akerlof, G., 50, 51
Akin, J.S., 661
Alderman, H., 677, 693
Algeria, 241, 483
Allen, F.: on interlinking, 801–802; on sharecropping, 120
Amman (Jordan), 428
Anderson, K.H., 597
Andhra Pradish (India), moneylending in, 792, 793, 794
Anthropometric data: in health measurement, 650–651; and labor productivity, 685, 686–687; and morbidity, 668; and mortality, 667–668; and schooling productivity, 688–689
Approaches to development: Marxist, 4–5; neoclassical, 3–4; structuralist, 5
Approaches to development economics, 39–68; economic policy and the state, 40, 63–66; income distribution and growth, 40, 51–57; institutions and resource allocation, 40, 45–51; Marxist, 40, 45; neoclassical, 40, 41–45; structuralist-institutionalist, 40; theory of the household, 40, 57–62; trade and development, 40, 57–62. *See also* Marxism; Neoclassical development economics
Argentina, 46, 181
Arida, Persio, 8, 61, 161–194, 199
Aristotle, 16, 19
Arrow, K.J., 4, 155, 359, 475, 765
Arroyave, G., 685
Arthur, B., 50
Asia: agriculture in, 286, 306–308; education in, 586; family planning in, 519; urban–rural remittances in, 433. *See also* East Asia; South Asia; West Asia
Atkinson, A.B., 369
Australia, agriculture in, 285, 308, 312
Austria, 481

Bacha, E., 55, 58, 61, 167, 172
Baer, W., 366
Bairagi, R., 667
Bairoch, P., 286, 304, 306, 310; on city growth, 428, 439
Balanced growth: consequences of abandoning, 90; and economic dualism, 83–86; and population, 85; and trade, 88–90
Balassa, B., 182, 235, 345
Baldwin, R., 684
Bangkok (Thailand), 596
Bangladesh, 292, 306, 483, 492; Bank of, 790; health in, 669; nutrition in, 676, 682, 690; population growth in, 500, 517, 519, 521, 525, 531
Bankruptcy, 805–806
Banks and institutions, role of in credit markets, 787–791; 795, 826
Baran, P., 58, 180
Bardhan, Pranab, 6, 39–71, 52, 60, 64, 727; on interlinking in India, 795, 798, 806, 816; labor recruitment model of, 728, 734, 736, 737
Barnum, H.N., 638, 719
Barrera, A., 605
Barro, R.J., 401, 412
Bartel, A., 638
Bartlett, W., 177
Basu, K., 165, 745–746, 767, 768; on credit markets, 778–779, 801
Bates, R.H., 326
Batina, G., 522
Bauer, P., 212
Baumol, W.J., 176
Becker, G.S., 42, 532, 577, 585
Behrman, J.R., 229, 434, 472, 500, 631–711; on fertility behavior, 509; on the self-employed, 596
Bell, Clive, 49, 763–830; on credit markets in LDCs, 474–475, 775, 793, 794, 796; on rural labor markets, 734, 736–737; on sharecropping, 741; on tenancy contracts, 742, 810, 822, 823
Bentham, Jeremy, 522
Bequests, influence on savings, 400–401, 409
Berg, A.D., 654
Bergsman, J., 348
Berry, A., 386, 439
Betancourt, R.R., 387
Bevan, J.W.L., 795
Bhaduri, A., 767, 768; on credit markets, 778, 780, 813–814
Bhagwati, J., 61, 263, 266, 344; on growth in large countries, 358; on TFP growth, 352
Bhalla, S.S., 387, 388, 396, 411
Binswanger, H.P., 104, 300; on complexity of rural decision-making, 315–316; on credit

markets, 768, 781, 792, 793; on plantations, 736
Biological–chemical innovations, 303–304; region of use, 312
Birdsall, J.R., 434, 500
Birdsall, Nancy, 470–471, 472, 526; on health care, 662
Births, 644–645
Black, R.E., 668
Blau, D.M., 661, 669–670
Blinder, A.S., on savings, 385, 392, 409
Bliss, C.J., 52, 644, 683; on Indian credit markets, 792–793, 795–796; on nutrition-based efficiency model, 720, 725
Bocock, P., 340
Boeke, 74
Bogota (Colombia), 428, 441
Boissiere, M., 587
Bongaerts, J., 689, 690
Borooah, V., 778
Borrowing: in LDCs, 392–394; and savings, 409–410. *See also* Credit markets
Boserup, E., 43, 492
Botswana, 752
Bottomley, A., 767, 768; on credit markets, 770, 775, 778, 794; on interest rates, 782
Boulier, B.L., 512, 521
Boutras–Ghali, Y., 172
Bowles, S., 51, 52
Bradley, D.J., 668
Brain drain: and educational policy, 613; and migration, 431–433
Braverman, A., 122, 148; model for tenancy and credit, 803–806, 814, 821–822, 825
Brazil, 12–13, 59, 179, 351, 448; agricultural growth in, 301; education in, 613; health in, 662; industrialization in, 337, 338, 339, 347, 348; low productivity in, 357; nutrition in, 676, 677, 693; population growth in, 500; production of cars, 188; rural–urban migrants in, 601; wage gaps in, 435
Breast feeding, and mortality, 668–671
Brenner, R., 50
Britain, 211, 218, 226; agriculture in, 285, 292, 309; role of services in, 460. *See also* England
Brown, Lester, 319–320
Bruno, M., 172
Buffie, E., 54, 167
Bukharin, N.I., 172
Burma, 59, 240
Burns, A.F., 188

Cain, M.T., 502, 517
Calcutta, 427
Calories: income elasticity for, 675–676; and labor productivity, 684–687

Calvo, G.A., 748
Cambodia, 266
Canada, 210, 308, 312, 754
Canavese, A., 170
Cantillon, Richard, 28, 34, 35
Capital: barriers to flow of, 146; foreign, 414, 451; human, and education, 577, 579, 581–582; human vs. physical, 395, 548–549; and lack of financial intermediaries, 144–146; shortage of in LDCs, 142–143; through saving, 382
Capital (Marx), 173
Capital formation, Kuznets on, 226
Capital market, constraint on mobility, 745–746
Capitalism, and Marx on unemployment, 174
Cardoso, F.H., 59, 170, 186
Carnoy, M., 588
Cavallo, D., 185, 186
Chad, 312
Chakravarty, S., 167
Chandhri, R., 683
Chayanov, A.K., 175, 729
Cheetham, R., 175, 215, 449
Chemicals, 243
Chen, L.C., 667
Chenery, Hollis B., 60, 179, 228, 242, 354; on agriculture, 276, 317; on basis for comparative analysis, 217; on growth, 212; on interindustry relations, 231; on savings and investment, 226; on structural change, 197–201, 208, 214, 342; two-gap model of, 172; on typology, 214; on use of models, 220, 237
Chernichovsky, D., 668
Cheung, S.N., 116
Chichilinsky, G., 177, 178
Child schooling, and fertility behavior, 515–516, 533. *See also* Education
Childhood, savings and dependency in, 404
Children: effect on savings, 405–407; health of, 699. *See also* Fertility; Health
Chile, 306, 387, 414, 415; credit markets in, 793, 794
China, 12–13, 181, 292, 483; birth rate in, 481; education in, 689; life expectancy in, 483; population growth in, 492, 527
Chomitz, K.M., 526
Chowdhury, A.K.M.A., 690
Chu, S.F., 360
Chuhan, P., 662
Cipolla, C.M., 336
Circular flow: in Schumpeter's theory of development, 163–164; other versions of, 164; structuralists on, 184
Cities: employment in, 439–441; limitations on growth of, 450; numbers of migrants to, 437–439; service sectors in, 440–441, 442, 460; and urban bias, 441–442. *See also* Urbanization

Clague, C., 359
Clark, C., 198, 213; on agriculture, 276, 288, 325
Clark, C.A.M., 668
Clark, P.B., 167
Climate, effect of variability in, 391–392. *See also* Seasonality
Coale, A.J., 489–490, 495, 524
Cobb–Douglas production function, 143, 310, 366, 562, 680, 685, 686, 821
Cochrane, S.H., 514, 609
Cole, W.C., 748
Cole, W.E., 446
Collateral, 778–782, 827; uses of, 768–769. *See also* Credit markets
Colombia, 387, 447, 481, 483; credit markets in, 794; earnings in, 599–601; education in, 607, 702; fertility in, 692; migration in, 753; nutrition in, 695
Commodities, primary and structural change, 259–260
Commodity markets, non-existence factor in underdevelopment, 7
Comparative analysis: basis for, 216–217; level of, 219–220; methodology of, 218–221; models vs. description, 220–221; in structural transformation, 216–223; time-series vs. cross-section, 221–223
Computable General Equilibrium (CGE), models for migration and city growth, 453–455
Congo, 241
Consumers: demand and relative prices, 259; durables, and saving, 387
Contraception: alternatives, 525; and education, 515, 608–609; in models of fertility behavior, 508, 509; and nutrition, 690; and size of population, 521. *See also* Fertility
Corden, W.M., 171, 443
Corporation, savings of, 411–412
Cortes, M., 340
Cost sharing, 122–123
Costa Rica, 481, 483
Crafts, N.F.R., 226, 239, 257
Credit: and savings, 393–394; and strategic default, 771, 777–778, 785, 787, 804, 827
Credit contracts, 769–782; differences in, 767–768; formulae for, 769–772; moral hazard and incentives, 774–778; pure screening, 772–774; usury and alienation of collateral, 778–782
Credit markets, 763–830; characteristics of, 766; credit contracts, 769–782; credit terms, 791, 793–794; evidence concerning, 791–797; and the government, 156, 412; innovation and interest rate, 782–783; and interlinked transactions, 797–826; and market structure, 791, 794–795; and other markets, 791,

795–796; public policy on, 783–791, 826; recurring themes in research on, 765–766; sources of funds, 791–793

Crimmins, E., 510

Crops, research for, 303–304

Cross-country studies, 228–229, 239; of fertility behavior, 512–513; of health and nutrition, 633, 672–674; of labor productivity, 687–688; of role of exports in growth, 356–357; of savings, 413

Culter, P., 654

Cultural milieu, as factor in economic growth, 267

Culture, and estimates of health, 652

Daniels, M.R., 359

Darling, M., 767, 768, 795, 797

Dasgupta, P., 94, 720, 724

Da Vanzo, J., 669

Deaton, A., 385

Debreu, G., 4, 155, 475

De Ferranti, D., 696, 703

De-industrialization, 239, 241

De Janvry, A., 44, 46, 54, 167; on agriculture, 287–288

Delgado, H., 690

Della Valle, P.A., 417

Demand: in developing economy, 211; functions, in health, 667

Demeny, P., 493, 530

Demographic Transition, 690–691

Demography: and national education systems, 551; and population growth, 531; recent changes in, 479–483; and synthesis model of fertility, 506–507

Denison, 254, 350, 355, 491

Denmark, 309

Deolalikar, A.B., 229, 472, 631–711

Desai, P., 358

Deutsch, J., 242

Developed economy: domestic determinants of productivity growth in, 351–352; role of industrial productivity in, 346–347; as stage of transformation, 246–248

Developing countries. *See* Less developed countries (LDCs)

Development: analytics of, 74–91; approaches to, 39–71; and education, 544; Marxist approach, 4–5; neoclassical approach, 3–4; and population growth, 529–535; role of agriculture in, 283–288; and saving, 381–419; Schumpeter on, 163–165; strategy for agricultural, 321–328; structuralist view of, 5

Development, concept of: early treatment of, 10–11; freedom and capability, 16–18;

functionings, 15–16; growth and development, 12–15 values, 20–23; weights and rankings, 18–20

Development economics: approaches to, 3, 5, 6, 39–68, 197, 205; broad view of, 162; defined, xi, 205; questions facing, 94–95; structural change in, 206, 211–214

Development process, 142–153; development strategies, 150–153; factor supplies, 142–147; impact of health and nutrition on, 636; role of government in, 153–156; technical change and entrepreneurship, 147–149

Development strategies, 150–153; innovators and imitators, 150–151; methods of learning, 151–153

Development theory, 27–37; background, 28; effect of organization, 34–36; overall balance, 31–34; sectoral imbalance, 28–31

Diamond, P., 406

Diaz-Alejandro, C., 359

Differential productivity model, 263

Disequilibrium, concept of, 207–208

Distribution, and GNP, 13–14

Dixit, A., 83, 175

Dobb, M., 56

Domar, E., 173

Domestic resource cost (DRC), 338, 347–348; in large countries, 357–358

Donald, 767

Drèze, J., 796

Dualism, 74–91, 211; and balanced growth, 83–86; defined, 74; intersectoral markets in closed economy, 77–80; modern analytics of closed, 76–86; in open economy, 86–91; organizational, 80–82, 86; place in economic history, 75–76

Duncan, G.J., 386

"Dutch disease", 90–91, 171, 182, 200, 241; in rural areas, 318

Dutt, A., 54, 166, 176, 185

East Africa, credit markets in, 797

East Asia: agriculture in, 44, 285, 328; city growth in, 428; industrialization in, 339, 371; ISI in, 349; labor policies in, 351; level of education in, 355, 546, 574, 576; population growth in, 483

Easterlin, R.A., 508, 510

Eckaus, R., 74, 177, 178, 188, 366, 594, 602

Economics: concept of dualism in, 75–76; growth and economic development, 12–15; orthodox vs. development, 40. *See also* Organization, economic

Economics of Welfare (Pigou), 19–20

Economist, 181

Ecuador, 387

Edirisinghe, N., 694
Education: alternative models of, 577–585; and
    asset choice, 394–396; conclusions concerning,
    615–617; and disincentives for population
    growth, 527; effect on saving, 309, 495; effect
    on transformation, 355, 364; financing of, 614;
    interactions with returns from, 605–606; and
    labor supply, 591–593; male–female return on,
    610–615; and migration, 436, 745; national
    systems of, 550–577; and nutrition, 678,
    688–689; and occupational choice, 593–597;
    and parental status, 587–589; and population
    growth, 497–499; private rate of return, 585,
    589–590, 602, 613; and productivity of
    farmers, 597–598; public policy on, 610–615;
    rates of return, 471, 575, 585–607; and skilled
    labor, 147; social rate of return, 585, 613;
    social value of, 471–472; and student ability,
    587; of women and fertility rate, 505, 509, 513,
    514, 533. *See also* National educational
    systems
Effective rate of protection (ERP), 338; and
    growth, 344–345, 348
Efficiency Wage Hypothesis, 683
Efficiency wage theories, 7–8, 129–131
Egypt, 241, 267, 308, 725; food subsidy in, 693,
    696; industrialization in, 337, 338; labor
    markets in, 732; tenancy contracts in, 739,
    741; TFP in, 363–364
Eicher, C.K., 315
Ellman, M., 172
Elster, J., 41–42
Emmanuel, A., 56, 58
Employment: and choice of technology, 366–369;
    creation of in manufacturing sector, 365–371;
    family enterprise model, 728–733; surplus
    labor, 715–728; and wage determination in
    rural labor markets, 715–733
Enforcement, in credit markets, 801–803
Engel, Ernst, 42, 187, 209, 213, 219, 335; on
    imperialism, 58; on consumption, 209
Engel's Law, 86, 165, 197, 216, 231, 297; and
    agriculture, 279; effects of, 251, 452, 459, 733
Engels, Friedrich, 426, 427; age of migrants in,
    431
England: agricultural revolution in, 276; birth
    rates in, 481; fertility behavior in, 517–518; in
    Malthusian theory, 487; manufacturing in, 426;
    urban growth in, 429–430, 448; wage gaps in,
    434, 435. *See also* Britain
English Corn Laws, 169; Malthus on, 170;
    Ricardo on, 170
Enke, S., 489
Entitlements, and fertility rates, 526–527
Entrepreneurs, Schumpeter on, 163
Environment, and population growth, 496–497

Equilibrium, concept of, 207–208
Equilibrium contracts, 117–118; efficiency of,
    123–124; extensions of theory, 118–119; and
    government policies, 140; non-competitive,
    121–122; uniformity in, 119–121
Equivalency theorem, 116–117, 122
Eswaren, M., 44–45, 737–738; tenancy model,
    740, 742
Europe: agricultural productivity in, 309; fertility
    decline in, 501
European Economic Community (EEC), 309
Evans, D., 181
Evenson, R.E., 679–680
Exchange-rate conversions, 262–265
Exchange-rate deviation index (ERD), 263
Exports: effect of growth in, 345; and growth
    rate, 183, 356–357; from light industry, 235;
    Smith on, 29; substitution of, 89–91
Externality, and GNP, 14

Fable of the Bees, The (Mandeville), 32
Factor-market distortions, 369–370
Factor supplies: barriers to flow of capital, 146;
    capital shortage, 142–143; and the
    development process in LDCs, 142–147;
    financial intermediaries, 144–146; in
    industrialization, 338–340; in schools, 571;
    undersaving, 143–144
Family: decisions on size of, 497–499; defined,
    469fn; and education, 605–606; effect of
    planning for, 489–490, 501; and intrafamily
    data, 670, 677; as labor market, 714–715; 718;
    in low-income urban settings, 756; in
    Malthusian theory, 486; model for family
    enterprise, 728–733; and population growth,
    493; and saving, 382, 401–403; and school
    quality, 590. *See also* Fertility
Family organization, 105–115; family-welfare
    models, 105, 106–112; household as a market,
    105; hybrids, 105, 114–115; market-oriented,
    112–114; and property rights. *See also*
    Household
Family planning, 489–490, 501; and education,
    606; and fertility, 519–521, 526, 533–534
Fane, G., 598
Farrell, M.J., 63, 360
Feder, G., 356
Fei, J.C.H., 175, 215, 288, 335; on industrial
    sector employment, 366; on motivation for
    migration, 449, 716; on rates of growth, 346
Feldman, G.A., 57, 173
Feldstein, N., 227
Fertility: determinants of, 501–523; economic
    models of fertility behavior, 503–512; and
    education, 605–606; empirical studies of,
    512–521; endogenous, and optimal population

size, 522; family decisions on, 469, 470, 475; and family planning, 519–521, 526; and female nutrition, 689–690; and health care, 663; and income distribution, 499–501; and market failure, 525–526; and nutrition, 678; and population growth, 478, 481, 483, 497; and savings, 495; and school expenditures, 571; and welfare policies, 523–529
Feudalism, transition from, 50
Fields, G.S., 147, 339, 351, 584, 748
Findlay, R., 60, 172, 443
First Industrial Revolution, and urban growth, 429–430
Fisher, A.G.B., 213
Fishlow, A., 261
Fleming, J.M., 165
Folbre, N., 512
Foley, D., 188
Food: in measurement of health, 658–659; price of, 260–261; prices and nutrient demand, 676–677; subsidies for, 692–696; world crisis in, 314. *See also* Nutrition
Food consumption, decline in GNP share during industrialization, 231
Foreign exchange, relation to growth, 30
Foreign trade, increase in, 224
Foster, S.O., 668
France, agriculture in, 285, 309
Friedman, M., 388
Friedmanites, 184
Frisch, R.E., 689
Fry, J., 750
Fry, M.J., 416
Functionings: and the better life, 15; and characteristics of commodities, 16; and capability, 17; freedom to choose, 16–18; refined, 18; weights and rankings, 18–20
Fundamental Theorem of Welfare Economics, 152
Furtado, C., 167

Gambia, 690
Gang of Four, 319, 340, 353, 371
Geertz, C., 44
Genetics, and health, 659
Geographic mobility: basic model of migration, 744–745; constraints on, 745–746; and heterogeneity, 753–754; risk, remittances, and family behavior, 751–753; and rural labor markets, 743–754; two-sector unemployment equilibrium models, 746–751
Geography, role of in agriculture, 296–297. *See also* Seasonality
Gerschenkron, A., 188; on factors for industrialization, 338–339; on paths of development, 210; on substitutability, 217

Gerschenkron effect, 260
Gersovitz, Mark, 219, 220, 381–424
Ghana, 792, 796
Ghodake, R.D., 734
Giovannini, A., 185, 385
Glover, D.R., 491
Gorman, W.M., 16
Government in agriculture, 294, 298–299, 320–321, 325, 328; consequences of policies, 140–142; as coordinator, 154–155; and credit markets, 826; and education, 586, 606, 610–615; and employment, 369; on fertility, 523; food subsidies, 692–696; impact of intervention, 344; in low-income labor markets, 714; and information problems, 155–156; role of in 18th century, 35–36; and savings, 412–413; in technical change for agriculture, 303. *See also* Public policy
Grameen Bank, 790
Granger, C.W.J., 350
Green Revolution, 484
Greenhalgh, S., 403
Gregory, P., 440
Griffin, C., 603
Griliches, Z., 587, 588–589, 597
Gross national product (GNP): and development economics, 12; distribution of, 13–14; and education, 553, 555, 610–611; inadequacy of, 14–15; investment vs. food consumption, 231
Growth, patterns of, 187–189; in agriculture and industry, 290, 301; demand-side, 250–254; effect of policy decisions on, 343–346; patterns of, 223–255; resources for, 319–320; sectoral contributions to, 244–248; and structural change, 197–199, 208, 210, 250–258; and stylized facts, 223; supply-side, 254–255. *See also* Development
Guasch, J.L., 821
Guatemala, 597, 668, 684
Gupta, K.L., 416

Habichi, J.P., 669
Haiti, 312
Hammer, J., 518
Handoussa, H., 363–364
Hanushek, E.A., 579
Harberger, A., 179–180
Harris, J., 584, 747
Harris–Todaro model, 141, 584, 747–749, 755
Harriss, B., 794, 797
Harrod–Dower formula, 173, 211, 212
Hart, G., 802
Hartwell, R.M., 209
Harvey, William, 31
Hawkins, D., 187, 188
Hay, J.M., 594

Hayami, Y., 215, 285, 288; on differences in productivity, 310–312, 327–328, 597; on history of agriculture, 306–310; model for agricultural productivity, 304–305, 306

Heady, E., 122

Health: changes in level of, 633–636; and contraception, 525, 533; cross-country studies of, 672–674; and education, 605, 608; as factor in productivity, 472; and investment, 495; measurement of, 650–653, 656–657; and migration, 436; and population growth, 497–499; questions for research, 702–704; and saving, 396–400, 409; studies on determinants of, 660–674

Health and nutrition: determinants of, 660–683; empirical studies of impact in LDCs, 683–692; and fertility, 689–690; full-income constraint, 645; future research on, 702–704; impact of macro adjustment policies on, 649–650, 697–698; measurement problems in, 650–660; model for, 638; production functions for, 640–645; reduced form demand relations, 646–648; and schooling productivity, 688–689; studies of supply considerations, 692–696; summary of studies, 698–701; and supplies, 649; theoretical framework for, 637–650

Health-care: demand functions for, 661–667; subsidies for, 696

Heckman, J.J., 588, 597, 604, 757

Heckscher–Ohlin model, 343, 345

Helminiak, T., 684

Herve, M.E.A., 366

Heston, A.W., 261

Hicks, J.R., 345

Hicks, N., 698

Hicks neutral shift factor, 356, 814

Higgins, B., 74

Higher education: and the brain drain, 613; costs of, 547

Hill, D.H., 386

Hirschman, A.O., 11, 66–67, 166, 178; on linkages, 210, 289; on population growth, 491

Hirschman hypothesis, 359–360

History, economic: structural change in, 209–211; and urban migration, 461

Ho, T.J., 667

Hobson, J.A., 182

Hoffmann, W.G., 213, 242

Hong Kong, 319, 340, 520. *See also* Gang of Four

Hooley, R.W., 414

Hoover, E.M., 489–490, 495, 524

Horioka, C., 227

Horton, S., 653, 664–665; cross-country studies of health, 672, 674; studies of nutrition, 681–682, 696

Hoselitz, B.F., 428; on overurbanization, 456–457; on urbanization, 439–440, 451

Hossain, M., 790

Hotz, V.J., 588, 757

Household: and credit markets, 792; decisions of, 470; defined, 469fn; on education, 549; in family enterprise model, 730; farm, 299–300; health and nutrition in, 637–640, 642–643, 644, 659–660; and measurement of health care, 663; non-market production in, and schooling, 607–610, 617; remittances of migrants to, 751–753; size of, and nutrition, 678, 680; surveys on savings of, 385–390; theory of, 6, 40–45; and uncertainty in saving, 390–392

Household demand model of fertility, 503–506; vs. synthesis model, 509–512

Housing: influence on migration, 450; in Third World cities, 428

Houthakker, H.S., 171, 227, 228; on Engel's law, 231

Hrubec, Z., 657

Huffman, W.E., 598

Hume, David, 28, 29–30, 32; on businessmen, 35; on money, 33–34; on wage level, 33

Hungary, 241

Imitation, vs. innovation, 150–151

Immink, M., 683–684

Import-substituting industrialization (ISI), 347–348, 349, 350

Imports: and economic dualism, 87–89; shift from exports, 91

Incentive-efficiency wage models, 129–131; reducing the amount of land, 129; reducing fixed payment, 130–131

Income: as determinant of saving, 388; and fertility rate, 504, 509–510, 512, 516–517; and migration, 745–746; and nutrient demand, 675, 700; and population growth, 482, 499, 501; and remittances from migrants, 751; and schooling, 576; share of agriculture in, 240; and welfare in interlinking, 816–823

Income distribution, 6; and aggregate savings, 407–411, 416, 417; and growth, 51–57; and high fertility, 499–501; long-run, 161–194; Marxists vs. neoclassicists on, 51–54; structuralists on, 54. *See also* Long-run income distribution

India, 59, 170, 178; agriculture in, 285, 290, 292, 310; city growth in, 453; credit markets in, 768, 791–796; family planning in, 520; fertility behavior in, 516, 609, 691; health care in, 664, 666; labor markets in, 732, 734; nutrition in, 654, 655, 668, 675, 676, 679, 685, 687, 700; and nutrition–wage efficiency theory, 725–727; population growth in, 483, 499, 521, 526; role of state in economic planning, 64–65; rural wage rates in, 743; savings in, 387, 396, 414; slow industrialization in, 166, 167, 337, 338; tenancy contracts in, 741, 742; urban employment in, 440

Indian National Sample Survey, 676

Indonesia, 279, 301, 308, 318, 483; health in, 670; industrialization in, 338; nutrition in, 675; rural labor markets in, 733; wage rates in, 725

Industrial Revolution: in England, 426, 429–430, 431, 434, 435, 460; and growth of dualism, 75–76

Industrialization: and agriculture, 281, 371; conditions preceding, 336–342; costs of protection, 347–348; employment creation in, 365–367; evolving studies of production, 342–346; impact of trade on, 346–358; micro studies of productivity, 358–365; as necessary stage, 94–95, 206; negative effects of, 335; policy on, 266–267; and rise in manufacturing, 251; as stage of transformation, 245–246; and trade, 334–372; and urbanization, 426, 440

Industry, vs. agriculture in economic transformation, 201

Industry and Trade in Some Developing Countries (Little, Scitovsky, and Scott), 179

Infant mortality, 669; and education, 607, 609; and fertility, 518–519, 533, 690–692, 701; in LDCs, 633, 662, 663; and seasonality, 679

Inflation: in models of circular flow, 168–169; tax for, 186

Information: and constraints on mobility, 745–746; in credit markets, 764, 768, 797, 827; and government, 155–156; and lack of capital, 145; problem for rural labor market, 734, 758

Information-theoretic approach to LDCs, 100–102, 156

Innovation: and education, 598; vs. imitation, 150–151; inappropriate, 149, 150; and interlinking, 813–816; and population growth, 491–493; resistance to, 148–149; in Schumpeter's theory, 163–164; as stage of development, 94

Institutional-historical approach to LDCs, 103

Institutions, and modern economic growth, 267–268. *See also* Banks

Insurance: children as, 517; by family, 402; by governments, 413; in rural context, 734; and saving, 382, 391

Interest: effect on saving, 385; government policies on, 826; in India, 793–796; and innovation, 782; rates of, 767. *See also* Credit contracts; Credit markets

Interindustry relations, 231

Interlinkage: causes of, 798–803; costs of, 798–799; in credit markets, 764, 767, 795–797,

797–803, 827; defined, 797–798; and innovation, 813–816; in LDCs, 102–103; moral hazard and incentives, 799–801; Nash bargaining solution, 810–813; and policy reforms, 823–826; screening, 801–803; of tenancy and credit, 803–809; welfare and income distribution, 816–823

International Comparisons Project (ICP), 261, 262, 673

International economy, function of in development, xi

International trade: and agriculture, 320–321; role of in industrialization, 341–342

Intersection technique; in value endogeneity, 22; in value heterogeneity, 20

Intertemporal productivity, 363–364

Investment: education as, 577; human capital theory of education as, 577, 580–582; post-schooling, on the job, 580; physical, and population growth, 494–495; rise during industrialization, 231; role of in developing economy, 212, 226; and savings, 410

Iran, 241, 739

Iraq, 241

Israel, 241, 266, 355

Italy, 231, 341, 351; agriculture in, 285, 286; production of cars, 188

Ivory Coast, 301, 605

Iyengar, N.S., 678

Izumi, Y., 339

Jamison, D.T., 597–598, 689

Japan, 62, 66, 215, 231; agriculture in, 44, 285, 292, 308, 312, 323, 325, 339; exports of, 235; fertility decline in, 501; industrial growth in, 177; labor productivity in, 258–259

Java, 292, 727. *See also* Indonesia

Jimenez, E., 697, 703

Jodha, N.S., 768

Johnson, D.G., 117, 282, 283

Johnston, B.F., 176, 280; on agriculture, 289–290, 324–325; "Johnston–Mellor environment", 282, 283, 284

Jones, W.O., 796

Jordan, 483

Jorgenson, D.W., 175, 290, 366, 449

Jung, W.S., 183, 357

Kakwani, N., 678

Kaldor, N., 169

Kalecki, M., 52, 165, 166, 169, 176

Kanbur, S.M.R., 60, 177

Kaneda, H., 177

Kannappan, S., 434, 447

Kaplan, S.L., 326

Katz, J.M., 351

Kelley, A.C., 175, 215, 387, 449; model for city growth, 454–455
Kendrick, D.A., 350, 471
Kenya, 301, 364–365, 495, 751; credit markets in, 792; educational policy in, 614
Keyder, C., 218
Keyfitz, N., 441, 455
Keumer, A., 668
Keynes, Maynard, 31; economic theory of, 184, 211, 224
Khaldi, N., 598
Khan, Q.M., 669
Kielman, A.A., 667, 668
Kim, Y.C., 353, 355
Kindleberger, C.P., 184, 215
King, Gregory, 10
Knight, J.B., 587
Korea, 267, 483, 520; agricultural productivity in, 308; exports from, 252; TFP in, 353, 357. *See also* South Korea
Kotlikoff, J., 752
Kotwal, A., 44–45, 737–738; tenancy model of, 740, 742
Kravis, I.B., 261, 262
Krueger, A.O., 180, 266, 352, 370
Krugman, P., 60
Kubisch, A., 698
Kuwait, 483
Kuznets, Simon, xi, 76, 86, 162, 177, 187, 205, 241–242; on accumulation, 226; on agriculture, 276, 285, 288, 297; on capital formation, 226; on cross-country studies, 228, 229, 239; on cross-section studies, 221; curve of income inequality, 257; on household nonmarket production, 549; on migration, 744; on policy, 265; on population growth, 478, 491, 499, 529; on prices, 261; research program of, 216–217; on savings, 416; on structural transformation, 198, 208, 342, 354; synthesis of modern economic growth, 213–214, 223; on use of models, 220
Kwon, J.K., 353

Labor: in agriculture, 241, 285, 304; creation of jobs for in LDCs, 365–371; and development, 7; and education, 558, 577, 591–593; and family organization, 107, 109; of farm household, 299–300; and management in agriculture, 294; and organizational dualism, 80–82; and productivity, 32, 358–359, 683–689, 701; relative productivity of, 256–257; skilled, 46–47; in urban labor markets, 442–448; and wages, 32–33
Labor markets: dual, 756–757; for education, 612–613; and fertility, 524; and geographic mobility, 743–754; labor contracts in rural,

733–743; in low-income countries, 714–759; measurements of, 584; summary of research on, 747–759; women in, 515, 603
Labor-tying arrangements, in agriculture, 48–49
Laborers, casual and permanent, 736–738
Lag structures, 350
Lagrange, Joseph Louis, 10
Laissez-faire, and Pareto optimum, 3–4
Land: and credit markets, 768, 789; economics of tenure, 35; effect of redistribution, 129; and labor, 739; ownership of, and migration, 746; productivity of, 304–306; tenancy contracts, 738–743; urban limits of, 450–451; and urban migration, 452, 457–458
"Land to the tiller," 823, 824–825
Landes, D., 211, 341
Landlessness: and migration, 746; and unemployment, 128, 129
Landlord–tenant relationship, 115–124; cost-sharing, 122–123; efficiency of market equilibrium, 123–124; equilibrium contracts, 117–118; equivalency result, 115–117; and innovation, 813–816; and interlinkage of markets, 133–134; and labor heterogeneity, 119; and moneylending, 795–796, 800–801, 803–809; outside wage opportunities, 118–119; public policy on, 823–826; and tenant contracts, 810–813; uniformity, 119–122. *See also* Sharecropping
Laos, 312
Lapham, R.J., 520, 521
Large countries, low productivity in, 357–358
Latin America, 66, 358, 448; agriculture in, 292; city growth in, 428; education in, 546, 568, 574–575, 576; labor in, 366; Marxism on agriculture in, 287–288; population growth in, 483; problems of industrialization in, 166, 167; social returns on education in, 586; theory of inflation in, 170; urban employment in, 440
Lau, L.J., 597–598, 638, 719
Lavoisier, Antoine, 10
Leff, N.H., 339, 415–416, 417
Leibenstein, H., 52, 348, 369, 487, 644, 683; on labor productivity, 683, 723
Leibowitz, A., 588
Lele, U., 178
Lenin, N., 43, 44, 58; on organization of production in agriculture, 176, 178, 286–287
Leontief, V., 188, 223, 229, 612
Leslie, J., 688
Less developed countries (LDCs): borrowing in, 393; choice of investment in, 395; conditions preceding industrialization in, 336–342; credit markets in, 745, 748; cross-country studies of saving in, 413–418; determination of fertility in, 502–523; development process in, 142–156;

disequilibrium in, 208–209; education in, 590, 610–615; empirical studies of health and nutrition in, 683–692; employment creation in manufacturing, 365–371; evolving structure of production in, 342–346, 371–372; food subsidies in, 692–696; health and nutrition in, 633, 652, 660–683; as imitators, 94; improvement in agriculture in, 310–312; industrial productivity in 346–347; industrialization in 334; information-theoretic approach to, 100–102; irrational-peasant hypothesis, 102–104; labor markets in, 714–759; neoclassical approach to, 96–100; population growth in, 479–483, 529; and public policy, 140–142; research on productivity in, 358–365; saving in, 382; subsidies in, 696–697; TFP in, 352–356, 358; theory of rural organization, 105–134; time-series vs. cross-section studies of, 221–222; transition from rural to industrial urban in, 205; urban sector of, 134–136. *See also* Third World

Lewis, Stephen, 348
Lewis, W. Arthur, xi, 6, 27–37, 44, 162, 165, 354, 366; on agriculture, 276, 279, 288; on dualism, 80, 81, 82; on investment, 212; labor surplus model of, 427; on Marx, 174–176; on manufacturing, 335; on motivation for migration, 449, 451, 715–716; on saving, 382; on sectoral differences, 213; on technological change, 371; on wage gaps, 434
Liberalization, effect of experiments in, 181–185
Liberia, 240
Libya, 241, 483
Life expectancy: cross-country studies of, 672–674; and GNP, 12–13; in LDCs, 633, 699; in measurement of health, 653
Limits to Growth (Meadows et al.), 470
Lin, W., 638
Linder, S.B., 233
Lindert, P.H., 500
Linkages: Bell on, 475; and structural change, 210–211. *See also* Interlinkage
Lipton, M., 441
Little, I.M.D., 61, 179, 260; on agriculture, 288; on structuralist view, 213
Living conditions: and freedom of choice, 17; and functionings, 15; and GNP, 12–15; as motivation for development, 11
Lluch, C., 175, 260
Loans. *See* Credit contracts
Lobdell, R.A., 432–433
Locke, John, 33, 34
Lockheed, M., 597
Long-run income distribution, 163–194; demand-driven models, 165–169; neoclassical

resurgence-trade, 178–184; patterns of growth, 187–189; resource limitations and reproduction, 169–174; Schumpeter's theory of, 163–165; structuralists vs. monetarists, 184, 187
Lopez, R., 733
Low, S.M., 652
Low-income countries, labor markets in, 714–759. *See also* Less developed countries
Lowenstein, M.S., 667
Lucas, R.E.B., 433, 752
Lunn, P.G., 690
Lustig, N., 54
Luxemburg, Rosa, 43, 58, 188

McCarthy, F.D., 183
MacCord, C., 667
McIntosh, J., 177
McKinnon, R.I., 144, 185
Maddison, A., 215, 241
Madras, 741
Magnani, R.J., 668
Mahalanobis, P.C., 57, 165; model of, 173; on capital, 212
Makali, 727
Malawi, 792
Malaysia, 59, 279, 301, 347, 447, 519; credit markets in, 795; education in, 581, 598; fertility in, 609, 692; family labor supply in, 719; health in, 669
Malenbaum, W., 687
Mali, 662
Malnourishment: and fertility, 689–690; measurement of, 654–655; and morbidity, 667; and mortality, 667–668, 700. *See also* Nutrition
Malthus, Thomas, 169, 170, 189; on fertility of household, 470, 501; on population growth, 75, 478, 486–490, 500; and Third World urbanization, 442, 452–453, 456; and urban decay, 426, 427
Mamalakis, M., 414, 415
Management: choice of, 153; and policy, 267
Manchester (England), 426, 427
Mandeville, Bernard, 32
Manufacturing: changes in during industrialization, 242–243; criticisms of results of, 334; as a sequence of phases, 252–254; shift of economy toward, 245–246, 251–252; and urban decay, 426; and urban growth, 457; and wage gaps, 434. *See also* Industrialization
Manufacturing production, redistribution of, 224
Mao (Tse-tung), 178
Marayana, 696
Margen, S., 655

Marglin, S., 52, 56
Market equilibrium, 136–140; special cases of, 138–140
Marriage, economic theories of, 502
Marshall, A., 806
Marshall, P.J., 183, 357, 491
Martorell, R., 667, 685
Marx, Karl, 15, 19, 23, 151, 173, 188; on imperialism, 58; on services, 460; shades of, 174–178
Marxism: on agriculture, 286–287; and development, 4–5, 6, 67–68; and imperialism, 58; on income distribution, 51–54, 55–56; on sharecropping, 48; on state and economic policy, 64, 65; and theory of household, 41–45; on trade and development, 57, 180
Mason, A., 416
Mason, E.S., 267
Mateus, A., 675–676, 695, 696, 703
Mauldin, W.P., 520, 521
Mauskopf, J., 691
Maximization, and the theory of the household, 40–41
Mayhew, H., 426
Mazumdar, D., 441, 644, 683
Meadows, D.H., 470
Mechanization, in agriculture, 295
Mellor, J.W., 178, 280; on agriculture, 289–290, 324–325
Menken, J., 689
Merrick, T.W., 662
Mexico, 12–13, 59, 279, 355; agricultural growth in, 301; education in, 588; liberalization experiments in, 181; low productivity in, 357; oil in, 318; population in, 483
Mexico City, 691
Middle-income countries, growth in, 224
Migrants: remittances from, 751–752; temporary, 751
Migration: and city growth, 449–459; and education, 598, 599–602; heterogeneity of, 753–754; motivation for, 435–437, 599; numbers of, 437–439; and property rights, 113–114; questions remaining, 459–461; and remittances, 113, 751–752; rural to urban, 96, 107–110; selectivity bias for, 430–433, 549; and urban wage, 136; and urbanization, 426–465. *See also* Geographic mobility; Third World; Urbanization
Miliband, R., 65
Mill, John Stuart, 522
Mincer, J., 532, 577, 579–580, 586, 591–592, 601
Minimum efficient size (MES), 349
Mirrlees, J., 105, 720
Mitra, A., 170, 805, 814
Mobility. *See also* Geographic mobility

Models: adaptation to empirical studies, 513; alternatives for education, 577–585; for changing agricultural productivity, 304–306, 326–327; Coale and Hoover, 489–490; conceptual limitations of, 509–512; for credit contracts, 772; of economic consequences of population growth, 484–486, 529; of educational system, 562–564, 616; family enterprise, 728–733; of fertility behavior, 503–509; future research for, 531; for health and nutrition, 638; household "demand", 503–506, 532; of Malthus, 486; for manpower needs of economy, 611–612; for migration, 744–745; for migration and city growth, 453–455; and problems with human capital, 580–582; on risks of agriculture, 734–735; structure of, 207; for surplus labor economies, 716, 717–720; synthesis, 506–509, 510, 532–533; tenancy and credit, 803–813; unemployment equilibrium, 746–751
Modigliani, F., 413, 415–416, 417
Monetarists: position of, 185; vs. structuralists, 184–187
Money: effect of on output, 33–34; structuralists on, 184; transition from metals to paper, 35. *See also* Credit contracts
Moneylenders: vs. banks, 787–791; costs of, 770; in India, 791–792, 794, 795; information of, 791; and public policy, 784; terms of, 771; views concerning, 767–768. *See also* Credit markets
Montgomery, M., 442
Moock, P.R., 688
Morbidity: and farm profits, 687; and malnourishment, 668; production functions and, 667; and seasonality, 679. *See also* Health and Nutrition
Morocco, 483, 676, 696
Morris, C.T., 239
Mortality: decline in, 481, 690–691; and income level, 483; infant, and fertility, 518–519; in measurement of health, 653; production functions governing, 640, 642, 667. *See also* Infant mortality
Mosher, Arthur, 280; environment of, 282, 283, 284
Mukherjee, A., 796
Multinational corporations (MNCs), 369
Musgrove, P., 387, 388
Myint, H., 89, 290
Myrdal, G., 66, 166

Nash bargaining solution, 810–813
Nasser, G.A., 289
National Bureau of Economic Research (NBER), 347, 352

National Council of Applied Economic Research
(NCAER), 387, 411
National educational systems, 550–577; cross-
sectional findings, 575–577; empirical
decomposition of expenditures, 564–568;
estimates of school expenditure equations,
568–571; model of, 562–564; regional patterns
in residuals, 573–575; sex differences in
enrollment, 571–573; and supply and demand,
557–562
National Research Council of the National
Academy of Sciences, 493, 530, 534
National savings, 403–418; aggregation over
cohorts, 404–407; corporate, 411–412;
evidence at aggregate level, 413–418; and
government, 412–413; income distribution and
aggregate savings, 407–411
Nationalization: of agriculture, 151; effect of
threat of, 146
Nehman, G.I., 794
Nehru, Jawaharlal, 289
Nelson, R.R., 356, 364, 487
Neoclassical development economics, 49, 50,
67–68, 211; on agriculture, 284, 288; approach
to policy, 267; on balance among sectors, 199;
on economic policy and the state, 63, 65; on
employment, 369; on income distribution,
51–54; and LDCs, 97–100; and Marx on
unemployment, 174–175; on population
growth, 487–488, 494; on trade and
development, 57, 61, 179–184; on theory of
household, 40–45, 284
Nepal, 688
Nerlove, N., 522
New Zealand, 212
Newbery, D., 740, 806
Newly industrializing countries (NICs), 339
Nicaragua, 240, 509, 596; health and nutrition
in, 661, 665, 669, 670, 675, 678
Nichols, W.H., 290
Nicolai-on, 54
Nicomachean Ethics (Aristotle), 16
Niger, 240, 241
Nigeria, 318, 712; industry in, 338
Nisbet, C.T., 793–794, 797
Nishimizu, M., 353, 363–364
Nkrumah, K., 289
North, D.C., 51, 64, 65
North America, population growth in, 478
Norway, 231
Noyola Vasquez, J.F., 170
Nogent, J., 518
Nurkse, R., 81, 165, 178; on consumer demand,
259; on sectoral differences, 213
Nutrients: demand for, 675–679; determinants
of, 674–683; and nutritional status, 653;

production functions, 679–680; questions for
research, 703
Nutrition: changes in level of, 633–636; and
health, 633, 671; measurement of, 653–656;
production functions of, 642, 644; and
productivity, 472–473; and saving, 396–400,
409; and surplus labor economies, 720–728.
See also Health and nutrition
Nutrition-based efficiency model, 720–728; tests
of, 725
Nutritional wage–productivity model in rural
unemployment, 125–129

O'Brien, P.K., 218
Ocampo, J.A., 58
Occam's Razor, 189
Occupation, choice of and education, 593–597
Oguchi, N., 417
Ohkawa, K., 215
Ohkawa thesis, 177
Oil: effect of imports of, 318; and urban
migration, 451
Okun, A.M., 49
Old-age security, and fertility behavior, 517–518
Olsen, R.J., 691, 692
Olson, M., 64
Organization, economic, 93–160; basic tenets,
96–104; development process, 142–156; and
government policies, 140–142; and market
equilibrium, 136–140; questions for, 94–95;
rural organization, 105–134; urban sector,
134–136
Organization of Petroleum Exporting Countries
(OPEC), 319, 428
*Origin of Family, Private Property and the State,
The* (Engels), 42
Output, and credit, 827
Overurbanization: future of, 456–457; meaning
of, 439–441

Pack, Howard, 181, 183, 201, 266, 333–380
Page, J.M., Jr., 363–364
Pakistan, 301, 308, 370, 483, 520; tenancy
contracts in, 739
Panama, 588
Papanek, G.F., 417
Papola, T.S., 448
Parental status, and returns on education,
587–589, 590
Pareto optimality, 3–4
Parikh, K., 188
Pasinetti, L.L., 187, 188
Patman, Wright, 185, 186
Patnaik, U., 176
Pawnbrokers, 794
Payne, P., 654, 655, 700

Peasants: and demography, 44; Marxism on, 43–44

Perkins, D.H., 222

Perroux, F., 166

Personal savings, 383–403; and bequests, 400–401; and borrowing, 392–394; education and asset choice, 394–396; and family, 401–403; and health and nutrition, 396–400; household surveys of, 385–390; simple model of individual saving, 384–390; uncertainty and, 390–392. *See also* National savings; Savings

Peru, 310, 387, 435, 525, 558

Petty, Sir William, 10, 28, 34

Philippines, 285, 301, 308, 310, 605; earnings of women in, 603–604; family planning in, 521, 609; health in, 661, 664–665, 668; low productivity in, 357, 364–365; nutrition in, 679–680, 684; sharecropping in, 741

Physiocrats: on agriculture, 288; and dualism, 75

Pigou, A.C., 19

Pinstrup-Andersen, P., 695, 696, 703

Pitt, M.M., 663–664, 670, 676–677; on health, 678, 687; on rural labor markets, 733

Polachek, S., 579

Policy. *See* Government policy; Public policy

Politics (Aristotle), 16

Popkin, B., 684

Population: and balanced growth, 85; economic approaches to, 477–521; growth and urbanization, 426, 453, 457–458; and rural–urban migration, 743; savings and changes in, 403–407, 415, 416

Population growth: conclusions concerning, 529–535; demographic changes, 479–483; and determinants of fertility, 501–502; Malthus and pessimists on, 486–490; methodology of future research on, 531, 534; models for, 484–486; optimists on, 490–493, 529; revisionists on, 493–501, 530; and rise in income, 482; and schools, 576; welfare policies and fertility, 523–529

Powell, A., 260

Prebisch, R., 74, 289

Prebisch–Singer effect, 259

Preobrazhensky, A., 56, 76, 169, 170, 171, 176, 189; on agriculture vs. industrialization, 260, 289

Preston, S.H., 428; on cross-country studies of health, 672–673; on health and nutrition, 697; on urban employment, 440; on urban growth, 429–430, 438, 455

Prices: changes in during development, 258; and exchange-rate conversions, 262–265; finding a "right", 182–183; and measurement of health, 657, 666–667; and nutrition, 699–700;

role of in agriculture, 294, 298. *See also* Relative prices

Primary production: shift to manufacturing, 251–252; as stage of transformation, 245

Primary schools, 547; expenditures per child in, 574; returns to women from, 604; sex differences in enrollment in, 572; vs. secondary, 567–568

Private schools, 555, 574

Production: domestic determinants of growth in, 351–352; evolving structure of, 342–346; household, 503; impact of policy intervention on, 344; nonmarket, and schooling, 607–610, 617

Productivity: and education, 545; micro studies of, 358–365; and sectoral reallocation, 355–356

Productivity, agricultural: and farmers' education, 597–598; historical record of, 306–310; model for, 304–306; and nutrition, 701; sources of differences in, 310–312

Property rights: and growth, 496–497; in market-oriented families, 113–114

Protection, and growth of productivity, 348–349

Proteins, and income elasticity, 675–676

Psacharopoulos, G., 604

Public policy: ceiling on interest rates, 785–787; on credit markets, 783–791, 823–826; on food subsidies, 692–696; on health and nutrition, 637, 677; questions for research, 703–704; and state-owned banks, 785, 787–791. *See also* Government policy

Pudassini, S.P., 598

Punjab (India), moneylending in, 792, 793, 794

Purchasing power parities (PPP), 262, 263

Pursell, G., 340, 357

Quesnay, Francois, 10, 31

Quigley, J.M., 579

Quisumbing, M.A.R., 169

Radhakishna, R., 676

Raju, P.T., 795

Rakshit, M., 414, 415

Ram, R., 385, 394, 416

Ramanathan, R., 387

Ramaswami, U.K., 61

Ranis, Gustav, 7, 73–92, 175, 215; on agriculture, 288; on approaches to typology, 248; on industrial sector employment, 366; on manufacturing, 335; on motivation for migration, 449, 715–716; on rates of growth, 346

Rao, J.M., 176, 778, 802

Rationality, factor in industrialization, 341

Ravenstein, E.G., 426

Ray, D., 720, 724

Razin, A., 522
Redford, A., 426
Relative prices, 259–262; consumer demand, 259; of food, 260–261; of investment goods, 261–262; of primary commodities, 259–260; of services, 262
Religion, as influence on status of women, 572–573
Remittances, urban–rural, 432–433, 751–752, 758
Rempel, H., 432–433
Research: agricultural, 302, 312; basis for comparative analysis, 216–217; on credit markets, 826–828; evolution of thought on agricultural, 313–315; diffusion of, 303; on fertility determinants, 531, 534; methodology of, 218–221; micro studies of production, 358–365; on population growth in LDCs, 484, 530–531, 534; problems in educational, 547–550, 586–587, 616; on productivity, 352–356; questions on health and nutrition, 636; on structural transformation, 216–223; time-series vs. cross-section, 221–223
Reserve Bank of India, 791, 793, 794, 797, 826
Resources: access to, and saving, 407; and agriculture, 290–291; allocation of, 6; effects of shifts in, 255–256; for growth and sustainability, 319–320; limitations and reproduction, 169–174; in Malthus model, 470; migration and transfers of, 449; and population growth, 496–497; reallocation of, 208–209, 257–258, 279
Reutlinger, S., 653, 654, 681
Reynolds, L.G., 290–291
Rhee, Y.W., 340, 357
Ricardo, David, 58, 75, 170, 263
Rice, and food subsidies, 694
Riley, J.G., 594
Rio de Janeiro (Brazil), 691
Risks: and credit contracts, 778–782, 827; family decisions on, 475; and migration, 752, 758; and rural labor markets, 734–735; and tenancy contracts, 739–740, 741–742
Robertson, 224
Robinson, C., 754
Robinson, Joan, 168
Robinson, S., 353
Roemer, J., 44, 178
Rogers, A., 431
Rosenstein-Roden, P.N., 165, 166, 178, 189; on sectoral differences, 213
Rosenzweig, M.R., 300, 647, 713–762; on credit markets, 781; on health care, 662–663, 666, 670, 702; on labor markets in LDCs, 473–474; on mobility, 741; on models of fertility behavior, 509, 515, 516, 521, 605, 692; on

nutrition, 677, 678, 687; on rural decision-making, 315–316, 401; on size of households, 499, 503
Ross-Larson, B., 340, 357
Rostow, W.W., 209, 212
Rothschild, M., 390, 773, 783
Rudra, A., 727, 767, 768; on interlinking in India, 795, 816
Rural labor, welfare of, 302, 304–305
Rural labor markets: casual laborers, 736–738; employment and wages, 715–733; labor contracts in, 733–743; models used for, 728, 733; permanent laborers, 736–738; tenancy contracts in, 738–743
Rural organization, theory of: and credit markets, 105; of the family, 105–115; rural section as a whole, 133–134; tenant–landlord relationship, 105, 115–124; unemployment, 125–132
Ruttan, V., 215, 288; on differences in productivity, 310–312, 327–328, 597; on history of agriculture, 306–310; model for agricultural productivity, 304–305, 306
Ryan, J.G., 685, 734
Rybezynski theorem, 167, 178, 344

Sabot, R.H., 439, 587
Sadka, E., 522
Sadoulet, E., 54, 167
Sah, R., 136, 142, 172, 289
St. Lucia, 684
Salter, W.E.G., 171
Samuelson, P.A., 406, 488
Sanders, J.H., 678
Sanders, R.D., 446, 748
San Jose (Costa Rica), 691
Saudi Arabia, 241
Savings: and accumulation, 225–226; barriers to flow of capital, 146; and development, 382; and lack of financial intermediaries, 144–146; in LDCs, 143–146; national, 403–418; personal, 383–403; and population growth, 494–495; problems remaining, 418–419. *See also* National savings; Personal savings
Saxonhouse, G.R., 339
Say's Law, 31
Schools: and nonmarket production, 607–610; quality of, and returns to, 589–591. *See also* Education; Primary schools; Secondary schools
Schultz, Paul, 471–472, 497, 543–630
Schultz, T.P., 543–630; on health care, 662–663, 666, 702; on infant mortality, 518–519, 691; on migration, 753; on models of fertility behavior, 509, 510, 515, 521, 524, 692; on nutrition, 678 ·

Schultz, T.W., 176, 394, 499, 605; on agriculture, 290, 321–322; on education as capital investment, 579; on liberalization of trade, 178; on life expectancy, 385; "Schultz–Ruttan environment", 282, 283

Schumpeter, J., 3, 5, 94; discussions of, 165–166, 169; on gains from trade, 180–181; followers of, 165; on technological change, 150; theory of development, 163–165

Scitovsky, T., 165, 179, 180–181, 260, 339

Scott, M., 179, 260

Seasonality: and agriculture, 295–296; and labor markets, 734; and nutrition, 678–679, 687

Seckler, D., 651, 655, 700

Secondary schooling: enrollment in, 576; expenditures for, 574; and fertility, 571; social rates of return for, 558; returns to women from, 604; sex differences in enrollment in, 572; vs. primary schools, 567–568

Sector proportions, changes in, 228–243; accounting framework, 230–231; in agriculture, 292; contributions to growth, 244–248; final demand, 231; intermediate demand, 231–232, manufacturing, disaggregated results, 242–243; post-war patterns, 239–242; and productivity growth, 355–356; and sectoral inclusiveness, 351; structure of production: broad sectors, 235–239; trade, 232–235; typology of developmental patterns, 248–250

Sectors: imbalance in, 29; and population growth, 494; transformation, in New Zealand, 212

Seiver, D., 515

Self-employed, the, wages and education of, 595–597

Selowsky, M., 653, 654

Sen, Amartya, 6, 9–26, 42, 56, 142, 176, 678; on agricultural labor markets, 716, 717, 725; on agricultural real wages, 82, 109; on nutrition, 678

Senegal, 240

Sengupta, S., 678

Seoul (Korea), 428

Services: informal vector in cities, 440–441, 442, 460; value of, 31

Sex differences: in employment, 734; in returns on education, 602–605, 617; in school enrollment rates, 571–573; in wages, 732, 743. *See also* Women

Shaban, R.A., 741

Shah, C.H., 654

Shanin, T., 43

Sharecropping, 7, 48; cost shares in, 122–123; in LDCs, 96, 102–103, 115–124; and interlinkage, 802, 823–826; persistence of, 119–122, 124;

and tenancy contracts, 739–741. *See also* Landlord–tenant relationship

Shaw, E.S., 185, 438

Shukla, V., 438

Sierra Leone, 675, 676, 685, 699, 719, 727

Simmons, A.B., 438

Simon, H., 176

Simon, Julian, 491, 492

Simultaneity, in health and nutrition studies, 658

Sinclair, S.W., 427–428

Singapore, 319, 340, 353, 527

Singer, H.W., 74

Singh, I., 638, 729, 732

Sismondi, 54

Sjaastad, L.A., 435–436

Skills, as necessary factor in industrialization, 339–340

Smith, Adam, 3, 10, 15, 19, 23, 28, 36; on businessmen, 35; on education as capital investment, 577; on LDCs, 97; on population growth, 491, 530; on sectoral imbalance, 29; on trade, 89; on value of labor, 30–31, 33

Smith, J.P., 581, 599

Sociometric data, in measurement of health, 650–651

Sociology, of fertility behavior, 511, 531

Soil erosion, 320

Solow, R.M., 8, 254, 350, 471

Somalia, 240, 241

Sommer, A., 667

South, the, as primary product exporter, 169, 171; wage gap in, 435

South Africa, 12, 418

South America, liberalization experiments in, 181. *See also* Latin America

South Asia: city growth in, 428; education in, 546, 574, 607; income and fertility rate in, 516; nutrition in, 678; remittances from migrants in, 751

South Korea, 59, 179, 319, 340, 355; agriculture in, 323; education in, 558, 598; on exports, 183; industrialization in, 337, 338, 339; protection in, 349; successes in, 353–355; trade and development in, 62, 65–66

Southern Cone of South America, 186

Soviet Union. *See* USSR

Spain, 359

Spivak, A., 752

Squire, L., 638, 719

Sri Lanka, 12–13, 301, 308, 483, 699; decline in mortality in, 481, 526; nutrition in, 694, 695

Srinivasan, T.N., 344, 358, 653, 700; on Indian credit markets, 793, 794, 796, 806, 813, 825; on labor markets, 734, 736–737; on tenancy contracts, 742, 823

Staatz, J.M., 315

"Stages approach", 209–210
Stalin, Josef, 172
Staples, and structural change, 210
Stark, O., 433, 438, 446, 752
State, the: economic policy and, 63–66; function of in development, xii, 3–4, 6; role in analysis of structural chance, 219
Steindl, J., 166
Stern, N.H., 52, 644, 683, 720, 725; on Indian credit markets, 792–793, 795–796
Steuart, James, 28, 29, 33, 34
Stiglitz, Joseph E., 7–8, 52, 53, 93–160, 172, 471, 475; on agriculture, 289; on cost sharing, 122; on credit markets, 769, 772–774, 775, 777, 782–783, 827; on employment, 369, 720; on equivalency, 116; on labor productivity, 644, 683, 728; model for tenancy and credit, 803–806, 821–822; model for unemployment equilibrium, 748–751; on saving, 390; on urban migration, 136
Stolper–Samuelson theorem, 178
Strauss, J., 605, 638, 676, 684; on family labor supply, 719; on nutrition, 685–686, 727–728
Streeten, P., 166
Structural transformation: accounting for, 250–258; in agriculture, 276–328; approaches to policy, 265–268; balance among sectors, 199–200; changes in sector proportions, 228–243; and development policy, 209; empirical research in, 216–223; exchange-rate conversions, 262–265; interdependence of policies, 200–201; micro and macro approaches to, 197; patterns of change, 198–199; patterns of growth and accumulation, 223–228; relative prices, 259–262; research program, 197–199; role of industrialization in, 334; structure and growth, 243–250; study of, 206–215
Structuralist-institutional theory, 40; and income distribution, 51, 54; and trade and development, 60–62
Structuralists: equations of, 184–185; vs. monetarists, 184–187
Structure: in development economics, 211–214; in economic history, 209–211; need for typology, 214–215; study of changes in, 206–215; use of concept, 206. *See also* Structural transformation
Stylized facts, 220; defined, 198, 223; of prices, 258; of urbanization, 427
Subsidies, 701; food, 692–696; other health goods, 696–697; targeting of, 695
Substitutability, in development process, 217
Sudan, 696
Sukarno, 289
Sukhatme, P.V., 655, 672, 700

Summers, R., 261
Sunkel, O., 170
Supply considerations and nutrition, 692–698; food subsidies, 692–696
Surplus labor economies, 715–728; absent labor markets, 717; models for, 716; nutrition-based efficiency model, 720–728; perfect labor markets, 717–720
Sussangkarn, C., 741
Svennilson, I., 215
Swan, T.W., 8, 171
Sweden, 66
Sweezy, P., 180
Sylos-Labini, P., 169, 174
Syrquin, Moshe, 198, 203–273; on agriculture, 276, 317; on patterns of change in production, 342–343; on sectoral reallocation, 355–356

Tableau Economique (Quesnay), 31
Taiwan, 59, 319, 340, 356; agriculture in, 308, 323, 325; education in, 613; exports of, 252; family in, 403; family labor supply in, 719; industrialization in, 337, 338, 339; protection in, 349; studies of fertility in, 521; successes of, 353–355; tenancy contracts in, 739
Talati, C., 183
Tanzania, 447, 614, 792
Taubman, P., 638, 657
Tavares, M.C., 167
Taxation, and savings, 413
Taylor, C., 668
Taylor, Lance, 8, 54, 55, 60, 161–194, 199, 242; on nutrition, 696
Teachers: and the educational system, 558–562; primary vs. secondary, 569–570; ratio with students, 568, 574; wages of, 574, 576
Technical change: frontier, 309; problems with, 312–321; sources of in agriculture, 302–313
Technology: in agriculture, 297, 314; choice of to increase employment, 366–369, 370–371; frontier of, 309; inappropriate, 149, 150; information costs of, 369–370; landlords' resistance to innovation, 148–149; and saving, 405; and urban growth, 459
Teilhet, S., 596
Teitel, S., 359
Tenancy contracts, 739–743; share vs. fixed-rent, 742
Tenants: credit for, 623; "land to the tiller" program, 824–825. *See also* Landlord–tenant relationship
TFP. *See* Total factor productivity
Thailand, 301, 483, 598, 694, 719
Third World: drives for migration and city growth, 449–459; growth rates in cities of, 427–430; research needed, 459–461; trade

patterns in, 179; urban employment in, 440, 447; urbanization in, 426–427, 440; wage gaps in, 431–435; wages in cities of, 446–448. *See also* Less developed countries

Thomas, V., 435

Timmer, Peter, 200, 201, 215, 275–331; on nutrition, 677, 683

Todaro, Michael P., 177, 427, 434, 436, 439; model on migration by, 141, 443–445, 460, 584, 746–747

Tomes, N., 754

Torrens, 224

Total factor productivity (TFP), 334; and city growth, 452–453; and growth, 224–225; in LDCs, 352–356, 358; and trade orientation, 348–352; and trade regime, 352–353

Trade: changes in commodity composition of, 234–235; and changes in sector proportions, 232–235; and development, 6; and developing economies, 40, 57–62; early writings on, 29–31; and economic dualism, 86; and industrialization, 334–372; liberalization of, 178; neutral trade regimes, 349, 350; patterns of, 233. *See also* International Trade

Trairatvorakul, P., 694

Transformation, stages of: developed economy, 245, 246–248; industrialization, 245–246; primary production, 245. *See also* Structural transformation

Transforming Traditional Agriculture (Schultz), 321

Transnational factors: comparative analysis of, 219; in growth process, 216–217. *See also* Cross-country studies

Trowbridge, F.L., 667

Tsao, Y., 353

Tuncer, B., 352

Turkey, 301, 352, 353, 418

Turnham, D., 447

Tversky, A., 104

Two-gap model (Chenery and Bruno), 172–173

Typology: approaches to, 248; Chenery on, 214–215; of development patterns, 248–250

Udall, A.T., 441

Ultimate Resource, The (J. Simon), 492

Underemployment, 723; in Third World cities, 442

Unemployment: and education, 593; incentive–efficiency wage models, 129–131; and labor supply, 591–593; Marx on, 174; nutritional wage–productivity model, 125–129; of rural migrants, 601; in rural sector, 125–132; rural vs. urban, 755; in surplus labor economies, 716–733; in Third World cities, 447; two-sector equilibrium models of,

746–751; urban, in LDCs, 96

Unemployment equilibrium, 51–52

Union Carbide, 647

Union of Soviet Socialist Republics (USSR), agriculture in, 285, 289

United Nations, 428, 457, 608

UNICEF, 701

United States, 226, 231, 495; agriculture in, 283, 285, 292, 308, 312; birth rates in, 481, 501; decline of fertility in, 508, 509; education and earnings in, 577, 594; education and fertility in, 609; education and production of farmers, 597, 598; immigrants to, 448, 601; labor productivity in, 358–359; unemployment equilibrium model for, 751

Urban labor markets, 754–757; diversity and unemployment, 754–755; urban dualism and dual labor markets, 756–757

Urban sector, 134–136; as dualistic, 756; equations in, 137

Urbanization: disequilibrating labor market shocks, 433–439; and industrialization, 440; migrant selectivity bias, 430–433; and migration, 426–465; motivations for, 449–459; a necessary stage, 94–95, 206; and overurbanization, 439–441; questions remaining, 459–461; Todaro model, 443–446; transition to, 427–433; urban bias, 441–442, 452; urban labor markets, 442–448; use of models for, 455–459

Uruguay, 181

Values, endogeneity and heterogeneity, 20–21

Van Wijnbergen, S., 185

Venezuela, 318, 483

Vijverberg, W.P.M., 594

Vines, D., 60

Visaria, P., 386

Viteri, F., 683–684

Von Braun, J., 693

Von Neumann, J., 211

Von Oppen, M., 795

Von Piscjke, J., 767

Vorontsov, 54

Wage contracts, 737

Wages: in dual urban settings, 756; and educational research, 616; efficiency wage model, 720–728; and employment in rural labor markets, 714–733, 736; Marxism vs. neoclassicism on, 51–54; and productivity effects, 110–112; and returns on education, 591–593; and schooling, 582, 587; and the self-employed, 595–596; of teachers, 558–562; of urban immigrants, 445, 447; of women and

effect on fertility behavior, 515; in urban
 sector, 134–136
Waldorf, W.H., 596
Wales, T.J., 657
Wallace, D., 685
Wallace, R., 28
Wallace, T.D., 691
Walrasian economics, 179, 184, 187, 199; and
 Schumpeter's theory, 165–166
Ward, J.O., 678
Watanabe, T., 228, 231
Water, safe supplies of, 633, 662
Wealth of Nations, The (Adam Smith), 10, 28
Weber, Max, 35
Weisbrod, B., 684
Weiss, A., 53, 728; on credit markets, 769,
 772–774, 775, 777, 782
Welch, F., 589, 598, 605
Welfare: and income distribution, 816–823; and
 public policy, 823–826
West Africa, 796–797
West Asia, educational expenses in, 574
West Bengal (India), 734, 736, 737, 741
Western Europe: agriculture in, 278, 283, 312;
 labor productivity in, 358–359; population
 growth in, 478
Westphal, L.E., 181, 183, 266, 340
Wharton, C.R., 794, 795
Wheeler, D., 512, 521, 672, 673–674; on labor
 productivity, 688; on nutrient demand, 681
White, B., 727
White, L.J., 370
Williams, A.D., 691
Williams, R.A., 260
Williamson, J.G., 175, 200, 201, 215, 425, 465,
 473; on fertility behavior, 517; model for city
 growth, 454–455; on motivation for migration,
 449; on population growth, 500; on saving,
 387

Williamson-Gray, C., 676, 677, 693
Willis, R.J., 445
Winter, S., 364
Wolfe, B.J., 509, 596; on nutrition, 652, 654, 657,
 665, 669, 670, 678, 690
Wolgemuth, J.C., 684
Wolpin, K.I., 387, 389, 401, 411; on family
 planning, 521; on migration, 753; on size of
 households, 499, 503, 516; on wage–education
 relationship, 594
Women: advantages of education for, 546;
 education of, and fertility rate, 505, 509, 513,
 514; education and health, 665, 671, 678, 701;
 expected years of enrollments by, 553; in labor
 force, 579–580; nutrition–fertility link in,
 689–690; returns on education, 602–605, 608,
 643, 699, 701; and school enrollment rates,
 571–573; wages of, and schooling, 592
World Bank, 347, 447; on agriculture, 277, 304;
 on education, 553; on nutrition, 700; on
 population growth, 493, 521, 530, 534
World Development Report (World Bank), 181,
 301, 304
Wu, C.C., 598

Yamey, B.S., 212
Yap, L., 436, 447–448, 743, 744
Ybanez-Gonzalo, 679–680
Yotopoulos, P.A., 638
Young, Allyn, 166
Yugoslavia, 241, 353, 364

Zambia, 240, 750
Zellner, A., 397
Zimbabwe, 279
Zusman, P., 49, 775, 810, 822

WARNER MEMORIAL LIBRARY
EASTERN COLLEGE
ST. DAVIDS, PA. 19087